Lecture Notes in Computer Science 551
Edited by G. Goos and J. Hartmanis

S. Prehn W. J. Toetenel (Eds.)

VDM '91 Formal Software Development Methods

4th International Symposium of VDM Europe
Noordwijkerhout, The Netherlands
October 21-25, 1991
Proceedings

Volume 1: Conference Contributions

Springer-Verlag
Berlin Heidelberg New York
London Paris Tokyo
Hong Kong Barcelona
Budapest

Series Editors

Gerhard Goos
GMD Forschungsstelle
Universität Karlsruhe
Vincenz-Priessnitz-Straße 1
W-7500 Karlsruhe, FRG

Juris Hartmanis
Department of Computer Science
Cornell University
Upson Hall
Ithaca, NY 14853, USA

Volume Editors

Søren Prehn
Computer Resources International A/S
Bregnerødvej 144, P. O. Box 173, DK-3460 Birkerød, Denmark

Hans Toetenel
Delft University of Technology, Faculty of Technical Mathematics and Informatics
P. O. Box 356, 2600 AJ Delft, The Netherlands

CR Subject Classification (1991): D.2, F.3.1

ISBN 3-540-54834-3 Springer-Verlag Berlin Heidelberg New York
ISBN 0-387-54834-3 Springer-Verlag New York Berlin Heidelberg

Typesetting: Camera ready by author
Printing and binding: Druckhaus Beltz, Hemsbach/Bergstr.
45/3140-543210 - Printed on acid-free paper

Preface

The proceedings of the fourth VDM Symposium, VDM '91, are published in two volumes, of which this is the first. Previous VDM symposia were held in March 1987 (in Brussels, Belgium), in September 1988 (in Dublin, Ireland) and in April 1990 (in Kiel, Germany). Proceedings from the previous symposia were also published by Springer-Verlag in the Lecture Notes in Computer Science series, as volumes 252, 328 and 428, respectively.

All Vienna Development Method symposia have been organised by VDM Europe. VDM Europe was formed in 1985 as an advisory board sponsored by the Commission of the European Communities. The VDM Europe working group consisted of researchers, software engineers and programmers, all interested in promoting the industrial usage of formal methods for software development. The group met three to four times a year to present, discuss and disseminate recent results, problems and experiences. VDM Europe focused on the industrial usage of model-oriented formal methods, in particular VDM and closely related methods such as MetaSoft and RAISE, and supported the efforts to standardise the VDM notation, first within BSI, and later within ISO.

While the two first VDM symposia were mainly dedicated to research and practise of VDM, the third symposium - VDM and Z - presented a broader view. This, the fourth VDM symposium, goes even further. In tutorials and in papers, a larger number of methods for formal software development are presented.
Parallel to this development, it has been decided to reshape VDM Europe into Formal Methods Europe (FME). FME will primarily be oriented towards technology transfer to ensure that industry is continuously aware of available formal methods, their documentation and their support tools.
The proceedings of this symposium clearly reflect this trend.

The *Tutorials* volume includes four introductory tutorials (on *LARCH*, *Refinement Calculus*, *VDM*, and *RAISE*) and four advanced tutorials (on *ABEL*, *PROSPECTRA*, *The B Method*, and *The Stack*). While there are certainly other methods available which are or could be used fruitfully in industry, we believe that the tutorials of VDM '91 present a comprehensive account of the current state of the art.

The *Conference* volume has four parts: contributions of invited speakers, papers, project reports and tools demonstration abstracts. The three invited talks cover three different aspects of formal software development. The 31 *papers* cover both theory and practice. However, as compared with earlier VDM symposia, the emphasis is more on *development*: methods and calculi for development, verification and verification tools support, experiences from doing developments, and the associated theoretical problems with respect to semantics and logic. The 7 *project reports* present (shorter) accounts of experiences from specific projects. The 14 *tools demonstration* abstracts highlight the capabilities of formal methods support tools, all of which are demonstrated during the symposium.
We trust that you will find the material available in these proceedings useful.

Delft
August 1991

Søren Prehn
Hans Toetenel

Acknowledgements

Many people have contributed to the planning, organisation and success of VDM '91.

Executive Programme Committee

Patrick Behm
Andrzej Blikle
Hans Langmaack
Peter Lucas
Søren Prehn (chair)
Hans Toetenel
Jim Woodcock

Organisation Commitee

Nico Plat
Kees Pronk
Hans Toetenel (chair)
Hans Tonino

Local Organiser

Lodewijk Bos

Invited Speakers

Michael Jackson
Robin Milner
John Guttag

Panelists

Wlad Turski
Martyn Thomas

In addition, the invaluable contributions of the following should be acknowledged: Dines Bjørner for advice, inspiration and persistence; Horst Hüncke, Karel de Vriendt and Alejandro Moya, CEC, for their continued support to VDM Europe and Formal Methods Europe; Nico Plat for the organisation of the Tools Demonstration, and Toos Brussee, Coby Bouwer and Trudy Stoute at the secretariat of the Faculty of Technical Mathematics and Informatics of the Delft University of Technology; Hans Wössner and Alfred Hofmann of Springer-Verlag for their continued interest in VDM publications.

Referees

The submitted papers - whether accepted or rejected - were refereed by the following external referees. This symposium would not have been possible without their voluntary and dedicated work.

Mark A. Ardis
Marek Bednarczyki
Dines Bjørner
Dominique Bolignano
Andrej Borzyszkowski
Heinz Brix
Hans Bruun
Peter Michael Bruun
Karl-Heinz Buth
Neil Butler
Christine Choppy
Bent Dandanell Holdt-Jørgensen
Tim Denvir
Jeremy Dick
Martin Fränzle
David Garlan
Chris George
Susan Gerhardt
Anthony Hall
Bo Stig Hansen
Michael Reichardt Hansen
Anne Haxthausen
Kees van Hee
Wolfgang Henhapl
Friedrich von Henke
Götz Hofmann
Bernard Hohlfeld
Ronald Huijsman
Cliff B. Jones
Ulrik Jörring
Jan van Katwijk
Steve King
Dirk Kinnaes
Beata Konikowska
Ryszard Kubiak
Yves Ledru
Jacek Leszczylowski
Peter Lupton
Hans Henrik Løvengreen
Lynn Marshall
Fernando Mejia
Kees Middelburg
Dave Neilson
Mogens Nielsen
Stephen O'Brien
Wieslaw Pawlowski
Jan Storbank Pedersen
Brian Ritchie
Gunter Schmidt
Uwe Schmidt
Pierre-Yves Schobbens
Chris Sennet
Stefan Sokolowski
Marian Srebrny
Werner Struckmann
Andrej Tarlecki
Karel de Vlaminck
Reinhard Völler
Jozef Winkowski
Chris van Westrhenen
William Wood
John Wordsworth
Raymond Zavodnik
Job Zwiers

Contents of Volume 1

Contents of Volume 2

Description Is Our Business

Michael Jackson
101 Hamilton Terrace
London NW8 9QX
England

1 Introduction

Formal development methods are arguably one of the most important advances in the business of creating useful software. And the VDM conference is certainly one of the most important formal conferences on formal development methods. So it is with a degree of surprise that someone so informal as I am finds himself here, addressing you now. But I am delighted to be here, and I thank the program committee for inviting me and so giving me this opportunity.

I would like to use it to offer you a general account of what software development is about, and, on the basis of that account, to suggest an area of research and activity that I think can be particularly fruitful. It is bold to offer a general account of a whole field; and it is doubly bold to suggest research topics to researchers who have already been so successful. But generality and boldness are surely the privileges of a keynote speech.

2 The Purpose Of A System

The purpose of a system is to bring about some useful relationships within and among some domains of interest in the world.

In a classic problem, often stated but seldom solved, there are patients in hospital beds, attached to analog devices that allow their temperature, blood pressure, and other vital factors to be read electrically. That is one domain. There is a station, equipped with a VDU, where the duty nurse works. That is another domain. There are safe ranges for each patient's vital factors, and periodicities for reading the factors, specified by medical staff. They are another domain. The purpose of the system is to ensure that when a reading of one of a patient's factors falls outside its safe range the nurse is notified. The nurse must also be notified when an analog device fails.

We have here the elements of a problem: a number of domains of interest; and a number of relationships that are required to hold within and among the domains.

The elements of a solution - of the kind we would like to be able to develop - are also twofold: appropriate connections between the domains and a machine we are to create; and the machine, created by describing its behaviour in software texts. The property of general-purpose computers, which we exploit in our solutions, is precisely that they are able to accept a symbolic description of a specialised behaviour and forthwith create a new machine by adapting themselves to behave in the way described.

3 The Software Development Problem

Our central task, as software developers, is to describe the required machine behaviour as a specialisation of the existing behaviour of an available machine. If this task is not entirely trivial, we need a development method.

A development method aims to answer the following questions:

(a) How can we organise the description of the required behaviour?

(b) What contributory descriptions should we make, as parts of our end product or to support our production activity?

(c) In what languages should we make our descriptions?

(d) In what order should we make our descriptions?

(e) By what operations, especially operations using existing descriptions from this or other developments, should we make each description?

There are many questions here, and I want to focus only one one: what contributory descriptions should we make? And I want to give only one part of a complete answer to that question: we should describe the domains of the system, fully and explicitly.

4 Describing Domains

I have spoken of a system as consisting of its domains together with its machine, each domain being connected to the machine. From this point of view, a specification of the usual kind can be thought of as describing the interface between the machine and the domains: that is, describing what must happen at the connections. This way of thinking about a specification is commonly adopted, but with a difference of terminology. Commonly, the term 'system' is used for what I am calling the 'machine'; and what I am calling the 'domains' are called the 'environment'.

This terminological difference has a substantial effect, because it is natural to think of ourselves as being concerned with something called 'the system', while the 'environment' will be the concern of other people. In the contractual view of state-based specifications, for example, it is the customer's reponsibility to ensure that the environment satisfies the preconditions; only if it does so do we then become responsible for satisfying the postconditions. Our view is therefore focussed on the machine: we stand outside the specification, and look inward at the machine. We may have the environment to some extent in mind, but our explicit descriptions will be descriptions of the machine.

I want to suggest that, for at least some of the time, we should instead stand inside the specification and look out at the domains. We may - or may not - have the eventual machine in mind, but our explicit descriptions should at this point be descriptions of the domains. There are several reasons for adopting this view.

First, a domain may have properties that are important for the system but are not representable in a machine-directed specification. For example, in a lift control system, turning the motor on will cause the lift to start in an upwards or downwards direction, depending on the setting of the motor polarity. This is not a relationship that the machine is required to bring about or to maintain: it is a property of the domain on which the system will rely. Where, in a specification based on a state and operation model, would this relationship between the event of switching on the motor and the subsequent behaviour of the lift in the shaft be described?

Second, the problem of implementation bias will cease to trouble us. If our specification describes the collection of books in a library as an ordered set, rather than an unordered set, then a domain-oriented specification must explicitly say what the ordering is. For instance, it may be the accession order of the books; or it may be an ordering of their shelf locations. If the described ordering is true of the domain, then all is well: we may have written down a piece of description that we did not need, but there is no implementation bias in that. If, on the other hand, the described ordering is not true of the domain, then our description is simply erroneous, and it is directly falsifiable by examining the domain. The question of implementation bias does not arise.

Third, we should devote effort to describing domains explicitly and directly because they are often rich, complex, and difficult to formalise. If we pay too little attention to the domains themselves, rushing eagerly to the formal world of the machine, we may find that our customer can not use the system we build: the customer assented to the specification; but it was wrong nonetheless, and the customer is entitled to hold us responsible.

Effort devoted to direct explicit description of domains will not be wasted. No one today needs to be convinced that an explicit description of the source program is an essential prerequisite for developing a compiler. This is because of a completely general property of systems: the machine is a model of each domain, and vice versa.

5 Descriptions And Models

My use of the term 'model' differs from the common uses among software developers, and I make no apology for that: I hope to convince you that my usage is justifiable. My attempts to convince you will be partly in what I shall say now, and partly in what I shall say later on in my talk.

I use the word 'model' somewhat as it is used when speaking of a model aeroplane. There are two objects: a large passenger plane that can transport two hundred people over thousands of miles, and a toy that a child might like for a birthday present. The two objects are related because one description is true of both.

A description is true of an object - or a domain - through the medium of what I shall call an 'abstraction'. To avoid distressing you by yet more terminological unorthodoxy, I invite you to think of an 'abstraction' as the inverse of what you would perhaps prefer to call an 'interpretation'. Whatever it may be called, it provides a mapping between the symbols used in the description and the observable phenomena of the described domain.

In this sense, a machine in a system is a model of each domain, and each domain is a model of the machine. Because the machine and the domain are connected - possibly as two interacting concurrent processes, possibly as two static structures between which there is some similarity of form, possibly in some combination of the dynamic and static - there must be some description that, with suitable interpretations, is true of them both. A grammar describes both the compiler's input and the behaviour of its recursive descent parser - provided, of course, that we understand that 'next' is to be interpreted spatially for the source text and temporally for the parser.

My main point here, then, is that effort devoted to describing a domain pays off by producing at least a partial description of the machine as its by-product. But I would also point out that the modelling relationship between machine and domains allows us - unless we are very careful - to drift into describing the one when we believe we are describing the other.

6 The Formal And The Informal

Machines, of course, are purely formal (unless they fail to operate correctly or lack a proper formal specification). But many domains of interest - perhaps even most domains of interest - are largely informal. Domains involving activities of human beings - those annoying creatures - are always totally informal; and even non-human domains must be partly informal if they are tangible.

I think of informality in this sense as a kind of unboundedness. Whatever we may decide about the meaning of a term, there is always more evidence that can be brought to cast doubt on our decision. Considerations can be shown to be relevant that previously we had thought could be safely ignored; hard cases can be invented to expose unintended anomalies. To deal with such domains in machine-based systems we must formalise: we must make formal descriptions of informal domains. I believe that this activity of formalisation is crucially important in software development; that is is intellectually challenging; and that it is sadly neglected.

Informality is not the same thing as ambiguity. Ambiguity is a purely technical linguistic failure, easily put right by logicians and lesser formalists. I recently saw two notices, side by side, at the foot of an escalator. One read 'Shoes Must Be Worn'. That seemed clear enough, and I was sure I understood it. But the other notice read 'Dogs Must Be Carried'. That gave me pause for a moment.

But only for a moment. I am not so completely informal that I could not resolve the ambiguity. The notice about shoes meant that:

"P travels on the escalator" => "P is wearing shoes"

while the notice about dogs meant that:

"D is a dog and D travels on the escalator" => "D is carried".

In their natural language form the notices might have been worded better as "Escalator users must wear shoes" and "Dogs must be carried". But resolving this ambiguity is only the easy part of the problem. Further questions arise immediately. Must dogs wear shoes? What counts as shoes? What counts as being carried? What counts as a dog?

A cartoon from Punch, printed in 1869, expounds the essence of the solution to this last question at least. A railway passenger, intending to travel with a collection of pet animals, has enquired about the fares to be charged for her pets. The porter is explaining to her how the formalism of the railway company's fare rules is to be applied in this case.

> "Station master say, Mum, as Cats is Dogs, and Rabbits is Dogs, and so's Parrots; but this 'ere Tortoise is an Insect, so there ain't no charge for it!"

We might be tempted to tell our customers that this is a trivial but disagreeable mess, and that they must deal with it themselves. They should work out for themselves whether cats are dogs and rabbits are dogs, and tortoises are dogs, and let us know when they have decided. We, for our part, want nothing to do with it.

I think that would be a great mistake. I think some interesting questions lie precisely at this interface between the formal and the informal. Not the social, personal, economic, or political questions involved in working out what system is best and obtaining a general consent to that system - although those questions are real enough. But rather the narrower and more intellectual concern of understanding how the formal and the informal interact, and how we can use elements of a formal approach to deal more effectively with informal domains.

7 Formalisation At Risk

We prefer formal descriptions to informal because formal descriptions can allow us to reason about the domains and their required relationships, and about the intended behaviour of the machine. For example, we would like to apply arithmetic to things that can be regarded as individuals. But we have to be sure that the formal manipulations will indeed be applicable to the description, given the denotations of terms on which we and our customer have decided.

Arithmetic, for example, is not always applicable even when we seem to be dealing with sets of individuals or with objects to which numerical values can apparently be assigned. It may not be clear whether some phenomenon - for example, a cherry in a variety that produces many Siamese twins - is one individual or two. Two raindrops, clearly distinct as they run down a window pane in driving rain, become one raindrop when they touch and surface tension takes its effect. Cash stored in a moneybox changes its nominal value when some denomination is demonetised, but the same cash stored in a bank account does not. A short flight on a scheduled service lands with more passengers than originally boarded, because one of them was a pregnant woman. Imperfect formalisation - and formalisation of the informal is always imperfect - can frustrate our reasoning.

Sometimes the only sensible response is to ignore the vanishingly infrequent exceptions - airlines don't usually allow pregnant women to fly, and demonetisation is comparatively rare - and just make sure that there is an escape clause somewhere: some overriding transaction that allows the system's users to put the books straight.

But often there is a problem in the customer's own conceptual and linguistic framework for dealing with a domain. Consider, for example, the notion of a telephone call. In the earliest days of the telephone system, the notion of a call was quite clear: subscriber A phones subscriber B, and the call begins when B's phone starts to ring and ends when either A or B puts the phone down. The word 'call', and some accompanying notion, has persisted in use until the present day, because it does serve some purposes quite adequately. But today's telephone system allows conference calls: A phones B; B adds C into the conversation by using the conference feature; then A puts the phone down and B and C continue talking: where is the call now?. Or someone phones a chat line, where a constantly changing set of adolescents conduct a continuous conversation 24 hours a day. Or you phone the directory enquiries service, and the operator not only tells you the number you want, but also connects you to that number, using the Directory Assistance Call Completion feature. In the face of these more complex features, the original notion of a call begins to look very difficult to define.

And so it is. Probably the single notion of a 'call' should now be abandoned; but replacements are needed for many of the purposes it serves. How are such replacements to be defined? This is an important question, and one that software developers can not ignore.

8 The Narrow Bridge

The bridge between the informal and the formal is provided by what I have called 'abstractions', which you may be more comfortable calling 'interpretations'. On one side of the bridge you have informal descriptions by which significant phenomena - perhaps classes of individuals, or events, or predicates - can be recognised in the domain. On the other side you have the symbols by which these phenomena will be denoted in our formal descriptions.

This bridge must be carefully sited, and should be as narrow as possible while still bearing the traffic. If it is sited in the wrong place, or is gratuitously broadened, or there is no visible bridge at all, the result will be a serious defect in our descriptions. In the rude world of informal development methods, this defect takes the form of a disseminated informality, showing itself as a smog hovering over all descriptions that make any reference at all to the application domains: nothing is clear, nothing is defined, nothing can be relied upon, and reasoning is dangerous.

In the more refined world of formal development methods, the defect takes the form of a denotational uncertainty. If we think of the specification as being, in part, a description of the domains, we can imagine it as a template to be fitted over the domains, as a map may be put into correspondence with the terrain it describes. The denotational uncertainty is this: we do not know which are the triangulation points on the map. So we do not know which reference points may be taken for granted in checking - and even questioning - whether the map is a correct description of the terrain. We have nowhere to stand: we can not move the world.

9 Ignoring The Real World

Whether we are looking inward through our specifications at the machine or outward at the domains is in some respects a subtle question: the modelling relationship makes it so. But certainly there are many things that are found frequently in domains but only rarely explicitly treated in formalisms.

One example is causality. It is, of course, a brilliantly successful idea to abstract from causality and to write specifications in terms of what an idiot could observe when the system is in operation. It is also brilliantly successful to write specifications in terms of operations on states, leaving unanswered the question of who is required or permitted to perform the operations. In Lamport's well-known account of the transition axiom method, he points out that the conventional formal specification of a Queue module would be satisfied by a module that occasionally performed a spontaneous Put operation without involving or informing the user. So he adds to his interface specification the stipulation that only the user is permitted to execute Get and Put Operations. But the reality of the connections between the machine and the domains is potentially far more complex than this, and demands a serious and coherent treatment.

Another example is the recognition of events as first-class citizens, and, as a consequence, a similarly liberal treatment of all kinds of aggregates of events. Events need to be classified: 'this dialling of the digit 1 was part of dialling a number, but that dialling of the same digit was a request to put a call on hold'. Episodes consisting of event sets also sometimes demand to be recognised as individuals: 'the game between A and B on board 3 has so far consisted of these moves'. Events, like all individuals in the real world, are simultaneously of several types: 'this transaction was a sale for dealer A, a purchase for dealer B, and a class 2 bargain for the stock exchange authorities'.

I am not claiming that these particular notions are universally ignored, or that they are not to be found in any formalisms whatsoever: I know that such a claim would be false. My point rather is that we could benefit from looking outward at domains as well as inward at the machine, and that we might be led thus to some fruitful additions to our conceptual repertoire.

Our present predilection for looking inward is clearly demonstrated by our language. The commonly accepted use of the word 'model', for example, views the real world as a model of a theory: it is the theory that is fundamental, and the world is secondary. The use of the word 'interpretation' has a similar import: instead of saying that symbolic logic describes the world, we say that the world is an interpretation of the logic. Instead of saying that an abstract type is a description that can be applied to certain things in the world, we say that those things are 'instantiations' of the type: the Larch stack is real - it is the wobbling pile of plates in the cafeteria that is secondary and insubstantial. This kind of usage may be unsurprising to logicians, but it would certainly surprise other people. One does not often hear a cartographer speaking of a country as a model of his map of it.

So let us, sometimes at least, look outward. The point at which formalisms meet informal realities seems to me to be like the junction of two dissimilar metals: there is a difference of temperature, and an electromotive force is generated. I think this force could be a source of real intellectual energy, and I hope we will not be backwards in exploiting it.

Michael Jackson
24 July 1991

Concurrent Processes as Objects

Robin Milner, University of Edinburgh

The topic of my lecture will be the π-calculus, an algebraic model for communicating processes. This model is in the tradition of process algebras [1, 3, 4, 5]. It goes a step further than these in one respect: it models processes whose configuration is dynamically varying. This enrichment gives the calculus status as a general computational model. Its main character is what may be called the *object* paradigm, since it most directly represents the action and reaction among independently existing agents. It also embraces the *function* paradigm, since both functions (the λ-calculus) and data can be accurately encoded as processes.

In the lecture I hope to cover the following: motivating examples; definition of π-calculus; reduction rules; process equivalence (bisimilarity); encoding data and functions as processes.

A basic knowledge of process algebra can be got from some of the books referred to above. The π-calculus is most clearly derived from CCS [5]; it evolved through work by Nielsen and Engberg [2], and the best introduction is the two-part paper by Milner, Parrow and Walker [7]. The encoding of λ-calculus is done in detail in [6].

References

[1] Baeten, J.C.M. and Weijland, W.P., **Process Algebra**, Cambridge University Press 1990.

[2] Engberg, U. and Nielsen, M., *A Calculus of Communicating Systems with Label Passing*, Report DAIMI PB-208, Computer Science Department, University of Århus, 1986.

[3] Hoare, C.A.R., **Communicating Sequential Processes**, Prentice Hall, 1985.

[4] Hennessy, M., **Algebraic Theory of Processes**, MIT Press, 1988.

[5] Milner, R., **Communication and Concurrency**, Prentice Hall, 1989

[6] Milner, R., *Functions as Processes*, Proc. ICALP '90, Lecture Notes in Computer Science, Vol. 443, pp167–180, Springer-Verlag, 1990.

[7] Milner, R., Parrow, J. and Walker, D., *A Calculus of Mobile Processes*, Reports ECS-LFCS-89-85 and -86, Laboratory for Foundations of Computer Science, Computer Science Department, Edinburgh University, 1989. (To appear in Journal of Information and Computation.)

The Larch Approach to Specification

John V. Guttag
MIT Laboratory for Computer Science
Cambridge, Massachusetts

Larch is one of many approaches to formal specification, and has much in common with many of them. It is distinguished form most others by

- Its two-tiered, definitional approach to specification.
- Its facilities for modularization on both tiers.
- Its provision for programming-language-specific checks on the relationship of code to specifications.
- Its emphasis on incrementally composing and analyzing specifications.

In Larch's two-tiered approach to specification, each specification has components written in two languages: one designed for a specific programming language and another independent of any programming language. A Larch *interface specification* describes the interface that a progam component provides to clients (programs that use it). Each interface specification is written in a programming-language-dependent Larch interface language. Each interface specification relies upon definitions from an auxilary specification, written in a programming-language-independent specification language, the Larch Shared Language (LSL).

Larch interface languages deal with what can be observed about the behavior of components written in a particular programming language. They incorporate programming-language-specific notations and semantics for features such as side effects, exception handling, iterators, and concurrency.

Larch Shared Language specifications are used to provide a semanties for the primitive terms used in interface specifications. Specifiers are not limited to a fixed set of primitive terms, but can use LSL to define specialized vocabularies suitable for particular interface specifications.

This talk presents an overview of Larch with an emphasis on what distinguishes it from other approaches to specification. Examples of both LSL specifications and LCL (an interface language for C) specifications will be shown.

Formal Specification in Metamorphic Programming

David A. Penny, Richard C. Holt, Michael W. Godfrey†

Department of Computer Science
University of Toronto

ABSTRACT

Formal specification methods have not been embraced wholeheartedly by the software development industry. We believe that a large part of industry's reluctance is due to *semantic gaps* that are encountered when attempting to integrate formal specification with other stages of the software development process. Semantic gaps necessitate a dramatic shift in a programmer's mode of thought, and undergoing many such shifts during the development of a software system is inefficient. We identify semantic gaps in the software development process and show how they can be minimized by an approach called *metamorphic programming* that operates in-the-large and in-the-small. The main contribution that metamorphic programming makes to formal specification is to clarify the ways in which specifications can be merged smoothly into the software development lifecycle.

1. Introduction

Many researchers in the field of formal methods would agree that formal specifications are not being used as much as they *ought* to be ([Meyer 85], [Neumann 89], [Wing 90]). Our background is in language design and operating systems construction. One of us has been instrumental in designing and producing a programming language, Turing, that has met with some success [Holt 88a]. Another is the major author of a 60,000 line 4.3BSD UNIX-compatible operating system for large-scale shared-memory multiprocessors written in the Turing language. Being academics, formal methods of all kinds appeal to us. Due to pragmatic reasons, however, we have not been able to apply these methods to our compiler and operating systems programming work as much as we might have liked. In this paper we present our views on why this is so, and put forward a proposal, called *metamorphic programming*, that addresses the problems as we see them.

Excellent work has been done on the foundations of formal specification, and on developing effective notations and tools. Our thesis, however, is that current formal specification methodologies do not fit into the software development cycle very well. We believe this is due to the presence of so-called *semantic gaps*.

The idea of a semantic gap [Holt 91] can be explained by analogy to writing a paper (the foremost topic in our minds at this instant!). Suppose an author were forced by his editor to write the outline in English, the first draft in Cantonese, and the final version in Arabic. Although compelling arguments might be made that English is most suitable for writing outlines, Cantonese an excellent language for first drafts, and Arabic ideal for writing final

† authors' email addresses: ynnep@turing.toronto.edu, holt@turing.toronto.edu, migod@turing.toronto.edu

versions, these arguments are unlikely to sway the practicing author. As preposterous as this situation may seem, we expect the software professional to be able to analyze and design using a CASE tool, specify with VDM, prototype with Smalltalk, and implement in C! Any proposed tool that introduces sizable semantic gaps into the software development process is likely to be rejected by the practitioner as inefficient, and this includes specification languages.

In this paper, we propose a method for minimizing semantic gaps from (our variant of) the software development process. This method allows the formal specification stage to be integrated gracefully with the other stages. We present the method in terms of the concepts and tools with which we are most familiar, but the general approach can be adapted to the work of others.

In the next section, we present our software development model and point out the semantic gaps that can result when existing tools are used. In the following section, we give an overview of how metamorphic programming can minimize these gaps. The subsequent two sections examine the requirements for supporting metamorphic programming, first discussing programming in-the-small and then generalizing to programming in-the-large. We then discuss software development environments, and we conclude by re-stating the ideas most relevant to making formal specification techniques more accessible to the software developer.

2. Semantic Gaps in the Software Development Process

Our model of the software development process, and one we hope will not be too controversial, is denoted by the acronym ASPIT — each letter stands for one of the five general stages in the process.

A) *Analysis* — the process of understanding (in the mind) what needs to be accomplished, and determining the external interfaces. This understanding is most aptly communicated using natural language and diagrams.

S) *Specification* — formally specifying precisely what needs to be accomplished.

P) *Prototyping* — writing a possibly incomplete, and perhaps inefficient, version of the software that can be executed.

I) *Implementation* — writing an efficient version of the software that is well-suited to execution on a standard computer architecture (*i.e.* producing machine-oriented code).

T) *Tuning* — meeting efficiency constraints by profiling the implementation to reveal trouble spots, and re-coding in a manner better adapted to the specific target computer architecture (*i.e.* producing machine-specific code).

Additionally, testing, validation, and verification are considered to occur wherever and as often as needed. When any of the stages proves to be too complex to be held in the mind all at once, decomposition (also called design) must be performed. Figure 1 gives an example of notations commonly used for each ASPIT stage.

Researchers and programmers generally agree that if only a development process such as ASPIT were followed carefully, high-quality software would result. Such a rigid process, however, is considered to be burdensome in practice, and hence is eschewed by many software developers [Parnas 86]. It would be perilous for us, as researchers, to ignore this sentiment, and simply admonish programmers to "get with it". It is far better to seek out the reasons behind the sentiment and address them directly.

Programmers feel they can work more efficiently without having to conform to a strict development process. We believe that, given the state-of-the-art, this observation is accurate. It is supported by anecdotal evidence relating how much faster individuals (who operate as best suit themselves) can work compared to large organizations (where the programmers are constrained to follow a formal development process). A major cause of the inefficiency associated

Stage	Typical notation
A: Analysis	Entity/relation diagram
S: Specification	VDM, Z, Larch
P: Prototype	SmallTalk, Prolog
I: Implementation	Pascal
T: Tuned implementation	C language

Figure 1: ASPIT Notations
Typical notations for the ASPIT stages of software development.

with the development process is the cognitive inefficiency of being forced to cross large semantic gaps between development stages over and over again.

There are two kinds of semantic gaps: those concerning programming in-the-small and those concerning programming in-the-large. In addition, there is a cognitive gap between the ideal development process (which operates as a time progression), and the way many programmers prefer to work (which appears more haphazard). We shall first discuss the semantic gaps in-the-small, and then the other gaps.

Figure 2 shows the semantic gaps that operate in-the-small. These gaps occur between the stages of the ASPIT development process.

1) *A-S gap (between analysis and specification)*: Typically, a programmer analyzes a problem by drawing diagrams and contemplating the appropriate sequence of operations. To formally specify a problem, however, the programmer must undergo a *paradigm shift* [Holt 91], and begin thinking in terms of model-oriented methods (or, worse still, property-oriented algebraic methods) that relate inputs to outputs using predicates. We admit that for some problems predicate-oriented specifications are very natural, but for many others they are not. This mismatch between a programmer's familiar thought processes and the thought process needed to formally specify a problem constitutes a semantic gap.
2) *S-P and P-I gaps (between specification, prototyping, and implementation)*: If a distinct prototyping language, such as Smalltalk, is used, it is typically radically different in syntax and concept from both the specification language and the implementation language. Having to shift frameworks when moving among these stages is inefficient.
3) *S-I gap (between specification and implementation)*: If a distinct prototyping language is not used, the gap between specification and implementation becomes very large. An implementation language, being by definition efficiently implementable on standard computer architectures, forces premature optimization, since only efficiently executable types and statements are legal. To implement a formal specification, a programmer must not only switch notations, but also "shift gears" mentally from the abstract mathematical world of sets, sequences, and predicates, to the concrete operational world of arrays, pointers, and statements. The absence of intermediate stages to smooth this transition entails a major semantic gap.†

† The two-tiered approach employed by Larch [Guttag 85] attempts to minimize the S-I gap by relating a (purely mathematical) specification with an implementation via a special interface language.

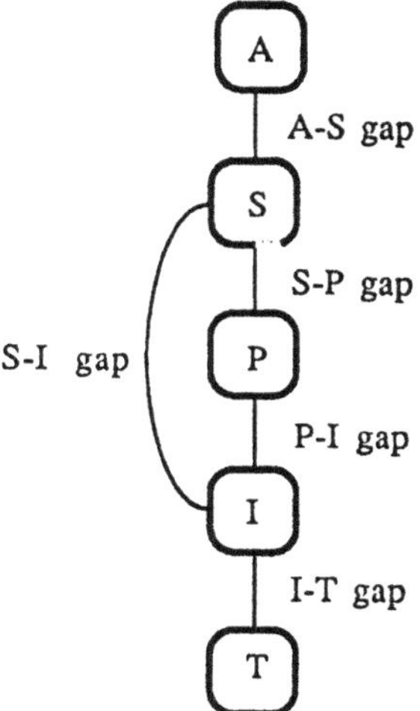

Figure 2: Interstage Semantic Gaps
Each gap incurs a paradigm shift and a need to validate consistency.

4) *I-T gap (between implementation and tuning)*: High-level programming languages featuring formal definitions, strong typing, and plenty of compile-time and run-time checking, such as Pascal or Turing, are natural initial targets when transforming specifications into programs. Such languages, however, are not generally suitable for systems programming, where machine-specific efficiency and access to the underlying implementation (such as the CPU registers) are important considerations. Unless two distinct programming languages are used (and this introduces another semantic gap), the gap between specification and tuned implementation becomes large.

Each of these *interstage* semantic gaps creates a barrier to the use of formal specification methods in the software development process, as well as creating a need to validate consistency. Because these gaps cause problems even when the size of the software to be developed is small, they are said to operate in-the-small. A semantic gap that shows up only when developing large software systems will now be considered.

In a large project the various stages of ASPIT, including specification, need to be decomposed into manageable chunks and these chunks glued together. There exist CASE tools that aid in software design, but they are typically not well-integrated with other tools. Moreover, there is usually no mechanism for helping the programmer keep the structure consistent between stages. For example, if a specification is decomposed in one way, and an implementation in another, then learning how the specification is structured is of no help in learning how the implementation is structured. This structural discontinuity between the stages of ASPIT is called the *design gap*. This gap is especially important because much of the time spent by programmers new to a project is devoted to understanding the overall structure of the system. If this has to be done more than once, a great deal of effort is wasted.

The design gap is an example of a semantic gap that operates only in-the-large. A problem with the development process that exists both in-the-large and in-the-small, however, is the idea of the development process as a time progression.

Large organizations often force programmers to follow the stages of ASPIT as a time progression in what is known as the *waterfall* model. The waterfall model allows feedback from a later stage to an earlier one, but in practice this is not encouraged ("You want to change the requirements NOW?"). The idea of the development process as a time progression is inconsistent with the way many programmers would operate by choice. For example, when creating a specification some programmers feel it is helpful to write some code first and then do the specification. Constraining programmers to progress linearly through the stages of ASPIT (including formal specification), whether or not they feel that is appropriate for their current project, creates another barrier to the use of formal specification.

By eliminating these problems, the cognitive cost of using formal specifications in the development process drops dramatically and formal specification can be integrated into the overall software development process.

3. Metamorphic Programming

In the remainder of the paper we discuss an approach that minimizes semantic gaps called *metamorphic programming*. In this section we explain some general concepts of metamorphic programming, and show how problems associated with viewing the development cycle as a time progression may be solved. In the following section, on metamorphic programming in-the-small, we show how interstage semantic gaps can be minimized by using a notation that operates over the entire range of expressibility, from analysis to formal specification to eventual tuned implementation. In the subsequent section, we reveal metamorphic programming in-the-small as the degenerate case of metamorphic programming in-the-large, and show how the design gap, which only operates in-the-large, may be minimized.

As the name implies, metamorphic programming strives to keep the outside view (the cocoon) of a software system complete and consistent despite gradual, but eventually radical, changes occurring within. Thus, all interfaces to the software under development remain constant after analysis has determined what they should be. After prototyping, when executable versions of the software become available, this "completeness" implies that all stages of the executable program implement the entire specification, albeit with vastly different performance characteristics.

Within the cocoon, gradual metamorphosis from any one ASPIT stage to an adjacent one is facilitated by minimizing interstage semantic gaps. Unlike a cocoon, however, all stages in the metamorphosis are considered to exist simultaneously. Work on the various stages may proceed sporadically and in any order. To complete an ASPIT version, all stages must be completed and be mutually consistent. This may be contrasted with the traditional view that the various stages of software development have as a goal the production of the final tuned implementation. Here the goal is to produce an ASPIT *version*, which records the entire development process as well as the final product.

Operating in this manner produces a development trail that can be followed by maintenance programmers, and aids the initial programmer in completely thinking out all aspects of the problem being solved. In terms of specification, this view holds that the benefit of producing a specification prior to coding is modest compared to the benefit of having a specification that is consistent with the documentation and code.

The idea that after analysis all interfaces to the code remain constant does not imply that changes to the requirements are not allowed. Rather, a requirements change is considered to create a new *configuration* of the system. Old, and possibly incomplete, configurations may be maintained, kept as historical records, or discarded. Related ideas will be discussed in more detail in the section on metamorphic programming in-the-large. First, however, we shall define metamorphic programming in-the-small, and show how it minimizes interstage semantic gaps.

4. Metamorphic Programming In-The-Small

When a problem is small enough that no explicit decomposition need be done to complete the ASPIT stages, we are considered to be operating in-the-small. Not being *explicitly decomposed* means that the programmer neither needs nor wants aid for recalling or describing the structure of the decomposition. For example, structure diagrams may be essential for understanding how the modules of a complex software system fit together. Similar diagrams showing how statements within a procedure fit together (such as *flowcharts*) are considered burdensome. When the capacity of the programmer's head is exceeded, we move to programming in-the-large.

Metamorphic programming in-the-small has as its goal the elimination of the semantic gaps between the stages of ASPIT. To achieve this, we introduce the idea of *notational continuity*, which means that the languages used to express each of the stages of ASPIT are conceptually and syntactically consistent.

The detailed design of languages satisfying notational consistency is considered to be of secondary importance to the prime objective. We propose a particular notation based on the Turing language, but the reader is encouraged to consider other possibilities, notably those based on VDM or Z [Di Giovanni 90]. Figure 3 illustrates notational consistency using our notation.

We consider that the best way to achieve notational consistency is to design dialects of a single language that blend together seamlessly [Goldberg 89]. The language, however, must achieve certain other goals which we shall now explain.

An overriding goal is that the language be capable of expressing concepts in the entire range from abstract mathematical specifications, to concrete machine-specific code. To bridge the initial gap between analysis (that uses natural language) and specification (that uses formal notation), the specification language must not stray too far from the proficient thought processes used by the programmer during analysis. Existing specification languages, such as VDM [Jones 90] and Z [Spivey 89], go a long way towards achieving this goal. Especially important in these languages is the ease with which predicates can be stated, and their use of high-level, abstract mathematical types such as sets sequences and maps, that more closely match a programmer's cognition than do machine-oriented data types.

To further minimize the gap between analysis and specification, formal specification must be made more *accessible* to the practitioner. One way to enhance accessibility is to introduce operational specifications. Sometimes it is easier to specify a problem as a predicate relating the input state to the output state, and sometimes it is easier to specify a problem as a sequence of sub-problems to be solved in a specified order. We do not argue that one approach is superior to the other, we simply recognize the fact that depending upon what is being specified, one may be more natural than the other, and therefore both should be allowed.

One aspect of many existing formal methodologies that limits accessibility is the need to include in predicates the fact that large parts of the state space remain unchanged. The mind naturally dwells on those things that change. To have to state explicitly that a thing remains unchanged may be mathematically convenient, but is contrary to natural thought. We shall propose a notation to solve this problem.

To bridge the gap between specification and prototyping, it is helpful for the specification language to support operational specification. An operational specification has the advantage that it is executable as a prototype. Thus, in metamorphic programming the prototyping language should be the same as the operational specification language, and should support the same data types, operations, and syntax as the specification language. In this way, the sole semantic gap between specification and prototype is the gap between predicate and operational specifications. To close this gap, the language should support a smooth transformation

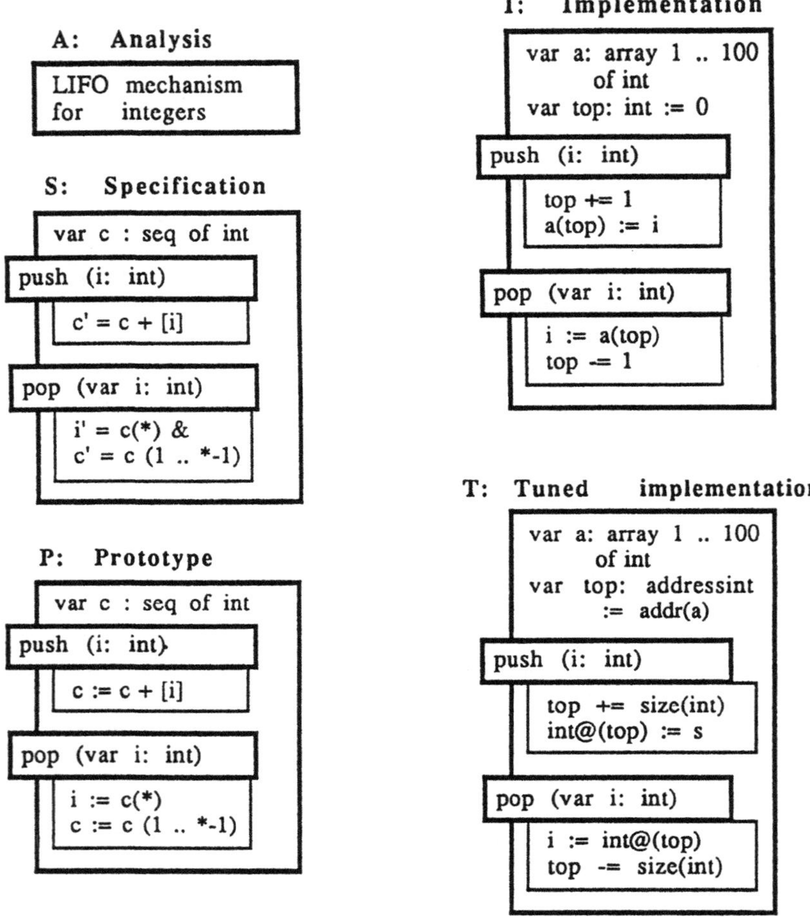

Figure 3: Notational Consistency
The ASPIT stages using a stack as an example.

between these two types of specifications. The closely related ideas of transformational programming [CIP 87], operational refinement ([Jones 90], [Morgan 90]) and predicative programming [Hehner 84], have been explored by others.

The smooth transformation from predicate to operational specification should be followed by a smooth transformation from prototype to efficient machine-oriented implementation. Machine-oriented in this context does not mean machine-dependent, but rather means formally defined but designed to be efficiently implementable on standard computer architectures.

In cases where machine-independent features are not efficient enough (as for parts of systems programs), the transformation must be allowed to continue to machine-specific code. Machine-specific language features typically have semantics that can be stated only with reference to a specific compiler implementation and target architecture.

By satisfying these goals, a single metamorphic programming language can support notational continuity in the full range of expressibility, from abstract mathematical specifications to machine-specific final code, yet remain accessible. The rest of the section discusses a notation designed to achieve these goals.

4.1. A Metamorphic Language: Dialects of Turing

Our specific example of designing a metamorphic notation concentrates on evolving a formally defined, machine-oriented language called Turing in two separate directions: towards more abstract mathematical features on one hand, and towards more machine specificity on the other. In this section, we introduce the notation and discuss the design of the existing dialects of Turing suitable for machine-oriented and machine-specific implementations. In the following subsections, we discuss the extension towards specification and prototyping. Figure 4 illustrates the evolution of *Turing* in the two directions.

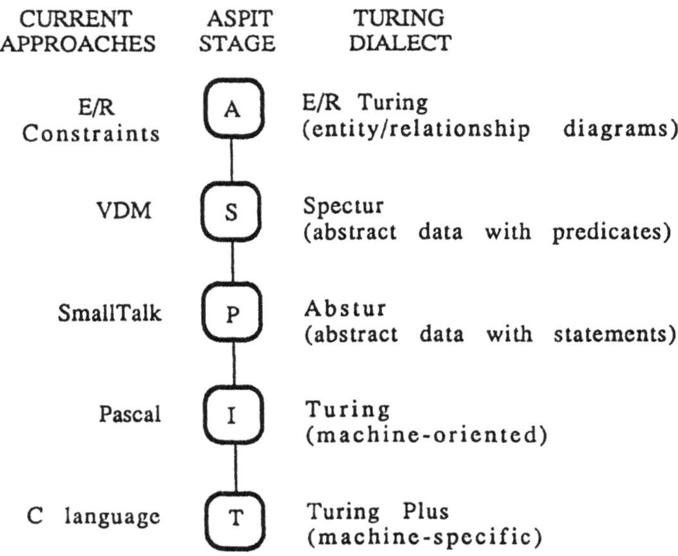

Figure 4: Notational Continuity
Semantic gaps are minimized using dialects of Turing in each ASPIT stage.

For machine specificity, we have taken as our goal to support the same expressibility, and run with the same efficiency, as the C language. For abstract mathematical features, we have taken as our goal to support the same level of expressibility as the VDM and Z notations. We start with Turing as the base, rather than VDM or Z, because we have a large community of Turing users and because we have expertise with Turing implementations. Thus our syntax is similar to Turing's syntax, and may not appeal to an expert in VDM or Z. The reader should bear in mind, however, that the ideas may be applied equally starting with VDM or Z as the base language.

The dialect of Turing called *Turing Plus* [Holt 88a] supports expressibility equivalent to that of the C language. The dialect called *Spectur* (Specification language for Turing), supports the same level of expressibility as VDM [Godfrey 90]. The *Abstur* dialect (Abstract

Turing) is the operational version of *Spectur*, and supports both operational specifications and prototyping at the same conceptual level as VDM. The dialect called *E/R* (Entity/Relation) *Turing* is used to record the major entities of a software system along with the relations between them and to provide a framework for recording the analysis (written in natural language) of these entities.

The base language, Turing (a direct descendant of the Pascal and Euclid languages), has a formally defined syntax and semantics [Holt 88b] — a complete formal specification of the Turing language has been published. The decomposition and writing of this large specification has given us some insights into the specification process. In addition to its formal definition, Turing supports complete and efficient legality checks at compile-time and run-time (this is called *faithful execution*) with descriptive error messages to indicate violations. Turing is designed to be efficiently implementable on standard computer architectures (*i.e.* runs as fast as C when checking is disabled), and at the same time be easy to learn and use (simple and consistent syntax and concepts). Turing implementations are available for many computers [Stephenson 90].

Turing, while useful as a general-purpose language, is not usable by itself for systems programming. Therefore, Turing has been extended by adding exception handlers, concurrency, and machine-dependent access to the underlying machine architecture. This extension to Turing, called Turing Plus, has been implemented on many different computers, in some cases by emitting C as the target language. So as not to confuse the formally-defined and machine-dependent parts of the language, the syntax is designed so that a programmer never gets machine-dependent features by default, but must explicitly write them in each case. Thus, a lexic scan of the program text is sufficient for determining if machine-dependent features are being used. One of the authors has used Turing Plus to write a 60,000 line 4.3BSD UNIX-compatible operating system for a large-scale multiprocessor. This operating system was developed by starting with an initial implementation written entirely with formally defined language features, and adapting (metamorphosing) it through the use of machine-specific features to the target architecture.

Thus, a consistent evolution of the Turing base language into one that supports machine-specific constructs has been completed successfully, with conceptual and syntactic consistency throughout. Our success in this direction encouraged us to try designing extensions in the opposite direction, towards the more abstract mathematical concepts used in VDM and Z, suitable for specification and prototyping.

This design has, in many cases, turned out to be more an exercise in removing mathematically arbitrary restrictions from Turing than in adding extra features.† We shall now describe the essential concepts of this design. Unlike the Turing and Turing Plus dialects, this evolution remains a paper exercise. First, we shall describe the Spectur dialect that is notationally continuous with respect to Turing and Turing Plus, and that supports model-oriented VDM-like specification. Following this we shall describe the Abstur dialect, which adds operational specification and prototyping to Spectur.

4.1.1. Spectur: Specification Language for Turing

To minimize semantic gaps between specification and implementation, we designed Spectur as a dialect of Turing [Godfrey 90]. Turing already supports **pre**, **post**, and **invariant** statements in modules and procedures, and a syntax for non-quantified boolean expressions. To evolve Turing towards a more VDM-like specification language, we have added quantification and abstract mathematical data types together with their constructors.

---

† De Man has described a similar experience [De Man 90].

The Turing language, which the reader may take to be a variant of Pascal, supports arrays, sets, and strings (character sequences). To provide Spectur with abstract types, we relax the restrictions that Turing makes on its types. To provide sequences of arbitrary types, we relax the restriction that a string is necessarily a sequence of characters. To provide sets of arbitrary types, we relax the Turing restriction that elements of sets must be index types (subranges and enumerated types). To provide maps, we relax the restriction that array subscripts must be index types. With these relaxations, the practitioner moves easily between the worlds of abstract specifications and efficient implementations.

To illustrate this concept, we give data types that can be used to specify an operating system disk cache. This example uses a map, which is effectively an array indexed by an arbitrary type. A disk cache keeps in-core copies of recently accessed disk blocks, so that disk requests can often avoid using the physical disk, which is comparatively slow. A particular disk block in a UNIX-like operating system is identified by a *DeviceAddress*, which lists the *major device identifier* (which disk driver to use), the *minor device identifier* (which disk controlled by that driver to use), and the *block address* (the block number on that disk). The in-core version of a disk block is kept in an array of bytes. With our extensions to allow maps and arbitrary sets, the cache's data can be declared as follows:

```
type Byte: 0..255

const BlockSize := 4096
type Block: array 0..BlockSize-1 of Byte

type DeviceAddress:
   record
       majorDeviceID: nat        /* A "nat" is a natural number */
       minorDeviceID: nat
       blockAddress : nat
   end record

/* Set of blocks currently controlled by the cache */
var cached: set of DeviceAddress

/* Block contents */
var cache: map DeviceAddress to Block
```

This disk cache, which the programmer may eventually implement by hashing *DeviceAddress* to find the associated 4K buffer, is specified easily and powerfully by allowing *DeviceAddress* to be the index type for the *cache* map, and by specifying currently active cache blocks using the *cached* set.

As another example, we shall use Spectur data types to specify a binary tree of integers. Each node of the tree is defined by its position relative to the root. A node's position is specified in terms of directions from the root of the tree to the node (*e.g.* go left, go right, go left). The nodes currently in the tree are given by the set *nodes*, the values of those nodes are given by the *data* map.

```
type Direction    : enum(left,right)
type Path   : sequence of Direction

var nodes   : set of Path
var data    : map Path to int
```

Since Spectur maps, sets, and sequences are generalizations of Turing arrays, sets, and strings, notational consistency is achieved by using the operators of the latter with the former.

A further restriction that may be removed from Turing to provide a more powerful language is the distinction between sets and types. If types are viewed as sets, and sets as types, this allows us to express the idea of variables only taking on values from a given set, as illustrated in this example (Hehner has expressed similar ideas [Hehner 84]).

type EvenInt: set of int := {i: int | i mod 2 = 0}
var x: EvenInt

In this section, we have shown how a specification language, Spectur, at the conceptual level of VDM or Z may be designed by extending a machine-oriented base language. The extensions consist of a handful of new features and a relaxation of Turing's existing context rules for types. These modifications result in a specification language which provides continuity with the programmer's thought processes used during analysis (through the use of data types such as those in VDM or Z), and with machine-oriented and machine-specific implementation languages (because the syntax and operators are all derived from the same base language). Spectur omits the operational parts of Turing, but the Abstur dialect, which will now be presented, includes them.

4.1.2. Abstur: For Operational Specifications and Prototyping

The *Abstur* (Abstract Turing) dialect of Turing is a prototyping language and a language used for operational specification. It is notationally consistent with the predicate specification language (Spectur) and the implementation languages (Turing and Turing Plus).

We mentioned earlier that one of our goals for a metamorphic programming language is the ability to merge operational specifications with predicate (pre/post) specifications. This is considered necessary to close the gap between analysis, where the programmer often thinks operationally, and specification. Furthermore, an operational specification language can also serve as a prototyping language.

Abstur inherits all the abstract data types of Spectur. The Spectur language does not allow procedures to have *bodies*, only pre and post-conditions. We could have designed Abstur to be the opposite, namely, to omit pre/post and to allow only bodies. Instead, to minimize the semantic gap between pre/post specification and prototyping, Abstur supports both pre/post and bodies. In Abstur, such a body can serve both as an operational specification and as a prototype implementation. Abstur is so closely blended with Turing on the one hand, and Spectur on the other, that the distinction is somewhat blurred. We consider this an advantage.

For example, to specify that the disk cache described above is to be flushed (written back to disk and invalidated), the following Abstur code could serve both as an operational specification and as a prototype implementation.

```
for deviceAddress: cached
   Device.WriteBlock(deviceAddress, cache(deviceAddress))
end for
cached := {}
```

In Turing proper, only index types are allowed as the bounds in for loops. However, when type restrictions of this sort are relaxed, and when types and sets are considered equivalent, this usage, which non-deterministically iterates through the members of the *cached* set, falls out naturally.

4.1.2.1. Handling Non-Determinism with the Pick Statement

One of the common criticisms levelled against operational specifications is that they overconstrain. To solve this difficulty, the **pick** statement, a non-deterministic assignment statement, is added to Abstur. This statement is used to specify non-determinism in operational specifications. The syntax of **pick** is:

pick *variableReference* [**:** *typeOrSet*]

For example, in specifying operating systems procedures, we found it common that successful completion is non-deterministic as it depends on unknown resource limitations [Godfrey 88]. This is specified as follows:

var success: boolean
pick success

The **pick** statement non-deterministically chooses a value for *success* from that variable's base type (boolean, in this case). The range of allowed values may be narrowed by specifying a particular set to pick from:

var j: int
pick j: {i: int | i mod 2 = 0}

This example non-deterministically chooses an even integer to assign to variable *i*. Note that **pick** is *not* the same as a random number generator — no particular distribution of results is guaranteed or even suggested. Using a **pick** in an operational specification specifies that any of the values in the given set is an acceptable solution to the problem being specified.

4.1.2.2. Mixing Predicates and Statements with the Attain Statement

So far the Abstur language allows operational specifications to be mixed with predicate specifications only at the level of a procedure. A more finely grained mixing is desirable, however, and so Abstur also includes the **attain** statement for inserting predicate specifications in-line with an operational specification.† The full syntax of **attain** is:

```
attain [import importedVariables]
  [pre preCondition]
  postCondition
  [by
     [pre preConditionForBy]
     Statements
  {elsby
     [pre preConditionForElsby]
     Statements}
  end by]
```

The simplest form of this statement gives nothing but the post-condition. First we shall discuss this post-condition then the optional parts of the statement.

The post-condition specifies a relationship between "before" and "after" values of the state. This does not have an immediate operational meaning (and hence cannot be used for prototyping) unless a **by** clause accompanies it (more on this later).

The values of variables after the **attain** are denoted using a prime ('), the values before are written without a prime. The prime may be attached to any reference that may be assigned to. The following example specifies a search of an integer array for an element with the value

† The specification statement of the Refinement Calculus [Morgan 90] is similar to Abstur's **attain** statement, but does not have an analogue of the **by** clause.

12:

```
var a: array 1..5 of int := init(14,12,15,43,2)
var i: 1..5
attain a(i') = 12 ∧ a'=a
```

This **attain** statement specifies that after completion, the new value of *i* should be set to the index of an element of *a* containing the value 12, and that the array *a* should not be changed.

An optional pre-condition may be attached to the **attain** statement to indicate explicitly the requirements for implementability of the predicate, and to record guaranteed knowledge of the state that an eventual implementation may assume. For example, the above predicate is not attainable unless a 12 exists in the array:

```
attain  pre ∃ i: 1..5 • a(i) = 12
   a(i') = 12  ∧  a'=a
```

Note that if the pre-condition is not actually met, an **attain** statement can be thought of as a *miracle* statement [Hehner 84] that attains the impossible.

4.1.2.3. The Frame Problem

Repeatedly stating those things that must remain unchanged, for example $a'=a$, becomes a significant nuisance when many large and complex data structures are involved. This is called the *frame problem*, and results from an insufficient narrowing of the scope of interest [Genesereth 87]. This problem can make pre/post specifications clumsier than the programmer wants to write or decipher.

To illustrate the frame problem, we present an example that we encountered when specifying a virtual memory manager. The major data types for this specification are:

```
type Descriptor: nat                    /* Each memory space has a unique Descriptor */
type VirtualAddress: nat

type SpaceRecord:
   record
      file  : File.Descriptor            /* File containing the initial memory image */
      bytes : map VirtualAddress to Byte  /* Contents of virtual memory */
   end record

var space: map Descriptor to SpaceRecord
```

The predicate used to state the simple concept of a given byte in a virtual memory space changing value (*i.e.* the *poke* operation) turns out to be rather tedious:

```
procedure poke (s: Descriptor, va: VirtualAddress, b: Byte)
   attain space(s).data(va)' = b ∧
      ∀ a: VirtualAddress •( a ≠ va  ⇒  space(s).bytes(a)' = space(s).bytes(a) ) ∧
      space(s).file' = space(s).file ∧
      ∀ d: Descriptor •( d ≠ s  ⇒  space(d)' = space(d) )
end poke
```

The first line of this post-condition is obvious and deals with change. The remaining lines (the confusing part) state simply that all the rest of the *space* data remains unchanged.

We shall outline three solutions to the frame problem, intended to make the use of pre/post specifications less tedious and hence more acceptable to the programmer. The first is the explicit use of an **import** list, which parallels import lists that Turing uses for procedures and modules. In this example, the **attain** can be simplified to:

attain import var space(s).data(va)
space(s).data(va)' = b

This import list effectively creates the additional predicates that specify that nothing but *space(s).data(va)* is allowed to change.

The second solution is the automatic creation of an import list based on a lexical scan of the predicate. This scan locates all primed (parts of) variables and effectively allows only them to be changed. In this example, the import would be implicitly created exactly as we have just given it explicitly.

The third solution is to implicitly define the import list based on the meaning (not just the lexic form) of the post-condition. This approach avoids a problem with lexically produced import lists, which is that semantically identical predicates may have have different import lists, and hence mean different things. This happens exactly when a primed item in a predicate can be removed by rewriting the predicate to another equivalent predicate.

To define an import list based on the meaning of the post-condition, we start by dividing the state into *atoms* of a language-defined granularity. Given a generic initial state, any atom which can possibly have an effect on the truth or falsity of the post-condition is included in the implicit import list. An atom would be, for example, an element of an array with a primitive type such as an integer.

We define the dependency relationship *dep(Q,a')* to be true when post-condition *Q* may possibly depend on the value of atom *a'*. Let *A'* be the set of all "after" atoms except *a'*.

$$dep(Q,a') \equiv \exists A' \bullet (\exists a' \bullet Q \wedge \exists a' \bullet not\ Q)$$

In other words, *Q* depends on *a'* for a given initial state if there exists a final state in which *Q* is true, and there exists another final state, differing only in the value of *a'*, in which *Q* is false. The implicit import list contains exactly those (parts of) variables that *Q* depends on. This import list can be written as a predicate stating which atoms remain unchanged as a function of the initial state, and this predicate should be considered to be implicitly conjoined with the post-condition. Using this technique, our example can be specified more concisely:

```
procedure poke (s: Descriptor, va: VirtualAddress, b: Byte)
   attain space(s).data(va)' = b
end poke
```

4.1.2.4. "By" Clauses to Maintain What-How Relationships

To complete the discussion of the **attain** statement, we now consider the use of the **by** clause which assigns an operational meaning to an **attain** statement. This feature is intended to provide a convenient path from predicate specifications to operational ones, and thus also to prototypes. The **by** clause maintains the *what-how* relationship between a predicate specification and an operational implementation. The *what* part is the predicate to be attained. The *how* part consists of the statements within the **by**. An example that uses the **by** clause is:

```
var a: array MIN..MAX of int
var i: MIN..MAX
const v := 12

attain pre ∃ j: MIN..MAX • a(j) = v
   a(i') = v
by
   i := 1
   loop
       exit when a(i) = 12
       i := i + 1
   end loop
elsby
   pre ∀ j: MIN..MAX-1 • a(j) <= a(j+1)
   binarySearch(a,MIN,MAX,v, i)
end by
```

Here, a predicate specification has been transformed into two alternative operational implementations, the first given in-line, and the second calling a procedure. The first **pre** describes the requirements for implementability of the predicate, and thus any operational specification must assume this. The first **by** clause is guaranteed to set *i* to an index of an element of *a* with value *v*, provided that such an element exists.

In general, *how* a predicate is attained may depend upon the context, and thus the precondition within the **elsby** clause in the example given above. The **elsby** clause provides an alternative implementation assuming, in addition to the implementability constraint, that the array is sorted.

The overall pre-condition for an **attain** statement is the conjunction of the explicit precondition for the **attain** with that of each of its **by** and **elsby** clauses. If the **attain**'s precondition is omitted, it is taken to be **true**.

In this section, we outlined the design of the Abstur operational specification and prototyping language. Abstur supports integrated operational and predicate specification through the use of Spectur data types, Turing statements and operators, and Abstur **pick** and **attain** statements.

5. Metamorphic Programming In-The-Large

Metamorphic programming in-the-small removes the semantic gaps between the stages of the ASPIT development process, serving to blend formal specifications smoothly into the development process. We have previously stated that when none of these ASPIT stages need to be decomposed explicitly, we are operating in-the-small. Conversely, if any of the stages do need to be decomposed, we are operating in-the-large.

All the ASPIT stages, including formal specification, require decomposition into parts when dealing with large systems. For example, the formal specification of the context conditions for the Turing language is based on seven distinct sub-specifications (of such things as type definitions), each of which is formally specified [Holt 88b]. Similarly, in any large system the other ASPIT stages eventually need to be broken into parts.

As we have mentioned before, when the decomposition into parts of one stage (such as specification) differs from the decomposition in another stage, we have a design gap. We call this difference in decomposition a *structural discontinuity*. Structural discontinuities are a particularly pernicious form of semantic gap, and a key goal of metamorphic programming in-the-large is to minimize them. Of the many problems to be solved in programming in-the-

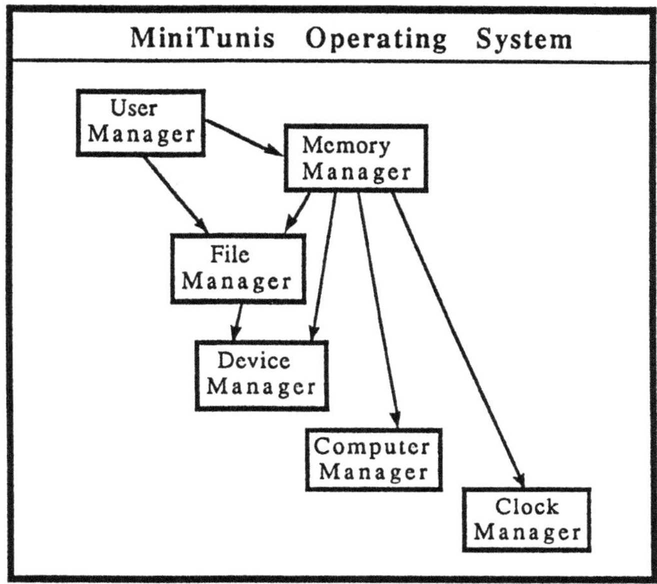

Figure 5: Design of a Software Object
The decomposition of the MiniTunis operating system.

large ([ISPW-4-88], [IWSCM-2-89]), we shall concentrate on this particular one, and its relationship to formal specifications.

Figure 5 shows an example of the decomposition of a piece of software. This shows the structure of the MiniTunis operating system, which is a model operating system used primarily for teaching about operating systems. MiniTunis [Penny 88] is essentially a simplified variant of UNIX. Even with simplification, it has an internal structure containing a number of subsystems. The development of the system as a whole goes through the ASPIT stages, and relies in turn on the completion of the ASPIT stages of its parts. This illustrates the fact that the ASPIT process is recursive, namely, a large software object goes through each of the A, S, P, I and T stages, and each of these in turn may require decomposition and further ASPIT development, and so on through the layers of decomposition.

In the fortuitous case, the parts into which one stage is decomposed (the specification, for example) will correspond exactly to the parts into which the other stages are decomposed. In simple systems, we can force this correspondence, but in large software systems we must recognize that complexity and changing requirements will eventually force discontinuities among the stages. Creating an underlying model that can accommodate such discontinuities during development, but which will in the end result in one structurally continuous version of the ASPIT process, is a goal of metamorphic programming in-the-large.

Figure 6 illustrates a particular software system called object *E*. The interface to the object, represented by its methods with their signatures, remains constant. However, there have been three distinct development cycles for the object, with distinct internal structures — version 1 is un-decomposed, version 2 is composed of sub-objects F1 and F2, and version 3 is composed of sub-objects G1, G2 and G3.

If *E* is an operating system, we can imagine that version 1 represents an initial naïve attempt to complete the entire project in-the-small (without decomposition). Versions 2 and 3 are two alternative decompositions. Version 2 is decomposed into a file manager (with embedded device management) and a memory manager. Version 3 is decomposed into a file manager, a distinct device manager, and a memory manager. Within a version, the decomposition of all stages is constrained to be identical to all others. Thus in each version the specification is structured in the same manner as the implementation. Indeed, we can take this to be the definition of a *version*, namely, that all of its ASPIT stages have the same structure.

The two basic reasons for beginning a new version are *structural decomposition* and *structural discontinuity*. In figure 6, versions 2 and 3 are structural decompositions of version 1. Version 2 and version 3 are structurally discontinuous.

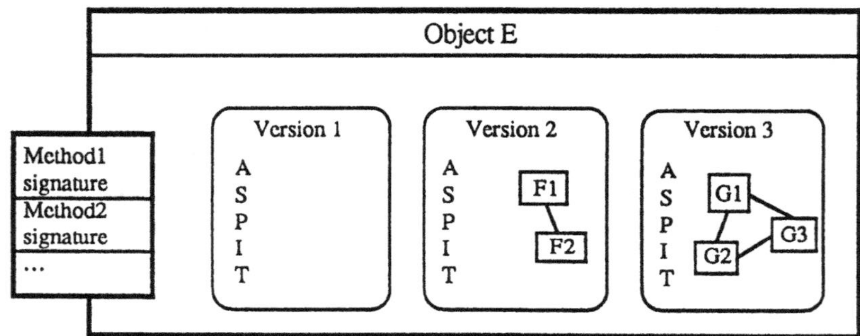

Figure 6: Structural Discontinuity
Object E has a particular signature and meaning.
There are three versions of E's internal structure.

In metamorphic programming, we typically start by assuming that any object can be completed in-the-small. Sometimes this works out, but often it does not. In the case of the MiniTunis operating system, it is feasible to perform the analysis entirely in-the-small. We may take version 1 in figure 6 to illustrate such an analysis.

To specify MiniTunis, however, the un-decomposed structure of version 1 is not suitable. Rather, it is necessary to decompose the specification into a *File Manager* object and a *Memory Manager* object.† Version 2 in figure 6 illustrates this case. Since the structure of the specification is more decomposed than that of the analysis, we have a mild form of structural discontinuity. To resolve this discontinuity, and produce a version of the ASPIT development process in which the specification is structurally continuous with respect to the other stages, we must complete version 2 using the same structure throughout all the stages. Completing version 2 entails writing ASPIT for sub-objects F1 and F2, and then writing the ASPIT for object *E* in terms of these sub-objects.

To implement MiniTunis, however, the structure of version 2 turns out to be inherently inefficient, because all access to the disk, including the heavily used paging access from the

† The formal specification of the MiniTunis file manager [Godfrey 88] can be contrasted with the formal specification of the UNIX file system that was done by Morgan and Sufrin using a Z-like notation [Morgan 84].

Memory Manager, is constrained to go through the *File Manager* object. During implementation of version 2 this fact was discovered, and thus version 3 was started. For version 3, the *Device Manager* object is moved up a level in the decomposition. Versions 2 and 3 now exhibit a strong form of structural discontinuity in that the decomposition of the specification from version 2 is different from that of the implementation from version 3. To resolve this discontinuity, and produce a version of the ASPIT development process in which all stages are structurally continuous, we must complete version 3. As for any other version, completing version 3 entails writing ASPIT for all its sub-objects (G1, G2, and G3), and then writing the ASPIT for object *E* in terms of these sub-objects.

Being recursive, whatever applies to an object applies equally to its sub-objects. Thus sub-objects will, in general, consist of several versions in various stages of completion. Note that an object is considered complete once *at least one* complete ASPIT version of that object, and all its sub-objects, has been produced.

From this discussion, the key conclusion with respect to formal specifications is that it is essential for the structure of the specification to match that of the rest of the version. If this is not the case, the programmer attempting to understand the structure of an object will waste time learning, in turn, the structures of each of the stages separately. The implication, therefore, is that the specification must be divided carefully into parts that are suitable for implementation. If this is not the case, the implementation will no doubt adopt a conflicting structure, at considerable cost in terms of the overall development. The usual case, when such a conflict occurs, is to abandon the specification and carry on modifying the implementation. The way to make sure the specification will continue to be of value is to update it repeatedly along with the implementation and all other stages. This in turn demands minimization of semantic gaps throughout all aspects of the development process.

Checking for the structural continuity of a version can be largely mechanized, given notational continuity among the stages. Lacking such support, the headache of repeated manual checking of the information in each stage is likely to be too much for the programmer to manage. In the following section we shall take a look at tools, such as ones to help solve this problem, required to support metamorphic programming.

6. Software Development Environment

Most professional software developers make extensive use of support tools, and there is a large amount of work in progress to integrate tools into software development environments [ISPW-4-88]. For formal specifications to be used widely in software development, they must be supported by tools that are well-integrated into these environments.

The metamorphic approach to programming provides a basis for accomplishing this integration. For development in-the-small, notational consistency immediately implies the possibility of a common computer representation for object interfaces across the ASPIT stages. For example, figure 3 shows that the methods of a object can be represented identically across the stages. This allows the environment to mechanically check consistency among stages, or even to automatically generate the interface part of an incomplete stage based on that of other stages.

Figure 3 gives five distinct views of a software object, corresponding to each of the ASPIT stages. Ideally, the programmer considers the object as a coherent whole that can be viewed in these various ways. The environment should support this concept by presenting a graphic icon representing the object, and allowing the programmer to view or expand it, by selecting, for example, the S (specification) option.

For development in-the-large, the environment should maintain the relationship among the sub-objects of an object, which in turn means there must be a mechanical record of the object's structure. There should be an option to display this structure graphically, in a format such as that shown in figure 5, as is already done in many CASE tools (such as [Coad 90]). Many of the structural relations, such as those given by import lists, have an obvious computerized representation and can be enforced automatically across the stages of a given version of an object. In other words, the environment can automatically prevent or detect structural discontinuities.

If we view the software development process as the continuing creation of software objects for installation in a re-use library, we see that the metamorphic programming approach provides considerable advantages beyond those provided to a single project. The new advantage is that we gain a single paradigm by which the software professional browses, understands, updates, etc., the rather large set of software objects available to be used in ongoing projects. This comes about because the library itself is organized as objects, each of which has an ASPIT organization and is in turn composed of more sub-objects of a similar nature.

Returning to the idea of object decomposition, we see that the designer should strive continually to divide an object into parts that already exist in the library, or conversely, to combine existing objects to create new objects of general utility.

The idea of a single development paradigm is one of the "holy grails" of object-oriented computing. What we have tried to clarify is how formal specification can be fitted smoothly and profitably into such a paradigm. In this view, a specification is not thought of as an end unto itself, but rather as a stage that is an integral part of a software development system.

7. Conclusions

In this paper we have argued that *semantic gaps* are a primary reason why formal specification techniques such as VDM or Z have not been accepted more generally by practitioners. These gaps correspond to *paradigm shifts* for the professional programmer, in other words, to significantly different ways of understanding the software under development. After having identified these gaps in the software development process, especially those related to specification, we showed how they can be minimized using an approach called *metamorphic programming* that operates both in-the-large and in-the-small.

The main contribution that metamorphic programming makes to formal specification is to clarify the ways in which specifications can be merged smoothly into the software development lifecycle.

References

[Bjorner90] D. Bjorner, C. A. R. Hoare and H. Langmaack (eds.), *VDM '90: VDM and Z — Formal Methods in Software Development — Proc. of the Third International Symposium of VDM Europe 1990, Kiel FRG*, Springer-Verlag LNCS #428, April 1990.

[CIP-87] *The Munich Project CIP — Volume 2: The Program Transformation System CIP-S*, Springer-Verlag LNCS #292, 1987.

[Coad90] Peter Coad and Edward Yourdon, *Object-Oriented Analysis*, Prentice Hall, Englewood Cliffs NJ, 1990.

[DeMan90] Jozef De Man, "Making Languages More Powerful by Removing Limitations", *Proc. of ACM SIGSOFT International Workshop on Formal Methods in Software Development*, ACM Software Engineering Notes, vol. 15, no. 4, September 1990.

[DiGiovanni90] R. Di Giovanni and P. L. Iachini, "HOOD and Z for the Development of Complex Software Systems", in [Bjorner et al 90].

[Genesereth87] Michael R. Genesereth and N. Nilsson, *Logical Foundations of Artificial Intelligence*, Morgan Kaufmann, Los Altos CA, 1987.

[Godfrey88] Michael W. Godfrey, *Toward Formal Specification of Operating System Modules*, M.Sc. thesis, Dept. of Computer Science, Univ. of Toronto, May 1988.

[Godfrey90] Michael W. Godfrey and Richard C. Holt, "Spectur — A Specification Language for the Programmer", Technical Report CSRI-241, Univ. of Toronto, June 1990.

[Goldberg89] A. Goldberg and D. Robson, *Smalltalk-80: The Language*, Addison-Wesley, Reading MA, 1989.

[Guttag85] J. V. Guttag, J. J. Horning, and J. M. Wing, "Larch in Five Easy Pieces", Technical Report 5, Digital Equipment Corporation Systems Research Center, July 1985.

[Hehner84] E. C. R. Hehner, "Predicative Programming, parts 1 and 2", *Communications of the ACM*, vol. 27, no. 2, February 1984.

[Holt88a] R. C. Holt and J. R. Cordy, "The Turing Programming Language", *Communications of the ACM*, vol. 31, no. 12, December 1988.

[Holt88b] R. C. Holt, P. A. Matthews, J. A. Rosselet, and J. R. Cordy, *The Turing Programming Language: Design and Definition*, Prentice Hall International, 1988.

[Holt91] R. C. Holt, Terry Stanhope and George Lausman, "Object Oriented Computing: Looking Forward to Year 2000", ITRC Tech. Report TR-9101, Information Technology Research Centre, Univ. of Toronto, April 1991.

[ISPW-4-88] *Proc. of the Fourth International Software Process Workshop* ACM SIGSOFT Engineering Notes, vol. 14, no. 4, June 1988.

[IWSCM-2-89] *Proc. of the Second International Workshop on Software Configuration Management*, ACM SIGSOFT Engineering Notes, vol. 17, no. 7, November 1989.

[Jones90] C. B. Jones, *Systematic Software Development Using VDM*, Second Edition, Prentice Hall International, 1990.

[Meyer85] B. Meyer, "On Formalism in Specification", *IEEE Software*, vol. 2, no. 1, January 1985.

[Morgan84] C. Morgan and B. Sufrin, "Specification of the UNIX Filing System", *IEEE Trans. on Software Engineering*, vol. 10, no. 2, March 1984, pp 128-142.

[Morgan90] Carroll Morgan, *Programming from Specifications*, Prentice Hall International, 1990.

[Neumann89] Peter G. Neumann, "Flaws in Specifications and What To Do About Them", *Proc. of the Fifth International Workshop on Software Specification and Design*, ACM SIGSOFT Engineering Notes, vol. 14, no. 3, May 1989.

[Parnas86] David L. Parnas and Paul C. Clements, "A Rational Design Process: How and Why to Fake it", *IEEE Trans. on Software Engineering*, vol. SE-12, no. 2, February 1986.

[Penny88] David A. Penny and Richard C. Holt, "The Concurrent Programming of Operating Systems using the Turing Plus Language", Course Notes, Dept. of Computer Science, Univ. of Toronto, 1988.

[Stephenson90] C. Stephenson and R. C. Holt, "Changing Trends is High School Programming", *Educational Computing Organization of Ontario Output*, vol. 11, no. 2, July 1990.

[Spivey89] J. M. Spivey, *The Z Notation: A Reference Manual*, Prentice Hall International, 1989.

[Wing90] Jeannette M. Wing, "A Specifier's Introduction to Formal Methods", *IEEE Computer*, vol. 23, no. 9, September 1990.

Formalizing Design Spaces: Implicit Invocation Mechanisms

David Garlan
School of Computer Science
Carnegie Mellon University
Pittsburgh, PA 15213 USA

David Notkin
Dept. of Computer Science & Engineering
University of Washington
Seattle, WA 98195 USA

Abstract

An important goal of software engineering is to exploit commonalities in system design in order to reduce the complexity of building new systems, support large-scale reuse, and provide automated assistance for system development. A significant roadblock to accomplishing this goal is that common properties of systems are poorly understood. In this paper we argue that formal specification can help solve this problem. A formal definition of a design framework can identify the common properties of a family of systems and make clear the dimensions of specialization. New designs can then be built out of old ones in a principled way, at reduced cost to designers and implementors.

To illustrate these points, we present a formalization of a system integration technique called implicit invocation. We show how many previously unrelated systems can be viewed as instances of the same underlying framework. Then we briefly indicate how the formalization allows us to reason about certain properties of those systems as well as the relationships between different systems.

1 Introduction

Software systems are rarely conceived in isolation. Instead, most systems represent a new instance of a product in some family of related systems, be they accounting systems, database products, or compilers. Each system typically shares with other applications in its family a common "framework" of behavioral and structural properties. An important goal of software engineering is to improve software productivity by exploiting these frameworks to reduce the complexity of building systems, support large-scale reuse, and provide automated assistance for system development.

Broadly speaking, we have not been very successful in doing this. With the exception of certain specialized domains (eg., spreadsheets, report generation, compiler construction), most systems are treated as an innovative development effort. Commonalities in design, if exploited at all, influence development primarily through past experience of builders who apply their knowledge in ad hoc and unstructured ways. As a result there is a proliferation of system designs and implementation mechanisms, even when the resulting products have many features in common.

There are two fundamental reasons for our failure to exploit commonalities in design. First, differences in system design often reflect important differences in system requirements. As an example, consider the diversity of tool integration mechanisms found in programming environments. Even though most modern environments share a common goal of integrating a set of program development tools, an environment that is required to incorporate existing tools may well lead to a different design for tool integration than one in which all tools are hand-crafted for the environment.

The second reason for the proliferation of designs, however, is that the common properties of those designs are poorly understood. Consequently it is hard to take advantage of previous experiences when designing a system, even though the new system may have much in common with existing systems. (Approaches such as object-oriented design, JSP/JSD, etc., do not directly address this problem, since they give guidance for how to construct specific designs rather than for understanding or relating families of designs.)

In this paper we argue that formal specification can help solve this problem. First, a formal definition of a design framework can identify the common properties of a family of systems. This makes it possible to see how previously unrelated systems can be treated as instances of the same underlying design. Second, if carried out properly, the formalization can make clear the dimensions of specialization that can be used to turn an abstract design framework into a design for a particular application. In this way, new designs can be built out of old ones in a principled way, at reduced cost to designers and implementors.

To illustrate these points, we present a formalization of a system integration technique, called implicit invocation. We show how many previously unrelated systems can be viewed as instances of the same underlying framework. Then we briefly indicate how the formalization allows us to reason about certain properties of those systems as well as the relationships between different systems.

2 Implicit Invocation Mechanisms

Complex systems are typically composed out of many components, such as data types, objects, tools, knowledge sources, etc. A fundamental issue in the development of these systems is the choice of mechanism for integrating those components. Certainly the most common integration mechanism is explicit invocation: components interact directly by calling routines in other components. These "routines" may be interface routines of abstract data types, invocation commands of tools, methods of objects, explicit queries of databases, etc.

However, there is another mechanism — implicit invocation — that is also becoming a widespread technique for organizing systems. The idea behind implicit invocation is that actions performed by one component in a system may cause the invocation of routines in other components in the system, without the original component having explicit static references to those other components. (We will make the definitions of the terms "action" and "component" precise later.)

For example, in the Field system [Reiss 90], tools such as editors and variable monitors can register interest in a debugger's actions related to breakpoints. Then, when the debugger stops at a breakpoint, it announces an event that allows the system to automatically invoke methods in those registered tools.[1] These methods might scroll an editor to the appropriate source line or redisplay the value of monitored variables. In this scheme, the debugger simply announces an event, but does not know what other tools (if any) are concerned with that event, or what they will do when that event is

[1]In the remainder of this paper we will refer to the interface routines of a component as its "methods".

announced.

The widespread interest in implicit invocation mechanisms arises for at least two reasons. First, implicit invocation mechanisms make it easier to build systems that relieve users from having to explicitly invoke related components. For example, a user interface might use implicit invocation to automatically update multiple views of the same data when the user changes that data. Implicit invocation makes systems like these easier to build because complex interactions between components need not be directly encoded in the components themselves. In this way, components can be built largely independently, but still work together in supporting a user's goals. Second, implicit invocation mechanisms reduce the cost of system evolution [Sullivan & Notkin 90]. In particular, because components are loosely coupled, it is possible to integrate new components without affecting the components that implicitly invoke the new components. This makes it possible to evolve an environment more easily over time, as well as to configure an environment dynamically.

Examples of systems with implicit invocation mechanisms abound. They are used in programming environments to integrate tools [Reiss 90, Gerety 89], in database management systems to ensure consistency constraints [Hewitt 69, Balzer 86], in user interfaces to separate presentation of data from applications that manage the data [Krasner & Pope 88], and by syntax-directed editors to support incremental semantic checking [Habermann & Notkin 86, Habermann et al. 91]. They also appear in spreadsheets, blackboard systems, attribute grammar systems, constraint-based systems, as well as many other kinds of systems.

Typically each such implicit invocation mechanism has been produced as a separate and innovative design, at significant intellectual and developmental cost. As we mentioned earlier, one of the reasons for this duplication of effort is that those mechanisms have rather different goals. However, a perhaps more significant reason is that commonalities between the mechanisms have not been understood, or, until recently, even recognized [Garlan et al. 90]. In the remainder of this paper we show how formal specification can help make these relationships clear. We present an abstract model of implicit invocation, based on the notion of event announcement. Then we illustrate how specific designs are obtained by elaborating this abstract model.

3 A Formal Model for Implicit Invocation

Abstractly, an implicit invocation mechanism can be modelled as a collection of components, each of which has an interface that specifies a set of methods and a set of events. As is traditionally the case, the methods define operations that other components can explicitly invoke. The events, however, define actions that the component promises to announce to other components in the system. The implicit invocation mechanism must also provide a way to associate events with methods that are to be invoked when those events are announced.

We now formalize these ideas in three steps using the Z specification language. First, we define the state space of the basic model. Next we define an abstract run-time model that explains how events are announced and handled by an implicit invocation system. Finally, we show how the model can be used to define existing systems, additionally illustrating how it allows us to reason about relationships between some of these systems.

3.1 The Basic Model

We begin by assuming there exist sets of events, methods, and component names, which, for the time being, we will simply treat as primitive types.

$[EVENT, METHOD, CNAME]$

A component is modelled as an entity that has a name and an interface consisting of a set of *methods* and a set of *events*.

Component

$name : CNAME$
$methods : \mathbb{P}\ METHOD$
$events : \mathbb{P}\ EVENT$

A particular event (or method) is identified by a pair consisting of the name of a component and the event (or method) itself. In this way we can talk about the same event or method appearing in different components. We use the type abbreviations *Event* and *Method* to refer to these pairs (respectively).

$Event == CNAME \times EVENT$
$Method == CNAME \times METHOD$

For convenience we define the functions *Events* and *Methods*, which extract the set of components and methods from a collection of components.

$Events : \mathbb{P}\ Component \rightarrow \mathbb{P}\ Event$
$Methods : \mathbb{P}\ Component \rightarrow \mathbb{P}\ Method$

$Events\ cs = \{c : cs;\ e : EVENT \mid e \in c.events \bullet (c.name, e)\}$
$Methods\ cs = \{c : cs;\ m : METHOD \mid m \in c.methods \bullet (c.name, m)\}$

An event system, *EventSystem*, consists of a set of components and an event manager. The event manager, *EM*, is a binary relation associating events and methods that should be invoked when that event is announced. Thus, as we will see later, when an event e is announced, all methods related to it by *EM* are invoked in the corresponding components.

EventSystem

$components : \mathbb{P}\ Component$
$EM : Event \leftrightarrow Method$

$\forall c_1, c_2 : components \bullet (c_1.name = c_2.name) \Leftrightarrow (c_1 = c_2)$
$\mathrm{dom}\ EM \subseteq Events\ components$
$\mathrm{ran}\ EM \subseteq Methods\ components$

The state invariant of *EventSystem* asserts that the components in the system have unique names, and that the event manager contains only events and methods that actually exist in the system.

This characterization of *EM* is an extremely general one. In particular, this model allows the same event to be associated with many different methods, and even with many methods in the same component. It also permits some events to be associated with no methods. Further, it leaves open the issue of what components can announce events, and whether there are any restrictions on the methods that can be associated with those events

3.2 Run-Time Model.

To give meaning to *EventSystem* it is necessary to say how it behaves. There are two basic operations to consider. The first operation allows a component to "announce" an event, and the second abstractly allows the system to choose an event and then invoke the methods associated with it.

Both operations are accommodated by a run-time model for an event system that associates a set of announced events with that system. This set contains events that have been raised but not yet been handled. We will insist, however, that announced events are in fact ones that the event manager can handle.

RunTimeSystem

$$\begin{array}{l} EventSystem \\ announced : \mathbb{P}\ Event \\ \hline announced \subseteq Events\ components \end{array}$$

Announcing an event is straightforward: an component can only announce one of its own events, and the effect is simply to add the event to *announced*.

Announce

$$\begin{array}{l} \Delta RunTimeSystem \\ announcer? : Component \\ event? : EVENT \\ \hline announcer? \in components \\ event? \in announcer?.events \\ \Xi EventSystem \\ announced' = announced \cup \{(announcer?.name, event?)\} \end{array}$$

The run-time behavior of an event system is determined largely by the run-time behavior of the components—that is, by the way they handle method invocations. There are many possible models for this behavior. However, for the purpose of abstractly modelling an event system, we simply assume the existence of a run-time operation *InvokeMethods* that, given a set of methods, invokes them in some system-specific way to change the state of the components in the system.

InvokeMethods

$$\begin{array}{l} \Delta RunTimeSystem \\ methods : \mathbb{P}\ Method \\ \hline methods \subseteq Methods\ components \end{array}$$

We assume as a precondition of *InvokeMethods* that the methods to be invoked are *bone fide* methods of the *EventSystem*, but say nothing about the result of having invoked those methods.

This definition naturally leaves open many aspects of *InvokeMethods*. Any implementation of such a system would have to make numerous decisions, such as the order in which the methods are invoked, whether methods can be invoked concurrently, whether methods can change the set of components in the system, how new events are announced as a side effect of method invocation, etc.

Events are handled in two phases. First, an event is selected and removed from the set of announced events. No other aspect of the run-time system changes during this phase. Second, the selected event is "propagated" by invoking the methods associated with that event.

$$\begin{array}{|l}\hline \textit{Select} \\ \Delta \textit{RunTimeSystem} \\ e' : \textit{Event} \\ \hline e' \in \textit{announced} \\ \textit{announced}' = \textit{announced} \setminus \{e'\} \\ \theta \textit{EventSystem} = \theta \textit{EventSystem}' \\ \hline \end{array}$$

We intentionally do not say how the event is chosen, but leave that decision to vary from system to system.

$$\begin{array}{|l}\hline \textit{Propagate} \\ \Delta \textit{RunTimeSystem} \\ e : \textit{Event} \\ \hline \exists\, \textit{methods} : \mathbb{P}\ \textit{Method} \mid \textit{methods} = \textit{EM}\,(\!|\{e\}|\!) \bullet \textit{InvokeMethods} \\ \hline \end{array}$$

Finally, we put the two parts together to obtain the operation *HandleEvent*.

$$\textit{HandleEvent} \mathrel{\widehat{=}} \textit{Select} \mathbin{;} \textit{Propagate}$$

In these definitions we do not place any restrictions on the computations performed by the components through explicit (method) invocation as a consequence of *HandleEvent*.

This definition of a run-time model is so abstract as to be of little direct practical use, although it is needed to make clear the context in which an event system is used. In fact, the schemas defining the model can be thought of as placeholders that would require specialization to define a given concrete system. However, rather than discuss these run-time specializations, in the remainder of the paper we focus instead on the specializations of *EventSystem* itself.

3.3 Specializations

To show how this general framework can be specialized we consider five specific systems. The first system is the basis for the user interface design of Smalltalk-80. The next two are examples associated with databases in programming environments. The last two are tool integration mechanisms for systems constructed out of existing Unix-based tools. For purposes of illustration and comparison we will focus primarily on programming environment examples, although the model applies equally well to a much broader class of systems [Garlan et al. 90]. In each case we will refine the definition of *EventSystem* in one of two ways: by elaborating the elements of *EVENT* and *METHOD*; and by constraining the way *EM* is defined.

Smalltalk-80 MVC. Our first specialization is the implicit invocation mechanism that supports the Smalltalk-80 Model-View-Controller (MVC) paradigm [Goldberg & Robson 83]. This mechanism is based on the notion that any object can register as a "dependent" of any other object. When an object announces the "changed" event, the "update" method is implicitly invoked in each of its dependents. Thus the MVC provides a fixed, predetermined set of events (namely the "changed" event) and associated methods (namely the "update" method).[2]

To model this mechanism formally we first state that the *changed* event and *update* method are elements of types *EVENT* and *METHOD*, respectively.

$$\begin{array}{l} changed : EVENT \\ update : METHOD \end{array}$$

Next, we model dependencies between objects as a relation between components. This dependency relation then precisely determines the *EM* relation as follows: first, the events associated with each component is restricted to the set $\{changed\}$; and second, *EM* simply pairs *changed* events with the appropriate *update* methods.

ST80

$$\begin{array}{l} EventSystem \\ dependents : Component \leftrightarrow Component \\ \hline \mathrm{dom}\ dependents \subseteq components \\ \mathrm{ran}\ dependents \subseteq components \\ \forall\, c : components \bullet c.events = \{changed\} \\ EM = \{c_1, c_2 : components \mid (c_1, c_2) \in dependents \bullet \\ \qquad ((c_1.name, changed), (c_2.name, update))\} \end{array}$$

Note that a consequence of the invariant of *EventSystem* is that each dependent in the system must have *update* as one its methods. We could formulate this as a lemma—albeit a simple one—to be proved about such a system. In its implementation, Smalltalk-80 supports this lemma by providing a default *update* method in the Object class, at the top of the class hierarchy.

APPL/A. The next specialization is the implicit invocation mechanism of APPL/A [Sutton, Heimbigner & Osterweil 90], an Ada-based language that supports process programming. APPL/A's implicit invocation mechanism was inspired by mechanisms to support consistency in entity-relation databases [Hewitt 69, Balzer 86]. Its event mechanism has two basic restrictions. First, relations—instances of a special type constructor in APPL/A—are the only components that can announce events. Other components, such as variables, packages, and tasks, communicate only through explicit invocation. Second, a relation can only announce one of the following predefined events: insert, delete, update, find.[3] These events correspond to the primitive operations that can be performed on relations.

To model this formally we declare the events specific to this mechanism.

$$insert\_e, delete\_e, update\_e, find\_e : EVENT$$

---

[2] Actually, there are three versions of the *changed* event: one with no parameters, one with one parameter, and one with two parameters. There are also three corresponding versions of the *update* method. Also, it should be pointed out that although Smalltalk-80 is flexible enough to program alternative implementations of an implicit invocation mechanism, the MVC paradigm does not take advantage of this flexibility.

[3] Actually, each of these four event types has two flavors: accept and complete.

Next, we identify a distinguished set of components, called *relations*. These are the only components that can announce events and hence all other components in the system have an empty set of events. These restrictions are summarized in the schema *APPL_A*.

$$
\begin{array}{l}
\textit{APPL\_A} \\
\hline
\textit{EventSystem} \\
\textit{relations} : \mathbb{P}\ \textit{Component} \\
\hline
\textit{relations} \subseteq \textit{components} \\
\forall r : \textit{relations} \bullet r.\textit{events} = \{\textit{insert\_e}, \textit{delete\_e}, \textit{update\_e}, \textit{find\_e}\} \\
\forall c : \textit{components} \setminus \textit{relations} \bullet c.\textit{events} = \varnothing \\
\hline
\end{array}
$$

Gandalf. The third mechanism is the "daemon" invocation mechanism of the Gandalf System [Habermann & Notkin 86]. Gandalf uses implicit invocation to provide (among other things) incremental, static semantic checking for programs. The user creates a program by incrementally building an abstract syntax tree. As nodes are added to the tree, daemons associated with those nodes are activated to do type checking, provide incremental code generation, etc.

Gandalf is similar to APPL/A insofar as it defines a fixed set of events. (Likewise, these events correspond to the primitive operations that can be performed on nodes in the abstract syntax tree.) For the purposes of this exposition, we adopt the same set. Gandalf also imposes some additional structure. First, as we have said, Gandalf has two kinds of components: abstract syntax trees (ASTs) and daemons. Second, only the nodes in an AST can announce events. Third, each node in an AST is paired with at most one daemon, which is responsible for handling all events announced by its node. Thus each daemon has a set of methods corresponding precisely to the events that a node can announce.

To model the Gandalf implicit invocation mechanism we define the names of methods supported by daemons (*insert*, *delete*, ...) , and then restrict the event mechanism as indicated.[4]

$$
\begin{array}{|l}
\textit{Node}, \textit{Daemon} : \mathbb{P}\ \textit{Component} \\
\textit{insert\_m}, \textit{delete\_m}, \textit{update\_m}, \textit{find\_m} : \textit{METHOD}
\end{array}
$$

[4]In these definitions we assume there exists a generic type constructor *TREE* and a function *nodes* that yields the set of nodes in a tree. These are easily added to the mathematical toolkit, in the style of the Z Reference Manual [Spivey 89].

$$
\begin{array}{l}
\textit{Gandalf} \\
\hline
\textit{EventSystem} \\
AST : TREE[Node] \\
daemons : \mathbb{P}\ Daemon \\
ND : Node \twoheadrightarrow Daemon \\
\hline
\mathrm{dom}\ ND \subseteq nodes\ AST \wedge \mathrm{ran}\ ND = daemons \\
daemons \cap AST = \varnothing \\
\forall n : AST \bullet n.events = \{insert\_e, delete\_e, update\_e, find\_e\} \\
\forall d : daemons \bullet d.methods = \{insert\_m, delete\_m, update\_m, find\_m\} \\
EM = \{n : \mathrm{dom}\ ND \bullet ((n.name, insert\_e), ((ND\ n).name, insert\_m))\} \cup \\
\quad \{n : \mathrm{dom}\ ND \bullet ((n.name, delete\_e), ((ND\ n).name, delete\_m))\} \cup \\
\quad \ldots
\end{array}
$$

Field. The next system is the tool integration mechanism developed by the Field System [Reiss 90]. Field was designed to make it relatively easy to incorporate existing Unix tools into a programming environment. In a Field environment tools communicate by "broadcasting" interesting events. Other tools can register patterns that indicate which events should be routed to them and which methods should be called when an event matches that pattern. When an event is announced, a pattern matcher checks all registered patterns, invoking the associated method whenever a pattern is matched. For example, if a program editor announces when it has finished editing a module, a compiler might register for such announcements and automatically recompile the edited module.

To describe this behavior in terms of our basic model, we first define a new type of basic entity, *PATTERN*.

$$[PATTERN]$$

Next we associate a pattern matcher (*match*) with *EventSystem*, and a *register* relation that, for each component, associates patterns with methods of that component. The register relation then uniquely determines *EM*.

$$
\begin{array}{l}
\textit{Field} \\
\hline
\textit{EventSystem} \\
match : EVENT \leftrightarrow PATTERN \\
register : Component \leftrightarrow (PATTERN \times METHOD) \\
\hline
\mathrm{dom}\ register \subseteq components \\
((c_1.name, e), (c_2.name, m)) \in EM \Leftrightarrow \\
\quad (\exists\, pat : PATTERN \bullet (c_2, (pat, m)) \in register \wedge (e, pat) \in match)
\end{array}
$$

The invariant guarantees that the Event/Method pairs in *EM* are those for which some registered pattern matches the event associated with the method.

Forest. Forest adapts the Field implicit invocation mechanism to allow each component to define a "policy" for deciding (dynamically) which methods to invoke when a pattern is matched [Garlan & Ilias 90]. Thus instead of always invoking the same method, a component's policy determines what method should be invoked. The policy evaluation may depend on some state variables maintained by the event system.

For example, incremental, implicit recompilation of edited modules—as illustrated for Field— may be appropriate at certain times but not others. Using Forest, it is possible to define a policy to control when the compiler should be invoked. For instance, such a policy might be defined in terms of a state variable "EditingManyModules": incremental recompilation will take place only if the value of this variable is false.

We model Forest by considering *STATE* to be a new primitive type, and by treating a *POLICY* as a function that returns a method when applied to a given *STATE*.

$[STATE]$
$POLICY == STATE \rightarrow METHOD$

Like Field, Forest has *register* and *match* relations, which together uniquely determine *EM* for the system.

Forest

$EventSystem$
$match : EVENT \leftrightarrow PATTERN$
$register : Component \leftrightarrow (PATTERN \times POLICY)$
$policy\_state : STATE$

$\mathrm{dom}\ register \subseteq components$
$((c_1.name, e), (c_2.name, m)) \in EM \Leftrightarrow$
$\quad (\exists\, pat : PATTERN;\ policy : POLICY \bullet$
$\qquad (c_2, (pat, policy)) \in register \land$
$\qquad (e, pat) \in match \land$
$\qquad policy(policy\_state) = m)$

As with Field, the invariant of Forest guarantees that the Event/Method pairs in *EM* are those for which both a pattern and a policy combine to map the event to the method.

3.4 Using the Model

The value of the implicit invocation model is its ability to provide insight into the space of designs that adopt implicit invocation mechanisms. At the very least, the formal abstractions greatly simplify comparisons between existing systems, and make clear how each of them can be viewed as a variation on a common underlying design. Designs that are typically realized as thousands of lines of code, can be examined and compared with relative ease in several pages of formal specification.

For example, similarities between Gandalf and APPL/A become apparent, even though the two systems were implemented completely independently, and with quite different goals. In particular, both generate events in response to operations on certain types of components—relations, in the case of APPL/A, and AST nodes, in the case of Gandalf. Both restrict the components in the system that can handle events, and both restrict the vocabulary of event announcements. Finally, both are similar to Smalltalk-80, which further restricts announcers and receivers of events.

However, the usefulness of a formal model extends beyond qualitative, high-level comparisons. Indeed, there are at least three important ways in which the model allows us to reason about different implicit invocation systems.

First, it makes explicit the restrictions that each system imposes on the general model. This in turn allows us to explain some of the limitations of existing systems, and to predict properties of new designs. For example, consider APPL/A's restriction that allows only relations to announce events. A consequence is that the programmer either must use standard, explicit invocation mechanisms (eg., procedure call) to connect components that are not relations, or else must model those components as relations. In the former case, the benefits of implicit invocation mechanisms—such as easier evolution—may not apply. In the latter case, system components are forced to be treated as relations, even when they have other, more natural representations.

As another example, consider Gandalf's restriction of *EM*. It is not hard to show that *EM* is a (partial) function. That is,

$$Gandalf \vdash EM \in Event \nrightarrow Method$$

Thus in the Gandalf System only a single component (viz., a daemon) can be associated with an event. As a consequence each implicitly invoked method is itself responsible for *explicitly* invoking methods of any other component that might be "interested" in the announced event. This restriction is a serious shortcoming: since these additional relationships must be encoded in the implicitly invoked daemons, these daemons can become quite complex. Moreover, many of the benefits of loose coupling of system components is lost, making it difficult, for example, to evolve the system. Our practical experiences with Gandalf environments had given us an intuitive understanding of this general issue, but it was the formalization that clarified the specific problem.

Second, the approach allows us to formally compare systems. For example, it is possible to precisely characterize the relationship between Field and Forest. The implicit invocation mechanisms of a Field programming environment can be viewed as a special case of a Forest programming environment in which each policy always returns the same method, regardless of the *policy_state* of the system. More formally, we can state the following lemma:

$$\begin{array}{l} f : Forest;\ g : Field \vdash \\ \qquad f.components = g.components \land f.match = g.match \land \\ \qquad (\forall\ (c, (pat, m)) \in g.register \bullet \exists\ policy \mid \\ \qquad\qquad (c, (pat, policy)) \in f.register \land policy(f.policystate) = m) \\ \qquad \Rightarrow f.EM = g.EM \end{array}$$

Third, the approach encourages the formal statement of properties that can be compared against the various specializations of the model. For instance, one such property is whether there are potential circularities in a system. In this case a circularity is a chain of implicit invocations that starts at one component and returns to that component. While the existence of circularities will, in general, depend on the specific *components* and *EM* relation in a particular *EventSystem*, for a system such as a Gandalf environment, it is possible to argue that no circularities can exist with respect to implicit invocation. (Nothing in the specification prohibits an implicitly invoked method from *explicitly* interacting with a node, which in turn may trigger the implicitly invoked method again, and so on.) More formally, given the following definition of *Circular*:

Circular

$$
\begin{array}{|l}
\textit{EventSystem} \\
\hline
\exists\ \textit{implicitly\_invokes} : \textit{components} \leftrightarrow \textit{components} \mid \\
\quad (c_1, c_2) \in \textit{implicitly\_invokes} \Leftrightarrow (\exists\ m : \textit{METHOD};\ e : \textit{EVENT} \bullet \\
\qquad ((c_1.\textit{name}, e), (c_2.\textit{name}, m)) \in \textit{EM}) \bullet \\
\quad \exists\ c : \textit{components} \bullet (c, c) \in \textit{implicitly\_invokes}^{+}
\end{array}
$$

we can show:

$$\textit{Gandalf} \vdash \neg\ \textit{Circular}$$

4 Discussion and Conclusions

As we have illustrated, formal specification can provide considerable insight into a design space. This application of formal methods, however, is not a traditional one. It is therefore appropriate to reflect on this use of formalization.

Traditionally applications of formal methods have focused on the problem of developing specifications for individual systems. Moreover, typically, the primary issue is one of correctness: is a given implementation correct with respect to the given specification. In contrast, the use of formal methods described in this paper (and elsewhere [Garlan & Delisle 90, Delisle & Garlan 90a]) is to extract the abstract the properties of a *family* of systems. Abstraction allows us to concentrate on the common design decisions, ignoring specific details of particular systems, so that different systems can be compared along certain dimensions. "Refinement" is then used to show how specific systems specialize the shared abstractions. However, in this case refinement is being used to elaborate an abstract design, rather than provide an implementation of a specification. The question that one asks of a refinement is then no longer "Is it correct?", but "What are its properties?", and "How do these properties compare with those obtained through other such refinements?" Furthermore, it becomes reasonable to talk about the *dimensions of refinement* that can be used to specialize an abstract design framework. In the examples above, we looked at refinements of *EVENTS*, *COMPONENTS*, and the associated event manager. This allowed us to compare disparate systems such as Gandalf, APPL/A, and Smalltalk in terms of their refinement along these specific dimensions.

A consequence of this different emphasis on abstraction and refinement, is that the quality of a formal specification is no longer simply a question of completeness and consistency. Instead, formal specification of a design space must be judged on its ability to reveal the important properties of a family of systems. To accomplish this a formal specification must balance the simplicity of an abstract model against the need to expose key properties. This can be a difficult balance to attain. In the case of implicit invocation mechanisms we chose to abstract the way in which events are announced. This simplifies the description, but makes it difficult, for example, to describe different schemes for passing parameters through an announced event. Similarly, we chose not to model the mechanism for explicit method invocation. Again that decision leads to simplicity, but also makes it difficult for us to talk about certain hybrid implicit invocation mechanisms that, for example, announce events automatically whenever certain methods are invoked.

A second consequence is that certain properties of a formal notation become crucial in carrying out the formalization of a design space. In particular, we relied heavily on the use of Z's schema calculus to first define a "kernel" design (*EventSystem*) and then later elaborate that design. In this respect, our use of Z is similar to Flinn and Sørensen's in their CAVIAR case study [Flinn & Ib. Sørensen]. Like our approach, they show how a specific system specification can be obtained by specializing (or instantiating) one or more reusable, abstract formal designs. The primary difference in approach, however, is that here we use the technique to support comparison of different systems. Additionally, the CAVIAR study makes heavy use of Z generic schemas to parameterize the basic building blocks. In our case study, however, we have found generics to be less useful, since the dimensions of specialization are not easily defined simply by "plugging in" the right type. This may very well point out the need for more powerful support for characterizing the parameterization of such frameworks, perhaps in the style of algebraic approaches [Goguen 86].

Acknowledgements

We would like to thank Kevin Sullivan and Robert Allen for their invaluable contributions to both the content and form of this paper. Kevin provided much of the initial insight into the underlying formal simplicity of implicit invocation mechanisms. Robert spotted numerous inconsistencies and deficiencies in earlier versions of the Z model.

References

[Balzer 86] R.M. Balzer. Living in the Next Generation Operating System. *Proceedings of the Fourth World Computer Conference.* (September, 1986).

[Delisle & Garlan 90a] N. Delisle and D. Garlan. Applying Formal Specification to Industrial Problems: A Specification of an Oscilloscope. *IEEE Software* (September 1990).

[Flinn & Ib. Sørensen] Bill Flinn and Ib. Sørensen. CAVIAR: A Case Study in Specification. In *Specification Case Studies*, ed. Ian Hayes, Prentice Hall International (1987).

[Garlan & Delisle 90] David Garlan and Norman Delisle. Formal Specifications as Reusable Frameworks. *Proceedings of the International Symposium: VDM'90 - VDM and Z.* Kiel, Germany (April 1990), Springer-Verlag, LNCS 428.

[Garlan & Ilias 90] D. Garlan and E. Ilias. Low-cost, Adaptable Tool Integration Policies for Integrated Environments. *Proceedings of ACM SIGSOFT90: Fourth Symposium on Software Development Environments*, pp. 1–10 (December 1990).

[Garlan et al. 90] David Garlan, Gail E. Kaiser, and David Notkin. On the Criteria to be Used in Composing Tools into Systems. Technical Report CUCS-034-90, Department of Computer Science, Columbia University (July 1990). To appear, *IEEE Computer.*

[Gerety 89] Colin Gerety. HP SoftBench: A New Generation of Software Development Tools. Technical Report SESD-89-25, Hewlett-Packard Software Engineering Systems Division, Fort Collins, Colorado (November 1989).

[Goguen 86] J.A. Goguen. Reusing and Interconnecting Software Components. *IEEE Computer* (February 1986).

[Goldberg & Robson 83] A. Goldberg and D. Robson. *Smalltalk-80: The Language and its Implementation.* Addison-Wesley (1983).

[Habermann et al. 91] A.N. Habermann, D. Garlan, and D. Notkin. Generation of Integrated Task-Specific Programming Environments. In *CMU Computer Science: 25th Anniversary Commemorative Symposium.* Addison-Wesley (January 1991).

[Habermann & Notkin 86] A.N. Habermann and D. Notkin. Gandalf Software Development Environments. *IEEE Transactions on Software Engineering SE-12*,12 (December 1986), pp. 1117–1127.

[Hewitt 69] Carl Hewitt. PLANNER: A Language for Proving Theorems in Robots. *Proceedings of the First International Joint Conference in Artificial Intelligence.*, Washington DC (1969).

[Krasner & Pope 88] G.E. Krasner and S.T. Pope. A Cookbook for Using the Model-View-Controller User Interface Paradigm in Smalltalk-80. *Journal of Object Oriented Programming 1*,3 (August/September 1988), pp. 26–49.

[Reiss 90] S.P. Reiss. Connecting Tools using Message Passing in the Field Environment. *IEEE Software* 7,4 (July 1990), pp. 57–66.

[Spivey 89] J.M. Spivey. *The Z Notation: A Reference Manual.* Prentice Hall International (1989).

[Sullivan & Notkin 90] K. Sullivan and D. Notkin. Reconciling Environment Integration and Component Independence. *Proceedings of ACM SIGSOFT90: Fourth Symposium on Software Development Environments*, pp. 22-33 (December 1990).

[Sutton, Heimbigner & Osterweil 90] S.M. Sutton, Jr., D. Heimbigner, & L.J. Osterweil. Language Constructs for Managing Change in Process-Centered Environments. *Proceedings of ACM SIGSOFT90: Fourth Symposium on Software Development Environments*, pp. 206–217 (December 1990).

On Type Checking in VDM and Related Consistency Issues

Flemming Damm Bo Stig Hansen Hans Bruun

Department of Computer Science,
Technical University of Denmark,
Building 344, DK-2800 Lyngby

Abstract

The variants of specification languages used with the Vienna Development Method (VDM) offer a rather expressive notion of types. Higher order function types, recursively defined types, and a notion of union types which does not require injection and projection are all included, not to mention subtypes characterized by arbitrary predicates.

Besides this, VDM specifications are in general not executable so dynamic type checking does not make sense. However, proof of their total consistency (satisfiability), as advocated by Cliff Jones [5], covers all type checking including what is usually considered "dynamic", e.g. index range checks. In addition, it ensures other desirable properties such as termination of recursively defined functions.

In this paper, we identify a number of general problems concerning automatic type checking of VDM specifications and the relation to consistency proofs. The authors are currently investigating different ways of handling the problems and the presentation includes outlines of some of these.

1 Introduction

With the Vienna Development Method (VDM), different specification language variants have been used over the years [2, 5] but one of their common characteristics has been a quite powerful notion of type. This relates to the important rôle of types as a modeling tool in VDM.

The other traditional rôle of types namely as an instrument for automatic consistency checking has, so far, mostly been ignored in connection with VDM. One of the reasons for this has, no doubt, been the inherent difficulties in doing automatic type checking with a type universe as rich as VDM's. In the work reported on here, we have investigated some of the problems related to VDM type checking. Our presentation is intended to give an overview of these problems as well as some proposals for dealing with them.

Traditionally, type checking is an activity undertaken to reveal certain kinds of inconsistencies within programs or, as in our case, within formal specifications. In general, many kinds of inconsistencies are possible. The specification might, e.g., prescribe: (1) that an integer number should be added to a boolean value; (2) that the first element of an empty list should be retrieved; (3) that a non-terminating evaluation of a recursively defined function should be performed.

In most programming languages, cases like (1) may all be detected by a static analysis. Cases like (2) and (3) are, however, generally undecidable, so there can be no algorithm which will detect them all. For this reason, static type checking is traditionally restricted to cover cases like (1) even though case (2) in some sense concerns the same kind of inconsistency: application of a function to an argument for which the function is not defined.

In VDM, all of the above cases are generally undecidable. Consider, e.g., the addition of an integer number to the value of a formal parameter which has the type of integers union booleans: $\mathbb{N} \mid \mathbb{B}$. In specific cases, it may be possible to deduce from the context that the value of the parameter is indeed an integer. For instance, expressions of the special form

if is-$t(e)$ then ... else ...

might be recognized and the knowledge that e has type t could then be exploited when checking the "then" branch of the conditional. However, the tests which in this way guard a subexpression may be arbitrary predicates so it is generally undecidable whether a context implies that an expression has a certain (sub)type. With VDM, static type checking must therefore necessarily be incomplete just like all attempts at automatically analyzing cases like (2) and (3) are deemed to be.

In search for an approach to type/consistency checking which is applicable under these circumstances, we will in the following discuss two different views of the problem.

Consistency Proof Obligations

The consistency proof obligations which are considered in the work by Cliff Jones [5] concern all three aspects of consistency. Due to the undecidability of the problem, such consistency proofs can in general not be constructed automatically. It is, however, possible to design a terminating theorem prover which will be able to automatically construct the proofs in some cases. In the context of VDM, static analysis might therefore be viewed as just that: an attempt at automatic discharge of consistency proof obligations.

In the cases where the automatic consistency proving fails, this approach to static analysis has not helped much. It is still unknown whether the failure was due to the incompleteness of the analysis or caused by the specification actually being inconsistent. In cases where the specification *is* inconsistent it would definitely be valuable to have this pointed out.

Traditional Type Checking

In traditional work on type checking, the usual approach is to define a decidable typing predicate $e:t$ which holds in the cases where the expression e is considered to have the type t. In order to achieve the decidability, the predicate is usually defined so it, in a sense, is too liberal. Considering, e.g., indexing beyond the length of an integer array, this does not yield an integer but, even so, a traditional typing predicate would be defined to hold in this case. The same is true regarding expressions whose evaluation implies non-termination. In other words, consistency is not guaranteed by traditional typing predicates. Their usefulness is due to another desirable property: if there are no types t for which $e:t$ holds then it is certain that the program (or specification) is inconsistent.

In summary, classical type checking allows rejection of some kinds of inconsistencies but acceptance of consistent programs/specifications is not directly supported. It is characteristic for the kinds of inconsistencies which are not detected that they may only arise from the use of certain syntactic constructs/schemes such as, e.g., array indexing, assignment, parameter passing (range errors) and recursive definition.

The problem of type checking in VDM is sufficiently different that such a traditional approach will not be viable. The VDM notion of union types makes it impossible to identify a restricted set of syntactic constructs as the only ones which may cause undetectable inconsistencies. As illustrated by the example above, almost any kind of composite expression may contain subexpressions which cannot be typed precisely enough by static analysis. Which inconsistencies to recognize and which to ignore is not obvious in this setting.

Several possible analyses are illustrated in the following section but there seems to be no "natural" place to stop in the search for a sufficiently advanced one. One way of coping with this problem is to define, as a base, a rather simple analysis and then suggest a number of more advanced tests which may be added to the base.

Above it was argued that not only acceptance of obviously consistent specifications, but also rejection of obviously inconsistent ones would be valuable. Viewing the problem in the light of traditional type checking, one might wonder whether it would be sufficient to *only* consider rejection and totally leave out acceptance. In this connection, it is worth noticing that VDM specifications are usually not executed (or even executable) as programs are. This difference may be seen as one of the motivations for also considering automatic acceptance. In traditional type checking, detection of inconsistencies through run-time checks is an important supplement to the incomplete static analysis. However, with non-executable VDM specifications this generally makes no sense. Therefore, confidence in the consistency of a specification can only be obtained through a more or less rigorous/formal consistency argument.

To support this, it is desirable that static analysis besides rejecting obviously inconsistent specifications also accepts obviously consistent ones and in the remaining cases generates conditions which, when proved by the user, ensures consistency. Note that in previous work on static semantics of VDM specifications [9, 8] the aspects of acceptance and generation of consistency conditions have not been considered.

Overview

In the light of the above discussion, we recommend that both consistency acceptance and rejection is considered when designing static analyses of VDM specifications. Generally, automatic detection of inconsistencies must be incomplete just like automatic consistency proving. So in both cases, the practical usefulness will depend on the degree of overlap between the specifications which are actually written and the ones which will be recognized.

Specific classes of consistency checks which may be performed automatically are exemplified in the following section. We admit that the choice of which checks to consider may seem somewhat ad-hoc. It has been guided mostly by our experience and intuition regarding typical VDM specifications and what kinds of analyses we have been inspired to come up with. Never the less, the material may have some relevance, at least as an illustration of the diversity of checks which may be considered.

When a specification neither can be automatically accepted nor rejected, it is up to the user (specifier) to prove the consistency. Even then, static analysis may help by automatically discharging trivial parts of the proof obligation thus leaving only the "difficult" subproblems to the user. In other words, it is a conditional consistency which is proved automatically and it then remains to be proved by the user that the conditions generated are actually fulfilled. Some considerations in this regard are presented in section 4.

The approach of proving conditional consistency may only be successful if the proof obligation can be decomposed into parts, some of which lending themselves to automatic proofs; this turns out not to be straight-forward when considering recursively defined functions. In Jones' proof system for VDM [5], termination is an integral part of type correctness. The proposition $e \in t$ states that the expression e denotes a value of the type t and for it to hold it is necessary that e really denotes a value, i.e. that it does not imply non-termination (or non-satisfiability). Termination is one of the difficult subproblems referred to above and we have therefore investigated the possibility of separating it from the purely type related consistency requirements. Our results in this respect are outlined in section 3.

Types play a special rôle in connection with functions which are specified implicitly by pre/post conditions. This style of specification opens for the possibility of not fixing the function results completely. For a given argument, there may be a range of possible results delimited by the required result type and the post-condition. For such a specification to be consistent, there must for each acceptable argument exist a result which both belongs to the result type and fulfills the post-condition. In this setting, it seems extremely limited what can be done with respect to automatic proofs of the consistency. Automatic rejection of some "obviously" inconsistent specifications turns out possible, however; both topics are considered in section 3.

2 Elements of VDM Type Checking

In this section, a number of different analyses are illustrated by examples but first we would like to give an overview of the essential type relations referred to here and in the following section.

Relationships between Types

In VDM, the sets of values denoted by different type expressions need not be disjoint. As examples consider: (1) the natural numbers $\mathbb{N}$ which is a subset of the integers $\mathbb{Z}$; (2) two union types which may have a common component type; (3) two union types where one has all the components of the other plus some more. So when considering whether an expression will evaluate to values in a given type or not it is essential to be able to relate type expressions: do they denote overlapping or disjoint sets of values or perhaps one set is totally included in the other (one type is a subtype of the other)?

We will not go into the topic here, but only note that previous work on subtypes has not dealt with the special problems related to having both recursively defined types and "real" union types as in VDM (see, e.g., the recent work by Amadio and Cardelli [1]). The topic is currently being investigated at the department of the authors.

In the following, the terms "subtype" and "smaller type" are used interchangeably.

Basic Acceptance and Rejection

A basic level of type checking might be achieved by solely checking synthesized expression types against the type constraints imposed by the context of the expressions. Considering, e.g., expressions with the union operator, if one operand has the type t_1-set and the other t_2-set for some types t_1 and t_2 then it can be accepted that the union is of type $(t_1 \mid t_2)$-set. This may be expressed by an inference rule:

$$(1) \quad \frac{A \vdash_{acc} e_1 : t_1\text{-set} \quad A \vdash_{acc} e_2 : t_2\text{-set}}{A \vdash_{acc} e_1 \cup e_2 : (t_1 \mid t_2)\text{-set}}$$

Here, A denotes a set of assumptions concerning the types of variables which may occur in the expression. This kind of rules may be used to decompose the problem of finding a type for some expression to one or more similar problems concerning the syntactic components of the expression. The process finishes when atomic pieces of syntax are reached: the types of constants are given as rules without premisses and the types of variables should follow from the assumptions. Applied (pre/post) defined functions are simply considered to have the type stated by the user (the relationship between types and termination/satisfiability is discussed in section 3).

It is possible to complete a set of rules following these lines and we would suggest this as the base level of acceptance.

Considering rejection, the result of a union cannot be a set if it can be shown that one of the operands is not a set. It turns out that rules of this kind may be formulated in (at least) two radically different ways. One approach is to define a rejection predicate $A \vdash^{\forall}_{rej} e : t$ which should hold only if it in all worlds where the assumptions A hold is true that e does not have type t. This predicate may be defined structurally over the different kinds of expressions by writing inference rules like the following for each kind:

$$(2) \quad \frac{A \vdash^{\forall}_{rej} e_i : t\text{-set}}{A \vdash^{\forall}_{rej} e_1 \cup e_2 : t\text{-set}} \quad 1 \leq i \leq 2 \qquad\qquad (3) \quad \frac{t \otimes w\text{-set}}{A \vdash^{\forall}_{rej} e_1 \cup e_2 : t}$$

The second of these rules uses a type variable w which, implicitly, is universally quantified and also a type disjointness predicate $\otimes$ which must be defined separately.

As a quite different approach it is possible to structurally define a predicate for non-rejectability, i.e. a predicate which describes that expressions *may* have certain types so it cannot be rejected that they actually have these types. When such a predicate is defined so it is decidable and complete it may be used for automatic rejection: if the predicate for a given expression cannot be shown to hold for any type then it can be rejected that the expression is consistent.

The rules for the non-rejection predicate will in many cases be quite similar to the acceptance rules for the same constructs, however with some differences regarding the non-strict expressions such as if-then-else, logical conjunction and disjunction. Another difference lies in the relationship to subtypes: If it cannot be rejected that an expression has a given type then it also cannot be rejected that it has a subtype of that type. With acceptance, the converse is true: if it can be accepted that an expression has a given type then it also can be accepted that it has any super-type of that type. The approach of defining a rejection in terms of the negation of a non-rejection predicate is considered in other work [4] by the authors.

Acceptance by Case Analysis

A structural definition of the acceptance predicate as suggested above turns out not to handle cases where only a union type can be inferred for a subexpression. Considering, e.g., the above rule for the union operator, this alone allows no conclusion to be drawn regarding the type of $e_1 \cup e_2$ if, say, e_1 is variable with type t-set | t'-set and e_2 has type t''-set. Likewise if e_1 is an application of a function whose result type is a union type.

In order to infer a precise type in such situations, it is necessary to consider the two cases arising from assuming that e_2 has one of the types in the type union. The resulting type is then the type union of the results of analyzing each case:

$$(4) \quad \frac{\begin{array}{l} A \vdash_{acc} e : t_1 \mid t_2 \\ e : t_1, A \vdash_{acc} e' : t_1' \\ e : t_2, A \vdash_{acc} e' : t_2' \end{array}}{A \vdash_{acc} e' : (t_1' \mid t_2')} \quad e \text{ is a subexpression of } e'$$

Using this rule on the above example, the type $(t \mid t''\text{-set}) \mid (t' \mid t''\text{-set})$ may be inferred.

It may be noticed that the above rule is a specialization of a general rule for case analysis known as "or-elimination" [5]. The restriction that only sum types of *subexpressions* may be used as a basis for the case analysis is not necessary from a theoretical point of view. In connection with automatic type inference, however, some guidance regarding the choice of e in the above rule is required and since the premisses of all the other rules concern subexpressions it seems reasonable to choose a subexpression.

Acceptance and Rejection by Specialized Function Typing

With user-defined function types it is sometimes the case that the result of a function application cannot be typed with the desired precision so neither acceptance nor rejection is possible. As an example, consider an identity function defined as follows:

$$f : \mathbb{N} \mid \mathbb{B} \to \mathbb{N} \mid \mathbb{B}$$
$$f(x) \triangleq x$$

Even if some variable y is known to be of type $\mathbb{N}$, the type correctness of an expression like $f(y)+1$ cannot be established from the limited information provided by the function's type: $(\mathbb{N} \mid \mathbb{B}) \to (\mathbb{N} \mid \mathbb{B})$.

This and similar cases may be handled by inferring a specialized type of the function body b and thus the result under the assumption that the formal parameter x has the same type as the actual parameter a:

$$(5) \quad \frac{A \models_{acc} a : t_1 \quad x : t_1, A \models_{acc} b : t_2}{A \models_{acc} f(a) : t_2}$$

Considering rejection, it may in a similar fashion be rejected that a function application has a given type if it can be rejected that the body has this type under the assumption that the formal parameter has the same type as the actual parameter.

Rejection of Function Types

In many cases, it is sufficient to consider a rejection predicate $A \models^{\forall}_{rej} e : t$ which should hold only if it in all worlds where the assumptions A hold is true that e does not have type t. Due to the (meta) quantification over all worlds we call this universal rejection and mark the sequent symbol accordingly. If we, e.g., would try to reject that some existential (object) quantification is boolean, this could be done by universally rejecting that the quantified expression is boolean:

$$(6) \quad \frac{v : t_1, A \models^{\forall}_{rej} e : \mathbb{B}}{A \models^{\forall}_{rej} (\exists v : t_1 \cdot e) : \mathbb{B}}$$

Regarding the variables introduced as formal parameters of functions, it turns out that the meta quantification over all worlds is sufficient but not necessary: if, for all possible arguments of the declared type, the function body does not have the declared result type then we may indeed reject that the function has the declared type. In fact, such a rejection is sound if there is just one argument value for which the body does not have the declared result type. The latter is obviously correct for total functions (they should be defined for all arguments). Partial functions are for some arguments allowed to be undefined due to non-termination but it is questionable whether undefinedness due to type errors should also be allowed. This problem is also touched upon in section 3.

For now we note that a new rejection predicate: $A \Vdash^{\exists}_{\mathrm{rej}} e : t$ called existential rejection is relevant and sound at least in connection with total functions. The predicate should hold only if there exists a world where the assumptions A hold and it is true that e does not have type t. Compared to universal rejection, the existential rejection predicate is more powerful in the sense that it may reject more of the inconsistent specifications.

With the alternative, indirect approach to specifying rejection, this more powerful rejection is obtained by introducing a new rule for non-rejectability: a function having a function type cannot be rejected if it, in all cases where the formal parameter has a subtype of the specified domain type, cannot be rejected that the body has the specified range type.

Fine-grained types

In many cases it is possible to infer and utilize type information which is so detailed that it cannot be expressed in terms of the usual VDM types (excluding invariants). Examples include the types of non-empty sets, sequences, etc., negative integers, and perhaps most importantly: one element types **true** and **false** for the boolean values true and false. The latter will provide a basis for a (limited) handling of cases like the one presented in the introduction: if is-$\mathbb{N}(y)$ then $y + 1$ else ...

3 Type Consistency versus General Consistency

In the previous section, type consistency has been the main topic. We have not given a precise definition of what exactly is covered by type consistency but relied on some intuitive understanding. In VDM specifications, it should, however, be clear that there are kinds of inconsistencies which need not necessarily be classified as type errors. Inconsistencies may be caused by recursively defined functions which either do not terminate or whose associated functionals are not continuous. Implicitly specified functions which are not satisfiable also cause inconsistency.

The draft dynamic semantics of BSI/VDM SL [6] does not distinguish between type errors and other errors. We think, however, that these classes of errors could be separated definitionally as done, e.g., in the classical work by Milner [7]. No matter whether a distinction is made in the dynamic semantics or not, it may still be desirable to do so in the static semantics. First of all, most users will see, e.g., type errors and non-termination as conceptually different and may therefore want to deal with these independently. In a draft specification a user may, e.g., only be concerned with type errors. Secondly, the distinction between type errors and other errors is technically important, since the techniques for determining type errors and the other errors are quite different. The distinction is also useful in connection with rejection of ill-formed specifications, since these may then be rejected solely because of one sort of error (typically a type error).

Establishing a distinction between type errors and other errors naturally leads to a corresponding distinction between bottom values in the model theory. We will let the usual bottom symbol $\perp$ denote error values which are not type errors, and let **wrong** denote a type error value. In accordance with Jones' proof system [5], we let the proposition $e \in t$ state that the expression e denotes a well-defined value of the type t, i.e., that it neither denotes $\perp$ nor **wrong**. Next, we let the proposition $e : t$ mean that the expression e is type correct with respect to the type t. More precisely, if $e : t$ holds then the expression e either denotes a value of the type t or the bottom value $\perp$ in the model theory, and $e : t$ holds if $e \in t$ holds. Thus, if $e : t$ holds then e does not denote **wrong**. We also introduce the proposition $\tau(e)$ which holds if the expression e does not yield $\perp$ in the model theory. The essential relationships between the 3 properties may be expressed by the following rules:

$$(7)\quad \frac{A \models_{acc} e \in t}{A \models_{acc} e : t} \qquad (8)\quad \frac{A \models_{acc} e \in t}{A \models_{acc} \tau(e)} \qquad (9)\quad \frac{A \models_{acc} e : t \quad A \models_{acc} \tau(e)}{A \models_{acc} e \in t}$$

It follows trivially that $e \in t$ holds if and only if $e : t$ and $\tau(e)$ holds.

In terms of these propositions, a whole specification is consistent if for each specified function f with a declared type t the proposition $f \in t$ holds. In the following subsections, we will take a closer look on what this definition means for directly defined respectively implicitly specified functions.

In previous work, **wrong** has been used exclusively for denoting the type errors which should be detected by some given analysis, whereas $\perp$ has been used as a denotation of all other errors including non-termination and so-called dynamic type errors. In VDM, the type checking of even simple expressions like $x + 1$ is generally undecidable and we have proposed to make an open ended definition of what could/should be detected by static analysis. In the dynamic semantics, we would, however, like that the cases resulting in **wrong** should be fixed once and for all. For this reason, we use **wrong** as a denotation of *all* type errors, i.e. errors resulting from the application of a function to an argument outside its domain of definition.

LPF (Logic for Partial Functions), which is a three valued logic, has in recent years played a central rôle in connection with VDM [5]. With our proposal of having two error values, $\perp$ and **wrong**, the question arises whether a four valued logic is now needed. We believe this not to be the case since the two error values may be considered indistinguishable from the point of view of the logic. In the model theory, there will at some level be a distinction with rules like:

$\perp \vee$ false $== \perp$
wrong $\vee$ false == **wrong**
$\perp \vee$ **wrong** $== \perp$

However, these rules become identical to those of LPF when viewed under an abstraction where $\perp$ and **wrong** are considered to be representations of a single undefinedness value. This means that the proof theory of LPF may be used without changes and that it still will be complete with respect to the model theory (viewed under the abstraction).

As a desirable consequence of this approach, an expression like, e.g., $x = [\,] \vee$ hd $x = b$ is consistent when x is some sequence, even if hd x denotes **wrong** in the case where x is the empty sequence. As a less desirable consequence, expressions like true $\vee$ hd 5 are also consistent. Such constructions could be flagged by a separate quality analysis but from a purely semantic point of view, we propose that they be regarded as consistent.

Termination Errors

To accept a directly defined function f as consistent, one has to prove $f \in t$, where t is the declared function type. The type t must either be a total or partial function type.

A function is total if it for each argument value of the argument type yields a well-defined value, i.e., neither **wrong** nor $\perp$. In other words, this means that a total function must be type consistent and terminate for all arguments. To clarify this, regard the following example:

$$f : \mathbb{N} \to \mathbb{N}$$
$$f(x) \;\triangleq\; \text{if } x = 0 \text{ then } 0 \text{ else } f(x+1)$$

This function is type consistent since the body of the function does not involve any type inconsistent function applications. On the other hand, it is not generally consistent since it is declared to be total, but for some (actually the most) arguments it does not terminate.

Partial functions are allowed not to terminate for some arguments. Consequently, the following function specification is consistent:

$$f : \mathbb{N} \xrightarrow{\sim} \mathbb{N}$$
$$f(x) \;\triangleq\; \text{if } x = 0 \text{ then } 0 \text{ else } f(x+1)$$

It is an open question whether partiality caused by type errors should be allowed. As an example, consider the following definition of a partial function for subtracting two natural numbers.

$$f : \mathbb{N} \times \mathbb{N} \xrightarrow{\sim} \mathbb{N}$$
$$f(x) \;\triangleq\; \text{if } y = 0 \text{ then } x \text{ else } f(x-1, y-1)$$

The *body* of this function definition will be type inconsistent for some argument pairs, e.g. $(0,1)$. We prefer to consider such function definitions inconsistent and this view is assumed in the following. Alternatively, one could have chosen to let cases like the above be flagged with warnings by a separate quality analysis.

Our view has the advantage that application of a function (total or partial) will never yield **wrong** if the function definition is type consistent and the argument belongs to the required argument type. This ensures soundness of the usual type inference rule for function application. Thus, we assume that partiality of functions may only be caused of non-termination and consequently $f \in t \stackrel{\sim}{\rightarrow} t'$ means that f must be type consistent. A function f with a formal parameter x is type consistent if its body E is type consistent under the assumptions that all specified functions $f_1, \ldots, f_n$ are type correct with respect to their declared type, i.e. the context of the function is assumed type consistent. This is formalized with the following rule:

$$(10)\ \frac{f_1 \in t_1 \stackrel{\sim}{\rightarrow} t_1', \ldots, f_n \in t_n \stackrel{\sim}{\rightarrow} t_n', x \in t, A \models_{acc} E : t'}{A \models_{acc} f_i \in t \stackrel{\sim}{\rightarrow} t'} \qquad 1 \leq i \leq n$$

This allows type inference for recursive as well as mutually recursive functions. Notice, that the assumptions of rule 10 do not prevent us from trying to infer more precise function types in connection with function applications. In the examples above, we saw that a function is total if its body is type correct and it terminates for all arguments. For directly defined functions:

$$f : t_1 \rightarrow t_2$$
$$f(x) \triangleq E$$

the rule may be expressed as follows:

$$(11)\ \frac{A \models_{acc} f \in t_1 \stackrel{\sim}{\rightarrow} t_2 \quad A \models_{acc} x \in t_1 \vdash \tau(E)}{A \models_{acc} f \in t_1 \rightarrow t_2}$$

As these rules shows, the general consistency requirement for directly defined functions can be partioned into two proof obligations for respectively type consistency and termination.

We will now give an outline of a proof system for termination. Firstly, we regard what we will call strong compound expressions. The evaluation of a strong compound expression terminates if and only if the evaluation of each subcomponent expression terminates. (This should not be confused with the notion of *strict* compound expressions [4].) As an example, consider addition, i.e., an expression of the form $e_1 + e_2$. Evaluation of this expression requires evaluation of both e_1 and e_2. For a strong compound expression $op(e_1, \ldots, e_n)$ we thus have the following rule:

$$(12)\ \frac{A \models_{acc} \tau(e_1) \quad \ldots \quad A \models_{acc} \tau(e_n)}{A \models_{acc} \tau(op(e_1, \ldots, e_n))}$$

Note, that a constant expression (literal) is a strong compound expression which has no subexpressions and thus trivially terminates. Secondly, remember $e \in t$ means that e denotes a value of type t and thus a well-defined value. Hence, we have the following rule:

$$(13)\quad \frac{}{x \in t, A \vdash_{\text{acc}} \tau(x)}$$

Next, regard function applications. Functions applications are not strong compound expressions since they do not necessarily terminate when the evaluation of both the function and the argument terminates. It is also required that the body of the function terminates. When f is a directly defined function, we may ensure termination of the function application $f(a)$ by requiring termination of the actual argument a and termination of the function body, say E, under the assumption that the formal argument, say x, terminates:

$$(14)\quad \frac{A \vdash_{\text{acc}} \tau(a) \quad \tau(x), A \vdash_{\text{acc}} \tau(E)}{A \vdash_{\text{acc}} \tau(f(a))}$$

With these rules it is possible to prove termination of non-recursive functions which are composed of strong compound expressions.

Contrary to function application whose termination requires more than termination of the subexpressions, the termination condition of boolean and conditional expressions is weaker. Boolean and conditional expressions are not strong compound expressions. E.g., a disjunction may only require evaluation of a one of the disjuncts. If one of the disjuncts denotes true, the disjunction denotes true no matter what the other disjunct denotes. Hence, we have the following set of rules for termination of a disjunction:

$$(15)\quad \frac{A \vdash_{\text{acc}} \tau(e_1) \quad A \vdash_{\text{acc}} \tau(e_2)}{A \vdash_{\text{acc}} \tau(e_1 \vee e_2)} \qquad (16)\quad \frac{A \vdash_{\text{acc}} e_i \in \mathbf{true}}{A \vdash_{\text{acc}} \tau(e_1 \vee e_2)} \quad 1 \le i \le 2$$

The assumption $e_i \in$ **true** of rule 16 most, however, be proved using the whole proof system. I.e. e_i must be type correct with respect to **true** and terminate (see rule 9).

Termination does not imply type consistency (although, as mentioned above, the proof of termination may require type consistency of a subexpression). This means that, e.g., an expression like $x = [\,] \vee \mathsf{hd}\, x = b$ terminates and can be proved to do so since both disjuncts terminates (x is assumed to be some variable and b a constant).

To prove termination of recursively defined functions it is in general necessary to use induction. It is no easy task to do this mechanically. In some cases it may, however, be possibly by utilizing some well-founded ordering on the formal argument type. Regard, e.g., the factorial function:

$$f : \mathsf{N} \rightarrow \mathsf{N}$$

$$f(x) \triangleq \mathsf{if}\ x = 0\ \mathsf{then}\ 1\ \mathsf{else}\ x \times f(x-1)$$

Here, we may mechanically recognize that the actual parameter in the recursive call is less than the formal parameter and that there is a least value (zero) of the argument. For this reason termination can be guaranteed. In a similar manner it could be proved that the previously defined function for subtracting two natural numbers terminates. This function is, however, not type consistent.

In general, heuristics could be built into the proof system to handle some classes of recursive functions. Other orderings which could be considered are, e.g., the length of sequences and the cardinality of sets. A similar approach is taken in the work by Boyer and Moore [3].

At last, we need to consider application of implicitly specified functions. These applications are regarded as expressions which always terminate, since we assume recursion is disallowed in connection with implicit specifications.

Even though it is not possible to prove termination of all functions mechanically, it may still be appropriate to distinguish errors caused by type inconsistency and non-termination. By extending the general proof theory with specialized proof rules for proving termination, it may also be possible to prove termination manually without considering type consistency. In the work by Cliff Jones [5], it is illustrated how one may systematically construct inference rules for reasoning about (some aspects of) directly defined functions. Likewise, one may in a systematic way define inference rules for reasoning specifically about termination. For the factorial function above, the following rules may be appropriate:

(17) $\dfrac{}{\tau(f(0))}$ (18) $\dfrac{x \neq 0 \quad \tau(f(x-1))}{\tau(f(x))}$

Satisfiability Errors

In VDM, functions may be specified implicitly in terms of pre-conditions and post-conditions which relate argument and result values. In general, there is for such specifications a requirement that for each argument value which satisfies the pre-condition there must exist a result value satisfying the post-condition. This is sometimes referred to as the requirement of satisfiability. Implicit function specifications are loose in the sense that there may be several result values which satisfy the post-condition for each argument value. In this connection, one should note that the declared result type of an implicitly specified function does not only play a describing rôle but also a defining rôle since extending the result type may add to the number of functions which fulfill the specification. This must be seen in contrast to a directly defined function whose declared result type only plays a rôle in connection with well-definedness.

Satisfiability is the only consistency requirement for implicit function definitions. Consider an implicitly specified function:

$g\,(x : t_d)\; y : t_r$
post $e(x, y)$

Note that no pre-condition is mentioned since this simply may be viewed as an invariant on the argument type when considering satisfiability. For the function f specified above, satisfiability may be formalized with the rule:

$$(19)\quad \frac{g_1 \in t_1 \xrightarrow{\sim} t_1', \ldots, g_n \in t_n \rightarrow t_n', A \vdash_{acc} \forall x \in t_d' \cdot \exists y \in t_r \cdot e(x,y) \in \mathbf{true}}{A \vdash_{acc} g \in t_d' \rightarrow t_r}$$

Here—as in rule 10—the context is assumed consistent, i.e. all other functions are assumed correct with respect to their declared type. This causes no problems if we assume that recursion is not allowed in connection with implicitly specified functions.

Note that the satisfiability requirement is stated in terms of the one element type **true** for the boolean value true. With this formulation we do not exclude automatic verification of the requirement by means of an extended type inference system even though it is clear that this will not be possible in many cases.

For explicit function definitions, we found a natural distinction between type errors and termination errors. Such a distinction is, however, not possible for implicitly specified functions. Requiring, e.g., that the post-condition must be type correct with respect to the boolean type for all possible result values is not correct since the requirement of satisfaction is fulfilled as long as the post-condition is true for at least one result value. There is no requirement that the the post-condition must be false for those values for which it is not true. One could then demand that the expression $\forall x \in t_d' \cdot \exists y \in t_r \cdot e(x,y)$ is type correct with respect to the boolean type. This is, however, not a sufficient requirement. Afterwards, satisfiability must be shown by proving the truth of the same expression, i.e. that it is correct with respect to the one value type **true**.

The type correctness of the post-condition with respect to the boolean type may, however, be used in connection with rejection. Thus, an implicit function definition may be rejected if it for all argument and results of the declared types may be rejected that the post-condition is boolean.

$$(20)\quad \frac{x \in t_d', y \in t_r, A \vdash^{\forall}_{rej} e(x,y) : \mathbb{B}}{A \vdash^{\forall}_{rej} g \in t_d' \rightarrow t_r}$$

Continuity Errors

As previously mentioned, inconsistencies may also be caused by non-continuity of the functions used in recursive definitions. Consider, e.g., the following functional:

$F(f : \mathbb{N} \xrightarrow{\sim} \mathbb{N})\, g : \mathbb{N} \xrightarrow{\sim} \mathbb{N}$

post true

The set of functions fulfilling this specification also includes non-continuous ones, unless these are explicitly excluded in the dynamic semantics. However, with an expression like

let $f = F(f)$ in ...

it is only possible to compute the least fixed point if F is continuous. Otherwise the specification must be considered inconsistent. A similar inconsistency may arise when the let ... be st ... in ... construction is used to define functionals.

We shall not go into further details here. We do, however, think that it possible to make some static checks of continuity as done for termination.

4 Generation of Proof Obligations

As we have already argued, consistency of VDM specifications is in general undecidable. Thus, we do not hope to develop a proof system for consistency which is complete, sound and decidable. The proof obligations for consistency are, however, well-defined. Hence, what we cannot prove mechanically with a given proof system, may be left for the user to prove. Turning this around means that we can mechanically prove consistency provided that the user has proved some parts of the proof obligations. In other words, it is a conditional consistency which is mechanically proved. The proof obligations which are left to user may be proved in the full theory, i.e. the general proof theory or the model theory.

In the cases where the mechanical consistency proving fails, this is either owing to the incompleteness of the proof system or caused by the specification actually being inconsistent. Since the detection of inconsistency also is incomplete, it cannot always be decided why the proof failed. It gives, however, no meaning to leave definitely unprovable proof obligations to the user. Thus we expect that the specification is not mechanically rejectable. In some sence, this means we only leave proof obligations to the user if there is some hope to prove them.

A proof may be represented as a proof tree which shows how the goal can be deduced from the axioms. Starting with the goal, i.e., the root of a proof tree, the task of proving can be regarded as building the tree until the leafs are reached. Thus, failing to prove means that it is not possible to complete a construction of a proof tree. The task of generating proof obligations for the user may then be viewed as pointing out which subtrees remain to complete the proof. To do this, a partial proof tree must first be constructed.

There may in general be several ways to deduce a goal. For each (sub)goal there may be several rules which can be applied, i.e., several ways to continue the construction of the proof tree. On the other hand, there may also be several rules which do not lead to completion in the sence that application of these rules leads to a contradicting subgoal, i.e. generally unprovable subgoal. To assist the search for a proof, applicability conditions may be added to the rules as side conditions. Applicability conditions may exclude application of some rules. For example, consider the following rule which may be used to prove that multiplication of two numbers yields a natural number:

$$(21)\quad \frac{A \vdash_{\mathrm{acc}} e_1 : \mathbb{N} \quad A \vdash_{\mathrm{acc}} e_2 : \mathbb{N}}{A \vdash_{\mathrm{acc}} e_1 \times e_2 : \mathbb{N}}$$

If it can be rejected that one of the operands e_1 or e_2 yields a natural number, the rule is not applicable.

Consider the applicable rules for a given goal. Some of these may have the property that the assumptions are provable whenever the conclusion holds. In other words, if we choose one of these rules there will be no risk of generating unprovable sub-goals provided that the original goal holds. This may be illustrated by the following rules for concluding that an addition yields a real number:

$$(22)\ \frac{A \vdash_{\overline{\text{acc}}} e : \mathsf{N}}{A \vdash_{\overline{\text{acc}}} e : \mathsf{R}} \qquad (23)\ \frac{A \vdash_{\overline{\text{acc}}} e_1 : \mathsf{R} \quad A \vdash_{\overline{\text{acc}}} e_2 : \mathsf{R}}{A \vdash_{\overline{\text{acc}}} e_1 + e_2 : \mathsf{R}}$$

Both rules may be applicable. But, if the addition yields a real number then the operands must also denote real numbers. Thus, if the goal is true then so are the assumptions of rule 23, and then nothing is done wrong when rule 23 is applied. We say that the rule is *selectable*. In some cases, rule 22 may also be selectable, because the addition will not yield non-natural numbers. In contrast to rule 23, the selection condition for rule 22 should, however, not be trivially true. Also, consider rule 21 again. If it can be rejected that both operands yield a non-natural, real number then this rule is selectable.

One could now ask whether the statement "A rule is selectable if it is the only applicable rule" is true. Under certain circumstances it is true, but not always, since there may be unformalized rules which are applicable. This leads us to the notion of local completeness. We say a set of rules is *locally complete* with respect to some goal when the goal holds if and only if the assumptions of one of the rules holds. E.g., rule 23 constitutes a singleton set which is locally complete.

Now, we may modify the above statement such that it becomes true: "A rule is selectable if it is the only applicable rule among a locally complete set of rules".

Having introduced the notion of local completeness, we may notice a correspondence between the proof systems for respectively rejection and acceptance. Consider a goal which is reached during the construction of a proof tree. If there is a locally complete set of rules for this goal and none of these rules are applicable then it seems reasonable to require that the specification is mechanically rejectable.

The proof obligations which should be left to the user may be generated by continuing the constructing the proof tree as long as there are selectable rules. If no rules are selectable, the goal is left as a proof obligations to the user. The applicability condition and the notion of local completeness may then be useful when assisting the user in proving the proof obligations. More precisely, this means that for given proof obligation a tool can show the user the possible ways to continue the proof construction by listing the applicable rules. Choosing one of these rules could then cause generation of a new set of proof obligations. When the set of rules for a goal which is left to the user is not locally complete then the user should be made aware of this. Contrary, if the set of rules for the considered goal is locally complete, one of the applicable rules must lead to a proof. Otherwise, the specification is inconsistent.

The proof obligations generated in this way will consequently be stated in terms of the predicates of our dedicated proof systems. These do not all have a correspondence in the general theory, so they must be transformed. Some typical examples are the type correctness predicate $e:t$, the fine-grained types and the termination predicate τ. Consider, e.g., the proof obligation $e:\mathbf{true}$. It may be transformed and generalized into an obligation which requires the truth of e. It is a generalisation because the truth of e includes termination. It may also be appropiate to merge some proof obligations. Typically, this could be two proof obligations for type correctness respectively termination of the same expression. These can be merged into one proof obligation which is expressed in terms of the membership relation: $e \in t$.

Another way of handling the generated proof obligations is to extend the general theory with proof rules for type consistency, termination and so forth. We have already considered this briefly with respect to termination.

At last one should notice that the assumptions of a proof obligation may be too weak. It could, e.g., be the case that a non-zero natural number is just assumed to be natural number. Under such too weak assumption it thus may not be possible to prove the desired proof obligation. Instead of these explicitly stated assumptions one should really use the current context. In other words, a proof obligation should rather be interpreted as: Show that the considered expression has the desired property *in its context*.

5 Conclusion

With VDM's notion of types, static type checking is not as straight-forward as is typically the case for programming languages. Type checking of even very simple expressions like $x + 1$, which in traditional programming languages may be handled by static analysis, is in VDM generally undecidable. So static type checking for VDM is necessarily incomplete and it is our observation that there is no "natural" place to stop in the search for "sufficiently" advanced analyses. We have therefore proposed a division of the static semantics into a basic analysis and a set of possible extensions which is open to future additions.

In traditional type checking, the statically undetectable type errors may be caught by dynamic checks carried out at run-time. VDM specifications are usually not executed or even executable, so dynamic checks are not possible. Therefore, the only way to gain confidence in the consistency of a specification is to construct a consistency proof or rigorous argument. For a specification to be consistent, one may identify several requirements which must be fulfilled: (1) the functionals associated with recursive function definitions must be continuous; (2) total, recursively defined functions must always terminate; (3) pre/post specified functions must be satisfiable; (4) functions must only be applied to arguments for which they are defined.

We have argued that these requirements can be justified independently and proposed the definition of automatic analyses for rejecting, respectively accepting that specifications fulfil requirement (4). In connection with acceptance, ideas have also been presented regarding the automatic generation of proof obligations which capture the consistency requirements not checked. The latter might concern requirements (1) to (3) and also "dynamic type checks" (range checks for sequence indexing and so forth).

Regarding requirement (2), the proof system of Jones [5] does not allow a separate justification of termination; instead this is considered an integral part of type consistency. We have presented proof rules and schemes for reasoning about termination separately so the user need not be concerned with the type consistency in cases where this is proved automatically.

References

[1] Robert M. Amadio and Luca Cardelli. Subtyping recursive types. Research Report 62, Systems Research Center, Digital Equipment Corporation, 1990.

[2] Dines Bjørner and Cliff B. Jones, editors. *The Vienna Development Method: The Meta-Language*, volume 61 of *Lecture Notes in Computer Science*. Springer-Verlag, 1978.

[3] Robert S. Boyer and J. Strother Moore. *A Computational Logic Handbook*, volume 23 of *Perspective in Computing*. Academic Press, Inc., 1988.

[4] Hans Bruun, Bo Stig Hansen, and Flemming Damm. An approach to the static semantics of VDM-SL. This volume.

[5] Cliff B. Jones. *Systematic Software Development Using VDM*. Series in Computer Science. Prentice-Hall International, 2. edition, 1990.

[6] Peter Gorm Larsen. The dynamic semantics of the BSI/VDM specification language. Draft version, August 1990.

[7] Robert Milner. A theory of type polymorphism in programming. *Journal of Computer and System Sciences*, 17:348–375, 1978.

[8] B. Monahan and A. Walsh. Context conditions for the STC VDM reference language. Technical Report 725 05308 ed. 2, STC plc/Manchester University, 1986.

[9] Nico Plat, Ronald Hiujsman, Jan van Katwijk, Gertjan van Oosten, Kees Pronk, and Hans Toetenel. Type checking BSI/VDM-SL. In *VDM '90, VDM and Z—Formal Methods in Software Development,* volume 428 of *Lecture Notes in Computer Science*, pages 399–425. VDM-Europe, Springer-Verlag, 1990.

Combining transformation and posit-and-prove in a VDM development

T. Clement
Department of Computer Science,
University of Manchester, Manchester M13 9PL.
e-mail: timc@uk.ac.man.cs

Abstract

We provide a rigorous development of a structure sharing unification algorithm from an abstract algorithm of established correctness. This is done by a mixture of transformation and posit-and-prove techniques. From this, some conclusions are drawn about a practical approach to rigorous development and the way in which it should be supported.

1 Introduction

The unification of terms has applications in several areas of computer science, including theorem proving [Rob65], the execution of Prolog programs [Llo87], and polymorphic type checking [Mil78]. Not surprisingly, there has been extensive work on the development of efficient unification algorithms, including [BM72, MM82]. It has also been used on previous occasions as an example for the application of formal methods [MW81, Fit90, Vad90]. Each of these is a development of an algorithm from a specification: in the first two cases, an intuitive but inefficient algorithm from a natural specification; and in the third case an efficient algorithm from a specification in which the data types were chosen in advance to support that algorithm.

In this paper, a rather different path will be taken. We shall begin with an "abstract algorithm", which is inefficient but which can readily be derived from a specification similar to Fitzgerald's by a process similar to that of Manna and Waldinger [Cle90]. Our goal is the production of an efficient algorithm together with a proof that it meets the original specification. The motivation is to explore the process of rigorous development through an example which is small but reasonably challenging.

VDM prescribes a fairly rigid approach to development. At each stage, a specification closer to an implementation is posited and then proved to meet the original specification. The proofs necessary are described by a set of proof obligations [Jon90]. In the case of a data reification step, the change in data representation is accounted for by the introduction of a retrieve function from the reification to the abstraction.

Transformation is an alternative approach, where the original specification is massaged by a series of correctness preserving steps to give the implementation. By taking the transformation rules as lemmas, we can interpret each step as simultaneously generating a new specification and a proof of its validity. However, the problem arises of providing a set of transformations *a priori*. One solution is to provide a small set of very general transformations, such as unfold and fold [BD77]. The resulting development steps are much smaller than those which would be taken in justifying a design in the VDM approach, but common patterns of transformation can be packaged into derived steps, as in CIP [B+88]. Folding and unfolding must also be supplemented by laws on the data types and the introduction of new definitions based on intuition (eurekas).

In our development, we shall feel free to use whichever approach seems more appropriate at each stage. In the conclusions, we shall review the choice of approaches made, try to account for them, and suggest a setting wherein they might be unified.

2 The abstract algorithm

A unification algorithm operates on pairs of terms and yields a substitution. We define the type *Term* as the union of the types *CompoundTerm* and *Variable*, where each of these is a composite type. In the case of a compound term, its components are its function symbol, drawn from some set which will not be further defined, and a sequence of argument terms. A variable has a single component, its variable symbol. The extra layer of structure is technically convenient in VDM when constructing definitions by cases.

$$\begin{array}{lrl} \mathit{CompoundTerm} :: & \mathit{op} : & \mathit{FnSymbol} \\ & \mathit{args} : & \mathit{Term}^* \end{array}$$

$$\mathit{Variable} :: v : \mathit{VarSymbol}$$

$$\mathit{Term} = \mathit{Variable} \mid \mathit{CompoundTerm}$$

At this stage, we can also define when a variable occurs in a term:

$$\_\mathsf{occurs\text{-}in}\_ : \mathit{VarSymbol} \times \mathit{Term} \to \mathbb{B}$$

$$\begin{array}{ll} v \ \mathsf{occurs\text{-}in}\ t \ \triangleq & \mathsf{cases}\ t\ \mathsf{of} \\ & \quad \mathit{mk\text{-}Variable}(v') \to v = v' \\ & \quad \mathit{mk\text{-}CompoundTerm}(f, \mathit{args}) \to \exists t' \in \mathsf{rng}\ \mathit{args} \cdot v\ \mathsf{occurs\text{-}in}\ t' \\ & \mathsf{end} \end{array}$$

Substitutions are usually formalized as maps from *VarSymbols* to *Terms*, subject to the condition that no variable maps to itself. The substitutions created by the abstract algorithm will have the stronger property that no variable in the domain occurs in the range. This will be important in the development, so we express it here in the invariant.

$$Substitution = VarSymbol \xrightarrow{m} Term$$

where

$$inv\text{-}Substitution(\theta) \;\triangleq\; \forall v \in \mathsf{dom}\,\theta \cdot \neg\exists t \in \mathsf{rng}\,\theta \cdot v \text{ occurs-in } t$$

We also need definitions for the values of variables in substitutions, the application of substitutions to terms, and the composition of substitutions.

$$\_[\_] : Substitution \times VarSymbol \to Term$$

$$\theta[v] \;\triangleq\; \mathsf{if}\ v \in \mathsf{dom}\,\theta\ \mathsf{then}\ \theta(v)\ \mathsf{else}\ mk\text{-}Variable(v)$$

$$\_ \bullet \_ : Term \times Substitution \to Term$$

$$\begin{aligned} t \bullet \theta \;\triangleq\; & \mathsf{cases}\ t\ \mathsf{of} \\ & \quad mk\text{-}Variable(v) \to \theta[v] \\ & \quad mk\text{-}CompoundTerm(f, args) \to mk\text{-}CompoundTerm(f, args \bullet^{*} \theta) \\ & \mathsf{end} \end{aligned}$$

$$\_ \bullet^{*} \_ : Term^{*} \times Substitution \to Term^{*}$$

$$\begin{aligned} ts \bullet^{*} \theta \;\triangleq\; & \mathsf{cases}\ ts\ \mathsf{of} \\ & \quad [\,] \to [\,] \\ & \quad \mathsf{cons}(t', ts') \to \mathsf{cons}(t' \bullet \theta, ts' \bullet^{*} \theta) \\ & \mathsf{end} \end{aligned}$$

$$\_ \circ \_\ (\theta_1 : Substitution, \theta_2 : Substitution)\ \theta : Substitution$$

$$\mathsf{pre}\ \exists \theta \in Substitution \cdot \forall t \in Term \cdot t \bullet \theta = t \bullet \theta_1 \bullet \theta_2$$

$$\mathsf{post}\ \forall t \in Term \cdot t \bullet \theta = t \bullet \theta_1 \bullet \theta_2$$

(The precondition on composition ensures that idempotence is preserved, and obviously guarantees implementability. All uses of composition below can be shown to respect it.) As a result of the invariant on substitutions we can prove the following idempotence property of composition, which will be used heavily later.

$$\theta \in Substitution \vdash \theta \circ \theta = \theta$$

The abstract algorithm can now be presented as a pair of mutually recursive functions. Termination can be argued using the variant proposed in [MW81] (the lexicographic combination of the number of distinct variables and the number of symbols in a pair of terms).

$mgu_1 : Term \times Term \to [Substitution]$

$mgu_1(t_1, t_2) \quad \triangleq$
    cases (t_1, t_2) of
        $(mk\text{-}Variable(v_1), mk\text{-}Variable(v_2)) \to$
            if $v_1 = v_2$ then $\{\ \}$ else $\{v_1 \mapsto t_2\}$
        $(mk\text{-}Variable(v_1), mk\text{-}CompoundTerm(f_2, args_2)) \to$
            if v_1 occurs-in t_2 then nil else $\{v_1 \mapsto t_2\}$
        $(mk\text{-}CompoundTerm(f_1, args_1), mk\text{-}Variable(v_2)) \to$
            if v_2 occurs-in t_1 then nil else $\{v_2 \mapsto t_1\}$
        $(mk\text{-}CompoundTerm(f_1, args_1), mk\text{-}CompoundTerm(f_2, args_2)) \to$
            if $f_1 = f_2 \wedge$ len $args_1 =$ len $args_2$ then $mgul_1(args_1, args_2)$ else nil
    end

$mgul_1 : Term^* \times Term^* \to [Substitution]$

$mgul_1(ts_1, ts_2) \quad \triangleq$
    cases (ts_1, ts_2) of
        $([\,],[\,]) \to \{\ \}$
        $(\text{cons}(t_1', ts_1'), \text{cons}(t_2', ts_2')) \to$
            let $\theta_H = mgu_1(t_1', t_2')$ in
                if $\theta_H =$ nil then nil
                else let $\theta_T = mgul_1(ts_1' \bullet^* \theta_H, ts_2' \bullet^* \theta_H)$ in
                    if $\theta_T =$ nil then nil else $\theta_H \circ \theta_T$
    end
pre len $ts_1 =$ len ts_2

3 Accumulating the substitution

The self-recursive call in $mgul_1$ is not tail recursive because the result must be tested and composed with θ_H. However, because composition is associative and has a unit there is a standard means of converting it to a tail-recursive form by adding an accumulating parameter [Coo66]. This will not of itself make a major difference to the efficiency of the algorithm, but will enable subsequent developments.

We define a new function with a parameter of (almost) the same type as the result:

$mgul_2 : Term^* \times Term^* \times Substitution \to [Substitution]$

$mgul_2(ts_1, ts_2, \theta) \quad \triangleq \quad$ let $\theta' = mgul_1(ts_1, ts_2)$ in
    if $\theta' =$ nil then nil else $\theta \circ \theta'$

pre len $ts_1 =$ len ts_2

From the unit property we have

$ts_1, ts_2 \colon Term^* \vdash mgul_1(ts_1, ts_2) = mgul_2(ts_1, ts_2, \{\ \})$

which will allow the replacement of the old definition by the new anywhere.

We can then convert this to an equivalent form by unfolding the definition of $mgul_1$, simplifying the resulting expression using properties of if, let, cases and associativity, and finally folding $(\theta \circ \theta_H) \circ mgul_1(ts_1 \bullet^* \theta_H, ts_2 \bullet^* \theta_H)$ into $mgul_2(ts_1 \bullet^* \theta_H, ts_2 \bullet^* \theta_H, \theta \circ \theta_H)$ to give

$mgul_2(ts_1, ts_2, \theta) \;\triangleq$
  cases (ts_1, ts_2) of
    $([\,],[\,]) \to \theta$
    $(\mathsf{cons}(t_1', ts_1'), \mathsf{cons}(t_2', ts_2')) \to$
      let $\theta_H = mgu_1(t_1', t_2')$ in
        if $\theta_H = \mathsf{nil}$ then nil else $mgul_2(ts_1' \bullet^* \theta_H, ts_2' \bullet^* \theta_H, \theta \circ \theta_H)$
  end
pre len ts_1 = len ts_2

which is tail-recursive as promised (but still includes an application of mgu_1).

An analogous definition of mgu_2

$mgu_2 : Term \times Term \times Substitution \to [Substitution]$

$mgu_2(t_1, t_2, \theta) \;\triangleq$
  let $\theta' = mgu_1(t_1, t_2)$ in
  if $\theta' = \mathsf{nil}$ then nil else $\theta \circ \theta'$

can be subjected to a similar process to obtain the equivalent form

$mgu_2(t_1, t_2, \theta) \;\triangleq$
  cases (t_1, t_2) of
    $(mk\text{-}Variable(v_1), mk\text{-}Variable(v_2)) \to$
      if $v_1 = v_2$ then θ else $\theta \circ \{v_1 \mapsto t_2\}$
    $(mk\text{-}Variable(v_1), mk\text{-}CompoundTerm(f_2, args_2)) \to$
      if v_1 occurs-in t_2 then nil else $\theta \circ \{v_1 \mapsto t_2\}$
    $(mk\text{-}CompoundTerm(f_1, args_1), mk\text{-}Variable(v_2)) \to$
      if v_2 occurs-in t_1 then nil else $\theta \circ \{v_2 \mapsto t_1\}$
    $(mk\text{-}CompoundTerm(f_1, args_1), mk\text{-}CompoundTerm(f_2, args_2)) \to$
      if $f_1 = f_2 \wedge$ len $args_1$ = len $args_2$ then $mgul_2(args_1, args_2, \theta)$ else nil
  end

where the substitution is accumulated continuously throughout the unification.

4 Representing the goal lazily

The major part of the work undertaken by mgu_2 is in substitution. One aspect of this is that when unifying two lists of terms, the entire tails of the lists are substituted after unifying the heads, although only the heads of the tails will be used before being substituted again. Thus the final elements of two n-element lists will be substituted n-1 times before being examined. When we observe that the accumulating substitution in $mgul_2$ is exactly the substitution that has been applied to the next terms by the time they are unified, it suggests representing the substituted terms by the original terms and the substitution, applying it only when necessary. This data representation change is our next step.

4.1 A transformational approach

Changes in data representations can be achieved by the transformation of a standard eureka definition [Dar84]. If we have an operation $op: X \to Y$ and a representation X_C of X with retrieve function $retr$, we define $op_C(x_C) = op(retr(op_C))$ to make the specification satisfaction diagram

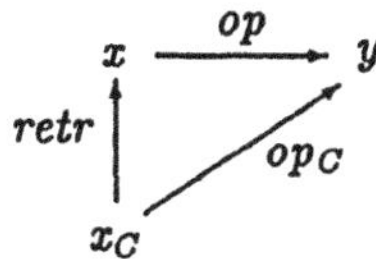

commute. If we have chosen a useful representation, we shall be able to transform the definition of op_C to a form which does not just apply $retr$ and apply the old operation to the abstraction.

In this case, we define

$$mgu_3(t_1, t_2, \theta) \quad \triangleq \quad mgu_2(t_1 \bullet \theta, t_2 \bullet \theta, \theta)$$

since the retrieval operation is the application of the substitution. Suppose we try unfolding the definition of $\_ \bullet \_$. The result is

$$
\begin{array}{l}
mgu_3(t_1, t_2, \theta) \ \triangleq \\
\quad \textsf{cases}\ (t_1, t_2)\ \textsf{of} \\
\quad\quad (\textit{mk-Variable}(v_1), \textit{mk-Variable}(v_2)) \to mgu_2(\theta[v_1], \theta[v_2], \theta) \\
\quad\quad (\textit{mk-Variable}(v_1), \textit{mk-CompoundTerm}(f_2, args_2)) \to \\
\quad\quad\quad mgu_2(\theta[v_1], \textit{mk-CompoundTerm}(f_2, args_2 \bullet^* \theta), \theta) \\
\quad\quad (\textit{mk-CompoundTerm}(f_1, args_1), \textit{mk-Variable}(v_2)) \to \\
\quad\quad\quad mgu_2(\textit{mk-CompoundTerm}(f_1, args_1 \bullet^* \theta), \theta[v_2], \theta) \\
\quad\quad (\textit{mk-CompoundTerm}(f_1, args_1), \textit{mk-CompoundTerm}(f_2, args_2)) \to \\
\quad\quad\quad mgu_2(\textit{mk-CompoundTerm}(f_1, args_1 \bullet^* \theta), \\
\quad\quad\quad\quad\quad \textit{mk-CompoundTerm}(f_2, args_2 \bullet^* \theta), \theta) \\
\quad \textsf{end}
\end{array}
$$

Then unfolding mgu_2 and simplifying the case expressions gives the expression of figure 1, where variable names have been chosen to make primes signify substituted values.

Our aim is to rewrite this definition in such a way that substitution is avoided where possible. It is clear from the fully unfolded form that we must substitute variables. Fortunately this can be made a cheap operation. It is also clear that many of the compound term substitutions are needed to construct the unifier, and cannot be avoided without changing the substitution representation. The remainder are in expressions of the form $\textsf{len}\ args_i \bullet^* \theta$ and in applications of $mgul_2$. The first of these can be trivially simplified using the rule

$$ts: Term^*; \theta: Substitution \vdash \textsf{len}\ ts \bullet^* \theta = \textsf{len}\ ts$$

The second suggests defining

```
mgu3(t1, t2, θ)  ≜
  cases (t1, t2) of
    (mk-Variable(v1), mk-Variable(v2)) →
      cases (θ[v1], θ[v2]) of
        (mk-Variable(v1'), mk-Variable(v2')) →
          if v1' = v2' then θ else θ ∘ {v1' ↦ θ[v2]}
        (mk-Variable(v1'), mk-CompoundTerm(f2', args2')) →
          if v1' occurs-in θ[v2] then nil else θ ∘ {v1' ↦ θ[v2]}
        (mk-CompoundTerm(f1', args1'), mk-Variable(v2')) →
          if v2' occurs-in θ[v1] then nil else θ ∘ {v2' ↦ θ[v1]}
        (mk-CompoundTerm(f1', args1'), mk-CompoundTerm(f2', args2')) →
          if f1' = f2' ∧ len args1' = len args2' then mgul2(args1', args2', θ)
          else nil
      end
    (mk-Variable(v1), mk-CompoundTerm(f2, args2)) →
      cases θ[v1] of
        mk-Variable(v1') →
          if v1' occurs-in mk-CompoundTerm(f2, args2 •* θ) then nil
          else θ ∘ {v1' ↦ mk-CompoundTerm(f2, args2) • θ}
        mk-CompoundTerm(f1', args1') →
          if f1' = f2 ∧ len args1' = len args2 •* θ
          then mgul2(args1', args2 •* θ, θ) else nil
      end
    (mk-CompoundTerm(f1, args1), mk-Variable(v2)) →
      cases θ[v2] of
        mk-Variable(v2') →
          if v2' occurs-in mk-CompoundTerm(f1, args1 •* θ) then nil
          else θ ∘ {v2' ↦ mk-CompoundTerm(f1, args1 •* θ)}
        mk-CompoundTerm(f2', args2') →
          if f1 = f2' ∧ len args1 •* θ = len args2'
          then mgul2(args1 •* θ, args2', θ) else nil
      end
    (mk-CompoundTerm(f1, args1), mk-CompoundTerm(f2, args2)) →
      if f1 = f2 ∧ len args1 •* θ = len args2 •* θ
      then mgul2(args1 •* θ, args2 •* θ, θ) else nil
  end
```

Figure 1: The fully unfolded mgu_3

$$mgul_3(ts_1, ts_2, \theta) \quad \triangleq \quad mgul_2(ts_1 \bullet^* \theta, ts_2 \bullet^* \theta, \theta)$$

pre len ts_1 = len ts_2

by analogy with mgu_3 and deriving an efficient implementation of that. This will fold immediately with the last case, and with the earlier subcases involving $mgul_2$ on using the idempotence property of substitutions. The result of using these two rewrites is

```
mgu3(t1, t2, θ) △
    cases (t1, t2) of
        (mk-Variable(v1), mk-Variable(v2)) →
            cases (θ[v1], θ[v2]) of
                ⋮
                (mk-CompoundTerm(f1', args1'), mk-CompoundTerm(f2', args2')) →
                    if f1' = f2' ∧ len args1' = len args2' then mgul3(args1', args2', θ)
                    else nil
            end
        (mk-Variable(v1), mk-CompoundTerm(f2, args2)) →
            cases θ[v1] of
                mk-Variable(v1') → ...
                mk-CompoundTerm(f1', args1') →
                    if f1' = f2 ∧ len args1' = len args2 then mgul3(args1', args2, θ)
                    else nil
            end
        (mk-CompoundTerm(f1, args1), mk-Variable(v2)) →
            cases θ[v2] of
                mk-Variable(v2') → ...
                mk-CompoundTerm(f2', args2') →
                    if f1 = f2' ∧ len args1 = len args2' then mgul3(args1, args2', θ)
                    else nil
            end
        (mk-CompoundTerm(f1, args1), mk-CompoundTerm(f2, args2)) →
            if f1 = f2 ∧ len args1 = len args2 then mgul3(args1, args2, θ) else nil
    end
```

Using idempotence to prepare for the fold imposes an extra (delayed) substitution of terms which have already been substituted, trading some speed for the convenience of a single abstraction.

The resulting expression remains complex. One strategy for achieving simplification is to introduce a eureka definition to abstract related terms. We can attempt to use this to obtain a definition of the same form as that of the first unfolding by finding a generalization of the expressions in the cases, under the laws on substitution, projections of composite types, and simplification of case expressions. This can then be used as the body of a function abstraction, applied at the appropriate instance in each case. In principle we could automate such a search. (Indeed, we could try to effect the entire simplification of the fully unfolded expression in the same way.) In practice, we see that it will help to adopt the case structure of the (variable,variable) case above, and then use idempotence to add extra $\bullet\theta$s, giving

$$
\begin{array}{l}
mgu_3(t_1, t_2, \theta) \quad \triangleq \\
\quad \textsf{cases } (t_1, t_2) \textsf{ of} \\
\quad\quad (mk\text{-}Variable(v_1), mk\text{-}Variable(v_2)) \rightarrow equate_1(\theta[v_1], \theta[v_2], \theta) \\
\quad\quad (mk\text{-}Variable(v_1), mk\text{-}CompoundTerm(f_2, args_2)) \rightarrow equate_1(\theta[v_1], t_2, \theta) \\
\quad\quad (mk\text{-}CompoundTerm(f_1, args_1), mk\text{-}Variable(v_2)) \rightarrow equate_1(t_1, \theta[v_2], \theta) \\
\quad\quad (mk\text{-}CompoundTerm(f_1, args_1), mk\text{-}CompoundTerm(f_2, args_2)) \rightarrow \\
\quad\quad\quad equate_1(t_1, t_2, \theta) \\
\quad \textsf{end}
\end{array}
$$

where

$$
\begin{array}{l}
equate_1(t_1, t_2, \theta) \quad \triangleq \\
\quad \textsf{cases } (t_1, t_2) \textsf{ of} \\
\quad\quad (mk\text{-}Variable(v_1), mk\text{-}Variable(v_2)) \rightarrow \\
\quad\quad\quad \textsf{if } v_1 = v_2 \textsf{ then } \theta \textsf{ else } \theta \circ \{v_1 \mapsto t_2 \bullet \theta\} \\
\quad\quad (mk\text{-}Variable(v_1), mk\text{-}CompoundTerm(f_2, args_2)) \rightarrow \\
\quad\quad\quad \textsf{if } v_1 \textsf{ occurs-in } t_2 \bullet \theta \textsf{ then nil else } \theta \circ \{v_1 \mapsto t_2 \bullet \theta\} \\
\quad\quad (mk\text{-}CompoundTerm(f_1, args_1), mk\text{-}Variable(v_2)) \rightarrow \\
\quad\quad\quad \textsf{if } v_2 \textsf{ occurs-in } t_1 \bullet \theta \textsf{ then nil else } \theta \circ \{v_2 \mapsto t_1 \bullet \theta\} \\
\quad\quad (mk\text{-}CompoundTerm(f_1, args_1), mk\text{-}CompoundTerm(f_2, args_2)) \rightarrow \\
\quad\quad\quad \textsf{if } f_1 = f_2 \wedge \textsf{len } args_1 = \textsf{len } args_2 \textsf{ then } mgul_3(args_1, args_2, \theta) \textsf{ else nil} \\
\quad \textsf{end}
\end{array}
$$

(The $\bullet\theta$ in the (variable,variable) case is not necessary, but gives a common form to the base cases.)

A further eureka definition

$$
\begin{array}{l}
expand_1(t, \theta) \quad \triangleq \\
\quad \textsf{cases } t \textsf{ of} \\
\quad\quad mk\text{-}Variable(v) \rightarrow \theta[v] \\
\quad\quad mk\text{-}CompoundTerm(f, args) \rightarrow t \\
\quad \textsf{end}
\end{array}
$$

(which is derivable in principle in the same way as $equate_1$) gives the final folded form

$$mgu_3(t_1, t_2, \theta) \quad \triangleq \quad equate_1(expand_1(t_1, \theta), expand_1(t_2, \theta), \theta)$$

We can finish the transformational development by providing an implementation of $mgul_3$. This is straightforward. Unfolding the definitions of $\_ \bullet^* \_$ and $mgul_2$ gives

$$
\begin{array}{l}
mgul_3(ts_1, ts_2, \theta) \quad \triangleq \\
\quad \textsf{cases } (ts_1, ts_2) \textsf{ of} \\
\quad\quad ([\,], [\,]) \rightarrow \theta \\
\quad\quad (\textsf{cons}(t_1', ts_1'), \textsf{cons}(t_2', ts_2')) \rightarrow \\
\quad\quad\quad \textsf{let } \theta_H = mgu_1(t_1' \bullet \theta, t_2' \bullet \theta) \textsf{ in} \\
\quad\quad\quad\quad \textsf{if } \theta_H = \textsf{nil then nil else } mgul_2(ts_1' \bullet^* \theta \bullet^* \theta_H, ts_2' \bullet^* \theta \bullet^* \theta_H, \theta \circ \theta_H) \\
\quad \textsf{end} \\
\textsf{pre len } ts_1 = \textsf{len } ts_2
\end{array}
$$

Now rewriting the let expression, using the definition of composition, and the new law

$$t_1, t_2\colon Term; \theta\colon Substitution \vdash mgu_2(t_1, t_2, \theta) = \mathsf{nil} \Leftrightarrow mgu_1(t_1, t_2) = \mathsf{nil}$$

gives folds using mgu_3 and $mgul_3$

$$
\begin{array}{l}
mgul_3(ts_1, ts_2, \theta) \;\; \triangleq \\
\quad \mathsf{cases}\ (ts_1, ts_2)\ \mathsf{of} \\
\quad\quad ([\,], [\,]) \rightarrow \theta \\
\quad\quad (\mathsf{cons}(t_1', ts_1'), \mathsf{cons}(t_2', ts_2')) \rightarrow \\
\quad\quad\quad \mathsf{let}\ \theta' = mgu_3(t_1', t_2', \theta)\ \mathsf{in} \\
\quad\quad\quad\quad \mathsf{if}\ \theta' = \mathsf{nil}\ \mathsf{then\ nil\ else}\ mgul_3(ts_1', ts_2', \theta') \\
\quad \mathsf{end} \\
\mathsf{pre\ len}\ ts_1 = \mathsf{len}\ ts_2
\end{array}
$$

4.2 A posit and prove approach

To develop the new version of mgu_3 by transformation required some insight beyond the original design of the data representation, in order to postulate the definitions of $equate_1$ and $expand_1$. Perhaps a similar amount of introspection at the start of the development would allow us to posit a definition of mgu_3 and *prove* the usual VDM specification satisfaction obligation

$$mgu_3(t_1, t_2, \theta) = mgu_2(t_1 \bullet \theta, t_2 \bullet \theta, \theta)$$

This posited definition will, of course, avoid as much substitution as possible by exploiting the data representation.

Our first idea is that compound terms input to mgu_3 do not need to be substituted to determine that they represent compound terms. (This was discovered by unfolding $\_ \bullet \_$ in the transformational development.) It suggests decomposing mgu_3 as

$$mgu_3(t_1, t_2, \theta) \;\; \triangleq \;\; equate_1(expand_1(t_1, \theta), expand_1(t_2, \theta), \theta)$$

where $expand_1$ substitutes only variables and $equate_1$ is to be suitably defined. We posit the $expand_1$ definition of the previous section as an obvious way to achieve its specification. The second insight is that we can define $equate_1$ as a variant of mgu_2 where compound terms are substituted before use in the bodies of the case expressions, since the extra substitution of compound terms derived from variables will have no effect. (The same insight gave $equate_1$ as a eureka in the transformational development.) If we again give the base cases a common form we arrive at

$$
\begin{array}{l}
equate_1(t_1, t_2, \theta) \ \triangleq \\
\quad \textsf{cases } (t_1, t_2) \textsf{ of} \\
\quad\quad (mk\text{-}Variable(v_1), mk\text{-}Variable(v_2)) \rightarrow \\
\quad\quad\quad \textsf{if } v_1 = v_2 \textsf{ then } \theta \textsf{ else } \theta \circ \{v_1 \mapsto t_2 \bullet \theta\} \\
\quad\quad (mk\text{-}Variable(v_1), mk\text{-}CompoundTerm(f_2, args_2)) \rightarrow \\
\quad\quad\quad \textsf{if } v_1 \textsf{ occurs-in } t_2 \bullet \theta \textsf{ then nil else } \theta \circ \{v_1 \mapsto t_2 \bullet \theta\} \\
\quad\quad (mk\text{-}CompoundTerm(f_1, args_1), mk\text{-}Variable(v_2)) \rightarrow \\
\quad\quad\quad \textsf{if } v_2 \textsf{ occurs-in } t_1 \bullet \theta \textsf{ then nil else } \theta \circ \{v_2 \mapsto t_1 \bullet \theta\} \\
\quad\quad (mk\text{-}CompoundTerm(f_1, args_1), mk\text{-}CompoundTerm(f_2, args_2)) \rightarrow \\
\quad\quad\quad \textsf{if } f_1 = f_2 \wedge \textsf{len } args_1 = \textsf{len } args_2 \textsf{ then } mgul_2(args_1 \bullet^* \theta, args_2 \bullet^* \theta, \theta) \\
\quad\quad\quad \textsf{else nil} \\
\quad \textsf{end}
\end{array}
$$

We can then complete the development by defining and transforming $mgul_3$ as before.

The proof of specification satisfaction can be carried out by considering the nine cases of figure 1, making the proof parts of the two developments identical. However, we can turn around the insight that led us to $equate_1$ and posit the theorem

$$
\frac{t_1, t_2\colon Term \quad \theta\colon Substitution \quad t_1\colon Variable \vdash t_1 \bullet \theta = t_1 \quad t_2\colon Variable \vdash t_2 \bullet \theta = t_2}{equate_1(t_1, t_2, \theta) = mgu_2(t_1 \bullet \theta, t_2 \bullet \theta, \theta)}
$$

which has an easy proof by cases. Then the specification satisfaction theorem follows from two properties of $expand_1$:

$$t\colon Term; \theta\colon Substitution \vdash expand_1(t, \theta) \bullet \theta = t \bullet \theta$$

$$t\colon Term; \theta\colon Substitution; expand_1(t, \theta)\colon Variable \vdash expand_1(t, \theta) = t \bullet \theta$$

Factoring the proof into properties of $expand_1$ and $equate_1$ gives us lemmas that we shall be able to re-use later.

5 Improving the substitution representation

The substitutions of terms left in mgu_3 are associated either with the occurs checks or with the construction of the unifier, both explicitly and implicitly in the composition of substitutions. The intermediate values of θ are used to expand variables and in the occurs check substitution. Each of these uses will involve only a few of the variables in the domain, so there seems to be scope for a lazy representation of substitutions where we can compute the values of these few variables when needed, rather than the value of every variable in advance.

By construction, every base case in $equate_1$ has a common form, which we could abstract by the (obvious) eureka

$$update_A : Variable \times Term \times Substitution \rightarrow Substitution$$

$$update_A(v, t, \theta) \ \triangleq \ \theta \circ \{v \mapsto t \bullet \theta\}$$

$$\textsf{pre } v \notin \textsf{dom}\, \theta \wedge \neg(v \textsf{ occurs-in } t \bullet \theta)$$

(The precondition is met by the uses, and is necessary to guarantee that the result is idempotent and to prove the results below.) The unifier is constructed by a series of applications of this operation to the empty substitution.

We can interpret this algebraically: *Substitution* is the carrier in a model of a sort with constant *empty*, represented in the model by $\{\}$, and constructor *update*, represented by $update_A$. We can also show that it satisfies the equation

$$update_A(v_1, t_1, update_A(v_2, t_2, \theta)) = update_A(v_2, t_2, update_A(v_1, t_1, \theta))$$

(for defined applications of $update_A$) by considering values of variables in the domain of the resulting substitutions and using

$$\neg(v_1 \text{ occurs-in } t_2 \bullet \theta \wedge v_2 \text{ occurs-in } t_1 \bullet \theta)$$

which is a consequence of the $update_A$ precondition.

Universal algebra [EM85] studies the categories of models of signatures with equational axioms. (To be precise, we need the extension to partial algebras [BW82].) The arrows in these categories are total functions from carrier set to carrier set which satisfy the specification satisfaction condition on the operations of the signature. If we can show that an arrow is epic, then it is a retrieve function and its source is an adequate representation of its target. (This amounts to a check that there is no junk in the original model.) An initial model in the category has a morphism to any other model.

An initial model of this signature and equation is provided by a subset of

$$Substitution\text{-}R = VarSymbol \xrightarrow{m} Term$$

with *empty* modelled by $\{\}$, and *update* modelled by

$$update_R(v, t, \theta) \;\triangleq\; \theta \cup \{v \mapsto t\}$$

$$\text{pre } v \notin \text{dom } \theta \wedge \neg(v \text{ occurs-in } t \bullet \theta)$$

The subset is precisely those values constructible by $update_R$ from $\{\}$: we could characterize them by an invariant as in [Vad90], but shall not need to. Let us call the morphism *retr-Substitution*. By using the specification satisfaction condition

$$\begin{aligned} &v\colon VarSymbol;\ t\colon Term;\ \theta\colon Substitution\text{-}R \vdash \\ &\qquad retr\text{-}Substitution(\theta \cup \{v \mapsto t\}) = \\ &\qquad retr\text{-}Substitution(\theta) \circ \{v \mapsto t \bullet retr\text{-}Substitution(\theta)\} \end{aligned}$$

together with idempotence and induction over sets, we can show *Substitution* is a subset of *Substitution-R*, and that any $\theta \in Substitution$ can be represented by itself, so an initial model is adequate. (This just confirms the intuition above that every *Substitution* can be generated by applying $update_A$ enough times to $\{\}$.) Similarly, [*Substitution_R*] will represent [*Substitution*] with *retr-Substitution* extended to map nil to nil.

We can introduce this new data representation with a eureka definition. In this case, the result type as well as an input type is affected by the change. Since the retrieve function is not an isomorphism, there is a choice of concrete output values to represent the abstract result. This can be expressed directly in VDM using postconditions:

$$mgu_4(t_1\colon Term, t_2\colon Term, \theta\colon Substitution\text{-}R)\ \theta'\colon [Substitution\text{-}R]$$

$$\text{post } retr\text{-}Substitution(\theta') = mgu_3(t_1, t_2, retr\text{-}Substitution(\theta))$$

(This is simpler than [Dar84], where a canonical representation function must be used to define the operation on the new data type.) Unfolding the function application in the post-condition gives

$mgu_4(t_1: Term, t_2: Term, \theta: Substitution\text{-}R)\ \theta': [Substitution\text{-}R]$

post $retr\text{-}Substitution(\theta') =$
$\quad equate_1(expand_1(t_1, retr\text{-}Substitution(\theta)),$
$\qquad expand_1(t_2, retr\text{-}Substitution(\theta)), retr\text{-}Substitution(\theta))$

which immediately suggests the eureka definitions

$equate_2(t_1: Term, t_2: Term, \theta: Substitution\text{-}R)\ \theta': [Substitution\text{-}R]$

post $retr\text{-}Substitution(\theta') = equate_1(t_1, t_2, retr\text{-}Substitution(\theta))$

$expand_2(t, \theta) \ \triangleq\ expand_1(t, retr\text{-}Substitution(\theta))$

Folding gives the specification

$mgu_4(t_1: Term, t_2: Term, \theta: Substitution\text{-}R)\ \theta': [Substitution\text{-}R]$

post $retr\text{-}Substitution(\theta') =$
$\quad retr\text{-}Substitution(equate_2(expand_2(t_1, \theta), expand_2(t_2, \theta), \theta))$

which is obviously satisfied by the implementation

$mgu_4(t_1, t_2, \theta) \ \triangleq\ equate_2(expand_2(t_1, \theta), expand_2(t_2, \theta), \theta)$

We can handle *equate*$_2$ in a similar way. Unfolding leads to a case expression. This can be rewritten using the specification satisfaction theorem and an obvious eureka definition

$mgul_4(ts_1: Term^*, ts_2: Term^*, \theta: Substitution\text{-}R)\ \theta': [Substitution\text{-}R]$

post $retr\text{-}Substitution(\theta') = mgul_3(ts_1, ts_2, retr\text{-}Substitution(\theta))$

to a form where the result is always a *retr-Substitution*(...) expression. Stripping out the *retr-Substitution* applications gives the obvious implementation

$equate_2(t_1, t_2, \theta) \ \triangleq$
cases (t_1, t_2) of
$\quad (mk\text{-}Variable(v_1), mk\text{-}Variable(v_2)) \rightarrow$
$\qquad$ if $v_1 = v_2$ then θ else $\theta \cup \{v_1 \mapsto t_2\}$
$\quad (mk\text{-}Variable(v_1), mk\text{-}CompoundTerm(f_2, args_2)) \rightarrow$
$\qquad$ if t_1 occurs-in $t_2 \bullet retr\text{-}Substitution(\theta)$ then nil else $\theta \cup \{v_1 \mapsto t_2\}$
$\quad (mk\text{-}CompoundTerm(f_1, args_1), mk\text{-}Variable(v_2)) \rightarrow$
$\qquad$ if t_2 occurs-in $t_1 \bullet retr\text{-}Substitution(\theta)$ then nil else $\theta \cup \{v_2 \mapsto t_1\}$
$\quad (mk\text{-}CompoundTerm(f_1, args_1), mk\text{-}CompoundTerm(f_2, args_2)) \rightarrow$
$\qquad$ if $f_1 = f_2 \wedge$ len $args_1 =$ len $args_2$ then $mgul_4(args_1, args_2, \theta)$ else nil
end

Deriving

$$
\begin{array}{l}
mgul_4(ts_1, ts_2, \theta) \quad \triangleq \\
\quad \textsf{cases } (ts_1, ts_2) \textsf{ of} \\
\qquad ([\,],[\,]) \rightarrow \theta \\
\qquad (\textsf{cons}(t_1', ts_1'), \textsf{cons}(t_2', ts_2')) \rightarrow \\
\qquad\quad \textsf{let } \theta' = mgu_4(t_1', t_2', \theta) \textsf{ in} \\
\qquad\qquad \textsf{if } \theta' = \textsf{nil then nil else } mgul_4(ts_1', ts_2', \theta') \\
\quad \textsf{end} \\
\textsf{pre len } ts_1 = \textsf{len } ts_2
\end{array}
$$

from its specification is a trivial exercise.

We now need to consider *expand*$_2$. Transformation of the specification above would lead us to define a function for obtaining the value of a variable from the substitution. Intuitively, this can be done by looking up the term that it is bound to, and substituting it recursively. Formally, we can show

$$
\begin{array}{l}
v\colon Variable; \theta\colon Substitution\text{-}R; v \in \textsf{dom}\,\theta \vdash \\
\qquad retr\text{-}Substitution(\theta)(v) = \theta(v) \bullet retr\text{-}Substitution(\theta)
\end{array}
$$

by induction on *Substitution-R* terms, using the specification satisfaction theorem and the precondition on $update_R$.

However, the same intuition suggests that this is more than is necessary. If we look up the variable and find a compound term, the result of further substitution will leave a compound term, and this substitution will be done anyway in *equate*$_1$ (or equivalently, delayed by *equate*$_2$). This suggests positing the definition

$$
\begin{array}{l}
expand_3(t, \theta) \quad \triangleq \\
\quad \textsf{cases } t \textsf{ of} \\
\qquad mk\text{-}Variable(v) \rightarrow \\
\qquad\quad \textsf{if } v \in \textsf{dom}\,\theta \textsf{ then } expand_3(\theta(v), \theta) \textsf{ else } mk\text{-}Variable(v) \\
\qquad mk\text{-}CompoundTerm(f, args) \rightarrow t \\
\quad \textsf{end}
\end{array}
$$

and proving the looser theorem

$$
\begin{array}{l}
t_1, t_2\colon Term; \theta\colon Substitution\text{-}R \vdash \\
\qquad equate_2(expand_3(t_1, \theta), expand_3(t_2, \theta), \theta) = \\
\qquad equate_2(expand_1(t_1, retr\text{-}Substitution(\theta)), \\
\qquad\qquad expand_1(t_2, retr\text{-}Substitution(\theta)), \theta)
\end{array}
$$

If we can establish the analogues of the *expand*$_1$ properties at the end of section 4.2

$$
\begin{array}{l}
t\colon Term; \theta\colon Substitution\text{-}R \vdash \\
\qquad expand_3(t, \theta) \bullet retr\text{-}Substitution(\theta) = t \bullet retr\text{-}Substitution(\theta)
\end{array}
$$

$$
\begin{array}{l}
t\colon Term; \theta\colon Substitution; expand_3(t, \theta)\colon Variable \vdash \\
\qquad expand_3(t, \theta) = t \bullet retr\text{-}Substitution(\theta)
\end{array}
$$

this proof can be presented as two copies of the specification satisfaction proof in that section, one for *expand*$_1$ and one for *expand*$_3$. These lemmas can be proved by induction on the number of $expand_3$ applications (which is bounded by the idempotence of the represented substitution), completing the justification of the change in representation. We observe that this has been accomplished without ever defining *retr-Substitution*, using only the properties it must have as a retrieve function. In essence, the choice of an initial model means that this is all the properties it does have.

6 Summary and conclusions

The development so far has been unusual in that the formal data types we end up with are very similar to those we began with, although the way we use them to represent terms and substitutions has changed. The common theme motivating the changes has been the delaying of substitutions until substituted values are needed (which turns out to be when we look at variables). The representations are lazy in the sense that they provide a recipe to compute a value rather than the value itself.

To complete the development, we should first need to implement the occurs-in relation, which has been left untouched through the various changes. A single definition such as

$$occurs\_in'(v, t, \theta) \;\;\triangleq\;\; v \text{ occurs-in } (t \bullet retr\text{-}Substitution(\theta))$$

could be transformed using the laws developed earlier. The result would still involve a time-consuming traversal of the represented term, which algorithms like that of [MM82] avoid. In Prolog, where this algorithm is usually used, the occurs check is omitted. Surprisingly, we can still regard the result as a unification algorithm for an extended definition of terms [Col82].

We should then need a series of reifications to represent the abstract types in more implementable ways. For example, we should like to achieve constant time access to variables in substitutions. One observation that we can make is that since no term is ever substituted in the final algorithm, the substitution must be built up from subterms of the original inputs. With suitable data structures, we can do this using pointers to the subterms rather than copies of them, which accounts for the description of the algorithm as structure sharing.

The development so far has been carried out by a mixture of transformation and posit-and-prove. The first step was a pure transformation, based on a eureka definition of a standard form for introducing tail recursion. The second step was also carried out by transformation, beginning with a eureka of another standard form for introducing data representation changes. Of the further eurekas, some also followed this pattern, but others, necessary to simplify the unfolded forms, were seen to require insight, if only to select them from a mechanically derived set of generalizations under equations. In the posit-and-prove version of the same development, the same intuition led directly to the new specification. It sufficed because the development was completed by a routine eureka and transformation: the positing of the entire set of final definitions would have been harder.

The final step begins as usual with an intuitive data representation change represented by a standard eureka definition (although the retrieve function itself is described by an initial property rather than directly). Substantial parts of the development are done by transformation, but a key change, introducing $expand_3$, was posited based on intuition derived from the proof of an earlier law. It is possible instead to keep unfolding the definition of mgu_4. The conditional in $\_[\_]$ gives rise to some very large terms, and it soon becomes apparent that there is an endless regress in unfolding the variable case. This may suggest an inductive generalization to give a eureka definition equivalent to $expand_3$. It may again be possible to mechanize the suggestion of such eurekas. However, we would still need to posit and prove a law such as that relating $equate_1$ to mgu_2 to complete the rewriting. The transformational approach seems a more roundabout way to achieve the final result.

In summary, transformation has been of great use in the straightforward parts of the development, where we use only "standard" eurekas and "obvious" laws. The rest of the development sketched above might well be of this type. In other places, although transformation provides a framework and a useful focussing onto the difficult parts, these parts are tackled more readily by posit-and-prove. There is a clear symbiosis between the approaches which makes the use of transformation techniques in VDM developments attractive.

It has been claimed (in [Bal81], for example) that transformational developments formalize the developer's intuition in a way that posit-and-prove developments do not. This claim does not seem to be supported by the parallel developments of sections 4.1 and 4.2. In each case, the intuition behind the data type reification is represented (only) by the retrieve function, and intuitions about the way to exploit the new data type are recorded in function definitions which are eurekas in one case and posited in the other. There is also unrecorded intuition behind the laws that we must prove for the data types. Further, the separate development of the proof of correctness in section 4.2 encouraged a decomposition into lemmas, reflecting an insight into the algorithm which was later exploited in section 5.

These results are perhaps not surprising. We are trying to construct and prove an implementation. Large parts of any proof are routine. In particular, when we are working with function definitions, β-conversion (in either direction) is likely to be commonplace, and almost automatic. It is precisely this which is captured by folding and unfolding. Similarly, common laws of data types, such as associativity, are applied so frequently as to be worth mentioning only in a fully formal proof. Simple developments, such as the first step here, use only these lemmas. In more complex proofs, they will leave gaps. These consist of the intuitively plausible but as yet unproven inferences which "make the proof go through". They are the posited components (both laws and definitions) of the development steps above.

In the light of this, we might regard transformation as one proof technique among many for conducting developments. In fact, it is a combination of two: forwards inference, which generates proven results that can be screened for interesting ones; and proof structuring through the use of lemmas, which enables us to re-use the effort we put into earlier proofs. Even when we abandon the first, as we have to when proofs get hard, practical use of rigorous development demands that we retain the second. In the inferences which complete complex proofs lie the generalizations which become the new lemmas, reusable in further developments or in later parts of the current one. Those who do not understand their proofs are condemned to repeat them.

Theorem proving for development tends to be broad rather than deep. We need to be able to store large numbers of definitions and theorems in a way which collects together related results so that we have a chance of finding them to re-use them. We need to be able to revise proofs as we understand better how to structure them. If we are to rely on lemmas, then the proofs should be formal, not rigorous. (One of the rigorous "proofs" in this paper had a counterexample that went undetected for some time.) These requirements can best be realized by mechanical support of the proof process. The MuRal system [J^+91] offers much of this support, and some of this development has been carried out using it. It is clear that formalizing some of the rest (the algebraic components of section 5, for example) will be challenging, but perhaps the wide applicability of the techniques will justify the effort involved.

References

[B+88] F.L. Bauer et al. *The Munich Project CIP: Volume II*, volume 292 of *Lecture Notes in Computer Science*. Springer-Verlag, 1988.

[Bal81] R. Balzer. Transformational implementation: An example. *IEEE Transactions on Software Engineering*, 7:3–14, 1981.

[BD77] R.M. Burstall and J. Darlington. A transformation system for developing recursive programs. *Journal of the ACM*, 24:44–67, 1977.

[BM72] R. S. Boyer and J. S. Moore. The sharing of structure in theorem-proving programs. In *Machine Intelligence 7*, pages 101–116, 1972.

[BW82] M. Broy and M. Wirsing. Partial abstract types. *Acta Informatica*, 18:47–64, 1982.

[Cle90] T. P. Clement. A CS212 case study: Unification. Unpublished lecture notes, 1990.

[Col82] A. Colmerauer. Prolog and infinite trees. In *Logic Programming*, pages 231–251. Academic Press, 1982.

[Coo66] D. C. Cooper. The equivalence of certain computations. *Computer Journal*, 9:45–52, 1966.

[Dar84] J. Darlington. The design of efficient data representations. In *Automatic Program Construction Techniques*, chapter 7, pages 139–156. Macmillan, 1984.

[EM85] H. Ehrig and B. Mahr. *Fundamentals of Algebraic Specification*, volume 6 of *EATCS Monographs*. Springer-Verlag, 1985.

[Fit90] J. S. Fitzgerald. Unification: Specification and development. In *Case Studies in Systematic Software Development*, pages 127–161. Prentice-Hall International, 1990.

[J+91] C. B. Jones et al. *mural: A Formal Development Support System*. Springer-Verlag, 1991.

[Jon90] C. B. Jones. *Systematic Software Development Using VDM*. Prentice-Hall International, 2nd edition, 1990.

[Llo87] J. W. Lloyd. *Foundations of Logic Programming*. Springer-Verlag, 2nd edition, 1987.

[Mil78] R. Milner. A theory of type polymorphism in programming. *Journal of Computer and Systems Sciences*, 17:348–375, 1978.

[MM82] A. Martelli and U. Montanari. An efficient unification algorithm. *ACM Transactions on Programming Languages and Systems*, 4:258–282, 1982.

[MW81] Z. Manna and R. Waldinger. Deductive synthesis of the unification algorithm. *Science of Computer Programming*, 1:5–48, 1981.

[Rob65] J. A. Robinson. A machine oriented logic based on the resolution principle. *Journal of the ACM*, 12:23–41, 1965.

[Vad90] S. Vadera. Building a theory of unification. In *Case Studies in Systematic Software Development*, pages 163–193. Prentice-Hall International, 1990.

A Case for Structured Analysis/Formal Design

Nico Plat
Jan van Katwijk
Kees Pronk

Delft University of Technology
Faculty of Technical Mathematics and Informatics
P.O. Box 356, NL-2600 AJ Delft, The Netherlands
E-mail: {nico, jan, kees}@dutiaa.tudelft.nl

abstract

Both formal methods and structured methods in software development have disadvantages inherent to the class of methods they belong to. A better method may be composed by taking the best of a formal method and the best of a structured method and constructing one, new method. In this paper two approaches to transforming data flow diagrams, the main system representation resulting from SA, to constructs in VDM are described. Each approach can be used as a basis for a combined SA/VDM method. A comparison is made between the two presented models by analyzing their characteristics. Some conclusions on the usability of the combination of SA and VDM are presented.

1 Introduction

The use of formal methods in software development can provide better complexity control, and may therefore make the production of software cheaper while resulting in higher quality products. Nevertheless, software development in professional communities often is completely *ad hoc*, or at best supported by structured methods such as OOD, SA/SD and JSD. A major issue for educational and research institutions therefore is to develop paradigms for software development with increased formality, and to teach the professional community its proper use. One of the problems with such paradigms seems to be the lack of a clear view on the transition from structured to formal methods. Although we agree with [Hall 90] in which is stated that, in general, one does not have to be a mathematician in order to be able to use formal methods, most professional software developers are scared by the apparent amount of mathematics which is an intrinsic part of formal methods. It is very hard to convince those professionals that using formal methods will lead to better specifications and programmes, and investments in that area are indeed cost-effective.

Based on class room experiences, experiences with potential software engineers and experiences with professionals in the field, we are convinced that a simple transition from the usage of structured methods on the one day to the usage of formal methods on the next day is too much to ask. What is needed is a method in which aspects of formal methods and structured methods are somehow combined. A quite natural approach to combining structured and formal methods for software development seems to be what is usually called a *parallel* approach. In this approach, the software system is developed using one of the classical structured approaches while in parallel a second development takes place using formal methods. Although such a parallel approach is extremely useful as a base for developing safe and reliable software systems [Leveson 91], we do not believe that the approach is very useful to convince people to use formal methods themselves. Since the parallel step will often be performed by people trained in formal methods, those who *have* to be convinced, i.e. the ones taking the classical approach, may not be impressed at all. On the contrary, the effect might even be negative [Kemmerer 90].

We therefore advocate a *sequential* approach, an approach in which different methods are used in different stages of the software production process, some of them formal, others structured. Of course the question then is: which formal methods to take and which part of a structured method to replace by which 'formal method'.

Structured Analysis/Structured Design (SA/SD) [DeMarco 79, Gane 79, Constantine 79, Yourdon 75, Myers 75] is one of the most widely used software development methods. When trying to achieve an increase of the use of formal methods, it seems worthwhile to investigate the possibilities to either *annotate* the analysis and design results (the most important ones are *data flow diagrams (DFDs))* or to exchange either SA or SD with a formal method, in our case the *Vienna Development Method (VDM)* [Bjørner 82, Jones 90]. For extensive descriptions of SA and VDM the reader is referred to the literature. Our first experiments with finding ways to combine VDM with SA/SD can be found in [Toetenel 90].

We started with some experiments in which we looked at the *annotation* of designs that were resulting from SD in the classical SA/SD development approach. Based on reports on combining JSD and VDM [Chedgey 87] we had some hopes that a combination of SD and VDM would turn out to be more practicable. The process of annotating turned out to be quite difficult while the resulting specifications were not found very helpful in understanding the design either. A brief analysis showed that these difficulties were caused by the fact that all design steps were already taken, while the semantics of the designs themselves were very intuitive. Therefore, we decided to extend our experiment with the development of a methodology in which we replaced the SD step altogether with a VDM driven development method. We deliberately moved the point in the development from where a formal description of the software under construction would be written, to the front of the development process. We envisage a combined sequential SA/VDM method as a software development method in which the first steps resemble the traditional SA approach (construction of a context diagram followed by refinement until an acceptable level of detail has been reached) followed by a process of transforming DFD constructs in a systematic way to VDM constructs, in this way generating a formal specification of the software system under construction. This process gives the following advantages over the original SA process:

- the analyst/designer is given structural guidance for the construction of a formal specification of the system. The formal specification should then be used as a starting point for the further development of the system;
- the analyst/designer has two views of the system (a *graphical view* provided by the DFD and a *textual view* provided by the formal specification) which allows him to concentrate on the aspects he is interested in only;
- the formal specification can be regarded as a formal semantics of the DFD, so:
  - the meaning of the DFD (which used to have an intuitive meaning only) has now become precise and unambiguous;
  - it is now possible to check the DFD for any inconsistencies.

In this paper we will describe the underlying principles of how DFDs can be transformed to VDM constructs. If certain restrictions to DFDs are applied, this transformation can be fully automated. A formal specification of such a transformation is described in [Larsen 91a]. The methodological aspects of our approach are described in [Larsen 91b]. A small case study of our approach is presented in [Plat 91].

Our approach to the construction of a formal specification is to formalize the intuitive semantics that can be given to DFDs in a structured way, which, in combination with knowledge of the representation of data in the system and knowledge of the control flow, will lead to a usable formal specification of the system. In section 2 we will first describe the informal semantics of DFDs and a strategy for transforming DFDs into VDM specifications. Section 3 contains a detailed description of two approaches for mapping DFD constructs onto VDM constructs, including a small example and a comparison of both approaches. Finally, in section 4 we draw some conclusions on the usability of SA as a starting point for the construction of a formal specification.

2 DFDs and VDM specifications combined

In this section we describe the strategy for mapping DFDs onto VDM constructs. First we give a brief 'informal' description of DFDs.

2.1 An informal description of DFDs

A DFD is a *directed graph* consisting of elementary building blocks. Each building block has a graphical notation (figure 1). Through the years a number of different dialects have evolved and extensions have been defined (e.g. SA/RT [Ward 85] and SSADM [Longworth 86]), but we will limit ourselves to a very elementary form of DFDs with a small number of different building blocks:

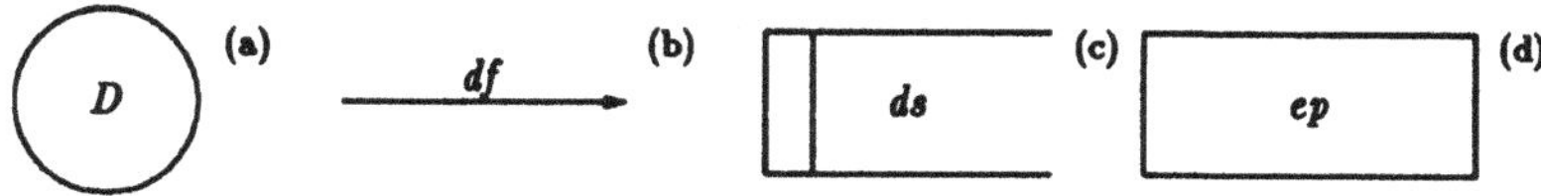

Figure 1: (a) Data transformer; (b) Data flow; (c) Data store; (d) External process

1. *Data transformers.* Data transformers are usually denoted as bubbles. They have any number of inputs, and any number of outputs.
2. *Data flows.* Data flows are represented as arrows, connecting one data transformer to another. They represent a flow of data between the data transformers they connect. The flow of data is unidirectional in the direction of the arrow.
3. *Data stores.* Data stores provide for (temporary) storage of data.
4. *External processes.* External process are processes that are not part of the system but belong to the outside world. They are used to show where the input to the system is coming from and where the output of the system is going to.

DFDs are used to model the *information flow* through a system. As such they provide a limited view of the system: in their most rudimentary form they neither show the control flow of the system nor any timing aspects. Therefore, DFDs are often combined with data dictionaries, control flow diagrams, state transition diagrams, decision tables and mini-specs to provide a more complete view of all the aspects of the system.

The process of constructing a DFD is an iterative one. Initially, the system to be designed is envisaged as one large data transformer, getting input from and providing output to external processes. This initial, high-level DFD is called a *context diagram.* The next step is the *refinement* (or *decomposition*) of the context diagram into a network of data transformers, the total network having the same functionality as the original context diagram. This process is repeated for each data transformer until the analyst/designer considers all the data transformers in the DFD to be primitive, i.e. each data transformer performs a well-defined, well-understood function.

Usually, the intermediate DFDs constructed in the refinement process are not discarded, but are kept as part of the system documentation. An analyst/designer can use them to study the system at different levels of abstraction. We call such a collection of DFDs, describing the same system but at different levels of abstraction, a *hierarchy of DFDs.*

2.2 A strategy for mapping DFDs onto VDM constructs

When discussing the transformation of DFDs to VDM specifications, a context has to be defined in which this transformation is a meaningful activity. Our strategy for the definition of this context first follows the traditional approach of SA to construct a model of the system (the DFD) by identifying data transformers and data flows, and refining the data transformers until all data transformers are considered to be primitive. We will refer to the DFD that is constructed in this way as the *low-level DFD.* Additionally, rules are provided for the transformation of a low-level DFD to appropriate VDM counterparts. Different transformations exist, two of which are described in section 3.

Other products of SA are not taken into account, e.g. it is assumed that *VDM domain definitions* have been provided for the *data descriptions of the data flows* between the data transformers in the DFD. In principle such domain definitions can, to some extent, be automatically derived from typical SA products as *data dictionaries* and *Entity Relationship Diagrams (ERDs)*.

Methodological aspects

Our strategy does *not* address the *methodological aspects* of mapping DFDs onto VDM. This aspect is, however, taken into account in [Larsen 91b], [Larsen 91a] and [Plat 91], in which an elaborate strategy is used for deciding in which order parts in a DFD are transformed, and in which VDM modules are used for structuring the different levels in the hierarchy of DFDs.

Characteristics of the problem domain

Some characteristics of the problem domain (e.g. timing aspects, knowledge about the implementation model of the system) can influence the way a DFD can best be mapped onto a VDM specification. In this paper we describe how to transform the most general form of DFDs, i.e. DFDs that only show the flow of data through the system, not making any assumptions on timing aspects or control flow. We call the execution of a transformation in which only the DFD (and some essential information on data types and functional aspects of the system) is taken into account a *primary-mapping step* in the transformation.

Since the VDM specifications resulting from a primary-mapping step can look rather complicated, we want to leave the possibility open to include characteristics of the problem domain (usually non-functional requirements imposed upon the system) in the transformation. We call this process the *secondary-mapping step.* As will be shown later on, the secondary-mapping step can influence the readability of the formal specification to a large extent. Executing the secondary-mapping step corresponds to applying restrictions to the DFDs we want to be able to transform. The primary-mapping step and the secondar-mapping step are shown in figure 2.

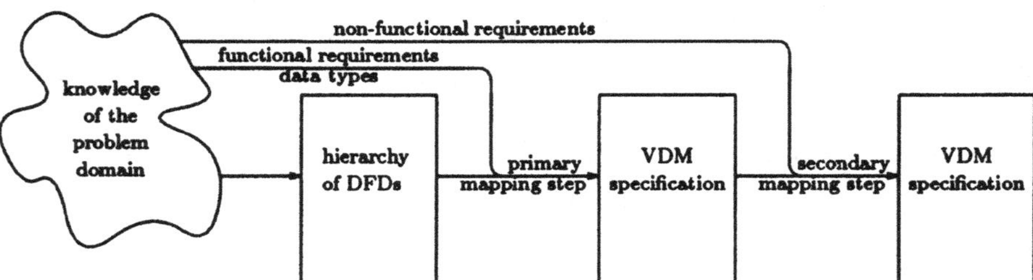

Figure 2: The primary-mapping step and the secondary-mapping step

The distinction between the primary-mapping step and the secondary-mapping step is made to allow for a semantically clean description of the two approaches in section 3. In practice both steps would be integrated into one single step in which the *informal* aspects of the system (captured in DFDs, data dictionary and auxiliary knowledge of the problem domain) are transformed to a complete *formal* specification of the system.

Relation to other work

When DFDs were introduced originally, they were presented as a graphical notation. The intended semantics of this notation was defined verbally. Since then, some work has been done on formalizing DFDs, with the intention either of disambiguating their meaning, or of using the formal semantics as a base for an integrated formal/structured method.

In [Randell 90] a translation back and forth between DFDs and Z specifications is described. [Alabiso 88] contains an explanation of how one can manually transform DFDs into an object-oriented design. The paper touches upon some of the problematic issues arising in a transformation from DFDs. In [Semmens 91] a small example of how a DFD can be transformed in Z is presented. However, no formal semantics of the DFDs is presented and it is not clear to what extent the transformation can be automated. In [Bruza 89] some guidelines for how semantics can be attached to DFDs are given. It is sketched how DFDs can be transformed to a Petri Net variant combined with path expressions. In [Adler 88] a semantic base for guiding the decomposition process in the construction of a hierarchy of DFDs is presented. This work is based on graph theory in an algebraic setting. In [Fraser 91] a rule-based approach for transforming SA products into VDM specifications is presented. Their VDM specifications are very explicit and hard to read, mainly because of the way decision tables have been taken into account.

Our work differs from the work of other authors in that we (in the primary-mapping step) do not assume any specific implementation model for DFDs; DFDs are envisaged as networks of connected processes through which the flow of data is shown, nothing more and nothing less. No assumptions are made on the way in which or when the data transformers execute. At the same time it is still possible to construct understandable VDM specifications, although mainly in the secondary-mapping step.

3 Mapping DFD constructs onto VDM constructs

Mapping the various DFD constructs onto VDM constructs can be done in a number of ways. More than two different mappings exist, but we we will concentrate on two approaches which are opposites of each other: the *PAC approach* and the *SAC approach*.

3.1 The PAC approach

In the PAC approach for mapping DFD constructs onto VDM constructs we make minimal assumptions on *how* data is transported from one data transformer to the other. We call this the *P*(arallel) *AC*(ces) *approach* (parallel as opposed to *sequential* access, assumed in the second approach which is discussed in section 3.2). In the PAC approach, the primary-mapping step consists of 4 activities, to be carried out sequentially:

1. Create a *VDM state component* for each *data store* in the DFD.
2. Create a *VDM operation* for each *data transformer* and for each *external process* in the DFD.
3. Create a *VDM operation* for each *(set of) data store(s)* and all the *data transformers* which access that same (set of) data store(s). Replace these data store(s) and data transformers in the DFD by one single data transformer. The newly created VDM operation is a model for this data transformer.
4. Create a *VDM operation* for each *data flow* and the (two) *data transformers* connected by the data flow. Replace each such data flow and the two data transformers in the DFD by one single data transformer. The newly created VDM operation is a model for this data transformer.

Steps 3 and 4 essentially correspond to a process of *composition* (in contrast to the *decomposition*-process during which the context diagram was refined into a low-level DFD, containing only primitive data transformers) of data transformers into higher-level data transformers until only one data transformer remains; this data transformer corresponds to the context diagram that was used as the starting point for the SA process. The details of the steps are explained below.

Data stores

The first activity in the primary-mapping step in the PAC approach is the mapping of *data stores* onto *VDM state components*. We refrain from specifying *how* access to a data store takes place nor do we make any assumption on the way in which data stores are accessed by data transformers. We will assume, however, that if two data transformers update the same data store, these updates are indivisible actions, i.e. they cannot occur simultaneously. An arrow between a data transformer and a data store means that the data transformer has access to the data store. Such an arrow is seen as a syntactical notation to make the data store visible to a data transformer, and therefore has no explicit VDM counterpart. If the arrow is directed from the data transformer to the data store it means that the data transformer may add objects to the data store. Write access also implies that the data store can be examined without affecting it. If the arrow is directed from the data store to the data transformer it means that the data transformer only has read access the data store, so the data transformer cannot change the data store.

Data transformers and external processes

In the PAC approach, data transformers and external processes are treated in exactly the same way, therefore we will limit the discussion to data transformers. Since we don't know how or when a data transformer is triggered (this is part of the control flow) the only semantics we can give to a data transformer is a description of the effect of the data transformer, taking into account the presence or absence of data on all or some of its inputs. The most obvious construct in VDM-SL onto which a *data transformer* can be mapped is a *VDM operation*. We use *implicit* VDM operations since our main interest lies in *what* the effect of the transformation is, instead of *how* the effect is achieved which is, after all, also not directly shown by the DFD.

Inputs and outputs of a data transformer are dealt with as follows:

- *Inputs to the data transformers* are transformed to *input parameters* of the VDM operation. The input parameters of a VDM operation are typed. We determine the type of an input parameter from the information we have of the data flow connected to the data transformer (presented by the user in the form of a VDM-like data dictionary).
- *Outputs from the data transformers* are transformed to *the result parameter* of the VDM operation. A tuple expression is constructed if a data transformer has more than one output. The types of the components are determined in the same way as the types of the inputs of the data transformer.

The order in which input and output parameters are presented in the signature of the operation is for the moment left unspecified, because talking about the 'order' of inputs and outputs of a data transformer in a *picture*, which the DFD after all is, is not very meaningful.

If a data transformation takes place we can neither assume that output values are generated for *all* the outputs of that data transformer nor that input values will be taken from *all* the inputs. Data transformers thus essentially are overloaded constructs that might show different behaviour, depending on the presence and the values of its inputs. Unfortunately, overloading of operations is not supported in VDM-SL. To simulate overloading, we introduce a syntactical extension to VDM-SL by adding a special value τ to the input and output domains of operations. We specify that this special value has been added to a domain by appending an subscript Θ to the domain. So, $\mathbb{N}_{\Theta}$ is the notation for the domain of natural numbers extended with the special value τ. The VDM-SL 'built-in' special value nil (created by the optional-domain constructor) cannot be used for this purpose due to the conflicts that can be caused by the possible use of optional domains in the data dictionary of the DFD.

Example 1

An example of a data transformer is shown in figure 3. A suitable VDM operation[1] to

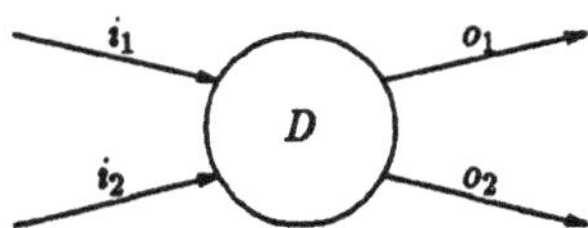

Figure 3: Data transformer with two inputs and two outputs

model this data transformer is:

1. For the specification of VDM constructs we will use BSI/VDM-SL as defined in [BSI/VDM], with a few minor lexical extensions.

$$D\,(i_1 : I_{1\Theta}, i_2 : I_{2\Theta})\ o : O_{1\Theta} \times O_{2\Theta}$$
$$\textsf{post let } mk\text{-}(o_1, o_2) = o \textsf{ in}$$
$$P_D(i_1, i_2, o_1, o_2)$$

The predicate P_D depends on the *functionality* of the data transformer D. It cannot be derived from the DFD and must therefore be provided by the analyst/designer. The most general form of P_D is the logical value true, which corresponds to a semantics for data transformer D disregarding information on the functionality of D: *any* implementation with a signature satisfying the types of the inputs i_1 and i_2 and outputs o_1 and o_2 will satisfy the post-condition true.

To illustrate a possible further development step of a specification as general as the one above, we will assume that we know that data transformer D produces an output o_1 for each input i_1 and an output o_2 for each input i_2. The corresponding VDM operation then becomes:

$$D\,(i_1 : I_{1\Theta}, i_2 : I_{2\Theta})\ o : O_{1\Theta} \times O_{2\Theta}$$
$$\textsf{post let } mk\text{-}(o_1, o_2) = o \textsf{ in}$$
$$(P_{1D}(i_1, o_1) \wedge o_2 = \tau) \vee$$
$$(P_{2D}(i_2, o_2) \wedge o_1 = \tau)$$

The disjunction in the post-condition allows the post-condition to be satisfied by arbitrarily choosing between either performing the transformation for i_1 (in which case no output needs to be constructed for o_2) or performing the transformation for i_2 (in which case no output needs to be constructed for o_1). The ability to express looseness in VDM enables us in this case to disregard control flow.
□

Data flows
Data flow arrows show a connection between two data transformers or between a data transformer and an external process. *When* or *how* data flows is not considered, the meaning of a connection is the *composition* of the data transformers that it combines. Since a composition of two data transformers is a (higher-level) data transformer itself, and since we have chosen to map data transformers onto VDM operations, we map *data flows* onto *VDM operations* as well. The post-condition of the resulting operation must show the *existence* of the connection between the two data transformers or the data transformer and the external process.

Example 2
We start with an example (figure 4) in which two data transformers D_1 and D_2, each with two inputs, are connected to each other by a data flow o_{1D1}. The semantics of such a construct becomes clear when we consider the higher-level data transformer $D_1\,ToD_2$, giving

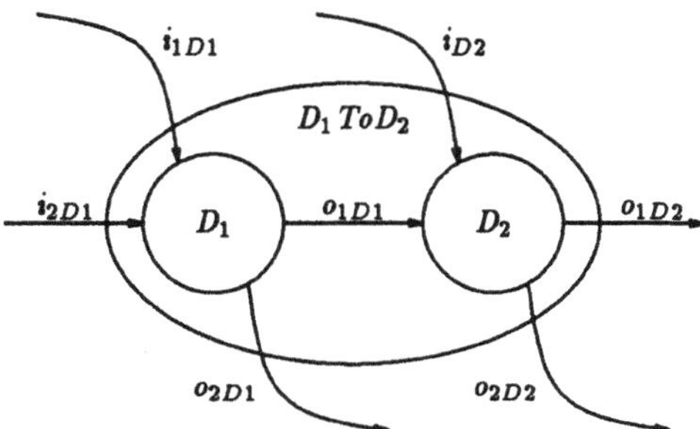

Figure 4: Combination of two data transformers

semantics to the data flow arrow. At first sight, the way to map this data transformer onto a VDM operation appears to be the following:

$$\begin{array}{l} D_1\,ToD_2\,(i_{1D1} : I_{1D1\theta}, i_{2D1} : I_{2D1\theta}, i_{D2} : I_{D2\theta})\ o : O_{2D1\theta} \times O_{1D2\theta} \times O_{2D2\theta} \\ \textsf{post let}\ mk\text{-}(o_{2D1}, o_{1D2}, o_{2D2}) = o\ \textsf{in} \\ \quad (\exists\, o_{1D1} : O_{1D1\theta} \cdot post\text{-}D_1(i_{1D1}, i_{2D1}, o_{1D1}, o_{2D1}) \wedge \\ \qquad\qquad post\text{-}D_2(i_{D2}, o_{1D1}, o_{1D2}, o_{2D2})) \end{array}$$

In this specification, the output value of D_1 is directly used as the input value for D_2. Unfortunately, this specification is too strict: since we make no assumptions on the control and speed of execution of data transformers, we cannot directly connect the output of D_1 to the input of D_2. Suppose e.g. that D_2 receives an input value on its input i_{D2} such that it can make a valid transformation, regardless of the input o_{1D1}. The specification above forces D_2 to take input o_{1D1} into account as well, therefore we must seek for a specification for $D_1\,ToD_2$ that is more 'loose'. We know, however, that the value of o_{1D1} must at one time have fulfilled the post-condition of D_1. The VDM operation corresponding to the combination shown in figure 4 is:

$$\begin{array}{l} D_1\,ToD_2\,(i_{1D1} : I_{1D1\theta}, i_{2D1} : I_{2D1\theta}, i_{D2} : I_{D2\theta})\ o : O_{2D1\theta} \times O_{1D2\theta} \times O_{2D2\theta} \\ \textsf{post let}\ mk\text{-}(o_{2D1}, o_{1D2}, o_{2D2}) = o\ \textsf{in} \\ \quad (\exists\, o_{1D1} : O_{1D1\theta} \cdot post\text{-}D_1(i_{1D1}, i_{2D1}, o_{1D1}, o_{2D1})) \wedge \\ \quad (\exists\, o_{1D1} : O_{1D1\theta}, o'_{2D1} : O_{2D1\theta}, i'_{1D1} : I_{1D1\theta}, i'_{2D1} : I_{2D1\theta} \cdot \\ \qquad post\text{-}D_1(i'_{1D1}, i'_{2D1}, o_{1D1}, o'_{2D1}) \wedge \\ \qquad post\text{-}D_2(i_{D2}, o_{1D1}, o_{1D2}, o_{2D2})) \end{array}$$

The post-condition of this operation can thus be satisfied by creating an o_{D1} which satisfies the post-condition of D_1 (in effect we execute D_1 to create such a o_{D1}), which can then be used to satisfy the post-condition of D_2. The total effect of $D_1\,ToD_2$ is the execution of both D_1 and D_2, denoted by the conjunction between the two quantified expressions. The specification of more inputs and/or outputs is done along the same lines.
□

Example 3
A slightly more complicated example is shown in figure 5. The corresponding VDM op-

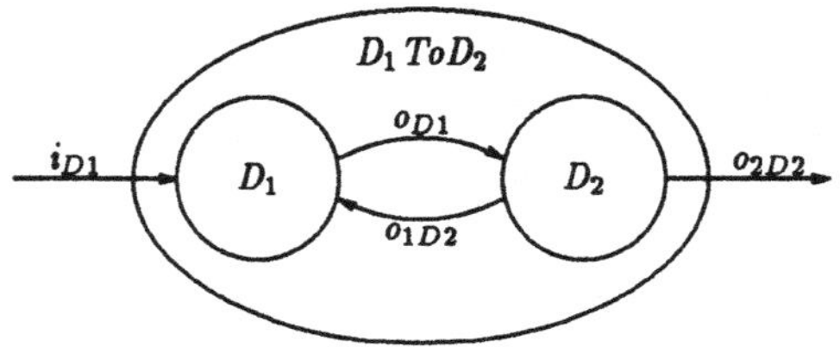

Figure 5: Fragment of a DFD containing a loop

eration is:

$$\begin{array}{l} D_1\,ToD_2\,(i_{D1} : I_{D1\Theta})\; o_{2D2} : O_{2D2\Theta} \\ \textbf{post}\; (\exists\, o_{D1}, o'_{D1} : O_{D1\Theta}, o_{1D2} : O_{1D2\Theta}, o'_{2D2} : O_{2D2\Theta} \cdot \\ \qquad \textit{post-}D_1(i_{D1}, o_{1D2}, o_{D1}) \wedge \textit{post-}D_2(o'_{D1}, o_{1D2}, o'_{2D2})) \wedge \\ \quad (\exists\, i'_{D1} : I_{D1}, o_{D1} : O_{D1\Theta}, o_{1D2}, o'_{1D2} : O_{1D2\Theta} \cdot \\ \qquad \textit{post-}D_2(o_{D1}, o_{2D2}, o_{1D2}) \wedge \textit{post-}D_1(i'_{D1}, o'_{1D2}, o_{D1})) \end{array}$$

This example shows how to deal with 'recursive' data transformers. Existential quantification is used to generate the data flowing between D_1 and D_2.
□

The order in which the combinations of data transformers are made can in the secondary-mapping step significantly influence the readability of the specification, and is therefore an important aspect of a combined SA/VDM method (see also [Larsen 91a]). In the primary-mapping step, however, this order is irrelevant, which increases the credibility of the belief that the PAC approach is a consistent approach for mapping DFD constructs onto VDM constructs. To support this thesis we present the following theorem.

Theorem
The composition of the data transformers D_1, D_2 and D_3 (figure 6) is associative.
□

Outline of proof: We can combine D_1, D_2 and D_3 in two different ways: D_1 and D_2 first and then combine the result with D_3, or D_2 and D_3 first and then combine the result with D_1. In this way two operations $(D_1\,ToD_2)\,ToD_3$ and $D_1\,To(D_2\,ToD_3)$ can be constructed following the earlier presented rules, which both specify the behaviour of the combination D_1, D_2 and D_3. To show the associativity we have to prove the following:

$$\forall\, i : I_\Theta, o : O_\Theta \cdot (\textit{post-}(D_1\,ToD_2)\,ToD_3(i, o) \;\Leftrightarrow\; \textit{post-}D_1\,To(D_2\,ToD_3)(i, o))$$

The proof itself is fairly straightforward and is therefore not given in this paper.
□

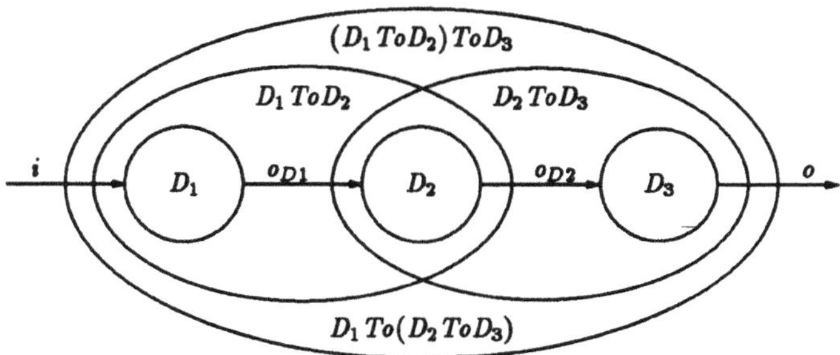

Figure 6: Combination of three data transformers

Data transformers in combination with data stores
Combinations of data transformers and data stores are modelled as operations accessing the state of the system.

Example 4
An example of a data transformer in combination with a data store is shown in figure 7. The corresponding VDM specification is:

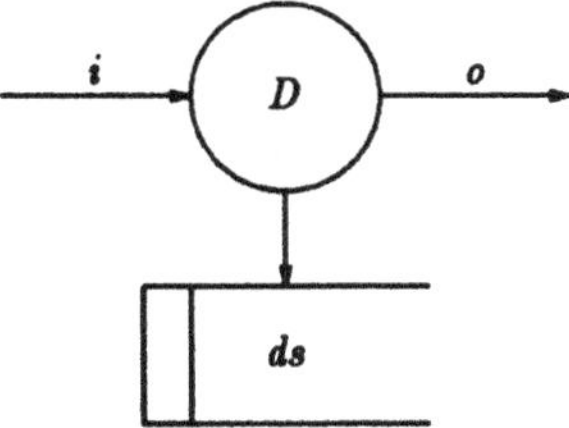

Figure 7: Access to a data store

$D\,(i : I_{\Theta})\; o : O_{\Theta}$
ext wr $ds : DS$

post $P_D(i, o, ds, \overleftarrow{ds})$

□

Example 5
Combining data transformers accessing the same data store is more complicated. Consider the configuration in figure 8. We know that both D_1 and D_2 can or will access data store ds, but we cannot make any assumption on the order in which these accesses take place. We are able to enumerate the possibilities, however. In this case we only have two possibilities: either D_1 uses the data store first and then D_2, or the other way around. $D_1\,To D_2$ must take both situations into account, which is achieved in the following specification:

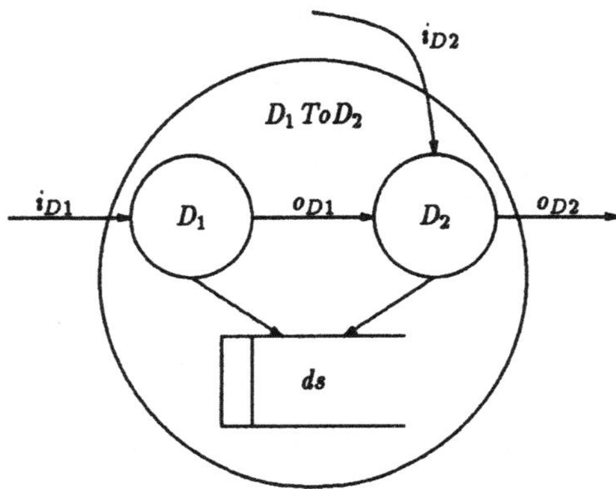

Figure 8: Combination of two data transformers and one data store

$D_1\,ToD_2\,(i_{D1} : I_{D1\Theta}, i_{D2} : I_{D2\Theta})\ o_{D2} : O_{D2\Theta}$
ext wr $ds : DS$

$$
\begin{aligned}
\textbf{post}\ \exists\ & ds_{D1_o}, ds_{D1_n}, ds_{D2_o}, ds_{D2_n}, ds_{dc} : DS \cdot \\
& (\exists\, o_{D1} : O_{D1\Theta} \cdot post\text{-}D_1(i_{D1}, o_{D1}, ds_{D1_n}, ds_{D1_o}) \wedge \\
& (\exists\, o_{D1} : O_{D1\Theta}, i_{D1} : I_{D1\Theta} \cdot post\text{-}D_1(i_{D1}, o_{D1}, ds_{D2_o}, ds_{dc}) \wedge \\
& \qquad\qquad post\text{-}D_2(o_{D1}, i_{D2}, o_{D2}, ds_{D2_n}, ds_{D2_o})) \wedge \\
& (ds = ds_{D1_n} \wedge \overleftarrow{ds} = ds_{D2_o} \wedge ds_{D1_o} = ds_{D2_n}) \vee \\
& (ds = ds_{D2_n} \wedge \overleftarrow{ds} = ds_{D1_o} \wedge ds_{D1_n} = ds_{D2_o}))
\end{aligned}
$$

In the specification of this operation the fact is used that during the transformation three synchronization points can be distinguished: the first synchronization point is the point *before* the transformation (characterized by $\overleftarrow{ds}$), the second synchronization point is either after D_1 has accessed data store ds or after D_2 has accessed data store ds (since access to a data store was characterized as an indivisible action), and the last synchronization point is *after* the transformation performed by the data transformer (characterized by ds). To characterize the second synchronization point we introduce an intermediate value ds_{dc} for the state in the post-condition. The effect of the transformation can then be characterized by specifying that either ds_{dc} is produced by D_1 and then used as an input value for D_2, or vice versa.

Because of the ordering problem, all data transformers that use the same data store (or even the same set of data stores!) have to be combined in one single data transformer. The more data transformers use the same data store, the more complicated the specification for the combined data transformer will be.
□

3.2 The SAC approach

In the second approach that we present, called the *S*(equential) *AC*(ces) *approach*, we use the fact that a data flow is a channel which can be used as an input or as an output by a data transformer, as a starting point. As in the PAC approach, the primary-mapping step in the SAC approach consists of a number of steps:

1. Map each *data store* onto a *VDM state component*.
2. For each *data flow* in the DFD, create a *state component* the type of which is a *sequence of the elements* that are transported by that data flow.
3. For each *state component modelling a data flow*, create two *VDM operations* which can be used to add and remove elements from those state components.
4. Create a *VDM operation* for each *data transformer* and for each *external process* in the DFD.

The details of these steps are explained below.

Data stores

Data stores are treated in the same way as in the PAC approach, i.e. they are mapped onto *state components*.

Data flows

A data flow arrow is viewed as an arbitrary large (but finite) channel (queue), receiving input on one side (the tail of the data flow arrow) and providing output on the other side (the head of the data flow arrow). A data transformer can provide output to a data flow or receive input from a data flow, depending on the direction of the connection. However, a data transformer cannot just arbitrarily access any data element that is currently in one of its input channels, it can only access the first such data element.

Since in this approach, *data flow* arrows are explicitly regarded as static elements which can hold data and deliver them on demand, the most obvious way to represent them is as part of the *state* of the specification. The order of the elements that flow through the channel is important, therefore we will model data flows as *sequences* of the type of the data elements. We also associate *access operations* with these state components to ensure their correct use.

Example 6

Consider again the data flow arrow in figure 1b. The corresponding component of the state, including operations for accessing this component, is:

state ... **of**
  $\ldots : \ldots$
  $df : DF^*$
  $\ldots : \ldots$
end

$$
\begin{array}{l}
\textit{Put-df}\ (i : DF) \\
\textbf{ext wr}\ df : DF^{*} \\
\textbf{post}\ df = \overleftarrow{df} \curvearrowright [i]
\end{array}
$$

$$
\begin{array}{l}
\textit{Get-df}\ ()\ r : DF_{\Theta} \\
\textbf{ext wr}\ df : DF^{*} \\
\textbf{post if}\ \overleftarrow{df} = [\,] \\
\qquad \textbf{then}\ r = \tau \wedge df = [\,] \\
\qquad \textbf{else}\ \overleftarrow{df} = [r] \curvearrowright df
\end{array}
$$

Note that for the specification of *Get-df* it is again necessary to use the syntactical Θ extension.

□

Data transformers and external processes

Data transformers and *external processes* are modelled as *VDM operations*, just as in the PAC approach. The difference is that now they have neither input nor result parameters, because the state elements implementing the data flows can be accessed directly.

Example 7

Consider again the data transformer shown in figure 3. The VDM counterpart[2] of the data transformer shown in figure 3, under the first interpretation used in example 1, is:

$$
\begin{array}{l}
D\,() \\
\textbf{ext wr}\ i_1 : I_1{}^{*} \\
\qquad \textbf{wr}\ i_2 : I_2{}^{*} \\
\qquad \textbf{wr}\ o_1 : O_1{}^{*} \\
\qquad \textbf{wr}\ o_2 : O_2{}^{*} \\
\textbf{post}\ \exists\, i_1' : I_{1\Theta}, i_2' : I_{2\Theta}, o_1' : O_{1\Theta}, o_2' : O_{2\Theta} \cdot \\
\qquad\qquad (\textit{post-Get-}i_1(i_1', i_1, \overleftarrow{i_1}) \wedge \textit{post-Get-}i_2(i_2', i_2, \overleftarrow{i_2}) \wedge \\
\qquad\qquad \textit{post-Put-}o_1(o_1', o_1, \overleftarrow{o_1}) \wedge \textit{post-Put-}o_2(o_2', o_2, \overleftarrow{o_2}) \wedge \\
\qquad\qquad P_D(i_1', i_2', o_1', o_2'))
\end{array}
$$

The data flows i_1, i_2, o_1 and o_2 are modelled as state components, made visible to the operation by an external clause. In the post-condition single elements for input and output are created by using quantified expressions. These single elements are then used as parameters to the *Get* and *Put* operations and to the predicate P_D describing the effect of the data transformer on different input values. The binary expressions stating that new

2. The definitions of the *Put* and *Get* operations are not explicitly given in the examples of the SAC approach.

state values should be the same as the old values (e.g. $i_2 = \overleftarrow{i_2}$) are necessary to ensure that when one specific input value is transformed, the other input/output pair remains unaffected.

As in example 1, assume that we have some additional knowledge: D will produce an o_1 if i_1 is present on its input, and an o_2 if an i_2 is present. Following the SAC approach the VDM operation then becomes:

$$
\begin{array}{l}
D\,()\\
\textsf{ext wr } i_1 : I_1{}^*\\
\quad \textsf{wr } i_2 : I_2{}^*\\
\quad \textsf{wr } o_1 : O_1{}^*\\
\quad \textsf{wr } o_2 : O_2{}^*\\
\textsf{post } \exists\, i : I_{1\Theta} \mid I_{2\Theta}, o : O_{1\Theta} \mid O_{2\Theta} \cdot\\
\qquad (\textit{post-Get-}i_1(i, i_1, \overleftarrow{i_1}) \wedge \textit{post-Put-}o_1(o, o_1, \overleftarrow{o_1}) \wedge\\
\qquad\; i_2 = \overleftarrow{i_2} \wedge o_2 = \overleftarrow{o_2} \wedge P_{1D}(i, o)) \vee\\
\qquad (\textit{post-Get-}i_2(i, i_2, \overleftarrow{i_2}) \wedge \textit{post-Put-}o_2(o, o_2, \overleftarrow{o_2}) \wedge\\
\qquad\; i_1 = \overleftarrow{i_1} \wedge o_1 = \overleftarrow{o_1} \wedge P_{2D}(i, o))
\end{array}
$$

As in the PAC approach, looseness (as implied by the disjunction between the two possibilities) is used to leave the choice which transformation is performed, which is after all part of the control flow of the system, unspecified.
□

Example 8
Consider the combination of two data transformers that was used in example 3. The VDM specification for this combination following the SAC approach is:

$$
\begin{array}{l}
\textsf{state} \ldots \textsf{ of}\\
\quad \ldots \;\; : \ldots\\
\quad i_{D1} \;\; : I_{D1}{}^*\\
\quad o_{D1} \;\; : O_{D1}{}^*\\
\quad o_{1D2} : O_{1D2}{}^*\\
\quad o_{2D2} : O_{2D2}{}^*\\
\quad \ldots \;\; : \ldots\\
\textsf{end}
\end{array}
$$

$$
\begin{array}{l}
D_1\,()\\
\textsf{ext wr } i_{D1} \;\; : I_{D1}{}^*\\
\quad \textsf{wr } o_{1D2} : O_{1D2}{}^*\\
\quad \textsf{wr } o_{D1} \;\; : O_{D1}{}^*
\end{array}
$$

$$\textbf{post}\ \exists\, i'_{D1} : I_{D1\theta},\, o'_{D1} : O_{D1\theta},\, o'_{1D2} : O_{1D2\theta} \cdot$$
$$\quad \textit{post-Get-}i_{D1}(i'_{D1}, i_{D1}, \overleftarrow{i_{D1}}) \wedge \textit{post-Get-}o_{1D2}(o'_{1D2}, o_{1D2}, \overleftarrow{o_{1D2}}) \wedge$$
$$\quad \textit{post-Put-}o_{D1}(o'_{D1}, o_{D1}, \overleftarrow{o_{D1}}) \wedge P_{D1}(i'_{D1}, o'_{1D2}, o'_{D1})$$

$D_2\,()$
ext wr $o_{D1}\ : O_{D1}{}^*$
wr $o_{1D2} : O_{1D2}{}^*$
wr $o_{2D2} : O_{2D2}{}^*$

$$\textbf{post}\ \exists\, o'_{D1} : O_{D1\theta},\, o'_{1D2} : O_{1D2\theta},\, o'_{2D2} : O_{2D2\theta} \cdot$$
$$\quad \textit{post-Get-}o_{D1}(o'_{D1}, o_{D1}, \overleftarrow{o_{D1}}) \wedge \textit{post-Put-}o_{1D2}(o'_{1D2}, o_{1D2}, \overleftarrow{o_{1D2}}) \wedge$$
$$\quad \textit{post-Put-}o_{2D2}(o'_{2D2}, o_{2D2}, \overleftarrow{o_{2D2}}) \wedge P_{D2}(o'_{D1}, o'_{1D2}, o'_{2D2})$$

This VDM specification as a whole is a specification for the higher-level DFD comprising the combination of D_1 and D_2.
□

3.3 Fragment from a spelling checker

To illustrate the PAC approach and the SAC approach we will show how a fragment from a DFD for a simple spelling checker can be transformed to VDM. The problem is used in [Sommerville 82] to explain the notions of data flow diagrams and structure charts. The component which we will use to illustrate both approaches will expect a *file_name*, and checks whether a file having this name is present in a file system *docs*. An indication *file_not_found* for the absence or presence of such a file is returned. If the file is present it is split into a sequence of words (each of which will be checked against a dictionary by another component). The DFD for this component is shown in figure 9. The following

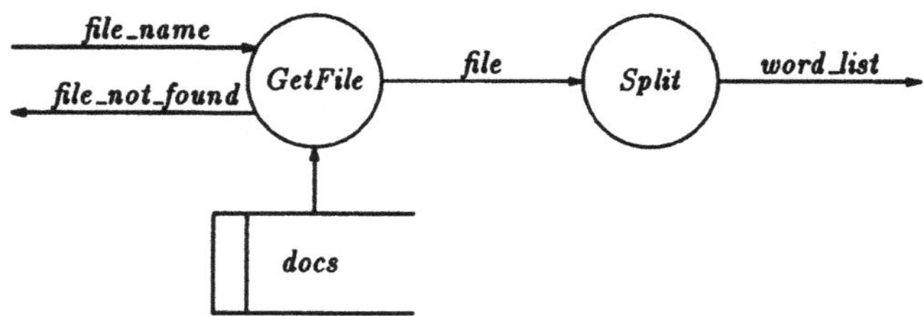

Figure 9: Fragment of the DFD for the spelling checker

VDM data types are used:

$$\begin{aligned} &\textit{Docs} &&= \textit{FileName} \xrightarrow{m} \textit{File} \\ &\textit{FileName} &&= \textsf{token} \\ &\textit{File} &&= \textsf{char}^* \\ &\textit{FileNotFound} &&= \mathbb{B} \\ &\textit{WordList} &&= \textit{Word}^* \\ &\textit{Word} &&= \textsf{char}^+ \end{aligned}$$

The spelling checker component according to the PAC approach
In the primary-mapping step, the following VDM specification can be derived for the spelling checker component following the PAC approach:

$$\textsf{state}\ \mathit{SpellingChecker}\ \textsf{of}$$
$$\quad \mathit{docs} : \mathit{Docs}$$
$$\textsf{end}$$

$$\mathit{GetFile}\,(\mathit{file\_name} : \mathit{FileName}_{\Theta})\ r : \mathit{FileNotFound}_{\Theta} \times \mathit{File}_{\Theta}$$
$$\textsf{ext rd}\ \ \mathit{docs} : \mathit{Docs}$$
$$\textsf{post let}\ \mathit{mk\text{-}}(\mathit{file\_not\_found}, \mathit{file}) = r\ \textsf{in}$$
$$\quad \textsf{if}\ \mathit{file\_name} \in \textsf{dom}\ \mathit{docs}$$
$$\quad \textsf{then}\ \mathit{file\_not\_found} = \textsf{false} \wedge \mathit{file} = \mathit{docs}(\mathit{file\_name})$$
$$\quad \textsf{else}\ \mathit{file\_not\_found} = \textsf{true} \wedge \mathit{file} = \tau$$

$$\mathit{Split}\,(\mathit{file} : \mathit{File}_{\Theta})\ \mathit{word\_list} : \mathit{WordList}_{\Theta}$$
$$\textsf{post if}\ \mathit{file} = \tau$$
$$\quad \textsf{then}\ \mathit{word\_list} = \tau$$
$$\quad \textsf{else}\ \mathit{word\_list} =$$
$$\qquad [\mathit{file}\,(i, \ldots, j) \mid i, j \in \textsf{inds}\ \mathit{file} \cdot i \leq j \wedge \neg \exists\, k \in \{i, \ldots, j\} \cdot \mathit{file}(k) = \text{' '}]$$

$$\mathit{GetFileToSplit}\,(\mathit{file\_name} : \mathit{FileName}_{\Theta})\ r : \mathit{FileNotFound}_{\Theta} \times \mathit{WordList}_{\Theta}$$
$$\textsf{ext rd}\ \ \mathit{docs} : \mathit{Docs}$$
$$\textsf{post let}\ \mathit{mk\text{-}}(\mathit{file\_not\_found}, \mathit{word\_list}) = r\ \textsf{in}$$
$$\quad \exists\, \mathit{file} : \mathit{File}_{\Theta} \cdot \mathit{post\text{-}GetFile}(\mathit{file\_name}, \mathit{mk\text{-}}(\mathit{file\_not\_found}, \mathit{file}), \mathit{docs}) \wedge$$
$$\quad \exists\, \mathit{file} : \mathit{File}_{\Theta}, \mathit{file\_name} : \mathit{FileName}_{\Theta}, \mathit{file\_not\_found} : \mathit{FileNotFound}_{\Theta} \cdot$$
$$\qquad \mathit{post\text{-}GetFile}(\mathit{file\_name}, \mathit{mk\text{-}}(\mathit{file\_not\_found}, \mathit{file}), \mathit{docs}) \wedge$$
$$\qquad \mathit{post\text{-}Split}(\mathit{file}, \mathit{word\_list})$$

The most apparent aspect of the specification is the complexity of the operation *GetFileToSplit*. The complexity is due to the looseness of the operation. When we take non-functional aspects of the problem into account, it soon becomes clear that the specification can be significantly improved in the secondary-mapping step. Suppose e.g. that we use the knowledge that the system can be implemented as a *sequential system*. This means that timing assumptions can be made about the connection between *GetFile* and *Split*, resulting in the elimination of the looseness in *GetFileToSplit*.

Another optimization results from an analysis of the data types used. The Θ extensions can be eliminated by changing the domain definitions such that special values are introduced the model the τ value. For the domain *File* the optional-domain constructor can be used because that constructor has not already been used in the definition of the domain *File*. For the domain *WordList*, the special value '[ ]' can be used to model the value τ, since the empty sequence will not in any other situation be used for that domain. For all the other domains used, the Θ extensions can simply be removed, because the value τ is not used for those domains in the specification. If no suitable replacements for τ can be found, it is always possible to eliminate the Θ extensions by constructing a union of the original domain with a special value denoted as a quote literal.

The specifications of *GetFile*, *Split* and *GetFileToSplit* can now be changed into:

$$
\begin{array}{l}
\mathit{GetFile}\,(\mathit{file\_name} : \mathit{FileName})\ r : \mathit{FileNotFound} \times [\mathit{File}] \\
\textsf{ext rd}\ \ \mathit{docs} : \mathit{Docs} \\
\textsf{post let}\ \mathit{mk}\text{-}(\mathit{file\_not\_found}, \mathit{file}) = r\ \textsf{in} \\
\quad \textsf{if}\ \mathit{file\_name} \in \textsf{dom}\ \mathit{docs} \\
\quad \textsf{then}\ \mathit{file\_not\_found} = \textsf{false} \wedge \mathit{file} = \mathit{docs}(\mathit{file\_name}) \\
\quad \textsf{else}\ \mathit{file\_not\_found} = \textsf{true} \wedge \mathit{file} = \textsf{nil}
\end{array}
$$

$$
\begin{array}{l}
\mathit{Split}\,(\mathit{file} : [\mathit{File}])\ \mathit{word\_list} : \mathit{WordList} \\
\textsf{post if}\ \mathit{file} = \textsf{nil} \\
\quad \textsf{then}\ \mathit{word\_list} = [\,] \\
\quad \textsf{else}\ \mathit{word\_list} = \\
\qquad [\mathit{file}\,(i, \ldots, j) \mid i, j \in \textsf{inds}\ \mathit{file} \cdot i \leq j \wedge \neg \exists\, k \in \{i, \ldots, j\} \cdot \mathit{file}(k) = \text{' '}]
\end{array}
$$

$$
\begin{array}{l}
\mathit{GetFileToSplit}\,(\mathit{file\_name} : \mathit{FileName})\ r : \mathit{FileNotFound} \times \mathit{WordList} \\
\textsf{ext rd}\ \ \mathit{docs} : \mathit{Docs} \\
\textsf{post let}\ \mathit{mk}\text{-}(\mathit{file\_not\_found}, \mathit{word\_list}) = r\ \textsf{in} \\
\quad \exists\, \mathit{file} : [\mathit{File}] \cdot \mathit{post}\text{-}\mathit{GetFile}(\mathit{file\_name}, \mathit{mk}\text{-}(\mathit{file\_not\_found}, \mathit{file}), \mathit{docs}) \wedge \\
\qquad\qquad\qquad \mathit{post}\text{-}\mathit{Split}(\mathit{file}, \mathit{word\_list})
\end{array}
$$

The specification resulting from the secondary-mapping step is easier to understand and more elegant than the specification resulting from the primary-mapping step.

The spelling checker component according to the SAC approach

A VDM specification constructed for the spelling checker component in the primary-mapping step, following the SAC approach, is as follows:

$$
\begin{array}{l}
\textsf{state}\ \mathit{SpellingChecker}\ \textsf{of} \\
\quad \begin{array}{ll}
\mathit{docs} & : \mathit{Docs} \\
\mathit{file\_name} & : \mathit{FileName}^* \\
\mathit{file\_not\_found} & : \mathit{FileNotFound}^* \\
\mathit{file} & : \mathit{File}^* \\
\mathit{word\_list} & : \mathit{WordList}^*
\end{array} \\
\textsf{end}
\end{array}
$$

$$
\begin{array}{l}
\mathit{GetFile}\,()\\
\textbf{ext rd } \mathit{docs} \quad : \mathit{Docs}\\
\quad \textbf{wr } \mathit{file\_name} \quad : \mathit{FileName}^*\\
\quad \textbf{wr } \mathit{file} \quad : \mathit{File}^*\\
\quad \textbf{wr } \mathit{file\_not\_found} : \mathit{FileNotFound}^*\\
\textbf{post let } \mathit{file\_name}' : \mathit{FileName}_\Theta \textbf{ be st}\\
\qquad\qquad \mathit{post\text{-}Get\text{-}file\_name}(\mathit{file\_name}', \mathit{file\_name}, \overleftarrow{\mathit{file\_name}}) \textbf{ in}\\
\quad \textbf{if } \mathit{file\_name}' = \tau\\
\quad \textbf{then } \mathit{file\_not\_found} = \overleftarrow{\mathit{file\_not\_found}} \wedge \mathit{file} = \overleftarrow{\mathit{file}}\\
\quad \textbf{else if } \mathit{file\_name}' \in \textbf{dom } \mathit{docs}\\
\qquad \textbf{then } \mathit{post\text{-}Put\text{-}file\_not\_found}(\textbf{false}, \mathit{file\_not\_found}, \overleftarrow{\mathit{file\_not\_found}}) \wedge\\
\qquad\qquad \mathit{post\text{-}Put\text{-}file}(\mathit{docs}(\mathit{file\_name}'), \mathit{files}, \overleftarrow{\mathit{files}})\\
\qquad \textbf{else } \mathit{post\text{-}Put\text{-}file\_not\_found}(\textbf{true}, \mathit{file\_not\_found}, \overleftarrow{\mathit{file\_not\_found}}) \wedge\\
\qquad\qquad \mathit{file} = \overleftarrow{\mathit{file}}
\end{array}
$$

$$
\begin{array}{l}
\mathit{Split}\,()\\
\textbf{ext wr } \mathit{file} \quad : \mathit{File}^*\\
\quad \textbf{wr } \mathit{word\_list} : \mathit{WordList}^*\\
\textbf{post let } \mathit{file}' : \mathit{File}_\Theta \textbf{ be st } \mathit{post\text{-}Get\text{-}file}(\mathit{file}', \mathit{file}, \overleftarrow{\mathit{file}}) \textbf{ in}\\
\quad \textbf{if } \mathit{file}' = \tau\\
\quad \textbf{then } \mathit{word\_list} = \overleftarrow{\mathit{word\_list}}\\
\quad \textbf{else let } \mathit{word\_list}' =\\
\qquad\qquad [\mathit{file}'(i, \ldots, j) \mid\\
\qquad\qquad\qquad i, j \in \textbf{inds } \mathit{file}' \cdot i \leq j \wedge \neg \exists k \in \{i, \ldots, j\} \cdot \mathit{file}'(k) = \text{' '}] \textbf{ in}\\
\qquad \mathit{post\text{-}Put\text{-}word\_list}(\mathit{word\_list}', \mathit{word\_list}, \overleftarrow{\mathit{word\_list}})
\end{array}
$$

The external clause in this specification shows the state components to which the operation has read- and/or write access. Unfortunately, it is possible to change the state components modelling the various data flows *without* using the appropriate *Put* and *Get* operations due to the lack of data hiding facilities in VDM.

VDM requires that if a state component remains unchanged, this must be explicitly marked as such in the post-condition. This is the case for *GetFile*: if a file having the user-supplied file name is not present in the file system, then the *file* data flow remains unchanged. If we 'forget' to specify that a specific state component remains unchanged, then the implementation of that operation is allowed to change the value of that state component into any (legal) value because every such value will satisfy the post-condition.

As in the PAC approach, during the secondary-mapping step a number of improvements can be made. The elimination of Θ extensions in this case can be realized by the observation that, since we had assumed that we were modelling a sequential system, both operations cannot perform any useful actions unless input values are present on their inputs. The τ values can then be modelled as empty sequences in combination with preconditions for the operations. The specifications for *GetFile* and *Split* then become:

GetFile ()
ext rd *docs* : *Docs*
  wr *file_name* : *FileName**
  wr *file* : *File**
  wr *file_not_found* : *FileNotFound**
pre $file\_name \neq [\,]$
post let $file\_name' : FileName$ **be st**
    $post\text{-}Get\text{-}file\_name(file\_name', file\_name, \overleftarrow{file\_name})$ **in**
  if $file\_name' \in \mathbf{dom}\ docs$
  then $post\text{-}Put\text{-}file\_not\_found(\mathsf{false}, file\_not\_found, \overleftarrow{file\_not\_found}) \land$
    $post\text{-}Put\text{-}file(docs(file\_name'), files, \overleftarrow{files})$
  else $post\text{-}Put\text{-}file\_not\_found(\mathsf{true}, file\_not\_found, \overleftarrow{file\_not\_found}) \land file = \overleftarrow{file}$

Split ()
ext wr *file* : *File**
  wr *word_list* : *WordList**
pre $file \neq [\,]$
post let $file' : File$ **be st** $post\text{-}Get\text{-}file(file', file, \overleftarrow{file})$ **in**
  let $word\_list' =$
    $[file'(i, \ldots, j) \mid$
      $i, j \in \mathbf{inds}\ file' \cdot i \leq j \land \neg \exists k \in \{i, \ldots, j\} \cdot file'(k) = \text{' '}]$ **in**
  $post\text{-}Put\text{-}word\_list(word\_list', word\_list, \overleftarrow{word\_list})$

The specification resulting from the secondary-mapping step is easier to understand and more elegant than the specification resulting from the primary-mapping step.

The spelling checker component directly specified

A VDM specification for the spelling checker component written directly from analyzing the problem description could be as follows:

state *SpellingChecker* **of**
  docs : *Docs*
end

GetFileToSplit (*file_name* : *FileName*) $r : FileNotFound \times [File]$
ext rd *docs* : *Docs*

$$
\begin{array}{l}
\textsf{post let } mk\text{-}(file\_not\_found, word\_list) = r \textsf{ in} \\
\quad \textsf{let } file\_not\_found = (file\_name \notin \textsf{dom } docs) \textsf{ in} \\
\quad \textsf{if } file\_not\_found \\
\quad \textsf{then } r = mk\text{-}(\textsf{true}, \textsf{nil}) \\
\quad \textsf{else let } file = docs(file\_name) \textsf{ in} \\
\qquad \textsf{let } word\_list = \\
\qquad\qquad [file\,(i, \ldots, j) \mid \\
\qquad\qquad\qquad i, j \in \textsf{inds } file \cdot i \leq j \wedge \neg \exists\, k \in \{i, \ldots, j\} \cdot file(k) = \text{' '}] \textsf{ in} \\
\qquad r = mk\text{-}(file\_not\_found, word\_list)
\end{array}
$$

Since no explicit decomposition step was made (due to the simplicity of the problem), the above specification is shorter than the ones constructed following the PAC approach or the SAC approach, which doesn't necessarily make it more understandable but does make the specification better manageable.

The quoting of post-conditions, which is present in the specifications constructed following the PAC or the SAC approach, is absent in the specification written from scratch. This is unfortunate, because the quotation mechanism provides handles for a further development of the specification into an implementation.

However, since the specification of the spelling checker component is just a toy problem, no final conclusions on the usability of the specification constructed using the PAC approach or the SAC approach, in comparison with the specification above, can be drawn.

3.4 A comparison of the PAC approach and the SAC approach

Both the PAC approach and the SAC approach provide a sound base for the complete and consistent modelling of DFDs. A significant difference between the two approaches is that in the PAC approach it is assumed that a data flow only expresses the existence of a (directed) connection between two data transforers, whereas in the SAC approach it is assumed that data flows are sequential channels which communicate data between two data transformers.

The PAC approach can perhaps best be seen as a means to provide a formal semantics for DFDs (although to validate this statement more characteristics of the approach should be examined) because it closely models the intuitive semantics most system analysts give to DFDs. The disadvantage is that its use results in rather complex specifications; the 'loose' interpretation of data flows complicates the post-condition associated with the operation modelling that data flow considerably. This becomes even worse when we take the influence of data stores into account: as we have seen in example 5, even the specification for only two data transformers accessing the same data store is hard to understand, and when the number of data stores involved increases, this complexity increases as well. The complexity of a combination of data transformers can be decreased by using explicit definitions instead of the implicit ones shown in this paper. Such definitions, however, are less abstract than their implicit counterparts.

The SAC approach provides a more operational approach for transforming DFDs, and therefore seems a more practical base for software development. A minor technical problem with the use of VDM for the specification of the result of the transformation is that, although we assume the presence of *Put* and *Get* operations, it is possible to violate the rule of sequential access by directly accessing the data flow through sequence indexing, and it is possible to use an input data flow as an output data flow. Consistency checking of DFDs when following the SAC approach is therefore more complicated, whereas when following the PAC approach the consistency of the DFD is largely induced by the syntax of VDM-SL. Furthermore, the specification of all *Put* and *Get* operations themselves forms a significant part of the overall specification.

By applying restrictions to the DFDs better specifications can be obtained. In the spelling checker example, we saw that under the assumption that we were modelling a sequential system, the specifications resulting from following both the PAC approach and the SAC approach could be significantly improved. Furthermore, the Θ extensions could be replaced by the standard VDM optional-domain constructor, or by other 'special' values.

4 Conclusions and future research

In this paper we have demonstrated that using formal methods, VDM in our case, to describe a design expressed as a DFD, is a viable option and can be done in a number of different ways. We introduced two approaches for transforming DFDs to VDM specifications: the PAC approach and the SAC approach.

The rules in the PAC approach are based on a minimum of timing assumptions, the only one being that a data transformer consumes input that was produced by a predecessor data transformer at some earlier time. The rules in the second approach, the SAC approach, are based on the assumption that data flows can be modelled as queues, thereby enforcing a sequential aspect on the data flow. Of course, there are many other possibilities as well. From the spectrum of possibilities we only chose two, based on distant sets of rules, to transform a DFD design to a complete formal specification.

VDM is useful as a formalism in which to express the semantics of DFDs. Especially the ability to express looseness in VDM is a powerful tool. The resulting specifications have a limited practical value due to the looseness involved. This changes rather drastically when restrictions upon the DFDs are imposed, thus leading to the conclusion that VDM is a useful component in a combined structured/formal method with SA. This can become even more apparent when other graphical notations from SA are formalized as well, and are incorporated in the transformation. We expect that using the 'method' in VDM will result in the addition of control information to the design in a similar way as the SD method introduces control information during the systematic transform of a DFD to a structure chart.

Future research

Future research should be concentrated on:

- an investigation of other models in the universe of models for mapping DFDs to VDM constructs. Such an investigation may provide other models having the same powerful properties as the PAC approach and the SAC approach, and in addition to this eliminate the less advantageous properties of these models;
- the investigation of formalizing other graphical notations which can be integrated in the combined method;
- a validation of the approach by professional software engineers for real-life problems (a prerequisite for this is the availability of elaborate guidelines for the approach);
- a more thorough analysis of the possibilities for the further development of a software system, starting from the formal specifications constructed by following a standard transformation from DFDs to VDM.

In spite of the recognition that much research will have to be carried out in order to get all questions answered, we believe that SD can be replaced by VDM, leading to an approach which, on one hand is acceptable to the professional software engineering community, and on the other hand is sufficiently formal to ensure increased confidence in the possibilities for validation and verification of the designs during the development process.

Acknowledgements

We acknowledge the valuable contributions of Hans Toetenel in long discussions on a variety of issues in combining VDM with less formal, but somehow well-established software development methods, and both him, Peter Gorm Larsen and Hans Tonino for their suggestions to improve this paper.

References

[Adler 88] Mike Adler. An Algebra for Data Flow Diagram Process Decomposition. *IEEE Transaction on Software Engineering*, 14(2):169–183, February 1988.

[Alabiso 88] Bruno Alabiso. Transformation of Data Flow Analysis Models to Object Oriented Design. In *OOPSLA'88 Proceedings*, pages 335–353, ACM, November 1988.

[Bjørner 82] D. Bjørner, C.B. Jones. *Formal Specification & Software Development. Series in Computer Science*, Prentice-Hall International, 1982.

[Bruza 89] P.D. Bruza, Th. P. van der Weide. *The Semantics of Data Flow Diagrams.* Technical Report 89-16, University of Nijmegen, The Netherlands, October 1989.

[BSI/VDM] BSI IST/5/-/50. VDM Specification Language: Proto-Standard. March 1991.

[Chedgey 87] Chr. Chedgey, S. Kearney, H.J. Kugler. Using VDM in an Object-oriented Development Method for Ada Software. In D. Bjørner, C.B. Jones, editor, *VDM - A Formal Method at Work; proc. of the 1st VDM-Europe Symposium*, pages 63–76, Springer-Verlag, Berlin, March 1987.

[Constantine 79] L.L. Constantine, E. Yourdon. *Structured Design*. Prentice Hall, Englewood Cliffs, New Jersey, 1979.

[DeMarco 79] Tom DeMarco. *Structured Analysis and System Specification*. Yourdon Press, Englewood Cliffs, New Jersey, 1979.

[Fraser 91] M.D. Fraser, K. Kumar, V.K. Vaishnavi. Informal and Formal Requirements Specification Languages: Bridging the Gap. *IEEE Transactions on Software Engeneering*, 17(5):454–466, May 1991.

[Gane 79] Chris Gane, Trish Sarson. *Structured Systems Analysis: Tools and Techniques*. Prentice Hall, Englewood Cliffs, New Jersey, 1979.

[Hall 90] Anthony Hall. Seven Myths of Formal Methods. *IEEE Software*, 7(5):11–19, September 1990.

[Jones 90] C.B. Jones. *Systematic Software Development using VDM (2nd edition). Series in Computer Science*, Prentice-Hall International, 1990.

[Kemmerer 90] Richard A. Kemmerer. Integrating Formal Methods into the Development Process. *IEEE Software*, 7(5):37–50, September 1990.

[Larsen 91a] Peter Gorm Larsen, Nico Plat, Hans Toetenel. *A Complete Formal Semantics of Data Flow Diagrams*. Technical Report, Delft University of Technology, September 1991.

[Larsen 91b] Peter Gorm Larsen, Jan van Katwijk, Nico Plat, Kees Pronk, Hans Toetenel. SVDM: An Integrated Combination of SA and VDM. *Submitted to the Methods Integration Workshop in Leeds, UK*, September 1991.

[Leveson 91] Nancy G. Leveson. Software Safety in Embedded Computer Systems. *Communications of the ACM*, 34(2):34–46, February 1991.

[Longworth 86] G. Longworth, D. Nicholls. *SSADM Manual*. NCC, December 1986.

[Myers 75] G.J. Myers. *Reliable Software through Composite Design*. Van Nostrand, New York, 1975.

[Plat 91] Nico Plat, Peter Gorm Larsen, Hans Toetenel. Formal Transformations: Using SA and VDM as different Views in Software Development. *Submitted to the International Conference on Computer Systems and Software Engineering (CompEuro'92), May 1992, The Hague, The Netherlands*, 1991.

[Randell 90] G.P. Randell. *Translating Data Flow Diagrams into Z (and Vice Versa)*. Technical Report 90019, Procurement Executive, Ministry of Defence, RSRE, Malvern, Worcestershire, UK, October 1990.

[Semmens 91] Lesley Semmens, Pat Allen. Using Entity Relationship Models as a basis for Z Specifications.

[Sommerville 82] I. Sommerville. *Software Engineering*. Addison-Wesley, London, 1982.

[Toetenel 90] Hans Toetenel, Jan van Katwijk, Nico Plat. Structured Analysis – Formal Design, using Stream & Object oriented Formal Specification. *Software Engineering Notes*, 15(4):118–127, 1990.

[Ward 85] Paul T. Ward, Stephen J. Mellor. *Structured Development for Real-Time Systems. Yourdon Press Computing Series*, Yourdon Press, Englewood Cliffs, New Jersey, 1985.

[Yourdon 75] E. Yourdon. *Techniques of Program Structure and Design*. Prentice Hall, Englewood Cliffs, New Jersey, 1975.

A Model-oriented Method for Algebraic Specifications using COLD-1 as Notation*

Reinder J. Bril
Philips Research Laboratories Eindhoven (PRLE),
P.O. Box 80.000, 5600 JA Eindhoven, The Netherlands
Tel: +31 40 74 29 05, Fax: +31 40 74 40 04,
Email: rjbril@prl.philips.nl

Abstract

A model-oriented method for algebraic specifications is described, using the design language COLD-1 as notation. The method is based upon standard algebraic concepts, such as equivalence relations, congruence relations and homomorphisms. The method makes a clear distinction between the abstract type being defined and the model used as representation. The advantage of this approach is that the problem of implementation bias does not apply and that the operations of the model do not need to satisfy a property usually termed representation invariant. As such, the method deviates in an essential way from model-oriented methods like VDM and Z. Conceivable tool support for the method is briefly sketched.

Keywords: Model-oriented methods, algebraic specifications, wide-spectrum languages, method support.

1 Introduction

Two classes of methods for the specification of abstract types are typically distinguished (see, for example, [18]): *model-oriented* methods and *property-oriented* methods.

Using a model-oriented method, the behaviour of an abstract type is specified by constructing a model of the type in terms of other data abstractions with known properties. The latter include the standard mathematical domains, like tuples, sets, sequences and maps. Other terms identifying the same area are *Specification by Representation* and *Abstract Model Approach.*

Using a property-oriented method, an abstract type is defined by stating a set of properties, usually in the form of a set of axioms, that the type must satisfy.

In this paper, a model-oriented method for algebraic specifications is presented, using the design language COLD-1[1] as notation. The method is based upon standard algebraic concepts, like equivalence relations, congruence relations and epimorphisms (i.e. surjective

*This work is partially supported by the ESPRIT II project ATMOSPHERE, ref #2565.

[1]COLD is an acronym for Common Object-oriented Language for Design.

homomorphisms, see [5]). Instead of considering total epimorphisms only, the more general case of partial epimorphisms is taken as a starting point for the method (a partial epimorphism is a weak homomorphism; see [3]). The method makes a clear distinction between the abstract type being defined and the model used as representation. The advantage of this approach is that the problem of implementation bias (see, for example, [10]) does not apply and that the operations of the model do not need to satisfy a property usually termed representation invariant (see, for example, [6]).

The organisation of this paper is as follows. In Section 2, an overview of the language COLD-1 is given. In Section 3, the model-oriented method is described. Section 4 presents a specification of bounded sequences[2] in terms of 2-tuples, natural numbers and sequences. The relation between the model used as representation and a conceivable implementation is touched upon in Section 5. Conceivable tool support for the method is described in Section 6. Finally, in Section 7, the conclusions are drawn, and directions for future work identified.

2 COLD-1

COLD is a formal wide-spectrum design language, which has been developed at Philips Research Laboratories Eindhoven (PRLE) within the framework of the ESPRIT I project METEOR, ref #432. COLD is a *formal* language, which means that the well-formedness and semantics of the language are defined mathematically. This guarantees that descriptions in the language leave no room for ambiguity and that a high level of tool support can be provided. COLD is a *wide-spectrum* language, which means that the language allows for descriptions at several levels of abstraction. COLD is a *design* language to emphasise that the language can be used for recording a (software) system in its intermediate stages of design, ranging from specification to implementation.

The language is in the tradition of VDM ([10]) and Z ([17]), but has been influenced by ASL ([19]), Module Algebra ([2]), Harel's dynamic logic ([7]), Scott's E-logic ([16]) and object-oriented languages. Furthermore, it contains a novel notion of "design" comparable with the structuring mechanisms provided by, e.g. HOOD.

Actually, COLD is not one language but a family of languages. Amongst these, the language COLD-K plays a special role, since it is a *kernel* language which serves as a fixed point in the development of the language. There is a mathematically defined syntax and semantics for COLD-K, for which we refer to [4] and [11]. All essential semantic features are contained in this kernel language, as well as high level constructs for modularisation, parameterisation and designs. COLD-K is meant to be used as the basis of application-oriented language versions, which are more user-friendly. An example of such an application-oriented language is COLD-1. The language COLD-1 ([13]) with accompanying tools ([15]) are developed at PRLE.

The language structure of COLD-1 is given in Figure 1.

The *descriptions* layer provides support for *Design In The Large*, like: modularisation, parameterisation, (software) components and descriptions.

The *definitions* layer provides support for *Design In The Small*, like: algebraic specifications, axiomatic specifications, inductive definitions, pre & postconditions, invariants, abstract

[2]The problem of how to specify bounded sequences algebraically was posed by C.B. Jones during a workshop of the ESPRIT I project METEOR (ref #432) at De Brug in Mierlo September 1989 ([1]).

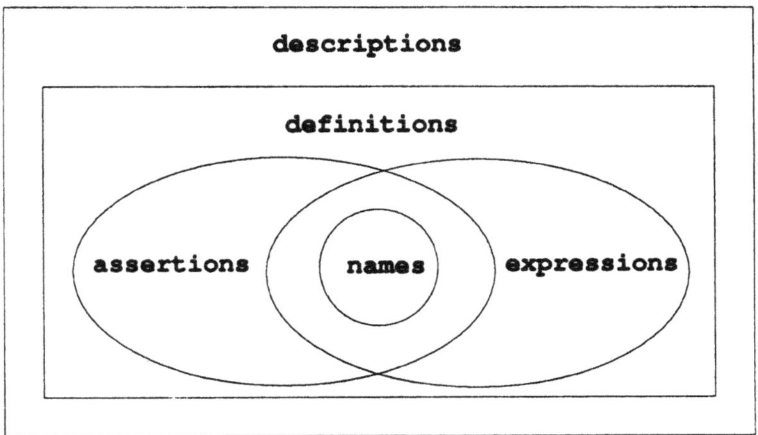

Figure 1: COLD-1 Language Structure

algorithmic descriptions and imperative programming constructs.

The *assertion language* is an extension of many-sorted-first-order predicate logic with equality (using the expressions as terms), a definedness predicate, operators from dynamic logic, an "initially" assertion (which refers to the initial state), a "prime" operator (which refers to the previous state), declaration assertions, binding assertions and block assertions, among others.

The *expression language* extends the usual term language of many-sorted predicate logic (object variables and function application) with application of partial functions (i.e. functions that may yield undefined values), application of procedures, the standard statement constructs (the empty statement `SKIP`, a guard (`A?`), sequential composition (`X;Y`), alternative choice (`X|Y`) and repetition (`X*`), where `A` is an assertion and `X` and `Y` are expressions), declaration expressions, binding expressions and block expressions, among others.

Specific details of COLD-1 deemed relevant for this paper are given in Appendix A.

3 Model-oriented Method

Using a model-oriented method the objects of an abstract type are represented in terms of other data abstractions with known properties. The operations of the abstract type can be specified in terms of the operations of the known abstractions selected as the representation. The (possibly partial) function mapping representations to their abstract counterpart is termed an abstraction function.

In Subsection 3.1, abstraction functions are considered. Subsection 3.2 describes how the set of abstract objects is defined by means of an abstraction function. The definition of the abstract operations in terms of the concrete operations on the representations using the abstraction function is dealt with in Subsection 3.3. Finally, in Subsection 3.4, an outline of the model-oriented method is given.

3.1 Abstraction Function

An abstraction function maps representations (i.e. "concrete" objects) to their abstract counterparts (i.e. "abstract" objects). Other terms to denote this function are retrieve function ([10]), interpretation function ([6]) or representation function ([8]). Four classes of abstraction functions are distinguished based upon the properties of being *injective* and *total* (see Table 1).

	injective	*total*
I	+	+
II	+	−
III	−	+
IV	−	−

Table 1: Classes of abstraction functions

For each of these classes, an example of a data type with a conceivable representation is given below (see Figure 2 as well):

I Stacks represented as sequences.

II Bounded natural numbers (i.e. natural numbers restricted to a subset characterised by an upperbound `max`) represented as natural numbers.

III Sets represented as sequences.

IV Rational numbers, viewed as a quotient of two integers, represented as 2-tuples of integers, where the first field reflects the numerator and the second field reflects the denominator.

An abstraction function `abs: Con -> Abs` is uniquely determined by means of a partial equivalence relation `eqv: Con # Con` (see Appendix B). Two representations `c1` and `c2` are mapped on the same abstract object iff they are equivalent, i.e.

```
FUNC abs: Con -> Abs

AXIOM FORALL c1,c2:Con( eqv(c1,c2) <=> abs(c1) = abs(c2) )
```

Note that the infix operator = represents *weak equality* in COLD-1 (see Subsection A.3).

Because a partial equivalence relation uniquely determines an abstraction function, the properties of the abstraction function are reflected by corresponding properties of the equivalence relation. If the abstraction function `abs` is total, one may derive from the equivalence given above that `eqv` is reflexive, and vice versa:

```
THEOREM FORALL c:Con( abs(c)! )          % abs is total
        <=> FORALL c:Con( eqv(c,c) )    % eqv is reflexive
```

A similar, but trivial, theorem may be derived if `abs` is injective. The domain of `abs` may be characterised by a predicate `is_abs` using `eqv`:

```
PRED is_abs: Con
IN   c
DEF  eqv(c,c)

THEOREM FORALL c:Con( is_abs(c) <=> abs(c)! )
```

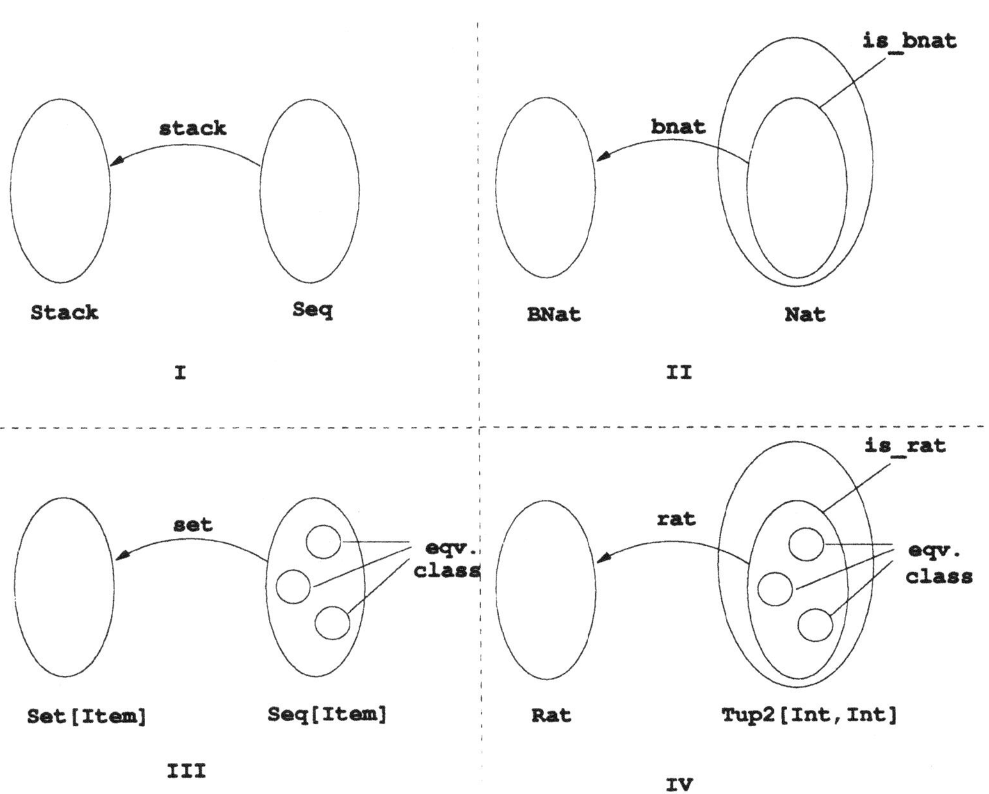

Figure 2: Examples of Conceivable Models

For the four examples given above, the corresponding equivalence relations are defined by means of inductive definitions below:

I Two sequences representing stacks are equivalent iff they are equal:

```
PRED eqv : Seq # Seq
IND  FORALL s1,s2: Seq
     ( s1 = s2 => eqv(s1,s2) )
```

II Two natural numbers representing bounded natural numbers are equal iff they are equal and less than or equal to `max`:

```
PRED eqv: Nat # Nat
IND  FORALL n,m:Nat
     ( n <= max AND n = m => eqv(n,m) )
```

III Two sequences representing sets are equal iff they contain the same items (irrespective of either the order of the items or the number of occurrences of the items in the sequence):

```
PRED eqv: Seq # Seq
IND  FORALL s1,s2:Seq
     ( FORALL i:Item( is_in(i,s1) <=> is_in(i,s2) ) => eqv(s1,s2) )
```

IV Two 2-tuples `t1` and `t2` representing rational numbers are equivalent iff they represent the same fraction:

```
PRED eqv: Tup2 # Tup2
IND  FORALL t1,t2:Tup2
     ( proj2(t1) /= 0 AND proj2(t2) /= 0
       AND proj1(t1)*proj2(t2) = proj1(t2)*proj2(t1) => eqv(t1,t2) )
```

3.2 Definition of the Abstract Sort

An abstraction function is *surjective* (i.e. its range and co-domain coincide). Stated in other words, the set of abstract objects is completely described by means of the set of concrete objects and the abstraction function.

3.3 Definition of the Abstract Operations

The abstract operations are defined in terms of the concrete operations using the abstraction function. Four classes of abstract (concrete) operations are distinguished based on the occurrence of abstract (concrete) objects as argument or result (see Table 2). The operations belonging to the class *i*, *ii*, and *iii* are termed *transformers*, *accessors* and *constructors*, respectively in [12]. Clearly, the operations belonging to class *iv* are irrelevant for the subject under consideration. In order to be able to define an abstract operation in terms of a concrete operation using the abstraction function, the concrete operation must "preserve" the equivalence classes as defined by the partial equivalence relation. Hence, given a concrete operation `cfi: Con -> Con` and two equivalent concrete objects `c1` and `c2`, the results `cfi(c1)` and `cfi(c2)` should either be equivalent, or both lack an abstract counterpart. Note that this property may conveniently be described by means of the abstraction function using the *strong equality* predicate of COLD-1 (see Subsection A.3):

	argument	*result*
i	+	+
ii	+	−
iii	−	+
iv	−	−

Table 2: Classes of operations

```
THEOREM FORALL c1,c2:Con( eqv(c1,c2) => abs(cfi(c1)) == abs(cfi(c2)) )
```

The behaviour of the concrete operation `cfi` is only of concern for those arguments `c` belonging to the domain of the abstraction function (i.e. for which the assertion `is_abs(c)` (or `eqv(c,c)`) holds). Furthermore, whenever `cfi(c1)` and `cfi(c2)` do not belong to the domain of `abs`, the actual values returned (or even their definedness) are of no importance. A similar theorem for a concrete function `cfii: Con -> Item` having a concrete object as argument is given below:

```
THEOREM FORALL c1,c2:Con( eqv(c1,c2) => cfii(c1) == cfii(c2) )
```

The property of the operations `cfi` and `cfii`, expressed by the theorems given above, is often called the *substitution property*. Note that this property is relevant for transformers and accessors only. Whenever the substitution property holds for all such operations given a (partial) equivalence relation, this relation is called a (partial) *congruence relation*. A (partial) congruence relation uniquely defines an (partial) *epimorphism* (i.e. a (partial) surjective homomorphism) mapping an algebra (i.e. the model) into a homologeous algebra (i.e. the abstract type to be defined). A partial epimorphism is a weak homomorphism (see [3]).

The abstract counterparts of conceivable concrete operations belonging to the classes *i* till *iii* are defined axiomatically below:

```
FUNC afi   : Abs  -> Abs
FUNC afii  : Abs  -> Item
FUNC afiii : Item -> Abs

AXIOM FORALL c:Con
      ( is_abs(c) => ( afi(abs(c))   == abs(cfi(c))
                     ; afii(abs(c))  == cfii(c)
                     )
      )
    ; FORALL i:Item( afiii(i) == abs(cfiii(i)) )
```

The predicate characterising the domain of the abstraction function is frequently termed *representation invariant* (see, e.g. [12]). Note that the definition of the concrete operations is not constrained by the representation invariant. In fact, whenever the substitution property is met, the construction of the abstract model by means of the abstraction function obviates the need to consider the representation invariant when defining the concrete operations, simplifying the construction of the model considerably.

3.4 Outline of the Method

The model-oriented method dealt with in this paper consists of the following steps:

1. Describe the signature and intended interpretation of the sorts, predicates and functions of the abstract type.
2. Define a model of the abstract type:
   (a) Choose an appropriate representation of the data.
   (b) Describe the signature of the model.
   (c) Define a partial equivalence relation on the representation chosen.
   (d) Formulate the substitution property for transformers and accessors.
   (e) Define the concrete operations in such a way that the substitution property holds.
3. Define the set of abstract objects and the abstract operations in terms of the set of concrete objects and the concrete operations using the abstraction function.

The definition of the abstract type in terms of the model is facilitated by the component `IPQ` from the standard COLD-1 library IGLOO[3] ([14]). The component `IPQ` provides the abstract sort, the abstraction function, and the predicate characterising the domain of the abstraction function, given the concrete sort and the partial equivalence relation (see Appendix D).

[3]IGLOO is an acronym for Incremental Generic Library Of Objects.

4 Example: Bounded Sequences

The component BSEQ[Item] specifies the parameterised abstract type of bounded sequences of objects of sort Item. The maximum length of a bounded sequence is a parameter of the operations constructing abstract objects. The abstract type is specified using a model in which bounded sequences are represented as 2-tuples, where the first field reflects the sequence and the second field reflects the maximum length of the sequence. Note that the maximum length of a bounded sequence is part of the representation. This makes it possible to differentiate between, for example, an empty sequence with a maximum length of m and one with a maximum length of n, when $m \neq n$.

The operations on the concrete objects representing bounded sequences are defined in terms of the operations provided by the following components from the standard COLD-1 library IGLOO:

- NAT, which specifies the data type of natural numbers;
- SEQ[Item], which specifies the parameterised data type of finite sequences of objects of the type Item (see Appendix C.1); and
- TUP2[Item1,Item2], which specifies the parameterised data type of 2-tuples of objects of the types Item1 and Item2 (see Appendix C.2).

4.1 Signature and Intended Interpretation

The intended interpretation of the component BSEQ is given in comment below. The signature of BSEQ, which is given explicitly in Subsection 4.3, may be derived from the informal description.

```
% BSEQ specifies the parameterized data type of bounded sequences.
%
% Interpretation (i:Item, s,t:BSeq, m:Nat):
%
% Itêm          : the set of objects contained in bounded sequences;
% BSeq          : the set of bounded sequences of objects of type Item;
% empty(m)      : the empty bounded sequence with maximum length m;
% cons(i,s,m)   : the bounded sequence with i appended at the head of
%                 s and maxmimum length m;
% hd(s)         : the head of s (= element with index 0);
% tl(s,m)       : the tail of s (= s with its head removed) with maximum
%                 length m;
% len(s)        : the length of s (= number of elements of s);
% maxlen(s)     : the maximum length of s.

COMPONENT BSEQ[Item] SPECIFICATION
```

4.2 Definition of the Model

4.2.1 Representation of the Data

A bounded sequence may be represented as a 2-tuple, consisting of a sequence and a natural number.

4.2.2 Signature of the Model

The component BSEQMODEL specifies a model of bounded sequences. The ABSTRACT clause contains the abbreviated component ITEM specifying the parameter Item of BSEQMODEL. The signature of BSEQMODEL is given after the keyword EXPORT. Note that this signature contains:

- a sort Tup2 representing bounded sequences;
- concrete operations for all abstract operations to be provided by the component BSEQ; and
- a partial equivalence relation eqv.

```
LET BSEQMODEL[Item] :=

ABSTRACT
  ITEM
EXPORT
  SORT Tup2
  FUNC empty  : Nat                    -> Tup2,
       cons   : Item # Tup2 # Nat -> Tup2,
       hd     : Tup2                   -> Item,
       tl     : Tup2 # Nat             -> Tup2,
       len    : Tup2                   -> Nat,
       maxlen : Tup2                   -> Nat
  PRED eqv    : Tup2 # Tup2
```

The specification of BSEQMODEL uses the components NAT, SEQ, TUP2 and IPQ. The component SEQ is instantiated with the sort Item, being the parameter of the model. The component IPQ is instantiated with the concrete sort Tup2 (provided by the instantiated component TUP2) and the partial equivalence relation eqv (which is defined in the model). The abstraction function ipq and predicate is_ipq provided by IPQ are renamed to bseq and is_bseq, respectively. The component IPQ is used to simplify the specification of the substitution property.

```
IMPORT
  NAT, SEQ[Item], TUP2[Seq[Item],Nat],
  IPQ[Tup2,eqv]
    RENAMING
      FUNC ipq    TO bseq
      PRED is_ipq TO is_bseq
    END
CLASS
```

4.2.3 Definition of the Equivalence Relation

A tuple tup(s,n) represents a bounded sequence iff the length of s is less than or equal to n. So we should define eqv in such a way that the following theorem holds:

```
THEOREM FORALL t:Tup2( is_bseq(t) <=> len(proj1(t)) <= proj2(t) )
```

This can be achieved by the following definition of eqv:

```
PRED eqv: Tup2 # Tup2
IN   t1,t2
DEF  len(proj1(t1)) <= proj2(t1) AND t1 = t2
```

Note that the abstraction function is injective, but not total (i.e. case II in Subsection 3.1).

4.2.4 Substitution Property

```
THEOREM % Substitution property:
        FORALL t1,t2: Tup2
        ( eqv(t1,t2)
          => ( hd(t1)      == hd(t2)
             ; len(t1)     == len(t2)
             ; maxlen(t1) == maxlen(t2)
             ; FORALL i:Item,n:Nat
               ( bseq(cons(i,t1,n)) == bseq(cons(i,t2,n)) )
             ; FORALL n:Nat( bseq(tl(t1,n)) == bseq(tl(t2,n)) )
             )
        )
```

The substitution property gives rise to proof obligations for transformers and accessors. In this particular example, however, the substitution property is trivially satisfied, because each (non-empty) equivalence class contains exactly one element.

4.2.5 Definition of the Concrete Operations

The concrete operations are defined in terms of the operations on sequences and 2-tuples.

```
FUNC empty: Nat -> Tup2
IN   n
DEF  tup(empty,n)

FUNC cons : Item # Tup2 # Nat -> Tup2
IN   i,t,n
DEF  tup(cons(i,proj1(t)),n)

FUNC hd : Tup2 -> Item
IN   t
DEF  hd(proj1(t))

FUNC tl : Tup2 # Nat -> Tup2
IN   t,n
DEF  tup(tl(proj1(t)),n)

FUNC len : Tup2 -> Nat
IN   t
DEF  len(proj1(t))

FUNC maxlen : Tup2 -> Nat
IN   t
DEF  proj2(t)

END
```

4.3 Definition of the Abstract Type

The signature of the component BSEQ is given below:

```
ABSTRACT
  ITEM
EXPORT
  SORT BSeq
```

```
FUNC empty  : Nat                  -> BSeq,
     cons   : Item # BSeq # Nat -> BSeq,
     hd     : BSeq                 -> Item,
     tl     : BSeq # Nat           -> BSeq,
     len    : BSeq                 -> Nat,
     maxlen : BSeq                 -> Nat
```

The definition of the abstract type is given in terms of the component BSEQMODEL and the component IPQ.

```
IMPORT
  BSEQMODEL[Item],
  IPQ[Tup2,eqv]
    RENAMING
      SORT Ipq    TO BSeq
      FUNC ipq    TO bseq
      PRED is_ipq TO is_bseq
    END
CLASS
```

The definitions of the abstract functions are straightforward.

```
  FUNC empty  : Nat                  -> BSeq
  FUNC cons   : Item # BSeq # Nat -> BSeq
  FUNC hd     : BSeq                 -> Item
  FUNC tl     : BSeq # Nat           -> BSeq
  FUNC len    : BSeq                 -> Nat
  FUNC maxlen : BSeq                 -> Nat

  AXIOM FORALL n:Nat( empty(n) == bseq(empty(n)) )
      ; FORALL t:Tup2
        ( is_bseq(t)
          => ( hd(bseq(t))     == hd(t)
             ; len(bseq(t))    == len(t)
             ; maxlen(bseq(t)) == maxlen(t)
             ; FORALL i:Item,n:Nat
               ( cons(i,bseq(t),n) == bseq(cons(i,t,n)) )
             ; FORALL n:Nat( tl(bseq(t),n) == bseq(tl(t,n)) )
             )
        )

END
```

5 Towards an Implementation of the Abstract Type

Unlike methods such as VDM and Z, the model used to specify an abstract type using the model-oriented method described in this paper will in general not be an implementation of the abstract type. This is an immediate consequence of the fact that the concrete operations need not satisfy the representation invariant.

Fortunately, construction of an implementation from the model is straightforward. Whenever a concrete operation yields an object c which does not belong to the domain of the abstraction function (i.e. the assertion NOT eqv(c,c) holds), the corresponding operation of the implementation should become undefined. Hence, by guarding the result of transformers and constructors by the condition eqv(c,c), the model may be used as an implementation of the abstract type.

Generation of an implementation of an abstract type is feasible whenever the models are constructed using:

- executable constructs of the language COLD-1; and
- components which have implementations associated with them.

Note that in the example given in Subsection 4.2, the model is defined using (very simple) executable constructs of the language COLD-1.

6 Towards Tool Support for the Method

Considering the model (e.g. `BSEQMODEL`) on the one hand and the abstract type (e.g. `BSEQ`) on the other hand, the following aspects may be noted:

- the `ABSTRACT` clauses of the model and the abstract type are identical;
- the `EXPORT` clauses of the model and the abstract type are identical, apart from:
  - the names of the sorts (e.g. `BSeq` instead of `Tup2`);
  - the equivalence relation `eqv`, which is lacking in the abstract type.
- the `IMPORT` clause of the abstract type contains:
  - the (instantiation of the) model;
  - the (instantiation and subsequent renaming of the) component `IPQ`.
- the definitions of the abstract type have a very regular pattern.

In the example presented, the concrete sort did neither occur as an argument nor as a result of any abstract operation. This is not typical, however. For example, assume bounded natural numbers were specified using natural numbers. Is such a case, an embedding function `nat : BNat -> Nat` mapping a bounded natural number on a natural number is conceivable. Hence, a clear distinction should be made between arguments and results which are meant to represent the abstract type, and those which do not. This problem is easily solved by an appropriate renaming of the sort chosen as representation and usage of the copy section, the detailed treatment of which falls outside the scope of this paper, however.

In the example presented, the concrete operations were given the same symbol as the abstract operations (using overloading). Whenever other symbols are chosen, an appropriate renaming is required.

In summary, the specification of the abstract type can be generated automatically given:

- the specification of the model;
- the names of the abstract sort and the concrete sort;
- the symbols of the abstract operations and the concrete operations (optionally); and
- the equivalence relation `eqv`.

Similarly, because the substitution property has a very regular pattern, it may be generated as a verification condition by means of tools as well. Finally, the construction of an implementation of the abstract type is feasible (see Section 5).

7 Conclusions & Directions for Future Work

A model-oriented method for algebraic specifications is described, using the design language COLD-1 as notation. The method is centered around the notion of a partial equivalence relation. The abstract sort, abstraction function and the representation invariant (i.e. the predicate characterising the domain of the abstraction function) are defined in terms of the partial equivalence relation. In fact, given a partial equivalence relation and a model satisfying the substitution property, the specification of the abstract type can be derived automatically. Because the assertion language of COLD-1 is based on classical two-valued logic, partial functions are treated quite naturally.

Unlike existing model-oriented methods like VDM and Z, which identify the abstract type to be defined and the model used as representation, the method presented makes a clear distinction between the abstract type and the model. The advantage of this approach is that the problem of "implementation bias" does not apply and that the operations of the model do not need to satisfy the representation invariant, simplifying the construction of the model considerably.

By explicitly using an abstraction function, the method is closely related to the concept of "abstract implementations" (which is based on [6], amongst others; see [9] for an in depth treatment of the subject). Because the method constructs the specification of the abstract type using the abstraction function, it should be clearly distinguished from this concept, however.

The model used as representation will in general not be usable as an implementation of the abstract type as such. Generation of an implementation using the model, however, is shown to be straightforward. The correctness of the implementation follows immediately from the construction.

Method support is provided through a dedicated component `IPQ` from the standard COLD-1 library IGLOO facilitating the construction of the specification of an abstract type, given a model and a partial equivalence relation.

Conceivable standard constructs to be used for the construction of the model are (where the corresponding COLD-1 component from IGLOO is given between brackets): n-tuples, i.e. Cartesian products consisting of n fields (`TUP`*n*), sets (`SET`), sequences (`SEQ`) and maps (`MAP`).

Tool support for the method has been identified in the following areas:

- generation of the substitution property as a verification condition;
- generation of the specification of the abstract type, given a model and a partial equivalence relation;
- generation of an implementation of the abstract type.

Although the model-oriented method presented concerns algebraic specifications only, extensions of the method to cover state-based specifications are feasible. This topic falls outside the scope of this paper, however.

8 Acknowledgements

I would like to thank Hans B.M. Jonkers for his many helpful comments and suggestions.

References

[1] J. Bergstra and L. Feijs, editors. *Algebraic Methods II: Theory, Tools and Applications.* Springer-Verlag, 1991. LNCS 490.

[2] J. Bergstra, J. Heering, and P. Klint. Module Algebra. *J. ACM*, 37(2):335 – 372, Apr. 1990.

[3] M. Broy and M. Wirsing. Partial abstract types. *Acta Informatica*, 18(1):47 – 64, 1982. Springer–Verlag, Berlin Heidelberg New York.

[4] L. Feijs, H. Jonkers, C. Koymans, and G. Renardel de Lavalette. Formal Definition of the Design Language COLD–K. Technical Report METEOR/t7/PRLE/7, Philips Research Laboratories (PRLE), P.O. Box 80.000, 5600 JA Eindhoven, the Netherlands, Apr. 1987. ESPRIT project 432.

[5] G. Grätzer. *Universal Algebra.* D. van Nostrand Company, Inc., 1968.

[6] J. Guttag. Abstract Data Types and the Development of Data Structures. *Commun. ACM*, 20(6):396 – 404, June 1977.

[7] D. Harel. *Handbook of Philosophical Logic*, volume II, chapter Dynamic Logic, pages 497 – 604. D. Reidel Publishing Company, 1984. ISBN 90-277-1604-8.

[8] C. Hoare. Proof of Correctness of Data Representation. *Acta Informatica*, 1(4):271 – 281, 1972.

[9] I. V. Horebeek and J. Lewi. *Algebraic Specifications in Software Engineering, An Introduction.* Springer-Verlag, Berlin Heidelberg New York, 1989. ISBN 3-540-51626-3.

[10] C. B. Jones. *Systematic Software Development Using VDM.* Series in Computer Science. Prentice-Hall International, 1986. ISBN 0-13-880725-6.

[11] H. Jonkers. A Concrete Syntax for COLD–K. Technical Report METEOR/t8/PRLE/2, Philips Research Laboratories (PRLE), P.O. Box 80.000, 5600 JA Eindhoven, the Netherlands, 1988. ESPRIT project 432.

[12] B. Meyer. *Object-oriented Software Construction.* Series in Computer Science. Prentice-Hall International, 1988. ISBN 0-13-629049-3.

[13] Philips Research, Information and Software Technology (IST), Bldg. WAY–1.21, P.O. Box 80.000, 5600 JA Eindhoven, the Netherlands. *Description of COLD-1*, May 1991. 12 NC: 4322 270 55341.

[14] Philips Research, Information and Software Technology (IST), Bldg. WAY–1.21, P.O. Box 80.000, 5600 JA Eindhoven, the Netherlands. *Igloo User's Manual*, May 1991. 12 NC: 4322 270 55321.

[15] Philips Research, Information and Software Technology (IST), Bldg. WAY–1.21, P.O. Box 80.000, 5600 JA Eindhoven, the Netherlands. *User's Manual ICE 0.4*, July 1991. 12 NC: 4322 270 55721.

[16] D. Scott. *Bertrand Russell, Philosopher of the Century*, chapter Existence and Description in Formal Logic, pages 181 – 200. Allen & Unwin, London, 1967.

[17] J. Spivey. *Understanding Z, a specification language and its formal semantics.* Cambridge Tracts in Theoretical Computer Science 3, 1988. ISBN 0-521-33429-2.

[18] J. Wing. A Specifier's Introduction to Formal Methods. *IEEE Computer*, 23(9):8–24, Sept. 1990.

[19] M. Wirsing. Structured Algebraic Specifications: a Kernel Language. Master's thesis, Technische Universität München, 1983.

[20] M. Wirsing and M. Broy. *Theoretical Foundations of Programming Methodology*, volume 91 of *C - Mathematical and Physical Sciences*, chapter An Analysis of Semantic Models for Algebraic Specifications, pages 351 – 413. D. Reidel Publishing Company, P.O.Box 17, 3300 AA Dordrecht, Holland, 1982. Lecture Notes of an International Summer School, directed by F.L. Bauer, E.W. Dijkstra and C.A.R. Hoare, ISBN 90-277-1460-6.

A Details of COLD-1

A.1 Definedness

A sort may be conceived as partitioned in two sets: a set of *defined* objects and a set of *undefined* objects (see Figure 3).

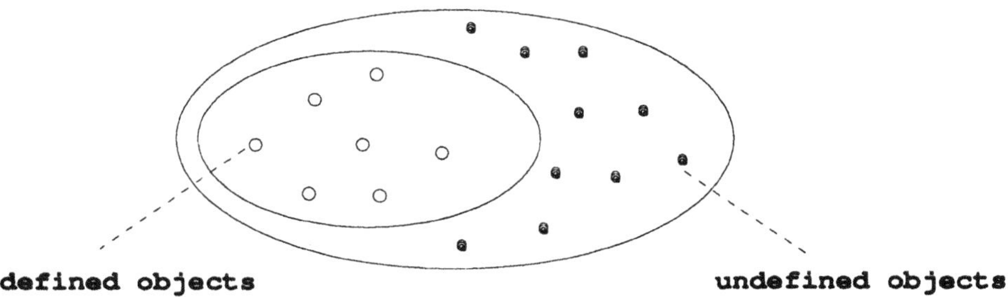

Figure 3: Defined and Undefined Objects

Functions in COLD-1 are *partial*: they may be *undefined* for certain elements.

The *definedness* (*undefinedness*) *predicate*, represented by the postfix operator ! (^), expresses that an object is defined (undefined), e.g.

```
THEOREM 0!;        % the natural number zero is defined
        pred(0)^   % the predecessor of zero is undefined
```

A.2 Strictness

Functions and (user-defined) predicates are *strict*. If we apply a function to an undefined argument, the result will also be undefined. If we apply a user-defined predicate to an undefined argument, the predicate will be false. Hence,

```
THEOREM x^ => f(x)^;
        x^ => NOT r(x)
```

A.3 Equality

There exist two kinds of equality in COLD-1: *weak* equality and *strong* equality. Weak equality, represented by the infix operator =, is strict. Strong equality, represented by the infix operator ==, may be expressed in terms of definedness and weak equality: two objects x and y are strongly equal iff they are either equal in the weak sense, or both undefined.

```
THEOREM x = y => x! AND y!;
        x == y <=> x = y OR (x^ AND y^)
```

Instead of "weak", the qualifier "existential" is used in [3]. Definedness can be expressed in terms of weak equality:

```
THEOREM x! <=> x = x
```

Similar to equality, there exist two kinds of inequality in COLD-1, which may be expressed directly in terms of the equality predicates:

```
THEOREM x  /= y <=> NOT x  = y;
        x =/= y <=> NOT x == y
```

A.4 Qualifiers

Qualifiers (`FORALL` and `EXISTS`) range over defined objects only. So we have the following tautology:

```
THEOREM FORALL t: T( t! );
        NOT EXISTS t: T( t^ )
```

B Equivalence Relations

An *equivalence relation* is a binary relation that is *reflexive*, *symmetric* and *transitive* (see, e.g. [5]). Given an equivalence relation, the set of all elements that are equivalent one to another is called an *equivalence class*. Equivalence classes do not intersect.

An equivalence relation `eqv` on a set `Item` defines a *natural mapping* from `Item` to the quotient set `Item/eqv` (see [5]). A natural mapping is a *total* function due to the fact that an equivalence relation is reflexive.

In order to be able to define a *partial natural mapping*, the notion of a *partial equivalence relation* is introduced. A partial equivalence relation is both *symmetric* and *transivitive*, but need not be *reflexive*. This should not come as a surprise. In [20], it is already mentioned that the congruence relation termed *existential equality* is not an equivalence relation in general, because it is not reflexive. A partial equivalence relation `eqv` on a set `Item` defines a partial natural mapping from `Item` to the partial quotient set `Item/eqv`. Note that because a partial equivalence relation need not be reflexive, the union of all equivalence classes need not be identical to the set of all elements, i.e. a partial equivalence relation need not define a partition. The union of all equivalence classes characterises the domain of the partial natural mapping.

To distinguish partial equivalence relations from equivalence relations, an equivalence relation is sometimes called a *strict equivalence relation* for emphasis. The qualifier "partial" will always be used when referring to partial equivalence relations.

Apart from being reflexive or not, equivalence relations may be classified as being either *weak* or *strong*, similar to equality (see Section A.3). Due to the fact that user-defined predicates are strict in COLD-1 (see Section A.2), user-defined equivalence relations are always weak.

The component `WPE` specifying a weak partial equivalence is given below.

```
% WPE specifies a weak partial equivalence relation.
%
% Interpretation (i,j:Item):
%
% Item      : the set of objects on which the equivalence relation
%             is defined;
% eqv(i,j)  : i and j are equivalent.

LET WPE :=

EXPORT
  SORT Item
  PRED eqv : Item # Item
CLASS

  SORT Item
  PRED eqv : Item # Item

  AXIOM  FORALL i,j,k:Item
  {WPE1} ( eqv(i,j) => eqv(j,i)                    % symmetric
  {WPE2} ; eqv(i,j) AND eqv(j,k) => eqv(i,k)  % transitive
         )

END
```

C Standard Mathematical Domains

Those parts of the parameterised components SEQ and TUP2 of the COLD-1 library IGLOO deemed relevant for this paper are given in this appendix. Their definitions are not shown.

C.1 Sequences

```
% SEQ specifies the parameterized data type of finite sequences.
%
% Interpretation (i:Item, s,t:Seq, m:Nat):
%
% Item      : the set of objects contained in sequences;
% Seq       : the set of finite sequences of objects of type Item;
% empty     : the empty sequence;
% cons(i,s) : the sequence s with i appended at the head of s;
% hd(s)     : the head of s (= element with index 0);
% tl(s)     : the tail of s (= s with its head removed);
% len(s)    : the length of s (= number of elements of s).

COMPONENT SEQ[Item] SPECIFICATION

ABSTRACT
  ITEM
EXPORT
  SORT Seq
  FUNC empty :              -> Seq,
       cons  : Item # Seq -> Seq,
       hd    : Seq          -> Item,
```

```
      tl    : Seq          -> Seq,
      len   : Seq          -> Nat
IMPORT
  NAT
CLASS
```

Definitions

```
END
```

C.2 Two-Tuples

```
% TUP2 specifies the parameterized data type of 2-tuples.
%
% Interpretation (i1:Item1, i2:Item2, t:Tup):
%
% Item1       : the set of objects acting as the first elements of tuples;
% Item2       : the set of objects acting as the second elements of tuples;
% Tup         : the set of tuples of objects of types Item1 and Item2;
% tup(i1,i2)  : the tuple consisting of i1 and i2;
% proj1(t)    : the first element of tuple t;
% proj2(t)    : the second element of tuple t.
%
% Note:
%
% This data type can be generalised in a straightforward way to
% the case of n-tuples (n > 0).

COMPONENT TUP2[Item1,Item2] SPECIFICATION

ABSTRACT
  ITEM1, ITEM2
EXPORT
  SORT Tup2
  FUNC tup : Item1 # Item2 -> Tup2,
       proj1 : Tup2 -> Item1,
       proj2 : Tup2 -> Item2
CLASS
```

Definitions

```
END
```

D Isomorphism to a Partial Quotient set

A partial equivalence relation `eqv` **on a set** `Item` **induces a partial quotient set** `Item/eqv`**. The component** `IPQ` **specifies an isomorphism to this subset.**

```
% IPQ defines a partial quotient set, as defined by a partial
% equivalence relation, as an abstract type.
%
% Interpretation (i,j:Item):
%
% Item       : the set of objects on which the partial equivalence
%              relation is defined;
% Ipq        : the set of objects isomorphic to the partial quotient set;
```

```
% eqv(i,j)   : i and j are partially equivalent;
% ipq(i)     : the object corresponding with the equivalence class [i]/eqv;
% is_ipq(i)  : i belongs to the domain of ipq.

LET IPQ[Item,eqv] :=

ABSTRACT
  WPE
EXPORT
  SORT Item,
       Ipq
  FUNC ipq    : Item -> Ipq
  PRED eqv    : Item # Item,
       is_ipq : Item
CLASS

  SORT Ipq
  FUNC ipq    : Item -> Ipq
  PRED is_ipq : Item
```

The partial natural mapping (or partial epimorphism) `ipq`, sort `Ipq` and predicate `is_ipq` are defined axiomatically in terms of `eqv`:

```
  DECL i,i1,i2:Item, b:Ipq

  AXIOM
  {IPQ1} ipq(i1) = ipq(i2) <=> eqv(i1,i2);
  {IPQ2} EXISTS j:Item( ipq(j) = b );        % ipq is surjective
  {IPQ3} is_ipq(i) <=> eqv(i,i)

END
```

A Mechanical Formalization of Several Fairness Notions

David M. Goldschlag

Computational Logic, Inc.
1717 West Sixth Street, Suite 290
Austin, Texas 78703-4776
U.S.A.
Telephone: (512) 322-9951
e-mail: dmg@cli.com

Abstract: Fairness abstractions are useful for reasoning about computations of non-deterministic programs. This paper presents proof rules for reasoning about three fairness notions and one safety assumption with an automated theorem prover. These proof rules have been integrated into a mechanization of the Unity logic [8, 9] and are suitable for the mechanical verification of concurrent programs. Mechanical verification provides greater trust in the correctness of a proof.

The three fairness notions presented here are unconditional, weak, and strong fairness [6]. The safety assumption is deadlock freedom which guarantees that no deadlock occurs during the computation. These abstractions are demonstrated by the mechanically verified proof of a dining philosopher's program, also discussed here.

1. Introduction

This paper presents a mechanical formalization of three fairness notions and one safety assumption. This formalization extends the mechanization of Chandy and Misra's Unity logic [5] described in [8, 9] and permits the mechanical verification of concurrent programs under the assumptions of unconditional, weak, and strong fairness [13], and the safety assumption of deadlock freedom. Deadlock freedom guarantees that no deadlock occurs during the computation.

These assumptions are useful for reasoning about computations of non-deterministic programs since they may permit delaying consideration of certain implementation issues at early stages of program design. This paper demonstrates these assumptions by the mechanically verified proof of a solution to the dining philosopher's problem.

These four assumptions are formalized as proof rules. These proof rules are either theorems of the operational semantics of concurrency presented here or are consistent with a restriction of that operational semantics. In the first case, the proof system is (relatively) complete, since all properties may ultimately be derived directly from the operational semantics. In the second case, completeness depends upon whether the proof rules in the literature are sufficient. However, the proof system is sound, since the restricted operational semantics justifies the new proof rules.

The mechanization presented here is an encoding of the Unity logic on the Boyer-Moore prover [2]. Proofs in this system resemble Unity hand proofs, but are longer, since all concepts are defined from first principles. This proof system is semi-automatic since complex proofs are guided by the user. Mechanical verification provides greater trust in the correctness of a proof.

This paper is organized in the following way: Since the mechanization here has been done on the Boyer-Moore prover, section 2 presents a brief introduction to the Boyer-Moore logic and its prover. Section 3 presents an operational semantics of concurrency that justifies the proof rules presented in section 5. That section also presents the intuition behind each of the fairness notions. Sections 4 and 6 present specification predicates for several types of correctness properties. Section 7 presents the specification and proof of a solution to the dining philosopher's problem which illustrates the use of the proof rules. Section 8 summarizes related work and offers some concluding remarks.

2. The Boyer-Moore Prover

2.1. The Boyer-Moore Logic

This proof system is specified in the Nqthm version of the Boyer-Moore logic [2]. Nqthm is a quantifier free first order logic with equality that permits recursive definitions. It also defines an interpreter function for the quotation of terms in the logic. Nqthm uses a prefix syntax similar to pure Lisp. This notation is completely unambiguous, easy to parse, and easy to read after some practice. Informal definitions of functions used in this paper follow:

- `T` is an abbreviation for `(TRUE)` which is not equal to `F` which is an abbreviation for `(FALSE)`.
- `(EQUAL A B)` is `T` if `A=B`, `F` otherwise.
- The value of the term `(AND X Y)` is `T` if both `X` and `Y` are not `F`, `F` otherwise. `OR`, `IMPLIES`, `NOT`, and `IFF` are similarly defined.
- The value of the term `(IF A B C)` is `C` if `A=F`, `B` otherwise.
- `(NUMBERP A)` tests whether `A` is a number.
- `(ZEROP A)` is `T` if `A=0` or `(NOT (NUMBERP A))`.

- `(ADD1 A)` returns the successor to `A` (i.e., `A+1`). If `(NUMBERP A)` is false then `(ADD1 A)` is `1`.
- `(SUB1 A)` returns the predecessor of `A` (i.e., `A-1`). If `(ZEROP A)` is true, then `(SUB1 A)` is `0`.
- `(PLUS A B)` is `A+B`, and is defined recursively using `ADD1`.
- `(LESSP A B)` is `A<B`, and is defined recursively using `SUB1`.
- Literals are quoted. For example, `'ABC` is a literal. `NIL` is an abbreviation for `'NIL`.
- `(CONS A B)` represents a pair. `(CAR (CONS A B))` is `A`, and `(CDR (CONS A B))` is `B`. Compositions of car's and cdr's can be abbreviated: `(CADR A)` is read as `(CAR (CDR A))`.
- `(LISTP A)` is true if `A` is a pair.
- `(LIST A)` is an abbreviation for `(CONS A NIL)`. `LIST` can take an arbitrary number of arguments: `(LIST A B C)` is read as `(CONS A (CONS B (CONS C NIL)))`.
- `'(A)` is an abbreviation for `(LIST 'A)`. Similarly, `'(A B C)` is an abbreviation for `(LIST 'A 'B 'C)`.[1]
- `(LENGTH L)` returns the length of the list `L`.
- `(MEMBER X L)` tests whether `X` is an element of the list `L`.
- `(APPLY$ FUNC ARGS)` is the result of applying the function `FUNC` to the arguments `ARGS`.[2] For example, `(APPLY$ 'PLUS (LIST 1 2))` is `(PLUS 1 2)` which is `3`.
- `(EVAL$ T TERM ALIST)` represents the value obtained by applying the outermost function symbol in `TERM` to the `EVAL$` of the arguments in `TERM`. If `TERM` is a literal atom, then `(EVAL$ T TERM ALIST)` is the second element of the first pair in `ALIST` whose first element is `TERM`.

2.2. Functional Instantiation

The theorem prover is directed by *events* submitted by the user. Definitions and theorems introduce newly defined functions and theorems, respectively. Partially constrained function symbols are defined by the *constrain* event which introduces new function symbols and their constraints. To ensure the consistency of the constraints, one must demonstrate that they are satisfiable. Therefore, the constrain event also requires the presentation of one old function symbol as a model for each new function symbol; the constraints, with each new symbol substituted by its model, must be provable [3]. There is no logical connection between the new symbols and their models, however; providing the models is simply a soundness guarantee.

---

[1] Actually, this quote mechanism is a facility of the Lisp reader.

[2] This simple definition is only true for total functions but is sufficient for this paper.

All extensions to the Boyer-Moore logic presented in this paper were added using either the definitional principle or the constrain mechanism. Furthermore, the admissibility of these definitions and constraints was mechanically checked using the Boyer-Moore prover. This guarantees that the resulting logic is a conservative extension of the Boyer-Moore logic, and is therefore sound. All theorems presented here were mechanically verified by the Boyer-Moore prover enhanced with Kaufmann's proof checker [10].

2.3. Definitions with Quantifiers

It is often useful to be able to include quantifiers in the body of a definition. Since the Boyer-Moore logic does not define quantifiers, the quantifiers must be removed by a technique called skolemization. If the definition is not recursive, adding the skolemized definition preserves the theory's consistency [11].

As a convenience, one may abbreviate nested `FORALL`'s by putting all consecutive universally quantified variables in a list. Therefore, `(FORALL X (FORALL Y (EQUAL X Y)))` may be abbreviated to `(FORALL (X Y) (EQUAL X Y))`. Nested `EXISTS`'s may be shortened similarly.

Notice that the quantifiers `FORALL` and `EXISTS` may occur only in non-recursive definitions and are automatically skolemized away by the theorem prover. For notational convenience, other quantified formulas are occasionally used in this paper (and were translated manually). In these cases, the quantifier symbols $\forall$ and $\exists$ are used instead.

3. The Operational Semantics

The operational semantics of concurrency used here is based on the transition system model [13, 5]. A *transition system* is a set of statements that effect transitions on the system state. A *computation* is the sequence of states generated by the composition of an infinite sequence of transitions on an initial state. *Fairness* notions are restrictions of the scheduling of statements in the computation. For example, if every program statement is a total function, then *unconditional fairness* requires that each statement be responsible for an infinite number of transitions in the computation (every statement is scheduled infinitely often). Other fairness notions introduce the concept of *enabled* transitions, where a statement can only effect a transition if it is enabled (the statement can produce a successor state). These notions will be formalized in Section 5. Stronger fairness notions restrict the set of computations that a program may generate; hence a program's behavior may be correct under one fairness notion and not under another.

The next sections present an operational characterization of an arbitrary computation.

3.1. A Concurrent Program

A program is a list of statements. Each statement is a relation from previous states to next states. We define the function **N** so the term **(N OLD NEW E)** is true if and only if **NEW** is a possible successor state to **OLD** under the transition specified by statement **E**. The actual definition of **N** is not important until one considers a particular program. For completeness, however, the definition of **N** is:

Definition: N

```
(N OLD NEW E)
  =
(APPLY$ (CAR E) (APPEND (LIST OLD NEW) (CDR E)))
```

N applies the **CAR** of the statement to the previous and next states, along with any other arguments encoded into the **CDR** of the statement. A state can be any data structure. Intuitively, a statement is a list with the first component being a function name, and the remainder of the list being other arguments. These arguments may instantiate a function representing a generic statement to a specific program statement. This encoding provides a convenient way to specify programs containing many similar statements that differ only by an index or some other parameter.

A statement **E** is *enabled* in state **OLD** if there exists some state **NEW** such that **(N OLD NEW E)** is true. That is, a statement is enabled if it can produce a successor state. We call such transitions *effective*. If a statement cannot effect any effective transitions from state **OLD** then it is *disabled* for that state. The *enabling* condition for a statement is the weakest precondition guaranteeing an effective transition. A statement's effective transition may be the identity transition, however (e.g., the **SKIP** statement).

3.2. A Computation

We now characterize a function, named **S**, representing an arbitrary, but fixed computation. The execution of a concurrent program is an interleaving of statements in the program. This characterization of **S** requires that every statement be scheduled infinitely often. Disabled statements effect the null transition. This formalization is equivalent to weak fairness. Furthermore, if all program statements are total functions, this reduces to unconditional fairness.

Introducing extra skip states can be considered stuttering and is legitimate since repeated states do not interfere with either the safety or liveness properties discussed in section 4. Fairness notions presented later will guarantee that a statement eventually executes an effective transition.

The term **(S PRG I)** represents the **I**'th state in the execution of program **PRG**. The function **S** is characterized by the following two constraints specifying the relationship between successive states in a computation:

Constraint: S-Effective-Transition[3]

```
(IMPLIES (AND (LISTP PRG)
              (∃ NEW (N (S PRG I) NEW (CHOOSE PRG I))))
         (N (S PRG I)
            (S PRG (ADD1 I))
            (CHOOSE PRG I)))
```

This constraint states that, given two assumptions, the state **(S PRG (ADD1 I))** is a successor state to **(S PRG I)** and the statement governing that transition is chosen by the function **CHOOSE** in the term **(CHOOSE PRG I)**. Additional constraints about **CHOOSE** will be presented later.

The two assumptions are:

- The program must be non-empty. This is stated by the term **(LISTP PRG)**. If the program has no statements, then no execution may be deduced.
- There is some successor state from **(S PRG I)** under the statement scheduled by **(CHOOSE PRG I)**. (If the statement is disabled, no effective transition is possible. The next constraint specifies that the null transition occurs in this case.)

The second constraint specifies the relationship between successive states when the scheduled statement is disabled:

Constrain: S-Idle-Transition[4]

```
(IMPLIES (AND (LISTP PRG)
              (NOT (∃ NEW (N (S PRG I) NEW (CHOOSE PRG I)))))
         (EQUAL (S PRG (ADD1 I))
                (S PRG I)))
```

This constraint states that if a disabled statement is scheduled, then no progress is made (i.e., a skip statement is executed instead).

---

[3]This constraint is equivalent to the following unquantified formula, because the existential may be moved outside the formula.

```
(IMPLIES (AND (LISTP PRG)
              (N (S PRG I) NEW (CHOOSE PRG I)))
         (N (S PRG I)
            (S PRG (ADD1 I))
            (CHOOSE PRG I)))
```

Indeed, the unquantified formula is used in the mechanization since it is easier to formalize in the Boyer-Moore logic. However, the quantified formula is simpler for exposition.

[4]This constraint is equivalent to the following unquantified formula, by introducing a skolem function **(NEWX E OLD)** which returns a successor state to **OLD** for statement **E** if possible. To prove that the null transition is effected, one must prove that **NEWX** is not a successor state. Since one knows nothing about **NEWX**, this is equivalent to demonstrating that no successor state exists. This formula is the one used in the formalization.

```
(IMPLIES (AND (LISTP PRG)
              (NOT (N (S PRG I)
                      (NEWX (CHOOSE PRG I)
                            (S PRG I))
                      (CHOOSE PRG I))))
         (EQUAL (S PRG (ADD1 I))
                (S PRG I)))
```

3.3. The Scheduler

The function **CHOOSE** is a scheduler. It is characterized by the following constraints:

Constraint: Choose-Chooses

```
(IMPLIES (LISTP PRG)
         (MEMBER (CHOOSE PRG I) PRG))
```

This constraint states that **CHOOSE** schedules statements from the non-empty program **PRG**.

We now guarantee that every statement is scheduled infinitely often. We do this without regard for enabled or disabled statements; effective transitions will be guaranteed by subsequent fairness notions.

Scheduling every statement infinitely often is equivalent to always scheduling each statement again. This property is specified by the function **NEXT** and its relationship to **CHOOSE**:

Constraint: Next-Is-At-Or-After

```
(IMPLIES (MEMBER E PRG)
         (NOT (LESSP (NEXT PRG E I) I)))
```

This constraint states that for statements in the program, **NEXT** returns a value at or after **I**. Furthermore, **(NEXT PRG E I)** returns a future point in the schedule when statement **E** is scheduled.

Constraint: Choose-Next

```
(IMPLIES (MEMBER E PRG)
         (EQUAL (CHOOSE PRG (NEXT PRG E I))
                E))
```

This completes the definition of the operational semantics of concurrency.[5] Since **S**, **CHOOSE**, and **NEXT** are characterized only by the constraints listed above, **S** defines an arbitrary computation of a concurrent program. **S** guarantees that every statement will be scheduled infinitely often; transitions need not be effective. Statements proved about **S** are true for any computation.[6] So theorems in which **PRG** is a free variable are really proof rules, and this is the focus of the next sections.

4. Specification Predicates

Before formalizing the three fairness notions and the safety notion of deadlock freedom, we must define predicates for specifying correctness properties. Proof rules for these notions will be theorems permitting the proof of correctness properties.

The interesting properties of concurrent programs are safety and liveness (progress).

---

[5]There are several other constraints that coerce non-numeric index arguments to zero and identify **NEXT**'s type as numeric.

[6]That is, **S**, **CHOOSE**, and **NEXT** are constrained function symbols, and theorems proved about them can be instantiated with terms representing any computation.

Safety properties are those that state that something bad will never happen; examples are invariant properties such as mutual exclusion and freedom from deadlock. Liveness properties state that something good will eventually happen; examples are termination and freedom from starvation. We borrow Unity's predicates for safety (**UNLESS**) and liveness (**LEADS-TO**) and present the definitions of these predicates in the context of this proof system.

4.1. Unless

The function **EVAL** evaluates a formula (its first argument) in the context of a state (its second argument). Its definition is:

Definition: Eval

```
(EVAL PRED STATE)
  =
(EVAL$ T PRED (LIST (CONS 'STATE STATE)))
```

When **EVAL** is used, the formula must use **'STATE** as the name of the "variable" representing the state. Notice that **EVAL** has the expected property:

Theorem: Eval-Or

```
(EQUAL (EVAL (LIST 'OR P Q) STATE)
       (OR (EVAL P STATE)
           (EVAL Q STATE)))
```

That is, **EVAL** distributes over **OR**. Similarly, **EVAL** distributes over the other logical connectives. The definition of **UNLESS** is:

Definition: Unless

```
(UNLESS P Q PRG)
  ⇔
(FORALL (OLD NEW E)
        (IMPLIES (AND (MEMBER E PRG)
                      (N OLD NEW E)
                      (EVAL (LIST 'AND P (LIST 'NOT Q)) OLD))
                 (EVAL (LIST 'OR P Q) NEW)))
```

(UNLESS P Q PRG) states that every statement in the program **PRG** takes states where **P** holds but **Q** does not to states where **P** or **Q** holds. Intuitively, this means that once **P** holds in a computation, it continues to hold (it is stable), at least until **Q** holds (this may occur immediately). A subtle point is that if the precondition **P** disables some statement, then **UNLESS** holds vacuously for that statement. This is consistent with the operational semantics presented earlier, since a disabled statement, if scheduled, will effect the null transition. Hence the successor state will be identical to the previous state and the precondition **P** will be preserved.

Notice that if **(UNLESS P '(FALSE) PRG)** is true for program **PRG** (that is **P** is a stable property) and **P** holds on the initial state (e.g., **(EVAL P (S PRG 0))**), then **P** is an invariant of **PRG** (that is, **P** is true of every state in the computation). In Unity, this implication is an equivalence: **P UNLESS FALSE** is true for every invariant. Unlike Unity's **UNLESS**, this **UNLESS** is not restricted to reachable states in the computation. This difference simplifies program composition and is key to the definition of the safety notion of deadlock freedom.

4.2. Leads-To

LEADS-TO is the general progress predicate. It is defined as follows:

Definition: Leads-To

```
(LEADS-TO P Q PRG)
   ⇔
(FORALL I (IMPLIES (EVAL P (S PRG I))
                   (EXISTS J
                           (AND (NOT (LESSP J I))
                                (EVAL Q (S PRG J))))))
```

(LEADS-TO P Q PRG) states that if **P** holds at some point in a computation of program **PRG**, then **Q** holds at that point or at some later point in the computation.

Unity's theorems about **LEADS-TO** are theorems in this proof system as well. For example, **LEADS-TO** is transitive (this theorem may be applied repeatedly, by induction):

Theorem: Leads-To-Transitive

```
(IMPLIES (AND (LEADS-TO P Q PRG)
              (LEADS-TO Q R PRG))
         (LEADS-TO P R PRG))
```

Curiously, **LEADS-TO** can be used to specify invariance properties. **(LEADS-TO P '(FALSE) PRG)** implies that the negation of **P** is invariant. This is deduced by contradiction: if **P** does hold at some point in the computation, then **'(FALSE)** would have to hold subsequently, which is impossible. Notice, that **(LEADS-TO P '(FALSE) PRG)** is only concerned with reachable states in the computation: it does not imply **(UNLESS (LIST 'NOT P) '(FALSE) PRG)**, even though **(LIST 'NOT P)** evaluates to the negation of **P**. (See section 4.1.)

5. Fairness

5.1. Unconditional Fairness

Fairness notions place restrictions on the scheduler, yielding more useful computations. The weakest fairness notion, *unconditional fairness*, requires that program states be always enabled (statements are total functions). Consequently, no restrictions are placed on the scheduler, other than that every statement be scheduled infinitely often (in no particular order). It is easy to imagine scenarios where starvation or deadlock occur under unconditional fairness.

The first requirement of unconditional fairness, that all program statements be total functions, is captured by defining the function **TOTAL**:

Definition: Total

```
(TOTAL PRG)
   =
(FORALL E (IMPLIES (MEMBER E PRG)
                   (FORALL OLD
                           (EXISTS NEW (N OLD NEW E))))))
```

(TOTAL PRG) is true only if every statement in **PRG** specifies at least one successor state for every previous state. The successor state may be unchanged (the statement may be a skip statement).

The proof rule for deducing the liveness properties of programs executed under unconditional fairness is supported by the following intuition. We wish to prove a simple **LEADS-TO** property: **(LEADS-TO P Q PRG)**. That is, every **P** state is followed by some **Q** state. Suppose that every program statement takes **P** states to states where **P** or **Q** holds. Then we know that **P** persists, at least until **Q** holds. (This is formalized by **(UNLESS P Q PRG)**.) Furthermore, if there exists some statement that transforms all **P** states to **Q** states, then, by fairness, we know that that statement will be eventually executed. If **Q** has not yet held, since **P** persists, **Q** will hold subsequent to the first execution of that statement. This notion of some statement transforming all **P** states to **Q** states is captured by the function **ENSURES** (borrowed from Unity):

Definition: Ensures

```
(ENSURES P Q PRG)
   ⇔
(EXISTS E (AND (MEMBER E PRG)
               (FORALL (OLD NEW)
                       (IMPLIES (AND (N OLD NEW E)
                                     (EVAL (LIST 'AND P
                                                 (LIST 'NOT Q))
                                           OLD))
                                (EVAL Q NEW))))))
```

Therefore, if a program is **TOTAL**, and **P** persists until **Q** and some statement transforms all **P** states to **Q** states, unconditional fairness implies that **(LEADS-TO P Q PRG)** holds as well. This argument is formalized in the following theorem, which is the proof rule for unconditional fairness:

Theorem: Unconditional-Fairness

```
(IMPLIES (AND (UNLESS P Q PRG)
              (ENSURES P Q PRG)
              (TOTAL PRG))
         (LEADS-TO P Q PRG))
```

Notice, that this theorem does not require any assumptions about the computation (other than what is implied by the characterization of **S**). This is because any arbitrary ordering of statements (provided every statement is scheduled infinitely often) is sufficient for unconditional fairness.

Notice also, that **ENSURES** is inappropriate if a program is not **TOTAL**, because if some statement is disabled by the precondition **P**, **(ENSURES P Q PRG)** is vacuously true.

5.2. Weak Fairness

Weak fairness is an extension of unconditional fairness for programs that are not **TOTAL**. Weak fairness excludes from consideration computations in which a statement is enabled continuously but is not scheduled effectively. That is, in order to guarantee that a statement will effect an effective transition under weak fairness, one must ensure that once it is enabled, it remains enabled (at least) until it is scheduled. Notice, however, that this is a simple property of the computation **S**: since, by fairness, every statement is scheduled again, if some statement is continuously enabled from some point in the computation, it will execute effectively the next time it is scheduled. Hence, the proof rule describing weak fairness is a theorem that requires some knowledge about statements' enabling conditions.

To specify this notion, we first introduce a predicate that identifies a statement's enabling condition.

Definition: Enabling-Condition

```
(ENABLING-CONDITION C E PRG)
   ⇔
(AND (MEMBER E PRG)
     (FORALL (OLD NEW)
             (IMPLIES (N OLD NEW E)
                      (EVAL C OLD)))
     (FORALL OLD (IMPLIES (EVAL C OLD)
                          (EXISTS NEW (N OLD NEW E)))))
```

(ENABLING-CONDITION C E PRG) states that **C** is the enabling condition for statement **E** in program **PRG**. That is, for all possible transitions, **C** holds on the previous state, and if **C** holds on the previous state, some successor state exists.

We now define a predicate similar to **ENSURES** that considers enabling conditions:

Definition: E-Ensures

```
(E-ENSURES P Q C PRG)
   ⇔
(EXISTS E
        (AND (MEMBER E PRG)
             (ENABLING-CONDITION C E PRG)
             (FORALL (OLD NEW)
                     (IMPLIES (AND (N OLD NEW E)
                                   (EVAL (LIST 'AND P
                                               (LIST 'NOT Q))
                                         OLD))
                              (EVAL Q NEW))))))
```

(E-ENSURES P Q C PRG) says that some statement take some **P** states to **Q** states (and is disabled for all the rest) and has enabling condition **C**.

The intuition behind the proof rule for weak fairness is as follows: We wish to prove **(LEADS-TO P Q PRG)**. Assume that **P** persists at least until **Q** holds (**(UNLESS P Q PRG)**). Also assume that some key statement transforms **P** states to **Q** states and has enabling condition **C**. Then, if **P** implies **C** during the interval starting when **P** first holds and ending when the key statement is scheduled (or when **Q** holds), we may deduce that **Q** ultimately occurs, for if **Q** has not yet held, then the key statement will be scheduled effectively and **Q** will hold subsequently. This argument is formalized in the following theorem:

Theorem: Weak-Fairness

```
(IMPLIES (AND (UNLESS P Q PRG)
              (E-ENSURES P Q C PRG)
              (IMPLIES (EVAL (LIST 'AND P (LIST 'NOT Q))
                             (S PRG (WITNESS P Q C PRG)))
                       (EVAL C (S PRG (WITNESS P Q C PRG)))))
         (LEADS-TO P Q PRG))
```

At first glance, this theorem seems not to follow the reasoning outlined above, for it appears to only check whether the key statement's enabling condition **C** holds at the single point **(WITNESS P Q C PRG)** and not whether **C** holds continuously over the appropriate interval. However, **WITNESS** is defined to inspect that interval and return the first point where the key statement is disabled. (If the key statement is enabled continuously, then **WITNESS** returns the first point when either **Q** holds or the key statement is scheduled.) In this theorem, the hypothesis requires that the key statement be enabled (or **Q** holds) even at that point. If that is the case, then we may deduce that the key statement is enabled continuously until the state before **Q** holds.

The advantage of defining **WITNESS** in this way is that it transforms an inductive argument (inspecting an arbitrary interval) to analysis at a single arbitrary point; this simplifies reasoning.

Notice, that weak fairness is more general than unconditional fairness since programs need not be **TOTAL**, yet does not require special scheduling not already guaranteed by the computation **S**. However, both starvation and deadlock are still possible under weak fairness.

5.3. Strong Fairness

Strong fairness guarantees freedom from starvation. Starvation occurs when a process needs a resource, which is available infinitely often (but not necessarily continuously), yet only requests the resource when it is unavailable. Strong fairness precludes computations where a statement that is enabled infinitely often is never scheduled effectively. Equivalently, strong fairness requires that if a statement is enabled infinitely often, it is scheduled effectively infinitely often.

The proof rule for deducing strong fairness properties is supported by the following intuition. Suppose that we wish to prove **(LEADS-TO P Q PRG)** and we know that **P** persists at least until **Q** holds (**(UNLESS P Q PRG)**). Suppose further that there exists some key statement with enabling condition **C** that transforms states where both **P** and **C** hold to **Q** states. Under strong fairness, to guarantee that the key statement is scheduled effectively, one must demonstrate that **P** and **C** occur often enough (e.g., could occur infinitely often). Therefore, to prove **(LEADS-TO P Q PRG)** it is sufficient to prove

(LEADS-TO P (LIST 'OR Q C)), since, by hypothesis, **P** persists until **Q**, and if **C** holds before, then the key statement could be scheduled effectively. If it is not scheduled at that point, then we repeat the argument. By strong fairness, eventually, the key statement will be scheduled effectively.

The proof rule formalizing this argument is:

Constraint: Strong-Fairness

```
(IMPLIES (AND (UNLESS P Q PRG)
              (E-ENSURES P Q C PRG)
              (LEADS-TO P (LIST 'OR Q C) PRG)
              (STRONGLY-FAIR PRG))
         (LEADS-TO P Q PRG))
```

The term **(STRONGLY-FAIR PRG)** introduces a new (undefined) function symbol that, essentially, tags uses of this proof rule. Since **(STRONGLY-FAIR PRG)** cannot be proved, it must be a hypothesis to any **LEADS-TO** property deduced using this proof rule. Furthermore, since reasoning directly about the operational semantics **S** yields nothing more than weak fairness, it is impossible to deduce stronger results about **S** without appealing to this proof rule. This proof rule is consistent with the rest of this theory because there exists a model for the function **STRONGLY-FAIR** satisfying this constraint: any unary function that is always false. Completeness and appropriateness is justified by the correctness of the supporting literature. [13, 12]

It may appear that this proof rule requires circular reasoning: it proves one **LEADS-TO** property by appealing to another. A clever answer is found in [13]: We can disregard the key statement when proving the **LEADS-TO** property in the hypothesis, since if it is ultimately scheduled effectively, we can ignore the **LEADS-TO** property in the hypothesis (since **Q** is then reached), and if it not scheduled effectively, we can ignore it when deducing that hypothesis (since it is equivalent to a skip statement). Other researchers emphasize this point by requiring that the **LEADS-TO** property in the hypothesis be proved with respect to a smaller program: the original less the key statement. [12]

5.4. Deadlock Freedom

Deadlock freedom guarantees the absence of deadlock in the computation. Deadlock occurs when a statement which ought to be able to execute remains disabled. More precisely, a deadlocked condition is a stable condition that disables some program statement.

The proof rule formalizing this notion is:

Constraint: Deadlock-Freedom

```
(IMPLIES (AND (UNLESS INV '(FALSE) PRG)
              (ENABLING-CONDITION C E PRG)
              (IMPLIES (EVAL INV (S PRG (SOME-INDEX)))
                       (NOT (EVAL C (S PRG (SOME-INDEX)))))
              (DEADLOCK-FREE PRG))
         (LEADS-TO INV '(FALSE) PRG))
```

This proof rules states that if **INV** is stable and **C** is statement **E**'s enabling condition, if **INV** is a stronger predicate than the negation of **C** then **INV** is false of every state in the computation. That is, the negation of **INV** is an invariant of the computation (section 4.2). Stating that **INV** is stronger than the negation of **C** with respect to computation states is more powerful than stating it with respect to all states (since computation states is a smaller set); the function **SOME-INDEX** is simply an arbitrary index. As with strong fairness, the new function **DEADLOCK-FREE** is an undefined function symbol which serves as a tag for uses of this proof rule. This proof rule is consistent with the rest of this theory because any unary function whose value is always false serves as a model for **DEADLOCK-FREE** satisfying this constraint.

In the next sections, the proof rules for weak fairness, strong fairness, and deadlock freedom are illustrated by the proof of a sample program.

6. More Specification Predicates

Before presenting the example program, it is helpful to introduce several additional specification predicates and proof rules, which will simplify both the statement and proof of the correctness theorems. The first predicate places assumptions on the initial state:

Definition: Initial-Condition

```
(INITIAL-CONDITION IC PRG)
    =
(EVAL IC (S PRG 0))
```

Stating **(INITIAL-CONDITION IC PRG)** in the hypothesis of a theorem, implies that **IC** holds on the initial state. Invariants are specified using the predicate **INVARIANT**:

Definition: Invariant

```
(INVARIANT INV PRG)
    =
(FORALL I (EVAL INV (S PRG I)))
```

(INVARIANT INV PRG) is true only if **INV** holds on every state in the computation. Often, it is proved by assuming that **INV** holds initially and proving **(UNLESS INV '(FALSE) PRG)**. Also, if **INV** is a consequence of any other invariant (and that invariant's necessary initial conditions are satisfied), then **(INVARIANT INV PRG)** is true as well.

The next predicate specifies properties that are eventually stable. Such properties are important, as they represent generalizations of the notion of fixed points in the computation. (Unity specifies such properties using **UNLESS** and **LEADS-TO** and adding auxiliary variables to the program [14].) In our example, we will show that deadlock, which is a stable property, is, under certain hypotheses, eventually reached in the computation. Since deadlock freedom guarantees that deadlock is avoided, the hypotheses must be false. This is a key step in the correctness proof.

Definition: Eventually-Stable

```
(EVENTUALLY-STABLE R PRG)
   =
(EXISTS I (FORALL J (IMPLIES (NOT (LESSP J I))
                             (EVAL R (S PRG J)))))
```

(EVENTUALLY-STABLE R PRG) states that there exists a point in the computation, after which **R** holds continuously. It is interesting to note that such properties are the negation of **LEADS-TO** properties, in the sense presented in the following theorem:

Theorem: Not-Eventually-Stable-Proves-Leads-To

```
(IMPLIES (AND (NOT (EVENTUALLY-STABLE NOT-Q PRG))
              (IMPLIES (NOT (EVAL NOT-Q
                                  (S PRG (JES (ILEADS P PRG Q)
                                              PRG NOT-Q))))
                       (EVAL Q (S PRG (JES (ILEADS P PRG Q)
                                           PRG NOT-Q))))))
         (LEADS-TO P Q PRG))
```

This theorem states that if predicate **NOT-Q** is not eventually stable, and the negation of **NOT-Q** implies **Q**, then **Q** states occur infinitely often in the computation (i.e., **Q** states eventually follow any **P** state). The term **(S PRG (JES (ILEADS P PRG Q) PRG NOT-Q))** represents that arbitrary state at which **NOT-Q** must imply **Q**. (It is obtained from the skolemization of the definition of **LEADS-TO**.)

7. An Example Program

In this section, we prove that the classically incorrect solution to the dining philosopher's problem is indeed correct under the assumptions of strong fairness and deadlock freedom. The solution has **N** philosophers in a ring, with a shared fork between each philosopher; a hungry philosopher picks up a fork if it is free when it checks, becomes eating when it has both forks, and subsequently simultaneously becomes thinking and releases both forks. The important observation is that both strong fairness (a hungry philosopher will eventually pick up a fork that becomes free infinitely often) and deadlock freedom (never do all philosophers own their left (right) forks simultaneously) are necessary in the proof, so this example demonstrates both proof rules.

We first present the statements for each philosopher:

Definition: Thinking-To

```
(THINKING-TO OLD NEW INDEX)
   =
(IF (THINKING OLD INDEX)
    (AND (OR (THINKING NEW INDEX)
             (HUNGRY NEW INDEX))
         (CHANGED OLD NEW (LIST (CONS 'S INDEX))))
  (CHANGED OLD NEW NIL))
```

This function represents the generic transition between thinking and hungry states for a philosopher with index **INDEX**. It states that a philosopher may take a transition between a thinking state and either another thinking state, or a hungry state. The function **CHANGED** states that only the variable **(CONS 'S INDEX)** representing the state of philosopher

INDEX may change value during this transition. Notice that this transition is always enabled: if it is executed when the philosopher is not thinking, then no values change.

The next function specifies the transition where a philosopher picks up its free left fork:

Definition: Hungry-Left

```
(HUNGRY-LEFT OLD NEW INDEX)
   =
(AND (HUNGRY OLD INDEX)
     (FREE OLD INDEX)
     (OWNS-LEFT NEW INDEX)
     (CHANGED OLD NEW (LIST (CONS 'F INDEX))))
```

This statement states that if, in the old state, the philosopher is hungry and its left fork is free, then in the new state it owns its left fork. If the philosopher is neither hungry nor is its left fork free, the statement is disabled. Again, all variables but the one capturing the status of the interesting fork remain unchanged.

The analogous function for picking up free right forks is:

Definition: Hungry-Right

```
(HUNGRY-RIGHT OLD NEW INDEX N)
   =
(AND (HUNGRY OLD INDEX)
     (FREE OLD (ADD1-MOD N INDEX))
     (OWNS-RIGHT NEW INDEX N)
     (CHANGED OLD NEW (LIST (CONS 'F (ADD1-MOD N INDEX)))))
```

The important observation in this statement is that forks are indexed in the following way: the **N** philosophers have indices `[0, ... , N-1]` and a philosopher's left fork shares its index. A right fork, consequently, has the index if the philosopher's right neighbor: **(ADD1-MOD N INDEX)**.

The next statement represents the transition from hungry and owning both forks, to eating. It is always enabled:

Definition: Hungry-Both

```
(HUNGRY-BOTH OLD NEW INDEX N)
   =
(IF (AND (HUNGRY OLD INDEX)
         (OWNS-LEFT OLD INDEX)
         (OWNS-RIGHT OLD INDEX N))
    (AND (EATING NEW INDEX)
         (CHANGED OLD NEW (LIST (CONS 'S INDEX))))
  (CHANGED OLD NEW NIL))
```

The final statement represents the transition between eating and thinking, with the simultaneous release of both forks:

Definition: Eating-To

```
(EATING-TO OLD NEW INDEX N)
   =
(IF (EATING OLD INDEX)
    (AND (THINKING NEW INDEX)
         (FREE NEW INDEX)
         (FREE NEW (ADD1-MOD N INDEX))
         (CHANGED OLD NEW (LIST (CONS 'S INDEX)
                                (CONS 'F INDEX)
                                (CONS 'F (ADD1-MOD
                                          N INDEX)))))
  (CHANGED OLD NEW NIL))
```

Each philosopher in the ring is specified by five statements, captured by the following function:

Definition: Phil

```
(PHIL INDEX N)
   =
(LIST (LIST 'THINKING-TO INDEX)
      (LIST 'HUNGRY-LEFT INDEX)
      (LIST 'HUNGRY-RIGHT INDEX N)
      (LIST 'HUNGRY-BOTH INDEX N)
      (LIST 'EATING-TO INDEX N))
```

The first component in each statement is a function name, the remaining components are arguments to that function (supplementing the implicit arguments of the old and new states).

The program for the entire ring of philosophers is the concatenation of instances of **(PHIL INDEX N)** for values of **INDEX** from **[0, ... , N-1]**. This is represented by the term **(PHIL-PRG N)**.

7.1. The Correctness Specification

The correctness specification will be a liveness property stating that every hungry philosopher eventually eats. This is captured by the following theorem:

Theorem: Correctness

```
(IMPLIES (AND (LESSP 1 N)
              (NUMBERP INDEX)
              (LESSP INDEX N)
              (INITIAL-CONDITION
               '(AND (PROPER-PHILS STATE (QUOTE ,N))
                     (PROPER-FORKS STATE (QUOTE ,N)))
               (PHIL-PRG N))
              (STRONGLY-FAIR (PHIL-PRG N))
              (DEADLOCK-FREE (PHIL-PRG N)))
         (LEADS-TO '(HUNGRY STATE (QUOTE ,INDEX))
                   '(EATING STATE (QUOTE ,INDEX))
                   (PHIL-PRG N)))
```

The conclusion of this theorem is a **LEADS-TO** statement, where the beginning predicate states that the **INDEX**'ed philosopher is hungry, and the ending predicate states that that same philosopher is eating. The hypotheses indicate that we are assuming both strong fairness and deadlock freedom. Also, there is more than one philosopher in the ring, and **INDEX** is some number less than the size of the ring. Finally, we assume two conditions about the initial state: **PROPER-PHILS** and **PROPER-FORKS**. These properties are also invariants of the program.

The term **(PROPER-FORKS STATE N)** states that every fork is either free, or is owned by a neighboring philosopher. The term **(PROPER-PHILS STATE N)** states that **(PROPER-PHIL STATE PHIL RIGHT)** holds for every **PHIL** in the range [0, ..., N-1], where **RIGHT** is **(ADD1-MOD N PHIL)**, where **PROPER-PHIL** is defined as follows:

Definition: Proper-Phil

```
(PROPER-PHIL STATE PHIL RIGHT)
  =
(AND (IMPLIES (THINKING STATE PHIL)
              (AND (NOT (EQUAL (FORK STATE PHIL) PHIL))
                   (NOT (EQUAL (FORK STATE RIGHT) PHIL))))
     (IMPLIES (EATING STATE PHIL)
              (AND (EQUAL (FORK STATE PHIL) PHIL)
                   (EQUAL (FORK STATE RIGHT) PHIL)))
     (OR (THINKING STATE PHIL)
         (HUNGRY STATE PHIL)
         (EATING STATE PHIL)))
```

This states that a philosopher is either thinking, hungry, or eating. Also, thinking philosophers own no forks, and eating philosophers own both forks.

The two conditions **(PROPER-PHILS STATE N)** and **(PROPER-FORKS STATE N)** represent legal states and are invariants. This is stated in the following theorem:

Theorem: Phil-Prg-Invariant

```
(IMPLIES (AND (LESSP 1 N)
              (INITIAL-CONDITION
               '(AND (PROPER-PHILS STATE (QUOTE ,N))
                     (PROPER-FORKS STATE (QUOTE ,N)))
               (PHIL-PRG N)))
         (AND (INVARIANT '(PROPER-PHILS STATE (QUOTE ,N))
                         (PHIL-PRG N))
              (INVARIANT '(PROPER-FORKS STATE (QUOTE ,N))
                         (PHIL-PRG N))))
```

This theorem states that if the initial state is legal, then both **PROPER-PHILS** and **PROPER-FORKS** are invariant.

7.2. The Correctness Proof

The invariant properties are proved by demonstrating that every statement preserves the invariant. The liveness property is a more interesting proof and is the focus of this section. To prove that a hungry philosopher eventually eats, we must prove that:

- A hungry philosopher eventually picks up its left fork.
- A hungry philosopher eventually picks up its right fork.
- A hungry philosopher that owns both forks eventually eats.

The last theorem is simple and is proved by appealing to the weak fairness proof rule. (Hungry and owns both forks is stable until eating, and one statement transforms hungry and owns both forks to eating.) The theorem is:

Theorem: Owns-Both-Leads-To-Eating

```
(IMPLIES (AND (LESSP 1 N)
              (LESSP INDEX N)
              (NUMBERP INDEX)
              (INITIAL-CONDITION
               '(AND (PROPER-PHILS STATE (QUOTE ,N))
                     (PROPER-FORKS STATE (QUOTE ,N)))
               (PHIL-PRG N)))
         (LEADS-TO '(AND (OWNS-LEFT STATE (QUOTE ,INDEX))
                         (OWNS-RIGHT STATE (QUOTE ,INDEX)
                                     (QUOTE ,N)))
                   '(EATING STATE (QUOTE ,INDEX))
                   (PHIL-PRG N)))
```

The remaining theorems depend upon forks becoming free infinitely often. A necessary intermediate theorem states that an eating process eventually frees both of its forks. This theorem is also proved by appealing to the weak fairness proof rule, and is stated in the following way:

Theorem: Eating-Leads-To-Free

```
(IMPLIES (AND (LESSP 1 N)
              (LESSP INDEX N)
              (NUMBERP INDEX)
              (INITIAL-CONDITION
               '(AND (PROPER-PHILS STATE (QUOTE ,N))
                     (PROPER-FORKS STATE (QUOTE ,N)))
               (PHIL-PRG N)))
         (LEADS-TO '(EATING STATE (QUOTE ,INDEX))
                   '(AND (FREE STATE (QUOTE ,INDEX))
                         (FREE STATE
                               (QUOTE ,(ADD1-MOD N INDEX))))
                   (PHIL-PRG N)))
```

To prove that forks become free infinitely often, we show that if any fork does not become free infinitely often then a deadlocked condition will eventually exist. For example, if some philosopher's left fork does not become free infinitely often, then all philosophers eventually own their right forks. Later, we take advantage of this result, by the deadlock freedom proof rule: since the conclusion cannot occur, then the hypotheses must be false, and the left fork must become free infinitely often. The theorem is:

Theorem: Eventually-Stable-Right-Implies-All-Rights

```
(IMPLIES (AND (LESSP 1 N)
              (LESSP J N)
              (NUMBERP J)
              (STRONGLY-FAIR (PHIL-PRG N))
              (INITIAL-CONDITION
               '(AND (PROPER-PHILS STATE (QUOTE ,N))
                     (PROPER-FORKS STATE (QUOTE ,N)))
               (PHIL-PRG N))
              (EVENTUALLY-STABLE '(AND (HUNGRY STATE (QUOTE ,J))
                                       (OWNS-RIGHT STATE
                                                   (QUOTE ,J)
                                                   (QUOTE ,N)))
                                 (PHIL-PRG N)))
         (EVENTUALLY-STABLE '(ALL-RIGHTS STATE
                                         (QUOTE ,N))
                            (PHIL-PRG N)))
```

The negation of the **EVENTUALLY-STABLE** term in the hypotheses implies that the philosopher's right fork becomes free infinitely often, or is owned by the philosopher's right neighbor. More succinctly, this is equivalent to (substituting **INDEX** for **J**):

```
(LEADS-TO '(TRUE)
          '(OR (FREE STATE (QUOTE ,(ADD1-MOD N INDEX)))
               (OWNS-LEFT STATE
                          (QUOTE ,(ADD1-MOD N INDEX))))
          (PHIL-PRG N))
```

The fact that the index is **(ADD1-MOD N INDEX)** is not important, since the range of that term is equivalent to **INDEX**'s domain. Hence, this is equivalent to the **LEADS-TO** property that is needed when appealing to the strong fairness proof rule, when proving that a hungry philosopher will eventually own its left fork.

To prove that every hungry philosopher eventually owns its left fork, we use the deadlock freedom proof rule to prove that a state in which every philosopher owns its right fork cannot occur:

Theorem: Never-All-Rights

```
(IMPLIES (AND (DEADLOCK-FREE (PHIL-PRG N))
              (LESSP 1 N))
         (INVARIANT '(NOT (ALL-RIGHTS STATE (QUOTE ,N)))
                    (PHIL-PRG N)))
```

This is proved by observing that an **ALL-RIGHTS** state is stable and disables (forever) any **HUNGRY-LEFT** statement. Hence, **ALL-RIGHTS** satisfies the criterion of a deadlocked state and is, by deadlock freedom, guaranteed never to occur.

These theorems imply the following, by appealing to the strong fairness proof rule:

Theorem: Hungry-Leads-To-Owns-Left

```
(IMPLIES (AND (LESSP 1 N)
              (NUMBERP INDEX)
              (LESSP INDEX N)
              (INITIAL-CONDITION
               '(AND (PROPER-PHILS STATE (QUOTE ,N))
                     (PROPER-FORKS STATE (QUOTE ,N)))
               (PHIL-PRG N))
              (STRONGLY-FAIR (PHIL-PRG N))
              (DEADLOCK-FREE (PHIL-PRG N)))
         (LEADS-TO '(HUNGRY STATE (QUOTE ,INDEX))
                   '(OWNS-LEFT STATE (QUOTE ,INDEX))
                   (PHIL-PRG N)))
```

A similar argument permits the proof that a hungry philosopher eventually owns its right fork. Combining these results with the facts that a hungry philosopher that owns its left fork persists in that state until it eats and that a hungry philosopher remains hungry until it eats, permits the proof of the correctness theorem:

Theorem: Correctness

```
(IMPLIES (AND (LESSP 1 N)
              (NUMBERP INDEX)
              (LESSP INDEX N)
              (INITIAL-CONDITION
               '(AND (PROPER-PHILS STATE (QUOTE ,N))
                     (PROPER-FORKS STATE (QUOTE ,N)))
               (PHIL-PRG N))
              (STRONGLY-FAIR (PHIL-PRG N))
              (DEADLOCK-FREE (PHIL-PRG N)))
         (LEADS-TO '(HUNGRY STATE (QUOTE ,INDEX))
                   '(EATING STATE (QUOTE ,INDEX))
                   (PHIL-PRG N)))
```

This proof has been mechanically verified on the Boyer-Moore prover. The proof entailed 33 definitions and 114 theorems, in addition to the theory defining the proof system itself and a library of theorems about integers. It is difficult to estimate the time it took to construct the proof of the correctness of this dining philosopher's algorithm, since the necessary theory in the underlying proof system was developed simultaneously.

8. Conclusion

This paper presents a formalization, in the Boyer-Moore logic, of three fairness notions, unconditional, weak, and strong fairness, and the safety notion of deadlock freedom. This formalization has been implemented on the Boyer-Moore prover and is suitable for the mechanical verification of concurrent programs. This was demonstrated by the mechanically verified proof of a solution to the dining philosophers program whose correctness depended upon strong fairness and deadlock freedom. Mechanical verification increases the trust one may place in a proof.

In general, it is not possible for a practical scheduler to always prevent deadlock. However, deadlock freedom may prove to be a useful abstraction for modeling those systems that do incorporate deadlock prevention schemes. At the most abstract level, deadlock situations would be identified, and then assumed to be avoided.

Other researchers have embedded one logic within another mechanized logic in order to prove soundness and provide mechanized support for the new logic. Hoare logic was embedded in LCF in [16], Dijsktra's weakest preconditions were embedded in HOL in [1], while CSP was embedded in HOL in [4]. These mechanized theories have not been used to mechanically prove the correctness of other programs. Manna's and Pnueli's framework for proving both invariance and eventuality properties, under weak fairness, were formalized on the Boyer-Moore prover in [15]; this system was used to verify an example program computing binomial coefficients and several other programs. Lamport has encoded the proof rules from his Temporal Logic of Actions [12] for weak and strong fairness on LP [7] and has used the system to verify a program.

This operational semantics of concurrency presented here provides justification for both unconditional and weak fairness and for a subset of the Unity logic, by providing a model for an arbitrary weakly fair trace. The proof rules for strong fairness and deadlock freedom are consistent with this theory. Since this theory is a conservative extension of a sound logic, it is sound as well. This methodology suggests two ways to develop sound proof systems: either prove the proof rules as theorems of some operational semantics, or tag the use of the proof rules by adding an undefined term in the hypothesis of the new proof rule. Since the undefined term could be equal to false, the new theory is a conservative extension of the old. This term will also need to be a hypothesis of every theorem proved using this proof rule, and may therefore be a useful bookkeeping device.

Acknowledgments

This work was supported in part at Computational Logic, Inc., by the Defense Advanced Research Projects Agency, ARPA Order 7406, and ONR Contract N00014-88-C-0454. The views and conclusions contained in this document are those of the author and should not be interpreted as representing the official policies, either expressed or implied, of Computational Logic, Inc., the Defense Advanced Research Projects Agency, the Office of Naval Research, or the U.S. Government.

References

[1] R.J.R. Back and J. von Wright.
Refinement Concepts Formalized in Higher Order Logic.
In M. Broy and C. B. Jones (editors), *Programming Concepts and Methods*. North Holland, Amsterdam, 1990.

[2] R. S. Boyer and J S. Moore.
A Computational Logic Handbook.
Academic Press, Boston, 1988.

[3] R.S. Boyer, D. Goldschlag, M. Kaufmann, J S. Moore.
Functional Instantiation in First Order Logic.
Technical Report 44, Computational Logic, Inc., 1717 West Sixth Street, Suite 290 Austin, TX 78703, May, 1989.
Published in proceedings of the 1989 Workshop on Programming Logic, Programming Methodology Group, University of Goteborg, West Germany.

[4] Albert Camilleri.
Reasoning in CSP via the HOL Theorem Prover.
IEEE Transactions on Software Engineering SE-16, September, 1990.

[5] K. Mani Chandy and Jayadev Misra.
Parallel Program Design: A Foundation.
Addison Wesley, Massachusetts, 1988.

[6] Nissim Francez.
Fairness.
Springer-Verlag, New York, 1986.

[7] S.J. Garland, J.V. Guttag, J.J. Horning.
Debugging Larch Shared Language Specifications.
IEEE Transactions on Software Engineering SE-16(9), September, 1990.

[8] David M. Goldschlag.
Mechanizing Unity.
In M. Broy and C. B. Jones (editors), *Programming Concepts and Methods.* North Holland, Amsterdam, 1990.

[9] David M. Goldschlag.
Mechanically Verifying Concurrent Programs with the Boyer-Moore Prover.
IEEE Transactions on Software Engineering SE-16(9), September, 1990.

[10] M. Kaufmann.
A User's Manual for an Interactive Enhancement to the Boyer-Moore Theorem Prover.
Technical Report ICSCA-CMP-60, Institute for Computing Science, University of Texas at Austin, Austin, TX 78712, 1987.
Also available through Computational Logic, Inc., Suite 290, 1717 West Sixth Street, Austin, TX 78703.

[11] Matt Kaufmann.
DEFN-SK: An Extension of the Boyer-Moore Theorem Prover to Handle First-Order Quantifiers.
Technical Report 43, Computational Logic, Inc., May, 1989.
Draft.

[12] Leslie Lamport.
A Temporal Logic of Actions.
Technical Report Research Report 57, DEC Systems Research Center, 130 Lytton Avenue, Palo Alto, CA 94301, April, 1990.

[13] Zohar Manna and Amir Pnueli.
Adequate Proof Principles for Invariance and Liveness Properties of Concurrent Programs.
Science of Computer Programming 4:257-289, 1984.

[14] Jayadev Misra.
Auxiliary Variables.
Technical Report Notes on UNITY: 15-90, Department of Computer Sciences, The University of Texas at Austin, July, 1990.

[15] David M. Russinoff.
Verifying Concurrent Programs with the Boyer-Moore Prover.
Technical Report Forthcoming, MCC, Austin, Texas, 1990.

[16] S. Sokolowski.
Soundness of Hoare's Logic: an Automatic Proof Using LCF.
TOPLAS 9:100-120, 1987.

Specification and stepwise development of communicating systems

Stephan Rössig Michael Schenke

Universität Oldenburg
Fachbereich Informatik
Ammerländer Heerstr. 114-118
D-2900 Oldenburg
Germany

Abstract

This paper deals with the specification of communicating systems and their stepwise transformation into occam-like programs. For communicating systems a model similar to Hoare's CSP is used. First a specification language is given, which is particularly suitable for describing communicating systems. A quite simple readiness semantics allows to specify the users' wishes in an exact but easily expressible manner. Secondly aspects of a development approach are shown, how to achieve programs satisfying these specifications. For this purpose transformation rules are given whose applicability can be checked syntactically. Their correctness can be proved on the basis of readiness semantics and predicative semantics for the programming language. The main characteristics of the approach are illustrated by examples.

1 Introduction

This paper reflects those parts of the ProCoS project[1] which deal with the specification of communicating systems and their transformation into occam-like [IN88] programs. Here, a communicating system interacts with its environment only by synchronous message passing on directed channels, a method like in CSP [Hoa85].

We shall first present a specification language, called $\mathbf{SL_0}$[JROR90], which is particularly suitable for describing communicating systems. We define a quite simple readiness semantics which allows to specify the users' wishes in an exact but easily expressible manner. We secondly show aspects of a development approach, how to achieve so called PL-programs satisfying these specifications, cf.[Ol91, Ol91a]. For this purpose we give transformation rules whose applicability can be checked syntactically. Their correctness can be proved on the basis of readiness semantics for the specification language and predicative semantics for the programming language, cf.[Heh84]. The latter semantics is more complex because it has to cope with additional details not considered in specifications. For instance programs may terminate or diverge, but in the readiness semantics no such issues are dealt with.

The main characteristics of the approach are illustrated by examples. To demonstrate the expressiveness of $\mathbf{SL_0}$ we specify a single lift system. In order to show the whole range from specifications via transformations to programs the example of a buffer will be used.

---

[1] ProCoS is an ESPRIT BRA project that covers all steps in the development of provably correct systems from a formal requirements' capture down to the implementation with help of a verified compiler [Bjo89].

2 Specification language

A communicating system is characterized by its interface and its communication behaviour. The interface shows the static aspect of how the system is embedded into the environment. This includes direction and type information for all communication channels. The dynamic behaviour describes the order in which communications must occur. This contains sequencing constraints on the channels involved in the communications as well as restrictions on the values which are exchanged.

The main idea of $\mathbf{SL_0}$ is to separate concerns in an uninterpreted trace part and an interpreted state part. The trace part makes use of regular expressions, projection and parallelism (intersection). The state part makes use of predicates to specify the effect of communications on directed channels as a pre-post-relation [Heh84].

For a formal treatment of the behaviour we use a readiness semantics [OH86]. Here, a communication is a pair consisting of a channel name and a value compatible with the associated channel type. The behaviour is then given as a set of so called *ready pairs.* Each ready pair consists of a *trace*, i.e. finite sequence of communications, and a *ready set*, i.e. a set of channel names. Intuitively, a ready pair (tr, Rdy) forces the system – after it has engaged with its environment in trace tr – to be ready for communication on all channels listed in Rdy.

An informal introduction to $\mathbf{SL_0}$ is given with the following examples of buffer specifications. After that the readiness semantics of $\mathbf{SL_0}$ is defined. Then as a larger example the specification of a lift system is given.

2.1 Syntax and informal semantics of $\mathbf{SL_0}$

In $\mathbf{SL_0}$ a system specification is given by listing a set of basic items. Each item either declares a static property of the system, i.e. a channel or a local variable, or it gives a behaviour requirement, i.e. a trace- or a communication assertion. The following specification of a one element buffer shows examples of all kinds of basic items.

```
buffer = spec input in of int
              output out of int
              trace one-elem-buffer on {in,out} in pref (in.out)*
              var buff of int
              com in  write {buff}  when true  then buff'=@in
              com out  read {buff}  when true  then @out=buff
         end
```

The channel declarations of the first two lines define the interface. The *buffer* is connected with the environment by two channels named *in* and *out.* Through a communication on *in* the buffer receives an integer from the environment while a communication on *out* sends an integer to the environment.

The third line shows a trace assertion which can be referred to by *one-elem-buffer.* It restricts the communication behaviour by giving sequencing constraints for *in* and *out.* The regular expression *pref (in.out)**, where *pref* denotes the prefix closure, forces the *buffer* to communicate on both channels in an alternating order starting with *in.* In general a trace assertion specifies sequencing constraints on a certain subset of channels by stating a regular expression over this subset. It restricts the order in which communications may take place on the different channels whereas the communicated values are ignored.

Constraints of the values are specified by communication assertions in connection with local variables. In the fourth line an integer variable *buff* is declared. The last two items are communication assertions for channels *in* and *out*, respectively. The first assertion states that a communication on *in* assigns the communicated value to *buff*. The latter requires that a communication on *out* always exchanges the current value of *buff* and that this variable must not change its value when performing an *out* communication. Generally, a communication assertion constrains the communication on a single channel with respect to the internal system state and describes the effect of such a communication on this internal state. A communication is only possible if the enable predicate, i.e. the boolean expression after **when**, is true in the current state. The effect predicate, i.e. the boolean expression after **then**, relates the internal state before and after the communication was performed. Here the channel name prefixed by @ refers to the communicated value, all unprimed variable names to values of state variables before, i.e. the old state, and the primed versions to the values after the communication, i.e. the new state. A variable may only occur in a predicate if it is mentioned in the list of the *read* variables or in the list of the *write* variables. In addition its value may only be changed if it is listed as a write variable. Generally, there may be more than one communication assertion for a channel. But in this case the union of all write and the union of all read variables must fit together, i.e must be disjoint sets.

The next specification *BUFFER* describes a buffer of capacity two. The idea here is to use a further channel *transfer* which is hidden from the environment. An *in* communication receives an integer and stores it in the first cell *buff1*. A communication on *out* exchanges the value of the second cell *buff2* with the environment. On the other hand the only effect of a *transfer* communication is to transfer the value of *buff1* to cell *buff2*.

BUFFER = **CHAN** *transfer* **in**
 spec **input** *in* **of** *int*
  output *out, transfer* **of** *int*
  trace *receive-data* **on** {*in,transfer*} **in** *pref (in.transfer)**
  trace *send-data* **on** {*transfer,out*} **in** *pref (transfer.out)**
  var *buff1, buff2* **of** *int*
  com *in* **write** {*buff1*} **when** *true* **then** *buff1'=@in*
  com *transfer* **read** {*buff1*} **write** {*buff2*}
   when *true* **then** *buff2'=buff1*
  com *out* **read** {*buff2*} **when** *true* **then** *@out=buff2*
 end

Specification *BUFFER* contains two trace assertions *receive-data* and *send-data*. This forces the system to obey both regular expressions in parallel. I.e. the system may only perform such traces *tr* where for each trace assertion *ta* the projection of *tr* onto its channel subset Ch_{ta} of *ta* is allowed by its regular expression re_{ta}. Thus a communication on *transfer* has to obey *receive-data* and *send-data*. In contrast channel *in* is only constrained by *receive-data* and channel *out* only by *send-data*. Of course they are synchronized by *transfer*.

An $\mathbf{SL}_0$ system specification describes the communication behaviour by the sets *TA* of all trace assertions and *CA* of all communication assertions. The former set gives global sequencing conditions by relating the occurrences of communications on the different channels. But *TA* makes neither constraints for the communicated values nor for the internal state transitions associated with the occurrences of communications. In contrast the latter set *CA* describes for each channel what the exact values are that can be exchanged and how the system state changes associated with a communication on this channel. The motivation for organizing the behaviour specification in these two parts is to ease the transformation of $\mathbf{SL}_0$ specifaications into programs. The first part yields a synchronization skeleton and the second part tells us how to complete this skeleton into a program by adding sequential processes.

2.2 Readiness semantics of $\mathbf{SL}_0$

In the following we view an $\mathbf{SL}_0$ specification as a tupel $S = (Chan, TA, Vars, CA)$, where $Chan$ is the interface of S, i.e. the set of all channels declared in S together with their direction and type, and $Vars$ the set of all local variables together with their type and possibly their initial values. An internal state $\sigma \in States$ maps each variable $x \in Vars$ onto a value of its associated type ty_x. An initial state of S maps every initialized variable $x \in Vars$ to its initial value and all others to any value of their types.

For a channel $ch \in Chan$ we denote its direction by dir_{ch} and its type by ty_{ch}. A trace assertion $ta \in TA$ is a pair (Ch, re) where its regular expression re is built up over its channel set Ch. A communication assertion in CA is a tupel $ca = (ch, R, W, wh, th)$. Here ch is the name of the channel which is constrained by ca. The possibly empty sets R and W denote the disjoint lists of read-only and write variables, respectively. Only variables from $R \cup W$ may occur within the enable predicate wh. We say that *enable predicate wh holds in a state σ* if it evaluates to $true$ when all its free variables get their values from σ. On the other hand the effect predicate th can additionally contain primed names w' for $w \in W$ and the name $@ch$ which refers to the communicated value. An *effect predicate th holds in a triple* (σ, σ', m) if its evaluation yields $true$ when all unprimed variables get their values from σ , all primed ones theirs from σ' and where m is the value of $@ch$.

For a given communication assertion ca we refer to its components by ch_{ca}, R_{ca}, W_{ca}, etc., and similarly for trace assertions and specifications.

A *communication* is a pair (ch, m) consisting of channel ch on which the communication takes place and the communicated value m, an element of the associated type ty_{ch}. For a set of channels Ch let $Comm(Ch) =_{df} \{(ch, m) | ch \in Ch \wedge m$ a value of type $ty_{ch}\}$ denote the set of all communications and $Comm(Ch)^*$ the *set of all traces*, i.e. finite sequences of these communications.

An *interface-behaviour pair* $Ch : Beh$ consists of a channel set Ch and a subset $Beh \subseteq Comm(Ch)^* \times Ch$ of *ready pairs* over Ch. The parallel synchronization $P \,||\, Q$ of such pairs $C_P : B_P$ and $C_Q : B_Q$ yields a pair with interface $C_P \cup C_Q$, namely

$$P \,||\, Q \;=_{df}\; C_P \cup C_Q : \{(tr, Rdy) | \exists (t_P, R_P) \in B_P, (t_Q, R_Q) \in B_Q :\; tr \downarrow C_P = t_P \wedge tr \downarrow C_Q = t_Q \\ \wedge Rdy = (R_P \cap R_Q) \cup ((R_P \cup R_Q) \setminus (C_P \cap C_Q)\ \}.$$

Here, the *projection* $tr \downarrow Ch$ of trace tr onto channel set Ch removes all those communications from tr whose channels are not mentioned in Ch. In the case of same interface Ch for P and Q we get a simplified formula:

$$P \,||\, Q \;=\; Ch : \{(tr, R_P \cap R_Q) \,|\, (tr, R_P) \in P \wedge (tr, R_Q) \in Q\}.$$

The readiness semantics $\mathcal{R}[\![\cdot]\!]$ identifies an $\mathbf{SL}_0$ specification $S = (Chan, TA, Vars, CA)$ with an interface-behaviour pair obtained by the synchronization of the interface-behaviour pairs $\mathcal{R}[\![TA]\!]$ for the trace assertions and $\mathcal{R}[\![CA]\!]$ for the communication assertions:

$$\mathcal{R}[\![S]\!] \;=_{df}\; \mathcal{R}[\![TA]\!] \,||\, \mathcal{R}[\![CA]\!].$$

Here, the interface of $\mathcal{R}[\![S]\!]$ is given by the set $Chan$ of all channels of S. Next we define $\mathcal{R}[\![TA]\!]$ and $\mathcal{R}[\![CA]\!]$.

The *channel word* $chan(tr)$ extracts the sequence of channels from trace tr. By $\mathcal{L}[\![re]\!]$ and $pc\mathcal{L}[\![re]\!]$ we denote the language generated by regular expression re (over alphabet Ch) and its prefix closure, respectively. The set of all *possible extensions* of $w \in Ch^*$ with respect to re is defined

$$ext(w, re) \;=_{df}\; \{b \in Ch |\ w.b \in pc\mathcal{L}[\![re]\!]\}$$

and the generalization to traces $tr \in Comm^*$ by $ext(tr, re) =_{df} ext(chan(tr), re)$.
For a single trace assertion $ta \in TA$ the readiness semantics allows all traces which obey its regular expression re_{ta} in its context Ch_{ta}.

$$\mathcal{R}[\![ta]\!] =_{df} Ch_{ta} : \{(tr, Rdy) | \; chan(tr) \in \mathcal{L}[\![re_{ta}]\!] \wedge Rdy = ext(tr, re_{ta})\}$$

The ready pairs allowed by a set of trace assertions have to fulfil each of them in parallel. By associativity of the synchronization operator and neutral element $\emptyset : \emptyset$ we can define

$$\mathcal{R}[\![TA]\!] =_{df} \|_{ta \in TA} \mathcal{R}[\![ta]\!] \qquad \text{with} \qquad \mathcal{R}[\![\emptyset]\!] = \emptyset : \emptyset.$$

The trace assertions restrict only the channel words of the traces and its semantics is given compositionally. Constraints on the communication values and internal state transitions are given by the communication assertions. To capture their semantics we first introduce a binary *transition relation* $\overset{(ch,m)}{\Longrightarrow}_{CA} \subseteq States \times States$ generated from a set CA of communication assertions.

$$\begin{aligned} \sigma \overset{(ch,m)}{\Longrightarrow}_{CA} \sigma' \Leftrightarrow_{df} & \forall ca \in CA : (\; ch = ch_{ca} \Rightarrow (wh_{ca} \text{ holds in } \sigma \wedge th_{ca} \text{ holds in } (\sigma, \sigma', m)) \;) \\ & \wedge \forall x \in Vars : (\sigma(x) \neq \sigma'(x) \Rightarrow (\; \exists ca \in CA : (ch_{ca} = ch \wedge x \in W_{ca}) \\ & \qquad \wedge \neg \exists ca \in CA : (ch_{ca} = ch \wedge x \in R_{ca})) \;) \end{aligned}$$

A transition from a state σ into new state σ' by a communication on channel ch with value m is only possible if the enable predicates of all communication assertions for ch hold in σ, further all effect predicates hold in (σ, σ', m) and if at most internal variables mentioned as write variables change their values but no one which is mentioned as read-only.

We extend this notion to traces $tr = (ch_1, m_1) \ldots (ch_n, m_n), 0 \leq n$, as follows:

$$\sigma \overset{tr}{\Longrightarrow}_{CA} \sigma' \Leftrightarrow_{df} \exists \sigma_0, \ldots, \sigma_n : \sigma_0 = \sigma \wedge \sigma_n = \sigma' \wedge \; \forall i \in 1..n : \sigma_{i-1} \overset{(ch_i,m_i)}{\Longrightarrow}_{CA} \sigma_i.$$

The behaviour requirements given by the communication assertions for a specification S lead to the following interface-behaviour pair:

$$\begin{aligned} \mathcal{R}[\![CA]\!] =_{df} Chan : \{(tr, Rdy) | \; & \exists \sigma_0, \sigma' : \sigma_0 \text{ is an initial state in } S \wedge \sigma_0 \overset{tr}{\Longrightarrow}_{CA} \sigma' \wedge \\ & Rdy = \{ch \in Chan | \forall ca \in CA : ch_{ca} = ch \Rightarrow wh_{ca} \text{ holds in } \sigma'\}\}. \end{aligned}$$

The following remarks give a hint how to achieve a unique communication assertion for each channel. The *neutral communication assertion* $(ch, \emptyset, \emptyset, true, true)$ of channel ch may be added to CA without changing the associated transition relation. Two assertions $ca_1 = (ch, W_1, R_1, wh_1, th_1)$ and $ca_2 = (ch, W_2, R_2, wh_2, th_2)$ with $(W_1 \cup W_2) \cap (R_1 \cup R_2) = \emptyset$ can be replaced in CA by the *combined assertion*

$$combine(ca_1, ca_2) \;_{df}= \; (ch, W_1 \cup W_2, R_1 \cup R_2, wh_1 \wedge wh_2, th_1 \wedge th_2)$$

without changing $\Longrightarrow_{CA}$.

The readiness semantics for specifications with hidden channels (cf. *BUFFER*) is obtained by defining a suitable hiding operator. The idea is that all hidden channels are removed from the interface and communication on hidden channels cannot be observed. Thus all communications on these channels are removed from the traces. Further the system can never be ready for a communication on a hidden channel. For this reason all ready pairs with ready sets containing at least one of these channels are excluded.

This intuitive meaning is formalized as follows. Let $Ch = \{ch_1, \ldots, ch_n\}$ be a set of channels and S a specification. Then the readiness semantics of S after hiding all channels of Ch is defined:

$$\begin{aligned} & \mathcal{R}[\![\textbf{CHAN}\, ch_1, \ldots, ch_n \,\textbf{in}\, S]\!] =_{df} \\ & \qquad Chan_S \backslash Ch : \{(tr \downarrow (Chan_S \backslash Ch), Rdy) \,|\, (tr, Rdy) \in \mathcal{R}[\![S]\!] \wedge Rdy \cap Ch = \emptyset\}. \end{aligned}$$

2.3 Specification of a lift system

As an example for the expressiveness of $\mathbf{SL}_0$ we specify the single lift system of [Bar87, Bro88]. The following informal requirements and constraints are given for a single lift system in [Bar87].

R1. The lift has a set of buttons, one button for each floor. The buttons illuminate when pressed and cause the lift to visit the corresponding floor. The illumination is cancelled when the floor is visited.

R2. Each floor has one request button. The buttons illuminate when pressed and cause the lift to stop at that floor at the next possible moment. The illumination is cancelled when the lift stops at the floor.

R3. When there are no outstanding requests for the lift, it should remain stationary at the last floor visited with the doors closed.

R4. (a) Every request for the lift must eventually be serviced.

(b) The lift should not stop at floors not requesting service.

R5. The lift should travel as far as possible without changing direction.

C1. All requests must eventually be serviced, and no floor should be stopped at when there is no unserviced request for that floor.

C2. The lift should not pass a floor for which there is an outstanding (unserviced) request.

C3. The lift should not change direction if there is an outstanding request whose service would cause the lift to continue in the same direction.

The specification of the lift system is given by specifying some subparts of the system and afterwards combining them together. In a first step the behaviour which can be observed from the i-th floor is given. ($1 \leq i \leq m$, where m is the number of floors.) Requirement R2 will be formalised by means of the following description: Each floor consists of a lift door, which can be opened and closed, a call button, which can be pressed, and a call light, which can be switched on and off. This informal description of floor i suggests the introduction of the following five channel names: $open_i$ (open the door in floor i), $close_i$ (close the door), on_c_i (switch the call light on), off_c_i (switch the call light off), c_i (press the call button). With these basic facts requirement R2 can be formalized. Assertion $call\&light_i$ expresses that the call light is switched on when the button is pressed.

$$\textbf{trace } call\&light_i \textbf{ on } \{\, c_i,\ on\_c_i,\ off\_c_i \,\} \textbf{ in } (c_i \cdot on\_c_i \cdot off\_c_i)^*$$

The light is only switched on after the call button was pressed and a further press action is only possible after the light was switched off.

R2 also requires that the door should be opened after the call button was pressed. But the door can also be opened without a preceding press action since the request for servicing floor i could also be given by another action (R1). Assertion $call\&door_i$ expresses that the call button can only be pressed when the door is closed and if it was pressed then the door shall be opened.

$$\textbf{trace } call\&door_i \textbf{ on } \{\, c_i,\ open_i,\ close_i \,\} \textbf{ in } (open_i \cdot close_i + c_i \cdot open_i \cdot close_i)^*$$

The light should only be switched on when the door is closed and switched off when the door is open. This interleaving is formalized in $light\&door_i$.

$$\textbf{trace } \mathit{light\&door}_i \textbf{ on } \{\ open_i,\ close_i,\ on\_c_i,\ off\_c_i\ \} \quad \textbf{in } (open_i \cdot close_i + on\_c_i \cdot open_i \cdot off\_c_i \cdot close_i)^*$$

And the light should immediately be switched on after the call button was pressed without opening the door in between.

$$\textbf{trace } \mathit{immediate\_lighting}_i \textbf{ on } \{\ c_i,\ open_i,\ on\_c_i\ \} \quad \textbf{in } (open_i + c_i \cdot on\_c_i \cdot open_i)^*$$

How to merge the trace assertions $call\&light_i$, $call\&door_i$, $light\&door_i$ and $immediate\_lighting_i$ together is shown in section 3.2. The result specifies the behaviour of the floor i as a subsystem of the whole lift system.

$$\textbf{trace } C\_floor\_behaviour_i \textbf{ on } \{\ c_i,\ open_i,\ close_i,\ on\_c_i,\ off\_c_i\ \} \quad \textbf{in } (open_i \cdot close_i + c_i \cdot on\_c_i \cdot open_i \cdot off\_c_i \cdot close_i)^*$$

Analogously to R2 requirement R1 describes the combination of the send button for floor i within the lift together with its corresponding send light and the door. By introducing the new channel names s_i (pressing the send button), on_s_i (switch the send light on) and off_s_i (switch the send light off) a formalization of R1 can be made in the same way. It results in

$$\textbf{trace } S\_floor\_behaviour_i \textbf{ on } \{\ s_i,\ open_i,\ close_i,\ on\_s_i,\ off\_s_i\ \} \quad \textbf{in } (open_i \cdot close_i + s_i \cdot on\_s_i \cdot open_i \cdot off\_s_i \cdot close_i\ )^*$$

The two assertions $C\_floor\_behaviour_i$ and $S\_floor\_behaviour_i$ ensure that a request for the i-th floor indicated by a press action c_i or s_i will eventually be serviced, what is supposed here to happen by opening the door of the i-th floor; i.e. R4(a) holds. But they do not require that a door may only be opened if a request is outstanding; i.e. R4(b) is not yet formalized.

This requirement R4 can be formalized by introducing a variable $request_i$ which indicates whether an outstanding request exists. Initially no request pending, the variable is initialized to false.

$$\textbf{var } request_i \textbf{ of } Bool \textbf{ init } false$$

This variable is set when service for the i-th floor is required by c_i or s_i and reset after the service was performed. The door can be opened only if $request_i$ is set. This is expressed by the following communication assertions.

com	s_i	**write**	$\{request_i\}$	**when**	*true*	**then**	$request_i'$
com	c_i	**write**	$\{request_i\}$	**when**	*true*	**then**	$request_i'$
com	$open_i$	**read**	$\{request_i\}$	**when**	$request_i$	**then**	*true*
com	$close_i$	**write**	$\{request_i\}$	**when**	*true*	**then**	$\neg\ request_i'$

[Bar87] characterizes the movements of the lift cage implicitly. In this $\mathbf{SL_0}$ specification the lift cage and its movement actions are explicitly introduced by a set of further channel names: dn_i (movement from floor $i+1$ down to floor i for all $i \in 1 \ldots m-1$) and up_i (movement from floor $i-1$ upwards to floor i for all $i \in 2 \ldots m$).

Additionally it can be observed whether the lift after a movement stops at the reached floor or passes onwards by $stop_i$ (for all $i \in 1 \ldots m$) and $pass_i$ (for all $i \in 2 \ldots m-1$). In the following trace assertions *cage_actions* is used as an abbreviation for the projection alphabet

$$cage\_actions =_{df} \{\ dn_j,\ up_k,\ stop_i,\ pass_{i'}\ \mid\ 1 \leq j < m, 2 \leq k \leq m, 1 \leq i \leq m, 2 \leq i' < m\ \}$$

and $rest_l, (1 \leq l \leq m)$, denotes the regular expression

$$rest_l =_{df} \left(\sum_{j \neq l, j \neq l-1} dn_j + \sum_{k \neq l, k \neq l+1} up_k + \sum_{i \neq l} stop_i + \sum_{i' \neq l} pass_{i'} \right)^*$$

describing all sequences of cage actions without any action related to floor l.
It is assumed that the cage is initially at floor 1.

$$\textbf{trace } lift_1 \textbf{ on } cage\_actions \textbf{ in } (\ up_2 \cdot rest_1 \cdot dn_1 \cdot stop_1\ )^*$$
$$\textbf{trace } lift_m \textbf{ on } cage\_actions \textbf{ in } (\ rest_m \cdot up_m \cdot stop_m \cdot dn_{m-1}\ )^*$$
$$\textbf{trace } lift_l \textbf{ on } cage\_actions \textbf{ in } (rest_l \cdot (\ up_l \cdot pass_l \cdot up_{l+1} + dn_l \cdot pass_l \cdot dn_{l-1} + (up_l + dn_l) \cdot stop_l \cdot (up_{l+1} + dn_{l-1})))^*$$

Now the interaction of all doors and the lift cage is specified:

(1) A door may only be opened after the cage has stopped at that floor (and before it has left it again).

$$\textbf{trace } safe\_opening \textbf{ on } \{\ open_i,\ stop_i,\ dn_j,\ up_k\ \mid 1 \le i \le m, 1 \le j < m, 2 \le k \le m\ \}$$
$$\textbf{in } open_1^* \cdot \left(move^* \cdot \left(\sum_{i=1}^{m} stop_i \cdot open_i^* \right) \right)^*$$

where $move =_{df} dn_1 + \ldots + dn_{m-1} + up_2 + \ldots + up_m$.

(2) Of course the lift may only be moved if all doors are closed.

$$\textbf{trace } safe\_move \textbf{ on } \{\ open_i,\ close_i,\ dn_j,\ up_k\ \mid 1 \le i \le m, 1 \le j < m, 2 \le k \le m\}$$
$$\textbf{in } \left(\left(\sum_{i=1}^{m} open_i \cdot close_i \right)^* \cdot move \right)^*$$

(3) The lift may only stop at floor i if there is an outstanding request (R4(b),C1).

$$\textbf{com } stop_i \textbf{ read } \{\ request_i\ \} \textbf{ when } request_i \textbf{ then } true$$

(4) The lift may only pass floor i if there is no outstanding request (C2).

$$\textbf{com } pass_i \textbf{ read } \{\ request_i\ \} \textbf{ when } \neg\ request_i \textbf{ then } true$$

(5) The lift may only move if there exists an outstanding request and may leave a floor only if there is no request for this floor (R3). This can be formalized by introducing enable predicates for all movement actions.

$$\textbf{com } dn_j \textbf{ read } \{\ request_1, \ldots, request_{j+1}\ \} \quad \textbf{when } \bigvee_{l=1}^{j} request_l \wedge \neg\ request_{j+1}$$

An analogous enable predicate must hold for upwards movements.

Now it remains to specify the maximally same direction travel property (R5, C3). For this reason the variable *curr_dir* is introduced which shall indicate the current travel direction.

$$\textbf{var } curr\_dir \textbf{ of } (up,\ down) \textbf{ init } up$$

Based on this variable the enable predicates for up_k and dn_j can be extended to guarantee the maximal travels.

$$\textbf{com } dn_j \textbf{ read } \{\ request_1, \ldots, request_m\ \} \textbf{ write } \{\ curr\_dir\ \}$$
$$\textbf{when } \bigvee_{l=1}^{j} request_l \wedge \neg\ request_{j+1} \wedge (curr\_dir = down \vee \bigwedge_{l=j+2}^{m} \neg\ request_l)$$
$$\textbf{then } curr\_dir' = down$$

The lift with current position at floor $j+1$ may only travel down, if there exists a request for a lower floor, if there is no request for current floor $j+1$ and if the lift came from above or there exists no request for any above floor.
Analogously the enable predicate for upwards movements are changed.

3 Transformation technique

This section deals with the development of an implementation for a given $\mathbf{SL}_0$ specification. Our target language PL can be roughly viewed as an occam 2 subset [IN88]. A PL program is built up by combination of basic processes which are assignment, synchronous communication on unidirected channels, and the special ones SKIP and STOP. As combining operators we have the sequence SEQ, the conditional IF, the alternation ALT, the iteration WHILE and the parallel PAR processes. While a PL program P is executed it may be either in a stable state, or has terminated or is diverging (cf. [Hoa85]). Stability means that P is ready for communication on a subset of its channels. A communication is performed on one of these channels if the environment is also ready for this channel.

$\mathbf{SL}_0$ specifications and PL programs are compared by a so called satisfaction relation *sat* [O191]. We write P *sat* S iff program P is a correct implementation of specification S. Intuitively, a correct implementation requires that for each trace tr which can be performed by P there exists a ready pair (tr, Rdy) in $\mathcal{R}[\![S]\!]$. And in the case that P has performed all communications of tr then the program has to be ready for the channels mentioned in Rdy.

Here, we neither give a formal semantics of PL nor the *sat* relation. They can be found in [OR91]. Instead we present a development strategy based on complex transformations steps. During the construction process we proceed by rearranging some parts of the specification or by replacing some parts by a bit of program syntax. By the correctness of the transformation rules it is guaranteed that the so constructed programs satisfy their specifications.

The applicability of these transformation rules can be checked on a syntactical level. Thus their automatically supported realisation is possible.

3.1 Syntax directed transformation

The design of $\mathbf{SL}_0$ was influenced by the aim to achieve a transformation technique which can split the program development in a part dealing with the program control structure and another one treating the implementation of individual communications. The syntax directed transformation rule (SDT) provides the possibility to generate for a given specification a correct implementation in only one transformation step. This advantage must be paid for by several strong syntactic restrictions which the source specification has to fulfil.

In the following we call this subset of $\mathbf{SL}_0$ the *SDT specifications.* The SDT rule deduces the program's control structure from the syntax of the trace assertions. For this reason we require that an SDT specification S has exactly one trace assertion ta where its channel set is the whole interface $Chan_S$ and where its regular expression re_{ta} is a so called *SDT suitable regular expression.* These regular expressions may only have channels $c \in Chan_S$ as basic expressions but not the empty word. They are of the special form $re_{ta}{=}pref\ r$ where the regular expression r may not contain nested stars. Further the first component r_1 of each subexpression $r_1.r_2$ must be star free and for each subexpression $r_1 + r_2$ both components r_1, r_2 must not be of the form r^* and their sets of initial symbols $Initials(r_1)$, $Initials(r_2)$ must be disjoint. Since occam does not allow output guards all channels of $Initials(r_1 + r_2)$ must be input channels.

For the implementation of the internal state transition associated with a single communication we assume a function $transition[\![\cdot]\!]$ which takes an effect predicate th and returns a program part. The program part $transition[\![th]\!]$ implements the effect specified by th as pre-post-relation. For the effect predicate th_{ch} of an output channel ch additionally the computation of the communication value and its assignment to the variable $@ch$ is contained in $transition[\![th_{ch}]\!]$.

There are two requirements on the communication assertions of an SDT specification: the existence of a unique communication assertion ca_{ch} in CA_S for each channel ch of $Chan_s$ and that $transition[\![th_{ch}]\!]$ can be generated automatically for each channel.

The syntax directed transformation rule is given as function *Program*[[·]]. Let S be an SDT specification (*Chan*, *TA*, *Vars*, *CA*) with $TA = \{(Chan, pref\ re)\}$ and $CA = \{ca_{ch} | ch \in Chan\}$.

Program[[S]] $=_{df}$ **system** *Declarations*[[*Chan* ∪ *Vars*]]
SEQ[*Initialization*[[*Vars*]], *Proc*[[*re*]], STOP]
end

Here, *Declarations*[[*Chan* ∪ *Vars*]] generates the declarations of all local variables, external (input, output) and local (chan) channels. *Initialization*[[*Vars*]] produces a multiple assignment which assigns to each variable of *Vars* its initial value in so far as it is given. The main work is done by the recursively defined function *Proc*[[·]]. It constructs from *re* a skeleton of the program's control structure and enriches this by implementations for the single communications. Essentially, the compound operators .,+ and * of regular expressions are translated into the operators SEQ, ALT and WHILE of occam programs. The channel names as basic regular expressions are transformed into communications on these channels guarded by their enable predicates.

Proc[[ch]] $=_{df}$ var @ch of ty_{ch}:IF[wh_{ch} → SEQ[ch?@ch, *transition*[[th_{ch}]]]]
or ... SEQ[*transition*[[th_{ch}]], ch!@ch] depending on dir_{ch}

Proc[[$r_1 + r_2$]] $=_{df}$ var @ch_1 of ty_{ch_1} ... var @ch_n of ty_{ch_n} :*Alt*[[$r_1 + r_2$]](SKIP),
where $\{ch_1, \ldots, ch_n\} = Initials(r_1 + r_2)$.

Proc[[$r_1.r_2$]] $=_{df}$ SEQ[*Proc*[[r_1]], *Proc*[[r_2]]]

Proc[[r^*]] $=_{df}$ WHILE($\bigvee_{ch \in Initials(r)} wh_{ch}$, *Proc*[[r]])

As arguments the ALT takes only guarded alternatives which are pairs of a guarded communiaction and a following process. For this reason an ALT process is not directly generated from *Proc*[[·]] but with the auxiliary function *Alt*[[·]](·). Additionally to the regular expression *alt* takes a process as second argument and returns an ALT with guarded communications for all initials of the regular expression. All following processes in these guarded alternatives end with the second argument process.

Alt[[ch]](p) $=_{df}$ ALT[wh_{ch}&ch?@ch → SEQ[*transition*[[th_{ch}]], p]
Alt[[$r_1 + r_2$]](p) $=_{df}$ ALT[*Alt*[[r_1]](p), *Alt*[[r_2]](p)]
Alt[[$r_1.r_2$]](p) $=_{df}$ *Alt*[[r_1]](SEQ[*Proc*[[r_2]], p])

A correctness proof of the SDT rule is given in [Ros90]. In the following we show its application on the *buffer* example.

```
Program[buffer] = system input in of int:
                         output out of int:
                         var buff of int:
                         SEQ[<>:=<>              --no variable has to be initialized
                             WHILE(true,
                                SEQ[var @in of int:
                                    IF[true→SEQ[in?@in, buff:=@in]],
                                    var @out of int:
                                    IF[true→SEQ[@out:=buff, out!@out]]],
                             STOP]
                   end
```

The WHILE process in the above program is generated by *Proc*[[(*in.out*)*]]. By applying algebraic laws of the programming language (cf. [RH88]) we achieve the following equivalent loop.

```
WHILE( true, SEQ[ in?buff, out!buff] )
```

3.2 Merging trace assertions

SL_0-specifications with more than one trace assertion cannot be handled by SDT-rules. Thus these assertions have to be merged into one. Therefore we solve here the following problem: Given several trace assertions of the form (Ch_{ta}, re_{ta}), where $ta \in TA$. Find one trace assertion $(Chan, re)$, where $Chan$ is the set of all channels in the specification and re is built over it, such that $\mathcal{R}[\![(Chan, re)]\!] = \|_{ta\in TA}\mathcal{R}[\![(Ch_{ta}, re_{ta})]\!]$ holds. Since in trace assertions no states are dealt with, the ready-sets can be calculated in a uniquely determined way and thus be dropped here. The task of merging trace assertions can hence be reformulated as a problem concerning regular languages alone:

Let A be an alphabet. We fix the following notations: Let $a, a_i, b_i \in A$, $x, y, z, x_i, y_i \in \text{Reg}A$, the set of regular expressions over A, $Ch_i \subseteq A$, $pr_1(Ch, x) = Ch$, $pr_2(Ch, x) = x$. The parallel operator $\|$ is an n-ary mapping that assigns to pairs (Ch_i, re_i) of a context $Ch_i \subseteq A$ and a regular expression re_i over Ch_i a pair (Ch, re). It is fairly easy to see that the second component of the result of this operation is a regular set. But it is a difficult task to actually find a regular expression for the resulting set, given pairs denoting the operands of the parallel operator. Here a method for finding such an expression is described: In the case that appropriate regular expressions start with a letter the parallel operator can be considered as given in an operational way:

$$(Ch_1, x_1) \| .. \| (Ch_{i_1}, a.x_{i_1}) \| .. \| (Ch_{i_m}, a.x_{i_m}) \| .. \| (Ch_n, x_n) \rightarrow$$
$$a.((Ch_1, x_1) \| .. \| (Ch_{i_1}, x_{i_1}) \| .. \| (Ch_{i_m}, x_{i_m}) \| .. \| (Ch_n, x_n)),$$

where $a \in Ch_k$ holds for all $k \in \{i_1, ..., i_m\}$, and $a \notin Ch_k$ for all $k \notin \{i_1, ..., i_m\}$. An expression $(Ch_1, a_1x_1) \| .. \| (Ch_n, a.x_n)$ can be calculated as the sum of all expressions, to which it can evolve.

The main problem is to handle the interplay between the operators $*$ and $\|$. The basic idea is to expand the regular expressions by using the equation $x^* = xx^* + \varepsilon$ repeatedly for initial expressions until we end up with a letter in the beginning of each regular expression. Then the operational view can be applied, such that the expressions with a parallel operator can be considered as unknown variables in a system of equations.

Applying the equation $x^* = xx^* + \varepsilon$ too mechanically, however, will lead into trouble, as is shown by

$$(a^*b^*)^* = a^*b^*(a^*b^*)^* + \varepsilon = aa^*b^*(a^*b^*)^* + b^*(a^*b^*)^* + \varepsilon = aa^*b^*(a^*b^*)^* + bb^*(a^*b^*)^* + (a^*b^*)^* + \varepsilon.$$

Here we end up in a circle, for the right-hand side contains the left-hand side properly. This is the reason for the somewhat complicated definition of the expanded form below. In future we shall drop the contexts, if they do not matter.

We shall call a regular expression re ε-free, if $\varepsilon \notin \mathcal{L}[\![re]\!]$. This can easily be decided on a purely syntactical level. For each regular expression re let the *expanded form* $\text{EF}(re)$ be defined as follows:

a.)	$\text{EF}(\varepsilon)$	$= \varepsilon$, $\text{EF}(a) = a$,	for all $a \in A$
b.)	$\text{EF}(ax)$	$= ax$,	
c.)	$\text{EF}((\sum x_i)y)$	$= \sum \text{EF}(x_iy)$,	including the case $y = \varepsilon$,
d.)	$\text{EF}(x^*y)$	$= \widetilde{\text{EF}}(x)x^*y + \text{EF}(y)$,	including the case $y = \varepsilon$,
e.)	$\widetilde{\text{EF}}(\varepsilon)$	$= \varepsilon$, $\widetilde{\text{EF}}(a) = a$,	
f.)	$\widetilde{\text{EF}}(\sum x_i)$	$= \sum \widetilde{\text{EF}}(x_i)$,	
g.)	$\widetilde{\text{EF}}(x^*)$	$= \widetilde{\text{EF}}(x)$,	
h1.)	$\widetilde{\text{EF}}(\prod x_i)$	$= \text{EF}(\prod x_i)$,	if $\prod x_i$ is ε-free, with $\prod x_i = x_1..x_n$ (concatenation)

h2.) $\widetilde{\mathrm{EF}}(\prod x_i) = \sum \widetilde{\mathrm{EF}}(x_i)$, if $\prod x_i$ is not ε-free,
i1.) $\overline{\mathrm{EF}}(x) = \mathrm{EF}(x)$, if x is ε-free,
i2.) $\overline{\mathrm{EF}}(x) = \widetilde{\mathrm{EF}}(x)$, if x is not ε-free,
j.) $\mathrm{EF}((Ch_1, x_1) \| .. \| (Ch_n, x_n)) = (Ch_1, \mathrm{EF}(x_1)) \| .. \| (Ch_n, \mathrm{EF}(x_n))$.

It is easy to show by induction on the structure of x that $\mathrm{EF}(x)$ is well-defined and has the form $\mathrm{EF}(x) = \sum a_i x_i (+\varepsilon)$. By means of automata theory one can show that $\mathcal{L}[\![x]\!] = \mathcal{L}[\![\mathrm{EF}(x)]\!]$ holds ([Sch90]).

Now the announced method for the construction of a system of recursive equations is presented. In order to determine $(Ch_1, x_1) \| .. \| (Ch_n, x_n)$, we shall establish a set of undetermined variables $L_1, .., L_k$ and the relations between them:

$$L_1 := pr_2((Ch_1, x_1) \| .. \| (Ch_n, x_n)),\ k := 1.$$

For readability's sake we shall not distinguish between the L_i, which are purely regular expressions, and the pairs consisting of a context and the L_i.

a.) Make the expanded form, i.e.: $\mathrm{EF}(L_k) = (Ch_1, \sum a_{1i} x_{1i} (+\varepsilon)) \| .. \| (Ch_n, \sum a_{ni} x_{ni} (+\varepsilon))$.
b.) Calculate the right-hand side by commutativity, distributivity and the operational law for initial letters, such that a new equation holds:

$$L_k = \mathrm{EF}(L_k) = \sum c_l z_l$$

with $c_l \in A$ and z_l of the form $z_l = (Ch_1, re_1) \| .. \| (Ch_n, re_n)$.
c.) Those z_l which have already been recognized as some of the variables L_i are replaced by them. For the remaining ones we introduce new variables. Thus b.) is developed into a new equation whose coefficients c_l are elements of A.
d.) Each of the expressions z_l, for which in c.) a new variable L_i has been introduced, is again treated as in a.), i.e. $k := i$.
e.) The algorithm finishes as soon as no more variables can be introduced.

This algorithm terminates after finitely many steps, what is proven by a somewhat tricky structural induction on the regular expressions ([Sch90]). The result is a uniquely solvable system of equations, such that L_1 is the language looked for. The question how to solve such equations, that obey to the Greibach - condition, has been studied in [Sal66].

Next we show, how the algorithm works by means of the following example, which describes the *C-floor-behaviour* of the lift from section 2.3: Given the expression $(Ch_1, x_1) \| .. \| (Ch_4, x_4)$ with $x_1 = (c.on\_c.off\_c)^*$ from trace assertion *call&light*, $x_2 = (open.close + c.open.close)^*$ from *call&door*, $x_3 = (open.close + on\_c.open.off\_c.close)^*$ from *light&door*, $x_4 = (open + c.on\_c.open)^*$ from *immediate_lighting* and Ch_i are the channel sets of these trace assertions. In the following we drop the Ch_i and by the algorithm get the equations:

$$L_1 = c.L_2 + open.L_3 + \varepsilon \qquad L_3 = close.L_1 \qquad L_5 = off\_c.L_3$$
$$L_2 = on\_c.L_4 \qquad L_4 = open.L_5$$

with

$$\begin{aligned} L_1 &= x_1 \| x_2 \| x_3 \| x_4 \\ &= c.on\_c.off\_c.x_1 + \varepsilon \| (open.close + c.open.close).x_2 + \varepsilon \| \\ &\quad (open.close + on\_c.open.off\_c.close).x_3 + \varepsilon \| (open + c.on\_c.open).x_4 + \varepsilon \end{aligned}$$

$$L_2 = on\_c.off\_c.x_1 \,\|\, open.close.x_2 + \,\|\, x_3 \,\|\, on\_c.open.x_4$$
$$L_3 = x_1 \,\|\, close.x_2 \,\|\, close.x_3 \,\|\, x_4$$
$$L_4 = off\_c.x_1 \,\|\, open.close.x_2 \,\|\, open.off\_c.close.x_3 \,\|\, open.x_4$$
$$L_5 = off\_c.x_1 \,\|\, close.x_2 \,\|\, off\_c.close.x_3 \,\|\, x_4.$$

The method how to solve the equations is standard. We shall end up with

$$x_1 \,\|\, x_2 \,\|\, x_3 \,\|\, x_4 \;=\; L_1 \;=\; (open.close \;+\; c.on\_c.open.off\_c.close)^*,$$

the required regular expression.

3.3 Parallel decomposition

Another development strategy is the parallel decomposition. Here, the given specification is splitt up into subsets of its basic items which form smaller specifications. From the following proposition it is clear that the synchronization of such a set of subsystems implements the whole specification.

Let S, S_1, S_2 be specifications with $Chans_{S_1} \cup Chans_{S_2} = Chans_S$ and where the trace assertions TA_{S_1}, TA_{S_2}, the variables $Vars_{S_1}, Vars_{S_2}$ and the communication assertions CA_{S_1}, CA_{S_2} of S_1 and S_2 are partitions of those sets of S. Then the following equation holds:

$$\mathcal{R}[\![S]\!] = \mathcal{R}[\![S_1]\!] \,\|\, \mathcal{R}[\![S_2]\!].$$

In restricted interface situations this synchronization can be implemented by the parallel composition operator **PAR** of the programming language. Each channel between subprocesses of a **PAR** connects exactly two of them and outside of the **PAR** process all these channels must be declared as local. Thus the parallel decomposition can only be applied if all communication between the intended subsystems occurs only on hidden channels.

For a set of basic items it may be impossible to find subsets which fulfil the above given constraints. Then it may be useful to break a single complex trace or communication assertions into more simpler ones. This can be seen as the reverse operation of trace merging or of combining communication assertions.

In the following we demonstrate the parallel decomposition technique roughly by developing an implementation for the *BUFFER* example. The idea is to construct two processes around the trace assertions *receive-date* and *send-data*. Both of them participate in communications on channel *transfer*. Since the communication assertion $ca_{transfer}$ associated to *transfer* accesses both variables *buff1* and *buff2* we have to split this assertion into two such that each of the new ones only accesses one variable. As a first step we strengthen the effect predicate of $ca_{transfer}$ by constraining the possible communication values.

ca_{trans} : **com** *transfer* **read** {*buff1*} **write** {*buff2*}
when *true* **then** *buff2'=@transfer* ∧ *@transfer=buff1*

The original assertion allows each integer as communication value for *@transfer* while the new version ca_{trans} forces a unique value. But since channel *transfer* is hidden this strengthening does not change the readiness semantics of the specification after hiding channel *transfer*.
Now we split ca_{trans} into the following two communication assertions.

ca_{trans1} : **com** *transfer* **read** {*buff1*} **when** *true* **then** *@transfer=buff1*
ca_{trans2} : **com** *transfer* **write** {*buff2*} **when** *true* **then** *buff2'=@transfer*

This step is immediately justified by the fact that $combine(ca_{trans1}, ca_{trans2})$ and ca_{trans} are equal.

Now a situation as described in the above proposition is achieved and we split the *BUFFER* specification into parallel composition *Buffer* with subcomponents *B*1 and *B*2.

```
Buffer = system input in of int:
                output out of int:
                chan transfer of int:
                PAR[ B1, B2 ]
         where B1 = spec input in of int
                         output transfer of int
                         trace receive-data on {in,transfer} in pref (in.transfer)*
                         var buff1 of int
                         com in  write {buff1}  when true  then buff1'=@in
                         com transfer  read {buff1}  when true  then @transfer=buff1
                    end
               B2 = spec input transfer of int
                         output out of int
                         trace send-data on {transfer,out} in pref (transfer.out)*
                         var buff2 of int
                         com out  read {buff2}  when true  then @out=buff2
                         com transfer  write {buff2}  when true  then buff2'=@transfer
                    end
         end
```

The specifications *B*1 and *B*2 can now be transformed by the SDT rule into processes. Using the results of section 3.1 we get the following implementation for *BUFFER*.

```
Bufferimpl = system input in of int:
                    output out of int:
                    chan transfer of int:
                    PAR[var buff1 of int:
                        WHILE( true, SEQ[in?buff1, transfer!buff1]),
                        var buff2 of int:
                        WHILE( true, SEQ[transfer?buff2, out!buff2])]
             end
```

Final remarks

In this paper we have defined a simple specification language and have shown some strategies for developing programs which satisfy the given specifcations. The demonstrated transformations cannot treat every specification. Further rules are under examination. E.g. the expansion strategy [Ol91a] is less restrictive than SDT but requires the introduction of auxiliary variables to control the program flow.

It should be pointed out that the transformation rules in section 3 have been proved correct, but the proofs have been left out due to lack of space, since this would require to present the PL-semantics and satisfaction relation between specification and programs formally.

Finally we should like to thank the collaborators of the ProCoS project for discussions and hints. In particular we acknowledge E.-R. Olderog for his ideas, without which the present paper could not have been written.

References

[Bar87] H. Barringer, Up and down the Temporal Way. The Computer Journal 30:2 pp. 134-148, 1987.

[Bjo89] D. Bjørner, A ProCoS project description, ESPRIT BRA 3104, Bulletin of the EATCS 39, pp. 60-73, 1989.

[Bro88] M. Broy, An example for the Design of Distributed Systems in a Formal Setting: The Lift Problem, Techn. Report MIP-8802, Univ. Passau, Germany, 1988.

[Heh84] E.C.R. Hehner, Predicative Programming, CACM 27 (2), 1984.

[Hoa85] C.A.R. Hoare, Communicating Sequential Processes, Prentice Hall, 1985.

[IN88] INMOS Ltd., occam 2 Reference Manual, Prentice Hall, 1988.

[JROR90] K.M. Jensen, H. Rischel, E.-R. Olderog, S. Rössig, Syntax and informal semantics for the ProCoS specification language 0, ProCoS Doc. Id. ID/DTH KMJ 4/2, Tech. Univ. Denmark, 1990.

[Ol91] E.-R. Olderog, Nets, Terms and Formulas: Three Views of Concurrent Processes and their Relationship, Cambridge University Press, 1991.

[Ol91a] E.-R. Olderog, Towards a design calculus for communicating programs, to appear in: Proc. CONCUR 91, Amsterdam, The Netherlands, Lecture Notes in Comput. Sci., Springer, 1991.

[OH86] E.-R. Olderog, C.A.R. Hoare, Specification-oriented semantics for communicating processes, Acta Inform. 23, pp. 9-66, 1986.

[OR91] E.-R. Olderog, S. Rössig, Predicative semantics of MIX, ProCoS Doc. Id. OLD ERO 3/1, Univ. Oldenburg, 1991.

[Ros90] S. Rössig, Transformation of SL_0 specifications into PL programs, ProCoS Doc. Id. OLD SR 1/4, Univ. Oldenburg, 1990.

[RH88] A.W. Roscoe, C.A.R. Hoare, The laws of occam programming, Theoret. Comput. Sci. 60 pp. 177-229, 1988.

[Sal66] A. Salomaa, Two complete axiom systems for the algbra of regular events, JACM vol.13, no.1, pp.158–169, 1966.

[Sch90] M. Schenke, Regular Languages and Parallel Operators, ProCoS Doc. Id. OLD MS 1/2, Univ. Oldenburg, 1990.

Writing Operational Semantics in Z: A Structural Approach

Marc Benveniste*
IRISA

e-mail: mbenveni@irisa.fr
Campus de Beaulieu, 35042 Rennes Cédex. FRANCE.

1 Introduction

As the title may suggest, this paper shows how to write, in **Z**, operational semantics in the Plotkin's tradition, i.e. based on transition systems [1]. Furthermore, it provides the necessary definitions and offers, in the form of an example, guidelines for doing so. The convenience of such a notational union should be obvious, let only mention type checking, proof writing, and more prospectively, stepwise refinement. The example we treat suggests that the use of schemas favour the uncovering of different conceptual layers that never show in traditional presentations.

The core of this paper is divided in four sections. The first one introduces generic definitions of labelled transition systems. The second one presents the parallel language for which a dynamic semantics is elaborated in the third. In the latter, special attention is paid to the conceptual stratification of the description. It is achieved through the almost systematical use of schema frames, logical connectives and projection. The fourth section indicates how proofs can be written taking advantage of the specification effort. Due to space limitations, familiarity with the **Z** notation is required.

2 Transition systems in Z

We introduce defining notations only for labelled transition systems because the corresponding definitions for unlabelled ones are easily derived from these by restricting the set of labels to be a singleton. We then present the notion of computation associated with labelled transition systems. The source of these definitions can be found in [2].

2.1 Labelled transition systems

A relation on a set X, labelled by elements of A is called a *labelled relation*. It is usually defined as a subset of $\mathbb{P}(X \times A \times X)$. Each tuple is called a *labelled transition*. For technical reasons, we specify this set of transitions as a generic schema where the tuple elements are named:

---

*Supported by a grant from the XII CONACYT–CEFI fellowship programme jointly held by MEXICO and FRANCE.

$$\begin{array}{|l} \hline \textit{LabTrans}[\, X, A\,] \\ \textit{from}, \textit{to} : X \\ \textit{by} : A \\ \hline \end{array}$$

A *labelled transition system* (LTS) over a set X of *configurations* is a labelled relation *Rel* defined by *generalised induction*. The essence of a LTS lies in this rigorously mathematical way of defining the relation. The generalised inductive definition of a set consists of a base set, or set of axioms, and of an inference relation, or set of rules. The general induction principle ensures that taken together they uniquely define a set. That set is the smallest set that includes the base and that is closed under the inference rule. We define a *closure* function to encompass this mathematical construction:

$$\begin{array}{|l} [\, X\,] \\ \hline \textit{closure} : \mathbb{F}\, X \times (X \leftrightarrow X) \rightarrow \mathbb{P}\, X \\ \hline \forall R : X \leftrightarrow X;\ I : \mathbb{F}\, X \bullet \\ \quad I \subseteq \textit{closure}\ (\, I, R\,) \wedge \\ \quad R (\!|\ \textit{closure}\ (\, I, R\,)\ |\!) \subseteq \textit{closure}\ (\, I, R\,) \wedge \\ \quad (\forall Q : \mathbb{P}\, X \mid I \subseteq Q \wedge R (\!|\ Q\ |\!) \subseteq Q \bullet \textit{closure}\ (\, I, R\,) \subseteq Q) \\ \hline \end{array}$$

We model the rules of a LTS as a binary relation among finite sets of transitions.

$$\textit{Rules}[\, X, A\,] == (\mathbb{F}\ \textit{LabTrans}[\, X, A\,]) \leftrightarrow \mathbb{F}\ \textit{LabTrans}[\, X, A\,]$$

We can now define a LTS as follows:

$$\begin{array}{|l} \textit{LTS}[\, X, A\,] \\ \hline \textit{Rel} : \mathbb{P}\ \textit{LabTrans}[\, X, A\,] \\ \hline \exists \mathcal{A} : \mathbb{F}_1\ \textit{LabTrans}[\, X, A\,];\ \mathcal{R} : \textit{Rules}[\, X, A\,] \bullet \\ \quad \textit{Rel} = \bigcup(\textit{closure}(\ \{\ \mathcal{A}\ \}, \mathcal{R}\ )) \\ \hline \end{array}$$

The *Rel* relation captures all the possible moves over the configuration space. Each move is called a *transition* and *Rel* a *transition relation*. The label is usually interpreted as the action through which the move was made.

In an operational semantics framework, a configuration is the state of some abstract machine. These abstract machines are often simple and they are informally presented as tuples. For example, let *mem* be a store, ρ an environment and s a statement, then a machine state is given by:

$$\langle\ \textit{mem}, \rho, s\ \rangle$$

and a typical transition by:

$$(\dagger)\quad \langle\ \textit{mem}, \rho, s\ \rangle \xrightarrow{\alpha} \langle\ \textit{mem}', \rho', s'\ \rangle$$

where the relationship between primed elements of the tuple and unprimed ones is either specified by pattern matching or as side formulæ. **Z** schemas seem to be a natural choice for a formal definition:

$$\textit{State} \mathrel{\widehat{=}} [\ \textit{mem} : \textit{store};\ \rho : \textit{environment};\ s : \textit{statement}\ ]$$

The main reason for preferring this **Z** notation to a free one is that the resulting transition system is subject to formal proofs, type checking, and more prospectively, refinement, all within the same notational framework. It is therefore brought closer to mechanisation. Furthermore, schemas seem to favour the uncovering of different conceptual layers that never show in traditional presentations.

If a generic parameter could be "forced" to be a schema, a trivial (and pleasant) way of writing transitions in **Z** would rely on the combined use of the Δ and Ξ conventions, and the framing technique that results from schema inclusion [3]. The previous example, marked with the dagger (†), would simply be:

$$
\begin{array}{|l}
\hline
\textit{AxiomFrame}[\ \textit{State}\ ] \\
\Delta \textit{State} \\
a : A \\
\hline
a = \alpha \\
\text{pre- and post-conditions for the action} \\
\hline
\end{array}
$$

This is however not possible in **Z** as defined in [4]. In order to keep both genericity and framing capabilities, the *LabTrans* schema was preferred over tuples to introduce labelled transitions. This schema will be used later as an axiom frame.

We can now provide a function that maps a set of axioms (written as schemas) and rules into the unique LTS they define:

$$
\begin{array}{|l}
\hline\hline
[\ X, A\ ] \\
\textit{mkLTS} : (\mathbb{F}_1\ \textit{LabTrans}[\ X, A\ ]) \times \textit{Rules}[\ X, A\ ] \rightarrow \textit{LTS}[\ X, A\ ] \\
\hline
\forall \mathcal{A} : \mathbb{F}_1\ \textit{LabTrans}[\ X, A\ ];\ \mathcal{R} : \textit{Rules}[\ X, A\ ] \bullet \\
\quad \textit{mkLTS}(\mathcal{A}, \mathcal{R}) = (\ \mu\ \textit{LTS}[\ X, A\ ] \mid \textit{Rel} = \bigcup(\textit{closure}(\ \{\ \mathcal{A}\ \}, \mathcal{R}\ )\ )) \\
\hline
\end{array}
$$

We need to specify reachable configurations in order to specify the set of *terminal configurations* of a LTS, i.e. those for which no more transitions are possible. For a given set of transitions, say *LR*, and a given configuration, say x, the set of reachable configurations from x by *LR* is given by:

$$
\begin{array}{|l}
\hline\hline
[\ X, A\ ] \\
\textit{succ} : (\mathbb{P}\ \textit{LabTrans}[\ X, A\ ]) \rightarrow X \rightarrow \mathbb{P}\ X \\
\hline
\forall \textit{LR} : \mathbb{P}\ \textit{LabTrans}[\ X, A\ ];\ x : X \bullet \\
\quad \textit{succ}\ \textit{LR}\ x = \{\ t : \textit{LR} \mid t.\textit{from} = x \bullet t.\textit{to}\ \} \\
\hline
\end{array}
$$

We finally define the set of *labelled terminal transition systems* (LTTS). A LTTS is a LTS for which a set T of terminal configurations has been defined:

$$
\begin{array}{|l}
\hline
\textit{LTTS}[\ X, A\ ] \\
\textit{LTS}[\ X, A\ ] \\
T : \mathbb{F}\ X \\
\hline
\forall x : T \bullet \textit{succ}\ \textit{Rel}\ x = \varnothing \\
\hline
\end{array}
$$

2.2 Computations

For a given start configuration, a computation captures all the individual steps which are performed up to the moment we observe the system. These notions of observation and of individual step are important for they are determined by the expected notion of behaviour. It is often difficult to choose the appropriate sets of configurations and labels for a LTS.

We can model an individual step as a couple formed with the resulting configuration and the associated label.

$$Step[\ X, A\ ] \mathrel{\hat{=}} LabTrans[\ X, A\ ] \setminus (from)$$

A computation for a given set of labelled transitions is either a finite or an infinite sequence of such steps. In case it is finite, it can be *partial* in the precise sense that the last configuration of the computation has at least one successor by the LTS; in any other case, it is *complete*. Let $\mathrm{seq}^{\omega} X$ stand for the set of infinite sequences of X elements, and $\mathrm{seq}^{\infty} X$ for the set of all sequences of X elements. Formally:

$$\mathrm{seq}^{\omega} X == \mathbb{N}_1 \to X$$
$$\mathrm{seq}^{\infty} X == \mathrm{seq}\, X \cup \mathrm{seq}^{\omega} X$$

We can remark that our definition of computation allows various notions of behaviour: those based on labels, on configurations or based on both.

A computation is meaningful only in the context of a given LTS, say $\mathcal{S}$, and a start configuration, say x_0. We capture this dependency through the definition of two relations: $\partial computes$ (∂ should be read *partially*), to characterise all computations and *Computes*, to select the completed ones.

$$
\begin{array}{l}
[\ X, A\ ] \\
\hline
\_\ \partial computes\ \_, \\
\_\ Computes\ \_ : (LTS[\ X, A\ ] \times X) \leftrightarrow \mathrm{seq}^{\infty}(Step[\ X, A\ ]) \\
\hline
\forall \mathcal{S} : LTS[\ X, A\ ];\ x_0 : X;\ C : \mathrm{seq}^{\infty}(Step[\ X, A\ ]) \bullet \\
\quad (\ (\ \mathcal{S}, x_0\ )\ \partial computes\ C \Leftrightarrow \\
\qquad C(1) = (\ \mu\ LabTrans[\ X, A\ ]\ | \\
\qquad\qquad from = x_0 \wedge \theta LabTrans \in \mathcal{S}.Rel \bullet \theta Step\ ) \wedge \\
\qquad (\forall k : \mathrm{dom}\, C \mid k > 1 \bullet \\
\qquad\quad C(k) = (\ \mu\ LabTrans[\ X, A\ ]\ | \\
\qquad\qquad from = (C(k-1)).to \wedge \theta LabTrans \in \mathcal{S}.Rel \bullet \theta Step\ ))\ ) \\
\quad \wedge\ (\ (\ \mathcal{S}, x_0\ )\ Computes\ C \Leftrightarrow \\
\qquad (\ \mathcal{S}, x_0\ )\ \partial computes\ C \wedge \\
\qquad (\ C \notin \mathrm{seq}^{\omega}(Step[\ X, A\ ]) \Rightarrow succ\ (\mathcal{S}.Rel)\ ((last\ C).to) = \varnothing\ )\ )
\end{array}
$$

We can now turn our attention to the utilisation of LTS.

3 The example at hand

As a working example, we "transcribe" excerpts from the formal definition of the POLYGOTH programming language, reported in [5], into the simplified version presented in the next section (SOOL for simple object oriented language). This version of the language is very close to the simplest member of the POOL family [6], whose operational and denotational semantics are reported in [7] and [8]. Both our **Z** descriptions can therefore be compared to the referred work. It can be noticed that POLYGOTH's essential concept (the *multiprocedure*[1]) and mechanism (*fragmentation*[2]) are not considered in the present description. These two features of the language render the description of configurations and transitions complex and originally called for a more formal notation.

3.1 Informal presentation

A SOOL programme describes the behaviour of a (logically) distributed system in terms of objects interacting by exchanging messages. Objects are protection units. Their data cannot be accessed by any other object of the system. Objects manage their data using *variables* called instance variables. Variables contain references either to other objects -since all data are objects-, to the object they belong to or to a special object denoted by *nil*. Assigning an object to a variable makes it refer to the assigned object.

Objects are characterised by the *class* they belong to, except that *nil* belongs to all classes. A class is the description of a set of objects that share the same body, variables and methods. The *new* operation provided for classes enables asynchronous dynamic object creation. This operation is the sole source of parallelism in this oversimplified version. The body of a class describes what should be done at instancing time: it is called as a procedure whenever an instance is created. As for any procedure, parameters may be declared; they are known as class parameters.

Objects have the ability to act on their data obeying very strict protocols known as their *methods*. Methods are procedures that can access instance variables. They can have local variables as well. Additionally, they may call any method offered by their object. These calls are known as internal and they are immediately executed.

Objects may only interact by sending messages to each other. The sending object must specify the receiving one. A message is a request for the designated object. If understood by the receiver -i.e. if a method is defined to accept that request-, it will be handled as soon as it becomes idle. Meanwhile, the sender is suspended, waiting for a result message.

There are some primitive objects in the language. Only integer and boolean objects will be presented in this semantics.

3.2 Syntax

The different finite sets of syntactic elements named hereafter are assumed to be given: a set VAR of variables, a set $NAME$ of names and a set $UID_\perp$ of unique identifiers with a distinguished member $\perp$. Furthermore, we define the sets $iVAR$ and $tVAR$ of instance and temporary variables as two non–empty subsets of VAR that partition it.

[1]A multiprocedure is to parallelism what a procedure is to sequential programming: the abstraction of a parallel command. It brings the ability to compose them, hence a novel and unique form of *parallel recursivity* [9].

[2]The *fragmentation* mechanism results from (one possible) integration of the multiprocedure concept in an object oriented language. A *fragmented* object is an object whose state is partitioned in *fragments* and whose methods are multiprocedures. A *fragment* is defined by a partial state and partial definitions of the associated methods [10, 11].

$$\begin{array}{|l} iVAR, tVAR : (\mathbb{P}\ VAR) \setminus \varnothing \\ \hline \langle\ iVAR, tVAR\ \rangle \text{ partition } VAR \end{array}$$

Similarly, *cNAME* (for class names) and *mNAME* (for method names) partition *NAME*. We assume there exists a function new_{UID} that provides unique identifiers until the set is exhausted and $\perp$ thereafter:

$$\begin{array}{|l} new_{UID} : \mathbb{F}\ UID_{\perp} \rightarrow UID_{\perp} \\ \perp : UID_{\perp} \\ \hline \perp = new_{UID}\ UID_{\perp} \\ \forall X : \mathbb{F}\ UID_{\perp} \bullet new_{UID}\ X \in X \Leftrightarrow X = UID_{\perp} \end{array}$$

Let *UID* be the set of unique identifiers but $\perp$.

Objects are not fully characterised. Instead, they are denoted as follows: *nil* denotes itself, *tt* and *ff* denote the boolean <u>true</u> and <u>false</u>, $int(i)$ denotes the integer $\underline{i}$ and $ref(\alpha)$ denotes a reference to object $\underline{\alpha}$. Let *OBJ* be the set of objects.

The set *EXP* of expressions is defined as a free type. By way of a detailed explanation, a typical item of the corresponding concrete syntax is written at the right of each rule:

$EXP ::= const\ \langle\!\langle\ OBJ\ \rangle\!\rangle\ \mid$	[**true**, *1*, *56*, **nil**]
$var\ \langle\!\langle\ VAR\ \rangle\!\rangle\ \mid$	[$x\ (\in iVAR), t\ (\in tVAR)$]
$call\ \langle\!\langle\ EXP \times mNAME \times \text{seq}\ EXP\ \rangle\!\rangle\ \mid$	[$e\ !\ m(e_1, .., e_n)$]
$new\ \langle\!\langle\ cNAME \times \text{seq}\ EXP\ \rangle\!\rangle\ \mid$	[$C\ !\ \mathbf{new}(e_1, .., e_n)$]
$self\ \mid$	[**self**]
$wait\ \langle\!\langle\ UID_{\perp}\ \rangle\!\rangle$	[not available]

The last rule introduces an auxiliary expression to ease the writing of the semantics. It is not available to the programmer. The intuitive meaning of the expression $wait(\underline{\beta})$ in an object $\underline{\alpha}$ is the value sent to $\underline{\alpha}$ by $\underline{\beta}$. That value is specified in $\underline{\beta}$ with a matching *send* that is also auxiliary and that is introduced in the set *STMT* of statements given hereafter.

$STMT ::= val\ \langle\!\langle\ EXP\ \rangle\!\rangle\ \mid$	[e]
$assign\ \langle\!\langle\ VAR \times EXP\ \rangle\!\rangle\ \mid$	[$x := e,\ t := e$]
$comp\ \langle\!\langle\ STMT \times STMT\ \rangle\!\rangle\ \mid$	[$s_1\ ;\ s_2$]
$if\ \langle\!\langle\ EXP \times STMT \times STMT\ \rangle\!\rangle\ \mid$	[**if** e **then** s_1 **else** s_2 **fi**]
$do\ \langle\!\langle\ EXP \times STMT\ \rangle\!\rangle\ \mid$	[**while** e **do** s **od**]
$send\ \langle\!\langle\ STMT \times UID\ \rangle\!\rangle$	[not available]

In order to define the semantics of a statement s, we need a notion of environment. Let the set of class and method declarations be captured by the following schema:

$$
\begin{array}{|l}
\multicolumn{1}{l}{\_\_DECL\_\_\_\_\_\_\_\_\_\_\_\_\_\_\_\_\_\_\_\_\_\_\_\_\_\_\_\_\_\_\_\_\_\_\_\_\_\_\_} \\
in : \mathrm{iseq}\ VAR \\
knows : \mathbb{F}\ mNAME \\
data : \mathbb{F}\ VAR \\
does : STMT \\
\hline
\mathrm{ran}\ in \subseteq data
\end{array}
$$

where *in* stands for the input formal parameters. *knows* is the empty set in the case of a method declaration, and the set of methods known by the class otherwise. *data* and *does* are self explanatory. It should be noticed that the invariant of this schema partly defines the well–formedness of our declarations. All the necessary conditions should be included in this invariant.

An environment may then be defined as a partial mapping from class and method names to their corresponding declarations:

$$
\begin{array}{|l}
\multicolumn{1}{l}{\_\_ENV\_\_\_\_\_\_\_\_\_\_\_\_\_\_\_\_\_\_\_\_\_\_\_\_\_\_\_\_\_\_\_\_\_\_\_\_\_\_\_} \\
env : NAME \rightarrow\!\!\!\!\!\!\!\!\rightarrow\!\!\!\!+ DECL \\
\hline
\forall c\_used : \mathbb{F}\ cNAME \mid c\_used = cNAME \cap \mathrm{dom}\ env \bullet \\
\quad \exists m\_used : \mathrm{seq}(\mathbb{F}\ mNAME) \bullet \\
\quad\quad \mathrm{ran}\ m\_used = (env \mathbin{;} (\lambda\, DECL \bullet knows))(\!|\ c\_used\ |\!) \land \\
\quad\quad \langle\ c\_used\ \rangle \frown m\_used\ \mathrm{partition}\ \mathrm{dom}\ env \\
\mathrm{ran}((mNAME \lhd env) \mathbin{;} (\lambda\, DECL \bullet knows)) = \{\ \varnothing\ \}
\end{array}
$$

The invariant requires that no method is shared among classes, no two classes are declared with the same name and that methods are not nested. Other validating conditions should be included as well.

Finally, a programme is an environment with a distinguished class name, bound to be instanced at execution time. We assume this class is parameterless.

$$
\begin{array}{|l}
\multicolumn{1}{l}{\_\_PROGRAMME\_\_\_\_\_\_\_\_\_\_\_\_\_\_\_\_\_\_\_\_\_\_\_\_\_\_\_\_\_\_\_\_\_\_\_\_\_\_\_} \\
ENV \\
main : cNAME \\
\hline
main \in \mathrm{dom}\ env \\
(env\ main).in = \varnothing
\end{array}
$$

4 Semantics

In order to describe the semantics, we first need to define what our configurations and labels are. We intend to keep the logically distributed aspect of the language at hand. The concepts underlying the programming model embraced by the language should appear somehow in its semantics. Individual transitions may then be arranged on a semantical basis. For instance, if we choose a configuration to be a set of representations of SOOL objects, we emphasise the underlying programming model of our language, i.e., communicating sequential agents. The configuration itself is made of a collection of *partial* configurations, each modelling one object. This choice immediately suggests a grouping of transitions: those that involve a single object (non-communicating) and those that involve pairs (communication and creation). These two groups should be dealt with separately. Indeed, in our description they correspond to different schema frames.

4.1 Configurations and labels

What should an object modelling be? It highly depends on the expected abstraction level of the resulting semantics. Our semantics is syntax-directed so a *STMT* component is required. We include a store component to model the current state of the object, an environment to capture the declarations and the object identity[3]:

$$
\begin{array}{|l}
\hline
OBJECT_{\mathrm{error}} \\
id : UID_{\perp} \\
stmt : STMT \\
mem : \mathrm{seq}_1(VAR \twoheadrightarrow\!\!\!\!\!\!\!+ \; OBJ) \\
ENV \\
\hline
\end{array}
$$

We introduce *error*, a distinguished element of the $OBJECT_{\mathrm{error}}$ schema to model any erroneous object. Let *OBJECT* be the set of all $OBJECT_{\mathrm{error}}$ bindings but *error*.

$$error == (\mu\, OBJECT_{\mathrm{error}} \mid id = \perp \wedge stmt = val(const(nil)) \wedge mem = \langle\varnothing\rangle \wedge env = \varnothing)$$
$$OBJECT \mathrel{\hat=} [\ OBJECT_{\mathrm{error}} \mid \theta OBJECT_{\mathrm{error}} \neq error\ ]$$

A configuration is a finite (non-empty) set of objects that are uniquely identified by their *id* component. Let *HasId* be the *id* projector for $OBJECT_{\mathrm{error}}$ schemas.

$$HasId == (\ \lambda\, OBJECT_{\mathrm{error}} \bullet id\ )$$

In order to ease the expression of this uniqueness of object identifiers, we add a redundant component to the modelling of configurations: the set of known object identifiers. Configurations are described by the *STATE* schema below

$$
\begin{array}{|l}
\hline
STATE \\
created : \mathbb{F}_1\, OBJECT_{\mathrm{error}} \\
known : \mathbb{F}_1\, UID_{\perp} \\
\hline
created \lhd HasId \in created \rightarrowtail\!\!\!\!\!\!\!+ \; known, \\
\hline
\end{array}
$$

where the invariant ensures that an object is uniquely identified by its *id* field and that they are all in *known*. This invariant reveals an important property of the system: no transition should lead to a configuration where an object has multiple identifiers or whose

[3]The absence of a class name is explained by the invariant of *ENV*: it ensures that a method is uniquely defined by its name. We could specify the environment at the configuration level, or even fix it for a given programme. We leave it at this level for the resulting object model is more general: the language could be extended to modify the environment.

identifier is unknown. In section 5, we show how such a property can be established taking advantage of the **Z** notation.

What should the labels be? Had we wanted to observe the system as a collection of intelligible communications, we would have chosen labels that capture method calls. However, we suppose that the system observer cannot fully understand the messages exchanged, but he can recognise the identity of the involved objects as well as their roles (sender, receiver or argument). This observer could very well be a garbage collector. This vision is rendered by the following set of labels:

$LABEL ::= \tau \mid$ [internal affairs]
$\quad meets \langle\!\langle\ UID_{\perp} \times \mathrm{seq}\ UID\ \rangle\!\rangle$ [$\underline{\beta_i}$ are acquaintances of $\underline{\alpha}$]

We are ready to undertake the definition of a labelled terminal transition system. The semantics of our language can then be given either directly, as the set of all the possible computations from the initial configuration defined for each programme, or indirectly, as an "interpretation" of these computations. The choice heavily depends on the expected notion of programme equivalence, i.e. the classes of distinguishable programmes.

Our labelled terminal transition system is the binding of $LTTS[\ STATE, LABEL\ ]$ for which the axioms and rules are specified in the following sections. Transition stratification is achieved through the observance of a three steps methodology that can be phrased as follows:

- specify the common properties of the transitions and use the resulting schema as a frame,
- specialise the frame, introducing auxiliary variables as needed, for each transition,
- summarise with the logical disjunction of individual transitions and project on the frame to hide the auxiliary variables.

4.2 Axioms

This set of transitions are described as specialisations of the *LabTrans* schema from the tool–kit presented in the first section, properly parameterised:

$\Phi Axiom \mathrel{\widehat=} LabTrans[\ STATE, LABEL\ ]$

This schema frame captures the most general property of our transitions: they model a change from the *from* configuration to the *to* configuration triggered by the action labelled *by*. The figure below provides a graphical representation of this schema frame. Only the *created* component of the configuration is depicted, the *known* being redundant.

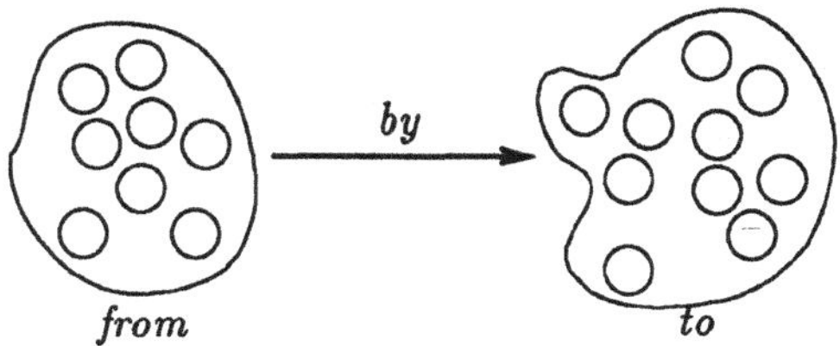

As it was explained in section 4, we introduce two specialisations of this schema frame to distinguish between transitions that involve a single object and those that involve two of them.

4.2.1 Single object transitions

In order to model a single object transition, we need to introduce a couple of objects: one to specify its before state and one for its state after the transition. Such changes are naturely modelled in **Z** with the Δ convention. The figure below depicts the modelling of this group of transitions.

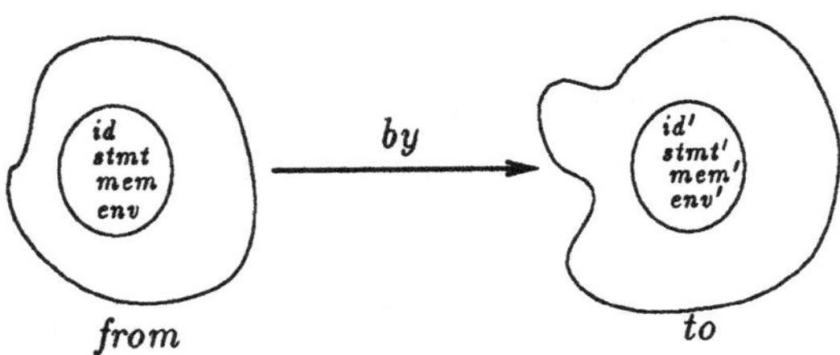

Each transition of this group is then simply determined by the way these two objects are related. Nevertheless, we can identify some properties common to all single object transitions. Surely, we should not allow the erroneous object, *error*, to start any legal transition. We define $\Delta OBJECT$ to explicitly show that no transition from the *error* state is possible, and that it may however be reached by any of them:

$$\Delta OBJECT \mathrel{\widehat{=}} OBJECT \land OBJECT'_{\text{error}}$$

Single object transitions preserve both the identity and the environment components of the involved object, except if the resulting object is *error*. All these transitions are *silent*, i.e. they are labelled with τ. Finally, as obvious as it may seem, they share the fact that they affect a single object. We use the schema $\Phi Single$ as a frame for this group of transitions to capture the common properties just mentioned[4]:

$$\begin{array}{|l}
\multicolumn{1}{l}{\Phi Single} \\
\hline
\Phi Axiom \\
\Delta OBJECT \\
\hline
(id' = id \land env' = env) \lor (\theta OBJECT' = error) \\
\theta OBJECT \in from.created \\
to.created = (from.created \setminus \{\ \theta OBJECT\ \}) \cup \{\ \theta OBJECT'\ \} \\
by = \tau \\
\hline
\end{array}$$

We further specialise these transitions according to the way the memory component (mem) of the involved object is affected. We group transitions that do not modify that component under the ΦNo_Store_Update schema,

$$\Phi No\_Store\_Update \mathrel{\widehat{=}} [\ \Phi Single \mid mem' = mem\ ],$$

and those that update it under the $\Phi Store\_Update$,

[4]Notice the implicit constraint placed on the *known* component by *STATE*'s invariant.

$$\begin{array}{|l}
\multicolumn{1}{l}{\Phi Store_Update} \\
\Phi Single \\
x : VAR;\ \gamma : OBJ;\ k : \mathbb{N}_1 \\
\hline
mem' = mem \oplus \{\ k \mapsto mem(k) \oplus \{\ x \mapsto \gamma\ \}\ \} \\
x \in iVAR \Rightarrow k = 1 \\
x \in tVAR \Rightarrow k = \#mem \\
\hline
\end{array}$$

that handles both a temporary variable, i.e. declared in a method, and an instance variable update[5].

No store update Examples of this family of axioms are method invocations on "built–in" objects such as integers or booleans. The schema calculus enables a systematic specification of *erroneous transitions.* An erroneous transition is one that leads to a configuration that includes the *error* object[6]. A *valid* transition is one that is not erroneous. One schema is written for each valid transition, one for the erroneous ones, and one to summarise. For instance, integer divisions (i ! **div**(j)) are specialised as valid or erroneous as follows: given

$$Div \mathrel{\widehat=} [\ \Phi No\_Store\_Update;\ i, j : \mathbb{Z} \mid stmt = val(call(const(int\ \ i), div, \langle\ const(int\ \ j)\ \rangle))\ ],$$

then valid divisions are given by:

$$OkDiv \mathrel{\widehat=} [\ Div \mid j \neq 0 \wedge stmt' = val(const(int(i \operatorname{div} j)))\ ]$$

and erroneous divisions by:

$$ErrDiv \mathrel{\widehat=} [\ Div \mid j = 0 \wedge \theta OBJECT' = error\ ]$$

...and the built–in (robust) transitions by:

$$Built\_In \mathrel{\widehat=} (OkDiv \vee ErrDiv \vee \ldots) \upharpoonright \Phi No\_Store\_Update$$

Another example is the evaluation of the expression *self* that returns the identity of the executing object:

$$OkSelf \mathrel{\widehat=} [\ \Phi No\_Store\_Update \mid stmt = val(self) \wedge stmt' = val(const(ref(id)))\ ]$$

Write We provide a single example of this subgroup of transitions. The assignment statement is trivially specified as a store update. The statement component of the resulting object holds the value just assigned.

$$Assign \mathrel{\widehat=} [\ \Phi Store\_Update \mid stmt = assign(x, const(\gamma)) \wedge stmt' = val(const(\gamma))\ ]$$

Other transitions of the Φ*Single* group include the (internal) call of an object's own method, through the *self* expression. We assume enough examples have already been shown to understand the two first steps of the proposed methodology. The third step is illustrated with the summarising schema *OneMove* written hereafter.

$$OneMove \mathrel{\widehat=} (Built\_In \vee OkSelf \vee Assign \vee \ldots) \upharpoonright \Phi Axiom$$

---

[5]Notice that the conjunction of the implications covers all the possibilities for x.

[6]Errors have to be dealt with at the object state level because *error* was introduced at this level. There is nothing absolute in the definition of erroneous transitions.

4.2.2 Double object transitions

In order to model this second group of axioms, we need to introduce two pairs of objects: one to specify the pair of objects before the transition and one to describe how they are affected. As we did for single object transitions, we use the Δ convention to model each object change. The figure below depicts our modelling.

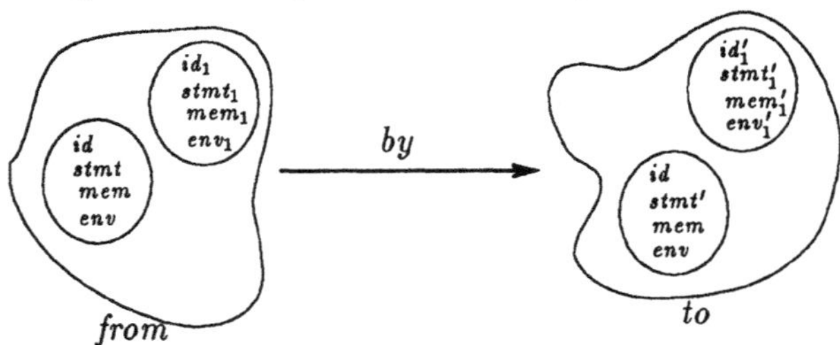

Most transitions in this group preserve the identity, environment and memory components of both the concerned objects. We introduce a schema to name the bindings obtained by dropping the *stmt* field of $OBJECT_{\text{error}}$:

$$OBJstate \mathrel{\widehat{=}} OBJECT_{\text{error}} \setminus (stmt)$$

Since the (class) instance creation description preserves these components for only one of the objects, the framing schema $\Phi Couple$ requires equality for only one of the pairs of *OBJstate* bindings. This requirement is naturally specified with the Ξ convention.

$\Phi Couple$
$\Phi Axiom$
$\Delta OBJECT;\ \Delta OBJECT_1$

$\Xi OBJstate$

$\{\ \theta OBJECT, \theta OBJECT_1\ \} \subseteq from.created$

$to.created = (from.created \setminus \{\ \theta OBJECT, \theta OBJECT_1\ \}) \cup$
$\qquad \{\ \theta OBJECT', \theta OBJECT_1'\ \}$

Each transition of this group is then simply determined by the value of its label and by the way the four object bindings are related.

Creation The creation of a class instance is described by two transitions. The first one "asks" for the creation. It provides the class name and the required initial parameter values. The second one provides the new object's identity, if possible. We only describe the first one, the second being an instance of the *communication* transitions group which is presented in the next subsection.

Φ*Create*

$$
\begin{array}{l}
\Phi Couple \\
c : cNAME;\ \overline{\gamma} : \mathrm{seq}\, OBJ;\ fresh : UID_{\perp} \\
\hline
\theta OBJECT = \theta OBJECT_1 \wedge fresh = new_{\mathrm{UID}}(from.known) \\
to.known = from.known \cup \{\ fresh\ \} \\
stmt = val(new(\ c\ ,\ \overline{\gamma}\,\S\, const\ ))
\end{array}
$$

The *OkCreation* and *ErrCreation* schemas described hereafter specialise the Φ*Create* transition frame to specify the transition's label and post-configuration when the creation is successful and when it fails respectively.

• The failure of an object creation, modelled by new_{UID} returning $\perp$, entails the immediate return of the *nil* result. The transition is silent and the resulting configuration comprises the *error* object.

ErrCreation

$$
\begin{array}{l}
\Phi Create \\
\hline
fresh = \perp \Rightarrow (\ by = \tau \wedge \\
\theta OBJECT_1' = error \wedge \\
stmt' = val(const(\ nil\ ))\ )
\end{array}
$$

• Otherwise, the successfully created object gets acquainted with the objects given as class parameters. The transition is labelled by the "meeting" of id_1' with the object identifiers present in the parameters, if any. A function is provided to extract this list of identifiers from the list of parameters:

$$takeUid == (\lambda\, \overline{\gamma} : \mathrm{seq}\, OBJ \bullet (\overline{\gamma} \upharpoonright ref(\!|\ UID\ |\!))\,\S\, ref^{-1})$$

Another auxiliary function is introduced to specify the initial store of the created object:

$$
\begin{array}{l}
memInit == (\lambda\, decl : DECL;\ actual : \mathrm{seq}\, OBJ \bullet \\
\qquad\qquad (\lambda\, x : decl.data \bullet nil) \oplus (decl.in^{-1}\,\S\, actual))
\end{array}
$$

The creator is temporarily blocked waiting for the identity of its child. The created object first sends its identity, obtained through the evaluation of the *self* expression, then executes the *does* statement associated with the named class in the creator's environment.

OkCreation

$$
\begin{array}{l}
\Phi Create \\
\hline
fresh \neq \perp \Rightarrow (\ by = meets(\ id_1', takeUid\ \overline{\gamma}\ ) \wedge \\
id_1' = fresh \wedge \\
stmt_1' = comp(\ send(\ val(self)\ ,\ id\ )\ ,\ (env\ c).does\ ) \wedge \\
env_1' = env \wedge mem_1' = \langle\ memInit(\ env\ c, \overline{\gamma}\ )\ \rangle \wedge \\
stmt' = val(wait(\ id_1'\ ))\ )
\end{array}
$$

Thus the first part of the creation is specified by:

$$Creation \mathrel{\widehat=} (OkCreation \wedge ErrCreation) \upharpoonright \Phi Axiom,$$

and the second one is an instance of the *communication* transitions group defined hereafter[7].

Communication Communications are based on the *client–server* model. A client "asks" a server to execute a method, say m, and provides a sequence of objects as argument, say $\overline{\gamma}$. The server "replies" by sending the result of the execution, say γ. These two communication phases are modelled by two transitions framed by ΦAsk and $\Phi Reply$ respectively. Both are specialisations of the $\Phi Couple$ frame that was depicted back in section 4.2.2. Furthermore, they both preserve the identity and environment components of the server, which is represented by the object decorated with a one subscript.

ΦAsk

$\Phi Couple$
$m : mNAME;\ \overline{\gamma} : \mathrm{seq}\ OBJ$

$id_1' = id_1 \wedge env_1' = env_1$
$by = meets(\ id_1, takeUid\ \overline{\gamma}\ )$

$\Phi Reply$

$\Phi Couple$
$\gamma : OBJ$

$id_1' = id_1 \wedge env_1' = env_1$
$by = meets(\ id, takeUid\ \langle\ \gamma\ \rangle\ )$

These transitions are labelled by the "meeting" of the receiver with the objects included in the argument of the call or the result. It should be noticed that a complete communication entails an even number of *meets*-labelled transitions. This fact is used in section 4.4 to characterise a deadlocked configuration.

The client and server objects are loosely specified. We tighten their specifications for the "ask" transition in the *Client1* and *Server1* schemas, constraining their statement and memory components.

$Client1$

ΦAsk
$dest : EXP$

$stmt = val(call(\ dest, m, \overline{\gamma} \mathbin{;} const\ ))$
$stmt' = val(wait(\ id_1\ ))$
$dest = const(ref(\ id_1\ ))$

$Server1$

ΦAsk
$any : OBJ$

$stmt_1 = val(const(\ any\ ))$
$stmt_1' = send(\ (env\ m).does\ ,\ id\ )$
$mem_1' = mem_1 \frown \langle\ memInit(\ env\ m, \overline{\gamma}\ )\ \rangle$

The client is required to issue the method call to the server named id_1 and to provide a sequence of constant values[8]. It is then blocked, waiting for the answer from the server. The server is required to be idle. This fact is characterised by its statement component

[7] Although it could be expressed in a single transition, this description is more flexible. It allows the specifier to switch from synchronous to asynchronous creations just by commuting the *send* and the *does* statements in the $stmt_1'$ component of *OkCreation*.

[8] The *dest* variable is just introduced to save horizontal space for the two columns layout.

being a constant value. Upon call acceptance, the server initiates and "pushes" a local store in its memory component. Then, it starts executing the body of the called method in order to send, later on, the result back to the client[9]. This transition is completely specified as follows:

$$Ask \mathrel{\widehat{=}} (Client1 \land Server1) \upharpoonright \Phi Axiom.$$

Reply Similarly, the *Client2* (resp. *Server2*) schema specialises the $\Phi Reply$ transition frame in the client (resp. server) components ...

```
┌─ Client2 ───────────────────────
│ ΦReply
├──────────────
│ stmt = val(wait( id₁ ))
│ stmt' = val(const( γ ))
└─────────────────────────────────
```

$$\begin{array}{|l} \textit{Client2} \\ \hline \Phi Reply \\ \hline stmt = val(wait(\ id_1\ )) \\ stmt' = val(const(\ \gamma\ )) \\ \hline \end{array}$$

$$\begin{array}{|l} \textit{Server2} \\ \hline \Phi Reply \\ \hline stmt_1 = send(\ val(const(\ \gamma\ ))\ ,\ id\ ) \\ stmt_1' = val(const(\ \gamma\ )) \\ mem_1' = front\ mem_1 \\ \hline \end{array}$$

...and the second group of communications is specified by:

$$Reply \mathrel{\widehat{=}} (Client2 \land Server2) \upharpoonright \Phi Axiom$$

4.2.3 Summarising

$$Axioms \mathrel{\widehat{=}} OneMove \lor Creation \lor Ask \lor Reply$$

It should be noticed that this schema expression clearly depicts our language underlying concepts. Furthermore, the schema calculus enables the stratification needed to uncover them through a rather systematic use of specialisation (expressed via schema inclusion) and generalisation (expressed via logical connectives and projection).

4.3 Rules

Rules are arranged according to their inference basis. Two groups are identified: those rules that infer on the configuration component and those that infer on the label.

4.3.1 *STATE* based rules

These rules are closely determined by the syntax structure of the programming language. They generally formalise the monotonic properties of the different injections of the abstract syntax with respect to the order induced by the transitions. Pictorially, these rules can be seen as a couple of single object transitions.

[9]The evaluation order for statements is specified by the rules presented in section 4.3.

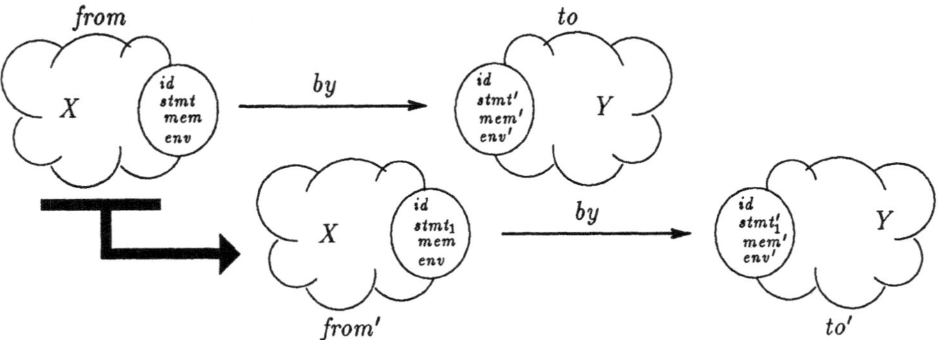

The objects in the top and the bottom transitions have identical components both in their before and after states except for the statement ones. We use $\Phi Progress$ as a frame for evaluation progress schemas. It is an auxiliary schema that characterises two single object transitions that only differ in the *stmt* component of their triggering object.

$$
\begin{array}{l}
\textbf{\_}\ \Phi Progress \\
\Phi Axiom;\ \Phi Axiom' \\
X, Y : \mathbb{F}\ OBJECT_{\mathrm{error}} \\
\Delta OBJECT;\ \Delta OBJECT_1 \\
\hline
from.created = X \cup \{\ \theta OBJECT\ \} \wedge to.created = Y \cup \{\ \theta OBJECT'_{\mathrm{error}}\ \} \\
from'.created = X \cup \{\ \theta OBJECT_1\ \} \wedge to'.created = Y \cup \{\ \theta OBJECT'_{\mathrm{error}\,1}\ \} \\
by = by' \\
id = id' \wedge \theta OBJstate = \theta OBJstate_1 \wedge \theta OBJstate' = \theta OBJstate'_1
\end{array}
$$

The statement components are left unspecified. Each rule is then simply determined by the way the statement components relate to each other.

We present two examples of these rules. They specify the evaluation order of an external method call. We can recall from the abstract syntax definition 3.2 that an external method call is made of the destination expression, the method name and a sequence of parameter expressions. To evaluate it, we need to evaluate the destination expression ...

$$
\begin{array}{l}
\textbf{\_}\ DestinationEval \\
\Phi Progress \\
m : mNAME;\ \overline{exp} : \mathrm{seq}\, EXP \\
\hline
stmt_1 = val(call(\ val^{-1}\ stmt\ ,\ m\ ,\ \overline{exp}\ )) \\
stmt'_1 = val(call(\ val^{-1}\ stmt'\ ,\ m\ ,\ \overline{exp}\ )),
\end{array}
$$

... and then evaluate actual parameters from left to right:

ActualsEval

$\Phi Progress$
$e : EXP;\ m : mNAME;\ \overline{\gamma} : \text{seq}\, OBJ;\ \overline{exp} : \text{seq}\, EXP$

$stmt_1 = val(call(\ e\ ,\ m\ ,\ (\overline{\gamma} \mathbin{;} const) \frown \langle\ val^{-1}\ stmt\ \rangle \frown \overline{exp}\ ))$
$stmt'_1 = val(call(\ e\ ,\ m\ ,\ (\overline{\gamma} \mathbin{;} const) \frown \langle\ val^{-1}\ stmt'\ \rangle \frown \overline{exp}\ )).$

Statement components are related by patterns formed of the injection *val* from expressions to statements. Moreover, they relate the evaluation of an argument expression to the evaluation of the injected expression. Other evaluation rules are defined similarly.

4.3.2 *LABEL* based rules

These rules do not mention specific objects, they are used to formalise more general properties of the system. Take parallelism for instance; it is easy to see that if two non–communicating transitions are valid, then their simultaneous occurrence is also valid, and the resulting configuration is the "union" of the individual results:

Parallelism

$\Phi Axiom_1;\ \Phi Axiom_2;\ \Phi Axiom'$

$from' = from_1 = from_2$

$to'.created = to_1.created \cup to_2.created$

$by' = \tau = by_1 = by_2$

Another important rule specifies under what conditions a configuration can be "extended" without interfering with a transition. If the configurations have no common objects neither before nor after the transition, than an extension is allowed:

Extension

$\Phi Axiom;\ \Phi Axiom'$
$extension : STATE$

$to.known \cap extension.known = \varnothing$
$from.known \cap extension.known = \varnothing$

$from'.created = from.created \cup extension.created$
$to'.created = to.created \cup extension.created$
$by' = by,$

4.3.3 Summarising

Rules that have a single numerator are summarised by:

$$Rule1 \mathrel{\widehat{=}} (DestinationEval \lor ActualsEval \lor Extension) \upharpoonright \Phi Axiom \land \Phi Axiom'$$

We describe the resulting inference rule as a global variable typed by the *Rules* defined in the proposed tool-kit, properly parameterised:

$$
\begin{array}{|l}
Rules : Rules[\ STATE, LABEL\ ] \\
\hline
Rules = \{\ Rule1 \bullet \{\ \theta\Phi Axiom\ \} \mapsto \{\ \Phi Axiom'\ \}\ \} \cup \\
\qquad\qquad \{\ Parallelism \bullet \{\ \theta\Phi Axiom_1, \theta\Phi Axiom_2\ \} \mapsto \{\ \theta\Phi Axiom'\ \}\ \}
\end{array}
$$

4.4 The system

Now that we have formally specified axioms and rules for every valid transition in SOOL, we let *SoolLTS* be the resulting labelled transition system:

$$SoolLTS == (mkLTS[\ STATE, LABEL\ ]\ (\{\ Axioms\ \}, Rules))$$

In order to characterise an execution that terminates deadlocked, we introduce a special configuration, denoted $\Box$ and defined by:

$$\Box == (\ \mu\, STATE \mid created = \{\ error\ \}\ )$$

Let *STEP* be the set of labelled configuration pairs that constitute a computation as defined in section 2.2.

$$STEP \mathrel{\widehat{=}} Step[\ STATE, LABEL\ ]$$

A configuration is deadlocked either if it is $\Box$ or if it is the last step of a finite and complete computation whose number of *meets(...)* labels is odd. A normally terminated configuration can be recognised by the fact that all its object states are idle, i.e. each of their *stmt* fields denotes a constant value.

$$
\begin{array}{|l}
Deadlock\_,\ TermOk\_ : \mathbb{F}\ STATE \\
\hline
\forall s : STATE \bullet \\
\quad (\ Deadlock\ s \Leftrightarrow \\
\qquad s = \Box \lor \\
\qquad (\ \exists s_0 : STATE;\ C : \mathrm{seq}\, STEP \mid (\ SoolLTS\ ,\ s_0\ )\ Computes\ C \bullet \\
\qquad\quad s = (last\ \ C).to \land \\
\qquad\quad (count(items\ \ C)(\ \mu\, STEP \mid by \in \mathrm{ran}\, meets\ ))\ \mathrm{mod}\ 2 = 1\ )\ ) \\
\land \\
\quad (\ TermOk\ s \Leftrightarrow \\
\qquad (\lambda\ OBJECT_{\mathrm{error}} \bullet stmt)(\!|\ s.created\ |\!) \subseteq (const \mathbin{;} val)(\!|\ OBJ\ |\!)\ )
\end{array}
$$

The resulting labelled terminal transition system is:

$$
\begin{aligned}
SoolLTTS == (\mu\, LTTS[\ STATE, LABEL\ ] \mid &\\
& Rel = SoolLTS.Rel \land \\
& T = \{\ s : STATE \mid TermOk\ s \lor Deadlock\ s\ \})
\end{aligned}
$$

A SOOL programme is rarely executed on its own. It is run within an operating system (*OS*). This *OS* is also modelled by a configuration. We define a function, *LL*, that denotes the loading and linking (or vice versa) of a programme in the presence of such a system.

This function has three possible outcomes: deadlock if the system is deadlocked, error if new_{UID} fails or a properly initiated configuration.

$$
\begin{array}{l}
LL : PROGRAMME \times STATE \rightarrow STATE \\
\hline
\forall P : PROGRAMME \bullet \\
\quad LL(\ P, \Box\ ) = \Box \land \\
\quad (\forall S : STATE \setminus \{\ \Box\ \} \bullet \\
\qquad LL(\ P, S\ ) = (\mu\, STATE \mid created = S.created \cup \{\ new_{\mathrm{OBJECT}}(\ P, S\ )\ \})\ )
\end{array}
$$

where new_{OBJECT} is defined by:

$$
\begin{array}{l}
new_{\mathrm{OBJECT}} : PROGRAMME \times STATE \rightarrow OBJECT_{\mathrm{error}} \\
\hline
\forall P : PROGRAMME;\ S : STATE \bullet \\
\quad (\ new_{\mathrm{UID}}(\ S.known\ ) = \bot \Rightarrow new_{\mathrm{OBJECT}}(\ P, S\ ) = error\ ) \land \\
\quad (\ new_{\mathrm{UID}}(\ S.known\ ) \neq \bot \Rightarrow new_{\mathrm{OBJECT}}(\ P, S\ ) = \\
\qquad (\mu\, OBJECT \mid id = new_{\mathrm{UID}}(\ S.known\ ) \land \\
\qquad\qquad stmt = ((P.env)(P.main)).does \land \\
\qquad\qquad mem = \langle\ memInit(\ (P.env)(P.main)\ ,\ \langle\rangle\ )\ \rangle \land \\
\qquad\qquad env = P.env)\ )
\end{array}
$$

Our linking is trivial ($env = P.env$), but a more elaborated scheme could be described in a similar manner.

Finally, the meaning of a SOOL programme is a function that maps the initial configuration, obtained with the LL function, to the set of all its possible executions. Only the configuration component of a step is needed in this case. Therefore, we introduce a projection operator to obtain the sequence of these components from a sequence of steps:

$$
\begin{array}{l}
\_^{\sigma} : \mathrm{seq}^{\infty}\, STEP \rightarrow \mathrm{seq}^{\infty}\, STATE \\
\hline
\forall C : \mathrm{seq}^{\infty}\, STEP \bullet \\
\quad C^{\sigma} = C\, ⨾\, (\ \lambda\, STEP \bullet to\ )
\end{array}
$$

Executions ending in a deadlocked configuration are tail-tagged with the special configuration $\Box$.

$$
\begin{array}{l}
[\![\ \_\ ]\!]_{\mathrm{Sool}} : PROGRAMME \rightarrow STATE \rightarrow \mathbb{P}(\ \mathrm{seq}^{\infty}\, STATE\ ) \\
\hline
\forall P : PROGRAMME \bullet \\
\quad [\![\ P\ ]\!]_{\mathrm{Sool}}(\Box) = \{\ \langle\ \Box\ \rangle\ \} \land \\
(\ \forall OS : STATE \setminus \{\ \Box\ \} \bullet \exists_1\, s_0 : STATE \mid s_0 = LL(\ P, OS\ ) \bullet \\
\qquad [\![\ P\ ]\!]_{\mathrm{Sool}}(OS) = \{\ C : \mathrm{seq}^{\omega}\, STEP \mid (\ SoolLTS\ ,\ s_0\ )\ Computes\ C \bullet C^{\sigma}\ \} \cup \\
\quad \{\ C : \mathrm{seq}\, STEP \mid (\ SoolLTS\ ,\ s_0\ )\ Computes\ C \land TermOk(\ last\ C^{\sigma}\ ) \bullet C^{\sigma}\ \} \cup \\
\quad \{\ C : \mathrm{seq}\, STEP \mid (\ SoolLTS\ ,\ s_0\ )\ Computes\ C \land Deadlock(\ last\ C^{\sigma}\ ) \bullet C^{\sigma} \frown \langle\ \Box\ \rangle\ \}\ )
\end{array}
$$

5 Proofs

This section is aimed at showing how to state and prove LTS properties in **Z**. A suitable generalised induction principle enables LTS induction proofs. This principle is used in the writing of a simple SOOL property proof. Only selected excerpts are presented due to space limitations.

5.1 Induction for LTS

As we have carefully defined labelled transitions as a schema, the set of transitions that satisfy a given property, say P, is trivially specified by:

```
┌─ ObeyP ──────────────────────────
│ LabTrans
├──────────
│ P
└──────────────────────────────────
```

Stating that a given LTS, say $\mathcal{S}$, obeys property P is formalised by the predicate:

$$\mathcal{S}.Rel \subseteq \{\ ObeyP\ \}$$

We cannot provide a generic definition of this predicate because *ObeyP* cannot be defined in this way, but we can introduce a set expression for it that has the same semantics. In **Z**, a property is denoted by the set of elements that satisfy it. Thus for any property P, the *ObeyP* schema is the set of *LabTrans* bindings identical to P. Let *Property* be the type of a property:

$$Property[\ X, A\ ] == \mathbb{P}\ LabTrans[\ X, A\ ]$$

The *Obeys* relation models the fact that a labelled transition system satisfies a property. It is defined as follows:

```
╒═[ X, A ]═══════════════════════════
│ _ Obeys _ : LTS[ X, A ] ↔ Property[ X, A ]
├──────────
│ ∀ 𝒮 : LTS[ X, A ]; P : Property[ X, A ] •
│   𝒮 Obeys P ⇔ 𝒮.Rel ⊆ P
└────────────────────────────────────
```

In order to establish that a LTS satisfies a property, it is only required to show that the defining axioms satisfy the property and that the rules preserve it. More formally,

Generalised induction principle For all the values of X and A,

$$\begin{array}{l} GIP[\ X, A\ ] \mathrel{\widehat{=}} \forall \mathcal{S} : LTS[\ X, A\ ];\ P : Property[\ X, A\ ] \bullet \\ \quad \exists \mathcal{A} : \mathbb{F}_1\ LabTrans[\ X, A\ ];\ \mathcal{R} : Rules[\ X, A\ ] \bullet \\ \quad ProofByInduction[\ X, A\ ] \Rightarrow [\ \mathcal{S} : LTS[\ X, A\ ];\ P : Property[\ X, A\ ] \mid \mathcal{S}\ Obeys\ P\ ], \end{array}$$

is *true* and a proof by induction can be characterised by:

$$\begin{array}{|l}
\multicolumn{1}{l}{_ \mathit{ProofByInduction}[\, X, A \,] _________________________} \\
\mathcal{S} : \mathit{LTS}[\, X, A \,];\ P : \mathit{Property}[\, X, A \,] \\
\mathcal{A} : \mathbb{F}_1\, \mathit{LabTrans}[\, X, A \,];\ \mathcal{R} : \mathit{Rules}[\, X, A \,] \\
\hline
\mathcal{S} = \mathit{mkLTS}(\mathcal{A}, \mathcal{R}) \\
\mathcal{A} \subseteq P \\
\forall p : \mathbb{F}_1\, P \bullet \mathcal{R}\ p \subseteq P \\
\hline
\end{array}$$

Justification The existence of axioms and rules is derived from LTS's definition,

1) $\mathcal{S} : \mathit{LTS}[\, X, A \,] \Leftrightarrow$ [LTS def]
$\exists \mathcal{A} : \mathbb{F}_1\, \mathit{LabTrans}[\, X, A \,];\ \mathcal{R} : \mathit{Rules}[\, X, A \,] \bullet \mathcal{S}.\mathit{Rel} = \bigcup(\mathit{closure}(\ \{\ \mathcal{A}\ \}, \mathcal{R}\ )\ ))$

Let $\mathcal{A}$ and $\mathcal{R}$ be those introduced in (1),

(2) $P : \mathit{Property}[\, X, A \,] \Rightarrow$ [sets fact]
(2.1) $\exists\, Q : \mathbb{P}\ \mathit{Property}[\, X, A \,] \bullet Q = \{\ T : \mathbb{F}\ \mathit{LabTrans}[\, X, A \,] \mid T \subseteq P\ \}$

(3) $\mathcal{A} \subseteq P \wedge (2.1)$
(3.1) $\Rightarrow \{\ \mathcal{A}\ \} \subseteq Q$ [$\mathcal{A}$ is finite]

(4) $\forall p : \mathbb{F}_1\, P \bullet \mathcal{R}\ p \subseteq P \wedge (2.1)$
(4.1) $\Rightarrow \mathcal{R}(\!|\ Q\ |\!) \subseteq Q$ [$\mathcal{R}$ preserves finiteness]

(5) (1) $\wedge$ (3.1) $\wedge$ (4.1)
(5.1) $\Rightarrow \mathit{closure}(\ \{\ \mathcal{A}\ \}, \mathcal{R}\ ) \subseteq Q$ [closure def (3rd inv's clause]
(5.2) $\Rightarrow \bigcup(\mathit{closure}(\ \{\ \mathcal{A}\ \}, \mathcal{R}\ )\ )) \subseteq \bigcup Q$ [$\bigcup$ law **Z** manual pp.92]
(5.3) $\Rightarrow \mathcal{S}.\mathit{Rel} \subseteq P$ [(1) & (2.1) & $\bigcup$ def]
(5.4) $\Rightarrow \mathcal{S}\ \mathit{Obeys}\ P$ [(5.3) & *Obeys* def]

□[10]

5.2 Proof style

We would like to establish that the semantics given to SOOL programmes preserves the invariant specified in the *STATE* schema. As a lemma, we need to show that every transition of the associated LTS, i.e. *SoolLTS*, maintains that invariant. We have already *required* that both the *from* state and the *to* state satisfy the configuration invariant, but we need to show that our requirements are consistent. We need to show that if the *from* state satisfies the *STATE* invariant then the *to* state, as defined by the transition, also satisfies it. We call that property *IdUniqueness*. It is specified as follows:

[10] The provided justification is incomplete. The uniqueness condition placed on the semantics of generic definitions in [12] has not been verified.

$$\begin{array}{|l}\hline \textit{IdUniqueness} \\ \Phi \textit{Axiom} \\ \hline (\exists\, \textit{STATE} \bullet \textit{from} = \theta \textit{STATE}) \Rightarrow (\exists\, \textit{STATE} \bullet \textit{to} = \theta \textit{STATE}) \\ \hline \end{array}$$

Theorem *SoolLTS Obeys* $\{$ *IdUniqueness* $\}$

We use the induction principle to prove it.

Lemma 1

$$\begin{array}{l} \exists\, \textit{ProofByInduction}[\,\textit{STATE}, \textit{LABEL}\,] \bullet \\ \quad \mathcal{S} = \textit{SoolLTS} \land P = \{\ \textit{IdUniqueness}\ \} \land \\ \quad \mathcal{A} = \{\ \textit{Axioms}\ \} \land \mathcal{R} = \textit{Rules} \end{array}$$

The proof by induction calls for three other lemmas.

Lemma 1.1 $\textit{SoolLTS} = \textit{mkLTS}(\{\ \textit{Axioms}\ \}, \textit{Rules})$

Proof 1.1 *SoolLTS*'s definition □

The base step of the induction proof, $\mathcal{A} \subseteq P$, is a corollary of its schema expression.

Lemma 1.2 $\forall\, \textit{Axioms} \bullet \textit{IdUniqueness}$

Corollary 1.2 (base step) $\{\ \textit{Axioms}\ \} \subseteq \{\ \textit{IdUniqueness}\ \}$

The structure of our specification is useful to prove this lemma. A straightforward decomposition stems from the definition of *Axioms*.

Lemma 1.2.1

$$\begin{array}{l} (\forall\, \textit{Axioms} \bullet \textit{IdUniqueness}) \\ \quad \Leftrightarrow (\forall\, \textit{OneMove} \bullet \textit{IdUniqueness}) \land (\forall\, \textit{Creation} \bullet \textit{IdUniqueness}) \land \\ \qquad (\forall\, \textit{Ask} \bullet \textit{IdUniqueness}) \land (\forall\, \textit{Reply} \bullet \textit{IdUniqueness}) \end{array}$$

Although we only provide the proof for the *Creation* transitions, the following lemma about *OneMove* transitions shows the benefits of a stratified specification. The following lemma says that if we prove that *OneMove* is consistent with $\Phi\textit{Single}$ –we have to, anyway–, then the *IdUniqueness* property holds for *OneMove* if it holds for $\Phi\textit{Single}$.

Lemma 1.2.2.1

$$\textit{Single} \mathrel{\widehat=} \Phi\textit{Single} \upharpoonright \Phi\textit{Axiom}$$

$$\textit{Consistent} \mathrel{\widehat=} \forall\, \textit{OneMove} \bullet \exists\, \Delta \textit{OBJECT} \bullet \Phi\textit{Single}$$

$$(\forall\, \textit{Single} \bullet \textit{IdUniqueness}) \land \textit{Consistent} \Rightarrow (\forall\, \textit{OneMove} \bullet \textit{IdUniqueness})$$

We do not need to prove the *IdUniqueness* property for each axiom of the *OneMove*; we only need to prove it for the framing schema.

The following lemma provides a more suitable formulation of the *IdUniqueness* property.

Lemma 1.2.3.1 $\forall \Phi Axiom \bullet$

$$IdUniqueness \Leftrightarrow (from.created \lhd HasId \in from.created \rightarrowtail\!\!\!\!\!\twoheadrightarrow from.known \Rightarrow to.created \lhd HasId \in to.created \rightarrowtail\!\!\!\!\!\twoheadrightarrow to.known)$$

Lemma 1.2.3.2 $\forall OBJECT;\ OBJECT_1 \bullet$

$$\theta OBJECT = \theta OBJECT_1 \Leftrightarrow \{\ \theta OBJECT, \theta OBJECT_1\ \} = \{\ \theta OBJECT\ \}$$

Lemma 1.2.3.3 $\forall fresh : UID_{\bot};\ \Phi Axiom \bullet$

$$fresh = new_{UID}(from.known) \Leftrightarrow (fresh = \bot \land fresh \in from.known) \lor (fresh \neq \bot \land fresh \notin from.known)$$

Lemma 1.2.3 $(\forall Creation \bullet IdUniqueness)$

Proof

$\forall \Phi Create \mid ErrCreation \land OkCreation \bullet$
$(fresh = \bot \land \theta OBJECT_1' = error) \lor (fresh \neq \bot \land id_1' = fresh)$
$\Leftrightarrow$ [lemma 1.2.3.3]
$\forall \Phi Create \mid ErrCreation \land OkCreation \bullet$
$(fresh = \bot \land fresh \in from.known \land \theta OBJECT_1' = error)$
$\lor (fresh \neq \bot \land fresh \notin from.known \land id_1' = fresh)$
$\Leftrightarrow$ [lemma 1.2.3.2 & $\Xi OBJstate$ & $to.known = from.known \cup \{\ fresh\ \}$]
$\forall \Phi Create \mid ErrCreation \land OkCreation \bullet$
$(\ fresh = \bot \land to.known = from.known$
$\land\ to.created \lhd HasId = from.created \lhd HasId\ )$
$\lor (\ fresh \neq \bot \land to.known \setminus from.known = \{\ id_1'\ \} \land$
$to.created \lhd HasId \setminus from.created \lhd HasId = \{\ \theta OBJECT_1' \mapsto id_1'\ \}\ )$
$\Rightarrow$ [bijection properties]
$\forall \Phi Create \mid ErrCreation \land OkCreation \bullet$
$(\ from.created \lhd HasId \in from.created \rightarrowtail\!\!\!\!\!\twoheadrightarrow from.known$
$\Rightarrow to.created \lhd HasId \in to.created \rightarrowtail\!\!\!\!\!\twoheadrightarrow to.known\ )$
$\lor (\ from.created \lhd HasId \in from.created \rightarrowtail\!\!\!\!\!\twoheadrightarrow from.known$
$\Rightarrow to.created \lhd HasId \in to.created \rightarrowtail\!\!\!\!\!\twoheadrightarrow to.known\ )$
$\Leftrightarrow$ [*Creation* definition & predicate laws]

$$\begin{array}{l}
\forall \mathit{Creation} \bullet \\
\quad \mathit{from.created} \lhd \mathit{HasId} \in \mathit{from.created} \rightarrowtail \mathit{from.known} \\
\quad \Rightarrow \mathit{to.created} \lhd \mathit{HasId} \in \mathit{to.created} \rightarrowtail \mathit{to.known} \\
\Leftrightarrow \qquad\qquad [\text{ lemma } 1.2.3.1] \\
\forall \mathit{Creation} \bullet \mathit{IdUniqueness}
\end{array}$$

□

Lastly, the induction step (obligation) of the proof is written as follows:

Lemma 1.3 (induction step)

$$\forall p : \mathbb{F}_1\{ \mathit{IdUniqueness} \} \bullet \mathit{Rules}\ p \subseteq \{ \mathit{IdUniqueness} \}$$

Due to space limitations (already quite overflown), the proof is omitted.

6 Concluding remarks

Z schemas were precious in obtaining a highly hierarchical description of the semantics. The structure of the specification mirrors the two different conceptual levels present in the language: internal working of objects and system behaviour of a collection of objects. A clear separation of concerns in the description is achieved through the use of schema frames. Take the assignment axiom (section 4.2.1) for instance: Φ*Store_Update* is focussed on the abstract machine move as *Assign* deals with the syntactical transformation. Readers may feel that schemas and related mathematical notations render descriptions harder and longer. Indeed, **Z** enforces that everything is said. Specifications are therefore verbose.

We are quite sure that inadequacies would be revealed by the undone proofs. This would only confirm our weakness in dealing with complex systems and strengthen our belief that formal methods are needed even if their use seems to complicate things. Tools are needed. The type checker was of great help. A theorem prover would be highly appreciated.

Another advantage of using **Z** lies in subsequent developments of the specified semantics. For instance, a graph of object dependencies can be defined (easily due to the labelling we chose) and used to specify the garbage collector or to identify localities among objects, all within the same notational framework. Changes in the language can be analyzed by formal transformations of its current specification.

Future work will investigate the idea of LTS refinements. In a very prospective way, a refinement of a LTS, say $\mathcal{S}$, would be a LTS, say $\mathcal{S}'$ such that there exists a foward simulation between them and the configurations of $\mathcal{S}'$ are refinements of $\mathcal{S}$'s. This relation among LTS is expected to be useful in the formal development of distributed systems and the stepwise implementation of programming languages. Lastly, the LaTeX source of the (*f*UZZ) reusable tool–kit for writing labelled transition systems is available from the author.

Acknowledgements I thank the programme committee for asking for the proof section. I ignore if it is what they expected. I am grateful to the anonymous referees for their finding of technical errors in the first submission. I acknowledge IRISA's support for this work . Lastly, I thank the members of the LSP team for many interesting discussions.

References

[1] G. Plotkin, "A structural approach to operational semantics," Department of computer science research report DAIMI FN-19, Aarhus University, Aarhus C, Denmark., Sept. 1981.

[2] W. Li, *An Operational Approach to Semantics and Translation for Concurrent Programming Languages.* PhD thesis, University of Edinburgh, 1982.

[3] I. Hayes, ed., *Specification Case Studies.* Prentice-Hall International, 1987. (contributions by B. Flinn, R. Gimson, C. Morgan, I. Sørensen and B. Sufrin).

[4] J. Spivey, *The Z Notation: A Reference Manual.* Prentice-Hall International, 1989.

[5] M. Benveniste, "Operational semantics of a distributed object-oriented language and its Z formal specification," Rapport de recherche 1230, INRIA, May 1990.

[6] P. America, "POOL-T: a parallel object-oriented language," in *[13]*, pp. 199–220, 1987.

[7] P. America, J. de Bakker, J. Kok, and J. Rutten, "Operational semantics of a parallel object-oriented language," in *13th Symposium on Principles of Programming Languages*, (St. Petersburg, Florida), pp. 194–208, 1986.

[8] P. America, J. de Bakker, J. Kok, and J. Rutten, "Denotational semantics of a parallel object-oriented language," *Information and Computation*, vol. 83, pp. 194–208, Nov. 1989.

[9] J.P. Banâtre, M. Banâtre, and F. Ployette, "The concept of multi-function: A general structuring tool for distributed operating systems," in *6th Conference on Distributed Computing Systems*, (Cambridge, Mass.), pp. 478–485, May 1986.

[10] P. Lecler, "Une approche de la programmation des systèmes distribués fondée sur la fragmentation des données et des calculs, et sa mise en œuvre dans le système GOTHIC.," thèse, Université de Rennes-I, Sept. 1989.

[11] M. Benveniste and V. Issarny, "Modèle de programmation," in *[14]*, pp. 17–41, 1991.

[12] J. Spivey, *Understanding Z: A specification language and its formal semantics.* No. 3 in Cambridge Tracts in Theoretical Computer Science, Cambridge University Press, 1988.

[13] A. Yonezawa and M. Tokoro, eds., *Object-Oriented Concurrent Programming.* Computer Systems, MIT Press, 1987.

[14] J.P. Banâtre and M. Banâtre, *Les systèmes distribués : l'expérience du système* GOTHIC. InterEditions, 1991.

EZ: A System for Automatic Prototyping of Z Specifications

Veronika Doma and Robin Nicholl[1]
Computer Science Department
The University of Western Ontario
London, Ontario
CANADA N6A 5B7

Abstract

Prototyping formal specifications can help capture accurately the requirements of real-world problems. We present a software system, called EZ, that generates executable prototypes directly from certain Z specifications. We first describe how nonmodular Z specifications can be mapped to search systems in C-Prolog. We then add modularity (schema referencing) and other features. A short comparison is made to other existing Z prototyping systems, with possibilities for future work being suggested.

1 Introduction

The goal of software engineering is to capture requirements of real-world problems in the form of programs that can be executed. For a particular problem, this process can involve several stages. In the earliest stage, or design process, a specifier may gather information about the problem and transfer this information to a non-procedural description, or *specification*, of the required input and output behaviour. An implementor may then convert the information in the specification to an executable program.

It is important that the implemented program be consistent with the specification, and that the specification be consistent with the real-world requirements. However, errors in understanding information and errors in encoding information are possible, and they can have serious ramifications. *Testing* of the implemented program helps to ensure that it is consistent with an implementor's understanding of a given specification. Also, *proving correctness* helps to ensure that the program is consistent with, or satisfies, its specification. These are methods for increasing confidence in the correctness of the *implementation* process. *Prototyping* a specification before the implementation process is begun can increase confidence in the design process.

Rather than refining a high-level description until it can be implemented efficiently, prototyping involves making a single mapping from a specification to a non-optimized implementation that exhibits the essential features of the specification. Viewing the execution of a prototype of an intended system can help a specifier to define and understand a real-word problem clearly, thus strengthening the correspondence between the true requirements of the desired system and its specification (see Figure 1). As does [3], we call the process of displaying the execution of a prototype *animation*.

[1]authors' email addresses: veru@csd.uwo.ca, robin@csd.uwo.ca

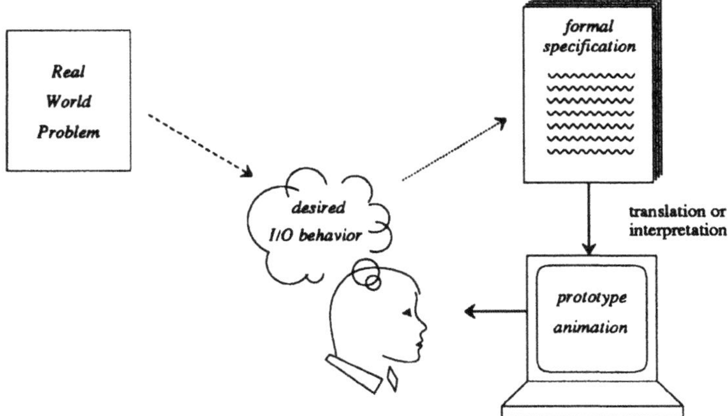

Figure 1: **Increasing the accuracy of transfer of user requirements to concrete specification**: Animation of prototypes generated from a specification can help capture accurately the requirements of a real-word problem by giving feedback about the properties of the specification.

Since specifications can be easier and less costly to modify than implemented systems, prototyping a specification is also likely to save development time. This is especially true if the prototypes are created automatically via some consistent mechanical translation method. If the "distance" between the non-procedural specification language and the executable prototyping language is not very large, and if the prototype is not required to perform efficiently, then *automatic* prototyping from a formal specification language is feasible. Unfortunately, the expressiveness of many specification languages makes them undecidable, making it impossible to determine whether any particular animation will terminate. Nevertheless, prototypes that do terminate can provide useful information.

We chose the name EZ (for *executing Z*) for our prototyping system. Z has two powerful features which make it concise and intuitive to use. The first of these we call *modularity* in this paper[2], which allows the organization of components of a specification into chunks, or *schemas*, and allows referencing of these schemas from other schemas. The second of these is called the *schema calculus*, which allows expressions to be formed over schemas involving logical and compositional operators. Section 4 shows a method of implementing modularity and operators of the schema calculus, as well as other important features of Z, by first mapping Z specifications to search systems in Prolog and then extending these search systems with features that Prolog provides. Section 5 describes an implementation of the EZ system based on these findings.

There has been previous success in animating Z with Prolog. In the Alvey Project SuZan [3, 10, 8, 9], Z is translated into Prolog semi-automatically and some specifications can be executed based on an extensive library of Prolog primitives that have been implemented. A generate-and-test method is used to generate variable values and test constraints over them. The direct execution of the resulting Prolog is very slow and

[2]This term is not to be confused with that of modularity in [13], which proposes some (more) modular extensions to Z .

transformations are made to increase execution efficiency before animation. Todd uses Z to specify a medical diagnostic problem and is successful in the implementation of a small prototype of this specification based on a hand-translation of his specification also into Prolog [17]. His system is slow, but acceptable in comparison to the length of time taken by hospital tests. King also maps Z specifications to Prolog (by hand) to animate them [6]. His prototypes execute more efficiently than those produced by the SuZan system, but more restrictions are made on the expressiveness of the Z notation that can be translated.

Though SuZan has a large library of primitives [8] and King's work executes quickly, none of the above systems have achieved as much success automating modularity and operators of the schema calculus as EZ, as far as we are aware. A comparison of EZ to previous systems is presented and directions for future work are suggested in section 6.

2 Example Problem

To provide a running example for the paper, we chose a simple robot navigation problem, depicted in Figure 2 and described below. Though not a typical systems specification, this problem illustrates the basic concepts of a model-oriented specification.

> **Informal description of a robot navigation problem:**
> A robot must navigate from a position (0,0) to a remote building at position (6,4) in a city which has streets all running in a north-south or east-west direction. All east-west roads have dead-ends on the east side.

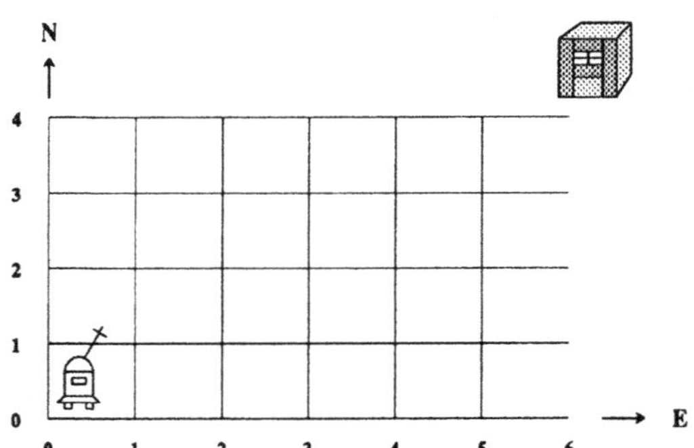

Figure 2: A simple robot navigation problem

For this problem, we may model the internal state as an ordered pair of x and y coordinates that represents the current location. We may view each operation as a relation between two particular states. Let E represent an operation of moving in the right-hand direction, and N represent an operation of moving upwards. The following shows a specification of this problem in Z with no schema referencing. *EastMove* and *NorthMove* are two possible operations on the internal state. *Init* and *Final* define the initial and final configurations of the internal state.

Init

$x, y : \mathbb{Z}$

$x = 0 \land y = 0$

Final

$x, y : \mathbb{Z}$

$x = 6 \land y = 4$

EastMove

$x, y, x', y' : \mathbb{Z}$

$x < 6 \land y \leq 4$
$x' = x + 1$
$y' = y$

NorthMove

$x, y, x', y' : \mathbb{Z}$

$x \leq 6 \land y < 4$
$x' = x$
$y' = y + 1$

3 Mapping Model-Oriented Specifications to AI Search Systems

Formal specifications are generally expressed as a set of operations to be implemented, together with some definition of the behaviour of each operation, giving *static* views of problems of interest. In particular, operators of model-oriented specifications describe relations between two state configurations, with no notion of time being necessary. However, to animate a specification, it must somehow be made dynamic. As in [3] and [6], we propose to *animate* the behaviour of individual operators by displaying the internal state components at a time t_i, before the operation takes place, and at time t_{i+1} after the operation has occurred. It would also be helpful to animate sequences of operators being applied at times $t_i \ldots t_n$. To achieve this, we propose to map Z specifications to AI search systems [1] and execute them via their *control systems*.

The major elements of an AI problem solving search system are one or more databases that comprise a global database, a set of rules or operators, and a control system. The global database is the central data structure used by the system and its possible configurations defines the state space. The rules operate on the global database, and the control system chooses rules to apply and applies them. We can map a description of the model of the internal state to the global database of the search system, map the operators to the operators of the search system, map the initial and final states to those of the search system, and animate individual operators and sequences of operators by selecting rules and applying them to the internal state with the control system.

Two kinds of control strategies for problem solving search systems are *tentative*, or noncommittal, and *irrevocable* [12]. With a tentative control strategy, alternative sequences of operators can be found, while with an irrevocable strategy, once an operator is applied, there is no provision made for returning to and proceeding from an earlier state. For example, with an irrevocable control strategy that prefers choosing *EastMove* over *NorthMove*, once the robot reaches (6,0), it will not be able to navigate further. However, with a tentative control strategy, it may be able to backtrack from (6,0) to (5,0) and proceed to the final state. While a tentative control strategy is memory intensive, it provides more informative animation. For instance, as a test for the safety of the set of operators of a specification, we could specify a final state to be an unsafe one, and test if it can be reached from an initial, or known reachable, state.

4 Mapping Z Specifications to Prolog Search Systems

The programming language Prolog provides the essentials for a tentative control system via its backtracking capability. Moreover, Prolog is based on first-order logic, which is the language of the predicate part of schemas. We show that there is a straightforward mapping of nonmodular Z specifications to AI search systems in Prolog. We continue by developing extensions to this mapping and show how a larger subset of Z, including schema referencing and some operators of the schema calculus, can be treated. The dialect of Prolog of our examples is C-Prolog.

A Prolog program consists of a set of clauses with one predicate on the left-hand side and zero or more on the right-hand side. We note that we can map schemas (as does SuZan) to Prolog in the following way:

- Map the name of the schema to the name of the Prolog predicate on the LHS.
- Make the arguments of this predicate those variables declared in the signature part.
- Map the Z predicates from the predicate part to the RHS of each clause.

We defer consideration of mapping the signature predicates of a schema to type checking predicates until section 4.2.

In mapping predicates, we cannot straightforwardly map the $=$ symbol in Z to the `=` symbol in Prolog. This is because Prolog's `=` operator checks for mere *syntactic* equality. However, the `is` predicate evaluates the expression on the right-hand side before checking for syntactic equality. It is restricted in that there can be only one argument on the left-hand side of an expression and it only works for arithmetic, but for now we will use `is` in this manner because of its simplicity. Hence, the following shows a possible mapping of the specification of section 2 into Prolog:

```
eastmove(X,Y,X2,Y2)     :- X < 6, Y =< 4, X2 is X + 1, Y2 is Y.
northmove(X,Y,X2,Y2)    :- X =< 6, Y < 4, X2 is X, Y2 is Y + 1.
init(X,Y)               :- X is 0, Y is 0.
final(X,Y)              :- X is 6, Y is 4.
```

4.1 Adding a Control System

A control system must know what the global state is, what the initial and final states are, and what the operators are. For the robot example, the parameters of the global state are x and y, which signify the robot's position. One possible way of determining what the initial states and operators are would be to type them in as a query to Prolog:

```
| ?- init(X,Y), eastmove(X,Y,X2,Y2).
| ?- eastmove(2,3,X2,Y2).
```

This strategy is an irrevocable one in which the user selects the operator to apply and also the particular state to apply it to. A tentative forward chaining control system would be provided by the following:

```
apply_rule(X,Y,X2,Y2) :- eastmove(X,Y,X2,Y2); northmove(X,Y,X2,Y2).
animate               :- init(X,Y), transitions(X,Y).
transitions(X,Y)      :- final(X,Y);
                         apply_rule(X,Y,X2,Y2), transitions(X2,Y2).
```

This control system would attempt to apply the rules in a depth-first order. The search space will be traversed in the manner shown in Figure 3. During execution the state components can be displayed by including a displaying predicate in `transitions`. Also, a predicate for checking if a state has already been visited could be added to prevent infinite cycles from occurring during animation. (See [4, 5]).

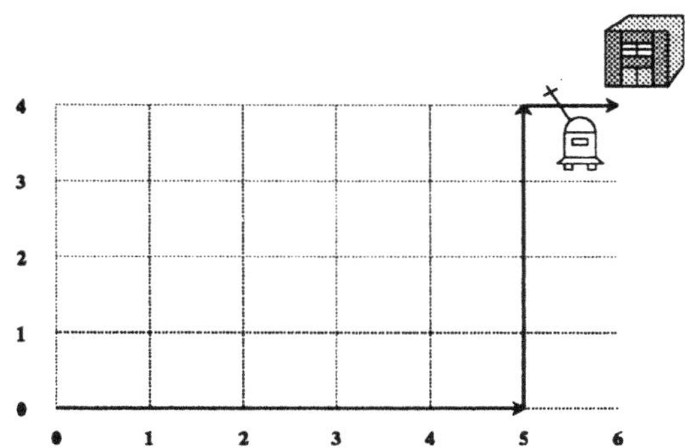

Figure 3: Depth-first traversal of search space.

By adding a variable to the predicate `animate`, for instance the anonymous variable:

```
animate(_)            :- init(X,Y), transitions(X,Y).
```

we also add the possibility of successively finding different search paths using Prolog's "retry" command (;) during execution. This gives us more complete information about the properties of the specification.

4.2 Constraint Satisfaction

The predicate part of a schema defines constraints over components of the internal state. We need a way to determine whether these constraints can be satisfied. For example, the schema *Init* can be defined equivalently as

$$\begin{array}{|l}\hline \textit{Init2} \\ x, y : \textit{integer} \\ \hline 0 = x + y \\ x \geq 0 \land y \geq 0 \\ \hline \end{array}$$

The three predicates of the predicate part uniquely determine x and y to have the value 0. However, Prolog is not able to conclude this result if *Init*2 were directly translated to:

```
init2(X,Y)                  :- 0 is X + Y, X >= 0, Y >= 0.
```

The above would cause a run-time error due to the fact that `is` requires that `X` and `Y` be instantiated before adding them together, but these values cannot be known at least until evaluating the conditions `X >= 0` and `Y >= 0`, which would also cause a run-time error if their values are uninstantiated. The solution to this problem we have undertaken is that also undertaken by SuZan [3]: a brute-force *generate-and-test* method. Type definitions in the signature part of a schema can be mapped to predicates which generate values of the appropriate type which can then be tested by the predicates mapped from the predicate part of a schema:

```
eastmove(X,Y,X2,Y2)      :- int(X), int(Y), int(X2), int(Y2),
                            X < 6, Y =< 4, X2 is X + 1, Y2 is Y.
```

It is important that the generation occur *before* testing; otherwise Prolog will encounter the same run-time error as described above.

This method also ensures that type constraints defined in the signature part of schemas are enforced – only values of the appropriate type can be generated. Unfortunately, it requires that variables be restricted to finite domains due to Prolog's depth-first search method. Indeed, it requires that variables be restricted to very small domains to prevent search spaces from becoming prohibitively large. For this example, we can restrict the domain *integer* to the set $\{0, 1, 2, 3, 4, 5, 6\}$ as we know that the robot will not be required to navigate beyond $(6, 4)$. The following will generate integers in this set:

```
int(X) :- member(X,[0,1,2,3,4,5,6]).
```

The generate-and-test method does have an advantage that can make our translation task easier. It allows us to simplify the translation of expressions because we know that all values will be instantiated when required for execution. Instead of using the `is` predicate to enforce evaluation of expressions and translating an expression such as $(x - y)/4 = 2 * x'$ to `V1 is X - Y, V2 is V1/4, V3 is 2 * X2, V2 = V3,` we can use Prolog's *operator* definitions and simply translate the expression to `equals((X - Y)/4, 2 * X')`, where `equals` is defined `equals(LHS,RHS) :- eval(LHS,V), eval(RHS,V),` and where the `eval` predicate is recursively defined to evaluate nested arithmetic expressions.

4.3 Schema Referencing

One of the strengths of the Z notation is that schemas have a referencing, or modular, capability. For example, for the robot specification we can separate out the components of the internal state and its invariants in a schema with name *Location*.

```
┌─ Location ─────────────────
│ x, y : integer
├──────────
│ 0 ≤ x ∧ x ≤ 6
│ 0 ≤ y ∧ y ≤ 4
└────────────────────────────
```

Init and *Final* can now refer to this state definition by including the name *Location* in their signature parts:

```
┌─ Init ─────────────────────
│ Location
├──────────
│ x = 0 ∧ y = 0
└────────────────────────────

┌─ Final ────────────────────
│ Location
├──────────
│ x = 6 ∧ y = 4
└────────────────────────────
```

Likewise, the operations can refer to two copies of *Location*; one for unprimed variables and one for primed variables:

```
┌─ EastMove ─────────────────
│ Location
│ Location'
├──────────
│ x' = x + 1
│ y' = y
└────────────────────────────

┌─ NorthMove ────────────────
│ Location
│ Location'
├──────────
│ x' = x
│ y' = y + 1
└────────────────────────────
```

Now we have two kinds of constructs in the signature part of schemas: type declarations and/or schema names. We can extend the translation procedure to simply map schema names in the signature part of schemas to predicates with corresponding names:

```
init(X,Y)              :- location(X,Y), equals(X,0), equals(Y,0).
eastmove(X,Y,X2,Y2)    :- location(X,Y), location(X2,Y2),
                          equals(X2,X+1), equals(Y2,Y).
```

Mapping modular specifications to clauses as above is, however, no longer a straightforward matter; it is necessary to find the variables that correspond to schema names that are referenced, or "imported", and place them wherever these schemas names are used. All variables that need to be accessed by imported predicates must be passed to these predicates by explicitly including them in all predicates that call the remote predicates. In this case, the variables x and y of the schema *Location* are declared only in the schema *Location*, but must be included as arguments of all the instances of the predicate `location` and in all of the predicates that call `location`.

One way to find these variables is to implement a two-pass translator: one pass to *flatten*, or unfold, a modular specification, or to create an internal data structure of schema names and associated variables, and a second pass to output the clauses as above.

If we find a way of implementing global variables in Prolog, however, a simpler single-pass translation is possible. A brute-force method of implementing such global variables is to give as arguments to each schema predicate a variable that stores all global variable names and their (possibly) instantiated values (in a list, say). Then, for each variable listed in the predicate part of the schema predicate, a look-up from the global-list of the schema predicate would be required before execution of the predicate. This would introduce some run-time inefficiency, but the extra time required to lookup each variable is insignificant compared to the possible combinatorial explosion caused by increasing the size of the domain of a variable.

In Z specifications of sequential systems [15], there are really *two* sets of variables at any time during execution: the variables that define the current state configuration, and the variables that define the next state configuration. So, for example, we could replace the arguments of the schema predicates of the previous example with merely two variables, say `S` and `S2`, and provide a look-up predicate, say `lookup`, for every variable from the predicate part of of the schema. The look-up would require reference to both the *name* of a variable and to its *value*. The name of the variable can be obtained by containing it within quote symbols[3]. For unprimed variables look-up would occur from `S`, while for primed variables this would occur from `S2`. For example:

```
location(S,S2)       :- int(X), int(Y),
                        lookup(S,'X'/X), lookup(S,'Y'/Y),
                        lequals(0,X), lequals(X,6),
                        lequals(0,Y), lequals(Y,4).
eastmove(S,S2)       :- location(S,S2), location(S2,_),
                        lookup(S,'X'/X), lookup(S,'Y'/Y),
                        lookup(S2,'X'/X2), lookup(S2,'Y'/Y2),
                        equals(X2,X+1), equals(Y2,Y).
```

We shift the names of the variables `(S,S2)` to `(S2,_)` for primed schema names such as *location* in **eastmove**. Schemas that do not have primed variables are still given both arguments, `(S,S2)`. This eliminates the need for a translator to make the distinction between state schemas and operator schemas — the variable `S2` for state schemas is simply ignored at run-time.

The `lookup` predicate can now be implemented:

```
lookup(List,Pair)          :- once_member(Pair,List).
once_member(X/Y,[X/Y|T])   :- !.
once_member(X/Y,[X/Z|T])   :- not(Y = Z), !, fail.
once_member(X/Y,[H/H2|T])  :- not(X = H), once_member(X/Y,T).
```

A useful side-effect of this definition is that the first time a variable is looked up, it is added to the look-up list. The second clause disallows a variable name to have more than one value, as in, for example, the list `['X'/4, 'Y'/3, 'X'/2]`.

[3]C-Prolog interprets capitalized names as variables. Putting quote symbols around Z variable names ensures that they are interpreted as constants.

4.4 The Δ Prefix

It is conventional to use the prefix Δ to abbreviate a reference to two copies of a state configuration, one for the current configuration, and one for the primed configuration. For example, *Location* $\wedge$ *Location'* can be abbreviated to Δ*Location* and the *EastMove* schema can be represented:

```
┌─ EastMove ──────────────────
│ ΔLocation
├────────────
│ x' = x + 1
│ y' = y
└─────────────────────────────
```

With an implementation of global variables, Δ can easily be implemented with the `call` predicate as follows:

```
delta(X) :- X =.. [Name,S,S2], call(X), X2 =.. [Name, S2, _], call(X2).
```

The `=..` predicate is used to extract the argument `S2` from the arguments of `X` in order to make it an argument of `X2` as well. Now we can map the new version of *EastMove* to

```
eastmove(S,S2)    :- delta(location(S,S2)),
                     lookup(S,'X'/X), lookup(S,'Y'/Y),
                     lookup(S2,'X'/X2), lookup(S2,'Y'/Y2),
                     equals(X2,X+1), equals(Y2,Y).
```

4.5 Boolean Connectives and Sequential Composition

Suppose we wanted to specify a set of possible operations with a schema

$$PossibleMove \;\widehat{=}\; EastMove \vee WestMove \vee NorthMove.$$

Now that we have a method for simulating global variables, we do not need to know the variables of these schema names when we come across them with a translator. We can simply translate the above to:

```
possiblemove(S,S2) :- eastmove(S,S2); westmove(S,S2); northmove(S,S2).
```

The $\vee$ symbol is translated to the semi-colon (;), C-Prolog's disjunction symbol. We can similarly translate the $\wedge$ operator to the comma (,).

The Z sequential composition operator is $⨟$ — it allows a single schema operator to be created from two sub-operations. With $⨟$ one can specify a specific (sub)traversal of the search space, for instance, $LeapNorth \;\widehat{=}\; NorthMove ⨟ NorthMove ⨟ NorthMove$. We could translate such a schema to the following:

```
leapnorth(S,S2) :- northmove(S,S3), northmove(S3,S4), northmove(S4,S2).
```

4.6 The Control System Revisited

The following modification of the tentative forward chaining Prolog control system described in section 4.1 would now produce a forward chaining control system to animate the translated Z components:

```
animate          :- init(S,_), transitions(S).
transitions(S)   :- final(S,_); possible_rule(S,S2), transitions(S2).
```

When **animate** is called, Prolog will cause an initial state to be instantiated and transitions to be made by applying one of the possible rules until the final state is satisfied. The predicate **init** must refer to the initial state, **final** to the final state, and **possible_rule** to the set of possible applicable rules.

A backward chaining control system would also be possible:

```
animate          :- final(S,_), transitions(S).
transitions(S)   :- init(S,_); possible_rule(S2,S), transitions(S2).
```

Such a control system could be useful in determining if particular states are reachable from a set of operators. For example, if *Final* refers to an unsafe state and *Init* refers to any known reachable state, then if backward chaining is successful in reaching *Init* we can conclude that our specification is unsafe.

5 EZ Implementation

The implementation of EZ is based on the discussion in section 4. The language of implementation is C-Prolog and a generate-and-test method of constraint satisfaction is used. Schema-referencing or modularity is implemented according to the method described in section 4.3. The Δ prefix and boolean schema connectives are implemented according to the methods described in sections 4.4 and 4.5, although the sequential composition operator is not yet implemented. Including a forward or backward chaining control system as described in section 4.6 results in a control system for the animator. (These can actually be written in Z-like notation and translated into the Prolog form [4, 5].)

We decided to use a public domain LaTeX [11] syntax for formatting and translating Z specifications [14, 7]. Since a LaTeX document includes text and macros that are informal explanations of the formal Z specification, they need to be removed before prototyping — this task is done automatically with a preprocessor. The translator, written in C-Prolog, is very simple (although not highly efficient) due to the similarity of our target syntax to the syntax of the input language. Input of a specification to the translator results in a Prolog prototype. The prototype is animated by running it in an environment that includes a library of implementations of primitive Z language constructs. Figure 4 sketches the components of EZ and their interaction.

To begin animation, a user types in the name of a schema from the names of all the schemas of the original specification that are listed. Typing the name of a schema will cause EZ to try to find a consistent instantiation of that schema given the current domain restrictions. If it succeeds, it will allow the user to find other possible instantiations and thus give him or her a more complete animation of the schema. Both irrevocable

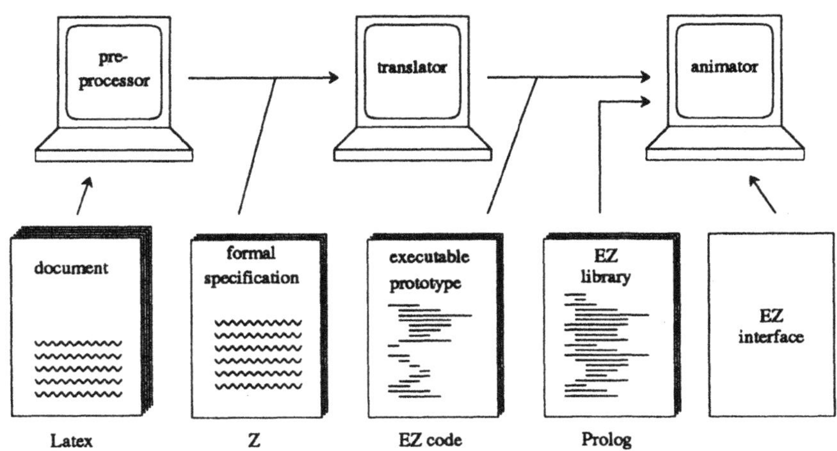

Figure 4: **The EZ System**: Three programs, a preprocessor, a translator, and an animator comprise the system components. A user may send a LaTeX document to the preprocessor, send its output to the translator, and then animate the result with an animator that has access to built-in primitives.

and tentative control strategies are also possible: the user may save a particular state configuration and continue, or allow the animator to automatically select a sequence of operators to apply.

Currently, the built-in types or domains are *integer*, *natural number*, and *character* along with *sequences* over these domains. Because the speed at which the animator runs depends on the search space it must traverse at any particular query, the animator allows a user to make domain restrictions before animation in order to help keep the search space at a manageable size.

6 Concluding Remarks

Feedback about the behaviour of eventual implementations of given specifications enables us to modify and refine them until we are confident that our requirements are met. A tool to help capture precisely and completely intended requirements before the implementation process is begun can prove very useful — once programs are written, requirement changes are much costlier. The EZ translator maps Z specifications into AI search systems in Prolog and then the EZ animator interprets them based on Prolog definitions of primitives from its library. A listing of features of EZ and those of other systems that have also mapped Z to Prolog is summarized in Table 1.

A weakness of all of these systems is that they do not provide a method for handling quantifiers, thus greatly limiting the expressiveness of the specifications that can be animated. King's implementation is even more restrictive — he restricts the interpretation of the "=" predicate and thus restricts all predicates in the predicate part of schemas to be essentially procedural assignment statements. Also, there is no general treatment of axiomatic or type definitions, and all animators must rely on some library of built-in

	King (1988)	**SuZan** (1990)	**EZ** (1991)
support tools	**implemented**: simple animator **proposed:** preprocessor, translator generator	**implemented**: editor, translator, transformation system **under development**: animator, graphical specification presenter	**implemented**: preprocessor, translator, simple animator
primitive types	sequences, sets, user defined types	finite sets, relations, functions, sequences, strings	bounded sequences, integers, strings
primitive operators	arithmetic, sequence, operators, operators over finite sets	arithmetic, sequence, set operators, operators over functions and relations	arithmetic, sequence operators
predicates over primitive types	$= \neq$	set relations, $=, \neq, \geq, \leq, <, >$	$=, \neq, \geq, \leq, <, >,$
predicate connectives	$\Rightarrow, \wedge, \vee$	$\wedge, \vee, \neg$	$\wedge, \vee, \neg$
quantifiers	none	none	none
constraint satisfaction method	none: predicate part limited to assignment and simple (in)equality test	generate-and-test	generate-and-test
modularity or schema referencing	referencing of *state* schemas	method suggested for both state and operators	both state and operators
schema connectives	none	$\neg, \wedge, \vee$	$\neg, \wedge, \vee,$ method suggested for $\fatsemi$
axiomatic definitions	no	method suggested	no
generic schemas	no	method suggested	no
control system	user chooses next rule to apply; irrevocable	user chooses next rule to apply and types in values of components of state configuration to apply it to	user may choose forward chaining or backward chaining control system, or make revocable choices via animator
case studies	alternating bit and preventative cyclic retransmission protocols	telephone network, lift system, vending machine, library system	convex hull problem

Table 1: Comparison of Z Animation Systems

predicates and types, with SuZan having the largest library (see Table 1) according to our references. If axiomatic and type definitions were translatable, then more flexibility in terms of specification "primitives" would be available, although it would be necessary to find a successful treatment of quantification as axiomatic definitions are often rich in quantifiers.

Obvious enhancements to EZ would be to extend the design of the implementation of the Δ prefix (as described in section 4.4) and implement the Ξ prefix so the specifier need not define Ξ schemas explicitly. A means of dealing with the sequential composition operator as described in section 4.5 should also be implemented. In implementing axiomatic definitions, we would also need to find a way to put a "hole" in the scope of schema variables with the same name as global variables [16, pp. 39-40].

A major shortcoming of EZ is that the generate-and-test constraint satisfaction solution causes the execution time of non-trivial specifications to be prohibitive. SuZan also has this problem, but provides a tool for transforming the programs generated by the translator into more efficient ones (see Table 1). Another possibility would be to add pruning to the search space by including logically equivalent but more efficient "assignment statement" versions of the predicates involving equality to the animator library, and then during animation executing as many assignment predicates as possible before executing their less efficient versions. Such pruning was added manually to make manageable our animation time of a specification of the convex hull problem [4, 5] and can be automated in a future version of EZ. Other possibilities would be to investigate the use of languages with built-in constraint satisfiers, such as those discussed in [2].

EZ's novel method for dealing with modularity by using a look-up list (section 4.3) made it unnecessary to "flatten" specifications to determine variable/schema bindings during translation to Prolog, and thus also simplified the implementation of schema connectives and the Δ prefix, as well as a that of a flexible control system. This method also gives a very strong syntactic correspondence between an EZ-generated Prolog program and its corresponding specification, allowing animation to follow closely a user's intuitive understanding of the specification being interpreted. It also presents possibilities for adding useful tracing features to the animator. Along with the method for implementing schema referencing, the generate-and-test method also makes the animator quite powerful: a user can select any schema from the translated specification and find one or all of its possible instantiations[4] without being required to know and type in the names of the state parameters pertinent to the schema.

In summary, we have implemented a system for animating the basic model-oriented constructs of a Z specification: states and operators, as well as schema referencing and schema combinators of the schema calculus. The translator is very simple, based on a close correspondence between Z and the target language, and the animator is powerful, allowing both irrevocable and tentative control strategies. By providing a tool for testing specifications against real world requirements, EZ contributes to the development of reliable and correct implementations — the end-product of the software development process.

[4]If a generate-and-test strategy is used, then limiting domains to finite sets can usually ensure that execution will halt (see [3] for pathological example), though not necessarily in reasonable time.

Acknowledgments

The helpful contributions made towards the preparation of this paper by Gilbert Verghese, Brian Nixon, Mike Godfrey, and John Tsotsos are gratefully acknowledged.

References

[1] A. Barr and E. A. Feigenbaum, editors. *The Handbook of Artificial Intelligence*, volume 1. William Kaufmann, Inc., 1981.

[2] J. Cohen. Constraint logic programming languages. *Communications of the ACM*, 33(7):52–68, July 1990.

[3] A. Dick, P. Krause, and J. Cozens. Computer aided transformation of Z into Prolog. *FACS FACTS, Series II*, 1(1):17–22, April 1990.

[4] V. Doma. EZ: A tool for automatic prototyping of Z specifications. MSc. Project Report, Computer Science Department, The University of Western Ontario, May 1991.

[5] V. Doma and R. Nicholl. Technical report on prototyping Z specifications with EZ. Computer Science Department, The University of Western Ontario, forthcoming 1991.

[6] P. King. Prototyping Z specifications. In G. Rose and I. Hayes, editors, *Second Half-yearly Report, UQ/OTC Collaborative Programme in Formal Description Techniques*, pages 5.1–5.23. Dept. of Computer Science, University of Queensland, February 1988.

[7] P. King. Printing Z and Object-Z LaTeX documents. A description of a public domain Z style option "oz.sty" for LaTeX , March 1990.

[8] R. Knott and P. J. Krause. Approach to animating Z using Prolog. Report A1.1, Alvey Project SE/065, Dept. Maths, University of Surrey, July 1988.

[9] R. Knott and P. J. Krause. Library system: An example of the rapid prototyping of a Z specification in Prolog. Report A1.2, Alvey Project SE/065, Dept. Maths, University of Surrey, June 1988.

[10] R. Knott and P. J. Krause. On the derivation of an effective animation: Telephone network case study. Report A1.3, Alvey Project SE/065, Dept. Maths, University of Surrey, November 1988.

[11] L. Lamport. *LATEX: A Document Preparation System*. Addison-Wesley, 1986.

[12] N. J. Nilsson. *Principles of Artificial Intelligence*. Tioga Publishing Co., 1980.

[13] A. Sampaio and S. Meira. Modular extensions to Z. In D. Bjorner, C. Hoare, and H. Langmaack, editors, *VDM '90, VDM and Z - Formal Methods in Software Development*, volume 428 of *Lecture Notes in Computer Science*. Springer-Verlag, 1990.

[14] J. M. Spivey. Printing Z with LaTeX . Programming Research Group, Oxford University, January 1987. A description of a public domain Z style option "zed.sty" for LaTeX .

[15] J. M. Spivey. *Understanding Z: A Specification Language and its Formal Semantics*, volume 3 of *Cambridge Tracts in Theoretical Computer Science*. Cambridge University Press, January 1988.

[16] J. M. Spivey. *The Z Notation: A Reference Manual*. International Series in Computer Science. Prentice-Hall, 1989.

[17] B. S. Todd. A model-based diagnostic program. *Software Engineering Journal*, 2(3):54–63, May 1987.

Z and high level Petri nets

K.M. van Hee L.J. Somers M. Voorhoeve

Department of Mathematics and Computing Science
Eindhoven University of Technology
Den Dolech 2, P.O. Box 513
5600 MB Eindhoven, the Netherlands
Email: wsinlou@win.tue.nl

Abstract

High level Petri nets have tokens with values, traditionally called colors, and transitions that produce tokens in a functional way, using the consumed tokens as arguments of the function application. Large nets should be designed in a top-down approach and therefore we introduce a hierarchical net model which combines a data flow diagram technique with a high level Petri net model. We use Z to specify this net model, which is in fact the metamodel for specific systems. Specific models we specify partly by diagrams and partly in Z. We give some advantages and disadvantages of using Z in this way. Finally we show how to specify systems by means of an example.

1 Introduction

The last years have shown a growing interest in the formal specification of distributed systems. Such a formal description should take care of the distribution aspects, the interaction between the distributed parts, the transitions between successive states of the system and the state space itself.

Petri nets, see e.g. [Jensen 91], have been used for quite a while to specify concurrent distributed systems. These nets have been augmented recently by a hierarchy to allow a systematic top-down design of a system specification. Such a design method is very similar to the common (informal) use of data flow diagrams [Yourdon 89].

Colored nets make it possible to attach values to tokens. For the specification of these values and the functionality of the transitions one needs a specification language. Usually a functional language is used for the specification of the transition functions. Recently, a few tools have been developed that offer hierarchical colored Petri nets as a specification formalism, cf. [Albrecht 89] and [Hee 89]. Our tool, ExSpect, is based upon a hierarchical timed net model and a functional language. This system has been in use for two years and we have gained a lot of experience in practical applications, e.g. [Aalst 90].

On the other hand, formalisms like Z and VDM are used frequently to specify reactive systems. They do not have mechanisms for treating concurrency and distribution in a straightforward way. However, a formalism like Z seems to be very well suited to specify the transitions in a colored Petri net, thereby replacing the functional language normally used.

There have been more attempts to integrate Z with graphical languages for the description of distributed systems. For instance, for HOOD such an integration is considered. In [Giovanni 90] it is noted that an integration with Petri nets is a point of research.

In the next sections we will use Z in two ways. Firstly for defining what a hierarchical Petri net is (section 2) and secondly for the specification of the state transitions of a Petri net (section 3). We will follow the notation of [Spivey 89]; if not we make a remark.

2 Hierarchical net model

Here we introduce the hierarchical net model that is being used in ExSpect [Hee 89] and that is closely related to hierarchical CP-nets [Jensen 91]. First, we define so called *flat nets*, which are in fact ordinary colored Petri nets. Then we define ***hierarchical nets*** and show how such a net determines a flat net.

We use the Z notation for the above definitions, thereby showing that Z is not only useful for modeling specific systems, but also for defining metamodels or model types. As observed in [Diepen 90], Z schemas can be interpreted as implicitly defined tables. So, if we give a schema for the net model, every flat net corresponds to one and only one element or tuple of the table determined by the schema.

2.1 Flat nets

A flat net has four basic types

$$[\mathit{Place}, \mathit{Transition}, \mathit{Connection}, \mathit{Value}].$$

The state of a flat net is determined by objects called *tokens*. Tokens reside at a place, an element of the type *Place*, and have a value belonging to the type *Value*. State changes are caused by transitions, elements of the type *Transition*. A transition can *fire*, consuming tokens from a specific set of places and producing tokens for another (not necessarily disjoint) set of places. A transition has a set of input and a set of output connections (elements of the type *Connection*). Connections are used to connect transitions to places.

A *flat net structure* is a directed labeled bipartite graph with places and transitions as nodes and connections as arcs. Traditionally, places are represented by circles and transitions by rectangles (cf. figure 1).

A flat net structure is defined by the following schema

FlatNetStructure

$P : \mathbb{P}\,\mathit{Place}$
$T : \mathbb{P}\,\mathit{Transition}$
$I : \mathit{Transition} \nrightarrow \mathbb{P}\,\mathit{Connection}$
$O : \mathit{Transition} \nrightarrow \mathbb{P}\,\mathit{Connection}$
$M : \mathit{Connection} \nrightarrow \mathit{Place}$

$\mathrm{dom}(I) = \mathrm{dom}(O) = T \land$
$(\bigcup \mathrm{rng}(I)) \cap (\bigcup \mathrm{rng}(O)) = \mathrm{dom}(M) \land$
$\mathrm{rng}(M) = P \land$
$\forall t_1, t_2 : T \mid t_1 \neq t_2 \bullet I(t_1) \cap I(t_2) = O(t_1) \cap O(t_2) = I(t_1) \cap O(t_2) = I(t_1) \cap O(t_1) = \emptyset$

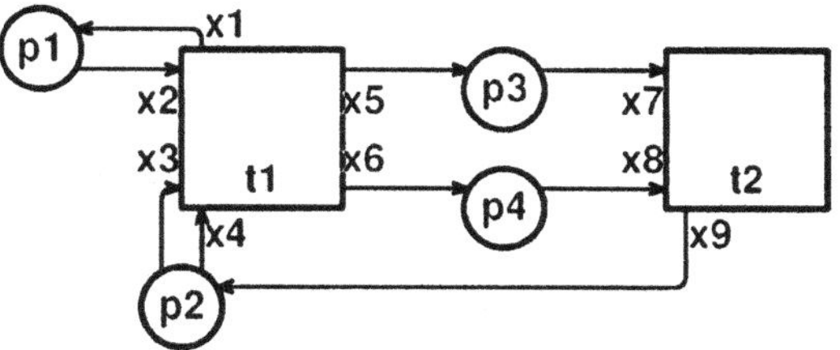

Figure 1: An example of a Petri net.

A net is determined by a set of places P, a set of transitions T, two functions I and O that assign to each transition t a set of connections through which it *consumes* tokens ($I(t)$) and a set of connections through which it *produces* tokens ($O(t)$). Each connection is assigned to a place [Hee 91]. So, when a transition t fires, it consumes as many tokens from a place as there are connections of $I(t)$ assigned to it. Furthermore, it produces for each connection in $O(t)$ one token or none, so if there are n connections in $O(t)$ assigned to a place, t may produce any number of tokens between 0 and n for this place. The last condition in the schema states that all connections are unique. In practice, we require only that connections between the same place and transition with the same direction have different labels. In that case we augment the label with a pair (t,p) for output connections and (p,t) for input connections (where t and p are the transition and the place involved) to obtain a unique label.

It is easy to define an instance of the type FlatNetStructure that describes e.g. the graph of fig. 1.

The flat net structure describes only the *static* aspects of a net model. The *dynamics* of such a model are described by an (unlabeled) *transition system.* Such a transition system has a state space S and a binary relation Tr over S. Each pair of Tr corresponds to a possible state transition of the whole system. In fact the transition system of the net model may be considered as an *operational semantics* of the flat net structure.

We define a derived type called *State*,

$$State == Place \nrightarrow (Value \nrightarrow \mathbb{N}).$$

So a state is a mapping that assigns to places a function counting the number of tokens per value. (Note that this function does not represent a bag since we allow numbers to be zero; however it is equivalent to one.)

For each place in a net structure, we define a subset of *Value* that represents the set of allowed token values for this place. We call this set the value *domain* of the place. In the next schema we define the *state space* of a net structure

StateSpace

$P : \mathbb{P}\, Place$

$S : \mathbb{P}\, State$

$D : Place \nrightarrow \mathbb{P}\, Value$

$\text{dom}(D) = P \land$

$\forall s : S \bullet \text{dom}(s) = P \land$

$\forall s : S \bullet \forall p : P \bullet \text{dom}(s(p)) \subset D(p)$

So component S defines the state space and D the function that assigns domains to places. The last predicate states that tokens at a certain place should have values in the domain of that place.

The next schema combines the state space and flat net structure schemas, adding two components. The first component is a function L that assigns to each transition a *local state transition function* which formalizes the consumption and production of tokens. The second component is the transition relation Tr over the state space.

$$
\begin{array}{|l}
\multicolumn{1}{l}{\mathit{NetModel}} \\
\hline
\mathit{FlatNetStructure} \\
\mathit{StateSpace} \\
L : \mathit{Transition} \nrightarrow (\mathit{State} \nrightarrow \mathit{State}) \\
\mathit{Tr} : \mathbb{P}(\mathit{State} \times \mathit{State}) \\
\hline
1\ \ \mathrm{dom}(L) = T \\
2\ \ \forall t : T \bullet \mathrm{dom}(L(t)) \subset S \\
3\ \ \forall t : T \bullet \forall s : \mathrm{dom}(L(t)) \bullet \forall p : \mathrm{dom}(s) \bullet \\
\qquad \Sigma(s(p)) = \#\{c : I(t) \mid M(c) = p\} \\
4\ \ \forall t : T \bullet \forall s : \mathrm{dom}(L(t)) \bullet \forall p : \mathrm{dom}(L(t)(s)) \bullet \\
\qquad \Sigma(L(t)(s)(p)) \leq \#\{c : O(t) \mid M(c) = p\} \\
5\ \ \forall x : \mathit{Tr} \bullet \mathrm{first}(x) \in S \wedge \mathrm{second}(x) \in S \\
6\ \ \forall s_1, s_2 : S \mid (s_1, s_2) \in \mathit{Tr} \bullet \exists t : T \bullet \exists s : S \bullet \\
\qquad \forall p : P \bullet s(p) \leq s_1(p) \wedge s \in \mathrm{dom}(L(t)) \wedge \\
\qquad \forall p : P \bullet s_2(p) = s_1(p) - s(p) + L(t)(s)(p) \\
\hline
\end{array}
$$

The third rule states that for each input connection one token is consumed; the fourth rule that for each output connection at most one token is produced. Rule six tells us how a (global) state transition is derived from a local state change caused by a transition in the net structure. Note that we add, subtract and compare functions; the generic function Σ summarizes the images of a function.

Given an initial state, the net model determines the set of paths of the net according to the transition law. If this law is deterministic, i.e. Tr is in reality of the type $State \nrightarrow State$, there is only one path. Note that for each state transition precisely one net transition should fire.

2.2 Hierarchical nets

Now we can introduce *net hierarchy*. For large systems it is too complicated to define a flat net structure in one step. One often uses a top-down design method similar to data flow diagram techniques [Yourdon 89] or HOOD [Giovanni 90].

Our hierarchical net structure allows us to decompose nets into places and *subnets* or *agents*. (Also compare channel/agency nets [Reisig 87]). At each level of the decomposition process we have to decide which subnets are *elementary* (i.e. are transitions) and which ones need further decomposition. When all subnets have been decomposed into elementary ones, we can proceed by defining a local state transition function for each elementary subnet.

The above hierarchical net structure is useful not only for the design process but also for documenting the net model, since it provides an overview of the flat net structure.

A subnet usually has connections like a transition. We always assume that the (one) subnet at the top of the hierarchy has no connections anymore. This means that if we want to describe a system that communicates with an environment (by exchanging tokens), we have to model that environment as a subnet and incorporate it at the top level. (Note that this was already the case in the flat net structure.) Figure 2 shows three levels of an example hierarchy.

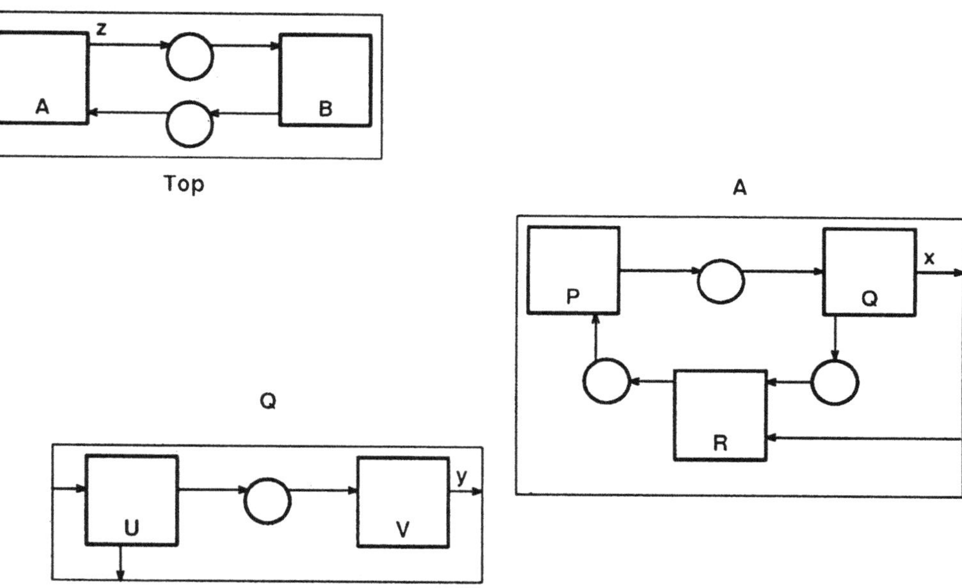

Figure 2: Hierarchical decomposition.

We see that every connection of a subnet is assigned to a place or connection in its supernet. In figure 2, y is assigned to x and x to z. In the next schema we define the hierarchical net structure, generalizing the flat net structure. Each subnet (except the top level one) and each place are mapped to precisely one supernet. These mappings constitute the components *HN* and *HP* in the schema. Component *Top* denotes the top level net. For subnets as well as transitions we use the same type

$$[Net]$$

replacing the earlier type *Transition*. Component N denotes all subnets, including transitions. Components *MP* and *MC* denote the assignment of connections. They replace component M of the flat net structure.

HierarchicalNetStructure

$$
\begin{array}{l}
P : \mathbb{P}\,Place \\
T : \mathbb{P}\,Net \\
N : \mathbb{P}\,Net \\
I : Net \rightarrowtail\!\!\!\!\rightarrow \mathbb{P}\,Connection \\
O : Net \rightarrowtail\!\!\!\!\rightarrow \mathbb{P}\,Connection \\
HN : Net \rightarrowtail\!\!\!\!\rightarrow Net \\
HP : Place \rightarrowtail\!\!\!\!\rightarrow Net \\
MP : Connection \rightarrowtail\!\!\!\!\rightarrow Place \\
MC : Connection \rightarrowtail\!\!\!\!\rightarrow Connection \\
Top : Net \\
\hline
1\ \ T \subset N \wedge Top \in N \backslash T \wedge \mathrm{dom}(I) = \mathrm{dom}(O) = N \backslash \{Top\} \\
2\ \ \mathrm{dom}(MP) \cap \mathrm{dom}(MC) = \emptyset \\
3\ \ \mathrm{dom}(MP) \cup \mathrm{dom}(MC) = (\bigcup \mathrm{rng}(I)) \cup (\bigcup \mathrm{rng}(O)) \\
4\ \ \forall n_1, n_2 : N \mid n_1 \neq n_2 \bullet I(n_1) \cap I(n_2) = O(n_1) \cap O(n_2) = I(n_1) \cap O(n_2) = \emptyset \\
5\ \ \mathrm{dom}(HN) = N \backslash \{Top\} \wedge \mathrm{rng}(HN) = N \backslash T \\
6\ \ \mathrm{dom}(HP) = P \wedge \mathrm{rng}(HP) = \mathrm{rng}(HN) \\
7\ \ \forall n : \mathrm{dom}(HN) \bullet \exists k : \mathbb{N} \bullet HN^k(n) = Top \\
8\ \ \forall n : \mathrm{dom}(HN) \bullet \forall c : I(n) \cup O(n) \bullet \\
\qquad c \in \mathrm{dom}(MP) \Rightarrow HP(MP(c)) = HN(n) \wedge \\
\qquad c \in \mathrm{dom}(MC) \wedge c \in I(n) \Rightarrow MC(c) \in I(HN(n)) \wedge \\
\qquad c \in \mathrm{dom}(MC) \wedge c \in O(n) \Rightarrow MC(c) \in O(HN(n))
\end{array}
$$

The first four rules of the above schema are straightforward modifications of rules of the flat net structure. Rules 5, 6 and 7 determine the mappings to the supernets; rule 7 guarantees that in the end everything is mapped to *Top*, so no cycles are possible. The last rule states that if a connection of a subnet is assigned to a place, then both the subnet and the place should be mapped to a common supernet. If it is assigned to a connection, this should be a connection of the supernet.

It is easy to derive a flat net structure from a hierarchical one, by assigning to each connection of a transition the place it is assigned to by the higher level subnets. The next axiomatic description defines a function *nettrans* that maps a hierarchical net structure onto a flat one.

$$
\begin{array}{l}
nettrans : HierarchicalNetStructure \rightarrow FlatNetStructure \\
\hline
\forall h : HierarchicalNetStructure \bullet \\
\quad \exists MN : Connection \rightarrowtail\!\!\!\!\rightarrow Place \bullet \\
\qquad \forall t : h.T \bullet \forall c : (h.I)t \cup (h.O)t \bullet \\
\qquad\quad c \in \mathrm{dom}(h.MP) \Rightarrow MN(c) = (h.MP)c \wedge \\
\qquad\quad c \in \mathrm{dom}(h.MC) \Rightarrow MN(c) = MN((h.MC)c) \\
\wedge \\
(nettrans(h)).P = h.P \wedge \\
(nettrans(h)).T = h.T \wedge \\
(nettrans(h)).I = h.T \lhd h.I \wedge \\
(nettrans(h)).O = h.T \lhd h.O \wedge \\
(nettrans(h)).M = h.MN
\end{array}
$$

Note that the function *MN* is defined recursively; it is however easy to see that this definition is sound.

In the development process, we start with the definition of a hierarchical net structure. This we transform into a flat net structure. Next we define a state space and finally a net model. In this section we have defined all these concepts, but we did not give a language to *specify* a net model. For the hierarchical net structure we advise a graphical representation such as the one we described and used in the example figures. For the specification of the state space and local state transition functions we advocate Z. This is the topic of the next section.

3 Specification of nets in Z

3.1 Places and transitions

In section 2 we have defined what a net model is. It is constructed from a hierarchical net structure which determines a flat net structure, a state space and local transition functions per net transition. In this section we show how the state space and the local transition function can be specified using Z. In fact we do more: we also specify the net model in Z. Using some examples, we present a method for specification of net models.

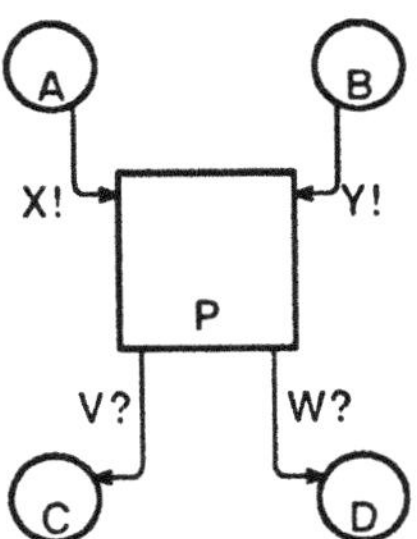

Figure 3: A flat net.

Consider the example of a flat net structure given in figure 3. To specify the value domains of the places we use type definitions. Let the types of the four places be T_A, T_B, T_C and T_D. We assume that all types have one common value, denoted by $\perp$ and called *bottom* or nil. The places of a net model are specified in one schema called *Places*. In our example we have the following schema for the places

Places

$A : T_A \twoheadrightarrow \mathbb{N}_1$
$B : T_B \twoheadrightarrow \mathbb{N}_1$
$C : T_C \twoheadrightarrow \mathbb{N}_1$
$D : T_D \twoheadrightarrow \mathbb{N}_1$

true

Note that all places are real bags now and not bags which allow frequency zero as in section 2.

Transitions are specified by three schemas called *front-end*, *body* and *back-end* that have to be combined by the pipe operator $\gg$. This operator has been introduced by [Hayes 87]. Later we will see that we only have to specify the body schema, the other schemas can be derived automatically from the body schema. For transition P in our example we define three schemas P_1, P_2 and P_3 and then $P \mathrel{\hat=} P_1 \gg P_2 \gg P_3$.

Schema P_1 describes the selection of tokens: one from place A and one from place B,

$$
\begin{array}{|l}
\multicolumn{1}{l}{P_1} \\
\hline
\Delta Places \\
\Xi(Places \backslash (A, B)) \\
X! : T_A \\
Y! : T_B \\
\hline
A \neq \emptyset \wedge B \neq \emptyset \wedge \\
X! \in \mathrm{dom}(A) \wedge Y! \in \mathrm{dom}(B) \wedge \\
A' = delete(X!, A) \wedge B' = delete(Y!, B) \\
\hline
\end{array}
$$

Note that both places should contain at least one token. The function *delete* is a generic function with type variable T. It updates a bag of type $T \pfun \mathbb{N}$ by deleting an arbitrary element from it.

$$
\begin{array}{|l}
\multicolumn{1}{l}{[T]} \\
\hline
delete : (T \times (T \pfun \mathbb{N})) \pfun (T \pfun \mathbb{N}) \\
\hline
\forall t : T \bullet \forall f : T \pfun \mathbb{N} \bullet t \in \mathrm{dom}(f) \Rightarrow \\
\quad (t, f) \in \mathrm{dom}(delete) \wedge \\
\quad f(t) > 1 \Rightarrow delete(t, f) = f \oplus \{t \mapsto f(t) - 1\} \wedge \\
\quad f(t) = 1 \Rightarrow delete(t, f) = \{t\} \ndres f \\
\hline
\end{array}
$$

The following schema of the specification of P is P_3.

$$
\begin{array}{|l}
\multicolumn{1}{l}{P_3} \\
\hline
\Delta Places \\
\Xi(Places \backslash (C, D)) \\
V? : T_C \\
W? : T_D \\
\hline
V? \neq \bot \Rightarrow C' = add(V?, C) \wedge \\
V? = \bot \Rightarrow C' = C \wedge \\
W? \neq \bot \Rightarrow D' = add(W?, D) \wedge \\
W? = \bot \Rightarrow D' = D \\
\hline
\end{array}
$$

This schema uses another generic function, called *add*, that adds one element to a bag.

$$
\begin{array}{|l}
\multicolumn{1}{l}{[T]} \\
\hline
add : (T \times (T \pfun \mathbb{N})) \pfun (T \pfun \mathbb{N}) \\
\hline
\forall t : T \bullet \forall f : T \pfun \mathbb{N} \bullet \\
\quad t \in \mathrm{dom}(f) \Rightarrow add(t, f) = f \oplus \{t \mapsto f(t) + 1\} \wedge \\
\quad t \notin \mathrm{dom}(f) \Rightarrow add(t, f) = f \oplus \{t \mapsto 1\} \\
\hline
\end{array}
$$

We take special care of the situation that the input has value $\bot$. This case occurs when a transition does not produce a token for a connection.

The schema P_2 specifies the functionality of the transition P. Since we are at this moment not interested in any particular functionality we leave it open by assuming a predicate E. Note that $V!$ or $W!$ may get the value $\perp$, which means that no token is produced.

$$
\begin{array}{|l}
\multicolumn{1}{l}{P_2} \\
\hline
X? : T_A \\
Y? : T_B \\
V! : T_C \\
W! : T_D \\
\hline
E \\
\hline
\end{array}
$$

The final schema P, defined by $P \mathrel{\hat{=}} P_1 \gg P_2 \gg P_3$ joins the three schemas and identifies components with ! and ? and leaves them out of the signature by introducing existential quantors for each of them, as illustrated in the example given in section 3.2. Of course we could have given a direct way to specify P. However, the schemas P_1 and P_3 can be derived from P_2: they do not require any decision from the designer; the designer only has to specify the schema P_2. If we consider $X?$ and $Y?$ as input connections of P and $V!$ and $W!$ as output connections, then we only need to know which places they are assigned to. This information can be derived from the graphical representation of the net structure. Similarly we derive the types of the places by giving the type of the tokens.

So, a full specification of a net model consists of a graphically represented hierarchical net structure, a schema with places and for each transition one schema (the body schema) with input and output connections as components, decorated with ? and ! respectively.

If we generate the front-end and back-end schemas for each transition then we have a complete Z specification with the following operational semantics: if an initial state is given then one of the transitions that is able to fire will do so. Then in the next state again one of the enabled transitions will fire. Note that a transition is enabled if the input places contain enough tokens. In the example this was checked by the first rule of schema P_1. It is possible that like in colored Petri nets there is a precondition based on input values. This can be expressed in the body schema of a transition. In our example the predicate E can have an expression, for instance $X? \neq Y?$.

Note that a specification in this way fits into the metamodel we presented in section 2. The diagram of figure 3 is an instance of the flat net structure schema. The state space is defined by the schema *Places*. To see this recall that in the metamodel a state is of the form $Place \nrightarrow (Value \rightarrow \mathbb{N})$. In the schema *Places* an instance is a tuple or a mapping that assigns to the places A, B, C and D a mapping from respectively T_A, T_B, T_C and T_D to $\mathbb{N}$. Hence T_A, T_B, T_C and T_D are subsets of *Value* and they determine the domains of the places. So we have defined in this way component D of schema *StateSpace*. The local transition function L of schema *NetModel* assigns to each transition a mapping from state to state. The transition schema P for transition P is in fact $L(P)$ since it defines a state transition that obeys the laws of the schema *NetModel*. Hence L is specified by a schema per transition. Finally the operational semantics discussed above and below satisfy the requirements for Tr in the schema *NetModel*.

All (serialized) execution paths of a net model can be obtained by constructing all possible lists containing firable transition schemas connected by the ; schema operator. For example for a net consisting of two transitions P and Q, we may get an execution path like

$$P$$
$$P; Q$$
$$P; Q; P$$
$$P; Q; P; P$$
$$P; Q; P; P; Q$$
$$\ldots$$

3.2 A small example

As a simple example we consider the net structure of figure 4. It consists of one transition

Figure 4: An example.

P that copies its input token to both output places. The schema representing the places is

$$\begin{array}{|l}
\multicolumn{1}{l}{Places[T]} \\
\hline
A : T \leftrightarrow \mathbb{N}_1 \\
B : T \leftrightarrow \mathbb{N}_1 \\
\hline
\text{true} \\
\hline
\end{array}$$

We have used an arbitrary type T for these places. The front-end, body an back-end schemas for the transition P are, according to the construction in the previous section

$$\begin{array}{|l}
\multicolumn{1}{l}{P_1[T]} \\
\hline
\Delta Places \\
\Xi(Places \backslash (A)) \\
X! : T \\
\hline
A \neq \emptyset \wedge \\
X! \in \operatorname{dom}(A) \wedge \\
A' = delete(X!, A) \\
\hline
\end{array}$$

$$\begin{array}{|l}
\multicolumn{1}{l}{P_2[T]} \\
\hline
X? : T \\
Y! : T \\
Z! : T \\
\hline
Y! = X? \wedge Z! = X? \\
\hline
\end{array}$$

$P_3[T]$

$$\begin{array}{|l}\Delta Places \\ Y? : T \\ Z? : T \\ \hline A' = add(Y?, A) \land \\ B' = add(Z?, B)\end{array}$$

Then P becomes, after removing most of the existential quantors

P

$$\begin{array}{|l}\Delta Places \\ \hline A' = A \land \exists Y : T \bullet B' = add(Y, B)\end{array}$$

3.3 Stores

In many applications it is useful to have a local state for a net transition. This can be modeled by a special place that always contains one token and that is both an input and an output place for the transition. We call such a place a *store*. (For stores we use a graphical representation differing from normal places.) Two transitions may have access to the same store; however only one at a time since there is only one token in the place representing the store. This avoids concurrent update problems. Usually a store has a rather complex type. It is not necessary to define the store as a bag since there is always one token; this will simplify the specifications considerably. So we may specify the type of a store just by the type of the token. In data base applications this token usually has a rather complex type that may be defined by several auxiliary schemas. As an example we construct for a store A a database type.

Person

$$\begin{array}{|l}name : NAME \\ address : NODE\ ADDRESS \\ age : \mathbb{N} \\ \hline age \geq 0\end{array}$$

Car

$$\begin{array}{|l}license : \mathbb{N} \\ kind : KIND \\ horsepower : \mathbb{N} \\ weigth : \mathbb{N} \\ \hline horsepower * 10 \geq weight\end{array}$$

Trip

$$\begin{array}{|l}driver : NAME \\ license : \mathbb{N} \\ starttime : \mathbb{N} \\ destination : PLACE \\ \hline \text{true}\end{array}$$

$$\begin{array}{|l}
\multicolumn{1}{l}{A} \\ \hline
person : \mathbb{P}(Person) \\
car : \mathbb{P}(Car) \\
trip : \mathbb{P}(Trip) \\ \hline
\forall t : trip \bullet t.driver \in \{x : person \bullet x.name\} \land \\
\qquad\qquad t.license \in \{x : car \bullet x.license\} \\ \hline
\end{array}$$

Note that the condition in schema A is a referential integrity constraint for the database.

3.4 An alternative place construction

We could have considered an alternative for the place construction. Up to here we followed the line of section 2. However, this leaves open how to choose tokens from the places. An alternative could be to replace the bags by queues. In fact this is the way we have implemented it in ExSpect. We have to replace the schema for the places by

$$\begin{array}{|l}
\multicolumn{1}{l}{Places} \\ \hline
A : \mathrm{seq} T_A \\
B : \mathrm{seq} T_B \\
C : \mathrm{seq} T_C \\
D : \mathrm{seq} T_D \\ \hline
\mathrm{true} \\ \hline
\end{array}$$

to account for the change of bag into queue. The front-end and back-end schemas for figure 3 now become equal to

$$\begin{array}{|l}
\multicolumn{1}{l}{P_1} \\ \hline
\Delta Places \\
\Xi(Places \setminus (A, B)) \\
X! : T_A \\
Y! : T_B \\ \hline
A \neq [\,] \land B \neq [\,] \land \\
X! = \mathrm{head}(A) \land Y! = \mathrm{head}(B) \land \\
A' = \mathrm{tail}(A) \land B' = \mathrm{tail}(B) \\ \hline
\end{array}$$

$$\begin{array}{|l}
\multicolumn{1}{l}{P_3} \\ \hline
\Delta Places \\
\Xi(Places \setminus (C, D)) \\
V? : T_C \\
W? : T_D \\ \hline
V? \neq \bot \Rightarrow C' = C \frown [V?] \land \\
V? = \bot \Rightarrow C' = C \land \\
W? \neq \bot \Rightarrow D' = D \frown [W?] \land \\
W? = \bot \Rightarrow D' = D \\ \hline
\end{array}$$

Note that P_2 does not have to be changed.

4 A distributed telephone index

To illustrate the concepts of the previous sections we present a simple distributed specification of a reactive system. It is a distributed telephone index: it receives questions for phone numbers and gives answers.

Let *NAME* be the set of all names and let *NUMBER* be the set of all valid telephone numbers. At the top level we may specify the index system (as seen from the environment of one node) as a schema *TI*. This is possible since we are dealing with a reactive system: it only produces tokens as a reaction upon an incoming token of the environment.

TI_2

$X? : NAME$
$Y! : NUMBER$
$index : NAME \rightarrow NUMBER$
$Y! = index(X?)$

The corresponding net is given in figure 5. In this net we have modeled the environment

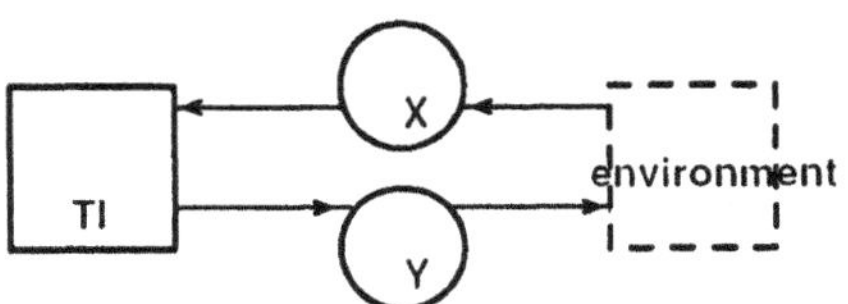

Figure 5: The toplevel of the index system.

as a subnet which we do not specify any further.

The next step is to decompose the net *TI* into several subnets *LTI*, each representing a local node. In a local node questions for numbers arrive from the local environment; if possible such a question is answered directly, if not a message is sent into a network of remote telephone indices. After a cycle through this network, an answer will arrive. The decomposition of the net *TI* is given in figure 6.

We use the following schema to represent the type of a message

mes

$name : NAME$
$number : NUMBER$
$address : NODE\ ADDRESS$

where *NODE ADDRESS* is the set of all node addresses. The *address* field denotes the node address from which the message originated and *name* denotes the name for which a number should be found.

We define the network of figure 7 as the decomposition of a local index system *LTI*. Each local index system i has stores containing its local index of names and numbers and its node address.

$Stores_i$

$address_i : NODE\ ADDRESS$
$index_i : NAME \nrightarrow NUMBER$
true

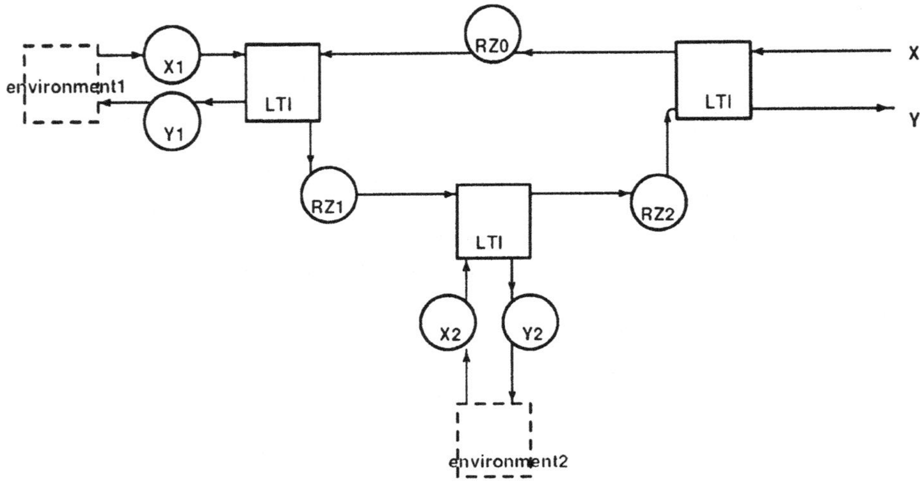

Figure 6: The decomposition of the toplevel *TI*.

The places we need are the following

Places
$R : mes \nrightarrow \mathbb{N}_1$
$X : NAME \nrightarrow \mathbb{N}_1$
$Y : NUMBER \nrightarrow \mathbb{N}_1$
$Z : mes \nrightarrow \mathbb{N}_1$
true

Questions enter the local index system at X, answers are given at Y and the incoming and outgoing network connections are supplied by R and Z. The specifications of the bodies of the two transitions P and Q in the local index system are given below.

P_2
$\Xi Stores_i$
$X? : NAME$
$Y! : NUMBER$
$Z! : mes$
$X? \in \mathrm{dom}(index_i) \wedge Y! = index_i(X?) \wedge Z! = \bot$
$\vee$
$X? \notin \mathrm{dom}(index_i) \wedge Y! = \bot \wedge Z!.name = X? \wedge Z!.address = address_i$

In reaction to a question on $X?$, transition P searches the local index and gives an answer on $Y!$ if the name is present. Otherwise it puts a message for information on $Z!$. The (local) index and address are never changed, so we have used $\Xi Stores_i$.

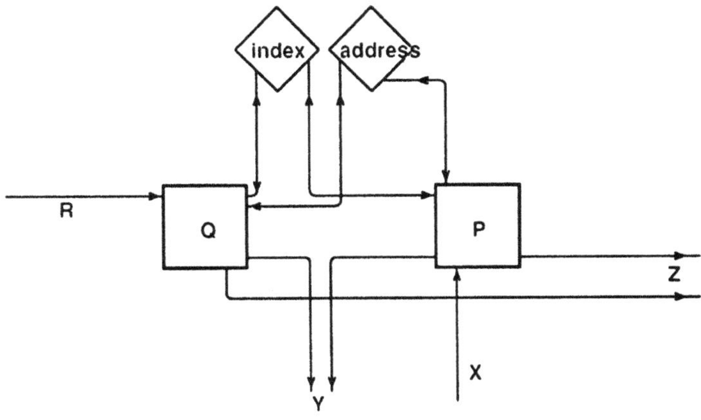

Figure 7: A local index system *LTI.*

Q_2

$\Xi Stores_i$
$R? : mes$
$Z! : mes$
$Y! : NUMBER$

$R?.address = address_i \wedge Y! = R?.number$
$\vee$
$R?.address \neq address_i \wedge R?.name \notin \mathrm{dom}(index_i) \wedge Z! = R?$
$\vee$
$R?.address \neq address_i \wedge R?.name \in \mathrm{dom}(index_i) \wedge$
$\quad Z!.name = R?.name \wedge Z!.address = R?.address \wedge Z!.number = index_i(R?.name)$

Transition Q takes an incoming *NAME,NUMBER,NODE ADDRESS* triple from $R?$ and sends the number to $Y!$ if the address matches the local address. This happens when a message sent by this node has traversed the whole network. Otherwise it searches the local index for the name and forwards the triple to the next node via $Z!$.

5 Conclusions

In this paper we have shown how Z can be used (a) to specify the metamodel of a hierarchical colored Petri net and (b) to specify the transitions in a specific colored Petri net. We have seen that Z is very well suited for such a specification. However, a few small comments remain. It is not possible to specify constants as parameters to schemas (types are possible). Therefore in our example in section 4 we have used a subscript i. Furthermore when one wants an executable specification, one needs to restrict the predicates in the body schemas of the transitions.

A method for constructing specifications of distributed systems starts by building a hierarchical net model in a graphical way and continues by specifying the primitive transitions by means of Z schemas. As a next design step, the Z schemas should be transformed into functions in order to get an executable specification as in ExSpect.

References

[Aalst 90] W.M.P.van der Alst and A.W.Waltmans, Modeling Logistic Systems with ExSpect, in: H.G.Sol, K.M.van Hee (eds.), Dynamic Modeling of Information Systems, North-Holland, 1991.

[Albrecht 89] K.Albrecht, K.Jensen and R.M.Shapiro, Design/CPN: A tool package supporting the use of Colored Petri Nets, Petri Net Newsletter 32, 1989.

[Diepen 90] M.J.van Diepen and K.M.van Hee, A Formal Semantics for Z and the link between Z and the Relational Algebra, in: D.Bjørner, C.A.R.Hoare, H.Langmaack (eds.), VDM'90, VDM and Z - Formal Methods in Software Development, Lecture Notes in Computer Science 428, Springer Verlag, 1990.

[Giovanni 90] R.Di Giovanni and P.L.Iachini, HOOD and Z for the Development of Complex Software Systems, in: D.Bjørner, C.A.R.Hoare, H.Langmaack (eds.), VDM'90, VDM and Z - Formal Methods in Software Development, Lecture Notes in Computer Science 428, Springer Verlag, 1990.

[Hayes 87] I.Hayes (ed.), Specification Case Studies, Prentice Hall, 1987.

[Hee 89] K.M.van Hee, L.J.Somers and M.Voorhoeve, Executable Specifications for Distributed Information Systems, in: E.D.Falkenberg, P.Lindgreen (eds.), Information system concepts: an in-depth analysis, North-Holland, 1989.

[Hee 91] K.M.van Hee and P.A.C.Verkoulen, Integration of a Data Model and Petri Nets, in: Proceedings 12th International Conference on Application and Theory of Petri Nets, Århus, Denmark, 1991.

[Jensen 91] K.Jensen, Colored Petri Nets: A High Level Language for System Design and Analysis, in: G.Rozenberg (ed), Advances in Petri Nets 1990, Lecture Notes in Computer Science 483, Springer Verlag, 1991.

[Reisig 87] W.Reisig, Petri Nets in Software Engineering, in: W.Brauer, W.Reisig, G.Rozenberg (eds.), Petri Nets: Applications and Relationships to other Models of Concurrency, in: Lecture Notes in Computer Science 255, Springer Verlag, 1987.

[Spivey 89] J.M.Spivey, The Z Notation: A Reference Manual, Prentice Hall, 1989.

[Yourdon 89] E.Yourdon, Modern structured analysis, Prentice-Hall 1989.

An Approach to the Static Semantics of VDM-SL

Hans Bruun Bo Stig Hansen Flemming Damm

Department of Computer Science,
Technical University of Denmark,
Building 344, DK-2800 Lyngby

Abstract

The work presented here concerns abstract specification of type checking for a specification language VDM-SL of the Vienna Development Method. Where previous work has focussed on rejection of "obviously" ill-typed specifications we do, in addition, consider acceptance of "obviously" well-typed expressions.

The presentation includes essential parts of the definition of several well-formedness predicates for increasingly advanced type analyses. In order to emphasize the similarities and symmetries, the different predicates are defined in terms of a single, parameterized predicate.

In other work, an independent definition of (type) consistency of VDM-SL specifications has been put forward. We discuss the necessary conditions for the correctness of our type checking with respect to this definition.

1 Introduction

VDM-SL is a formal specification language which has its roots in previous specification language variants used with the Vienna Development Method [3, 7]. The language is being defined by a British Standards Institute committee and the standardization has been accepted as an ISO work item (ISO working group SC22/WG19-VDM-SL). A mathematical definition of the language syntax and semantics is close to being completed [8] and the semantics part includes a model theoretic definition of a type universe [12]. Moreover, the (dynamic) semantics ($\mathcal{DS}$) of specifications is defined as a total function which for each specification yields the set of models fulfilling the specification. Termination errors, type errors etc. result in the empty set of models so in this sense the $\mathcal{DS}$ definition may be seen as also defining a notion of consistency.

The work reported on here concerns another aspect of VDM-SL which is sometimes called the static semantics (SS). This includes definitions of type checking and related consistency analyses which are decidable (i.e. may be implemented by a terminating algorithm).

In the related field of programming language semantics, theories of data types and type checking are topics which have been extensively studied. Considering VDM-SL, the notion and rôle of types and type checking is, however, somewhat different from

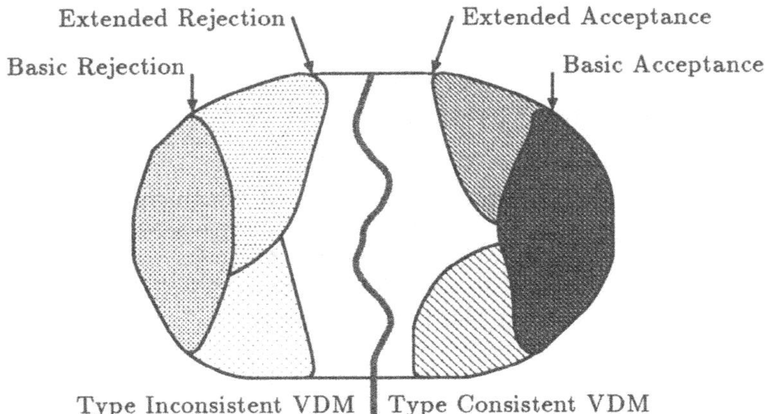

Figure 1: Rejected and accepted subsets of specifications.

what is usually found in programming languages. Some important differences and their implications are discussed in other work by the authors [5]. Following the approach suggested there, we propose a basic rejection and acceptance analysis and also a number of extensions. The set of possible extensions is open to future additions. The relationship between the different acceptance and rejection analyses is illustrated in figure 1.

As indicated above, there are many possible choices regarding which specifications to recognize as being consistent or inconsistent. Since there already exists an independent definition of consistency, namely the dynamic semantics of VDM-SL, it could, however, seem reasonable to require that: (A) only specifications which actually are inconsistent according to the dynamic semantics may be rejected; and (B) only specifications which actually are consistent may be accepted.

For a specification to be consistent according to the dynamic semantics, several requirements must be fulfilled: (1) the functionals associated with recursive function definitions must be continuous; (2) total, recursively defined functions must always terminate; (3) pre/post specified functions must be satisfiable; (4) functions must only be applied to arguments for which they are defined. In related work [5], we have argued that these requirements can be justified independently and we will in the following focus on item (4), the issue of type consistency.

1.1 Relation to Previous Work

In work by Nico Plat and others [11], an approach to the definition of a static semantics for VDM is outlined. Brian Monahan and A. Walsh [10] have also worked on this topic. In both works, only rejection (not acceptance) is considered. Moreover, the open-ended approach of defining more and more advanced analyses seems to be unique for our work. Another distinguishing characteristic is our clear commitment to correctness of the static semantics with respect to a definition of the dynamic semantics.

Regarding the style of definition, we have chosen to give the definition in terms of predicates relating expressions to their acceptable as well as to their non-rejectable types. There are cases where the set of such types for an expression is infinite. For this reason we have found it less desirable to take the more direct approach of defining functions for synthesizing sets of possible types as done in the works referred to above.

There is a tradition in the literature for defining type systems by stating type inference rules [9]. In the work reported on here, we have chosen to use VDM-SL itself for expressing the typing rules. Some may at a first look find that this leads to decreased clarity of the exposition. However, the freedom to use higher order functions and predicates have in our work given inspiration to a more pronounced structuring and parameterization of the typing rules than is usually seen.

1.2 Overview

In the following, we present essential parts of a definition of acceptance and rejection. Acceptance is defined in terms of a predicate for *definite well-formedness*. The relationship between the definite well-formedness predicate and the dynamic semantics is discussed in section 3.

Rejection is defined in terms of a predicate for *possible well-formedness*. When an expression is possibly well-formed with respect to a type, we will not reject that it may have this type. The predicate for possible well-formedness is defined so it is complete in the sense that all expressions which may evaluate to a value of a given type are also possibly well-formed with respect to that type. In addition, possible well-formedness is defined so: (1) it is decidable; and (2) the question whether there exists any type t for which an expression is possibly well-formed is also decidable.

The decidability and completeness allows us to define rejection as the case where an expression is not possibly well-formed with respect to any type.

The presentation is organized as follows. First, a representative collection of VDM-SL types is identified and relations among types, such as the subtype relation, are introduced. Next, a basic level of type checking is defined; this is done in a common framework for both possible and definite well-formedness which emphasizes the similarities and symmetries of the two notions. Last, some extended checks are considered; these include a flow analysis which, e.g., allows separate type checking of the branches of if-then-else expressions.

It should be noted that the analyses are clearly related to work in abstract interpretation [1]; we do, however, not elaborate on the relationship in this presentation.

2 Types and Type Representations

In the abstract syntax for VDM-SL [8] *Type* is the domain of type expressions. Types are used in a specification in two ways. First of all, types are used as part of type definitions. Next they are used to explicitly specify the type, for instance parameter and result types in function definitions and types of bindings.

In the $\mathcal{DS}$, a type defined in the type definitions at the top level of a VDM-SL specification denotes a VDM domain:

$$A = (\mid A \mid, \sqsubseteq_A, \|A\|)$$

where $(| A |, \sqsubseteq_A)$ is a CPO and $\|A\| \subseteq | A | \setminus \{\perp_A\}$. Here $\|A\|$ is the set of values belonging to the type when the constraints from invariants are taken into account.

When the SS checks for type consistency it makes approximations of the set of possible values to which the expressions in a specification may evaluate. However, the SS does not operate directly on these (often infinite) sets of values, but with some abstract representation of the sets. The domain for these abstract representations is called *TypeR* (for Type Representation). For the considered subset of VDM-SL it is defined as follows:

1.0 $\mathit{TypeR} = \mathit{BasicTypeR} \mid \mathit{SetTypeR} \mid \mathit{ProductTypeR} \mid$
.1 $\qquad \mathit{FnTypeR} \mid \mathit{TypeRId} \mid \mathit{UnionTypeR}$

2.0 $\mathit{BasicTypeR} = \mathrm{BOOL} \mid \mathrm{NAT}$

3.0 $\mathit{SetTypeR} :: \mathit{elemtp} : \mathit{Type0R}$

4.0 $\mathit{Type0R} = \mathit{TypeR} \mid \mathrm{EMPTYTYPE}$

5.0 $\mathit{ProductTypeR} :: \ \mathit{TypeR}^+$

6.0 $\mathit{FnTypeR} :: \mathit{dom} : \mathit{TypeR}$
.1 $\qquad \mathit{rng} \ : \mathit{TypeR}$

7.0 $\mathit{TypeRId} :: \ \mathit{Id}$

8.0 $\mathit{UnionTypeR} :: \ \mathit{TypeR}\text{-set}$
.1 inv $\mathit{mk}\text{-}\mathit{UnionTypeR}(\mathit{ts}) \triangleq$ card $\mathit{ts} \geq 1$

The above defined domain *TypeR* is closely related to the abstract syntax domain *Type*. In fact, for each *Type* object there is a corresponding *TypeR* object. This *TypeR* object is in the SS used as an abstract representation of the same set of values as the corresponding *Type* object denotes in the $\mathcal{DS}$ (i.e. $| A |$).

In a full specification of the SS there are more *TypeR* objects than *Type* objects such that more subsets of values can be represented. In the considered subset of VDM-SL we have just added a type representation EMPTYTYPE which represents the empty set of values. The type EMPTYTYPE may, however, only be used as the element type for a set type thereby providing a type representation *mk-SetTypeR*(EMPTYTYPE) which represents exactly the empty set value. Furthermore, for technical reasons, the representation of union types (*UnionTypeR*) is allowed to have just a single member whereas the abstract syntax requires at least two members.

In section 4.2.3 we show an example of increasing the granularity of the type representation system and exploiting the more detailed type information.

Environment. A type representation may contain identifiers which then should be defined in a type definition at the top level of the considered specification. To interpret a type representation, information about the type definitions must be available.

9.0 $\mathit{TypeREnv} = \mathit{Id} \xrightarrow{m} \mathit{TypeR}$

10.0 $\mathit{ValEnv} = \mathit{Id} \xrightarrow{m} \mathit{TypeR}$

11.0 $\mathit{Env} :: \mathit{tenv} : \mathit{TypeREnv}$
.1 $\qquad \mathit{venv} : \mathit{ValEnv}$

In the SS, an environment (i.e. an object from *Env*) is used to hold information about all defined/declared identifiers. An environment has a type representation environment (*TypeREnv*) and a value environment (*ValEnv*) as subcomponents.

The type representation environment maps the type identifiers defined in the type definitions to the corresponding type representation. The type representation environment remains constant throughout the analysis of a VDM-SL specification.

The value environment maps declared value identifiers (i.e. function names, parameter names, let-defined names etc.) to their corresponding type representations. The value environment may vary when analyzing different parts of a specification.

The set of values of a type. In the sequel, the set of proper values in the $\mathcal{DS}$ represented by a type representation t in a given environment *env* is denoted by $\mathcal{T}(t)(env)$, and the set is called *the set of values of the type t* (in the given environment). We will not formally define $\mathcal{T}(t)(env)$, but just refer to the above given informal description of the meaning of type representations. Note, however, that the set of values of a type does not include bottom values.

The SS relies on the following property of the defined type representation system:

(1) $\forall t_1, t_2 : TypeR \cdot \mathcal{T}(t_1)(env) \cap \mathcal{T}(t_2)(env) \neq \{\} \Rightarrow$
$\qquad \exists t_3 : TypeR \cdot \mathcal{T}(t_1)(env) \cap \mathcal{T}(t_2)(env) = \mathcal{T}(t_3)(env)$

i.e. if the sets of values for two types have a non-empty intersection then a type exists whose set of values is equal to the intersection. (For a use of this property see among others section 2.2).

In the remaining part, the word "type" (rather than type representation) will be used to mean a *TypeR* object. Furthermore, when making examples, "type"s (i.e. *TypeR* objects) will be shown using the concrete syntax notation for the corresponding *Type* object if there is such a corresponding *Type* object, i.e. we write B instead of BOOL, N × B instead of *mk-ProductTypeR*([NAT, BOOL]), etc..

2.1 Subtypes

In order to define the well-formedness functions, it is necessary first to formalize the notion of one type being a subtype of another. We do this in terms of the *is_subtype* predicate defined below. In relation to the $\mathcal{DS}$ we have that $is\_subtype(type_1, type_2)(env)$ must be true if and only if the set of values of $type_1$ is a subset of the set of values of $type_2$, i.e.

(2) $is\_subtype(type_1, type_2)(env) \Leftrightarrow \mathcal{T}(type_1)(env) \subseteq \mathcal{T}(type_2)(env)$

The following definition of the *is_subtype* predicate is inspired of the algebra of symbolic types presented in [2].

12.0 $is\_subtype : Type0R \times Type0R \rightarrow Env \rightarrow \mathbb{B}$
.1 $is\_subtype\,(type_1, type_2)(mk\text{-}Env(tenv, \text{-})) \triangleq$
.2 $\quad \exists\, strel : (Type0R \times Type0R)\text{-set} \cdot$
.3 $\qquad is\_subtype\_rel(strel)(tenv) \wedge (type_1, type_2) \in strel$

The definition of *is_subtype* relies on the *is_subtype_rel* defined below. The type $type_1$ is a subtype of type $type_2$ if there exists a subtype relation *strel* conforming to the given type environment such that $(type_1, type_2)$ is in that relation.

The following predicate *is_subtype_rel* defines the requirements which a type relation *strel* must fulfil in order to be a subtype relation satisfying the requirement (2). It is commented afterwards.

```
13.0 is_subtype_rel : (Type0R × Type0R)-set → TypeREnv → B
 .1  is_subtype_rel (strel)(tenv) ≜
 .2    ∀(t1, t2) ∈ strel ·
 .3       cases (t1, t2) :
 .4         (mk-TypeRId(id1), -)       → id1 ∈ dom tenv ∧ (tenv(id1), t2) ∈ strel,
 .5         (-, mk-TypeRId(id2))       → id2 ∈ dom tenv ∧ (t1, tenv(id2)) ∈ strel,
 .6         (mk-UnionTypeR(ts1), -) → ∀ t1 ∈ ts1 · (t1, t2) ∈ strel,
 .7         (-, mk-UnionTypeR(ts2)) → ∃ t2 ∈ ts2 · (t1, t2) ∈ strel,
 .8         (mk-SetTypeR(et1), mk-SetTypeR(et2)) →
 .9              (et1, et2) ∈ strel,
 .10        (mk-ProductTypeR(ts1), mk-ProductTypeR(ts2)) →
 .11             len ts1 = len ts2 ∧ ∀ i ∈ inds ts1 · (ts1(i), ts2(i)) ∈ strel,
 .12        (mk-FnTypeR(at1, rt1), mk-FnTypeR(at2, rt2)) →
 .13             (rt1, rt2) ∈ strel ∧ (at1, at2) ∈ strel ∧ (at2, at1) ∈ strel,
 .14        (NAT, NAT)                 → true,
 .15        (BOOL, BOOL)               → true,
 .16        (EMPTYTYPE, -)             → true,
 .17        others                     → false
 .18      end
```

A subtype relation is determined from two parts: (1) the type equations represented in the type environment and (2) the structure of the types:

1. To conform with the type equations, a subtype relation *strel* must fulfil the following requirements (13.4-5):
   If $(typeid, t_2)$ is in *strel* and the type equations define $typeid = type$ then $(type, t_2)$ must also be in *strel*. In a similar way, if $(t_1, typeid)$ is in *strel* and the type equations define $typeid = type$ then $(t_1, type)$ must also be in *strel*.

2. To conform with the type structure, a subtype relation *strel* must fulfil the following conditions (13.6-16):
   (13.6) If $(mk\text{-}UnionTypeR(\{t_1, t_2\}), t)$ is in *strel* then (t_1, t) and (t_2, t) must also be in *strel*.
   (13.7) If $(t, mk\text{-}UnionTypeR(\{t_1, t_2\}))$ is in *strel* then at least one of (t, t_1) and (t, t_2) must also be in *strel*. Note, it is important that this rule is after the previous rule.
   (13.8) If $(mk\text{-}SetTypeR(et_1), mk\text{-}SetTypeR(et_2))$ is in *strel* then the element type et_1 must be a subtype of et_2, i.e., (et_1, et_2) must also be in *strel*.
   (13.10) and so on ...
   (13.12) If $(mk\text{-}FnTypeR(at_1, rt_1), mk\text{-}FnTypeR(at_2, rt_2))$ is in *strel* then the range type rt_1 must be a subtype of the range type rt_2, i.e., (rt_1, rt_2) must also be in *strel*. Furthermore, the argument types at_1 and at_2 must be *equivalent*, i.e., both (at_1, at_2) and (at_2, at_1) must be in *strel*.
   (13.16) The type EMPTYTYPE represents the empty set of values and consequently must be a subtype of any type.

Example. To show examples of subtype relations we assume the following type definitions:

14.0 $S = S \times \mathsf{N} \mid \mathsf{N} \mid \mathsf{B}$

15.0 $T = T \times \mathsf{N} \mid \mathsf{N}$

In the environment corresponding to these type definitions the type S has an infinite number of subtypes some of which are:

$S \times \mathsf{N}$, N , B
$(S \times \mathsf{N}) \times \mathsf{N}$, $\mathsf{N} \times \mathsf{N}$, $\mathsf{B} \times \mathsf{N}$
$((S \times \mathsf{N}) \times \mathsf{N}) \times \mathsf{N}$, $(\mathsf{N} \times \mathsf{N}) \times \mathsf{N}$, $(\mathsf{B} \times \mathsf{N}) \times \mathsf{N}$

With the above shown definitions the set of values of type T is a subset of the set of values of type S, i.e. T must be a subtype of S, and then of course the type $T \times \mathsf{N}$ which is a subtype of T must also be a subtype of S. To show that *is_subtype*$(T \times \mathsf{N}, S)(env)$ is true, we must show that a finite set of type pairs *strel* exists which contains the pair $(T \times \mathsf{N} \preceq S)$ and which fulfils the requirements for a subtype relation as defined in 13. In the following table, the left column shows all the type pairs $(t_1 \preceq t_2)$ in this *strel*. In each row, the second column indicates the requirement which must be fulfilled for the type pair in the first column to be in *strel*. If the requirement is a request for other type pairs to be in *strel* then these type pairs are shown in the first column of the next row.

type pairs $(t_1 \preceq t_2)$ in *strel*	requirements
$(T \times \mathsf{N} \preceq S)$	13.5
$(T \times \mathsf{N} \preceq S \times \mathsf{N} \mid \mathsf{N} \mid \mathsf{B})$	13.7
$(T \times \mathsf{N} \preceq S \times \mathsf{N})$	13.10
$(\mathsf{N} \preceq \mathsf{N})$	13.14
$(T \preceq S)$	13.4
$(T \times \mathsf{N} \mid \mathsf{N} \preceq S)$	13.5
$(T \times \mathsf{N} \mid \mathsf{N} \preceq S \times \mathsf{N} \mid \mathsf{N} \mid \mathsf{B})$	13.6
$(T \times \mathsf{N} \preceq S \times \mathsf{N} \mid \mathsf{N} \mid \mathsf{B})$	already in set
$(\mathsf{N} \preceq S \times \mathsf{N} \mid \mathsf{N} \mid \mathsf{B})$	13.7
$(\mathsf{N} \preceq \mathsf{N})$	already in set

□

2.2 Non-disjoint Types

Another type relation needed by the SS is the *overlapping* relation. In relation to the $\mathcal{DS}$ we have that *overlapping*$(type_1, type_2)(env)$ must be true if the sets of values of $type_1$ and $type_2$ are non-disjoint, i.e.

(3) $\mathcal{T}(type_1)(env) \cap \mathcal{T}(type_2)(env) \neq \{\} \Rightarrow overlapping(type_1, type_2)(env)$

By using property (1) of the type representation system and property (2) of *is_subtype* we have that if two types t_1 and t_2 have a common subtype, then they are overlapping:

16.0 $overlapping : TypeR \times TypeR \to Env \to \mathsf{B}$
.1 $overlapping\,(t_1, t_2)(env) \triangleq$
.2 $\quad \exists\, st : TypeR \cdot is\_subtype(st, t_1)(env) \wedge is\_subtype(st, t_2)(env)$

Note that EMPTYTYPE is not a *TypeR* object.

3 Well-formedness of Expressions

The static semantics (SS) defines two main predicates, one for acceptance of expressions and one for rejection of expressions. The two predicates could be defined by two separate sets of formulae. An expression is accepted if it is well-formed according to a predicate for definite well-formedness, whereas an expression is rejected if it is *not* well-formed according to a predicate for possible well-formedness. Because both acceptance and rejection is defined in terms of predicates for *well-formedness*, the two sets of formulae will be quite similar. The definition of the SS exploits this property and merges the two sets of formulae for possible and definite well-formedness. Consequently, there will be *one* basic well-formedness predicate for each expression construct defining acceptance as well as rejection:

17.0 $wf\_Expr : \Pi \rightarrow Expr \rightarrow TypeR \rightarrow Env \rightarrow \mathbb{B}$
.1 $wf\_Expr_{\pi}(e)(t)(env) \triangleq$
.2 cases e :
.3 $mk\text{-}IdExpr(\text{-}) \rightarrow wf\_IdExpr_{\pi}(e)(t)(env),$
.4 $mk\text{-}IfExpr(\text{-},\text{-},\text{-}) \rightarrow wf\_IfExpr_{\pi}(e)(t)(env),$
.5 $mk\text{-}FctApply(\text{-},\text{-}) \rightarrow wf\_FctApply_{\pi}(e)(t)(env),$
.6 $mk\text{-}SetEnumeration(\text{-}) \rightarrow wf\_SetEnumeration_{\pi}(e)(t)(env),$
.7 $\vdots \rightarrow \vdots$
.8 end

The choice of possible and definite well-formedness is conveyed to the predicates via a parameter of type Π. This parameter also holds information about whether the acceptance or rejection should be based on a minimum check or an extended check:

18.0 $\Pi = POS \mid DEF$

19.0 $POS :: checkset : PCheck\text{-}\mathsf{set}$

20.0 $DEF :: checkset : DCheck\text{-}\mathsf{set}$

The *checkset* component indicates the wanted checks by mentioning a set of possible checks. An empty check set corresponds to a minimum check. The examples of well-formedness predicates shown in this section are simplified so they only correspond to the minimum check. The discussion is, however, independent of the actual check set. In section 4, we will consider some of the checks that has been added beyond the minimum check.

A well-formedness predicate for expressions corresponding to some specific check π (of type Π) has the type WFE where

21.0 $WFE = Expr \rightarrow TypeR \rightarrow Env \rightarrow \mathbb{B}$

In addition to all of the above mentioned basic well-formedness predicates, the SS defines derived well-formedness predicates based on some general typing rules (to be discussed in sections 3.3.1, 3.3.2 and 4.2). These general typing rules are defined in terms of functions of the type $\Pi \rightarrow WFE \rightarrow WFE$ which transform a well-formedness predicate to a more general or powerful version.

In the following wf_D denotes a definite well-formedness predicate, i.e. a well-formedness predicate corresponding to a check of the form $mk\text{-}DEF(c)$. Furthermore, wf_P

denotes a possible well-formedness predicate, i.e. a well-formedness predicate corresponding to a check of the form *mk-POS*(c). We also use D and P as shorthand notations for *mk-DEF*(c) respectively *mk-POS*(c). In the above, c is some check set.

3.1 General Soundness Requirements

When the SS for some well-formedness predicate $wf : WFE$, some expression $e : Expr$, type $t : TypeR$ and environment $env : Env$ defines $wf(e)(t)(env)$ to be true, the set of values of type t in some way represents an approximation of the possible values of the expression e in the dynamic semantics ($\mathcal{DS}$). So from the value of $wf(e)(t)(env)$ we must be able to make some conclusion about the value which the expression e denotes in the $\mathcal{DS}$. Exactly which conclusion depends on whether wf is a definite or possible well-formedness predicate.

In order to relate type consistency to the $\mathcal{DS}$ it is necessary to distinguish bottom errors caused by type inconsistency and other sorts of inconsistencies. This is discussed further in other work by the authors [5]. Here we will just assume the existence of two bottom values $\perp$ and **wrong** in the $\mathcal{DS}$ where **wrong** denotes a type error value and $\perp$ denotes other errors such as, e.g., non-termination.

In order to understand this relationship of the well-formedness predicates to the $\mathcal{DS}$ we first introduce the following concept. Free identifiers in the expression parameter of the well-formedness predicate must have a description in the environment parameter env. If we bind these identifiers to all possible values which fulfil the description in the environment env, e will evaluate to a set of possible values. This set of possible values including **wrong**, but excluding $\perp$ will be denoted by $\mathcal{E}(e)(env)$ and is called *the set of expression values* for e (in the given environment).

In relation to the $\mathcal{DS}$, the definition of the well-formedness predicates wf must be sound as described below. We consider definite and possible well-formedness separately.

Definite Well-formedness: For a definite well-formedness predicate wf_D the following relationship between the SS and the $\mathcal{DS}$ must be satisfied:

(4) $\quad wf_D(e)(t)(env) \;\Rightarrow\; \mathcal{E}(e)(env) \subseteq \mathcal{T}(t)(env)$

Consequently, $wf_D(e)(t)(env)$ is not true when **wrong** is in the set of expression values for e. Requirement (4) forms the basis for acceptance:

Acceptance rule 1: If we in the SS for some type t have that $wf_D(e)(t)(env)$ is true, then we may *accept* that all the values to which e may evaluate are inside the set of values of type t.

This is illustrated by a Venn-diagram in figure 2 (left part). The irregular shaped dotted area represents the set of expression values $\mathcal{E}(e)(env)$ and the surrounding sharp circle t represents the set of values $\mathcal{T}(t)(env)$ of a type t for which $wf_D(e)(t)(env)$ is true.

Possible Well-formedness: A possible well-formedness predicate wf_P is used for *rejection*. In order not to reject correct expressions the definition of wf_P must satisfy the following soundness requirement:

(5) $\quad \mathcal{E}(e)(env) \subseteq \mathcal{PT}(wf_P)(e)(env) \cup \{\mathbf{wrong}\}$

where $\mathcal{PT}$ is defined by

(6) $\quad \mathcal{PT}(wf_P)(e)(env) \;=\; \bigcup\{\mathcal{T}(t)(env) \mid t : TypeR \cdot t \in PT(wf_P)(e)(env)\}$

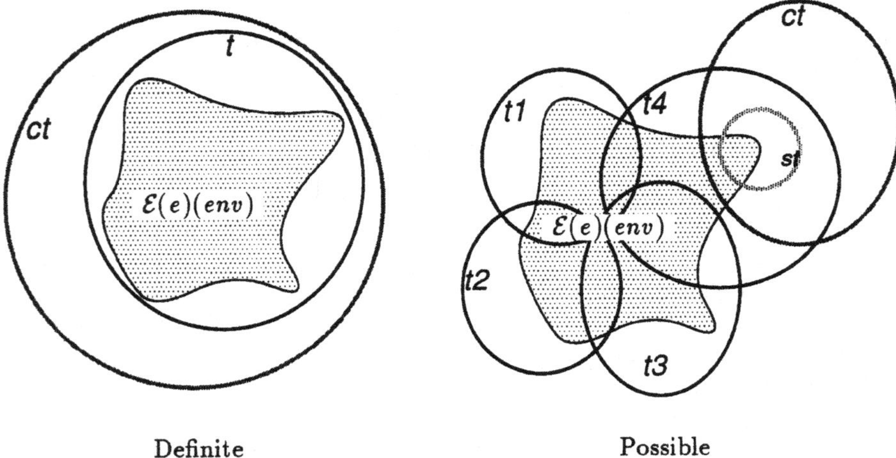

Figure 2: Soundness of well-formedness predicates for expressions.

(7) $PT(wf_P)(e)(env) \quad = \quad \{t \mid t : \mathit{TypeR} \cdot wf_P(e)(t)(env)\}$

The set of types $PT(wf_P)(e)(env)$ is called *the possible types* of e. The set of values $\mathcal{PT}(wf_P)(e)(env)$ is called *the set of values of the possible types* for e. In words the soundness requirement says that the set of values of the possible types for e must cover the set of expression values for e. In other words, it is required that for each value v to which the expression e may evaluate in the environment env there exists a type t such that $v \in \mathcal{T}(t)(env)$ and $wf_P(e)(t)(env)$ is true. The requirement (5) forms the basis for the following kind of rejection:

Rejection rule 1: If we in the SS have

$$\neg \exists\, t : \mathit{TypeR} \cdot wf_P(e)(t)(env)$$

i.e. $\mathcal{PT}(wf_P)(e)(env) = \{\,\}$ then we in the $\mathcal{DS}$ have $\mathcal{E}(e)(env) \subseteq \{\textbf{wrong}\}$ and we may *reject* that e evaluates to any value (in the given environment env).

This is illustrated by the Venn-diagram in figure 2 (right part). The irregular shaped dotted area represents the set of expression values $\mathcal{E}(e)(env)$. The possible types are $t1$, $t2$, $t3$ and $t4$, i.e. the types t for which $wf_P(e)(t)(env)$ holds. The ellipses labeled with these types then represent the corresponding sets of values of these types, so the union of these sets is *the set of values of the possible types* and must cover the set of expression values.

3.2 Examples of Basic Well-formedness Predicates

We show the definition of a few of the basic well-formedness predicates for expressions and argue for their soundness.

Example. We consider variables occurring as expressions.

22.0 $wf\_IdExpr : \Pi \rightarrow IdExpr \rightarrow TypeR \rightarrow Env \rightarrow \mathbb{B}$
.1 $wf\_IdExpr_{\pi}(mk\text{-}IdExpr(id))(type)(env) \triangleq$
.2 $\quad$ let $valueenv = env.venv$ in
.3 $\quad id \in \text{dom } valueenv \wedge type = valueenv(id)$

Here $wf\_IdExpr_{\pi}(mk\text{-}IdExpr(id))(type)(env)$ is (independent of π) true for exactly one type which is the type to which the identifier id is mapped in the environment env. We have the best possible approximation: $\mathcal{E}(mk\text{-}IdExpr(id))(env) = \mathcal{T}(type)(env)$. □

Example. We consider the well-formedness predicate for boolean literals.

23.0 $wf\_BoolLit : \Pi \rightarrow BoolLit \rightarrow TypeR \rightarrow Env \rightarrow \mathbb{B}$
.1 $wf\_BoolLit_{\pi}(mk\text{-}BoolLit(bv))(type)(env) \triangleq$
.2 $\quad type = \text{BOOL}$

This predicate is (for both definite and possible well-formedness) true for the type BOOL. The soundness requirements are fulfilled by $\mathcal{E}(mk\text{-}BoolLit(bv))(env) \subseteq \{\text{true}, \text{false}\} = \mathcal{T}(\text{BOOL})(env)$. □

Example. This example concerns if-then-else expressions.

24.0 $wf\_IfExpr : \Pi \rightarrow IfExpr \rightarrow TypeR \rightarrow Env \rightarrow \mathbb{B}$
.1 $wf\_IfExpr_{\pi}(mk\text{-}IfExpr(e_0, e_1, e_2))(type)(env) \triangleq$
.2 $\quad In\_type_{\pi}(wf\_Expr_{\pi})(e_0)(\text{BOOL})(env) \wedge$
.3 $\quad$ cases π :
.4 $\quad\quad mk\text{-}DEF(\text{-}) \rightarrow \exists\, t_1, t_2 : TypeR \cdot$
.5 $\quad\quad\quad wf\_Expr_{\pi}(e_1)(t_1)(env) \wedge wf\_Expr_{\pi}(e_2)(t_2)(env) \wedge$
.6 $\quad\quad\quad mk\text{-}UnionTypeR(\{t_1, t_2\}) = type,$
.7 $\quad\quad mk\text{-}POS(\text{-}) \rightarrow wf\_Expr_{\pi}(e_1)(type)(env) \vee wf\_Expr_{\pi}(e_2)(type)(env)$
.8 $\quad$ end

The check of the condition e_0 (24.2) is based on the *In_type* rule which will be explained in section 3.3.2. From the $\mathcal{DS}$ of the if-then-else expression we have that

(8) $\quad \mathcal{E}(mk\text{-}IfExpr(e_0, e_1, e_2))(env) \subseteq \mathcal{E}(e_1)(env) \cup \mathcal{E}(e_2)(env)$

In the following, it is assumed that the soundness requirements (4) and (5) are fulfilled for wf_Expr_{π} applied to the subcomponent expressions e_1 and e_2.

At the basic level of checking, we do not make a separate analysis of the two cases arising from e_0 being false respectively true. Consequently, the type of the if-then-else expression must cover both possibilities (24.4-6) For definite well-formedness we then have:

$$
\begin{aligned}
&\mathcal{E}(mk\text{-}IfExpr(e_0, e_1, e_2))(env) \\
&\subseteq \mathcal{E}(e_1)(env) \cup \mathcal{E}(e_2)(env) && \text{(from (8))} \\
&\subseteq \mathcal{T}(t_1)(env) \cup \mathcal{T}(t_2)(env) && \text{(from soundness req. (4))} \\
&= \mathcal{T}(mk\text{-}UnionTypeR(\{t_1, t_2\}))(env) && \text{(from } \mathcal{T}(mk\text{-}UnionTypeR(tset))(env)\text{)} \\
&= \mathcal{T}(type)(env) && \text{(from 24.6)}
\end{aligned}
$$

Hence, the soundness requirement is fulfilled for wf_IfExpr_D. Similarly, the if-then-else expression is possibly well-formed for all the types for which either e_1 or e_2 is possibly well-formed. The soundness requirement for wf_IfExpr_P is fulfilled by:

$$\mathcal{PT}(wf\_IfExpr_\pi)(mk\text{-}IfExpr(e_0, e_1, e_2))(env) \cup \{\textbf{wrong}\}$$
$$= \mathcal{PT}(wf\_Expr_\pi)(e_1)(env) \cup \mathcal{PT}(wf\_Expr_\pi)(e_2)(env) \cup \{\textbf{wrong}\} \qquad \text{(from (6) and 24.7)}$$
$$\supseteq \mathcal{E}(e_1)(env) \cup \mathcal{E}(e_2)(env) \qquad \text{(from soundness req. (5))}$$
$$\supseteq \mathcal{E}(mk\text{-}IfExpr(e_0, e_1, e_2))(env) \qquad \text{(from (8))}$$

Consider the following examples of a if-then-else expressions:

$F\,(n : \mathsf{N}, x : \mathsf{N} \mid \mathsf{B}) \triangleq$
 ...if ... then n else true...
 ...if ... then $x + 1$ else true...

For the two if-then-else expressions in the above shown function body we have: The first expression is definitely well-formed for the type $\mathsf{N} \mid \mathsf{B}$ and possibly well-formed for the two types N and B. The second expression is not definitely well-formed for any type since $x + 1$ is not definitely well-formed in the given context. On the other hand, the expression is possibly well-formed for both N and B. □

3.3 Expressions in Context

Expressions occur as components in larger constructs (such as other expressions, function bodies etc.). An expression e occurring in a given context is in the $\mathcal{DS}$ required to yield values within some given set of values depending on the given context. In the SS, such a set of allowed result values may be expressed by a type ct.

When checking for definite well-formedness, the SS must require that all the expression values $\mathcal{E}(e)(env)$ are inside the set of values $\mathcal{T}(ct)(env)$ of type ct. When checking for possible well-formedness, the SS must—informally speaking—require that some of the expression values $\mathcal{E}(e)(env)$ are in the set of values $\mathcal{T}(ct)(env)$. We consider the formulation of this check in the SS for definite and possible well-formedness.

Definite Well-formedness. In the previous section it was shown that for definite well-formedness many of the basic well-formedness predicates are defined in such a way that they will be fulfilled for at most one type. As an example, consider a boolean literal bl occurring as an actual parameter to a function defined with a formal parameter of the type $\mathsf{N} \mid \mathsf{B}$. The definite well-formedness of this actual parameter cannot simply be checked by $wf\_Expr_D(bl)(ct)(env)$ where ct in the considered example is $\mathsf{N} \mid \mathsf{B}$. The predicate $wf\_Expr_D(bl)(ct)(env)$ will only be true for $ct = \mathsf{B}$. Consequently, it is false for the considered example.

When checking that an expression yields values within some specific type ct required by the context, the following more general rule for acceptance should be used:

Acceptance rule 2: If we in the SS for some specific type ct have

$$\exists\, t : TypeR \cdot wf_D(e)(t)(env) \wedge is\_subtype(t, ct)(env)$$

where wf_D satisfies the soundness requirement (4) then in the $\mathcal{DS}$ we have $\mathcal{E}(e)(env) \subseteq \mathcal{T}(ct)(env)$, i.e. we may accept that all the values to which e may evaluate are inside the set of values of type ct.

This is illustrated by the left part of figure 2. The proof of this is shown in [4].

Possible Well-formedness. For possible well-formedness we have a problem similar to the above described for definite well-formedness. Consider the example:

$F(x : \mathsf{N\text{-}set} \mid \mathsf{N}) \triangleq \ \ldots$
$F(\mathsf{if}\ \ldots\ \mathsf{then}\ 1\ \mathsf{else}\ \mathsf{true})$

The function application of F should not be rejected because the actual parameter of the function application may yield a value of type N which is a subtype of the formal parameter type N-set | N. However, $wf\_Expr_P(\mathsf{if}\ \ldots\ \mathsf{then}\ 1\ \mathsf{else}\ \mathsf{true})(ct)(env)$ is only true for $ct = \mathsf{N}$ and $ct = \mathsf{B}$, so for the considered example where $ct = \mathsf{N\text{-}set} \mid \mathsf{N}$ it is false.

To reject that an expression e evaluates to a value belonging to some specific type ct required by the context must be based on the following observation. If the set of values of type ct does not overlap the set of values of the possible types for e, i.e. $\mathcal{T}(ct)(env) \cap \mathcal{PT}(wf_P)(e)(env) = \{\}$ where wf_P satisfies the soundness requirement (5), then we may conclude that $\mathcal{T}(ct)(env) \cap \mathcal{E}(e)(env) = \{\}$:

Rejection rule 2: If we in the SS for some specific type ct have

$$\neg \exists\, t : TypeR \cdot overlapping(t, ct)(env) \wedge wf_P(e)(t)(env)$$

where wf_P satisfies the soundness requirement (5), then we in the $\mathcal{DS}$ have $\mathcal{E}(e)(env) \cap \mathcal{T}(ct)(env) = \{\}$, i.e. we may *reject* that e in the environment env evaluates to a value in the set of values of type ct.

This is illustrated by the right part of figure 2. We assume that the shown types ($t1, t2, t3$ and $t4$) are the possible types for a well-formedness predicate wf_P which satisfies the soundness requirement (5). For this reason the union of the corresponding sets of values of the types covers the set of expression values. If the set of values of the specific type ct does not overlap one of these possible types, it cannot overlap the set of expression values. A general proof of this is shown in [4].

3.3.1 The Subsumption Rule

Rather than using the two new rules for acceptance and rejection we introduce a new typing rule which will make the well-formedness predicates more appropriate for the above discussed checks of expressions in a context. As mentioned previously, typing rules are defined in the terms of functions of the type $\Pi \rightarrow WFE \rightarrow WFE$ which transform a well-formedness predicate to a more general or powerful version.

The typing rule which is needed for definite well-formedness is in the literature (see, e.g. [6]) some times called the subsumption rule. Actually, we define two versions which, however, only differ in the case of possible well-formedness. The first version defined below does not quite correspond to what one might expect from the above discussion, but it turns out to be the most appropriate.

25.0 $Subsumption : \Pi \rightarrow WFE \rightarrow WFE$
.1 $Subsumption_{\pi}(wf)(e)(type)(env) \triangleq$
.2 $\quad \exists\, et : TypeR \cdot$
.3 $\qquad wf(e)(et)(env) \wedge$
.4 $\qquad \mathsf{cases}\ \pi :$
.5 $\qquad\quad mk\text{-}DEF(\text{-}) \rightarrow is\_subtype(et, type)(env),$
.6 $\qquad\quad mk\text{-}POS(\text{-}) \rightarrow is\_subtype(type, et)(env)$
.7 $\qquad \mathsf{end}$

The alternative version is defined in section 3.3.2. We analyze the rule for definite and possible well-formedness separately:

Definite Well-formedness. If $wf_D(e)(t)(env)$ is true for a type t and ct is a supertype of t, then $Subsumption_D(wf_D)(e)(ct)(env)$ is true. (See the left part of figure 2). It is easy to see that if wf_D satisfies the soundness requirement (4) then $Subsumption_D(wf_D)$ also satisfies the soundness requirement (4), i.e.

(9) $Subsumption_D(wf_D)(e)(t)(env) \Rightarrow \mathcal{E}(e)(env) \subseteq \mathcal{T}(t)(env)$

From the definition of *Subsumption* it is seen that $Subsumption_D(wf_D)(e)(ct)(env)$ is equivalent to the check in acceptance rule 2. We thus have the following general rule for acceptance which is a reformulation of rule 2:

Acceptance rule 3: If we in the SS have that $Subsumption_D(wf_D)(e)(ct)(env)$ is true for some specific type ct and wf_D fulfils the soundness requirement (4), then we in the $\mathcal{DS}$ have $\mathcal{E}(e)(env) \subseteq \mathcal{T}(ct)(env)$.

Possible Well-formedness. If $wf_P(e)(t)(env)$ is true for a type t and st is subtype of t then $Subsumption_P(wf_P)(e)(st)(env)$ is true. In figure 2 (right part), besides being true for the possible types $t1, \ldots, t4$ the transformed well-formedness predicate now also becomes true for all their subtypes including the shown subtype st.

It is easy to see that if wf_P satisfies the soundness requirement (5), the soundness requirement is also satisfied for $Subsumption_P(wf_P)$, i.e.

(10) $\mathcal{E}(e)(env) \subseteq \mathcal{PT}(Subsumption_P(wf_P))(e)(env) \cup \{\textbf{wrong}\}$

Using *Subsumption* we have a new rejection rule:

Rejection rule 3: If we in the SS for some type ct have

$$\neg \exists\, st : \mathit{TypeR} \cdot is\_subtype(st, ct)(env) \wedge Subsumption_P(wf_P)(e)(st)(env)$$

where wf_P satisfies the soundness requirement (5), then we in the $\mathcal{DS}$ have $\mathcal{E}(e)(env) \cap \mathcal{T}(ct)(env) = \{\}$.

From the definition of *Subsumption* (def. 25) and the definition of *overlapping* (def. 16) it is seen that the check in rejection rule 3 is equivalent to the check in rejection rule 2.

This is also illustrated in figure 2 (right part). Among the types for which the well-formedness predicate transformed with *Subsumption* is true, we have the shown type st which is a subtype of ct. Consequently, with the information available in the possible types we cannot reject that the expression e evaluates to a value inside the set of values of type ct (and in the example e actually does).

3.3.2 An Alternative Subsumption Rule

If the just defined subsumption rule in the case of possible well-formedness is defined a little bit different we can get a simpler rejection rule. We call this modified subsumption rule *In_type*:

26.0 $In\_type : \Pi \rightarrow WFE \rightarrow WFE$
.1 $In\_type_{\pi}(wf)(expr)(type)(env) \triangleq$
.2 $\quad \exists\, et : TypeR \cdot$
.3 $\quad\quad wf(e)(et)(env) \land$
.4 $\quad\quad$ cases π :
.5 $\quad\quad\quad mk\text{-}DEF(\text{-}) \rightarrow is\_subtype(et, type)(env),$
.6 $\quad\quad\quad mk\text{-}POS(\text{-}) \rightarrow overlapping(type, et)(env)$
.7 $\quad\quad$ end

If $wf_P(e)(t)(env)$ is true then $In\_type_P(wf_P)(e)(ct)(env)$ is true for any type ct for which $overlapping(ct, t)(env)$ is true. In the right part of figure 2, the transformed well-formedness predicate is in addition to the possible types $t1, \ldots, t4$ also true for all their overlapping types including the shown overlapping type ct. Rejection can now be based on the following simple rule:

Rejection rule 4: If we in the SS for some type t have $\neg\, In\_type_P(wf_P)(e)(t)(env)$ where wf_P satisfies the soundness requirement (5), then we in the $\mathcal{DS}$ have $\mathcal{E}(e)(env) \cap \mathcal{T}(t)(env) = \{\}$.

There are, however, good reasons for using this rule with care. The used type relation *overlapping* is not transitive. In compound expressions where the type of a component expression may influence the result type of the compound expression, the possible well-formedness predicate will end up using *overlapping* in a transitive manner and in this way make too liberal conclusions about the possible types.

Therefor *In_type* should only be used to express that a component expression must have some specific type (usually BOOL as in the already considered example concerning if-then-else expressions) which has no influence on the compound expressions' result type. This will be discussed further in section 3.4.

3.4 Strict Compound Expressions

A strict compound expression is an expression whose evaluation in the $\mathcal{DS}$ requires the evaluation of all the subcomponent expressions. In the VDM-SL there are more than 50 expression constructs and/or operators which are strict. In the SS it is possible to treat all the strict compound expressions according to the same scheme shown in the following.

We consider a compound expression $SCExpr$ having n subcomponent expressions:

$$Expr = \ldots \mid SCExpr \mid \ldots$$

$$\begin{aligned} SCExpr :: {} & s1 : Expr_1 \\ & \vdots \\ & sn : Expr_n \end{aligned}$$

The form of the well-formedness predicate for such a construct is sketched below:

27.0 $wf\_SCExpr : \Pi \rightarrow SCExpr \rightarrow TypeR \rightarrow Env \rightarrow \mathbb{B}$
.1 $wf\_SCExpr_{\pi}(mk\text{-}SCExpr(e_1, \ldots, e_n))(rtype)(env) \triangleq$
.2 $\quad$ let $TP(t_1, \ldots, t_n : TypeR)(rt : TypeR)(env : Env) : \mathbb{B} =$
.3 $\qquad$ "A basic type predicate characteristic for the *SCExpr* construct which states the relationship between the types t_i of the component values and the type rt of the result value."
.4 $\qquad$ in
.5 $\quad wf\_SCompExpr_{\pi}(TP)(e_1, \ldots, e_n)(rtype)(env)$

where $wf\_SCompExpr$ is a general function used to check the well-formedness of strict compound expressions based on the basic type predicate TP:

28.0 $wf\_SCompExpr : \Pi \rightarrow TPredicate \rightarrow Expr \times \ldots \times Expr \rightarrow TypeR \rightarrow Env \rightarrow \mathbb{B}$
.1 $wf\_SCompExpr_{\pi}(TP)(e_1, \ldots, e_n)(rtype)(env) \triangleq$
.2 $\quad \exists\, ct_1, \ldots, ct_n : TypeR \cdot$
.3 $\qquad Subsumption_{\pi}(wf\_Expr_{\pi})(e_1)(ct_1)(env) \wedge$
.4 $\qquad \vdots$
.5 $\qquad Subsumption_{\pi}(wf\_Expr_{\pi})(e_n)(ct_n)(env) \wedge$
.6 $\qquad TP(ct_1, \ldots, ct_n)(rtype)(env)$

The function $wf\_SCompExpr$ is actually defined in 3 versions:

$$wf\_SCompExprn : \Pi \rightarrow TnPredicate \rightarrow Expr^{*} \rightarrow TypeR \rightarrow Env \rightarrow \mathbb{B}$$
$$wf\_SCompExpr2 : \Pi \rightarrow T2Predicate \rightarrow Expr \times Expr \rightarrow TypeR \rightarrow Env \rightarrow \mathbb{B}$$
$$wf\_SCompExpr1 : \Pi \rightarrow T1Predicate \rightarrow Expr \rightarrow TypeR \rightarrow Env \rightarrow \mathbb{B}$$

The first version can take an arbitrary number of component expressions. The next two versions are specialized versions of the first one for two respectively one component expressions.

In order to illustrate the use of $wf\_SCompExpr$, especially the interplay between the type requirements expressed in lines 28.3-5 and that in line 28.6 we show a few instantiations of the general scheme wf_SCExpr.

Example. We consider the well-formedness predicate for the union operator for sets:

29.0 $wf\_SETUNION : \Pi \rightarrow BinaryExpr \rightarrow TypeR \rightarrow Env \rightarrow \mathbb{B}$
.1 $wf\_SETUNION_{\pi}(mk\text{-}BinaryExpr(e_1, \mathrm{SETUNION}, e_2))(type)(env) \triangleq$
.2 $\quad$ let $TP(t_1, t_2 : TypeR)(rt : TypeR)(env : Env) : \mathbb{B} =$
.3 $\qquad \exists\, et_1, et_2 : TypeR \cdot t_1 = mk\text{-}SetTypeR(et_1) \wedge t_2 = mk\text{-}SetTypeR(et_2) \wedge$
.4 $\qquad\qquad rt = mk\text{-}SetTypeR(mk\text{-}UnionTypeR(\{et_1, et_2\}))$ in
.5 $\quad wf\_SCompExpr2_{\pi}(TP)(e_1, e_2)(type)(env)$

In $wf\_SCompExpr2$ (see def. 28) the well-formedness predicate $Subsumption_{\pi}(wf\_Expr_{\pi})$ is used to check the component expressions e_1 and e_2. Informally speaking, this means that for definite well-formedness the component types are generalized if possible to the necessary super-type in order to be accepted by the TP predicate.

Consider the following concrete example of an expression involving the union operator for sets:

$$D\,(x : (\mathbb{B} \times \mathbb{B})\text{-set} \mid \mathbb{B}\text{-set}) : \ldots \triangleq$$
$$\ldots\; x \cup \{1\}\; \ldots$$

When checking the expression $x \cup \{1\}$ for definite well-formedness, the type predicate

TP for the union operator expects a set type, so the type of the left argument (x) is lifted to at least ($\mathbb{B} \times \mathbb{B} \mid \mathbb{B}$)-set. Consequently the least result type will be ($\mathbb{B} \times \mathbb{B} \mid \mathbb{B} \mid \mathbb{N}$)-set.

For possible well-formedness, however, the type of a component expression can be any subtype of the type provided by *wf_Expr*; the argument type is *not* lifted. Consequently, the type predicate *TP* must be able to accept (some of the) subtypes of the expected type. Consider also this example:

$$mytype = \mathbb{B}\text{-set} \mid \mathbb{N}$$

$$P\,(x : (\mathbb{N} \mid \mathbb{N} \times \mathbb{N})\text{-set} \mid mytype) : \ldots \;\triangleq$$
$$\ldots\; x \cup \{1\} \;\ldots$$

When checking the expression $x \cup \{1\}$ for possible well-formedness, the types provided for the type predicate *TP* for the left argument will be any of the subtypes for the declared type of x, i.e. ($\mathbb{N} \mid \mathbb{N} \times \mathbb{N}$)-set, $\mathbb{N}$-set, ($\mathbb{N} \times \mathbb{N}$)-set, $\mathbb{B}$-set and $\mathbb{N}$ of which *TP* will accept one of the set types depending on the result type. □

Example. This example concerns the well-formedness predicate for function applications:

```
30.0  wf_FctApply : Π → FctApply → TypeR → Env → B
  .1  wf_FctApply_π (mk-FctApply(fe, ae))(type)(env) ≜
  .2    let TP(fet, aet : TypeR)(rt : TypeR)(env : Env) : B =
  .3          cases fet :
  .4            FnTypeR(fat, frt) → is_subtype(aet, fat)(env) ∧ frt = rt,
  .5            others → false
  .6          end in
  .7    wf_SCompExpr2_π (TP)(fe, ae)(type)(env)
```

Here we consider the function definition:

$$F\,(f : (\mathbb{N} \mid \mathbb{N} \times \mathbb{N}) \rightarrow \mathbb{N}, x : \mathbb{N} \mid \mathbb{B}) \;\triangleq$$
$$\ldots\; f(x) \;\ldots$$

When checking the expression $f(x)$ for possible well-formedness, the type predicate *TP* for application gets the component types ($\mathbb{N} \mid \mathbb{N} \times \mathbb{N}$) $\rightarrow \mathbb{N}$ and $\mathbb{N} \mid \mathbb{B}$ and their subtypes. Here *TP* for the second component (the argument) must be able to accept the defined argument type $\mathbb{N} \mid \mathbb{N} \times \mathbb{N}$ *and* all subtypes of the defined argument type, i.e. also $\mathbb{N}$. See def. 30.4. □

For the two just shown examples we see that the type predicate for set union naturally accepts the necessary subtypes by accepting all set types, whereas in the definition of the type predicate for function application the subtypes of the defined argument type should be added to the accepted types. We give a more formal description of the requirements to the type predicate *TP* in section 3.4.1.

If in the definition of *wf_SCompExpr*, the alternative subsumption rule *In_type* (see section 3.3.2) was applied in place of *Subsumption*, the component types would be generalized to the necessary super-types both for definite and possible well-formedness and no precautions would be necessary in the definition of *TP* for possible well-formedness. This replacement does not violate the soundness requirement but far too many illegal specifications would not be rejected. As an example consider:

$$F\,(f : \mathbb{B}\text{-set} \rightarrow \mathbb{N}) \;\triangleq$$
$$\ldots\; f(\{1\} \cup \{2\}) \;\ldots$$

When checking the shown expression for possible well-formedness the type N-set of the left argument $\{1\}$ could be lifted to (N | B)-set. Hence, a possible result type of the set union expression could be (N | B)-set of which the subtype B-set would be accepted as a possible argument type in the function application. The misery is caused by an implicit double application of *overlapping* which is *not* transitive.

However, even when using *Subsumption* rather than *In_type*, the above shown function application will *not* be rejected by the possible well-formedness predicates which is shown until now. One of the possible types of $\{1\} \cup \{2\}$ when *Subsumption* is used, is the empty set type EMPTYTYPE-set which is also a subtype of the defined argument type B-set of f. This may be handled by introducing types for non-empty sets.

3.4.1 The Characteristic Type Predicate *TP*

The basic type predicate *TP* characteristic for a *SCExpr* construct must satisfy some relations to the $\mathcal{DS}$ in order to assure that *wf_SCompExpr* satisfies the soundness requirements (4) and (5). As the VDM-SL allows looseness in specifications, a specification may have several models in the $\mathcal{DS}$. To manage this, the $\mathcal{DS}$'s definition of semantics of expressions is organized in several levels but at the innermost level each expression construct is defined by a function *Apply* which for strict compound expressions have a definition like

$$ApplySCExpr(v_1 : VAL, \ldots, v_n : VAL) : VAL \triangleq \ldots$$

Here *VAL* is the domain of values in the $\mathcal{DS}$. The domain *VAL* includes bottom values, i.e. both $\perp$ and **wrong**.

The SS does not distinguish between the different models in the $\mathcal{DS}$, but merge them all together. This means that when estimating types for expressions we consider the union of all possible values from all models:

(11) $\mathcal{E}(mk\text{-}SCExpr(e_1, \ldots, e_n))(env) =$

$$\{ApplySCExpr(v_1, \ldots, v_n) \mid v_1 \in \mathcal{E}(e_1)(env), \ldots, v_n \in \mathcal{E}(e_n)(env)\} \setminus \{\perp\}$$

In accordance with the previously informal definition of $\mathcal{E}$ we exclude $\perp$ from the set of expression values but include **wrong**. We consider definite and possible well-formedness separately.

Definite Well-formedness. Let $ct_1, \ldots, ct_n$ be some component types and rt a result type. The definition of *TP* must satisfy the requirement:

(12) $TP(ct_1, \ldots, ct_n)(rt)(env) \;\Rightarrow\; V\_SCExpr(ct_1, \ldots, ct_n)(env) \subseteq \mathcal{T}(rt)(env)$

where *V_SCExpr* is defined by

(13) $V\_SCExpr(ct_1, \ldots, ct_n)(env) =$

$$\{ApplySCExpr(v_1, \ldots, v_n) \mid v_1 \in \mathcal{T}(ct_1)(env), \ldots, v_n \in \mathcal{T}(ct_n)(env)\} \setminus \{\perp\}$$

So, if $TP(ct_1, \ldots, ct_n)(rt)(env)$ is true for some component types $ct_1, \ldots, ct_n$ and result type rt, then all possible combinations of component values belonging to the component types must be legal, i.e. type consistent component values and must result in a value belonging to the result type. Since **wrong** $\notin \mathcal{T}(t)(env)$ for any type t, it follows from requirement (12) that

$$\mathbf{wrong} \in V\_SCExpr(ct_1, \ldots, ct_n)(env) \;\Rightarrow\; \neg\, TP(ct_1, \ldots, ct_n)(rt)(env)$$

If the characteristic type predicate TP for a $SCExpr$ construct satisfies the requirement (12), then wf_SCExpr_D also satisfies the soundness requirement (4), i.e.

$$wf\_SCExpr_D(mk\text{-}SCExpr(e_1, \ldots, e_n))(type)(env) \Rightarrow \\ \quad \mathcal{E}(mk\text{-}SCExpr(e_1, \ldots, e_n))(env) \subseteq \mathcal{T}(type)(env)$$

A proof of this is shown in [4].

Possible Well-formedness. We say that a type vt is the minimal type for a value $v \in VAL$ if vt is one of the least types which contains v:

(14) $is\_min\_type(v : VAL)(vt : TypeR)(env : Env) =$
$$v \in \mathcal{T}(vt)(env) \wedge \\ \forall\, t : TypeR \cdot v \in \mathcal{T}(t)(env) \Rightarrow is\_subtype(vt, t)(env)$$

For possible well-formedness the type predicate TP characteristic for a $SCExpr$ construct must now respect the following requirement:

(15) $\forall\, v_1, \ldots, v_n, rv \in VAL \setminus \{\mathbf{wrong}, \bot\} \cdot$
$$rv = ApplySCExpr(v_1, \ldots, v_n) \Rightarrow \\ \exists\, ct_1, \ldots, ct_n, rt : TypeR \cdot \\ \quad TP(ct_1, \ldots, ct_n)(rt)(env) \wedge rv \in \mathcal{T}(rt)(env) \wedge \\ \quad is\_min\_type(v_1)(ct_1)(env) \wedge \ldots \wedge is\_min\_type(v_n)(ct_n)(env)$$

In words this means that for all possible type consistent combinations of component values $v_1, \ldots, v_n$ and corresponding result value rv there exist component types $ct_1, \ldots, ct_n$ and a result type rt such that they satisfy the type predicate TP and the result value belongs to the result type and each component type is a minimal type of the corresponding component value.

As mentioned previously, because argument types are communicated to TP using *Subsumption*, the argument types are not "lifted" up to TP, but TP must be able to get down to the possible argument subtypes; this is ensured by the third requirement mentioned above.

If the characteristic type predicate TP for a $SCExpr$ construct satisfies the requirement (15), then wf_SCExpr_P satisfies the soundness requirement (5), i.e.

$$\mathcal{E}(mk\text{-}SCExpr(e_1, \ldots, e_n))(env) \subseteq \\ \quad \mathcal{PT}(wf\_SCExpr_P)(mk\text{-}SCExpr(e_1, \ldots, e_n))(env) \cup \{\mathbf{wrong}\}$$

A proof of this is shown in [4]. For most of the strict compound expressions, only a single type predicate TP is defined which satisfies both of the above defined requirements.

3.4.2 Examples of Strict Compound Expressions

In this section we show a few more examples of basic well-formedness predicates for strict compound expressions in order to illustrate the versatility of this approach to defining static semantics.

Example. The well-formedness predicate for function composition may be defined by:

31.0 $wf\_FCTCOMPOSE : \Pi \rightarrow BinaryExpr \rightarrow TypeR \rightarrow Env \rightarrow \mathbb{B}$
.1 $wf\_FCTCOMPOSE_{\pi}(mk\text{-}BinaryExpr(f, \text{FCTCOMPOSE}, g))(type)(env) \triangleq$
.2 $\quad \text{let } TP(t_1, t_2 : TypeR)(rt : TypeR)(env : Env) : \mathbb{B} =$
.3 $\qquad\quad \exists\, gat, grt, fat, frt : TypeR \cdot$
.4 $\qquad\qquad t_1 = mk\text{-}FnTypeR(fat, frt) \wedge t_2 = mk\text{-}FnTypeR(gat, grt) \wedge$
.5 $\qquad\qquad rt = mk\text{-}FnTypeR(gat, frt) \wedge$
.6 $\qquad\qquad is\_subtype(grt, fat)(env) \text{ in}$
.7 $\quad wf\_SCompExpr2_{\pi}(TP)(f, g)(type)(env)$

As examples of function compositions consider:

32.0 $F(f_1 : A \rightarrow (B \mid C), f_2 : (B \mid C \mid D) \rightarrow E,$
.1 $\quad f_3 : N \mid (B \mid E) \rightarrow F \mid (C \mid F) \rightarrow G : \ldots) \triangleq$
.2 $\quad \ldots f_2 \circ f_1 \ldots$
.3 $\quad \ldots f_3 \circ f_1 \ldots$

The first shown function composition is definitely well-formed with respect to the function type $A \rightarrow E$. Since f_1 is possibly well-formed with respect to the type $A \rightarrow B$ and $A \rightarrow C$ (using *Subsumption*), the second function composition is possibly well-formed with respect to the function types $A \rightarrow F$ and $A \rightarrow G$. It is, however, not definitely well-formed for any type.

The use of implicit definitions makes it easy to define function composition, whereas a more direct definition method which, for instance, is based on synthesizing sets of types from the component expressions may require more elaborate formulae for stating the relationship between the components' possible function types and the composed function type. □

Example. We consider the well-formedness predicate for set enumerations.

33.0 $wf\_SetEnumeration : \Pi \rightarrow SetEnumeration \rightarrow TypeR \rightarrow Env \rightarrow \mathbb{B}$
.1 $wf\_SetEnumeration_{\pi}(mk\text{-}SetEnumeration(exprset))(type)(env) \triangleq$
.2 $\quad \text{let } TP(list\_of\_elementtypes : TypeR^*)(rt : TypeR)(env : Env) : \mathbb{B} =$
.3 $\qquad\quad \text{let } tset = \text{elems } list\_of\_elementtypes \text{ in}$
.4 $\qquad\quad \neg \exists\, t \in tset, ft : FnTypeR \cdot type\_dep(t, ft)(env.tenv) \wedge$
.5 $\qquad\quad \text{let } et = (\text{if } tset = \{\,\}$
.6 $\qquad\qquad\qquad \text{then EMPTYTYPE}$
.7 $\qquad\qquad\qquad \text{else } mk\text{-}UnionTypeR(tset)) \text{ in}$
.8 $\qquad\quad rt = mk\text{-}SetTypeR(et) \text{ in}$
.9 $\quad wf\_SCompExprn_{\pi}(TP)([e \mid e \in exprset])(type)(env)$

This is an example with an arbitrary number of components. Note that the elements in a set enumeration must not have a type which depends on a function type (see 33.4). Consider the following concrete example of a enumerated set:

$$G(x : \mathbb{N} \mid \mathbb{N} \times \mathbb{N} \mid (\mathbb{N} \rightarrow \mathbb{N})) : \ldots \triangleq$$
$$\ldots \{\text{true}, x\} \ldots$$

The shown set enumeration is not definitely well-formed for any type, but possibly well-formed with respect to the set types $(\mathbb{B} \mid \mathbb{N})$-**set** and $(\mathbb{B} \mid \mathbb{N} \times \mathbb{N})$-**set**. □

4 Non-basic Checks

In this section, we describe how some checks can be added beyond the minimum check. By adding more checks we want to be able to reject a larger set of the ill-formed specifications and accept a larger set of the well-formed specifications. The soundness requirements (4) and (5) only assures soundness but of course not completeness. If we define $wf_D(e)(t)(env)$ to be false for all types t the soundness requirement (4) is trivially satisfied and no expressions will be accepted. If we define $wf_P(e)(t)(env)$ to be true for all types t the soundness requirement (5) is trivially satisfied and no expressions will be rejected.

Let wf_{DEF1} and wf_{DEF2} be two definite well-formedness predicates. Then wf_{DEF1} is at least as powerful for acceptance as wf_{DEF2} if $Subsumption_D(wf_{DEF1})(e)(t)(env)$ is true for at least as many types t as $Subsumption_D(wf_{DEF2})(e)(t)(env)$ (See acceptance rule 3). Formally this means

$$DT(wf_{DEF1})(e)(env) \supseteq DT(wf_{DEF2})(e)(env)$$

where DT is the counterpart to PT which is defined for possible well-formedness. The function DT is defined by:

(16) $DT(wf_D)(e)(env) = \{t \mid t : TypeR \cdot Subsumption_D(wf_D)(e)(t)(env)\}$

This means that wf_{DEF1} is *more* powerful than wf_{DEF2} if wf_{DEF1} either is able to accept a more precise (i.e. smaller) type than wf_{DEF2} or wf_{DEF1} is able to accept a type while wf_{DEF2} is not.

In a similar way let wf_{POS1} and wf_{POS2} be two possible well-formedness predicates for which

$$\mathcal{PT}(wf_{POS1})(e)(env) \subseteq \mathcal{PT}(wf_{POS2})(e)(env)$$

When using rejection rule 3, wf_{POS1} will be able to reject at least as many types ct as wf_{POS2}. We say that wf_{POS1} is at least as powerful for rejection as wf_{POS2}.

To have a specification checked beyond the minimum check one must add one or more of the possible checks to the check sets which are part of the well-formedness predicates π parameter defined in section 3 (def. 17 and 18). The checks which we define for definite well-formedness respectively possible well-formedness, are

34.0 $DCheck = \text{UNIONCLOSE} \mid \text{FLOWANALYZE} \mid \ldots$

35.0 $PCheck = \text{LOCALCONTEXT} \mid \text{FLOWANALYZE} \mid \ldots$

4.1 Union Close

The check which we are going to consider in this section concerns an improvement of the way the strict compound expressions are checked in the case of definite well-formedness. However, as before the checking is still based on the characteristic type predicates TP defined for each construct (section 3.4).

As an example where improved checking is required, consider a function D defined as follows:

$$D\,(x : (\mathsf{B} \times \mathsf{B})\text{-}\mathbf{set} \mid \mathsf{B}\text{-}\mathbf{set}) : \ldots \triangleq$$
$$\ldots\ E(x \cup \{1\})\ \ldots$$

As we have seen (in section 3.4 def. 29), the characteristic type predicate $TP_{\cup}$ for the set union operator only accepts set types for the component types. Accordingly (by using the *Subsumption* rule) the union type of the left argument x must be lifted to at least $(\mathsf{B}\times\mathsf{B} \mid \mathsf{B})$-set and consequently the least result type for $x \cup \{1\}$ will be $(\mathsf{B}\times\mathsf{B} \mid \mathsf{B} \mid \mathsf{N})$-set.

That type is, however, a poor approximation of the values of the considered expression. In the given context, $x \cup \{1\}$ will always yield either a set of booleans and the natural number 1 or a set of boolean pairs and the natural number 1, but never a set containing both booleans, boolean pairs and the natural number 1. It is, however, possible with the type representations we have at our disposal to suggest a better type, namely $(\mathsf{B} \times \mathsf{B} \mid \mathsf{N})$-set $\mid$ $(\mathsf{B} \mid \mathsf{N})$-set. If the function E which is applied to $x \cup \{1\}$ is defined as

$$E(set : (\mathsf{B} \times \mathsf{B} \mid \mathsf{N})\text{-set} \mid (\mathsf{B} \mid \mathsf{N})\text{-set}) \triangleq \ldots$$

then $E(x \cup \{1\})$ will only be definitely well-formed if $x \cup \{1\}$ as a result type can have this suggested better type.

The conclusion of the above analysis is that

if $TP_{\cup}$ accepts
$TP_{\cup}((\mathsf{B} \times \mathsf{B})\text{-set}, \mathsf{N}\text{-set})((\mathsf{B} \times \mathsf{B} \mid \mathsf{N})\text{-set})(env)$ and
$TP_{\cup}(\mathsf{B}\text{-set}, \mathsf{N}\text{-set})((\mathsf{B} \mid \mathsf{N})\text{-set})(env)$
then $TP_{\cup}$ should also accept
$TP_{\cup}((\mathsf{B} \times \mathsf{B})\text{-set} \mid \mathsf{B}\text{-set}, \mathsf{N}\text{-set})((\mathsf{B} \times \mathsf{B} \mid \mathsf{N})\text{-set} \mid (\mathsf{B} \mid \mathsf{N})\text{-set})(env)$

Another example which demonstrates the weakness of the characteristic type predicates as defined until now is as follows:

$$G(f : \mathsf{N} \to \mathsf{B}, g : (\mathsf{N} \mid \mathsf{B}) \to \mathsf{N}) : \ldots \triangleq$$
$$\ldots(\text{if } \ldots \text{ then } f \text{ else } g)(5)\ldots$$

We will analyze the function application in the body of G for definite well-formedness. The characteristic type predicate $TP_{()}$ for function application only accepts function types for the first component expression (see section 3.4 def. 30). The function expression (if.... then f else g) is definitely well-formed for the union type $\mathsf{N} \to \mathsf{B} \mid (\mathsf{N} \mid \mathsf{B}) \to \mathsf{N}$ and—due to the subsumption rule—all greater types. However, there is no function type above this union type. Two function types are only related if they have equivalent domain types (see section 2 def. 12 and 13)). So the function application is not definitely well-formed for any type. In the $\mathcal{DS}$ the shown function application is type consistent, all values in $\mathcal{T}(\mathsf{N} \to \mathsf{B} \mid (\mathsf{N} \mid \mathsf{B}) \to \mathsf{N})(env)$ are functions which accepts a natural number as argument.

The conclusion of the above analysis is that

if $TP_{()}$ accepts
$TP_{()}(\mathsf{N} \to \mathsf{B}, \mathsf{N})(\mathsf{B})(env)$ and
$TP_{()}((\mathsf{N} \mid \mathsf{B}) \to \mathsf{N}, \mathsf{N})(\mathsf{N})(env)$
then $TP_{()}$ should also accept
$TP_{()}(\mathsf{N} \to \mathsf{B} \mid (\mathsf{N} \mid \mathsf{B}) \to \mathsf{N}, \mathsf{N})(\mathsf{B} \mid \mathsf{N})(env)$

The above two shown examples of improvements of a TP predicate is in general done by a function *UnionClose* which transforms a TP predicate to the improved version. As shown by the examples, the improved TP predicate holds for some union types if and only if the original version holds for all combinations of the *member* types. So we define (informally):

36.0 $is\_member\_type : TypeR \times TypeR \rightarrow Env \rightarrow \mathbf{B}$
.1 $is\_member\_type\,(mt, t)(env) \triangleq$
.2 $\quad mt = t \vee$
.3 $\quad t = (t_1 \mid \ldots \mid mt \mid \ldots) \vee$
.4 $\quad t$ is typename defined by $t = mt \vee$
.5 $\quad \exists\, t' : TypeR \cdot is\_member\_type(mt, t')(env) \wedge is\_member\_type(t', t)(env)$

and then

37.0 $UnionClose : TPredicate \rightarrow TPredicate$
.1 $UnionClose\,(TP)(ct_1, \ldots, ct_n)(rt)(env) \triangleq$
.2 $\quad \forall\, mct_1, \ldots, mct_n : TypeR \cdot$
.3 $\qquad is\_member\_type(mct_1, ct_1)(env) \wedge$
.4 $\qquad \vdots$
.5 $\qquad is\_member\_type(mct_n, ct_n)(env) \Rightarrow$
.6 $\qquad \exists\, mrt : TypeR \cdot TP(mct_1, \ldots, mct_n)(mrt)(env) \wedge$
.7 $\qquad\qquad is\_member\_type(mrt, rt)(env)$

If TP satisfies the requirement (12) for definite well-formedness then $UnionClose(TP)$ also satisfies this requirement. We can justify this as follows. Assume we have

$$TP(t_1, \ldots, t_{i1}, \ldots, t_n)(rt_1)(env) \quad \text{and}$$
$$TP(t_1, \ldots, t_{i2}, \ldots, t_n)(rt_2)(env)$$

then from requirement (12) we have

$$V\_SCExpr(t_1, \ldots, t_{i1}, \ldots, t_n)(env) \subseteq \mathcal{T}(rt_1)(env) \quad \text{and}$$
$$V\_SCExpr(t_1, \ldots, t_{i2}, \ldots, t_n)(env) \subseteq \mathcal{T}(rt_2)(env)$$

From the definition of V_SCExpr (13) and

$$\mathcal{T}(t_{i1} \mid t_{i2})(env) = \mathcal{T}(t_{i1})(env) \cup \mathcal{T}(t_{i2})(env)$$

we get

$$\begin{aligned}
& V_SCExpr(t_1, \ldots, t_{i1} \mid t_{i2}, \ldots, t_n)(env) \\
& = V_SCExpr(t_1, \ldots, t_{i1}, \ldots, t_n)(env) \cup V_SCExpr(t_1, \ldots, t_{i2}, \ldots, t_n)(env) \\
& \subseteq \mathcal{T}(rt_1)(env) \cup \mathcal{T}(rt_2)(env) \\
& = \mathcal{T}(rt_1 \mid rt_2)(env)
\end{aligned}$$

Hence, it is in accordance with requirement (12) to state that

$$UnionClose(TP)(t_1, \ldots, t_{i1} \mid t_{i2}, \ldots, t_n)(rt_1 \mid rt_2)(env)$$

The definition of $wf\_SCompExpr$ (section 3.4 def. 28) may now be modified to use the improved TP when asked for:

38.0 $wf\_SCompExpr : \Pi \rightarrow TPredicate \rightarrow Expr \times \ldots \times Expr \rightarrow TypeR \rightarrow Env \rightarrow \mathsf{B}$
.1 $wf\_SCompExpr_{\pi}(TP)(e_1, \ldots, e_n)(rtype)(env) \triangleq$
.2 $\quad \exists\, ct_1, \ldots, ct_n : TypeR \cdot$
.3 $\quad\quad Subsumption_{\pi}(wf\_Expr_{\pi})(e_1)(ct_1)(env) \wedge$
.4 $\quad\quad \vdots$
.5 $\quad\quad Subsumption_{\pi}(wf\_Expr_{\pi})(e_n)(ct_n)(env) \wedge$
.6 $\quad\quad$ cases π :
.7 $\quad\quad\quad mk\text{-}DEF(\{\text{UNIONCLOSE}\} \cup \text{-}) \rightarrow$
.8 $\quad\quad\quad\quad UnionClose(TP)(ct_1, \ldots, ct_n)(rtype)(env),$
.9 $\quad\quad\quad$ others $\rightarrow TP(ct_1, \ldots, ct_n)(rtype)(env)$
.10 $\quad\quad$ end

4.2 Sub-environment Based Checks

The checks we are going to consider in this section concerns expressions which occur in the scope of locally defined identifiers. The general idea of all the checks is to analyze the expression in one or more sub-environments where the locally defined identifiers are mapped to smaller more specific types. We will define the different concepts and typing rules during the following description of the first and most obvious of this checks: LOCALCONTEXT.

4.2.1 Local Context

Expressions are analyzed in some local environment. However, in the basic well-formedness predicates all subexpressions in the given environment are analyzed independently thereby failing to see obviously conflicting uses of identifiers:

$F(f : \mathsf{N} \rightarrow (\mathsf{N} \mid \mathsf{B}), n : \mathsf{N}) : \ldots \triangleq$
$\quad$ let $x = f(n)$ in
$\quad \{x + 1, \text{if } x \text{ then } 1 \text{ else } 0, \neg(\text{if } x + 1 > 5 \text{ then } x + 1 \text{ else } x)\}$

Here the body of the let expression is checked in a value environment which besides mapping f and n to the defined parameter types, maps x to the result type of $f(n)$, i.e. $\mathsf{N} \mid \mathsf{B}$. Due to the independent checks of occurrencies of x, the body of the let expression (a set enumeration) is possibly well-formed. The first expression in which x occurs is possibly well-formed for the possible type N of x and the second expression is possibly well-formed for the possible type B of x. The last expression is also possibly well-formed because the else-branch is possibly well-formed with respect to the type B (when checked independently of the condition of the if-then-else expression).

When the let expression is evaluated in the $\mathcal{DS}$, x is of course bound to either a natural number or a boolean value so the evaluation causes a type error. A necessary requirement in order to evaluate the let expression in the $\mathcal{DS}$ is that there must be at least one value to which x may be bound without causing type inconsistencies in the body of the let expression. In the SS we now approximate this by requiring the existence of at least one *sub-environment* (with respect to x) for which the body of the let expression is possibly well-formed. With this new requirement the body in the example must be possible well-formed in an environment where x is bound to N *or* in an environment where x is bound to $\mathbb{B}$. But this requirement is not fulfilled, so now the let expression is *not* possibly well-formed.

In order to formalize this check we first define

39.0 $is\_subEnv : Id\text{-set} \rightarrow Env \times Env \rightarrow \mathbb{B}$
.1 $is\_subEnv\,(lids)(senv, env) \triangleq$
.2 $\quad senv.tenv = env.tenv \wedge$
.3 $\quad \text{let } svenv = senv.venv,$
.4 $\qquad venv = env.venv \text{ in}$
.5 $\quad \text{dom } svenv = \text{dom } venv \wedge$
.6 $\quad \forall\, id \in (\text{dom } venv - lids) \cdot svenv(id) = venv(id) \wedge$
.7 $\quad \forall\, id \in lids \cdot is\_subtype(svenv(id), venv(id))(env) \wedge is\_specific\_type(svenv(id))$

An environment *senv* is a sub-environment of the environment *env* (with respect to some local identifiers *lids*) if and only if they have the same type environment part and also the same value environment part *except* that the value environment of *senv* maps the local identifiers *lids* to subtypes of the corresponding types in *env*. However, if that was the only condition for sub-environments every environment would have itself as a sub-environment and nothing was obtained. The important point is that the subtypes in *senv* must be so-called *specific types*: In a specific type, component types representing a single element is not a union type or a type identifier.

The two next examples show the point about sub-environments and specific types.

$$F\,(H : \mathbb{N} \rightarrow \mathbb{N} \times (\mathbb{N} \mid \mathbb{B}), f : \mathbb{N} \times \mathbb{N} \rightarrow \mathbb{N}, g : \mathbb{N} \times \mathbb{B} \rightarrow \mathbb{N}, n : \mathbb{N}) \;\; : \mathbb{N}\text{-set} \triangleq$$
$$\text{let } x = H(n) \text{ in } \{f(x), g(x)\}$$

Here, the body of the let expression is checked in an environment where x is mapped to $\mathbb{N} \times (\mathbb{N} \mid \mathbb{B})$. With the LOCALCONTEXT check the body must be possibly well-formed in one of the sub-environments which are $\{\ldots, x \mapsto \mathbb{N} \times \mathbb{N}\}$ and $\{\ldots, x \mapsto \mathbb{N} \times \mathbb{B}\}$. Notice that the original environment is not a sub-environment of itself, because the second component of the product type represents a single value and is a union type. Consequently, the body of the let expression is not possibly well-formed.

The second example is

$$F\,(G : \mathbb{N} \rightarrow \mathbb{N} \rightarrow (\mathbb{N} \mid \mathbb{B}), n : \mathbb{N}) \;\; : \mathbb{N}\text{-set} \triangleq$$
$$\text{let } g = G(n) \text{ in } \{g(n) + 1, \text{if } g(n+1) \text{ then } 1 \text{ else } 0\}$$

The body of the let expression is checked in an environment where g is mapped to $\mathbb{N} \rightarrow (\mathbb{N} \mid \mathbb{B})$. So, with the LOCALCONTEXT check the body must be possibly well-formed in one of the sub-environments. Now the original environment is among the sub-environments because the union type in $\mathbb{N} \rightarrow (\mathbb{N} \mid \mathbb{B})$ is not a component representing a single value; one and the same function may yield a natural number for one application and a boolean value for another application. Consequently, as the body of the let expression is possibly well-formed in this original environment it is still possibly well-formed with the LOCALCONTEXT check (as it should be).

We define our new rule for expressions in the scope of local identifiers according to the previously used style as a function which transforms a well-formedness predicate to another more powerful version:

```
40.0 In_scope : Π → Id-set → WFE → WFE
  .1 In_scope_π(local_ids)(wf)(expr)(type)(env) ≜
  .2    cases π :
  .3       mk-POS({LOCALCONTEXT} ∪ -) →
  .4           ∃ subenv : Env ·
  .5               is_subEnv(local_ids)(subenv, env) ∧ wf(expr)(type)(subenv),
  .6       others → wf(expr)(type)(env)
  .7    end
```

In a subsequent section (4.2.3) *In_scope* is extended to include other kinds of sub-environment based checks.

We will discuss properties of the *In_scope* transformed well-formedness predicates in section 4.2.4.

4.2.2 Examples of Expressions in the Scope of Local Identifiers

In this section we show the well-formedness predicates for some of the constructs which introduce a new scope and hence has the opportunity to use the *In_scope* rule.

Example. We consider simplified let expressions, i.e. let expression with just an identifier on the left-hand side (no pattern) and no recursion.

```
41.0 wf_LetExpr : Π → LetExpr → TypeR → Env → B
  .1 wf_LetExpr_π(mk-LetExpr(id, rhs_expr, in_expr))(type)(env) ≜
  .2    let mk-Env(tenv, venv) = env in
  .3    ∃ rhs_t : TypeR ·
  .4        wf_Expr_π(rhs_expr)(rhs_t)(env) ∧
  .5        let newenv = mk-Env(tenv, venv † {id ↦ rhs_t}) in
  .6        In_scope_π({id})(wf_Expr_π)(in_expr)(type)(newenv)
```

□

Example. At the top level of a specification we have the function definitions.

```
42.0 wf_FnDef : Π → FnDef → Env → B
  .1 wf_FnDef_π(mk-FnDef(fnhead, body))(env) ≜
  .2    let mk-Env(tenv, venv) = env in ...
  .3    let local_venv = ...fnhead...env...,
  .4        restype = ...fnhead...env... in
  .5    let newenv = mk-Env(tenv, venv † local_venv),
  .6        locids = dom loc_venv in
  .7    ((In_scope_π(locids)) ∘ (In_type_π)) (wf_Expr_π)(body)(restype)(newenv)
```

The function body is checked in a new environment *newenv* which is the global environment *env* overridden by the local value environment *local_venv* emanating from parameter definitions in the function heading *fnhead*. The body must have a value in the set of values of the defined result type *restype*. Because the type of the body does not propagate further we can use the alternative subsumption rule *In_type* without any risk (see section 3.3.2 and 3.4). Notice, we use two rules ($In\_scope_\pi(locids)$ and In_type_π) to transform the basic well-formedness predicate (wf_Expr_π). □

4.2.3 Flow Analysis

To show the nature of the improved checks which will be described in this section we first analyze two examples which demonstrate some obvious deficiencies of the basic well-formedness predicates:

43.0 $P\,(f : \mathsf{B} \rightarrow \mathsf{N}, x : \mathsf{N} \mid \mathsf{B}) : \mathsf{N} \triangleq$
.1 if is-$\mathsf{N}(x)$ then $f(x)$ else $x + 1$

44.0 $D\,(x : \mathsf{N} \mid \mathsf{B}, n : \mathsf{N}) : \mathsf{N} \mid \mathsf{B} \triangleq$
.1 if $x = n$ then $x + 1$ else x

The type representation system as described in section 2 does not provide enough information to estimate which of the branches of an if-then-else expression will be evaluated. Consequently, in the well-formedness predicate for the if-then-else expression (in section 3.2, def. 24) the then-branch and else-branch are checked for well-formedness in the same environment independently of the actual value of the condition part of the if-then-else expression.

Accordingly, when the if-then-else expression in the body of P is checked for possibly well-formedness both $f(x)$ and $x + 1$ is checked in an environment where x is bound to $\mathsf{N} \mid \mathsf{B}$. It is therefore estimated to be possibly well-formed, i.e. it is not rejected as we would prefer it to be.

In a similar way when checking the if-then-else expression in the body of D for definite well-formedness the then-branch $x + 1$ is checked in an environment where x is bound to $\mathsf{N} \mid \mathsf{B}$ and consequently cannot be definitely well-formed, i.e. it is not accepted as we would prefer it to be.

To make it possible to estimate the flow through an if-then-else expression when analyzing for possible and definite well-formedness it is in the first place necessary to increase the granularity of the type representation system so we have types representing the values **true** and **false**. The domain of basic type representations *BasicTypeR* defined in section 2 is extended as follows:

45.0 $BasicTypeR = \text{BOOL} \mid \text{TRUE} \mid \text{FALSE} \mid \text{NAT}$

Here the new types TRUE and FALSE represents the values **true** respectively **false**. In accordance with this, the subtype relation (section 2 def. 13) is extended in a straightforward way such that the types TRUE and FALSE both become a subtype of themselves and BOOL.

In order to make flow analysis possible two more steps need to be done. The well-formedness predicates for expressions having boolean components or yielding boolean results must be defined so they make use of the increased type information (about **true** and **false**). Especially the well-formedness predicate for the if-then-else expression must be redefined to utilize the increased type information from the condition expression in order to estimate which branch will be evaluated. However, if that was the only change we would just have constant folding of boolean expressions.

A simple form of flow analysis may be based on the notion of sub-environment introduced in section 4.2.1. So, another step is to define the mechanism which analyzes the expression in one or more sub-environments. We do that below by extending *In_scope* with a sub-environment based check for possible and definite well-formedness with FLOWANALYZE in the check set:

46.0 $In\_scope : \Pi \to Id\text{-}\mathsf{set} \to WFE \to WFE$
.1 $In\_scope_{\pi}(local\_ids)(wf)(expr)(type)(env) \triangleq$
.2 $\quad \mathsf{cases}\ \pi :$
.3 $\quad\quad mk\text{-}POS(\{\text{LOCALCONTEXT}\} \cup \text{-}), mk\text{-}POS(\{\text{FLOWANALYZE}\} \cup \text{-}) \to$
.4 $\quad\quad\quad \exists\, subenv : Env \cdot$
.5 $\quad\quad\quad\quad is\_subEnv(local\_ids)(subenv, env) \wedge wf(expr)(type)(subenv),$
.6 $\quad\quad mk\text{-}DEF(\{\text{FLOWANALYZE}\} \cup \text{-}) \to$
.7 $\quad\quad\quad \forall\, subenv : Env \cdot$
.8 $\quad\quad\quad\quad is\_subEnv(local\_ids)(subenv, env) \Rightarrow$
.9 $\quad\quad\quad\quad \exists\, st : TypeR \cdot wf(expr)(st)(subenv) \wedge is\_subtype(st, type)(env),$
.10 $\quad\quad \mathsf{others} \to wf(expr)(type)(env)$
.11 $\quad \mathsf{end}$

For possible well-formedness with FLOWANALYZE in the check set, the check is the same as for LOCALCONTEXT in the check set: there must exist at least one sub-environment where the considered expression is possibly well-formed. For definite well-formedness with FLOWANALYZE in the check set, the expression must in all sub-environments be (definitely) well-formed for some type. Standing alone this requirement adds nothing. However, with FLOWANALYZE put in the check set at the top level the well-formedness predicate *wf* is supposed to make a much better approximation of the types.

Consequently, the final step is to define the well-formedness predicates for constructs having boolean components or yielding boolean results such that they utilize the more detailed type information (about true and false) in the considered sub-environments. We show a few examples:

Example. We reconsider the if-then-else expressions.

47.0 $wf\_IfExpr : \Pi \to IfExpr \to TypeR \to Env \to \mathbb{B}$
.1 $wf\_IfExpr_{\pi}(mk\text{-}IfExpr(e_0, e_1, e_2))(type)(env) \triangleq$
.2 $\quad \exists\, t_0 : TypeR \cdot$
.3 $\quad\quad wf\_Expr_{\pi}(e_0)(t_0)(env) \wedge is\_compatible_{\pi}(t_0, \text{BOOL})(env) \wedge$
.4 $\quad\quad \mathsf{let}\ a_1 = \text{FLOWANALYZE} \in check\_set(\pi) \Rightarrow is\_subtype(\text{TRUE}, t_0)(env),$
.5 $\quad\quad\quad a_2 = \text{FLOWANALYZE} \in check\_set(\pi) \Rightarrow is\_subtype(\text{FALSE}, t_0)(env)\ \mathsf{in}$
.6 $\quad\quad \mathsf{cases}\ \pi :$
.7 $\quad\quad\quad mk\text{-}DEF(\text{-}) \to$
.8 $\quad\quad\quad\quad \exists\, t_1, t_2 : TypeR, tset : TypeR\text{-}\mathsf{set} \cdot$
.9 $\quad\quad\quad\quad\quad (a_1 \Rightarrow wf\_Expr_{\pi}(e_1)(t_1)(env)) \wedge$
.10 $\quad\quad\quad\quad\quad (a_2 \Rightarrow wf\_Expr_{\pi}(e_2)(t_2)(env)) \wedge$
.11 $\quad\quad\quad\quad\quad tset = \{t \mid t : TypeR \cdot a_1 \wedge (t = t_1) \vee a_2 \wedge (t = t_2)\} \wedge$
.12 $\quad\quad\quad\quad\quad type = mk\text{-}UnionTypeR(tset),$
.13 $\quad\quad\quad mk\text{-}POS(\text{-}) \to$
.14 $\quad\quad\quad\quad (a_1 \wedge wf\_Expr_{\pi}(e_1)(type)(env)) \vee (a_2 \wedge wf\_Expr_{\pi}(e_2)(type)(env))$
.15 $\quad\quad \mathsf{end}$

where *is_compatible* is defined by:

```
48.0 is_compatible : Π → TypeR × TypeR → Env → B
  .1 is_compatible_π(t1, t2)(env) ≜
  .2    cases π :
  .3       mk-POS(-) → overlapping(t1, t2)(env),
  .4       mk-DEF(-) → is_subtype(t1, t2)(env)
  .5    end
```

We will make no formal proof but only make probable that the new well-formedness predicate for if-then-else expressions is sound:

The values of a_1 and a_2 (47.4 and 47.5) indicates whether the type of the then-branch respectively else-branch will influence on the result type of the if-then-else expression. If FLOWANALYZE is not in the check set then both branches will be considered as the expression to be evaluated. Consequently, both a_1 and a_2 are true and the new version of the well-formedness predicate is then identical to the provisional version in section 3.2 (def. 24). If FLOWANALYZE is in the check set then a_1 and a_2 depends on how small a type is estimated for the condition expression e_0.

For definite well-formedness we have: If t_0 is estimated to BOOL both a_1 and a_2 are true and (just as when FLOWANALYZE $\notin$ *checkset*) the type of the if-then-else expression will be the union of the two types for which e_1 respectively e_2 are definitely well-formed (47.11-12). If t_0 can be estimated to some smaller type, assume for instance TRUE i.e. $a_1 =$ true and $a_2 =$ false, then only e_1 needs to be definitely well-formed for some type, and the type of the if-then-else expression will be exactly that type (or technically the union of it).

For possible well-formedness (47.14) we have in a similar way: If the estimated type t_0 is BOOL then the if-then-else expression will be possibly well-formed for all the types for which either e_1 or e_2 will be possibly well-formed. If t_0 can be estimated to some smaller type, assume as before TRUE, then the if-then-else expression will only be possibly well-formed for the types for which e_1 will be possibly well-formed. □

Example. This examples concerns the equality operator:

```
49.0 wf_EQ : Π → BinaryExpr → TypeR → Env → B
  .1 wf_EQ_π(mk-BinaryExpr(le, EQ, re))(type)(env) ≜
  .2    let TP(t1, t2 : TypeR)(rt : TypeR)(env : Env) : B =
  .3          ∀ t ∈ {t1, t2} · ¬ ∃ ft : FnTypeR · type_dep(t, ft)(env.tenv) ∧
  .4          rt = (if FLOWANALYZE ∈ check_set(π)
  .5                then if same_value(t1, t2)(env) then TRUE
  .6                     elseif ¬ overlapping(t1, t2)(env) then FALSE
  .7                     else BOOL
  .8                else BOOL) in
  .9    wf_SCompExpr2_π(TP)(le, re)(type)(env)
```

The equality operator EQ yields a boolean value. If FLOWANALYZE is in the check set, then we try in the SS to infer which boolean value the expression yields. In other words we try to infer a better estimation than BOOL. For both definite and possible well-formedness, the result type is TRUE if the two operand types represent exactly the same value (*same_value*). With the granularity of the type representations this is only true for the types representing the values true, false and the empty set. If the two operand types represent disjoint set of type values then the result type is false. Otherwise BOOL is estimated as the result type.

The two operand types to the equality operator may not depend on a function type (49.3). □

Example. We consider the recognizer function, i.e. the function which tests whether an expression yields a value of some specific type.

50.0 $wf\_IsExpr : \Pi \rightarrow IsExpr \rightarrow TypeR \rightarrow Env \rightarrow \mathsf{B}$
.1 $wf\_IsExpr_{\pi}(mk\text{-}IsExpr(testty, expr))(type)(env) \triangleq$
.2 $\quad$ let $ttype = make\_TypeR(testty)(env)$ in
.3 $\quad$ let $TP(t : TypeR)(rt : TypeR)(env : Env) : \mathsf{B} =$
.4 $\qquad rt =$ (if FLOWANALYZE $\in check\_set(\pi)$
.5 $\qquad\quad$ then if $is\_subtype(t, ttype)(env)$ then TRUE
.6 $\qquad\qquad$ elseif $\neg\, overlapping(t, ttype)(env)$ then FALSE
.7 $\qquad\qquad$ else BOOL
.8 $\qquad\quad$ else BOOL) in
.9 $\quad wf\_SCompExpr1_{\pi}(TP)(expr)(type)(env)$

The recognizer function yields a boolean value. If (in the $\mathcal{DS}$) the value of the operand expression is in the set of values of the test type *testty*, the test holds and otherwise it does not. In the SS this is approximated as follows. If the operand type is a subtype of the test type then the result type is TRUE. If the operand type and the test type are disjoint then the result type is FALSE, and in the remaining cases is BOOL the best possible approximation. □

Now we can reanalyze the two examples (def. 43 and 44) shown in the beginning of this section with FLOWANALYZE in the check set.

To check the body of the function definition of P (def. 43) for possible well-formedness we must among all the sub-environments with respect to the formal parameters f and x find one in which it it possibly well-formed:
(1) In the sub-environment $\{\ldots, x \mapsto \mathsf{N}\}$ is the condition $is\text{-}\mathsf{N}(x)$ only possibly well-formed for the type TRUE, i.e. in the well-formedness predicate for the if-then-else expression we have that $a_1 = \mathsf{true}$ and $a_2 = \mathsf{false}$. Consequently, the if-then-else expression is possibly well-formed (in the considered environment) only if $f(x)$ is possibly well-formed, but it is not.
(2) In the sub-environment $\{\ldots, x \mapsto \mathsf{B}\}$ is the condition $is\text{-}\mathsf{N}(x)$ only possibly well-formed for the type FALSE, i.e. in the well-formedness predicate for the if-then-else expression we have that $a_1 = \mathsf{false}$ and $a_2 = \mathsf{true}$. Consequently, the if-then-else expression is possibly well-formed (in the considered environment) only if $x + 1$ is possibly well-formed, but it is not.
From the above analysis we conclude that the body is not possibly well-formed, so it is rejected.

To check the body of the function definition of D (def. 44) for definite well-formedness we must show that it is definitely well-formed in all sub-environments with respect to the formal parameters x and n:
(1) In the sub-environment $\{\ldots, x \mapsto \mathsf{N}\}$ the smallest type for which the condition $x = n$ is definitely well-formed is B, i.e. in the well-formedness predicate for the if-then-else expression we have that $a_1 = \mathsf{true}$ and $a_2 = \mathsf{true}$. So, in order to be definitely well-formed both branches must be definitely well-formed in the considered environment for some type, and so they are.

(2) In the sub-environment $\{\ldots, x \mapsto \mathsf{B}\}$ the smallest type for which the condition $x = n$ is definitely well-formed is FALSE, i.e. in the well-formedness predicate for the if-then-else expression we have that $a_1 = \mathsf{false}$ and $a_2 = \mathsf{true}$. Consequently, only the else-branch (x) have to be definitely well-formed in the considered sub-environment, and so it is. From the above analysis we conclude that the body is definitely well-formed, so it is accepted.

4.2.4 Properties of *In_scope*

In this section we round off the discussion and the use of *In_scope* by stating its properties concerning soundness and power. In the following let wf_{DF} be a well-formedness predicate corresponding to a check of the form $mk\text{-}DEF(c)$ where c is some check set which contains FLOWANALYZE, and let wf_{PLF} be a well-formedness predicate corresponding to a check of the form $mk\text{-}POS(c)$ where LOCALCONTEXT $\in c \vee$ FLOWANALYZE $\in c$. Furthermore, we use the following shorthand notations: DF denotes $mk\text{-}DEF(c)$ where c is some check set which contains FLOWANALYZE. PLF denotes $mk\text{-}POS(c)$ where c is some check set which contains LOCALCONTEXT or FLOWANALYZE. Finally, let *lids* be some set of (locally defined) identifiers.

If the definite well-formedness predicate wf_{DF} satisfies the soundness requirement (4) then $In\_scope_{DF}(lids)(wf_{DF})$ also satisfies the soundness requirement, i.e.

$$In\_scope_{DF}(lids)(wf_{DF})(expr)(type)(env) \Rightarrow \mathcal{E}(expr)(env) \subseteq \mathcal{T}(type)(env)$$

The transformed well-formedness predicate will be at least as powerful for acceptance as the original predicate, i.e.

$$DT(In\_scope_{DF}(lids)(wf_{DF}))(expr)(env) \supseteq DT(wf_{DF})(expr)(env)$$

The discussion in the previous section of the function definition for D (def. 44) demonstrated that there actually *are* expressions and environments for which the *In_scope* transformed predicate is *more* powerful for acceptance: For the body of the function D and the environment *env* (which includes the parameters of D) we have that

$$wf\_IfExpr_{DF}(\mathsf{if}\ x = n\ \mathsf{then}\ x + 1\ \mathsf{else}\ x)(t)(env)$$

is not true for any type t, i.e. $DT(wf\_IfExpr)(\ldots)(env) = \{\}$. On the other hand

$$In\_scope_{DF}(\{x, n\})(wf\_IfExpr_{DF})(\mathsf{if}\ x = n\ \mathsf{then}\ x + 1\ \mathsf{else}\ x)(t)(env)$$

is true for $t = \mathsf{N} \mid \mathsf{B}$ (or technically for $t = \mathsf{N} \mid (\mathsf{N} \mid \mathsf{B})$).

If the predicate for possible well-formedness wf_{PLF} satisfies the soundness requirement (5) then $In\_scope_{PLF}(lids)(wf_{PLF})$ also satisfies the soundness requirement, i.e.

$$\mathcal{E}(expr)(env) \subseteq \mathcal{PT}(In\_scope_{PLF}(lids)(wf_{PLF}))(expr)(env) \cup \{\mathbf{wrong}\}$$

The transformed well-formedness predicate $In\_scope_{PLF}(lids)(wf_{PLF})$ is at least as powerful for rejection as wf_{PLF}, i.e.

$$\mathcal{PT}(In\_scope_{PLF}(lids)(wf_{PLF}))(expr)(env) \subseteq \mathcal{PT}(wf_{PLF})(expr)(env)$$

As for definite well-formedness, some of the examples in the previous sections demonstrated that there actually *are* expressions and environments for which the *In_scope* transformed predicate is *more* powerful for rejection. For the body of the function P (def. 43) and the environment *env* we have that:

$$wf\_IfExpr_{PLF}(\mathsf{if}\ is\text{-}\mathsf{N}(x)\ \mathsf{then}\ f(x)\ \mathsf{else}\ x + 1)(t)(env)$$

is true for $t = \mathsf{N}$, i.e. $\mathcal{T}(\mathsf{N})(env) \subseteq \mathcal{PT}(wf\_IfExpr)(\ldots)(env)$. On the other hand

$$In\_scope_{PLF}(\{f, x\})(wf\_IfExpr_{PLF})(\text{if } is\text{-}\mathsf{N}(x) \text{ then } f(x) \text{ else } x+1)(t)(env)$$

is not true for any type t, i.e. $\mathcal{PT}(wf\_IfExpr)(\ldots)(env) = \{\}$.

A proof of the above stated properties is shown in [4].

5 Conclusion

Transparency has been a main goal of our work on defining a static semantics for VDM-SL. The utilization of implicit specification and structuring by use of higher order functions has been motivated by this goal. It is our observation that the implicit style emphasizes the aspect of *which* specifications to accept/reject rather than the more procedural aspect of *how* to compute an acceptance or rejection result.

Compared with the approach of defining static semantics by type inference systems, our style of definition may be considered a bit more operational since the order of application of typing rules to a certain extent is fixed. On the other hand, we have found it valuable to be able to use higher order functions and predicates for structuring the definition; this would not fit so well into the framework of type inference systems.

Another goal for our work has been to define the static semantics with a set of extended checks such that the rejected and accepted specifications from a practical point of view get quite close to the border between inconsistent and consistent specifications, thus leaving only a few proof obligations to the user (re. figure 1).

One can easily imagine a definition where the more advanced checks obscure the basic typing rules. However, it has turned out possible with our approach to separate most of the extended checks from the basic definition. Only checks which result in increased granularity of the type representation system seem to require redefinition of the basic well-formedness predicates.

The relationship to the dynamic semantics is another important issue. We have in this presentation identified the proof obligations for correctness of the static semantics with respect to the dynamic semantics.

When defining a static analysis, decidability is essential; there must exist a terminating procedure which will perform exactly the analysis specified. So, having used implicit specifications, we must justify that these do not lead to undecidability. This justification is part of related work at our department. The static semantics presented here is currently being transformed/refined to a constructive version and finally implemented as part of a language sensitive structure editor for VDM-SL.

5.1 Further Work

One of the future research topics related to this project is to find more classes of decidable checks which may be specified in a simple an transparent manner without interfering with the basic checking and which recognize commonly occurring situations of consistency and inconsistency in specifications.

Due to the undecidability of type consistency there are no limits to the search for type consistent and type inconsistent specifications. The static semantics may analyze an arbitrary number of special situations. We will always be able to come up with new "obvious" examples which should be detected. In the following we mention some extensions to the checks described in section 4.

1. The granularity of the type representation system may be increased in different ways beyond what has been done in section 4.2.3. Types for representing non-empty sets and non-empty sequences are clear candidates.

2. In an explicitly defined function, the body must be type consistent for any value of the formal parameters. This may easily be expressed by requiring that the function body must be possibly well-formed with respect to the formal parameters in all subenvironments.

3. The sub-environment based checks may be improved. Consider, e.g., the two function definitions

   $$F1\,(H : \mathsf{N} \rightarrow \mathsf{N} \times (\mathsf{N} \mid \mathsf{B}), f : \mathsf{N} \times \mathsf{N} \rightarrow \mathsf{N}, g : \mathsf{N} \times \mathsf{B} \rightarrow \mathsf{N}, n : \mathsf{N}) \triangleq$$
   $$\quad \mathsf{let}\ x = H(n)\ \mathsf{in}\ \{f(x), g(x)\}$$
   $$F2\,(H : \mathsf{N} \rightarrow \mathsf{N} \times (\mathsf{N} \mid \mathsf{B}), f : \mathsf{N} \times \mathsf{N} \rightarrow \mathsf{N}, g : \mathsf{N} \times \mathsf{B} \rightarrow \mathsf{N}, n : \mathsf{N}) \triangleq$$
   $$\quad \{f(H(n)), g(H(n))\}$$

   Here, the inconsistent use of x in $F1$ will be detected by the LOCALCONTEXT check described in section 4.2.1, but the inconsistent use of $H(n)$ in $F2$ will not be detected. Inconsistent typing of expressions may be managed by having an environment which maps expressions to types. This will ensure that two occurrences of the same expression will have the same type assigned.

4. In the well-formedness predicate for function application (section 3.4, def. 30), the resulting expression type is always the defined function result type independent of the actual argument type. Here, a first simple step for improvement is to let the resulting application type depend on the type of the function body. The second more serious step is to let the type of the function body depend on the actual parameter types so the type of a function application depends on the type of the actual parameter.

   This step is theoretically more difficult and requires a more profound change of the static semantics: now function definitions in the specifications considered must be represented by type functions (from argument type to result type) determined as some fixed point.

References

[1] Samson Abramsky and Chris Hankin, editors. *Abstract Interpretation of Declarative Languages.* Ellis Horwood Series in Computers and Their Applications. Ellis Horwood Limited, 1987.

[2] Marek Bednarczyk, Andrzej M. Borzyszkowski, and Wiesław Pawłowski. Towards the semantics of the definitional language of MetaSoft. In *VDM '90, VDM and Z—Formal Methods in Software Development,* volume 428 of *Lecture Notes in Computer Science*, pages 477–503. VDM-Europe, Springer-Verlag, 1990.

[3] Dines Bjørner and Cliff B. Jones, editors. *The Vienna Development Method: The Meta-Language*, volume 61 of *Lecture Notes in Computer Science*. Springer-Verlag, 1978.

[4] Hans Bruun, Bo Stig Hansen, and Flemming Damm. An approach to the static semantics of VDM-SL. Technical Report 1991-90, Department of Computer Science, The Technical University of Denmark, 1991.

[5] Flemming Damm, Bo Stig Hansen, and Hans Bruun. Type checking in VDM and related consistency issues. This volume.

[6] Robert Harper and Benjamin Pierce. A record calculus based on symmetric concatenation. Technical report, School of Computer Science, Carnegie Mellon University, 1990.

[7] Cliff B. Jones. *Systematic Software Development Using VDM.* Series in Computer Science. Prentice-Hall International, 2. edition, 1990.

[8] Peter Gorm Larsen. The dynamic semantics of the BSI/VDM specification language. Draft version, August 1990.

[9] Robert Milner, Mads Tofte, and Robert Harper. *The Definition of Standard ML.* MIT Press, 1990.

[10] B. Monahan and A. Walsh. Context conditions for the STC VDM reference language. Technical Report 725 05308 ed. 2, STC plc/Manchester University, 1986.

[11] Nico Plat, Ronald Hiujsman, Jan van Katwijk, Gertjan van Oosten, Kees Pronk, and Hans Toetenel. Type checking BSI/VDM-SL. In *VDM '90, VDM and Z—Formal Methods in Software Development,* volume 428 of *Lecture Notes in Computer Science*, pages 399–425. VDM-Europe, Springer-Verlag, 1990.

[12] Andrzej Tarlecki and Morten Wieth. A naive domain universe for VDM. In *VDM '90, VDM and Z—Formal Methods in Software Development,* volume 428 of *Lecture Notes in Computer Science*, pages 552–579. VDM-Europe, Springer-Verlag, 1990.

Behavioural Extension for CSP

Michael J. Butler
Programming Research Group
Oxford University Computing Laboratory
8 - 11 Keble Road
OX1 3QD

August 2, 1991

Abstract

The notion of behavioural extension is important for system evolution, incremental design and, inheritance in object-orientation. Behavioural extension as relations between CSP processes is investigated. A number of different extension relations are developed motivated by some examples of behavioural extension from the telecoms domain. Each extension relation is characterised in terms of CSP operators and a number of algebraic laws stated. The results are then transferred to the action system approach to CSP and rules for behavioural extension in action systems are developed.

1 Introduction and Background

The motivation for a formal investigation of the notion of behavioural extension came from a number of sources. It is common practice to develop a new computer system by modifying an existing system. The author previously undertook some work [But90] on adding new features to an existing PABX (telephone system) by taking a formal Z [Spi89] specification of the original PABX and extending it to incorporate the new features. A requirement was that the new PABX should have all the features of the original PABX as well as the extra features. A set of rules to be followed when extending a Z specification were developed, but the only basis for these rules was informal.

Another source of motivation comes from the practice of incremental design which is common in software engineering. We start off by specifying a system which satisfies a subset of the requirements and then extend the system until all the requirements are met. In the design of many systems it is common to firstly specify the normal operation and then extend the system to deal with exceptional conditions. In the design of communications networks it is common to firstly specify the service to be provided to the normal users and then extend the system to deal with management of the network. The question is how does an extension affect the original specification?

The idea of object-oriented design is very much in vogue in software engineering, and an important concept in object orientation is the notion of inheritance. [Cus90] advocates the use of an extension relation defined for LOTOS [BS86] as a definition of inheritance. Basically a process *P2* inherits the behaviour of *P1* if *P2* has all the behaviour of *P1* plus some extra behaviour.

This paper develops four forms of extension relation for CSP [Hoa85] processes. We use the notation $P1 \sqsubseteq_X P2$ to say that *P2* is an X-extension of *P1*. In each case the alphabet of *P2* (written A_2) contains the alphabet of *P1* (written A_1), that is $A_1 \subseteq A_2$, and we usually use E to denote $A_2 - A_1$.

A simplified example from the telecoms domain is presented for each extension relation. This motivates the intuitive understanding of the extension form. The extension relation is characterised algebraically using CSP operators and a set of algebraic laws developed. Using these algebraic laws it is verified that the example presented satisfies the extension relation. In order to define the fourth extension relation it will be necessary to introduce a new CSP operator.

By deriving the failures-divergences characterisation of an extension relation we can shift our attention to the Action System approach to CSP of Morgan [Mor90]. For two of the extension relations some rules are developed which guarantee that one action system is an extension of another. One of the examples used in the algebraic approach is recast as an action system and verifying that it satisfies the appropriate extension relation is straightforward.

2 CSP Processes

A CSP process (P) consists of an alphabet (αP) of events and a set of behaviours described in one of three increasingly rich models: *traces* ($\mathcal{T}$), *failures* ($\mathcal{F}$), and *failures-divergences* ($\mathcal{F}, \mathcal{D}$). We will only be concerned with the failures-divergences model.

A CSP process can be specified using an algebraic notation in which terms are formed from elements of αP and operators such as "$\rightarrow$" (event-prefixing), ";" (sequential composition of processes), "$\Box$" (deterministic choice), "$\sqcap$" (non-deterministic choice), "$\|$" (parallel composition), "$|||$" (interleaving composition) and, "\" (hiding). The behavioural meaning of a term P is given by the semantic functions $\mathcal{T}[\![P]\!]$, $\mathcal{F}[\![P]\!]$ and, $\mathcal{D}[\![P]\!]$.

Two terms in the algebra are equal if they have the same semantic model. Also of importance is the notion of refinement (inequality). In the failures-divergences model P is refined by Q (written $P \sqsubseteq Q$) whenever:

$$\mathcal{F}[\![P]\!] \supseteq \mathcal{F}[\![Q]\!] \ \wedge \ \mathcal{D}[\![P]\!] \supseteq \mathcal{D}[\![Q]\!]$$

Semantic equality and inequality give rise to a rich set of algebraic laws many of which are listed in [Hoa85].

A process can be defined recursively using the notation $P = \mu X : A \bullet F(X)$, where, for any term X, $F(X)$ defines a term. The meaning of a recursive definition is given by the least (w.r.t. the refinement relation) fixed point of the function F. In the failures-divergences model the bottom element used to find the least fixed point is the process *CHAOS*.

In the examples presented we will need to differentiate input and output events: "$c?x$" represents input of value x on channel c, meaning a process is prepared to engage in *any* event $c.x$; "$c!v$" represents output of value x on channel c, meaning a process is prepared to engage in *some* event $c.v$.

3 Blockable Extension

The simplest form of extension to be presented is termed *blockable extension.* The idea is that if *P1* is replaced by *P2* and the environment never engages in any of the extra events (E) of *P2* then the environment shouldn't notice any change in behaviour. The example we choose is that of adding an abbreviated dialling feature to a telephone system. A very simplified specification of the system is:

$$TN = dial?q \rightarrow Request(q)\,;\,TN$$

The user dials a number q and the system then enters a state where it is requesting a connection with phone q. When the request is complete the system reverts to behaving as *TN*. *TN* is now extended in order to allow a single number to be stored and requested at any time by simply pressing the *abbr_dial* button. An extra operation to allow the stored number to be set and reset is also provided:

$$\begin{aligned} TNAD &= (\ dial?q \rightarrow Request(q)\,;\,TNAD \\ &\quad\ \Box abbr\_set?a \rightarrow TNAD(a)\ ) \\ TNAD(a) &= (\ dial?q \rightarrow Request(q)\,;\,TNAD(a) \\ &\quad\ \Box abbr\_dial \rightarrow Request(a)\,;\,TNAD(a) \\ &\quad\ \Box abbr\_set?b \rightarrow TNAD(b)\ ) \end{aligned}$$

To say that *TNAD* is a blockable extension of *TN* will mean that any user of *TNAD* who never makes use of the abbreviated dialling feature will experience the same behaviour as if it was using *TN*. The algebraic characterisation of blockable extension will say that if we block the events *abbr_dial* and *abbr_set* in *TNAD* we get the same behaviour as *TN*. The required blocking operator is defined using $STOP_E$ (the process that refuses all events E):

Definition 1 $P\ \underline{\text{block}}\ E \mathrel{\hat{=}} (P \parallel STOP_E), \qquad \textit{where } E \subseteq \alpha P$

So we could say that *P2* is a blockable extension of *P1* whenever $P2\ \underline{\text{block}}\ E = P1$. However these two terms cannot be equated since the alphabet of ($P2\ \underline{\text{block}}\ E$) may be bigger than the alphabet of *P1*. We need to increase the alphabet of *P1* without affecting its behaviour using the following CSP operator:

Definition 2 $P_{+E} \mathrel{\hat{=}} (P \parallel STOP_E), \qquad \textit{where } \alpha P \cap E = \emptyset$

Rather than using equality between the terms we use refinement in the definition of blockable extension:

Definition 3 (Blockable Extension)

$$\begin{aligned} P1 \sqsubseteq_B P2 \ &\mathrel{\hat{=}}\ P1_{+E} \sqsubseteq (P2\ \underline{\text{block}}\ E) \\ &\qquad \textit{where } A_1 \subseteq A_2, E = A_2 - A_1 \end{aligned}$$

This definition means that with all the events E blocked $P2$ offers the same or better (more deterministic, less divergent) behaviour than $P1$. The following six laws can easily be proven using already available algebraic laws of CSP:

B.E. 1 $\sqsubseteq_B$ *is a partial order:*

$$\begin{array}{l} P \sqsubseteq_B P \\ P1 \sqsubseteq_B P2 \land P2 \sqsubseteq_B P3 \;\Rightarrow\; P1 \sqsubseteq_B P3 \\ P1 \sqsubseteq_B P2 \land P2 \sqsubseteq_B P1 \;\Rightarrow\; P1 = P2 \end{array}$$

B.E. 2 $P1 \sqsubseteq P2 \;\Rightarrow\; P1 \sqsubseteq_B P2$

B.E. 3 $P \sqsubseteq_B P_{+E}, \qquad \text{where } \alpha P \cap E = \emptyset$

B.E. 4 $P1 \sqsubseteq_B P2 \;\Rightarrow\; (a \rightarrow P1) \sqsubseteq_B (a \rightarrow P2), \qquad \text{where } a \in A_1$

B.E. 5 $P1 \sqsubseteq_B P2 \;\Rightarrow\; (P1 \parallel Q) \sqsubseteq_B (P2 \parallel Q), \qquad \text{where } \alpha Q \cap E = \emptyset$

B.E. 6 $P1 \sqsubseteq_B P2 \;\Rightarrow\; (P1 \sqcap Q) \sqsubseteq_B (P2 \sqcap Q_{+E}), \qquad \text{where } \alpha Q = A_1$

For example, the proof of **B.E. 5** is as follows:

$P1 \sqsubseteq_B P2$

$\Leftrightarrow P1_{+E} \sqsubseteq P2$ <u>block</u> E — by definition

$\Leftrightarrow P1 \parallel STOP_E \sqsubseteq P2 \parallel STOP_E$ — by definition

$\Rightarrow P1 \parallel STOP_E \parallel Q \sqsubseteq P2 \parallel STOP_E \parallel Q$ — since $\parallel$ monotonic

$\Leftrightarrow P1 \parallel Q \parallel STOP_E \sqsubseteq P2 \parallel Q \parallel STOP_E$ — laws of $\parallel$

$\Leftrightarrow (P1 \parallel Q)_{+E} \sqsubseteq (P2 \parallel Q)$ <u>block</u> E — since $\alpha Q \cap E = \emptyset$

$\Leftrightarrow P1 \parallel Q \sqsubseteq_B P2 \parallel Q$ □

Many CSP processes are defined recursively so the following law is important:

B.E. 7

$$\frac{\begin{array}{l} P1 = \mu X : A_1 \bullet F(X) \\ P2 = \mu Y : A_2 \bullet G(Y), \qquad \text{where } F \text{ and } G \text{ are Continuous} \\ X \sqsubseteq_B Y \Rightarrow F(X) \sqsubseteq_B G(Y) \end{array}}{P1 \sqsubseteq_B P2}$$

We will see that the other three extension relations satisfy laws similar to **B.E.1** to **B.E.7**. The following two laws are not satisfied by the other extension relations:

B.E. 8 $P1 \sqsubseteq_B P2 \;\Rightarrow\; (P1 \,\Box\, Q) \sqsubseteq_B (P2 \,\Box\, Q_{+E}), \qquad \text{where } \alpha Q = A_1$

B.E. 9 $P1 \sqsubseteq_B P2 \;\Rightarrow\; P1 \sqsubseteq_B (P2 \,\Box\, Q),$
$\text{where } Q = (x : E' \rightarrow Q'(x)),\; E' \subseteq E$

4 Interleaving Extension

The second extension relation is termed *interleaving extension.* If *P2* is an interleaving extension of *P1* then even if the environment does engage in one of the extra events (E) of *P2*, *P2* should still offer similar behaviour to *P1*. The example we choose is the addition of a billing function to a data transmission channel. The basic channel is:

$$Chan \;=\; in?x \rightarrow out!x \rightarrow Chan$$

Chan is extended so that it increments a counter each time a data package is transmitted and an extra operation is provided to query and reset the billing counter at any time:

$$\begin{aligned} BChan &= BChan(0) \\ BChan(b) &= (\; in?x \rightarrow BChan(b,x) \\ &\qquad \Box q!b \rightarrow BChan(0)\;) \\ BChan(b,x) &= (\; out!x \rightarrow BChan(b+1) \\ &\qquad \Box q!b \rightarrow BChan(0,x)\;) \end{aligned}$$

To say that *BChan* is an interleaving extension of *Chan* will mean that reading and resetting of the counter will never interfere with the data transmission service.

$SOMETIMES_E$ is the most non-deterministic process over the alphabet E which never diverges. Any process with alphabet E which never diverges is a refinement of $SOMETIMES_E$. If *P1* is interleaved with $SOMETIMES_E$ we get a process which is always prepared to behave as *P1* and may be prepared sometimes to engage in events from E without affecting the state of *P1*. Interleaving extension is defined as:

Definition 4 (Interleaving Extension)

$$P1 \sqsubseteq_I P2 \;\widehat{=}\; (P1 \;|||\; SOMETIMES_E) \sqsubseteq P2$$
$$\text{where } A_1 \subseteq A_2, E = A_2 - A_1$$

Interleaving extension satisfies the following algebraic laws:

I.E. 1..7 *as* **B.E. 1..7**

I.E. 8 $P1 \sqsubseteq_I P2 \;\Rightarrow\; P1 \sqsubseteq_I (P2 \Box e \rightarrow P2)$, $\quad$ *where* $e \in E$

I.E. 9 $P1 \sqsubseteq_I (\mu Y : A_2 \bullet G(Y)) \;\Rightarrow\; P1 \sqsubseteq_I (\mu Y : A_2 \bullet G(Y) \Box e \rightarrow Y)$,
where $e \in E$

We are now in a position to prove that $Chan \sqsubseteq_I BChan$. To simplify the proof we ignore the data values and just concentrate on the events:

$$\begin{aligned} Chan &= \mu X \bullet i \rightarrow o \rightarrow X \\ BChan &= (\mu Y \bullet i \rightarrow (\mu Z \bullet o \rightarrow Y \Box q \rightarrow Z) \Box q \rightarrow Y) \end{aligned}$$

Proof:

$X \sqsubseteq_I Y$ assumption
$\Rightarrow\ o \rightarrow X\ \sqsubseteq_I\ o \rightarrow Y$ by **I.E. 4**
$\Rightarrow\ o \rightarrow X\ \sqsubseteq_I\ (\mu Z \bullet o \rightarrow Y \square q \rightarrow Z)$ by **I.E. 9**
$\Rightarrow\ i \rightarrow o \rightarrow X\ \sqsubseteq_I\ i \rightarrow (\mu Z \bullet o \rightarrow Y \square q \rightarrow Z)$ by **I.E. 4**
therefore, discharging our assumption
$(\mu X \bullet i \rightarrow o \rightarrow X)\ \sqsubseteq_I\ (\mu Y \bullet i \rightarrow (\mu Z \bullet o \rightarrow Y \square q \rightarrow Z))$ by **I.E. 7**
and
$(\mu X \bullet i \rightarrow o \rightarrow X)\ \sqsubseteq_I\ (\mu Y \bullet i \rightarrow (\mu Z \bullet o \rightarrow Y \square q \rightarrow Z) \square q \rightarrow Y)$ by **I.E. 9**
□

5 Concealable Extension

Law **I.E. 8** is useful for an understanding of interleaving extension:

$$P1 \sqsubseteq_I P2 \ \Rightarrow\ P1 \sqsubseteq_I (P2 \square e \rightarrow P2), \qquad \text{where } e \in E$$

The environment is offered the choice of *P2* or doing a single *e* and then *P2*. But sometimes we may wish for the extended process to engage in a sequence of events before returning to the original behaviour:

$$P1 \sqsubseteq_X P2 \ \Rightarrow\ P1 \sqsubseteq_X (P2 \square e \rightarrow f \rightarrow P2), \qquad \text{where } e, f \in E$$

This law is not satisfied by interleaving extension since after engaging in *e* the extended process is no longer prepared to engage in any of the events of A_1. Yet after engaging in *f*, the extended process does revert to offering the original behaviour again. The next extension relation deals with this situation. The example we choose is a data transmission channel with a disrupt-resume mechanism:

$$\begin{aligned} DChan \ = \ & (\ in?x \rightarrow out!x \rightarrow DChan \\ & \square disrupt \rightarrow resume \rightarrow in?x \rightarrow out!x \rightarrow DChan\ ) \end{aligned}$$

For example, the Session Layer protocol of the OSI reference model (see [HS88]) has a disrupt-resume mechanism which may be used to allow traffic of higher priority to temporarily take over an established session. But the only effect this should have would be to delay the original transmission not to prevent any of it.

Our algebraic characterisation of this form of extension says that if we conceal the *E* events in the extended process we get similar behaviour to the original process:

Definition 5 (Concealable Extension)

$$\begin{aligned} P1 \sqsubseteq_C P2 \ \ \widehat{=}\ \ & P1 \sqsubseteq (P2 \setminus E) \\ & \textit{where } A_1 \subseteq A_2, E = A_2 - A_1 \end{aligned}$$

Laws:

C.E. 1..7 *as* **B.E. 1..7**

C.E. 8 $P1 \sqsubseteq_C P2 \;\Rightarrow\; P1 \sqsubseteq_C (e \rightarrow P2), \qquad where\ e \in E$

C.E. 9 $P1 \sqsubseteq_C P2 \;\Rightarrow\; P1 \sqsubseteq_C (P2 \,\Box\, \hat{e} \rightarrow P2),$
$where\ \hat{e} \mathrel{\hat{=}} e_0 \rightarrow e_1 \rightarrow \cdots \rightarrow e_n, \qquad e_i \in E,\ 0 \leq i \leq n$

These laws allow us to prove that $Chan \sqsubseteq_C DChan$. Again we ignore data values and rewrite $DChan$ as:

$$DChan \;=\; (\mu Y \bullet i \rightarrow o \rightarrow Y \,\Box\, d \rightarrow r \rightarrow i \rightarrow o \rightarrow Y)$$

Proof:

Now $X \sqsubseteq_C Y$
$\Rightarrow (i \rightarrow o \rightarrow X) \sqsubseteq_C (i \rightarrow o \rightarrow Y)$ — by **C.E. 4** twice
$\Rightarrow (i \rightarrow o \rightarrow X) \sqsubseteq_C (i \rightarrow o \rightarrow Y \,\Box\, d \rightarrow r \rightarrow i \rightarrow o \rightarrow Y)$ — by **C.E. 9**
So $Chan \sqsubseteq_C DChan$ — by **C.E. 7**

□

There is a problem with our definition of concealable extension in that a *resume* cannot be followed immediately by a *disrupt*. But consider *ADChan* which always allows transmission to be disrupted:

$$ADChan \;=\; (\ in?x \rightarrow ADChan(x)\ \Box disrupt \rightarrow resume \rightarrow ADChan\ )$$

$$ADChan(x) \;=\; (\ out!x \rightarrow ADChan\ \Box disrupt \rightarrow resume \rightarrow ADChan(x)\ )$$

This time *ADChan* diverges if *disrupt* and *resume* are hidden, i.e.

$$ADChan \setminus \{disrupt, resume\} = CHAOS$$

so that $Chan \not\sqsubseteq_C ADChan$. But in reality *disrupt* and *resume* are not hidden – we just assume that if *disrupt* occurs then, at some later stage, *resume* will occur and the process reverts back to offering the original behaviour. Our definition of concealable extension says that after the *resume*, the process must revert back to offering the original behaviour *and* refuse to engage in either *disrupt* or *resume* until some event A_1 is engaged in. This is too restrictive – there is no reason why the extended process shouldn't always offer some events from E provided it doesn't infinitely refuse the original behaviour. We introduce a new CSP operator called *fair-concealment* written $P \downharpoonleft C$, though we don't present its formal definition here.

Unlike the normal CSP concealment operator, fair-concealment only introduces divergence if it is possible for P to engage in an infinite number of events from C while always refusing *all* of $(\alpha P - C)$. The fourth extension, termed *fair-concealable extension*, is defined as:

Definition 6 (Fair-Concealable Extension)

$$P1 \sqsubseteq_{FC} P2 \quad \widehat{=} \quad P1 \sqsubseteq (P2 \downharpoonright E) \quad \text{where } A_1 \subseteq A_2, E = A_2 - A_1$$

The $\downharpoonright$ operator satisfies laws similar to the \ operator which allows us to show that fair-concealable extension satisfies the following laws:

F.E. 1..7 *as* **B.E. 1..7**

F.E. 8 $P1 \sqsubseteq_{FC} P2 \;\Rightarrow\; P1 \sqsubseteq_{FC} (e \rightarrow P2), \qquad \text{where } e \in E$

F.E. 9 $P1 \sqsubseteq_{FC} P2 \;\Rightarrow\; P1 \sqsubseteq_{FC} (P2 \,\Box\, \hat{e} \rightarrow P2),$
$\quad \text{where } \hat{e} \mathrel{\widehat{=}} e_0 \rightarrow e_1 \rightarrow \cdots \rightarrow e_n, \qquad e_i \in E,\ 0 \leq i \leq n$

These are similar to **C.E. 1** to **C.E. 9** but $\sqsubseteq_{FC}$ also satisfies the following law which is not satisfied by $\sqsubseteq_C$:

F.E. 10 $P1 \sqsubseteq_{FC} (\mu\, Y : A_2 \bullet G(Y)) \;\Rightarrow\; P1 \sqsubseteq_{FC} (\mu\, Y : A_2 \bullet G(Y) \,\Box\, \hat{e} \rightarrow Y),$
provided P1 never deadlocks
$\quad \text{where } \hat{e} \mathrel{\widehat{=}} e_0 \rightarrow e_1 \rightarrow \cdots \rightarrow e_n, \qquad e_i \in E,\ 0 \leq i \leq n$

The proviso is because if *P1* does deadlock (refuse all events A_1) then $P2 \downharpoonright E$ may diverge as it may engage in an infinite number of E events while always refusing all of A_1. A diverging process is not a refinement of a deadlocked one.

We can now prove that *ADChan* is an Fair-Concealable extension of *Chan*. Rewriting *ADChan* as:

$$ADChan \;=\; (\mu\, Y \bullet i \rightarrow (\mu\, Z \bullet o \rightarrow Y \,\Box\, d \rightarrow r \rightarrow Z) \,\Box\, d \rightarrow r \rightarrow Y)$$

The proof that $Chan \sqsubseteq_{FC} ADChan$ is similar to the proof that $Chan \sqsubseteq_I BChan$ except that we now use $d \rightarrow r$ instead of q and **F.E. 10** instead of **I.E. 9**.

Some further remarks can be made about the new concealment operator that has been introduced. It shares some similarities with the CCS [Mil89] treatment of internal events. For example, in CCS, the following two processes are weakly equivalent ($\approx$):

$$(a \rightarrow P) \approx (\mu X \bullet (a \rightarrow P) \,\Box\, (\tau \rightarrow X))$$

Here τ is the special silent event. Similarly, in CSP

$$(a \rightarrow P) = (\mu X \bullet (a \rightarrow P) \,\Box\, (c \rightarrow X)) \downharpoonright \{c\}$$

It is known that the 'absorption' of some cases of divergence by CCS weak equivalence involves an implicit fairness assumption (see [BS86]).

It should be pointed out that fair-concealment is not a *continuous* operator and so cannot be used within a recursive definition. This is not a problem for our use of it in defining $\sqsubseteq_{FC}$. It is never intended that the events E be actually concealed – the $\downharpoonright$ operator is only being used to characterise $\sqsubseteq_{FC}$. Also, all of the laws **F.E. 1** to **F.E 10** are proven without requiring $\downharpoonright$ to be continuous.

6 Action Systems and Extension

6.1 Action systems

An action system $\mathcal{P}$ consists of an alphabet of labels A, a set of labelled actions $\{\mathcal{P}_x \mid x \in A\}$ and an initialisation $\mathcal{P}_\iota$. An *action* consists of a guard (g) and a command (com); a *guard* is a predicate while a *command* is a program fragment in Dijkstra's language of guarded commands [Dij76]. For convenience we write $\mathcal{P}_x$ as "$x : g \longrightarrow com$" where $\mathcal{P}$ is understood from context. An action is said to be enabled when its guard is true. An *initialisation* is simply a command. Again for convenience we write $\mathcal{P}_\iota$ as "**initially** com".

An action system proceeds by firstly executing the initialisation; then, repeatedly, an enabled action is selected and executed. An action system deadlocks if no action is enabled, and diverges whenever some command aborts.

6.2 The CSP – action system correspondence

For action S and predicate R, the formula $\overline{wp}(S, R)$ (conjugate weakest precondition) characterises those initial states from which action S could *possibly* establish R. It is defined as [Mor90]

$$\overline{wp}(S, R) \;\; \widehat{=} \;\; \neg\, wp(S, \neg\, R)$$

For any trace t, we write $\mathcal{P}_t$ for the sequential composition of the actions of $\mathcal{P}$ labelled from t, with $\mathcal{P}_{\langle\rangle} = \textbf{skip}$. For any set of labels X, we write $gd_{\mathcal{P}} X$ for the *disjunction* of the guards of actions labelled from X.

[Mor90] shows the correspondence between the CSP of [Hoa85] and action systems by defining the failures and divergences of an action system as conjugate weakest precondition formulae over the initialisation and the labelled actions. We repeat those definitions here:

Definition 7 (failures) *For an action system $\mathcal{P} = (A, \mathcal{P}_\iota, \{\mathcal{P}_x \mid x \in A\})$ the failures of $\mathcal{P}$ (failures$[\![\mathcal{P}]\!]$) are those $(s, X) \in (A^* \times \mathbf{P}\, A)$ which satisfy*

$$\overline{wp}(\mathcal{P}_{\langle\iota\rangle s}, \neg\, gd_{\mathcal{P}} X).$$

Definition 8 (divergences) *For an action system $\mathcal{P} = (A, \mathcal{P}_\iota, \{\mathcal{P}_x \mid x \in A\})$ the divergences of $\mathcal{P}$ (divergences$[\![\mathcal{P}]\!]$) are those $s \in A^*$ which satisfy*

$$\overline{wp}(\mathcal{P}_{\langle\iota\rangle s}, false).$$

[WM90] defines forward simulation between two action systems $\mathcal{A}$ and $\mathcal{C}$. This consists of an invariant I between the state-space of $\mathcal{A}$ and the state-space of $\mathcal{C}$ and of a set of conditions on each of the actions of $\mathcal{A}$ and of $\mathcal{C}$. If a forwards simulation exists then $\mathcal{A}$ is refined by $\mathcal{C}$, i.e.

$$failures[\![\mathcal{A}]\!] \supseteq failures[\![\mathcal{C}]\!] \;\wedge\; divergences[\![\mathcal{A}]\!] \supseteq divergences[\![\mathcal{C}]\!]$$

We present rules similar to [WM90] for blockable and interleaving extension.

6.3 Blockable Extension

In the following theorem it is assumed that the state-space of $\mathcal{P}1$ is characterised by state-variable a and that of $\mathcal{P}2$ by state-variable c.

Theorem 1 *If for any predicate ϕ not containing abstract variable a there is a relation I between a and c such that*

1. $(\exists\, c \bullet \overline{wp}(\mathcal{P}2_\iota, \phi)) \;\Rightarrow\; (\exists\, a \bullet \overline{wp}(\mathcal{P}1_\iota, (\exists\, c \bullet I \wedge \phi)))$
2. *for all* $\alpha \in A_1$*:*
   $(\exists\, c \bullet I \wedge \overline{wp}(\mathcal{P}2_\alpha, \phi)) \;\Rightarrow\; \overline{wp}(\mathcal{P}1_\alpha, (\exists\, c \bullet I \wedge \phi))$
3. *for all* $\alpha \in A_1$*:*
   $(\exists\, a \bullet I \wedge gd_{\mathcal{P}1}\alpha) \;\Rightarrow\; gd_{\mathcal{P}2}\alpha$

then $\mathcal{P}1 \sqsubseteq_B \mathcal{P}2$.

In order to prove theorem 1 we need the following theorem which characterises blockable extension in failures-divergences terms and which can be derived using the algebraic definition (definition 3):

Theorem 2 (Blockable Extension: Failures-Divergences)

$$\begin{aligned} P1 \sqsubseteq_B P2 \;\Leftrightarrow\; \forall\, s \in A_1^* \,;\, X \subseteq A_1 \bullet \\ (s, X) \in \mathcal{F}[\![P2]\!] \Rightarrow (s, X) \in \mathcal{F}[\![P1]\!] \\ s \in \mathcal{D}[\![P2]\!] \Rightarrow s \in \mathcal{D}[\![P1]\!] \end{aligned}$$

Note that this is not the same as CSP refinement since here we are only quantifying over A_1 and not A_2. However the proof that the conditions of theorem 1 imply the right-hand side of theorem 2 is very similar to the proof given in [WM90] that forwards-simulation implies refinement.

6.4 Interleaving Extension

For interleaving extension we also need to constrain the actions labelled from E (condition 2b):

Theorem 3 *if for any predicate ϕ not containing abstract variable a there is a relation I between a and c such that*

1. $(\exists\, c \bullet \overline{wp}(\mathcal{P}2_\iota, \phi)) \;\Rightarrow\; (\exists\, a \bullet \overline{wp}(\mathcal{P}1_\iota, (\exists\, c \bullet I \wedge \phi)))$

2a. *for all* $\alpha \in A_1$*:*
   $(\exists\, c \bullet I \wedge \overline{wp}(\mathcal{P}2_\alpha, \phi)) \;\Rightarrow\; \overline{wp}(\mathcal{P}1_\alpha, (\exists\, c \bullet I \wedge \phi))$

2b. *for all* $\beta \in E$*:*
   $(\exists\, c \bullet I \wedge \overline{wp}(\mathcal{P}2_\beta, \phi)) \;\Rightarrow\; (\exists\, c \bullet I \wedge \phi)$

3. *for all* $\alpha \in A_1$*:*
   $(\exists\, a \bullet I \wedge gd_{\mathcal{P}1}\alpha) \;\Rightarrow\; gd_{\mathcal{P}2}\alpha$

then $\mathcal{P}1 \sqsubseteq_I \mathcal{P}2$.

The failures-divergences characterisation of interleaving extension is given by:

Theorem 4 (Interleaving Extension: Failures-Divergences)

$$P1 \sqsubseteq_I P2 \;\Leftrightarrow \forall\, s \in A_2^* \,; X \subseteq A_2 \bullet$$
$$(s, X) \in \mathcal{F}[\![P2]\!] \Rightarrow (s \restriction A_1, X \cap A_1) \in \mathcal{F}[\![P1]\!]$$
$$s \in \mathcal{D}[\![P2]\!] \Rightarrow (s \restriction A_1) \in \mathcal{D}[\![P1]\!]$$

Here $(s \restriction A)$ is the trace resulting from restricting the trace s to elements in the set A preserving number of occurrences and order. Like theorem 2, theorem 4 is derived using the algebraic characterisation of $\sqsubseteq_I$.

Proof of theorem 3:

Observe the following lemma which can be proven using condition 1 and 2 of theorem 3 and induction over traces s:

Lemma 1 $(\exists\, c \bullet \overline{wp}(\mathcal{P}2_{\langle i \rangle s}, \phi)) \;\Rightarrow\; (\exists\, a \bullet \overline{wp}(\mathcal{P}1_{\langle i \rangle (s \restriction A_1)}, (\exists\, c \bullet I \wedge \phi)))$

Also, the following lemma can be proven from condition 3 of theorem 3:

Lemma 2 $(\exists\, c \bullet I \wedge \neg\, gd_{\mathcal{P}2}\; Y) \Rightarrow \neg\, (gd_{\mathcal{P}1}\; Y)$, all $Y \subseteq A_1$

Now we show the consequent of theorem 3 by showing that conditions 1...3 of theorem 3 imply the right-hand side of theorem 4:

$(s, X) \in \mathit{failures}[\![\mathcal{P}2]\!]$
$\Leftrightarrow (\exists\, c \bullet \overline{wp}(\mathcal{P}2_{\langle i \rangle s}, \neg\, gd_{\mathcal{P}2} X))$ Defn. 7
$\Rightarrow (\exists\, c \bullet \overline{wp}(\mathcal{P}2_{\langle i \rangle s}, \neg\, gd_{\mathcal{P}2}(X \cap A_1)))$ Defn. of $gd_{\mathcal{P}} X$
$\Rightarrow (\exists\, a \bullet \overline{wp}(\mathcal{P}1_{\langle i \rangle (s \restriction A_1)}, (\exists\, c \bullet I \wedge \neg\, gd_{\mathcal{P}2}(X \cap A_1))))$ Lemma 1
$\Rightarrow (\exists\, a \bullet \overline{wp}(\mathcal{P}1_{\langle i \rangle (s \restriction A_1)}, \neg\, gd_{\mathcal{P}1}(X \cap A_1)))$ Lemma 2
$\Leftrightarrow (\; s \restriction A_1 \;,\; X \cap A_1 \;) \in \mathit{failures}[\![\mathcal{P}1]\!]$

To show

$$s \in \mathit{divergences}[\![\mathcal{P}2]\!] \Rightarrow (s \restriction A_1) \in \mathit{divergences}[\![\mathcal{P}1]\!]$$

simply replace predicate ϕ with *false* in lemma 1 □

There is a special case of theorem 3 where the variables of $\mathcal{P}2$ consist of the variables of $\mathcal{P}1$ plus some extra variables. Actions labelled from A_1 are almost the same except that they may also affect the new variables while the E actions should *only* affect the new variables:

Corollary 1 *if P1 and P2 have the form*

$\mathcal{P}1 \mathrel{\widehat{=}}$
var a
initially $a := a_0$
$\alpha : G_\alpha(a) \longrightarrow a := f_\alpha(a), \qquad \text{all } \alpha \in A_1$

$\mathcal{P}2 \mathrel{\widehat{=}}$
var a, b
initially $a, b := a_0, b_0$
$\alpha : G_\alpha(a) \longrightarrow a, b := f_\alpha(a), f'_\alpha(a, b), \qquad \text{all } \alpha \in A_1$
$\beta : H_\beta(a, b) \longrightarrow b := f''_\beta(a, b), \qquad \text{all } \beta \in E$

then $\mathcal{P}1 \sqsubseteq_I \mathcal{P}2$.

We can check syntactically that $\mathcal{P}1$ and $\mathcal{P}2$ are of this form and it can be easily shown that any pair of action systems of this form satisfy conditions 1...3 of theorem 3, hence $\mathcal{P}1 \sqsubseteq_I \mathcal{P}2$. The syntactic relationship between $\mathcal{P}1$ and $\mathcal{P}2$ as defined in corollary 1 is the same as *superposition* in UNITY [CM88], and so we provide a more rigorous justification for the definition of UNITY superposition.

To illustrate the use of corollary 1 we look again at the example of adding a billing function to a data transmission channel. This time the channel is an infinite buffer instead of a buffer of length 1. The following notation is used to describe a family of similar actions:

$$\begin{aligned} \langle l.x \mid x \in T : G_x \longrightarrow Com_x \rangle \;\equiv\;\; & l.a : G_a \longrightarrow Com_a \\ & l.b : G_b \longrightarrow Com_b \\ & \;\;\vdots \qquad\qquad \text{where } a, b, \ldots \in T \end{aligned}$$

This can be used to describe CSP synchronous communication with l representing a channel name and x representing the value communicated. For our purposes, if G_x is independent of x then l is an input channel. While if G_x depends on x then l is an output channel.

The channel is specified by the following action system:

$BufChan \mathrel{\widehat{=}}$
var $\mathsf{c} : \text{seq } Data \bullet$
initially $\mathsf{c} := \langle\rangle$
$\langle in.x \mid x \in Data : \quad true \longrightarrow (\mathsf{c} := \mathsf{c}^\frown\langle x\rangle) \rangle$
$\langle out.x \mid x \in Data : \quad (\#\mathsf{c} > 0 \wedge head(\mathsf{c}) = x) \longrightarrow (\mathsf{c} := tail(\mathsf{c})) \rangle$

To add the billing feature a second state component is added to act as a billing counter, and an extra action schema to read and reset the billing counter:

$$\begin{array}{lll} \mathit{BillBufChan} \mathrel{\widehat{=}} & & \\ \textbf{var}\ \mathsf{c} : \mathrm{seq}\, \mathit{Data}\ ; \mathsf{b} : \mathbb{N} \bullet & & \\ \textbf{initially}\ \ \mathsf{c}, \mathsf{b} := \langle\rangle, \mathit{0} & & \\ \langle \mathit{in.x} \mid x \in \mathit{Data} : & \mathit{true} \longrightarrow (\mathsf{c} := \mathsf{c}^\frown\langle x \rangle)\ \rangle & \\ \langle \mathit{out.x} \mid x \in \mathit{Data} : & (\#\mathsf{c} > \mathit{0} \wedge \mathit{head}(\mathsf{c}) = x) \longrightarrow (\mathsf{c}, \mathsf{b} := \mathit{tail}(\mathsf{c}), \mathsf{b} + \mathit{1})\ \rangle & \\ \langle \mathit{q.v} \mid v \in \mathit{Data} : & (v = \mathsf{b}) \longrightarrow (\mathsf{b} := \mathit{0})\ \rangle & \end{array}$$

We can check syntactically that the conditions of corollary 1 are met so that *BufChan* $\sqsubseteq_I$ *BillBufChan*.

7 Conclusions

A number of behavioural extension relations have been presented whose definitions were motivated by examples from the telecoms domain. Firstly we looked at the extension relations in terms of the algebraic approach to CSP and then in terms of the action system approach. The extension relations could be useful when upgrading systems (adding new features); in incremental design, or; as definitions of inheritance in object-orientation (cf [Cus90]). The choice of which relation to use will depend on our particular needs *and* on ease of verification. Although the four relations do not form a linear hierarchy, they do form a linear hierarchy in terms of ease of verification (starting with the least difficult):

$$\sqsubseteq_B \qquad \sqsubseteq_I \qquad \sqsubseteq_{FC} \qquad \sqsubseteq_C$$

A corollary conclusion from the investigation is the strength, in certain ways, of the action system approach over the algebraic approach. The examples demonstrate that extending an action system is more straightforward: basically some new state-variables and some new actions are added, rather than having to embed the extension in various places in the algebraic description. The notation used here to describe action systems may be cumbersome for large systems, but we could equally use a state-based notation such as VDM [Jon86] or Z [Spi89] to describe action systems.

Even if we use the action system approach, the algebraic laws are still useful. For example, transitivity is important for incremental design, while the following law is important for extending embedded systems:

$$P1 \sqsubseteq_X P2 \ \Rightarrow\ (P1 \parallel Q) \sqsubseteq_X (P2 \parallel Q)$$

The algebraic laws are also useful in terms of coming to an intuitive understanding of the extension relations. The algebraic laws are easier concepts to grasp than the rules relating action systems. This will help in deciding which extension relation is required for our particular purposes.

Acknowledgements

Thanks to my supervisor Carroll Morgan for a number of helpful suggestions. Broadcom Ltd. Dublin and the RACE ARISE project provided funding.

References

[BS86] Ed Brinksma and Giuseppe Scollo. *Formal Notions of implementation and conformance in LOTOS.* Memorandum INF-86-13, University of Twente, Netherlands, December 1986.

[But90] Michael J. Butler. *Service Extension at the Specification Level.* In *Proceedings Z User Meeting, Oxford*, December 1990.

[CM88] K. Mani Chandy and Jayadev Misra. *Parallel Program Design - A Foundation.* Addison–Wesley, 1988.

[Cus90] Elspeth Cusack. *Refinement, Conformance and Inheritance.* Workshop on the Theory and Practice of Refinement, Open University, August 1990.

[Dij76] E. W. Dijsktra. *A Discipline of Programming.* Prentice-Hall, 1976.

[Hoa85] C. A. R. Hoare. *Communicating Sequential Processes.* Prentice–Hall, 1985.

[HS88] John Henshall and Sandy Shaw. *OSI Explained.* Ellis–Horwood, 1988.

[Jon86] C.B. Jones. *Systematic Software Development using VDM.* Prentice–Hall, 1986.

[Mil89] Robin Milner. *Communication and Concurrency.* Prentice–Hall, 1989.

[Mor90] Carroll Morgan. Of wp and csp. In W.H.J. Feijen, A.J.M. van Gasteren, David Gries, and Jayadev Misra, editors, *Beauty is our business: a birthday salute to Edsger W. Dijkstra.* Springer–Verlag, 1990.

[Spi89] J.M. Spivey. *The Z Notation - A Reference Manual.* Prentice–Hall, 1989.

[WM90] J.C.P. Woodcock and Carroll Morgan. *Refinement of State-Based Concurrent Systems.* In *Proceedings VDM '90, Kiel*, April 1990.

Cpo's do not form a cpo, and yet recursion works*

Marek A. Bednarczyk
Andrzej M. Borzyszkowski

Institute of Computer Science, Polish Academy of Sciences†

Abstract

We consider type universes as examples of regular algebras in the area of the denotational semantics of programming languages. The paper concentrates on our method which was used implicitly in the studies of the domain universes underlying MetaSoft, cf. [BBP90], and BSI/VDM, cf. [TW90].
Technically speaking the method allows to prove that a given algebra, e.g., an algebra of types, is regular. It is demonstrated by means of an example that the method applies even to universes which are *essentially regular*, i.e., which are neither cpo's, nor the images of the initial regular algebra.

1 Introduction

1.1 The Problem

It is a usual practice in the area of programming languages to assign *types* to the manipulated *objects*. The typing procedure yields the first, but somewhat *naive*, explanation of the notion of type: *each type stands for the* set *of objects that have the type assigned to them.* Consequently, one should demand that the type forming operators be interpreted as operations on sets. Indeed, it was discovered early that most programming concepts have natural set-theoretical explanations. Accordingly, *records* should belong to the Cartesian product of the field types, *variant records* should belong to the disjoint sum of the field types, *functions* should be mathematical functions, etc.

The simple set-theoretical approach was advocated in the Vienna Development Method (VDM), see [BJ78], [BJ82], with the now emerging standard BSI/VDM, see [Mon87], [TW90] and [Gor90]. The approach was also taken by related approaches like MetaSoft,

*Sponsored by the Polish Academy of Sciences, project MetaSoft, grant CPBP 02.17
†Address: ul. Jaśkowa Dolina 31, P.O.Box 562, 80 252 Gdańsk, POLAND, tel. +(48)(58) 41 90 15 ext. 26, tlx. 512233

[Bli87], [BBP90], or RAISE, see [NHWG88]. The idea was to stick to the naive, but natural, set-theoretical interpretation of types.

The problems start when one insists on having *recursion* around, i.e., when one allows to define recursively either types or their objects or both. In general, to make sense of a recursive definition of an element of a set one has to be able to solve certain fixpoint equations in the set. However, a given fixpoint equation may have many solutions in the given set, or may have no solutions at all. Thus, one has to guarantee that each interesting equation has at least one solution, and that there is some method of choosing one of the solutions from the many.

To achieve the above one usually augments the sets with some extra structure, to require all operations appearing in the equations to preserve the structure and, finally, to choose some *canonical* fixpoints of the equations as the meaning of the corresponding definition.

Two well-known such structures were developed by mathematicians: *complete partial orders* with *bottom*, abbr.: *cppo*, and *complete metric spaces.* In both cases the extra structure serves to distinguish a class of *convergent sequences: chains* and *Cauchy sequences*, respectively. The completeness requirement in both cases stipulates the existence of *limits* of convergent sequences. Now, the admissible operations have to transform convergent sequences into convergent sequences, and to preserve their limits. Fixpoint equations are solved by constructing convergent sequences, and taking their limits.

Each of the two approaches has its advantages and drawbacks. It should be mentioned that M. Smyth has recently proposed a generalization, cf. [Smy87], in an attempt to have the best of both worlds.

In the programming languages practice recursion may appear on two levels: one may wish to define recursively types and/or their elements.

Recursive Types

The class of all sets has a natural structure of a cppo: it is ordered (by the inclusion relation: $\subseteq$), has a bottom (the empty set: $\emptyset$), and limits (unions) of all chains. Still, it was discovered early that some interesting operations on sets are not continuous. Let us consider the following type definition:

$$D = D \to \omega \tag{1}$$

where ω stands for the set of natural numbers, and $D \to \omega$ stands for the set of all functions from D to ω. Existence of non-empty solutions of (1) is impossible in the standard Zermelo-Fraenkel set theory simply for cardinality reasons. Therefore, it would not help if one allows the solutions to be defined up to isomorphism (bijection) rather than up to equality.

Recursive Objects

It would be nice to have a type system with all types allowing for recursive definitions of their objects and types themselves forming a Cartesian closed category with coproducts. In other words, the type system would have three type forming operations: product types (record types), disjoint union of types (variant record types) and function types. Unfortunately, it is impossible to have such a type system even if we disallow type recursion, see [HP90] for details. In particular, one cannot expect to come up with a type system consisting of cpo's with bottoms, "full" products, "full" function spaces and "full" coproducts of cppo's — this explains the problems in the construction of the type universe for the BSI/VDM specification language as reported in [TW90].

The problem of providing a denotational semantics to languages with recursion was first addressed by Scott and Strachey at Oxford. They wanted to give mathematical meaning to Algol 60. In that language functions can be applied to themselves — one can easily define an Algol 60 function which, intuitively, is of the type satisfying equation (1). Therefore, a non-standard interpretation of the function space constructor was required. To cope with the problem Scott developed a theory of *reflexive domains.*

It was noticed, however, that the need for solving type equations like (1) does not arise when it comes to consider the denotational semantics of most modern programming languages, like Pascal, Modula, C, etc. On this ground Blikle and Tarlecki argued, cf. [BT83], that in most cases one can adopt the naive view rather than the mathematically sophisticated machinery of reflexive domains. One has to abandon, however, type definitions like (1) in which the non-continuous operators appear in the essentially recursive way.

1.2 Naive Denotational Semantics

In the MetaSoft project we have faced the problem of providing a naive denotational semantics for the kernel language of the MetaSoft system. From this perspective the MetaSoft project provided a testing ground for the ideas presented in [BT83]. The preliminary results of this experiment are presented in [BBP90]. These results justify expectations expressed in [BT83] — at least to some extent.

On one hand one can indeed give a set-theoretical semantics for a functional language with a syntactically restricted form of recursive definitions of both types and objects. On the other hand, some of these expectations were too naive. For instance, it is necessary to impose complete partial ordering on *all* domains and require *all* the function objects involved to be order preserving, and in fact continuous. Thus, the interpretation of the partial function space constructor may not, unlike suggested in [BT83], be taken as the set of *all* partial functions.

From [HP90] it follows that there are problems with recursive definitions of the elements of coproduct types — coproduct types can be used to define e.g., natural numbers. But has ever anybody attempted to define a single natural number recursively? Recursion is good for defining functions (like factorial), and tuples of functions (mutual recursion). Only some of the types that appear in programming practice have a *natural* structure of a complete partial order with bottom — enough to define their elements recursively. The factorial function is an element of the function type: it is the set of order preserving partial functions from the *flat* poset of natural numbers to itself; the functions are ordered by inclusion, the empty (totally undefined) function is the bottom. In case of the type of natural numbers the natural ordering is flat: no bottom, different elements are incomparable.

The authors believe that there is some ground to talk about *natural denotational semantics.* Its main tenet would be to interpret types as complete partial orders, not necessarily with bottoms, and look for the ordering that comes naturally from the structure of the sets. In particular, the non-trivial orderings would be introduced either by the constant types, or by operations like partial function type constructor. All the other type-forming operations preserve the ordering of the argument types in the natural way. The semantics presented in [BBP90] is natural.

This is in marked contrast to the usual practice when all domains are equipped with artificial bottoms, see e.g., [TW90]. It should be added that an approach to denotational semantics similar to ours was first suggested by Plotkin, see [Plo85] and later taken up by Gunter and Jung, cf. [GJ88].

2 Domain equations and continuous algebras

In the MetaSoft project we had to propose a programming language which features, among others, product types, disjoint union of types and function types and allows for recursive definitions of types and functions. Naturally, only those recursive type definitions are allowed in which the function type constructor appears in essentially non-recursive way.

This is sufficient to define, for instance, the set ω of natural numbers since it is (isomorphic to) the least solution of the equation

$$N = \mathsf{unit} + N. \tag{2}$$

Throughout the paper we identify isomorphic solutions of recursive type equations.

In MetaSoft we can also work with sets of binary trees of natural numbers, lists of natural functions, etc. For instance the type of lists of natural functions can be identified with the L-component of the least solution of the following regular system of recursive type equations

$$\begin{cases} N & = & \mathsf{unit} + N \\ L & = & \mathsf{unit} + (N \to N) \times L \end{cases}$$

2.1 Algebras of sets and algebras of partial orders

As the collection of denotations of recursively defined types, in the first approximation, one can take *any* family $\mathcal{D}omain$ of sets which is closed under suitable type-forming operations, and which is ordered by the set-theoretic inclusion. In what follows we assume only that $\mathcal{D}omain$ contains sets $A+B = \{\mathbf{tt}\} \times A \cup \{\mathbf{ff}\} \times B$ corresponding to the disjoint union, and the Cartesian product $A \times B = \{\langle a,b\rangle \mid a \in A, b \in B\}$, for any $A, B \in \mathcal{D}omain$. Let us remind the reader that an ordered pair is defined by $\langle x,y\rangle = \{\{x\},\{x,y\}\}$. Thus, $\mathcal{D}omain$ is an algebra over a signature consisting of two binary operation symbols $+$ and $\times$ which stand for the disjoint union and the Cartesian product of sets, respectively. Moreover, $\mathcal{D}omain$ should allow solving recursive domain equations, like (2) above.

The first approach towards a theory of recursive definitions in arbitrary algebras was that taken by the ADJ group, cf. [ADJ77]. They introduced the notion of an ω-continuous algebra. An *ω-continuous algebra* has an ω-cppo as the carrier and continuous functions as the operations. By an *ω-cppo*, abbr. cppo, we mean an ω-complete pointed poset, i.e., a poset with least upper bounds of all ω-chains and with the bottom as the distinguished (least) element. Cppo's are usually referred to as cpo's, but we reserve the name *cpo* to those ω-complete posets which may have no bottom at all. Functions between posets which preserve the existing least upper bounds of ω-chains are called *continuous*. *Strict* functions between cppo's are those preserving bottoms.

Note that in our case operations $+$ and $\times$ are continuous. The requirement of completeness of a carrier is easy to fulfill — we just assume that $\emptyset \in \mathcal{Domain}$ and that the union of any ω-chain of elements of $\mathcal{Domain}$ is also in $\mathcal{Domain}$. The existence of such families of sets can be established within set theory without problems.

This first approximation is not what one really wants. At least some of the types should allow for recursive definitions of their elements. In fact we want them to be cppo's. The practical consequence of the above requirement is that *all* types must be cpo's, see [BBP90].

A poset $\mathbf{P} = \langle P, \leq \rangle$ is *included* in a poset $\mathbf{Q} = \langle Q, \preceq \rangle$, notation $\mathbf{P} \subseteq \mathbf{Q}$, if $P \subseteq Q$ and $\leq \subseteq \preceq$. Every ω-chain of posets $\mathbf{Q}_n = \langle Q_n, \leq_n \rangle$ has a least upper bound equal $\mathbf{Q} = \langle Q, \preceq \rangle$ where $Q = \bigcup \{Q_n \mid n \in \omega\}$ and $\preceq = \bigcup \{\leq_n \mid n \in \omega\}$.

The operations of disjoint union and Cartesian product extend to operations on posets in the usual way.

$\langle P, \leq \rangle + \langle Q, \preceq \rangle = \langle P + Q, \sqsubseteq \rangle$ where

$$\langle \mathbf{tt}, x \rangle \sqsubseteq \langle \mathbf{tt}, y \rangle \iff x \leq y \quad \text{and} \quad \langle \mathbf{ff}, x \rangle \sqsubseteq \langle \mathbf{ff}, y \rangle \iff x \preceq y$$

$$\text{with } \langle \mathbf{tt}, x \rangle \text{ and } \langle \mathbf{ff}, y \rangle \text{ incomparable}$$

$\langle P, \leq \rangle \times \langle Q, \preceq \rangle = \langle P \times Q, \sqsubseteq \rangle$ where

$$\langle p, q \rangle \sqsubseteq \langle p', q' \rangle \iff p \leq p' \wedge q \preceq q'.$$

Obviously, these operations are continuous with respect to the poset inclusion. Let $\mathcal{Order}$ possess the same properties as $\mathcal{Domain}$. That is, let $\mathcal{Order}$ be *any* family of posets containing $\emptyset$, closed w.r.t. $\times$ and $+$ and unions of ω-chains of posets ordered by inclusion.

If $\mathcal{Order}$ contains a one element poset the equation (2) has the least solution in $\mathcal{Order}$ isomorphic to the *flat* poset of natural numbers. The latter means the set of natural numbers ordered by the equality relation.

Our minimal assumptions do not guarantee that the minimal algebra $\mathcal{Order}$ will contain non-trivially ordered types. In fact, the minimal algebra is empty. The non-trivial orders are introduced either by throwing them into a particular algebra $\mathcal{Order}$ one-by-one as constants, or systematically, when $\mathcal{Order}$ is assumed to be closed under a type-forming operation which introduces non-trivial ordering. The second situation took place in the MetaSoft project where we assumed that our type universe is closed under the partial functions type constructor.

2.2 Algebra of complete partial orders

Let $\mathcal{Cpo} = \{\mathbf{P} \in \mathcal{Order} \mid \mathbf{P} \text{ is a cpo}\}$ be the family of all cpo's in $\mathcal{Order}$. It is a subalgebra since the disjoint union of cpo's is a cpo and the Cartesian product of cpo's is a cpo too.

The problem is that $\mathcal{Cpo}$ is not a sub-cpo of $\mathcal{Order}$ in general, i.e., that the least upper bound of an ω-chain of cpo's calculated in $\mathcal{Order}$ may fail to be a cpo.

Moreover, *Cpo* may fail to be complete at all. All the claims made above are demonstrated by the following example.

Example 1 *In set theory it is customary to identify a natural number n with the set of all natural numbers strictly smaller than n. Thus, we have* $0 = \{\}$, $1 = \{0\}$, $\ldots$, $\omega = \{0, 1, \ldots\}$. *Under this identification the usual ordering coincides with set inclusion*

$$m \leq n \iff m \subseteq n.$$

Let $[n] = \langle n, \subseteq \rangle$, *for* $n \in \omega$, *and* $[\omega] = \langle \omega, \subseteq \rangle$. *Then posets* $[n]$, $n \in \omega$, *are cpo's, in fact, complete lattices, while* $[\omega]$ *is not a cpo.*

Let Order_ω *be the least set of posets such that*

- $[n] \in \mathit{Order}_\omega$,
- $\mathbf{P}, \mathbf{Q} \in \mathit{Order}_\omega$ *implies* $\mathbf{P} + \mathbf{Q}$, $\mathbf{P} \times \mathbf{Q} \in \mathit{Order}_\omega$,
- *if* $\mathbf{P}_n \in \mathit{Order}_\omega$, $n \in \omega$, *form a chain then* $\bigcup \{\mathbf{P}_n \mid n \in \omega\} \in \mathit{Order}_\omega$.

Let $\mathit{Cpo}_\omega = \{\mathbf{P} \in \mathit{Order}_\omega \mid \mathbf{P}$ *is a cpo*$\}$. *We also assume that* tt *and* ff *are neither pairs nor equal to* $[n]$, $n \in \omega$.

Proposition 2.1 $\mathit{Cpo}_\omega \subseteq \mathit{Order}_\omega$ *is not a sub-cpo of* Order_ω.

Proof. Consider the ω-chain $\{[n] \mid n \in \omega\} \subseteq \mathit{Cpo}_\omega$. It has $[\omega]$ as the least upper bound in Order_ω, but $[\omega] \notin \mathit{Cpo}_\omega$. □

Proving that the algebra Cpo_ω of the above example is not complete requires more effort.

Lemma 2.2 *If* $0 \in \mathbf{P} \in \mathit{Order}_\omega$ *then* $\mathbf{P} \subseteq [\omega]$.

Proof. The proof goes by induction on the resason behind $\mathbf{P} \in \mathit{Order}_\omega$.

If $\mathbf{P} = [n]$, for some $n \in \omega$, then certainly $\mathbf{P} \subseteq [\omega]$.

If $\mathbf{P} = \mathbf{Q}_1 + \mathbf{Q}_2$ or $\mathbf{P} = \mathbf{Q}_1 \times \mathbf{Q}_2$ then $0 = \{\} \notin \mathbf{P}$ since every element of such $\mathbf{P}$ is a pair $\langle x, y \rangle = \{\{x\}, \{x, y\}\} \neq \{\}$

Finally, if $\mathbf{P} = \bigcup \{\mathbf{P}_i \mid i \in \omega\}$ is the least upper bound of a chain $\{\mathbf{P}_i \mid i \in \omega\}$ then $0 \in \mathbf{P}$ implies $0 \in \mathbf{P}_i$ for some natural i. Hence, $0 \in \mathbf{P}_k$ for all $k \geq i$. By induction hypothesis it follows that $\mathbf{P}_k \subseteq [\omega]$, for $k \geq i$. On the other hand, $\mathbf{P}_k \subseteq [\omega]$ for all $k \leq i$, since $\{\mathbf{P}_i \mid i \in \omega\}$ form a chain. Hence, $\mathbf{P} = \bigcup \{\mathbf{P}_i \mid i \in \omega\} \subseteq [\omega]$. □

Proposition 2.3 Cpo_ω *is not a cpo, and hence it is not a cppo as well.*

Proof. From Lemma 2.2 it follows that the only upper bound of the chain $\{[n] \mid n \in \omega\}$ in Order_ω is $[\omega]$. Therefore the chain has no upper bounds in Cpo_ω at all. □

3 Regular Algebras

The theory of regular algebras, see [Tiu78], allows systems of recursive equations to be used as definitions of elements of algebras. Simplifying the idea a bit, one can say that the carrier of a regular algebra is a poset with a bottom. Moreover, it is assumed that the *important* ω-chains have their least upper bounds, and that the operations of the algebra preserve these least upper bounds.

Clearly, an ω-continuous algebra is a regular algebra.

An important example of a regular but non-continuous algebra is the algebra of regular trees over a signature. Essentially, this algebra is built from the syntax in a *minimal way* that ensures its initiality, cf. [Tiu78].

3.1 The definition

Let $\Sigma = \langle \mathsf{Op}, \mathsf{ar} \rangle$ be a one-sorted signature with the set of operation symbols $\sigma\colon \mathsf{Op}$ and the arity function $\mathsf{ar}\colon \mathsf{Op} \to \omega$. The set of all terms over Σ with variables from a set X is denoted by $\mathcal{T}_\Sigma(X)$. Let $\mathbf{A} = \langle A, \mathsf{Op}_A \rangle$ be a Σ-algebra. The value $[\![t]\!] : A^n \to A$ of a term $t \in \mathcal{T}_\Sigma(\{x_1, \ldots, x_n\})$ with n variables is called the *polynomial function* induced by t or the *derived operator* corresponding to t, cf. [ADJ77].

Above, by abuse of the language, we identify the Cartesian product A^n with the set of functions $\{x_1, \ldots, x_n\} \to A$. In this way the function $[\![x_i]\!]$ corresponds to the i-th projection under the identification. In general, polynomial functions are compositions of projections and operations in the algebra. If constant functions enter into a composition, the resulting function is called *algebraic*.

The definition given below is slightly less general than the original definition given in [Tiu78] but it is sufficient for our purposes.

Definition 3.1 A *regular* Σ-algebra is an algebra $\mathbf{A}$ whose carrier A is a poset with a bottom $\perp$ and whose operations are monotone, such that

> for any n-tuple $\vec{H} = \langle H_1, \ldots, H_n \rangle : A^n \to A^n$ of algebraic functions, the chain $\left\{ \vec{H}^\ell(\vec{\perp}) \mid \ell \in \omega \right\}$ has the least upper bound which, moreover, is a fixpoint of $\vec{H}$.

In the above $\vec{\perp} = \langle \perp, \ldots, \perp \rangle : A^n \to A^n$.

If $\vec{H} = \langle [\![t_1]\!], \ldots, [\![t_n]\!] \rangle$ where $t_i \in \mathcal{T}_\Sigma(\{x_1, \ldots, x_n\})$, $i{=}1, \ldots, n$ and $\langle a_1, \ldots, a_n \rangle \in A^n$ is its fixpoint then the latter is a solution of the following regular system of equations

$$\begin{cases} x_1 &= t_1 \\ & \vdots \\ x_n &= t_n \end{cases}$$

In [Tiu78] it is shown that regular trees form an initial regular Σ-algebra. More recent [Cou83] is a good reference on trees over a signature, and regular trees in particular.

Examples of non-ω-continuous algebras given in [Tiu78] are algebras of regular and context-free languages, and of functions computable by Ianow and monadic recursive schemes. All of them are images of initial regular Σ-algebras in ω-continuous algebras for appropriate Σ.

3.2 Complete partial orders form a regular algebra

Now, let us proceed to show that *Cpo*, although it is not ω-continuous, is a regular algebra. We start with the introduction of a suborder of the inclusion order.

Definition 3.2 Let $\mathbf{P} = \langle P, \leq \rangle$ and $\mathbf{Q} = \langle Q, \preceq \rangle$ be posets with $\mathbf{P} \subseteq \mathbf{Q}$. Then $\mathbf{P}$ is called a *direct summand* of $\mathbf{Q}$, denoted $\mathbf{P} \trianglelefteq \mathbf{Q}$, provided that

$$(\forall\, p, q \in Q)\ ((p \in P \vee q \in P) \wedge p \preceq q) \Rightarrow (p \in P \wedge q \in Q \wedge p \leq q).$$

The terminology above stems from the observation that given $\mathbf{P} \subseteq \mathbf{Q}$, $\mathbf{P} \trianglelefteq \mathbf{Q}$ iff $\mathbf{Q}$ is isomorphic to $\mathbf{P} + \mathbf{P}'$, for some $\mathbf{P}'$.

Below we show that appropriate conditions discussed in the introduction are fulfilled.

Lemma 3.1 *Algebraic functions are monotone with respect to* $\trianglelefteq$.

Proof. First we have to check that $\mathbf{P} \trianglelefteq \mathbf{Q}$ and $\mathbf{P}' \trianglelefteq \mathbf{Q}'$ implies $\mathbf{P} + \mathbf{P}' \trianglelefteq \mathbf{Q} + \mathbf{Q}'$ and $\mathbf{P} \times \mathbf{P}' \trianglelefteq \mathbf{Q} \times \mathbf{Q}'$. This is straightforward from definitions.

Algebraic functions are compositions of the above with projections and constant functions, hence the claim. □

The crucial property of the order $\trianglelefteq$ is that the least upper bound in *Order* of any ω-chain $\mathbf{P}_0 \trianglelefteq \mathbf{P}_1 \trianglelefteq \cdots$ in *Cpo* is a cpo. In the subsequent lemma $\trianglelefteq$ on *Order*^{n} denotes, abusing the notation, the n-th power of $\trianglelefteq$ on *Order*.

Lemma 3.2 *Let* $\vec{\mathbf{P}}_0 \trianglelefteq \vec{\mathbf{P}}_1 \trianglelefteq \cdots$ *be a chain in* *Cpo*^{n}. *Then the least upper bound of the chain calculated in* *Order*^{n} *belongs, in fact, to* *Cpo*^{n}.

Proof. Let $\vec{\mathbf{Q}}$ be the union of all $\vec{\mathbf{P}}_\ell$, $\ell \in \omega$, taken coordinatewise. Let $a_0 \preceq a_1 \preceq \ldots$ be a chain of elements of one of coordinates $\langle Q, \preceq \rangle$ of $\mathbf{Q}$. Let i be a natural number such that $a_0 \in P_i$, $\mathbf{P}_i = \langle P_i, \leq \rangle$. By definition 3.2, $a_1 \in P_i$ and $a_0 \leq a_1$ in P_i. Hence, by induction, $a_0 \leq a_1 \leq \ldots a_\ell \leq a_{\ell+1} \leq \ldots$ in P_i. But then $a_0, a_1, \ldots$ has its limit in $P_i \subseteq Q$ since P_i is a cpo. □

It follows from the lemma that the carrier of *Cpo* is ω-complete with respect to $\trianglelefteq$ and also that the least upper bounds in *Cpo* with respect to the order $\trianglelefteq$ and the standard inclusion order $\subseteq$ coincide.

The required result follows easily from the lemmas.

Theorem 3.3 *Let* $\vec{H} : \mathit{Order}^n \to \mathit{Order}^n$ *be a tuple of algebraic functions. Let* $\vec{\mathbf{X}}$ *be its least fixpoint. Then* $\vec{\mathbf{X}} \in \mathit{Cpo}^n$.

Proof. Let us build up the sequence of iterations $\left\{\vec{H}^\ell(\vec{\emptyset}) \mid \ell \in \omega\right\}$. Because $\vec{H}$ is $\subseteq$-monotone and $\emptyset$ is the least element of *Order*, the sequence is an ω-chain with respect to $\subseteq$ ordering. Its limit in *Order*^{n} is the least fixpoint of $\vec{H}$. Furthermore, all elements of the sequence are in *Cpo*^{n}, for $\emptyset$ is a cpo and $\vec{H} : \mathit{Cpo}^n \to \mathit{Cpo}^n$.

According to Lemma 3.1, algebraic functions are $\trianglelefteq$-monotone. Since $\vec{\emptyset}$ is a direct summand of $\vec{H}(\vec{\emptyset})$, the whole chain is also an ω-chain in $\langle \mathit{Cpo}^n, \trianglelefteq \rangle$. We see that Lemma 3.2 can be applied to yield the result. □

In this way we have shown that *Cpo* is a regular algebra.

Now we return to example 1 to show that Cpo_ω is not an image of the algebra of regular trees, even if all $[n]$, $n \in \omega$ are added to a signature as constants.

Lemma 3.4 *Let $A, B \in \mathcal{O}rder_\omega$. If $A \neq \emptyset$ or $B \neq \emptyset$ then for any $C, D \in \mathcal{O}rder_\omega$,*

- $A + B \neq C \times D$,
- $A + B \neq [n]$
- $A + B = C + D$ *implies* $A = C$, $B = D$,
- $A \times B \neq [n]$,
- $[n] = [\ell]$ *implies* $n = \ell$. □

Proposition 3.5 *$\mathcal{C}po_\omega$ is not an image of the initial regular $\{+, \times, [n] \mid n \in \omega\}$-algebra.*

Proof. $\mathcal{C}po_\omega$ ordered by $\trianglelefteq$ is ω-continuous. Hence it contains images of the following infinite trees T_n, $n \in \omega$,

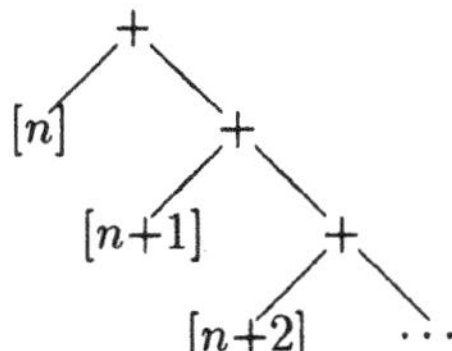

Let A_n, $n \in \omega$, denote the sets corresponding to images of T_n in $\mathcal{C}po$. It follows from the lemma that no A_n can be a solution of a finite system of equations. □

Let us also remark that the plan used in the paper cannot be used to show that regular trees themselves form a regular algebra.

Conclusions

All the regular algebras mentioned in [Tiu78] are images of the algebras of regular trees in suitable continuous algebras. Some of them are not complete, like the algebra of regular languages ordered by inclusion.

Our example regular algebra $\langle \mathcal{C}po_\omega, \subseteq \rangle$ is neither complete nor an image of the algebra of regular trees. In fact, it is similar to the algebra of the denotations of (closed) type expressions studied in [BBP90]. The latter algebra is closed, additionally, w.r.t. the mappings space and partial functions space operations. It can be shown that mappings space operation does preserve direct summands (i.e. is $\trianglelefteq$-monotone) while the partial functions space operation does not. Also, the first operation is continuous while the other one is not. What is important, though, both map cpo's to cpo's. Hence, in the appropriate $\mathcal{C}po$, one can solve regular systems of equations in which partial functions space operation appears in an essentially non-recursive way.

Obviously, other direct summand preserving, continuous operations can be easily added. Other operations, even non-continuous, can be added under proviso that they be not used recursively in systems of equations.

Acknowledgements

The authors would like to thank Andrzej Tarlecki for urging us to *prove* the main theorem instead of waving hands. We also thank other members of the MetaSoft group for stimulating discussions and comments.

References

[ADJ77] J. Goguen, J. W. Thatcher, E. G. Wagner, and J. B. Wright. An initial algebra semantics and continuous algebras. *Journal of the ACM*, 24(1):68–95, January 1977.

[BBP90] Marek A. Bednarczyk, Andrzej M. Borzyszkowski, and Wiesław Pawłowski. Towards the semantics of the definitional language of MetaSoft. In Dines Bjørner, editor, *VDM & Z: Formal Methods in Software Development, 3rd VDM-Europe Symposium, Kiel*, pages 477–503. LNCS, vol. 428, Springer-Verlag, 1990.

[BJ78] Dines Bjørner and Cliff B. Jones. *The Vienna Development Method: The Meta-Language*, volume 61 of *LNCS*. Springer-Verlag, 1978.

[BJ82] Dines Bjørner and Cliff B. Jones. *Formal Specification of Software Development*. Prentice Hall, Englewood Cliffs, 1982.

[Bli87] Andrzej J. Blikle. *MetaSoft Primer. Towards a Metalanguage of Applied Denotational Semantics*, volume 288 of *LNCS*. Springer-Verlag, 1987.

[BT83] Andrzej J. Blikle and Andrzej Tarlecki. Naive denotational semantics. In *Proceedings IFIP Congress 1983*. North Holland, 1983.

[Cou83] Bruno Courcelle. Fundamental properties of infinite trees. *Theoretical Computer Science*, 25:95–169, 1983.

[GJ88] Carl Gunter and Achim Jung. Coherence and consistency in domains. In *3rd IEEE Symposium on Logic in Computer Science*, pages 309–317. IEEE, 1988.

[Gor90] Peter Gorm Larsen, editor. *The dynamic semantics of the BSI/VDM specification language*. Technical report, IFAD, Munkebjærgvænget 17, DK–5230 Odense M, Denmark, July 1990.

[HP90] Hagen Huwig and Axal Poigné. A note on inconsistencies caused by fixedpoints in a cartesian closed category. *Theoretical Computer Science*, 73:101–112, 1990.

[Mon87] Brian Q. Monahan. A type model for VDM. In Dines Bjørner and Cliff B. Jones, editors, *VDM—A Formal Method at Work, VDM-Europe Symposium, Brussels*, pages 210–236. LNCS, vol. 252, Springer-Verlag, 1987.

[NHWG88] M. Nielsen, K. Havelund, K. R. Wagner, and C. George. The RAISE language, methods and tools. In R. Bloomfield, R. Jones, and L. Marshall, editors, *VDM: The Way Ahead, 2nd VDM-Europe Symposium, Dublin*, pages 376–405. LNCS, vol. 328, Springer-Verlag, 1988.

[Plo85] Gordon Plotkin. Domains. Postgraduate Course—Lecture Notes, Edinburgh University, 1985.

[Smy87] M. B. Smyth. Quasi-uniformities: Reconciling domains with metric spaces. LNCS vol. 298, 1987.

[Tiu78] J. Tiuryn. Fixed points and algebras with infinitely long expressions. Part I. *Fundamenta Informaticæ*, 2(1):103–128, 1978. also in *Proceedings* MFCS'77, LNCS, vol. 53, 1977.

[TW90] Andrzej Tarlecki and Morten Wieth. A naive domain universe for VDM. In Dines Bjørner, editor, *VDM & Z: Formal Methods in Software Development, 3rd VDM-Europe Symposium, Kiel*, pages 552–579. LNCS, vol. 428, Springer-Verlag, 1990.

LPF and MPL_ω — A Logical Comparison of VDM SL and COLD-K

C.A. Middelburg* and G.R. Renardel de Lavalette**

Abstract

This paper compares the finitary three-valued logic LPF and the infinitary two-valued logic MPL_ω, the logics underlying VDM SL and COLD-K. These logics reflect different approaches to reasoning about partial functions and bringing recursive function definitions into proofs. The purpose of the comparison is to acquire insight into the relationship between these approaches. A natural translation from LPF to MPL_ω is given. It is shown that what can be proved remains the same after translation, in case strictness axioms are added to LPF or removed from MPL_ω. The translation from LPF to MPL_ω is extended to recursive function definitions and this translation is next used to justify some ways of bringing the definitions of partial functions into proofs using LPF.

1 Introduction

Functions specified in VDM SL [Jon90, JS90] or COLD-K [Jon89] are generally partial functions. Partial functions give rise to non-denoting terms. This makes reasoning about partial functions problematic in classical first-order logic. The underlying logics of VDM SL and COLD-K, viz. LPF [BCJ84, Che86] and MPL_ω [KR89], have different approaches to solve this problem.

Classical first-order logic has been used fruitfully to describe and formalize mathematical concepts and theories. But there was always the problem of non-denoting terms: terms that do not refer to objects in the intended domain (they are also called undefined terms). The classical example is division by zero. In most formalizations, this problem is sidestepped by considering division not as a binary function but as a ternary relation D, where $D(x,y,z)$ means that x divided by y yields z, or by restriction of the language: allowing t/t' as a term only if $t' \neq 0$. In recursion theory, however, it became clear that partial functions are essential in any decent theory of recursive functions.

*Dept. of Computer Science, PTT Research, Dr. Neher Laboratories, P.O. Box 421, 2260 AK Leidschendam, The Netherlands; e-mail: CA.Middelburg@pttrnl.nl.

**Software Engineering Research Centre, P.O. Box 424, 3500 AK Utrecht, The Netherlands and Section Applied Logic, University of Utrecht, P.O. Box 80126, 3508 TC Utrecht, The Netherlands; e-mail: renardel@serc.nl.

Scott provided a formal basis for reasoning about partial functions in [Sco67], later extended to intuitionistic logic with sheaf semantics in [Sco79]. Semantically, the situation is as follows: the intended domain is extended with an object $\perp$ (undefined) to which the undefined terms refer. This idea has been adopted by, for example, Beeson in [Bee85] and the second author in [Ren84]. This approach has also been followed in MPL_ω, the logic underlying COLD-K. It can be characterized as follows:

- there is a definedness predicate $\downarrow$, where $t\downarrow$ means that t is denoting (or is defined, exists, refers to a defined object);
- if an atomic formula is true, then all terms occurring in it are defined (the strictness property).

Another approach has been followed in LPF, the logic underlying VDM SL. Here the possibility of undefinedness is extended to the formulae by adding a truth value N (neither-true-nor-false), so terms and formulae are in this respect treated on an equal footing. This makes LPF a non-classical logic with three truth values. So the definition of the logical connectives has to be extended. This is done by taking the definitions obtained by extending the classical truth-conditions and falsity-conditions with a clause yielding N for the other cases. In other words, Kleene's strong three-valued connectives [Kle52] are taken. For example, we have for any propositions A and A':

$$A \wedge A' = \begin{array}{ll} \mathsf{T} & \text{if } A = \mathsf{T} \textit{ and } A' = \mathsf{T}, \\ \mathsf{F} & \text{if } A = \mathsf{F} \textit{ or } A' = \mathsf{F}, \\ \mathsf{N} & \text{otherwise.} \end{array}$$

This extension to the three-valued case yields monotonic operators with respect to the ordering $\mathsf{N} \preceq \mathsf{T}, \mathsf{F}$, the ordering of information contents. Furthermore, there is only a weak strictness property:

if an atomic formula $t = t'$ is true or false, then both t and t' are defined.

One might expect the following strong version here:

if an atomic formula is true or false, then all terms occurring in it are defined.

There are reasons to think that such a version of strictness is an intended property of LPF. It is strongly suggested in Section 3.3 of [Jon86, Jon90], as is shown in [Tho89] (see Section 7 of the current paper for LPF with strictness axioms).

In this paper we consider these two ways of dealing with undefinedness more closely, in a comparison of the underlying logics of the specification languages VDM SL and COLD-K. In Section 2, these logics are described in broad outline. Some other logics which handle partial functions are discussed in Section 3. Sections 4–8 constitute the body of this paper. In Section 4 we present $\mathrm{ML}^=$, many-sorted classical logic with equality, by giving definitions of the language, the proof system, and the interpretation of $\mathrm{ML}^=$. It is used as the starting point for the presentations of LPF and MPL_ω in Sections 5 and 6. LPF is embedded into MPL_ω in Section 7. Section 8 is concerned with recursive function definitions in LPF and MPL_ω. Conclusions and final remarks are given in Section 9.

In [CJ90], Cheng and Jones compare the usability of different logics in handling partial functions. Their brief treatment of logics based on Scott's idea and their way of bringing the definitions of partial functions into proofs using LPF provided an important stimulus to write this paper.

2 Overview of LPF and MPL$_\omega$

LPF and MPL$_\omega$ reflect different approaches to deal with non-denoting terms in formulae. This section describes these logics informally and in broad outline.

2.1 LPF

LPF is a non-classical finitary first-order logic of partial functions with equality. Its typical features are obtained by rather drastic changes to classical first-order logic. Classical reasoning is invalidated on a large scale. A mathematically precise presentation of LPF is given by Cheng in [Che86].

The logic LPF adopts an approach to solve the problem with non-denoting terms in formulae, which does not stay within the realm of classical, two-valued logics. Atomic formulae that contain non-denoting terms may be logically neither-true-nor-false. Thus, the assumption of the "excluded middle" is given up. Yet, the classical truth-conditions and falsehood-conditions for logical connectives and quantifiers are adopted. The formula concerned is classified as neither-true-nor-false exactly when it cannot be classified as true or false by these conditions. Likewise, an equation $t_1 = t_2$ is classified as neither-true-nor-false exactly when t_1 or t_2 is non-denoting.

This approach leaves open the treatment of free variables. In contrast with MPL$_\omega$, free variables are always denoting — just as bound variables.

A definedness connective Δ guarantees expressive completeness of the connectives of LPF for three-valued truth functions. ΔA is true if the formula A can be classified as either true or false, and false otherwise.

LPF lacks countably infinite conjunctions, which we shall see in MPL$_\omega$. Neither is there another feature in LPF that allows recursive or inductive definitions to be expressed as formulae. LPF lacks descriptions, which would also give rise to non-denoting terms, as well.

The formation rules for LPF are the usual formation rules with an additional rule for formulae of the form ΔA. The proof system of LPF presented in [Che86] is a Gentzen-type sequent calculus that does not resemble a classical one. Even so, adding one axiom schema — stating the assumption of the excluded middle — would make it a complete proof system for classical first order logic with equality.

The formulae that contain only function and predicate symbols from a certain set Σ constitute the language of LPF over Σ. The structures used for interpretation of the language of LPF over Σ consist of an interpretation of every symbol in Σ as well as an interpretation of the equality symbol that is in accordance with the above-mentioned treatment of non-denoting terms in equations. The connectives and quantifiers are always interpreted according to the outlined classification of formulae. The interpretation of the language in the structures concerned is sound with respect to the proof system. The proof system is complete with respect to the interpretation of the language in these structures.

The outlined version of LPF is the one-sorted version presented in [Che86]. In the current paper, that version is generalized to a many-sorted version of LPF. For convenience, the many-sorted version is compared with MPL$_\omega$.

2.2 MPL$_\omega$

MPL$_\omega$ is a many-sorted infinitary first-order logic of partial functions with equality. Its typical features are mainly obtained by additions to language and proof system of classical first-order logic. Classical reasoning is only invalidated on a small scale. The language, proof system and interpretation of MPL$_\omega$ are introduced by Koymans and Renardel de Lavalette in [KR89].

The logic MPL$_\omega$ adopts an approach to solve the problem with non-denoting terms in formulae, which stays within the realm of classical, two-valued logics. Atomic formulae that contain non-denoting terms are logically false. In this way, the assumption of the excluded middle does not have to be given up. When a formula cannot be classified as true, it is inexorably classified as false. No further distinction is made. However, denoting terms and non-denoting terms can be distinguished. $t =_S t$ means that t is denoting (for terms t of sort S), which is also written $t\downarrow_S$. There is a standard undefined constant symbol $\uparrow_S$ for every sort symbol S. $\uparrow_S$ is a non-denoting term of sort S.

If $A_0, A_1, A_2, \ldots$ are countably many formulae, then the formula $\bigwedge_n A_n$ can be formed. This allows a large class of recursive and inductive definitions of functions and predicates to be expressed as formulae of MPL$_\omega$. This was first sketched in [KR89, Section 4] and later worked out in detail by Renardel de Lavalette in [Ren89].

If A is a formula, then the term $\iota x\colon S\,(A)$ can be formed which is called a description. Its intended meaning is the unique value x of sort S that satisfies A if such a unique value exists and undefined otherwise. This means that not every description will be denoting. Descriptions can be eliminated: it is possible to translate formulae containing descriptions into logically equivalent formulae without descriptions.

The formation rules for MPL$_\omega$ are the usual formation rules with an additional rule for descriptions and with the rule for binary conjunctions replaced by the rule for countably infinite conjunctions from L$_\omega$ [Kar64, Kei71] (classical first-order logic with countably infinite conjunctions). The proof system of MPL$_\omega$ presented in [KR89] is a Gentzen-type sequent calculus that resembles one for L$_\omega$. Obviously, there are additional axioms for equality, undefined, and description.

The formulae that contain only sort, function and predicate symbols from a certain set Σ constitute the language of MPL$_\omega$ over Σ. The structures used for interpretation of the language of MPL$_\omega$ over Σ consist of an interpretation of every symbol in Σ as well as an interpretation of each of the equality symbols associated with the sort symbols in Σ. These interpretations have to be in accordance with the outlined treatment of non-denoting terms. The classical interpretation of the connectives and quantifiers is used. This means that, unlike free variables, bound variables are always denoting. The interpretation of the language in the structures concerned is sound with respect to the proof system. The proof system is complete with respect to the interpretation of the language in these structures.

3 Other Logics for Partial Functions

There are other logics for partial function. They differ from LPF and MPL_ω in various ways. The key differences are discussed in this section.

3.1 Other Three-valued Logics

The key differences between the various three-valued logics are with respect to:

- what logical connectives and quantifiers are taken as basic,
- whether equality of some kind is taken as basic and if so which kind,
- what model-theoretic notion of logical consequence is taken to underlie the proof system.

Negation, disjunction, and existential quantifier are basic in the version of LPF presented in [Che86]. Each behaves according to its classical truth-condition and falsehood-condition; only if neither of them meets, it will yield neither-true-nor-false. This is Kleene's way of extending the classical connectives and quantifiers to the three-valued case [Kle52]. In addition, there are two basic connectives which have no classical counterparts: a nullary connective designating neither-true-nor-false and a unary connective for definedness of formulae. All possible connectives for three-valued logics are definable by the above-mentioned four basic connectives. The definable connectives include McCarthy's connectives [McC67] and Łukasiewicz's connectives [Luk67]. McCarthy's quantifiers are also definable. Quantifiers which bind variables that may be non-denoting are not definable, but such quantifiers are uncommon in a three-valued setting.

There are several ways of extending classical equality to the three-valued case. Admissible kinds of equality only differ in their treatment of non-denoting terms:

- *weak equality*: if either t_1 or t_2 is non-denoting, then $t_1 = t_2$ is neither-true-nor-false;
- *strong equality*: if either t_1 or t_2 is non-denoting, then $t_1 = t_2$ is true whenever both t_1 and t_2 are non-denoting and false otherwise;
- *existential equality*: if either t_1 or t_2 is non-denoting, then $t_1 = t_2$ is false.

Weak equality is basic in LPF. Due to the presence of the definedness connective, strong equality and existential equality are also definable. Thus, LPF encompasses most three-valued logics with respect to their connectives, quantifiers and equality predicates.

The following are the intuitive ideas that underlie sensible notions of logical consequence for three-valued logics:

- from premises that are not false, one can draw conclusions that are not false;
- from premises that are true, one can draw conclusions that are not false;
- from premises that are true, one can draw conclusions that are true;
- from premises that are true, one can draw conclusions that are true, and conclusions that are false must arise from premises that are false.

Note that "from premises that are not false, one can draw conclusions that are true" does not correspond to a sensible notion of logical consequence, since not every formula will be a consequence of itself.

Logical consequence for three-valued logics according to the first idea amounts to logics in which the definedness of any formula (i.e. the property that the formula is either true or false) can be treated as true. It means that a separate proof is needed to establish the definedness. For formulae formed with Kleene's or McCarthy's connectives and Kleene's quantifiers, logical consequence for three-valued logics according to the second idea reduces to classical logical consequence for two-valued logics. For formulae formed with Kleene's connectives and Kleene's quantifiers, logical consequence for three-valued logics according to the third idea coincides with classical logical consequence for two-valued logics except for the absence of what depends anyhow on the excluded middle. That is, it is lacking exactly what does not leave room for formulae which are neither true nor false. This is what one naturally expects from a three-valued logic where the additional truth value is interpreted as neither true nor false. The last idea actually combines the first idea and the third idea. The corresponding notion of logical consequence seems too strong for a logic for the formal specification and verified design of software systems, which is only concerned with drawing true conclusions from true premises.

For LPF, the underlying notion of logical consequence is the third one of the above-mentioned notions. The first notion underlies Owe's weak logic [Owe84]. The second notion underlies the logic PFOL which is presented in [GL90] together with reflections on the semantic options for three-valued logics and their relationships. Amongst other things, it is shown in [GL90] that logical consequence according to the first or second notion can be defined over logical consequence according to the third notion (in the latter case, it can only be defined provided that the definedness connective is available). Similar reflections are also presented in [KTB88], but there a definedness connective is not mentioned. In [KTB88], attention is also paid to McCarthy's connectives. The last notion of logical consequence underlies Blamey's partial logic [Bla86]. It follows immediately that the above-mentioned definability results extend to this notion. Because of these definability results for other notions of logical consequence, LPF also encompasses most three-valued logics with respect to their underlying notion of logical consequence.

3.2 Other Two-valued Logics

The various two-valued logics for partial functions are quite similar with respect to their connectives and their underlying notion of logical consequence. The quantifiers differ slightly in the treatment of the bound variables.

The key differences between the various two-valued logics are with respect to:

- the treatment of free variables and bound variables,
- whether equality of some kind is taken as basic and if so which kind,
- whether two levels of truth values are used.

In MPL_ω, free variables may not denote but bound variables always do. The same happens in Scott's free logic [Sco67], Plotkin's PFL (Partial Function Logic) [Plo85] and other free logics (for a discussion of free logics, see [Ben86]). Due to this treatment of free and bound variables, frequent reasoning about the definedness of terms can be avoided. This contrasts with Scott's LCF (Logic of Computable Functions), which was renamed PPλ [GMW79, Pau87], where bound variables may as well not denote: frequent reasoning about undefined is customary. The treatment of variables in PPλ is a consequence of the decision not to differ from classical first-order logic with respect to logical axioms and inference rules. Quantifications, where the bound variable may be non-denoting, can be treated as abbreviations in MPL_ω. Both free variables and bound variables always denote in Beeson's LPT (Logic of Partial Terms) [Bee88]. Thus, LPT is kept closer to classical first-order logic than the free logics.

MPL_ω is a two-valued logic with existential equality. Strong equality is definable. Note that weak equality makes no sense in two-valued logics. All of this is the same as in Scott's free logic and Beeson's LPT. But PPλ is a logic with strong equality. This means that it does not differ from classical logic with respect to its kind of equality as well.

PPλ is the only one of the above-mentioned logics which is classical, but nevertheless it handles partial functions. That result is reached by adopting a layered approach which give rise to two levels of truth values. Terms, which are intended to represent computable objects, can be undefined (as computations commonly involve applications of partial functions). Thus, three "computational truth values", including an undefined truth value, is made provision for. Formulae, which are meant to be assertions about computable objects, must be either true or false (which corresponds to the truth or falsehood, respectively, of the assertions). So there are only two "logical truth values".

Roughly speaking, there are two main approaches of handling partial functions in a two-valued logic: the approach adopted by free logics and the layered approach adopted by PPλ. MPL_ω adopts the former approach; it encompasses most free logics with respect to their treatment of free and bound variables and their predicates concerning equality. Although MPL_ω does not adopt the latter approach, it is shown in the current paper that it allows for a layered approach: formulae of LPF can be treated as terms of MPL_ω.

4 Many-sorted Classical Logic with Equality

MPL_ω and LPF are quite different. Nevertheless, $\text{ML}^=$, many-sorted classical logic with equality, provides a convenient starting point for a presentation of both logics. Hence, language, proof system and interpretation of $\text{ML}^=$ are presented first.

4.1 Signatures

A language of $ML^=$ is constructed with sort symbols, function symbols and predicate symbols that belong to a certain set, called a signature. For a given signature, say Σ, the language concerned is called the language of $ML^=$ over signature Σ or the language of $ML^=(\Sigma)$. The corresponding proof system and interpretation are analogously called the proof system of $ML^=(\Sigma)$ and the interpretation of $ML^=(\Sigma)$, respectively.

We assume a set $SORT$ of *sort symbols*, a set $FUNC$ of *function symbols*, and a set $PRED$ of *predicate symbols*. f, g range over $FUNC$, P, Q range over $PRED$, and $S, S_1, S_2, \ldots$ range over $SORT$. Every $f \in FUNC$ has a *function type* $S_1 \times \cdots \times S_n \rightarrow S_{n+1}$ and every $P \in PRED$ has a *predicate type* $S_1 \times \cdots \times S_n$ ($S_1, \ldots, S_{n+1} \in SORT$). To indicate this, we use the notation $f: S_1 \times \cdots \times S_n \rightarrow S_{n+1}$ and $P: S_1 \times \cdots \times S_n$. Function symbols of function type $\rightarrow S$ are also called *constant symbols* of sort S. For every $S \in SORT$, there is a standard predicate symbol $=_S: S \times S$, called *equality*.

A *signature* Σ is a finite subset of $SORT \cup FUNC \cup PRED$ such that

$$\text{for all } f \in \Sigma, f: S_1 \times \cdots \times S_n \rightarrow S_{n+1} \;\Rightarrow\; S_1, \ldots, S_{n+1} \in \Sigma;$$
$$\text{for all } P \in \Sigma, P: S_1 \times \cdots \times S_n \;\Rightarrow\; S_1, \ldots, S_n \in \Sigma.$$

We write $\mathrm{S}(\Sigma)$ for $\Sigma \cap SORT$, $\mathrm{F}(\Sigma)$ for $\Sigma \cap FUNC$, $\mathrm{P}(\Sigma)$ for $\Sigma \cap PRED$, $\mathrm{SP}(\Sigma)$ for $\{=_S \mid S \in \mathrm{S}(\Sigma)\}$. $SIGN$ denotes the set of all signatures for $ML^=$.

We also assume a set VAR of *variable symbols*. $x, y, z, x_1, x_2, \ldots$ range over VAR. Every $x \in VAR$ has a *sort* S ($S \in SORT$).

We write $\mathcal{V}$ for $SORT \cup FUNC \cup PRED \cup VAR$. We write $w \equiv w'$, where $w, w' \in \mathcal{V}$, to indicate that w and w' are identical symbols.

Furthermore, it is assumed that $SORT$, $FUNC$, $PRED$, and VAR are four disjoint sets and $=_S \notin \mathcal{V}$ for all $S \in SORT$.

4.2 Language of $ML^=(\Sigma)$

Terms and Formulae

The language of $ML^=(\Sigma)$ contains terms and formulae. They are constructed according to the formation rules which are given below. $t, t', t_1, t_1', t_2, t_2', \ldots$ range over terms and $A, A_0, A_0', A_1, A_1', \ldots$ range over formulae.

The terms of $ML^=(\Sigma)$ are inductively defined by the following formation rules:

1. variable symbols of sort S are terms of sort S, for any $S \in \mathrm{S}(\Sigma)$;

2. if $f \in \mathrm{F}(\Sigma)$, $f: S_1 \times \cdots \times S_n \rightarrow S_{n+1}$ and $t_1, \ldots, t_n$ are terms of sorts $S_1, \ldots, S_n$, respectively, then $f(t_1, \ldots, t_n)$ is a term of sort S_{n+1}.

The formulae of $ML^=(\Sigma)$ are inductively defined by the following formation rules:

1. $\top$ and $\bot$ are formulae;

2. if $P \in \mathrm{P}(\Sigma) \cup \mathrm{SP}(\Sigma)$, $P: S_1 \times \cdots \times S_n$ and $t_1, \ldots, t_n$ are terms of sorts $S_1, \ldots, S_n$, respectively, then $P(t_1, \ldots, t_n)$ is a formula;

3. if A is formula, then $\neg A$ is a formula;

4. if A_1 and A_2 are formulae, then $A_1 \wedge A_2$ is a formula;

5. if A is a formula and x is a variable of sort S, $S \in \mathrm{S}(\Sigma)$, then $\forall x: S\,(A)$ is a formula.

The string representation of formulae as suggested by these formation rules can lead to syntactic ambiguities. Parentheses are used to avoid such ambiguities.

For every set Γ of formulae of $\mathrm{ML}^{=}(\Sigma)$, $sig(\Gamma)$, the signature of Γ, is the smallest signature such that for every formula $A \in \Gamma$, A is a formula of $\mathrm{ML}^{=}(sig(\Gamma))$.

$\mathcal{T}_{ML^{=}}(\Sigma)$ denotes the set of all terms of $\mathrm{ML}^{=}(\Sigma)$.
$\mathcal{L}_{ML^{=}}(\Sigma)$ denotes the set of all formulae of $\mathrm{ML}^{=}(\Sigma)$.

Notational Conventions

Constant symbols may be used as terms, i.e. in terms of the form $f(t_1, \ldots, t_n)$ the parentheses may be omitted whenever $n = 0$.

The equality symbols ($=_S$) are used in infix notation. Moreover, they are used without subscript when this causes no ambiguity.

Sometimes $\forall x_1: S_1\,(\cdots \forall x_n: S_n\,(A)\cdots)$ is simply written as $\forall x_1: S_1, \ldots, x_n: S_n\,(A)$.

Absent from the language of $\mathrm{ML}^{=}(\Sigma)$ are disjunction, existential quantification, etc. They are defined as abbreviations:

$$\begin{array}{lll} A_1 \vee A_2 & := & \neg(\neg A_1 \wedge \neg A_2), \\ A_1 \rightarrow A_2 & := & \neg A_1 \vee A_2, \\ A_1 \leftrightarrow A_2 & := & (A_1 \rightarrow A_2) \wedge (A_2 \rightarrow A_1), \\ \exists x: S\,(A) & := & \neg \forall x: S\,(\neg A). \end{array}$$

The need to use parentheses in the string representation of formulae is reduced by ranking the precedence of the logical symbols $\neg$, $\wedge$, $\vee$, $\rightarrow$, $\leftrightarrow$. The enumeration presents this order from the highest precedence to the lowest precedence.

Free Variables and Substitution

For a term or formula E of $\mathrm{ML}^{=}(\Sigma)$, $free(E)$ denotes the set of *free variable* of E, which is defined as usual. We write $free(\Gamma)$, where Γ is a set of formulae, for $\bigcup\{free(A) \mid A \in \Gamma\}$. A variable symbol x is called *free in* Γ if $x \in free(\Gamma)$.

Substitution for variables is also defined as usual. Let x be a variable symbol, t be a term (x and t of the same sort) and E be a term or formula. Then $[x := t]E$ is the result of replacing the term t for the free occurrences of the variable symbol x in E, avoiding that free variables in t become bound by means of renaming of bound variables.

4.3 Proof System of $\mathrm{ML}^{=}(\Sigma)$

Sequents

The proof system of $\mathrm{ML}^{=}(\Sigma)$ is formulated as a Gentzen-type sequent calculus.

A *sequent* is an expression of the form $\Gamma \vdash \Delta$, where Γ and Δ are finite sets of formulae of $ML^=(\Sigma)$. Instead of $\{\} \vdash \Delta$ we write $\vdash \Delta$, and instead of $\Gamma \vdash \{\}$ we write $\Gamma \vdash$.

The intended meaning of the sequent $\Gamma \vdash \Delta$ is that the conjunction of the formulae in Γ entails the disjunction of the formulae in Δ. A sequent is proved by a derivation obtained by using the axiom schemas and rules of inference given below.

Axiom Schemas and Rules of Inference

$\Gamma, \Delta, \Gamma', \Delta', \ldots$ stand for arbitrary finite sets of formulae of $ML^=(\Sigma)$.
A, A_1, A_2 stand for arbitrary formulae of $ML^=(\Sigma)$.
t, t_1, t_2 stand for arbitrary terms (of appropriate sorts) of $ML^=(\Sigma)$.
x, y, z stand for arbitrary variable symbols (of appropriate sorts).
S stands for an arbitrary sort symbol in Σ.

We write Γ, Δ for $\Gamma \cup \Delta$ and A for $\{A\}$.

The proof system of $ML^=(\Sigma)$ is defined by the following axiom schemas and rules of inference:

Logical Axioms:

(⊤) $\vdash \top$

(⊥) $\bot \vdash$

(taut) $A \vdash A$

Non-logical Axioms:

(eqv) $\vdash \forall x{:}\,S\,(x = x) \wedge \forall x{:}\,S, y{:}\,S, z{:}\,S\,(x = y \wedge x = z \rightarrow y = z)$

(sub) $t_1 = t_2, [x := t_1]A \vdash [x := t_2]A$

Rules of Inference:

$(\neg L)\ \dfrac{\Gamma \vdash \Delta, A}{\Gamma, \neg A \vdash \Delta}$ $(\neg R)\ \dfrac{\Gamma, A \vdash \Delta}{\Gamma \vdash \Delta, \neg A}$

$(\wedge L)\ \dfrac{\Gamma, A_i \vdash \Delta}{\Gamma, A_1 \wedge A_2 \vdash \Delta}$ for $i = 1, 2$ $(\wedge R)\ \dfrac{\Gamma \vdash \Delta, A_1 \quad \Gamma \vdash \Delta, A_2}{\Gamma \vdash \Delta, A_1 \wedge A_2}$

$(\forall L)\ \dfrac{\Gamma, [x := t]A \vdash \Delta}{\Gamma, \forall x{:}\,S(A) \vdash \Delta}$ $(\forall R)\ \dfrac{\Gamma \vdash \Delta, A}{\Gamma \vdash \Delta, \forall x{:}\,S(A)}$

$(\text{cut})\ \dfrac{\Gamma \vdash \Delta, A \quad \Gamma', A \vdash \Delta'}{\Gamma, \Gamma' \vdash \Delta, \Delta'}$ $(\text{weak})\ \dfrac{\Gamma \vdash \Delta}{\Gamma, \Gamma' \vdash \Delta, \Delta'}$

Restriction on the rule $(\forall R)$: x not free in $\Gamma \cup \Delta$.

Multiple instances of axiom schema (eqv) for the same sort symbol are superfluous. In $ML^=$, the axiom schema (sub) is equivalent to $\vdash \forall x{:}\,S, y{:}\,S\,(x = y \wedge A \rightarrow [x := y]A)$. The rule (weak) becomes a derived rule when the axiom schemas are replaced by weakened versions (axiom schemas $\vdash A$ are replaced by axiom schemas $\Gamma \vdash \Delta, A$, etc.).

The deduction theorem holds in $ML^=$:

$$\frac{A_1 \vdash A_2}{\vdash A_1 \rightarrow A_2} \quad \text{is a derived rule.}$$

LPF does not have this property in common with $ML^=$.

Derivations

A *derivation* (or *proof*) is a finitely branching tree with branches of finite length, where the nodes are labelled with sequents in such a way that the labels of terminal nodes are instances of axiom schemas and the label of any non-terminal node is obtained from the labels of its immediate descendants by applying an inference rule.

A sequent $\Gamma \vdash \Delta$ is *derivable* if there exists a derivation with its root labelled by $\Gamma \vdash \Delta$. We write $ML^=(\Sigma)$: $\Gamma \vdash \Delta$ (and sometimes just $\Gamma \vdash \Delta$ without more ado) to indicate that $\Gamma \vdash \Delta$ is derivable.

4.4 Interpretation of $ML^=(\Sigma)$

Structures

The structures used for interpretation of terms and formulae of $ML^=(\Sigma)$ consist of an interpretation of every symbol in the signature Σ as well as an interpretation of the equality symbols.

A structure $\mathbf{A}$ with signature Σ consists of:

1. for every $S \in \mathrm{S}(\Sigma)$, a non-empty set $S^{\mathbf{A}}$;
2. for every $f \in \mathrm{F}(\Sigma)$, $f\colon S_1 \times \cdots \times S_n \rightarrow S_{n+1}$, a total map $f^{\mathbf{A}}\colon S_1^{\mathbf{A}} \times \cdots \times S_n^{\mathbf{A}} \rightarrow S_{n+1}^{\mathbf{A}}$;
3. for every $P \in \mathrm{P}(\Sigma)$, $P\colon S_1 \times \cdots \times S_n$, a total map $P^{\mathbf{A}}\colon S_1^{\mathbf{A}} \times \cdots \times S_n^{\mathbf{A}} \rightarrow \{\mathsf{T}, \mathsf{F}\}$;
4. for every $S \in \mathrm{S}(\Sigma)$, a total map $=_S^{\mathbf{A}}\colon S^{\mathbf{A}} \times S^{\mathbf{A}} \rightarrow \{\mathsf{T}, \mathsf{F}\}$ such that

$$\textit{for all } d, d' \in S^{\mathbf{A}},\ =_S^{\mathbf{A}}(d, d') = \begin{array}{ll} \mathsf{T} & \text{if } d = d', \\ \mathsf{F} & \text{if } d \neq d'. \end{array}$$

Instead of $w^{\mathbf{A}}$ we write w when it is clear from the context that the interpretation of symbol w in structure $\mathbf{A}$ is meant.

Assignment

An assignment in a structure $\mathbf{A}$ with signature Σ assigns to variables of sorts in Σ elements of the corresponding domains in $\mathbf{A}$. The interpretation of terms and formulae of $ML^=(\Sigma)$ in $\mathbf{A}$ is given with respect to an assignment α in $\mathbf{A}$.

Let $\mathbf{A}$ be a structure with signature Σ. Then an *assignment* in $\mathbf{A}$ is a function α which maps variables of sort $S \in \mathrm{S}(\Sigma)$ to elements of $S^{\mathbf{A}}$.

For every assignment α in $\mathbf{A}$, variable symbol x of sort $S \in \mathrm{S}(\Sigma)$ and element $d \in S^{\mathbf{A}}$, we write $\alpha(x \rightarrow d)$ for the assignment α' such that $\alpha'(y) = \alpha(y)$ if $y \not\equiv x$ and $\alpha'(x) = d$.

Interpretation

The interpretation of terms is given by a function mapping term t of sort S, structure $\mathbf{A}$ and assignment α in $\mathbf{A}$ to the element of $S^{\mathbf{A}}$ that is the value of t in $\mathbf{A}$ under assignment α. Similarly, the interpretation of formulae is given by a function mapping formula A, structure $\mathbf{A}$ and assignment α in $\mathbf{A}$ to the element of $\{\mathsf{T},\mathsf{F}\}$ that is the truth value of A in $\mathbf{A}$ under assignment α. We write $[\![t]\!]^{\mathbf{A}}_{\alpha}$ and $[\![A]\!]^{\mathbf{A}}_{\alpha}$ for these interpretations. The superscripts are omitted when it is clear from the context which structure is meant.

The interpretation functions for terms and formulae are inductively defined by:

$$
\begin{array}{ll}
[\![x]\!]_{\alpha} & = \alpha(x), \\
[\![f(t_1,\ldots,t_n)]\!]_{\alpha} & = f([\![t_1]\!]_{\alpha},\ldots,[\![t_n]\!]_{\alpha}),
\end{array}
$$

$$
\begin{array}{lll}
[\![\top]\!]_{\alpha} & = \mathsf{T}, & \\
[\![\bot]\!]_{\alpha} & = \mathsf{F}, & \\
[\![P(t_1,\ldots,t_n)]\!]_{\alpha} & = P([\![t_1]\!]_{\alpha},\ldots,[\![t_n]\!]_{\alpha}), & \\
[\![t_1 = t_2]\!]_{\alpha} & = =_S([\![t_1]\!]_{\alpha},[\![t_2]\!]_{\alpha}), & \\
[\![\neg A]\!]_{\alpha} & = \mathsf{T} & \text{if } [\![A]\!]_{\alpha} = \mathsf{F}, \\
 & \ \mathsf{F} & \text{if } [\![A]\!]_{\alpha} = \mathsf{T}, \\
[\![A_1 \wedge A_2]\!]_{\alpha} & = \mathsf{T} & \text{if } [\![A_1]\!]_{\alpha} = \mathsf{T} \textit{ and } [\![A_2]\!]_{\alpha} = \mathsf{T}, \\
 & \ \mathsf{F} & \text{if } [\![A_1]\!]_{\alpha} = \mathsf{F} \textit{ or } [\![A_2]\!]_{\alpha} = \mathsf{F}, \\
[\![\forall x{:}\, S\,(A)]\!]_{\alpha} & = \mathsf{T} & \text{if } \textit{for all } d \in S,\ [\![A]\!]_{\alpha(x\to d)} = \mathsf{T}, \\
 & \ \mathsf{F} & \text{if } \textit{for some } d \in S,\ [\![A]\!]_{\alpha(x\to d)} = \mathsf{F}.
\end{array}
$$

We write $\mathbf{A} \models A[\alpha]$ for $[\![A]\!]^{\mathbf{A}}_{\alpha} = \mathsf{T}$.

For finite sets Γ and Δ of formulae of $\mathrm{ML}^{=}(\Sigma)$, Δ is a *consequence* of Γ, written $\Gamma \models \Delta$, iff for all structures $\mathbf{A}$ with signature Σ, for all assignments α in $\mathbf{A}$, if $\mathbf{A} \models A[\alpha]$ for all $A \in \Gamma$ then $\mathbf{A} \models A'[\alpha]$ for some $A' \in \Delta$.

$\mathrm{ML}^{=}$ has the following soundness and completeness properties:

soundness: if $\Gamma \vdash \Delta$, then $\Gamma \models \Delta$; *completeness*: if $\Gamma \models \Delta$, then $\Gamma \vdash \Delta$.

LPF and MPL_{ω} have these properties in common with $\mathrm{ML}^{=}$.

5 Many-sorted Partial Infinitary Logic

MPL_{ω} is introduced by Koymans and Renardel de Lavalette in [KR89], where a mathematically precise presentation is given. In this section, language, proof system and interpretation of MPL_{ω} are presented by describing the differences with language, proof system and interpretation of $\mathrm{ML}^{=}$. These differences are consequences of the features that MPL_{ω} has in addition to those of $\mathrm{ML}^{=}$, viz. coverage of undefinedness, descriptions and countably infinite conjunctions. The assumptions and definitions about symbols and signatures for $\mathrm{ML}^{=}$ also apply to MPL_{ω}, except that additional standard symbols — needed for the coverage of undefinedness — are assumed.

5.1 Additional Standard Symbols for $\mathbf{MPL}_\omega$

For every $S \in SORT$, there is a standard function symbol $\uparrow_S\colon \rightarrow S$, called *undefined*. We write SF(Σ) for $\{\uparrow_S | \; S \in \mathrm{S}(\Sigma)\}$. It is assumed that $\uparrow_S \notin \mathcal{V}$ for all $S \in SORT$.

5.2 Language of $\mathbf{MPL}_\omega(\Sigma)$

The language of $\mathrm{MPL}_\omega(\Sigma)$ differs from the language of $\mathrm{ML}^=(\Sigma)$. The language of $\mathrm{ML}^=(\Sigma)$ requires adaptations to each of the additional features of MPL_ω.

Terms and Formulae

The terms and formulae of $\mathrm{MPL}_\omega(\Sigma)$ are simultaneously and inductively defined by the formation rules which are obtained from the formation rules for terms and formulae of $\mathrm{ML}^=(\Sigma)$ as follows:

a. replace formation rule 2 for terms by the following rule to adapt for undefinedness:

   2′. if $f \in \mathrm{F}(\Sigma) \cup \mathrm{SF}(\Sigma)$, $f\colon S_1 \times \cdots \times S_n \rightarrow S_{n+1}$ and $t_1, \ldots, t_n$ are terms of sorts $S_1, \ldots, S_n$, respectively, then $f(t_1, \ldots, t_n)$ is a term of sort S_{n+1};

b. add the following formation rule for terms to adapt for descriptions:

   3′. if A is a formula and x is a variable of sort S, $S \in \mathrm{S}(\Sigma)$, then $\iota x\colon S\,(A)$ is a term of sort S;

c. replace the formation rule 4 for formulae by the following rule to adapt for countably infinite conjunctions:

   4′. if $\langle A_n \rangle_{n<\omega} = \langle A_0, A_1, \ldots \rangle$ are formulae, then $\bigwedge_n A_n$ is a formula.

So we have countable conjunctions instead of binary conjunctions and descriptions as additional terms. Similar to the treatment of standard predicate symbols in the formation of (atomic) formulae, the standard function symbols are treated in the formation of terms in the same way as the function symbols from the signature Σ.

The terms and formulae of $\mathrm{MPL}_\omega(\Sigma)$, that can be constructed from the signature Σ according to the formation rules which are given above, include ill-formed terms and formulae. Only terms and formulae with a finite number of free variables are well-formed. In what follows, terms and formulae are always assumed to be well-formed.

A term or formula E of $\mathrm{MPL}_\omega(\Sigma)$ is *well-formed* iff *free*(E) is finite.

$\mathcal{T}_{MPL_\omega}(\Sigma)$ denotes the set of all well-formed terms of $\mathrm{MPL}_\omega(\Sigma)$.
$\mathcal{L}_{MPL_\omega}(\Sigma)$ denotes the set of all well-formed formulae of $\mathrm{MPL}_\omega(\Sigma)$.

Notational Conventions

The undefined symbols ($\uparrow_S$) are used without subscript when this causes no ambiguity.

Countable disjunctions, binary conjunctions, definedness, and non-existential equality are defined as abbreviations:

$$\begin{array}{ll} \bigvee_n A_n & := \neg \bigwedge_n \neg A_n, \\ A_1 \wedge A_2 & := \bigwedge_n A'_n, \text{where } A'_0 = A_1 \text{ and } A'_n = A_2 \text{ for } 0 < n < \omega, \\ t{\downarrow}_S & := t =_S t \\ t_1 \simeq_S t_2 & := (t_1{\downarrow}_S \vee t_2{\downarrow}_S) \rightarrow t_1 =_S t_2. \end{array}$$

Binary disjunction, existential quantification, etc. are defined as abbreviations as for $\mathrm{ML}^{=}$.

The definedness symbols ($\downarrow_S$) and non-existential equality symbols ($\simeq_S$) are used without subscript when this causes no ambiguity.

In [KR89], definedness of terms is taken as a primitive notion: the definedness symbols are additional standard symbols. Here, definedness of t is defined as abbreviation of a formula. This difference is not essential, since $\vdash t{\downarrow} \leftrightarrow t = t$ holds.

5.3 Proof System of $\mathbf{MPL}_\omega(\boldsymbol{\Sigma})$

The proof system of $\mathrm{MPL}_\omega(\Sigma)$ differs from the proof system of $\mathrm{ML}^{=}(\Sigma)$. The proof system of $\mathrm{ML}^{=}(\Sigma)$ also requires adaptations to each of the additional features of MPL_ω.

The proof system of $\mathrm{MPL}_\omega(\Sigma)$ is defined by the axiom schemas and rules of inference which are obtained from the axiom schemas and rules of inference of $\mathrm{ML}^{=}(\Sigma)$ as follows:

a. add the following non-logical axiom schemas to adapt for undefinedness:

$(S{\uparrow})$ $\vdash \neg({\uparrow}_S{\downarrow})$

$(f{\downarrow})$ $\vdash f(t_1,\ldots,t_n){\downarrow} \rightarrow t_1{\downarrow} \wedge \ldots \wedge t_n{\downarrow}$

$(P{\downarrow})$ $\vdash P(t_1,\ldots,t_n) \rightarrow t_1{\downarrow} \wedge \ldots \wedge t_n{\downarrow}$

$(={\downarrow})$ $\vdash t_1 = t_2 \rightarrow t_1{\downarrow} \wedge t_2{\downarrow}$;

b. replace the rules of inference $(\forall L)$ and $(\forall R)$ by the following rules to adapt for undefinedness:

$$(\forall L)\ \frac{\Gamma \vdash \Delta, t{\downarrow}_S \quad \Gamma, [x := t]A \vdash \Delta}{\Gamma, \forall x{:}\, S(A) \vdash \Delta} \qquad (\forall R)\ \frac{\Gamma, x{\downarrow}_S \vdash \Delta, A}{\Gamma \vdash \Delta, \forall x{:}\, S(A)}\ ;$$

c. add the following non-logical axiom schema to adapt for descriptions:

(ι) $\vdash \forall y{:}\, S(y = \iota x{:}\, S(A) \leftrightarrow \forall x{:}\, S(A \leftrightarrow x = y))$;

d. replace the rules of inference $(\wedge L)$ and $(\wedge R)$ by the following rules to adapt for countably infinite conjunctions:

$$(\bigwedge L)\ \frac{\Gamma, A_i \vdash \Delta}{\Gamma, \bigwedge_n A_n \vdash \Delta} \text{ for all } i \quad (\bigwedge R)\ \frac{\langle \Gamma \vdash \Delta, A_n \rangle_{n<\omega}}{\Gamma \vdash \Delta, \bigwedge_n A_n}\ .$$

Restriction on the axiom schema (ι): y not free in A. The restriction on the rule $(\forall R)$, viz. x not free in $\Gamma \cup \Delta$, remains.

Furthermore, the sets of formulae in a sequent $\Gamma \vdash \Delta$ may be countably infinite, but only finitely many different variables may occur free, i.e. *free*(Γ) and *free*(Δ) are finite. Derivations may be infinitely (but countably) branching.

This sequent calculus resembles a Gentzen-type sequent calculus for infinitary classical first-order logic with equality. There are additional non-logical axiom schemas concerning definedness for the function and predicate symbols (including the undefined and equality symbols). There is also an axiom schema for descriptions. The slightly adapted rules for the universal quantifier are due to the treatment of free and bound variables: free variables may not denote but bound variables always do.

In [KR89], a proof system of $\mathrm{MPL}_\omega(\Sigma)$ is presented whose axiom schemas are weakened versions of equivalent axiom schemas for the axiom schemas of the proof system presented above (axiom schemas $\Gamma \vdash \Delta, A$ instead of axiom schemas $\vdash A$, etc.) and whose rules of inference do not include the weakening rule. However, the weakening rule is a derived rule. The rules of the proof system presented above include the weakening rule, because it is no longer a derived rule. On the other hand, when the weakening rule is included, the weakened versions of the axiom schemas become derivable. In other words, the proof systems are equivalent.

5.4 Interpretation of $\mathbf{MPL}_\omega(\boldsymbol{\Sigma})$

The interpretation of $\mathrm{MPL}_\omega(\Sigma)$ differs from the interpretation of $\mathrm{ML}^=(\Sigma)$. The interpretation of $\mathrm{ML}^=(\Sigma)$ requires adaptations to each of the additional features of MPL_ω. This includes the structures used for interpretation.

Structures

The structures used for MPL_ω differ from the structures used for $\mathrm{ML}^=$. The differences (for a structure $\mathbf{A}$ with signature Σ) are:

- for every $S \in \mathrm{S}(\Sigma)$, $S^{\mathbf{A}}$ is such that $\bot \in S^{\mathbf{A}}$;
- for every $S \in \mathrm{S}(\Sigma)$, $=_S^{\mathbf{A}}$ is such that
  for all $d, d' \in S^{\mathbf{A}}$, $=_S^{\mathbf{A}}(d,d') = \begin{cases} \mathsf{T} & \text{if } d \neq \bot \textit{ and } d' \neq \bot \textit{ and } d = d', \\ \mathsf{F} & \text{if } d = \bot \textit{ or } d' = \bot \textit{ or } d \neq d'; \end{cases}$
- for every $f \in \mathrm{F}(\Sigma)$, $f\colon S_1 \times \cdots \times S_n \to S_{n+1}$, $f^{\mathbf{A}}$ is such that
  for all $d_1 \in S_1^{\mathbf{A}}, \ldots, d_n \in S_n^{\mathbf{A}}$, $d_1 = \bot$ *or* ... *or* $d_n = \bot \Rightarrow f^{\mathbf{A}}(d_1,\ldots,d_n) = \bot$;
- for every $P \in \mathrm{P}(\Sigma)$, $P\colon S_1 \times \cdots \times S_n$, $P^{\mathbf{A}}$ is such that
  for all $d_1 \in S_1^{\mathbf{A}}, \ldots, d_n \in S_n^{\mathbf{A}}$, $d_1 = \bot$ *or* ... *or* $d_n = \bot \Rightarrow P^{\mathbf{A}}(d_1,\ldots,d_n) = \mathsf{F}$.

In other words, the interpretations of sort symbols must be sets containing a special element $\bot$. When a term is non-denoting, $\bot$ is used as its interpretation. The interpretation of every symbol concerned is in accordance with the following treatment of non-denoting terms: atomic formulae that contain non-denoting terms are logically false.

Interpretation

The interpretation functions for terms and formulae are simultaneously and inductively defined by the interpretation rules obtained from the interpretation rules of $\mathrm{ML}^{=}$ as follows:

a. add the following interpretation rule to adapt for undefinedness:

$$[\![\uparrow s]\!]_\alpha \;=\; \bot,$$

b. replace the interpretation rule for universal quantifications by the following rule to adapt for undefinedness:

$$[\![\forall x\colon S\,(A)]\!]_\alpha \;=\; \begin{cases} \mathsf{T} & \text{if } \textit{for all } d \in S - \{\bot\},\ [\![A]\!]_{\alpha(x\to d)} = \mathsf{T}, \\ \mathsf{F} & \text{if } \textit{for some } d \in S - \{\bot\},\ [\![A]\!]_{\alpha(x\to d)} = \mathsf{F}; \end{cases}$$

c. add the following interpretation rule to adapt for descriptions:

$$[\![\iota x\colon S\,(A)]\!]_\alpha \;=\; \begin{cases} \textit{the unique } d \in S - \{\bot\} \textit{ such that } [\![A]\!]_{\alpha(x\to d)} = \mathsf{T} & \text{if it exists,} \\ \bot & \text{otherwise;} \end{cases}$$

d. replace the interpretation rule for binary conjunctions by the following rule to adapt for countably infinite conjunctions:

$$[\![\textstyle\bigwedge_n A_n]\!]_\alpha \;=\; \begin{cases} \mathsf{T} & \text{if } [\![A_n]\!]_\alpha = \mathsf{T} \textit{ for all } n < \omega, \\ \mathsf{F} & \text{if } [\![A_n]\!]_\alpha = \mathsf{F} \textit{ for some } n < \omega. \end{cases}$$

So the interpretation of binary conjunctions is extended to countable conjunctions and the interpretation of descriptions is added. The interpretation of universal quantifications is slightly adapted in order to guarantee that bound variables always denote.

LPF needs predicate symbols to be interpreted as truth-valued functions and the interpretation of formulae to be given by a truth-valued function. This is already anticipated in the presentation of $\mathrm{ML}^{=}$ and MPL_ω. In this way, the essential differences between LPF and MPL_ω can be emphasized.

In [KR89], structures for $\mathrm{MPL}_\omega(\Sigma)$ are used whose interpretations of predicate symbols are n-ary relations. In the structures used here, these relations can be thought of as being replaced by the truth-valued functions that are their characteristic functions. This view agrees with the interpretation of formulae of the forms $P(t_1, \ldots, t_n)$ and $t_1 = t_2$ in such structures, which is given by the interpretation function described here. That is, the truth-valued functions used as interpretations of predicate symbols are consistently identified with the relations for which they are the characteristic functions. In other words, the truth of formulae is invariant under the replacement. Furthermore, the interpretation of formulae of $\mathrm{MPL}_\omega(\Sigma)$ is given in [KR89] by an interpretation relation. The interpretation function described here is the characteristic function of that relation. So it gives essentially the same interpretation of formulae.

5.5 Properties of MPL_ω

Some interesting properties of this logic, are presented below.

1. The deduction theorem holds in MPL_ω:

   $\dfrac{A_1 \vdash A_2}{\vdash A_1 \rightarrow A_2}$ is a derived rule.

2. MPL_ω is weaker than $\mathrm{ML}_\omega^=$, $\mathrm{ML}^=$ with binary conjunctions replaced by countable conjunctions:

   for every sequent $\Gamma \vdash \Delta$ of $\mathrm{ML}_\omega^=(\Sigma)$: $\mathrm{MPL}'_\omega(\Sigma): \Gamma \vdash \Delta$ iff $\mathrm{ML}_\omega^=(\Sigma): \Gamma \vdash \Delta$.

   $\mathrm{MPL}'_\omega(\Sigma)$ is $\mathrm{MPL}_\omega(\Sigma)$ extended with the axiom schema $\vdash t\downarrow$ where t is an arbitrary term without occurrences of undefined symbols ($\uparrow s$).

   That is, adding the assumption of definedness to MPL_ω yields a complete proof system for $\mathrm{ML}_\omega^=$. The proof is obvious.

   MPL_ω is even strictly weaker than $\mathrm{ML}_\omega^=$: $\vdash t\downarrow$, where t is an arbitrary term without occurrences of undefined symbols, is in general not derivable in MPL_ω.

3. MPL_ω can be reduced to $\mathrm{L}_\omega^=$, classical first-order logic with equality and countably infinite conjunctions:

   $\mathrm{MPL}_\omega(\Sigma)$: $\vdash A$ iff $\mathrm{L}_\omega^=(\Sigma^*)$: $\mathrm{Ax}(\Sigma) \vdash A^*$

   for appropriate mappings $\bullet^*$ (for signatures and formulae) and an appropriate mapping Ax (mapping signatures of MPL_ω to sets of formulae of $\mathrm{L}_\omega^=$).

   A proof is given in [Ren89, Appendix C.1].

6 Logic for Partial Functions

LPF is introduced by Barringer, Cheng and Jones in [BCJ84], where it is presented in broad outline. A mathematically precise presentation is given by Cheng in [Che86]. In this section, language, proof system and interpretation of LPF are presented by describing the differences with language, proof system and interpretation of $\mathrm{ML}^=$. These differences are consequences of the feature that LPF has in addition to the features of $\mathrm{ML}^=$, viz. coverage of undefinedness with three truth values. The assumptions and definitions about symbols and signatures for $\mathrm{ML}^=$ also apply to LPF.

In [Che86], the connectives $*, \Delta, \neg, \vee$ and the quantifier $\exists$ are considered to be basic. In this section, $\top, \bot, *, \Delta, \neg, \wedge$ and $\forall$ are considered to be basic. In either case, all non-basic connectives and quantifiers can be defined with the basic ones. In [Che86], a one-sorted version of LPF is presented. In order to make a comparison with MPL_ω easier, a many-sorted version of LPF is presented in this section.

6.1 Language of LPF(Σ)

The language of LPF(Σ) differs from the language of $\mathrm{ML}^{=}(\Sigma)$. The language of $\mathrm{ML}^{=}$ requires adaptations to the additional feature of LPF.

Terms and Formulae

The formation rules for terms of LPF(Σ) and formation rules for terms of $\mathrm{ML}^{=}(\Sigma)$ are the very same. The formulae of LPF(Σ) are inductively defined by the formation rules which are obtained from the formation rules for formulae of $\mathrm{ML}^{=}(\Sigma)$ as follows:

a. replace formation rule 1 by the following rule:

  1″. $\top$, $\bot$, and $*$ are formulae;

b. add the following formation rule:

  6″. if A is formula, then ΔA is a formula.

So we have $*$ and Δ as additional connectives (nullary and unary, respectively).
$\mathcal{T}_{LPF}(\Sigma)$ denotes the set of all terms of LPF(Σ).
$\mathcal{L}_{LPF}(\Sigma)$ denotes the set of all formulae of LPF(Σ).

Notational Conventions

Several kinds of definedness and equality are defined as abbreviations:

$$
\begin{array}{lll}
\delta A & := & A \vee \neg A, \\
E_S(t) & := & t =_S t, \\
t{\downarrow}_S & := & \Delta E_S(t), \\
t_1 \overset{\exists}{=}_S t_2 & := & t_1 =_S t_2 \wedge \Delta(E_S(t_1) \wedge E_S(t_2)), \\
t_1 ==_S t_2 & := & (t_1{\downarrow}_S \vee t_2{\downarrow}_S) \rightarrow t_1 \overset{\exists}{=}_S t_2 .
\end{array}
$$

Binary disjunction, existential quantification, etc. are defined as abbreviations as for $\mathrm{ML}^{=}$.

The definedness and equality symbols E_S, ${\downarrow}_S$, $\overset{\exists}{=}_S$ and $==_S$ are used without subscript when this causes no ambiguity.

Both $E(t)$ and $t{\downarrow}$ mean that t is denoting. If t is non-denoting, then $E(t)$ is neither-true-nor-false but $t{\downarrow}$ is false as in MPL_ω. If either t_1 or t_2 is non-denoting, then $t_1 \overset{\exists}{=} t_2$ is either true or false and $t_1 == t_2$ is false. $\overset{\exists}{=}$ is existential equality and $==$ is strong equality (see Section 3.1). $==$ is essentially the same as $\simeq$ in MPL_ω.

6.2 Proof System of LPF(Σ)

The proof system of LPF(Σ) differs from the proof system of $\mathrm{ML}^{=}(\Sigma)$. The proof system of $\mathrm{ML}^{=}$ also requires adaptations to the additional feature of LPF. The differences are great.

The proof system of LPF(Σ) is defined by the axiom schemas and rules of inference which are obtained from the axiom schemas and rules of inference of ML$^=$(Σ) as follows:

a. add the following logical axiom schemas:

(*) $\quad * \vdash$

($\neg$*) $\quad \neg * \vdash$

(contr) $\quad A, \neg A \vdash$;

b. add the following non-logical axiom schemas:

(var) $\quad \vdash E(x)$

(=E) $\quad t_1 = t_2 \vdash E(t_1) \wedge E(t_2)$

($\neg$=E) $\quad \neg(t_1 = t_2) \vdash E(t_1) \wedge E(t_2)$

(comp) $\quad E(t_1), E(t_2) \vdash t_1 = t_2, \neg(t_1 = t_2)$;

c. add the following rules of inference:

$$(\Delta L)\ \frac{\Gamma, \neg A \vdash \Delta \quad \Gamma, A \vdash \Delta}{\Gamma, \Delta A \vdash \Delta} \qquad (\Delta R)\ \frac{\Gamma \vdash \Delta, A}{\Gamma \vdash \Delta, \Delta A} \quad \frac{\Gamma \vdash \Delta, \neg A}{\Gamma \vdash \Delta, \Delta A}$$

$$(\neg \Delta L)\ \frac{\Gamma \vdash \Delta, A}{\Gamma, \neg \Delta A \vdash \Delta} \quad \frac{\Gamma \vdash \Delta, \neg A}{\Gamma, \neg \Delta A \vdash \Delta} \qquad (\neg \Delta R)\ \frac{\Gamma, \neg A \vdash \Delta \quad \Gamma, A \vdash \Delta}{\Gamma \vdash \Delta, \neg \Delta A}\ ;$$

d. replace all rules of inference except (cut) and (weak) by the following rules:

$$(\neg\neg L)\ \frac{\Gamma, A \vdash \Delta}{\Gamma, \neg\neg A \vdash \Delta} \qquad (\neg\neg R)\ \frac{\Gamma \vdash \Delta, A}{\Gamma \vdash \Delta, \neg\neg A}$$

$$(\wedge L)\ \frac{\Gamma, A_i \vdash \Delta}{\Gamma, A_1 \wedge A_2 \vdash \Delta} \text{ for } i = 1, 2 \qquad (\wedge R)\ \frac{\Gamma \vdash \Delta, A_1 \quad \Gamma \vdash \Delta, A_2}{\Gamma \vdash \Delta, A_1 \wedge A_2}$$

$$(\neg\wedge L)\ \frac{\Gamma, \neg A_1 \vdash \Delta \quad \Gamma, \neg A_2 \vdash \Delta}{\Gamma, \neg(A_1 \wedge A_2) \vdash \Delta} \qquad (\neg\wedge R)\ \frac{\Gamma \vdash \Delta, \neg A_i}{\Gamma \vdash \Delta, \neg(A_1 \wedge A_2)} \text{ for } i = 1, 2$$

$$(\forall L)\ \frac{\Gamma \vdash \Delta, E_S(t) \quad \Gamma, [x := t]A \vdash \Delta}{\Gamma, \forall x{:}\, S(A) \vdash \Delta} \qquad (\forall R)\ \frac{\Gamma \vdash \Delta, A}{\Gamma \vdash \Delta, \forall x{:}\, S(A)}$$

$$(\neg\forall L)\ \frac{\Gamma, \neg A \vdash \Delta}{\Gamma, \neg\forall x{:}\, S(A) \vdash \Delta} \qquad (\neg\forall R)\ \frac{\Gamma \vdash \Delta, E_S(t) \quad \Gamma \vdash \Delta, \neg[x := t]A}{\Gamma \vdash \Delta, \neg\forall x{:}\, S(A)}\ .$$

The restriction on the rule ($\forall R$), viz. x not free in $\Gamma \cup \Delta$, remains and also applies to the rule ($\neg\forall L$).

This sequent calculus does not resemble a Gentzen-type sequent calculus for classical first-order logic. Adding the axiom schema $\vdash A, \neg A$, corresponding to the law of the excluded middle, would make it a complete proof system for ML$^=$. Because this law does not hold, the rules ($\neg L$) and ($\neg R$) are replaced by the axiom schema (contr) and the special rules concerning negation for each of the basic connectives and the universal quantifier. The additional axiom schemas for equality are due to the extension of equality to the three-valued case. The axiom schema $(= E)$ is similar to the axiom schema $(=\downarrow)$ of MPL_ω. Axiom schemas and rules concerning the connectives without a classical counterpart are added. The usual rules for the universal quantifier are slightly adapted, because bound variables always denote. The adapted rules also differ from the corresponding rules of MPL_ω, because, unlike there, free variables always denote in LPF. The axiom schema (var) expresses that free variables always denote. Note that the rules $(\wedge L)$ and $(\wedge R)$ are not changed.

In [Che86], a proof system of LPF is presented with rules concerning disjunction and existential quantification instead of rules concerning conjunction and universal quantification as in the proof system presented above, since different connectives and quantifiers are taken as basic there. In either case, the other rules are derived rules. The axiom schemas of the proof system presented above also include the additional axiom schemas $(\top)$ and $(\bot)$. However, these axiom schemas are derivable. In other words, the proof systems are equivalent.

6.3 Interpretation of LPF(Σ)

The interpretation of LPF(Σ) differs from the interpretation of $\mathrm{ML}^=(\Sigma)$. The interpretation of $\mathrm{ML}^=$ requires adaptations to the additional feature of LPF. This includes the structures used for interpretation.

Structures

The structures used for LPF differ from the structures used for $\mathrm{ML}^=$. The differences (for a structure $\mathbf{A}$ with signature Σ) are:

- for every $S \in \mathrm{S}(\Sigma)$, $S^{\mathbf{A}}$ is such that $\bot \in S^{\mathbf{A}}$ and $S^{\mathbf{A}} - \{\bot\}$ is non-empty;
- for every $P \in \mathrm{P}(\Sigma) \cup \mathrm{SP}(\Sigma)$, $P^{\mathbf{A}}$ maps to $\{\mathsf{T}, \mathsf{F}, \mathsf{N}\}$;
- for every $S \in \mathrm{S}(\Sigma)$, $=_S^{\mathbf{A}}$ is such that

$$\textit{for all } d, d' \in S^{\mathbf{A}},\ =_S^{\mathbf{A}}(d,d') = \begin{cases} \mathsf{T} & \text{if } d \neq \bot \textit{ and } d' \neq \bot \textit{ and } d = d', \\ \mathsf{F} & \text{if } d \neq \bot \textit{ and } d' \neq \bot \textit{ and } d \neq d', \\ \mathsf{N} & \text{otherwise.} \end{cases}$$

In other words, the interpretations of sort symbols are extended with a special element $\bot$ and the domain of truth values is extended with another special element N. When a term is non-denoting, $\bot$ is used as its interpretation. Analogously, when a formula is neither T (*true*) nor F (*false*), N is used as its interpretation. We can think of N as corresponding to the classification *neither-true-nor-false*. The interpretation of every symbol concerned is in accordance with the treatment of non-denoting terms where equations $t_1 = t_2$ are logically neither-true-nor-false when t_1 or t_2 is non-denoting.

In contrast with MPL_ω, the interpretation of sort symbols may not be sets that only contain $\bot$. Functions and predicates may be non-strict. However, these are minor differences. The main difference is that predicates may yield the truth value N.

Assignment

The definition of assignment is also changed. Let **A** be a structure with signature Σ. Then an *assignment* in **A** is a function α which maps variables of sort $S \in \mathrm{S}(\Sigma)$ to elements of $S^{\mathbf{A}} - \{\bot\}$. This means that variables are never mapped to $\bot$. This restriction is in accordance with the treatment of free and bound variables: both free and bound variables always denote. Without the redefinition of assignment, a redefinition of consequence would have been necessary.

Interpretation

The interpretation function for terms and formulae are inductively defined by the interpretation rules obtained from the interpretation rules of $\mathrm{ML}^=$ as follows:

a. add the following interpretation rules:

$$\begin{array}{lcll} [\![*]\!]_\alpha, & = & \mathsf{N}, & \\ [\![\Delta A]\!]_\alpha & = & \mathsf{T} & \text{if } [\![A]\!]_\alpha = \mathsf{T} \textit{ or } [\![A]\!]_\alpha = \mathsf{F}, \\ & & \mathsf{F} & \text{otherwise;} \end{array}$$

b. replace the interpretation rules for negations, binary conjunctions, and universal quantifications by the following rules:

$$\begin{array}{lcll} [\![\neg A]\!]_\alpha & = & \mathsf{T} & \text{if } [\![A]\!]_\alpha = \mathsf{F}, \\ & & \mathsf{F} & \text{if } [\![A]\!]_\alpha = \mathsf{T}, \\ & & \mathsf{N} & \text{otherwise,} \\ [\![A_1 \wedge A_2]\!]_\alpha & = & \mathsf{T} & \text{if } [\![A_1]\!]_\alpha = \mathsf{T} \textit{ and } [\![A_2]\!]_\alpha = \mathsf{T}, \\ & & \mathsf{F} & \text{if } [\![A_1]\!]_\alpha = \mathsf{F} \textit{ or } [\![A_2]\!]_\alpha = \mathsf{F}, \\ & & \mathsf{N} & \text{otherwise,} \\ [\![\forall x{:}\, S\,(A)]\!]_\alpha & = & \mathsf{T} & \text{if } \textit{for all } d \in S - \{\bot\},\ [\![A]\!]_{\alpha(x \to d)} = \mathsf{T}, \\ & & \mathsf{F} & \text{if } \textit{for some } d \in S - \{\bot\},\ [\![A]\!]_{\alpha(x \to d)} = \mathsf{F}, \\ & & \mathsf{N} & \text{otherwise.} \end{array}$$

So the classical T/F-conditions for connectives and quantifiers are adopted; only the assumption is given up that all formulae under all assignment have to be either true or false. The interpretation of the new connectives is added.

6.4 Properties of LPF

Some properties, that are relevant to the use of this logic, are presented here.

1. LPF has the following expressiveness property:

   All functions of type $\{\mathsf{T},\mathsf{F},\mathsf{N}\}^n \to \{\mathsf{T},\mathsf{F},\mathsf{N}\}$ are definable by the basic connectives of LPF.

   A proof is given in [Che86, Section 3.1].

2. A weak version of the deduction theorem holds in LPF:

$$\frac{A_1 \vdash A_2 \quad \vdash \delta(A_1)}{\vdash A_1 \rightarrow A_2}$$ is a derived rule.

A proof is given in [Jon90, Section 1.3].

3. LPF is weaker than $ML^=$:

   for every sequent $\Gamma \vdash \Delta$ of $ML^=(\Sigma)$: $\quad LPF'(\Sigma): \Gamma \vdash \Delta \quad$ iff $\quad ML^=(\Sigma): \Gamma \vdash \Delta$.

   $LPF'(\Sigma)$ is $LPF(\Sigma)$ extended with the axiom schema $\vdash A, \neg A$.

   That is, adding the law of the excluded middle to LPF yields a complete proof system for $ML^=$. A proof for propositional LPF without equality (in the one-sorted case) is given in [Avr88, Section 4.1]. That proof extends directly to the general case.

   LPF is even strictly weaker than $ML^=$: $\vdash A, \neg A$ is in general not derivable in LPF.

7 Reducing LPF to MPL_ω

The relationship between LPF and $ML^=$ is clearly characterized by property (3) of Section 6.4. The relationship between MPL_ω and $ML^=_\omega$ is similarly characterized by property (2) of Section 5.5. Besides, the relationship between MPL_ω and the one-sorted fragment of $ML^=_\omega$, i.e. $L^=_\omega$, is characterized by property (3) of Section 5.5. That property is a reducibility result.

In this section, the relationship between LPF and MPL_ω will also be characterized by a reducibility result. The mappings concerned provide a uniform embedding of LPF into MPL_ω.

7.1 Translation

The translation given below simplifies the translation of the logical expressions of VVSL (which are roughly the formulae of LPF) in [Mid90].

We write:

$\mathcal{T}_{LPF}$	for $\bigcup\{\mathcal{T}_{LPF}(\Sigma) \mid \Sigma \in SIGN\}$,	$\mathcal{L}_{LPF}$	for $\bigcup\{\mathcal{L}_{LPF}(\Sigma) \mid \Sigma \in SIGN\}$,
$\mathcal{T}_{MPL_\omega}$	for $\bigcup\{\mathcal{T}_{MPL_\omega}(\Sigma) \mid \Sigma \in SIGN\}$,	$\mathcal{L}_{MPL_\omega}$	for $\bigcup\{\mathcal{L}_{MPL_\omega}(\Sigma) \mid \Sigma \in SIGN\}$.

For the translation of formulae two mappings are used:

$$\langle\!\!\langle \bullet \rangle\!\!\rangle : \mathcal{L}_{LPF} \rightarrow \mathcal{T}_{MPL_\omega}, \quad \langle\!\!\langle \bullet \rangle\!\!\rangle : \mathcal{T}_{LPF} \rightarrow \mathcal{T}_{MPL_\omega}.$$

For a formula A of LPF, the formula $\langle\!\!\langle A \rangle\!\!\rangle = tt$ is the translation of A to MPL_ω. Intuitively, $\langle\!\!\langle A \rangle\!\!\rangle = tt$ is a formula of MPL_ω stating that the formula A of LPF is true in LPF. Likewise, $\langle\!\!\langle A \rangle\!\!\rangle = ff$ is a formula of MPL_ω stating that the formula A of LPF is false in LPF. In case both $\langle\!\!\langle A \rangle\!\!\rangle = tt$ and $\langle\!\!\langle A \rangle\!\!\rangle = ff$ are false in MPL_ω, A is neither-true-nor-false in LPF.

The syntactic variables that are used in the definition of these mappings, range over syntactic objects as follows (subscripts and primes are not shown):

S ranges over $SORT$, f ranges over $FUNC$, P ranges over $PRED$,
x ranges over VAR, t ranges over $\mathcal{T}_{LPF}$, A ranges over $\mathcal{L}_{LPF}$.

It is assumed that $\mathsf{B} \in SORT$, $\mathit{tt}, \mathit{ff} \in FUNC$, $\mathit{tt}, \mathit{ff}: \rightarrow \mathsf{B}$, and $\boldsymbol{b} \in VAR$, $\boldsymbol{b}$ of sort B.

We assume a total mapping from $\mathcal{V}$ to $\mathcal{V}$; for each $w \in \mathcal{V}$, we write $\boldsymbol{w}$ for the symbol to which w is mapped. Furthermore, the mapping is assumed to be injective and such that

each sort symbol S is mapped to a sort symbol $\boldsymbol{S}$,
each function symbol $f: S_1 \times \cdots \times S_n \rightarrow S_{n+1}$ is mapped to a function symbol $\boldsymbol{f}: \boldsymbol{S}_1 \times \cdots \times \boldsymbol{S}_n \rightarrow \boldsymbol{S}_{n+1}$,
each predicate symbol $P: S_1 \times \cdots \times S_n$ is mapped to a function symbol $\boldsymbol{P}: \boldsymbol{S}_1 \times \cdots \times \boldsymbol{S}_n \rightarrow \mathsf{B}$,
each variable symbol x of sort S is mapped to a variable symbol $\boldsymbol{x}$ of sort $\boldsymbol{S}$,
the set $\{\mathsf{B}, \mathit{tt}, \mathit{ff}, \boldsymbol{b}\}$ and its image are disjoint.

The translation mappings are inductively defined by:

$$
\begin{aligned}
\{\!|x|\!\} &= \boldsymbol{x},\\
\{\!|f(t_1,\ldots,t_n)|\!\} &= \boldsymbol{f}(\{\!|t_1|\!\},\ldots,\{\!|t_n|\!\}),\\[1ex]
\{\!|*|\!\} &= \uparrow,\\
\{\!|P(t_1,\ldots,t_n)|\!\} &= \boldsymbol{P}(\{\!|t_1|\!\},\ldots,\{\!|t_n|\!\}),\\
\{\!|t_1 = t_2|\!\} &= \iota\, \boldsymbol{b}{:}\,\mathsf{B}(\ \{\!|t_1|\!\}\!\downarrow \wedge \{\!|t_2|\!\}\!\downarrow \rightarrow (\{\!|t_1|\!\} = \{\!|t_2|\!\} \ \leftrightarrow\ \boldsymbol{b} = \mathit{tt})\ ),\\
\{\!|\Delta A|\!\} &= \iota\, \boldsymbol{b}{:}\,\mathsf{B}(\ \{\!|A|\!\} = \mathit{tt} \vee \{\!|A|\!\} = \mathit{ff} \ \leftrightarrow\ \boldsymbol{b} = \mathit{tt}\ ),\\
\{\!|\neg A|\!\} &= \iota\, \boldsymbol{b}{:}\,\mathsf{B}(\ (\{\!|A|\!\} = \mathit{tt} \ \leftrightarrow\ \boldsymbol{b} = \mathit{ff}) \wedge\\
&\qquad\qquad\quad (\{\!|A|\!\} = \mathit{ff} \ \leftrightarrow\ \boldsymbol{b} = \mathit{tt})\ ),\\
\{\!|A_1 \wedge A_2|\!\} &= \iota\, \boldsymbol{b}{:}\,\mathsf{B}(\ (\{\!|A_1|\!\} = \mathit{tt} \wedge \{\!|A_2|\!\} = \mathit{tt} \ \leftrightarrow\ \boldsymbol{b} = \mathit{tt}) \wedge\\
&\qquad\qquad\quad (\{\!|A_1|\!\} = \mathit{ff} \vee \{\!|A_2|\!\} = \mathit{ff} \ \leftrightarrow\ \boldsymbol{b} = \mathit{ff})\ ),\\
\{\!|\forall x{:}\,S\,(A)|\!\} &= \iota\, \boldsymbol{b}{:}\,\mathsf{B}(\ (\forall \boldsymbol{x}{:}\,\boldsymbol{S}(\{\!|A|\!\} = \mathit{tt}) \ \leftrightarrow\ \boldsymbol{b} = \mathit{tt}) \wedge\\
&\qquad\qquad\quad (\exists \boldsymbol{x}{:}\,\boldsymbol{S}(\{\!|A|\!\} = \mathit{ff}) \ \leftrightarrow\ \boldsymbol{b} = \mathit{ff})\ ).
\end{aligned}
$$

These translation rules strongly resemble the interpretation rules of LPF that are given in Section 6.3. Only the translation rule for equations does not resemble the corresponding interpretation rule. The interpretation rule concerned gives explicitly a truth-condition and a falsehood-condition. The corresponding translation rule, unlike the other ones, could be simplified by leaving this style.

A translation for sequents of LPF(Σ) can also be devised:

$$\{\!|\Gamma \vdash \Delta|\!\} := \mathrm{Ax}(\Sigma) \cup \mathrm{Bax} \cup \{\{\!|A|\!\} = \mathit{tt} \mid A \in \Gamma\} \vdash \{\{\!|A'|\!\} = \mathit{tt} \mid A' \in \Delta\},$$

where
$$
\begin{aligned}
\mathrm{Ax}(\Sigma) &= \{\exists \boldsymbol{y}_S{:}\,\boldsymbol{S}(\boldsymbol{y}_S\!\downarrow) \mid S \in \mathrm{S}(\Sigma)\},\\
\mathrm{Bax} &= \{\forall\, \boldsymbol{b}{:}\,\mathsf{B}(\boldsymbol{b} = \mathit{tt} \vee \boldsymbol{b} = \mathit{ff}), \neg(\mathit{tt} = \mathit{ff})\}.
\end{aligned}
$$

Here, it is assumed that $\boldsymbol{y}_S$ is a variable symbol of sort $\boldsymbol{S}$ for all $S \in SORT$.

7.2 Reducibility

Roughly speaking, LPF can be reduced to MPL$_\omega$ in the sense that what can be proved in LPF remains the same after translation. Unfortunately, MPL$_\omega$ only deals with strict functions and predicates whilst LPF deals with non-strict functions and predicates as well. Therefore "MPL$_\omega$ without strictness axioms" and "LPF with strictness axioms" are introduced.

MPL_ω^- is MPL_ω with its proof system restricted by removing the axiom schema $(f\downarrow)$ and the axiom schema $(P\downarrow)$.

LPF^+ is LPF with its proof system extended by adding the axiom schema $(f\downarrow)$ and the following axiom schema:

$$(P\downarrow') \quad \vdash \Delta\, P(t_1, \ldots, t_n) \rightarrow t_1\downarrow \wedge \ldots \wedge t_n\downarrow \; .$$

Structures for LPF with strict maps as interpretations of function and predicate symbols are called strict structures.

Theorem

1. LPF^+ can be reduced to MPL_ω, i.e.:

   $$LPF^+(\Sigma)\colon \Gamma \vdash \Delta \quad \text{iff} \quad MPL_\omega(\Sigma \cup \{\mathsf{B}, tt, ff\})\colon \langle\!|\Gamma \vdash \Delta|\!\rangle;$$

2. LPF can be reduced to MPL_ω^-, i.e.:

   $$LPF(\Sigma)\colon \Gamma \vdash \Delta \quad \text{iff} \quad MPL_\omega^-(\Sigma \cup \{\mathsf{B}, tt, ff\})\colon \langle\!|\Gamma \vdash \Delta|\!\rangle.$$

Proof:
1. $\Rightarrow$ is proved by induction over the length of a derivation of $\Gamma \vdash \Delta$. For $\Leftarrow$, it suffices to show that for some strict structure $\mathbf{A}$ of LPF with signature Σ that is a counter-model for $\Gamma \vdash \Delta$, there exists a structure $\mathbf{A}^*$ of MPL_ω with signature $\Sigma \cup \{\mathsf{B}, tt, ff\}$ that is a counter-model for $\langle\!|\Gamma \vdash \Delta|\!\rangle$.
2. is proved similarly. □

It is assumed that the translation of sequents is extended to inference rules in the obvious way.

Corollary
The translation of the inference rules of LPF are derived rules in MPL_ω.

8 Recursively Defined Functions

In the previous section, LPF is embedded into MPL_ω. Besides, recursive function definitions can be represented in MPL_ω. All that allows the rules that are used to reason about recursively defined functions in LPF to become derived rules of MPL_ω.

8.1 LPF and Recursive Function Definitions

The logic LPF is used in VDM [Jon86, Jon90, JS90] to reason about recursively defined functions. The feature for recursive function definitions in VDM is made precise below by defining a conservative extension of LPF, referred to by LPF^R.

The following additional formation rule for terms is required:

3″. if A is a formula and t_1 and t_2 are terms of sort S, then **if** A **then** t_1 **else** t_2 is a term of sort S, for any $S \in \mathrm{S}(\Sigma)$.

Terms of this form are called *conditionals*. In [BCJ84, Jon86], conditionals are also regarded as terms of an extension of LPF.

The following additional formation rule for formulae is required:

7″. if $f \in F(\Sigma)$, $f: S_1 \times \ldots \times S_n \rightarrow S_{n+1}$, $x_1, \ldots, x_n$ are distinct variables of sorts $S_1, \ldots, S_n$, respectively, and t is a term of sort S_{n+1} with $free(t) \subseteq \{x_1, \ldots, x_n\}$, then $f(x_1, \ldots, x_n) \triangleq t$ is a formula.

Formulae of this form are called *recursive function definitions*.

A recursive function definition $f(x_1, \ldots, x_n) \triangleq t$ defines f directly in terms of a defining term t in which the function being defined may be recursively used.

The following additional inference rules are needed:

$$\text{(if-E)} \quad \frac{\vdash A \quad \vdash t == \textsf{if } A \textsf{ then } t_1 \textsf{ else } t_2}{\vdash t == t_1} \qquad \frac{\vdash \neg A \quad \vdash t == \textsf{if } A \textsf{ then } t_1 \textsf{ else } t_2}{\vdash t == t_2}$$

$$(\triangleq\rightarrow==) \quad \frac{}{f(x_1, \ldots, x_n) \triangleq t \vdash \forall x_1 : S_1, \ldots, x_n : S_n \, (f(x_1, \ldots, x_n) == t)} \, .$$

Restriction on the rule $(\triangleq\rightarrow==)$: $f: S_1 \times \cdots \times S_n \rightarrow S_{n+1}$.

These rules for conditionals and recursive function definitions are essentially the same as those postulated in [BCJ84]. However, recursive function definitions are not treated as formulae there.

The following substitution rules for reasoning about recursively defined functions are introduced by Jones in [Jon86]:[1]

$$(\triangleq\text{-subs}) \quad \frac{\vdash t = t \quad \vdash [y := [x := t]t']A}{\vdash [y := f(t)]A} \qquad \text{given a recursive function definition } f(x) \triangleq t'$$

$$\text{(if-subs)} \quad \frac{\vdash A \quad \vdash E(t) \quad \vdash [y := [x := t]t_1]A'}{\vdash [y := f(t)]A'} \quad \frac{\vdash \neg A \quad \vdash E(t) \quad \vdash [y := [x := t]t_2]A'}{\vdash [y := f(t)]A'} \qquad \text{given a recursive function definition } f(x) \triangleq \textsf{if } A \textsf{ then } t_1 \textsf{ else } t_2$$

These rules can be regarded as derived rules of LPF^R. They permit proofs to avoid use of and reasoning about strong equality, provided that there are no nested conditionals involved.

In [Jon90], Jones informally explains how a recursive definition of a partial function can be rendered into inference rules. The inference rules concerned resemble the appropriate rules of an inductive definition of the function (for partial functions, such rules usually need to be of a particular form). Given the recursive definition, the inference rules can also be regarded as derived rules of LPF^R.

In structures for LPF, a partial function is modelled by a total map whose argument domains and result domain contain a special element $\perp$. An argument tuple is mapped to $\perp$ if the function concerned is undefined for that argument tuple. This suggests the following definition, which is used in the additional interpretation rules given below.

[1] Only the simple case of unary functions is shown; extension to the general case of n-ary functions is straightforward.

For total maps F and G, $F, G: \mathcal{S}_1 \times \cdots \times \mathcal{S}_n \to \mathcal{S}_{n+1}$ $(\bot \in \mathcal{S}_1, \ldots, \mathcal{S}_{n+1})$, F is called *less defined than* G iff

$$\textit{for all } d_1 \in \mathcal{S}_1, \ldots, d_n \in \mathcal{S}_n, F(d_1, \ldots, d_n) \neq \bot \Rightarrow F(d_1, \ldots, d_n) = G(d_1, \ldots, d_n).$$

The following additional interpretation rules are required:

$$\begin{aligned}
[\![\textsf{if } A \textsf{ then } t_1 \textsf{ else } t_2]\!]^{\mathbf{A}}_{\alpha} &= [\![t_1]\!]^{\mathbf{A}}_{\alpha} \text{ if } [\![A]\!]^{\mathbf{A}}_{\alpha} = \mathsf{T}, \\
& [\![t_2]\!]^{\mathbf{A}}_{\alpha} \text{ if } [\![A]\!]^{\mathbf{A}}_{\alpha} = \mathsf{F}, \\
& \bot \text{ otherwise}, \\
[\![f(x_1, \ldots, x_n) \triangleq t]\!]^{\mathbf{A}}_{\alpha} &= \mathsf{T} \text{ if } f^{\mathbf{A}} \text{ is the least defined } F: S_1^{\mathbf{A}} \times \cdots \times S_n^{\mathbf{A}} \to S_{n+1}^{\mathbf{A}} \text{ such} \\
& \text{that } \textit{for all } d_1 \in S_1^{\mathbf{A}} - \{\bot\}, \ldots, d_{n+1} \in S_{n+1}^{\mathbf{A}} - \{\bot\}, \\
& [\![t]\!]^{\mathbf{A}'}_{\alpha(x_1 \to d_1)\cdots(x_n \to d_n)} = d_{n+1} \Rightarrow F(d_1, \ldots, d_n) = d_{n+1}, \\
& \mathsf{F} \text{ otherwise;}
\end{aligned}$$

assuming that $f: S_1 \times \cdots \times S_n \to S_{n+1}$ and where $\mathbf{A}'$ is the structure with signature Σ such that $w^{\mathbf{A}'} = w^{\mathbf{A}}$ if $w \not\equiv f$ and $f^{\mathbf{A}'} = F$ $(w \in \Sigma \cup \mathrm{SP}(\Sigma))$.

It can easily be checked that the least defined F satisfying a condition of the given form always exists.

The extended interpretation is sound with respect to the extended proof system. However, the extended proof system is not complete with respect to the extended interpretation. Because the inference rules do not cover the "leastness" of recursively defined functions, they are not sufficient to prove all properties that hold for those functions. Their undefinedness properties cannot be proved.

8.2 MPL$_\omega$ and Recursive Function Definitions

Just like terms of LPF, conditionals can be mapped to terms of MPL$_\omega$. That is, the definition of the translation mappings for LPF can be extended to LPF with conditionals by the addition of the following translation rule for conditionals:

$$\langle\!\langle \textsf{if } A \textsf{ then } t_1 \textsf{ else } t_2 \rangle\!\rangle = \iota \boldsymbol{y}: \boldsymbol{S}((\langle\!\langle A \rangle\!\rangle = \mathit{tt} \to \boldsymbol{y} = \langle\!\langle t_1 \rangle\!\rangle) \wedge (\langle\!\langle A \rangle\!\rangle = \mathit{ff} \to \boldsymbol{y} = \langle\!\langle t_2 \rangle\!\rangle)),$$

assuming that if A then t_1 else t_2 is a term of sort S and where $\boldsymbol{y}$ is a variable symbol of sort $\boldsymbol{S}$ not free in $\langle\!\langle A \rangle\!\rangle$, $\langle\!\langle t_1 \rangle\!\rangle$, and $\langle\!\langle t_2 \rangle\!\rangle$.

Just like formulae of LPF, recursive function definitions can be mapped to terms of MPL$_\omega$. That is, the definition of the translation mappings for LPF with conditionals can further be extended to LPF^R by the addition of the following translation rule for recursive function definitions:

$$\begin{aligned}
&\langle\!\langle f(x_1, \ldots, x_n) \triangleq t \rangle\!\rangle = \\
&\quad \iota \boldsymbol{b}: \mathsf{B}(\boldsymbol{f} :\stackrel{\mathrm{I}}{=} \forall \boldsymbol{x}_1: \boldsymbol{S}_1, \ldots, \boldsymbol{x}_n: \boldsymbol{S}_n, \boldsymbol{y}: \boldsymbol{S}_{n+1}(\langle\!\langle t \rangle\!\rangle = \boldsymbol{y} \to \boldsymbol{f}(\boldsymbol{x}_1, \ldots, \boldsymbol{x}_n) = \boldsymbol{y}) \leftrightarrow \boldsymbol{b} = \mathit{tt}),
\end{aligned}$$

assuming that $f: S_1 \times \cdots \times S_n \to S_{n+1}$ and where $\boldsymbol{y}$ is a variable symbol of sort $\boldsymbol{S}_{n+1}$ not free in $\langle\!\langle t \rangle\!\rangle$.

For a recursive function definition $f(x_1, \ldots, x_n) \triangleq t$, the formula $\langle\!\langle f(x_1, \ldots, x_n) \triangleq t \rangle\!\rangle = \mathit{tt}$ is its translation to MPL$_\omega$. Intuitively, $\langle\!\langle f(x_1, \ldots, x_n) \triangleq t \rangle\!\rangle = \mathit{tt}$ is a formula of MPL$_\omega$ stating that f is the least defined function such that the value of that function for arguments $x_1, \ldots, x_n$ is the value that is yielded by evaluation of t when f denotes that function.

This translation simplifies the translation of the explicit function definitions of VVSL in [Mid90].

For function symbol $f \in \mathrm{F}(\Sigma)$, $f\colon S_1 \times \cdots \times S_n \rightarrow S_{n+1}$, and formula A of $\mathrm{MPL}_\omega(\Sigma)$, $f :\stackrel{\mathrm{I}}{=} A$ is defined as an abbreviation of a formula of MPL_ω by

$$f :\stackrel{\mathrm{I}}{=} A \;:=\; \forall x_1 : S_1, \ldots, x_n : S_n \,(f(x_1, \ldots, x_n) \simeq (\delta f.A)(x_1, \ldots, x_n)).$$

$(\delta f.A)(t_1, \ldots, t_n)$ abbreviates a term of $\mathrm{MPL}_\omega(\Sigma)$. It can be regarded as function application, with $(\delta f.A)$ denoting the least defined function f such that A (under the conditions that A is admissible for f and A is functionality preserving for f). This notation and the accompanying conditions are defined in [Mid90, Section 4.7]. It can be defined as abbreviations because MPL_ω is a logic with countably infinite conjunctions.

The meaning of $\delta f.A$ is reflected in the following derived rules, which are proved in [Ren89, Appendix D.4]:

$$\frac{\vdash \mathrm{Adm}(f, A)}{\vdash \mathrm{Func}(f, A) \rightarrow [f := \delta f.A]A} \qquad \frac{\vdash \mathrm{Adm}(f, A)}{\vdash \mathrm{Func}(f, A) \rightarrow (A \rightarrow \delta f.A \subseteq f)}\,.$$

$\mathrm{Adm}(f, A)$ and $\mathrm{Func}(f, A)$ abbreviate formulae of MPL_ω stating the above-mentioned conditions concerning admissibility and preservation of functionality. $\delta f.A \subseteq f$ abbreviates a formula stating that $\delta f.A$ is less (or equally) defined than f.

The rules ($\triangleq\!\rightarrow\!==$) and (if-E) of LPF^R become derived rules of MPL_ω after translation. Consequently, the same holds for the substitution rules ($\triangleq$-subs) and (if-subs) as well as the rules generated from recursive function definitions according to [Jon90].

Theorem
The translation of the rules ($\triangleq\!\rightarrow\!==$) and (if-E) are derived rules of MPL_ω.
Proof:
Straightforward. □

9 Conclusions and Final Remarks

Classical reasoning can be used in the positive fragment of LPF. Generally, classical reasoning cannot be used out of the positive fragment. In particular, the deduction theorem does not hold in LPF. The departures from classical reasoning are consequences of giving up the assumption of the excluded middle.

In MPL_ω, reasoning only differs from classical reasoning with respect to variables and equality. The differences are direct consequences of embodying non-denoting terms. Such differences are also present in LPF. But unlike formulae of LPF, formulae of MPL_ω do not inherit the possibility of being non-denoting.

Free variables and bound variables are treated the same in LPF (variables always denote). The different treatment of free variables and bound variables in MPL_ω is usual in free logics, e.g. in Scott's free logic. Owing to the different treatment of free variables and bound variables, many references to undefined (i.e. non-denoting terms) can be avoided.

In both logics, equality is such that non-denoting terms are not equal, not even when they are identical (for non-denoting terms t, $t = t$ is neither-true-nor-false in LPF and false in MPL_ω). But the kind of equality that equates all non-denoting terms can be expressed in both logics. The substitution rules ($\triangleq$-subs) and (if-subs), which can be regarded as derived rules of LPF extended with recursive function definitions, permit proofs of properties concerning simple recursively defined functions to avoid use of two kinds of equality. Similar derived rules can be devised for MPL_ω.

In this paper, it is shown that LPF can be reduced to MPL_ω and that recursive function definitions in VDM style can be represented in MPL_ω. Formulae of LPF can be treated as terms of MPL_ω. Thus, LPF-formulae's truth, falsehood or either lack can be expressed in MPL_ω. Because recursive definitions of partial functions can also be expressed in MPL_ω, reasoning about these functions can be done within MPL_ω. Even properties that depend upon the leastness of the functions can be proved.

First of all, these results demonstrate that three-valued logics such as LPF are not necessary to deal with partial functions: formulae can be translated to formulae of a two-valued logic and what can be proved remains the same after translation. What is more, the results demonstrate that MPL_ω allows for a layered approach to handle partial functions: formulae of LPF can be regarded as abbreviations of terms of MPL_ω. Thereby, it becomes possible to switch between reasoning in LPF and reasoning in MPL_ω. In that case, reasoning in LPF should be taken for being derived from reasoning in MPL_ω.

LPF has to be extended for reasoning about recursively defined function. The results about recursive definitions of partial functions justify the additional rules ($\triangleq\!\to\!==$) and (if-E) (thus, they also justify the generation of rules from recursive function definitions according to [Jon90]). LPF has also to be extended for reasoning about the data types used in VDM (e.g. natural numbers, finite sets, composite objects), see also [Jon90]. The rules concerned can be justified in the same vein. The required translations are already worked out in [Mid90].

References

[Avr88] A. Avron. Foundations and proof theory of 3-valued logics. LFCS Report ECS-LFCS-88-48, University of Edinburgh, Department of Computer Science, 1988.

[BCJ84] H. Barringer, H. Cheng, and C.B. Jones. A logic covering undefinedness in program proofs. *Acta Informatica*, 21:251–269, 1984.

[Bee85] M.J. Beeson. *Foundations of Constructive Mathematics.* Springer Verlag, 1985.

[Bee88] M.J. Beeson. Towards a computation system based on set theory. *Theoretical Computer Science*, 60:297–340, 1988.

[Ben86] E. Bencivenga. Free logics. In D. Gabbay and F. Guenther, editors, *Handbook of Philosophical Logic, Volume III*, chapter III.6. D. Reidel Publishing Company, 1986.

[Bla86] S. Blamey. Partial logic. In D. Gabbay and F. Guenther, editors, *Handbook of Philosophical Logic, Volume III*, chapter III.1. D. Reidel Publishing Company, 1986.

[Che86] J.H. Cheng. *A Logic for Partial Functions.* PhD thesis, University of Manchester, Department of Computer Science, 1986. Technical Report UMCS-86-7-1.

[CJ90] J.H. Cheng and C.B. Jones. On the usability of logics which handle partial functions. Technical Report UMCS-90-3-1, University of Manchester, Department of Computer Science, 1990.

[GL90] A. Gavilanes-Franco and F. Lucio-Carrasco. A first order logic for partial functions. *Theoretical Computer Science*, 74:37–69, 1990.

[GMW79] M.J.C. Gordon, R. Milner, and C. Wadsworth. *Edinburgh LCF.* Springer Verlag, LNCS 78, 1979.

[Jon86] C.B. Jones. *Systematic Software Development Using VDM.* Prentice-Hall, first edition, 1986.

[Jon89] H.B.M. Jonkers. An introduction to COLD-K. In M. Wirsing and J.A. Bergstra, editors, *Algebraic Methods: Theory, Tools and Applications*, pages 139–205. Springer Verlag, LNCS 394, 1989.

[Jon90] C.B. Jones. *Systematic Software Development Using VDM.* Prentice-Hall, second edition, 1990.

[JS90] C.B. Jones and R.C.F. Shaw. *Case Studies in Systematic Software Development.* Prentice-Hall, 1990.

[Kar64] C. Karp. *Languages with Expressions of Infinite Length.* North-Holland, 1964.

[Kei71] H.J. Keisler. *Model Theory for Infinitary Logic.* North-Holland, 1971.

[Kle52] S.C. Kleene. *Introduction to Metamathematics.* North-Holland, 1952.

[KR89] C.P.J. Koymans and G.R. Renardel de Lavalette. The logic MPL_ω. In M. Wirsing and J.A. Bergstra, editors, *Algebraic Methods: Theory, Tools and Applications*, pages 247–282. Springer Verlag, LNCS 394, 1989.

[KTB88] B. Konikowska, A. Tarlecki, and A. Blikle. A three-valued logic for software specification and validation. In R. Bloomfield, L. Marshall, and R. Jones, editors, *VDM '88*, pages 218–242. Springer Verlag, LNCS 328, 1988.

[Łuk67] J. Łukasiewicz. On three-valued logic. In S. McCall, editor, *Polish Logic 1920–1939.* Oxford University Press, 1967.

[McC67] J. McCarthy. A basis for a mathematical theory of computation. In P. Braffort and D. Hirschberg, editors, *Computer Programming and Formal Systems*, pages 33–70. North-Holland Publishing Company, 1967.

[Mid90] C.A. Middelburg. *Syntax and Semantics of VVSL — A Language for Structured VDM Specifications.* PhD thesis, University of Amsterdam, September 1990. Available from PTT Research, Dr. Neher Laboratories.

[Owe84] O. Owe. An approach to program reasoning based on a first-order logic of partial functions. Computer Science Technical Report CS-081, University of California, San Diego, 1984.

[Pau87] L.C. Paulson. *Logic and Computation.* Cambridge University Press, Cambridge Tracts in Theoretical Computer Science 2, 1987.

[Plo85] G.D. Plotkin. Partial function logic. Lectures at Edinburgh University, 1985.

[Ren84] G.R. Renardel de Lavalette. Descriptions in mathematical logic. *Studia Logica*, 43:281–294, 1984.

[Ren89] G.R. Renardel de Lavalette. COLD-K^2, the static kernel of COLD-K. Report RP/mod-89/8, SERC, 1989.

[Sco67] D.S. Scott. Existence and description in formal logic. In R. Schoenman, editor, *Bertrand Russell, Philosopher of the Century*, pages 181–200. Allen & Unwin, 1967.

[Sco79] D.S. Scott. Identity and existence in intuitionistic logic. In M.P. Fourman, C.J. Mulvey, and D.S. Scott, editors, *Applications of Sheaves*, pages 660–696. Springer Verlag, Lecture Notes in Mathematics 753, 1979.

[Tho89] S. Thompson. A logic for Miranda. *Formal Aspects of Computing*, 1(4):339–365, 1989.

Tactical Tools for Distributing VDM Specifications

Thierry Cattel
Digital Equipement, Centre Technique Europe Sarl
Chemin du Levant, 01210 Ferney-Voltaire
Laboratoire d'Informatique, URA CNRS 822
Université de Franche-Comté
25030 Besançon cedex
France
Phone : +33 81.66.64.58 Fax : +33 81.66.61.77
E-mail : cattel@emc2.enet.dec.com

Abstract

A major issue in software engineering is the mastery of sofware design. The increasing distributed programming facilities open lots of new possibilities but make the task of designers more complex. Our work is to contribute to a rational design of real-sized distributable applications. We propose an approach based on the VDM formal method as support for the design phase and based on the Conic distributed language and environment as target for the implementation. We apply successive refinements on a VDM model so as to modify its distributability. The refinements are formalized, their validity is proved and they are tactical tools for a support environment of distributable software design. We express the general architecture of the resulting application into Conic.

Keywords

Formal specification, refinement, distributable application, programming in the large, reliability, tactical tools, virtual node, module, port, communication.

1. Introduction

The aim of software engineering is clearly to find means to build quality software [13]. Rigourous approaches like formal methods are more and more accepted as aiming in that direction. The development of workstations and communication networks proves that distributed programming is now a reality and makes the task of designers more complex. The support available is mainly distributed operating systems like Amoeba[17] or Chorus[15], parallel languages like Ada or Occam or distributed environments like Conic[10]. Regarding methods, works are mostly algorithmic based. Approaches of rigorous program development like program transformations[6] and program derivation support tools are numerous. To our knowledge, only few attempts are done towards distributable applications[14].

The aim of our work is to contribute to the design of distributable applications. We propose a rational approach applicable to real-sized applications. It is part of a general development approach and focusses on step refining a formal specification and leading to the architecture of the application. More precisely (Fig.1) from an initial VDM specification[8], it leads to the architectural structure of the application compatible with the underlying model of Conic[10].

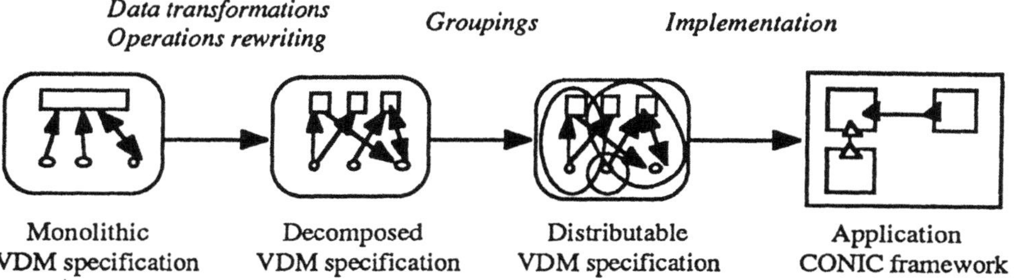

Fig.1 - Rational design steps

The basic mean of our approach is the essential feature of VDM : the *refinement technique*. We apply transformations to the data of the model so as to make it more suitable for distribution. These transformations are particular data refinements and their validity may be prooved (data reification adequacy). The goal of some works done around B[11] or MURAL is to provide support tools for the development of VDM design. Their concern is more particularly the validation of the design, thanks to theorem proving techniques, rather than the design itself. Indeed once a design is input into the system, the validation properties are generated and it is possible to carry out its formal justification selecting logical rules from a theory store ; new theories, proofs and strategies defined with tactics languages may be added, thus allowing design reuse. Regarding specification construction and refinement, when existing, the provided support is limited to syntactic editors.

Our work is an enrichment proposal for this lacking support. In imitation to the quoted theorem prover techniques, we formalise the data refinements as inference rules that will be the tactical tools of our system for designing distributable applications ; we will later provide general rules of transformation application strategy. The originality of this work is firstly the application of formal techniques on *programming in the large* problems, and secondly the explicit expression of the designer *savoir-faire*, including it in the tools so that the approach is extensible at the tactical level as at the strategic level.

In the following paragraphs we describe each step of the approach illustrating it with an example. We first give a brief overview of the VDM method and give an initial VDM model of the example. We study the general problem of distribution, show how it appears inside a VDM model, how it may be modified by means of transformations. We consider transformations, present their formalism, show which property to be proved to ensure their validity and give some examples. We study application strategy issues. We apply transformations on our example, obtaining a new model. We show how to sum up the model structure with a graph, describe the grouping phase (logical configuration) and finally give hints for implementing the architecture of the resulting model into Conic environment.

2. Formal specification in VDM

The main framework of our work is the VDM formal method[8]. VDM has been chosen because it is one of the most used in industry and research to specify large systems[12], and some tools are now available[2], [16].

2.1. General philosophy

VDM is based on a formal language and a stepwise method. The language allows to write model-oriented specifications in terms of a state and operations acting on this state. The state is an instance of an abstract data type described by high level constructors such as set, seq, map, composite structures and basic types such as integer, boolean ; the state may be constrained by an invariant property. The operations have input and output parameters, and may use the model state ; they are described with a precondition and a postcondition which are expressions of the set theory and the first order logic. The classical VDM stepwise method consists in writing a first specification, successively refining it until the distance to a possible implementation is negligible. The validity of the first model must be proved with regard to a set of certain properties : *operation satisfiability, state invariant preservation by each operation*, etc. ; then refinements are applied. The validity of the new model must be proved with regard to another set of properties : *data reification adequacy, domain rule, result rule.* Among various VDM dialects, the British Standard Institute has defined a general standard included in [8], which we took as a reference. We slightly modified the language, changing the symbols into names, etc. We do not formally explicit the syntax used, it is illustrated with an example below.

2.2. Example

2.2.1. Requirements

This example is inspired of [7] and consists in the management of a flyingclub. The characteristics of each pilot (address, account, log book) and airplane must be recorded. The arrival of new pilots and airplanes must be taken into account. The pilots may credit or debit their account. Each flight must be recorded on the log book of the pilot and of the airplane ; an accounting movement must be recorded for the person who will pay for the flight. Requests like *the list of all the flights between two dates* may be submitted. Parts of the related specification is given below. Its state is composed of three datas : *pilots, airplanes, mvts* respectively recording information related to pilots, airplanes and accountancy. Four operations are detailed ; *AIRPLANEFLIGHTS* returns all the flights for a given plane between two dates ; *PILOTREGISTRATION* takes into account the registration of a new pilot ; *PILOTCREDIT* records the deposit of money on the account of a pilot ; *FLIGHT* records a flight on the log book of the pilot, on the log book of the plane, and in the accountancy.

2.2.2. Specification

```
module flying_club
   state
     record
          pilots      : Pname   -> Pilot
          airplanes   : Aname   -> Airplane
          mvts        : Date    -> Acmvts
     end
     inv λx.all pn in dom(pilots(x)), d in dom(book(pilots(x)(pn))),
                pf in book(pilots(x)(pn))(d) .
                exists  an in dom(airplanes(x)), d in dom(book(airplanes(x)(an))),
                    af in book(airplanes(x)(an))(d) .
                    pilot(af)=pn and aircraft(pf)=an and deph(af)=deph(pf) and ...
     init (pilots->{}, airplanes->{}, mvts->{})
```

```
types
    Pilot = record
                char    : Pchar
                book    : Pflightm
            end
    Airplane = record
                char    : Achar
                book    : Aflightm
                price   : Money
            end
    Pflightm = Date -> Pflights
    Pflights = Pflight-set
    Aflightm = Date -> Aflights
    Pflight = record
                payer     : Pname
                airplane  : Aname
                deph      : Hour
                arrh      : Hour
            end
    Aflights = Aflight-set
    Acmvts = Acmvt-set     inv λx.x<>{}
    Sort = @CRED / @DEB / @FLIGHT
    Aflight = record
                pilot     : Pname
                payer     : Pname
                deph      : Hour
                arrh      : Hour
            end
    Acmvt = record
                pilot   : Pname
                sort    : Sort
                val     : Money
            end
    Acflight = record
                airplane  : Aname
                pilot     : Pname
                payer     : Pname
                deph      : Hour
                arrh      : Hour
            end
    Pinf = record
                name   : Pname
                char   : Pchar
            end
operations
    AIRPLANEFLIGHTS(an:Aname, begind:Date, endd:Date) afm:Afligthm
        ext    rd airplanes
        pre    an in dom(airplanes)
        post   afm={d->afs in book(airplanes(an)) / begind≤d≤endd}
    PILOTREGISTRATION(pi:Pinf)
        ext    wr pilots
        pre    name(pi) notin dom(pilots)
        post   pilots=pilots' union {name(pi)->(char->char(pi), book->{})}
    PILOTCREDIT(pn:Pname, m:Money, d:Date)
        ext    wr mvts
        pre    pn in dom(pilots)
        post   case   d in dom(mvts')      -> mvts=mvts' overwrite {d->mvts'(d) union{c}}
                      d notin dom(mvts')   -> mvts=mvts' union {d->{c}}
               end  and  c=(sort->@CRED, pilot->pn, val->m)
    FLIGHT(af:Aflight, d:Date)
        ext    wr pilots, airplanes, mvts
        pre    pilot(af) in dom(pilots) and payer(af) in dom(pilots)
        post   pilots=pilots' overwrite {pilot(af)->(char->char(opil),book->npbook)} and
               opil=pilots'(pilot(af))
               ...
    ...
end
```

2.3. Structure graph

The underlying structure of a specification does not appear directly when looking at the VDM text but could be graphically represented (Fig.2) as a bipartite graph with two sorts of vertices : one corresponding to data and one to operations ; there is as much data as there are fields in the state definition. The egdes linking the vertices correspond to the way the operations use the data and may be of two kinds : read and/or write.

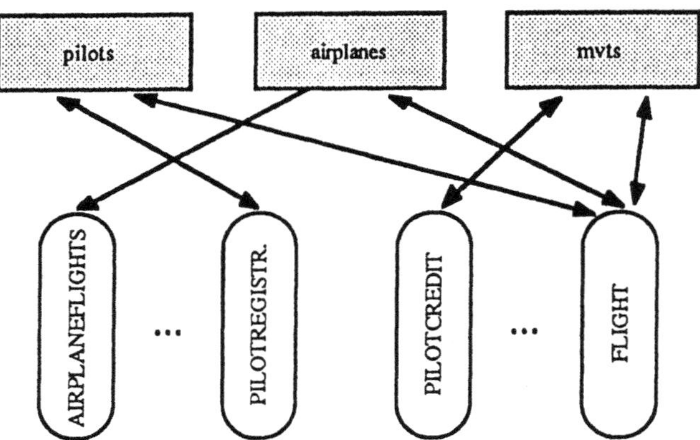

Fig.2 - Flyingclub initial structure graph

3. Distribution

3.1. Preliminary

The distribution is applicable to an objet, and is composed of a division phase consisting in splitting the object into fragments, a grouping phase consisting in mapping the fragments onto a network of virtual machines and a configuration phase consisting in mapping the virtual machines onto a network of physical machines. These steps are dependent of the object divisibility, the grouping and configuration criterions. Unless the object is totally indivisible, it always exists several distribution choices. A finer division allows to reach all the distribution choices resulting of a coarser division ; it is necessary to divide the object as much as possible to get a better chance to reach a good distribution solution.

In our topic, the object to be distributed is a software application. The incentive of the distribution is the good utilization of the available machines for the particular application to be built ; it may be the calculation time minimization, the balance of calculation load on the machine network, etc. The division and grouping steps will be detailed. We do not intend to develop the configuration phase any further.

We now consider how to distribute a VDM specification, composed of a state and a set of operations. We only focus on state division. The state is a data structure built by means of VDM basic data types and constructors and its divisibility depends on them. We consider that data not totally defined or defined as integer, boolean, quote literal, union is not divisible. Data defined as a record or a set could be considered as divisible. Map and sequence may be expressed in terms of sets and records, then their divisibility is the concern of what is said upper. In fact, the application distribution normally takes place before its execution. However it might evolve during the execution ; this situation is called dynamic configuration and is supported by environment such as Conic[10]. We deliberately decide to totally define the distribution of an application before its execution for sake of simplicity. For this reason we only consider data expressed by the record constructor as directly divisible.

The state structuration choice of the initial model is partly arbitrary for there always exists multiple intuitively equivalent possibilities. Among these possibilities, some are more suitable for distribution since they are more divisible. The following state definition has a single field, a map whose elements of the codomain are separate maps :

```
state
    record m:M end
    init (m->{})
types
    M = T1->(T2->T3)
    inv λx.all (x1,x2) in dom(x) . x1<>x2 => dom(x(x1)) inter dom(x(x2)) = {}
```

It is intuitively equivalent to the following one. The initial map has been split into two maps and the state has now two fields and so is more divisible :

```
state
    record m1:M   m2:T2->T3 end
    inv λx.union(rng(m1(x)))=dom(m2(x))
    init (m1->{}, m2->{})
types
    M = T1->(T2-set)
        inv λx.all (x1,x2) in dom(x) . x1<>x2 => x(x1) inter x(x2) = {}
```

More formally the intuitive idea of data type equivalence must be related to the VDM concept of data refinement. A data refinement is characterized by the transformation of a data type into another one and the inverse transformation called *retreive function*. Any inept data refinement might be expressed and the so called *data reification adequacy* property allows the identification of valid ones. A valid data refinement in fact formally expresses the intuitive idea of data type equivalence.

These observations suggest us to take an inventory of all the possible data refinements and to identify those that will lead to a more suitable structuration of the state. We will dispose on a set of tactic tools, the basic bricks of our design system, and, it will be possible to find application strategies complying with the ideas exposed above that will provide more suitable isomorphic models. The data refinements are defined as data transformations rules whose denotational semantics is presented in the natural semantics style[9].

3.2. State refinements

3.2.1. Notation conventions

The data refinements will act on types presented in abstract syntax which we do not detail. All manipulated types will be unfold. For convenience, since abstract syntax is not very readable we will use concrete syntax for denoting lambda functions. The type of the following state:

```
state
    record f1:Number_set end
    init ...
types
    Number_set=Number-set inv λx.card(x)<20
    Number=integer invλx.x>10
```

will be written :

```
t( rect[  fd(id f1, t(   sett(   t(  intt(),
                                     λx.x>10)),
                         λx.card(x)<20))],        λx.true)
```

3.2.2. Data refinement formalization

The data refinements (Fig.3) are presented in the natural semantics style as a formal system (called *T*) of inference rules of the form :

$$\frac{\vdash_P PRED \ \ldots \ \vdash_T \ldots}{\vdash_T TYPE1 \rightarrow TYPE2,\ RETF}$$

where *TYPE1* is of the form *t(D1, I1)* and *TYPE2* is of the form *t(D2, I2)*. The rule means that any instance *d1* of *D1* verifying the invariant *I1* may be transformed, under some conditions, into an instance *d2* of type *D2* that verifies *I2* ; the retreive function *RETF* is such that *d1=RETF(d2)*. Applicability conditions may reference other transformation rules or first order predicates ; in this latter case we express them as a theorem prover with another formal system (called *P*) whose judgments are of the form : *⊢P—PRED*

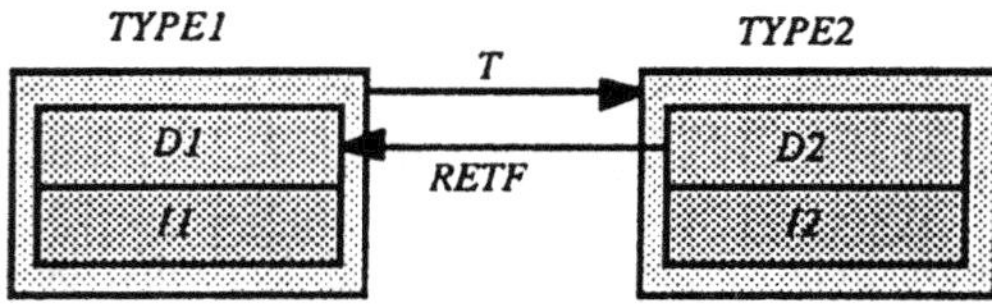

Fig.3 - Data refinement

3.2.3. Rules examples

We give few examples of transformation rules. The ***set-into-seq*** rule expresses a very classical VDM refinement : a set is represented with a non repetitive sequence. Some rules like ***weak map-constr*** or ***dom field-migration*** should be generalised but are not for the sake of clarity.

⊢T— t(sett(D), λx.true) → t(seqt(D), λx.card(rng(x))=len(x)), λx.rng(x) **set-into-seq**

⊢T— t(sett(t(rect[fd(F1,D1), fd(F2,D2)], RI)), λx.true) **weak-map-constr**
→ t(mapt(D1, t(sett(D2), SI)), MI), RETF
where
SI = λx.x<>{}   MI = λx. all x1 in RETF(x).RI(x1)
RETF = λx.{ (F1->d1,F2->d2) / d1->cds in x and d2 in cds }

⊢T— t(mapt(D, CD), λx.true) **weak-map-inv**
→ t(mapt(CD, t(sett(D), λx.x<>{})), MI), RETF
where
RETF = λx.{ d->cd / d in ds and cd->ds in x}
MI = λx. all (x1, x2) in dom(x) . x1<>x2 => x(x1) inter x(x2) = {}

⊢P— CDI(x)=>x<>{} **map-set-inv**

⊢T— t(mapt(D, t(sett(CD), CDI)), λx.true) → t(mapt(CD,t(sett(D), CDI1)), MI) , RETF
where
CDI1 = λx. x<>{}   MI =λx. all x1 in rng(RETF(x)) . CDI(x1)
RETF = λx.{ d->cds / cd->ds in x and d in ds and cd in cds}

```
⊢P–  SI(x)=>x<>{}                                                    dom-field-migration
──────────────────────────────────────────────────
⊢T–  t( mapt(t( rect[fd(F1,D1),fd(F2, D2)], RI), t(sett(CD),SI)), λx.true)
       → t(  mapt(D1, t( sett(t( rect[fd(F2,D2),fd(F3, CD)], RI1)), SI1)), MI) , RETF
where
       RI1 = λx.true    SI1 = λx.x<>{}
       MI = λx. ( all x1 in dom(RETF(x)).RI(x1) )  and  ( all x1 in rng(RETF(x)).SI(x1) )
       RETF = λx.{ (F1->d1,F2->d2)->ds
                           | d1->mds in x and (F2->d2, F3->d) in mds and d in ds}

⊢T–  t( mapt(t( uniont[t(D1,I1), t(D2,I2)], UI), CD), λx.true)       uniom-dom-map-split
       → t(  rect[   fd(F1, t(mapt(t(D1, DI1), CD), λx.true)),
                     fd(F2, t(mapt(t(D2, DI2), CD), λx.true))], RI1) ,  RETF
where DI1 = I1 and UI    DI2 = I2 and UI    RI1 = λx.true    RETF = λx.F1(x) union F2(x)

⊢T– t(mapt(quotet(Q), CD), λx.true) → CD, λx.{Q->x}                  quote-dom-map-simpl

⊢T–  t( mapt(D, t( rect[fd(F1,CD1),fd(F2, CD2)], RI)), λx.true)     rec-codom-map-split
       → t(  rect[   fd(F1, t(mapt(D,CD1), λx.true)),
                     fd(F2, t(mapt(D,CD2), λx.true))], RI1), RETF
where
       RI1 = λx.dom(F1(x))=dom(F2(x)) and all x1 in rng(RETF(x)) . RI(x1)
       RETF = λx.{ d->(F1->F1(x)(d),F2->F2(x)(d)) | d in dom(F1(x)) }

⊢T–  t( rect[  fd(F1, D1),                                                      rec-flat
               ..., fd(Fi,  t(  rect[fd(Fi1, Di1), ..., fd(Fim, Dim)], RI)), ...,
               fd(Fn, Dn)], λx.true)
       → t(  rect[   fd(F1, D1), ..., fd(Fi1, Di1), ..., fd(Fim, Dim), ..., fd(Fn, Dn)], RI),
       λx.(F1->F1(x), ..., Fi->(Fi1->Fi1(x), ..., Fim->Fim(x)), ..., Fn->Fn(x))

⊢T–  Di → Di', RETFi                                                            rec-subst
──────────────────────────────────────────────────
⊢T–  t(  rect[fd(F1, D1), ..., fd(Fi, Di), ..., fd(Fn, Dn)], λx.true)
       → t(  rect[fd(F1, D1), ..., fd(Fi, Di'), ..., fd(Fn, Dn)], λx.true),
       λx.(F1->F1(x), ..., Fi->RETFi(Fi(x)), ..., Fn->Fn(x))

⊢P–  I(x)=>I1(x)    ⊢T–   t(D, I1) → t(D1, I2), RETF                    inv  weak-csq
──────────────────────────────────────────
⊢T–  t(D, I) → t(D1, I2 and I∘RETF), RETF

⊢T–  t(D0, I0) → t(D1, I1), RETF1    ⊢T– t(D1, I1) → t(D2, I2), RETF2          ref-comp
──────────────────────────────────────────────────────
⊢T–  t(D0, I0) → t(D2, I2), RETF1∘RETF2
```

3.2.4. Soundness

The *data refinement adequacy* property insures the soundness of a data refinement rule. It formally expresses the meaning of the associated inference rule, namely :

all x in { d1 in D1 | I1(x) } . (exists y in { d2 in D2 | I2(d2) } . x=RETF(y)) or in an equivalent way, according to classical logic rules :

all x in D1 . (I1(x) => (exists y in D2 . I2(y) and y=RETF(x))

We present the validity proof of the ***inv-weak-csq*** rule as in [8], thanks to boxes. All the quoted rules are included in [8], we only explicit the ***exists-inst*** rule but not its justification. It must be proved :

all d in D.I(d)=>(exists d1 in D1 . (I2 and I∘RETF)(d1) and d=RETF(d1))

knowing :

all d in D.I(d)=>I1(d) *all d in D.I1(d) =>(exists d1 in D1.I2(d1) and d=RETF(d1))*

Lemma

exists x in X. E(x) ***exists-inst***

---

xa in X and E(xa)

Proof

from *all d in D . I(d)=>I1(d),*
all d in D . I1(d)=>(exists d1 in D1. I2(d1) and d=RETF(d1))
1 *all d in D . I(d)=>I1(d)* ***h***
2 *all d in D . I1(d)=>(exists d1 in D1. I2(d1) and d=RETF(d1))* ***h***
3 ***from*** *da in D*
3.1 *I(da)=>I1(da)* ***all-E(1,h3)***
3.2 *I1(da)=>(exists d1 in D1. I2(d1) and da=RETF(d1))* ***all-E(2,h3)***
3.3 *I(da)=>(exists d1 in D1. I2(d1) and da=RETF(d1))* ***=>-transitivity(3.1,3.2)***
3.4 ***from*** *I(da)*
3.4.1 *exists d1 in D1. I2(d1) and da=RETF(d1)* ***=>-E(h3.4,3.3)***
3.4.2 *d1 in D1 and I2(d1) and da=RETF(d1)* ***exists-inst(3.4.1)***
3.4.3 *da=RETF(d1)* ***and-E(3.4.2)***
3.4.4 *I(RETF(d1))* ***h3.4,3.4.3***
3.4.5 *I∘RETF(d1)* ***lambda-fonction***
3.4.6 *d1 in D1* ***and-E(3.4.2)***
3.4.7 *I2(d1) and da=RETF(d1)* ***and-E(3.4.2)***
3.4.8 *I2(d1) and I∘RETF(d1) and da=RETF(d1)* ***and-I(3.4.5,3.4.7)***
3.4.9 *(I2 and I∘RETF)(d1) and da=RETF(d1)* ***lambda-fonction***
infer *exists d1 in D1 .* ***exists-I(3.4.6,3.4.9)***
(I2 and I∘RETF)(d1) and da=RETF(d1)
3.5 *I(da) in* ***boolean*** ***invariant***
infer *I(da)=>exists d1 in D1 .* ***=>-I(3.4,3.5)***
(I2 and I∘RETF)(d1) and da=RETF(d1)
infer *all d in D. I(d)=>exists d1 in D1 . (I2 and I∘RETF)(d1) and d=RETF(d1)* ***all-I(3)***

3.2.5. Examples

We present a detailed application of the ***inv-weak-csq*** rule to throw light on the transformation mecanism. We then globally explain how to transform the flyingclub example.

3.2.5.1. Detailed application of inv-weak-csq

Let a map whose elements of the domain and the codomain are of the same type, let say *Name*, and whose codomain is a subset of the domain :

t(mapt(t(id Name, λx.true), t(id Name, λx.true)), λx. rng(x) subset dom(x))

According to the ***inv-weak-csq*** rule, since *(rng(x) subset dom(x))* => ***true*** the ***map-weak-inv*** rule is applicable and the result is :

t(mapt(t(id Name, λx.true), t(sett(t(id Name, λx.true)), λx.x<>{})), I)

where I is given by :

I = λx. (all (x1, x2) in dom(x) . x1<>x2 => x(x1) inter x(x2) = {}) and
(λx. rng(x) subset dom(x)) •(λx.{ d->cd / d in ds and cd->ds in x})

I = λx. (all (x1, x2) in dom(x) . x1<>x2 => x(x1) inter x(x2) = {}) and
(rng({ d->cd / d in ds and cd->ds in x}) subset
dom({ d->cd / d in ds and cd->ds in x}))

and using the properties of VDM operators and constructors dom, rng, subset, map, etc.:

I = λx. (all (x1, x2) in dom(x) . x1<>x2 => x(x1) inter x(x2) = {}) and
dom(x) subset (union rng(x))

3.2.5.2. Application to the example

We show how to apply the refinements on our example and give the general form of the obtained results. Obvious transformations like changing the order of the fields inside a record are ommitted. Writing all the details would be cumbersome and long. We are currently implementing a support tool for this task. The unfold state of the initial specification is :

```
record
    pilots    : Pname->record
                          char   : Pchar
                          book   : Date->(record
                                          payer     : Pname
                                          airplane  : Aname
                                          deph      : Hour
                                          arrh      : Hour     end)-set
                      end
    airplanes : Aname->record
                          char   : Achar
                          book   : Date->(record
                                          pilot     : Pname
                                          payer     : Pname
                                          deph      : Hour
                                          arrh      : Hour     end)-set
                          price  : Money
                      end
    mvts  : Date->(record
                   pilot  : Pname
                   sort   : @CRED | @DEB | @FLIGHT
                   val    : Money
               end)-set
end
inv λx.  all pn in dom(pilots(x)), d in dom(book(pilots(x)(pn)))
    ...
```

Two applications of the rules ***rec-codom-map-split***, ***ref-comp***, ***rec-subst*** and ***rec-flat*** on the *pilots* map leads to two maps. The *airplanes* map may also be split into three maps :

```
record
    pilotchars      : Pname->Pchar
    pilotbooks      : Pname->(Date->(record
                                            payer       : Pname
                                            airplane    : Aname
                                            deph        : Hour
                                            arrh        : Hour      end)-set)
    airplanechars   : Aname->Achar
    airplanebooks   : Aname->(Date->(record
                                            pilot   : Pname
                                            payer   : Pname
                                            deph    : Hour
                                            arrh    : Hour          end)-set)
    airplaneprices  : Aname->Money
    ...
end
inv λx.    ... and dom(pilotchars(x))=dom(pilotbooks(x))
                and dom(airplanechars(x))=dom(airplanebooks(x))=dom(airplaneprices(x)) ...
```

The field called *mvts* is a map whose elements of the codomain (§2.2.2) are non empty sets. The corresponding unfold abstract syntax form is :

```
t(  mapt(  t(id Date, ...),
           t(  sett(  t(  rect[  fd(id sort, t(uniont[  quotet(id CRED), quotet(id DEB),
                                                        quotet(id FLIGHT)], ...)),
                                 fd(id val, t(id Money, ...)),
                                 fd(id name, t(id Pname, ...))], ...)),  λx.x<>{})), ...)
```

thus the rule ***map-set-inv*** is applicable and gives :

```
t(  mapt(  t(  rect[  fd(id sort, t(uniont[quotet(id CRED), quotet(id DEB),
                                            quotet(id FLIGHT)], ...)),
                      fd(id val, t(id Money, ...)),
                      fd(id name, t(id Pname, ...))], ...),
           t(  sett(  t(id Date, ...)), λx.x<>{})), ...)
```

on which the rule ***dom-field-migration*** is applicable and gives :

```
t(  mapt(  t(  uniont[quotet(id CRED), quotet(id DEB), quotet(id FLIGHT)], ...),
           t(  sett(  t(  rect[  fd(id date, t(id Date, ...)),
                                 fd(id val, t(id Money, ...)),
                                 fd(id name, t(id Pname, ...))], ...)),  λx.x<>{})), ...)
```

On this last result, the rule ***union-dom-map-split*** is applicable, and we obtain two maps :

```
t(  rect[  fd( id moneymvts,
               t(  mapt(  t(  uniont[quotet(id CRED), quotet(id DEB)], ...),
                          t(  sett(  t( rect[fd(id date, t(id Date, ...)),
                                             fd(id val, t(id Money, ...)),
                                             fd(id name, t(id Pname, ...))], ...)), ...)), ...)),
           fd( id flightmvts,
               t(  mapt(  t(  quotet(id FLIGHT)),
                          t( sett( t( rect[fd(id date, t(id Date, ...)),
                                           fd(id val, t(id Money, ...)),
                                           fd(id name, t(id Pname, ...))], ...)), ...)), ...))], ...)
```

The map called *flightmvts* may be simplified using the rule ***quote-dom-map-simpl*** :

```
t(  sett(  t(  rect[  fd(id date, t(id Date, ...)),
                      fd(id val, t(id Money, ...)),
                      fd(id name, t(id Pname, ...))], ...)), ...)
```

and retransformed into a map, using the ***weak-map-constr*** rule :

```
t( mapt( t( id Pname, ...),
         t( sett( t( rect[ fd(id date, t(id Date, ...)),
                           fd(id val, t(id Money, ...))], ...)), λx.x<>{})), ...)
```

We arbitrarily stop the development at this point. Combining these results with the application of the rules ***ref-comp*** and ***rec-subst*** will eventually produce the state :

```
record
    pilotchars     :Pname->Pchar
    pilotbooks     :Pname->(Date->(record
                                      payer      :Pname
                                      airplane   :Aname
                                      deph       :Hour
                                      arrh       :Hour     end)-set)
    airplanechars  :Aname->Achar
    airplanebooks  :Aname->(Date->(record
                                      pilot      :Pname
                                      payer      :Pname
                                      deph       :Hour
                                      arrh       :Hour     end)-set)
    airplaneprices :Aname->Money
    moneymvts      :(@CRED|@DEB)->(record
                                      date   :Date
                                      val    :Money
                                      pilot  :Pname        end)-set
    flightmvts     :Pname->(record
                              date   :Date
                              val    :Money                end)-set
end
inv λx.   ...
```

The state (Fig.4) is now composed of seven fields instead of only three initially. The data of the specification is now more divisible and some operations, like *AIRPLANEFLIGHTS* are now decoupled from data they do not use any more and it will be interesting for the distribution of the application.

3.2.6. Refinement application strategies

We have presented some tactical means for refining the data of a VDM specification. We have formalized them as inference rules and a prototype tool for supporting their application is being developped. With this tool we will experiment how to apply the successive refinements in order to bring out elements of strategy. We know that a possible criterion is the obtention of a state record composed of more fields but it may depend on the problem. Experimenting with the tool we are developping will give some new answers. We plan to integrate means for defining application stategies like in B or Theo[5]

3.3. Operations rewriting

When the data is refined, the operations using them must be rewritten. Without detailing more this point here, *PILOTREGISTRATION* after the refinement of §3.2.5.2 could become :

PILOTREGISTRATION(pi:Pinf)
ext *wr pilotchars, pilotbooks*
pre *name(pi) notin dom(pilotchars)*
post *pilotchars=pilotchars' union {name(pi)->char(pi)} and*
pilotbooks=pilotbooks' union {name(pi)->{}}

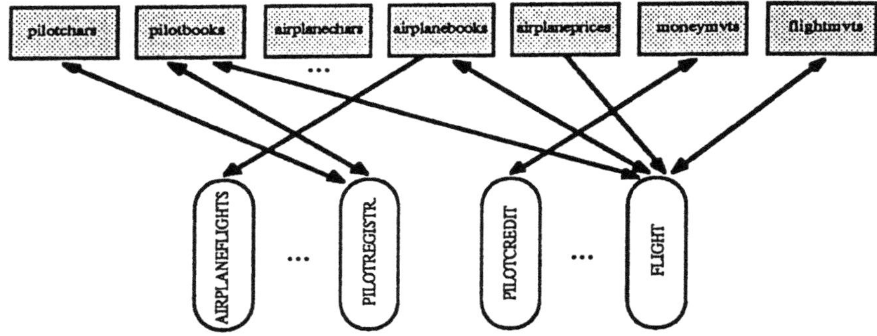

Fig.4 - Flyingclub final structure graph

4. Groupings and implementation

4.1. Presentation

The following phase is very important since it concerns the configuration of the application onto a virtual logical architecture. It consists in grouping the fragments of the application into several groups. From the structure graph, we produce a set of extracted graphs applying ad hoc grouping locality criterions for example. Without going into the details, we present a possible grouping of our refined example (Fig.5). Each group will correspond to a Conic module at the implementation level, and the egdes going from one group to another clearly show the future message exchanges. Intuitively, the groupe called *1* is composed of the data *pilotchars* and in particular of the operation *PILOTREGISTRATION* ; it will be dedicated to manage the registration of new pilots. The groupe called *3* manages the flights ; the group called *2* may correspond to a query submitted from a remote terminal.

The last phase consists in producing the Conic architecture code of the distributable application from the last VDM specification and the groupings choices. This transition is systematic and brings the executable semantics of Conic to the application. Conic[10] is a technical environment based on a distributable application model including the virtual node concept. Its essential features are modularity, abstraction and communication. A distributable application is a network of interconnected modules ; a module may itself be a network of modules. Each module has a well-defined interface composed of input output ports and communicates with the modules it is linked to by messages passing. There are two different communication semantics and then two kinds of communication ports : an asynchronous one and a synchronous one. In the asynchronous mode, the sender sends a message and waits until it has been taken into account by the system, but does not care if the message arrives at the receiver or not. In synchronous mode, the sender waits an answer of the receiver. All topologies are possible including bipoint, broadcasting and merge connections, except for synchronous ports which do not support broadcasting. In the case of a port receiving messages from several senders (merge), messages are buffered and treated in FIFO order.

Our goal is to provide the architecture of a distributable application but not its detailed construction, so we do not consider VDM operation decomposition. The technique we adopt is straightforward. It consists in doing a module of every data, operation, and group. Each data module will be a server for the data it encapsulates ; it will be interfaced with two ports : a synchronous one for reading the value of the data, an asynchronous one for writing the data. Each operation module possesses the corresponding ports for the data it uses. Inside a group, the modules are connected according to their data utilization. The module communications of a group towards a data out of this group are gathered and the group module then owns as much ports as needed for these communications. This solution illustrate the upstream approach but it is not efficient nor reliable : the data is always manipulated globally and the parallelism grain of the application is thiner than an operation and mutual exclusion or deadlock issues may arise. Some solutions exist for these problems but we do not develop this point in this paper.

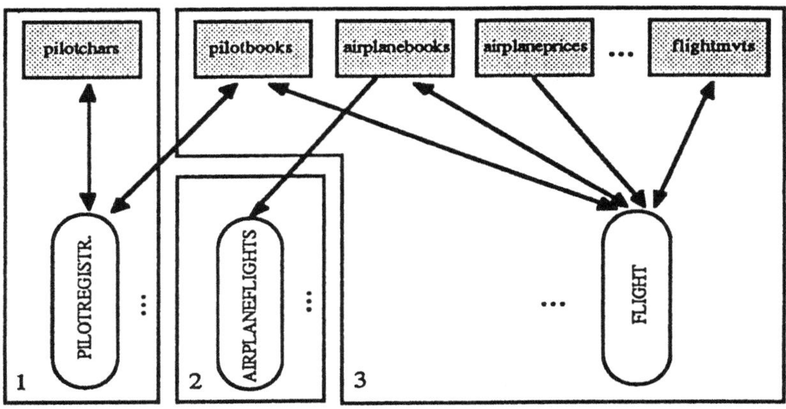

Fig.5 - Flyingclub groupings

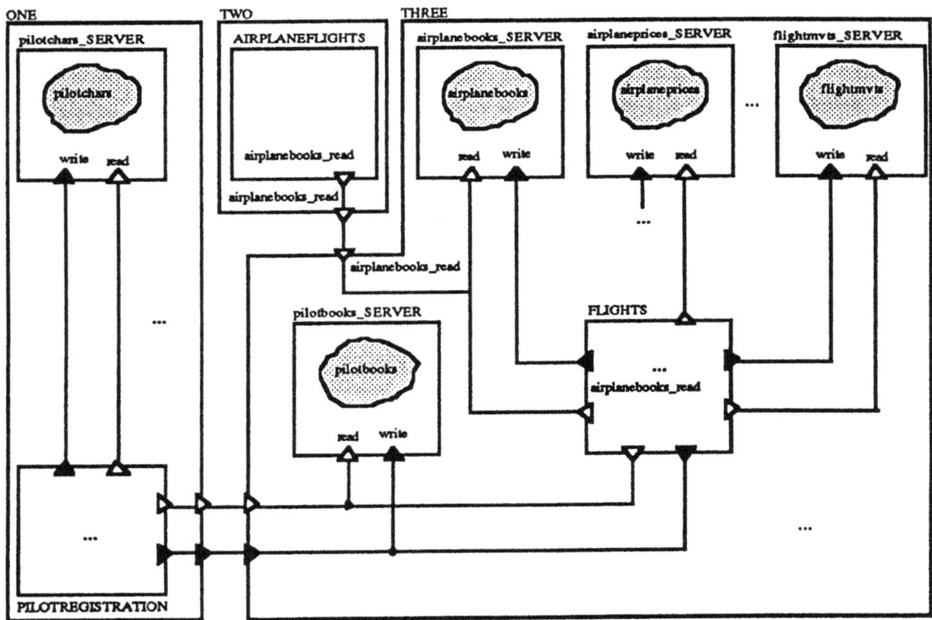

Fig.6 - Flyingclub CONIC implementation

4.2. Flyingclub example

We use the Conic graphical representation of the application architecture since it clearly shows the modules, ports and connections and drop the module code (Fig.6). Each module and port is named. The synchronous ports are represented with empty triangles, asynchronous ones with filled triangles. The direction of the communication is in the direction of the arrows.

Conclusion

In this paper, we have sketched out a possible approach for designing distributable applications starting from a VDM specification. We have given a precise framework with concrete steps and intermediary formalisms. We have proposed a first solution for solving the issues occurring at each step. We have treated a medium-sized example and presented a few transformation rules ; some more details may be found in [3] and [4]. We are currently implementing prototype tools with CENTAUR[1] and we plan to integrate in our development environment, complementary tools like B or Theo. One objective of this tool is to test refinements suitability on bigger examples, to discover relevant application strategies and to enrich the approach itself.

References

[1] P.Borras, D.Clément, T.Despeyroux : *CENTAUR : The system* ; Proc. of SIGSOFT'88 third annual symposium on sotfware development environments, Boston, 1988.

[2] R.Bloomfield, P.Froome, B.Monahan : *Specbox : a toolkit for BSI-VDM* ; Adelard, internal report, February 1989.

[3] T.Cattel : *Rational Design of Distributed Applications ;* Third European Software Engineering Conference ,Milano, Italy, 21-24 October 1991.

[4] T.Cattel, G.-R.Perrin : *A stepwise refinement for distributed applications ;* Sixth International Workshop on Soft. Specif. & Design, Como, Italy, 25-26 October 1991.

[5] J.Despeyroux : *Theo : an interactive proof development system* ; INRIA RR116, 1990.

[6] M.S.Feather : *A survey of classification of some program transformation approaches and techniques* ; Program specif. and transf., p.165-195, Elsevier publishers, Holland, 1987.

[7] Anna GRAM : *Raisonner pour programmer* ; Dunod informatique, Paris 1986.

[8] C.B.Jones : *Systematic Software Development Using VDM* ; Prentice Hall Inter., 1990.

[9] G.Kahn : *Natural Semantics* ; Proc. of STACS'87, LNCS 247, 1987.

[10] J.Kramer : *Configuration programming - A framework for the development of distributable systems* ; Proc. of Computer syst. and soft. eng., Tel Aviv, May 1990.

[11] C.Lafontaine, Y.Ledru, P.Y.Schobbens : *An experiment in formal software development : using the B theorem prover on a VDM case study* ; Proc. 12th Int. Conf. on Software Engineering, IEEE Computer society press, 1990.

[12] Y.Ledru, P.Y.Schobbens : *Applying VDM to large developments* ; Proc. ACM SIGSOFT Int. Workshop on Formal methods in soft. devel., pp.55-58, Napa, May 1990.

[13] B.Meyer : *Object-oriented Software Construction* ; Prentice Hall, 1988.

[14] M.Mühlhäuser : *Software engineering in distributed systems - Approaches and issues* ; Proc. of Phoenix conf. on computers and communications, Scottsdale, March 1990.

[15] M.Rozier, V.Abrossimov, F.Armand et al. : *Chorus Distributed Operating Systems* ; Chorus systèmes, technical report 88-7.5, 1988.

[16] *RAISE overview* ; RAISE/CRI/DOC/9/V2, CRI, Denmark, June 1990.

[17] A.S.Tanenbaum, R.V.Renesse, H.VanStaveren et al. : *Experiences with the AMOEBA distributed operating system* ; Com. of the ACM Vol. 33, N°12, December 1990.

An Attempt to Reason about Shared-State Concurrency in the Style of VDM

Ketil Stølen*
Department of Computer Science, Manchester University,
Oxford Road, Manchester, M13, 9PL

Abstract

The paper presents an attempt to develop a totally correct shared-state parallel program in the style of VDM. Programs are specified by tuples of five assertions (P, R, W, G, E). The pre-condition P, the rely-condition R and the wait-condition W describe assumptions about the environment, while the guar-condition G and the eff-condition E characterise commitments to the implementation.
The pre-, rely- and guar-conditions are closely related to the similarly named conditions in Jones' rely/guarantee method, while the eff-condition corresponds to what Jones calls the post-condition. The wait-condition is supposed to characterise the set of states in which it is safe for the implementation to be blocked; in other words, the set of states in which the implementation, when it becomes blocked, eventually will be released by the environment. The implementation is not allowed to be blocked during the execution of an atomic statement.
Auxiliary variables are introduced to increase the expressiveness. They are used both as a specification tool; to characterise a program that has not yet been implemented, and as a verification tool; to show that a given algorithm satisfies a specific property. However, although it is possible to define history-variables in this approach, the auxiliary variables may be of any type, and it is up to the user to define the auxiliary structure he prefers. Moreover, the auxiliary structure is only a part of the logic. This means that auxiliary variables do not have to be implemented as if they were ordinary programming variables.

1 Introduction

VDM, the Vienna Development Method, has been used successfully for the development of software in a wide variety of areas (see for example [JS90]). However, VDM is basically a technique for the design of sequential programs. The object of this paper is to describe a method that can be used to reason about shared-state concurrency in a similar way.

The first attempt to develop shared-state parallel programs in a VDM-style was due to Cliff Jones [Jon81], [Jon83]. In his approach, often called the *rely/guarantee* method, a proof tuple is of the form

$$z \ \underline{\text{sat}} \ (P, R, G, Q),$$

where z is a program, and (P, R, G, Q) is a specification consisting of four assertions P, R, G and Q. The pre-condition P and the rely-condition R constitute *assumptions* about the *environment*. In return the *implementation* z must satisfy the guar(antee)-condition G, the post-condition Q and terminate, when operated in an environment which fulfills the assumptions.

The pre-condition characterises a set of states to which the implementation is applicable. Any uninterrupted state transition by the environment is supposed to satisfy the rely-condition, while any atomic

*Address from September 1st 1991:Institut für Informatik, der Technischen Universität, postfach 20 24 20, Arcisstrasse 21, D-8000 München 2. email:stoelen@lan.informatik.tu-muenchen.de

state-transition by the implementation must satisfy the guar-condition. Finally, the post-condition characterises the overall effect of executing the implementation in such an environment.

The rely/guarantee method allows erroneous interference decisions to be spotted and corrected at the level where they are taken. Moreover, specifications are decomposed into subspecifications. Thus programs can be developed in a top-down style.

Unfortunately, the rely/guarantee method cannot be used for the development of algorithms whose correctness depends upon *synchronisation*. Furthermore, many valid developments are excluded because sufficiently strong intermediate assertions cannot be *expressed*. This paper, based on the authors PhD-thesis [Stø90], presents a method called LSP (Logic of Specified Programs), which can be thought of as an extension of the rely/guarantee approach, and which does not suffer from the two weaknesses pointed out above. (There are a number of minor changes with respect to [Stø90]; most notably, transitivity and reflexivity constraints have been removed.)

The paper is organised as follows: You are currently reading the introduction. Sections 2 and 3 give a brief overview of LSP. Some simplifying notation is introduced in section 4, while a non-trivial algorithm is developed in section 5. Finally, in section 6, some possible extensions are discussed, and LSP is compared with related approaches known from the literature.

2 Logic of Specified Programs

A *program* is a finite, nonempty list of symbols whose context-independent syntax is characterised in the well-known BNF-notation: Given that $\langle vl \rangle$, $\langle el \rangle$, $\langle dl \rangle$, $\langle ts \rangle$ denote respectively a list of variables, a list of expressions, a list of variable declarations, and a Boolean test, then any program is of the form $\langle pg \rangle$, where

$$\begin{array}{rcl}
\langle pg \rangle & ::= & \langle as \rangle \mid \langle bl \rangle \mid \langle sc \rangle \mid \langle if \rangle \mid \langle wd \rangle \mid \langle pr \rangle \mid \langle aw \rangle \\
\langle as \rangle & ::= & \langle vl \rangle := \langle el \rangle \\
\langle bl \rangle & ::= & \textsf{blo}\ \langle dl \rangle ; \langle pg \rangle\ \textsf{olb} \\
\langle sc \rangle & ::= & \langle pg \rangle ; \langle pg \rangle \\
\langle if \rangle & ::= & \textsf{if}\ \langle ts \rangle\ \textsf{then}\ \langle pg \rangle\ \textsf{else}\ \langle pg \rangle\ \textsf{fi} \\
\langle wd \rangle & ::= & \textsf{while}\ \langle ts \rangle\ \textsf{do}\ \langle pg \rangle\ \textsf{od} \\
\langle pr \rangle & ::= & \{\langle pg \rangle \parallel \langle pg \rangle\} \\
\langle aw \rangle & ::= & \textsf{await}\ \langle ts \rangle\ \textsf{do}\ \langle pg \rangle\ \textsf{od}
\end{array}$$

The main structure of a program is characterised above. However, a syntactically correct program is also required to satisfy some supplementary constraints:

- Not surprisingly, the assignment-statement's two lists are required to have the same number of elements. Moreover, the j'th variable in the first list must be of the same type as the j'th expression in the second, and the same variable is not allowed to occur in the variable list more than once.

- The block-statement allows for declaration of variables. A variable is *local* to a program, if it is declared in the program; otherwise it is said to be *global*. For example, $\textsf{blo}\ x{:}\,N, y{:}\,N; x, y := 5{+}w, w\ \textsf{olb}$ has two local variables, x and y, and one global variable w. To avoid complications due to name clashes, it is required that the same variable cannot be declared more than once in the same program, and that a local variable cannot appear outside its block. The first constraint avoids name clashes between local variables, while the second ensures that the set of global variables is disjoint from the set of local variables.

- To simplify the deduction rules and the reasoning with auxiliary variables, it is required that variables occurring in the Boolean test of an if- or a while-statement cannot be updated by any process running in parallel. (If- and while-rules for a language without this requirement can be found in [Stø91b].) This constraint does of course not reduce the number of implementable algorithms. If x is a variable that can be updated by another process, then it is for example always possible to write $\textsf{blo}\ y{:}\,N; y :=$

x; if $y = 0$ then z_1 else z_2 fi olb instead of if $x = 0$ then z_1 else z_2 fi. Similar constraints are stated in [Sou84], [XH91]. For any program z, let *hid*[z] denote the set of variables that occur in the Boolean test of an if- or a while-statement in z.

Since it is beyond the scope of this paper to give a soundness proof for LSP (a detailed proof can be found in [Stø90]), no formal semantics will be given. However, there are a few important requirements which must be pointed out. Assignment-statements and Boolean tests are atomic. The environment is restricted from interfering until the await-statement's body has terminated if an evaluation of its Boolean test comes out true, and the execution of the await-statement's body is modeled by one atomic step. A *state* is defined as a mapping of all programming variables to values. The expressions in the assignment-statement's expression-list are evaluated in the same state. The assignment of an empty list of expressions to an empty list of variables corresponds to the usual skip-statement and will be denoted by skip.

No *fairness* constraint is assumed. In other words, a process may be *infinitely overtaken* by another process. A program is *blocked* in a state, if the program has not terminated, and its subprocesses have either terminated or are waiting in front of an await-statement whose Boolean test is false (in the actual state).

Since the object of LSP is to prove total correctness, a *progress* property is needed; namely that a program will always progress unless it is infinitely overtaken by the environment, it is blocked, or it has *terminated*. Finally, to avoid unnecessary complications, all functions are required to be total.

The base logic L is a μ-calculus. In the style of VDM [Jon90] hooked variables will be used to refer to an earlier state (which is not necessarily the previous state). This means that, for any *unhooked* variable x of type Σ, there is a *hooked* variable $\overleftarrow{x}$ of type Σ. Hooked variables are restricted from occurring in programs.

Given a structure and a valuation then expressions in L can be assigned meanings in the usual way. $\models A$ means that A is valid (in the actual structure), while $(s_1, s_2) \models A$, where (s_1, s_2) is a pair of states, means that A is true if each hooked variable x in A is assigned the value $s_1(x)$ and each unhooked variable x in A is assigned the value $s_2(x)$. The first state s_1 may be omitted if A has no occurrences of hooked variables.

Thus, an assertion A can be interpreted as the set of all pairs of states (s_1, s_2), such that $(s_1, s_2) \models A$. If A has no occurrences of hooked variables, it may also be thought of as the set of all states s, such that $s \models A$. Both interpretations will be used below. To indicate the intended meaning, it will be distinguished between *binary* and *unary* assertions. When an assertion is binary it denotes a set of pairs of states, while a unary assertion denotes a set of states. In other words, an assertion with occurrences of hooked variables is always binary, while an assertion without occurrences of hooked variables can be both binary and unary.

A specification is of the form

$$(\vartheta, \alpha) :: (P, R, W, G, E),$$

where the *pre-condition* P, and the *wait-condition* W are unary assertions, and the *rely-condition* R, the *guar-condition* G, and the *eff-condition* E are binary assertions. The *glo-set* ϑ is the set of global programming variables, while the *aux-set* α is the set of auxiliary variables. It is required that the unhooked version of any hooked or unhooked free variable occurring in P, R, W, G or E is an element of $\vartheta \cup \alpha$, and that $\vartheta \cap \alpha = \{\,\}$. The *global state* is the state restricted to $\vartheta \cup \alpha$.

A specification states a number of assumptions about the environment. First of all, the initial state is assumed to satisfy the pre-condition. Moreover, it is also assumed that any atomic step by the environment, which changes the global state, satisfies the rely-condition. For example, given the rely-condition $x < \overleftarrow{x} \wedge y = \overleftarrow{y}$, then it is assumed that the environment will never change the value of y. Moreover, if the environment assigns a new value to x, then this value will be less than or equal to the variable's previous value.

Thirdly, it is assumed that if the implementation can be blocked only in states which satisfy the wait-condition, and can never be blocked inside the body of an await-statement, then the implementation will always eventually be released by the environment — in other words, under this condition, if the implementation becomes blocked, then the environment will eventually change the state in such a way that the implementation may progress. (The wait-condition can also be interpreted as a commitment to the implementation. See [Stø90], [Stø91a] for a detailed explanation.)

Finally, it is assumed that the environment can only perform a finite number of consecutive atomic steps. This means that the environment can only perform infinitely many atomic steps, if the implementation performs infinitely many atomic steps. Thus, this assumption implies that the implementation will not be infinitely overtaken by the environment. Observe that this is not a fairness requirement on the programming language, because it does not constrain the implementation of a specification. If for example a parallel-statement $\{z_1 \parallel z_2\}$ occurs in the implementation, then this assumption does not influence whether or not z_1 is infinitely overtaken by z_2. Moreover, this assumption can be removed. The only difference is that an implementation is no longer required to terminate, but only to terminate whenever it is not infinitely overtaken by the environment (see [Stø90]).

A specification is of course not only stating assumptions about the environment, but also commitments to the implementation. Given an environment which satisfies the assumptions, then an implementation is required to terminate. Moreover, any atomic step by the implementation, which changes the global state, is required to satisfy the guar-condition, and the overall effect of executing the implementation is constrained to satisfy the eff-condition. Observe, that interference both before the implementation's first atomic step and after the implementation's last atomic step is included in the overall effect. This means that given the rely-condition $x > \overleftarrow{x}$, the strongest eff-condition for the program skip is $x \geq \overleftarrow{x}$.

The auxiliary variables are employed to ensure the needed expressiveness. They are not first implemented and then afterwards removed by a specially designed deduction-rule as in the Owicki/Gries method [OG76]. Instead, the auxiliary variables are only a part of the logic. Moreover, they can be used in two different ways:

- To strengthen a specification to eliminate undesirable implementations. In this case auxiliary variables are used as a *specification tool*; they are employed to characterise a program that has not yet been implemented.
- To strengthen a specification to make it possible to prove that a certain program satisfies a particular specification. Here auxiliary variables are used as a *verification tool*, since they are employed to show that a given algorithm satisfies a specific property.

The auxiliary variables may be of any type, and it is up to the user to define the auxiliary structure he prefers.

To characterise the use of auxiliary variables it is necessary to introduce a new relation

$$z_1 \overset{(\vartheta,\alpha)}{\hookrightarrow} z_2,$$

called an *augmentation*, which states that the program z_2 can be obtained from the program z_1 by adding auxiliary structure constrained by the set of global programming variables ϑ and the set of auxiliary variables α. There are of course a number of restrictions on the auxiliary structure. First of all, to make sure that the auxiliary structure has no influence on the algorithm, auxiliary variables are constrained from occurring in the Boolean tests of if-, while- and await-statements. Furthermore, they cannot appear in an expression on the right-hand side in an assignment-statement, unless the corresponding variable on the left-hand side is auxiliary. Moreover, since it must be possible to remove some auxiliary variables from a specified program without having to remove all the auxiliary variables, it is important that they do not depend upon each other. This means that if an auxiliary variable a occurs on the left-hand side of an assignment-statement, then the only auxiliary variable that may occur in the corresponding expression on the right-hand side is a. However, the right-hand side expression may have any number of occurrences of elements of ϑ. This means that to eliminate all occurrences of an auxiliary variable a from a program, it is enough to remove all assignments to a. Finally, it is necessary to update auxiliary variables only in connection with assignment- and await-statements.

Before giving a more formal definition, it is necessary to introduce some helpful notation. If l and k are finite lists, then $\langle l \rangle$ denotes the set of elements in l, while $l \frown k$ denotes the result of prefixing k with l. Finally, if a is a list of variables, u is a list of expressions, and ϑ and α are two sets of variables, then

$a \leftarrow_{(\vartheta,\alpha)} u$ denotes that a and u have the same number of elements, that $\langle a \rangle \subseteq \alpha$, and that any variable occurring in u's j'th expression is either an element of ϑ, or equal to a's j'th variable. An augmentation can then be defined (recursively) as follows:

- Given two programs z_1, z_2 and two sets of variables ϑ and α, then $z_1 \stackrel{(\vartheta,\alpha)}{\hookrightarrow} z_2$, iff z_2 can be obtained from z_1 by substituting
  - a statement of the form

    $$v \frown a := r \frown u,$$

    where $a \leftarrow_{(\vartheta,\alpha)} u$, for each occurrence of an assignment-statement $v := r$, which does not occur in the body of an await-statement,
  - a statement of the form

    $$\text{await } b \text{ do } z'; a := u \text{ od},$$

    where $z \stackrel{(\vartheta,\alpha)}{\hookrightarrow} z'$ and $a \leftarrow_{(\vartheta,\alpha)} u$, for each occurrence of an await-statement await b do z od, which does not occur in the body of another await-statement.

A *specified program* is a pair of a program z and a specification ω, written z sat ω. It is required that for any variable x occurring in z, x is an element of ω's glo-set iff x is a global variable with respect to z. A specified program

$$z_1 \ \underline{\text{sat}} \ (\vartheta, \alpha) :: (P, R, W, G, E)$$

is valid iff there is a program z_2, such that $z_1 \stackrel{(\vartheta,\alpha)}{\hookrightarrow} z_2$, and

- z_2 terminates,
- any atomic step by z_2, which changes the global state, satisfies the guar-condition G,
- the overall effect of executing z_2 satisfies the eff-condition E,

whenever the environment is such that

- the initial state satisfies the pre-condition P,
- any atomic step by the environment, which changes the global state, satisfies the rely-condition R,
- if z_2 cannot be blocked in a state which does not satisfy the wait-condition, and z_2 cannot be blocked inside the body of an await-statement, then z_2 will always eventually be released by the environment,
- z_2 is not infinitely overtaken by the environment.

As an example, consider the task of specifying a program which adds a constant A to a global buffer called Bf. If the environment is restricted from interfering with Bf, then this can easily be expressed as follows:

$$(\{Bf\}, \{\}) :: (\text{true}, \text{false}, \text{false}, Bf = [A] \frown \overleftarrow{Bf}, Bf = [A] \frown \overleftarrow{Bf})$$

The pre-condition states that an implementation must be applicable in any state. Moreover, the rely-condition restricts the environment from changing the value of Bf, which means that the eff-condition can be used to express the desired change of state. Finally, the guar-condition specifies that the concatenation step takes place as one atomic step, while the falsity of the wait-condition implies that a correct implementation cannot become blocked.

If the environment is allowed to interfere freely with Bf, then the task of formulating a specification becomes more difficult. Observe that the actual concatenation step is still required to be atomic; the only difference from above is that the environment may interfere immediately before and (or) after the concatenation takes place. Since there are no restrictions on the way the environment can change Bf, and because interference due to the environment, both before the implementation's first atomic step, and after its last, is included in the overall effect, the eff-condition must allow anything to happen. This means that the eff-condition is no longer of much use. The specification

$$(\{Bf\},\{\})::(\mathsf{true},\mathsf{true},\mathsf{false},Bf=[A]\frown\overleftarrow{Bf},\mathsf{true})$$

is almost sufficient. The only problem is that there is no restriction on the number of times the implementation is allowed to add A to Bf. Hence, skip is for example one correct implementation, while $Bf:=[A]\frown Bf; Bf:=[A]\frown Bf$ is another correct implementation.

One solution is to introduce a Boolean auxiliary variable called Dn, and use Dn as a flag to indicate whether the implementation has added A to Bf or not. The program can then be specified as follows:

$$(\{Bf\},\{Dn\})::(\neg Dn, Dn\Leftrightarrow\overleftarrow{Dn},\mathsf{false},Bf=[A]\frown\overleftarrow{Bf}\wedge\neg\overleftarrow{Dn}\wedge Dn, Dn).$$

Since the environment cannot change the value of Dn, the implementation can add A to Bf only in a state where Dn is false, the concatenation transition changes Dn from false to true, and the implementation is not allowed to change Dn from true to false, it follows from the pre- and eff-conditions that the implementation adds A to Bf once and only once.

So far there has been no real need for the wait-condition. However, if an implementation is restricted from adding A to Bf until the environment has switched on a Boolean flag Rd, it is necessary to use the wait-condition to express that a valid environment will eventually switch on Rd:

$$(\{Bf, Rd\},\{Dn\})::(\neg Dn, Dn\Leftrightarrow\overleftarrow{Dn},\neg Rd, Bf=[A]\frown\overleftarrow{Bf}\wedge\neg\overleftarrow{Dn}\wedge\overleftarrow{Rd}\wedge Dn, Dn)$$

The guar-condition implies that the implementation cannot change the value of Rd from false to true, and moreover that the implementation can add A to $Buff$ only when Rd is switched on.

3 Deduction Rules

The object of this section is to formulate a number of deduction-rules for the development of valid specified programs. Additional rules needed for the completeness proof, and some useful adaptation rules are given as an appendix.

Given a list of expressions r, a set of variables ϑ, and three assertions A, B and C, where at least A is unary, then $\overleftarrow{r}$ denotes the list of expressions that can be obtained from r by hooking all free variables in r, $\overleftarrow{A}$ denotes the assertion that can be obtained from A by hooking all free variables in A, I_ϑ denotes the assertion $\bigwedge_{x\in\vartheta} x=\overleftarrow{x}$, while $B \mid C$ denotes an assertion characterising the 'relational composition' of B and C, in other words, $(s_1,s_2)\models B\mid C$ iff there is a state s_3 such that $(s_1,s_3)\models B$ and $(s_3,s_2)\models C$. Moreover, B^+ denotes an assertion characterising the transitive closure of B, B^* denotes an assertion characterising the reflexive and transitive closure of B, while A^B denotes an assertion characterising any state that can be reached from A by a finite number of B steps. This means that $s_1\models A^B$ iff there is a state s_2 such that $(s_2,s_1)\models\overleftarrow{A}\wedge B^*$.

The *consequence*-rule

$$\frac{\begin{array}{l} P_2 \Rightarrow P_1 \\ R_2 \Rightarrow R_1 \\ W_1 \Rightarrow W_2 \\ G_1 \Rightarrow G_2 \\ E_1 \Rightarrow E_2 \\ z \ \underline{\text{sat}} \ (\vartheta, \alpha) :: (P_1, R_1, W_1, G_1, E_1) \end{array}}{z \ \underline{\text{sat}} \ (\vartheta, \alpha) :: (P_2, R_2, W_2, G_2, E_2)}$$

is perhaps the easiest to understand. It basically states that it is always sound to strengthen the assumptions and weaken the commitments.

The *assignment*-rule is formulated in two steps. The first version

$$\frac{\overleftarrow{P^R} \wedge v = \overleftarrow{r} \wedge I_{\vartheta \setminus \{v\}} \Rightarrow (G \vee I_\vartheta) \wedge E}{v := r \ \underline{\text{sat}} \ (\vartheta, \{\}) :: (P, R, \text{false}, G, R^* \mid E \mid R^*)}$$

is sufficient whenever the set of auxiliary variables is empty. Since the assignment-statement is atomic, there is only one atomic step due to the actual program. Moreover, the environment may interfere a finite number of times both before and after. Since the initial state is assumed to satisfy the pre-condition P, and any change of global state due to the environment is assumed to satisfy the rely-condition R, it follows that the atomic step in which the actual assignment takes place satisfies $\overleftarrow{P^R} \wedge v = \overleftarrow{r} \wedge I_{\vartheta \setminus \{v\}}$. But then it is clear from the premise that this atomic step satisfies G if the state is changed, and I_ϑ otherwise. Moreover, it follows that the overall effect is characterised by $R^* \mid E \mid R^*$.

To grasp the intuition behind the general rule

$$\frac{\overleftarrow{P^R} \wedge v = \overleftarrow{r} \wedge I_{\vartheta \setminus \{v\}} \wedge a = \overleftarrow{u} \wedge I_{\alpha \setminus \{a\}} \Rightarrow (G \vee I_{\vartheta \cup \alpha}) \wedge E}{v := r \ \underline{\text{sat}} \ (\vartheta, \alpha) :: (P, R, \text{false}, G, R^* \mid E \mid R^*)} \qquad a \leftarrow_{(\vartheta,\alpha)} u$$

remember that the execution of an assignment-statement $v := r$ actually corresponds to the execution of an assignment-statement of the form $v \frown a := r \frown u$ where $a \leftarrow_{(\vartheta,\alpha)} u$. Thus, the only real difference from the above is that the premise must guarantee that the assignment-statement can be extended with auxiliary structure in such a way that the specified changes to both the auxiliary variables and the programming variables will indeed take place.

The *parallel*-rule is also easier to understand when designed in several steps. The first rule

$$\frac{\begin{array}{l} z_1 \ \underline{\text{sat}} \ (\vartheta, \alpha) :: (P, R \vee G_2, \text{false}, G_1, E_1) \\ z_2 \ \underline{\text{sat}} \ (\vartheta, \alpha) :: (P, R \vee G_1, \text{false}, G_2, E_2) \end{array}}{\{z_1 \parallel z_2\} \ \underline{\text{sat}} \ (\vartheta, \alpha) :: (P, R, \text{false}, G_1 \vee G_2, E_1 \wedge E_2)}$$

is sufficient whenever neither of the two processes can become blocked. The important thing to realise is that the rely-condition of the first premise allows any interference due to z_2, and similarly that the rely-condition of the second premise allows any interference due to z_1. Thus since the eff-condition covers interference both before the implementation's first atomic step and after the implementation's last atomic step, it is clear from the two premises that $\{z_1 \parallel z_2\}$ terminates, that any atomic step by the implementation, which changes the global-state, satisfies $G_1 \vee G_2$, and that the overall effect satisfies $E_1 \wedge E_2$.

The next version

$$\frac{\begin{array}{l}\neg(W_1 \wedge E_2) \wedge \neg(W_2 \wedge E_1) \wedge \neg(W_1 \wedge W_2) \\ z_1 \ \underline{\text{sat}}\ (\vartheta, \alpha)::(P, R \vee G_2, W_1, G_1, E_1) \\ z_2 \ \underline{\text{sat}}\ (\vartheta, \alpha)::(P, R \vee G_1, W_2, G_2, E_2)\end{array}}{\{z_1 \parallel z_2\} \ \underline{\text{sat}}\ (\vartheta, \alpha)::(P, R, \text{false}, G_1 \vee G_2, E_1 \wedge E_2)}$$

is sufficient whenever $\{z_1 \parallel z_2\}$ cannot become blocked. It follows from the second premise that z_1 can be blocked only in a state which satisfies W_1 when executed in an environment characterised by P and $R \vee G_2$. Moreover, the third premise implies that z_2 can be blocked only in a state which satisfies W_2 when executed in an environment characterised by P and $R \vee G_1$. But then, since the first premise implies that z_1 cannot be blocked after z_2 has terminated, that z_2 cannot be blocked after z_1 has terminated, and that z_1 and z_2 cannot be blocked at the same time, it follows that $\{z_1 \parallel z_2\}$ cannot become blocked in an environment characterised by P and R.

This rule can easily be extended to deal with the general case:

$$\frac{\begin{array}{l}\neg(W_1 \wedge E_2) \wedge \neg(W_2 \wedge E_1) \wedge \neg(W_1 \wedge W_2) \\ z_1 \ \underline{\text{sat}}\ (\vartheta, \alpha)::(P, R \vee G_2, W \vee W_1, G_1, E_1) \\ z_2 \ \underline{\text{sat}}\ (\vartheta, \alpha)::(P, R \vee G_1, W \vee W_2, G_2, E_2)\end{array}}{\{z_1 \parallel z_2\} \ \underline{\text{sat}}\ (\vartheta, \alpha)::(P, R, W, G_1 \vee G_2, E_1 \wedge E_2)}$$

The idea is that W characterises the states in which the overall program can be blocked. This rule can of course be generalised further to deal with more than two processes:

$$\frac{\begin{array}{l}\neg(W_j \wedge \bigwedge_{k=1,k\neq j}^{m}(W_k \vee E_k))_{1\leq j\leq m} \\ z_j \ \underline{\text{sat}}\ (\vartheta, \alpha)::(P, R \vee \bigvee_{k=1,k\neq j}^{m} G_k, W \vee W_j, G_j, E_j)_{1\leq j\leq m}\end{array}}{\|_{j=1}^{m} z_j \ \underline{\text{sat}}\ (\vartheta, \alpha)::(P, R, W, \bigvee_{j=1}^{m} G_j, \bigwedge_{j=1}^{m} E_j)}$$

Here, $\|_{j=1}^{m} z_j$ denotes any program that can be obtained from $z_1 \parallel \ldots \parallel z_m$ by adding curly brackets. The 'first' premise ensures that whenever process j is blocked in a state s, such that $s \models \neg W \wedge W_j$, then there is at least one other process which is enabled. The last rule is 'deducible' from the basic rules of LSP.

The *await*-rule is related to the assignment-rule. Again the explanation is split into two steps. The first version

$$\frac{z \ \underline{\text{sat}}\ (\vartheta, \{\,\})::(P^R \wedge b, \text{false}, \text{false}, \text{true}, (G \vee I_\vartheta) \wedge E)}{\text{await } b \text{ do } z \text{ od } \underline{\text{sat}}\ (\vartheta, \{\,\})::(P, R, P^R \wedge \neg b, G, R^* \mid E \mid R^*)}$$

is sufficient whenever the set of auxiliary variables is empty. The statement can be blocked only in a state which does not satisfy the Boolean test b and can be reached from a state which satisfies the pre-condition P by a finite number of R-steps. This motivates the conclusion's wait-condition. The environment is syntactically constrained from interfering with the await-statement's body, which explains the choice of rely- and wait-conditions in the premise. Moreover, the await-statement's body is required to terminate for any state which satisfies $P^R \wedge b$. The rest should follow easily from the discussion above.

With respect to the general version

$$\frac{\begin{array}{l}E_1 \mid (I_\vartheta \wedge a = \overleftarrow{u} \wedge I_{\alpha\setminus\{a\}}) \Rightarrow (G \vee I_{\vartheta\cup\alpha}) \wedge E_2 \\ z \ \underline{\text{sat}}\ (\vartheta, \alpha)::(P^R \wedge b, \text{false}, \text{false}, \text{true}, E_1)\end{array}}{\text{await } b \text{ do } z \text{ od } \underline{\text{sat}}\ (\vartheta, \alpha)::(P, R, P^R \wedge \neg b, G, R^* \mid E_2 \mid R^*)} \qquad a \leftarrow_{(\vartheta,\alpha)} u$$

remember that the execution of an await-statement await b do z od corresponds to the execution of a statement of the form await b do $z'; a := u$ od, where $z \overset{(\vartheta,\alpha)}{\hookrightarrow} z'$ and $a \leftarrow_{(\vartheta,\alpha)} u$. Thus, given the assumptions about the environment, the effect of z' is characterised by E_1, while E_2 characterises the effect of $z'; a := u$. Moreover, the atomic step representing the 'execution' of $z'; a := u$ satisfies G if the state is changed, and $I_{\vartheta\cup\alpha}$ otherwise. This explains the 'new' premise.

4 Simplifying Notation

To make specifications more readable, a *process* scheme

> *Name*(*In*) *Out*
> glo g_dcl
> aux a_dcl
>
> pre P
> rely R
> wait W
> guar G
> eff E,

which corresponds to VDM's operation concept, has been found helpful. Not surprisingly, *Name* is the name of the process, *In* is the list of input parameters, while *Out* is the list of output parameters. Moreover, global variables are declared in g_dcl, while *a-dcl* is used to declare auxiliary variables. Finally, P, R, W, G and E denote respectively the pre-, rely-, wait-, guar- and eff-conditions. Input and output parameters should be interpreted in the same way as in [Jon90].

In VDM [Jon90] it is indicated in the declaration of a variable whether the operation has write access to the variable or only read access. If an operation has no write access to a variable, clearly its value will be left unchanged. An obvious generalisation to the concurrent case is to declare variables according to whether

- both the process and the environment have write access,
- the process has write access and the environment has only read access,
- the environment has write access and the process has only read access,
- both the process and the environment have only read access.

However, because of the existence of the await-statement, a process may update a global variable x in such a way that this is invisible from the outside, namely by ensuring that x always has the same value when an atomic statement terminates as x had when the same atomic statement was entered. Thus, it seems more sensible to use the following convention: For any variable x (global or auxiliary), then

- icec x (internal change, external change) — means that both the process and the environment can do observable changes to x,
- ices x (internal change, external stable) — means that only the process can do observable changes to x,
- isec x (internal stable, external change) — means that only the environment can do observable changes to x,
- ises x (internal stable, external stable) — means that neither the process nor the environment can do observable changes to x.

In the style of VDM, if it is clear from g_dcl or a_dcl that a particular variable cannot be changed (in an observable way) by a process, its environment or both, then this will not be restated in the rely-, guar- and eff-conditions of the process. For example, if isec x is a declaration in g_dcl, then it is clear that any atomic change of state by the process will satisfy $x = \overleftarrow{x}$, but to keep the specifications as simple as possible, this does not have to be restated in the guar-condition, although it may be added as an extra conjunct when proofs are undertaken.

When proving properties of programs it is often helpful to insert assertions into the code. For example, the sequential program

$$\{\mathsf{true}\}\ \mathsf{while}\ x > 0\ \mathsf{do}\ \{x > 0\}\ x := x - 1\ \mathsf{od}\ \{x \leq 0\}$$

has three such assertions. The first and last characterise respectively the initial and final states, while the one in the middle describes the state each time the program counter is 'situated' between the Boolean test and the assignment-statement. Programs will be annotated in a similar style below, but because the assertions may have occurrences of hooked variables, and because the environment may interfere, it is necessary to discuss the meaning of such assertions in more detail. Observe that annotated programs are not a part of the formal system LSP; annotated programs are introduced here only to make it easier for the reader to follow the argumentation.

The annotations will have occurrences of hooked variables when this is convenient. The hooked variables are supposed to refer to the initial state with respect to the particular piece of code in which the annotation occur. Moreover, the truth of the annotations is supposed to be maintained by the environment. For example, if the environment is restricted from updating x, then the annotated program

$$\{x = \overleftarrow{x}\}\ x := x + 5;\ \{x = \overleftarrow{x} + 5\}\ x := x + 3\ \{x = \overleftarrow{x} + 8\},$$

states that x equals its initial value until the first assignment-statement is executed, that the difference between the value of x and its initial value is 5, when the program counter is situated between the first and the second assignment-statement, and that the difference between the value of x and its initial value is 8 after the second assignment-statement has terminated. If the rely-condition is changed to $x > \overleftarrow{x}$, the annotations must be updated as below

$$\{x \geq \overleftarrow{x}\}\ x := x + 5;\ \{x \geq \overleftarrow{x} + 5\}\ x := x + 3\ \{x \geq \overleftarrow{x} + 8\}.$$

5 Set Partition

Given two non-empty, disjoint sets of natural numbers, S and L; the task is to design a program which terminates in a state where the maximum element of S is less than the minimum element of L. The sizes of the two sets must remain unchanged. Moreover, after termination, the union of S and L is required to equal the union of their initial values. It is assumed that the program will only be used in an environment which does not interfere with S and L.

This informal specification can be translated into a more mathematical notation:

Sort()
glo ices S: set of $\mathbb{N}$, L: set of $\mathbb{N}$
aux

pre $S \cap L = \{\,\} \wedge S \neq \{\,\} \wedge L \neq \{\,\}$
rely false
wait false
guar true
eff $\#S = \#\overleftarrow{S} \wedge \#L = \#\overleftarrow{L} \wedge$
$S \cup L = \overleftarrow{S} \cup \overleftarrow{L} \wedge max(S) < min(L).$

It follows from the declarations of S and L (and also from the rely-condition) that they will not be updated by the environment. The wait-condition implies that a correct implementation will never become blocked. The guar-condition allows the implementor to update S and L as he likes. The rest should be clear from the informal specification.

The algorithm (inspired from [Bar85], [Dij82]) employs two processes called respectively *Small* and *Large*. The basic idea is as follows:

- The process *Small* starts by finding the maximum element of S. This integer is sent on to *Large* and then subtracted from S. The task of *Large* is to add the received integer to L, and thereafter send the minimum element of L (which by then contains the integer just received from *Small*) back to *Small* and remove it from L. The process *Small* adds the element sent from *Large* to S. Then, if the maximum of S equals the integer just received from *Large*, it follows that the maximum of S is less than the minimum of L and the algorithm terminates. Otherwise, the whole procedure is repeated. Since the difference between the maximum of S and the minimum of L is decreased at each iteration, it follows that the program will eventually terminate.

The variables Mx: N and Mn: N simulate respectively 'the channel' from *Small* to *Large* and 'the channel' from *Large* to *Small*. To secure that the two processes stay in step, the Boolean variable Flg: B is introduced. When *Small* switches on Flg, it means that *Large* may read the next value from Mx, and when *Large* makes Flg false, it signals that Mn is ready to be read by *Small*. The adding, finding the maximum and sending section of *Small* is mutually exclusive with the adding, finding the minimum and sending section of *Large*. The only thing the process *Small* is allowed to do while Flg is true, is to remove from S the integer it just sent to *Large*. Similarly, when Flg is false, *Large* is only allowed to remove the element it just sent to *Small*.

This means that an implementation should be of the form

blo $Mx: \mathbb{N}, Mn: \mathbb{N}, Flg: \mathbb{B}; Init(); Conc()$ olb

where *Init* initialises the local state, and *Conc* represents the parallel composition of *Small* and *Large*.

To make it easier to formulate and reason about properties satisfied by the concurrent part of the implementation, *Init* will simulate the first iteration of the algorithm; in other words, perform the first interchange of values. This means that:

Init()
glo ices S: set of $\mathbb{N}$, L: set of $\mathbb{N}$, $Mx: \mathbb{N}, Mn: \mathbb{N}, Flg: \mathbb{B}$
aux

pre $S \cap L = \{\} \wedge S \neq \{\} \wedge L \neq \{\}$
rely false
wait false
guar true
eff $\#S = \#\overleftarrow{S} \wedge \#L = \#\overleftarrow{L} \wedge S \cup L = \overleftarrow{S} \cup \overleftarrow{L} \wedge$
$Mn \leq Mx \wedge S \cap L = \{\} \wedge Mx = max(S) \wedge$
$Mn \in S \wedge Mn < min(L) \wedge \neg Flg.$

Basically, *Init* simulates 'the sending' of one element in both directions. Thus, the next process to transfer a value (if necessary) is *Small*, which explains the restriction on Flg. Moreover, *Small* has already determined the 'new' maximum of S. The implementation of *Init* is not very challenging. The program below is obviously sufficient:

$$Mx := max(S); L := L \cup \{Mx\}; S := S - \{Mx\};$$
$$Mn := min(L); S := S \cup \{Mn\}; L := L - \{Mn\};$$
$$Flg := \text{false}; Mx := max(S).$$

The next step is to characterise a few properties that will be invariantly true for the concurrent part of the implementation. Since for both processes the previously sent element is removed before the actual process starts to look for a new integer to send, and since the processes stay in step, it follows that

$$S \cap L \subseteq \{Mn, Mx\}.$$

Moreover, because *Large* will return the integer just received if the maximum of S is less than the minimum of L, it is also true that

$$Mn \leq Mx.$$

To simplify the reasoning, let *uInv* (from now on called the *unary* invariant) denote the conjunction of these two assertions.

To ensure maintenance of the original integers it is required that any atomic change of state satisfies

$$S \cup L \cup \{Mx, Mn\} = \overleftarrow{S} \cup \overleftarrow{L} \cup \{\overleftarrow{Mx}, \overleftarrow{Mn}\}.$$

This is of course not enough on its own; however, if the conjunction of the eff-conditions of the two processes implies that $\{Mx, Mn\} \subseteq S \cup L$, it follows easily from the eff-condition of *Init* that the desired maintenance property is satisfied by the overall program.

Since the first interchange of elements has already taken place in *Init*, it is clear that any transition by either *Small* or *Large* will satisfy

$$Mx \leq \overleftarrow{Mx} \wedge Mn \geq \overleftarrow{Mn}.$$

The only possible change of state due to *Large* while *Flg* is false, is that *Mn* is removed from L, and the only possible change of state due to *Small* while *Flg* is true, is that *Mx* is removed from S. Moreover, since *Small* never updates *Mn* and L, and *Large* never updates *Mx* and S, it follows that any atomic step satisfies the two assertions

$$\neg\overleftarrow{Flg} \Rightarrow Mn = \overleftarrow{Mn} \wedge (L \cup \{Mn\} = \overleftarrow{L} \vee L = \overleftarrow{L}),$$
$$\overleftarrow{Flg} \Rightarrow Mx = \overleftarrow{Mx} \wedge (S \cup \{Mx\} = \overleftarrow{S} \vee S = \overleftarrow{S}).$$

To prove that the number of elements in S, when *Small* terminates, equals the set's initial size, and similarly for L, any atomic step should also satisfy the following two assertions:

$$\neg\overleftarrow{Flg} \wedge Flg \Rightarrow (Mx = Mn \vee Mx \notin L) \wedge Mn \in S,$$
$$\overleftarrow{Flg} \wedge \neg Flg \Rightarrow (Mx = Mn \vee Mn \notin S) \wedge Mx \in L.$$

Let *bInv* (from now on called the *binary* invariant) denote the conjunction of these six assertions.

It may be argued that *uInv* and *bInv* should have had arguments indicating which part of the global state they affect. However, this has been ignored here because of the large number of arguments needed. One way to reduce the number of arguments is to introduce records in the style of VDM.

The process *Small* will become blocked only when it is ready to enter its critical section and *Large* has not yet finished its critical section. This means that *Small* will wait only in a state which satisfies *Flg*. Similarly, it is clear that *Large* will be held back only in a state characterised by $\neg Flg$. The conjunction of these two assertions is obviously inconsistent, which means that *Small* and *Large* cannot be blocked at the same time. One way to make sure that neither of the processes can be blocked after the other process has terminated, is to introduce an auxiliary variable $Trm\colon \mathbb{B}$, which is required to be false initially and is first switched on when *Small* leaves its critical section for the last time; in other words, when *Mx* equals *Mn*. If the unary invariant *uInv* is strengthened with the conjunct

$$Trm \Rightarrow Flg,$$

and the binary invariant *bInv* is strengthened with the two conjuncts

$$\neg\overleftarrow{Trm} \wedge Trm \Leftrightarrow \neg\overleftarrow{Flg} \wedge Flg \wedge Mx = Mn,$$
$$\overleftarrow{Trm} \Rightarrow Trm.$$

it follows that *Trm* is true after *Large* has terminated, and that *Flg* is true after *Small* has terminated. But then, since *Small* can become blocked only in a state which satisfies $Flg \wedge \neg Trm$, and *Large* can become blocked only in a state which satisfies $\neg Flg$, it follows that deadlock is impossible.

From the discussion above it is clear that *Small* does not need write access to *L* and *Mn*. Similarly, *Large* will never have to change the values of *S*, *Mx* and *Trm*. To secure mutual exclusion *Large* must maintain the falsity of *Flg*, while *Small* in return must guarantee never to make *Flg* false. Thus, in a more formal notation:

Small()
glo ices $S\colon$ set of $\mathbb{N}, Mx\colon \mathbb{N}$
isec $L\colon$ set of $\mathbb{N}, Mn\colon \mathbb{N}$
icec $Flg\colon \mathbb{B}$
aux ices $Trm\colon \mathbb{B}$

pre $Mx = max(S) \wedge Mx \notin L \wedge Mn \in S \wedge \neg Flg \wedge \neg Trm \wedge uInv$
rely $(\neg\overleftarrow{Flg} \Rightarrow \neg Flg) \wedge bInv \wedge uInv$
wait $Flg \wedge \neg Trm$
guar $(\overleftarrow{Flg} \Rightarrow Flg) \wedge bInv \wedge uInv$
eff $\#S = \#\overleftarrow{S} \wedge Mx = Mn \wedge Mx = max(S) \wedge Flg,$

Large()
glo isec $S\colon$ set of $\mathbb{N}, Mx\colon \mathbb{N}$
ices $L\colon$ set of $\mathbb{N}, Mn\colon \mathbb{N}$
icec $Flg\colon \mathbb{B}$
aux isec $Trm\colon \mathbb{B}$

pre $Mx \notin L \wedge Mn \in S \wedge Mn < min(L) \wedge \neg Flg \wedge \neg Trm \wedge uInv$
rely $(\overleftarrow{Flg} \Rightarrow Flg) \wedge bInv \wedge uInv$
wait $\neg Flg$
guar $(\neg\overleftarrow{Flg} \Rightarrow \neg Flg) \wedge bInv \wedge uInv$
eff $\#L = \#\overleftarrow{L} \wedge Mx = Mn \wedge Mn < min(L) \wedge Trm.$

Since the wait-conditions of both processes are inconsistent with the wait- and eff-conditions of the other process, it follows by the eff- (see appendix), consequence-, and parallel-rules that the concurrent part of the implementation satisfies:

Conc()
glo ices $S\colon$ set of $\mathbb{N}, L\colon$ set of $\mathbb{N}, Mx\colon \mathbb{N}, Mn\colon \mathbb{N}, Flg\colon \mathbb{B}$
aux ices $Trm\colon \mathbb{B}$

pre $Mx = max(S) \wedge Mx \notin L \wedge Mn \in S \wedge Mn < min(L) \wedge \neg Flg \wedge \neg Trm \wedge uInv$
rely false
wait false
guar true
eff $\#S = \#\overleftarrow{S} \wedge \#L = \#\overleftarrow{L} \wedge Mx = Mn \wedge Mx = max(S) \wedge Mn < min(L) \wedge bInv^{*} \wedge uInv,$

which together with *Init* gives the desired overall effect.

How should *Small* and *Large* best be decomposed? Obviously, in both cases a while-construct is needed. One possible strategy is the following:

```
blo V_S: B;                                blo V_L: B;
    V_S := (Mx ≠ Mn);                          await Flg do skip od;
    while V_S do                               V_L := (Mx ≠ Mn);
        Sml(); V_S := (Mx ≠ Mn)                while V_L do
    od;                                            Lrg(); V_L := (Mx ≠ Mn)
    Flg := true                                od
olb,                                       olb.
```

For both loops the obvious termination expression is $Mx - Mn$. Moreover, since

$$\overleftarrow{Mn} < \overleftarrow{Mx} \wedge (Mx < \overleftarrow{Mx} \vee Mx = Mn) \wedge bInv \wedge uInv \Rightarrow 0 \leq Mx - Mn < \overleftarrow{Mx} - \overleftarrow{Mn},$$
$$\overleftarrow{Mn} < \overleftarrow{Mx} \wedge Mn > \overleftarrow{Mn} \wedge bInv \wedge uInv \Rightarrow 0 \leq Mx - Mn < \overleftarrow{Mx} - \overleftarrow{Mn},$$

it follows easily that both loops terminate, and that the specifications of *Small* and *Large* are satisfied, if it can be proved that *Sml* and *Lrg* are characterised by:

Sml()

glo	ices	S: set of $\mathbb{N}$, Mx: $\mathbb{N}$
	isec	L: set of $\mathbb{N}$, Mn: $\mathbb{N}$
	icec	Flg: $\mathbb{B}$
aux	ices	Trm: $\mathbb{B}$

pre	$Mn < Mx \wedge Mx = max(S) \wedge Mx \notin L \wedge Mn \in S \wedge \neg Flg \wedge \neg Trm \wedge uInv$
rely	$(\neg\overleftarrow{Flg} \Rightarrow \neg Flg) \wedge bInv \wedge uInv$
wait	$Flg \wedge \neg Trm$
guar	$(\overleftarrow{Flg} \Rightarrow Flg) \wedge bInv \wedge uInv$
eff	$\#S = \#\overleftarrow{S} \wedge Mx = max(S) \wedge Mn \in S \wedge (Mx < \overleftarrow{Mx} \vee Mx = Mn) \wedge \neg Flg \wedge \neg Trm$,

Lrg()

glo	isec	S: set of $\mathbb{N}$, Mx: $\mathbb{N}$
	ices	L: set of $\mathbb{N}$, Mn: $\mathbb{N}$
	icec	Flg: $\mathbb{B}$
aux	isec	Trm: $\mathbb{B}$

pre	$Mn < Mx \wedge Mx \notin L \wedge Mn \in S \wedge Mn < min(L) \wedge Flg \wedge \neg Trm \wedge uInv$
rely	$(\overleftarrow{Flg} \Rightarrow Flg) \wedge bInv \wedge uInv$
wait	$\neg Flg$
guar	$(\neg\overleftarrow{Flg} \Rightarrow \neg Flg) \wedge bInv \wedge uInv$
eff	$\#L = \#\overleftarrow{L} \wedge Mn < min(L) \wedge Mn > \overleftarrow{Mn} \wedge (Mx = Mn \Leftrightarrow Trm)$.

It can be shown that *Sml* is satisfied by the following annotated program:

$$\{\#S = \#\overleftarrow{S} \wedge Mx = \overleftarrow{Mx} \wedge Mn < Mx \wedge Mx = max(S) \wedge Mn \in S \wedge Mx \notin L \wedge \neg Flg \wedge \neg Trm \wedge bInv^* \wedge uInv\}$$

Flg: = true;

$$\{\#S = \#\overleftarrow{S} \wedge Mx = \overleftarrow{Mx} \wedge Mx = max(S) \wedge (\neg Flg \Rightarrow Mx = Mn \vee (Mn \notin S \wedge Mx \in L)) \wedge \neg Trm \wedge bInv^* \wedge uInv\}$$

$S := S \setminus \{Mx\}$;

$$\{\#S = \#\overleftarrow{S} - 1 \wedge Mx = \overleftarrow{Mx} \wedge (S \neq \{\,\} \Rightarrow Mx > max(S)) \wedge (\neg Flg \Rightarrow Mx = Mn \vee (Mn \notin S \wedge Mx \in L)) \wedge \neg Trm \wedge bInv^* \wedge uInv\}$$

await $\neg Flg$ do skip od;

$$\{\#S = \#\overleftarrow{S} - 1 \wedge Mx = \overleftarrow{Mx} \wedge (S \neq \{\,\} \Rightarrow Mx > max(S)) \wedge (Mx = Mn \vee (Mn \notin S \wedge Mx \in L)) \wedge \neg Flg \wedge \neg Trm \wedge bInv^* \wedge uInv\}$$

$S := S \cup \{Mn\};$

$$\{\#S = \#\overleftarrow{S} \wedge Mx = \overleftarrow{Mx} \wedge ((Mx > max(S) \wedge Mx \in L) \vee (Mx = max(S) \wedge Mx = Mn)) \wedge Mn \in S \wedge \neg Flg \wedge \neg Trm \wedge bInv^* \wedge uInv\}$$

$Mx := max(S);$

$$\{\#S = \#\overleftarrow{S} \wedge ((Mx < \overleftarrow{Mx} \wedge Mx \notin L) \vee Mx = Mn) \wedge Mx = max(S) \wedge Mn \in S \wedge \neg Flg \wedge \neg Trm \wedge bInv^* \wedge uInv\}.$$

Similarly, *Lrg* can be implemented as below:

$$\{\#L = \#\overleftarrow{L} \wedge Mn = \overleftarrow{Mn} \wedge Mn < Mx \wedge Mx \notin L \wedge Mn \in S \wedge Mn < min(L) \wedge Flg \wedge \neg Trm \wedge bInv^* \wedge uInv\}$$

$L := L \cup \{Mx\};$

$$\{\#L = \#\overleftarrow{L} + 1 \wedge Mn = \overleftarrow{Mn} \wedge Mx \in L \wedge Mn \in S \wedge Mn < min(L) \wedge Flg \wedge \neg Trm \wedge bInv^* \wedge uInv\}$$

$Mn := min(L);$

$$\{\#L = \#\overleftarrow{L} + 1 \wedge Mn > \overleftarrow{Mn} \wedge Mx \in L \wedge (Mx = Mn \vee Mn \notin S) \wedge Mn = min(L) \wedge Flg \wedge \neg Trm \wedge bInv^* \wedge uInv\}$$

$Flg :=$ false;

$$\{\#L = \#\overleftarrow{L} + 1 \wedge Mn > \overleftarrow{Mn} \wedge (Flg \Rightarrow Mx = Mn \vee (Mx \notin L \wedge Mn \in S)) \wedge Mn = min(L) \wedge (Flg \Rightarrow (Mx = Mn \Leftrightarrow Trm)) \wedge bInv^* \wedge uInv\}$$

$L := L \setminus \{Mn\};$

$$\{\#L = \#\overleftarrow{L} \wedge Mn > \overleftarrow{Mn} \wedge (Flg \Rightarrow Mx = Mn \vee (Mx \notin L \wedge Mn \in S)) \wedge Mn < min(L) \wedge (Flg \Rightarrow (Mx = Mn \Leftrightarrow Trm)) \wedge bInv^* \wedge uInv\}$$

await Flg do skip od

$$\{\#L = \#\overleftarrow{L} \wedge Mn > \overleftarrow{Mn} \wedge (Mx = Mn \vee (Mx \notin L \wedge Mn \in S)) \wedge Mn < min(L) \wedge Flg \wedge (Mx = Mn \Leftrightarrow Trm) \wedge bInv^* \wedge uInv\}.$$

6 Discussion

It has been shown above how LSP can be employed to reason about shared-state concurrency in the style of VDM. The use of two invariants, a unary invariant, which is true initially and maintained by each atomic step, and a binary invariant, which is satisfied by any atomic change to the global state, simplified the design of the set-partition algorithm. This way of structuring a development has also been used on other examples with similar effect [Stø90]. Related invariant concepts are discussed in [Jon81], [GR89], [XH91].

This paper has only proposed a set of *program-decomposition* rules. How to formulate sufficiently strong *data-refinement* rules is still an open question. Jones [Jon81] proposed a refinement-rule for the rely/guarantee-method which can easily be extended to deal with LSP specifications. Unfortunately, as pointed out in [WD88], this refinement-rule is far from complete.

In [Stø90] LSP is proved to be sound with respect to an operational semantics, and it is also shown that LSP is relatively complete under the assumptions that structures are admissible, and that for any first order assertion A and structure π, it is always possible to express an assertion B in L, which is valid in π iff A is well-founded on the set of states in π.

Because the programming language is unfair, the system presented in this paper cannot deal with programs whose algorithms rely upon busy waiting. Thus LSP is incomplete with respect to a *weakly* fair language and even more so for a *strongly* fair programming language. However, this does not mean that fair languages cannot be dealt with in a similar style. In [Stø91b] it is shown how LSP can be modified to handle both weakly fair and strongly fair programming languages.

The program constructs discussed in this paper are deterministic (although they all have a nondeterministic behaviour due to possible interference), and all functions have been required to be total. These constraints are not necessary. It is shown in [Stø90] that LSP can be extended to facilitate both nondeterministic program constructs and partial functions.

The parallel-rule in the Owicki/Gries method [OG76] depends upon a number of tests which only can be carried out after the component processes have been implemented and their proofs have been constructed. This is unacceptable when designing large software products in a top-down style, because erroneous design decisions, taken early in the design process, may remain undetected until the whole program is complete. In the worst case, everything that depends upon such mistakes will have to be thrown away.

To avoid problems of this type a proof method should satisfy what is known as the principle of *compositionality* [dR85] — namely that a program's specification always can be verified on the basis of the specifications of its constitute components, without knowledge of the interior program structure of those components.

LSP can be thought of as a compositional reformulation of the Owicki/Gries method. The rely-, guar- and wait-conditions have been introduced to avoid the final non-interference and freedom-from-deadlock proofs (their additional interference-freedom requirement for total correctness is not correct [AdBO90]). However, there are some additional differences. The programming language differs from theirs in several respects. First of all, variables occurring in the Boolean test of an if- or a while-statement are restricted from being updated by the environment. In the Owicki/Gries language there is no such constraint. On the other hand, in their language await- and parallel-statements are constrained from occurring in the body of an await-statement. No such requirement is stated in this paper. The handling of auxiliary variables has also been changed. Auxiliary variables are only a part of the logic. Moreover, they can be employed both as a verification tool and as a specification tool, while in the Owicki/Gries method they can only be used as a verification tool.

Jones' system [Jon83] can be seen as a restricted version of LSP. There are two main differences. First of all, LSP has a wait-condition which makes it possible to deal with synchronisation. Secondly, because auxiliary variables may be employed both as specification and verification tools, LSP is more expressive.

Stirling's method [Sti88] employs a proof tuple closely related to that of Jones. The main difference is that the rely- and guar-conditions are represented as sets of invariants, while the post-condition is unary, not binary as in Jones' method. Auxiliary variables are implemented as if they were ordinary programming variables, and they cannot be used as a specification tool. Although this method favours top-down development in the style of Jones, it can only be employed for the design of partially correct programs.

Soundararajan [Sou84] uses CSP inspired history variables to state assumptions about the environment. Unfortunately, on many occasions, the use of history variables seems excessive. One advantage with LSP is therefore that the user is free to choose the auxiliary structure he prefers. Another difference is that LSP is not restricted to partial correctness.

Barringer, Kuiper and Pnueli [BKP84] employ temporal logic for the design of parallel programs. Their method can be used to develop nonterminating programs with respect to both safety and general liveness properties, and this formalism is therefore much more general than the one presented in this paper. However, although it is quite possible to employ the same temporal logic to develop totally correct sequential programs, most users would prefer to apply ordinary Hoare-logic in the style of for example VDM [Jon90]. The reason is that Hoare-logic is designed to deal with the sequential case only, and it is therefore both simpler to use and easier to understand than a formalism powerful enough to handle concurrency. A similar distinction can be made between the development of terminating programs versus programs that are not supposed to terminate and regarding different fairness constraints. LSP should be understood as a method specially designed for the development of totally correct shared-state parallel programs.

The Xu/He approach [XH91] is (as pointed out in their paper) inspired by LSP's tuple of five assertions. However, instead of a wait-condition they use a run-condition — the negation of LSP's wait. Another difference is their specification oriented semantics. Moreover, auxiliary variables are dealt with in the Owicki/Gries style. This means that auxiliary variables are implemented as if they were ordinary programming variables and cannot be used as a specification tool.

In LSP, and in most of the methods mentioned above, the syntactic structure of the programming language is used to direct the decomposition of a specification into subspecifications. Some argue that the syntactic structure of a programming language is too close to machine architecture and therefore less suited to guide the design of algorithms — at least at the most abstract levels. Ideas like this have lead to the proposal of action based formalisms like [Bac88], [CM88], [Lam90].

7 Acknowledgements

As mentioned above, this paper is based on the author's PhD-thesis, and I would first all like to thank my supervisor Cliff B. Jones for his help and support. I am also indebted to Howard Barringer, John S. Fitzgerald, Mathai Joseph, Wojciech Penczek and Xu Qiwen. Financial support has been received from the Norwegian Research Council for Science and the Humanities and the Wolfson Foundation.

References

[AdBO90] K. R. Apt, F. S. de Boer, and E. R. Olderog. Proving termination of parallel programs. In W. H. J. Feijen, A. J. M. van Gasteren, D. Gries, and J. Misra, editors, *Beauty Is Our Business, A Birthday Salute to Edsger W. Dijkstra*. Springer-Verlag, 1990.

[Bac88] R. J. R. Back. A calculus of refinments for program derivations. *Acta Informatica*, 25:593–624, 1988.

[Bar85] H. Barringer. *A Survey of Verification Techniques for Parallel Programs*, volume 191 of *Lecture Notes in Computer Science*. Springer-Verlag, 1985.

[BKP84] H. Barringer, R. Kuiper, and A. Pnueli. Now you may compose temporal logic specifications. In *Proc. Sixteenth ACM Symposium on Theory of Computing*, pages 51–63, 1984.

[CM88] K. M. Chandy and J. Misra. *Parallel Program Design, A Foundation*. Addison-Wesley, 1988.

[Dij82] E. W. Dijkstra. A correctness proof for communicating processes: A small exercise. In *Selected Writings on Computing: A Personal Perspective*. Springer-Verlag, 1982.

[dR85] W. P. de Roever. The quest for compositionality, formal models in programming. In F. J. Neuhold and G. Chroust, editors, *Proc. IFIP 85*, pages 181–205, 1985.

[GR89] D. Grosvenor and A. Robinson. An evaluation of rely-guarantee. Unpublished Paper, March 1989.

[Jon81] C. B. Jones. *Development Methods for Computer Programs Including a Notion of Interference.* PhD thesis, Oxford University, 1981.

[Jon83] C. B. Jones. Specification and design of (parallel) programs. In Mason R.E.A., editor, *Proc. Information Processing 83*, pages 321–331, 1983.

[Jon90] C. B. Jones. *Systematic Software Development Using VDM, Second Edition.* Prentice-Hall International, 1990.

[JS90] C. B. Jones and R. C. F. Shaw, editors. *Case Studies in Systematic Software Development.* Prentice Hall International, 1990.

[Lam90] L. Lamport. A temporal logic of actions. Technical Report 57, Digital, Palo Alto, 1990.

[OG76] S. Owicki and D. Gries. An axiomatic proof technique for parallel programs. *Acta Informatica*, 6:319–340, 1976.

[Sou84] N. Soundararajan. A proof technique for parallel programs. *Theoretical Computer Science*, 31:13–29, 1984.

[Sti88] C. Stirling. A generalization of Owicki-Gries's Hoare logic for a concurrent while language. *Theoretical Computer Science*, 58:347–359, 1988.

[Stø90] K. Stølen. *Development of Parallel Programs on Shared Data-Structures.* PhD thesis, University of Manchester, 1990.

[Stø91a] K. Stølen. A method for the development of totally correct shared-state parallel programs. Accepted for CONCUR'91, proceedings will appear in Lecture Notes in Computer Science, 1991.

[Stø91b] K. Stølen. Proving total correctness with respect to fair (shared-state) parallel languages. In preparation, 1991.

[WD88] J. C. P. Woodcock and B. Dickinson. Using VDM with rely and guarantee-conditions. Experiences from a real project. In R. Bloomfield, L. Marshall, and R. Jones, editors, *Proc. 2nd VDM-Europe Symposium, Lecture Notes in Computer Science 328*, pages 434–458, 1988.

[XH91] Q. Xu and J. He. A theory of state-based parallel programming by refinement:part 1. In J. Morris, editor, *Proc. 4th BCS-FACS Refinement Workshop*, 1991.

Additional Rules Needed in Completeness Proof

if: :

$$\frac{z_1 \ \underline{\text{sat}}\ (\vartheta,\alpha)::(P \wedge b, R, W, G, E) \quad z_2 \ \underline{\text{sat}}\ (\vartheta,\alpha)::(P \wedge \neg b, R, W, G, E)}{\text{if } b \text{ then } z_1 \text{ else } z_2 \text{ fi } \underline{\text{sat}}\ (\vartheta,\alpha)::(P, R, W, G, E)}$$

pre: :

$$\frac{z \ \underline{\text{sat}}\ (\vartheta,\alpha)::(P, R, W, G, E)}{z \ \underline{\text{sat}}\ (\vartheta,\alpha)::(P, R, W, G, \overleftarrow{P} \wedge E)}$$

while: :

$$\frac{\begin{array}{l} E \text{ is well-founded} \\ z \ \underline{\text{sat}}\ (\vartheta, \alpha) :: (P \wedge b, R, W, G, P \wedge E) \end{array}}{\text{while } b \text{ do } z \text{ od } \underline{\text{sat}}\ (\vartheta, \alpha) :: (P, R, W, G, (E^{+} \vee R^{*}) \wedge \neg b)}$$

access: :

$$\frac{\begin{array}{l} x \in hid[z] \\ z \ \underline{\text{sat}}\ (\vartheta, \alpha) :: (P, R \wedge x = \overleftarrow{x}, W, G, E) \end{array}}{z \ \underline{\text{sat}}\ (\vartheta, \alpha) :: (P, R, W, G, E)}$$

sequential: :

$$\frac{\begin{array}{l} z_1 \ \underline{\text{sat}}\ (\vartheta, \alpha) :: (P_1, R, W, G, P_2 \wedge E_1) \\ z_2 \ \underline{\text{sat}}\ (\vartheta, \alpha) :: (P_2, R, W, G, E_2) \end{array}}{z_1; z_2 \ \underline{\text{sat}}\ (\vartheta, \alpha) :: (P_1, R, W, G, E_1 \mid E_2)}$$

elimination: :

$$\frac{\begin{array}{l} x \notin \vartheta \\ z \ \underline{\text{sat}}\ (\vartheta, \alpha) :: (P, R, W, G, E) \end{array}}{z \ \underline{\text{sat}}\ (\vartheta, \alpha \setminus \{x\}) :: (\exists x : P, \forall \overleftarrow{x} : \exists x : R, W, G, E)}$$

block: :

$$\frac{z \ \underline{\text{sat}}\ (\vartheta, \alpha) :: (P, R \wedge \bigwedge_{j=1}^{n} x_j = \overleftarrow{x_j}, W, G, E)}{\text{blo } x_1 : T_1, \ldots, x_n : T_n; z \text{ olb } \underline{\text{sat}}\ (\vartheta \setminus \bigcup_{j=1}^{n} \{x_j\}, \alpha) :: (P, R, W, G, E)}$$

Some Useful Adaptation Rules

eff: :

$$\frac{z \ \underline{\text{sat}}\ (\vartheta, \alpha) :: (P, R, W, G, E)}{z \ \underline{\text{sat}}\ (\vartheta, \alpha) :: (P, R, W, G, E \wedge (R \vee G)^{*})}$$

rely: :

$$\frac{z \ \underline{\text{sat}}\ (\vartheta, \alpha) :: (P, R, W, G, E)}{z \ \underline{\text{sat}}\ (\vartheta, \alpha) :: (P, R^{*}, W, G, E)}$$

invariant: :

$$\frac{\begin{array}{l} P \Rightarrow K \\ \overleftarrow{K} \wedge (R \vee G) \Rightarrow K \\ z \ \underline{\text{sat}}\ (\vartheta, \alpha) :: (P, R, W, G, E) \end{array}}{z \ \underline{\text{sat}}\ (\vartheta, \alpha) :: (P, R, K \wedge W, \overleftarrow{K} \wedge G, E)}$$

augment: :

$$\frac{\begin{array}{l} z_2 \overset{(\vartheta \setminus \alpha, \alpha)}{\hookrightarrow} z_1 \\ z_1 \ \underline{\text{sat}}\ (\vartheta, \{\,\}) :: (P, R, W, G, E) \end{array}}{z_2 \ \underline{\text{sat}}\ (\vartheta \setminus \alpha, \alpha) :: (P, R, W, G, E)}$$

stutter: :

$$\frac{z \ \underline{\text{sat}}\ (\vartheta, \alpha) :: (P, R, W, G, E)}{z \ \underline{\text{sat}}\ (\vartheta, \alpha) :: (P, R \vee I_{\vartheta \cup \alpha}, W, G, E)}$$

glo: :

$$\frac{\begin{array}{l} x \notin \vartheta \cup \alpha \\ z \ \underline{\text{sat}}\ (\vartheta, \alpha) :: (P, R, W, G, E) \end{array}}{z \ \underline{\text{sat}}\ (\vartheta \cup \{x\}, \alpha) :: (P, R, W, G \wedge x = \overleftarrow{x}, E)}$$

aux: :

$$\frac{\begin{array}{l} x \notin \vartheta \cup \alpha \\ z \ \underline{\text{sat}}\ (\vartheta, \alpha) :: (P, R, W, G, E) \end{array}}{z \ \underline{\text{sat}}\ (\vartheta, \alpha \cup \{x\}) :: (P, R, W, G \wedge x = \overleftarrow{x}, E)}$$

Reasoning about VDM specifications

Morten Elvang-Gøransson

Department of Computer Science, Building 344

Technical University of Denmark, DK–2800 Lyngby

Abstract

The paper suggests a technique for representing partial recursive functions in Logic for Partial Functions. The technique preserves the least fixed point interpretation of such functions, and in this sense improves the technique hitherto applied to represent VDM specifications.

1 Introduction

A prerequisite for reasoning about a VDM specification is to represent it in a logic by the rules of which reasoning can take place. As pointed out by Cheng and Jones [2] finding good representations is not a trivial job. Cheng and Jones present a problem with their technique for representing VDM functions in Logic for Partial Functions (LPF) [1]. Their representation technique is too loose to capture the least fixed point properties of the represented function.

In this paper we, without any claim of originality, show how a well known technique, independently advocated by Owe [4, 7] and Constable [3], can solve the problem described by Cheng and Jones. The technique allows to represent partial (or general) recursive functions in a way such that their least fixed point properties are preserved. The defining axioms can be extracted directly from the function definitions written in the specification, and it should thus be straight forward to implement it as part of the mural system [6] or similar VDM development support systems.

The reason for restricting the logical interpretation of a partial recursive function to the least fixed point of its defining equation is, from one view point, that the least fixed point contains exactly the information that can be retrieved from the function (definition) through computations. This is the basic motivation for the school of 'least fixed point semantics'. The reader not acquainted with least fixed point semantics is referred to Schmidts book [8], but it is not essential for the understanding of this paper.

We expect the reader to be familiar with VDM in the style of Jones [5].

Outline of paper

Following a short description in §2 of VDM, LPF, and the particular problem we are going to solve, we in §3 adapt Constables theory of General Recursive Arithmetic [3] to our context. §4 gives a solution to the problem of §2, and §5 shows briefly how the more interesting 'challenge problem' stated by Cheng and Jones [2] can be treated with the technique presented in this paper. Some final remarks are placed in §6.

Acknowledgement

I'm grateful to Dr. Olaf Owe for many hints and comments. It was from Olaf that I first learned about the idea described in this paper. I'm also grateful to Professor Cliff B. Jones and to my supervisor Professor Dines Bjørner for their continuous interest in my work.

2 VDM, LPF, and the problem

We will restrict our selves to a subset of VDM by considering only the data type of integers, with the usual arithmetical operators and the conditional (if-then-else), and the booleans, with the usual connectives and quantifiers. The logic for VDM is LPF, where the connectives and quantifiers are given the Kleene interpretation. The turn style, $\vdash$, is given the following interpretation: $P \vdash Q$ if and only if Q is true whenever P is. This is all well known from Jones' book [5]. In this paper we stay as close to Jones' notation as possible, and thus we shall not spend more time on introducing the notation etc.

Consider the following partial function from [2]:

$evenp : \mathsf{Z} \rightarrow \mathsf{B}$

$evenp(i) \ \triangleq \ \textsf{if } i = 0 \textsf{ then true else } evenp(i-2)$

With the usual least fixed point interpretation of function definitions this function definition denotes a function, which will return true for all non-negative even numbers, and which is undefined otherwise.

Following the representation technique described in [2] *evenp* is represented by the following rules:

$$\text{evenp-b}\ \frac{}{evenp(0)}$$

$$\text{evenp-i}\ \frac{evenp(i-2)}{evenp(i)}$$

As pointed out in [2] the problem with this representation is that it is consistent for all fixed points of the definition of *evenp*, not only the least one.

One example highlighting this problem is, still following [2], that:

$$evenp(i) \vdash (i \ \mathsf{mod}\ 2 \ = \ 0),$$

which is obviously true for a least fixed point interpretation of *evenp*, is not provable from the above representation.

Thus, the representation technique applied by Cheng and Jones is too loose, but, as we shall see next, this looseness can be tightened by adopting Constables technique [3].

3 Representation of partial recursive functions

The following section is basically a modification of some results from Constables theory of General Recursive Arithmetic (GRA) [3] to the VDM style. Constable asserts that the representation technique applied in GRA is faithful to the whole class of partial recursive functions. We will concentrate on exposing the actual machinery. The small changes we have imposed on Constables theory do not have any effect on the meta logical results. Constable gives another interpretation of the connectives in the logic, and a more elaborate definition of function definitions, proofs, etc. In this paper we have no need for this extra machinery and the difference in the interpretation of the logical connectives is without importance. We will restrict the presentation to only cover unary functions and predicates, but the extension to the n-ary case is without problems.

Assume that we have a partial recursive function:

$$f : T \rightarrow T$$

$$f(x) \triangleq exp(x).$$

$exp(x)$ is defined by composition of the basic arithmetical operators, other defined functions, and possibly f is self. T may be any VDM data type in principle, but we will only consider functions defined over the integers.

For any such partial recursive function, f, there will be some, possibly empty, subset of T for which f is total, i.e. has a well defined value for each argument in the subset. This observation is the key point in Constables (and Owes) representation technique(s) for partial recursive functions. Let $\mathbf{D}_f$: $T \rightarrow \mathsf{B}$ be a total predicate that, for each object x in T, is true whenever f is defined for x, and false otherwise. From the definition of a partial recursive function, f, it is possible to extract an inductive definition of $\mathbf{D}_f$. $\mathbf{D}_f$ is called the characteristic predicate for f. By guarding any application of f by its characteristic predicate it is forced to behave as the least fixed point of its defining equation. Characteristic predicates are not allowed to occur in function definitions.

3.1 Well definedness

An inductive definition of well definedness is given for all syntactic constructs in the language of LPF. For instance, for an application, $f(t)$, to be well defined, written $\triangle[f(t)]$, it is sufficient that t is defined, $\triangle[t]$, and that f has a well defined value at t, i.e. that $\mathbf{D}_f(t)$ holds.

Since we only give examples of functions over the integers, there is no need to distinguish different types. It is, however, straight forward to index the $\triangle$-symbols with types to define a many typed version. The characteristic predicates for the basic arithmetical operators over the integers are assumed to be known a priori. For instance we have that $\mathbf{D}_+(x, y)$ is true, whenever x and y are integers. For defined functions all we will have are inductive definitions of their characteristic predicates. In order to extract information from these definitions, an induction rule will be added for each such inductive definition.

The $\triangle$-symbol is a syntactical meta operator not part of the basic language. For each formula P (term t) we read $\triangle[P]$ ($\triangle[t]$) as 'P is well defined' ('t is well defined').

From the Kleene interpretation (refer to [1]) of the logical connectives we have:

$$
\begin{array}{lll}
\triangle[\neg P] & \text{iff} & \triangle[P] \\
\triangle[P \wedge Q] & \text{iff} & (\triangle[P] \wedge \neg P) \vee (\triangle[Q] \wedge \neg Q) \vee (\triangle[P] \wedge \triangle[Q]) \\
\triangle[P \vee Q] & \text{iff} & (\triangle[P] \wedge P) \vee (\triangle[Q] \wedge Q) \vee (\triangle[P] \wedge \triangle[Q]) \\
\triangle[P \Rightarrow Q] & \text{iff} & (\triangle[P] \wedge \neg P) \vee (\triangle[Q] \wedge Q) \vee (\triangle[P] \wedge \triangle[Q]) \\
\triangle[P \Leftrightarrow Q] & \text{iff} & \triangle[P] \wedge \triangle[Q] \\
\triangle[\forall x{:}\, T \cdot P] & \text{iff} & (\exists x{:}\, T \cdot \triangle[P] \wedge \neg P) \vee (\forall x{:}\, T \cdot \triangle[P]) \\
\triangle[\exists x{:}\, T \cdot P] & \text{iff} & (\exists x{:}\, T \cdot \triangle[P] \wedge P) \vee (\forall x{:}\, T \cdot \triangle[P])
\end{array}
$$

For the rest of the syntactic forms in the language we have:

$$
\begin{array}{lll}
\triangle[t{:}\, T] & \text{iff} & \triangle[t] \\
\triangle[t_1 = t_2] & \text{iff} & \triangle[t_1] \wedge \triangle[t_2] \\
\triangle[\textsf{if } c \textbf{ then } t_1 \textbf{ else } t_2] & \text{iff} & \triangle[c] \wedge (c \Rightarrow \triangle[t_1]) \wedge (\neg c \Rightarrow \triangle[t_2]) \\
\triangle[f(t)] & \text{iff} & \triangle[t] \wedge \mathbf{D}_f(t) \\
\triangle[\mathbf{D}_f(t)] & \text{iff} & \triangle[t]
\end{array}
$$

Equality, non-logical functions, and characteristic predicates are required to be strict, in the sense that they are undefined for undefined arguments. In the same sense the conditional (if-then-else) and the logical connectives and quantifiers are non-strict.

By applying the above definitions as rewrite rules from left to right, we have got a confluent and terminating rewrite system, where the irreducible formulas are free for $\triangle$-symbols. The $\triangle$-symbol is not part of the basic language, and whenever it occurs, it abbreviates the irreducible formula that can be achieved through rewriting.

In the paper on LPF [1] there is defined a (primitive) $\triangle$-connective, which suits essentially the same purpose as the (meta) $\triangle$-symbol defined in this paper. Their differences are unessential[1] to our presentation. The $\triangle$-connective from [1] is not part of the logic defined in [5]. The above inductive definition of well definedness is a conservative extension of the logic defined in [5], in the sense that it does not violate the consistency of the logic.

3.2 Representation

A partial recursive function

$$f : T \rightarrow T$$

$$f(x) \triangleq exp(x),$$

where $exp(x)$ may not contain any characteristic predicates, is represented by the following axioms:

- $\forall x: T \cdot \mathbf{D}_f(x) \Rightarrow (f(x) = exp(x))$
- $\forall x: T \cdot \mathbf{D}_f(x) \Leftrightarrow F_f[\mathbf{D}_f, x]$
- $(\forall x: T \cdot F_f[P, x] \Rightarrow P(x)) \Rightarrow (\forall x: T \cdot \mathbf{D}_f(x) \Rightarrow P(x))$ (P total)

where $F_f[\mathbf{D}_f, x] = \triangle[exp(x)]$ following Constables notation. $F_f[\mathbf{D}_f, x]$ means that we have two place-holders, the first holding all the places where $\mathbf{D}_f$ syntactically occurs, and similarly for x. The first axiom represents a function definition in a way similar to the representation technique of Cheng and Jones [2], but the equality is here guarded by the characteristic predicate of the defined function. The second axiom gives an inductive definition of the characteristic predicate, and the third axiom ensures that the inductive definition of the characteristic predicate is interpreted as the minimal one (w.r.t. implication!). The requirement that P must be total in the third axiom is stronger than absolutely necessary, but is sufficient for our purposes. Whether P can be allowed to be partial or not depends on the concrete form of $F[P, x]$.

[1]The $\triangle$-connective in LPF is non-monotonic in the sense defined in [1], whereas all the connectives applied in this paper are monotonic. Since the $\triangle$-symbol in this paper is defined it is less expressive than the $\triangle$-connective from [1].

For LPF extended with a theory for the integers, we have the following result. The definition of provability is the usual one.

Theorem 3.1 (Constable) *For all n, m in Z and all recursively defined $f: \mathsf{Z} \rightarrow \mathsf{Z}$,*

- *f is defined at n if and only if $\mathbf{D}_f(n)$ is provable, and*
- *$f(n) = m$ if and only if $f(n) = m$ is provable.*

This result straight forwardly generalizes to the class of VDM data types with a countable set of objects. Be aware that the left hand sides of the 'if and only if' statements presuppose a least fixed point interpretation of the function definitions.

The above three axioms can be expressed in a more familiar style as LPF rules.

$$\text{f-def}\ \frac{\mathbf{D}_f(x) \qquad x: T}{f(x) = exp(x)}$$

$$\mathbf{D}_f\text{-def}\ \frac{x: T}{\mathbf{D}_f(x) \ \Leftrightarrow \ F_f[\mathbf{D}_f, x]}$$

$$\mathbf{D}_f\text{-ind}\ \frac{x: T, F_f[P, x] \ \vdash \ P(x)}{x: T \ \vdash \ \mathbf{D}_f(x) \ \Rightarrow \ P(x)}\ P \text{ total}$$

For any partial recursive function these rules are consistent extensions of LPF.

3.3 Modification of LPF

Since all true formulas are well defined in LPF, we have the following rule (scheme):

$$\Delta\text{-I}\ \frac{P}{\Delta[P]}$$

for all formulas P. All rules of LPF, as defined in [5], are left unchanged, and in the next section we freely apply the rules from [5, Appendix C].

4 A solution

Using the technique from §3 we get the following representation of the *evenp* function from §2. The characteristic predicate is defined as $\mathbf{D}_{ev}$, and from the definition of *evenp* we get:

$$\begin{aligned}
& F_{ev}[\mathbf{D}_{ev}, i] \\
= \; & \Delta[\mathsf{if}\ i = 0\ \mathsf{then\ true\ else}\ evenp(i-2)] \\
= \; & \Delta[i = 0] \wedge \\
& ((i = 0) \Rightarrow \Delta[\mathsf{true}]) \wedge \\
& ((i \neq 0) \Rightarrow \Delta[evenp(i-2)]) \\
= \; & ((i \neq 0) \Rightarrow (\Delta[i-2] \wedge \mathbf{D}_{ev}(i-2))) \\
= \; & ((i \neq 0) \Rightarrow \mathbf{D}_{ev}(i-2)),
\end{aligned}$$

by using the facts that $\Delta[i = 0]$, $\Delta[\mathsf{true}]$, and $\Delta[i-2]$ are always well defined. This follows from the facts that variables in LPF can only bind well defined values and that the constants 'true', '0', and '2' are well defined. This results in the following representing rules:

$$evenp\text{-def}\ \frac{\mathbf{D}_{ev}(i) \qquad i{:}\,\mathsf{Z}}{evenp(i) = \mathsf{if}\ i = 0\ \mathsf{then\ true\ else}\ evenp(i-2)}$$

$$\mathbf{D}_{ev}\text{-def}\ \frac{i{:}\,\mathsf{Z}}{\mathbf{D}_{ev}(i) \Leftrightarrow (i \neq 0 \Rightarrow \mathbf{D}_{ev}(i-2))}$$

$$\mathbf{D}_{ev}\text{-ind}\ \frac{i{:}\,\mathsf{Z}, (i \neq 0 \Rightarrow P(i-2)) \vdash P(i)}{i{:}\,\mathsf{Z} \vdash \mathbf{D}_{ev}(i) \Rightarrow P(i)}\ P \text{ total}$$

Applying the VDM theory defined in [5] we can now prove a number of intermediate results and finally, as an immediate consequence of these, that:

$$evenp(i) \vdash (i \mathsf{mod} 2 = 0).$$

The proofs are given in the 'box' style of Jones [5]. To simplify the proofs we let $EV(i)$ abbreviate $(i \bmod 2 = 0)$.

1st lemma

$EV(i) \wedge (i \geq 0)$ well defined for all i:Z (exercise)

H from i: Z, $i \neq 0 \Rightarrow EV(i-2) \wedge (i-2 \geq 0)$

$(i = 0) \vee (i \neq 0)$ property of Z

from $i = 0$

infer $EV(0) \wedge (i \geq 0)$

from $i \neq 0$

$EV(i-2)$ $\Rightarrow$-E and $\wedge$-E on H

$i \geq 2$ (similarly)

$EV(i)$ property of mod

$i \geq 0$ property of Z

infer $EV(i) \wedge (i \geq 0)$ $\wedge$-I

infer $EV(i) \wedge (i \geq 0)$ by cases

i: Z $\vdash$ $\mathbf{D}_{ev}(i) \Rightarrow EV(i) \wedge (i \geq 0)$ $\mathbf{D}_{ev}$-ind

2nd lemma

IH from i: N, $\forall j$: N $\cdot$ $j < i \Rightarrow (EV(j) \wedge j \geq 0) \Rightarrow \mathbf{D}_{ev}(j)$

$(i = 0) \vee (i = 1) \vee (i \geq 2)$ property of N

from $i = 0$

$\neg (i \neq 0)$

infer $(EV(i) \wedge i \geq 0) \Rightarrow \mathbf{D}_{ev}(i)$ $\Rightarrow$-vac (twice) and $\mathbf{D}_{ev}$-def

from $i = 1$

$\neg (EV(i) \wedge i \geq 0)$ $\neg\wedge$-I

infer $(EV(i) \wedge i \geq 0) \Rightarrow \mathbf{D}_{ev}(i)$ $\Rightarrow$-vac

from $i \geq 2$

$\delta(EV(i) \wedge i \geq 0)$ (exercise)

from $EV(i) \wedge i \geq 0$

$EV(i-2) \wedge i - 2 \geq 0$ property of Z since $i \geq 2$

$\mathbf{D}_{ev}(i-2)$ IH

$i \neq 0 \Rightarrow \mathbf{D}_{ev}(i-2)$ $\Rightarrow$-vac

infer $\mathbf{D}_{ev}(i)$ $\mathbf{D}_{ev}$-def

infer $(EV(i) \wedge i \geq 0) \Rightarrow \mathbf{D}_{ev}(i)$ $\Rightarrow$-I

infer $(EV(i) \wedge i \geq 0) \Rightarrow \mathbf{D}_{ev}(i)$ by cases

i: N $\vdash$ $(EV(i) \wedge i \geq 0) \Rightarrow \mathbf{D}_{ev}(i)$ N-*cind*

3rd lemma

from $i{:}\,\mathsf{Z}$
    $(i \geq 0) \vee (i < 0)$ — property of Z
    from $i \geq 0$
    infer $(EV(i) \wedge i \geq 0) \Rightarrow \mathbf{D}_{ev}(i)$ — 2nd lemma
    from $i < 0$
        $\neg\,(EV(i) \wedge i \geq 0)$ — $\neg\wedge$-I
    infer $(EV(i) \wedge i \geq 0) \Rightarrow \mathbf{D}_{ev}(i)$ — $\Rightarrow$-vac
infer $(EV(i) \wedge i \geq 0) \Rightarrow \mathbf{D}_{ev}(i)$ — by cases

$i{:}\,\mathsf{Z} \vdash (EV(i) \wedge i \geq 0) \Rightarrow \mathbf{D}_{ev}(i)$

The 3rd lemma simply extends the result established in the 2nd lemma to hold for all integers.

Main result

$i{:}\,\mathsf{Z} \vdash \mathbf{D}_{ev}(i) \Leftrightarrow EV(i) \wedge (i \geq 0)$ — 1st lemma and 3rd lemma

Solution

from $evenp(i)$
    $\Delta[evenp(i)]$ — Δ-I
    $\mathbf{D}_{ev}(i)$ — $\mathbf{D}_{ev}$-def
    $EV(i) \wedge (i \geq 0)$ — the main result
infer $EV(i)$ — $\wedge$-E

$evenp(i) \vdash (i \bmod 2 = 0)$

From the main result a solution to the problem described in §2 was easily found. Thus, the problem described in §2 can be solved by application of the representation technique described in §3.

The results of Constable [3] ensure that this is not the only case, but that the representation technique will have the same nice properties for the class of partial recursive functions.

Be aware that results like the 'main result' above are not always possible to establish. Finding a logical equivalent for the characteristic predicate of some partial recursive function corresponds to solving the 'halting problem'.

5 The challenge problem revisited

Cheng and Jones [2] defined the following problem as a challenge for logics claiming to support reasoning about partial functions. To meet this challenge we give a brief outline on how the problem can be solved by the method advocated in this paper. The challenge problem is defined as follows. Given the VDM specification of the partial function:

$$subp : \mathsf{Z} \times \mathsf{Z} \rightarrow \mathsf{Z}$$

$$subp(i,j) \quad \triangleq \quad \textsf{if } i = j \textsf{ then } 0 \textsf{ else } subp(i, j+1) + 1$$

prove that it has the following property:

$$\forall i,j \colon \mathsf{Z} \cdot (i \geq j) \;\Rightarrow\; subp(i,j) = (i - j)$$

The problems involved in establishing results like this are well understood, cf. Cheng and Jones [2].

The *subp* function is represented by the following rules:

$$subp\text{-def}\ \frac{\mathbf{D}_{su}(i,j) \qquad i,j \colon \mathsf{Z}}{subp(i,j) \;=\; \textsf{if } i = j \textsf{ then } 0 \textsf{ else } subp(i,j+1)+1}$$

$$\mathbf{D}_{su}\text{-def}\ \frac{i,j \colon \mathsf{Z}}{\mathbf{D}_{su}(i,j) \;\Leftrightarrow\; (i \neq j) \;\Rightarrow\; \mathbf{D}_{su}(i,j+1)}$$

$$\mathbf{D}_{su}\text{-ind}\ \frac{i,j \colon \mathsf{Z},\ (i \neq j \;\Rightarrow\; P(i,j+1)) \vdash P(i,j)}{i,j \colon \mathsf{Z} \vdash \mathbf{D}_{su}(i,j) \;\Rightarrow\; P(i,j)}\ P \text{ total}$$

With an approach similar to the one taken in §4 we can establish the following main result:

$$i,j \colon \mathsf{Z} \vdash \mathbf{D}_{su}(i,j) \;\Leftrightarrow\; (i \geq j).$$

With this at hand, the proof of the *subp* property proceeds as in [2] with few modifications.

From this we can see, that working with the improved theory for VDM as defined in this paper is not significantly more complicated than working in Jones' theory for VDM. All we have done is to add more expressive rules for representing definitions of functions. Everything else is left unchanged.

6 Final remarks

We have shown how partial recursive functions can be represented in LPF by application of Constables (or Owes) method. The consistency of the resulting logical system can be established by application of well known meta logical methods, but we have not done so in this paper.

Adopting the representation technique described in this paper as the 'official' representation technique for VDM would not have any great influence on the LPF based theory for VDM defined by Jones in [5]. The presentation technique described in this paper simply fills some gaps in the theory hitherto used for VDM, without violating anything.

One place where the representation technique could be useful is in the VDM support tool of the mural system [6]. It would be possible to extract the representing rules directly from the function definitions, much in the same way as it is done presently. For more details about the mural system, the reader is referred to [6].

To what extend does the new representation technique increase the complexity of the theory for VDM? In the present VDM instantiation of the mural system, which seems to be the one of richest theories for VDM at the moment, 'formation' rules like:

$$\frac{x : \mathsf{Z} \qquad y : \mathsf{Z}}{x + y : \mathsf{Z}}$$

are already defined. Such rules are necessary in order to establish the consistency of specifications, and they are very similar to rule schemes of the form:

$$\frac{\triangle[x] \qquad \triangle[y]}{\triangle[x + y]}$$

Although the $\triangle$-symbol is a meta operator, there are no problems in using it in the syntax of the proof system, provided that the sufficient number of rules are added for its introduction and elimination. Thus, much of the technical machinery are in this sense already present in the mural theory for VDM. Also the characteristic predicates have some correspondence with traditional VDM, since for any partially defined function, f, it must hold for its precondition, pre-f, that:

$$\text{pre-}f(x) \;\Rightarrow\; \mathbf{D}_f(x)$$

for all elements x in the domain of f. It thus seems that an adoption of the described representation technique will not significantly increase the complexity of the logical system for VDM.

References

[1] H. Barringer, J.H. Cheng, C.B. Jones. *A Logic Covering Undefinedness in Program Proofs.* Acta Informatica 21, pp. 251-269. 1984.

[2] J.H. Cheng, C.B. Jones. *On the usability of logics which handle partial functions.* In: C. Morgan and J.C.P. Woodcock. *3rd Refinement Workshop*, pp. 51-72. Springer-Verlag. 1991.

[3] R.L. Constable. *Partial functions in constructive formal theories.* In: A.B. Cremers and H.P. Kriegel. *Theoretical Computer Science.* LNCS 145, pp. 1-18. Springer-Verlag. 1983.

[4] O.-J. Dahl, D.F. Langmyhr, O. Owe. *Preliminary Report on the Specification and Programming Language ABEL.* Research Report. No. 106. Department of Informatics. University of Oslo. 1986.

[5] C.B. Jones. *Systematic Software Development Using VDM.* 2nd ed. Prentice Hall International 1990.

[6] C.B. Jones, K.D. Jones, P.A. Lindsay, R. Moore. *mural: A Formal Development Support System.* Springer-Verlag. 1991.

[7] O. Owe. *An approach to program reasoning based on a first order logic for partial functions.* Research Report. No. 89. Department of Informatics. University of Oslo. 1985. (Also available as: Computer Science Technical Report Number CS-081, Dep. of Electrical Engineering and Computer Science, University of California, San Diego, U.S.A., June 1984.)

[8] D.A. Schmidt. *Denotational Semantics: a methodology for language development.* Allyn and Bacon. 1986.

On Formal Specification of a Proof Tool

R.D. Arthan
ICL Secure Systems,
Eskdale Road,
Winnersh,
Berks. RG11 5TT

1 Introduction

1.1 Background

Tools and methods for the specification and design of computer systems are increasing in sophistication. Much current research and development is attempting to exploit this sophistication to improve the effectiveness of systems development practices. It is becoming feasible to offer much higher assurance than hitherto that systems meet critical requirements, e.g. concerning safety or security. Standards such as [7] are evolving to demand the use of formal specification *and verification* of designs (and, one day, perhaps implementations). Thus, tools giving cost-effective means for providing formal proofs of critical requirements are of increasing importance. ICL Secure Systems, as part of its role as lead partner in the DTI-sponsored FST project, is attempting to improve the technology base for formal verification.

The main enabling technology with which ICL is concerned is the HOL theorem proving system, [1, 8]. A public domain version of HOL has been distributed by Cambridge University and has been used with some success both in academia and in industry. ICL plans to offer an industrial quality implementation of HOL and to use it to provide proof support for other formalisms such as Z. An experimental Z proof tool based on a prototype reimplementation of HOL has recently been produced for use by ICL and its collaborators.

This paper gives a simplified case study, in Z, illustrating some of the techniques being used. The case study is concerned with two main themes. The first theme is concerned with the integrity of the proof tool, the second is concerned with the consistency of the specifications about which we wish to reason and with the extension mechanisms which the logics used should support. The work on integrity is fairly recent work carried out within the FST project. The treatment of consistency is based on much earlier work of ICL on using HOL to reason about Z specifications which was first described in an ICL internal document, [6] and which resulted in the inclusion of a new facility supporting loose specifications in the Cambridge HOL system.

1.2 Integrity

One issue in industrialising HOL which is felt to be of particular importance is its integrity, i.e., the level of confidence that users and their customers can have in the correctness of the proof tool itself. While research continues to ameliorate the problem, the production of fully formal proofs is a difficult and time-consuming activity. The expense of producing such proofs is not justifiable unless one can be confident that they are correct. Commercial proofs involve millions of primitive inference steps (mostly automatically performed, one hopes!); human checking of each step is inconceivable.

The basic approach to the integrity problem is to specify formally the logic used in the tool and to give an abstract specification of the critical requirements for the tool. The proof tools we are concerned with follow the LCF paradigm, described in [2], which encapsulates all critical code inside an abstract data type. In our approach the implementation of this critical kernel is based on a formal design which, we assert, meets the critical requirements. This assertion may be rigorously formalised and so is susceptible both to informal analysis and to fully formal proof. Finding the proofs is eased by constructing the design to facilitate a top-down decomposition of the critical requirements into requirements on its subsystems. The main goal of all of this is to minimise the amount of proof work which must be carried out. The critical requirements deliberately fall short of a fully formal functional specification (the design is much closer to that), since what we wish to prove is not that the tool does everything the user wants correctly, but that it cannot be used to prove 'false'. A proof of full functional correctness would be both unnecessary and unfeasible. We believe that this method of reducing the complexity of a high-assurance problem by concentrating effort on what is critical is a very important part of making formal verification possible in real situations.

An important aspect of the LCF paradigm is that, once we have the kernel of the proof tool, development of facilities to make the tool effective to use can be produced freely without prejudicing the integrity of the system. So, for example, an automatic proof procedure may be transferred from a research and development environment into actual industrial use without requiring more extensive verification of its correctness than would be required for any other software engineering tool — infelicitous behaviour of the proof procedure cannot compromise the integrity of the system. The construction of these higher level facilities is outside the scope of this paper.

1.3 Consistency of Specifications

We wish to use the proof tool to reason about specifications written in languages such as Z. Such specification languages include features which at first sight may compromise the integrity of the proof tool. In this paper we describe a practical solution to one such problem which arises with Z.

Informal proof work with Z usually treats the specification as a collection of axioms. This approach has the inherent disadvantage that one may prove anything on the basis of an inconsistent set of axioms. It is therefore necessary to relate proof to specification in such a way that an incorrect specification does not give rise to this problem.

One reason for allowing what are apparently arbitrary axiomatic extensions in Z, is to allow the user to make loose specifications. A variable can be defined by stating a property which does not have to define the variable uniquely. This feature helps us to avoid cluttering specifications with irrelevant details and to make our specifications more general.

The underlying logical mechanism we propose to solve this problem for the axiomatic and generic boxes in Z is a rule of *conservative extension* allowing new objects to be defined provided an appropriate consistency proposition has been proved. The apparent disadvantage with this is that we must interleave our specification activity with proof work to supply the necessary consistency propositions. Fortunately some fairly straightforward automated proof techniques allows us to defer the proof obligations (essentially by approximating a loose specification by one which can automatically be proved consistent and which is equivalent to the original one if it can be proved consistent).

In fact, to ease this problem further, ICL have developed machinery for HOL which can automatically discharge the consistency proof obligations for quite a useful class of specification idioms. Work is in progress on extending this machinery to the prototype Z proof tool.

1.4 Overview of the Case Study

The bulk of the sequel comprises a formal specification in Z of the following:

1. the language and deductive system of a simple logic (section 2);
2. an abstract model of a proof tool for the logic and a statement of its critical properties (section 3);
3. a design for the kernel of a proof tool for the logic, believed to satisfy the critical properties (section 4).

Section 5.1 discusses how one might informally or formally verify the "belief" mentioned in item 3 above; Sections 5.2 and 5.3 consider how such a kernel might be implemented and discuss its use to support specification activities.

The Z specification is presented in definition-before-use order. Those who prefer to read top-down are invited to read section 2.1 first, to set the scene, and then sections 3 and 4, in that order, skipping back to section 2 when necessary. An index to the specification may be found at the end of the paper.

Our use of the Z notation is intended to follow [5]. The forms of Z paragraph such as free type definitions which do not come in boxes are high-lighted by a bar in the left margin. Defining occurrences of global variables are shown in **bold** type.

The source text of this document is in fact a script from which the Z paragraphs can be extracted for machine processing. The type-correctness of the specification has been checked using the prototype Z proof support tool referred to in section 1.1 above. No formal proof work has been carried out on the material in this document, however proof work has begun on the HOL specification of the proof tool for HOL on which this paper has been based.

2 The Logic

The logic used in our example will be classical first order logic. The treatment is fairly close to that which may be found in [3], the main departure being that we envisage variable names and the like being character strings rather than single letters with superscripts and subscripts. Also since we are interested in tools which help a user to build particular theories of interest, later on we are very explicit about mechanisms with which axioms are introduced.

2.1 Language

Names The language with which we shall work contains names whose structure we do not wish to specify here. In an implementation these might be character strings. For the specification, we introduce the set of names as a given set.

z

$$[\mathbf{name}]$$

Terms The terms of our language are variables or are formed from simpler terms by function application. It is technically convenient to treat constants as functions with no arguments.

z

$$\begin{array}{lll} \mathbf{term} & ::= & \mathbf{var}\langle\langle name \rangle\rangle \\ & | & \mathbf{app}\langle\langle name \times seq\ term \rangle\rangle \end{array}$$

Formulae A formula is either an application of an atomic predicate to a list of formulae or is formed from other formulae via negation, implication or universal quantification.

z

$$\begin{array}{lll} \mathbf{form} & ::= & \mathbf{prd}\langle\langle name \times seq\ term \rangle\rangle \\ & | & \mathbf{neg}\langle\langle form \rangle\rangle \\ & | & \mathbf{imp}\langle\langle form \times form \rangle\rangle \\ & | & \mathbf{all}\langle\langle name \times form \rangle\rangle \end{array}$$

Theories A theory is just a set of formulae. We will think of the theory as specifying the functions and predicates which appear in it.

z

$$\textbf{theory} == \mathbb{P}\, form$$

Well-Formedness of Terms We will say that a formula is well-formed with respect to a theory if all the functions and predicates it contains appear in the theory. Note that this is a rather different use of terminology from [3], where the idea of a wff just corresponds to our representation of the syntax as a free type.

If a function (or predicate) name appears in two places in a formula or a theory with differing numbers of arguments we think of the different instances as being distinct functions (or predicates). (We might expect a proof tool to protect the user from getting into this situation, lest it be confusing in practice).

We use the following auxiliary definitions to define well-formedness:

z

$$\begin{array}{l}
\textbf{term_funcs} : term \rightarrow \mathbb{F}\,(name \times \mathbb{N});\\
\textbf{form_funcs} : form \rightarrow \mathbb{F}\,(name \times \mathbb{N});\\
\textbf{form_preds} : form \rightarrow \mathbb{F}\,(name \times \mathbb{N})
\end{array}$$

$$\begin{array}{ll}
\multicolumn{2}{l}{\forall n{:}name;\ ts{:}seq\ term;\ p,\ q{:}form \bullet}\\
 & term_funcs\ (var\ n) = \{\}\\
\wedge & term_funcs\ (app(n, ts)) = \{(n, \#\, ts)\} \cup \bigcup(ran\ (term_funcs \circ ts))\\
\wedge & \\
 & form_funcs\ (prd(n, ts)) = \bigcup(ran\ (term_funcs \circ ts))\\
\wedge & form_funcs\ (neg\ p) = form_funcs\ p\\
\wedge & form_funcs\ (imp(p, q)) = form_funcs\ p \cup form_funcs\ q\\
\wedge & form_funcs\ (all(n, p)) = form_funcs\ p\\
\wedge & \\
 & form_preds(prd(n, ts)) = \{(n, \#\, ts)\}\\
\wedge & form_preds\ (neg\ p) = form_preds\ p\\
\wedge & form_preds\ (imp(p, q)) = form_preds\ p \cup form_preds\ q\\
\wedge & form_preds\ (all(n, p)) = form_preds\ p
\end{array}$$

Now we can define *wff*, the function which assigns to a theory the set of formulae which are well-formed with respect to it.

z

$$\textbf{wff} : theory \rightarrow \mathbb{P}\, form$$

$$\begin{array}{lll}
\multicolumn{3}{l}{\forall thy{:}theory;\ p{:}\quad form \bullet}\\
 & \multicolumn{2}{l}{p \in wff\ thy}\\
\Leftrightarrow & (& form_funcs\ p \subseteq \bigcup(form_funcs(\!|thy|\!))\\
 & \wedge & form_preds\ p \subseteq \bigcup(form_preds(\!|thy|\!)))
\end{array}$$

2.2 Operations on Syntax

This section contains the definitions of certain operations on syntax which we shall need. The operations are extraction of free variables, substitution of terms for variables and some derived formula constructors. We define substitution in terms of a matching operation. This section contains the definitions of these operations.

Free Variables The functions which extract the free variables of terms and formulae are defined as follows:

z

$$\begin{array}{l}
\textbf{term_frees}: term \rightarrow \mathbb{F}\ name;\\
\textbf{form_frees}: form \rightarrow \mathbb{F}\ name
\end{array}$$

$$\begin{array}{ll}
\multicolumn{2}{l}{\forall n{:}name;\ ts{:}seq\ term;\ p, q{:}form \bullet}\\
 & term_frees\ (var\ n) = \{n\}\\
\wedge & term_frees(app(n, ts)) = \bigcup(ran\ (term_frees \circ ts))\\
\wedge & \\
 & form_frees(prd(n, ts)) = \bigcup(ran\ (term_frees \circ ts))\\
\wedge & form_frees\ (neg\ p) = form_frees\ p\\
\wedge & form_frees\ (imp(p, q)) = form_frees\ p \cup form_frees\ q\\
\wedge & form_frees\ (all(n, p)) = form_frees\ p \setminus \{n\}
\end{array}$$

Matching We will need to define the notion of substituting a term for a variable in a formula. This is an idea which is frequently defined vaguely or incorrectly and so it is worth specifying formally. To do this in a reasonably abstract way, we first of all define a notion of matching. The definition is quite technical and readers are invited to skip this section, if they wish.

We wish to define a partial function *form_match*. Given two formulae, p_1 and p_2, say, such that p_2 is a substitution instance of p_1 under some assignment, *match*, of terms to the free variables of p_1, *form_match* should return *match*. Here we wish to allow renaming of bound variables in order to avoid variable capture problems. So for example, under the assignment which sends y to $x + 1$, we wish $\forall x \bullet x = y$ to match $\forall x' \bullet x' = x + 1$ (but not $\forall x \bullet x = x + 1$).

First of all we define matching for terms and sequences of terms. It turns out that matching is easiest to specify if we introduce an auxiliary argument which records the correspondence between bound variables in the two terms.

z

$$\begin{array}{l}
\textbf{term_match}: (term \times term \times (name \twoheadrightarrow\!\!\!\!\!\!\mapsto term)) \rightarrow\!\!\!\!\!\!\mapsto (name \twoheadrightarrow\!\!\!\!\!\!\mapsto term);\\
\textbf{seq_term_match}: (seq\ term \times seq\ term \times (name \twoheadrightarrow\!\!\!\!\!\!\mapsto term)) \rightarrow\!\!\!\!\!\!\mapsto (name \twoheadrightarrow\!\!\!\!\!\!\mapsto term)
\end{array}$$

$$\begin{array}{l}
(\forall t1, t2{:}\ term;\ env, match{:}name \twoheadrightarrow\!\!\!\!\!\!\mapsto term \bullet\\
\quad (t1, t2, env) \mapsto match \in term_match \Leftrightarrow\\
\quad\quad (\exists n{:}name \bullet t1 = var\ n\\
\quad\quad \wedge \quad (env\ n = t2 \vee n \notin dom\ env)\\
\quad\quad \wedge \quad match = \{n \mapsto t2\})\\
\\
\quad \vee \quad (\exists n{:}name;\ ts1, ts2{:}seq\ term \bullet t1 = app(n, ts1) \wedge t2 = app(n, ts2)\\
\quad\quad \wedge \quad (ts1, ts2, env) \mapsto match \in seq_term_match))\\
\wedge\\
(\forall ts1, ts2{:}seq\ term;\ env, match{:}name \twoheadrightarrow\!\!\!\!\!\!\mapsto term \bullet\\
\quad (ts1, ts2, env) \mapsto match \in seq_term_match \Leftrightarrow\\
\quad\quad\quad dom\ ts1 = dom\ ts2\\
\quad\quad \wedge \quad (\exists matches : seq(name \twoheadrightarrow\!\!\!\!\!\!\mapsto term) \bullet\\
\quad\quad\quad \forall i : dom\ ts1 \bullet\\
\quad\quad\quad\quad (ts1\ i, ts2\ i, env) \mapsto matches\ i \in term_match\\
\quad\quad\quad \wedge \quad disjoint\ matches \wedge match = \bigcup(ran\ matches)))
\end{array}$$

form_match is now defined as follows:

z

$$\mathbf{form\_match} : (form \times form \times (name \mathrel{+\!\!\!\!\twoheadrightarrow} term)) \mathrel{+\!\!\!\!\rightarrow} (name \mathrel{+\!\!\!\!\twoheadrightarrow} term)$$

$$\begin{array}{l}
\forall p1, p2: form; env, match: name \mathrel{+\!\!\!\!\twoheadrightarrow} term \bullet \\
\quad (p1, p2, env) \mapsto match \in form_match \\
\Leftrightarrow \\
\qquad (\exists n: name; ts1, ts2: seq\ term; matches : seq\ (name \mathrel{+\!\!\!\!\twoheadrightarrow} term) \bullet \\
\qquad\qquad p1 = prd(n, ts1) \land p2 = prd(n, ts2) \\
\qquad \land \quad (ts1, ts2, env) \mapsto match \in seq_term_match) \\
\quad \lor \quad (\exists q1, q2: form \bullet \\
\qquad\qquad p1 = neg\ q1 \land p2 = neg\ q2 \\
\qquad \land \quad (q1, q2, env) \mapsto match \in form_match) \\
\quad \lor \quad (\exists q1, r1, q2, r2: form; matchq, matchr: name \mathrel{+\!\!\!\!\twoheadrightarrow} term \bullet \\
\qquad\qquad p1 = imp(q1, r1) \land p2 = imp(q2, r2) \\
\qquad \land \quad (q1, q2, env) \mapsto matchq \in form_match \\
\qquad \land \quad (r1, r2, env) \mapsto matchr \in form_match \\
\qquad \land \quad disjoint\langle matchq, matchr\rangle \\
\qquad \land \quad match = matchq \cup matchr) \\
\quad \lor \quad (\exists n1, n2: name; q1, q2: form \bullet \\
\qquad\qquad p1 = all(n1, q1) \land p2 = all(n2, q2) \\
\qquad \land \quad (q1, q2, env \oplus \{n1 \mapsto var\ n2\}) \mapsto match \in form_match)
\end{array}$$

Substitution This is now easy to specify in terms of matching. Note that the fact that we make it a total function implies that the given set *name* must be infinite (so that the supply of names for use in renaming bound variables is never exhausted).

z

$$\mathbf{subst} : (name \mathrel{+\!\!\!\!\twoheadrightarrow} term) \times form \rightarrow form$$

$$\forall subs: name \mathrel{+\!\!\!\!\twoheadrightarrow} term; p: form \bullet form\_match(p, subst(subs, p), \varnothing) = subs$$

Derived Formula Constructors To define our rule of conservative extension, we require two derived formula constructors ('derived' as opposed to the 'primitive' constructors, *prd*, *neg*, *imp* and *all*).

z

$$\mathbf{exists} : (name \times form) \rightarrow form$$

$$\forall n: name; p: form \bullet exists(n, p) = neg(all(n, neg\ p))$$

We also need a function to form the universal quantification of a formula over a list of variables:

z

$$\mathbf{list\_all} : seq\ name \times form \rightarrow form$$

$$\begin{array}{l}
\forall p: form; n: name; ns: seq\ name \bullet \\
\qquad list_all(\langle\rangle, p) = p \\
\quad \land \quad list_all(\langle n\rangle \frown ns, p) = all(n, list_all(ns, p))
\end{array}$$

2.3 Inference

The two inference rules are exactly as in [3]. They are the rule of *modus ponens,* and the rule of generalisation. We formalise these and the axioms of first order logic in this section and also define the notion of derivability.

Modus Ponens This rule says that from $p \Rightarrow q$ and p we may infer q:

z

$$\mathbf{mp} : (form \times form) \mathrel{+\!\!\!\to} form$$

$$dom\ mp = \{p, q{:}form \mid true \bullet (imp(p, q), p)\}$$
$$\land \quad (\forall p, q{:}form \bullet mp(imp(p, q), p) = q)$$

Generalisation This rule says that from p we may infer $\forall x \bullet p$ for any variable x.

z

$$\mathbf{gen} : (name \times form) \rightarrow form$$

$$\forall n{:}name; p{:}form \bullet gen(n, p) = all(n, p)$$

Logical Axioms We also need the logical axioms for first order logic with equality[1]. See [3] for a description of these. Since their formalisation is not particularly illuminating we omit the details here.

z

$$\mathbf{logical\_axioms} : \mathbb{P}\, form$$

....

Direct Derivability We now wish to say formally how the inference rules and the logical axioms are used to construct the consequences of a set of formulae. This notion is defined using the following idea of a direct consequence.

z

$$\mathbf{direct\_consequences} : \mathbb{P}\, form \rightarrow \mathbb{P}\, form$$

$$\forall hyps{:}\mathbb{P}\, form; p{:}form \bullet p \in direct\_consequences\ hyps \Leftrightarrow$$
$$p \in logical\_axioms$$
$$\lor \quad p \in hyps$$
$$\lor \quad (\exists q, r{:}hyps \bullet p = mp(q, r))$$
$$\lor \quad (\exists n{:}name; q : hyps \bullet p = gen(n, q))$$

Derivability The consequences of a set, *hyps* say, of formulae comprise the smallest set containing *hyps* which is closed under taking direct consequences.

z

$$\mathbf{consequences} : \mathbb{P}\, form \rightarrow \mathbb{P}\, form$$

$$\forall hyps{:}\mathbb{P}\, form \bullet consequences\ hyps = \bigcap\{ps : \mathbb{P}\, form \mid hyps \subseteq ps \land direct\_consequences\ ps \subseteq ps\}$$

We shall often use the term *theorem* to describe a formula which is a consequence of a particular theory under discussion.

[1] Building in the equality axioms makes it easier to pretend that the proof tool we are presenting would be of practical use, since we do not supply a mechanism by which the user could introduce an infinite set of axioms. In a proof system such as HOL, polymorphism and the ability to define higher order functions allow most, if not all, theories of practical interest to be finitely axiomatised and the introduction of infinite axiom schemes is not required.

2.4 Extending Theories

In this section we define two mechanisms for extending a theory. The first mechanism, *new_axiom*, supports addition of an arbitrary formula as an axiom. The second mechanism *new_specification* is parameterised by a formula of a particular form, which must be a theorem of the theory we are extending. This theorem constitutes a proof of the consistency of an implicit specification of a new function. Given such a theorem, *new_specification* adds a defining axiom for the new function which, in fact, constitutes a *conservative* extension of the theory.

Examples of definitions in actual use are very frequently conservative. For example, all of the definitions in this document are intended to be conservative over the sort of axiom system one imagines should be provided for Z (allowing Z to be viewed as a many-sorted variant of Zermelo set theory).

2.4.1 Axiomatic Extension

An arbitrary formula may be introduced into a theory by the function *new_axiom*:

Z

$$\text{new\_axiom} : \mathit{theory} \to \mathit{form} \to \mathit{theory}$$

$$\forall \mathit{thy}{:}\mathit{theory};\ p{:}\mathit{form} \bullet \mathit{new\_axiom}\ \mathit{thy}\ p = \mathit{thy} \cup \{p\}$$

We take the view that, in practice, the user will wish to work within a fixed set of axioms, and part of the critical properties we identify for the kernel of the proof system asserts that axioms introduced with *new_axiom* are clearly distinguished from the axioms introduced by *new_specification*.

2.4.2 Conservative Extension

Our conservative extension mechanism allows us to introduce a new function satisfying a specified property. Assume, for example, that we were working in the theory of real numbers and that we wished to define the ceiling functions. That is to say we wish to define a function, *ceil*, say, with one parameter satisfying the property

Example

$$\forall x \bullet (\mathit{ceil}\ x \in \mathbb{Z} \wedge \mathit{ceil}\ x \geq x \wedge (\forall m \bullet (m < \mathit{ceil}\ x \wedge m \in \mathbb{Z}) \Rightarrow m < x))$$

To introduce such a function we must first demonstrate that the above definition is conservative (and hence, *a fortiori* consistent). To do this we would first prove the theorem:

Example

$$\forall x \bullet \exists \mathit{ceil} \bullet (\mathit{ceil} \in \mathbb{Z} \wedge \mathit{ceil} \geq x \wedge (\forall m \bullet (m < \mathit{ceil} \wedge m \in \mathbb{Z}) \Rightarrow m < x))$$

It is fairly easy to see that the theoremhood, and hence the truth, of the above assertion implies that for any element, x, of any model of the theory, there is an element, *ceil*, such that the above holds. It follows that in any model we can find an interpretation for the desired new function symbol *ceil* (provided the set theory in which we do the model theory has the axiom of choice). Note that the argument relies on the fact that the assertion contains no free variables.

Thus, in essence, our rule says that given a theorem of the form:

Example

$$\forall x1 \bullet \forall x2 \bullet \ldots \forall xk \bullet \exists c \bullet P$$

where the x_i are distinct variables, we may introduce a new function, f say, of k arguments, with the defining axiom

Example

$$\forall x1 \bullet \forall x2 \bullet \ldots \forall xk \bullet P[f(x1, x2, \ldots, xk)/c]$$

where the notation in the square brackets denotes substitution.

Our principle of definition is then given by the following function, *new_specification*, in which we assume, for simplicity that the name of the new function is the same as the existentially quantified variable in the theorem:

z

$$\textsf{new\_specification} : \mathit{theory} \rightarrow \mathit{form} \twoheadrightarrow \mathit{theory}$$

$$\begin{array}{l}
\forall \mathit{thy}{:}\mathit{theory} \bullet \ \mathit{dom}\,(\mathit{new_specification}\ \mathit{thy}) \\
\quad = \ \{ \ \mathit{xs}{:}\ \mathit{seq}\ \mathit{name};\ c{:}\mathit{name};\ p{:}\mathit{wff}\ \mathit{thy} \\
\qquad \mid \ \mathit{form_frees}\ p \subseteq \{c\} \cup \mathit{ran}\ \mathit{xs} \\
\qquad \land \ \mathit{xs} \in \mathbb{N} \rightarrowtail\!\!\!\!\twoheadrightarrow \mathit{name} \\
\qquad \land \ (c, \#\mathit{xs}) \notin \bigcup(\mathit{form_funcs}(\!|\mathit{thy}|\!)) \\
\qquad \land \ \mathit{list_all}(\mathit{xs}, \mathit{exists}(c, p)) \in \mathit{consequences}\ \mathit{thy} \\
\qquad \bullet \ \mathit{list_all}(\mathit{xs}, \mathit{exists}(c, p)) \quad \} \\
\land \ (\forall\, \mathit{xs}{:}\ \mathit{seq}\ \mathit{name};\ c{:}\mathit{name};\ p{:}\mathit{wff}\ \mathit{thy} \\
\qquad \mid \ \mathit{list_all}(\mathit{xs}, \mathit{exists}(c, p)) \in \mathit{dom}\,(\mathit{new_specification}\ \mathit{thy}) \\
\qquad \bullet \ \mathit{new_specification}\ \mathit{thy}\ (\mathit{list_all}(\mathit{xs}, \mathit{exists}(c, p))) \\
\qquad = \ \mathit{thy} \cup \{\mathit{subst}(\{c \mapsto \mathit{app}(c, \mathit{var} \circ \mathit{xs})\}, p)\})
\end{array}$$

3 Critical Properties of the Proof Tool

We envisage a tool which assists the user in building theories and proving theorems. We now give a rather abstract model of such a tool. It is intended to make visible only those features which are necessary to state the critical requirements on such a tool. For simplicity, we assume that the tool works with a single theory. Extending the present specification to cater for a tool managing a collection of named theories is straightforward.

States The state of the proof tool is a triple, (*thy*, *defs*, *thms*) say. *thy* gives the set of non-logical axioms which have been introduced using one of the two extension mechanisms. *defs* gives the subset of *thy* comprising the axioms introduced using *new_specification*. *thms* records the theorems which have been proved by the user. The following defines the allowable states of the abstract proof tool, which we sometimes refer to as 'abstract states':

z

STATE

$$\begin{array}{ll}
\mathit{thy} & : \mathit{theory}; \\
\mathit{defs} & : \mathbb{F}\,\mathit{form}; \\
\mathit{thms} & : \mathbb{F}\,\mathit{form}
\end{array}$$

$$\mathit{defs} \subseteq \mathit{thy} \land \mathit{thms} \subseteq \mathit{wff}\ \mathit{thy}$$

The Kernel Let us say that a 'kernel' is a transition function equipped with an interpretation function allowing us to view its state space as an abstract state. We formalise this property by the following definition (which is generic in the state space, ST, inputs, IP, and outputs, OP, of the transition function):

z

KERNEL[ST, IP, OP]

$$\begin{array}{ll}
\mathit{tr_f} & : (IP \times ST) \rightarrow (OP \times ST); \\
\mathit{int} & : ST \rightarrow STATE
\end{array}$$

We may now formulate two critical properties which we would like the proof system to have.

Critical Property 1 The first critical property is intended to ensure that the tool contains a correct implementation of the rules of inference and to place some constraints on the mechanisms which modify the theory (e.g. it would prevent an operation which deleted an arbitrary axiom). It says that states in which all the alleged theorems are indeed consequences of the axioms are mapped to states with the same property:

z

$$
\begin{array}{l}
[ST, IP, OP] \\
\quad \mathbf{derivability\_preserving} : \mathbb{P}\ KERNEL[ST, IP, OP] \\
\hline
\quad \forall\, ker{:}KERNEL[ST, IP, OP] \bullet \\
\qquad ker \in derivability\_preserving \\
\quad \Leftrightarrow \quad (\forall st1, st2 : ST;\ ip{:}\ IP;\ op{:}OP \mid (op, st2) = ker.tr\_f(ip, st1) \bullet \\
\qquad\qquad (ker.int\ st1).thms \subseteq consequences((ker.int\ st1).thy) \\
\qquad \Rightarrow \quad (ker.int\ st2).thms \subseteq consequences((ker.int\ st2).thy))
\end{array}
$$

Critical Property 2 The second critical property demands that the tool makes a proper distinction between conservative and axiomatic extensions. It asks that every transition of the tool which changes the definitions component of the abstract state does so via *new_specification*. For the want of a better word, we use the term *standard* for this property.

z

$$
\begin{array}{l}
[ST, IP, OP] \\
\quad \mathbf{standard} : \mathbb{P}\ KERNEL[ST, IP, OP] \\
\hline
\forall\, ker{:}KERNEL[ST, IP, OP] \bullet \\
\quad ker \in standard \\
\Leftrightarrow \quad (\forall st1, st2 : ST;\ ip{:}\ IP;\ op{:}OP \mid (op, st2) = ker.tr\_f(ip, st1) \bullet \\
\qquad (ker.int\ st2).defs \neq (ker.int\ st1).defs \\
\quad \Rightarrow \quad (\exists p{:}form \bullet \\
\qquad\qquad (ker.int\ st2).thy = new\_specification\ ((ker.int\ st1).thy)\ p \\
\qquad \wedge \qquad (ker.int\ st2).defs \\
\qquad = \qquad (ker.int\ st1).defs \cup ((ker.int\ st2).thy \setminus (ker.int\ st1).thy)))
\end{array}
$$

4 Design of the Kernel

In this section we give the design of the critical kernel for a very simple proof tool, which, we believe, satisfies the specification we have given. The design deliberately underspecifies certain aspects, and in section 5.2 below we consider how a simple program could be implemented which realises it and also discuss some shortcomings arising from our simplification of the actual work done for HOL.

States In the design we use finite functions over names to represent the sets which appear in the abstract state. We also decide to hold the 'conservative axioms' and the 'axiomatic axioms' separately.

Thus, the state in the design will range over the following set:

z

$$
\begin{array}{l}
\mathbf{C\_STATE} \\
\quad axs, defs, thms \quad : name \twoheadrightarrow\!\!\!\!\!\!\shortmid\ \ form \\
\hline
\quad ran\ thms \subseteq wff(ran\ axs \cup ran\ defs)
\end{array}
$$

(Here $C\_$ and, later, $c\_$ stand for 'concrete'.)

Interpretation Function This is very straightforward:

z

$$\mathbf{int\_c\_state} : C\_STATE \rightarrow STATE$$

$$\begin{array}{ll} \forall c\_st{:}C\_STATE \bullet & \\ & (int\_c\_state\ c\_st).thy = ran\,(c\_st.axs) \cup ran\,(c\_st.defs) \\ \land & (int\_c\_state\ c\_st).defs = ran\,(c\_st.defs) \\ \land & (int\_c\_state\ c\_st).thms = ran\,(c\_st.thms) \end{array}$$

Inputs and Outputs Since our specification is defined purely in terms of the state of the system, we do not wish to specify the inputs or outputs in detail. We represent them both as given sets:

z

$$[\mathbf{C\_IP}, \mathbf{C\_OP}]$$

Inference rules The function *infer* maps inputs to state transitions which correspond to various forms of proof activity. None of the transitions computed by *infer* change the axioms and definitions components of the state. To allow *infer* to reject input which is invalid, it may also fail to change the theorems component. Otherwise it adds a new entry in the theorems component associating a formula with some name. The formula is either a logical axiom, or an axiom or definition of the theory, or is obtained by applying *modus ponens* or generalisation to some arguments in which any formulae occur in the theorems component.

z

$$\mathbf{infer} : C\_IP \rightarrow C\_STATE \rightarrow C\_STATE$$

$$\begin{array}{llll} \multicolumn{4}{l}{\forall ip{:}C\_IP;\ st1, st2 : C\_STATE \mid st2 = infer\ ip\ st1 \bullet} \\ & st2.axs = st1.axs & & \\ \land & st2.defs = st1.defs & & \\ \land & (& st2.thms = st1.thms & \\ & \lor & (\exists p{:}logical\_axioms;\ pn{:}name \bullet & \\ & & & pn \notin dom(st1.thms) \land st2.thms = st1.thms \cup \{pn \mapsto p\}) \\ & \lor & (\exists p{:}ran(st1.axs) \cup ran(st1.defs);\ pn{:}name \bullet & \\ & & & pn \notin dom(st1.thms) \land st2.thms = st1.thms \cup \{pn \mapsto p\}) \\ & \lor & (\exists p, q{:}form;\ rn{:}name \mid \{p, q\} \subseteq ran(st1.thms) \bullet & \\ & & & rn \notin dom(st1.thms) \land st2.thms = st1.thms \cup \{rn \mapsto mp(p, q)\}) \\ & \lor & (\exists p{:}form;\ n, qn{:}name \mid p \in ran(st1.thms) \bullet & \\ & & & qn \notin dom(st1.thms) \land st2.thms = st1.thms \cup \{qn \mapsto gen(n, p)\})) \end{array}$$

Note that there is a close correspondence between the definition of *infer* and the definition of *direct_consequence* in section 2.3 above.

Extending Theories The function *extend* maps inputs to state transitions which introduce new axioms or definitions. Such transitions do not change the theorems component of the state. *new_axiom* or *new_specification* is used to compute an updated axioms or definitions component. Note that the defining predicate for *C_STATE* ensures that the formula passed to *new_specification* is indeed a consequence of the axioms and definitions of the theory.

z

$$\mathbf{extend}: C\_IP \rightarrow C\_STATE \rightarrow C\_STATE$$

$$\begin{array}{l}
\forall ip{:}C_IP;\ st1, st2 : C_STATE \mid st2 = extend\ ip\ st1 \bullet \\
\qquad st2.thms = st1.thms \\
\wedge \quad (\quad (\exists p{:}form \bullet \\
\qquad\qquad ran(st2.axs) = new_axiom\ (ran(st1.axs) \cup ran(st1.defs))\ p \\
\qquad\qquad\qquad \setminus ran(st1.defs) \\
\qquad \wedge \quad st2.defs = st1.defs) \\
\quad \vee \quad (\exists p{:}ran(st1.thms) \bullet \\
\qquad\qquad ran(st2.defs) = new_specification(ran(st1.axs) \cup ran(st1.defs))\ p \\
\qquad\qquad\qquad \setminus ran(st1.axs) \\
\qquad \wedge \quad st2.axs = st1.axs))
\end{array}$$

Transition Function This is very straightforward:

z

$$\mathbf{c\_trans\_fun}: C\_IP \times C\_STATE \rightarrow C\_OP \times C\_STATE$$

$$\begin{array}{l}
\forall ip{:}C_IP;\ op{:}C_OP;\ st1, st2 : C_STATE \mid (op, st2) = c_trans_fun\ (ip, st1) \bullet \\
\qquad st2 = infer\ ip\ st1 \vee st2 = extend\ ip\ st1
\end{array}$$

Kernel Construction The design of our proof tool is completed by combining the transition and interpretation functions to give an instance of the type *KERNEL*:

z

$$\mathbf{c\_ker}: KERNEL[C\_STATE, C\_IP, C\_OP]$$

$$c\_ker.tr\_f = c\_trans\_fun \wedge c\_ker.int = int\_c\_state$$

5 Discussion

5.1 Verification Issues

Now we have given a design as an instance of the type *KERNEL*, we can state the critical requirements for it formally. Thus, the overall correctness proposition for the design is the conjecture:

$1.\quad ?\vdash c\_ker \in derivability\_preserving \cap standard$

We would like to reduce this to conjectures about the inference and extension subsystems. The proof of this reduction of the problem would precede along the following lines:

We would expand conjecture 1 using the definitions of *derivability_preserving*, *standard*, *c_ker*, *int_c_state* and *trans_fun* and then observe that inference and *new_axiom* transitions must be standard (because they do not change the definitions) and that extension transitions preserve derivability (because they do not change the theorems component and do not remove any axioms or definitions). Thus the conjecture reduces to the following conjectures, which, in effect, assert that inference transitions preserve derivability and that *new_specification* transitions are standard.

2. $?\vdash \forall ip{:}C\_IP;\ st1, st2 : C\_STATE \mid st2 = infer\ ip\ st1 \bullet$
$\quad ran(st1.thms) \subseteq consequences(ran(st1.axs) \cup ran(st1.defs))$
$\Rightarrow \quad ran(st2.thms) \subseteq consequences(ran(st2.axs) \cup ran(st2.defs))$

3. $?\vdash \forall ip{:}C\_IP;\ st1, st2 : C\_STATE \mid st2 = extend\ ip\ st1 \bullet$
$\quad ran(st2.defs) \neq ran(st2.defs)$
$\Rightarrow \quad (\exists p{:}form \bullet$
$\qquad ran(st2.axs \cup st2.defs) = new\_specification\ (ran(st1.axs) \cup ran(st1.defs))\ p$
$\quad \wedge \qquad ran(st2.defs)$
$\qquad = \quad ran(st1.defs) \cup (ran(st2.axs \cup st2.defs)$
$\qquad\qquad \setminus (ran(st1.axs) \cup ran(st1.defs))))$

Thus, we have reduced the correctness proposition for the complete system to properties of its subsystems taken separately. Continuing this decomposition process would lead fairly quickly to an informal proof of correctness for the system in an example of this kind (probably after one or more rounds of corrections to the design, and perhaps the specification, where the proof attempt revealed flaws). Although the sketch given in the previous paragraph deliberately omits many details (e.g. the justification of the definitions of *infer* and *extend* against the defining property of *C_STATE*), a fully formal proof using a real-life proof development system such as HOL would be quite feasible.

5.2 Implementation Issues

The actual implementation of the system would follow the LCF paradigm. The kernel would be implemented as an abstract data type in an interactive functional programming language such as Standard ML (see [4]). Implementing the types and functions defined in sections 2.1 and 2.2 is very straightforward in such a language. Assuming this to have been done, and also assuming a type *'a dict* implementing string-indexed lookup tables for items of type *'a* with operations *empty*, *enter* etc., the abstract data type might start as follows:

Standard ML Example

```
abstype theorem = mk_theorem of form
with    local   val c_state:
                        {axs:form dict ref, defs:form dict ref, thms:form dict ref}
                = {axs = ref empty, defs = ref empty, thms = ref empty};
        in      fun new_axiom (n:string, p:form) : theorem = (
                        #axs c_state := enter (n, p)(!(#axs c_state));
                        mk_theorem p
                );
        (* .... *)
        end;
end;
```

The user interacts with the system using ML as a command language (usually referred to as the metalanguage in this context). Thus from the point of view of our design the input to the system would be the metalanguage commands, and the outputs might be taken as the values printed by the ML system. Note that there is no explicit implementation of the functions *infer* and *extend*, which were introduced in the design just to identify a decomposition of the kernel into subsystems. In a fully formal treatment of the implementation, one would have to display an interpretation function describing how the implementation realised the design

One very naive aspect of our design is that it stores the result of every inference in the theory. In practice, the design should allow the inference rules to be coded as functions returning values of type *theorem* and theorems would only be saved when the user made an explicit request for the system to do so. For this reason, it is arguable that the design does not really capture the "essence of LCF". To do this properly the design needs to model the metalanguage store in which the results of inferences reside. Our actual work on HOL addresses this issue as well as others which arise in supporting the features we wish for in a real system (e.g. management of a hierarchy of named theories allowing deletion of theories, and of definitions and axioms within them).

5.3 Supporting Specification

In section 1.3, we mentioned that the conservative extension mechanism was intended to help in treating specifications without prejudicing logical consistency. In this section we sketch how this works in practice and how we arrange to defer the proof obligations until specification work is completed.

The idea is to have (non-critical) code which does a certain amount of automatic proof while the specification is loaded into the system to build the corresponding theory. In our example, one might consider processing Z-like implicit, possibly loose, definitions of the form:

Example

$$\begin{array}{|l} \cdot\ c \\ \hline P \end{array}$$

where c is the name of a new function to be introduced and P is its desired defining property (in which $x_1, \ldots, x_k$ occur free, say). This would be handled by a procedure which automatically proved the following trivial theorem:

Example

$$\vdash \forall x1 \bullet ... \forall xk \bullet \exists c \bullet ((\forall x1 \bullet ... \forall xk \bullet \exists c' \bullet P[c'/c]) \Rightarrow P)$$

Passing this to *new_specification* gives the defining axiom:

Example

$$\vdash \forall x1 \bullet ... \forall xk \bullet \exists c \bullet ((\forall x1 \bullet ... \forall xk \bullet \exists c' \bullet P[c'/c]) \Rightarrow P[c(x1, ... xk)/c])$$

where the second last c is the new function symbol rather than a variable. This defining axiom is clearly equivalent to $P[c(x1, ... xk)/c]$ if we can prove the *consistency* proposition for the definition, namely the conjecture:

Example

$$?\vdash \forall x1 \bullet ... \forall xk \bullet \exists c' \bullet P[c'/c]$$

Thus a specification may be used to construct a theory by means of conservative extensions each of which introduces a defining axiom which is logically equivalent to the desired axiom provided the corresponding consistency proposition is provable.

In fact, the ideas we have outlined would not be of much use in first order logic, in general. However in Z or in a higher-order system like HOL, it becomes quite powerful. In many useful cases it is possible to automate the proof of the consistency proposition. For example, definitions by recursion over a free type or definitions of a set like the definition of *wff* in section 2.1 above may usefully be handled in this way.

6 Conclusions

Work in progress within ICL to construct a high integrity proof tool is beginning to get a good grip on the problem using methods which we have illustrated in this paper in a much-simplified example. A key aspect of the approach is explicit specification of a formal object modelling the kernel of the system of which one can postulate formally the desired critical properties. A formal verification of the design for the kernel against these critical properties seems feasible and work on this is in progress. In the future, it may be possible to bridge the gap between the design and the implementation by means of a formalisation of the implementation language semantics.

A major part of the problem of how specifications are handled in the proof tool has been solved using the conservative extension mechanism which we have discussed. While this technique caters well for implicit definitions of values, we do not yet have a usable, elegant and effective analogue for implicitly defining types in typed systems such as Z or HOL. Moreover, Z has a facility for a user to introduce an arbitrary predicate as a constraint. It is not yet clear how in practice one can handle all of Z in a conservative way. Work on these topics is in progress.

Acknowledgments

The FST project (IED project 1563) is jointly funded by International Computers Limited and by the Information Engineering Directorate of the UK Department of Trade and Industry.

References

[1] Michael J.C. Gordon. HOL:A Proof Generating System for Higher-Order Logic. In G. Birtwistle and P. A. Subrahmanyam, editors, *VLSI Specification, Verification and Synthesis.* Kluwer, 1987.

[2] Michael J.C. Gordon, Arthur J. Milner, and Christopher P. Wadsworth. *Edinburgh LCF. Lecture Notes in Computer Science. Vol. 78.* Springer-Verlag, 1979.

[3] Elliot Mendelson. *Introduction to Mathematical Logic.* Wadworth and Brook/Cole, third edition, 1987.

[4] Robin Milner, Mads Tofte, and Robert Harper. *The Definition of Standard ML.* MIT Press, 1990.

[5] J.M. Spivey. *The Z Notation: A Reference Manual.* Prentice-Hall, 1989.

[6] DS/FMU/INFRA/001. *Infra Project Overview Document.* K. Blackburn, ICL Secure Systems, WIN01.

[7] Interim Defence Standard 00-55(Draft). *Requirements for the Procurement of Safety Critical Software in Defence Equipment.*

[8] *The HOL System: Description.* SRI International, 4 December 1989.

Index of Z Names

Reasoning about VDM Developments using The VDM Support Tool in Mural

J.C. Bicarregui and B. Ritchie
Systems Engineering Division
Informatics Department
Rutherford Appleton Laboratory

Abstract

Mural is an interactive mathematical reasoning environment designed to assist the kind of theorem proving tasks that arise when following a formal methods approach to software engineering. It is the result of work carried out at Manchester University and the Rutherford Appleton Laboratory under the Alvey IPSE 2.5 project.

Considerable design emphasis has been placed upon the user interface, using the power of workstation technology to present information and to give the user freedom of action backed up by careful dependency tracking. Through this emphasis on the user interface it is hoped to enable users to maintain their intuition of the problem domain and hence guide the proof in the right direction, whilst the mechanical symbolic manipulation of the machine can maintain the integrity of the proof.

The Mural proof assistant is generic in that it can be instantiated for reasoning in a variety of logics. Logical theories are constructed in a hierarchical store where collections of declarations and axioms are structured along with derived rules and their proofs. Some effort has been spent on the instantiation of the proof assistant for the formal method VDM. This instantiation includes theories of the logic LPF upon which VDM is based, and of the basic types and functions of VDM.

The system includes tools for the construction of VDM specifications and reifications between them and for the generation of the proof obligations that provide the basis of the formal verification of the refinement relationship. It also supports the construction of theories in the proof assistant where it is possible to reason about specifications, reifications and proof obligations. Though there are many more features that would be desirable in a complete environment for VDM, this degree of support has shown that the Mural proof assistant could be used as an integral part of a generic support environment including provision for the formal development of software.

This paper concentrates upon the VDM support aspects of Mural: how users can build specifications and reifications between them; and how these are "translated" into Mural theories including the generation of the corresponding proof obligations.

Keywords: formal methods, formal specification, refinement, proof, integrated support environments.

1 Introduction

One frequently cited reason for the slow take-up of formal methods in industry is the lack of tools for supporting the processes involved. Tools are required that can provide integrated support for the full formal development method, including the construction of specifications, incremental refinement of specifications to implementations, the generation of proof obligations for the verification of the refinements and the formal reasoning required to discharge them. Such tools could also address the management of the formal objects involved. However, fully integrated tools for all the processes of formal software development may still be some way off.

The Mural system, developed by Manchester University and Rutherford Appleton Laboratory under the Alvey funded IPSE 2.5 project, is primarily concerned with providing generic support for what is perhaps the most intricate of these processes, that is the construction of fully formal mathematical proofs. The project has also concerned itself with how this proof assistant could be integrated with support for the other processes of formal development. To this end, support facilities for specification and verification for the formal development method VDM have been built alongside the formal reasoning assistant. With this combined facility it is possible to construct VDM specifications and reifications between them and generate the theories in which proof obligations can be discharged, thus providing a level of integration not previously available.

This paper discusses the support for VDM provided by the Mural system. We assume some knowledge of VDM, including data reification and operation modelling.

2 Background

2.1 The Mural System

The major component of Mural is a generic mathematical reasoning environment designed to assist in the theorem proving tasks that arise when following a formal methods approach to software engineering. Using a carefully specified and constructed kernel, and through the use of "state-of-the-art" user interface design, Mural is intended to harness the mechanical precision of the computer in combination with the intuitive insight of the user. Mural is founded on a generic logic that can be instantiated to a variety of logics [1] and thus is capable of providing support for the reasoning required in many formal development methods. Logical theories are organised in a hierarchical store where collections of declarations and axioms are structured along with derived rules and their proofs. Proofs are constructed interactively in a natural deduction style. The user is given the freedom to construct the proof in any manner – top-down, bottom-up, middle-out,. . . , with Mural providing assistance in determining which existing rules in the theory store are applicable at each stage, and checking correctness of the reasoning in the proof.

The second component of Mural is a support facility for VDM, the VDM Support Tool (VST). This facility provides support for the construction of VDM specifications and refinements between them. It also generates theories in the hierarchy in which the specifications can be reasoned about together with the proof obligations that must be discharged to verify the design decisions. Considerable effort has also gone into populating the proof assistant with the theories of the basic constructs of VDM. By intention, the Mural VDM support tool does not provide full support for specification and refinement in VDM, as the primary reason for its development was to investigate how a fuller support facility could be integrated with the proof assistant. Only a small part of the VDM specification language is catered for, and only a limited notion of reification is supported. Operation decomposition is not addressed. At present, the only way to determine the status of proofs about a specification or reification is by looking at the status of the rules in the corresponding Mural theories. The VST does however provide a level of integration of support for the processes of specification refinement and proof that was not previously available. Though limited in its original objectives, the degree of support provided has attracted much interest and the system has been used on several non-trivial specifications as part of evaluation work.

2.2 Related Work

Following almost twenty years of development and practical use in a wide variety of applications, work is currently under way to develop a BSI standard for the VDM specification language [2]. The standardisation effort concentrates upon the abstract and concrete syntaxes but also addresses semantics and context conditions. It is hoped that this work will be adopted by ISO. The standardisation effort, however, does not consider issues related to refinement and proof.

The use of VDM as a development method including refinement and proof is described in [3]. There have been a number of papers addressing semantic issues in VDM. In [4, 5], the formulation of the proof obligations are justified with respect to a semantic model for VDM. Monahan [6] has presented a semantic model for VDM type definitions; this has been used by Arentoft and Larsen as the starting point for a semantic model for BSI-VDM [7]. Operation decomposition has been addressed by Milne [8] and Ah-Kee [9]. A new formulation of some of the proof rules for operation decomposition is presented in [3].

In addition to Mural, there are a number of other tools for the construction of VDM specifications. STC's VDM Toolset [10] provides a structure editor for specifications, which performs some static type-checking and syntax conformance. Adelard's SpecBox provides a parser for BSI-VDM which performs arity checking. IST's GENESIS has been instantiated for VDM, giving a structure editor and static semantics checker; there is also a proof editor for LPF, but proof obligations are not generated from VDM specifications.

A number of tools exist which provide support for specification construction and (patent) type-checking in Z, including Spivey's "Fuzz". Several proof tools have been used to discharge Z "proof opportunities" (including the "B" tool [13] and the Boyer-Moore theorem prover). There have been some recent interesting developments in reasoning about Z specifications by embedding the notation in other systems, in the "zedB" rule base for the B tool, and in the FST project's work on Z in HOL.

The RAISE project [14] developed a "wide-spectrum" specification language in which specifications can be written in both model-oriented and algebraic styles. Part of the RAISE work has involved the design of tools to support the construction of specifications, though little or no support for formal proof is provided.

3 A Small Example

In this section we give an example of a small development in the VDM support tool. The example is a simple address book with a lookup operation.

Figure 1 shows the development browser, which comprises two (duplicate) lists of specifications ("abstract" and "concrete", relative to the reifications) and a list of reifications. Each reification links two specifications, with the intention of showing that one specification can be considered a "more concrete" version of the other. When a specification is selected in the

lookup

(Abstract) specifications	Reifications	(Concrete) specifications
lookup lev 1	lookup reification	lookup lev 1
lookup lev 2		lookup lev 2
lookup reification aux. spec.		lookup reification aux. spec.

Figure 1: **A development browser**

"abstract" list, the list of reifications is filtered to show only those reifications "from" that specification, and similarly for the "concrete" list. When a specification is selected in each list, it is possible to add a new reification between them (in addition to any already present). Selecting a reification causes its abstract and concrete specifications to be selected in the two lists, as in the figure.

From the development browser, we can add, browse and edit specifications using a specification browser. Figure 2 shows the specification browser on the level 1 (most abstract) specification of "lookup". This consists of lists of the type, constant, function and operation definitions in the specification, a button to show the state, and a "noticeboard" in which the definitions can be displayed and edited in individual "notices". (The noticeboard is a miniature window environment in which notices may be moved, resized, iconised and exposed). The visible notices here show definitions of the types $ADDR$ and $AddrBook$, and the specification of the $LOOKUP$ operation. At this level, the address book is simply a map from names to addresses, and $LOOKUP$ is specified in terms of map functions. These definitions were constructed using a structure editor which uses an abstract syntax drawn from the BSI draft standard.

Another instance of the browser on the "level 2 lookup" specification is shown in figure 3. The address book in this case is a sequence of pairs of names and addresses. To ensure that it is still "map-like" we need to restrict this by an invariant that no two distinct elements of the sequence can have the same name. To simplify the specification of the new operation $LOOKUP2$, we choose to define two auxiliary function definitions, $addrFor$ (which is

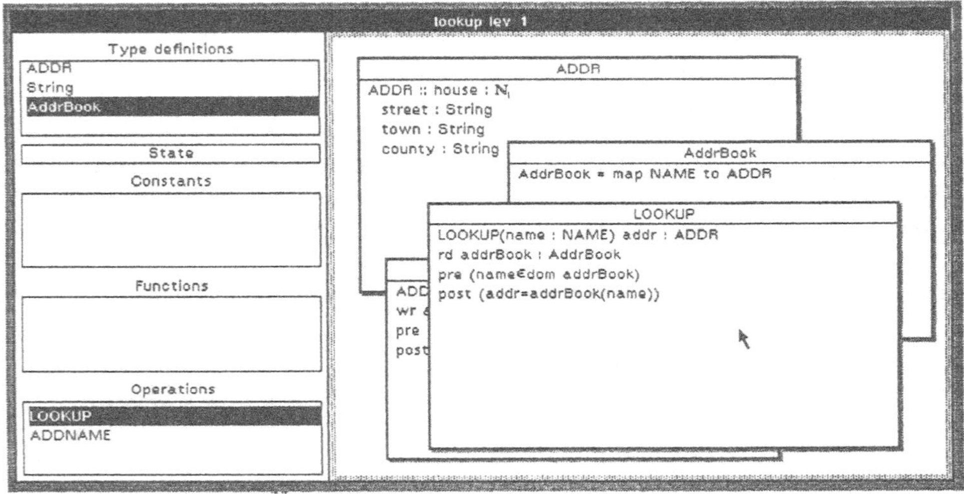

Figure 2: **Specification browser on the "abstract" lookup specification**

implicitly defined) and *existsAddr* (which is explicitly[1] defined).

When we construct a reification between two specifications, or look at an existing reification, it is presented in a reification browser (figure 4). This contains component lists for the two specifications, and lists for definitions specific to the reification (e.g. auxiliary functions used to define retrieve functions). Components of specifications may be viewed via notices in an attached noticeboard. At present, the reification browser is incomplete; the only interesting thing we can do here is to select an operation in each specification and create an operation model between them. Doing this for the operations *LOOKUP* and *LOOKUP*2 gives us an operation modelling browser (figure 5). This lists the arguments, read and write externals and result of the two operations (the operation may also be viewed as a notice in the attached noticeboard), and a central list which is a "pool" of available data reifications. The component lists of the two operations are tied, so that when (for example) the (single) read-only state component of the abstract operation is selected, the corresponding component of the concrete operation is also selected. The intention is to link each of these component-pairs by a data retrieval describing how the type of the concrete component can be viewed as a data reification of the type of its abstract counterpart. When a pair is selected, this can be done by selecting a data reification in the central list and "tying" it to the pair. These links are used in the generation of the domain and result obligations arising from the operation model. The noticeboard in the example shows a data reification between *AddrBook* and *AddrBook*2; in addition to the abstract and concrete types, this contains the definition of the retrieve function from *AddrBook*2 to *AddrBook*, here defined in terms of an auxiliary function *mapFromSeq*. Note that we permit interface refinement (i.e. reification of argument and result types); and that our reification model is restricted to those cases where the abstract and concrete operations have the same number of read and write components.

[1]Note: though explicit, this definition is non-constructive, through its use of existential quantification; however, the function is "clearly implementible" in this case.

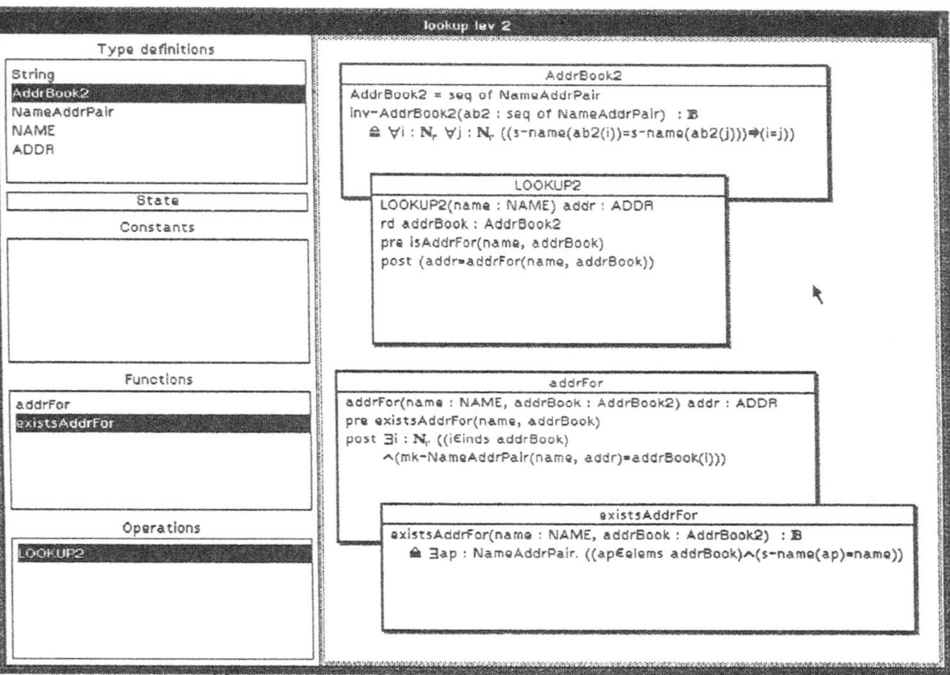

Figure 3: **Specification browser on the "concrete" lookup specification**

We are free to construct abstract and concrete specifications in any order, and the components of each specification can be added in any order. It is even possible to begin building a reification between two specifications before they are complete (indeed, we have done so here).

4 Theories from Developments

In this section we describe the approach taken in the translation of VDM specifications and reifications into the Mural theory store, to create theories within which we can reason about the proof obligations that arise. As Mural is generic, there is a "once-off" effort to instantiate the theory store for VDM, creating a hierarchy of theories (propositional and predicate LPF, numbers, sets, maps, sequences etc.) culminating in a "VDM Primitives" theory. This theory should be an ancestor of every theory generated from a specification or reification in the VDM support tool. Such a theory store is not static: not only will new theories be created corresponding to new specifications and reifications, but more derived rules can be added to the VDM Primitives hierarchy as required.

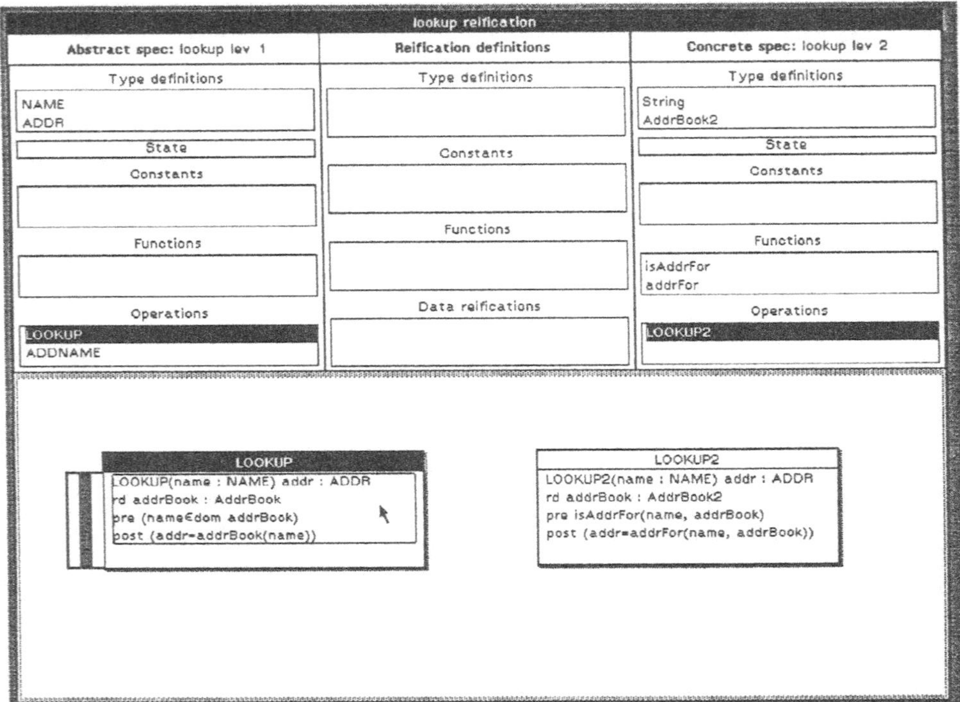

Figure 4: **A reification browser**

4.1 Notation used for Mural theory components

There is insufficient space in this paper to describe Mural's generic logic; here we give only a brief summary of the notation used in this paper to describe components of Mural theories.

The Mural theory store is organised as a hierarchy of individual "theories". Each theory can declare new type and expression symbols, which can be defined either through axioms or by direct definitions. The syntax permits higher-order metavariables and includes dependent type constructs, but beta-reduction is not built-in (to make matching of proof rules decidable). In addition to axioms, a theory can also contain derived rules; each rule may have an associated proof which justifies it with respect to the axioms or other derived rules. (It is possible to use derived rules in proofs before they have been proven; Mural's dependency tracking can determine the set of unproven rules used in a proof (directly or indirectly), and will also prevent circular arguments). A theory can have one or more parent theories, in which case all the declarations, definitions, axioms and rules of these theories (and their ancestors) may be used in the theory.

We will use the following notation to describe components of Mural theories[2].

A Mural *declaration* such as

[2]This notation is not precisely the same notation as used in Mural, and does not capture the full power of Mural's declaration mechanism and inference rules (for example, an inference rule may also contain sequent hypotheses), but is sufficient for our purposes.

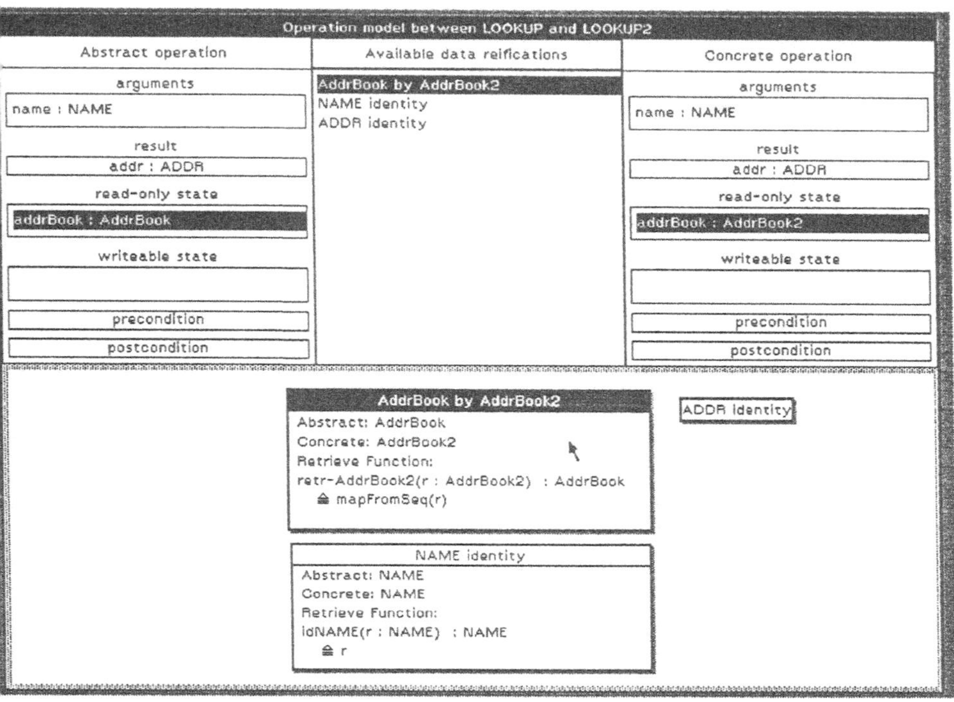

Figure 5: **An operation model browser**

$mk\text{-}T \mapsto [2,0]$

declares a constant symbol $mk\text{-}T$ of expression arity 2 and type arity 0. We will use this notation for both expression and type declarations. If $mk\text{-}T$ is an expression constant declared as above, then we may construct expressions such as $mk\text{-}T[x,y]$ for any expressions x and y. Whether or not such an expression is meaningful depends upon axioms (e.g. formation rules) given in the theory[3].

Expression and type symbols may be bound to *definitions*, e.g.

$\wedge \mapsto \neg(\neg(\llbracket e1 \rrbracket) \vee \neg(\llbracket e2 \rrbracket))$

defines $\wedge$ as an expression constant of (expression) arity 2 (using $\llbracket e1 \rrbracket$ and $\llbracket e2 \rrbracket$ as "placeholders" in the definition). Instances of definitions in expressions may be folded and unfolded; for example the expressions

$\wedge[P,Q]$ and $\neg(\neg P \vee \neg Q)$

are interchangeable. (In Mural, it is also possible to specify a "pretty-printing" format for each constant (declared or defined). For $\wedge$, this is defined as $(\llbracket e1 \rrbracket \wedge \llbracket e2 \rrbracket)$, so $\wedge[P,Q]$ will actually appear as $(P \wedge Q)$. In much of what follows, we will use pretty-printed notation without introduction.)

[3]All of the constants we will declare during the translation of specifications and reifications will have type arity 0. An example of a constant with a non-zero type arity is the set type constructor X-set, which is declared as $setof \mapsto [0,1]$ (i.e. it takes one type as an argument).

We will use the following notation for inference rules:

$$\boxed{\text{mk-T formn}}(a, b)\frac{a: A, b: B}{mk\text{-}T(a, b): T}$$

defines an inference rule (which may be either an axiom or a derived rule) called "mk-T formn". This rule has expression metavariables a and b (which may be "instantiated" to any expressions when applying the rule). It has two hypotheses (which in this case are typing assertions) and a conclusion. This rule states that if we have two expressions a and b of types A and B respectively, then the expression $mk\text{-}T[a, b]$ is of type T.

4.2 Theories from Specifications

How best to divide the objects corresponding to specifications into theories is largely a matter of taste. For example, we could try to place each type definition in a theory of its own; this would allow reuse of the type definition when reasoning about other specifications. However, we would then have to make the theory structure reflect the inter-dependency of type definitions. We choose a simpler approach where each specification becomes a single Mural theory. If a "finer-grained" structure is required, then the theories must be rebuilt by hand.

The "translated theory" of a specification is a single Mural theory, with the VDM Primitives theory as its parent. The theory contains:

- Mural type definitions, type formation and checking axioms corresponding to the type definitions of the specification;
- definitions of any constants and explicit functions;
- definitions of the pre- and post-conditions of implicit functions and operations;
- (initially unproven) rules corresponding to proof obligations and type-checking (including invariant checking) of functions and operations

As we shall see later, many proof obligations can be presented as extra hypotheses to axioms, rather than as unproven rules. In such cases, the axiom can then be used in practice only when the proof obligation is discharged.

The translation of specifications is incremental, but demand-driven: for example, if a function definition is modified after translation, then its translation is undone, but will be regenerated if the specification is subsequently re-translated.

4.3 Translation of types and type definitions

Generally, a type definition in a specification will be translated to a similar type definition in Mural. Most of the type constructors of VDM can be described in "general" theories which form part of the VDM Primitives theory. Sets, maps, sequences, (binary) type unions and optional types are in this category. Type definitions using these constructors can be translated as Mural definitions using instances of the generic constructors. N-ary type unions can be translated as a composition of binary unions.

4.3.1 Invariants

For a definition of type T with an invariant where the type shape uses the above constructors, translation is straightforward. First, the definition of the invariant *inv-T* (an explicit function definition) is translated (as will be described later). Then the type definition is translated to a *SubType* definition. For example, the type definition:

$$T = Texp$$

where

inv-T(v) $\triangleq$ P(v)

is translated to a definition of *inv-T* and to the Mural definition of the type symbol T:

$$T \mapsto < v\colon Texp' \mid inv\text{-}T(v) >$$

where $Texp'$ is the translation of the type shape $Texp$. This defines type T as a subtype of type $Texp'$ such that all values v of type T satisfy the predicate $inv\text{-}T(v)$. Note that we adopt the view that the invariant is an intrinsic part of the type T, and that there is no intermediate type "T without the invariant".

4.3.2 Composite types

Composite type definitions require an alternative treatment. As different composite type definitions may have different numbers of fields, and as Mural does not allow constants of variable arities, it is not possible (or rather, not easy) to define a general "composite type constructor" in Mural. Therefore composite type shapes cannot be translated into Mural type expressions directly. Furthermore, a greater amount of information is associated with composite types than other type constructions, in that a composite type definition also defines constructor and destructor functions. Instead, we create an axiomatic definition, with formation and typing rules for expressions involving the constructor and destructors.

For example, the composite type definition

$$\begin{aligned} T :: f1 &: A \\ f2 &: B \end{aligned}$$

should be "translated" to:

a declaration of the constructor function (an expression constant with expression arity two):

$$mk\text{-}T \mapsto [2, 0];$$

declarations of the destructor functions (expression constants with expression arity one):

$$s\text{-}f1, s\text{-}f2 \mapsto [1, 0];$$

appropriate typing axioms:

$$\boxed{\text{s-f1 formn}}(t)\frac{t\colon T}{s\text{-}f1(t)\colon A}$$

$$\boxed{\text{s-f2 formn}}(t)\frac{t: T}{s\text{-}f2(t): B}$$

$$\boxed{\text{mk-T formn}}(a, b)\frac{a: A, b: B}{mk\text{-}T(a, b): T}$$

and axioms defining $s\text{-}f1$ and $s\text{-}f2$:

$$\boxed{\text{s-f1 intro}}(a, b)\frac{mk\text{-}T(a, b): T}{s\text{-}f1(mk\text{-}T(a, b)) = a}$$

$$\boxed{\text{s-f2 intro}}(a, b)\frac{mk\text{-}T(a, b): T}{s\text{-}f2(mk\text{-}T(a, b)) = b}$$

(note the use of typing assertions to ensure that $mk\text{-}T(a, b)$ is well-formed)

$$\boxed{\text{mk-T intro}}(t)\frac{t: T}{mk\text{-}T(s\text{-}f1(t), s\text{-}f2(t)) = t}$$

When a composite type definition has an associated invariant, this must also be declared and mentioned in the $mk\text{-}T$ formation axiom, e.g.:

$$inv\text{-}T \mapsto [2, 0]$$

$$\boxed{\text{mk-T formn}}(a, b)\frac{a: A, b: B, inv\text{-}T(a, b)}{mk\text{-}T(a, b): T}$$

and we must also provide an axiom for asserting the invariant:

$$\boxed{\text{inv-T intro}}(a, b)\frac{mk\text{-}T(a, b): T}{inv\text{-}T(a, b)}$$

It should be pointed out that this is only a partial translation, as an induction scheme for T is not generated.

4.4 Translation of function definitions

4.4.1 Definition of pre- and post-conditions

A VDM definition of a function f declares a new function name for use in expressions. Therefore the first part of the translation creates a Mural declaration of an expression symbol f of the appropriate arity. If the function has a pre-condition, then a definition of the symbol *pre-f* is also created; similarly for the post-condition of an implicit function. For example, given:

$f\ (x: \mathbb{N}, y: \mathbb{N})\ r: \mathbb{N}$
pre $x \geq y$
post $r = x - y$

then the following definitions will be created in translation:

$$pre\text{-}f \triangleq ([\![1]\!] \geq [\![2]\!])$$
$$post\text{-}f \triangleq [\![3]\!] = [\![1]\!] - [\![2]\!]$$

The symbols *pre-f* and *post-f* can then be used in the definition axiom for the function. We must guard against ill-formed pre- and post-conditions; though some of these checks could be performed by the VST, we prefer to phrase these checks as proof obligations in the translated theory. Given arguments of the correct types, the pre-condition must be a Boolean expression:

$$\boxed{\text{wf-pre-f}}(x, y)\frac{x: \mathbb{N}, y: \mathbb{N}}{pre\text{-}f(x, y): \mathbb{B}}$$

It may be argued that this is overstrict, in that it forces pre-conditions to be total; however, for approaches such as animation, it may be useful to determine when a function or operation *cannot* be applied or invoked, in addition to determining when it can.

Given arguments of the correct types such that the pre-condition holds, the post-condition must also be a Boolean expression:

$$\boxed{\text{wf-post-f}}(x, y, r)\frac{x: \mathbb{N}, y: \mathbb{N}, r: \mathbb{N}, pre\text{-}f(a, b)}{post\text{-}f(a, b, r): \mathbb{B}}$$

4.4.2 Translation of explicit function definitions

An explicit function definition such as:

$$f : \mathbb{N} \times \mathbb{N} \to \mathbb{N}$$
$$f(x, y) \quad \triangleq \quad x - y$$

could be translated into a Mural definition $f \mapsto [\![e1]\!] - [\![e2]\!]$ where instances of x and y in the function body have been replaced in the Mural definition by $[\![e1]\!]$ and $[\![e2]\!]$ respectively.

(Note that this function is ill-defined when $x < y$; this will be reflected in the inability to complete the proof of the well-formedness obligation given later.)

However if the body of a function does not refer to some argument, then such a simple translation would not work, as the Mural definition would be ill-formed. (The expansion of any Mural definition must mention all of its arguments; this allows us to treat definition folding and unfolding as proper inverses. It also prevents us from replacing a non-denoting term by a denoting term.) The only well-formed definition we can make will have an arity which is less than that of the original function; this would greatly complicate the translation process. Therefore we have chosen to translate explicit functions into symbol declarations and axioms rather than direct definitions. This has the further advantage of making the translation of explicit functions similar to that for implicit functions.

For an explicitly-defined function:

$$f : \mathbb{N} \times \mathbb{N} \to \mathbb{N}$$
$$f(x, y) \quad \triangleq \quad x - y$$
$$\text{pre } x \geq y$$

we want to be able to substitute occurrences in expressions of applications of the function by the body of the definition (with suitable substitutions). However, we should only be allowed to do this when the function application is well-formed, that is, when the arguments are of the correct types and satisfy the pre-condition. Thus, we want a rule of the form

$$\boxed{\text{"f defn"}}(x, y)\frac{x: \mathbb{N}, y: \mathbb{N}, \textit{pre-f}(x, y)}{f(x, y) = x - y}$$

Note that instances of x and y in the body of the function are translated to meta-variables.

However, this is not strict enough: we must also ensure that the function definition is itself well-formed. When the arguments are of the correct type and satisfy the pre-condition, then the body should have the same type as the result type claimed for the definition. In theory, the VDM support tool could perform some of the well-formedness checks on explicit function definitions, but for some cases — those where the result type of the function has an associated invariant — this cannot be done mechanically, and the well-formedness check must be presented as a rule to the proof assistant. Such a rule might appear as:

$$\boxed{\text{f well-formed}}(x, y)\frac{x: \mathbb{N}, y: \mathbb{N}, \textit{pre-f}(x, y)}{x - y: \mathbb{N}}$$

In preference to giving this as a separate (unproven) rule, we add its conclusion as an extra hypothesis to the final definition axiom, to make the dependency clear:

$$\boxed{\text{f defn}}(x, y)\frac{x: A, y: B, \textit{pre-f}(x, y), x - y: \mathbb{N}}{f(x, y) = x - y}$$

The "working version" of this axiom can then be derived by proving the general well-formedness obligation rule and discharging the new hypothesis.

4.4.3 Translation of implicit function definitions

Given an implicit function definition:

$f\ (x: \mathbb{N}, y: \mathbb{N})\ r: \mathbb{N}$
pre $x \geq y$
post $r = x - y$

we need rules for reasoning about expressions which contain subexpressions of the form $f(e_1, e_2)$.

If f is implicitly defined as above, then we know that the expression $f(x, y)$ is of type $\mathbb{N}$ when x, y are of type $\mathbb{N}$ and *pre-f* holds for them; i.e., we need a rule such as:

$$\boxed{\text{"f-formn"}}(x, y)\frac{x: \mathbb{N}, y: \mathbb{N}, \textit{pre-f}(x, y)}{f(x, y): \mathbb{N}}$$

As f is implicitly defined, we cannot, in general, give a precise value z such that $f(x, y) = z$; the most we can say is that $f(x, y)$ satisfies its post-condition (given the same conditions as above):

$$\boxed{\text{"f-prop"}}(x, y)\frac{x: \mathbb{N}, y: \mathbb{N}, \textit{pre-f}(x, y)}{\textit{post-f}(x, y, f(x, y))}$$

Before we can use these rules, we should discharge the implementibility proof obligation for f (otherwise, there is no guarantee that the expression $f(x, y)$ denotes a value). The implementibility obligation can be described as the (initially unproven) rule:

$$\boxed{\text{f implementible}}(x, y)\frac{x\colon \mathbb{N}, y\colon \mathbb{N}, \textit{pre-f}(x, y)}{\exists r\colon \mathbb{N} \cdot \textit{post-f}(x, y, r)}$$

In preference to generating the first two rules in translation, we create two axioms which incorporate "one-point" versions of the implementibility obligation:

$$\boxed{\text{f-formn}}(x, y)\frac{x\colon \mathbb{N}, y\colon \mathbb{N}, \textit{pre-f}(x, y), \exists r\colon \mathbb{N} \cdot \textit{post-f}(x, y, r)}{f(x, y)\colon \mathbb{N}}$$

$$\boxed{\text{f-prop}}(x, y)\frac{x\colon \mathbb{N}, y\colon \mathbb{N}, \textit{pre-f}(x, y), \exists r\colon \mathbb{N} \cdot \textit{post-f}(x, y, r)}{\textit{post-f}(x, y, f(x, y))}$$

Thus, before we can derive any properties of an expression which applies f to a particular x and y, we must show that f is implementible for those particular arguments. Note that if we prove the more general implementibility obligation, we can then use it to discharge the one-point versions in the axioms and thus derive the "working versions" first given.

4.5 Translation of operation definitions

As operation decomposition is not supported by the VST, only implicit operation definitions are translated. The pre- and post-conditions are translated in a similar manner as for function definitions. Their translation is slightly more complicated in that the pre-condition can refer to the "initial state" of an operation, and the post-condition can refer to the initial and final states, in addition to the arguments and result.

The implementibility obligation for an operation

$OP\ (x\colon X)\ r\colon R$
ext rd rd : Rd
  wr wr : Wr
pre ...expression in x, rd and wr...
post ...expression in x, r, rd, $\overleftarrow{wr}$ and wr...

is translated as an unproven rule[4]:

$$\boxed{\text{OP implementibility}}(x, rd, \overleftarrow{wr})\frac{x\colon X, rd\colon Rd, \overleftarrow{wr}\colon Wr, \textit{pre-OP}(x, r, rd, \overleftarrow{wr})}{\exists r\colon R \cdot \exists wr\colon Wr \cdot \textit{post-OP}(x, r, rd, \overleftarrow{wr}, wr)}$$

4.6 Theories from Reifications

In order to reason about a reification of one specification by another, we need the information contained in the two specifications. Therefore, the theory within which we reason about the

[4]If operation decomposition were supported, then the conclusion could appear as a hypothesis to an axiom concerning calls of the operation within an "explicit" operation, by analogy with the definition axiom for an implicit function definition.

reification should inherit from both their theories. This is achieved by making the theories of the two specifications parents of the reification theory.

Roughly, the theory of a reification will contain definitions of the retrieve functions used in the data reifications, together with all the concomitant proof obligations of data reification and operations modelling. It will also contain definitions of auxiliary types and functions used.

4.6.1 Translation of data reifications

Within a reification, a particular data reification from a concrete type C to an abstract type A via a retrieve function *retr-A* translates to:

- a definition or declaration of the retrieve function (in the same manner as for explicit function definitions), as a function from C to A:

  $$\mathit{retr\text{-}A} \mapsto [1, 0];$$

- and an unproven rule expressing the adequacy obligation for the data reification:

$$\boxed{\text{retr-A adequacy}}(c)\frac{c\colon C}{\exists a\colon A \cdot \mathit{retr\text{-}A}(c) = a}$$

Both of these are situated in the theory of the overall reification.

4.6.2 Translation of operation models

Recall that an operation modelling refers to the abstract and concrete operations and a number of *DataReifs*. Translation of the *OpModel* amounts to the translation of each of these along with the creation of two unproven rules in the reification theory: one expressing the domain obligation, and another expressing the result obligation.

Suppose an abstract operation AOP is modelled by a concrete operation COP:

$AOP\ (aa\colon AA)\ ar\colon AR$	$COP\ (ca\colon CA)\ cr\colon CR$
ext rd $ard\ :\ ARD$	ext rd $crd\ :\ CRD$
wr $awr\ :\ AWR$	wr $cwr\ :\ CWR$
pre ...	pre ...
post ...	post ...

and that *retr-a*, *retr-r*,..., *retr-wr* are the retrieve functions associated with each component. Then the domain proof obligations generated is of the form:

$$\boxed{COP \text{ domain obln}}(ca, crd, cwr)\frac{ca\colon CA,\ crd\colon CRD,\ cwr\colon CWR,\quad \mathit{pre\text{-}AOP}(\mathit{retr\text{-}a}(ca), \mathit{retr\text{-}rd}(crd), \mathit{retr\text{-}wr}(cwr))}{\mathit{pre\text{-}COP}(ca, crd, cwr)}$$

that is, the concrete pre-condition should hold whenever the abstract pre-condition holds for the retrieved values. The generated result proof obligation has the form:

$$\boxed{OP_C \text{ result obligation}}(ca, \ldots, cwr)\frac{\begin{array}{c}a_c: A_C, r_c: R_C, rd_c: RD_C, \overleftarrow{wr_c}: WR_C, wr_c: WR_C,\\ pre\text{-}OP_A(retr\text{-}a(a_c), retr\text{-}rd(rd_c), retr\text{-}wr(\overleftarrow{wr_c})),\\ post\text{-}OP_C(a_c, r_c, rd_c, \overleftarrow{wr_c}, wr_c)\end{array}}{\begin{array}{c}post\text{-}OP_A(retr\text{-}a(a_c), retr\text{-}r(r_c), retr\text{-}rd(rd_c),\\ retr\text{-}wr(\overleftarrow{wr_c}), retr\text{-}wr(wr_c))\end{array}}$$

that is: the abstract post-condition should hold on the retrieved values whenever the abstract pre-condition and concrete post-condition hold. The generalisation to multiple arguments and state references is straightforward.

4.7 An example

An important design decision in the development of Mural was to preserve as far as possible the freedom of the user to construct objects (such as theories, proofs, specifications and refinements) in any order. However (partly as a consequence of this freedom of construction order) care must be taken when we come to translate specifications and reifications into the Mural theory store. For example, an attempt to translate (say) an operation which refers to a function or type which has no definition in the specification will fail; a reification cannot be translated before its abstract and concrete specifications; and before an operation model can be translated, all of its component-pairs must be tied to data reifications. Furthermore, the VDM support tool's translation mechanism does not track dependencies, so the user must ensure that components of specifications and reifications are translated in the correct order.

With these provisos in mind (and with the addition of "identity retrievals" on *NAME* and *ADDR* in our example operation model), we can translate our mini-development into the Mural store. This creates a Mural theory for each specification, extending the basic VDM theory, containing translations of the type, function and operation definitions (including well-formedness and implementibility proof obligations). Translating the reification creates a theory which inherits from the theories of the two specifications and contains definitions of the retrieve functions, the corresponding adequacy proof obligations, and the domain and result obligations of the operation model. Figure 6 shows a Mural theory browser on the theory generated from our reification. Its parent theories are the theories generated from the two specifications (which in turn have the basic "VDM" theory as a common parent). Thus the reification theory inherits all the declarations and definitions in the two specification theories (e.g. definitions of the pre- and post-conditions of *LOOKUP* and *LOOKUP2*). The reification theory contains declarations and definitions of the retrieve functions used in our operation model, together with their adequacy obligations. The noticeboard contains notices showing the statements of the domain and result obligations for our operation model, together with the statement of the adequacy obligation for *retr-AddrBook*.

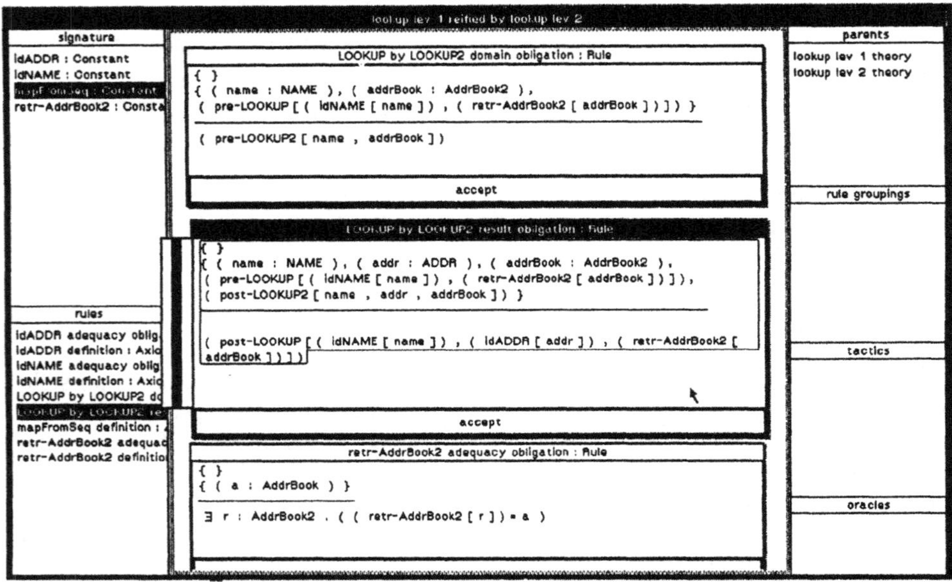

Figure 6: **A theory browser on the *LOOKUP* reification theory**

5 Conclusions

As stated earlier, the VDM support tool component of Mural is not a fully-fledged support environment for VDM. There are many ways in which it could be improved or extended, for example:

- Only a small subset of VDM is catered for.
- Many well-formedness checks could be carried out prior to the translation phase (including, for example, "patent" type-checking, detection of references to undeclared types/functions).
- The theory structure should be finer-grained, allowing re-use of common type definitions or even common data reifications.
- The support tool does not "keep track" of proof obligations etc, so users cannot easily determine which obligations are still outstanding for a particular specification or reification (or component thereof). (This would be easy to remedy.)
- The reification model chosen greatly limits the kinds of operations that can be modelled.
- There is no support for operation decomposition; much work needs to be done to determine a practical interface model for this.

However, the VDM support tool has satisfied our original intentions of providing "interesting" proof obligations to exercise the Mural proof assistant, and of demonstrating that a generic formal reasoning environment can be extended and instantiated to provide support for a particular development method.

References

[1] Lindsay, P. *A formal system with inclusion polymorphism.* IPSE 2.5 working document 060/pal014/2.3, 1987.

[2] BSI IST/5/50. *VDM Specification Language Proto-Standard.* Working paper IST/5/50/170, 1990.

[3] Jones, C. *Systematic Software Development Using VDM.* Prentice-Hall, 1990 (second edition).

[4] Jones, C. *Program Specification and Verification in VDM.* Technical report UMCS-86-10-5, Department of Computer Science, Manchester University, 1986.

[5] Jones, C. VDM Proof Obligations and Their Justification. In: *VDM '87: VDM — A Formal Method at Work.* LNCS 252, Springer-Verlag, 1987.

[6] Monahan, B. A Type Model for VDM In: *VDM '87: VDM — A Formal Method at Work.* LNCS 252, Springer-Verlag, 1987.

[7] Arentoft, M.M. and Larsen, P.G. *The Dynamic Semantics of the BSI/VDM Specification Language.* M.Sc.E.-thesis, Department of Computer Science, Technical University of Denmark, 1988.

[8] Milne, R. Proof Rules for VDM Statements. In *VDM '88: VDM — The Way Ahead.* LNCS 328, Springer–Verlag 1988.

[9] Ah-Kee, J.A. *Operation Decomposition Proof Obligations for Blocks and Procedures.* Ph.D. thesis, Department of Computer Science, Manchester University, 1989.

[10] Crispin, R.J. Experience Using VDM in STC. In: *VDM '87: VDM — A Formal Method at Work.* LNCS 252, Springer-Verlag, 1987.

[11] Spivey, J.M. *The Z notation.* Prentice–Hall, 1989.

[12] Spivey, J.M. *Understanding Z.* Cambridge University Press, 1988.

[13] Abrial, J-R. The B Tool (Abstract). In *VDM '88: VDM — The Way Ahead.* LNCS 328, Springer–Verlag 1988.

[14] Nielson, M, Klaus, H, Wagner, K.R and George, C. The RAISE Language, Method and Tools. *Formal Aspects of Computing* Vol.1 No.1 pp 85-114, 1989.

EVES: An Overview

Dan Craigen, Sentot Kromodimoeljo, Irwin Meisels,
Bill Pase, and Mark Saaltink*

ORA Corporation
265 Carling Avenue, Suite 506
Ottawa, Ontario K1S 2E1
Canada

Internet: eves@ora.on.ca
Telephone: (613) 238 7900

Abstract

In this paper we describe a new formal methods tool called EVES. EVES consists of a set theoretic language, called Verdi, and an automated deduction system, called NEVER. We present an overview of Verdi, NEVER, and the underlying mathematics; and develop a small program, to demonstrate the basic functionality of EVES.
Keywords: Automated deduction, EVES, formal methods, logic of programs, NEVER, Verdi.

1 Introduction

In previous papers [Cra 87, CKM* 88] we presented our views on the putative benefits accruing from the application of verification systems, and we identified various problems with many of the existing verification systems. In particular, many verification systems have poor automated deduction support and lack demonstrable soundness. The primary purpose of the EVES project was to develop a verification system, integrating techniques from automated deduction, mathematics, language design and formal methods, so that the system is both sound and useful. The development of the prototype verification system m-EVES [CKM* 88] and various experimental applications of m-EVES allowed us to gain experience before finally committing to the particular design for EVES.

The development of EVES has followed two principal directions: (1) the design of a new specification and implementation language, called Verdi (which included the development of the formal semantics and proof system with demonstration of soundness), and (2) the implementation of a new theorem prover called NEVER.

*The development of EVES was sponsored by the Canadian Department of National Defence through DSS contract W2207-8-AF78 and various other contracts. This paper is a revised version of ORA Conference Paper CP–91–5402–43, March 1991.

In this paper, we will present an overview of various aspects of EVES, and present a flavour of EVES through a small example. Other reports (such as [Cra 90, Saa 89, Saa 90, SC 90, KP 90]) present detailed descriptions of Verdi, the underlying mathematics, and other applications of EVES (embedding a version of simple type theory in EVES, and a verified implementation of an interpreter for a small programming language).

For the purposes of this paper, a verification system consists of a language or languages that allow the formal specification and implementation of programs, a proof obligation generator, and some form of automated deduction support.

2 Verdi

Verdi [Cra 90] is a formal notation that may be used to write programs that are to be verified formally using the EVES verification system. Consequently, Verdi consists of syntactic forms for expressing specifications (what effect a program is to have), implementations (how a program is to cause an effect), and proofs (justification that a program meets its specification).

Verdi is based on a version of untyped set theory [Fra 68], which can be used to express rigorous mathematical concepts [Saa 89]. For example, Verdi can be used to prove theorems of set theory (e.g., Schroeder-Bernstein, Cantor), to prove the functional correctness of hardware designs (e.g., an n-bit adder), or to prove security-critical properties (e.g., versions of non-interference).

The syntax of Verdi is similar to the s-expressions of LISP.

While Verdi is, in general, an untyped language, typing information is necessary for syntactic forms that are to be executed. In proofs, types denote sets of values.

The Bool, Int and Char types are defined by the initial theory. The Bool type denotes the logical truth values. The Int type denotes the set of mathematical integers. The Char type denotes the ASCII character set. Other types are introduced through an enumeration declaration, an array declaration, or a record declaration. Verdi type sameness is a variant of structural sameness (since the structures of records and enumerations are not used in sameness checking). Hence, Verdi type sameness is a compromise between the extremes of name sameness and structural sameness.

The various function declarations introduce functions. Functions that are used in an executable context must have been introduced by a "typed function declaration." Such a declaration associates type information with the parameters and the result of the function. The result of evaluating an executable function application is predictable only if the application is legal. By "legal" it is meant that the parameters satisfy certain constraints. Non-executable functions may be defined recursively and, by using function recursion groups, through mutual recursion.

A procedure declaration introduces a procedure and is always executable. Procedures may be defined recursively and, by using procedure recursion groups, through mutual recursion.

An axiom declaration expresses a fact and may include heuristic information.

An expression is a Verdi sentence that can be evaluated to produce a value. The expressions are character literals, numerals, strings, identifiers (denoting variables), function applications, and quantifications.

A statement is a Verdi sentence that denotes one or more execution steps and determines, in part, the ordering of the execution steps. Through the execution of statements, the values associated with the observables and states are modified. The Verdi statements are exit (from a loop), return (from a procedure), abort (the program), note (a form of annotation), assignment, procedure call, block, conditional, case, loop, and two forms of *for* loop.

A library is a repository for library objects and is the main means for large scale modularization and abstraction. Libraries can be used to save reusable theories, programs and specifications. Library objects are collections of Verdi declarations that, through the use of the `load` command, may depend upon other library objects. The `load` command introduces the declarations of the associated library specification object (and any necessary subsidiary library specification objects) to a current theory. The EVES library mechanism is further described in Appendix A.

3 NEVER

The theorem prover NEVER is an integral component of EVES. It is an interactive theorem prover capable of automatically performing large proof steps. Its design had been influenced by earlier theorem provers, specifically the Bledsoe-Bruell prover [Ble 73], the Stanford Pascal Verifier [Luc 79], the Boyer-Moore theorem prover [BM 79], and the Affirm theorem prover [Tho 81].

NEVER is neither a fully automatic nor an entirely manual theorem prover. Although NEVER provides powerful deductive techniques for the automatic proof of theorems, it also includes simple user steps that permit its use as a system more akin to a proof checker than a theorem prover. This idea of combining the manual and automatic capabilities is most closely related to the ideas involved in the work of Bledsoe and Bruell. It represents a tacit admission that, for some proofs, it may be essential for the user to resort to hand steps, since the automatic capabilities of NEVER may be inadequate.

Combining the manual and automatic functions within a single system creates the possibility of a synergy between abilities of the system (speed and accuracy) and the user (insight). By allowing the user to back up and selectively override specific decisions that the prover may make, we hope to enhance this synergy between the user and machine.

Proof Steps

To prove a formula, the formula must first be made *current*. Subsequently, proof steps are used to transform the current formula to a new formula.

Use of Axioms

Axioms can be assumed during a proof of some other conjecture with the `use` or `apply` commands. In addition, axioms declared as rewrite or forward rules may be applied automatically by NEVER. A rewrite rule specifies the conditional replacement of an expression by another equivalent expression. A grule specifies a formula to be assumed whenever the rule is "triggered." A forward rule supports forward chaining.

With the `invoke` command, the user can explicitly invoke function definitions. In addition, function definitions may be automatically invoked. By "invoked" we mean that the defining axiom for the function is used as a rewrite rule.

Simplification attempts to replace an expression with an equivalent expression which the system considers to be simpler. Propositional tautologies are always detected. In addition, simplification reasons about equalities, inequalities, integers, and quantifiers; and it applies forward rules and grules.

Rewriting consists of the application of rewrite rules as well as simplification. While traversing a formula, an attempt is made to match patterns of rewrite rules against subexpressions of the formula. If a pattern matches a subexpression, an attempt is made to apply the associated rewrite rule.

Reduction consists of a single traversal of a proposition, invoking function definitions, applying rewrite rules, and performing simplification.

The induction technique used by NEVER is based on that of the Boyer-Moore prover [BM 79]. Normally, induction schemes are heuristically chosen, based on calls to recursive functions within the current formula. However, the user may direct the prover by providing an explicit term on which to induct.

4 Verdi Interpreter

The EVES system incorporates an interpreter for executable Verdi code. With the interpreter, the user can print values of expressions and call Verdi procedures. Interpreter variables may be declared, assigned to, and passed as actuals to procedures and functions.

The interpreter also provides the ability to trace routines, set breakpoints, interrupt the interpretation and examine routine locals and formals, and print tracebacks.

5 EVES

EVES is written in Common LISP and has been successfully run on Symbolics, Sun 3s, SPARCstations, Data General AViiONs, VAXes and the Apple Macintosh IIx. The system is about 43,000 lines of Common LISP in size.

Interaction with EVES may occur through either an editor interface or a command processor. The most common use is through an Emacs interface.

Conceptually, the development process is one of theory extension (through Verdi declarations). Development starts with the Verdi initial theory, which embodies the concepts that are built into Verdi. As declarations are added, information representing the declarations are entered into the EVES database. The result is a new current theory, which consists of the previous theory extended to include the new declarations. Declarations may result in the generation of proof obligations. Proof obligations, when proven, guarantee that a declaration results in a conservative extension. The system supports a degree of incrementality in that declarations may be added or removed.

6 The Flow Modulator Example

Below, we will present the Flow Modulator example. Through this example we demonstrate the use of the EVES library mechanism for structuring formally developed systems.

The development of the Flow Modulator is structured as follows:

- "fmenv:" A specification of parameters to the flow modulator.
- "fmio:" The specification of the I/O routines to be used by the Flow Modulator. I/O procedures, such as those described in "fmio," would be implemented in a language other than Verdi.
- "seq:" A small theory of sequences that is used in the specification of the I/O routines and the Flow Modulator program. This is one of the standard EVES theories.
- "flow:" The main program for the Flow Modulator along with a simple little property about the specification.

Suppose there are two computer systems, Public and Private. It is intended that messages will be allowed to flow from the Private system to the Public system if the messages satisfy a particular predicate.

The program described herein specifies and implements a *flow modulator*. The flow modulator will sequentially read a message from the Private System, determine whether that message satisfies an appropriate predicate and, based upon the result, will either release the message to the Public System or will log the rejected message.

The first set of declarations pertain to messages flowing from the Private system to the Public system. The actual structure of the message datatype is left unspecified, as is the implementation detail for the function "ok." The function "ok" determines whether a message can be released by the Private system. Finally, for this portion of the program, we introduce an executable function that stipulates the maximum number of messages that will be processed by the program. The grules "about number of messages" stipulate that this value must be non-negative and representable.[1]

As we are developing a specification, there are no proof obligations required. In general, consistency of an axiomatic specification is demonstrated through the existence of a model for the specification. Such a demonstration is usually performed within the EVES system. (Note: All user input is prefaced by the system prompt character ">".)

```
> (TYPE-STUB message)
> (TYPED-FUNCTION-STUB ok (((msg) (message))) (bool)  ())
> (TYPED-FUNCTION-STUB number_of_messages () (int) ())

>(GRULE about_number_of_messages_1 ()
  (>= (number_of_messages) 0))

>(GRULE about_number_of_messages_2 ()
  (<= (number_of_messages) (int.last)))

>(MAKE fmenv spec)
```

[1]This approach is a bit artificial. It would have been more reasonable to posit the existence of a finite sequence of messages that would represent the sequence of messages to be read by the Flow Modulator.

The following sequence of declarations specify the I/O routines that may be used by the flow modulator. Two procedures are specified that, respectively, output and input messages. Invocation of each process results in the processing of a single message.

A history of messages is associated with each port. This history is the sequence of messages that have flowed through the port. An abstraction function, "port history," is used to capture this intent. Note that we load a sequence specification called "seq." This specification is omitted from the paper (for space reasons), but is described in [Cra 90].

```
> (RESET)
> (LOAD seq)
> (LOAD fmenv)

> (TYPE-STUB a_port)
> (FUNCTION-STUB port_history (port))

> (PROCEDURE-STUB output_port
                 ((MVAR (port) (a_port)) (LVAR (msg) (fmenv!message)))
                 ( (INITIAL (port_0 port))
                   (PRE (true))
                   (POST (= (port_history port)
                            (seq!tack msg (port_history port_0))))))

> (PROCEDURE-STUB input_port
                 ((MVAR (port) (a_port)) (PVAR (msg) (fmenv!message)))
                 ( (INITIAL (port_0 port))
                   (PRE (true))
                   (POST (= (port_history port)
                            (seq!tack msg (port_history port_0))))))

> (MAKE fmio spec)
```

Having structured our development as above, we are now in position to develop the main Flow Modulator program.

```
> (RESET)
> (LOAD fmio)
```

The two functions "accepted messages" and "rejected messages" determine subsequences based on the truth or falsity, respectively, of the "ok" predicate on sequence elements.

```
> (FUNCTION accepted_messages (seq)
    ((MEASURE (seq!length seq)))
  (IF (seq!emptyp seq)
      (seq!empty)
      (IF (fmenv!ok (seq!head seq))
          (seq!tack
            (seq!head seq)
            (accepted_messages (seq!tail seq)))
          (accepted_messages (seq!tail seq)))))
> (REDUCE)
```

```
> (GRULE accepted_messages_are_seqp (seq)
   (seq!seqp (accepted_messages seq)))
> (PROVE-BY-INDUCTION)

> (FUNCTION rejected_messages (seq)
    ((MEASURE (seq!length seq)))
  (IF (seq!emptyp seq)
      (seq!empty)
      (IF (NOT (fmenv!ok (seq!head seq)))
          (seq!tack
            (seq!head seq)
            (rejected_messages (seq!tail seq)))
          (rejected_messages (seq!tail seq)))))
> (REDUCE)
```

"Security property" of a sequence is true if every element of a sequence satisfies the "ok" predicate.

```
> (FUNCTION security_property (seq)
    ((MEASURE  (seq!length seq)))
  (IF (seq!emptyp seq)
      (true)
      (AND (security_property (seq!tail seq))
           (fmenv!ok (seq!head seq)))))
> (REDUCE)
```

The following assertion states that the security property holds for the sequence derived from the "accepted messages" function. This is a simple example of a proof of a specification property. The proof proceeds by induction. Note that we allow the prover to proceed automatically.

```
> (AXIOM accepted_message_sequence_is_secure (seq)
    (security_property (accepted_messages seq)))
> (PROVE-BY-INDUCTION)

Beginning proof of ACCEPTED_MESSAGE_SEQUENCE_IS_SECURE ...
(SECURITY_PROPERTY (ACCEPTED_MESSAGES SEQ))

Inducting using the following scheme ...
(AND (IMPLIES (SEQ!EMPTYP SEQ)
              (*P* SEQ))
     (IMPLIES (AND (FMENV!OK (SEQ!HEAD SEQ))
                   (NOT (SEQ!EMPTYP SEQ))
                   (*P* (SEQ!TAIL SEQ)))
              (*P* SEQ))
     (IMPLIES (AND (NOT (FMENV!OK (SEQ!HEAD SEQ)))
                   (NOT (SEQ!EMPTYP SEQ))
                   (*P* (SEQ!TAIL SEQ)))
              (*P* SEQ)))
```

The prover instantiates the above schema as below and reduces the formula to (TRUE):

```
produces ...
(AND (IMPLIES (SEQ!EMPTYP SEQ)
              (SECURITY_PROPERTY (ACCEPTED_MESSAGES SEQ)))
     (IMPLIES (AND (FMENV!OK (SEQ!HEAD SEQ))
                   (NOT (SEQ!EMPTYP SEQ))
                   (SECURITY_PROPERTY (ACCEPTED_MESSAGES (SEQ!TAIL SEQ))))
              (SECURITY_PROPERTY (ACCEPTED_MESSAGES SEQ)))
     (IMPLIES (AND (NOT (FMENV!OK (SEQ!HEAD SEQ)))
                   (NOT (SEQ!EMPTYP SEQ))
                   (SECURITY_PROPERTY (ACCEPTED_MESSAGES (SEQ!TAIL SEQ))))
              (SECURITY_PROPERTY (ACCEPTED_MESSAGES SEQ))))

Which simplifies
with invocation of SECURITY_PROPERTY, ACCEPTED_MESSAGES
forward chaining using SEQ!TACK-HEAD-TAIL, ELEM-TYPE-P.TYPE-P
with the assumptions SEQ!TACK-NOT-EMPTY, SEQ!SEQP-TACK, SEQ!HEAD-TACK,
SEQ!TAIL-TACK-SEQ, SEQ!SIZE-TAIL, SEQ!EMPTYP-EMPTY, SEQ!SEQP-EMPTY,
ACCEPTED_MESSAGES_ARE_SEQP, ELEM-TYPE-P.CHAR, ELEM-TYPE-P.INT,
TYPE-P.BOOL to
(TRUE)
```

The following three functions are used to annotate the main procedure. As none of these functions are recursive, no proof obligations need to be satisfied.

```
> (FUNCTION pre_condition (down reject input)
          ()                                ;no measure expression
          (AND (= (fmio!port_history down)   (seq!empty))
               (= (fmio!port_history reject) (seq!empty))
               (= (fmio!port_history input)  (seq!empty))))

> (FUNCTION post_condition (down reject input)
          ()                                ;no measure expression
          (AND (= (fmio!port_history down)
                  (accepted_messages (fmio!port_history input)))
               (= (fmio!port_history reject)
                  (rejected_messages (fmio!port_history input)))
               (= (seq!length (fmio!port_history input))
                  (fmenv!number_of_messages))))

> (FUNCTION loop_invariant
          (down reject input number_of_messages_read)
          ()                                ;no measure expression
          (AND (seq!seqp (fmio!port_history input))
               (= (fmio!port_history down)
                  (accepted_messages (fmio!port_history input)))
```

```
            (= (fmio!port_history reject)
               (rejected_messages (fmio!port_history input)))
            (= (seq!length (fmio!port_history input))
               number_of_messages_read)
            (>= (fmenv!number_of_messages) number_of_messages_read)
            (>= number_of_messages_read 0)))
```

Finally, the main procedure is presented. The implementation is straightforward.

```
> (PROCEDURE flow_modulator ((MVAR (down reject input) (fmio!a_port)))
          ((PRE  (pre_condition  down reject input))
           (POST (post_condition down reject input)) )
          (BLOCK ((PVAR (msg) (fmenv!message))
                  (PVAR (number_of_messages_read) (int) 0))
                 (LOOP
                  ((INVARIANT
                    (loop_invariant down reject input
                                    number_of_messages_read))
                   (MEASURE (- (fmenv!number_of_messages)
                               number_of_messages_read)))
                  (EXIT (= number_of_messages_read
                           (fmenv!number_of_messages)))
                  (fmio!input_port input msg)
                  (:= number_of_messages_read
                      (+ number_of_messages_read 1))
                  (COND ((fmenv!ok msg) (fmio!output_port down msg))
                      ((true)   (fmio!output_port reject msg))))
                 ))
```

As the proof obligation generated by the above declaration is long, we have not include it here. It should be noted, however, that though the proof obligation is textually lengthy, its structure follows that of the program; hence, one can become adept at reading such propositions. One recent change to EVES allows for separate case analyses of appropriately structured propositions.

Our first effort is to apply the non-inductive portion of the prover to the proof obligation. As is apparent from the information presented, the prover performs a substantial amount of work and the resulting proof obligation is shown in Figure 1.

```
> (WITHOUT-INSTANTIATION (REDUCE))

Which simplifies
with invocation of M<, FMIO!OUTPUT_PORT.POST, FMIO!OUTPUT_PORT.PRE,
FMENV!OK.PRE, +.PRE, FMIO!INPUT_PORT.POST, FMIO!INPUT_PORT.PRE,
POST_CONDITION, LOOP_INVARIANT, SEQ!LENGTH, REJECTED_MESSAGES,
ACCEPTED_MESSAGES, PRE_CONDITION
when rewriting with RANGE.DEFINITION
forward chaining using SEQ!TACK-HEAD-TAIL, >=.SAME.TYPE,
```

```
ELEM-TYPE-P.TYPE-P
with the assumptions SUCC.INT, SUCC.TYPE-OF, -.TYPE-OF, FMENV!OK.TYPE-OF,
ORD.CHAR.LAST.1, ORD.CHAR.LAST.2, INT.BOUNDS.2, INT.BOUNDS.3,
FMENV!ABOUT_NUMBER_OF_MESSAGES_2, INT.BOUNDS.1, INT.BOUNDS.4, +.TYPE-OF,
SEQ!TACK-NOT-EMPTY, SEQ!SEQP-TACK, SEQ!HEAD-TACK, SEQ!TAIL-TACK-SEQ,
FMENV!ABOUT_NUMBER_OF_MESSAGES_1, SEQ!LENGTH-NON-NEGATIVE,
ACCEPTED_MESSAGES_ARE_SEQP, FMENV!MESSAGE.TYPE-P, SEQ!EMPTYP-EMPTY,
SEQ!SEQP-EMPTY, FMIO!A_PORT.TYPE-P, ELEM-TYPE-P.CHAR, ELEM-TYPE-P.INT,
TYPE-P.BOOL to ... (see accompanying figure)
```

Next, we have the prover heuristically choose a set of equality substitutions and then reduce the formula.

```
> (EQUALITY-SUBSTITUTE)

Substituting
(= (FMIO!PORT_HISTORY DOWN-0)
   (ACCEPTED_MESSAGES (FMIO!PORT_HISTORY INPUT-0)))
(= (FMIO!PORT_HISTORY REJECT-0)
   (REJECTED_MESSAGES (FMIO!PORT_HISTORY INPUT-0)))
(= NUMBER_OF_MESSAGES_READ (SEQ!LENGTH (FMIO!PORT_HISTORY INPUT-0)))
(= (FMIO!PORT_HISTORY INPUT-1)
   (SEQ!TACK MSG-1 (FMIO!PORT_HISTORY INPUT-0)))
(= (FMIO!PORT_HISTORY DOWN-1)
   (SEQ!TACK MSG-1
        (ACCEPTED_MESSAGES (FMIO!PORT_HISTORY INPUT-0))))
(= (FMIO!PORT_HISTORY REJECT-1)
   (SEQ!TACK MSG-1
        (REJECTED_MESSAGES (FMIO!PORT_HISTORY INPUT-0))))
produces ...output omitted...

> (REDUCE)

Which simplifies
with invocation of SEQ!LENGTH, REJECTED_MESSAGES, ACCEPTED_MESSAGES
forward chaining using SEQ!TACK-HEAD-TAIL, >=.SAME.TYPE,
ELEM-TYPE-P.TYPE-P
with the assumptions +.TYPE-OF, SEQ!SIZE-TAIL, FMENV!OK.TYPE-OF,
SEQ!TACK-NOT-EMPTY, SEQ!SEQP-TACK, SEQ!HEAD-TACK, SEQ!TAIL-TACK-SEQ,
FMENV!ABOUT_NUMBER_OF_MESSAGES_1, SEQ!LENGTH-NON-NEGATIVE,
ACCEPTED_MESSAGES_ARE_SEQP, FMENV!MESSAGE.TYPE-P, SEQ!EMPTYP-EMPTY,
SEQ!SEQP-EMPTY, FMIO!A_PORT.TYPE-P, ELEM-TYPE-P.CHAR, ELEM-TYPE-P.INT,
TYPE-P.BOOL to ...
(TRUE)
```

Finally, we save the result of our labours in a library.

```
> (MAKE flow model)
```

```
(IMPLIES
 (AND (= (TYPE-OF DOWN) (FMIO!A_PORT))
      (= (TYPE-OF REJECT) (FMIO!A_PORT))
      (= (TYPE-OF INPUT) (FMIO!A_PORT))
      (= (FMIO!PORT_HISTORY DOWN) (SEQ!EMPTY))
      (= (FMIO!PORT_HISTORY REJECT) (SEQ!EMPTY))
      (= (FMIO!PORT_HISTORY INPUT) (SEQ!EMPTY))
      (SOME (MSG) (= (TYPE-OF MSG) (FMENV!MESSAGE))))
 (ALL
  (INPUT-0 NUMBER_OF_MESSAGES_READ DOWN-0 REJECT-0 INPUT-1 MSG-1)
  (IMPLIES
   (AND (= (TYPE-OF INPUT-0) (FMIO!A_PORT))
(= (TYPE-OF NUMBER_OF_MESSAGES_READ) (INT))
(= (TYPE-OF DOWN-0) (FMIO!A_PORT))
(= (TYPE-OF REJECT-0) (FMIO!A_PORT))
(SEQ!SEQP (FMIO!PORT_HISTORY INPUT-0))
(= (ACCEPTED_MESSAGES (FMIO!PORT_HISTORY INPUT-0))
   (FMIO!PORT_HISTORY DOWN-0))
(= (FMIO!PORT_HISTORY REJECT-0)
   (REJECTED_MESSAGES (FMIO!PORT_HISTORY INPUT-0)))
(= (SEQ!LENGTH (FMIO!PORT_HISTORY INPUT-0)) NUMBER_OF_MESSAGES_READ)
(>= (FMENV!NUMBER_OF_MESSAGES) NUMBER_OF_MESSAGES_READ)
(NOT (= NUMBER_OF_MESSAGES_READ (FMENV!NUMBER_OF_MESSAGES)))
(= (TYPE-OF INPUT-1) (FMIO!A_PORT))
(= (TYPE-OF MSG-1) (FMENV!MESSAGE))
(= (FMIO!PORT_HISTORY INPUT-1)
   (SEQ!TACK MSG-1 (FMIO!PORT_HISTORY INPUT-0))))
   (IF (FMENV!OK MSG-1)
       (ALL (DOWN-1)
     (IMPLIES (AND (= (TYPE-OF DOWN-1) (FMIO!A_PORT))
  (= (FMIO!PORT_HISTORY DOWN-1)
     (SEQ!TACK MSG-1 (FMIO!PORT_HISTORY DOWN-0))))
     (AND (= (ACCEPTED_MESSAGES (FMIO!PORT_HISTORY INPUT-1))
     (FMIO!PORT_HISTORY DOWN-1))
  (= (FMIO!PORT_HISTORY REJECT-0)
     (REJECTED_MESSAGES (FMIO!PORT_HISTORY INPUT-1)))
  (= (SEQ!LENGTH (FMIO!PORT_HISTORY INPUT-1))
     (+ NUMBER_OF_MESSAGES_READ 1)))))
       (ALL (REJECT-1)
    (IMPLIES (AND (= (TYPE-OF REJECT-1) (FMIO!A_PORT))
  (= (FMIO!PORT_HISTORY REJECT-1)
     (SEQ!TACK MSG-1 (FMIO!PORT_HISTORY REJECT-0))))
     (AND (= (ACCEPTED_MESSAGES (FMIO!PORT_HISTORY INPUT-1))
     (FMIO!PORT_HISTORY DOWN-0))
  (= (FMIO!PORT_HISTORY REJECT-1)
     (REJECTED_MESSAGES (FMIO!PORT_HISTORY INPUT-1)))
  (= (SEQ!LENGTH (FMIO!PORT_HISTORY INPUT-1))
     (+ NUMBER_OF_MESSAGES_READ 1)))))))))
```

Figure 1: Proof obligation for Flow Modulator after reduction

7 Other Examples

In this section we discuss two further applications of EVES, though we will not present any portions of the proofs.

PICO Interpreter

The PICO Interpreter example [KP 90] is a specification and verification of an interpreter for the PICO programming language [BHK 89] (a language for "while" programs). The interpreter interprets PICO programs in abstract syntax form, and consists of a type checker and an evaluator.

We took an algebraic specification of a PICO interpreter as described by Bergstra, Heering, and Klint [BHK 89], and translated it into Verdi. The translation was mostly syntactic (we had to add extra axioms to capture the initial algebra semantics assumed by their specification). We provided a model for the specification. Except for the part that deals with possible non-termination of PICO programs, the model was relatively straightforward.

We then proceeded with a verified procedural implementation of the interpreter. We specified abstraction functions from the concrete data structures manipulated by the procedures to the abstract data structures used in the algebraic specification. Each procedure was annotated with a post specification that relates the abstraction of the result with the algebraic specification. Currently, all data structure manipulation procedures and all type checking procedures have been implemented and verified. We have also implemented and verified the evaluator procedures for PICO declarations and PICO expressions. We have yet to implement and verify the evaluator procedures for statements.

The PICO Interpreter example used the EVES library facility extensively. Each ASF module is translated into an EVES library unit. (ASF is the algebraic specification language used by Bergstra, Heering, and Klint [BHK 89]). In addition, each procedural implementation of a library unit is also made into a library unit.

Z Mathematical Library

We have investigated [Saa 91a] the possibility of supporting the Z notation in EVES, and we have built library units [Saa 91b] comprising most of the "Mathematical Toolkit" as described in Spivey's Z Reference Manual [Spi 87]. Many additional laws (beyond those explicitly mentioned in the Toolkit) are needed to complete the proofs of the laws in the Toolkit. In the course of this work, some minor errors in the laws were found.

We have also experimented with the transcription of Z text into Verdi, allowing for formal proofs of assertions made in the Z specification. Early results of the experiments indicate that the translation is a bit too messy to perform reliably by hand, so we would probably want to automate it. On the positive side, we have been able to complete a number of proofs of transcribed theorems.

Relating Z to EVES is not completely straightforward, for several reasons:

- EVES makes a sharp distinction between axiomatic assumptions and definitions; Z does not. In the absence of additional annotations in the Z text, every axiomatic box must be considered an additional environmental assumption.

- The Z notation does not define a way of stating theorems. Coupled with the previous point, this makes a direct transcription of a Z text into EVES a sequence of axiomatic assumptions. This gives EVES nothing to do.
- To use EVES effectively, it is necessary to furnish the axioms of a theory with some heuristic hints. These are not present in Z text.
- EVES provides untyped ZFC set theory, while Z is typed. There are several different ways to transcribe typed theories into untyped theories; it is, at present, unclear which approach will be the most successful in EVES.

If support for Z is provided, it is not likely that the proofs will be as automatic as one might hope. EVES works best in theories where expressions can be normalized to a canonical form. The Toolkit is rich in algebraic laws, and it is therefore difficult to define normal forms for expressions. It seems likely that, as a result, the Toolkit will be expressed in such a way that many of the laws will not be used heuristically by EVES.

8 Conclusions

Since EVES is a relatively new system, the set of examples to which it has been applied is still fairly small. The PICO interpreter example is the largest to which we have applied either EVES or the predecessor system m-EVES. The size of the PICO interpreter (for specifications, implementation, and system commands) is approximately 11,000 lines and successfully demonstrated the utility of the library mechanism.

For completeness, we note that the examples performed in m-EVES can be modified and proven in EVES. The m-EVES examples have included, amongst others, security proofs [Cra 88], code proofs (such as for variations of the UNIX TR and WC programs [Mei 89a, Mei 89b]), various mathematical theory developments (e.g., [SC 90]), and a small hardware example [PS 89].

As stated in the introduction, the primary purpose of the EVES project was to develop a verification system, integrating techniques from automated deduction, mathematics, language design and formal methods, so that the system is both sound and useful. We believe that the development has been successful in achieving these aims. This has been demonstrated, in part, by our ability to specify, implement and prove a substantial application: the PICO interpreter.

The main EVES development was completed in 1990. Current work has us investigating further techniques for enhancing NEVER and, as alluded to above, considering whether a Z-mode to EVES is feasible. Future work will be directed at significantly enhancing system documentation, the rigorous development of a compiler for Verdi, and the application of EVES to substantial applications.

References

[BHK 89] J.A. Bergstra, J. Heering, P. Klint, editors. *Algebraic Specification.* ACM Press, 1989.

[Ble 73] W.W. Bledsoe, P. Bruell, A man-machine theorem proving system. In *Proceedings of the 3rd IJCAI*, Stanford U., 1973; also *Artificial Intelligence* 5(1):51-72, 1974.

[BM 79] R.S. Boyer, J S. Moore, *A Computational Logic*, Academic Press, NY, 1979.

[CKM* 88] Dan Craigen, Sentot Kromodimoeljo, Irwin Meisels, Andy Nielson, Bill Pase, and Mark Saaltink. m-EVES: A Tool for Verifying Software. In *Proceedings of the 11th International Conference on Software Engineering (ICSE'11)*, Singapore, April 1988.

[Cra 87] Dan Craigen. Strengths and Weaknesses of Program Verification Systems. In *Proceedings of the 1st European Software Engineering Conference*, Strasbourg, France. Springer-Verlag, September 1987.

[Cra 88] Dan Craigen. An Application of the m-EVES Verification System. In *Proceedings of the 2nd Workshop on Software Testing, Verification and Analysis*, Banff, Alberta, July 1988.

[Cra 90] Dan Craigen. *Reference Manual for the Language Verdi.* Technical Report TR-90-5429-09, Odyssey Research Associates, Ottawa, February 1990.

[Fra 68] Abraham Fraenkel. *Abstract Set Theory.* North-Holland, 1968.

[KP 90] Sentot Kromodimoeljo, Bill Pase. *Using the EVES Library Facility: A PICO Interpreter.* Technical Report TR-90-5444-02, Odyssey Research Associates, Ottawa, February 1990.

[Luc 79] D.C. Luckham, et al., *Stanford Pascal verifier user manual*, Report STAN-CS-79-731, Stanford U. Computer Science Department, March 1979.

[Mei 89a] Irwin Meisels. *TR Program Example.* Technical Report TR-89-5443-02, Odyssey Research Associates, Ottawa, August 1989.

[Mei 89b] Irwin Meisels. *WC Program Example.* Technical Report TR-89-5443-03, Odyssey Research Associates, Ottawa, October 1989.

[PS 89] Bill Pase and Mark Saaltink. Formal Verification in m-EVES. In *Current Trends in Hardware Verification and Automated Theorem Proving,* G. Birtwistle, and P.A. Subrahmanyam, editors, Springer-Verlag, 1989.

[Saa 89] Mark Saaltink. *A Formal Description of Verdi.* Technical Report TR-89-5429-10, Odyssey Research Associates, Ottawa, October 1989.

[Saa 90] Mark Saaltink. *Alternative Semantics for Verdi.* Technical Report TR-90-5446-02, Odyssey Research Associates, Ottawa, November 1990.

[Saa 91a] Mark Saaltink. *Z and EVES.* Technical Report TR-91-5449-02, ORA Corporation, Ottawa, July 1991.

[Saa 91b] Mark Saaltink. *The EVES Library.* Technical Report TR-91-5449-03, ORA Corporation, Ottawa, July 1991.

[SC 90] Mark Saaltink and Dan Craigen. Simple Type Theory in EVES. In *Proceedings of the 4th Workshop on Higher Order Logic.* G. Birtwistle, editor, Springer-Verlag, 1991.

[Spi 87] J.M. Spivey. *The Z Notation: A Reference Manual.* Prentice Hall, 1987.

[Tho 81] D.H. Thompson, R.W. Erickson, editors. *AFFIRM Reference Manual.*, USC Information Sciences Institute, Marina Dey Ray, CA, 1981.

A Library Commands

Below, we present an edited version of the on-line help for libraries. We describe the commands for manipulating libraries, present a conceptual background, and also show the kind of information available through the EVES help facility.

Libraries

The library facility allows for the storage, retrieval and deletion of units from libraries. The main purpose of this facility is to provide a modularization mechanism. There are three kinds of units: spec units, containing axiomatic specifications; model units, containing implementations; and freeze units, containing incomplete sessions.

Spec units may be loaded into EVES using the `load` command. When loaded, declarations created by these units are assumed to be proven elsewhere. Specifically, they must be proven in their corresponding model unit. By loading only the specification unit, implementation detail is suppressed and, consequently, proofs should be less complex.

Set Library `(SET-LIBRARY string)`

Sets the current library to the specified directory.

Delete `(DELETE identifier kind)`

Deletes the library unit specified. Other units that depend on this unit are also deleted.

Edit `(EDIT identifier kind)`

Puts the database in the same state as when the make of the object was performed.

Load `(LOAD identifier)`

Loads the spec unit specified by the identifier. The unit's declarations are added to the database.

Make `(MAKE identifier kind)`

Writes the contents of the database as a library unit specified by the identifier. The kind determines whether the unit is to be a spec, model or freeze unit. The command has no effect if the addition of the unit to the library would result in a circularity or if the resulting unit is not consistent with a corresponding specification or model unit (if one exists).

Print library status (PRINT-LIBRARY-STATUS)
Prints the status of the current library. The names of the units in the library are listed together with their kind (e.g., spec, model, or freeze).

B Prover Commands

In this appendix, a selection of the prover commands available to users of EVES is presented. Once again, these descriptions are derived from the on-line help.

Equality Substitute Command (EQUALITY-SUBSTITUTE [EXPRESSION])
The `equality substitute` command substitutes, for the expression, its equal in appropriate contexts of the current formula. The expression must appear as the left or right side of an equality within the current formula (otherwise, the command has no effect). In the absence of the expression, a heuristic is used to substitute equalities automatically.

Induct Command (INDUCT [expression])
The `induct` command attempts to apply an induction scheme to the current formula. In the absence of the optional expression, an induction scheme is heuristically chosen based on calls to recursive functions occurring in the current formula. If the optional expression is present, then EVES attempts an induction using the expression.

Instantiate Command (INSTANTIATE (identifier expression)+)
The `instantiate` command performs the given instantiations on the current formula. To allow the instantiations to occur, the scopes of quantifiers in the formula may be modified. Logical equivalence is maintained by keeping the uninstantiated subexpressions as extra conjuncts or disjuncts.

Invoke Command (INVOKE expression)
The `invoke` command replaces the application of a function, as specified by the expression, by its defining expression (instantiated by the actual parameters to the function application). The `invoke` command works for functions that have been disabled. In addition, the `invoke` command may be applied to an expression rather than to a function, in which case, it works like a selective invoke in that occurrences of the expression in the formula are replaced by the expanded version.

Open Command (OPEN)
The `open` command removes leading universal quantifiers from the current formula and the quantified variables are consequently free variables.

Prenex Command (PRENEX)
The `prenex` command converts the current formula into prenex form (as far as possible). If the result of this command is a completely prenexed formula with only universal quantifiers, then the `open` command may be used to make the formula quantifier-free.

Reduce Command (REDUCE)
The `reduce` command applies the non-inductive heuristics of the prover to the current formula. This consists of simplification, rewriting, and invocation.

Rewrite Command (REWRITE)
The `rewrite` command rewrites and simplifies the current formula. Conditional rewrite rules may be applied, provided their condition can be proven using only simplification and rewriting.

Simplify Command (SIMPLIFY)
The `simplify` command simplifies the current formula. This may, for example, perform the substitution of equalities, apply forward rules and grules, and instantiate variables.

Use Command (USE identifier (identifier expression)*)
The `use` command adds the axiom associated with the identifier to the current formula as an assumption. This results in a new formula of the form

```
(IMPLIES assumption formula)
```

where the assumption is the axiom instantiated with the instantiations.

Deriving Transitivity of VDM-Reification in DEVA

Matthias Weber
Institut für Programmstrukturen und Datenorganisation
Universität Karlsruhe
Postfach 6980, D-7500 Karlsruhe, Germany
e-mail: weberm@ira.uka.uucp

Abstract

This paper reports on an exercise to study how a typical fundamental property of a development technique, viz. transitivity of data-reification in VDM, is formally derived as a property of a method formalization in a meta-calculus, viz. DEVA. To this end, an existing DEVA-formalization of the VDM-reification has been generalized such that its axiom set becomes independent from the number of reification steps performed. This generalized formalization allows to prove transitivity of reification. The formalization and the transitivity proof are performed completely inside DEVA.

1 Introduction

The development and application of systematic methods for the construction of safe software systems is a wide and active area of research in computer science. In particular, several "rigorous" methodologies such as VDM and Z have been developed up to a point where they start to enter industrial application.

These rigorous methodologies start from abstract formal specifications of software systems and define systematic transitions to construct concrete implementations. The transitions give rise to a number of *proof obligations*, e.g. the proof of applicability conditions of transformation rules or correctness conditions of refinement steps. These proof obligations ensure the correctness of the concrete implementation wrt. the abstract specification. Computer support systems for such methodologies have been developed, however most of them concentrate on supporting various *syntactic issues* of the involved languages, e.g. by editors, formatters, and analysis tools, while often neglecting to support the crucial *correctness issue* of these methods, i.e. the proof obligations to ensure the correctness of implementations wrt. the given specification.

This work is part of an ongoing research effort to investigate the formalization of development methods and program developments in the DEVA meta-calculus in order to obtain semantically adequate support systems. This paper reports on an exercise to study how a typical fundamental property of a development technique, viz. transitivity of data-reification in VDM, is formally derived as a property of a method formalization in a meta-calculus, viz. DEVA [SWGC89]. To this end, an existing DEVA-formalization of the VDM-reification [Laf90] has been generalized such that its axiom set becomes independent from the number of reification steps performed. This generalized formalization allows to prove transitivity of reification. The formalization and the transitivity proof are performed completely inside DEVA.

The DEVA meta-calculus was originally developed within the ESPRIT-project #519, ToolUse [SWGC89]. As a result of the application of DEVA in the ToolUse project there exist several examples of method formalizations, e.g. [Laf90], [Web90]. Prototype support systems for DEVA [Gab90] have been developed on which the formalizations have been validated in varying degrees. The language theory for a kernel language of DEVA, corresponding to Nederpelt calculus extended by a notion of context, has been investigated in [Gro90], the (current) full DEVA is defined and investigated in [Web91].

This paper is organized as follows: First, the DEVA meta-calculus is briefly introduced by some examples. Then, VDM-reification is formalized in DEVA and the transitivity proof in DEVA is presented. Finally, some conclusions of the exercise are drawn.

2 The DEVA meta-calculus

This section contains a very brief introduction of the DEVA meta-calculus. As such, it does not serve as a replacement of a detailed and precise decription [Web91]. The purpose of DEVA is to formally describe rigorous software development methods and software developments within these methods. The essential requirements driving the design of DEVA have been the following:

- DEVA should be sufficiently general and logically default-free, so as to encompass a wide range of development methods,
- the correctness of the developments relative to the given method must be ensured,
- long and complex formalizations must be presentable in a structured way, and
- the omission of details in developments must be allowed, where gaps could reach from omitted instantiations to partially presented proofs.

The approach taken to meet the first condition (i.e. generality) was inspired by theoretical work on logical frameworks, i.e. higher-order metasystems based on λ-calculi with dependent types (e.g. [Bru80], [HHP86]). Technically, DEVA can be seen as an extension of *Nederpelt calculus* [Ned80], a logical framework which evolved from the Automath project [Bru80]. These frameworks allow to formalize theories of logic and mathematics and to perform theorem-proving based on these theories. The connection between these systems and DEVA consists of viewing *software development methods as theories*, *software developments as proofs*, and *results of developments as theorems*. These frameworks usually define a notion of *type correctness* or *validity* as a concept to ensure that proofs have been correctly constructed according to the formalized theory. This notion is thus used in DEVA to satisfy the second condition. The class of DEVA-expressions representing proofs is called *texts*. DEVA-texts can be seen as extended typed λ-terms. To meet the third condition, a notion of theory and operations upon theories (e.g. concatenation, importation, instantiation) has been internalized into DEVA. The class of DEVA-expressions representing theories is called *contexts*. DEVA-contexts can be seen as lists of declarations and definitions, plus simple operations such as the above. The fourth condition has been partially met by defining a range of possible gaps allowed in *implicit descriptions*. For example, parameters for the application of a rule, the choice between several rules, and the number of times a rule is applied, may be left open.

Some language features can be briefly sketched on the description of a very general scheme of stepwise development as a DEVA-context:

part *development* :=
⟦ < *DECLARATION OF OBJECTS* >
; < *ASSUMPTION OF LAWS* >
; < *STEPWISE DEVELOPMENT* >
⟧

The description is split into three parts: the declaration of the development objects, the assumption of the development laws, and the actual stepwise development process. The above context introduces two constructs: A *context definition* **part** $p := c$ introduces the variable p as an abbreviation of the context c, and a *context join* $[\![c_1;\ c_2]\!]$ composes two contexts c_1, c_2 sequentially. The following equivalent notation ($\xrightarrow{EN}$) has been used:

$$[\![c_1;\ c_2;\ \ldots;\ c_n]\!] \quad \xrightarrow{EN} \quad [\![c_1;\ [\![c_2;\ \ldots c_n]\!]]\!]$$

In the above context < *name* > stands for some DEVA context, identified by *name*, which will be detailed below. The purpose of this notation is to *present* DEVA descriptions in a natural way, however, it is not a *construct* of the DEVA language. The development objects are declared as follows:

< *DECLARATION OF OBJECTS* > ≡

⟦ *prop* : **prim**
; res_0, res_1, res_2 : *prop*
⟧

The notation < *name* > ≡ ... is used to present the details of the expression abbreviated by *name*, Again, this notation is not a construct of the DEVA language. The first declaration introduces the set of propositions *prop* as being of type **prim**. A *declaration* $x : t$ is a context which introduces the variable x and asserts the text t as its type. The *primitive text* **prim** serves to introduce primitive types, i.e. types for which neither there exist subtypes nor supertypes. The remaining three declarations introduce three propositions res_1, res_2, res_3, which will appear as intermediate results of the development. The following notation has been used:

$$(x_1, \ldots, x_n : t) \quad \xrightarrow{EN} \quad [\![x_1 : t;\ \ldots;\ x_n : t]\!]$$

The following two development laws are assumed:

< *ASSUMPTION OF LAWS* > ≡

$$
\begin{array}{lll}
[\![& dev\_step_1 : & [res_0 \vdash res_1] \\
; & dev\_step_2 : & [res_1 \vdash res_2] \\
; & init\_dev : & res_0 \\
]\!] & &
\end{array}
$$

These laws state that res_0 implies res_1, and that res_1 implies res_2. Further, it is assumed that the proposition res_0 holds. The new DEVA construct in this example is *abstraction.* In its most general form, written $[c \vdash t]$, the context c is *assumed* within the derivation t. The specific notation $[res_1 \vdash res_2]$ in the above example is shorthand for $[x : res_1 \vdash res_2]$, a very common notation in languages with dependent types. The development structure can now be described as follows:

< *STEPWISE DEVELOPMENT* > ≡

$$
\begin{array}{lll}
[\![& dev := & init\_dev \\
 & & \qquad\qquad \therefore\ res_0 \\
 & & \backslash\ dev\_step_1 \\
 & & \qquad\qquad \therefore\ res_1 \\
 & & \backslash\ dev\_step2 \\
 & & \qquad\qquad \therefore\ res_2 \\
]\!] & &
\end{array}
$$

Starting from res_0, the two results res_1 and res_2 are successively derived by applying the assumed laws. The following constructs are introduced: A *definition* $x := t$ is a context which introduces the variable x as an abbreviation for the text t. A *judgement* $t_1 \therefore t_2$ is a text t_1 together with the assertion that its type is t_2. In a *direct application* $t_1 \backslash t_2$, t_1 serves as an argument for t_2. As a type constraint, it is required that the type of t_1 matches with the type of the domain in t_2. The development is assumed to be bracketed left-associative, i.e. it is equivalent to write $((((init\_dev \therefore res_0) \backslash dev\_step_1) \therefore res_1) \backslash dev\_step2) \therefore res_2$.

The following very simple property is used in the development:

$$
\frac{a \therefore t_1 \qquad\qquad f \therefore [t_1 \vdash t_2]}{a \backslash f \therefore t_2.}
$$

Finally, all parts of the example can be combined and presented as follows:

$$
\begin{array}{llll}
\multicolumn{4}{l}{\textbf{part}\ development :=} \\
[\![& prop & : & \textbf{prim} \\
; & res_0, res_1, res_2 & : & prop \\
; & dev\_step_1 & : & [res_0 \vdash res_1] \\
; & dev\_step_2 & : & [res_1 \vdash res_2] \\
; & init\_dev & : & res_0 \\
; & dev & := & init\_dev \\
 & & & \qquad\qquad \therefore\ res_0
\end{array}
$$

$$
\begin{array}{l}
\quad \backslash\ dev\_step_1 \\
\qquad\qquad \therefore\ res_1 \\
\quad \backslash\ dev\_step2 \\
\qquad\qquad \therefore\ res_2 \\
]\!]
\end{array}
$$

This *flat* presentation is equivalent to the above structured presentation, thanks to the *associativity* of the context join. A more specific development scheme is to *refine* an initial version of a system in a stepwise process in order to reach a concrete version of a system:

$$
\begin{array}{lll}
\multicolumn{3}{l}{\textbf{part}\ refinement :=} \\
[\![\ [\![\ prop, version & : & \textbf{prim} \\
\quad ;\ v_1, v_2, v_3 & : & version\ ]\!] \\
\quad ;\ (\cdot) \sqsubset (\cdot) & : & [version;\ version \vdash prop] \\
\quad]\!] & & \\
;\ [\![\ law_1 & : & v_1 \sqsubset v_2 \\
\quad ;\ law_2 & : & v_2 \sqsubset v_3 \\
\quad ;\ refine & : & [cv, av, iv : version \vdash [cv \sqsubset av \vdash \left|\frac{av \sqsubset iv}{cv \sqsubset iv}\right.]] \\
\quad ;\ init\_refine & : & v_3 \sqsubset v_3 \\
\quad]\!] & & \\
;\ dev\_refine := init\_refine & & \\
\qquad\qquad \therefore\ v_3 \sqsubset v_3 & & \\
\qquad \backslash\ refine(cv := v_2, av := v_3, iv := v_3, law_2) & & \\
\qquad\qquad \therefore\ v_2 \sqsubset v_3 & & \\
\qquad \backslash\ refine(cv := v_1, av := v_2, iv := v_3, law_1) & & \\
\qquad\qquad \therefore\ v_1 \sqsubset v_3 & & \\
]\!] & &
\end{array}
$$

$cv \sqsubset av$ denotes that a concrete version cv is a refinement of an abstract version av (iv denotes an initial version). The rule *refine* states transitivity of $\sqsubset$, a property which is necessary to compose development steps. This description introduced some new notations:

$$
\begin{array}{llll}
\left|\frac{c}{t}\right. & \xrightarrow{EN} & [c \vdash t] & \\
[c_1;\ c_2 \vdash t] & \xrightarrow{EN} & [[\![c_1;\ c_2]\!] \vdash t] & \\
t_1 \backslash t_2 & \xrightarrow{EN} & t_2(t_1) & (\backslash \text{ is left-associative}) \\
(\cdot)op(\cdot) : t & \xrightarrow{EN} & op : t & \text{where } op \text{ is used in infix notation} \\
t_1\ op\ t_2 & \xrightarrow{EN} & (op(t_1))(t_2) & \text{if } op \text{ is declared as infix operator}
\end{array}
$$

A generalized form of the direct application $t_1(t_2)$ has been used in the description: An *application* $t_1(x := t_2)$ is similar to a direct application, except that now it is possible to specify the formal parameter to be instantiated. Thus, for example, a direct application $[x : t \vdash x](a)$ is equivalent to the application $[x : t \vdash x](x := a)$. Expressions such as $t(t_1, x := t_2)$ are equivalent syntax for $(t(t_1))(x := t_2)$. The following kind of property has been used in the above development:

$$\frac{p_2 \ \therefore\ prog \qquad f \ \therefore\ [l, r : prog \vdash [l = r \vdash \ldots]]}{f(r := p_2) \ \therefore\ [l : prog \vdash [l = p_2 \vdash \ldots]]}$$

Some instantiation details in the refinement process can be suppressed using *implicit definitions*: An implicit definition $x\ ?\ t$ introduces the variable x and asserts t as its type. Thus, it resembles a declaration $x : t$. However, x is assumed to be implicitly defined from the types of other texts, appearing in the overall expression, and hence it does not need to be explicitly instantiated. For example, using implicit definitions, *refine* could also be declared as:

$$refine : [cv, av, iv\ ?\ version \vdash [cv \sqsubset av \vdash \left|\frac{av \sqsubset iv}{cv \sqsubset iv}\right]]$$

Thanks to this declaration of *refine*, many arguments may dissapear in its applications. For example, in the above development one may now write $refine(law_1)$ instead of $refine(cv := v_1, av := v_2, iv := v_3, law_1)$.

Parametric equality

As an example of a theory formalization in DEVA, consider parametric equality: It is formalized by stating properties for reflexivity, substitutivity, symmetry and transitivity. Only the first two are really needed, i.e. they are appear as declarations, the others can be derived, see [Web91] for proofs. The primitive type of proposition *prop* and the type of sorts *sort* are introduced in the theory about sorted logic (see appendix A).

part *equality* $:=$

$[\![\ (\cdot) = (\cdot) : \quad [s\ ?\ sort \vdash [s;\ s \vdash prop]]$

$;\ refl \quad : \quad [s\ ?\ sort;\ x\ ?\ s \vdash x = x]$

$;\ subst \quad : \quad [s\ ?\ sort;\ x, y\ ?\ s;\ P\ ?\ [s \vdash prop] \vdash [x = y \vdash \left|\frac{P(x)}{P(y)}\right]]$

$;\ sym \quad : \quad [s\ ?\ sort;\ x, y\ ?\ s \vdash \left|\frac{x = y}{y = x}\right]$

$;\ trans \quad : \quad [s\ ?\ sort;\ x, y, z\ ?\ s \vdash \left|\frac{x = y;\ y = z}{x = z}\right]$

$]\!]$

Natural numbers

The formalization of the Peano axioms for natural numbers consists of the constant 0, the unary operator *succ*, and the last three of Peano's axioms. The first two are implicit in the typing of 0 and *succ*.

part *naturals* :=
$$
\begin{array}{lll}
[\![\ nat & : & sort \\
;\ 0 & : & nat \\
;\ succ & : & [nat \vdash nat] \\
;\ peano_0 & : & [x\ ?\ nat \vdash \neg(succ(x) = 0)] \\
;\ peano_1 & : & [x, y\ ?\ nat \vdash \left|\dfrac{succ(x) = succ(y)}{x = y}\right.] \\
;\ induction & : & [P\ ?\ [nat \vdash prop] \vdash \left|\dfrac{P(0);\ [x : nat \vdash [P(x) \vdash P(succ(x))]]}{[x : nat \vdash P(x)]}\right.] \\
]\!]
\end{array}
$$

This concludes the illustration of some DEVA constructs and their properties. Further constructs will be introduced along the way in the next sections. All DEVA constructs used in this paper are summarized in appendix B.

3 Formalization of VDM-reification in DEVA

The formalization and proof exercise presented in this paper is built up as follows:

part *vdm_exercise* :=
[[**import** *pred_logic* (*see appendix A*)
; **import** *equality* (*see previous section*)
; **import** *naturals* (*see previous section*)
; **part** *vdm_data_reification* := (*see below*)
; **part** *transitivity_of_reification* := (*see next section*)
]]

The formalization starts by assuming a number of basic theories (i.e. classical calculus with equality and natural numbers). These theories are presented outside this section. After that, the VDM data reification is defined, imported, and proven to be transitive. A *context inclusion* **import** *p* includes the context abbreviated as *p* into the current context.

The definition of the VDM data reification itself consists of defining VDM operations, VDM versions, and finally the notion of reification between two versions:

part *vdm_data_reification* :=
[[**part** *vdm_operations* := (*see below*)

; **import** *vdm_operations*
; **part** *vdm_versions* := *(see below)*
; **import** *vdm_versions*
; **part** *vdm_reification* := *(see below)*
; **import** *vdm_reification*
$]\!]$

Operations

Operations in VDM transform a given input state and input parameter into an output state and output parameter. A precondition is imposed on the input parameter and the input state, and a postcondition relates the given input parameter and input state to an output parameter and output state. The signature of VDM-operations can be described in DEVA as follows:

part *vdm_operations* :=
$[\![$ $(\cdot) \times (\cdot)$:= $[s_1, s_2 : sort \vdash [par := s_1, st := s_2]]$
; *param* := $[in := sort, out := sort]$
; *op_type* := $\left| \dfrac{state : sort;\ par : param}{\begin{array}{l}[\,pre \;:= [par.in \times state \vdash prop] \\ ,\,post \;:= [par.in \times state;\ par.out \times state \vdash prop] \\ ]\end{array}} \right.$

For given sorts s_1, s_2, the text $s_1 \times s_2$ denotes the product $[par := s_1, st := s_2]$ of the (input or output) parameter sort and the state sort. *param* denotes the type of a parameter sort, i.e. a product of sorts labeled *in* and *out*. For an operation with a given state sort *state* and parameter sort *par*, the text *op_type*(*state*, *par*) denotes the signatures of the pre- and postcondition of that operation.

The above definitions introduced two new constructs for texts: A *named product* $[x_1 := t_1, \ldots, x_n := t_n]$ describes the finite sequence $t_1, \ldots, t_n$ of texts each identified by names $x_1, \ldots, x_n$. Some or all identifiers of a product can be omitted, e.g. one may write $[x := nat, y := prop]$ or $[x := nat, prop]$ or just $[nat, prop]$. A *projection* $t.x$ projects a product to the text identified by x in the product t.

In VDM, operations do not work on all states, but only on those satisfying an invariant. For any operation *op*, two correctness conditions involving invariants, pre- and postconditions are defined:

- For a given input of *op* on which the precondition holds and whose state component satisfies the invariant, there exists an output of *op* which is related to the input by the postcondition (*impl_cond*).
- For given input and output on which pre- and postcondition hold, the operation *op* preserves the invariants (*inv_cond*).

These conditions can be formally stated as follows:

$$; \ impl\_cond := \frac{st \ ? \ sort; \ par \ ? \ param; \quad op : op\_type(st, par); \ inv : [st \vdash prop]}{[in : par.in \times st \vdash \frac{inv(in.st); \ op.pre(in)}{\exists[out : par.out \times st \vdash op.post(in, out)]}]}$$

$$; \ inv\_cond := \frac{st \ ? \ sort; \ par \ ? \ param; \quad op : op\_type(st, par); \ inv : [st \vdash prop]}{[in : par.in \times st; \ out : par.out \times st \vdash \frac{op.pre(in); \ op.post(in, out)}{[inv(in.st) \vdash inv(out.st)]}]}$$

]]

Versions

A version is a list $op_1 +\!\!< (op_2 +\!\!< \ldots (op_n +\!\!< \langle\rangle) \ldots)$ of operations together with an invariant *inv*. The invariant can be seen as a parameter of that list. The type of versions with invariant *inv* (*version*(*inv*)) and the constructors $\langle\rangle, +\!\!<$ to build versions can be introduced in DEVA as follows:

part *vdm_versions* :=

$$[\![\ version : [st \ ? \ sort \vdash [[st \vdash prop] \vdash \mathbf{prim}]]$$

$$; \ \langle\rangle : [st \ ? \ sort; \ inv \ ? \ [st \vdash prop] \vdash version(inv)]$$

$$; \ (\cdot) +\!\!< (\cdot) : \frac{st \ ? \ sort; \ par \ ? \ param; \ inv \ ? \ [st \vdash prop]}{[op\_type(st, par); \ version(inv) \vdash version(inv)]}$$

A version *v* with invariant *inv* is *valid* (denoted by *v*✓), if all its operators *op* satisfy the two correctness conditions *impl_cond*(*op.inv*) and *inv_cond*(*op.inv*) for operations. *v*✓ can be defined as follows:

$$; \ (\cdot)\checkmark : [st \ ? \ sort; \ inv \ ? \ [st \vdash prop] \vdash [version(inv) \vdash prop]]$$

$$; \ \checkmark\_def : \frac{st \ ? \ sort; \ inv \ ? \ [st \vdash prop]; \ v \ ? \ version(inv); \quad par \ ? \ param; \ op \ ? \ (st, par)}{\begin{array}{l}[\ empty := \langle\rangle\checkmark \\ , cons := \dfrac{(op +\!\!< v)\checkmark}{[\ v\checkmark, \ inv\_cond(op, inv), \ impl\_cond(op, inv)\ ]} \\ ]\end{array}}$$

The definition introduced a new notation to denote equivalent texts.

$$\frac{t_1}{t_2} \ (\text{double line}) \quad \xrightarrow{EN} \quad [up := \frac{t_2}{t_1}, down := \frac{t_1}{t_2}]$$

The *length* $|v|$ of a version *v* is defined as the number of operations in *v*.

$$; \ |(\cdot)| \quad : \quad [st ? sort;\ inv ? [st \vdash prop] \vdash [version(inv) \vdash nat]\,]$$

$$; \ length\_def \quad : \quad \left|\begin{array}{l} st ? sort;\ inv ? [st \vdash prop];\ v ? version(inv); \\ par ? param;\ op ? (st, par) \\ \hline [\ empty := |\langle\rangle| = 0,\ cons := |op \dashv\!< v| = s(|v|)\ ] \end{array}\right.$$

A principle of structural induction on versions can be defined as follows:

$$; \ ver\_induction \quad : \quad \left|\begin{array}{l} P : [st ? sort;\ inv ? [st \vdash prop] \vdash [version(inv) \vdash prop]\,] \\ \hline empty := P(\langle\rangle); \\ cons \ := \left|\begin{array}{l} st ? sort;\ inv ? [st \vdash prop];\ par ? param \\ \hline [v : version(inv);\ op : (st, par) \vdash \dfrac{P(v)}{P(op \dashv\!< v)}] \end{array}\right. \\ \hline [st ? sort;\ inv ? [st \vdash prop] \vdash [v : version(inv) \vdash P(v)]\,] \end{array}\right.$$

$]\!]$

Reification

Reification is the transition from a valid abstract version, with operations working on an abstract state, to a valid concrete version, with operations working on a concrete state. Every concrete state is related to a unique abstract state via a *retrieve* function. Wrt. the invariants *ainv* and *cinv* of the abstract version and the concrete version, the retrieve function has to satisfy the following correctness conditions (*retr_cond*):

- The retrieve function preserves the invariants (*inv_cond*).
- The retrieve function is complete, in the sense that it reaches all abstract states satisfying the abstract invariant from concrete states satisfying the concrete invariant (*compl_cond*).

part *vdm_reification* :=

$$[\![\ retr\_cond := \left|\begin{array}{l} cst, ast ? sort; \\ cinv : [cst \vdash prop];\ ainv : [ast \vdash prop];\ retr : [cst \vdash ast] \\ \hline [\ inv\_cond \quad := [cs ? cst \vdash \dfrac{cinv(cs)}{ainv(retr(cs))}] \\ ,\ compl\_cond := [as ? ast \vdash \dfrac{ainv(as)}{\exists[cs : cst \vdash cinv(cs) \wedge retr(cs) = as]}] \\ ] \end{array}\right.$$

For every operation *aop* of the abstract version there must be a corresponding operation *cop* of the concrete version which satisfies the following operation reification conditions:

- The precondition must be preserved, when going from the abstract state to the concrete state (*domain_cond*).

- The postcondition must be preserved, when going from the concrete state to the abstract state (*result_cond*).

$$
;\ \mathit{op\_reif\_cond} := \left|\begin{array}{l}
\mathit{cst}, \mathit{ast}\ ?\ \mathit{sort};\ \mathit{par}\ ?\ \mathit{param} \\
;\ \mathit{cop} : \mathit{op\_type}(\mathit{cst}, \mathit{par});\ \mathit{aop} : \mathit{op\_type}(\mathit{ast}, \mathit{par}) \\
;\ \mathit{cinv} : [\mathit{cst} \vdash \mathit{prop}];\ \mathit{retr} : [\mathit{cst} \vdash \mathit{ast}] \\
;\ \mathit{abs} := [p\ ?\ \mathit{sort};\ i : p \times \mathit{cst} \vdash [i.\mathit{par}, \mathit{retr}(i.\mathit{st})]] \\
\hline
[\ \mathit{Cin}\ ?\ \mathit{par.in} \times \mathit{cst};\ \mathit{Ain} := \mathit{abs}(\mathit{Cin}) \\
;\ \mathit{Cout}\ ?\ \mathit{par.out} \times \mathit{cst};\ \mathit{Aout} := \mathit{abs}(\mathit{Cout}) \\
\vdash \left|\begin{array}{l}
\mathit{cinv}(\mathit{Cin.st});\ \mathit{aop.pre}(\mathit{Ain}) \\
\hline
[\ \mathit{domain\_cond} := \mathit{cop.pre}(\mathit{Cin}) \\
,\ \mathit{result\_cond} := \dfrac{\mathit{cop.post}(\mathit{Cin}, \mathit{Cout})}{\mathit{aop.post}(\mathit{Ain}, \mathit{Aout})}\ ]
\end{array}\right. \\
]
\end{array}\right.
$$

The operation reification condition is lifted to a version reification condition (*reif_cond*), by requiring that the n-th operation of the abstract version satisfies the operation reification condition wrt. the n-th operation of the concrete version.

$$
;\ \mathit{reif\_cond} : \left|\begin{array}{l}
\mathit{cst}, \mathit{ast}\ ?\ \mathit{sort};\ \mathit{par}\ ?\ \mathit{param} \\
;\ \mathit{cinv}\ ?\ [\mathit{cst} \vdash \mathit{prop}];\ \mathit{ainv}\ ?\ [\mathit{ast} \vdash \mathit{prop}] \\
\hline
[\mathit{version}(\mathit{cinv});\ \mathit{version}(\mathit{ainv});\ [\mathit{cst} \vdash \mathit{ast}] \vdash \mathit{prop}]
\end{array}\right.
$$

$$
;\ \mathit{reif\_cond\_def} : \left|\begin{array}{l}
\mathit{cst}, \mathit{ast}\ ?\ \mathit{sort};\ \mathit{par}\ ?\ \mathit{param} \\
;\ \mathit{aop}\ ?\ \mathit{op\_type}(\mathit{ast}, \mathit{par});\ \mathit{ainv}\ ?\ [\mathit{ast} \vdash \mathit{prop}] \\
;\ \mathit{cop}\ ?\ \mathit{op\_type}(\mathit{cst}, \mathit{par});\ \mathit{cinv}\ ?\ [\mathit{cst} \vdash \mathit{prop}] \\
;\ \mathit{av}\ ?\ \mathit{version}(\mathit{ainv});\ \mathit{cv}\ ?\ \mathit{version}(\mathit{cinv});\ \mathit{retr}\ ?\ [\mathit{cst} \vdash \mathit{ast}] \\
\hline
[\ \mathit{empty} := \mathit{reif\_cond}(\langle\rangle, \langle\rangle, \mathit{retr}) \\
,\ \mathit{cons} := \left|\begin{array}{l}
\mathit{reif\_cond}(\mathit{cop} +\!\!< \mathit{cv}, \mathit{aop} +\!\!< \mathit{av}, \mathit{retr}) \\
\hline\hline
[\ \mathit{op\_cond} := \mathit{op\_reif\_cond}(\mathit{cop}, \mathit{aop}, \mathit{cinv}, \mathit{retr}) \\
,\ \mathit{recur} := \mathit{reif\_cond}(\mathit{cv}, \mathit{av}, \mathit{retr})\ ]
\end{array}\right. \\
]
\end{array}\right.
$$

Finally, all these conditions can be put together to define the predicate $cv \sqsubset av$ **with** *retr*, which states that the concrete version *cv* is a reification of the abstract version *av*, and related by the retrieve function *retr*.

$$
;\ (\cdot) \sqsubset (\cdot)\ \mathbf{with}\ (\cdot) := \left|\begin{array}{l}
\mathit{cst}, \mathit{ast}\ ?\ \mathit{sort};\ \mathit{cinv}\ ?\ [\mathit{cst} \vdash \mathit{prop}];\ \mathit{ainv}\ ?\ [\mathit{ast} \vdash \mathit{prop}] \\
;\ \mathit{cv} : \mathit{version}(\mathit{cinv});\ \mathit{av} : \mathit{version}(\mathit{ainv});\ \mathit{retr} : [\mathit{cst} \vdash \mathit{ast}] \\
\hline
[\ \mathit{version\_verif} := [\mathit{concr} := \mathit{cv}\checkmark, \mathit{abstr} := \mathit{av}\checkmark] \\
,\ \mathit{retr\_verif} := \mathit{retr\_cond}(\mathit{cinv}, \mathit{ainv}, \mathit{retr}) \\
,\ \mathit{reif\_verif} := \mathit{reif\_cond}(\mathit{cv}, \mathit{av}, \mathit{retr})\ ]
\end{array}\right.
$$

]

4 Proof of transitivity of reification in DEVA

This section presents a proof that reification, as defined in the previous section, is transitive. More precisely, for versions v_1, v_2, v_3 and retrieve functions $retr_{12}$ and $retr_{23}$, the following property is proven:

$$\begin{array}{|c} v_1 \sqsubset v_2 \textbf{ with } retr_{12}; \qquad v_2 \sqsubset v_3 \textbf{ with } retr_{23} \\ \hline v_1 \sqsubset v_3 \textbf{ with } (retr_{12} \mathbin{\diamond\!\!>} retr_{23}) \end{array}$$

$t_1 \mathbin{\diamond\!\!>} t_2$ denotes the *direct cut* of t_1 with t_2, a composition of texts at the functional level. Depending on the kind of use, it can play the role of functional composition or that of the logical cut, i.e. the cutting-out of the conclusion of t_1 and the assumption of t_2. The basic property underlying the use of the cut is the following:

$$\frac{f \therefore [t_1 \vdash t_2] \qquad g \therefore [t_2 \vdash t_3]}{f \mathbin{\diamond\!\!>} g \therefore [t_1 \vdash t_3]}$$

Thus, the above property states that successive reifications can be composed by composing their retrieve functions.

Frequently used contexts

In order to formally state and prove the above property without long and boring object declarations, it is useful to systematically abbreviate a number of frequently used contexts introducing implicitly defined identifiers. These contexts describe situations in which (combinations of) triples of invariants, operations, versions, and retrieve functions are considered.

part *frequent_contexts* :=

$$\left[\!\left[\; \begin{array}{|llll|} \hline \multicolumn{4}{|l|}{\textbf{part } op\_cont :=} \\ [\![& st_1, st_2, st_3 & ? & sort \\ ; & par & ? & param \\ ; & op_1 & ? & op\_type(st_1, par) \\ ; & op_2 & ? & op\_type(st_2, par) \\ ; & op_3 & ? & op\_type(st_3, par) \\ ]\!] & & & \\ \hline \end{array} \right.$$

$$; \quad \begin{array}{|llll|} \hline \multicolumn{4}{|l|}{\textbf{part } retr\_cont :=} \\ [\![& st_1, st_2, st_3 & ? & sort \\ ; & retr_{12} & ? & [st_1 \vdash st_2] \\ ; & retr_{23} & ? & [st_2 \vdash st_3] \\ ; & retr_{13} & := & retr_{12} \mathbin{\diamond\!\!>} retr_{23} \\ ; & abs_{12} & := & [p \; ? \; sort; \; i : p \times st_1 \\ & & & \quad \vdash [i.par, retr_{12}(i.st)]] \\ ; & abs_{23} & := & [p \; ? \; sort; \; i : p \times st_2 \\ & & & \quad \vdash [i.par, retr_{23}(i.st)]] \\ ]\!] & & & \\ \hline \end{array}$$

$$; \quad \begin{array}{|llll|} \hline \multicolumn{4}{|l|}{\textbf{part } inv\_cont :=} \\ [\![& st_1, st_2, st_3 & ? & sort \\ ; & inv_1 & ? & [st_1 \vdash prop] \\ ; & inv_2 & ? & [st_2 \vdash prop] \\ ; & inv_3 & ? & [st_3 \vdash prop] \\ ]\!] & & & \\ \hline \end{array}$$

$$; \quad \begin{array}{|llll|} \hline \multicolumn{4}{|l|}{\textbf{part } ver\_cont :=} \\ [\![& \multicolumn{3}{l|}{\textbf{import } inv\_cont} \\ ; & v_1 & ? & version(inv_1) \\ ; & v_2 & ? & version(inv_2) \\ ; & v_3 & ? & version(inv_3) \\ ]\!] & & & \\ \hline \end{array}$$

; **part** *ver_op_cont* :=
$[\![$ st_1, st_2, st_3 ? *sort*
; **import** $ver\_cont(st_1 := st_1, st_2 := st_2, st_3 := st_3)$
; **import** $op\_cont(st_1 := st_1, st_2 := st_2, st_3 := st_3)$
$]\!]$

; **part** *ver_retr_cont* :=
$[\![$ st_1, st_2, st_3 ? *sort*
; **import** $ver\_cont(st_1 := st_1, st_2 := st_2, st_3 := st_3)$
; **import** $retr\_cont(st_1 := st_1, st_2 := st_2, st_3 := st_3)$
$]\!]$

$]\!]$

The last two components were constructed by means of a *context application* $c(x := t)$, which replaces the first declaration $x : t_1$ or implicit definition $x ? t_1$ to the definition $x := t$. Boxes have been used to clarify the structure of the description.

Simultaneous induction on version triples

In order to lift properties of operation triples to properties of version triples, an induction principle of simultaneous induction on version triples is needed. This principle can be derived using structural induction on versions (section 2).

part *ver_induction* :=
$[\![$ *ver_triple_induction* :=

import *inv_cont*; $P : \dfrac{version(inv_1);\ version(inv_2);\ version(inv_3)}{[p, q \ ?\ prop \vdash [p;\ q \vdash prop]]}$

empty := $P(\langle\rangle, \langle\rangle, \langle\rangle)$

< ... > ∴ ; *cons* := **import** *ver_op_cont* $(inv_1 := inv_1, inv_2 := inv_2, inv_3 := inv_3)$ ⊢ $\dfrac{P(v_1, v_2, v_3)}{P(op_1 +\!\!< v_1, op_2 +\!\!< v_2, op_3 +\!\!< v_3)}$

[**import** *ver_cont* $\vdash \dfrac{|v_1| = |v_2|;\ |v_2| = |v_3|}{P(v_1, v_2, v_3)}$]

< ... > stands for the omitted text representing the proof of the induction principle. Note, that the induction principles is parametrized over invariant triples and achieves induction over version triples. The predicates for which it can be instantiated have the form $[p;\ q \vdash r]$, where p, q, and r are any propositions. Further note, that it is required that all three versions are of equal length. It is easy to see that this condition holds for pairs of versions which satisfy the version reification condition.

; *equal_length* :=

$$<\ldots> \therefore \left|\begin{array}{l} st_1, st_2 \;?\; state;\; inv_1 \;?\; [st_1 \vdash prop];\; inv_2 \;?\; [st_2 \vdash prop];\\ v_1 \;?\; version(inv_1);\; v_2 \;?\; version(inv_2);\; retr \;?\; [st_1 \vdash st_2] \\ \hline \qquad \left|\begin{array}{c} reif\_cond(v_1, v_2, retr) \\ \hline |\, v_1 \,| = |\, v_2 \,| \end{array}\right. \end{array}\right.$$

]]

Global proof scheme

The proof of the transitivity property will be constructed purely from the reification formalization, the frequently used contexts, and the induction principle for version triples. In the DEVA calculus, this means that, using the contexts *vdm_data_reification*, *frequent-contexts*, and *version_induction*, a text *refine* can be constructed which proves reification transitivity, i.e.

part *transitivity_of_reification* :=
[[**import** *vdm_data_reification* := (*see above*)
; **part** *frequent_contexts* := (*see above*)
; **import** *frequent_contexts*
; **part** *version_induction* := (*see above*)
; **import** *version_induction*

$$; \; refine := (see\ below) \therefore \left\|\begin{array}{c} \textbf{import}\ ver\_retr\_cont \\ \hline v_1 \sqsubset v_2 \ \textbf{with}\ retr_{12}; \quad v_2 \sqsubset v_3 \ \textbf{with}\ retr_{23} \\ \hline v_1 \sqsubset v_3 \ \textbf{with}\ retr_{13} \end{array}\right.$$

]]

The structure of *refine* is very analogous to that of its type, i.e. it assumes the premises of transitivity of reification, that is, a given version v_1 is a reification of a version v_2 wrt. the retrieve function $retr_{12}$, and v_2 is a reification of a version v_3 wrt. a retrieve function $retr_{23}$:

$$refine := \left\|\begin{array}{c} \textbf{import}\ ver\_retr\_cont \\ \hline reif_{12} : v_1 \sqsubset v_2 \ \textbf{with}\ retr_{12}; \quad reif_{23} : v_2 \sqsubset v_3 \ \textbf{with}\ retr_{23} \\ \hline < PROOF\ OF\ v_1 \sqsubset v_3 \ \textbf{with}\ retr_{13} > \end{array}\right.$$

The proof that v_1 is a reification of a version v_3 wrt. the retrieve function $retr_{12} \mathbin{\diamond\!\!>} retr_{23}$ is decomposed as follows into proofs of three lemmas:

$$< PROOF\ OF\ v_1 \sqsubset v_3 \ \textbf{with}\ retr_{13} > \;\equiv$$

< *VERIFICATION OF THE RETRIEVE CONDITION* >
; < *TRANSITIVITY OF OPERATOR REIFICATION* >
; < *TRANSITIVITY OF THE REIFICATION CONDITION* >

< *PUTTING THINGS TOGETHER* > $\therefore\ v_1 \sqsubset v_3$ **with** $retr_{12} \Leftrightarrow retr_{23}$

Lemma1: Verification of the retrieve condition

The first proposition to be shown is that the composed retrieve function $retr_{13}$ satisfies the retrieve condition.

- The invariant condition *inv_cond* is derived by the logical cut of the invariant components of the two assumptions $reif_{12}$ and $reif_{23}$.
- Similarly, the completeness condition *compl_cond* can be derived from the completeness components of these assumptions. This time, the second assumption is used inside an existential quantification, making necessary an additional monotonicity rule (*ex_weaken*). After that, a number of simplification steps are required to reach the desired result. The details of these steps are suppressed by repeatedly applying the simplification tactic *ex_simpl* (defined in appendix A).

< *VERIFICATION OF THE RETRIEVE CONDITION* > $\equiv$

$$
\begin{array}{l}
[\![\ retr_{13}\_verif := \\
\quad [\ inv\_cond := \\
\qquad reif_{12}.retr\_verif.inv\_cond \\
\qquad\quad \therefore [s_1 ? st_1 \vdash \dfrac{inv_1(s_1)}{inv_2(retr_{12}(s_1))}] \\
\qquad \Leftrightarrow reif_{23}.retr\_verif.inv\_cond \\
\qquad\quad \therefore [s_1 ? st_1 \vdash \dfrac{inv_1(s_1)}{inv_3(retr_{13}(s_1))}] \\
\quad ,\ compl\_cond := \\
\qquad reif_{23}.retr\_verif.compl\_cond \\
\qquad\quad \therefore [s_3 ? st_3 \vdash \dfrac{inv_3(s_3)}{\exists[s_2 : st_2 \vdash retr_{23}(s_2) = s_3 \wedge inv_2(s_2)]}] \\
\qquad \Leftrightarrow ex\_weaken(reif_{12}.retr\_verif.compl\_cond) \\
\qquad\quad \therefore [s_3 ? st_3 \vdash \dfrac{inv_3(s_3)}{\exists [s_2 : st_2 \vdash retr_{23}(s_2) = s_3 \ \wedge \exists[s_1 : st_1 \vdash retr_{12}(s_1) = s_2 \wedge inv_1(s_1)]]}] \\
\qquad \Leftrightarrow \mathbf{loop}\ ex\_simpl \\
\qquad\quad \therefore [s_3 ? st_3 \vdash \dfrac{inv_3(s_3)}{\exists[s_1 : st_1 \vdash inv_1(s_1) \wedge retr_{13}(s_1) = s_3]}] \\
\quad] \\
\quad \therefore retr\_cond(inv_1, inv_3, retr_{13}) \\
]\!]
\end{array}
$$

An *iteration* $t_1 \Leftrightarrow$ **loop** $t_2 \therefore t_3$ denotes the iterated cut with t_2 in order to produce a text of type t_3 starting from t_1. Thus, it stands for some expansion $t_1 \Leftrightarrow t_2 \Leftrightarrow \ldots \Leftrightarrow t_2 \therefore t_3$.

Lemma2: Transitivity of operator reification

The second property needed is a lemma stating transitivity of the operator reification condition. Assuming this condition to hold for operator pairs op_1, op_2 and op_2, op_3 respectively, the condition must be shown for the pair op_1, op_3:

$< TRANSITIVITY\ OF\ OPERATOR\ REIFICATION > \equiv$

$$op\_refine := \left| \begin{array}{l} \textbf{import}\ op\_cont(st_1 := st_1, st_2 := st_2, st_3 := st_3) \\ \hline \left\| \begin{array}{l} hyp_{12} : op\_reif\_cond(op_1, op_2, inv_1, retr_{12}); \\ hyp_{23} : op\_reif\_cond(op_2, op_3, inv_2, retr_{23}) \\ \hline < PROOF\ OF\ op\_reif\_cond(op_1, op_3, inv_1, retr_{13}) > \end{array} \right. \end{array} \right.$$

A proof of the latter proposition, is presented below:

$< PROOF\ OF\ op\_reif\_cond(op_1, op_3, inv_1, retr_{13}) > \equiv$

$$\begin{array}{l} [\ \ in_1 : par.in \times st_1 \quad ;\ in_2 := abs_{12}(in_1) \quad ;\ in_3 := abs_{23}(in_2) \\ ;\ out_1 : par.out \times st_1;\ out_2 := abs_{12}(out_1);\ out_3 := abs_{23}(out_2) \\ \left| \begin{array}{lll} \quad inv_1\_hyp & : & inv_1(in_1.st) \\ ;\ op_3\_pre\_hyp & : & op_3.pre(in_3) \\ ;\ inv_2\_proof & := & (see\ below)\ \therefore inv_2(in_2.st) \\ ;\ op_2\_pre\_proof & := & (see\ below)\ \therefore op_2.pre(in_2) \end{array} \right. \\ \vdash \left| \begin{array}{l} [\ domain\_cond := hyp_{12}(inv_1\_hyp, op_2\_pre\_proof).domain\_cond \\ \qquad\qquad \therefore op_1.pre(in_1) \\ ,\ result\_cond := hyp_{12}(inv_1\_hyp, op_2\_pre\_proof).result\_cond \\ \qquad\qquad \therefore [op_1.post(in_1, out_1) \vdash op_2.post(in_2, out_2)] \\ \qquad \Rightarrow hyp_{23}(inv_2\_proof, op_3\_pre\_hyp).result\_cond \\ \qquad\qquad \therefore [op_1.post(in_1, out_1) \vdash op_3.post(in_3, out_3)] \\ ] \end{array} \right. \\ ] \\ \therefore op\_reif\_cond(op_1, op_3, inv_1, retr_{13}) \end{array}$$

Its assumptions have the same structure as that of the definition of *op_reif_cond*, i.e. it is assumed that the concrete invariant (inv_1_hyp) and that the precondition of the abstract operation holds ($op_3\_pre\_hyp$). In order to make use of the assumptions about operation reification (hyp_{12}, hyp_{23}), it is necessary to first derive the intermediate invariant (inv_2_proof) and the precondition of the intermediate operation ($op_2\_pre\_proof$). These two conditions are proven below. Note, that the first proof makes use of the overall hypothesis $reif_{12}$. More precisely, it needs the assumption that $retr_{12}$ preserves the invariants. In fact, without that condition, VDM-reification would not be transitive.

$$\begin{array}{ll} inv_2\_proof & := (reif_{12}.retr\_verif.inv\_cond)(inv_1\_hyp) \\ op_2\_pre\_proof & := hyp_{23}(inv_2\_proof, op_3\_pre\_hyp).domain\_cond \end{array}$$

The fact that the precondition is preserved (*domain_cond*) follows from the corresponding fact contained in the assumption hyp_{12}. The fact that the postcondition is preserved (*result_cond*) can be shown by functional composition of the corresponding facts contained in the two assumptions hyp_{12} and hyp_{23}. Note the use of all preparatory derivations to satisfy the preconditions of these assumptions.

Lemma3: Transitivity of the reification condition

To lift transitivity of operator reification (which is true regardless which operators are involved) to the level of transitivity of the version reification condition, the induction principle for version triples is instantiated to transitivity of the version reification condition.

< TRANSITIVITY OF THE REIFICATION CONDITION > ≡

$$[\![\; trans\_reif\_cond := \left| \frac{\textbf{import } ver\_cont(inv_1 := inv_1, inv_2 := inv_2, inv_3 := inv_3)}{\left| \frac{reif\_cond(v_1, v_2, retr_{12});\; reif\_cond(v_2, v_3, retr_{23})}{reif\_cond(v_1, v_3, retr_{13})} \right.} \right.$$

$$;\; trans\_reif\_cond\_induction := \; ver\_triple\_induction(trans\_reif\_cond)$$

For the base case of empty versions, it suffices to use the case of empty versions in the definition of the reification condition (*reif_cond_def.empty*). For the inductive step, it is necessary to prove transitivity of the "consed" versions under the assumption of transitivity of the original versions (*ihyp*).

$$;\; trans\_reif\_cond\_verif_0 :=$$

$$trans\_reif\_cond\_induction$$

$$(\; empty := \boxed{\begin{array}{l} \left| \dfrac{reif\_cond(\langle\rangle, \langle\rangle, retr_{12});\;\; reif\_cond(\langle\rangle, \langle\rangle, retr_{23})}{reif\_cond\_def.empty} \right. \\ \therefore\;\; trans\_reif\_cond(\langle\rangle, \langle\rangle, \langle\rangle) \end{array}} \;,$$

$$cons := \boxed{\left\| \frac{\textbf{import } ver\_op\_cont(inv_1 := inv_1, inv_2 := inv_2, inv_3 := inv_3)}{\left| \dfrac{ihyp : trans\_reif\_cond(v_1, v_2, v_3)}{\begin{array}{l} < PROOF\ OF\ trans\_reif\_cond(op_1 \twoheadleftarrow v_1, op_2 \twoheadleftarrow v_2, op_3 \twoheadleftarrow v_3) > \\ \therefore \left| \dfrac{trans\_reif\_cond(v_1, v_2, v_3)}{trans\_reif\_cond(op_1 \twoheadleftarrow v_1, op_2 \twoheadleftarrow v_2, op_3 \twoheadleftarrow v_3)} \right. \end{array}} \right.} \right.} \;)$$

$$\therefore \left| \frac{\textbf{import } ver\_cont(inv_1 := inv_1, inv_2 := inv_2, inv_3 := inv_3)}{\left| \dfrac{|v_1| = |v_2|;\; |v_2| = |v_3|}{trans\_reif\_cond(v_1, v_2, v_3)} \right.} \right.$$

For the proof of the inductive step (figure 1), the main part (*op_cond*) consists of showing the operation reification condition for the operator pair op_1 and op_3. The idea is to use transitivity of operator reification, that was shown above (*op_refine*). The remaining part of the condition (*recur_cond*) follows from the induction hypothesis. Finally, the conditions requiring equal lengths must be resolved:

$< PROOF\ OF\ trans\_reif\_cond(op_1 \prec v_1, op_2 \prec v_2, op_3 \prec v_3) > \equiv$

$$
\begin{array}{|l|}
\hline
\quad reif_{12}\_hyp : reif\_cond(op_1 \prec v_1, op_2 \prec v_2, retr_{12}); \\
\quad reif_{23}\_hyp : reif\_cond(op_2 \prec v_2, op_3 \prec v_3, retr_{23}) \\
\hline
[\ op\_cond \quad := op\_refine \\
\qquad\qquad (reif\_cond\_def.cons.down(reif_{12}\_hyp).op\_cond, \\
\qquad\qquad reif\_cond\_def.cons.down(reif_{23}\_hyp).op\_cond) \\
\qquad\qquad\quad \therefore op\_reif\_cond(op_1, op_3, inv_1, retr_{13}) \\
,\ recur\_cond := ihyp \\
\qquad\qquad (reif\_cond\_def.cons.down(reif_{12}\_hyp).recur, \\
\qquad\qquad reif\_cond\_def.cons.down(reif_{23}\_hyp).recur) \\
\qquad\qquad\quad \therefore reif\_cond(v_1, v_3, retr_{13}) \\
] \\
\backslash reif\_cond\_def.cons.up \\
\quad \therefore \quad reif\_cond(op_1 \prec v_1, op_3 \prec v_3, retr_{13}) \\
\hline
\end{array}
$$

$\therefore trans\_reif\_cond(op_1 \prec v_1, op_2 \prec v_2, op_3 \prec v_3)$

Figure 1: Inductive step of the proof of Lemma3

$$
\begin{array}{l}
;\ trans\_reif\_cond\_verif := trans\_reif\_cond\_verif_0(equal\_length(reif_{12}.reif\_verif), \\
\qquad\qquad\qquad\qquad\qquad\qquad equal\_length(reif_{23}.reif\_verif)) \\
\qquad\qquad\qquad \therefore \boxed{trans\_reif\_cond}
\end{array}
$$

]

Proof of transitivity of reification

Now, the above results can be put together to prove that version v_1 is a reification of version v_3 wrt. the retrieve function $retr_{13}$. Remember that, according to the definition of reification, there are three conditions to be satisfied: the version verification condition (which follows directly from the reification assumptions), the conditions for the composed retrieve function (which have been verified as Lemma1), and the version reification condition (which follows from Lemma3, using the version reification conditions of the assumptions).

$< PUTTING\ THINGS\ TOGETHER > \equiv$

$$
\begin{array}{l}
trans\_reif\_proof := \\
\quad [\ version\_verif := [\ concr \ := reif_{12}.version\_verif.concr \\
\qquad\qquad\qquad\qquad ,\ abstr \ := reif_{23}.version\_verif.abstr] \\
\qquad\qquad\qquad\qquad \therefore \boxed{[v_1\checkmark, v_3\checkmark]} \\
\quad ,\ retr\_verif \quad := retr_{13}\_verif \\
\qquad\qquad\qquad\qquad \therefore \boxed{retr\_cond(inv_1, inv_3, retr_{13})}
\end{array}
$$

, *reif_verif* := *trans_reif_cond_verif*(*reif*$_{12}$.*reif_verif*, *reif*$_{23}$.*reif_verif*)

$\therefore$ $\boxed{reif\_cond(v_1, v_3, retr_{13})}$

]

$\therefore$ $\boxed{v_1 \sqsubset v_3 \textbf{ with } retr_{13}}$

]]

This concludes the proof of transitivity of refinement. Remember, that there were only two assumptions about the reification from v_3 to v_2 and from v_2 to v_1. Thus, within the general proof outline given above, it holds that

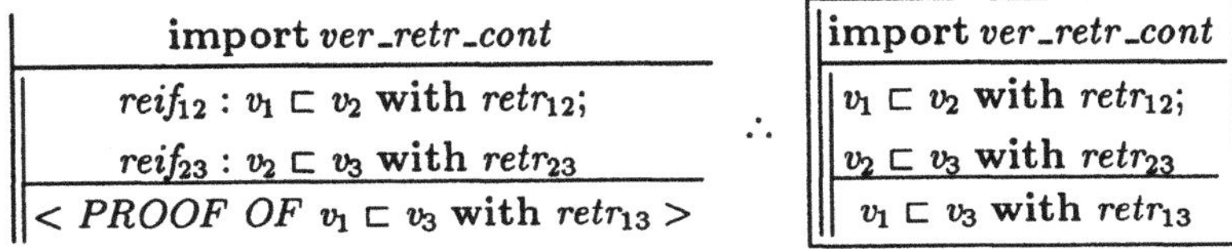

5 Conclusions

This paper has reported on an exercise to formally prove transitivity of VDM-reification wrt. a VDM-formalization, both performed in the formal development language DEVA. As a consequence, a strong formal support system for VDM-reification is obtained, which rigorously ensures the satisfaction of proof obligations and thus the credibility of reification chains.

Transitivity of VDM-reification is neither deep nor trivial to prove. The author has elaborated the proof in a mathematical style on paper, before formalizing it in DEVA. The formalization process introduced considerable formal overhead, mainly due to the explicit type declaration of all involved objects. In addition, the DEVA notation is not self-explanatory. However, the type system of this notation is essential for the logical control of the proof (i.e. no cheating) and an effort was made to reduce the formal overhead by a good proof structuration.

Proving properties like transitivity of reification helps to better understand formal methods. For example, it turned out at one point in the proof that the property of operator reification does not hold unless the retrieve function preserves the invariants (see Lemma 2). Further research aims at performing significant VDM development examples (with complete machine-checked proofs) inside DEVA.

Acknowledgements

My thanks go to Christine Lafontaine, Viktor Friesen, and the anonymous referees for their helpful comments.

Appendix A: Classical Many-Sorted Logic

The classical propositional calculus is formalized in DEVA in a natural deduction style. The formalization begins by introducing the basic propositional constant *false* and the logical connectives together with their corresponding introduction and elimination laws:

part *prop_logic* :=

$$
\begin{array}{lll}
[\![\ \mathit{prop} & : & \mathbf{prim} \\
; \ \mathit{false} & : & \mathit{prop} \\
; \ (\cdot) \Rightarrow (\cdot), (\cdot) \wedge (\cdot), (\cdot) \vee (\cdot) & : & [\mathit{prop};\ \mathit{prop} \vdash \mathit{prop}] \\
; \ \mathit{false\_elim} & : & [p\ ?\ \mathit{prop} \vdash [\mathit{false} \vdash p]] \\
; \ \mathit{imp} & : & [p, q\ ?\ \mathit{prop} \vdash [\mathit{intro} := \left|\frac{[p \vdash q]}{p \Rightarrow q}\right., \mathit{elim} := \left|\frac{p;\ p \Rightarrow q}{q}\right.]] \\
; \ \mathit{conj} & : & [p, q\ ?\ \mathit{prop} \vdash [\mathit{intro} := \left|\frac{p;\ q}{p \wedge q}\right., \mathit{eliml} := \left|\frac{p \wedge q}{p}\right., \mathit{elimr} := \left|\frac{p \wedge q}{q}\right.]] \\
; \ \mathit{disj} & : & [p, q, r\ ?\ \mathit{prop} \vdash [\mathit{introl} := \left|\frac{p}{p \vee q}\right., \mathit{intror} := \left|\frac{q}{p \vee q}\right., \\
 & & \qquad \mathit{elim} := \left|\frac{p \vee q;\ [p \vdash r];\ [q \vdash r]}{r}\right.]]
\end{array}
$$

Negation, the constant *true* and equivalence are defined in terms of the preceding declarations.

$$
\begin{array}{lll}
; \ \neg(\cdot) & := & [p : \mathit{prop} \vdash p \Rightarrow \mathit{false}] \\
; \ \mathit{true} & := & \neg \mathit{false} \\
; \ (\cdot) \Leftrightarrow (\cdot) & := & [p, q : \mathit{prop} \vdash (p \Rightarrow q) \wedge (q \Rightarrow p)]
\end{array}
$$

Finally, the law of the excluded middle is added, which effects the transition from the *intuitionistic* propositional calculus to the *classical* propositional calculus considered here.

$$
\begin{array}{lll}
; \ \mathit{excluded\_middle} & : & [p\ ?\ \mathit{prop} \vdash p \vee \neg p] \\
]\!]
\end{array}
$$

The predicate calculus is obtained by adding laws for the two quantifiers.

part *pred_logic* :=

$$
\begin{array}{lll}
[\![\ \mathbf{import}\ \mathit{prop\_logic} \\
; \ \mathit{sort} & : & \mathbf{prim} \\
; \ \forall(\cdot), \exists(\cdot) & : & [a\ ?\ \mathit{sort} \vdash [[a \vdash \mathit{prop}] \vdash \mathit{prop}]] \\
; \ \mathit{univ} & : & [a\ ?\mathit{sort};\ P\ ?\ [a \vdash \mathit{prop}] \vdash \\
 & & \qquad [\mathit{intro} := \left|\frac{[x : a \vdash P(x)]}{\forall P}\right., \mathit{elim} := [x : a \vdash \left|\frac{\forall P}{P(x)}\right.]]] \\
; \ \mathit{ex} & : & [a\ ?\ \mathit{sort};\ P\ ?\ [a \vdash \mathit{prop}] \vdash
\end{array}
$$

$$[intro := [x : a \vdash \frac{P(x)}{\exists P}], elim := [p\ ?\ prop \vdash \frac{[x : a \vdash \frac{P(x)}{p}];\ \exists P}{p}]]]$$

Three simple laws, useful for the proofs of this paper, involving existential quantification, can be derived (however, proofs are not given).

$$;\ and\_comm\ := <\ldots> \therefore\ [p, q\ ?\ prop \vdash \frac{p \wedge q}{q \wedge p}]$$

$$;\ ex\_weaken\ := <\ldots> \therefore\ \frac{a\ ?\ sort;\ P, Q, R\ ?\ [a \vdash prop]}{\frac{\exists[x : a \vdash P(x) \wedge Q(x)];\ [y : a \vdash [Q(y) \vdash R(y)]]}{\exists[x : a \vdash P(x) \wedge R(x)]}}$$

$$;\ ex\_swap\ := <\ldots> \therefore\ \frac{a, b\ ?\ sort;\ P\ ?\ [a \vdash prop];\ Q\ ?\ [b \vdash prop];\ R\ ?\ [a;\ b \vdash prop]}{\frac{\exists[x : a \vdash P(x) \wedge \exists[y : b \vdash Q(y) \wedge R(x, y)]]}{\exists[y : b \vdash Q(y) \wedge \exists[x : a \vdash P(x) \wedge R(x, y)]]}}$$

$$;\ ex\_fold\ := <\ldots> \therefore\ \frac{a, b, c\ ?\ sort;\ f\ ?\ [a \vdash b];\ g\ ?\ [b \vdash c];\ x\ ?\ a;\ z\ ?\ c}{\frac{\exists[y : b \vdash g(y) = z \wedge f(x) = y]}{(f \diamond g)(x) = z}}$$

Finally a deduction principle is added (as an axiom), stating that equivalent propositions may be substituted inside a proposition without changing its validity. Note, that this principle is at the meta-level wrt. predicate calculus, and therefore it could not be derived from the given axioms, unless e.g. a principle of structural induction on proposition schemas S is added to the formalization.

$$;\ psubst\ :\ [S\ ?\ [prop \vdash prop];\ p, q\ ?\ prop \vdash [\frac{p}{q} \vdash \frac{S(p)}{S(q)}]]$$

Finally, a simple tactic, useful for one of the proofs of this paper, can be defined:

; *ex_simpl*:= **alt**[*psubst*(*ex_weaken*), *psubst*(*ex_swap*), *psubst*(*and_commut*)]
]]

The *alternative* **alt**$[t_1, t_2]$ denotes the alternative choice between two texts.

Appendix B: DEVA constructs used in this paper

Basic Alphabets

$\{x, x_1, x_2, \ldots\}$ the set of *text identifiers*
$\{p, p_1, p_2, \ldots\}$ the set of *context identifiers*

Notations

texts $t, t_1, t_2, \ldots$
contexts $c, c_1, c_2, \ldots$

Context-constructs		*Text-constructs*	
$x : t$	declaration	**prim**	primitive text
$x := t$	definition	x	text identifier
$x\ ?\ t$	implicit definition	$[c \vdash t]$	abstraction
part $p := c$	context definition	$t_1(t_2)$	direct application
import p	context inclusion	$t_1(x := t_2)$	application
$[\![c_1;\ c_2]\!]$	context join	$[x_1 := t_1, \ldots, x_n := t_n]$	named product
$c(x := t)$	context application	$t.x$	projection
		$t_1 \triangleright t_2$	direct cut
		$t_1 \therefore t_2$	judgement
		alt$[t_1, t_2]$	alternative
		loop t	iteration

Literature

Bru80 N.G. de Bruijn, *A Survey of the Project AUTOMATH.* In: J.P. Seldin and J.R. Hindley (eds), *To H.B. Curry: Essays in Combinatory Logic, Lambda Calculus, and Formalism*, p.589-606, Academic Press, 1980.

Gab90 R. Gabriel (ed.), *ESPRIT Project ToolUse, Final Report of the Deva Support Task: Retrospective and Manuals*, Arbeitspapiere der GMD, no.425, GMD Karlsruhe, 1990.

Gro90 Ph. de Groote, *Définition et Properiéetés d'un métacalcul de répresentation de théories*, Thèse d'Etat, Université Catholique de Louvain, Belgium 1990.

HHP86 R. Harper, F.A. Honsell, and G. Plotkin. *A Framework for Defining Logics.* Proceedings of the 2nd Symposium on Logic in Computer Science, p. 194-204, IEEE, 1986.

Laf90 C. Lafontaine, *Formalization of the VDM Reification in the DEVA Meta Calculus. The Human-Leucocyte-Antigen case study.* In: M. Broy and C.B. Jones (editors), *Programming Concepts and Methods*, p.333-368, North-Holland, 1990.

Ned80 R.P. Nederpelt, *An Approach to Theorem Proving on the Basis of a Typed Lambda Calculus*, LNCS 87, p.181-190, Springer, 1980.

SWGC89 M. Sintzoff, M. Weber, Ph. de Groote, J. Cazin, *Definition 1.1 of the Generic Development Language Deva.* ToolUse-project, Research report, Unité d'Informatique, Université Catholique de Louvain, Belgium, 1989.

Web90 M. Weber, *Formalization of the Bird-Meertens Algorithmic Calculus in the DEVA Meta-Calculus*, In: M. Broy and C.B. Jones (editors), *Programming Concepts and Methods*, p.201-232, North-Holland, 1990.

Web91 M. Weber, *A Meta-Calculus for Formal System Development*, doctoral thesis, Oldenburg press Vol.195, München-Wien 1991.

Upgrading the pre- and postcondition technique

H.B.M. Jonkers*

Philips Research Laboratories Eindhoven
P.O. Box 80000, 5600 JA Eindhoven, The Netherlands

Abstract

This paper gives a reconstruction of the classical pre- and postcondition technique from its roots and extends it with several features. A number of problems in connection with pre- and postcondition specifications are discussed and solutions presented. Problems that are discussed include: framing, dynamic object creation, non-atomic actions and user-friendly syntax. The technique as described is part of the specification language COLD-1 and has been used in several industrial applications.

1 Introduction

The subject of this paper is so old that, as a researcher, one would almost feel embarassed writing about it. The pre- and postcondition technique is among the oldest and most frequently used specification techniques. Though its exact roots are hard to trace, the technique as such was given a more formal basis by Hoare in his well-known paper on the axiomatic basis of computer programming [5]. In his paper he introduced the pre- and postcondition formalism by means of formulae of the following form:

$$A \{ P \} B$$

specifying that, if *precondition* A is true before execution of the program fragment P, then the *postcondition* B will be true on its completion. This formulation contains the essence of pre- and postconditions, though many variations on the theme have been developed since. Examples are weakest preconditions [1] and dynamic logic [4]. The particular angle from which we shall approach the technique here is that of specifying state transitions of *systems* rather than programs. What is meant by this will be explained in Section 2.

Nowadays the pre- and postcondition technique is considered a standard technique in software development and it is being taught in almost every basic software engineering course. This gives the impression that the technique has fully matured and that it can readily be applied in everyday software development practice. The fact that this is not really the case is camouflaged by the sloppy and informal way pre- and postconditions are generally used in practice. When applying pre- and postconditions in the *formal* way to real-life systems, several problems come to light. A few examples of such problems are:

*This work has been performed within the framework of ESPRIT project 2565 (ATMOSPHERE).

- how to deal with dynamic object creation?
- how to specify a system hierarchically, given the fact that information in lower system levels may be hidden?
- how to combine pre- and postconditions with operational specification techniques?
- how to deal with non-atomic actions?
- how to choose a user-friendly syntax for pre- and postconditions?

The last point may seem obvious, but should not be underestimated. Formality is often felt as a straightjacket by the practitioner. A flexible syntax providing naturalness of expression can do a lot to remove this feeling.

For several years now, we have been working in Philips trying to make formal techniques useful in the industrial software development process. Our main vehicle in doing so has been the specification and design language COLD (Common Object-oriented Language for Design) developed at Philips Research Laboratories Eindhoven. COLD is a state-based, model-oriented wide-spectrum language in the tradition of VDM, but with a clear algebraic background and a stronger focus on techniques for 'design in the large'. In three successive ESPRIT projects (FAST, METEOR, ATMOSPHERE) an equal number of language versions were developed (COLD-S [7], COLD-K [2], COLD-1 [9]). COLD-S was a feasibility study, COLD-K is a *kernel language*, providing the basic semantic primitives of a wide-spectrum language, and COLD-1 is a *user-oriented language* defined on top of COLD-K, providing a user-friendly syntax (which COLD-K lacks). The following exemplifies the differences between COLD-1 and COLD-K: COLD-1 provides prefix, infix and postfix notations for user-defined operations (rather than the prefix notation of COLD-K), it provides standard templates for modular descriptions (rather than the algebraic modularization operators of COLD-K) and standard formats for pre- and postcondition style definitions (rather than the dynamic logic of COLD-K).

In the design of COLD-1, a number of lessons learned from the use of COLD in several industrial applications was taken into account. In particular, a number of problems with the practical use of pre- and postconditions were addressed, including the problems mentioned above (in fact, some of these problems were already addressed in COLD-K). In this paper we discuss the pre- and postcondition formalism as included in COLD-1, but the discussion is self-contained and independent of COLD-1. We start with the basic pre- and postcondition formalism and gradually extend it with new features, until a fully-fledged notation has been obtained. The focus is on the *practical use* of pre- and postconditions and not on the underlying theory. Nevertheless we shall define the meaning of the concepts that are used in a semi-formal way. For the formal meaning, we refer to [9] that defines the meaning of the pre- and postcondition formalism explained in this paper in terms of COLD-K.

2 Basic concepts

We are concerned with the specification of the state transitions of *systems*. A system consists of a collection of *states*, an *initial state* and a number of state transformers which we shall refer to as *procedures*. Procedures represent the state transitions that the system can make and are the things we want to specify using pre- and postconditions. Before going into the pre- and postcondition formalism, it makes sense to discuss in more detail what we mean by states and procedures and to say something about the assertion and expression language we shall use for describing them.

2.1 States

We shall use a very general model of states that can be paraphrased as "states are algebras". More precisely, we shall model states as *many-sorted algebras.* This sounds more complicated than it is; it simply means that a state is described by the following items:

1. a number of *sorts*, which are sets containing *objects*; the fact that T is a sort will be indicated as follows:

   SORT T

2. a number of *predicates*, which are relations defined on the sorts; the fact that r is a predicate defined on the sorts $T_1, \ldots, T_n$ will be indicated as follows:

   PRED r : T_1 # ... # T_n

3. a number of *functions*, which are partial mappings from a number of sorts to other sorts; the fact that f is a function from the sorts $T_1, \ldots, T_n$ to the sort V will be indicated as follows:

   FUNC f : T_1 # ... # T_n -> V

We shall refer to the sorts, predicates and functions that constitute the state of a system as the *state components* of the system.

Not much imagination is required to see that the above algebraic view of states is flexible enough to model almost any kind of information that is part of the state of a system. For example, if we think of a file system, we could have the following state components (among many others):

```
SORT File
PRED eof : File
FUNC contents : File # Nat -> Byte
```

Here the sort `File` represents the collection of all files in the system, the predicate value `eof(f)` indicates whether the 'end of file' condition is true for file `f`, and the function value `contents(f,i)` indicates which byte is stored at position `i` in the file `f`.

The set of possible states of a system will generally contain more than one state. We shall assume that all states of a system have the same *signature*, implying that they all have the same number of state components of the same name and type. In the file system example this implies that in each state of the system we have (at least) a sort `File`, a predicate `eof` and a function `contents` of the type indicated above.

The value of certain state components may vary from state to state. Those state components that may vary will be called *variables.* The fact that a state component is variable will be indicated by postfixing its declaration with the keyword `VAR`. Note that 'ordinary' programming variables can be viewed in a natural way as nullary functions. For example, an (unsigned) integer programming variable `x` corresponds to:

```
FUNC x : -> Nat   VAR
```

Note also that functions may be partial, implying that the variable `x` may be undefined.

Below we give the complete state signature of the file system example that we shall use extensively in the rest of the paper:

```
SORT File                                VAR
PRED eof      : File                     VAR
FUNC contents : File # Nat -> Byte       VAR
FUNC length   : File -> Nat              VAR
FUNC offset   : File -> Nat              VAR
FUNC cre_date : File -> Date
```

Note that the sort `File` is variable, which implies that the number of files may vary from state to state. The reason is that we want to be able to create files dynamically. The `length` function indicates the number of bytes in a file. The `offset` function indicates the position in the file where the next byte will be read or written. The creation date of a file, modelled by the function `cre_date`, is not variable but *constant* (in a sense that will be explained later): we cannot change it for the same reasons we cannot change our own birthday.

2.2 Procedures

Given the set of states of a system as spanned by its state components, let us now consider the state transitions of the system as represented by its associated procedures. A procedure p can be viewed as a mechanism that can be applied in a system state s in order to bring the system in a new state t. One of two things can happen when applying p in state s. The first is that p indeed brings the system in a new state t, in which case we say that p *succeeds* in state s and *transforms* s to t. The state t need not be uniquely determined. In other words, procedures may be *non-deterministic*. The second thing that can happen is that p does not succeed in bringing the system in a new state, and then we say that p *fails* in state s.

The state transitions established by procedures will be considered pure *atomic actions*. This implies that during a procedure application there is no interference with possible other procedure applications, and that a failing procedure application can be treated as if it never happened. The behaviour of the system as a whole can thus be viewed as the collection of all sequences of the following form:

$$s_0 \xrightarrow{p_1} s_1 \xrightarrow{p_2} \dots \xrightarrow{p_{n-1}} s_{n-1} \xrightarrow{p_n} s_n$$

where s_0 is the initial state and p_i denotes a successful procedure application transforming state s_{i-1} to state s_i ($i = 1, \dots, n,\ n \geq 0$). The question how to deal with non-atomic actions will be elaborated upon in Section 3.11.

The above is a somewhat operational and informal description of procedures. We can also define somewhat more abstractly and formally what we mean by them. We view procedures as binary *relations* between states, i.e. as subsets of $S \times S$, where S is the set of all system states. The fact that a procedure p transforms a state s to a state t is the same as saying that:

$$(s, t) \in p$$

or, in other words, that the relation p holds between states s and t. The fact that a procedure p succeeds in state s amounts to:

$$\exists\, t \in S\ (\ (s,t) \in p\ )$$

and then, of course, the fact that p fails in s is equivalent to:

$$\neg\exists\, t \in S\ (\ (s,t) \in p\ )$$

The above model of procedures corresponds to the simplest form of procedures. In practice, procedures can take objects as their inputs and yield objects as their outputs. The fact that p is a procedure that takes objects from the sorts $T_1, \ldots, T_n$ as its inputs and yields objects from the sorts $V_1, \ldots, V_m$ as its outputs will be indicated as follows:

PROC p : T_1 # ... # T_n -> V_1 # ... # V_m

What we have discussed so far was the case where $n = 0$ and $m = 0$, but the generalization is obvious. We shall view a procedure p as declared above as a relation between states *and* objects, i.e. as a set containing tuples of the form:

$$(s, x_1, \ldots, x_n, t, y_1, \ldots, y_m)$$

where s and t are states, x_i is an object of sort T_i in state s $(i = 1, \ldots, n)$ and y_i is an object of sort V_i in state t $(i = 1, \ldots, m)$. We shall say that p transforms a state s and input values $x_1, \ldots, x_n$ to a state t, *yielding* output values $y_1, \ldots, y_m$, if:

$$(s, x_1, \ldots, x_n, t, y_1, \ldots, y_m) \in p$$

If for given s and $x_1, \ldots, x_n$ corresponding t and $y_1, \ldots, y_m$ exist as above, we say that p succeeds in state s for the input values $x_1, \ldots, x_n$; otherwise we say that it fails.

Bringing together the algebraic view of states and the relational view of procedures, we obtain a system model where the state transitions as established by procedures are transitions from one algebraic structure to another. In such transitions the different components (sorts, predicates and functions) of the algebraic structure representing the state may be *modified.* For example, in the case of the file system we could have the following procedures:

```
PROC new   : -> File
PROC read  : File -> Byte
PROC write : File # Byte ->
```

The `new` procedure has no input parameters and yields a new file as its output, thus modifying the sort `File`. The `read` procedure takes a file as its input, reads the byte at the current offset from the file, increments the offset and yields the byte read as its output. In so doing it will not only modify the `offset` function, but (possibly) also the `eof` predicate. Of course, the `read` procedure will succeed only if the `eof` predicate is false. The `write` procedure takes a file and a byte as its arguments, writes the byte at the current position in the file and increments the offset without yielding an output. Among other things, it will modify the `contents` function.

2.3 Assertions

In order to formulate pre- and postconditions, we introduce *assertions* that allow us to express facts about states. The basic assertions we shall use are listed below:

$\texttt{TRUE}$
$\texttt{FALSE}$
$\texttt{NOT}\ A$
$A_1\ \texttt{AND}\ A_2$
$A_1\ \texttt{OR}\ A_2$
$A_1\ \texttt{=>}\ A_2$
$A_1\ \texttt{<=>}\ A_2$
$\texttt{FORALL}\ x_1{:}T_1,\ \dots\ ,x_n{:}T_n\ (\ A\ )$
$\texttt{EXISTS}\ x_1{:}T_1,\ \dots\ ,x_n{:}T_n\ (\ A\ )$
$r(t_1,\dots,t_n)$
$t\,!$
$t_1 = t_2$

where A, A_1, A_2 are assertions, $x_1, \dots, x_n$ are logical variables, $T_1, \dots, T_n$ are sorts, r is a predicate and $t, t_1, \dots, t_n$ are *terms*, i.e. constructs of one of the following two forms:

x
$f(t_1, \dots, t_n)$

where f is a function. From the above list it is clear that our assertion language is essentially first-order (typed) predicate logic, with two special predicates: ! (definedness) and = (equality). Besides the assertions listed above, we shall introduce some other assertions later on.

Assertions should always be interpreted with respect to a given state, where the sort, predicate and function symbols in the assertion denote the corresponding state components. This implies that the legal assertions associated with a given system are determined by the state signature of the system. The interpretation of assertions is as usual, except for the following. Since functions may be partial, terms may be written down that are undefined. This raises the question how assertions containing such undefined terms should be interpreted. Rather than introducing artefacts such as 'undefined objects' for every sort, we solve this by assuming *strictness*:

1. a term of the form $f(t_1, \dots, t_n)$, where f is a function symbol, should be interpreted as *undefined* if one of the terms $t_1, \dots, t_n$ is undefined;
2. an assertion of the form $r(t_1, \dots, t_n)$, where r is a predicate symbol, should be interpreted as *false* if one of the terms $t_1, \dots, t_n$ is undefined.

This implies that for all functions f and predicates r (including the built-in predicates ! and =) we have the following tautologies:

$r(t_1, \dots, t_n)\ \ \texttt{=>}\ t_1!\ \texttt{AND}\ \dots\ \texttt{AND}\ t_n!$
$f(t_1, \dots, t_n)!\ \texttt{=>}\ t_1!\ \texttt{AND}\ \dots\ \texttt{AND}\ t_n!$

Note that terms of the form x, where x is a logical variable introduced by one of the quantifiers FORALL or EXISTS, are by definition always defined: the quantifiers range over all objects in a sort and there is no such thing as an undefined object in a sort.

An example of an assertion is:

```
FORALL f:File ( NOT eof(f) => contents(f,offset(f))! )
```

which states that if we are not at the end of file `f`, position `offset(f)` in the file contains a well-defined value (byte). Another example of an assertion is:

```
EXISTS f:File,i:Nat ( i < length(f) AND contents(f,i) = 0 )
```

which states that there is a file `f` that contains a zero byte. In this assertion the predicate $<$ on `Nat` $\times$ `Nat` is used, with the obvious meaning.

2.4 Expressions

Besides assertions, we shall also need some way of denoting state transitions, for which we introduce *expressions.* The reasons why we need expressions will become clear later. Expressions can be viewed as binary relations between states. Analogous to procedures, we say that an expression E *succeeds* in a state s if there is a state t such that E *transforms* s to t, i.e. that $(s,t) \in E$. If there is no such state t we say that E *fails* in s. The basic expressions that we shall use are listed below:

$$\begin{array}{l} A\ ? \\ E_1\ ;\ E_2 \\ E_1 \mid E_2 \\ E\ * \\ p(t_1,\ldots,t_n) \end{array}$$

where A is an assertion, E, E_1, E_2 are expressions, p is a procedure and $t_1,\ldots,t_n$ are terms. The meaning of expressions as relations between states is indicated below:

$$\begin{array}{lll} A\ ? & = & \{\ (s,s) \mid s \in S \wedge A \text{ is true in } s\ \} \\ E_1\ ;\ E_2 & = & \{\ (s,t) \mid \exists\, u \in S\ (\ (s,u) \in E_1 \wedge (u,t) \in E_2\ )\ \} \\ E_1 \mid E_2 & = & \{\ (s,t) \mid (s,t) \in E_1 \vee (s,t) \in E_2\ \} \\ E\ * & = & \{\ (s,t) \mid \exists\, u_0,\ldots,u_n \in S\ (\ u_0 = s \wedge u_n = t \wedge \\ & & \qquad (u_{i-1},u_i) \in E\ (i = 1,\ldots,n)\ )\ \} \\ p(t_1,\ldots,t_n) & = & \{\ (s,t) \mid \exists\, x_1,\ldots,x_n\ (\ (s,x_1,\ldots,x_n,t) \in p \wedge \\ & & \qquad t_i \text{ denotes } x_i \text{ in } s\ (i = 1,\ldots,n)\ )\ \} \end{array}$$

In the above definitions we assumed that expressions have a 'side effect' only and yield no values as their result. The procedure p above should therefore be a procedure that yields no output values. In the examples to be discussed, we shall also use expressions that yield values. The generalization of the above definitions to the case of expressions that yield values requires the addition of terms and procedure applications as expressions. This generalization is straightforward and will be omitted here. A detail that should be noted is that the result yielded by the sequential composition $E_1\ ;\ E_2$ of two expressions is the concatenation of the results yielded by E_1 and E_2 (in contrast with some other languages that have value-returning expressions, such as C).

Note that the above definitions imply that procedure expressions (i.e. expressions of the form $p(t_1,\ldots,t_n)$) are also *strict*: the procedure p will fail if one of the terms t_i is undefined ($i = 1,\ldots,n$). Besides the expressions discussed in this section, a few other kinds of expressions will be introduced later on.

The following is an example of an expression:

```
write(f,0)*; eof(f) ?
```

It describes a state transition that changes all bytes of file `f` from the current offset to the end of the file to zeros. The following is an example of an expression that yields a value (besides establishing a side effect):

```
( eof(f)     ?; 0
| NOT eof(f) ?; read(f)
)
```

This expression corresponds to a traditional 'if-then-else' construct and can be read as such: if the end of file condition is true for `f`, the expression yields the zero byte (without side effect), otherwise it reads a byte from `f` and yields it (with the side effect of incrementing `offset(f)`).

3 Pre- and postcondition specifications

We have now made all necessary preparations for the discussion of the pre- and postcondition technique. We shall take Hoare's original formulation of pre- and postconditions [5] as a starting point and gradually extend the formalism.

3.1 The basic notation

As stated before, we intend to use pre- and postconditions for specifying procedures. At first, let us restrict ourselves to procedures that have no inputs and no outputs. Using Hoare's format, a pre- and postcondition specification of such a procedure p would look like this:

$$A \{ p \} B$$

We shall use a somewhat stylized version of this, and combine the specification and the declaration of the procedure, as indicated below:

```
PROC p : ->
PRE  A
POST B
```

If we require that procedures are declared only once (as we do), the above format implies that the complete pre- and postcondition specification is given in a single definition. This allows us to speak about *the* precondition A and *the* postcondition B of the procedure p. On the other hand, in Hoare's formulation we could have several pre- and postcondition specifications making statements about p, such as:

$$A_1 \{ p \} B_1$$
$$A_2 \{ p \} B_2$$

Whether this is what we want or not has to do with the question what we want to use pre- and postcondition specifications for. The formalism used by Hoare and later formalisms derived from it (such as various 'Hoare logics') are primarily meant for proving facts about program fragments, i.e. as a basis for *proof systems* of programming languages. Our primary purpose here is to provide a practical formalism that allows one to specify procedures in a concise and clear way, independent of any programming language. From this practical point of view, it is desirable that a procedure is specified in a single definition, rather than that the specification is spread over an entire description (such as in some forms of axiomatic specification).

According to the original interpretation of pre- and postcondition specifications, the above (stylized) specification of procedure p should be interpreted as follows:

1. p is a procedure with no inputs and no outputs;
2. if A is true in system state s and p succeeds in s, transforming state s to state t, then B is true in state t;

This interpretation does not guarantee that p succeeds if applied in a state s where A is true, which is generally what we want. We therefore make the following addition to the interpretation:

3. if A is true in system state s, then p succeeds in s;

The interpretation of pre- and postconditions thus obtained is the classical one, and is similar to the interpretation as used in e.g. VDM [6]. Yet we shall make another addition to the interpretation:

4. if p succeeds in system state s, then A is true in s.

This addition makes the precondition *equivalent* to the assertion that the procedure succeeds. This strong interpretation of the precondition is something that could be debated. The main objection that one could raise against it is that it unnecessarily limits the implementation freedom of the procedure. But is that really so?

In a program that uses procedure p as specified above, there are at least two different ways the precondition can be interpreted operationally (i.e. during program execution):

(a) as an assertion that should be true whenever the procedure is called during the execution of the program; if the precondition is false, this is considered an error and the program is aborted;

(b) as an assertion that may be true or false whenever the procedure is called during the execution of the program; if the precondition is false, the call fails without side-effects and some form of backtracking takes effect.

In case (a), the only safe way to implement p is to perform a run-time check on the precondition whenever p is called, but this amounts to implementing p in such a way that (4) is satisfied: the precondition is a necessary condition for successful execution of the procedure. In case (b), calling a procedure with a false precondition is considered a legal action and (4) should be satisfied anyhow. This case is certainly not artificial: it may e.g. occur if we use procedures to model events and implement them in an event-based language providing some form of backtracking. In that case we do not only want to express under what condition an event will occur (i.e. the procedure will succeed), but also under what condition an event will *not* occur (i.e. the procedure will fail).

We shall not commit ourselves here to any of the above two operational interpretations of preconditions (or any other interpretation): we want to keep things as independent as possible of the programming language used for implementing the procedures. In either interpretation, (4) does not unnecessarily limit implementation freedom in any practical sense. In interpretation (b), (4) is even essential to the proper specification of a procedure, which is the main reason why we require it. We note, by the way, that for the rest of this paper item (4) of the interpretation of pre- and postcondition specifications could simply be skipped: with very few exceptions all examples and definitions remain valid, though with a slightly different meaning.

The fact that we want to keep things independent of any programming language or execution model is also reflected by the fact that we so far carefully avoided the use of the word *termination*. The notion of termination is associated with *programs*, and occurs only in the implementation of procedures. At the specification level we have the notion of *success*, which is different from that of termination. The relation between the two can be indicated as follows. Procedures are atomic actions, which implies that if a procedure succeeds in a state s, the piece of code implementing it should by definition terminate if executed in state s. We are not concerned with specifying procedures that correspond to non-terminating or possibly non-terminating pieces of code, since such procedures would not correspond to atomic actions. We come back to this issue in Section 3.11.

3.2 Input and output parameters

The format for pre- and postcondition specifications discussed in the previous section assumed that procedures had neither inputs nor outputs. In practice, most procedures will have input and/or output parameters and it should be possible to refer to the input parameters in the precondition and to the input and output parameters in the postcondition. To accommodate input and output parameters we extend the format with an optional list of input parameters (prefixed by the keyword `IN`) and an optional list of output parameters (prefixed by the keyword `OUT`), as exemplified by the following specification:

```
PROC read : File -> Byte
IN   f
OUT  b
PRE  offset(f) < length(f)
POST b = contents(f,offset(f)-1)
```

The input parameters represent the values that are passed to the procedure when applying it and the output parameters represent the values yielded by the procedure after it has been successfully applied. Hence `b` represents the byte read from file `f` by means of the procedure application `read(f)`. The required generalization of the interpretation of pre- and postcondition specifications is straightforward. The above specification should, for example, be read as follows:

1. `read` is a procedure that takes an object of sort `File` as its input and yields an object of sort `Byte` as its output;
2. in a given state s and for a given object `f` of sort `File` in s, `read(f)` succeeds iff the following assertion is true in s:

   ```
   offset(f) < length(f)
   ```

3. if `read(f)` succeeds, it will bring the system in a state t and yield an object `b` of sort `Byte` in t such that the following assertion is true in t:

   ```
   b = contents(f,offset(f)-1)
   ```

3.3 Referring to the previous state

The specification of the **read** procedure discussed in the previous section is still quite unsatisfactory. A procedure described by a pre- and postcondition specification may, in principle, modify all variable parts of the system state. The postcondition of **read** makes a statement about the output value of the **read** procedure only. This implies that the implementer of **read** is free to change the variables of the file system in whatever way he desires, which is of course not what is intended. We want **read(f)** to affect (increment) the value of **offset(f)** only, and leave all other variables and parts of variables unmodified, with the exception of **eof(f)** which may become true if **offset(f)** becomes greater than or equal to **length(f)**.

In order to express the above additional requirements in the postcondition of **read**, we need some way of relating the 'old' values of variables to the 'new' values. The postcondition is always interpreted in the 'new' state (after successful application of the procedure), so we *can* refer to the new values of variables. In order to refer to the old values of variables, we allow variable names to be 'primed' (in the postcondition only). A primed variable name should be interpreted in the 'old' state (immediately before the application of the procedure). The prime notation corresponds to the hook notation of VDM. The additional requirements mentioned above can now be expressed as follows:

```
PROC read : File -> Byte
IN   f
OUT  b
PRE  offset(f) < length(f)
POST b = contents(f,offset(f)-1);
     offset(f) =  offset'(f) + 1;
     eof(f)    <=> offset(f) >= length(f);
     FORALL g:File
     ( g /= f =>
       ( offset(g) =  offset'(g)
       ; eof(g)    <=> eof'(g)
       )
     ; FORALL i:Nat ( contents(g,i) == contents'(g,i) )
     ; length(g) = length'(g)
     )
```

Here the semicolons used in the postcondition should be interpreted as **AND** operators, the only difference being that the operator priority of ; is much lower than that of **AND**. The operators **/=** and **==** are shorthands defined by:

$$t_1 \texttt{ /= } t_2 \quad \equiv \quad \texttt{NOT } t_1 \texttt{ = } t_2$$
$$t_1 \texttt{ == } t_2 \quad \equiv \quad t_1 \texttt{ = } t_2 \texttt{ OR (NOT } t_1\texttt{! AND NOT } t_2\texttt{!)}$$

In the specification we have assumed (for the time being) that sorts remain constant when making a transition from one state to another. We shall drop this assumption in Section 3.10. Note that we could replace the first line in the postcondition by:

```
b = contents(f,offset'(f));
```

3.4 Framing using modification rights

Though the specification of `read` above now contains all necessary requirements to be put on the `read` procedure, it can hardly be called a concise and clear specification. The major part of the postcondition consists of assertions stating that the value of certain variables or parts of variables is not affected. The situation becomes even worse if we add new variables to the system specification. Even if the new variables are completely unrelated to the file system variables, we would have to add assertions to the postcondition of `read` (and any other file system operation) stating that the procedure does not modify these variables. Otherwise `read` would be free to modify the new variables. This problem is known as the *framing problem.*

The solution to the problem is the association of *modification rights* with procedures. Modification rights indicate which variables may be modified by a procedure. By definition, all other variables are *not* modified by the procedure, including any variables introduced later. Variables in our model of states are sorts, predicates and functions, but using entire predicates and functions as units of modification would only solve part of the problem. For example, if we specified that `read` has modification rights with respect to the variables `offset` and `eof` (implying that the variables `File`, `contents` and `length` are not affected), we would still have to specify explicitly that `read(f)` does not affect `offset(g)` and `eof(g)` for all files `g /= f`.

What we need is a more refined way of identifying parts of the system state. When looking in more detail at the algebraic structure represented by the state, we can see that it is completely described by:

1. the sets of objects associated with the sort symbols;
2. the values (true/false) of all *predicate terms* $r(x_1, \ldots, x_n)$, where r is a predicate symbol and $x_1, \ldots, x_n$ are objects from the sorts;
3. the values of all *function terms* $f(x_1, \ldots, x_n)$, where f is a function symbol and $x_1, \ldots, x_n$ are objects from the sorts.

Instead of indicating which entire sorts, predicates or functions are modified by a procedure, we could indicate which sorts, predicate terms and function terms are affected. For this purpose we introduce so-called *entities.* An entity has one of the following forms: T, r, $r(t_1, \ldots, t_n)$, f or $f(t_1, \ldots, t_n)$, where T is a sort symbol, r is a predicate symbol, f is a function symbol and t_i is a term ($i = 1, \ldots, n$). The part of a state s identified by an entity is explained below:

1. T: the sort T in s;
2. r: the set of all predicate terms $r(x_1, \ldots, x_n)$, where x_i is an object in s ($i = 1, \ldots, n$);
3. $r(t_1, \ldots, t_n)$: the predicate term $r(x_1, \ldots, x_n)$, where x_i is the object denoted by t_i in s ($i = 1, \ldots, n$);
4. f: the set of all function terms $f(x_1, \ldots, x_n)$, where x_i is an object in s ($i = 1, \ldots, n$);
5. $f(t_1, \ldots, t_n)$: the function term $f(x_1, \ldots, x_n)$, where x_i is the object denoted by t_i in s ($i = 1, \ldots, n$).

When specifying the modification rights of a procedure we should give a list of entities. Only the parts of the state identified by these entities may be modified by the procedure; other parts are by definition not affected. Modification rights are specified in a clause of the following form:

```
MOD e1,...,en
```

where $e_1, \ldots, e_n$ are entities. This *modification clause* is placed between the precondition and the postcondition. In Section 3.7 we shall come back to this notation and slightly revise it.

Using modification rights, the specification of **read** can be written more concisely as:

```
PROC read : File -> Byte
IN   f
OUT  b
PRE  offset(f) < length(f)
MOD  offset(f), eof(f)
POST b = contents(f,offset'(f));
     offset(f) =  offset'(f) + 1;
     eof(f)   <=> offset(f) >= length(f)
```

Note that the notion of modification rights we have introduced differs from the access rights of VDM in that no read access of variables is specified. The reason is that the notion of *access* of variables is meaningless here, since it is an operational aspect that we abstract from. The only interpretation that we could give to the notion of read access of a variable is that of the variable name being *visible*. The visibility of names is controlled in COLD-1 by the modularization mechanisms (import, export, etc.).

3.5 Dependent and independent variables

Up till now we have assumed that all parts of the system state could vary independently, apart from those parts that were assumed to be constant (such as the function **cre_date**). Quite frequently variables are not really independent of each other, particularly if we use variables for recording auxiliary information. If we have a variable y which is dependent on another variable x, then it will probably accompany x in the modification rights of most procedures that modify x. In the postconditions of these procedures, besides specifying how x is affected, we have to specify how y is affected. If the dependency is such that we can *express* y in terms of x, this is somewhat of a pity. It would be much better if we could express the precise dependency of y on x once, and for the rest forget about y in modification rights and postconditions; y would then vary 'automatically' with x according to the specified dependency.

For this purpose we allow variables to be defined *explicitly* in terms of other variables. A variable defined in this way will be called a *dependent* variable and should no longer be mentioned in modification rights. All other variables will be called *independent variables*. An example is provided by the **eof** variable which was originally declared as an independent variable by:

```
PRED eof : File   VAR
```

We replace this definition by:

```
PRED eof : File
IN   f
DEF  offset(f) >= length(f)
```

This defines the predicate **eof** by stating that (in all system states) **eof(f)** is equivalent to the assertion:

```
offset(f) >= length(f)
```

The specification of the **read** procedure can now be simplified to:

```
PROC read : File -> Byte
IN   f
OUT  b
PRE  offset(f) < length(f)
MOD  offset(f)
POST b = contents(f,offset'(f));
     offset(f) = offset'(f) + 1
```

Note that from the fact that a certain variable does not occur in the modification rights of a procedure we can no longer infer immediately that the variable is not modified. It is still true for independent variables, but for dependent variables we have to infer this from the modification rights *and* the definitions of the variables.

By introducing the distinction between dependent and independent variables more concise and clearer specifications can be written. There is also a certain danger in it. To a certain extent the choice of the independent variables 'spanning' the state space can be viewed as a choice of *representation*. Quite often, the same system can be specified in different ways using different selections of independent variables. The particular choice made could be interpreted as a suggestion to implement the independent variables as *storage structures* and to implement the dependent variables as *algorithmic structures*. There is nothing wrong with this, as long as we bear in mind that the primary purpose of the specification is to clarify the desired behaviour of the system and *not* to describe a possible implementation. The danger can further be reduced by choosing variables that are sufficiently abstract (e.g. choose sets instead of bit sequences as the values of variables), thus specifying an *abstract model* of the system.

Insofar as the file system example is concerned, we shall assume that we have the following independent variables:

```
SORT File                                  VAR
FUNC contents : File # Nat -> Byte         VAR
FUNC offset   : File -> Nat                VAR
```

and the following dependent variables and constants:

```
PRED eof      : File
FUNC length   : File -> Nat
FUNC cre_date : File -> Date
```

The definition of the **length** function will be given in Section 3.9.

As a final note we remark that if we speak about 'variables' in the sequel, we generally mean independent variables. If we say that a procedure modifies only the variables $v_1, \ldots, v_n$, we mean that the procedure modifies only the variables $v_1, \ldots, v_n$ *and* the variables dependent on them. Similarly, if we say that two states are the same except for the values of the variables $v_1, \ldots, v_n$, we mean that they are the same except for the variables $v_1, \ldots, v_n$ *and* the variables dependent on them.

3.6 Wild cards in modification rights

The use of 'entities' in modification rights and the distinction between dependent and independent variables leads to a considerable reduction in the size of both modification clauses and postconditions. Yet there are still situations where the modification rights are too coarse in indicating which parts of the state space are affected by a procedure. This is not so much the case in a procedure such as `write`, specified by:

```
PROC write : File # Byte ->
IN   f, b
PRE  TRUE
MOD  contents(f,offset(f)), offset(f)
POST contents(f,offset'(f)) = b;
     offset(f)              = offset'(f) + 1
```

The reason is that it modifies exactly two function terms in the state space of the file system, and they can be enumerated in a simple way. If we have a procedure such as:

```
PROC rewrite : File ->
```

that is supposed to clear the contents of a given file, say `f`, the entities to be listed in the modification clause would be:

```
contents(f,0), contents(f,1), contents(f,2), ..., offset(f)
```

Since we cannot indicate an infinite number of function terms other than by indicating the entire function, we have no other choice than to specify `rewrite` as follows:

```
PROC rewrite : File ->
IN   f
PRE  TRUE
MOD  contents, offset(f)
POST FORALL i:Nat ( NOT contents(f,i)! );
     FORALL g:File,i:Nat
     ( g /= f => contents(g,i) == contents'(g,i) );
     offset(f) = 0
```

The fact that we have to state in the postcondition that the `contents` of files other than `f` is not modified is a nuisance. We overcome this problem by allowing (value-yielding) *expressions* to be used in entities instead of terms, where we restrict ourselves to expressions without side effects but *with* (possible) non-determinism. Such expressions can be viewed as denotations of *sets* of objects, i.e. the sets of objects that can be yielded by the expressions. An example is the following entity:

```
contents(f,(0|1|2|3))
```

which is equivalent to:

```
contents(f,0), contents(f,1), contents(f,2), contents(f,3)
```

This would not bring us very far if we did not have some way of writing down an expression that can yield an arbitrary object of a given sort. Such an expression is the *random selection* construct:

SOME x:T (A)

It succeeds if and only if there exists an object x of sort T such that assertion A is true. If it succeeds, it yields an arbitrary object of sort T satisfying A, without affecting the state. Hence the set of possible values yielded by the following expression:

SOME x:T (TRUE)

is the set of all objects of sort T. We shall use the 'wild card' character **$** as a shorthand for this expression. Which sort T is meant in this shorthand should be reconstructed from the context. (The overloading resolution mechanism in COLD-1 takes care of this.) Using the wild card notation, the `rewrite` procedure can be specified more concisely as follows:

```
PROC rewrite : File ->
IN   f
PRE  TRUE
MOD  contents(f,$), offset(f)
POST FORALL i:Nat ( NOT contents(f,i)! );
     offset(f) = 0
```

3.7 Framing using expressions

In reconstructing the pre- and postcondition formalism, we have up till now kept more or less to the beaten track. Apart from the different treatment of states, the way we deal with 'entities' and some technicalities, the pre- and postcondition formalism we have introduced is similar to that of VDM. This is not surprising: the formalism in this form has a proven track record. Yet the use of the formalism in practice runs up against a number of difficulties. We shall address a number of these difficulties in subsequent sections and enhance the formalism to cope with them.

First we shall focus on a problem that occurs when we apply the technique in hierarchical system specifications. Suppose we have given a complete specification of the file system. We want to use the file system as a building block for more complex systems. In accordance with good information hiding principles, we want to keep the internal representation details away from the user and make only those sorts and operations available to him that should be externally visible. For example, we do not want to make the `contents` function available to him, because it acts as the representation of the *internal* state of a file. The user should use the `read` operation to read data from a file. The information hiding can be achieved by some form of 'export' that makes only the external sort and operation names visible to the user.

Now suppose in some other system where we have 'imported' the file system module, we want to specify a procedure that performs a certain complex action on a file:

```
PROC complex : File ->
```

On first impulse we could try and specify it like this:

```
PROC complex : File ->
IN   f
PRE  ...
MOD  contents(f,$), offset(f)
POST ...
```

Apart from the fact that the `contents` function is not even visible, this would imply that we use the fact that `contents` and `offset` are (independent) variables, which is internal representation detail of the file system specification. Even worse, if we could specify the `complex` function in the above way, we would be able to change the variables of the file system in arbitrary ways, possibly violating all invariants of the file system. What we want is to view the file system as a true *abstract data type*, i.e. as a closed system that characterizes the objects of sort `File` completely by the operations defined on them. No composite operations on files should be possible other than those that can be performed by means of the operations defined in and exported by the module.

The key to a solution of the problem is contained in the last sentence: we should be able to 'frame' an operation, not in terms of the variables that it may modify, but in terms of the operations it may use to change the state. This could be accommodated by introducing a second form of framing besides the `MOD` mechanism, using a clause of the following form:

`USE` $p_1, \ldots, p_n$

where $p_1, \ldots, p_n$ are procedure names, representing a set of *use rights.* This clause specifies that the procedure being specified should be such that it establishes a state transformation that does not go beyond the effects that can be achieved by using the procedures $p_1, \ldots, p_n$ (in arbitrary ways). This was the solution chosen in COLD-K.

A more general solution to the problem can be obtained by taking a closer look at the notion of *framing*. Framing a procedure p amounts to specifying an upper limit, or *frame*, for the relation defined by p. That is, if p is a procedure with no input and output parameters, a frame F for p can be viewed as a subset of $S \times S$, where S is the set of all system states. Framing the procedure with respect to frame F amounts to requiring that $p \subseteq F$. If it is the case that $p \subseteq F$, we say that p *satisfies* the frame F. For example, the following clause in the definition of p:

`MOD` $e_1, \ldots, e_n$

specifies that p should satisfy the following frame:

$$\{ (s,t) \in S \times S \mid s \text{ is equal to } t \text{ except for the values of } e_1, \ldots, e_n \}$$

If we would have a flexible way of denoting relations between states, we could use that for denoting frames as well. Indeed we have such a notation: expressions denote relations between states and they have sufficient flexibility, as we will show. We therefore introduce the following notation for specifying that a procedure should satisfy a frame:

`SAT` E

where E is an expression. By putting this *satisfaction clause* between the pre- and postcondition of a procedure p, we specify that p should satisfy the frame denoted by E, i.e. that p as a relation should be a subset of E. This concept is easily generalized to the case where we have procedures with inputs and outputs. For example, if p has input parameters $x_1, \ldots, x_n$, it specifies that the relation described by the expression $p(x_1, \ldots, x_n)$ is a subset of E for all $x_1, \ldots, x_n$.

The use of the satisfaction clause is demonstrated in the specification of the complex function below:

```
PROC complex : File ->
IN   f
PRE  ...
SAT  ( rewrite(f) | write(f,$) )*
POST ...
```

The satisfaction clause specifies that complex(f), as a relation between states, should be a subset of the relation specified by the expression:

```
( rewrite(f) | write(f,$) )*
```

In other (more operational) words, this implies that complex(f) may modify the state in arbitrary ways, as long as the final state is such that it *could have been* obtained by repeated application of the rewrite(f) and write(f,$) operations. Given the fact that rewrite(f) and write(f,$) affect only the file f, we can infer from this that complex(f) will also affect only f. Note that this example shows another useful application of the 'wild card' expression $.

The specification of complex should not be interpreted in the sense that it prescribes that complex should be implemented in terms of the rewrite and write procedures. The frame expression is merely used to indicate a relation between states. complex may be implemented using any other procedure, provided that the states immediately before and after application of the procedure satisfy the relation specified by the frame.

By introducing an expression of the following form:

MOD $e_1, \ldots, e_n$

specifying an arbitrary change of state modifying the entities $e_1, \ldots, e_n$ (and no other entities, except the entities dependent on $e_1, \ldots, e_n$), the 'modification clause' introduced before can be replaced by:

SAT MOD $e_1, \ldots, e_n$

thus obtaining a uniform framing mechanism. The specification of the rewrite procedure from Section 3.6 should now be rewritten to:

```
PROC rewrite : File ->
IN   f
PRE  TRUE
SAT  MOD contents(f,$), offset(f)
POST FORALL i:Nat ( NOT contents(f,i)! );
     offset(f) = 0
```

The same holds for the read procedure from Section 3.5, but there we have to take some care. read yields a value, implying that the expression read(f) does not denote a simple binary relation between states, but a ternary relation between states and objects. Hence the specified frame should also denote a ternary relation, which can be achieved as follows:

```
PROC read : File -> Byte
IN   f
OUT  b
PRE  offset(f) < length(f)
SAT  MOD offset(f); $
POST b = contents(f,offset'(f));
     offset(f) = offset'(f) + 1
```

The flexibility of the framing mechanism described above is to a large extent based on the fact that we have very simple operators in our expression language. This allows us, for example, to use a kind of regular expressions in frames (see the specification of the `complex` function). The mechanism also allows us to frame procedures in much more subtle ways than can be done by means of modification rights or use rights. For example, the fact that a certain operation should increment a counter by an even number could be indicated by the frame:

```
( incr; incr )*
```

We can go even further and use the framing mechanism to put more and more algorithmic details in the frame of a procedure. Strictly speaking, a frame is an expression and expressions are relations and not algorithms. However, the more detailed the expressions become, the more they suggest a certain algorithm. This feature can be used as an *implementation technique*, by gradually transforming an axiomatic specification of a procedure to an algorithmic description. It can also be used as a *specification technique*, because it allows a mixed axiomatic/algorithmic style of specification. Such a semi-operational style of specification is often a good compromise in practice, though there are a number of dangers that should be kept in mind.

3.8 Giving names to objects

There are still a number of things that can be improved with respect to the user-friendliness of the pre- and postcondition notation. If we look at the specification of the `read` operation, we see for example that it contains three references to the 'old' value of the offset of file `f`: one in the precondition (`offset(f)`) and two in the postcondition (`offset'(f)`). The clarity of the specification could be improved if we had some mechanism of giving a name to this object, such that the name could be used throughout the pre- and postcondition specification. In COLD-1 this is supported by the *declaration* and *binding* mechanisms that allow names to be introduced and objects to be bound to these names. These mechanisms can be used in assertions as well as in expressions. Here we shall only discuss the combined declaration and binding which looks as follows (in its simplest form):

LET x := t

where x is a symbol and t is a term. This construct is considered a normal assertion or expression. As an assertion it is true iff the term t is defined. As an expression it succeeds iff the term t is defined, and if it succeeds it transforms any state to itself. In both cases it has the 'syntactic side effect' of introducing a new name x to which the object denoted by the term t is bound. This name can be used to denote that object in the context logically following the LET construct. So, in the following assertion:

LET x := t; A

the name x may be used in the assertion A to refer to the object denoted by the term t. We note that binding should not be confused with *assignment.* Object names are not variables: the binding of an object to a name is permanent and cannot be changed. In COLD, variables and assignment are modelled by *functions* and *procedures*, respectively.

Using the LET construct, the specification of **read** can be rewritten to:

```
PROC read : File -> Byte
IN   f
OUT  b
PRE  LET i := offset(f);
     i < length(f)
SAT  MOD offset(f); $
POST b = contents(f,i);
     offset(f) = i + 1
```

Here we see that the name **i** introduced in the precondition is used in the postcondition as well. It may also be used in the satisfaction clause, as exemplified by the following rewritten version of **write**:

```
PROC write : File # Byte ->
IN   f, b
PRE  LET i := offset(f)
SAT  MOD contents(f,i), offset(f)
POST contents(f,i) = b;
     offset(f)     = i + 1
```

Note that the occurrence of **offset(f)** in the satisfaction clause cannot be replaced by **i**, because **offset(f)** does not denote an object here, but an *entity*, i.e. a component of the state space.

The general rule is that any object name declared in the precondition may be used in the satisfaction clause and in the postcondition. Any object name declared in the satisfaction clause may be used in the postcondition (but not in the precondition). This explains why the satisfaction clause has been placed *between* the precondition and the postcondition. The above rule derives from what we formulated above as the fact that an object name declared in a construct may be used in any context 'logically following' that construct.

Defining precisely what 'logically following' means would bring us beyond the scope of this paper. The intuition behind it is easy to explain. A context logically follows an assertion A, if we may assume that A is true in that context. A context logically follows an expression E, if we may assume that E has succeeded in that context. The pre- and postcondition specification:

```
PROC p : ->
PRE  A
SAT  E
POST B
```

can be read as follows: if precondition A is true in state s, then p will behave as if expression E was executed, bringing the system in a state t where B is true. This implies that we may assume in E and B that assertion A is true in s, and in B we may assume that expression E has succeeded.

The precise semantics of the naming mechanism used in pre- and postcondition specifications is described in [9], where the pre- and postcondition formalism of COLD-1 is defined in terms of the assertion language of COLD-K. The assertion language of COLD-K is based on a generalized version of predicate logic with more liberal scope rules for existentially quantified names and is defined in [2] by translation to a logic with 'classical' scope rules [10]. The logic was independently described in [3], where it was referred to as *dynamic predicate logic.*

Since the assertion language of COLD-1 is based on that of COLD-K, it 'inherits' the liberal scope rules of COLD-K. This freedom can often be used to write more natural pre- and postcondition specifications, without sacrificing formality. (It is not a coincidence that dynamic predicate logic stems from the field of natural language processing.) A typical case is the following. Quite frequently, we have to state in a precondition that an object satisfying a certain property should exist. In the postcondition, or even the satisfaction clause, we often have to refer to that object again. This can now be done without having to redeclare that object.

Suppose, for example, that we have to specify a **next** procedure on files, that finds the next byte in a file that is identical to the byte at the current offset. The precondition is that such a byte exists. This can be specified as follows:

```
PROC next : File ->
IN   f
PRE  LET i := offset(f);
     LET b := contents(f,i);
     EXISTS j:Nat ( j > i AND contents(f,j) = b )
SAT  seek(f,$)
POST offset(f) = j;
     FORALL k:Nat ( i < k AND k < j => contents(f,k) /= b )
```

where **seek** is specified by:

```
PROC seek : File # Nat ->
IN   f, i
PRE  i <= length(f)
SAT  MOD offset(f)
POST offset(f) = i
```

The specification of **next** could even be written like this:

```
PROC next : File ->
IN   f
PRE  LET i := offset(f);
     LET b := contents(f,i);
     EXISTS j:Nat ( j > i AND contents(f,j) = b )
SAT  seek(f,j)
POST FORALL k:Nat ( i < k AND k < j => contents(f,k) /= b )
```

Note that this can be read in a very natural way: if there is a position j at the right of the current offset i containing a byte equal to the byte b at position i, then **next(f)** will seek such a position, choosing the *first* such position (as expressed by the postcondition).

As a final remark we note that the above examples show that the use of the LET construct in preconditions can considerably reduce the need to use prime notation in postconditions for referring to the previous state. In the examples, the names introduced by means of LET are essentially used as so-called *freeze variables* that 'freeze' certain state information affected by the operation. The declaration and binding mechanism is more general than freeze variables, however.

3.9 Dependencies

As in VDM, it is useful to extend the pre- and postcondition formalism also to the specification of functions, in particular to functions that are dependent variables. This extension seems obvious, because functions can be viewed as a kind of deterministic procedures without side effects. We can keep the same format for pre- and postcondition specifications. The only thing we have to do is to replace the keyword PROC by FUNC and drop the satisfaction clause. The precondition then expresses when the function is defined and the postcondition expresses a relation between the input and output parameters. There is no need to use 'primes' in the postcondition, since a function does not affect the state. The length function defined on files could, for example, be defined as follows:

```
FUNC length : File -> Nat
IN   f
OUT  n
PRE  TRUE
POST FORALL i:Nat ( contents(f,i)! <=> i < n )
```

Note that this definition not only puts constraints on the length function itself (it even completely characterizes it), but also on the contents function (which is an independent variable).

At first sight there is no problem with the above definition. Now consider another example. Suppose in the file system specification we want to specify that a one-byte CRC (Cyclic Redundancy Check) is associated with every file, without making a commitment yet as to which kind of CRC is to be used. Since the value of the CRC depends on the contents of a file, we want to treat the CRC as a dependent variable that could be specified by:

```
FUNC crc : File -> Nat
IN   f
OUT  n
PRE  TRUE
POST n < 256
```

In contrast with the length function, the crc function is not uniquely characterized by its specification.

The problem with the above specification is the following. Suppose we have a procedure p, either from the file system or from another system using the file system. If p does not affect the contents of any file, we would like to be able to infer that p does not affect the CRC of any file. This cannot be derived from the specification of `crc`, so we would have to express it in the specification of p. In practice this would mean that we would have to express this in the specification of each procedure that does not affect the contents of a file. This is not only a nuisance, but conflicts with the reason why the distinction between dependent and independent variables was introduced in the first place.

Defining `crc` as an independent variable does not help either. First of all, we have to add `crc` to the modification rights of all file system procedures that modify the `contents` function, which is still a nuisance. Secondly, if `crc` is introduced as an independent variable *outside* the file system (in some other module), we would have to modify the specifications of the procedures *inside* the file system. This conflicts with the idea of an abstract data type as a closed system. Finally, we are able to express only a part of the dependency of `crc` on `contents` this way. The fact that `crc(f)` does not change if the contents of `f` is changed and then restored cannot be captured this way.

The solution is to require that in the pre- and postcondition specification of a dependent variable, the dependency is explicitly specified. For that purpose the *dependency clause* is introduced, which has the following form:

DEP $e_1, \ldots, e_n$

where $e_1, \ldots, e_n$ are entities (which may be dependent variables themselves). Similar to the satisfaction clause of procedures, this clause should be put between the precondition and postcondition of a function specification, implying that the names of formal parameters of the function may be used in the entities $e_1, \ldots, e_n$. It expresses two things:

1. the function f being specified is a dependent variable;
2. for any pair of states s, t and values $x_1, \ldots, x_m$ of the formal parameters of f, the fact that $e_1, \ldots, e_n$ have the same values in s and t, implies that $f(x_1, \ldots, x_m)$ has the same value in s and t.

Note that the second point implies that $f(x_1, \ldots, x_n)$ will not change unless at least one of the values of $e_1, \ldots, e_n$ changes.

The proper specification of `crc` now becomes:

```
FUNC crc : File -> Nat
IN   f
OUT  n
PRE  TRUE
DEP  contents(f,$)
POST n < 256
```

If we have an arbitrary procedure p that does not affect the contents of a file `f`, we can now simply derive that `crc(f)` remains the same because none of the entities of the form `contents(f,i)` is affected by p.

If the list of entities in a dependency clause is empty, it follows from the meaning of the dependency clause that the function being specified will have the same value in all system states. In other words, the function is *constant*, implying that we can view it as a true mathematical function. In that case the dependency clause may also be omitted. The definition of the `length` function should therefore also be adjusted:

```
FUNC length : File -> Nat
IN   f
OUT  n
PRE  TRUE
DEP  contents(f,$)
POST FORALL i:Nat ( contents(f,i)! <=> i < n )
```

One could argue that the dependency clause provides redundant information in this case, because the `length` function is already uniquely characterized by the pre- and postcondition. If indeed a function is fully characterized by the pre- and postcondition, one could also consider specifying the function explicitly, *provided* this does not affect the level of abstractness of the specification too much. Suppose, for example, that we want to specify a function that indicates the remaining number of bytes from the current offset to the end of the file. This function could be specified as follows:

```
FUNC rest : File -> Nat
IN   f
OUT  n
PRE  TRUE
DEP  length(f), offset(f)
POST offset(f) + n = length(f)
```

but the following explicit definition is shorter and just as clear:

```
FUNC rest : File -> Nat
IN   f
DEF  length(f) - offset(f)
```

In explicit function definitions no dependency clauses are required: the dependencies follow immediately from the function body.

3.10 Dynamic object creation

So far we have assumed that sorts remain constant when making a transition from one state to another. We want to use pre- and postcondition techniques also for specifying operations of object-oriented systems and operations on dynamic data structures. In such systems and data structures we have to deal with the phenomenon of *dynamic object creation* and hence with variable sorts. In our model of states as algebras, the way to deal with variable sorts seems quite obvious. Simply view them as variable sets of objects that can vary from state to state and treat them in the same way as other variables. For example, if we want to specify procedures that create files dynamically, we could (and in fact already did) define the sort `File` as an independent variable:

```
SORT File   VAR
```

In the satisfaction clause of a procedure that creates files we could then, by means of the following expression, specify that this sort is modified:

```
MOD File
```

The problem with the above is that sorts are not simply sets of objects that can vary arbitrarily: sorts also act as the domains and ranges of predicates and functions. If a sort is modified, in principle all predicates and functions defined on the sort are modified. This would mean that we would have to extend the list of entities following the `MOD` keyword above with all predicates and functions that have the sort `File` in their domain or range. Apart from being very impractical, this conflicts with the idea that `File` is an independent variable: modification of one independent variable should not affect another.

The first part of the solution of this problem is already indicated in Section 3.4, which introduced a fine-grain notion of modification. If we specify that a predicate or function f is not modified in a transition from a state s to a state t, we shall interpret this as the fact that each predicate or function term of the form $f(x_1, \ldots, x_n)$ in s has the same value as in t. Note that this is not the same as saying that f should be the same in s and t, because there may be predicate or function terms in t that are not predicate or function terms in s. Such terms arise if in the transition from s to t new objects are created. The fact that a predicate or function f is *constant* (such as the function `cre_date` of the file system) can now more precisely be defined as the fact that f is not modified (in the above sense) in any state transition.

The above more liberal notion of modification is only well-defined if we assume that each legal predicate or function term in s is also a legal predicate or function term in t. The second part of the solution, therefore, is to require that for each transition from a state s to a state t, the sorts in s are subsets of the corresponding sorts in t. In other words, we shall assume that objects cannot be deleted from sorts. This may seem a severe restriction, but in reality it is not. The fact that an object may not be deleted from a sort does not mean that, in an implementation of the system, the object should be kept in memory. The abstract notion of *existence* of an object should not be confused with the operational notion of *being allocated.*

The notion of modification as defined above leads to a quite natural way of dealing with dynamic object creation in pre- and postcondition specifications. This is demonstrated by the following example, specifying a procedure that creates a new (empty) file:

```
PROC new : -> File
OUT  f
PRE  TRUE
SAT  MOD File; $
POST ISNEW f;
     FORALL g:File ( ISNEW g => f = g );
     length(f)   = 0;
     offset(f)   = 0;
     cre_date(f) = current_date
```

Here `ISNEW` is a (pseudo-)predicate expressing that an object exists in the state immediately after the application of the procedure, but not in the state immediately before it. `ISNEW` may be used in postconditions only. The first two lines of the postcondition express that exactly one new object `f` of sort `File` is created. The rest of the postcondition is concerned with specifying the values of the new function terms that arise from the creation of the new object `f`, including the value of the term `cre_date(f)` of the function `cre_date` that was defined as a constant. Due to the way we defined modification, the satisfaction clause of `new` puts no constraints whatsoever on these terms, in contrast with terms such as `offset(g)` for files `g /= f` which should keep their old values. Note that we can derive from the pre- and postcondition specification of the `length` function that the file `f` created by `new` is indeed empty, i.e. that:

```
FORALL i:Nat ( NOT contents(f,i)! )
```

3.11 Non-atomic actions

The pre- and postcondition formalism has its limitations. These limitations derive from the fact that it is essentially a formalism for specifying *atomic actions*. The behaviour of sequential systems can be structured in a natural way around the concept of procedures as atomic actions. This makes the formalism ideally suited for specifying the behaviour of sequential systems. The situation becomes different if we turn to concurrent systems, or more generally, *reactive systems*. In such systems classical procedures are no longer sufficient for structuring system behaviour. Higher level concepts are required, in particular some notion of *process*. Processes may run indefinitely and interact with their environment, so they can certainly not be viewed as atomic actions. Is there still some way we can make pre- and postcondition specifications useful in specifying such systems?

What we could try and do is to extend the pre- and postcondition formalism such that it can be used for specifying non-atomic actions. This can be done by generalizing the notion of procedure in such a way that it coincides with the notion of process. This is essentially what we do if we extend a sequential language such as C with process control primitives. The fact that procedures are no longer atomic actions implies that we cannot view them as relations between states any more. A more complicated model is required, such as the model of procedures as sets of computation sequences. In specifications of procedures we must be able to make statements about the intermediate states that procedures can go through. An approach to do this by adding so-called *inter-conditions* to pre- and postcondition specifications is described in [11].

The problem with the above approach is that the inherent simplicity of the pre- and postcondition technique gets almost completely lost. This simplicity is the main strength of the technique and should, in my opinion, not be sacrificed for the sake of more general applicability. It is better to recognize the limitations of the technique and to investigate how it can be made useful in the context of specifying the behaviour of reactive systems. In efforts to broaden the scope of COLD, originally developed as a language for specifying sequential systems, to cover the specification of reactive systems, we at first followed the course of generalizing procedures to processes. The consequence of pursuing this course would be that the semantics of the language would have to be revised completely. Rather than going this way, we investigated how the existing language could be used for specifying reactive systems by a proper re-interpretation of the concepts already available in the language. The surprising conclusion of this investigation was that very little is necessary to achieve this, and least of all a revision of the semantics. The approach on which this is based relies heavily on the use of the pre- and postcondition technique, as we shall explain below.

The units of structuring in COLD are called *classes*. Each class in itself can be viewed as a *system* in the sense we used the word before. That is, a class consists of a set of states, an initial state and a number of procedures. The states and the state transitions determined by the procedures together determine a *state transition graph*, describing the complete behaviour of the class. In this graph, state transitions are labelled by the successful procedure applications that accomplish them. By interpreting the state transition graph as a *process graph*, we can view classes as processes. The behaviour of a class as a process is the collection of all possible paths (= sequences of successful procedure applications) through the process graph, starting from the initial state.

As it turns out in the interpretation of classes as processes, the COLD *import* operator on classes coincides with the *parallel composition* operator on processes, according to the interleaving model of concurrency. That is, the process graph of the class D obtained by importing a class C_1 into another class C_2 is obtained by *merging* the process graphs of C_1 and C_2. Thus, process structure coincides with modular structure in a way very similar to e.g. SDL [12]. This also has the advantage that all structuring mechanisms that are available for classes (such as import, export, renaming, parameterization) can be applied equally well to processes.

The only thing that is lacking in the above picture of classes as processes is how classes should be interpreted in the operational sense or, in other words, how do we 'execute' a class? A class as such is a transition system that will not perform any actions by itself. The graph of the transition system can be viewed as a kind of road map, but we need additional rules on how to choose a route on the map. This can be done in a very simple way by distinguishing between *active procedures*, that are supposed to 'happen' autonomously, and *passive procedures*, that are supposed to 'happen' only if explicitly applied. Successful applications of active procedures can be viewed as actions of the process itself (*internal actions*), while successful applications of passive procedures can be viewed as actions of the environment of the process (*external actions*).

We illustrate the above approach by means of a very simple example. Suppose we have a device, consisting of a panel and a controller. The panel contains a single push button, that will set an internal event flag when pushed. At the interface side of the panel, a mechanism is provided to detect that the event flag is set and at the same time reset it. A class modelling the panel can be specified as follows:

```
CLASS
  FUNC flag : -> UpDown   VAR
  AXIOM INIT => flag = down
  PROC push : ->
  PRE  flag = down
  SAT  MOD flag
  POST flag = up
  PROC event : ->
  PRE  flag = up
  SAT  MOD flag
  POST flag = down
END
```

Here we use an axiom to characterize the initial state; `INIT` is a built-in predicate that is true iff the class is in its initial state. Note that in this specification it is essential that the precondition is a sufficient *and* necessary condition for the success of a procedure: the `event` procedure is supposed to succeed only if the flag is up.

The controller should react to the push button events triggered from the panel, dependent on one of two states s1 and s2 it can be in. If it is in state s1, it should react to a push button event by performing an external action action1 and going to state s2. If it is in state s2, it should react to a push button event by performing an external action action2 and going to state s1. This can be specified as follows:

```
CLASS

  FUNC state : -> State   VAR

  AXIOM INIT => state = s1

  PROC react1 : ->
  PRE  state = s1
  SAT  MOD state; action1
  POST state = s2

  PROC react2 : ->
  PRE  state = s2
  SAT  MOD state; action2
  POST state = s1

  PROC control : ->
  DEF  ( state = s1 ?; event; react1
       | state = s2 ?; event; react2
       )

END
```

Here the control procedure is meant as an active procedure, while all other procedures are passive. The device specification can be put together by importing the panel specification into the controller specification, which in terms of processes amounts to putting the panel and the controller in parallel. The fact that control is an active procedure implies that it will be applied 'automatically' in a state where control succeeds. Of course, it will only succeed after a push action has been performed in the environment, implying that the behaviour of the device consists of an interleaving of push and control operations.

Note that all procedures, except the control procedure, have been specified by means of pre- and postconditions. A complete software development method based on the above approach has been developed within Philips and applied successfully in practice. A detailed discussion of the method goes beyond the scope of this paper, but it shows that the pre- and postcondition technique can play an important role even in the specification of reactive systems. The main limitations of a pre- and postcondition based approach as sketched here are that:

- liveness and real-time properties cannot be expressed;
- history information (if required) must be recorded in variables.

One could say that the approach is essentially a means of specifiying a state transition system without making any commitment as to the underlying execution model. This abstraction from operational details should make it easy to deal with liveness and real-time properties in an add-on way, e.g. using a dedicated formalism such as temporal logic.

4 Conclusion

The pre- and postcondition technique in the form presented here is part of the formal specification and design language COLD-1, which is supported by the ICE tool set developed by the Information and Software Technology department of Philips Research. As such the technique has been used in several industrial applications within Philips where it has shown its effectiveness. As a matter of fact, several of the features that were presented grew out of the needs arising from experimental industrial applications.

The strength of the pre- and postcondition technique remains its simplicity. No complex mathematical theory or deep understanding of formal logic is required to apply the technique. It appeals directly to the intuition of the average system developer. All this makes it an ideal entry point for introducing formal techniques in industry. As we hope to have shown in this paper, the technique can be upgraded in such a way that it is able to cope with all requirements that arise from its application in the development of real-life systems. Despite its age, we are therefore convinced that the pre- and postcondition technique is more alive than ever!

References

[1] E.W. DIJKSTRA, *A Discipline of Programming*, Prentice Hall (1976).

[2] L.M.G. FEIJS, H.B.M. JONKERS, C.P.J. KOYMANS, G.R. RENARDEL DE LAVALETTE, *Formal Definition of the Design Language COLD-K*, Technical Report, ESPRIT project 432 (1987).

[3] J.G. GROENENDIJK, M. STOKHOF, *Dynamic Predicate Logic*, University of Amsterdam (1989).

[4] D. HAREL, *First-order Dynamic Logic*, Lecture Notes in Computer Science 68, Springer-Verlag (1979).

[5] C.A.R. HOARE, *An axiomatic basis for computer programming*, Communications of the ACM 12 (1969), 576-580.

[6] C.B. JONES, *Systematic Software Development using VDM, Second Edition*, Prentice Hall (1989).

[7] H.B.M. JONKERS, *The single linguistic framework*, Technical Report, ESPRIT pilot project FAST (1984).

[8] H.B.M. JONKERS, *An Introduction to COLD-K*, in: M. WIRSING, J.A. BERGSTRA (Eds.), *Algebraic Methods: Theory, Tools and Applications*, LNCS 394, Springer-Verlag (1989), 139-205.

[9] H.B.M. JONKERS, *Description of COLD-1*, Technical Report, ESPRIT project 2565 (1991).

[10] C.P.J. KOYMANS, G.R. RENARDEL DE LAVALETTE, *The Logic* MPL_ω, in: M. WIRSING, J.A. BERGSTRA (Eds.), *Algebraic Methods: Theory, Tools and Applications*, LNCS 394, Springer-Verlag (1989), 247-282.

[11] C.A. MIDDELBURG, *Syntax and Semantics of VVSL*, Ph.D. Thesis, University of Amsterdam (1990).

[12] R. SARACCO, J.R.W. SMITH, R. REED, *Telecommunications Systems Engineering using SDL*, North-Holland (1989).

The Formal Development of a Secure Transaction Mechanism

Paul Smith and Richard Keighley
Secure Information Systems Limited, Sentinel House, Harvest Crescent,
Ancells Park, Fleet, Hampshire, GU13 8UZ,UK

Abstract

This paper reports on the use of formal refinement in the development of a Transaction Processing (TP) mechanism for a secure database management system called SWORD. The SWORD specification, written in Z, defines the semantics of concurrent transactions which operate on shared databases without interfering. The specification is quite abstract: in contrast, our design for the TP mechanism (also specified in Z) is extremely complex since it achieves non-interference without using data locks. This paper describes our experience of using formal specification and refinement to develop the TP mechanism in a manner which is amenable to reasoning about its correctness.

1. Introduction

This paper investigates the application of mathematics to the development of a novel transaction processing mechanism for a multi-level secure database management system (DBMS), called SWORD [Wood90, Wiseman90a]. SWORD exemplifies the development of secure applications for an experimental computer called SMITE (Secure Multiprocessing of Information by Type Enforcement) [Harrold89], which is being developed by the Defence Research Agency (DRA) Electronics Division (formerly the Royal Signals and Radar Establishment). SMITE facilitates very high assurance in secure applications by providing a verified set of basic security mechanisms [Wiseman90b]. A security policy model [Terry89] defines the class of systems that could be built securely on SMITE; but achieving a secure system not only depends on complying with the security model, but also on the correctness of implementations (the 'refinement').

The SWORD implementation has been deliberately structured to minimise the complexity of design steps, in an attempt to make refinement tractable. Much of the formal development process has involved straightforward 'functional' data reification or simple operation decomposition [Smith90], but one step in particular combines 'non-functional' data reification with complex operation refinement: the implementation of a secure transaction mechanism. The complexity of the mechanism stems from the need to maintain many distinct views of a database, in order to facilitate multi-transaction access to shared databases without explicit data locking. No transaction may interfere with the view of any other transaction, which means that changes made by a transaction only affect that transaction, so called 'read-consistent views', or 'read consistency'.

Read consistency is quite straightforward to specify, and so it is possible to validate the formal specification of transaction processing. In contrast, the implementation of read consistency requires an extremely complex mechanism. Although it is straightforward to specify, it is difficult to be convinced that the transaction mechanism works properly in all circumstances. This view is sustained by the number of counter-examples discovered during the development of the transaction mechanism. Our confidence in the mechanism has increased steadily as flaws have been corrected, and the detection of new flaws has abated. Clearly, a greater degree of confidence in the correctness of the transaction mechanism is required. Having used formal methods as a design tool, it seems appropriate to prove that our novel transaction mechanism correctly refines the more comprehensible transaction processing specification.

In the next section, the need for a novel transaction processing mechanism is motivated. Our formal model of transaction processing is detailed in Section 3, followed by the formal specification of the mechanism itself in Section 4. The relationship between the abstract specification and its refinement is non-functional, i.e. any implementation state ambiguously corresponds to many abstract states. This invalidates assumptions made in some of the published formal methods, an issue which is taken up in Section 5.

2. Secure Transaction Processing

The need for a novel notion of multi-transaction processing is motivated in this section by introducing the multi-level security requirements for SWORD, particularly the need to avoid data-locking protocols. Then, an informal semantics for concurrent transactions called read-consistency is defined.

Multi-level Security in the SWORD Relational Database

SWORD is a multi-level secure relational database management system which supports SQL [SQL89] as far as possible. The usual notions of table, row, and key are supported, with extensions for storing and processing classified information at the field level in an extension to SQL, known as SQL⁺. The security controls in SWORD are aimed at preserving the confidentiality of information according to the rules of a mandatory security policy. In a multi-level secure system, each user operates with a clearance, which determines an upper bound on the classification of information that may be observed. In addition to direct retrieval, information can be signalled indirectly by modulating the use of shared resources. The SWORD security controls must prevent highly classified information flowing to users with a low clearance either directly or indirectly. To prevent information flowing directly, each field of a table carries a classification attribute, and any query must be sanitised on the basis of the requester's clearance. For example, consider a table of system faults, perhaps maintained by a computing service (see Figure 1).

System	*Faults*	*CPU Hrs.*	*Size (Kbytes)*
*X (**u**)*	*90 (**u**)*	*10000 (**u**)*	*500 (**u**)*
*Y (**u**)*	*60 (**c**)*	*999 (**r**)*	*200 (**u**)*
*Z (**u**)*	*100 (**u**)*	*15000 (**u**)*	*500 (**u**)*

Figure 1: System Faults Database

System 'X' has had 90 reported faults in 10000 hours of operation and occupies 500 kilobytes, and so on. The rows of the table are uniquely identified by the system name (its 'primary key'). Suppose three categories of user access the system faults table: the ***c***omputer department, which is responsible for providing services on the systems; ***r***equisitioners, who sponsor the use of the systems by end users; and the end ***u***sers themselves. These classifications form a hierarchy in the sense that the computer department should be able to see more information than the requisitioners, who in turn should be able to see more than the end users. The problem with the faults database is that some of the information is sensitive. For example, potential requisitioners should not discover that system Y has experienced a large number of problems in proportion to its life-time and size. Systems X and Z have typical fault profiles and hence any user cleared to at least ***u*** can see all the information associated with it. To prevent the requisitioners (and hence the users) from finding out about Y's unreliability, the number of faults is kept to the computer department. The requisitioner can see the rest of the information, but users are restricted to the size information. (Field classifications are bracketed in the figures.) If an end user (operating with clearance ***u***), attempted to select the faults column, SWORD would obscure the sensitive value for Y using a special sanitisation value.

More esoteric controls are required in order to prevent users from signalling information indirectly by creating, modifying and destroying objects which are visible to all users: so-called 'covert channels' [Kemmerer83].

The SWORD Architecture

The SWORD implementation is structured in strictly hierarchical service layers (see Figure 2). The purpose of choosing such an architecture was to isolate the 'trusted' security functions, and to encourage a fine-grained, incremental development approach which would ease individual refinement steps. In order to achieve these objectives, the trusted functionality needed to be contained to the lower layers (which are shaded below), with untrusted behaviour promoted to the higher layers.

The intermediate Tables layer provides a fairly primitive secure service for maintaining tables with classified entries. Beneath the Tables layer, the ISAM (Indexed Sequential Access Method) layer stores unstructured keyed records for rapid searching. The

Storage layer indexes bucket chains on physical disk, and these are used by the ISAM layer refinement to store ISAM structures efficiently and flexibly. The Relations and Database layers support alternate and foreign keys.

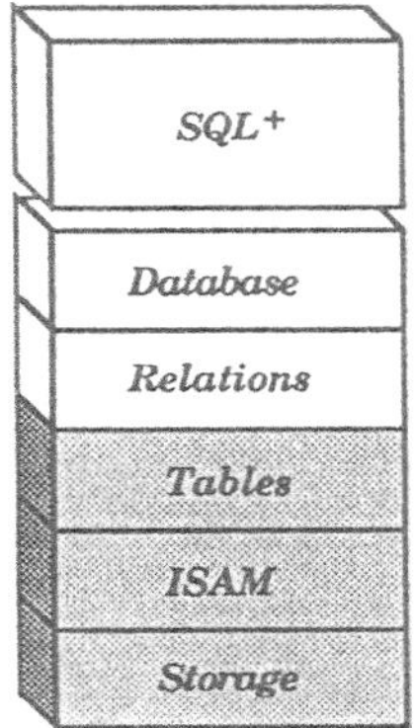

Figure 2: The SWORD Implementation Hierarchy

Additionally, each layer specifies the semantics of shared access to its structures by concurrent transactions, although the transaction mechanism is realised in the ISAM layer refinement, where tentative updates are recorded in 'edit lists' before being committed to physical disk. Each layer maintains broadly 'tabular' structures, which are contrived to support the layer above by facilitating serial processing of its structures using 'selectors' to point to horizontal elements. The selected element can be updated or deleted, for example. New elements can be inserted, and the selector can be reset or advanced through the table, and particular elements can be located by their key. The usual transaction management commands are supported, and transactions can be nested in a novel way using 'inner queries'. A query processor would translate structured queries (SQL^+) into serialised SWORD commands.

Concurrency Control without Data Locking : Read-Consistent Transactions

To maximise transaction throughput, transactions are conventionally executed concurrently in an interleaved manner. Transaction scheduling is normally the responsibility of the DBMS, but the scheduling policy must ensure that any two concurrent transactions have the same effect as running one to completion, before running the other (so-called 'serialisation' [SQL89]). Conventionally, transactions enforce serialisation using a locking protocol.

Clearly, transactions cannot be trusted to use such a locking protocol securely, because they could signal by modulating the status of locks. Instead, the responsibility for concurrency integrity lies with SWORD, which is a departure from the conventional DBMS technology. Each transaction must be provided with its own independent view of a database, which is not interfered with by any other transaction. Each transaction is allowed to make tentative changes to the database transparently (which prevents transactions from interfering, but does not guarantee serialisation in general). A transaction can discard its tentative changes ('rollback'), or make them visible to future transactions ('commit'). A transaction becomes active when it is explicitly started, and becomes inactive when it is explicitly finished, i.e. either committed or rolled back. A model of read-consistent views is introduced in the remainder of this section, drawing on examples expressed in an informal notation. The formal specification is introduced in the next section.

The view of the database seen by any (active) transaction is a 'snapshot' of its view at start time, incorporating the tentative changes made by that transaction. For example, suppose that a database contains five records. The first record, *a*, is keyed by *A*, *b* by *B*, and so on:

Database:	<Aa,	Bb,	Cc,	Dd,	Ee	>	

Assume that no other transactions are active. Now, if transaction *X* starts, the view is:

Transaction X:	<Aa,	Bb,	Cc,	Dd,	Ee	>	

Then, *X* changes the data in the first record from *a* to *α*, i.e. *Aa* becomes *Aα*. Also, *X* deletes *Ee* and inserts the new record *Ff*, (new or changed items are underlined):

Database:	<Aa,	Bb,	Cc,	Dd,	Ee	>		
Transaction X:	<A$\underline{\alpha}$,	Bb,	Cc,	Dd,			$\underline{\text{Ff}}$	>

When transaction *X* commits, its changes to the database are consolidated, as follows:

Database:	<Aα,	Bb,	Cc,	Dd,	Ff	>	

However, if a transaction *Y* became active before *X* committed, the system would need to remember that *Ee* remained in *Y's* view, whilst *Ff* is excluded, but *Aa* remains unchanged:

Database:	<Aα,	Bb,	Cc,	Dd,			Ff	>
Transaction X:	<A$\underline{\alpha}$,	Bb,	Cc,	Dd,			$\underline{\text{Ff}}$	>
Transaction Y:	<Aa,	Bb,	Cc,	Dd,	Ee	>		

For specification convenience, these separate views are unified within a single representation, recording which transactions see each record (and why). This is called the *dynamic* state of a record. Additionally, each record remembers whether or not it is visible to a newly activated transaction (i.e. committed). This is called the *stable* state of a record.

When a transaction becomes active, each record is either **visible** or **invisible** to the transaction, depending on whether or not it has been committed. The stable state of each record with respect to the starting transaction is either **vis** or **inv**. A record is visible to an active transaction if it has inserted it (**vis**), or alternatively if its stable state was **vis** when the transaction started, and the transaction has not changed or deleted the record. This passive dynamic state is denoted **exi** (for existing). If the transaction has deleted the record, it is invisible (**inv**). The dynamic state of a record remembers, for each transaction which started whilst the record was visible, a visibility attribute (**vis**, **exi**, or **inv**). For example, if transaction X has deleted the record in question, transaction Y has not deleted it, and transaction Z started when the record was not visible, the dynamic component of that record is:

$$\{X \mapsto \mathbf{inv}, Y \mapsto \mathbf{exi}\}$$

In this informal notation, the record R with dynamic and stable components d and s respectively, is denoted as follows:

$$R^{s}_{d}$$

When no transactions are active, the dynamic component of each record is empty. Suppose there are three records, with values represented by A, B and C. If no transactions are active, this is denoted:

$$< A^{\mathbf{vis}}_{\{\}},\ B^{\mathbf{vis}}_{\{\}},\ C^{\mathbf{vis}}_{\{\}} >$$

Any transaction which starts in this state sees all the values in the database, i.e. $<A,B,C>$. Note that a record with stable state **inv** and dynamic state {} is visible to no transaction. Such unreachable records are 'garbage collected' by SWORD, but details of this are omitted to simplify the presentation.

At the start of a transaction, X, '$X \mapsto$ ***exi***' is added to the dynamic state of each record with stable state **vis**. For example, if transaction X starts, the above database becomes:

$$< A^{\mathbf{vis}}_{\{X \mapsto \mathbf{exi}\}},\ B^{\mathbf{vis}}_{\{X \mapsto \mathbf{exi}\}},\ C^{\mathbf{vis}}_{\{X \mapsto \mathbf{exi}\}} >$$

An update by transaction X is represented by the addition of a new record, visible only to X. Thus the new record has stable state **inv**, and dynamic state $\{X \mapsto \mathbf{vis}\}$. The original record remains for the other active transactions, and subsequent transactions, for which the change is transparent. Additionally, the permanence of the old record provides a convenient basis for rollback. For example, if transaction X changes B to B_1, the above representation is as follows:

$$< A^{\mathbf{vis}}_{\{X \mapsto \mathbf{exi}\}},\ B^{\mathbf{vis}}_{\{X \mapsto \mathbf{inv}\}},\ B_1{}^{\mathbf{inv}}_{\{X \mapsto \mathbf{vis}\}},\ C^{\mathbf{vis}}_{\{X \mapsto \mathbf{exi}\}} >$$

The view seen by X is now $<A,B_1,C>$. Suppose transaction Y starts:

$$< A^{\mathbf{vis}}_{\{X \mapsto \mathbf{exi},\ Y \mapsto \mathbf{exi}\}},\ B^{\mathbf{vis}}_{\{X \mapsto \mathbf{inv},\ Y \mapsto \mathbf{exi}\}},\ B_1{}^{\mathbf{inv}}_{\{X \mapsto \mathbf{vis}\}},\ C^{\mathbf{vis}}_{\{X \mapsto \mathbf{exi},\ Y \mapsto \mathbf{exi}\}} >$$

Transactions proceed in an arbitrarily interleaved fashion. For example, transaction Y may change C to C_1:

$$\begin{array}{llllll} < & A^{\mathbf{vis}}, & B^{\mathbf{vis}}, & B_1^{\mathbf{inv}}, & C^{\mathbf{vis}}, & C_1^{\mathbf{inv}} > \\ & \{X\mapsto\mathbf{exi}, & \{X\mapsto\mathbf{inv}, & \{X\mapsto\mathbf{vis}\} & \{X\mapsto\mathbf{exi}, & \{Y\mapsto\mathbf{vis}\} \\ & \ Y\mapsto\mathbf{exi}\} & \ Y\mapsto\mathbf{exi}\} & & \ Y\mapsto\mathbf{inv}\} & \end{array}$$

Rollback is facilitated by removing the transaction from the dynamic state of each record. Commit copies the dynamic state of each record changed by the transaction (**vis** or **inv**) to the corresponding stable state. Future transactions then see new records, but no longer see deleted records.

This model of multi-transactions provides a comprehensible basis for specifying read-consistent database views. For concurrent updates or deletes, the new records corresponding to the updated views must be tracked, so they can be merged together once the transactions have committed, in spite of competing key updates. For example, assume that the database contains a single record:

$$\begin{array}{lll} < & Rr^{\mathbf{vis}} & > \\ & \{\} & \end{array}$$

Transaction X starts and changes the record to $R\underline{\alpha}$, changing just the data. A link is established between the original record and the updated record, shown below:

$$\begin{array}{llll} < & [Rr]^{\mathbf{vis}}, & [R\underline{\alpha}]^{\mathbf{inv}} & > \\ & \{X\mapsto\mathbf{inv}\} & \{X\mapsto\mathbf{vis}\} & \end{array}$$

Now transaction Y starts and changes Rr to $\underline{S}r$ altering the key, followed by transaction Z, which deletes the record Rr. The connection is extended to $\underline{S}r$ as follows:

$$\begin{array}{lllll} < & [Rr]^{\mathbf{vis}}, & [R\underline{\alpha}]^{\mathbf{inv}}, & [\underline{S}r]^{\mathbf{inv}} & > \\ & \{X\mapsto\mathbf{inv}, & \{X\mapsto\mathbf{vis}\} & \{Y\mapsto\mathbf{vis}\} & \\ & \ Y\mapsto\mathbf{inv}, & & & \\ & \ Z\mapsto\mathbf{inv}\} & & & \end{array}$$

Any transaction which commits must merge the effects of its update with the truly visible (i.e. visible stable state) record at the point of the commit. This ensures that concurrent updates are eventually merged together. If two transactions update the same part of a record, then the transaction which commits last takes precedence. However, if any active transaction deletes a record, the deletion persists, so-called 'delete persistency'. In the previous example, the physical record Rr is deleted, regardless of the order in which transactions X, Y and Z commit. This complex scenario is modelled in the following section.

The model is simple to understand because of its uniform treatment of extant records alongside tentatively updated, inserted and deleted records. However, this idealistic view is far removed from the archetypal transaction mechanism (the 'two-phase' commit) in which tentative changes are accommodated quite separately from the database, in temporary storage. The formal specification of our transaction mechanism is introduced in Section 4, and the two disparate representations of read-consistent views reconciled in Section 5.

3. The Formal Semantics of Read-Consistent Transactions

The formal semantics of read-consistent transactions in the ISAM, Tables and Relations Layers are specified in this section. We use the Z notation [Spivey89] with some extensions facilitated by the Zadok tool [Randell90]. Some minor liberties are taken with the tool syntax, such as unparenthesised expressions. The specification is written in a largely reusable form, but the presentation is specialised for the ISAM layer.

Transactions

A transaction is an indivisible sequence of commands performed on behalf of a user. Transactions can be nested and therefore have an associated depth. The outer-level transaction for a user u is identified by the pair $(u,1)$, and nested queries by $(u,2)$ etc.

[USER]
TRANS == USER × $\mathbb{N}$
nest == λ t:TRANS • (fst t, (snd t)+1)

Recall that a record is **vis**ible if tentatively inserted or updated by the transaction, **inv**isible if deleted, and **exi**sting if globally visible when the transaction started.

VISIBILITY ::= **vis** | **inv** | **exi**

The *dynamic* and *stable* attributes of each record are recorded in a composite transaction processing structure (*TP*), along with an indication of the extent of the *amend*ment: only the key; only the data; both the key and the data; or no change at all. Changes to an extant record are *link*ed together to facilitate key and/or data merging as well as to maintain delete persistency.

[LINK]
CTYPE ::= **keyonly** | **dataonly** | **keyanddata** | **none**

TP
dynamic: TRANS ⇸ VISIBILITY
stable: {**vis**, **inv**}; amend: CTYPE; link: $\mathbb{P}$ LINK

(stable = **vis** ⇒ **vis** ∉ ran dynamic) ∧ ...

Several conditions apply to the TP components: for example, a record which is visible to all newly invoked transactions cannot be dynamically visible to an active transaction.

The State

An ISAM is a sequence of keyed records (*index*), the contents of which are uninterpreted (*RAW*), and stored in a non-decreasing order (*leq*). A separate list of TPs (*tps*) mirrors the record sequence. This 'transaction mask' provides a basis for calculating read-consistent views of the index. A *pool* of allocated change connectors links competing key updates.

[RAW]

Record $\widehat{=}$ [key, data: RAW]

| _leq_ : $total\_order_{[RAW]}$

```
┌── ISAM ─────────────────────────────────────────────
│ index : seq Record
│ tps : seq TP
│ pool : ℙ LINK
├──────────
│ index ⨾ (λ Record · key) ∈ {s:seq RAW | (∀i:(2..#s) · s(i-1) leq (s i))}
│ #tps = #index
│ ⋃(ran (tps ⨾ (λ TP · link))) = pool
└─────────────────────────────────────────────────────
```

The ISAM layer identifies and maintains all the ISAMs in the system as well as recording the current depth of each transaction, which is initially zero. A transaction requesting an operation only sees its read-consistent view of an index: this is called the *aspect*. An aspect is determined from the set of indices of visible TPs, defined by the function *view*:

$$\begin{aligned} view == \lambda\ tps{:}seq\ TP;\ t{:}TRANS\ \cdot \\ dom\ (tps \rhd \{TP \mid (snd\ t = 0 \wedge stable = \mathbf{vis}) \vee \\ (snd\ t > 0 \wedge dynamic\ t \in \{\mathbf{vis}, \mathbf{exi}\})\}) \end{aligned}$$

A transaction (*t*) therefore sees the following aspect:

$$view\ (t, tps) \upharpoonright index$$

Transaction Operations

Operations are specified with respect to an ISAM and a transaction identifier, with the corresponding effect on the state of the layer described by a series of promotion schemas (not shown here), which also increment the nesting level and specify garbage collection. Only partial operations are shown here. The function *exists* modifies a TP to make the corresponding record dynamically visible to a fresh transaction.

$\phi visibilities\ \widehat{=}\ [\Delta TP \mid amend' = amend \wedge link' = link]$

$$
\begin{aligned}
exists == \lambda\ t{:}TRANS\ \cdot\ & \\
& (\lambda\ TP \mid stable = \mathbf{vis}\ \cdot \\
& \quad (\mu\ TP' \mid \phi visibilities \wedge dynamic' = dynamic \oplus \{t \mapsto \mathbf{exi}\})) \cup \\
& ((\{TP \mid stable \neq \mathbf{vis}\} \lhd id\ TP)
\end{aligned}
$$

When a transaction starts, its initial view of an index is calculated by applying *exists* to each TP in the TP list.

Start_transaction

$\Delta ISAM;\ t{:}TRANS$

$snd\ t = 0$
$tps' = tps \fatsemi (exists\ (nest\ t))$
$index' = index$
$pool' = pool$

Changes are committed by consigning the dynamic states to their stable states. When an update is committed, partial updates on key and/or data are *merge*d as follows:

$$
\begin{aligned}
merge == \lambda\ a, b{:}\ Record\ \cdot\ & (\lambda\ amend{:}\ \{\mathbf{none}\}\ \cdot\ a) \cup \\
& (\lambda\ amend{:}\ \{\mathbf{keyonly}\}\ \cdot\ (\mu\ Record' \mid key' = b.key \wedge data' = a.data) \cup \\
& (\lambda\ amend{:}\ \{\mathbf{dataonly}\}\ \cdot\ (\mu\ Record' \mid key' = a.key \wedge data' = b.data) \cup \\
& (\lambda\ amend{:}\ \{\mathbf{keyanddata}\}\ \cdot\ b)
\end{aligned}
$$

The altered record only *overwrites* those parts of the existing record that have changed. Each record which contains a committing update is merged with the original version of the record to which it is linked.

$$
\begin{aligned}
& \phi amend \mathrel{\widehat=} [\Delta TP \mid stable' = stable \wedge dynamic' = dynamic \wedge link' = link] \\
& overwrite == \lambda\ pairs{:}seq\ (Record \times TP)\ \cdot\ (\lambda\ t{:}\ TRANS\ \cdot \\
& \qquad (\lambda\ rec{:}\ Record;\ TP \mid amend = \mathbf{none}\ \cdot\ (rec, \theta TP)) \cup \\
& \qquad (\lambda\ rec{:}\ Record;\ TP \mid (t, \mathbf{vis}) \in dynamic \wedge amend \neq \mathbf{none}\ \cdot \\
& \qquad\quad ((merge\ (rec,\ change)\ amend), \\
& \qquad\qquad (\mu\ TP' \mid \phi amend \wedge amend' = \mathbf{none})) \\
& \qquad\qquad \textit{where}\quad original == (\mu\ tp{:}TP \mid tp \in ran\ (pairs \fatsemi snd) \wedge \\
& \qquad\qquad\qquad tp.link = link \wedge stable = \mathbf{vis}) \\
& \qquad\qquad\qquad change == fst(pairs\ ((pairs \fatsemi snd)^{-1}\ original\ ))\ \ ))
\end{aligned}
$$

Delete persistency can be maintained by verifying that each tentative change still refers to a physical record. If not, then the **vis**ible dynamic state is changed to one that **exi**sts.

$$delp == id\ VISIBILITY \oplus \{\mathbf{vis} \mapsto \mathbf{exi}\}$$

Upon deletion, the corresponding TP structure is *stabilise*d by ensuring (via the links), that the record does not spuriously re-appear when a competing transaction subsequently commits.

$$
\begin{array}{l}
\text{stabilise} == \lambda\ \text{trs: seq TP} \bullet \\
\qquad (\lambda\ \text{TP} \mid \text{link} = \{\} \bullet \theta\text{TP}) \cup \\
\qquad (\lambda\ \text{tp.TP} \mid \text{tp.link} \neq \{\} \wedge \textbf{vis} \in \text{stable}\,(\!|\text{changes}|\!) \bullet \theta\text{TP} \\
\qquad\quad \textit{where}\ \ \text{changes} == \{\text{tr: ran trs} \mid \text{tr.link} = \text{tp.link}\} \qquad) \cup \\
\qquad (\lambda\ \text{tp.TP} \mid \text{tp.link} \neq \{\} \wedge \textbf{vis} \notin \text{stable}\,(\!|\text{changes}|\!) \bullet \\
\qquad\qquad (\mu\ \text{TP}' \mid \text{stable}' = \text{tp.stable} \wedge \text{dynamic}' = (\text{tp.dynamic}) \mathbin{;} \text{delp} \wedge \\
\qquad\qquad\qquad \text{amend}' = \textbf{none} \wedge \text{link}' = \{\}\ ) \\
\qquad\quad \textit{where}\ \ \text{changes} == \{\text{tr: ran trs} \mid \text{tr.link} = \text{tp.link}\} \qquad)
\end{array}
$$

The dynamic view of a TP structure is consigned to the stable state, with the *expose* function:

$$
\begin{array}{l}
\text{expose} == \lambda\ \text{t:TRANS} \bullet (\lambda\ \text{TP} \bullet \\
\qquad (\mu\ \text{TP}' \mid \phi\text{visibilities} \wedge \text{dynamic}' = \{\text{t}\} \lhd \text{dynamic} \wedge \\
\qquad\qquad (\text{dynamic t} \in \{\textbf{vis}, \textbf{inv}\} \Rightarrow \text{stable}' = \text{dynamic t}) \wedge \\
\qquad\qquad (\text{dynamic t} \notin \{\textbf{vis}, \textbf{inv}\} \Rightarrow \text{stable}' = \text{stable}\ )\,))
\end{array}
$$

Therefore, when a transaction is committed, the index is updated and the transaction mask amended to reflect the changes.

$$
\begin{array}{|l}
\text{—— Commit\_transaction ——} \\
\Delta\text{ISAM; t:TRANS} \\
\hline
\text{snd t} = 1 \\
\quad \text{index}' = \text{changed} \mathbin{;} \text{fst} \\
\quad \text{tps}' = \text{exposed} \mathbin{;} (\text{stabilise exposed}) \\
\textit{where} \\
\quad \text{pairs} == \lambda\ \text{i:dom index} \bullet (\text{index i, tps i}) \\
\quad \text{changed} == \text{pairs} \mathbin{;} (\text{overwrite pairs t}) \\
\quad \text{exposed} == \text{changed} \mathbin{;} \text{snd} \mathbin{;} (\text{expose t})
\end{array}
$$

When a transaction is rolled back, the views of the current transaction and its ancestors are removed from the transaction mask, thus revoking the changes.

$$
\begin{array}{l}
\phi\text{dynamic} \mathrel{\widehat=} [\Delta\text{TP} \mid \text{stable}' = \text{stable} \wedge \text{amend}' = \text{amend} \wedge \text{link}' = \text{link}] \\
\text{remove} == \lambda\ \text{ts:}\mathbb{P}\ \text{TRANS} \bullet (\lambda\ \text{TP} \bullet (\mu\ \text{TP}' \mid \phi\text{dynamic} \wedge \text{dynamic}' = \text{ts} \lhd \text{dynamic}))
\end{array}
$$

$$
\begin{array}{|l}
\text{—— Rollback\_transaction ——} \\
\Delta\text{ISAM; t:TRANS} \\
\hline
\text{snd t} > 0 \\
\quad \text{tps}' = \text{tps} \mathbin{;} (\text{remove ancestors}) \\
\textit{where} \\
\quad \text{ancestors} == (\text{nest}^{-1\,*})\,(\!|\{\text{t}\}|\!)
\end{array}
$$

The uniform treatment of all changes is the principal abstraction in this specification, but the detailed level of design necessarily entails some 'implementation bias' [Jones86]. In section 4, tentative changes are dealt with using a more plausible representation.

4. Designing the Secure Transaction Mechanism

The transaction mechanism is specified in the ISAM layer refinement using a 'two-level store'. The services of the Storage layer are used to store permanent records on physical disk, whereas tentative changes are maintained separately in 'edit lists', notionally stored in main memory. The Storage layer also uses a (separate) two-level store as the basis of a 'two-phase' commit, but this is treated transparently here. The edit list representation is introduced, and the commit operation is partially refined to illustrate the complexity of the mechanism.

Edit Lists

An edit list describes the tentative changes to a stored index, using a distinct type of entry to represent the different types of change: an unchanged record is mirrored by a **take** entry; an update is represented by an **updates** entry; a (committed) deletion by a **ghost** entry; an insertion by a **new** entry. In addition, multiple instantiations of records which arise from competing key updates are represented by **visible** entries, the corresponding physical record being masked by a special **invisible** entry.

The commit operation is illustrated here for the most complex scenario: competing key updates. As such, only **take** and the **updates**, **visible** and **invisible** entries are discussed. A **take** edit list entry specifies that the corresponding record remains unchanged. Updates to a record are superimposed for each transaction by an **updates** entry. Each transaction's change is recorded in a separate structure, which holds the new value of the record and distinguishes the changed field numbers:

$$\text{CHANGE} \mathrel{\widehat=} [\ \text{trn: TRANS; rec: Record; kfields, dfields: } \mathbb{P}\,\mathbb{N}_1\ ]$$

The collective changes to a single record are identified within the updates entry, where 'deleters' and 'ignorers' (to whom the record is invisible) are identified. An **updates** entry represents non-key updates directly, and key updates indirectly. Each transaction can only perform one type of update per entry, so the sets of transactions must be disjoint.

UPDATES

changes: TRANS $\rightarrowtail\!\!\!\!\!\!\nrightarrow$ CHANGE

deletes, ignores: $\mathbb{P}$ TRANS

---

disjoint <dom changes, deletes, ignores>

Key-updates potentially move the position of a record. A moved record is obscured by an **invisible** entry, and a corresponding **visible** entry marks the new position for the mover. The modification is stored within a 'floating' indirect structure, uniquely identified and referenced from the **visible** and **invisible** entries. An **invisible** entry identifies the transactions that have updated the key, along with the indirection identifier.

[IID]
INVISIBLE ≙ [trans: ℙ TRANS; iid: IID]

An indirection contains a copy of the record currently on the disk, along with its updates.

INDIRECT ≙ [rec: Record; u: UPDATES]

When the key is changed, a **visible** entry is inserted at the new location, pointing to the same indirection as the corresponding **invisible** entry.

VISIBLE ≙ [trans: ℙ TRANS; iid: IID]

The set of all edit list entries is the disjoint sum of the entry structures.

EDIT ::= **take** | updates«UPDATES» |
visible«VISIBLE» | invisible «INVISIBLE» | ...

Refining the State

The ISAM implementation (hence the subscript ι below) *store*s an index on disk, and a separate edit list (*es*) holds the tentative changes. An indirection mapping (*ind*) links competing updates.

```
┌── ISAMι ──────────
│ store: seq Record
│ es: seq EDIT
│ ind: IID ⇸ INDIRECT
└───────────────────
```

Initially the ISAM implementation contains no records and the edit list is empty. Operations are specified relative to the current record accessed (r, r'), the corresponding edit entry (e, e'), and current positions in the store and edit list (mk, mk' and $epos$, $epos'$).

```
┌── ISAM_Abbrevsι ────
│ r, r' : Record
│ e, e': EDIT
│ mk, mk', epos, epos': ℕ
└─────────────────────
```

A position n in a record sequence is directly related to the position *conv es n* within the edit list *es*, which is calculated as follows:

conv==λes:seq EDIT ·
(λ epos:ℕ · #((1..epos) ↿ es) ⊳ {**take**, ran invisible, ran updates}))

The abbreviations above are calculated in the following framing schema:

```
┌── φISAM_ι ─────────────────────────────
│ ΔISAM_ι
│ ISAM_Abbrevs_ι
│ t: TRANS
│ extant: ℙ TRANS
├──────────
│ t ∈ extant
│ mk = conv es epos ∧ r = store (mk+1) ∧ e = es (epos+1)
│ mk' = conv es' epos' ∧ r' = store' (mk'+1) ∧ e' = es' (epos'+1)
└─────────────────────────────────────
```

Further schemas frame changes to the store or edit list, and are included in the operation schemas in a flexible fashion.

ϕRemove_disk $\widehat{=}$ [ϕISAM$_\iota$ | store'=((1..mk) $\upharpoonleft$ store)$\frown$(((mk+2)..#store)$\upharpoonleft$ store)]
ϕUpdate_disk $\widehat{=}$ [ϕISAM$_\iota$ | store' = store $\oplus$ {(mk+1) $\mapsto$ r'}]
ϕRemove_edit $\widehat{=}$ [ϕISAM$_\iota$ | es'=((1..epos) $\upharpoonleft$ es)$\frown$(((epos+2)..#es)$\upharpoonleft$ es)]
ϕUpdate_edit $\widehat{=}$ [ϕISAM$_\iota$ | es' = es $\oplus$ {(epos+1) $\mapsto$ e'}]

Additional framing schemas are used to specify which of the state components remain unchanged.

ϕentry $\widehat{=}$ [ΔISAM$_\iota$ | store' = store $\wedge$ ind' = ind $\wedge$ epos' = epos]
ϕeditlist $\widehat{=}$ [ΔISAM$_\iota$ | store' = store $\wedge$ epos' = epos]
ϕdiskentry $\widehat{=}$ [ΔISAM$_\iota$ | epos' = epos $\wedge$ ind' = ind]

Refining the Commit Operation

The Commit operation is considered here for competing key updates: i.e. the **updates** and **invisible** entries only.

When an **updates** entry is read from the edit list, one of three disk operations is performed. Either the record is deleted, a non-key change is made on the record, or the record is preserved. If the **updates** entry contains changes for more than one transaction, the change is made to the record and the transaction removed from the entry. If there are no more changes then the entry reverts to a **take**. A function *scope*, determines what transactions are in an **updates** entry, and *urem* removes a transaction from the entry.

scope == λ UPDATES $\cdot$ (dom changes) $\cup$ ignores $\cup$ deletes
urem == λ UPDATES $\cdot$ (λ t: TRANS $\cdot$ (μ UPDATES' | changes' = {t} $\lessdot$ changes $\wedge$
ignores' = ignores \ {t} $\wedge$ deletes' = deletes \ {t}))

```
┌── Commit_uchanges ──────────────────
│ φdiskentry; φUpdate_disk;φUpdate_edit
├──────────
│ e ∈ ran updates
│    t ∈ dom u.changes
│    r' = (u.changes t).rec
│    (scope u) \ {t} = {} ⇒ e' = take
│    (scope u) \ {t} ≠ {} ⇒ e' = updates (urem u t)
│ where
│    u == updates⁻¹ e
└─────────────────────────────────────
```

If an **updates** entry specifies that more than one transaction ignores the record, the committing transaction is removed from the entry, otherwise the entry reverts to **take**.

```
┌── Commit_uignores ──────────────────
│ φentry; φUpdate_edit
├──────────
│ e ∈ ran updates
│    t ∈ u.ignores
│    (scope u) \ {t} = {} ⇒ e' = take
│    (scope u) \ {t} ≠ {} ⇒ e' = updates (urem u t)
│ where
│    u == updates⁻¹ e
└─────────────────────────────────────
```

A similar schema is used for deletions. These are conjoined to produce a total operation:

Commit_updates ≙ Commit_uchanges ∨ Commit_uignores ∨ ...

An **invisible** entry occurs when a record is visible to some transactions, but invisible to others because of either a key change or an uncommitted deletion. When committing a key change the **invisible** entry is changed to **visible** for extant transactions.

```
vis == λ INVISIBLE · (λ extant: ℙ TRANS ·
            (μ VISIBLE' | trans' = extant \ trans ∧ iid' = iid) )
```

Read-only changes are created (*creads*) for transactions still seeing the original of a deleted record. Such changes are added to the indirection changes using *ireads*:

```
creads == λ extant: ℙ TRANS · (λ rec: Record · (λ t: TRANS ·
            (μ CHANGE' | trn' = t ∧ rec' = rec ∧ kfields = {} ∧ dfields = {} ) ) )
ireads == λ INDIRECT · (λ extant: ℙ TRANS · (λ r: Record ·
            (μ INDIRECT' | rec' = rec ∧ u' =
                  (μ UPDATES' | ignores' = u.ignores ∧ deletes' = u.deletes ∧
                        changes' = u.changes ∪ (creads extant r) ) ) ))
```

When a key change is committed, the record is deleted from its current position on the disk, and the entry replaced by a **visible** for all other extant transactions. Read changes are inserted into the indirection for the other extant transactions so that they still 'see' the old version of the record at this location.

```
── Commit_inv_changes_key ──────────────────────────────
│ ΦRemove_disk;ΦUpdate_edit
├──────────
│ e ∈ ran invisible
│    t ∈ inv.trans ∧ t ∈ dom invu.changes ∧ (invu.changes t).kfields ≠ {}
│    e' = visible (vis inv extant)
│    ind' = ind ⊕ {inv.iid ↦ (ireads (ind inv.iid) (extant \ inv.trans) r)}
│ where
│    inv == invisible⁻¹ e
│    invu == (ind inv.iid).u
│ epos' = epos
└────────────────────────────────────────────────────────
```

If a non-key change is committed, either the record is updated and the transaction is removed from both the entry and the indirection, or if the entry only contains the committing transaction, both the entry and the indirection are removed.

```
── Commit_inv_changes_nonkey ───────────────────────────
│ ΦUpdate_disk;ΦUpdate_edit
├──────────
│ e ∈ ran invisible
│    t ∈ inv.trans ∧ (invu.changes t).kfields = {} ∧
│    (invu.changes t).dfields = {} ⇒ r' = r ∧
│    (invu.changes t).dfields ≠ {} ⇒ r' = (invu.changes t).rec ∧
│    (#(scope invu) > 1 ⇒
│                 e' = invisible (irem inv t) ∧
│                 ind'= ind ⊕ {inv.iid ↦ (indrem (ind inv.iid) t)}) ∧
│    (#(scope invu) =1 ⇒
│                 e' = take ∧
│                 ind'= {invu.iid} ⩤ ind)
│ where
│    inv == invisible⁻¹ e
│    invu == (ind inv.iid).u
│ epos' = epos
└────────────────────────────────────────────────────────
```

The complete operation for committing an **invisible** entry is the disjunction of the above schemas, along with other schemas describing the effects of other entry types:

$$\text{Commit\_invisible} \ \widehat{=}\ \text{Commit\_inv\_changes\_key} \vee \text{Commit\_inv\_changes\_nonkey} \vee \ldots$$

The 'Commit Entry' operation consists of all of the possible types of committal for each edit list entry, thus:

$$\text{Commit\_entry} \ \widehat{=}\ \text{Commit\_updates} \vee \text{Commit\_invisible} \vee \ldots$$

To commit a transaction, the Commit_entry operation is applied to all edit list entries.

Refining the View

An aspect of the edit list is calculated for any given transaction, using a view function for each type of entry, to define the refined *view* function ($view_\iota$). For example, a transaction can see an **updates** (*uview*) if it has not altered the record or if it is visible in the scope of the entry.

$$\begin{aligned}
\text{uview} == \lambda\ \text{UPDATES} \cdot (\lambda\ \text{rec:Record} \cdot \\
&(\lambda\ \text{t:TRANS} \mid t \in \text{deletes} \vee t \in \text{ignores} \cdot \langle\rangle) \cup \\
&(\lambda\ \text{t:TRANS} \mid t \in \text{dom changes} \cdot \langle(\text{u.changes t}).\text{rec}\rangle) \cup \\
&(\lambda\ \text{t:TRANS} \mid t \notin \text{scope u} \cdot \langle \text{rec} \rangle\ ))
\end{aligned}$$

The $view_\iota$ function uses the viewing functions to determine the aspect, illustrated here for **take** and **updates** entries.

$$\begin{aligned}
view_\iota == \lambda\ \text{store:seq Record} \cdot (\lambda\ \text{ind:(ID} \nrightarrow \text{INDIRECT)} \cdot \\
&(\lambda\ \text{el:seq EDIT} \cdot (\lambda\ \text{t:TRANS} \cdot {}^\frown/(\lambda\ \text{epos: dom el} \cdot \\
&\quad (\mu\ \text{e: \{el epos\}} \mid e = \textbf{take} \cdot \langle \text{rec} \rangle) \cup \\
&\quad (\mu\ \text{e: \{el epos\}} \mid e \in \text{ran updates} \cdot \text{uview}\ (\text{updates}^{-1}\ e)\ \text{rec t}\ ) \cup \\
&\qquad \vdots \\
&\qquad \textit{where} \quad \text{rec} == \text{store}\ ((\text{conv es epos}) + 1)\ )\ ))\ )
\end{aligned}$$

This function is used to calculate the aspect of the ISAM implementation for a transaction, *t*.

$$view_\iota \ \text{store ind es t}$$

The edit list implementation and the TP list mechanism are reconciled in the next section.

5. Refinement

Fragments of the formal semantics of read-consistency were introduced in Section 3, and corresponding fragments of the transaction mechanism were formally specified in Section 4. The semantics treats tentative changes and stored records idealistically in a uniform manner, using TP lists. In contrast, the transaction mechanism separates tentative changes from stored records using edit lists. This section addresses the problem of showing that edit lists refine TP lists correctly.

Exponents of the programming calculus approach [Morgan90] would argue that we should have calculated the mechanism from the formal specification of the ISAM layer. However, we are constrained by the service layer architecture, and the need to produce specifications of each layer in parallel. Therefore, we needed to adopt an 'invent-and-verify' approach. Following [Jones86] the first step is to formally describe the 'coupling' relationship [Morgan90] between the states of the two specifications: TP lists versus edit lists.

The 'text-book' approach is to contrive a functional coupling relation, or 'retrieve function' [Jones86], which identifies each concrete state with at most one abstract state, i.e. each edit list must correspond to at most one TP list. This simplifies refinement proofs since concrete state variables can be substituted directly for the definition of the retrieve function. Unfortunately, this cannot be the case with the transaction mechanism, because both TP lists and edit lists arbitrarily interleave the views of all active transactions.

The problem is not simply that it is difficult to construct a TP list from a given edit list, but that a TP list must be selected from the set of TP lists represented by that edit list. This apparent ambiguity stems from 'implementation bias' [Jones86] in the semantics of read-consistency. Technically, the operations cannot distinguish between some distinct TP lists. For instance, if two transactions are active, with the following distinct views of the stored records,

< Aa, Bb, Ff >
< Aa, Bc, Ff >

the following TP lists are indistinguishable:

< Aa, Bb, Bc, Ff >
< Aa, Bc, Bb, Ff >

Edit list representations are also non-unique. For example, if two transactions, *X* and *Y*, see only the record *Aa*, except that both *X* and *Y* have changed the key to *A'*, the following two distinct edit lists both describe this scenario:

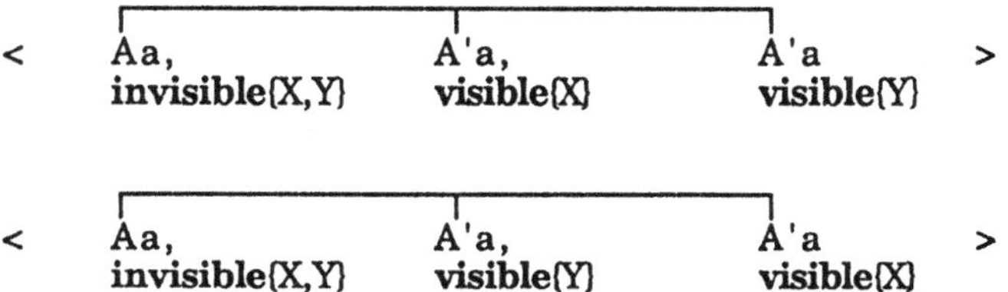

There appears to be a trade-off between the sheer convenience of the biased representation in specifying operations non-deterministically, in contrast with the difficulty of constructing a coupling relation and discharging the proof obligations without the luxury of direct substitutions. However, having conceded that the coupling relation must be non-functional, the relation need not be expressed constructively: the 'observational equivalence' [Sannella84] of corresponding transaction views is all that is required[1]. For each active transaction, its view of the records masked by the TP list must be identical to its view of the edit list superimposed on the store.

```
┌── ISAM_coupling ──────────────────────────────────
│ trns : USER → ℕ
│ ISAM; ISAMι
├──────────
│ ∀ t:trns • view (tps, t) ↿ index = viewι store indirect edits t
└───────────────────────────────────────────────────
```

In addition, the coupling must interpret place-markers within an edit list as pointers into TP lists and the store. The coupling specification for the ISAM layer promotes the above ISAM coupling accordingly.

6. Conclusions

The semantics of read-consistent transactions have been formally specified for the SWORD secure database management system, and a transaction mechanism has been developed using the Z notation. Even though the use of a mathematical design technique is prescribed by the SMITE approach to the development of high-assurance, secure systems, there is a more compelling need for mathematical verification: since the transaction mechanism is extremely complex, it is difficult to reason about its correctness informally.

Following the standard literature on refinement, we have attempted to construct a functional coupling relation between the states of the mechanism and the semantic domains. However, both formal specifications were simplified by devising non-unique state representations, i.e. a given state can have more than one representation, forcing the coupling relation to be non-functional. This complicates the refinement proof obligations, since terms denoting abstract states cannot be substituted for terms denoting abstracted concrete states in the proofs. Quite how this impacts on the difficulty of discharging the proof obligations remains to be seen. We have already determined that it is impractical to discharge such a large number of proof obligations manually, so we must mechanise the refinement steps and the proof obligations first.

The use of a formal notation has greatly assisted in defining the semantics of secure transaction processing. The structuring facilities of the Z notation were exploited to achieve a concise, comprehensible and reusable model. Similar structuring techniques

[1]Behavioural equivalence also provides us with a proof obligation for a notion of "Secure Refinement" [Smith91], which is sufficient to show that refinements do not introduce extraneous behaviours which could be exploited as signalling channels.

helped us to define the edit-list abstraction, and to specify operations in a succinct and flexible manner. However, this specification is extremely detailed, and is not particularly amenable to human reasoning, owing to the explosion of formalism inherent in very detailed design.

Acknowledgements

This work has been carried out with the support of Procurement Executive Ministry of Defence (UK), under Contract No. SLS42c/719, for which Peter Bottomley, Simon Wiseman and Andrew Wood of the DRA Electronics Division provided support and guidance. The authors are grateful to the referees for their detailed and helpful observations.

References

[Harrold89] Harrold, C.L., "An Introduction to the SMITE approach to Secure Computing", Computers and Security, pp 495–505, Vol. 8, October 1989.

[Jones86] Jones, C.B., "Systematic Software Development Using VDM", Prentice Hall International, 1986.

[Kemmerer83] Kemmerer, R.A., "Shared Resource Matrix Methodology: An Approach to Identifying Storage and Timing Channels", ACM Transactions on Computer Systems, Vol. 1, No. 3, August 1983.

[Morgan90] Morgan, C., "Programming from Specifications", Prentice Hall, 1990.

[Randell90] Randell, G.P., "Zadok User Guide", RSRE Memorandum No. 4356,1990.

[Sannella84] Sannella, D., Tarlecki, A., "On Observational Equivalence and Algebraic Specification", JCSS 34, pp150-178, 1984.

[Smith90] Smith, P., "Refinement in the Large", The SafetyNet'90 Conference Proceedings, October 1990.

[Smith91] Smith, P., "Secure Refinement", RSRE Report No. 91019, February 1991.

[Spivey89] Spivey, J.M., "The Z Notation A Reference Manual", Prentice Hall International, 1989.

[SQL89] "Information processing systems — Database Language SQL with integrity enhancement", ISO/IEC 9075 1989(E).

[Terry89] Terry, P.F., Wiseman, S.R., "A 'New' Security Policy Model", Proceedings of the 1989 IEEE Symposium on Security and Privacy, Oakland, 1989.

[Wiseman90a] Wiseman, S., "Control of Confidentiality in Databases", Computers and Security, Volume 9, No. 6, October 1990.

[Wiseman90b] Wiseman, S., "Basic Mechanisms for Computer Security", RSRE Report No. 89024, January 1990.

[Wood90] Wood, A.W., "The SWORD Model of Multilevel Secure Databases", RSRE Report No. 90008, June 1990.

FORMAL DEVELOPMENT OF A SERIAL COPY MANAGEMENT SYSTEM

Gerard R. Renardel de Lavalette
University of Groningen, Department of Computing Science
P.O. box 800, 9700 AV Groningen, The Netherlands

Abstract
In this paper we present and discuss specification, conceptual and technical design of a Serial Copy Management System (SCMS), devised to control copying of digital audio signals by DAT recorders. The specification and designs presented in this paper are written in the formal wide spectrum design language COLD-K. The work was performed in relation to the development of the Digital Audio Interface Standard.

1 Introduction

The ultimate gain of using formal specification and design languages lies in their ability to yield precise and unambiguous descriptions of models and systems. Such descriptions can profitably be employed in the development process of digital hardware and software. The work we report on in this paper is in essence of that nature, but in the somewhat less usual context of standardisation, viz. application of the wide spectrum design language COLD-K in the development of an Amendment to the Digital Audio Interface Standard (IEC-958) by the International Electrotechnical Commission (IEC). Part of the development of this Amendment took place at Philips Consumer Electronics (Eindhoven, the Netherlands) via representation in the Technical Committee No. 84 of the IEC. An important aspect of this Amendment is the Serial Copy Management System (SCMS, also called *Single* Copy Management System), devised to control copying of digital audio signals by DAT recorders. This paper addresses the specification, conceptual and technical design of the SCMS. As it turned out, the SCMS in the definitive Amendment is not in a direct way based on the designs presented here. Our designs, however, did play a role in the clarification of several issues involving the SCMS.

1.1. Amendment to the Digital Audio Interface Standard

An important and controversial aspect of the Amendment to the Digital Audio Interface Standard is formed by the restrictions on Digital Audio Tape (DAT) recorder copying. As a compromise between parties who wanted unrestricted copying (manufacturers of blank tapes and DAT recorders) and those who wanted severe limitations (copyright owners, producers of pre-recorded digital audio tapes), it was decided that *serial* copying (making copies of copies) of copyrighted material shall in principle be forbidden by the standard. The SCMS is proposed to regulate the copying behaviour of DAT recorders. The working document [USA89] contains a detailed functional description. We quote from Section 2 of [USA89]:

(e) under SCMS, the circuitry which controls the functions of a DAT recorder will be programmed to read certain coding information accompanying the source material and, based on the particular combination of code it reads, will permit unrestricted copying, permit copying but label the copy with a code to restrict further digital-to-digital copying, or disallow such copying;

(f) under SCMS, a DAT recorder will not be prevented from making first-generation digital-to-digital copies of original prerecorded music and other material from compact discs, prerecorded DAT cassettes, digital broadcasts, and other digital sources entering through a digital input, but will be prevented from making second-generation digital-to-digital copies of the copies;

(g) under SCMS, in recognition of the fact that a DAT recorder at present will be unable to determine whether original prerecorded music or other material entering through an analog input has been coded for copyright protection, a DAT recorder will not be prevented from making first-generation and second-generation digital-to-digital copies of the source material, but will be prevented from making third-generation digital-to-digital copies of the second-generation copies;

In this paper, we shall give a formal specification SPEC of this description of the SCMS, followed by a conceptual design CDESIGN which provably implements SPEC. Together with some coding requirements formalised in CODING, CDESIGN shall be extended to a technical design TDESIGN. All formal descriptions are given in COLD-K.

As has been stated in the Introduction, the specification and design of the SCMS given here is only one of the alternatives that have been studied in relation to the development of the Amendment to the IEC standard. The final version of the Amendment contains a description of a Serial Copy Management System that is based on other principles, but it behaves essentially the same as the SCMS described here. One difference between the standardized SCMS and our SCMS is that, in the former, recording devices have a more active role: they have to decide whether a signal can be copied or not, the signal only has to identify itself. This can be seen in contrast to the situation in our SCMS, where recording rights are attributed to signals (which can be interpreted as a more active role for signals).

1.2. Outline of the rest of this paper

§ 2 contains a short introduction into the design language COLD-K, concentrating on the features used in this paper. In § 3 we describe our universe of discourse consisting of signals, signal carriers, devices, etc. in the class BASICS. The functional description of the SCMS as given in [USA89] is formalised in § 4 in the class SPEC. A conceptual design of the SCMS, based on the notion of *record rights* is given in the class CDESIGN in § 5 and it is shown that it satisfies the specification SPEC. In § 6 the coding principles for signals are described in the class CODING. The technical design is given and investigated in the class TDESIGN in § 7, and some final remarks and conclusions are presented in § 8.
The inclusion diagram of the classes in this paper is given in fig. 1. The $\leq$ sign between the classes SPEC and CDESIGN indicates that the latter implements the former (see the end of §2).

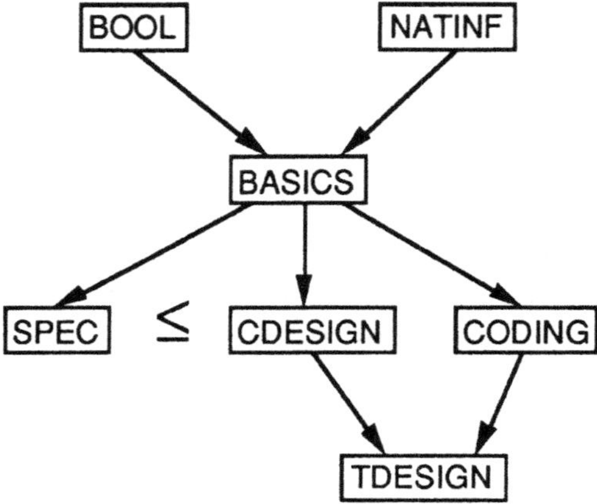

Fig. 1. Class inclusion diagram

1.3. Acknowledgements

The work reported here stemmed from the involvement of Philips Consumer Electronics (Eindhoven, the Netherlands) in the development of an Amendment to the Digital Audio Interface Standard (IEC-958) by the International Electrotechnical Commission. The work was performed while the author was at Utrecht University (Department of Philosophy, Applied Logic Group) and SERC (Software Engineering Research Centre, Utrecht); at the first affiliation, he received partial support from Philips Research Eindhoven.

The author thanks L. Feijs, H. Jonkers (both Philips Research Eindhoven) and W.J. Christis (Philips Consumer Electronics, Eindhoven) for fruitful collaboration, G. Wirtz (also Philips Consumer Electronics) for providing useful information on SCMS and the IEC standard, and K. Middelburg (PTT Research) and P. Hendriks (SERC) for comment on a draft of this paper.

2 The design language COLD-K

The specification and designs in this paper are presented as class descriptions in the formal wide spectrum design language COLD-K (COLD is an acronym of Common Object-oriented Language for Design, K stands for kernel). COLD-K is developed at Philips Research Laboratories Eindhoven, mainly in the ESPRIT projects FAST and METEOR, and is intended to serve as the kernel language for a family of wide-spectrum languages to be used for the specification, design and implementation of software systems. See [F*87] for the complete definition of COLD-K and [J89] for a good introduction. A more user-oriented member of the COLD-family based on COLD-K is COLD-1: see [J91a] for the definition and [B91], [J91b] in these Proceedings for applications.

The central notion of COLD-K is the *class*. A class can be seen as an abstract machine having a collection of states. These states are many-sorted algebras with predicates and (partial) functions, all states of a class having the same signature. States can be modified nondeterministically by procedures which belong to the class: the basic change actions are the creation of a new object (not to be used in this paper) and the modification of a function or a predicate. A procedure has zero or more parameters and returns zero or more objects. (In the

class descriptions of this paper, the only procedure is record in the class BASICS; it is used to model the recording of a signal on a digital audio tape by a state change. See 3.1, 3.2.)
Classes can be described by giving definitions of the sorts, functions and predicates of its states and of the procedures that can modify the states, and also by giving axioms. These definitions and axioms take roughly the form of sentences of an extension of first-order dynamic logic: so there are formulae

[E]A (meaning: after every execution of expression E assertion A holds)
<E>A (meaning: there is an execution of E after which A holds)

These dynamic expressions are formed using procedures, tests on assertions and programming constructs: sequential composition, alternative choice, repetition. (Here we only use the expression record(d,s,c), viz in axiom 1 of BASICS and in 3.3.(ii).)
Class descriptions can be subjected to modularisation and parametrisation operations, and this results in schemes. Finally schemes can be combined to form components which constitute systems. (The only modularisation operation we use here is import of a class in another class.)
In this paper, the Helvetica font will be used for COLD-K. Comment is written between curly brackets { }.

2.1. Semantics of COLD-K

COLD-K has a logical semantics, defined in [F*87]. This definition uses MPL_ω (Many-sorted Partial infinitary Logic), an extension of classical first-order logic with sorts, definedness predicates $\downarrow$ and undefined objects $\uparrow$ for every sort S ($t\downarrow$ means: t is a defined term; $\uparrow\downarrow$ is always false), partial functions (i.e. $f(x)\downarrow$ does not hold automatically), descriptions $\iota x{:}S(A)$ (meaning: the unique x of sort S satisfying A if such an x exists, otherwise undefined) and countably infinite conjunctions $\bigwedge_n A_n$ and disjunctions $\bigvee_n A_n$. The infinite disjunctions are used to make inductive definitions explicit. We refer to [KR89a], [R89], [M90] for more information on MPL_ω, and to [KR89b] for an account of the treatment of inductive definitions.
MPL_ω has undefined objects, but it is classical in that there are only two truth values: in this, it differs from e.g. the three-valued Logic of Partial Functions (LPF, with truth values **true**, **false** and **undefined**) on which VDM is based (see [J90]). However, a three-valued logic can be modeled in MPL_ω by adding a sort Bool having one undefined element (like every sort) and the two defined elements true and false. Here we shall do so in the context of COLD-K (see the class BOOL in the Appendix). See [MR91] in these Proceedings for a comparison of the logical frameworks of VDM and COLD-K.
All functions and atomic predicates in MPL_ω are *strict*, i.e. we have

$$f(t_1,\ldots,t_n)\downarrow \rightarrow t_1\downarrow \wedge \ldots \wedge t_n\downarrow \quad \text{for function symbols } f,$$
$$P(t_1,\ldots,t_n) \rightarrow t_1\downarrow \wedge \ldots \wedge t_n\downarrow \quad \text{for predicate symbols } P.$$

We shall try to give a feeling for the semantics by a few examples. Consider the following class description:

```
LET C :=
CLASS
      SORT A
      SORT B
      FUNC f : A -> B  VAR
      PRED Q : A # B
      PROC p : A # B ->
      AXIOM FORALL a : A b : B (Q(a,b)  =>  [p(a,b)](f(a) = b))
END
```

The class C contains the sorts A and B, the function f and the predicate Q. A, B, f and Q induce a collection of many-sorted algebras which act as the states of C. A, B and Q are the same in all states of this class: only f can vary in state transitions (as is indicated by the keyword VAR). The procedure p acts as a state transformer with two input parameters and no output parameters: the axiom says that, whenever Q(a,b) holds and p is applied with parameters a and b, then the value of f in a is changed (if necessary) in b.
All this is formalized explicitly in the logical semantics:

sem(C) = $<\Sigma,T>$, consisting of a signature Σ and a theory T in MPL_ω, where
$\Sigma = \{A, B, \textbf{state}, f : A \times \textbf{state} \rightarrow B, Q : A \times B \times \textbf{state}, p : A \times B \times \textbf{state} \times \textbf{state}\}$ and
$T = Cl(\Sigma,\{\varphi_1,\varphi_2\})$, with
$\varphi_1 = \forall a{:}A\ \forall b{:}B\ \forall s,t{:}\textbf{state}\ (Q(a,b,s) \rightarrow Q(a,b,t))$ (Q is state-independent),
$\varphi_2 = \forall a{:}A\ \forall b{:}B\ \forall s{:}\textbf{state}\ (Q(a,b,s) \rightarrow \forall t{:}\textbf{state}\ (p(a,b,s,t) \rightarrow f(a,t) = b))$
(the meaning of AXIOM).

This definition of φ_2 closely resembles the standard semantics of dynamic logic (see [H84]). $Cl(\Sigma,\Gamma)$, the closure of Γ under Σ, is the collection of all consequences of Γ in the signature Σ:

$$Cl(\Sigma,\Gamma) = \{\psi \mid MPL_\omega : \Gamma \vdash \psi,\ sig(\psi) \subseteq \Sigma\},$$

here $sig(\psi)$ denotes the signature elements occurring in ψ. Observe that the signature Σ of the interpretation is obtained from the signature of C by adding the sort **state**, extending functions and predicates with one state parameter (modeling their potential state dependence), and extending procedures with two state parameters (modeling their ability to change states, i.e. to go from one state to another).

To illustrate the use of implicit (and usually inductive) definitions, we consider the definition of the predicate finite in the class NATINF given in the Appendix:

```
PRED finite : Natinf
      IND finite(0) AND FORALL n : Natinf (finite(n) => finite(S(n)))
```

Now let φ(pred) (pred an arbitrary unary predicate of type Natinf) be the formula defined by

$\varphi(\text{pred}) =_{def} \text{pred}(0) \wedge \forall n{:}\text{Natinf}\ (\text{pred}(n) \rightarrow \text{pred}(S(n))).$

The effect of this definition is that finite is the *smallest* predicate satisfying φ, i.e.

$\varphi(\text{finite})$, and
$\varphi(\text{pred}) \rightarrow \forall n{:}\text{Natinf}\ (\text{finite}(n) \rightarrow \text{pred}(n))$ for any predicate pred.

The same applies to inductive definitions of functions: the unary function f inductively defined by the formula φ(f) is the smallest (in terms of graphs of functions: recall that functions are partial) function satisfying φ, i.e.

$\varphi(f)$, and
$\varphi(g) \rightarrow \forall xy\ (f(x) = y \rightarrow g(x) = y)$ for any unary function g.

Now consider two classes C1 and C2 with sem(C1) = <Σ1,T1> and sem(C2) = <Σ2,T2>. They can be combined by importing the one in the other:

LET C := IMPORT C1 INTO C2

the semantics of the result C is obtained by taking the pointwise union (and closing off):

$\text{sem}(C) = \langle \Sigma1 \cup \Sigma2, \text{Cl}(\Sigma1 \cup \Sigma2, T1 \cup T2) \rangle.$

Another thing one can do is compare C1 and C2, and we have the notation

C1 ≤ C2 (C2 *implements* C1, or: C1 *is implemented by* C2)

with the meaning

$\Sigma1 \subseteq \Sigma2$ and $T1 \subseteq T2$.

In words: the signature of C2 extends the signature of C1, and all consequences of C1 are consequences of C2.

3 Signals, carriers and devices

Before giving the specification SPEC of the SCMS in § 4, we fix a universe of discourse. This will be done formally in the class description BASICS, but first we give an informal description illustrated with a diagram.

3.1. Informal description
We consider three kinds of things:

digital audio *signals* available to the consumer,
signal *carriers* (e.g. digital audio tape (DAT), compact discs)
devices that work upon these.

For simplicity, we assume that a carrier *contains* (at most) one signal. Some signals are created by a device (e.g. a music instrument with digital output, a broadcast receiver, an analog-digital converter): that device is called the *source* of the signal. Other signals are obtained by *apply*ing a device (e.g. a DAT recorder, a CD player or a digital-digital converter) to another signal (the signal *on DAT*, on the CD or offered on the input of the converter): in this case, the signal has no source.
The Serial Copy Management System (SCMS) is a signal transformer, applied to signals before they are *record*ed on a carrier (in fact only on digital audio tape). This application of the SCMS to a signal may fail: then the signal will not be recorded. Successfully recording a signal on a DAT changes the state of the DAT: the signal it contains is changed, and it is no longer *original.*

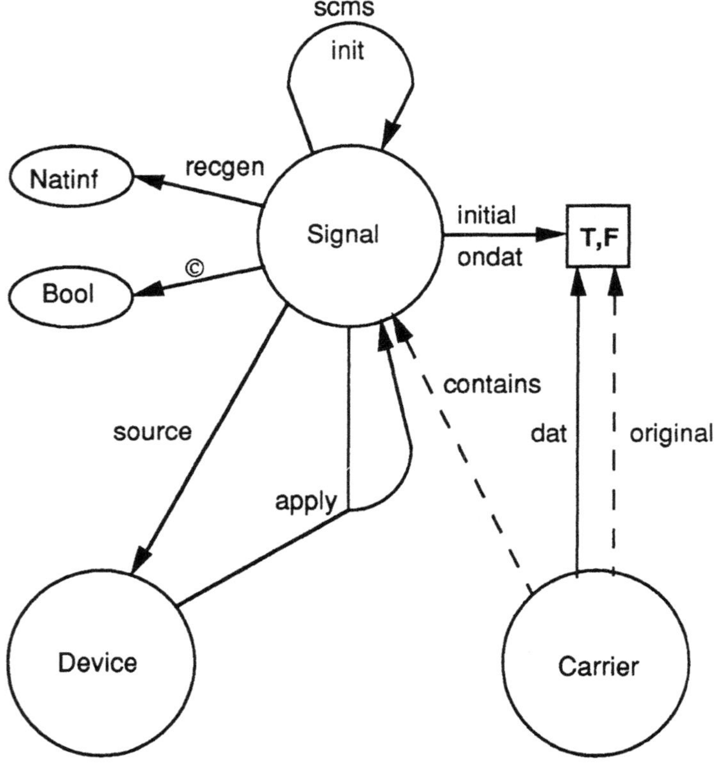

Fig. 2. Diagram of sorts, predicates and functions.

See fig. 2. The box with T,F in it represents the two truth values, the arrows pointing to it represent predicates, the other arrows represent functions. The dashed arrows correspond to functions that can be modified by the state-transforming procedure record.

Fig. 2 illustrates that we use both two- and three-element truth value sets. For intrinsic properties represented by the predicates dat (being a digital audio tape), original (containing its original pre-recorded signal), initial (being a prerecorded or created signal) and ondat (being on digital audio tape), only two truth values suffice; for the predicate © (to be considered as copyrighted), the third truth value **undefined** is used in case it follows from the type code of the signal whose copyright status is unknown, e.g. if the signal comes from an analog-digital converter (contrary to digital signals, analog signals - not present in our universe of discourse - do not contain any code for e.g. copyright status). The sort Bool is defined in the Appendix, together with Natinf (natural numbers with infinity).

3.2. Formal description

We now describe the universe of discourse formally in the class BASICS. The class descriptions BOOL and NATINF imported by BASICS are given in the Appendix.

```
LET BASICS :=
IMPORT BOOL NATINF INTO
CLASS

        SORT Signal
        SORT Device
        SORT Carrier

        FUNC contains : Carrier -> Signal  VAR
        FUNC apply : Device # Signal -> Signal
        FUNC source : Signal -> Device
        FUNC scms : Signal -> Signal
        FUNC © : Signal -> Bool

        PRED dat : Carrier
        PRED ondat : Signal
              PAR s : Signal DEF EXISTS c : Carrier (dat(c) AND contains(c) = s)
        PRED original : Carrier  VAR

        PROC record : Device # Signal # Carrier ->
              MOD contains original

{1}     AXIOM FORALL d : Device s : Signal c : Carrier
              ((<record(d,s,c)>TRUE => scms(s)! AND dat(c)) AND
              [record(d,s,c)](contains(c) = scms(s) AND NOT original(c)))
```

{Axiom 1 states: a signal s can only be recorded if scms(s) is defined; after recording signal s on device d, the signal on c is scms(s) and the carrier is no longer original.
Given a signal s, it is sometimes convenient to know the initial signal init(s) from which s is obtained by digital transformations and recordings, and its recording generation recgen(s), the number of recordings that have occurred between init(s) and s. In order to define these

functions, we need an inductive definition of the sort Signal, which is obtained in a standard way, using the inductively defined predicate ind and an axiom that states that all signals are in ind.}

```
PRED initial : Signal
    PAR s : Signal
        DEF source(s)! OR EXISTS c : Carrier (original(c) AND s = contains(c))
```

{So a signal is initial if it has a source or if it is on an original carrier.}

```
{2}    AXIOM FORALL s : Signal d : Device
           NOT initial(apply(d,s)) AND NOT initial(scms(s))
```

{This axiom enforces that signals made by a device or the SCMS are not initial.}

```
PRED ind : Signal
    IND FORALL s : Signal
        ((initial(s)  =>  ind(s))
        AND
        FORALL d : Device (ind(s) AND apply(d,s)!  =>  ind(apply(d,s)))
        AND
        (ind(s) AND scms(s)!  =>  ind(scms(s))))
```

```
{3}    AXIOM FORALL s : Signal ind(s)
```

{This axiom states that all signals are either initial or obtained from initial signals by finitely many applications of some device or the SCMS. It allows us to prove universal properties of signals by induction: if some property holds for all initial signals and is preserved under application of devices and under scms, then it holds for all signals.
Now we can define recgen and init inductively.}

```
FUNC recgen : Signal -> Natinf
    IND FORALL s : Signal
        ((initial(s) => recgen(s) = 0)
        AND
        FORALL d : Device (apply(d,s)! => recgen(apply(d,s)) = recgen(s))
        AND
        (scms(s)! => recgen(scms(s)) = recgen(s) + 1))
FUNC init : Signal -> Signal
    IND FORALL s : Signal
        ((initial(s) => init(s) = s)
        AND
        FORALL d : Device (apply(d,s)! => init(apply(d,s)) = init(s))
        AND
        (scms(s)! => init(scms(s)) = init(s)))

END {BASICS}
```

This describes formally the universe of discourse to be used in subsequent class descriptions. Before doing so, we prove some properties:

3.3. Lemma. The following assertions are true in BASICS:
i) FORALL s : Signal (initial(init(s)) AND finite(recgen(s))) (finite is defined in Natinf)
ii) FORALL s : Signal d : Device c : Carrier [record(d,s,c)] recgen(contains(c)) = recgen(s) + 1
iii) FORALL s : Signal d : Device NOT source(apply(d,s))!
Proof. (i) Induction over Signal, using the definition of ind and {3}.
(ii) Combine [record(d,s,c)](contains(c) = scms(s)) from {1} and recgen(scms(s)) = recgen(s) + 1 from the definition of recgen.
(iii) Combine NOT initial(apply(d,s)) from {2} and source(apply(d,s))! => initial(apply(d,s)) from the definition of initial.

4 Specification of the SCMS

Based on the functional descriptions given in [USA89] and quoted in § 1, we now specify the SCMS as follows:

```
LET SPEC :=
IMPORT BASICS INTO
CLASS

{4}     AXIOM FORALL s : Signal
                NOT scms(s)! <=>
                        (recgen(s) = 1 AND ©(init(s)) = true)
                        OR
                        (recgen(s) = 2 AND NOT ©(init(s))!)

END {SPEC}
```

In words: a digital signal cannot be recorded if and only if it is either a first-generation copy of an original digital signal with copyright or a second-generation copy of an original digital signal from a device which is unable to register copyright information. Axiom {4} has the following immediate consequences:

4.1. Lemma. The following assertions are true in the class SPEC:
i) FORALL s : Signal (©(init(s)) = false => scms(s)!)
ii) FORALL s : Signal (recgen(s) = 0 => scms(s)!)
iii) FORALL s : Signal (recgen(s) = 1 AND NOT ©(init(s))! => scms(s)!)
Proof. Follows straightforwardly from {4} (using elementary properties like $1 \neq 2$ and strictness of ©).

5 Conceptual design

We now give the conceptual design for the implementation of the requirements in the class SPEC. It uses the notion of *record rights* (as suggested by W.J. Christis), indicating how many record generations are allowed to be made from a signal. The range of record right values is N ∪ {inf} = {0,1,2,...,inf}, which is specified in the class NATINF given in the Appendix.

```
LET CDESIGN :=
IMPORT BASICS INTO
CLASS

        FUNC rr : Signal -> Natinf
                IND FORALL s : Signal
                        (initial(s) =>
                                ©(s) = false  <=>  rr(s) = inf      AND
                                NOT ©(s)!     <=>  rr(s) = 2        AND
                                ©(s) = true   <=>  rr(s) = 1)
                        AND
                        FORALL s : Signal d : Device  apply(d,s)! => rr(apply(d,s)) = rr(s)
                        AND
                        FORALL s : Signal  scms(s)! => rr(scms(s)) = pd(rr(s))
```

{So rr is defined with induction over Signal. On initial signals rr depends on the copyright status, its value remains unchanged under application of devices but is decremented (using the partial predecessor function pd defined in Natinf: pd(0) is undefined) after applying scms.}

{5} AXIOM FORALL s : Signal (NOT scms(s)! => rr(s) = 0)

{This axiom states that scms can only fail if no record rights are left.}

END {CDESIGN}

Before we show that CDESIGN implements SPEC, first some useful properties of rr.

5.1. Lemma. The following assertions are true in the class CDESIGN:
i) FORALL s : Signal (rr(s) = 0 OR rr(s) = 1 OR rr(s) = 2 OR rr(s) = inf)
ii) FORALL s : Signal rr(s) + recgen(s) = rr(init(s))
iii) FORALL s : Signal (NOT rr(init(s)) = 0)
iv) FORALL s : Signal (rr(s) = 0 <=> NOT scms(s)!)
v) FORALL s : Signal (rr(s) = inf <=> rr(init(s)) = inf)
Proof. (i),(ii) Induction over Signal.
(iii) Follows from the definition of rr and 3.3.(i).

(iv) The <= direction is just {5}, the other follows from scms(s)! => pd(rr(s))! (a consequence of the definition of rr) and NOT pd(0)! (a consequence of the definition of pd).
(v) Induction over Signal, using pd(inf) = inf.

5.2. Theorem. CDESIGN implements SPEC, i.e. all consequences of SPEC are consequences of CDESIGN.
Proof. It suffices to show that {4} holds in CDESIGN. This is shown as follows.

NOT scms(s)!	<=>	rr(s) = 0	(by 5.1(iv))
	<=>	rr(s) = 0 AND recgen(s) = rr(init(s))	(by 5.1(ii))
	<=>	rr(s) = 0 AND	
		((recgen(s) = 0 AND rr(init(s)) = 0) OR	
		(recgen(s) = 1 AND rr(init(s)) = 1) OR	
		(recgen(s) = 2 AND rr(init(s)) = 2) OR	
		(recgen(s) = inf AND rr(init(s)) = inf))	(by 5.1(i))
	<=>	rr(s) = 0 AND	
		((recgen(s) = 1 AND rr(init(s)) = 1) OR	
		(recgen(s) = 2 AND rr(init(s)) = 2))	(by 5.1(iii,v))
	<=>	(recgen(s) = 1 AND rr(init(s)) = 1) OR	
		(recgen(s) = 2 AND rr(init(s)) = 2)	(by 5.1(ii))
	<=>	(recgen(s) = 1 AND ©(init(s)) = true) OR	
		(recgen(s) = 2 AND NOT ©(init(s))!)	(def. of rr and 3.3.(i))

6 Coding

The technical design of the SCMS to be given in the next section involves the coding of the function rr defined in the conceptual design. First, however, we have to look at the requirements and restrictions that are imposed upon any such coding. They follow mainly from other standards and existing hardware. It is here that things get a bit messy. Before we go on, we quote from [USD89] (the technical reference document of [USA89]) a passage which gives an informal but rather precise technical description of the SCMS. It will serve as a benchmark for our technical design in § 7; at the same time, it gives an impression of some of the complications involved (there are more in the unquoted part).

> 1. Digital audio input signals in which the C bit is set as "0" shall not be recorded, except for the cases specified below in paragraphs 2, 4 and 5.
> 2. A DAT recorder may record a digital audio input signal in which the C bit is set as "0", where the Category Code of the signal is listed in the "Category Code White List" set forth below. The DAT recorder shall record "10" in ID6 on the tape in this case.
> 3. For digital audio input signals in which the C bit is set as "1", the DAT recorder shall record "00" in ID6 on the tape except for those cases specified below in paragraphs 4 and 5.
> 4. For digital audio input signals that contain Category Code information that is not defined in this Memorandum, the DAT recorder shall record "10" in ID6, regardless of the status of the C bit or the L bit.

5. For digital audio input signals originating from an A/D converter with the Category Code "01100XXL", or from other sources such as from A/D converters with the Category Code for "General" ("00000000"), the DAT recorder shall record "11" in ID6, regardless of the status of the C bit or the L bit. This requirement shall be applied to digital input signals that do not contain source information of the original signal before digitization, e.g., an A/D converter that does not deliver source information.

6. For digital input signals originating from an A/D converter with the Category Code "01101XXL", which can deliver original source code information concerning the C bit and L bit even if the source is in analog format, the requirement stated above in paragraph 5 shall not be applied. The "Category Code White List" set forth below includes this Category Code.

7. A digital audio tape of "original" generation status over which copyright protection has been asserted shall contain "11" in ID6. A digital audio tape of "original" generation status over which no copyright protection has been asserted shall contain "00" in ID6.

[USD89], part of Mandatory Standards for Recording Function

The C bit (on position 2 in the signal) is intended to indicate copyright protection. The Category Code (a string of eight bits on position 8 to 15) of a signal consists of two parts: the type code (position 8 to 14) and the L bit (position 15). The type code characterizes the type of device the signal comes from, the L bit is intended to code whether the signal is original or not. The White List has to do with the the fact that there exist already DAT recorders and other digital audio devices, with generation coding and copy limitations based on different conventions: some Category Codes in the White List have 1 as L bit, others have 0, but all signals with a Category Code from the White List are original. The standard under development has to comply with these conventions (and others not mentioned here).

```
LET CODING :=
IMPORT BASICS INTO
CLASS

    SORT Code              {this is the collection of codes: bits and bit strings}

    FUNC cbit : Signal -> Code
    FUNC lbit : Signal -> Code
    FUNC id6 : Signal -> Code
    FUNC catcode : Signal -> Code
    FUNC typecode : Signal -> Code
    FUNC typecode : Device -> Code
    FUNC lb : Code -> Code
    FUNC tc : Code -> Code
    FUNC cc : Code # Code -> Code
    FUNC 0 : -> Code
    FUNC 1 : -> Code
    FUNC 00 : -> Code
    FUNC 10 : -> Code
```

```
FUNC 11 : -> Code

PRED whitelist : Code
PRED undef : Code
PRED no©inf : Code

{6}   AXIOM FORALL s : Signal      lb(catcode(s)) = lbit(s) AND
                                   tc(catcode(s)) = typecode(s) AND
                                   cc(typecode(s),lbit(s)) = catcode(s)
```

{This axiom expresses that a Category Code has two parts: a type code and an L bit.}

```
{7}   AXIOM FORALL s : Signal
        (ondat(s) OR whitelist(typecode(s)) OR undef(typecode(s)) OR no©inf(typecode(s)))
        AND
        FORALL s1,s2,s3,s4 : Signal
        (ondat(s1) AND whitelist(typecode(s2)) AND
        undef(typecode(s3)) AND no©inf(typecode(s4))
            => NOT (s1=s2 OR s1=s3 OR s1=s4 OR s2 =s3 OR s2=s4 OR s3=s4))
```

{This is an inevitably cumbersome way to formalize that any signal is either on DAT, or its type code satisfies exactly one of the predicates whitelist, undef, or no©inf.}

```
{8}   AXIOM FORALL s : Signal
        (whitelist(catcode(s)) => whitelist(typecode(s))) AND
        (undef(catcode(s)) <=> undef(typecode(s))) AND
        (no©inf(catcode(s)) <=> no©inf(typecode(s)))
```

{This axiom states that ant type code contained in a category code on the White List is also assumed to be on that list, and furthermore that the L bit (the difference between the category code and the type code) is irrelevant for the predicates undef and no©inf.}

```
{9}   AXIOM FORALL s : Signal d : Device
        (source(s)! => typecode(s) = typecode(source(s))) AND
        (apply(d,s)! => typecode(apply(d,s)) = typecode(d))
```

{So a signal gets the type code of the device it comes from.}

```
END {CODING}
```

7 Technical design

Now we can give the technical design as an extension of the conceptual design combined with the coding requirements. The obvious idea is to code the value of rr with two bits (recall that rr can have four different values, see 5.1(i)). For signals not on DAT, the C bit and the L bit are used; signals on DAT use the two-bit field ID6.

```
LET TDESIGN :=
IMPORT CDESIGN CODING INTO
CLASS

        FUNC wlbit : Code -> Code
                IND FORALL c : Code (whitelist(c)  =>  wlbit(tc(c)) = lb(c))
```

{This function yields (if any) the L bit that completes a type code to a category code in the White List.}

```
        FUNC inv : Code -> Code
                IND  inv(0) = 1  AND  inv(1) = 0

{10}    AXIOM FORALL s : Signal
                (ondat(s)  =>
                        (rr(s) = inf     =>  id6(s) = 00)  AND
                        (rr(s) = 1       =>  id6(s) = 11)  AND
                        (rr(s) = 0       =>  id6(s) = 10))
                AND
                (whitelist(typecode(s))  =>
                        (rr(s) = inf  =>        cbit(s) = 1  AND  lbit(s) = 0)  AND
                        (rr(s) = 2  =>          cbit(s) = 1  AND  lbit(s) = 1)  AND
                        (rr(s) = 1  =>          cbit(s) = 0  AND  lbit(s) = wlbit(typecode(s)))  AND
                        (rr(s) = 0  =>          cbit(s) = 0  AND  lbit(s) = inv(wlbit(typecode(s)))))
                AND
                (undef(typecode(s))  =>  rr(s) = 1)
                AND
                (no©inf(typecode(s))  =>  rr(s) = 2)

END {TDESIGN}
```

We formulate the behaviour of scms in the class TDESIGN in a way comparable with the quoted part of the Mandatory Standard of [USD89].

7.1. Lemma. In TDESIGN the following holds (the bracketed numbers and the underlining are for later use):

```
FORALL s : Signal (NOT ondat(s)  =>
{1}     (cbit(s) = 0  AND NOT whitelist(catcode(s))   AND
                NOT undef(catcode(s))  AND  NOT no©inf(catcode(s))   =>  NOT scms(s)! )  AND
{2,6}   (cbit(s) = 0  AND whitelist(catcode(s))  =>  id6(scms(s)) = 10)  AND
{3}     (cbit(s) = 1  AND  lbit(s) = 0  AND
                NOT undef(catcode(s))  AND  NOT no©inf(catcode(s))   =>  id6(scms(s)) = 00)  AND
```

(cbit(s) = 1 AND lbit(s) = 1 AND
NOT undef(catcode(s)) AND NOT no©inf(catcode(s)) => id6(scms(s)) = 11) AND
{4} (undef(catcode(s)) => NOT id6(scms(s)) = 10) AND
{5} (no©inf(catcode(s)) => NOT id6(scms(s)) = 11))
AND
FORALL c : Carrier
{7} (dat(c) AND original(c) AND ©(contains(c)) = true => id6(contains(c)) = 11) AND
(dat(c) AND original(c) AND ©(contains(c)) = false => id6(contains(c)) = 00)

Proof. Follows from axiom {10}, using the partition of signals in four categories given by axiom {7}, the four possible values of rr given in 5.1(i) and the relation between rr and scms given in the definition of rr.

The non-underlined part of lemma 7.1 reflects the quoted part of [USD89] rather faithfully (the bracketed numbers correspond to the paragraphs); however, the underlined parts have not in any way been represented in [USD89]. They concern the behaviour of the SCMS on signals s with $rr(s) \geq 2$ coming from a device mentioned in the White List. Now the problem is that there are devices with type code in the White List that transform signals (e.g. D/D converters). These devices will receive signals of every possible rr-value (0,1,2 or inf): they should not change the rr value, so their output can have any of these four values. These values can be coded with the C and the L bit, but as a consequence every combination of values of these bits will have a different meaning and should be treated differently by other devices, such as a DAT recorder. By [USD89] (see paragraphs 1 and 2 of the quoted part in § 6), the value 0 for the C bit has to be used for the case that rr(s) = 0 or rr(s) = 1, so a C bit with value 1 indicates rr(s) = 2 or rr(s) = inf; the L bit will have to distinguish between these cases. But this is not reflected in any part of the description in [USD89].
Consider e.g. signals s from an A/D converter (so rr(s) = 2) that have passed a D/D converter. According to [USD89] (paragraph 3 of the quoted part in § 6), they can be recorded on DAT with rr-value inf! This would mean a serious leakage of the SCMS. Of course, it is very well possible that this has to do with the fact that a fully correct implementation of the SCMS according to the specifications is impossible without requirements on the behaviour of digital signal transformers, and they fall outside the scope of the Amendment in this version.
So either all signal transformers behave according to TDESIGN and the SCMS described in [USD89] is defective, or there are signal transformers that do not code the rr value properly in the C and the L bit, which makes any attempt to an implementation of the SCMS satisfying SPEC of no avail.

We end with a few other consequences of TDESIGN.

7.2. Lemma. In TDESIGN the following assertions hold:
i) FORALL d : Device s : Signal (undef(typecode(d)) AND apply(d,s)! => rr(s) = 1)
ii) FORALL d : Device s : Signal (no©inf(typecode(d)) AND apply(d,s)! => rr(s) = 2)
iii) FORALL s : Signal (undef(typecode(source(s))) => ©(s) = true)
iv) FORALL s : Signal (no©inf(typecode(source(s))) => NOT ©(s)!)

Proof. Straightforward, apply axioms {9}, {10} and the definition of rr.

These properties can be interpreted as requirements imposed on devices with type code satisfying undef and no©inf. E.g. (i,ii) say that such devices should not be able to transform digital signals (at least not in a invertible way), otherwise the SCMS is circumvented by applying them to signals that should not be recorded (rr(s) = 0), inverting their transformation of the signal (if necessary) and then recording (which is possible, for the rr-value is 1 or 2).

8 Final remarks

We have demonstrated above that it is very well possible to use the formal design language COLD-K adequately in the development of a design for the SCMS. It yields the well-known benefits of formal development: clarity, generality, precision and verifiability. Moreover, it reveals shortcomings of the original standard (see §7). On the other hand, these formal designs did not play a major role in the actual development process of the SCMS standard, as we explained in 1.1. The main reasons for this are:
- the usability of formal methods is restricted, due to lack of expertise;
- aspects of politics and negotiating are very important in the process of developing a standard with controversial aspects like the SCMS, and they may be at odds with the precision inherent in formalization;
- the work reported here is in fact an example of retroactive formalization and this is a notoriously problematic activity: we quote from [B*90, p. 67]:

> While retroactively applying formal methods is possible when an existing standard requires revision, perhaps updating and clarification, such retroactive application of formal methods can cause major problems. ... In most cases, it might be more sensible simply to abandon a nonformal standard and start again from scratch. After all, exercises in retroactive formalization tend to reveal such a lack of conceptual integrity and clarity in a standard that the revised standard would bear little resemblance to the original.

Nevertheless, we think that is it worthwhile to perform case studies with formal design languages in the context of standardisation. This can take place in the first phase of the three-phase-plan to introduce formal methods into standards, recommended by the International Standards Organization in [ISO87] (see also [B*90]).

Could this exercise in formal development also have been performed with another specification language (e.g. VDM or Z) instead of COLD-K? The answer is: yes, of course, for these three languages (and others) have a lot in common. The next question: does the choice for another language lead to a different design process, or is this roughly language-independent? This question probab;y has an affirmative answer, too; however, it is well imaginable that interesting information concerning the use and applicability of several features of these languages can be obtained from a comparison of case studies based on the same subject matter. We think that this case study could very well act as starting point for such a comparison.

References

[B*90] D. Blyth, C. Boldyreff, C. Ruggles, N. Tetteh-Lartey, *The case for formal methods in standards*, IEEE Software (September 1990) 65 - 67

[B91] R.J. Bril, *A model-oriented method for algebraic specification using COLD-1 as notation*, these Proceedings (1991)

[F*87] L.M.G. Feijs, H.B.M. Jonkers, C.P.J. Koymans, G.R. Renardel de Lavalette, *Formal definition of the design language COLD-K*, Technical Report, ESPRIT project 432, Doc.Nr. METEOR/t7/PRLE/7 (1987)

[H84] D. Harel, *Dynamic logic*, in: Handbook of Philosophical logic, vol. II (D. Gabbay, F. Guenthner, eds.) Reidel (1984) 497 - 604

[ISO87] *JTC1 Statement of Policy on Formal Description Techniques*, ISO/IEC JTC1 N145 and ISO/IEC JTC1/SC18 N1333, International Standard Organization, Geneva (1987)

[J89] H.B.M. Jonkers, *An introduction to COLD-K*, in: *Algebraic methods: Theory, Tools and Applications* (M. Wirsing, J.A. Bergstra, eds.) Lecture Notes in Computer Science 394, Springer-Verlag (1989) 139 - 205

[J90] C.B. Jones, *Systematic Software Development using VDM (second edition)*, Prentice-Hall (1990)

[J91a] H.B.M. Jonkers, *Description of COLD-1*, Technical Report, ESPRIT 2565 (1991)

[J91b] H.B.M. Jonkers, *Upgrading the pre- and post-condition technique*, these Proceedings (1991)

[KR89a] C.P.J. Koymans, G.R. Renardel de Lavalette, *The logic MPL_ω*, in: *Algebraic methods: Theory, Tools and Applications* (M. Wirsing, J.A. Bergstra, eds.) Springer Lecture Notes in Computer Science 394, Springer-Verlag (1989) 247 - 282

[KR89b] C.P.J. Koymans, G.R. Renardel de Lavalette, *Inductive definitions in COLD-K*, Logic Group Preprint Series 50, Department of Philosophy, University of Utrecht (1989)

[M90] C.A. Middelburg, *Syntax and semantics of VVSL, a language for structured VDM specifications*, Ph.D. thesis, University of Amsterdam (1990)

[MR91] C.A. Middelburg, G.R. Renardel de Lavalette, *LPF and MPL_ω - A logical comparison of VDM-SL and COLD-K*, these Proceedings (1991)

[R89] G.R. Renardel de Lavalette, *COLD-K^2, the static kernel of COLD-K*, Report RP/mod-89/8, Software Engineering Research Centre, Utrecht (1989)

[USA89] *United States Delegation Submission to the International Electrotechnical Commission regarding Digital Audio Interface Standards and Digital Audio Tape Recorders*

[USD89] *United States Digital Audio Tape Recorder Act*, Draft 11/16/89

Appendix

Here we give the definition of two class descriptions: the Booleans true and false, and the natural numbers extended with the infinite value inf.

```
LET BOOL :=
CLASS
      SORT Bool
      FUNC true : Bool
      FUNC false : Bool
      AXIOM true! AND false! AND NOT true = false AND
            FORALL b : Bool (b = true OR b = false)
END

LET NATINF :=
CLASS

      SORT Natinf

      FUNC 0 : -> Natinf
      FUNC 1 : -> Natinf
      FUNC 2 : -> Natinf
      FUNC inf : -> Natinf
      FUNC S : Natinf -> Natinf

      AXIOM NOT S(0) = 0
      AXIOM S(0) = 1 AND S(1) = 2 AND S(inf) = inf
      AXIOM FORALL n : Natinf S(n)!
      AXIOM FORALL m,n : Natinf (S(m) = S(n) => m = n)

      PRED finite : Natinf
            IND finite(0) AND FORALL n : Natinf (finite(n) => finite(S(n)))

      AXIOM FORALL n : Natinf (finite(n) OR n=inf)
```

{This axiom makes induction over the finite numbers possible.}

```
      FUNC pd : Natinf -> Natinf
            IND FORALL n : Natinf pd(S(n)) = n
```

{So pd, the predecessor function, is undefined on 0 and leaves inf unchanged.}

```
      FUNC _+_ : Natinf # Natinf -> Natinf
            IND FORALL m,n : Natinf (0+n = n AND S(m)+n = S(m+n) AND inf+n = inf)

END
```

Specification and Refinement in an Integrated Database Application Environment*

Klaus-Dieter Schewe, Joachim W. Schmidt, Ingrid Wetzel
Universität Hamburg, Fachbereich Informatik
Schlüterstr. 70, D-W2000 Hamburg 13, FRG

Abstract

Traditionally, substantial portion of database application semantics are captured through static and dynamic integrity constraints. The work reported in this paper exploits this fact by interpreting such database constraints as invariants and pre- and postconditions in the style of 'Z' [ScPi87,Spi88].

Database applications are specified by a conceptual modelling language close to TAXIS [MBW80], which has been enriched by constructs for a predicative specification style. Conceptual designs of database applications are formally analyzed for consistency and are refined, step by step, into efficient extended relational implementations. The reification of designs into implementations uses the formal framework of Abrial's Abstract Machines and generalized substitutions [Ab89].

It is shown that a small set of standard refinement rules is sufficient for a wide class of refinements. Furthermore, it is argued that the proposed *proof*-based approach has significant advantages over the traditional database technique, which *tests* constraints expensively at transaction commit time.

1 Introduction

Most of the semantics of data-intensive information systems can be captured in terms of integrity constraints as well as pre- and postconditions. This makes database applications a good candidate for the application of formal specifications. The complexity of the programs (transactions) to be specified may be small, but the data they act upon are very large, long-lived, sharable by many programs, and subject to numerous rules of consistency. These requirements result directly from the fact that databases serve as (partial) representations of some organizational unit or physical structure that exist in their own constraining context and on their own time-scale independent of any computer system. Hence, in contrast to applications like numerics or process control, the emphasis is on the preservation of data consistency.

This paper reports about results achieved in the FIDE* project which extend our previous efforts** [BMSW89] on the reification of conceptual designs in the semantic data

*This work has been supported in part by research grants from the E.E.C. Basic Research Action 3070 FIDE: "Formally Integrated Data Environments".

**DAIDA ("Development of Advanced Interactive Data-intensive Applications") was an ESPRIT project funded by the E.E.C under research contract 892.

and transaction language *TDL* [BMS87] based on formal specifications and stepwise refinement in Abstract Machines [Ab89]. Exploiting the fact that predicative specifications can be expressed by equivalent substitutions, we outline an automatic transformation of a TDL design into an Abstract Machine. Refinements of this initial machine can be achieved using a set of standard refinement rules, which depend on the chosen target language *DBPL* [SEM88], an efficiency-oriented extended relational database programming language.

1.1 The Conceptual Design Language TDL

TDL is a language that describes data as classes of objects related by attributes. Database states correspond to the extent of these data classes. A variety of different data classes is supported: basic classes are predefined and enumerated classes are used to model simple value sets. Complex values denoting tuples of other values are modelled by aggregate classes. Entities in the application domain are modelled by *entity classes.* Specific integrity constraints may be assigned to the attributes of entity classes such as attribute categories, range constraints and general invariants.

Attribute categories can be used to characterize the values of an object to be changing or unchanging during the object's lifetime or unique within the class. Range restrictions require the values of the attribute to belong to some other class.

Atomic state transitions are modelled as instances of *transaction classes*, where the input/output of a transaction and its actions are described by appropriate attributes and logical formulas. The body of a transaction is specified using the pre-/post style of 'VDM' or 'Z' [BjJo82,Spi88,ScPi87]. Preconditions are given via the keyword *GIVEN*, whereas postconditions require the keyword *GOALS*.

Inheritance is supported for data classes as well as for transaction classes, allowing the organization of objects and the reuse of transaction specifications.

We give the TDL description for a small database example dealing with project management:

```
TDLDESIGN ResearchCompanies IS
  ENUMERATED CLASS Agencies = {'ESPRIT, 'DFG, 'NSF, ...};
  ENTITY CLASS Companies WITH
    UNIQUE, UNCHANGING name : Strings;
    CHANGING engagedIn : SetOf Projects;
  END Companies;
  ENTITY CLASS Employees WITH
    UNCHANGING name : Strings;
    CHANGING belongsTo : Companies; worksOn : SetOf Projects;
    INVARIANTS onEmpProj: True IS
        ( THIS.worksOn ⊆ THIS.belongsTo.engagedIn);
  END Employees;
  ENTITY CLASS Projects WITH
    UNIQUE, UNCHANGING name : Strings; getsGrantFrom : Agencies;
    CHANGING consortium : SetOf Companies;
    INVARIANTS onProjComp: True Is
        ( THIS.consortium = { EACH x ∈ Companies : THIS ∈ x.engagedIn});
```

```
  END Projects;
  TRANSACTION CLASS HireEmployee WITH
    IN name : Strings; belongs : Companies; works : SetOf Project;
    OUT, PRODUCES e: Employees;
    GOALS (e'.name = name) AND (e'.worksOn = works) AND
         (e'.belongsTo = belongs);
  END HireEmployee;
END ResearchCompanies;
```

Briefly summarized, TDL is a language for describing the management of data maintained as *classes of objects related by attributes.* The state of the database is reflected by the extents of the classes, and the values of objects' attributes, which are subject to certain integrity constraints. *Transactions* are atomic state changes. TDL also introduces *functions* to aid in the expression of assertions, *scripts* to aid the description of global control constraints and *communication* facilities to support the frequent needs of information systems for message passing, coordination and timing constraints.

1.2 The Implementation Language DBPL

The database programming language DBPL [SEM88] integrates an extended relational view of database modelling into the programming language Modula-2. Based on integrated programming language and database technology, it offers a uniform framework for the implementation of data-intensive applications.

DBPL provides a new data type *relation* which allows to introduce relational database modelling to be coupled with the expressiveness of the programming language. This new datatype is orthogonal to the existing types of Modula-2, hence sets of arrays, arrays of relations, records of relations, etc. can be modelled.

Complex *access expressions* as usual in relational databases allow to abstract from iteration. Modules can be qualified to be database modules, which turns the variables in them to be persistent and shared. Specific procedures are characterized to be *transactions* denoting atomic state changes on persistent data. Therefore, DBPL provides mechanisms for controlled concurrent access to such data and for recovery.

Let us now illustrate the simple TDL-example above in DBPL notation:

```
DEFINITION MODULE ResearchCompaniesModule;
  IMPORT Identifier,String;
  TYPE
    Agencies = (ESPRIT, DFG, NSF, ..);
    CompNames, EmpNames,ProjNames = String.Type;
    EmpIds = Identifier.Type;
    ProjIdRecType =
         RECORD projName : ProjNames; getsGrantFrom : Agencies END;
    ProjIdRelType = RELATION OF ProjIdRecType;
    CompRelType = RELATION compName OF
         RECORD compName : CompNames; engagedIn : ProjIdRelType END;
    EmpRelType = RELATION employee OF
         RECORD employee : EmpIds; empName : EmpNames;
```

```
            belongsTo : CompNames; worksOn : ProjIdRelType END;
    ProjRelType = RELATION projId OF
        RECORD projId : ProjIdRecType;
            consortium : RELATION OF CompNames END;
  TRANSACTION hireEmployee(empName:EmpNames;belongs:CompNames;
        works:ProjIdRelType) : EmpIds;
END ResearchCompaniesModule
```

```
DATABASE IMPLEMENTATION MODULE ResearchCompaniesModule;
  IMPORT Identifier;
  VAR compRel : CompRelType;
      empRel : EmpRelType;
      projRel : ProjRelType;
  TRANSACTION hireEmployee (name:EmpNames;belongs:CompNames;
        works:ProjIdRelType) : EmpIds;
    VAR tEmpId : EmpIds;
    BEGIN
      IF SOME c IN compRel (c.compName = belongs) AND
        ALL w IN works (SOME p IN compRel[belongs].engagedIn (w = p))
      THEN tEmpId := Identifier.New;
        empRel :+ EmpRelType{{tEmpId,name,belongs,works}};
        RETURN tEmpId
      ELSE RETURN Identifier.Nil
      END
    END hireEmployee;
END ResearchCompaniesModule
```

2 A Formal Framework for the Reification Process

In order to produce high-quality database application systems, we have to guide users in mapping TDL-designs to DBPL-implementations:

- for a given TDL-design there are many substantially different DBPL-implementations, and it needs human interaction to make and justify decisions that lead to efficient implementations;
- the decisions are too complex to be made all at once; it needs a series of refinement steps referring to both data and procedural objects;
- the objects and decisions relevant for the refinement process need to have formally assured properties that should be recorded to support overall product consistency and evolution.

To meet the above requirements we have chosen Abrial's Abstract Machines [Ab89] as a formal basis for the mapping and the B-Tool for the verification of proof obligations.

2.1 The Abstract Machine Formalism

An Abstract Machine specification consists of two components, namely its state space specification, and its state transition specification.

2.1.1 The Static Component of an Abstract Machine

The specification of a state space is given by a list of variable names, called the **state variables** and by a list of well-founded formulas of a many-sorted first-order language $\mathcal{L}$ called the **invariant** and denoted by $\mathcal{I}$. Free variables occurring in $\mathcal{I}$ must be state variables. Each state variable belongs to a unique **basic set**, which has to be declared in some context. Hence, in order to complete the state space specification we must give a list of **contexts** that can be seen by the machine.

Such a context is defined by a list of *basic sets*, a list of *constant names* and a list of closed formulas over the language $\mathcal{L}$ called *properties*. A basic set may be either the set of natural numbers, an abstract set given only by its name, a set given by the enumeration of its elements or a constructed set, where cartesian product, powerset and partial function space are the only allowed constructors. We may then assume to have a fixed preinterpretation of these sorts s by sets $\mathcal{D}_s$. Then the state space of an Abstract Machine with state variables $x_1, ..., x_n$ is semantically denoted by the set

$$\Sigma \;=\; \{\sigma : \{x_1, .., x_n\} \rightarrow \mathcal{D} \mid \sigma(x_i) \in D_{s_i} \; for \; all \; i\},$$

where each s_i is the sort of the variable x_i and $\mathcal{D}$ denotes the union of the sets $\mathcal{D}_s$.

The language $\mathcal{L}$ associated with an Abstract Machine can then easily be formalized. The basic sorts of $\mathcal{L}$ are NAT and the other non-constructed basic sorts. The set of sorts is recursively defined using the basic sorts and the sort constructors *pow*, $\times$, $\mapsto$ denoting powerset construction, cartesian products and partial functions.

Since we use a fixed preinterpretation of the sorts as sets, one may regard the elements of these sets as constant symbols in $\mathcal{L}$ of the corresponding sort. Other function symbols are given by the usual functions $+$, $*$ on NAT, $\cup$, $\cap$, $\setminus$ on powersets or by the constant declarations in some context. The terms and formulas in $\mathcal{L}$ are defined in the usual way. The semantics of $\mathcal{L}$ is given by an interpretation $(\mathcal{A}, \sigma)$, where $\mathcal{A}$ is a structure extending the preinterpretation on sorts and σ is a variable binding.

We assume $\mathcal{A}$ to be fixed and write $\models_\sigma \mathcal{R}$, iff $\mathcal{R}$ is true under the interpretation $(\mathcal{A}, \sigma)$.

A wff $\mathcal{R}$ of $\mathcal{L}$ such that the free variables of $\mathcal{R}$ are state variables denotes a subset of Σ, namely

$$\Sigma_{\mathcal{R}} \;=\; \{\sigma \mid \models_\sigma \mathcal{R}\}.$$

Hence the invariant serves as a means to distinguish legal states in $\Sigma_{\mathcal{I}}$ from others.

2.1.2 The Dynamic Component of an Abstract Machine

The specification of *state transitions* is given through an **initialization** assigning initial values to each of the state variables and **transactions** that update the state space. Both kinds of state transitions are specified using the substitutions introduced by Dijkstra [DiSc89] with the additional possibility of unbounded choice:

$@z\bullet(P \rightarrow S)$ used as an abbreviation for an IF with an infinite list of guarded commands of the form $P(z) \rightarrow S(z)$, i.e. select any value for z such that P is true and execute the operation S' resulting from S by replacement of all free occurrences of z in S by the selected value. Clearly, if such a value for z does not exist, the @-substitution fails to terminate.

The semantics of substitutions S is given by means of two specific predicate transformers $wlp(S)$ and $wp(S)$, which satisfy the *pairing condition*, i.e. for all predicates $\mathcal{R}$

$$wp(S)(\mathcal{R}) \equiv wlp(S)(\mathcal{R}) \wedge wp(S)(true)$$

and the *conjunctivity condition*, which states for any family $(R_i)_{i \in I}$ of predicates

$$wlp(S)(\forall i \in I.\, R_i) \equiv \forall i \in I.\, wlp(S)(R_i)\ .$$

These conditions imply the conjunctivity of $wp(S)$ over non-empty families of predicates. As usual $wlp(S)$ will be called the **weakest liberal precondition** of S, and $wp(S)$ will be called the **weakest precondition** of S. The notation f^*, which we shall use later, denotes the **conjugate predicate transformer** of f. It is defined by

$$f^*(\mathcal{R}) \equiv \neg f(\neg\mathcal{R})\ .$$

The definitions of $wlp(S)$ and $wp(S)$ for all the substitutions that we allow are given in [DiSc89] or can be easily derived from there. For more details see [SSW+91]. In addition to the properties stated above we have for any substitution S

$$wp(S)(false) \equiv false\ .$$

This is the **Law of Excluded Miracles**. The related work by the PRG group [MRG88] and by J.-R. Abrial dispenses with this law. The main reason not to follow them is that we do not see any need for miracles. A more detailed discussion on the consequences implied by the introduction of miracles can be found in [SWS91].

2.1.3 On the Semantics of Abstract Machines

First we may associate a set-theoretic meaning to the substitutions of an Abstract Machine in terms of the state space. For this purpose we introduce the **characteristic predicate** P_σ of a state $\sigma \in \Sigma$ as

$$P_\sigma \equiv x_1 = \sigma(x_1) \wedge \cdots \wedge x_n = \sigma(x_n).$$

Characteristic predicates have only one model, i.e. $\Sigma_{P_\sigma} = \{\sigma\}$. Then we may associate with a substitution S the following set of state pairs

$$\Delta(S) = \{(\sigma_1, \sigma_2) \in \Sigma \times \Sigma \mid\models_{\sigma_1} wlp(S)^*(P_{\sigma_2})\}.$$

Since $wlp(S)^*(P\sigma_2)$ characterizes the states σ_1 such that there exists a computation of S in σ_1 leading to σ_2, $\Delta(S)$ describes the set of possible state transitions on Σ under control of S.

In addition, we need to know the subset of Σ that allows some computation of S not to terminate, this is given by

$$\Sigma_0(S) = \{\sigma \in \Sigma \mid \models_\sigma wp(S)^*(false)\}.$$

Summarizing, the set-theoretic semantics for substitutions is captured by a pair of assignement functions (Δ, Σ_0), with signature

$$\begin{aligned} \Delta &: S \rightarrow pow(\Sigma \times \Sigma) \; and \\ \Sigma_0 &: S \rightarrow pow(\Sigma). \end{aligned}$$

Then the global semantics of an Abstract Machine can be given in terms of traces on Σ, i.e. a set of finite of infinite sequences $\sigma = \sigma_o, \sigma_1, \sigma_2, \cdots$ of states $\sigma_i \in \Sigma$ such that the following conditions are satisfied:

(i) for all $\sigma_{-1} \in \Sigma$ we have $(\sigma_{-1}, \sigma_0) \in \Delta(S_0)$, where S_0 is the initialization,

(ii) for each $i > 0$ there is a transaction in S with $(\sigma_{i-1}, \sigma_i) \in \Delta(S)$,

(iii) if $t = \sigma_0, \sigma_1, \cdots, \sigma_n$ is finite, then there is a transaction S with $\sigma_n \in \Sigma_0(S)$.

2.2 Verification

In the following we describe which properties must be verified to assure transaction consistency and correct refinement. Then we indicate how to use a mechanical theorem proving assistant to guide the proofs.

2.2.1 Transaction Consistency Proof Obligation

The invariant component of an Abstract Machine states properties defining the set of legal states. Therefore, it is necessary to check that the transactions of the Abstract Machine always preserve the invariant.

In fact, if S is a transaction, it should be sufficient to require each terminating execution starting from a state satisfying the invariant $\mathcal{I}$ to result also in a state satisfying $\mathcal{I}$. As to the initialization S_0, we should require that any computation results in a state satisfying $\mathcal{I}$ no matter which was the initial state. Hence the following formal definition.

Definition 2.1 (Consistency) *Let M be an Abstract Machine with invariant $\mathcal{I}$.*

(i) A substitution S in M is consistent *$\mathcal{I}$ iff $\mathcal{I} \Rightarrow wlp(S)(\mathcal{I})$.*

(ii) M is consistent *iff all transactions S in M are consistent with respect to $\mathcal{I}$ and the initialization S_0 satisfies $wp(S_0)(\mathcal{I})$.*

2.2.2 Refinement Proof Obligation

Refinement is used as a means to map specifications down to implementations. This includes refining the operations as well as transforming the state space into a more suitable form. We shall first address operational refinement.

The intention behind refinement of an operation S is to eliminate step by step all non-terminating computations under control of S and to cancel some of the non-deterministic computations. Moreover, the remaining computations of S should establish at least the same final states. These considerations lead to the following formal definition:

Definition 2.2 (Operational Refinement) *Let S and T be two substitutions on the same state variables. Then T* **refines** *S iff the following three conditions hold for all predicates $\mathcal{R}$:*

(i) $wlp(S)^*(true) \Longrightarrow wlp(T)^*(true)$

(ii) $wlp(S)^*(true) \Longrightarrow (wlp(S)(\mathcal{R}) \Rightarrow wlp(T)(\mathcal{R}))$

(iii) $wp(S)(\mathcal{R}) \Longrightarrow wp(T)(\mathcal{R})$

We shall now give another form of these proof obligations that does not require a universal quantification over predicates.

Proposition 2.1 (Normal Form Proof Obligation) *Let S and T be substitutions with state variables $x_1, \ldots, x_n$. Let $z_1, \ldots, z_n$ be another bunch of variable names such that the x_i and the z_j are mutually different. Let x and z be the usual abbreviations for these bunches of variables. Then T refines S iff:*

(i) $(z = x) \wedge wlp(S)^*(true) \Longrightarrow wlp(T)^*(true) \wedge wlp(\{x/z\}.T)(wlp(S)^*(z = x))$ *and*

(ii) $(z = x) \wedge wp(S)(true) \Longrightarrow wp(T)(true)$

As to data refinement, the usual approach taken by [Ab89] [MRG88] is to use an abstract predicate $\mathcal{A}$ involving the state variables of both the substitutions of S and T. Assume that these state variables are mutually different. According to proposition 2.1 we define in this spirit:

Definition 2.3 *Let M, N be Abstract Machines with mutually different state variables x and z. Let $\mathcal{A}$ be some predicate on x and z. Then N* **refines** *M iff there is a bijection σ from the transactions of M to those of N such that for all pairs S, $T = \sigma(S)$ of transactions we have:*

(i) $\mathcal{A} \wedge wlp(S)^*(true) \Longrightarrow wlp(T)^*(true) \wedge wlp(T)(wlp(S)^*(\mathcal{A}))$ *and*

(ii) $\mathcal{A} \wedge wp(S)(true) \Longrightarrow wp(T)(true)$.

Syntactically, the abstraction predicate $\mathcal{A}$ is used in data refinement is added to the specification of the refined machine N using the additional keyword $CHANGE$.

2.2.3 The B Proof Assistent

The B-Tool [GAM+88] is a general proof assistant and uses a goal-oriented proof technique based on Gentzen's calculi. The built-in logic performs simple and multiple substitution and is designed to suit best the calculus of substitutions.

For the practical work with the B-Tool it is essential that proofs can be organized such that any unreducable goals (e.g., in lack of appropriate theories or in case of not provable predicates) are generated as lemmata. The proof of a lemma can be postponed, and the initial proof can go on. Typical examples of such delayed proof obligations refer to lemmata that express type assertions or arithmetic properties. Therefore, as a result of a proof, some lemmata may be left, which may be proven by the tool in a further step using additional theories. The B-tool can been used for two purposes:

- We used the built-in rewriting capability for a purely syntactical transformation of the TDL design into a first Abstract Machine. By this we exploited the fact that pre-post-specifications as they are used in TDL are equivalent to substitutions.
- We used B's capability as a theorem prover in order to prove the consistency of a machine and the refinement relation between two machines.

3 The Reification of TDL Designs

The purpose of designs is the exact representation of application semantics without taking care of efficiency criteria. For this purpose we used the design language TDL.

The purpose of implementations is to represent applications such that they can be executed efficiently. DBPL is a database programming language satisfying this requirement. The goal of the mapping process is to close the conceptual gap between these two layers by the exploitation of standard refinement steps. In order to use the Abstract Machines for this purpose we have to address three problems:

- represent designs in Abstract Machines, i.e. transform a TDL-description into an Abstract Machine,
- identify final specifications in Abstract Machines that can be transformed automatically into DBPL-programs, and
- identify standard refinement steps within Abstract Machines that are directed towards such final specifications.

3.1 Transformation of TDL-Designs into Abstract Machines

The transformation of a TDL-design into an Abstract Machine can be realized in a straightforward way. Each basic class and each each enumerated class in TDL gives rise to a basic set. The same applies to aggregate classes. The difference is that basic sets corresponding to enumerated classes are themselves given by enumeration, whereas basic sets corresponding to aggregate classes are constructed as cartesian products. Moreover, entity classes e constitute abstract basic sets E, but in addition they also give rise to state variables e of sort $pow(E)$. As usual with Abstract Machines [Ab89] these sort constraints are formulated as invariants.

Each attribute a of each entity class e will be transformed into a state variable plus an integrity constraint restricting the possible values of a to functions $a \rightarrow b$, where b is either the state variable associated with the range of the attribute or a basic set. In either case the associated sort is $A \mapsto B$, where A, B are the corresponding sorts. In order not to loose the naming information, B may be renamed, i.e. we introduce further constructed basic sets.

The attribute qualifier UNIQUE gets transformed into an invariant stating that the function associated with the attribute is injective. CHANGING can be neglected, since all state variables in Abstract Machines can be updated. UNCHANGING, however, would give rise to a dynamic constraint. Such constraints can not be formalized in Abstract Machines, but in an extension to them [SWS91]. Invariants in TDL can be translated directly into AM invariants.

As to transaction classes they can be translated into substitutions exploiting a weak equivalence between substitutions and pre-/post-specifications [Ab89,SSW+91]. However, inheritance on transaction classes affords another extension to Abstract Machines, i.e. the specialization of substitutions. This problem has been handled in [SWS91].

Then the initial Abstract Machine resulting from our previous TDL example looks as follows:

```
CONTEXT researchCompanies1.ctx
  BASIC SETS
    Agencies = { ESPRIT, DFG, NSF, ...};
    Companies;
    Employees;
    Projects;
    STRING = ...;
    CompNames, EmpNames, ProjNames = STRING;
END researchCompanies1.ctx

MACHINE researchCompanies1.mch
  SEES researchCompanies1.ctx
  VARIABLES companies, compName, engagedIn,
    employees, empName, belongsTo, worksOn,
    projects, projName, getsGrantFrom, consortium
  INVARIANTS companies ∈ pow(Companies);
    compName ∈ (companies → CompNames);
    engagedIn ∈ (companies → pow(projects));

    employees ∈ pow (Employees);
    empName ∈ (employees → EmpNames);
    belongsTo ∈ (employees → companies);
    worksOn ∈ (employees → pow (projects));

    projects ∈ pow(Projects);
    projName ∈ (projects → ProjNames);
    getsGrantFrom ∈ (projects → Agencies);
    consortium ∈ (projects → pow(companies));

    ∀x,y. x,y ∈ companies ⇒ (compName(x) = compName(y) ⇒ x = y);
    ∀x. x ∈ employees ⇒ (worksOn(x) ⊆ engagedIn(belongsTo(x));
    ∀x,y. x,y ∈ projects ⇒ (projName(x) = projName(y)
        ∧ getsGrantFrom(x) = getsGrantFrom(y) ⇒ x = y);
    ∀x. x ∈ projects ⇒ (consortium(x) = {y | y ∈ companies ∧ x ∈ engagedIn(y)});
  OPERATIONS e ⟵ hireEmployee (name, belongs, works) =
      IF ( name ∈ EmpNames ∧ belongs ∈ companies ∧
            works ∈ pow (engagedIn(belongs)) ⟶
      ( @ e • (e ∈ (Employees - employees)) ⟶
        empName(e), worksOn(e), belongsTo(e) := (name, works, belongs) ||
        employees := employees ∪ {e} ))
      FI
```

END hireEmployee;
End researchCompanies1.mch

3.2 Standard Refinement Steps

Let us now describe a bunch of different standard refinement steps that turned out to be sufficient for the mapping task from TDL to DBPL.

3.2.1 Data Identification Rules

The first refinement rules address the basic issues of *data identification*. The transformation process introduced abstract surrogates for classes in the initial abstract machine. However, data identification in our target language is only possible via keys, since DBPL is completely value-oriented. Therefore we have to replace the surrogates by identifying attributes.

More formally, in the initial context we have an abstract basic set, say A and in the initial Abstract Machine we have a state variable, say a together with an invariant $a \in pow(A)$. If there exists another state variable y together with invariants

$$y \in a \rightarrow B \text{ and } \forall x_1, x_2.(x_1 \in a \wedge x_2 \in a \Rightarrow (y(x_1) = y(x_2) \Rightarrow x_1 = x_2)) \, ,$$

i.e. that y defines a key constraint, we introduce a new variable a' in our refined machine together with the invariants $a' \in pow(B)$ and $\forall x.(x \in a' \Rightarrow y(x) = x)$. The context will be extended by $A = B$, i.e. the abstract set A will be replaced by a constructed set, and the CHANGE-predicate simply gets $x = x'$. This rule can be easily generalized to the case of more than one function y serving as a combined key.

In case there is no such state variable y, i.e. there is no key attribute, we use a second rule, which introduces a new abstract basic set B and a new state variable y together with the invariant $y \in a \rightarrow B$ and an injectivity constraint on y. We may then apply the first rule to the result of the second one.

In our example we applied the first rule to $A = Companies$, $a = companies$, $y = compName$ and $B = Companies$. The generalization of the first rule has been applied to $A = Project$, $a = projects$, $y_1 = projName$, $B_1 = ProjNames$, $y_2 = getsGrantFrom$ and $B_2 = Agencies$. We applied the second rule to $A = Employees$ and $a = employees$ introducing $B = EmpIds$, and $y = empId$. Then we could apply rule 1 to the result introducing $a' = empIds$. Hence, the result of the complete data identification step is as follows (we omit the effect on the *hireEmployee* operation):

BASIC SETS EmpIds;
Companies = CompNames;
Projects = ProjNames × Agencies;
Employees = EmpIds; ...

VARIABLES compnames, projectIds, empId, empIds...

CHANGE companies = compnames;
employees = empIds;
project = projIds;

INVARIANTS compnames ∈ pow(CompNames);

$\forall x.\ x \in compnames \Rightarrow (compName(x) = x);$

$empIds \in pow\ (EmpIds);$
$empid \in (empIds \rightarrow EmpIds);$
$\forall x.\ x \in empIds \Rightarrow (empId(x) = x);$

$projIds \in pow(Projects);$
$\forall x.\ x \in projIds \wedge \exists x_1, x_2.\ x = (x_1, x_2) \Rightarrow (projName(x) = x_1 \wedge$
$getsGrantFrom(x) = x_2);$

In general, data identification transforms unique attributes to keys and introduces artificial keys in case there is no identifying attribute.

3.2.2 Identifier Generation Rule

Substitutions in the initial Abstract Machine may involve an unbounded non-deterministic choice (@-substitution). Data identification does not affect this, it only transforms the condition on the value to be selected into the selection of fresh key values. Moving down to our target language we have to introduce a deterministic operation that delivers a fresh key. The corresponding refinement rule replaces the @-substitution by a sequence of the identifier generating operation followed by the previous assignment.

More formally, the substitution $@z \bullet (z \in Id \longrightarrow S(z))$ will be replaced by $z \leftarrow NewId(); S(z)$, where NewId is the identifier generating substitution, which has no input-parameter, but produces the output z.

Another operational refinement rule can be used to replace the parallel assignment in S by a sequence of assignments.

In our example the operation *hireEmployee* becomes more deterministic. The new operation in researchCompanies3.mch looks as follows:

```
tEmpId ⟵ hireEmployee (name, belongs, works) =
    IF ( name ∈ EmpNames ∧ belongs ∈ compnames ∧
          works ∈ pow (engagedIn(belongs))  ⟶
       tEmpId ⟵ NewEmpId() ;
       empIds := empIds ∪ {tEmpId} ;
       empId(tEmpId) := tEmpId ;
       empName(tEmpId) := name ;
       worksOn(tEmpId) := works ;
       belongsTo(tEmpId) := belongs )  FI
```

3.2.3 Data Structuring Rules

The data identification step introduced keys. However, another fundamental difference between the underlying data models of TDL and DBPL concerns the functional view in TDL in contrast to the relational view in DBPL. So far, we have state variables that are either subsets of some basic set or functions defined on such a set. Moving towards a relational view we have to combine functions having the same domain and to introduce more complex ranges.

More formally, we are given state variables $a, y_1, \ldots, y_n$ together with invariants $a \in pow(A)$ and $y_i \in a \rightarrow B_i$. The first idea is to replace the y_i by a new state variable y with the invariant $y \in x \rightarrow B_1 \times \ldots \times B_n$. However, due to data identification we know more about the functions y_i. The first m of these functions are simple projections to the components of a. Hence the new invariant on y is

$$y \in b_1 \times \ldots \times b_m \rightarrow B_{m+1} \times \ldots \times B_n .$$

As CHANGE-predicates we get $b_i = range(y_i)$ for $i = 1, \ldots m$ and $y_j = \pi_{j-m} \circ y$ for $j = m+1, \ldots, n$, where π_k denotes the k-th natural projection on $B_{m+1} \times \ldots \times B_n$.

In our example we apply this rule to $a = empIds$, $a = compnames$ and $a = projectIds$. In the first case the result is as follows:

VARIABLES empClass, ...
CHANGE empName = $\pi_1 \circ$ empClass;
    belongsTo = $\pi_2 \circ$ empClass;
    worksOn = $\pi_3 \circ$ empClass;
INVARIANTS empClass $\in$ empIds $\rightarrow$ EmpNames $\times$ compnames $\times$ pow(projIds);

Another refinement rule may be used to flatten the state variables, i.e. to remove set-valued attributes. To be more precise, assume the existence of an invariant $y \in a \rightarrow B_1 \times \ldots \times B_n$ with $B_i = pow(B)$ for some i (say $i = n$ without loss of generality), where a may be any domain (not necessarily a state variable). Then we may introduce two new state variables y_{flat} and y_{B_n} together with the invariants

$$y_{flat} \in a \rightarrow B_1 \times \ldots \times B_{n-1} \text{ and } y_{B_n} \in a \leftrightarrow B_n$$

and the CHANGE-predicates

$$y_{flat} = \pi_{1,\ldots,n-1} \circ y \text{ and } y_{B_n} = \{(x, b) \mid b \in \pi_n \circ y(x)\}$$

In our example this could be applied to $y = empClass$. However, our target language DBPL does not force us to use only first normal form relations. Hence it is an explicit decision to use this second rule or not. We omit the details concerning the example. Especially we omit the straightforward effect on the operation *hireEmployee*.

3.2.4 Data Typing Rules

Since DBPL is a strongly and statically typed database programming language, the next refinement step has to introduce *data types*. The main effect is on the basic sets. Each function invariant, say $y \in a \rightarrow b$ gives rise to a new constructed basic set $R = A \mapsto B$. In addition we get a new state variables y' together with the invariant $y \in R$ and the CHANGE-predicate $domain(y') = a$ and $\forall x . x \in a \Rightarrow y(x) = y'(x)$. In our example this leads to the introduction of basic sets that are equivalent to relation types in DBPL:

BASIC SETS ProjIdRecType = ProjNames × Agencies;
  ProjIdRelType = pow (ProjIdRecType);
  CompRelType = (CompNames +→ ProjIdRelType);
  EmpRelType = (EmpIds +→ EmpNames × CompNames × ProjIdRelType);
  ProjRelType = (ProjIdRecType +→ pow (CompNames));

VARIABLES compRel, empRel, projRel
CHANGE compRel = compClass ;
empRel = empClass ;
projRel = projClass ;
INVARIANTS compRel $\in$ *CompRelType;*
empRel $\in$ *EmpRelType;*
projRel $\in$ *ProjRelType;*

The effect on the *hireEmployee* operation is straightforward:

```
tEmpId ⟵ hireEmployee (name, belongs, works) =
    IF ( ∃ c . belongs ∈ domain(compRel) ∧
      ∀ w . w ∈ works ⇒ w ∈ π1(compRel(belongs)) ) ⟶
      tEmpId ⟵ NewEmpId() ;
      empIds := empIds ∪ {tEmpId} ;
      empId(tEmpId) := tEmpId ;
      empName(tEmpId) := name ;
      worksOn(tEmpId) := works ;
      belongsTo(tEmpId) := belongs ) FI
```

4 Conclusion

Database applications require the conceptual specification of highly structured and interrelated data. It is the complexity of data that makes database application development a hard task, whereas most operations on the data are rather easy such as simple insert, delete and update operations. Integrity constraints on the data are normally expressed by first-order predicates. Thus, the possibility to explicitly represent such constraints makes TDL a good choice for conceptual database design.

The reification of TDL designs in an extended relational database programming language is too complex to be automated, thus requires a mapping process. Based on the experience of the DAIDA project we used the formalism of Abstract Machines as a formal framework for this task, since they allow at the same time the semantics of TDL-designs to be captured and the procedurality required by efficiency-oriented database programs to be introduced via refinement.

Moreover, most commercial database systems do not offer any sophisticated mechanism in order to prove consistency. Integrity checking is done at run-time before transaction commit. In our approach, however, we were able to prove the consistency already at specification time. Transactions are modeled via operations in Abstract Machines, and consistency is semi-automatically verified using the B proof assistent.

Another positive experience we made with Abstract Machines is the possibility to refine a specification within one and the same language. This poses the strong requirement on formal specification languages to capture at the same time the semantics of a high-level conceptual design language and of an efficient implementation language. Moreover, we could show that mapping TDL designs to DBPL programs only requires a small set of standard refinement rules.

Our current work is built upon this preserving the style of transaction specifications. We are working on a new formal specification language that essentially allows to structure and modularize specifications and to capture particular classes of constraints by its type system. First intermediate results on this new language have been reported in [SWS91].

References

[Ab89] J. R. Abrial: *A Formal Approach to Large Software Construction*, in J.L.A. van de Snepscheut (Ed.): *Mathematics of Program Construction*, Proc. Int. Conf. Groningen, The Netherlands, June 89, Springer LNCS 375, 1989

[BjJo82] D. Bjørner, C. B. Jones: *Formal Specification and Software Development*, Prentice Hall, 1982

[BMS87] A. Borgida, J. Mylopoulos, J. W. Schmidt: *Final Version on TDL Design*, DAIDA deliverable

[BMSW89] A. Borgida, J. Mylopoulos, J. W. Schmidt, I. Wetzel: *Support for Data-Intensive Applications: Conceptual Design and Software Development*, Proc. of the 2nd Workshop on Database Programming Languages, Salishan Lodge, Oregon, June 1989

[DiSc89] E. W. Dijkstra, C. S. Scholten: *Predicate Calculus and Program Semantics*, Springer-Verlag, 1989

[GAM+88] P. Gardiner, J.-R. Abrial, C. C. Morgan, J. M. Spivey, T. N. Vickers: *The logic of 'B'*, Technical Report, Oxford Programming Research Group, September 1988

[MRG88] C. Morgan, K. Robinson, P. Gardiner: *On the Refinement Calculus*, Technical Monograph PRG-70, Oxford University Computing Labaratory, Oktober 1988

[MBW80] J. Mylopoulos, P. A. Bernstein, H. K. T. Wong: *A Language Facility for Designing Interactive Database-Intensive Applications*, ACM ToDS, vol. 5 (2), April 1980, pp. 185 – 207

[SSW+91] K.-D. Schewe, J. W. Schmidt, I. Wetzel, N. Bidoit, D. Castelli, C. Meghini: *Abstract machines revisited*, FIDE technical report 1991/11

[SWS91] K.-D. Schewe, I. Wetzel, J. W. Schmidt: *Towards a Structured Specification Language for Database Applications*, Proc. Int. Workshop on the Specification of Database Systems, Glasgow, July 1991

[SEM88] J. W. Schmidt, H. Eckhardt, F. Matthes: *DBPL Report*, DBPL-Memo 111-88, University of Frankfurt, 1988

[ScPi87] S. A. Schuman, D. H. Pitt: *Object-Oriented Subsystem Specification*, in L. Meertens, (Ed.): *Program Specifiation and Transformation*, The IFIP TC2/WG2.1 Working Conference, Bad Tölz, FRG, April 1986, North Holland Publishing Co, 1987

[Spi88] J. M. Spivey: *Understanding Z, A Specification language and its Formal Semantics*, Cambridge University Press, 1988

Techniques for Partial Specification and Specification of Switching Systems

Pamela Zave
AT&T Bell Laboratories
Murray Hill, New Jersey 07974

Michael Jackson
101 Hamilton Terrace
London NW8 9QX

Abstract

This paper reports on results obtained by specifying the connection patterns within a small PBX using Z. We discuss techniques for specification of switching systems, including how to model the state space of a feature-rich switching system, how to use the schema calculus for organizing a complex operation set, and how to realize the potential benefits of a partial specification. We also outline a new approach to constructing a specification as a composition of partial specifications written in different formal languages.

1 Introduction

We are engaged in a research project with two goals: to understand how to specify real switching systems, and to understand how to specify systems as compositions of partial specifications (with each partial specification being written in the language best suited to the properties it is intended to describe). The project includes construction and validation of a formal specification of a small PBX;[1] this PBX is based on a popular product line.

The PBX offers a variety of features to its users, including the ability to make several different types of connection within the switch. (Section 2 gives an overview of these features.) Certain patterns of connection are illegal, however. This aspect of the system is difficult to understand because there are many illegal patterns and they can be formed in many different ways. There is Morgan's precedent for using Z to represent connections in switching systems [6], so we decided to specify this aspect of the PBX in Z. This paper reports on the results of the case study.

Section 3 focuses on techniques for specification of switching systems. We present a formal model of the state space of connections that is significantly different from Morgan's, but more appropriate for specifying the feature-rich switching systems being produced today. We explain several sources of complexity in the operation set, and show how aggressive use of the schema calculus can be used to manage it. We also show how a partial specification such as ours—covering only one, narrow aspect of the system—can be used to enhance software quality and productivity.

[1] A Private Branch eXchange is a private switching system; it enables a group of telephones to share lines connecting the PBX to a central telephone exchange.

Constructing specifications as compositions of partial specifications written in different languages would have many important advantages, but there are difficult unsolved problems standing between us and that goal. Section 4 enumerates the problems, outlines a new approach to composition of partial specifications, and shows how the approach addresses the problems. The presentation is illustrated with examples from the PBX specification. This section is a sketchy, preliminary report, both because of lack of space and because our work in this area is not yet mature.

This case study is a good application for state-oriented specification languages such as Z and VDM. For the most part we are satisfied with Z. Its deficiencies, as indicated by this case study, are discussed along with related topics in Sections 3 and 4. The notation of Spivey's reference manual [7] is used throughout.

2 Connection Features of the PBX

The PBX that is the subject of this case study supports *stations* (telephones) with the capacity to participate in many connections simultaneously. Each connection in which a station participates must be associated with a resource (consisting of both hardware and software) through which the connection is identified and controlled. The hardware portion of this resource includes two lights for displaying the status of the connection and a button for selecting that connection. Because the capabilities and functions of this resource are similar to those of an ordinary household telephone, we call each instance of the resource a *virtual telephone* (VT).

At any time one VT (and sometimes more than one; see below) at a station is *selected*, and therefore has control of station resources such as the voice channel, speaker, microphone, and dialpad. This multiplexing leads to significant complications. The user can accomplish the equivalent of taking a household telephone offhook, for instance, either by taking the station offhook and then selecting the desired VT, or by selecting the desired VT and then taking the station offhook. Either way, we call the second event of the sequence an *open* with respect to the VT. Similarly, the effect of hanging up a household telephone is achieved by going onhook or by selecting a different VT than the one now selected (either way, we call it a *close* with respect to the VT). In the latter case, selecting a different VT closes the current VT and opens the new VT simultaneously.

When a VT is engaged in a connection, it can be put on *hold*. It is then possible to hang up or select a different VT without disturbing the connection of the held VT. The user can return to the held connection by re-opening it.

There are two types of VT. An *intercom virtual telephone* (IVT) is used for making calls between stations attached to the PBX; each station has two of these resources. To make a simple intercom call the user opens an IVT, gets an intercom dialtone, and dials the intercom number of the desired station. The call is received by the first idle IVT at the dialed station, if any, where it rings with a special intercom ringing cadence.

A *trunk* is a line from the PBX to a central telephone exchange (from the viewpoint of the central exchange the trunks behave exactly like ordinary household lines). The PBX may have a number of trunks, and for any trunk, any station may have a *trunk virtual telephone* (TVT) used exclusively for access to that trunk. If a TVT is open, then it is automatically connected to its trunk. Several TVTs on different stations can be

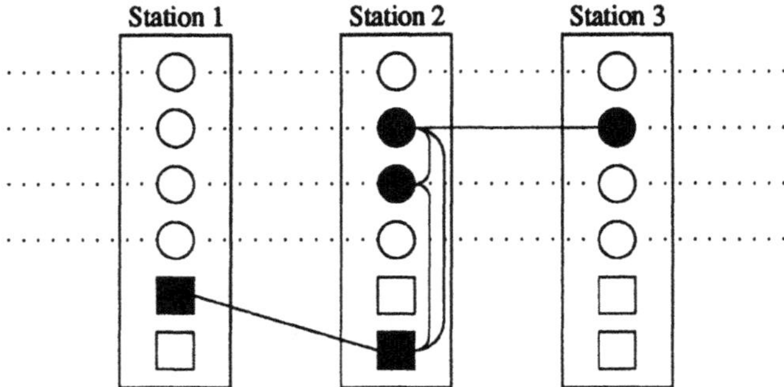

Figure 1: Examples of all three types of connection. Circles represent TVTs, while squares represent IVTs. Dotted lines represent trunks, and solid lines represent direct connections between VTs. Black VTs are connected.

connected to the same trunk simultaneously, which provides a multiparty feature called *bridging*. There is a *privacy* feature, however, that prevents a TVT from bridging onto a trunk whenever any station already connected to the trunk has privacy turned on.

The *conference* feature is used to connect several VTs at the same station, so that the parties they are connected to will also be connected. When a VT is already in a talking (and therefore selected) state, a conference is formed by pressing the station's conference button and then selecting another VT to be added to the conference. Afterwards both VTs are selected, and even more VTs can be added to the conference. A VT can be *dropped* from a conference by pressing the station's drop button and then selecting the VT to be dropped.

Figure 1 illustrates these concepts using a schematic notation. There is an intercom connection between Stations 1 and 2, and a conference at Station 2. Stations 2 and 3 are both connected to the same trunk, and therefore connected to each other.

3 Techniques for Specification of Switching Systems

3.1 State-Space Modeling for Feature-Rich Switching Systems

Almost all the formal specifications of switching systems that we have seen assume Plain Old Telephone Service (POTS), in which a telephone can only be connected to one other telephone (there are recent examples written in Timed CSP [5], LOTOS [2], and functional notation [1]). Although this is understandable—most people have nothing more than POTS at home—the fact is that current switching systems offer hundreds of features, and manufacturers of switching systems are under tremendous pressure to provide ever more features, faster, to their customers. It is clear that techniques for specifying feature-rich switches are needed.

An exception to the POTS rule is provided by Morgan's specification [6], which represents a connection as a set of telephones. Morgan points out that a conference call is a connected set whose size is greater than two. This model is faithful to the idea that all connections are alike because they all enable users of different telephones (actual or virtual) to talk to each another. But connections formed by different features are rarely alike in the constraints they must satisfy, or in the protocols for their creation and destruction. Connected sets alone are not adequate for specifying feature-rich switches, because it is necessary to use a representation of connections capable of distinguishing between connections made by different features. Our first modeling decision was to represent intercom connections (formed by intercom calls), trunk connections (formed by trunk calls and bridging), and conference connections (controlled by the conference and drop features) separately.

Each type of connection could be represented as a set of sets of VTs (this is Morgan's approach) or as a symmetric binary relation on VTs. Since the characteristics of the types of connection are different, some types are more easily represented as sets of sets, while the others are more easily represented as binary relations. The deciding factor is the need to combine the three representations. In Figure 1, for instance, the black VTs in Stations 1 and 3 are connected to each other because there is a path between them made up of connections of all three types. If connections of the three types are all represented as binary relations, then the relation of the black VT in Station 1 to the black VT in Station 3 is expressed effortlessly as the transitive closure of the union of the three relations.

The final modeling decision concerns the binary relations representing the different types of connection. Should they be transitively closed, or should they include only the direct connections created by the features? There are minor differences in ease of manipulation, but the biggest difference between these alternatives is that the closed relations include the identity relations on their domains, but the direct-connection relations do not. Direct-connection relations are more convenient because they allow us to determine whether a VT is connected simply by testing whether it is in the domain of the appropriate relation. Any query or constraint concerning connections, of course, must be phrased in terms of the transitive closure of the appropriate relation.

The basic types of the Z specification are *STATION* (the set of stations), *TRUNK* (the set of trunks), *IVT*, and *TVT*. *VT* is the set of all virtual telephones, defined as the union of *IVT* and *TVT*.

There are two global variables that represent the configuration of the PBX, *i.e.*, which stations and trunks the VTs are assigned to. There is also a global variable representing the privacy status of the stations. Changes to these variables are outside the scope of this specification.

$$\textit{ivt-assignment}: IVT \rightarrowtail\!\!\!\!\twoheadrightarrow STATION \times \{\ 1,\ 2\ \}$$

$$\textit{tvt-assignment}: TVT \rightarrowtail STATION \times TRUNK$$

$$\textit{private}: STATION \rightarrow \{\ \textit{true},\ \textit{false}\ \}$$

Two auxiliary functions are helpful in accessing these global variables while defining predicates.

$$\textit{station}: VT \rightarrow STATION$$
$$\textit{station} == (\textit{ivt-assignment} \cup \textit{tvt-assignment}) \mathbin{;} \textit{first}$$

$$\textit{trunk}: TVT \rightarrow TRUNK$$
$$\textit{trunk} == \textit{tvt-assignment} \mathbin{;} \textit{second}$$

There is a schema for each of the direct-connection relations (all of which are initially empty). The predicates in these schemas state that the relations are symmetric and irreflexive (as explained above), and give other properties of the relations based on how the features of the PBX work.

Intercom-Connections

$ic\text{-}conn\colon IVT \leftrightarrow IVT$

$\forall v1,v2{:}IVT \bullet (v1,v2) \in ic\text{-}conn \Rightarrow (v2,v1) \in ic\text{-}conn$
$ic\text{-}conn \cap id\ IVT = \emptyset$
$\forall v1,v2{:}IVT \bullet (v1,v2) \in ic\text{-}conn^* \Rightarrow (v1 = v2) \vee (station(v1) \neq station(v2))$
$\forall v{:}IVT \bullet \#\ ic\text{-}conn^* (\!|\ \{ v \}\ |\!) \leq 2$

Trunk-Connections

$tk\text{-}conn\colon (TRUNK \leftrightarrow TVT) \cup (TVT \leftrightarrow TRUNK)$

$\forall v{:}TVT,\ t{:}TRUNK \bullet (v,t) \in tk\text{-}conn \Leftrightarrow (t,v) \in tk\text{-}conn$
$\forall v1,v2{:}TVT \bullet (v1,v2) \in tk\text{-}conn^* \Rightarrow trunk(v1) = trunk(v2)$
$\forall v1,v2{:}TVT \bullet (v1,v2) \in tk\text{-}conn^* \Rightarrow (v1 = v2) \vee (station(v1) \neq station(v2))$

Conference-Connections

$conf\text{-}conn\colon VT \leftrightarrow VT$

$\forall v1,v2{:}VT \bullet (v1,v2) \in conf\text{-}conn \Rightarrow (v2,v1) \in conf\text{-}conn$
$conf\text{-}conn \cap id\ VT = \emptyset$
$\forall v1,v2{:}VT \bullet (v1,v2) \in conf\text{-}conn^* \Rightarrow station(v1) = station(v2)$

Note that direct trunk connections connect TVTs to their trunks; it is only by transitivity that TVTs become trunk-connected to each other. A direct trunk connection can also be thought of as a voice connection between the TVT and the outside party that the trunk is connected to through the central telephone exchange.

The *conn* relation (representing all connections) is simply the union of *ic-conn, tk-conn,* and *conf-conn.* Just as in Morgan's specification, it is often important to represent a maximal set of VTs, all of which are connected. Instead of representing connected sets explicitly, however, we derive them from the connection relations by means of the following function:

$$connected\text{-}set: \mathbb{P}\, VT \rightarrow \mathbb{P}\, VT$$
$$connected\text{-}set(vs) == conn^* \,(\!|\; vs \;|\!)\, \cap VT$$

It is also necessary to represent the set of stations involved in a connected set, which is:

$$station\text{-}set: \mathbb{P}\, VT \rightarrow \mathbb{P}\, STATION$$
$$station\text{-}set(vs) == station \,(\!|\; connected\text{-}set(vs) \;|\!)$$

The state space of the specification is defined by the following schema, combining the three direct-connection relations. The predicates in this schema state the five constraints restricting the connection patterns of the PBX. These constraints are all global, in the sense that they all involve more than one type of connection. They are also different from the predicates of the previous schemas in that they require active enforcement by the PBX—a user may request illegal connections, but the system must refuse those requests.

Connections

Intercom-Connections
Trunk-Connections
Conference-Connections

$\forall\, v{:}VT \bullet \#\, (conf\text{-}conn^* \,(\!|\; \{\, v \,\} \;|\!)\, \cap TVT) \leq 2$
$\forall\, v1,v2{:}IVT \bullet v1 \in \mathbf{dom}\; conf\text{-}conn \wedge (v1,v2) \in ic\text{-}conn^* \Rightarrow$
$\quad (v1 = v2) \vee (v2 \notin \mathbf{dom}\; conf\text{-}conn)$
$\forall\, v1,v2{:}TVT \bullet v1 \in \mathbf{dom}\; conf\text{-}conn \wedge (v1,v2) \in tk\text{-}conn^* \Rightarrow$
$\quad (v1 = v2) \vee (v2 \notin \mathbf{dom}\; conf\text{-}conn)$
$\forall\, v1,v2{:}VT \bullet \{\, v1,v2 \,\} \subseteq (connected\text{-}set(\{\, v1 \,\}) \setminus \mathbf{dom}\; conf\text{-}conn) \Rightarrow$
$\quad (v1 = v2) \vee (station(v1) \neq station(v2))$
$\forall\, v{:}VT \bullet \#\, station\text{-}set(\{\, v \,\}) \leq 3$

The first constraint is that a conference (*i.e.,* a conference-connected set of VTs) cannot include more than two TVTs. The second constraint says that an intercom connection cannot be involved in conferences at both ends, while the third constraint says that a trunk cannot be involved in more than one conference. Because of the second and third constraints, all of the conference-connected VTs in a connected set must be located at one station. The fourth constraint concerns the subset of a connected set that is not involved in conference connections, and says that all its members must be assigned to different stations. The fifth constraint is simply that a connected set cannot involve more than three stations. Figures 2, 3, and 4 illustrate connection patterns that violate the second, third, and fourth constraints, respectively.

3.2 Using the Schema Calculus for Organizing a Complex Operation Set

Our specification must include operations covering every situation in which a connection is created or destroyed, specifying the correct changes in the system state. The operations

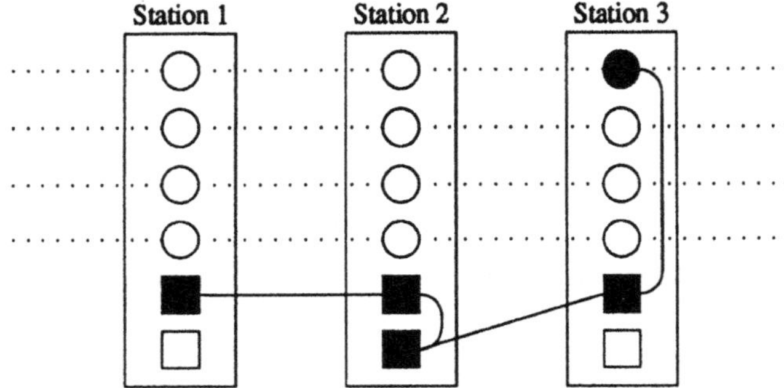

Figure 2: The intercom connection from Station 2 to Station 3 is involved in conferences at both ends, which is illegal.

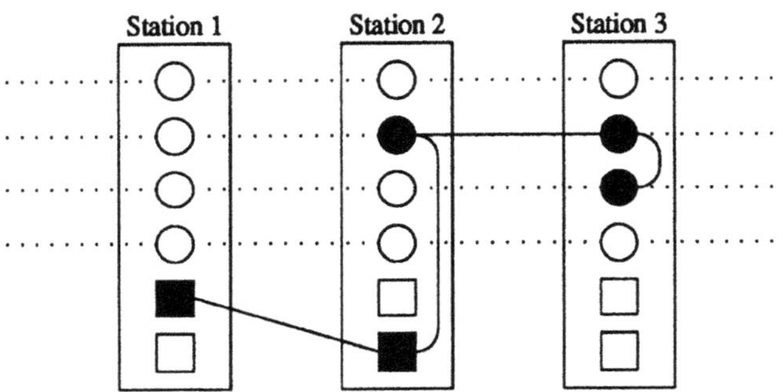

Figure 3: The second trunk is involved in conferences at two different stations, which is illegal.

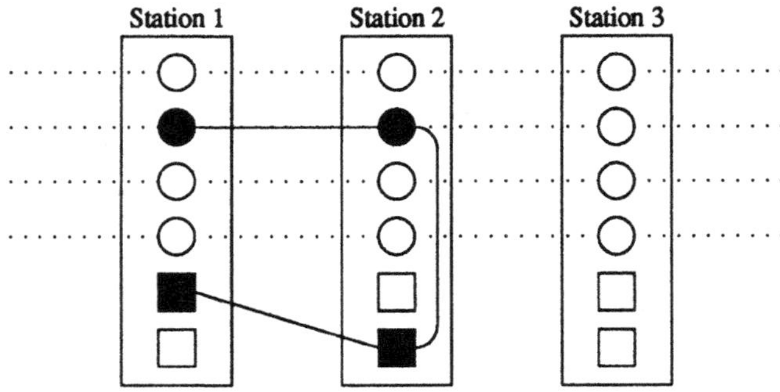

Figure 4: Two VTs at Station 1 are connected to each other but not conference-connected, which is illegal.

concerned with creation of connections must actually cover all *requests* for connections; they must check whether the requested connections would violate any constraints, and only create the requested connections if they are legal. There is a staggering number of situations to cover. We began our work on this specification by enumerating interesting situations, and found over a hundred of them indispensable to understanding the problem and designing the operation set.

Published examples of Z specifications often show the use of schema operators to separate successful operations from error cases (as in Spivey's tutorial introduction [7]). The techniques presented in this section share the same spirit, but push the use of the schema calculus much further in the interest of managing the complexity of the operation set.

Each operation of the specification must specify a new value for all three direct-connection relations. It is highly desirable, however, to specify updates to each relation separately. This simplifies proofs of all theorems having to do with individual relations. It also makes the basic update schemas reusable in different operations. So we begin by defining three simple schemas for each direct-connection relation: one to create connections of that type (*-Connect*), one to destroy them (*-Disconnect*), and one to specify that the relation does not change (*-Identity*).[2] Creation of an intercom connection is specified by:

$$ic\text{-}conn' = ic\text{-}conn \cup \{\ (v1?,v2?),\ (v2?,v1?)\ \}$$

where $v1?$ and $v2?$ are the two IVTs being intercom-connected. Creation of a trunk connection is specified by:

$$tk\text{-}conn' = tk\text{-}conn \cup \{\ (v?,trunk(v?)),\ (trunk(v?),v?)\ \}$$

where $v?$ is the TVT being connected to its trunk. Finally, creation of a conference connection is specified by:

$$conf\text{-}conn' = conf\text{-}conn \cup (\{\ v?\ \} \times vs?) \cup (vs? \times \{\ v?\ \})$$

where $v?$ is the new VT being added to the conference, and $vs?$ is the conference-connected set of VTs to which it is being added. Note that $v?$ is directly connected to every member of $vs?$, as there is no member of $vs?$ to which $v?$ is more directly connected than any other.

An operation that updates (at most) a single relation, such as *Trunk-Connect-Attempt*, can now be specified as:

$$Trunk\text{-}Connect\text{-}Attempt \mathrel{\widehat=} \ldots \wedge Intercom\text{-}Identity \wedge Conference\text{-}Identity$$

where the ellipsis replaces a schema expression for the attempted trunk-connection operation. The more complex operation *Trunk-and-Conference-Connect-Attempt* occurs when a user of a station has made a talking connection, then presses the conference button followed by the selection button of a TVT. If the TVT is not already connected and held, and the operation is successful, then this operation forms a trunk connection and a conference connection simultaneously. It is therefore specified as:

[2] At this point we must begin to omit portions of the specification, for lack of space. The entire operation set is specified in 14 operation schemas and 18 schema definitions using the schema calculus, and is available from the authors.

Trunk-and-Conference-Connect-Attempt $\hat{=}$... *Intercom-Identity*

where the ellipsis replaces a potential update to both *tk-conn* and *conf-conn*.

Previous case studies have shown the value of using separate schemas to specify successful and failing operations, such as (in this case) legal and illegal connection attempts. We also separate the preconditions for a legal connection attempt from the connection operation itself, so that successful connection operations are defined by schema expressions such as:

Effective-Trunk-Connect-Attempt $\hat{=}$ *Legal-Trunk-Connect-Attempt* $\wedge$ *Trunk-Connect*

Effective-Conference-Connect-Attempt $\hat{=}$
Legal-Conference-Connect-Attempt $\wedge$ *Conference-Connect*

This has the advantage that the preconditions for an illegal attempt, which are extensive in themselves, are defined simply by negating the *Legal- ... -Connect-Attempt* schemas.

We also make a further distinction between *effective* and *ineffective* operations, where an ineffective operation may be legal in itself but cannot be carried out because a companion operation is not legal. This enables us to deal with failures of operations that update two relations, which can occur because the preconditions for either update are not satisfied. Thus the definition of *Trunk-and-Conference-Connect-Attempt* is:

Trunk-and-Conference-Connect-Attempt $\hat{=}$
(*Effective-Trunk-and-Conference-Connect-Attempt* $\vee$
Ineffective-Trunk-and-Conference-Connect-Attempt) $\wedge$ *Intercom-Identity*

Effective-Trunk-and-Conference-Connect-Attempt $\hat{=}$
Effective-Trunk-Connect-Attempt $\wedge$ *Effective-Conference-Connect-Attempt*

Ineffective-Trunk-and-Conference-Connect-Attempt $\hat{=}$
(*Illegal-Trunk-Connect-Attempt* $\vee$ *Illegal-Conference-Connect-Attempt*)
$\wedge$ *Trunk-Identity* $\wedge$ *Conference-Identity*

Finally, there are situations (described in Section 2) in which a single button push simultaneously closes one VT and opens another. In some of these situations, the close is a disconnection and the open is a connection attempt. These situations are covered by operations defined in terms of sequential composition of schemas, for example

Disconnect-then-Intercom-Connect-Attempt $\hat{=}$
Disconnect $\fatsemi$ *Intercom-Connect-Attempt*

This construction enables us to make a new operation out of two previously defined operations, both of which are designed to update the entire state space. It is also appropriate to use sequential composition of schemas because the disconnection may make the connection attempt legal, even if it would not have been legal before the disconnection; by handling this case as if the disconnection preceded the connection attempt, we make the specified services as permissive as possible. No matter how we look at it, however, the formal semantics of *Disconnect-then-Intercom-Connect-Attempt* is that of an atomic operation on the state space.

Z provides no formal means of representing the operation set of a specification (by which we mean the set of operations that the state space may be subjected to at any time, at the whim of the specified system's environment). For instance, a specification may contain operation schemas P and Q, and also the definition $R \mathrel{\widehat{=}} P \wedge Q$, but there is no way to specify formally whether the operation set is $\{ R \}$ (in which case P and Q were invented simply to make R easier to define) or $\{ P, Q, R \}$.

In our specification these distinctions are extremely important, because so many operation schemas are combined in so many different ways. *Intercom-Connect-Attempt*, for example, is an operation of the specification in its own right, and is also used as a component of the schema expression defining *Disconnect-then-Intercom-Connect-Attempt*. We have taken care to use comments to identify the exact operation set, but it is disturbing that a property so essential to the real meaning of the specification is not part of its formal semantics.

3.3 Realizing the Potential Benefits of a Partial Specification

Proofs of the properties of direct-connection relations, such as these properties of *tk-conn*,

$$\forall\, v1, v2{:}TVT \bullet (v1,v2) \in tk\text{-}conn^* \Rightarrow trunk(v1) = trunk(v2)$$
$$\forall\, v1, v2{:}TVT \bullet (v1,v2) \in tk\text{-}conn^* \Rightarrow (v1 = v2) \vee (station(v1) \neq station(v2))$$
$$tk\text{-}conn^* = tk\text{-}conn^2$$

have proven valuable in establishing the consistency and completeness of the specification. We are less satisfied, however, with the utility of proofs of the global constraints in the *Connections* schema.

The problem is illustrated by the preconditions needed to ensure that an attempted conference connection does not violate this constraint:

$$\forall\, v{:}VT \bullet \#\, station\text{-}set(\{ v \}) \leq 3$$

There are three cases to consider. In the broadest case of adding VT $v?$ to the conference-connected set $vs?$, it must be true that

$$\#\, station\text{-}set(vs? \cup \{ v? \}) \leq 3$$

which is straightforward enough. If $v?$ is an idle IVT, however, then it must be true that

$$\#\, station\text{-}set(vs? \cup \{ v? \}) \leq 2$$

The reason is that the user's usual next step is to place a new intercom call connecting $v?$ to another IVT. Since the other IVT cannot be located at a station in $station\text{-}set(vs? \cup \{ v? \})$, due to other constraints, the new intercom connection is guaranteed to increase the size of the station set by one. Finally, if $v?$ is an idle TVT, and if there is a TVT $v1?$ already connected to $v?$'s trunk, then it must be true that

$$\#\, station\text{-}set(vs? \cup \{ v1? \}) \leq 3$$

The reason for this precondition is that when $v?$ becomes connected, $v1?$ will automatically become part of its connected set.

If only the first precondition of these three were needed, the proof of the global constraint could be written in a calculational style [3], and would enjoy the attendant succinctness, rigor, and mathematical insight. But, as the other preconditions show, the required reasoning is heavily dependent on case analysis in the application domain. Since there is a limit to our ability to map the complexities of the application domain onto standard mathematics, there is also a limit to the extent to which mathematics can assist our powers of reasoning.

The preceding observations may be interesting, but they digress from the actual topic of this section. A partial specification such as ours cannot possibly be refined into an implementation, because too much is missing. What else is it good for?

We chose this aspect of the PBX to specify in Z because it is difficult to understand, and seemed likely to benefit from a rigorous treatment. This is precisely the source of the specification's value. The understanding it provides can improve the documentation and user-interface design of the system, simplify the implementation, and lead to highly effective testing.

As evidence for these claims, we used the Z specification to find a number of flaws in the popular PBX on which our specification is based. Of the five global constraints, only two are documented and widely known in the organization responsible for developing the software. We discovered three major ways that the user interface could be made more consistent and forgiving. We tested the PBX in the hundred situations mentioned at the beginning of Section 3.2, and found bugs in 75% of the situations in which the fourth global constraint is violated. Furthermore, we found the general behavior of the PBX in enforcing the global constraints to be highly inconsistent; even when benign, these inconsistencies suggest that the implementation is far more complex and *ad hoc* than it needs to be.

Just as the Z specification enabled us to discover these flaws, it could have enabled the developers of the PBX software to prevent them.

4 An Approach to Composition of Partial Specifications

4.1 Unsolved Problems

The need to construct specifications as compositions of partial specifications, with each partial specification written in the language best suited to the properties it is intended to describe, is an urgent one. Unfortunately, difficult unsolved problems stand between us and this goal. It is necessary to compose specifications written in many different languages, and to enable them to build on each other (in the sense that a mathematical theory is built on a structure of axioms and lemmas). Specifications constructed as compositions of partial specifications must have the same desirable properties as single-language specifications, including implementation-independence and susceptibility to validation operations (such as algorithmic analysis, verification, and simulation). Finally, even though a partial specification may be written in isolation from other specifications (or before they are written), it is necessary to delimit its scope so that it will dovetail with other specifications, and to choose its concepts so that they will be semantically compatible with other specifications.

One possible approach to composition is to treat each partial specification as an executable module that interacts concurrently with other modules [8]. Although this is a natural way to think about multilanguage implementations, it has several serious disadvantages for specification.

The disadvantages of the concurrent-module approach originate in the fact that the interfaces between the modules are operational, *i.e.*, are defined in terms of an execution semantics. This introduces significant implementation bias in a specification: it will be difficult to show that an implementation is correct unless it has exactly the same internal, operational interface. An operational interface is also sensitive to all details, so that it will be very difficult to determine the scope and interface of an early partial specification so that it will work properly with the ones that are written later. A partial specification may have to be changed many times as the work progresses and its interface evolves.

The example of the concurrent-module approach is significant because Z is not designed to be composed in any other way. Consider, for example, the case of successful and failing attempts to create connections in the PBX. Our Z specification determines which attempts should succeed and fail, and there is no doubt that this decision must be communicated to other partial specifications. But since all of the semantics of Z are focused on the state and state changes, there is no way to communicate a decision except to set the value of a result variable. This result variable is an internal, operational interface between specifications. We shall return to this example several times in the next few sections.

4.2 Direct Description

Our new approach is grounded in the notion that the subject of any specification is the observable phenomena of some application domain. The domain of the PBX includes individual objects[3] such as stations and trunks, and individual events such as button pushes, offhooks, and onhooks. The domain also includes conditions of these individuals, such as a condition that a particular TVT is assigned to a particular station and a particular trunk, a condition that a particular station is offhook, or a condition that a particular indicator light is on. Note that all individuals are considered unique and distinguishable, as if they all had names.

A partial specification, regardless of the language it is written in, is simply a description of some relationships in the domain. For instance, it would be easy to use a regular expression or finite-state machine to say that offhook and onhook events at a particular station alternate. The formal semantics of the description is an assertion about certain events and about the *precedes* condition on them. (The precedes condition is automatically defined as true or false for all event pairs in any domain; if it is true for an event pair, then the event playing the *before* role occurs at an earlier time than the event playing the *after* role.)

As for the semantics of the Z specification, the signature of total injection ***tvt-assignment*** in Section 3.1 can be thought of as making an assertion about a domain condition ***is-tvt-assignment*** with roles TVT, station, and trunk. The assertion is that for every individual TVT, ***is-tvt-assignment*** holds with exactly one pair of individuals playing the station and trunk roles, and that this pair is not the assignment of any other TVT.

[3]We do *not* mean "object" as in "object-oriented programming," but simply a thing that exists over time (as opposed to an event, which is instantaneous). We are desperate to find a less overloaded word, and welcome all suggestions.

It is very important to know exactly which domain phenomena are in the scope of a description. The assertion that offhooks and onhooks alternate, for instance, is useless and meaningless if it can be interpreted as constraining some of the offhook and onhook events at a station, but not all of them. We address this issue with the concept of a *selection rule*. A selection rule identifies a set of phenomena as being in the scope of a description.[4] If the description is not true of all the phenomena in its scope, it is simply incorrect.

Given the framework presented so far, composition of partial specifications is simply logical conjunction of their assertions over the domain. The partial specifications are related to each other only because they are all assertions over the same set of phenomena.

Even though our presentation is still incomplete, it is already possible to see how some of the problems enumerated in Section 4.1 are solved by this approach. A language is composable as long as its semantics can be reduced to assertions about a domain of individuals and conditions; this includes all the specification languages we can think of. The scope of a partial specification is not critical because assertions can overlap or even underspecify without the drastic consequences of an operational interface whose gears do not mesh. Implementation independence is guaranteed because nothing is said about anything unless it is part of the application domain and observable to users of the system. The result variable used by Z to indicate the success or failure of a request, for instance, does not fit into this framework because there is no such variable in the PBX domain. In the PBX domain users can only deduce whether their connection requests succeeded from the states of the system after the requests, as indicated by lights and tones.

4.3 Indirect Description and Modality

The framework as presented so far is insufficient because it does not allow partial specifications to build on one another. This section discusses two ways in which partial specifications can be interdependent without compromising any of the advantages claimed in Section 4.2.

A partial specification can take advantage of terminology defined in another partial specification. For instance, a selection rule can identify the domain condition *is-tvt-assignment* in the informal domain, and indicate that it is in the scope of a partial specification written in Z. The Z specification uses it to define a new condition *is-trunk* (as in Section 3.1) with TVT and trunk roles. Another selection rule can identify *is-trunk* as a new condition, and provide it as part of the scope of another partial specification.

For another example, a finite-state machine with offhook, onhook, and some button-push events in its scope (an expanded version of the one mentioned in Section 4.2) can classify some of these events as opens, closes, or both (as explained in Section 2). Just as "offhook" refers to a set of individual domain events, the new term "open" also refers to a set (which just happens to overlap with "offhook," neither containing it nor being contained in it). Another selection rule can identify the new event set as part of the scope of another specification, which will be much easier to write because of the new terminology. Note that this selection rule identifies the set "open" not in the informal

[4]The selection rule can also bind the selected set of phenomena to a name local to the description. This can make a description re-usable in many different contexts.

domain, as before, but in the formal semantics of a finite-state machine. (Typically a finite-state machine classifies events in its scope according to its own local state when the events occur.)

Classification creates new sets of individuals but does not create new individuals themselves. Since we have been careful to ensure the validity of scopes and selection rules when new terminology is being defined, a partial specification with opens and closes in its scope can describe their relation to other domain phenomena, and even constrain further when they can occur. Because opens and closes are defined in a partial specification rather than observed directly in the domain, further constraints on them would be an example of *indirect description.*

Besides making partial specifications easier to write, defined terminology and indirect description also greatly alleviate the problem of writing a set of specifications all based on compatible concepts. The concepts used by different specifications need not be the same at all—they need only be unambiguously definable, by direct or indirect means, from the observable phenomena of the domain.

Classification of events should be used to communicate the results of operations in our Z specification to other partial specifications (if only classification were supported by Z.) Say that some opens are also classified as trunk-connect attempts, and are therefore in the scope of our Z specification. The Z specification could divide this set of events into two subsets, one consisting of successful attempts and the other of failing ones. Other specifications might have one, both, or neither of these event sets in their scopes.

The other way that one partial specification can depend on another is to rely on the truth of its assertions. This is not a simple matter, however, because the meaning of each partial specification is dependent on its *mode.* Modality in specifications addresses questions such as, "Who gets to make the choices?" and "Is this assertion guaranteed by the environment, required of the implementation, or hoped for as an implication of other properties?"

Fortunately, these questions are largely independent of composition itself. Consider, for instance, two partial specifications in different modes: one describes all possible sequences of events that a station can generate (and is therefore guaranteed by the system's environment), and the other describes certain responses to these stimuli that the switching system is required to produce. *If* these descriptions are consistent, then their composition is the conjunction of their assertions, as before. It is the criterion for consistency between them that is determined by their modes; here the criterion is that the second description must allow all the sequences of stimuli that the first one does. The system cannot restrict the stimuli that the environment can generate, nor can it fail to recognize and respond appropriately to all of them.

4.4 Other Observations on the Approach

We are in the midst of formalizing the framework for description and composition, including domain phenomena, scopes, and selection rules. We do not claim to understand modality yet, but are convinced that it is separable from description and composition, and have collected examples of descriptions with many different modes.

One obvious way to compose specifications written in different languages is to translate them all into some suitable logic, as if logic were the "assembly language" of specification.

Our approach is not inconsistent with this simple idea, but adds several not-so-obvious ideas to it:

1. The concepts of domain phenomena, scope, and selection make the relationship between a partial specification and an application domain explicit and precise. Without this rigor, many errors of over- and under-specification are easy to make and difficult to detect [4].

2. New terminology can be defined using the syntax of any specification language; the definition does not have to be translated into logic to be useful.

3. Modality (some notion of which is implicit in every approach to specification) is elucidated so that it can be manipulated explicitly and flexibly.

4. In the long term, we fully expect to define and implement useful operations on sets of partial specifications (such as consistency checks and construction of executable compositions) without first translating all the partial specifications into logic. It will not be possible to do this, however, until the relationships among the partial specifications are better understood. The concepts of description, composition, and modality presented briefly here are leading us steadily toward the necessary level of understanding.

References

[1] Jozef De Man. Description of telecommunication systems by means of a functional language. In *Proceedings of the International Conference on Software Engineering for Telecommunication Switching Systems*, Bournemouth, England, July 1989.

[2] M. Faci, L. Logrippo, and B. Stépian. Formal specifications of telephone systems in LOTOS. Technical Report TR-89-07, Computer Science Department, University of Ottawa, Ottawa, Ontario, Canada, February 1989.

[3] David Gries. Teaching calculation and discrimination: A more effective curriculum. *Communications of the ACM* XXXIV(3):44-55, March 1991.

[4] Michael Jackson. Description is our business. In this volume.

[5] A. Kay and J. N. Reed. A specification of a telephone exchange in Timed CSP. Technical Report PRG-TR-19-90, Programming Research Group, Oxford University Computing Laboratory, Oxford, England, 1990.

[6] Carroll Morgan. Telephone network. In Ian Hayes, editor, *Specification Case Studies*, pages 73-87, Prentice-Hall International, 1987.

[7] J. M. Spivey. *The Z Notation: A Reference Manual.* Prentice-Hall International, 1989.

[8] Pamela Zave. A compositional approach to multiparadigm programming. *IEEE Software* VI(5):15-25, September 1989.

Specification of the MAA Standard in VDM

G I Parkin & G O'Neill
Division of Information Technology and Computing,
National Physical Laboratory, Teddington, Middlesex,
TW11 0LW

August 1991

Abstract

A detailed example is given of how a formal specification language has been used to specify an international banking standard on message authentication. It illustrates how a specification language can be used to specify and validate a standard.

1 Introduction

This paper gives an outline of how a formal specification language was used to specify and validate an international (ISO) banking standard on message authentication (MAA) [1].

The purpose of this paper is to illustrate why standards should be formally specified. It also shows some of the ambiguities in the current version of the message authentication standard.

The remainder of this introduction briefly describes the standard, why it was chosen, the formal language used for the specification and the approach taken in developing the specification. Other sections in the paper give some details of the formal specification, list possible interpretation problems with the standard, and discuss those features in the specification which could give rise to implementation problems. The NPL Report [2] contains the complete formal specification of this standard.

1.1 The MAA standard

The application area of this standard is that of data security in banking and the scope of the standard is message authentication.

A Message Authentication Code (MAC) [3] is a data field (typically a number) attached to a set of data (or message) passing between correspondent financial institutions and transmitted along with that set of data. It is derived from all of the message or from those parts of the message which require protection against any alteration, whether accidental or intentional. The MAC must be the result of an agreed method of calculation known to both the sender and the receiver. One of the algorithms approved in [3] for this purpose is the Message Authenticator Algorithm (MAA) [1] and this is the standard which is the subject of this paper.

1.2 The choice of standard

The work in this paper arose partly out of the wish of members of the National Physical Laboratory staff to gain experience in the application of formal specification languages to data security standards, in the construction of implementations and in the development of conformance tests from these formally defined standards.

The MAA standard was suggested for several reasons. Firstly it is one of the few ISO standards in the data security area which is algorithmic in nature. This would make it relatively easy to write a formal specification of the standard and to implement the specification in a functional, logic or imperative programming language. Secondly staff at NPL were involved in some of the early development work [4] (but did not take part in drafting the standard) and so the topic was a familiar one. Thirdly it has been extensively used for about two years but nevertheless a formal specification of the standard and a validation of that specification would add to the confidence of users in the standard.

1.3 The specification language

The language chosen to specify the MAA was VDM (Vienna Development Method) which is based on discrete mathematics, is documented [5], and has the additional advantages of being in the process of becoming an international (ISO) standard and of being a methodology capable of formalising the software design process.
Since this work was done the MAA has also been specified in Z [6] and LOTOS [7].

1.4 Approach Taken

The approach taken in specifying the MAA took the following steps: 1) Redraft the MAA standard in VDM; 2) Translate the VDM specification into an executable language; 3) Test the implementation of the MAA standard using tests contained in the annex to the standard; and 4) Document the above.

The final document consisted of: The VDM specification along side the text from the MAA standard; and The VDM specification along side its implementation.

The document was designed such that: Any alterations to the VDM specification was automatically reflected through out the document; and Any alterations to the implementation was automatically reflected in the document when reproduced. The above document has been published as an NPL Report [2].

It is clear that there is an analogy between software development and the process of making a standard, see [8] for further details of this.

2 Specification of MAA in VDM

2.1 VDM Style

The following simple guidelines were used in redrafting the MAA in VDM. Firstly write the VDM in a purely functional way so that it could be implemented in a functional, logic or imperative programming language to provide a means of checking the specification using the test data contained in the Annex to the MAA standard. Secondly retain as much of the naming, structure etc. used in the MAA standard as possible. Thirdly follow the style of VDM in [5] and use the LaTeX macros from [9] designed to typeset specifications written in this style. In this paper we have rewritten the VDM in the emerging standard for VDM as described in [10] using a new set of LaTeX macros from [11].

2.2 The Specification

This section, containing an annotated version of the specification with comments on how it was derived from the MAA standard, is divided into the following subsections: **Values**– Global constants used throughout the specification; **Types**– Global types used throughout the specification; **Sections**– Sections in the MAA standard itself referred to by #Section number (where the Section Number is that of the MAA standard).

The VDM will be introduced by text quoted directly from the MAA standard[1], written in sans serif type style and highlighted by a double vertical bar. Comments on the standard or on the VDM specification are highlighted by a single vertical bar and any quotations from the standard inside comments are written in sans serif type.

2.2.1 Values

3.2 Technical

All numbers manipulated in this algorithm shall be regarded as 32-bit unsigned integers, unless otherwise stated. For such a number $N, 0 \leq N < 2^{32}$.

Word-length = 32;

Maximum-Number-Size = (2 ↑ *Word-length*) − 1;

Maximum-Number-Size-plus-1 = *Maximum-Number-Size* + 1;

Maximum-Number-Size-plus-1-*div*-2 = *Maximum-Number-Size-plus*-1 div 2;

Messages shall be input to the algorithm as a sequence of 32 bit numbers, $M_1, M_2, - M_n$, of which there are n, called message blocks ... This algorithm shall not be used to authenticate messages with more than 1 000 000 blocks, i.e. $n \leq 1\,000\,000$.

This extract from the standard defines numbers and message blocks (see 2.2.2 for the corresponding VDM types) and gives the upper limit in blocks for a message.

Maximum-No-of-Message-blocks = 1000000;

4.2.2 The main loop

The numbers A, B, C, D are constants which are, in hexadecimal notation:

Constant A:	0204	0801
Constant B:	0080	4021
Constant C:	*BFEF*	'*7FDF*
Constant D:	*7DFE*	*FBFF*

$A = 2 \times 2 \uparrow 24 + 4 \times 2 \uparrow 16 + 8 \times 2 \uparrow 8 + 1;$

$B = 0 \times 2 \uparrow 24 + 128 \times 2 \uparrow 16 + 64 \times 2 \uparrow 8 + 33;$

[1]Thanks to P Danvers, BSI, Linford Wood, Milton Keynes, MK14 6LE for permission to quote from the standard.

$C = 191 \times 2 \uparrow 24 + 239 \times 2 \uparrow 16 + 127 \times 2 \uparrow 8 + 223;$

$D = 125 \times 2 \uparrow 24 + 254 \times 2 \uparrow 16 + 251 \times 2 \uparrow 8 + 255;$

5 Specification of the mode of operation

Messages longer than 1 024 bytes shall be divided into blocks of 1 024 bytes and chained as follows.

For the first block of 1 024 bytes the MAC (4 bytes) shall be formed. The MAC value shall be prefixed to (but not transmitted in) the second block and the resultant 1 028 bytes authenticated. This procedure shall continue, with the MAC of each block prefixed to the next, until the last block, which need not be of size 1 024 bytes, and the final MAC shall be used as the transmitted MAC for the whole message.

Here the standard defines a message as a sequence of bytes and a block as a sequence of 1024 bytes (this definition of a block can be confused with the definition of a message block as a single 32 bit number, given in #3.2, see section 3.4 for problems of interpretation). Since the specification does not use bytes as a VDM type, the value of the following constant is given in terms of 32 bit numbers.

$\textit{Maximum-No-of-blocks-for-MAC} = 256;$

$\textit{Maximum-No-of-blocks-for-MAC-plus-}1 = \textit{Maximum-No-of-blocks-for-MAC} + 1$

2.2.2 Types

For the definition of a number, see the quoted text from the MAA standard at the start of section 2.2.1.

$\textit{Number} = \mathbb{N}$
inv $N \triangleq N < \textit{Maximum-Number-Size-plus-}1;$

3.2 Technical

Messages to be authenticated may originate as a bit string of any length ... The calculation can be performed on messages as short as one block ($n = 1$).

A message is described above as a sequence of bits with the implication that it has at least one bit in it (see section 3.1 for a discussion of this interpretation).

$\textit{Bit} = \mathbb{N}$
inv $B \triangleq B \in \{0, 1\};$

$\textit{Message-in-bits} = \textit{Bit}^*$
inv $M \triangleq$
  if (len M mod $\textit{Word-length}) = 0$
  then ((len M div $\textit{Word-length}) \leq \textit{Maximum-No-of-Message-blocks}) \wedge$
    (len $M > 0)$
  else ((len M div $\textit{Word-length}) + 1) \leq \textit{Maximum-No-of-Message-blocks};$

Note that the next type, defining the message in blocks to include the empty message, has only been done to simplify the VDM by reducing the amount of VDM needed to define the function *Main-loop* (see section 2.2.7). This function has been defined recursively with the stopping condition being the detection of a message of zero length. Without the additional data type, the recursion would have to stop on the detection of the last block and this block would have to be processed outside the loop by repeating the coding of the loop except for the recursive function call.

Message-in-blocks-plus-empty-Message $=$ *Number**
inv $M \triangleq$ len $M \leq$ *Maximum-No-of-Message-blocks*;

Message-in-blocks $=$ *Message-in-blocks-plus-empty-Message*
inv $M \triangleq 1 \leq$ len M;

3.2 Technical
The key shall comprise two 32 bit numbers J and K and thus has a size of 64 bits.
4.1.2 Definition of multiplication functions
To explain the multiplications, let the 64 bit product of X and Y be $[U, L]$. Here the square brackets mean that the values enclosed are concatenated, U on the left of L. Hence U is the upper (most significant) half of the product and L the lower (least significant) half.
Double-Number corresponds to the use of $[U, L]$. This type is used through out the standard.

Double-Number $=$ *Number**
inv $D \triangleq$ len $D = 2$;

Key $=$ *Double-Number*;

The next type is derived from the results of the **prelude** (see quote of #4.2.1 in section 2.2.7) which are then passed on to the main loop (see quote of #4.2.2 in section 2.2.7).

Key-Constant :: $X0$: *Number*
$Y0$: *Number*
$V0$: *Number*
W : *Number*
S : *Number*
T : *Number*

2.2.3 #3.2 Technical

3.2 Technical
They shall be input to the algorithm as a sequence of 32 bit numbers, $M_1, M_2, - M_n$, of which there are n, called message blocks. The detail of how to pad out the last block M_n to 32 bits is not part of the algorithm but shall be defined in any application.
The following specifies that the padding out of a message adds the required number of bits to the end of the message.

Pad-out-Message : *Message-in-bits* $\rightarrow$ *Message-in-bits*

Pad-out-Message $(M) \triangleq$
let *No-Extra-bits* $=$ *Word-length* $-$ (len M mod *Word-length*) in
if *No-Extra-bits* $=$ *Word-length*
then M
else $M \frown$ *Get-Application-defined-bits*$(M$, *No-Extra-bits*$)$;

The following is derived from **The detail ....** Note that *Message-in-bits* is included in the parameters to the function, although not explicitly used, to indicate that it might be used to generate the result of the function.

Get-Application-defined-bits $(M$: *Message-in-bits*, *No-bits* : $\mathbb{N})$ E : *Message-in-bits*
pre *No-bits* $<$ *Word-length*

post len $E = \textit{No-bits}$;

The following functions specify how to take a message as a sequence of bits and transform it into a sequence of **message blocks**. See section 3.2 for a discussion of the interpretation problems in this part of the standard.

Form-Message-into-blocks : *Message-in-bits* → *Message-in-blocks*

$\textit{Form-Message-into-blocks}\,(M) \triangleq$
  if len $M = \textit{Word-length}$
  then $[\textit{Form-Number}(M)]$
  else $[\textit{Form-Number}(\textit{Get-head-in-bits}(M, \textit{Word-length}))] \frown$
    $\textit{Form-Message-into-blocks}(\textit{Get-tail-in-bits}(M, \textit{Word-length}))$
pre (len $M \geq \textit{Word-length}$) $\wedge$ (len M mod $\textit{Word-length} = 0$);

Form-Number : *Message-in-bits* → *Number*

$\textit{Form-Number}\,(M) \triangleq$
  if len $M = 1$
  then hd M
  else hd $M + 2 \times (\textit{Form-Number}(\text{tl } M))$
pre len $M \leq \textit{Word-length}$;

2.2.4 #4.1.1 General definitions

We shall illustrate this section with two examples of the possible six functions (see [2] for the missing specifications).

4.1.1 General Definitions
A number of functions are used in the description of the algorithm. In the following, X and Y are 32 bit numbers and the result is a 32 bit number except where stated otherwise.

The following six functions are used in #4.2.1 and #4.4.2.

The following five functions describe the bitwise logical operations to be carried out on pairs of 32 bit numbers. These functions are also used to define the multiplication functions in #4.1.2. The functions *AND*, *OR*, *XOR* use recursion. For each, a function has been found to simulate the corresponding one bit logical operation. The recursion is used to separate out the corresponding bits from X and Y, do the one bit function and reconstruct the 32 bit result. The functions *ADD* and *CAR* follow directly from the standard.

$AND(X, Y)$ is the result of the logical AND operation carried out on each of 32 bits.

AND : *Number* × *Number* → *Number*

$AND\,(X, Y) \triangleq$
  if $(X = 0) \vee (Y = 0)$
  then 0
  else $(X \text{ mod } 2) \times (Y \text{ mod } 2) + 2 \times (AND(X \text{ div } 2, Y \text{ div } 2))$;

$CAR(X, Y)$ is the value of the carry from the 32nd bit when X is added to Y; it has the value 0 or 1.

$CAR : Number \times Number \rightarrow Number$

$CAR(X, Y) \triangleq$
$(X + Y)$ div $(Maximum\text{-}Number\text{-}Size\text{-}plus\text{-}1)$;

2.2.5 #4.1.2 Definition of multiplication functions

We shall illustrate this section with one example of the possible three functions (see [2] for the missing specifications).

4.1.2 Definition of multiplication functions
To explain the multiplications, let the 64 bit product of X and Y be $[U, L]$. Here the square brackets mean that the values enclosed are concatenated, U on the left of L. Hence U is the upper (most significant) half of the product and L the lower (least significant) half.

Note how in each of the following multiplication functions, U and L have to be explicitly defined.

#4.1.2.1 To calculate MUL1(X,Y)

Multiply X and Y to produce $[U, L]$. With S and C as local variables,

$$S := ADD(U, L); \qquad \ldots(1)$$
$$C := CAR(U, L); \qquad \ldots(2)$$
$$MUL1(X, Y) := ADD(S, C). \qquad \ldots(3)$$

That is to say, U shall be added to L with end around carry.
Numerically the result is congruent to $X * Y$, the product of X and Y, modulo $(2^{32} - 1)$.
It is not necessarily the smallest residue because it may equal $2^{32} - 1$.

$MUL1 : Number \times Number \rightarrow Number$

$MUL1(X, Y) \triangleq$
let $L = (X \times Y)$ mod $(Maximum\text{-}Number\text{-}Size\text{-}plus\text{-}1)$,
$U = (X \times Y)$ div $(Maximum\text{-}Number\text{-}Size\text{-}plus\text{-}1)$ in
let $S = ADD(U, L), C = CAR(U, L)$ in
$ADD(S, C)$

2.2.6 #4.1.3 Definitions of the functions BYT[X,Y] and PAT[X,Y]

A procedure is used in the prelude to condition both the keys and the results in order to prevent long strings of ones and zeros. It produces two results which are the conditioned values of X and Y and a number $PAT[X, Y]$ which records the changes that have been made. $PAT[X, Y] \leq 255$ so it is essentially an 8 bit number.

X and Y are regarded as strings of bytes. Using the notation $[X, Y, \ldots]$ for concatenating,

$$[X, Y] = [B_0, B_1, B_2, B_3, B_4, B_5, B_6, B_7]$$

Thus bytes B_0 to B_3 are derived from X and B_4 to B_7 from Y.
The procedure is best described by a procedure where each byte B_i is regarded as an integer of length 8 bits.

```
    begin
    P := 0;
    for i := 0 to 7 do
    begin
        P := 2*P;
        if B[i] = 0 then
        begin
            P := P + 1;
            B'[i] := P
        end
    else if B[i] = 255 then
        begin
            P := P + 1;
            B'[i] := 255 - P
        end
    else
    B'[i] := B[i];
    end
end;
```

NOTE – The procedure is written in the programming language PASCAL (see ISO 7185), except that the non-standard identifier B' has been used to maintain continuity with the text. The symbols $B[i]$ and $B'[i]$ correspond to B_i and B'_i in the text

The results are

$$BYT[X, Y] = [B'_0, B'_1, B'_2, B'_3, B'_4, B'_5, B'_6, B'_7]$$

and

$$PAT[X, Y] = P$$

The functions $BYT[X, Y]$ and $PAT[X, Y]$ were the most difficult to specify (probably because of trying to make the specification functional).
The first two **lets** of BYT and PAT correspond to where it says X and Y are regarded ...and B_4 to B_7 from Y., that is the transformation of X and Y into a sequence of bytes. See section 3.3 for problem of interpretation.
The last **let** of BYT is the transformation of the conditioned sequence (conditioned values) back into the numbers X and Y. The function *Condition-Sequence* modifies the sequence of bytes.

$BYT : Double\text{-}Number \rightarrow Double\text{-}Number$

$BYT\,(K) \triangleq$
 let X = hd K,
  Y = hd tl K in
 let $X' = [Byte(X,3), Byte(X,2), Byte(X,1), Byte(X,0)]$,
  $Y' = [Byte(Y,3), Byte(Y,2), Byte(Y,1), Byte(Y,0)]$ in
 let $XY = X' \frown Y'$,
  $P = 0$ in
 let $XY' = Condition\text{-}Sequence(XY, P)$ in
 let $X'' = Get\text{-}head\text{-}in\text{-}blocks(XY', 4)$, $Y'' = Get\text{-}tail\text{-}in\text{-}blocks(XY', 4)$ in
 $[Convert\text{-}Bytes\text{-}to\text{-}Number(X'')] \frown [Convert\text{-}Bytes\text{-}to\text{-}Number(Y'')]$;

$Byte : Number \times \mathbb{N} \rightarrow Number$

$Byte\,(N, B) \triangleq$
 if $B = 0$
 then N mod $2 \uparrow 8$
 else $Byte((N \text{ div } 2 \uparrow 8), B - 1)$
pre $(B \geq 0) \wedge (B \leq 3)$;

The following function modifies the sequence of bytes starting at the head of the sequence. Modification is done through the function *Condition-value* and depends on the changes already done on previous elements of the sequence as recorded in the function *Changes*.

$Condition\text{-}Sequence : Message\text{-}in\text{-}blocks \times Number \rightarrow Message\text{-}in\text{-}blocks$

$Condition\text{-}Sequence\,(M, P) \triangleq$
 if len $M = 1$
 then $[Condition\text{-}value(\text{hd } M, P)]$
 else $[Condition\text{-}value(\text{hd } M, P)] \frown Condition\text{-}Sequence(\text{tl } M, Changes(\text{hd } M, P))$;

The next two functions are derived from the PASCAL program in the above extract from the standard.

$Condition\text{-}value : Number \times Number \rightarrow Number$

$Condition\text{-}value\,(B, P) \triangleq$
 let $P' = 2 \times P$ in let $P'' = P' + 1$ in if $B = 0$
 then P''
 else if $B = 2 \uparrow 8 - 1$
  then $(2 \uparrow 8 - 1) - P''$
  else B;

$Changes : Number \times Number \rightarrow Number$

$Changes\,(B, P) \triangleq$
 let $P' = 2 \times P$ in let $P'' = P' + 1$ in if $(B = 0) \vee (B = 2 \uparrow 8 - 1)$
 then P''
 else P';

$Convert\text{-}Bytes\text{-}to\text{-}Number : Message\text{-}in\text{-}blocks \rightarrow Number$

$Convert\text{-}Bytes\text{-}to\text{-}Number\,(M) \triangleq$
if len $M = 1$
then hd M
else $Convert\text{-}Bytes\text{-}to\text{-}Number$(tl M) + (hd M) $\times 2 \uparrow 8 \times$ (len $M - 1$);

The function *Record-Changes* records what elements of the sequence are modified (records the changes).

$PAT : Double\text{-}Number \rightarrow Number$

$PAT\,(D) \triangleq$
let $X =$ hd D,
$Y =$ hd tl D in
let $X' = [Byte(X,3), Byte(X,2), Byte(X,1), Byte(X,0)]$,
$Y' = [Byte(Y,3), Byte(Y,2), Byte(Y,1), Byte(Y,0)]$ in
let $XY = X' \frown Y'$,
$P = 0$ in
$Record\text{-}Changes(XY, P)$;

$Record\text{-}Changes : Message\text{-}in\text{-}blocks \times Number \rightarrow Number$

$Record\text{-}Changes\,(M, P) \triangleq$
if len $M = 1$
then $Changes$(hd M, P)
else $Record\text{-}Changes$(tl M, $Changes$(hd M, P));

2.2.7 #4.2 Specification of the algorithm

#4.2.1 The prelude

See [2] for text of standard and for the specification of *Prelude*.

#4.2.2 The main loop

4.2.2 The main loop

This loop shall be performed in turn for each of the message blocks M_i. In addition to M_i, the principal values employed shall be X and Y and the main results shall be the new values of X and Y. It shall also use V and W and modify V at each performance. X, Y and V shall be initialized with the values provided by the prelude. In order to use the same keys again, the initial values of X, Y and V shall be preserved, therefore they shall be denoted X_0, Y_0 and V_0 and there shall be an initializing step $X := X_0$, $Y := Y_0$, $V := V_0$, after which the main loop shall be entered for the first time. The coda, which shall be used after all message blocks have been processed by n cycles of the loop, is described in 4.2.3.

NOTE – The program is shown in columns to clarify its parallel operation but it should be read in normal reading order, left to right on each line.

$$
\begin{array}{lll}
V := CYC(V); & & \\
E := XOR(V, W); & & \ldots(21) \\
X := XOR(X, M_i); & Y := XOR(Y, M_i); & \ldots(22) \\
F := ADD(E, Y); & G := ADD(E, X); & \\
F := OR(F, A); & G := OR(G, B); & \\
F := AND(F, C); & G := AND(G, D); & \ldots(23) \\
X := MUL1(X, F); & Y := MUL2A(Y, G). & \ldots(24)
\end{array}
$$

The numbers A, B, C, D are constants which are, in hexadecimal notation:

Constant A:	0204	0801
Constant B:	0080	4021
Constant C:	*BFEF*	*7FDF*
Constant D:	*7DFE*	*FBFF*

NOTE – Lines (21) are common to both paths. Line (22) introduces the message block M_i. Lines (23) prepare the multipliers and line (24) generates new X and Y values. Only X, Y and V are modified for use in the next cycle. F and G are local variables. Since the constant D has its most significant digit zero, $G < 2^{31}$ and this ensures that $MUL2A$ in line (24) will give the correct result.

This is directly derived from the above. It works recursively on each message of the block.

Main-loop : *Message-in-blocks-plus-empty-Message* × *Key-Constant* → *Number*

Main-loop $(M, KC) \triangleq$
  let $mk\text{-}Key\text{-}Constant(X, Y, V, W, S, T) = KC$ in
  if len $M = 0$
  then $XOR(X, Y)$
  else let $Mi =$ hd M in
    let $V' = CYC(V)$ in
    let $E = XOR(V', W)$,
      $X' = XOR(X, Mi)$, $Y' = XOR(Y, Mi)$ in
    let $F = ADD(E, Y')$, $G = ADD(E, X')$ in
    let $F' = OR(F, A)$, $G' = OR(G, B)$ in
    let $F'' = AND(F', C)$, $G'' = AND(G', D)$ in
    let $X'' = MUL1(X', F'')$, $Y'' = MUL2A(Y', G'')$ in
    $Main\text{-}loop($tl $M, mk\text{-}Key\text{-}Constant(X'', Y'', V', W, S, T))$;

#4.2.3 The coda

4.2.3 The coda

After the last message block M_n has been processed, the main loop shall be performed with message block S, then again with block T, i.e. $M_{n+1} = S, M_{n+2} = T$.

After this, the Message Authentication Code (MAC) shall be calculated as $Z = XOR(X, Y)$ and the algorithm shall then be complete.

NOTE – in order to calculate further MAC values without repeating the prelude (key calculation) until the keys are changed the values X_0, Y_0, V_0, W, S and T should be retained.

Note here the simplicity of the VDM. $XOR(X, Y)$ has been placed in the function *Main-loop* to simplify the VDM of the main loop.

MAC : *Message-in-blocks* × *Key* → *Number*

MAC (*M*, *K*) △
let *KC* = *Prelude*(*K*) in
let *S* = *KC.S*,
T = *KC.T* in
let *M'* = *M* ⌢ [*S*] ⌢ [*T*] in
Main-loop(*M'*, *KC*);

2.2.8 #5 Specification of the mode of operation

5 Specification of the mode of operation

Messages longer than 1 024 bytes shall be divided into blocks of 1 024 bytes and chained as follows.

For the first block of 1 024 bytes the MAC (4 bytes) shall be formed. The MAC value shall be prefixed to (but not transmitted in) the second block and the resultant 1 028 bytes authenticated. This procedure shall continue, with the MAC of each block prefixed to the next, until the last block, which need not be of size 1 024 bytes, and the final MAC shall be used as the transmitted MAC for the whole message.

This function pulls together all the rest of the VDM to produce the message authenticator algorithm. It starts with a message modelled as a sequence of bits and pads out this sequence (through the function *Pad-out-Message*) so that it can be transformed into a sequence of numbers (through the function *Form-Message-into-blocks*). It then does what is described above. See section 3.4 for problem of interpretation.

MAA : *Message-in-bits* × *Key* → *Number*

MAA (*M*, *K*) △
let *M'* = *Pad-out-Message*(*M*) in
let *M''* = *Form-Message-into-blocks*(*M'*) in
if len *M''* ≤ *Maximum-No-of-blocks-for-MAC*
then *MAC*(*M''*, *K*)
else let *M'''* = [*MAC*(*Get-head-in-blocks*(*M''*, *Maximum-No-of-blocks-for-MAC*), *K*)]
⌢ *Get-tail-in-blocks*(*M''*, *Maximum-No-of-blocks-for-MAC*) in
Block-MAC(*M'''*, *K*, *Maximum-No-of-blocks-for-MAC-plus-1*);

$Block\text{-}MAC : Message\text{-}in\text{-}blocks \times Key \times \mathbb{N} \rightarrow Number$

$Block\text{-}MAC\,(M, K, No\text{-}blocks) \triangleq$
  if len $M \leq No\text{-}blocks$
  then $MAC(M, K)$
  else let $M' = [MAC(Get\text{-}head\text{-}in\text{-}blocks(M, No\text{-}blocks), K)] \frown$ $Get\text{-}tail\text{-}in\text{-}blocks(M, No\text{-}blocks)$ in
    $Block\text{-}MAC(M', K, No\text{-}blocks)$;

3 Interpretation Problems

The following discussion demonstrates that the standard contains ambiguities.

3.1 Length of messages

The following extracts from section #3.2 of the standard were seen as having a bearing on the definition of the length of a message.

Messages to be authenticated may originate as a bit string of any length.
They shall be input to the algorithm as a sequence of 32 bit numbers, $M_1, M_2, - M_n$, of which there are n, called message blocks.
This algorithm shall not be used to authenticate messages with more than 1 000 000 blocks, i.e. $n \leq 1\,000\,000$.
The calculation can be performed on messages as short as one block ($n = 1$).

The first statement can be seen as permitting any length of message, including zero length, whereas the last statement seems to imply that a message must contain at least one block and therefore at least one bit. However, in terms of the language used in standards documents [12], "may" denotes a possible course of action while "can" refers to the ability of a user of the standard or to a possibility open to him. Neither of these statements is a mandatory requirement or even a recommendation and therefore only the second and third extracts from the standard are relevant. It is not clear from this whether you can have a message of zero length. It was decided to use the following definition of message length (see section 2.2.2) where M is a message constructed of message blocks:

$1 \leq$ len $M \wedge$ len $M \leq Maximum\text{-}No\text{-}of\text{-}Message\text{-}blocks$

3.2 Forming a message from bits.

The following extracts from section #3.2 of the standard are relevant as to how the message should be structured:

Messages to be authenticated may originate as a bit string of any length.
They shall be input to the algorithm as a sequence of 32 bit numbers, $M_1, M_2, - M_n$, of which there are n, called message blocks.

As discussed in section 3.1 only the second statement is mandatory and so a message is taken to be a sequence of 32 bit numbers. It is not defined how to construct a sequence of 32 bit numbers from a bit string. The VDM specification given starts from a message as a sequence of bits and constructs from this the message as a sequence of 32 bit numbers.

3.3 Transformation of Numbers into bytes

The following extract comes from section #4.1.3 of the standard:

X and Y are regarded as strings of bytes. Using the notation $[X, Y, \ldots]$ for concatenating,
$[X, Y] = [B_0, B_1, B_2, B_3, B_4, B_5, B_6, B_7]$
Thus bytes B_0 to B_3 are derived from X and B_4 to B_7 from Y.

This does not specify whether B_0 is the least significant byte of X or the most significant.

From the test examples given in the Annex to the standard it turns out that B_0 is the most significant byte of X. It could be argued that from section #4.1.2

To explain the multiplications, let the 64 bit product of X and Y be $[U, L]$. Here the square brackets mean that the values enclosed are concatenated, U on the left of L. Hence U is the upper (most significant) half of the product and L the lower (least significant) half.

that the left most element of a concatenation is the most significant part of a number and hence the correct interpretation could be derived.

3.4 Mode of operation

The following two extracts from sections #3.2 and #5 of the standard are relevant to the following discussion:

3.2 Technical
The mode of operation (see clause 5) is an essential feature of the implementation of this algorithm.
5 Specification of the mode of operation
Messages longer than 1 024 bytes shall be divided into blocks of 1 024 bytes and chained as follows.
For the first block of 1 024 bytes the MAC (4 bytes) shall be formed. The MAC value shall be prefixed to (but not transmitted in) the second block and the resultant 1 028 bytes authenticated. This procedure shall continue, with the MAC of each block prefixed to the next, until the last block, which need not be of size 1 024 bytes, and the final MAC shall be used as the transmitted MAC for the whole message.

Note the following: 1) These are the only references to the mode of operation in the standard; 2) The figure included in the standard does not show the mode of operation; 3) The Annex to the standard has tests for the rest of the standard but none for the mode of operation; and 4) As already noted in section 2.2.1 there is confusion over what blocks are because the message can now be viewed as a sequence of bytes.

The problems of interpretation stem from how the mode of operation is fitted in with the rest of the standard. Two possible alternative interpretations to the standard other than that of section 2.2 are given below. Annex E of the new draft international standard [13], of [3], contains a test for the mode of operation of the MAA and this confirms the interpretation given in section 2.2.

In the following interpretations a message block is assumed to be a 32 bit number, as in the standard, and the 1024 byte block is called a macro block.

3.4.1 Interpretation 1

From section #4.2.3 of the standard:

After the last message block M_n has been processed, the main loop shall be performed with message block S, then again with block T, i.e. $M_{n+1} = S, M_{n+2} = T$.
After this, the Message Authentication Code (MAC) shall be calculated as $Z = XOR(X, Y)$ and the algorithm shall then be complete.

Section #5 of the standard states how the total message is split up into macro blocks and how the MAC is used on them. M_n is used in #3.2 to refer to the last message of the total message so what can it mean in the above extract? The VDM in section 2.2 takes it to mean the last message block of each macro block so that S and T are included in each macro block when the MAC is formed. Another interpretation is that only the last macro block of the total message will include S and T. We show below how the VDM in section 2.2 would be modified to allow this:

| *Prelude* has to be included in *MAA* and removed from *MAC*.

$MAA : Message\text{-}in\text{-}bits \times Key \rightarrow Number$

$MAA\,(M, K) \triangleq$
  let $M' = Pad\text{-}out\text{-}Message(M)$ in
  let $M'' = Form\text{-}Message\text{-}into\text{-}blocks(M')$ in
  let $KC = Prelude(K)$ in
  if len $M'' \leq Maximum\text{-}No\text{-}of\text{-}blocks\text{-}for\text{-}MAC$
  then let $S = KC.S$,
        $T = KC.T$ in
     let $M''' = M'' \frown [S] \frown [T]$ in
     $MAC(M''', KC)$
  else let $M''' =$
        $[MAC(Get\text{-}head\text{-}in\text{-}blocks(M'', Maximum\text{-}No\text{-}of\text{-}blocks\text{-}for\text{-}MAC), KC)]$
        $\frown\ Get\text{-}tail\text{-}in\text{-}blocks(M'', Maximum\text{-}No\text{-}of\text{-}blocks\text{-}for\text{-}MAC)$ in
     $Block\text{-}MAC(M''', KC, Maximum\text{-}No\text{-}of\text{-}blocks\text{-}for\text{-}MAC\text{-}plus\text{-}1)$;

$Block\text{-}MAC : Message\text{-}in\text{-}blocks \times Key\text{-}Constant \times \mathbb{N} \rightarrow Number$

$Block\text{-}MAC\,(M, KC, No\text{-}blocks) \triangleq$
  if len $M \leq No\text{-}blocks$
  then let $S = KC.S$,
        $T = KC.T$ in
     let $M' = M \frown [S] \frown [T]$ in
     $MAC(M', KC)$
  else let $M' = [MAC(Get\text{-}head\text{-}in\text{-}blocks(M, No\text{-}blocks), KC)] \frown$
        $Get\text{-}tail\text{-}in\text{-}blocks(M, No\text{-}blocks)$ in
     $Block\text{-}MAC(M', KC, No\text{-}blocks)$;

$MAC : Message\text{-}in\text{-}blocks \times Key\text{-}Constant \rightarrow Number$

$MAC\,(M, KC) \triangleq$
  $Main\text{-}loop(M, KC)$;

3.4.2 Interpretation 2

The main loop (*Main-loop*, see section 2.2.7), is performed in turn for each of the message blocks of a macro block. It produces six values X, Y, V, W, S and T (the last three are not changed). A MAC formed on a macro block could use the initial values, X_0, Y_0, V_0,

W, S, T (produced by the *Prelude*) or the values left over from the last application of *MAC*. The latter is what you would expect in a data security application (see Chapter 4 of [14] for a discussion on this). It is shown below how the VDM in section 2.2 could be modified to allow for this interpretation:

A new type *MAC-Main-loop-Results* is introduced to pass back up the values from the *Main-loop*. *Prelude* has to be included in *MAA*.

```
MAC-Main-loop-Results :: MAC-Result        : Number
                         Main-loop-Result : Key-Constant

MAA : Message-in-bits × Key → Number

MAA(M, K) ≜
  let M′ = Pad-out-Message(M) in
  let M″ = Form-Message-into-blocks(M′),
      KC = Prelude(K) in
  if len M″ ≤ Maximum-No-of-blocks-for-MAC
  then MAC-Result(MAC(M″, KC))
  else let mk-MAC-Main-loop-Results(MR, MlR) =
             MAC(Get-head-in-blocks(M″, Maximum-No-of-blocks-for-MAC), KC) in
       let M‴ =
             [MR] ⌢ Get-tail-in-blocks(M″, Maximum-No-of-blocks-for-MAC) in
       Block-MAC(M‴, MlR, Maximum-No-of-blocks-for-MAC-plus-1);

Block-MAC : Message-in-blocks × Key-Constant × ℕ → Number

Block-MAC(M, KC, No-blocks) ≜
  if len M ≤ No-blocks
  then MAC-Result(MAC(M, KC))
  else let mk-MAC-Main-loop-Results(MR, MlR) =
             MAC(Get-head-in-blocks(M, No-blocks), KC) in
       let M′ = [MR] ⌢
              Get-tail-in-blocks(M, No-blocks) in
       Block-MAC(M′, MlR, No-blocks);

MAC : Message-in-blocks × Key-Constant → MAC-Main-loop-Results

MAC(M, KC) ≜
  let S = KC.S,
      T = KC.T in
  let M′ = M ⌢ [S] ⌢ [T] in
  Main-loop(M′, KC);
```

$$\begin{array}{l} \textit{Main-loop} : \textit{Message-in-blocks-plus-empty-Message} \times \textit{Key-Constant} \\ \qquad \to \textit{MAC-Main-loop-Results} \end{array}$$

$$\begin{array}{l} \textit{Main-loop}\,(M, KC) \triangleq \\ \quad \textsf{let } \textit{mk-Key-Constant}(X, Y, V, W, S, T) = KC \textsf{ in} \\ \quad \textsf{if len } M = 0 \\ \quad \textsf{then } \textit{mk-MAC-Main-loop-Results}(XOR(X, Y), KC) \\ \quad \textsf{else let } Mi = \textsf{hd } M \textsf{ in} \\ \qquad \textsf{let } V' = CYC(V) \textsf{ in} \\ \qquad \textsf{let } E = XOR(V', W), \\ \qquad\quad X' = XOR(X, Mi), Y' = XOR(Y, Mi) \textsf{ in} \\ \qquad \textsf{let } F = ADD(E, Y'), G = ADD(E, X') \textsf{ in} \\ \qquad \textsf{let } F' = OR(F, A), G' = OR(G, B) \textsf{ in} \\ \qquad \textsf{let } F'' = AND(F', C), G'' = AND(G', D) \textsf{ in} \\ \qquad \textsf{let } X'' = MUL1(X', F''), Y'' = MUL2A(Y', G'') \textsf{ in} \\ \qquad \textit{Main-loop}(\textsf{tl } M, \textit{mk-Key-Constant}(X'', Y'', V', W, S, T)); \end{array}$$

4 Implementations

The above VDM was translated by hand into *C*[15], *Miranda*[16] and *Modula*-2[17]. All these implementations have passed the tests in the Annex to the standard and the tests in Annex E of [21]. See [2] for the complete *C* and *Miranda* implementations in parallel with the VDM and [18] contains the *Modula*-2 implementation.

Below we indicate some problems that can be encountered when producing an implementation from the VDM specification:

Types Types in VDM are more expressive than those used in most programming languages and so invariants (*inv*) on types would have to be implemented explicitly in the program code. Note that the invariants on types in VDM are passed around with the types and an object of a given type, wherever it appears in the specification, must always satisfy the corresponding invariant.

Multibyte arithmetic It is not immediately clear from the specification, but any implementation will require 32 bit integer arithmetic, in particular for multiplication and addition (see section 2.2.4). For most programming languages (on 16 bit or 32 bit machines) it will be necessary to either implement or acquire an implementation of these functions.

Entry level of implementation in terms of message in bits This problem has been discussed in section 3.2. A decision will have to be taken on the form in which the message will be delivered to the MAA (in fact how the hardware is mapped onto the software).

Sequences The specification makes extensive use of sequence type which is one of the data types allowed in VDM but not supported by most programming languages. This would have to be implemented.

Recursion Recursion is used throughout the VDM specification and can use up considerable memory space, the amount depending on the depth of recursion.

5 Conclusions

To a prospective user the standard would seem quite clear until an attempt was made to implement it, when the interpretation problems described in section 3 would arise. The advantage of using a well defined specification language such as VDM (rather than the mixture of programming language, mathematics and English used in the standard) is that it gives an unambiguous description of the standard. It can also uncover possible interpretation problems at the specification level rather than at the implementation level. The agreed formal specification can then be used for producing diverse but equivalent implementations, as in the case of the MAA, or reference implementations for conformance testing, as is being done for Modula-2 [19].

On comparing the standard with the VDM specification it can be seen that they are comparable in size and complexity, assuming a basic knowledge of VDM. Any increase in the size of the VDM over the standard arises from the need to define the ambiguities in the MAA standard.

When doing this work the main problems encountered were which version of VDM to use (as yet no standard exists although one is being produced [20]) and whether any tools were available. The version of VDM used in the original work has a published book [5] illustrating its use and also has a set of LaTeX macros. There was no way to check the VDM except by hand and even then the implementation process uncovered several syntactic errors in the specification. This would be a more serious problem with larger VDM specifications such as the formal definition of Modula-2 [17].

The work described in this report demonstrates the application of formal methods to the standards area and it is recommended that formal methods should be used in the formulation and description of appropriate standards.

References

[1] BS 7102 (2):1989, 8731-2:1987. *Banking - Approved algorithm for message authentication - Part 2: Message authenticator algorithms.* Obtainable from: Sales Department, BSI, Linford Wood, Milton Keynes, MK14 6LE.

[2] G.I. Parkin and G. O'Neill. *Specification of the MAA Standard in VDM.* NPL Report DITC 160/90. February 1990.

[3] BS 7101:1989, ISO 8730:1986. *Protecting authentic wholesale messages between financial institutions.* Obtainable from: Sales Department, BSI, Linford Wood, Milton Keynes, MK14 6LE.

[4] D.W. Davies and D.O. Clayden. *The Message Authenticator Algorithm (MAA) and its Implementation.* NPL Report DITC 109/88. February 1988.

[5] C.B. Jones. *Systematic Software Development Using VDM.* Prentice-Hall International, 1986.

[6] M.K.F. Lai. *A formal interpretation of the MAA standard in Z.* NPL Report DITC 184/91. June 1991.

[7] H.B. Munster. *LOTOS specification of the MAA standard.* NPL Report to be published.

[8] C.L.N. Ruggles (Ed.). *Formal Methods in Standards, A Report from the BCS Working Group.* Springer-Verlag, 1990.

[9] M. Wolczko. *Typesetting VDM in* LaTeX. Dept. of Computer Science, The University, Manchester, M13 9PL. March 1988.

[10] BSI IST/5/19. *VDM Specification Language Proto-Standard.* British Standards Institution, 29 March 1990.

[11] I.P. Dickinson. *Typesetting VDM-SL with* VDM-SL *macros.* National Physical Laboratory, Teddington, Middlesex, TW11 0LW. 20 February 1991.

[12] IEC/ISO. *Rules for the drafting and presentation of International Standards.* 1986.

[13] ISO/DIS 8730, *Banking - Requirements for message authentication (wholesale).* 1987.

[14] D.W. Davies and W.L. Price. *Security for Computer Networks, An Introduction to Data Security in Teleprocessing and Electronic Funds Transfer.* John Wiley & Sons, 1984.

[15] B.W. Kernighan and D.M. Ritchie. *The C Programming Language.* Prentice-Hall, 1978.

[16] D.A. Turner. *An Overview of Miranda.* SIGPLAN Notices, December 1986.

[17] ISO/IEC JTC1 SC22/WG13/D106. *Modula-2 Standard, Third Working Draft.* British Standards Institution, 29 October 1989.

[18] R.P. Lampard. *An implementation of MAA from a VDM specification.* NPL Technical Memorandum DITC 50/91. January 1991.

[19] D.J.Andrews, A. Garg, S.P.A. Lau, J.R. Pitchers. *The Formal Definition of Modula-2 and Its Associated Interpreter.* Lecture Notes in Computer Science, Vol 328, Springer-Verlag 1988.

[20] D.J. Andrews. *Report from the BSI Panel for the Standardisation of VDM (IST/5/50).* Lecture Notes in Computer Science, Vol 328, Springer-Verlag 1988.

[21] ISO/DIS 8731-2, *Banking - Approved algorithm for message authentication - Part 2: Message authenticator algorithms*, 1990.

Unintrusive Ways to Integrate Formal Specifications in Practice

Jeannette M. Wing and Amy Moormann Zaremski
School of Computer Science
Carnegie Mellon University
Pittsburgh, Pennsylvania 15213

Abstract

Formal methods can be neatly woven in with less formal, but more widely-used, industrial-strength methods. We show how to integrate the Larch two-tiered specification method [GHW85a] with two used in the waterfall model of software development: Structured Analysis [Ros77] and Structure Charts [YC79]. We use Larch traits to define data elements in a data dictionary and the functionality of basic activities in Structured Analysis data-flow diagrams; Larch interfaces and traits to define the behavior of modules in Structure Charts. We also show how to integrate loosely formal specification in a prototyping model by discussing ways of refining Larch specifications as code evolves. To provide some realism to our ideas, we draw our examples from a non-trivial Larch specification of the graphical editor for the Miró visual languages [HMT+90].

1. A Different Picture of Software Development

Most pictures of the software development process are variations of the one shown in Figure 1(a) where we name the standard phases *requirements analysis*, *design*, *implementation*, and *validation*. Each phase results in at least one tangible product, e.g., a requirements specification, a design notebook, executable code, and test suites.

The software engineering community is beginning to acknowledge the need to use and the potential benefits obtained from using more formal methods for developing software. How then do formal methods fit in the picture? In 1980 Guttag and Horning proposed that formal specifications be used in program design [GH80]. This idea suggests revising Figure 1(a) to that in Figure 1(b) by inserting the phase *formal specification*. This revised picture implies that given a set of informally described requirements, a *system specifier* (a brand new player on the software development team [Win85]) writes a formal specification of the system to be built. After the system is built, formal *verification* is possible

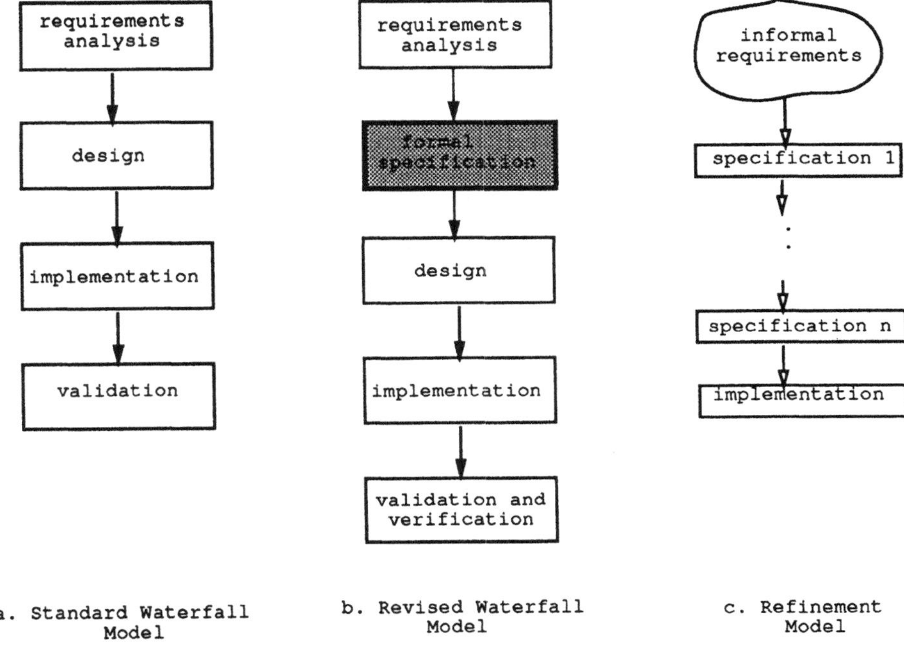

Figure 1: Software Development Models

since in principle the implementation can be proven correct with respect to the formal specification. We call this overall development process the *waterfall* model.

Zooming in at the design phase of the waterfall model gives rise to another common picture shown in Figure 1(c). Here, some initial formal specification codifies the informal requirements, shown as a cloud in the picture. Then, by applying a series of well-defined correctness-preserving transformations, the system specifier refines a specification from one step to the next, perhaps generating proof obligations along the way. The transformation process ends when an implementation with acceptable performance is reached. Discharging proof obligations in parallel with applying stepwise refinement dispenses with the need of a separate verification phase. A proof of correctness is generated as the program is developed [Dij76, Gri81, Jon86]. We call this development process the *refinement* model.

Software engineers who interpret at face value these pictures of software development might get the wrong impression that formal specifications have a fixed, well-defined, and rigid role in the software development process. The problem with the waterfall model picture is that it implies that a formal specification should be written before implementation begins. It implies that without doing verification, the developer would never be certain that an implementation is correct. The problem with the refinement model picture is that it implies that the design process can be accomplished completely systematically

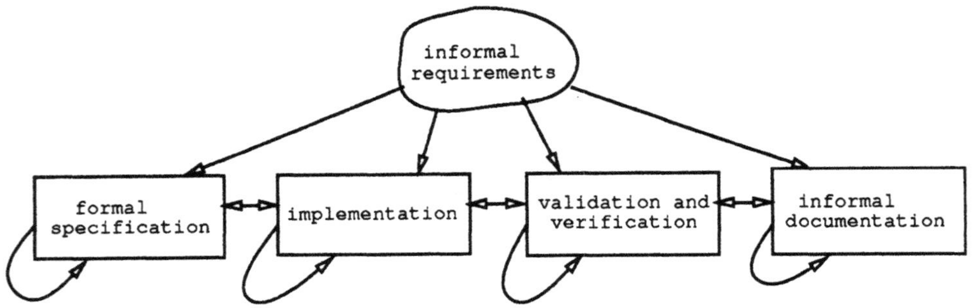

Figure 2: A Parallel-Iterative Model of Software Development

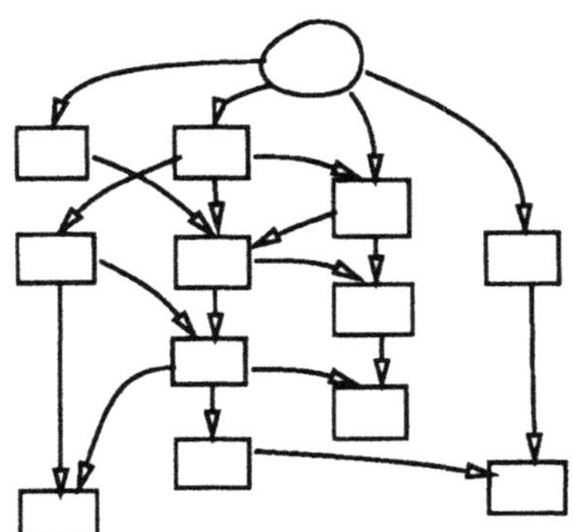

Figure 3: An Unrolling of the Parallel-Iterative Model

through stepwise refinement. The only creativity needed is to choose what to refine at each step and which of many provably correct transformations to apply. It requires that such transformations exist. These are all strong requirements and implications that can result from forgetting that these pictures are just abstractions of what occurs in practice. They idealize the software development process by hiding false starts, feedback loops, and parallel development strategies.

We propose a different picture shown in Figure 2. Here, starting from a set of informally described requirements, four iterative activities occur in parallel: formal specification, implementation, validation and verification, and writing informal documentation[1]. Unrolling each of the parallel activities (e.g., see Figure 3) shows that iterations of each need not occur in lockstep and that each can affect subsequent iterations of another.

Our picture not only accommodates different software development models, including the waterfall and refinement models, but also reflects more realistically how software is developed in practice. It explicitly shows iterations through specifications and implemen-

[1]In order not to clutter the picture, we do not draw the implicit arrows between non-adjacent boxes, e.g., between formal specification and informal documentation.

tations, and how results of one phase can influence and provide feedback to others. It makes more explicit the role of informal documentation rather than relegating it to be an invisible by-product of each phase. It allows the first use of formal methods to occur at any time during the development process: before, during, or after the system is built. The point of our picture is to convey to software engineers that applying formal methods need not be an intimidating or burdensome task. Applying formal methods is not something done by a group of people sitting off in a corner by themselves, but rather, more importantly, could and should be done alongside conventional software development activities. More significantly, with care and foresight specific formal methods can be neatly woven in with less formal, but more widely-used, industrial-strength methods. Thus, we use our picture to help illustrate natural and convenient ways of unintrusively integrating formal methods in the software development process: the main subject and contribution of this paper. Henceforth we will focus on the interplay between specification and implementation, though many of our remarks hold for the interplay between the other phases, e.g., formal specification and validation and verification.

Specifically, we present two ways to integrate formal methods in the current practice of software engineering. First, we show in Section 3 how to integrate the Larch two-tiered specification method [GHW85a] with methods used in a traditional waterfall model. Larch specifications fit in with Structured Analysis [Ros77], a typical requirements analysis method, and Structure Charts [YC79], a typical design method. Next in Section 4, we explain how we can integrate Larch in a prototyping model where versions of specifications and implementations evolve in parallel. Although we make our points using specific techniques, our approach is generally applicable to other requirements analysis and design methods such as SADT [Ros85] and JSM [Jac83] and other formal methods such as VDM [Jon86] and Z [Spi88]. To provide some realism to our ideas, instead of illustrating them using small examples, we extract pieces from a non-trivial Larch specification, that of the Miró graphical editor [Zar91]. We begin with an overview of the specificand (Miró) and specification language (Larch) in the next section. We conclude in Section 5 with some general words of advice to interested practitioners.

2. Miró and Larch

2.1. Specificand: Miró

The goal of the Miró Project is to provide language and tool support for letting users specify formally through pictures the security configuration of file systems (i.e., which users have access to which files) and general security policy constraints (i.e., rules to which a configuration must conform).

Miró consists of two visual languages, the *instance* language and the *constraint* language, both defined in [HMT+90]. An *instance picture* graphically denotes an access matrix that defines which users have which accesses to which files. Instance pictures model the specific security configuration between a set of users and a set of files, e.g., Alice cannot read Bob's mail file. A *constraint picture* denotes a set of instance pictures (or equivalently, the corresponding set of access matrices) that satisfies a particular security constraint, e.g., users with write access to a file must also have read access. When an instance picture, *IP*, is in the set denoted by a constraint picture, *CP*, we say *IP* "matches" *CP*.

The basic elements in the instance language are *boxes* and *arrows*. Boxes that contain no other boxes represent users and files. Boxes can contain other boxes to indicate groups of users and directories of files. User group boxes may overlap to indicate a user is in more than one group. Labeled arrows go from user (group) boxes to file (group) boxes; the label indicates the access mode, e.g., read or write. Access rights are inherited by corresponding pairs of boxes contained within boxes connected by arrows, thus minimizing the number of arrows necessary to draw. Arrows may be negated to indicate the denial of the labeled access.

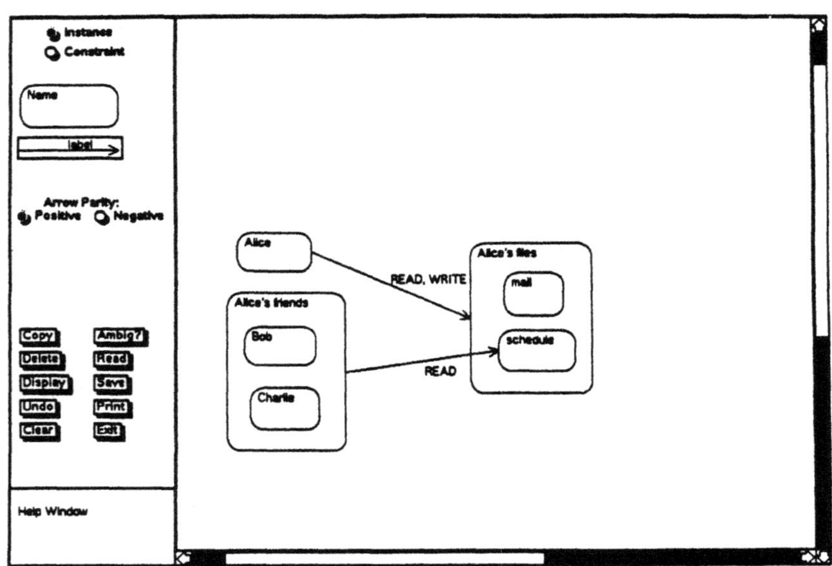

Figure 4: The Miró editor and a sample instance picture

Figure 4 shows an instance picture, as drawn in the Miró editor. The positive arrow from `Alice` to `Alice's files` indicates that Alice has read and write access to her files. The positive arrow from `Alice's friends` to Alice's `schedule` file indicates that both Bob and Charlie have read access to Alice's schedule. By default, since there are no arrows between Alice's friends and her other files, Bob and Charlie do not have read access to Alice's mail file. We could also show this property with an explicit negative arrow between Alice's friends and her mail file. The presence of both positive and negative arrows can lead to possibly *ambiguous* pictures, a property formally defined in [MTW90].

The *constraint* language also consists of boxes and arrows, but here the objects have different meanings. A box labeled with an expression defines a set of instance boxes. E.g., the left-hand box in Figure 5 denotes the set of instance boxes of type User. There are three sorts of arrows, allowing us to describe three different relations between boxes in an instance picture, *IP*: syntactic (solid horizontal) - whether an arrow explicitly appears in *IP*; semantic (dashed horizontal) - whether an access right exists in the matrix denoted by *IP*; and containment (solid vertical with head inside box) - whether a box is nested within another in *IP*. Additionally, the *thickness* attribute of each constraint object is key in defining a constraint picture's meaning: in general, for each set of instance objects that matches the thick part of the constraint, there must be another set of objects (disjoint from the set matching the thick part) that matches the thin part. Figure 5 shows a constraint picture that specifies that users who have write access to a file must have read access to it as well.

Figure 5: A sample constraint picture

The Miró editor provides facilities to create, view, and modify both instance and constraint pictures. The left-hand side of the window in Figure 4 displays a menu from which users can select the type of picture and object they wish to draw. The editor also serves as an interface to other Miró tools: an *ambiguity checker* that determines whether an instance picture is ambiguous, a *constraint checker* that determines whether an instance picture matches a constraint picture, a *prober* that creates a representation of an instance picture for a given file system, and a *verifier* that determines whether the result of the prober matches an instance picture. We revisit the relationship among these tools in Section 3.

2.2. Specification Language: Larch

We present a brief refresher of Larch here and give further details as necessary. See [GHW85b, GHM90] for more details.

Larch provides a "two-tiered" approach to specification. In one tier, the specifier writes *traits* in the Larch Shared Language (LSL) to assert state-independent properties of a program. Each trait introduces *sorts* and *operators* and defines equality between terms composed of the operators (and variables of the appropriate sorts). E.g., the *Box* trait in Figure 6 introduces the sort *B*, which is a **tuple of** six fields, and the operator *copy_box*. By our use of LSL's **tuple of** constructor, we implicitly introduce four

$Box(B)$: **trait**
  B **tuple of** $pos : CoordPair, size : CoordPair, b\_label : Label,$
    $thickness : LineThickness, starred : Bool, box\_type : BoxType$
  introduces
    $copy\_box : B \rightarrow B$

  asserts $\forall\ b : B$
    $copy\_box(b).pos == b.pos$
    $copy\_box(b).size == b.size$
    $copy\_box(b).thickness == b.thickness$
    $copy\_box(b).starred == b.starred$
    $copy\_box(b).box\_type == b.box\_type$

Figure 6: The Box Trait

other sorts (*CoordPair*, *Label*, *LineThickness*, and *BoxType*[2]) and the *__.field_name* and *set_field_name* operators for each of the six *field_names* in the tuple. Five equations constrain the meaning of *copy_box* and together imply that a box *b* is not necessarily equal to *copy_box(b)* since they may differ in the values set in their corresponding *b_label* fields.

In the second tier, the specifier writes *interfaces* in a Larch interface language (here, we use Lerner's extensions [Ler91] to the Generic Interface Language (GIL) [Che89]), to describe state-dependent effects of a program. An *operation interface* includes the operation's header and a body with three clauses: a **requires** clause states the operation's pre-condition; a **modifies** clause lists those objects whose value the operation may possibly change; an **ensures** clause states the operation's post-condition. The assertion language for the pre- and post-conditions is drawn from LSL traits.

An *object interface* contains a **based on** clause and a set of operation interfaces, one for each operation exported by the object. Through **based on** clauses, Larch interfaces link to LSL traits by specifying a correspondence between (programming-language specific) types and LSL sorts. An object has a type and a value that ranges over terms of the corresponding sort. An object interface also may contain **invariant** clauses that state properties of the object preserved by its operations.

Part of the interface specification for the Miró editor shown in Figure 7 defines the type *Editor*, which is based on the sort *Ed* introduced in the EditorState trait. The **private** clause declares an object *e* of *Editor* type that is local to this interface. It is treated as an implicit argument and result of each operation in the object's interface. ResizeBox's precondition requires that the set of selected objects be exactly the singleton set containing ResizeBox's argument *b* of Box type (*box_to_O* is an operator that coerces a box sort to a more generic object sort). Its post-condition updates the size and position of the box being resized (using *set_size* and *set_pos*) and unselects all objects. In a post-condition an

[2] *Bool* is built-in to all LSL traits.

```
object miro_editor
...
   type Editor based on Ed from EditorState
   private e : Editor

   invariant ...

   operation ResizeBox (b : Box, pos : Cp, size : Cp)
      requires e.selected_objs = {box_to_O(b)}
      modifies (e_obj)
      ensures  b' = set_size(set_pos(b,pos),size) ∧ e'.selected_objs = {}
...
```

Figure 7: Part of the Miro Editor Interface Specification

undecorated formal, *e*, stands for the initial value of the object; a primed one, *e'*, stands for the final value. The **modifies** clause states that MoveBoxes may change only the editor and no other object.

We used the LSL Checker and the GIL Checker to check all specifications in this paper for syntactic and sort/type correctness. [Zar91] contains the full specifications for the excerpts we give in this paper.

3. Formal Methods Integrated in the Waterfall Model

We assume some familiarity with the two software development techniques discussed in this section, Structured Analysis and Structure Charts, and show how we can integrate Larch with both.

3.1. Requirements Phase: Larch and Structured Analysis

Structured Analysis, developed by DeMarco [DeM78], is a common technique used to record a system's functional requirements. There are three components to a structured analysis document: data-flow diagrams, data dictionaries, and activity specifications. In a data-flow diagram, circles represent activities (processing elements) and arrows drawn between circles represent data elements flowing between their corresponding activities. A system specifier refines each activity in a data-flow diagram to a lower-level data-flow diagram; refinement continues until a set of basic activities is reached. A data dictionary provides the definition of all data elements flowing in a data-flow diagram (at each level of refinement). Activity specifications provide the definition of each basic activity.

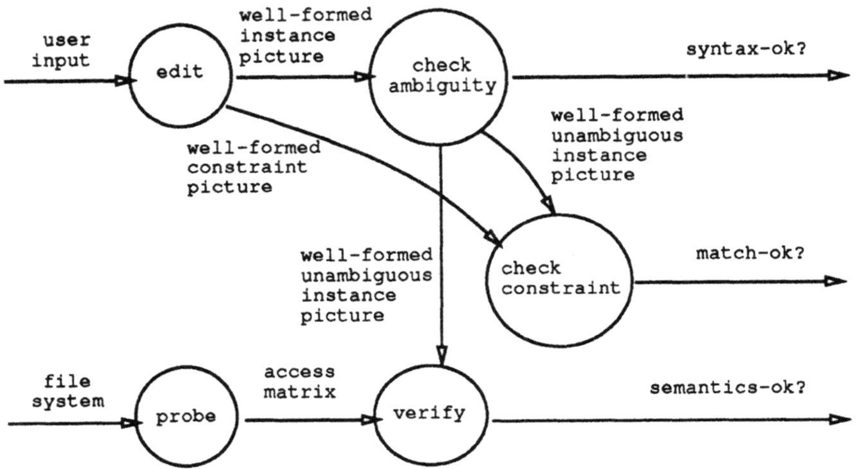

Figure 8: Data-Flow Diagram of the Miró Tools

For example, Figure 8 shows a top-level data-flow diagram of some of the functionality supported by the Miró tools. The *editor* takes user commands and creates well-formed instance pictures and well-formed constraint pictures. The *ambiguity checker* outputs well-formed unambiguous pictures that the *constraint checker* can check against given constraint pictures. The *prober* extracts an access matrix from a given file system directory that the *verifier* can then check against a given well-formed unambiguous instance picture.

Whereas notation and its interpretation for data-flow diagrams are standard, they are not for data dictionaries nor activity specifications. Here is one explicit point where Larch can be integrated in Structured Analysis:

Use the Larch Shared Language to define	(1) data elements in a data dictionary and (2) the functionality of basic activities.

3.1.1. Data Dictionaries Written in LSL

A data dictionary defines the data elements in a data-flow diagram. Many software engineering textbooks [Myn90, Pfl91, ED89] recommend using BNF-like notation, such as + for concatenation and {} for repetition, to describe how to form new data elements out of basic ones. For example,

Miro picture = Instance picture | Constraint picture
Instance picture = { Box | Arrow }

indicates that a Miro picture can be either an instance picture or constraint picture and an instance picture can be a collection of boxes and arrows. BNF-like notation forces the specifier to model data completely in terms of a few basic sorts of data elements like numbers, characters, and strings. This approach is at best inconvenient, e.g., how would we say that a box is the "concatenation" of four lines, but at worst too low-level in that the model forces the specifier to make design decisions prematurely. For example, we do not care that a box is composed of four lines since the implementor could choose to represent it as a set of pixels; rather we want to specify only those attributes of boxes that are necessary to describe the behaviors of the activities that manipulate boxes. In short, we cannot use BNF-like notation to describe the abstract properties of the data elements, e.g., those that would distinguish constraint boxes from instance boxes.

Instead, we can use the Larch Shared Language to write the data dictionary by specifying the sorts of data elements labeling the arrows in a data-flow diagram such as the one in Figure 8. Let us build up to a trait that describes well-formed instance pictures by beginning with one that describes basic pictures.

Figure 9 shows the sorts and operators introduced in the BasicPicture trait. A picture (sort *Pic*) is a collection of boxes and arrows. The renamings of sort identifiers in the two uses of the *Set* trait (from the Larch Handbook [GHW85b]) gives us the sorts *BSet* and *ASet* for sets of boxes and arrows, and, among others, the operators $\{\}{:}\rightarrow BSet$ and $\{\}{:}\rightarrow ASet$ to denote respectively the empty set of boxes and the empty set of arrows. The **generated by** clause says that all terms denoting values of pictures are expressed in terms of the operators *create_picture*, *insert_box*, and *insert_arrow*. The **partitioned by** clause says that if for two pictures their corresponding sets of *boxes* and sets of *arrows* are the same, then the pictures are the same. Through an **implies** clause, LSL provides a place to record explicitly consequences of the first-order theory denoted by a trait. The **converts ... exempting** clause states a property about the trait related to *sufficient-completeness* [Gut75]; it says that a term using any operator listed in the **converts** clause can be shown equal to either a term not using any convertible operator or an **exempt** term.

The equational axioms defining the operators are straightforward and given in the standard style of "algebraic" specifications (define the meaning of each non-constructor operator in terms of each constructor operator). For example, as shown in the equations below, we define *move_all_boxes(pic,delta)* to move each box in the picture *pic* by some amount *delta*. The picture is either empty, the result of inserting a box, or the result of inserting an arrow (since these are the three generating operators). The second equation states that the result of moving all boxes in a picture *pic* to which we have just inserted a box *b* is the same as (recursively) moving all boxes in *pic* and adding to it the result of changing *b*'s position by *delta*. The third equation similarly recurses through a picture's boxes without changing any inserted arrows.

$$
\begin{aligned}
&move\_all\_boxes(create\_picture, delta) == create\_picture\\
&move\_all\_boxes(insert\_box(pic, b), delta) ==\\
&\quad insert\_box(move\_all\_boxes(pic, delta), set\_pos(b, b.pos + delta))\\
&move\_all\_boxes(insert\_arrow(pic, a), delta) ==\\
&\quad insert\_arrow(move\_all\_boxes(pic, delta), a)
\end{aligned}
$$

```
BasicPicture(Pic) : trait
  includes Box, Set(B, BSet), Arrow, Set(A, ASet)
  introduces
      create_picture : → Pic
      insert_box : Pic, B → Pic
      insert_arrow : Pic, A → Pic
      move_all_boxes : Pic, CoordPair → Pic
      copy_picture : Pic → Pic
      delete_box : Pic, B → Pic
      delete_arrow : Pic, A → Pic
      boxes : Pic → BSet
      arrows : Pic → ASet
      arrows_attached_to_box : Pic, B → ASet
      arrows_attached_to_boxes : Pic, BSet → ASet

  asserts
      Pic generated by create_picture, insert_box, insert_arrow
      Pic partitioned by boxes, arrows
      . . . < Equations go here. > . . .
  implies
      converts move_all_boxes, copy_picture, delete_box, delete_arrow,
          boxes, arrows, arrows_attached_to_box, arrows_attached_to_boxes
          exempting ∀ b : B, a : A
              delete_box(create_picture, b), delete_arrow(create_picture, a)
```

Figure 9: Part of the BasicPicture Trait

```
WFPicture(Pic) : trait
  includes BasicPicture(Pic), Obj
  introduces
      arrows_attached : Pic, ASet → Bool
      arrow_attached : Pic, A → Bool
      well_formed : Pic → Bool
      delete_objs : Pic, ObjSet → Pic
      delete_wf_box : Pic, B → Pic
      delete_wf_arrow : Pic, A → Pic
      delete_arrows : Pic, ASet → Pic
      extract_wf : ObjSet → Pic

  asserts ∀ pic : Pic
      well_formed(pic) == arrows_attached(pic, arrows(pic))
      . . . < Other equations go here. > . . .
```

Figure 10: Part of the WFPicture Trait

Next we define a trait that builds upon basic pictures to define well-formedness for pictures. The *WFPicture* trait in Figure 10 introduces the *well-formed* operator among others. A well-formedness condition that is common to both instance and constraint pictures is that all arrows must be attached to boxes (no dangling arrows). We define the *arrows_attached* operator to capture this condition. *Arrows_attached* checks that a picture's set of arrows is attached by using *arrow_attached* to check each arrow in the set. An arrow is attached in a picture if the boxes at each of its ends are both in the picture.

$$
\begin{aligned}
&arrows\_attached(pic, \{\}) == true\\
&arrows\_attached(pic, insert(as, a)) ==\\
&\quad arrow\_attached(pic, a) \wedge arrows\_attached(pic, as)\\
&arrow\_attached(pic, a) ==\\
&\quad (((a.to\_box) \in boxes(pic)) \wedge ((a.from\_box) \in boxes(pic)))
\end{aligned}
$$

We then succinctly define the well-formedness condition common to instance and constraint pictures as:

$$well\_formed(pic) == arrows\_attached(pic, arrows(pic))$$

The operator *delete_objs* uses *delete_wf_box* and *delete_wf_arrow* to return a picture that is the result of deleting a set of objects. We define elsewhere the sort (O) for objects to be a union of the sorts (B and A) for boxes and arrows. For each object in the set of objects to be deleted, *delete_objs* checks whether the object is a box, i.e., $tag(obj) = box$, or an arrow and then uses the appropriate operator, *delete_wf_box* or *delete_wf_arrow*. Deleting just a box may violate the well-formedness condition since it could result in dangling arrows. Hence, if the box, b, being deleted is in the picture, *delete_wf_box* must delete all attached arrows before deleting b. *Delete_wf_arrow* operator deletes the arrow a from the picture only if a is in the picture.

$$
\begin{aligned}
&delete\_objs(pic, \{\}) == pic\\
&delete\_objs(pic, insert(os, obj)) == \textbf{if } tag(obj) = box\\
&\quad \textbf{then } delete\_objs(delete\_wf\_box(pic, obj.box), os)\\
&\quad \textbf{else } delete\_objs(delete\_wf\_arrow(pic, obj.arrow), os)\\
&delete\_wf\_box(pic, b) == \textbf{if } b \in boxes(pic)\\
&\quad \textbf{then } delete\_box(delete\_arrows(pic, arrows\_attached\_to\_box(pic, b)), b)\\
&\quad \textbf{else } pic\\
&delete\_wf\_arrow(pic, a) == \textbf{if } a \in arrows(pic) \textbf{ then } delete\_arrow(pic, a) \textbf{ else } pic
\end{aligned}
$$

Extract_wf returns a picture that is the maximal well-formed subset of a set of objects. The interface specification for the editor uses *extract_wf* to describe the behavior of the editor operation that copies objects (CopyObjs). The set of objects to be copied is a sub-picture, which may or may not be well-formed. The result of *extract_wf(os)* is a well-formed picture that contains all the objects of *os* except the dangling arrows, i.e., arrows that are not attached to boxes in *os*. We define *extract_wf* indirectly by defining what *boxes* and *arrows* are in the resulting picture:

$boxes(extract\_wf(os)) == boxes(os)$
$a \in arrows(extract\_wf(os)) ==$
$(a \in arrows(os)) \wedge ((a.to\_box) \in boxes(os)) \wedge ((a.from\_box) \in boxes(os))$

Instance pictures have an additional well-formedness condition that constraint pictures do not: each arrow must start from a box of type User (see the sixth field labeled *box_type:BoxType* of Figure 6) and end at a box of type File. Figure 11 shows the WFInstancePic trait that includes the WFPicture trait and adds this additional well-formedness condition. This example shows how one trait (WFInstancePic) can place further constraints on an operator, e.g., *well_formed*, introduced and defined elsewhere (WFPicture).

WFInstancePic : **trait**
includes *WFPicture*(*IPic*, *create_instance_pic* **for** *create_picture*)
introduces
$users\_to\_files : IPic, IASet \rightarrow Bool$
$user\_to\_file : IPic, IA \rightarrow Bool$

asserts $\forall$ *ipic* : *IPic*
$users\_to\_files(ipic, \{\}) == true$
$users\_to\_files(ipic, insert(as, a)) ==$
$user\_to\_file(ipic, a) \wedge users\_to\_files(ipic, as)$
$user\_to\_file(ipic, a) ==$
$(a.from\_box).box\_type = User \wedge (a.to\_box).box\_type = File$
$well\_formed(ipic) == users\_to\_files(ipic, arrows(ipic))$

Figure 11: Part of the WFInstancePic Trait

Returning to Figure 8 we now know more formally what "well-formed instance picture" means: in all pictures each arrow is attached to boxes at both ends and each goes from a User to a File box. We define other traits for defining distinguishing characteristics of constraint pictures and unambiguous (instance) pictures similarly and omit the details here. In summary, we see that LSL traits give a more precise definition of the sorts of data elements labeling the arrows in data-flow diagrams.

3.1.2. Activity Specifications Written in LSL

Activity specifications are usually written in English, pseudo-code, or using decision tables. Since we can interpret each basic activity as a mathematical function that takes data elements as input and returns them as output, we can write for an activity specification of function f an LSL trait that introduces and defines through equations the function f. For example, after refining the *edit* activity of the data-flow diagram of Figure 8, we may find we need to define a basic activity called *adjust_arrows* whose effect is to ensure that the well-formedness property of instance pictures is maintained.

We define *adjust_arrows* on pictures with the following equations, where *set_tail_pos* (*set_head_pos*) sets the position information for an arrow's tail (head) and *find_tail_pos* (*find_head_pos*), given a picture and two boxes, determines the appropriate coordinate pair of the tail (head) of the arrow being adjusted.

$$
\begin{aligned}
& adjust\_arrows(create\_picture, b) == create\_picture \\
& adjust\_arrows(insert\_box(pic, b1), b) == insert\_box(adjust\_arrows(pic, b), b1) \\
& adjust\_arrows(insert\_arrow(pic, a), b) == \\
& \quad \textbf{if } a.from\_box = b \textbf{ then } insert\_arrow\ (\ adjust\_arrows\ (\ pic, \mathrm{b}), \\
& \qquad\qquad set\_tail\_pos(a, find\_tail\_pos(pic, b, a.to\_box))) \\
& \quad \textbf{else if } a.to\_box = b \textbf{ then } insert\_arrow\ (\ adjust\_arrows\ (\ pic, \mathrm{b}), \\
& \qquad\qquad set\_head\_pos(a, find\_head\_pos(pic, b, a.to\_box))) \\
& \quad \textbf{else } insert\_arrow(adjust\_arrows(pic, b), a)
\end{aligned}
$$

In general, for any basic activity we can write its functional definition since LSL provides a conditional construct, function composition, and recursion.

3.2. Design Phase: Larch and Structure Charts

Yourdon and Constantine developed a structured design method that lets software developers express system designs using *Structure Charts* [YC79]. Developers may even choose to transform data-flow diagrams created in the requirements analysis phase to produce Structure Charts in the design phase. A Structure Chart is a hierarchical diagram in which rectangular boxes represent modules in a system and arrows connecting boxes represent the calling relationships among the modules.

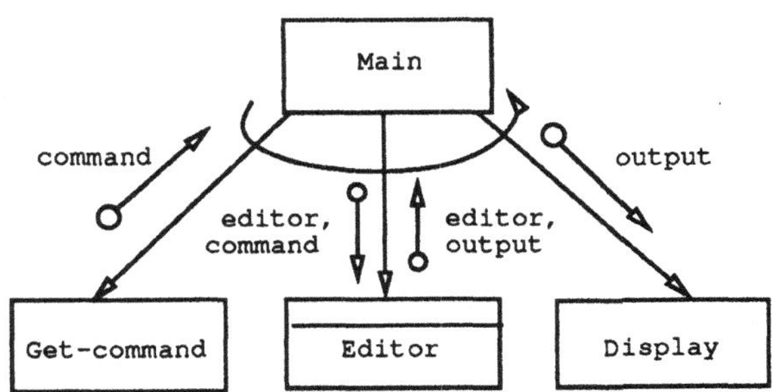

Figure 12: A Structure Chart Using the Editor Module

For example, the Structure Chart in Figure 12 shows the top-level control structure between four modules we have identified for the Miró editor[3]. The Main module loops receiving input commands from the user through the Get-command module, calling an Editor module that accepts different user commands initializing or transforming the editor state accordingly, and calling a Display module to output the transformed editor state. The short, labeled arrows represent the direction in which data flows between modules. We

[3]Here, we focus on just the "edit" activity in the data-flow diagram of Figure 8.

show the Editor module as a *data abstraction module* by drawing a double horizontal bar; more typically, we could depict it as a *procedural abstraction module* (single horizontal bar) that serves as a dispatcher (denoted by a diamond superimposed on the lower horizontal bar) to each of the operations exported by the data abstraction.

Structure Charts and Larch interface specifications are ideal complements of each other. Larch interface specifications are appropriate for specifying the behavior of each module. Larch provides no means of showing the interconnection among modules; structure charts do. Here is the explicit point where Larch can be integrated in the software development technique based on Structure Charts:

Use Larch interface language specifications to describe the behavior of modules in a Structure Chart.

To flesh out the editor example in more detail, we present pieces of the Larch interface specification of the editor data abstraction specified as a GIL object interface. We begin by describing editor state at the trait level and then describe the editor's operations at the interface level.

3.2.1. LSL Specification of Editor State

The *EditorState* trait (Figure 13) introduces the tuple sort *Ed* to stand for editor state. The *pos* and *size* fields indicate the location and size of the editor window on the screen. The *picture* field contains the current Miró picture, of sort *P* (introduced in the *PicUnion* trait), and *selected_objs* is the set of currently selected objects in the picture. The remainder of the tuple describes the current mode of the editor (as indicated in the menus): *picture_type* indicates whether the current picture is an instance or constraint picture; *object_type* is either box or arrow; *arrow_kind* is the kind of arrow – syntactic, semantic or containment (which is relevant only for constraint pictures); the rest of the attributes are self-explanatory. We introduce only one operator, *display_window*, but leave it unspecified here; we could use it to define a mapping from the abstract editor state to an actual mapping of screen pixels.

3.2.2. Part of the Larch Interface for the Editor

In Figure 7 we presented part of the Miró editor interface specification. We explain it in more detail here. We first establish using the **based on** clause a correspondence between the type of object being specified and the sort of values the object ranges over. We give elsewhere object specifications for other types, e.g., object sets (ObjSet) and coordinate pairs (Cp), on which the editor operation's depends. An **invariant** specifies properties that must be true after every procedure and before all procedures except those named in the **initialized by** clause. In this case, the first invariant states that the editor maintains

EditorState : **trait**
  includes *PicUnion*(*ObjType_Obj* **for** *O*, *Box_Obj* **for** *B*,
    Arrow_Obj **for** *A*), *PixelMap*

  OT **enumeration of** *box*, *arrow* % object type

  Ed **tuple of**
    pos : *CoordPair*, *size* : *CoordPair*, % position info
    picture : *P*, % graphical objects
    picture_type : *PicType*, % picture type
    object_type : *OT*, % object mode info
    arrow_kind : *ArrowKind*,
    arrow_parity : *Parity*,
    thickness : *LineThickness*,
    starred : *Bool*,
    selected_objs : *OS* % selection

  introduces
    display_window : *Ed* → *PixelMap* % not defined here

Figure 13: The EditorState Trait

the well-formedness of a picture and the second states that the set of selected objects must be a subset of all objects in the editor's picture.

object miro_editor
  type Editor **based on** Ed **from** EditorState
  private e : Editor

  invariant (well_formed(e.picture))
  invariant (e.selected_objs ⊆ objects(e.picture))

  initialized by CreateEditor

  . . . < Interface specifications of the twelve exported operations go here. > . . .

The complete editor specification contains interfaces for twelve operations. The operations include creating an editor (CreateEditor), drawing a box (DrawBox), drawing an arrow (DrawArrow), selecting an object (Select), selecting a group of objects (GroupSelect), unselecting objects (Unselect), moving boxes (MoveBoxes), resizing boxes (ResizeBox), deleting objects (DeleteObjs), copying objects (CopyObjs), changing an object's attribute (ChangeAttribute), and clearing the editor (Clear). We present only three here (another was given in Section 2).

CreateEditor's effects are to return a new object (**newobj**) of type editor and to initialize various fields of the tuple representing the editor's state. ([...] is the tuple constructor operator.)

operation CreateEditor (posn, size : Cp)
  requires true
  ensures (**newobj**(e_{obj})) ∧
    (e' = ([posn, size, create_picture(inst_pic),
      inst_pic, box, syn, positive, thin, false,{}]))

Miró editor users can select or unselect objects in three ways: individual select/unselect, group select, and global unselect. For example, GroupSelect requires that its argument, *os*, be a subset of objects in the picture and has the effect of adding *os* to the currently selected set. If an object in *os* is already selected, it remains selected.

operation GroupSelect (os : ObjSet)
  requires (os ⊆ objects(e.picture))
  modifies (e_{obj})
  ensures (e'.selected_objs = (e.selected_objs ∪ os))

The copy operation in the editor is somewhat complex because of the well-formedness constraint. Copy operates on only a subset of the currently selected objects, namely the maximal well-formed subset (i.e., all objects except dangling arrows). The **ensures** clause of CopyObjs thus specifies a new picture object, *newpic*, whose value is the result of copying the well-formed subset of the selected objects of *e.picture*. *e'.picture* is then the result of combining the existing picture with *newpic*, which has been moved by *delta*[4]. CopyObjs has the side effects of creating a new object for each of the copied objects in the well-formed subset and of unselecting all objects.

operation CopyObjs (delta : Cp)
  requires true
  modifies (e_{obj})
  ensures
    ∃ newpic : Picture ∀ o:ObjType
      newobj (newpic) ∧
      newpic!post = copy_picture(extract_wf(e.picture_type,e.selected_objs)) ∧
      (o ∈ objects(newpic!post) => **newobj** (o)) ∧
      e'.picture = pic_union(e.picture,
        move_all_boxes(newpic!post, delta)) ∧
      e'.selected_objs = {}

---

[4]GIL notation requires us to represent the final value of an object *a* as *a'* if *a* is a parameter or global variable and as *a*!post if *a* is a quantified variable.

3.3. Larch Tools and CASE Tools

In teaching the undergraduate software engineering course during the Spring 1991 semester, we loosely integrated the Larch Shared Language Checker and a Larch/C Checker with the CASE tool, *Software Through Pictures* (STP) [5]. STP supports graphical editors for many software analysis and design methods including Structured Analysis and Structure Charts. Where "annotations" are normally attached to data elements, e.g., in a data-flow diagram, users can in addition attach LSL specifications. Similarly, users can attach Larch/C specifications as annotations of modules in Structure Charts. A similar or even tighter integration is possible with many other CASE tools.

4. Formal Methods Integrated in a Prototyping Model

4.1. A Loose (Unintrusive) Integration

The prototyping model of software development has not reached the same maturity as the waterfall model. Software developers typically design and build prototypes in the implementation language itself rather than choosing a separate language. Alternatively, they can write prototypes in an executable formal specification language, e.g., PAISley [Zav72] and OBJ [FGJM85], and then rewrite the "final" prototype in a more efficient implementation language. This approach suggests a tight coupling between the specification and implementation, at least between the last specification and the first "efficient" implementation; it is roughly similar to the refinement model where the prototypes are specifications.

Although the use of an executable formal specification language is a valid way to integrate some classes of formal methods in a prototyping model, we explore here a looser integration in which a specification and an implementation are each written in their own notation and refined in different ways. This approach treats both the specification and implementation as dynamically changing by-products of each of the specifying and coding phases. Developing a specification and an implementation in parallel means that they can directly affect each other's next version. Each newer version of the specification (implementation) is influenced by earlier versions of the implementation (specification) and can influence the later versions.

When we developed both the Larch specification and the implementation of the Miró editor we followed a prototyping approach rather than the conventional waterfall or refinement approaches. Since our particular specificand has a heavy user interface component, prototyping was an appropriate and useful means of exploring and validating the graphical and device handling aspects of the Miró editor.

---

[5]Copyright 1990. IDE Software Through Pictures is a registered trademark of Interactive Development Environment.

The unrolling shown in Figure 3 matches the actual development of the Miró editor. We began writing formal specifications in parallel with designing and implementing the editor. We wrote three major versions of the specification where the last version was written after the implementation had already passed into the maintenance phase. We specified in the first version a subset of the editor's functionality and handled only instance pictures. The second version was more comprehensive and also dealt with constraint pictures, but we invented new syntactic constructs to make the Larch traits more concise. Finally, we added yet more functionality in the current version, but reverted to standard Larch syntax by translating our syntactic inventions. The current version itself went through at least eight minor iterations. The entire development effort, which also included changes to the instance and constraint languages, lasted two years.

4.2. Larch and Prototyping

Since there are no well-known or widely-used counterparts to Structured Analysis and Structure Charts for a prototyping model of software development, we cannot as concretely describe as we did for the waterfall model how Larch or any similar formal method fits in with prototyping. A specification, whether written in Larch or not, can evolve in many ways: by making it more complete, abstracting, generalizing, and improving its presentation. In this section we focus on these four kinds of changes in the context of Larch and point out places where cross-fertilization between specification and implementation can occur.

4.2.1. Make it more complete.

Write signatures of operations; introduce new types.

One way to start writing a Larch interface specification is to define the signatures of each operation. The signatures determine what other types of objects, hence data abstractions, need to be specified and implemented. For example, the GroupSelect operation takes a set of objects as its argument, introducing the need to implement an ObjSet (set of objects) type. This type information in the specification imposes constraints on other parts of specification too, in particular what is required by the **based on** trait: a type is based on some sort that must be introduced by some trait.

Fill in bodies of interfaces.

Once we have an operation's signature we can flesh out its body by writing **requires/modifies/ensures** clauses. Each clause has a direct influence on the implementation. The inclusion of a non-trivial **requires** clause (something other than "true") says the implementor need not check the system's state for whether the pre-condition holds since the client code is responsible for checking. The omission of a **modifies** clause (equivalent to saying **modifies nothing**) is a strong assertion that the implementor must uphold. Not only may no input argument be modified, but no global variable may be modified. All operations in the editor specification except CreateEditor may modify the editor's state. An **ensures** clause summarizes three important effects of an operation: what updates are made to any object listed in the **modifies** clause, what new objects are created, and what exceptional termination conditions are possible (error handling). CreateEditor, DrawBox, DrawArrow, and CopyObjs are the only editor operations that add new objects to the system's state. In contrast, ResizeBox does not delete an old box and create a new one; it just changes the properties of the old one.

Fill in trait information.

Just as interfaces can be fleshed out from one specification step to the next; traits can be fleshed out in a similar way. Signatures for trait operators can be given first; equations defining their meaning later. **Generated by**, **partitioned by**, and **converts** clauses can be added later, as necessary. Filling in details at the trait level may also affect the implementation. For example, **exempt** terms of a sort S usually stand for "error" values, which should be handled by a pre-condition in any operation referring to an object whose type is based on S. Alternatively, they could be handled by raising some exception (see discussion in Section 4.2.3 on removing pre-conditions).

4.2.2. Abstract.

An extreme example of applying abstraction is to consider the implementation as a specification. This viewpoint often makes sense when following the approach of developing a specification in parallel with an implementation. We use the implementation as an appropriate starting point for a specification and then abstract from it until we reach a high-level enough description of the system; this abstraction process goes in the opposite direction of that followed in the refinement model. The danger with this approach is that without sufficient abstraction the specification may reflect too faithfully the original implementation model and perhaps exclude other acceptable implementations.

For example, our implementation is written in a frame-based knowledge representation language and so we naturally represent each type of object in the editor as a *frame* with various *slots*. This record-like representation greatly influenced our initial specification in which we used LSL **tuples** for boxes and arrows and drew a one-to-one correspondence between slots in a frame and fields in the corresponding tuple. We include, for example, a field called *selected* used to determine whether that box or arrow is currently selected. Every operation in the editor's interface except CreateEditor tested and toggled this field explicitly. Later we removed the *selected* field from the tuple upon realizing that we already maintained the relevant information with the set of selected objects in the editor state (*selected_objs*).

One way to abstract from a concrete model is to state a property of the model and ask whether it is an essential behavioral characteristic of the desired system. If the property is irrelevant then it can be left out, making the specification more abstract. Removing irrelevant detail from a specification may sometimes result in a complete redesign of the abstractions themselves. Again, influenced by the record representation for all objects, we used **tuples** for describing pictures; later, upon realizing that the essential properties of pictures in which we are interested are similar to those for graphs, we changed the BasicPicture trait to build upon sets of boxes (nodes) and sets of arrows (edges). We recursively generate values for pictures with *create_picture*, *insert_box* and *insert_arrow* instead of a **tuple of** constructor. This change also made it easier to prove a consequence of this trait stated in its **implies** clause (see discussion in Section 4.2.4 on **implies** clauses).

4.2.3. Generalize.

Remove pre-conditions; handle error conditions.

Removing a pre-condition implies that an operation can be invoked from more states than before. An earlier specification of the MoveBoxes operation had a pre-condition that only one object be selected; hence moving objects had to be done by selecting and moving them one at a time. Removing the pre-condition allows MoveBoxes to operate on a set of objects, e.g., the set of selected objects. Removing a pre-condition in general may imply that the implementation now needs to check explicitly for a case that was safely ignored before. It often results in introducing an exceptional termination case in the post-condition, which now the implementor must **signal** under the appropriate condition.

Add type genericity.

An earlier specification had an operation each for deleting boxes, deleting arrows, copying boxes, copying arrows, changing attributes of a box, and changing attributes of an arrow. Realizing that deleting, copying, and changing attributes are operations whose effects are independent of whether their argument is a box or arrow led us to add a more generic object type to stand for boxes and arrows. This change led to the current version which has only three generic operations instead of six specific ones. In reality, the actual implementation influenced our addition of type genericity to these operations: Garnet [M+89], the graphical system on which Miró runs, supports the notion of an *object* on which many common editing operations can be performed.

In this instance, adding type genericity had the side effect of changing the underlying traits as well. We introduced a union sort for objects to stand for the corresponding box or arrow sorts. This change actually complicated the trait equations since we had to define some trait operators as lengthy "case" statements depending on an object's tag (recall the equations for *delete_objs* in Section 3.1); however, this complexity in the trait is completely hidden at the interface level in the specification. For example, what appears in the ChangeAttribute operation as a simple function call to the *change_attr* trait operator actually expands to its half-page long, nested **if-then-else** definition.

Add parameters to operations/operators.

We add parameters to an operation at the interface level, and similarly an operator at the trait level, to capture intentional incompleteness in a specification (delaying a design decision till binding time) and to add a degree of generality to the specification. For example, in the first version of the specification we explicitly modeled the mouse as an input device that provided coordinate pair information. In post-conditions of the earlier versions of DrawBox and DrawArrow we referred explicitly to this mouse's coordinate information to determine where the box or arrow is to be drawn. In contrast, our current version of the entire editor specification makes no reference to a mouse at all. DrawBox and DrawArrow each take coordinate pairs as parameters and do not care what or how that information is generated.

4.2.4. Improve presentation.

Add invariants.

Adding an invariant to a Larch interface specification is a way to capture explicitly in one place information that may be either implicit or scattered throughout the rest of the interface specification. In the Editor specification the invariant that all pictures be well-formed arose from factoring out what in an earlier version of the specification was in each of the operation's pre- and post-conditions. It is an example of an explicit statement of a property that the Miró editor is required to maintain. Adding this invariant had the side benefit of making the specification tidier.

Add **implies** *to traits.*

Stating explicit consequences of a trait is similar to stating explicit **invariants** in an interface. After writing a barebones trait with just equations and perhaps **generated by** and **partitioned by** clauses, often we add an **implies** clause as a way of formally documenting what else a trait intends to state. For example, since we can think of each Miró picture as being a graph where boxes are nodes and arrows are edges, we add the following **implies** clause to the WFPicture trait:

implies
Graph(B, A, Pic, *create_picture* **for** *empty*, *insert_box* **for** *addNode*,
insert_arrow **for** *addEdge*, *boxes* **for** *nodes*, *arrows* **for** *edges*)

where *Graph* is a Larch Handbook trait. This implication is a strong assertion. In terms of LSL semantics, it says that the first-order theory of graphs is a subset of the theory of well-formed instance pictures; any property of graphs holds for well-formed instance pictures.

We can take this one step further in our WFInstancePic trait. Since we add the well-formed requirement that each arrow goes from a User box to a File box, we can also add the implication that a well-formed instance picture is a bipartite graph. Here is a case where explicitly stating this as an implication caused us to realize a discrepancy between the specification and the implementation; the editor does not currently enforce this well-formedness property.

Make more readable and modular.

Many of the minor iterations of each major version of the specification improved the readability of the specification. Factoring large traits into smaller, reusable ones yields more modular specifications. For example, we define single traits each for boxes, arrows, and well-formed pictures; we reuse each twice: once for their version for instance pictures and once for constraint pictures. We also introduce many trait operators solely to shorten interface pre- and post-conditions.

5. Further Work and Final Remark

Based on our more realistic model of software development drawn in Figure 2, we suggest two practical directions for the software engineering community to pursue: (1) Begin to use formal methods now. The earlier the better, but it's never too late. Many specification case studies published are *post facto* specification exercises (e.g., [Win90, MS84]). A project can gain benefits from using formal methods no matter when they are introduced in the overall project's development plan. (2) Expand CASE technology to include tools that support formal methods. Integrating syntax and type checkers is easy; integrating semantic analyzers like proof checkers, proof debuggers, and theorem provers is harder, but possibly where the greatest payoff from using formal methods lies.

Our purpose in writing this paper is to provide concrete advice to practitioners on how formal methods can be integrated unintrusively in software engineering today. With the growing concern by the software engineering community to alleviate the "software crisis" by trying formal methods and with the growing interest by industry in formal methods, we hope our advice helps to bridge the gap between inventors of formal methods and their intended users.

6. Acknowledgments

We are grateful to Rick Lerner for his implementation of the GIL checker; to Rick, Allan Heydon, Mark Maimone, and Doug Tygar for their helpful comments on the Miró editor specification; and to Rod Nord for integrating the Larch tools with STP.

This research was sponsored by the Avionics Lab, Wright Research and Development Center, Aeronautical Systems Division (AFSC), U. S. Air Force, Wright-Patterson AFB, OH 45433-6543 under Contract F33615-90-C-1465, Arpa Order No. 7597. A. M. Zaremski is also supported by a fellowship from the Office of Naval Research. The views and conclusions contained in this document are those of the authors and should not be interpreted as representing the official policies, either expressed or implied, of the U.S. Government.

References

[Che89] J. Chen. The Larch/Generic Interface Language. S.B. Thesis, MIT, May 1989.

[DeM78] T. DeMarco. *Structured Analysis and System Specification.* Yourdon Press, New York, 1978.

[Dij76] E.W. Dijkstra. *A Discipline of Programming.* Prentice-Hall, 1976.

[ED89] C. Easteal and G. Davies. *Software Engineering: Analysis and Design.* McGraw-Hill, London, 1989.

[FGJM85] K. Futatsugi, J.A. Goguen, J.-P. Jouannaud, and J. Meseguer. Principles of OBJ2. In *Proceedings of ACM POPL*, pp. 52–66, 1985.

[GH80] J.V. Guttag and J.J. Horning. Formal specification as a design tool. In *Proceedings of the* 7th *Symposium on Principles of Programming Languages*, pp. 251–261, Las Vegas, Jan. 1980.

[GHM90] J.V. Guttag, J.J. Horning, and A. Modet. Report on the Larch Shared Language: Version 2.3. TR, DEC-SRC, 1990.

[GHW85a] John V. Guttag, James J. Horning, and Jeannette M. Wing. The Larch family of specification languages. *IEEE Software*, pp. 24–36, Sept. 1985.

[GHW85b] J.V. Guttag, J.J. Horning, and J.M. Wing. Larch in five easy pieces. TR, DEC-SRC, 1985.

[Gri81] D. Gries. *The Science of Programming.* Springer-Verlag, New York, 1981.

[Gut75] J.V. Guttag. *The Specification and Application to Programming of Abstract Data Types.* PhD thesis, University of Toronto, Toronto, Canada, Sept. 1975.

[HMT+90] A. Heydon, M. W. Maimone, J.D. Tygar, J. M. Wing, and A. M. Zaremski. Miró: Visual specification of security. *IEEE TSE*, 16(10):1185–1197, Oct. 1990.

[Jac83] M. Jackson. *System Development.* Prentice-Hall, Englewood Cliffs, 1983.

[Jon86] C.B. Jones. *Systematic Software Development Using VDM.* Prentice-Hall International, 1986.

[Ler91] R.A. Lerner. *Modular Specifications of Concurrent Programs.* PhD thesis, CMU, 1991. TR CS-91-131.

[M+89] B.A. Myers et al. The Garnet toolkit reference manuals: Support for highly-interactive , graphical user interfaces in Lisp. TR CS-89-196, CMU, Nov. 1989.

[MS84] C. Morgan and B. Sufrin. Specification of the UNIX filing system. *IEEE TSE*, 10(2):128–142, 1984.

[MTW90] M. W. Maimone, J. D. Tygar, and J. M. Wing. Formal semantics for visual specification of security. In S.K. Chang, ed., *Visual Languages and Visual Programming*. Plenum Publishing Corporation, 1990.

[Myn90] B.T. Mynatt. *Software Engineering with Student Project Guidance*. Prentice-Hall, Englewood Cliffs, 1990.

[Pfl91] S.L. Pfleeger. *Software Engineering: The Production of Quality Software*. Macillan, N.Y., 1991. Second edition.

[Ros77] D.T. Ross. Structured analysis (SA): A language for communicating ideas. *IEEE TSE*, pp. 16–34, Jan. 1977.

[Ros85] D.T. Ross. Applications and extensions of SADT. *IEEE Computer*, pp. 25–34, April 1985.

[Spi88] J.M. Spivey. *Introducing Z: a Specification Language and its Formal Semantics*. Cambridge University Press, 1988.

[Win85] J.M. Wing. Specification firms: A vision for the future. In *Proceedings of the* 3rd *International Workshop on Software Specification and Design*, pp. 241–243, 1985.

[Win90] J. Wing. Using Larch to specify Avalon/C++ objects. *IEEE TSE*, 16(9):1076–1088, Sept. 1990.

[YC79] E. Yourdon and L. Constantine. *Structured Design*. Prentice-Hall, Englewood Cliffs, 1979.

[Zar91] A.M. Zaremski. A Larch specification of the Miro editor. TR CS-91-111, CMU, 1991.

[Zav72] P. Zave. An operational approach to requirements specification for embedded systems. *IEEE TSE*, 8(3):250–269, May 1972.

An Overview of HP-SL

Stephen Bear

Hewlett-Packard Laboratories,
Filton Road,
Stoke Gifford,
Bristol BS12 6QZ.
United Kingdom

sb@hplb.hpl.hp.com

X.400 address: G=steve;S=bear;OU1=hpl;OU2=unix;O=hp;P=hp;A=gold 400;C=gb

ABSTRACT

The Software Engineering Department of HP Labs is developing and applying a small but powerful specification language, *HP-SL*. This project report provides an overview of the language, its supporting tools and the way in which it is being applied.

1 Introduction

The Software Engineering Department of HP Labs in Bristol is working to apply, extend and transfer the use of formal methods in an industrial environment.

Two programmes of work are underway to achieve these goals. One programme is developing an *industrial* specification language, HP-SL. The other programme is establishing and supporting the use of formal specification on real product developments.

This short paper reports some of our experience. Section 2 is the main part of the report; it provides an informal overview of the specification language HP-SL. Section 3 describes the tools developed to support HP-SL. Section 4 sketches our approach to transferring formal specification into HP.

1.1 Specification for Industry

Industrial training in formal specification must address two issues simultaneously.

- The idea of specifying a system by giving mathematical definitions.
- The details of a language in which to express such definitions.

Training at the start of a project is a visible cost, so it is important to be able to present these ideas quickly and efficiently. An industrial specification language must reduce the 'language overhead' as much as possible. However, the language must not be overly restricted. It must be flexible enough and powerful enough to define varied products in a natural way. In particular the language should not impose a single idiom.

HP-SL has been designed to address these concerns. It is a small and regular language. Two concepts are fundamental: abstract types and underspecified total functions. Building upon this foundation, the language provides the usual specification concepts. It is also flexible. Definitions may be given in assertional, pre-post or explicit styles. These different approaches are integrated in a uniform framework, so a single function may be specified in any mixture of the styles.

Polymorphic functions and 'new' type constructors may be defined. This makes it possible to effectively extend the language and to create new idioms. A very successful example, *'History Specification'* is described in [3].

A complete definition of HP-SL is beyond the scope of this paper, but a more detailed description of the language may be found in [5]

2 An Overview of HP-SL

The objective of this section is to give an overview of the HP-SL language and the specification style that it supports. We assume that the reader is familiar with other model oriented specification languages, such as VDM [1].

An HP-SL specification consists of a collection of definitions—definitions of types, values of types, functions or relations over the types, and assertions about types or values. The definitions may be interspersed with narrative text.

2.1 Basics

Predefined Types

HP-SL provides a number of pre-defined types including *Bool, Char* and *Real*. Values of these types may be defined explicitly or implicitly.

val $ten : Real \triangleq 10$
val $delta : Real$ **sat** $delta > 0 \wedge delta \leq 0.05$
val $number : Real$

These definitions introduce three named values: *ten* is an explicitly defined value of type *Real*; *delta* is an underspecified value of type *Real* which satisfies the constraint $delta > 0 \wedge delta \leq 0.05$; *number* is an underspecified value of type *Real* which is not constrained.

Predefined Type Constructors

HP-SL provides a number of pre-defined type constructors. These include the set and sequence type constructors *Set*, *Seq*, the map and function type constructors $\xrightarrow{m}$, $\rightarrow$ and the tuple type constructor $\times$. Later, we will see how new type constructors may be defined.

val *realset* : *Set Real* $\triangleq$ { 1, 2, 3, 4 }
val *realseq* : *Seq Real* $\triangleq$ $\ll$ 1, 2, 3, 4 $\gg$
val *realmap* : *Real* $\xrightarrow{m}$ *Real* $\triangleq$ [1 $\mapsto$ 1, 2 $\mapsto$ 4, 3 $\mapsto$ 9]
val *realfun* : *Real* $\rightarrow$ *Real* $\triangleq$ (λ *x* : *Real* $\cdot$ *x***x*)
val *realpair* : *Real* $\times$ *Real* $\triangleq$ (1, 2)

This fragment of HP-SL defines values of a number of types: *realset* is the set of real numbers 1,2,3 and 4. *realseq* is the sequence of real numbers 1,2,3,4. *realmap* is the map of the real numbers 1,2,3 to their squares. *realfun* is the function of the real numbers to their squares. Finally *realpair* is the pair of real numbers (1, 2).

Synonym Types

It is often convenient to give a name to an existing type or a type expression. In HP-SL this is done by a synonym type definition.

syntype *RealPair* $\triangleq$ *Real* $\times$ *Real*

This definition introduces a new name *RealPair* for the type denoted by the expression *Real* $\times$ *Real*. The definition does not introduce a distinct type. A value of type *RealPair* may be used wherever a value of type *Real* $\times$ *Real* could be used, and vice-versa.

Subtypes

Sometimes it is useful to define those elements of a type which satisfy some property. Such a collection is called a *subtype*. The property satisfied by elements of the subtype is called the invariant.

In HP-SL a subtype is defined by a type expression with an invariant clause. A subtype is often named by a synonym type definition.

syntype *Positive* $\triangleq$ *Real* **inv** $r \cdot r > 0$

This fragment of HP-SL defines a subtype of type *Real* which consists of all real numbers which are strictly greater than zero. The subtype is defined by the type expression *Real* **inv** $r \cdot r > 0$. The invariant clause is introduced by the language word **inv** which is followed by a pattern r and then the invariant predicate $r > 0$.

HP-SL provides a number of predefined subtypes, including *Int*, *Nat0* and *Nat1*.

2.2 Functions

Functions may be defined using a typed lamda calculus.

```
val realsqr  : Real → Real ≜ ( λ x : Real · x*x )
```

realsqr is a function of type *Real* → *Real* defined by the lambda expression $\lambda\ x : Real \cdot x{*}x$.

As a derived form, HP-SL provides a syntax which is closer to that used in programming languages, and is more familiar to engineers.

```
fn realsqr  : Real → Real is
   realsqr( x )  ≜  x*x
```

These two definitions of *realsqr* are equivalent.

Strictly, HP-SL functions have precisely one argument—multiple arguments are combined by the tuple type constructor. However, function application is by juxtaposition, so the resulting syntax is simple and looks natural.

```
fn realmultiply  : Real × Real → Real is
   realmultiply( x, y )  ≜  x*y

val six ≜ realmultiply( 2, 3 )
```

HP-SL functions are higher-order. Functions may accept other functions as arguments. In particular, functions may be defined in a 'curried' form.

```
fn realmultiply  : Real → Real → Real is
   realmultiply( x )( y )  ≜  x*y
```

Curried functions may be partially applied.

```
val double: Real → Real ≜ realmultiply(2)
```

double is a function of one real which doubles its argument.

Implicit Definitions

Implicit definitions are frequently more convenient than explicit definitions. HP-SL implicit definitions are conventional—a post-condition is given to define the relationship between the value returned by a function and the values of its arguments.

```
fn prime_factors : Nat1 → Seq Nat1 is
     prime_factors(n)
     return s
  post
     product(s) = n ∧
     ( ∀ p ∈ elems(s) · is_prime(p) )
```

This is equivalent to defining a value of the function type which satisfies the post condition.

```
val prime_factors : Nat1 → Seq Nat1 sat
   ( ∀ n : Nat1 ·
     let val s ≜ prime_factors(n) in
        product(s) = n ∧
        ( ∀ p ∈ elems(s) · is_prime(p) )
     endlet
   )
```

Partial Functions

Functions are not always well-defined for every value in the domain type, for example standard real division is not well-defined for divisor 0.

In HP-SL all functions are *total* functions, but a pre-condition may be used to explicitly indicate where a definition applies. For example, a *divide* function could be defined as follows

```
fn divide  : Real → Real → Real is
    divide(divisor)(numerator)
  pre divisor ≠ 0
    return quotient
  post quotient * divisor = numerator
```

The pre-condition in this definition does not restrict the *domain* of the function, it indicates where the definition constrains the function. It is equivalent to

```
fn divide  : Real → Real → Real is
     divide(divisor)(numerator)
     return quotient
  post
     divisor ≠ 0 ⇒ quotient * divisor = numerator
```

The application of a function to a value which does not satisfy the pre-condition is a valid expression. The following definition

```
val divide_by_zero : Real → Real ≜ divide 0
```

is valid. The function *divide_by_zero* is some function of type *Real* → *Real* but it is not constrained by the above definition of *divide*.

2.3 Incremental Definitions

When dealing with large systems it is convenient to be able to present specifications 'bit by bit'. In HP-SL, values may be defined by a series of definitions. Consider the following trivial example.

```
val zero : Real
assert non_positive ≜ zero ≤ 0
assert non_negative ≜ zero ≥ 0
```

This fragment of HP-SL consists of three definitions. The first definition introduces *zero* an unconstrained value of type *Real*.

The next definition is an 'assertion' called *non_positive*. An assertion is not a statement of some property which can be proved from other definitions. It is a definition which imposes a constraint on the specification. In this case it constrains the value *zero* to be less than or equal to 0. The second assertion, *non_negative* further constrains the value to be greater than or equal to 0. The overall effect is to define a value which satisfies both constraints.

Above we gave a definition of the function *divide* which constrained the function for non-zero divisors. We can give an assertion which ensures that division by zero always returns the value 0.

assert *zero_divisors* $\triangleq$ ($\forall$ *x:Real* · *divide(0)(x)* = *0*)

An alternative approach is to give *multiple* definitions. The following further definition of *divide* constrains the function for zero divisors. It has the same effect as the assertion—it ensures that division by zero returns the value 0.

```
fn divide  : Real → Real → Real is
   divide (divisor)(numerator)
      pre divisor = 0
   ≜ 0
```

2.4 Abstract Types

Defining New Types

In HP-SL, a 'new' type is introduced by an (abstract) type definition. This should be contrasted with a synonym type definition which just introduces a new name for an existing type.

```
type Person
type Contents
```

The type *Person* and the type *Contents* are new types which are distinct from all other types.

Such types are called *abstract types* because they have no 'internal structure', other than that implied by functions operating on the type. If there are no functions which operate on *Person* and *Contents* we know nothing more about them. This is equivalent to stating that properties and attributes of the type are irrelevant to the specification.

Abstract Types and Explicit Assertions

We can impose some structure on an abstract type by defining functions, and explicitly constraining the functions by assertions. We will explain this by presenting an example in detail. Afterwards, we will discuss some shorthand which makes such definitions much easier to write.

```
type Message

fn message : Person × Set Person × Contents → Message
fn sender : Message → Person
fn recipients : Message → Set Person
fn contents : Message → Contents
```

These definitions introduce a new abstract type, called *Message*, and four unconstrained functions: one which constructs values of type *Message* and three which 'project' into other types. We can constrain these functions by giving an assertion.

```
assert message_projectors ≜
  ( ∀ ( p:Person, sp:Set Person, c:Contents ) ·
      sender( message(p,sp,c) ) = p ∧
      recipients( message(p,sp,c) ) = sp ∧
      contents( message(p,sp,c) ) = c )
```

The assertion ensures that, for any value of type *Message* constructed by the *message* function, the projector functions return the appropriate components.

A consequence of this assertion is that there is no 'confusion' between values constructed by *message*. Two values $message(p_1,sp_1,c_1)$ and $message(p_2,sp_2,c_2)$ of type *Message* are equal if and only if $p_1 = p_2$ and $sp_1 = sp_2$ and $c_1 = c_2$.

We may also want to say that *all* values of type *Message* can be constructed by the constructor function. This is ensured by the following definition.

```
assert no_junk_message ≜
  ( ∀ m:Message · ( ∃ ( p:Person, sp:Set Person, c:Contents ) ·
      message(p,sp,c) = m ) )
```

This example shows that an abstract type may be defined by giving underspecified functions and then constraining the functions by assertions. This is a powerful approach, but it is too complex for routine industrial use. In the next section we will look at some 'shorthand' derived syntax which provides easy ways to give common definitions.

Record Types

The abstract type *Message* was defined by giving a constructor function, projectors, and explicit assertions which ensured that the type was isomorphic to *Person* × *Set Person* × *Contents*. One way to think of such a definition is as a 'tagged record' type. This is a very common kind of definition, and HP-SL provides a convenient short syntax.

```
type Message ≜
  [ message ▷
      ( sender : Person,
        recipients : Set Person,
        contents : Contents )   ]
```

This definition of the type *Message* is equivalent to that given in the previous section. The constructor function, projector functions and the assertions are derived systematically from the syntax.

The details of the type are contained within special brackets [...]. The name of the constructor function *message* is followed by a delimiter ▷. This is followed by the names and type of the 'components'. These names allow us to derive the signatures of the constructor and projector functions.

```
fn message : Person × Set Person × Contents → Message
fn sender : Message → Person
fn recipients : Message → Set Person
fn contents : Message → Contents
```

A number of other functions are also derived. These include an *'is'* function.

```
fn is_message : Message → Bool is
   is_message(m) ≜
     (∃ (p:Person, sp:Set Person, c:Contents) · message(p,sp,c) = m )
```

The *projectors* assertion and the *no junk* assertion may also be derived systematically. The *no junk* assertion may be stated in terms of the *is* function.

```
assert no_junk_message ≜
  ( ∀ m:Message · is_message(m) )
```

So the 'record type' syntax is a shorthand for the full definition of the abstract type, the constructor and projectors, and the assertions. We will call the derived functions and assertions, 'default' functions and assertions. They may be used just as if they had been defined explicitly.

Multiple Constructors

It is straightforward to extend this approach to allow more than one constructor. Syntactically, constructors are just separated by a vertical bar |.

type *RealTree* $\triangleq$
  [*leaf* ⊳ *leaf_value* : *Real*] |
  [*node* ⊳
    (*left* : *RealTree*,
      right : *RealTree*)]

This definition defines a type of tree where values are stored at the *leaves.*

A number of default functions and assertions are derived from the definition. Firstly, there are *two* constructors

fn *leaf* : *Real* $\rightarrow$ *RealTree*
fn *node* : *RealTree* $\times$ *RealTree* $\rightarrow$ *RealTree*

and their associated projectors.

fn *leaf_value* : *RealTree* $\rightarrow$ *Real*
fn *left* : *RealTree* $\rightarrow$ *RealTree*
fn *right* : *RealTree* $\rightarrow$ *RealTree*

The default *projector* and *no junk* assertions are derived. The *projector* assertions apply to each constructor separately. The *no junk* assertion applies jointly—it ensures that all values of type *RealTree* are constructed by either *leaf* or *node*. It may be stated using the default *is* functions.

assert *no_junk_realtree* $\triangleq$ ($\forall$ *t* : *RealTree* · *is_leaf*(*t*) $\vee$ *is_node*(*t*))

Two further default assertions are derived: *no confusion* and *induction.*

If a type has multiple constructors, the *projector* assertions are not enough to ensure that there is no confusion. We need to ensure that the values constructed by different constructors are distirct. This is achieved by the *no confusion* assertion.

```
assert no_confusion_realtree ≜
  ( ∀ t:RealTree · ¬ ( is_leaf(t) ∧ is_node(t) ))
```

Together with the projector assertions, this ensures that values of *RealTree* are equal if and only if they are constructed by the same constructor *and* the corresponding constructor arguments—components—are equal.

If a type is 'recursive'—that is, if a constructor function includes the type in its domain—then the *no junk* assertion is not enough to ensure that we can reason about *all* values of the type. This is achieved by the *induction* assertion.

```
assert induction_realtree ≜
  ( ∀ p : RealTree → Bool ·
     (∀ x:Real · p(leaf(x)) ) ∧
     (∀ (t1:RealTree, t2:RealTree) · p(t1) ∧ p(t2) ⇒ p(node(t1,t2)))
     ⇒
     (∀ t:RealTree · p(t))
  )
```

Constant constructors

Often, we wish to give constants as well as constructor functions. This is done by allowing the constructors to be named constants.

```
type RealStack ≜
  [ empty ] |
  [ push ▹
      ( pop : RealStack,
        top : Real )     ]
```

The type *RealStack* has two constructors: the constant *empty* and the function
$push : RealStack \times Real \rightarrow RealStack$.

The constant *empty* does not have any projectors. The constructor *push* has two projectors: *pop* and *top*.

Together with the default derived assertions, this is essentially equivalent to the usual initial algebra definition of a stack abstract datatype.

Enumerated Types

Sometimes, we want to define a type by enumerating its values. In HP-SL we simply give the constructor constants.

$$\textbf{type}\ \mathit{Colour} \triangleq [\ \mathit{red}\ ] \mid [\ \mathit{green}\ ] \mid [\ \mathit{blue}\ ]$$

The type *Colour* consists of precisely the constants *red, green* and *blue*. The default no junk assertion ensures that there are no other values, and the default no confusion assertion ensures that they are distinct values.

2.5 Relations

Specifying relationships between values is a fundamental specification technique. The basic approach is to define relationships by Boolean valued functions. For example, consider

$$\begin{array}{l}\textbf{fn}\ \mathit{less\_than} : \mathit{Int} \times \mathit{Int} \rightarrow \mathit{Bool}\ \textbf{is} \\ \quad \mathit{less\_than}(x,y) \triangleq x < y\end{array}$$

The values x and y are related, if and only if the expression $\mathit{less\_than}(x,y)$ is *true*.

In model oriented specification, such definitions are very common. HP-SL provides a derived syntax which emphasises the fact that we are interested in the *relationship* rather than the value returned by the function. For example the function *less_than* may be written as follows.

$$\begin{array}{l}\textbf{reln}\ \mathit{less\_than} : \mathit{Int} \times \mathit{Int}\ \textbf{is} \\ \quad \mathit{less\_than}(x,y) \triangleq x < y\end{array}$$

2.6 State and Operations

A typical model oriented specification of a system provides definitions of system state and operations which can update that state.

In HP-SL the system state is modelled by a type; operations on the system state are modelled.by functions or relations.

HP-SL does not distinguish the system state type—it is defined and referenced in exactly the same way as other types. Its special role in the specification is explained by the narrative text and not by the syntax. One consequence of this approach is that there is no 'frame-condition'—if an operation leaves part of the state unchanged, then the definition must say so.

To illustrate this style we give a specification of a trivial spell-checker system. The system maintains a dictionary of known words and has two operations. The first checks whether or not a given word is in the dictionary; the second will add a given word to the dictionary.

The dictionary contains words. We do not need to know anything about the properties of words, so they are modelled by an abstract type, *Word*.

type *Word*

The system dictionary is a collection of words, modelled as a set of words.

syntype *Dictionary* $\triangleq$ *Set Word*

The *checkword* operation takes a single word and checks whether or not it is in the dictionary. If it is in the dictionary, it returns the value *true*; if not, it returns the value *false*. In either case, the system dictionary is not changed. We will model this operation as a function.

fn *checkword* : *Word* $\times$ *Dictionary* $\rightarrow$ *Bool* **is**
checkword(*word*, *sys_dictionary*) $\triangleq$ *word* $\in$ *sys_dictionary*

In this definition, the word to be checked is *word* and the system dictionary is *sys_dictionary*. Since this is a function, the system dictionary is not changed.

The *addword* operation takes a single word and adds it to the dictionary. We model this operation by a relation.

reln *addword* : *Dictionary* $\times$ *Word* $\times$ *Dictionary* **is**
addword(*sys_dictionary*, *word*, *sys_dictionary'*)
$\triangleq$ *sys_dictionary'* $=$ *sys_dictionary* $\cup$ $\{$*word*$\}$

In this definition, the initial value of the system dictionary is *sys_dictionary*, the word to be added is *word* and the final value of the system dictionary is *sys_dictionary'*. The choice of names for the formal parameters of the relation are, of course, quite arbitrary. Current use of HP-SL follows the convention that the name of the initial value of system state is undecorated, and the final value is decorated by a prime.

2.7 Polymorphism

Polymorphic Functions

In HP-SL, it is possible to give *polymorphic* definitions. For example, the following defines a polymorphic function which returns the *last* element of a sequence. (The operator *elem* turns the sequence into a function).

```
fn ⦇ T ⦈ last_element : Seq T → T is
   last_element( s )
     pre len s ≠ 0
     ≜ (elem s)(len s)
```

The special brackets ⦇ ⦈ at the start of the definition introduce a *type variable, T*, which represents *any* type.

A polymorphic definition may be thought of as a finite representation of an infinite family of definitions—one for each binding of the type variable to a type. The above polymorphic definition introduces, amongst others, the functions

```
fn last_element : Seq Real → Real
fn last_element : Seq Bool → Bool
fn last_element : Seq (Real × Real) → Real × Real
...
```

Type Constructors

Polymorphism also allows us to give new *type constructors*. For example we can define a general *Tree* type constructor.

```
type ⦇ T ⦈ Tree ≜
        ⟦ leaf ▷ leaf_value : T ⟧ |
        ⟦ node ▷
             ( left : Tree T,
               right : Tree T ) ⟧
```

This introduces an abstract type constructor, and associated polymorphic default functions and assertions.

A new type constructor may be used in exactly the same way as a pre-defined type constructor. In the following example, notice that there is no distinction between the pre-defined constructor *Set* and the new type constructor *Tree*.

```
fn ⦇ T ⦈ leafvalues : Tree T → Set T is
   leafvalues( tree ) ≜
     if is_leaf(tree) then {leaf_value(tree)}
     else leafvalues( left(tree) ) ∪ leafvalues( right(tree) )
     endif
```

The function *leafvalues* collects the set of values associated with the leaves of a tree.

We can also define *synonym type* constructors, and give associated functions explicitly.

```
syntype ⦇ T ⦈ Bag ≜ T →m Nat1

fn ⦇ T ⦈ count_element : T × Bag T → Nat0 is
   count_element ( elem, bag ) ≜
     if elem ∈ dom bag then lookup bag(elem) else 0 endif
```

3 Tools to support HP-SL

The HP-SL toolset supports a style of *literate specification* by allowing the production of documents containing both formal specification and narrative text. Specifications written in HP-SL can be easily incorporated into documents written using the LaTeX document preparation system.

The toolset provides syntax and incremental typechecking, via an interface built upon the GNU Emacs editor [4]. A document is prepared in, or read into, a normal Emacs buffer. Commands bound to Emacs key-sequences invoke the parser and, optionally, the type checker. The parser and type checker work upon an item or region, which contain one or more HP-SL definitions. Definitions may be parsed in isolation; the type checker maintains an 'environment' of type information.

Incremental checking provides fast response and encourages developers to check their work as they write it. Any errors message from the parser or type checker are displayed in a separate Emacs window. Commands are available to move the editor cursor to the point at which each error is detected.

A specification document is formatted by a filter which replaces HP-SL Ascii syntax with appropriate LaTeX commands, and then invokes the normal LaTeX to DVI translator. The resulting document may be printed, or previewed at a workstation.

The toolset also provides a network-transparent database which allows several different documents, perhaps written by several members of a project, to share the same pieces of HP-SL specification. Items in the database are under version control and a document may refer to a particular version of an item, or to the 'latest' version, simplifying the task of keeping several separate but related documents in step during the design process.

4 Technology Transfer

A major objective of the Software Engineering Department is to demonstrate that the appropriate use of formal specification results in faster development of better quality software. We are working with a series of projects which can be used internally as examples and case studies.

Our current partners include two medical products, a CAD system and a pure software system. These are real product developments, not investigations or feasibility studies.

We have established a technology transfer model which helps to ensure that, even in the short term, the process of learning and using the technology is a net benefit.

The most important aspect is that we provide *project centred* training and support. We do not give general courses in the hope that some people might try out the ideas. We establish a close contact with a project team and work with them throughout the product development.

The process begins by identifying a suitable project. The criteria which we apply include the following.

- The project should be a mainstream product development involving new software.
- The project should be scoped, but work on the software must be at an early stage.
- The software team should be reasonably small, and enthusiastic about using a better development approach

Once a project has been identified, there is an investigation phase, which we use to develop an understanding of the application area. As a result of the investigation a joint proposal is made; this explains how formal specifications will be applied to the project and what benefits are expected. It is important that the management chain supports the collaboration.

The collaboration is launched with a two week visit by two people from HP Labs. The first week is a training course which covers simple discrete maths and the HP-SL language. The last day of the course is used to develop a prepared case study. The second week is a workshop which begins the process of applying HP-SL to the project itself. By the end of the workshop there is a firm technical strategy, and the project is using the specification language independently.

After the project launch we stay in contact with the project. We provide support by regular use of telephone, electronic mail and teleconference links. Further visits, by both sides, take place as the project proceeds.

All of our collaborations are still in progress, and none has yet reached product release, but initial results have been very encouraging. The language and the approach are transferable and help provide a faster, more efficient development process.

5 Acknowledgements

HP-SL is a model oriented specification language in the tradition of VDM, [1] and RAISE [2]. The concept and the detailed design of HP-SL are due to Patrick Goldsack. Errors and omissions in this presentation are mine.

6 References

[1] Jones C B. *Systematic Software Development Using VDM.* Prentice-Hall, Second edition, 1990.

[2] Havelund K. and Haxthausen A. RSL Reference Manual. Technical Report RAISE/CRI/DOC/2/V1, Computer Resources International, 1990.

[3] Harry P. History Specifications. HP Labs Internal Report, 1991.

[4] Stallman R. The extensible, customizable, self documenting, display editor. In *Interactive Programming Environments.* McGraw-Hill, 1984.

[5] Rush T., Harry P., Ferguson T., and Oliver H. Case studies in HP-SL. Technical Report HPL-90-137, Hewlett-Packard Laboratories, Bristol, 1990.

CICS project report

Experiences and results from the use of Z in IBM

Iain Houston
IBM United Kingdom Laboratories Ltd *

Steve King
Oxford University Computing Laboratory †

This paper describes some experiences and results arising from the use of Z in two major projects at the Hursley Park laboratory of IBM[1] United Kingdom Laboratories Ltd. The first project involved the use of Z in the development of a major new release of IBM's transaction processing system CICS[1] (Customer Information Control System), while the second project is a more recent one, concerning the formal specification of the CICS Application Programming Interface (API). The version of CICS which used Z in its development process was released to selected customers on an Early Support Programme in June 1989, and was made generally available in June 1990. Many process measurements were made during the development of the product, and early results show an encouraging improvement in quality, particularly in the parts of the release that were formally specified. The API specification project involved the description of an already existing interface, currently described informally in various manuals in the CICS library. Since this is purely a specification project, no figures are available for the success of the work in terms of reduction of errors, but the motivation for and experiences from the work are described below. Thus this report concentrates on describing results from the use of Z for the development of the CICS product, and experiences from the use of Z for the specification of the CICS API.

Development of a major new release of CICS

CICS is an online transaction processing system with many thousands of installations worldwide. It was originally developed in 1968, and since then it has undergone much development, greatly increasing its scope and power. It now consists of over 800,000 lines of code, some written in Assembler and some in an internal high level systems programming language, PLAS. As a result of these many years of development, it was decided in 1983 that it was necessary to invest resources in a major restructuring of the internals of CICS, to clarify internal interfaces and to provide the basis for future development of CICS. After much research, it was decided to use a development method based on Z for the development of most of the new code required.[2] Some of the remaining code

*IBM United Kingdom Laboratories Ltd, Hursley Park, Winchester, Hampshire SO21 2JN
†Oxford University Computing Laboratory, Programming Research Group, 11 Keble Road, Oxford OX1 3QD
[1] A trademark of the IBM Corporation
[2] For details of the other methods considered, see [1].

was developed into PLAS using traditional software engineering techniques without formal methods, and the rest of the development involved only changes to existing (usually Assembler) code. The development method adopted in this work concentrated on the use of Z as a notation for recording specifications and designs. Specifications were written in Z, followed by one or more levels of design in Z, and an abstract version of the required algorithm in Dijkstra's language of guarded commands, and finally code was produced. In most cases, there was no formal relationship between the documents produced at different levels of abstraction, and so very little proof work was done, although the preconditions of operations were recorded.

Results of the use of Z for code development

The primary aims of this use of formal methods were to improve the quality of the product, as seen by the customer, and to reduce development costs. This was to be achieved by reducing the overall number of errors in the product, and by identifying the remaining errors as early as possible in the development cycle: it is well known that it is much more expensive to correct a problem found late in the cycle than it is to correct one found earlier. Many measurements were taken throughout the development process: time spent producing specification and design documents, size of documents, resources spent on inspections, as well as number and severity of problems found. Since similar measurements were made on the non-Z developed code on this release, and on all the code in previous releases, meaningful comparisons are possible.

In order to interpret the figures on error rates, it is important to understand the scale of the software being produced. CICS/ESA V3.1 is the largest release of CICS that IBM has so far produced. The release consisted of 268,000 lines of new and modified code (together with over 500,000 lines of unchanged code). Of the new and modified code, approximately 37,000 lines were produced from Z specifications and designs, and a further 11,000 lines were partially specified in Z. Some 2000 pages of formal specifications were produced.

The figures which have been released show that both of the above objectives have been met: the overall quality of the product has been improved, with a reduction in the number of errors found, and the use of formal methods was a great benefit in causing errors to be found earlier in the development cycle. The graph in figure 1 shows a comparison between the rates of problem detection in Z specified code and non-Z specified code, at various stages in the product life cycle. The first impression is that the problem rate is lower in the Z specified code. However, when we look more closely, we can see that, in fact, the error rate for Z specified code is actually higher at the PLD stage. This is understandable because of the precision which is forced on the writer of the formal specification: he cannot ignore difficult issues, and so is more prone to making a wrong decision. However, it is beneficial that these errors are trapped at an early stage in the process, since a later recognition of the problem would be far more expensive. In fact, the graph shows a worrying number of problems caught only at the system test stage for the non-Z specified code: correction of these errors is not likely to be cheap.

IBM has also calculated that there is a reduction in the total development cost of the release. Based on the reduction in programmer days spent fixing problems, they estimate a 9% reduction, as compared to developing the 37,000 lines without Z specifications.

There also seems to have been a reduction in the number of errors reported by customers on the

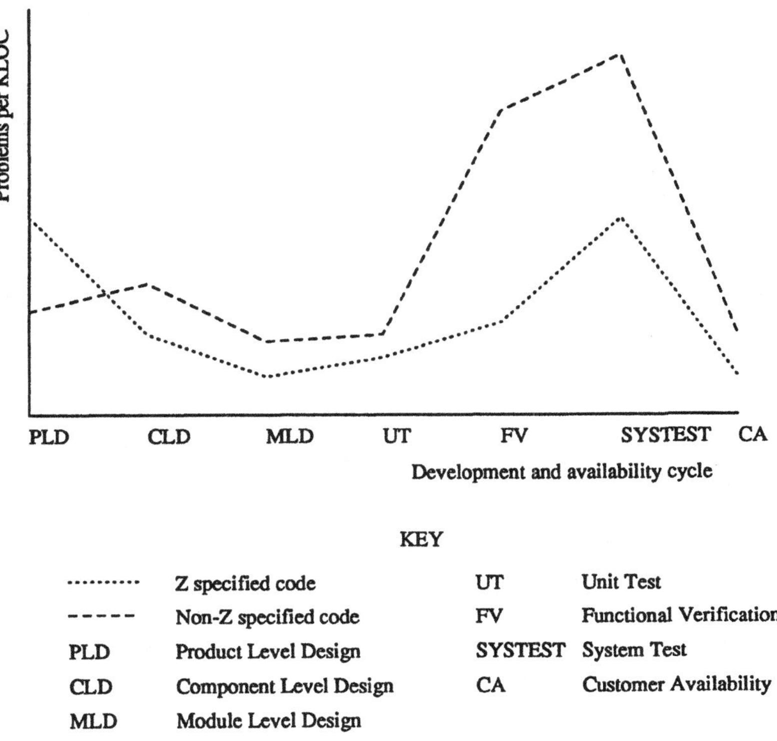

Figure 1: Comparison of problems found with two development methods in CICS/ESA V3.1

new release. This is important because this is an obvious way for the customer to judge quality. However, the length of time and the size of the sample mean that figures available so far should be treated with some caution. CICS/ESA V3.1.1 was only made generally available to customers at the end of June 1990, and it is IBM's experience that many customers do not change immediately to a new release when it is made available, unless there is some new functionality which they particularly need, or they are working at the limits of the capacity of the previous release. However, bearing those two provisos in mind, the figures on number of problems reported by customers are extremely encouraging: in the first 8 months after the release was made available, the code which was specified in Z seems to have approximately $2\frac{1}{2}$ times fewer problems than the code which was not specified in Z. These figures are even more encouraging when it is realised that the overall number of problems reported is much lower than on previous releases. There is also evidence to show that the severity of the problems for code specified in Z is much lower than for the other problems.

Taken as a whole, the quantitative results for the use of Z in CICS are very encouraging. However, a word of caution is in order here: it should be noted that IBM do not claim to have been running a carefully designed scientific experiment to test the merits of formal methods—there are no control cases, where we can look at the results of developing the same piece of code with formal methods, and without. All we can see are the results of applying formal methods in certain specific cases, and we should give only tentative interpretations of the figures. There are many other possible interpretations: for instance, it is possible that Z was used on only the least complex parts of the restructure work, thus making any comparison of error rates meaningless. However, IBM themselves have been encouraged enough by the figures to decide to continue to use Z on the next release of CICS.

The retrospective specification of the API

The CICS application programming interface (API) consists of a number of commands that an application programmer can embed in a PL/1, COBOL or C program to access the resources of a CICS system. A language preprocessor, supplied as a part of CICS, is used to translate embedded commands into calls, in the language of the program, to the CICS command processor.

The syntax of about 100 commands is described in the IBM reference manual [3]: the meaning of these commands is described informally in this and several other of the 30 volumes of the CICS/ESA reference library. There are several CICS products available on five different operating system, including MVS/ESA, and although each product has its own library, the behaviour of a core set of CICS commands is supposed to be the same in all the products. It has been the aim of this project to define formally this command base consisting of about 60 commands, arriving at a precise description of their effects. As well as this base, there are a number of towers that have not, at this stage, been treated formally. The towers include commands that are not implemented in all the different CICS products and the different behaviour of base commands when executed in a system of communicating CICS systems.

Various sources of information were used by the specifiers to discover what the behaviour of CICS should be. These included the manuals, the designers and module owners, the program code and the results of running experiments in which the behaviour of the API was observed. Finding the appropriate abstract model with which to describe the details of this information often proved to be an interesting challenge (see below). The purpose of the specifications is to give a definitive statement of the behaviour that CICS guarantees of its API.

Each specification was written by a single author—five different writers were involved in the project at various stages—but several other people were also involved in providing feedback and information for the specifier. After spending some time researching the behaviour of the commands in his area, the specifier called a meeting at which he presented a model for the state of the system, together with some indications of how the commands could be described in terms of this state. Those present at this meeting included both CICS experts, who could advise on the behaviour of the commands, and Z experts, who could advise on notation and modelling. Based on the feedback received, the specifier then produced a draft version of the complete specification, which was circulated to the same interested parties for comment. The next stage was a formal inspection: a new version of the document was produced and circulated one week before the meeting, to allow time for preparation. At the inspection, the document was read, from first line to last, and problem areas were identified. After the inspection, the specifier produced yet another version of the document, and, when the moderator of the inspection was satisfied that all the inspection points had been dealt with, the specification was deemed to be completed.

The API specifications are intended to be read by designers and developers, whether as CICS customers or vendors of CICS-based applications. Two other important kinds of audience are the teachers of CICS application programming and those who are interested in the application of formal methods to the specification of interfaces. It is also intended that the specifications will be of value within the Hursley development laboratory as a way of more rapidly and precisely communicating the behaviour of CICS between the designers and developers of the various CICS products.

An understanding of the specifications is expected to contribute to an improvement in the quality of the design and implementation of CICS applications and should help in resolving many of the sort of problems caused today by the various possible interpretations of existing informal descriptions of the behaviour of CICS.

Not only do the specifications establish a precise vocabulary for talking about the behaviour of the application programming interface, but they provide a structure in which knowledge about the interface can be organised. The value of this—formal—method of managing the complexity of the information communicated about CICS is not to be underestimated. A good deal of attention has been paid to trying to find the simplest data structures and the smallest schemas and to using Z's schema calculus to compose the specifications to communicate their meaning in the most obvious way.

All of the specifications resulting from this project are published as IBM Hursley Technical Reports and are available from the Communications Department at Hursley.

Experiences from the use of Z for specification

One of the most difficult problems facing the specifier of a large system is how to keep the complexity under control. If the complexity is not successfully managed, then the resulting specification is unlikely to achieve its purpose, which is to communicate an abstract view of the system to the reader. In a large specification project such as this one, there are important decisions to be made about how to divide up the interface, so that it can be described in portions of a reasonable size. Once these decisions have been taken, there are structuring decisions to be made at a lower level, working out how best to present a particular specification. These two aspects of structuring are discussed below, together with a few words on the problems of deciding exactly which behaviours to model, and on the lessons that were learnt.

Large scale structuring

One of the first decisions to be made on the project was how to divide up the API into sections of manageable size: at least to start with, the intention was to produce a number of specifications describing parts of the API, rather than an enormous document describing the entire interface. The first attempt at subdividing the interface involved using the traditional divisions: the Programmer's Reference Manual [3] grouped the commands of the API into categories for ease of description. In many cases, this modular structure was sufficient: for example, the code covered by the File Control specification is responsible for managing state data which is quite separate from the state data of other CICS resource managers. However, in a few cases, the traditional categorisation of commands was not satisfactory: there were relationships between categories which made separate specification unnecessarily complicated. For instance, the Condition Handling mechanism can be easily described within the Program Control specification, although they are not grouped together in [3]. In other cases, extremely complex data structures have evolved in the implementation, either where the original designers could see no obvious separation, or where subsequent generations have obscured the originally intended structure. Sometimes data structures have been merged with the intention of serving highly performance critical programs. In any case neither were state invariants written down nor were the preconditions of any of the operations. In some of the specification work, completely new boundaries needed to be drawn through existing components, and operations at a newly created interface had to be invented so that the precise meaning of some API commands could be explained. This was the case with the EXEC CICS START and EXEC CICS RETRIEVE commands of Interval Control, for example.

Smaller scale structuring

There are also some interesting observations to be made about data structuring at a lower level, that is, within the individual specifications. There are two main reasons why the data structures of a specification are required to be simple. Firstly the writer should make it blindingly obvious to the reader what behaviour he is requiring of the system, and secondly he should be able to prove, at least informally, that the system is well-behaved in the conventional sense of ensuring that operations respect the invariants of the state upon which they act and that any theorems stated about the system do hold. It has been found that the properties of state schemas with as few as three components can soon become too complicated for either the reader or the writer to be sure about. In this case, it is the writer's responsibility to recast the exposition of the specification.

Fortunately, the Z language provided a good deal of help as simpler data structures were abstracted from the complex existing structures of the implementation. Although it was necessary to break down the state into pieces small enough to be manageable, it was also necessary to present an interface whose behaviour was precisely that of the part of CICS which was being modelled. As more was understood about the behaviour of CICS, so it was possible to explain it in independent pieces, and to use the schema calculus to combine the smaller parts and to present them as a whole.

Combining disjoint states As was mentioned above, some parts of CICS are obviously separate from others. However, the separation between Task Control, Transaction Management and Terminal Control, for instance, was not so obvious. As schemas describing small aspects of CICS were combined, it emerged that the behaviour of a large part of CICS could be described as the behaviour of several quite independent systems with well-defined communications between them. The implementation, on the other hand, is singularly large and complex.

Promoting component states The most useful device for containing the complexity of all the specifications that were written was promotion. Often, the simplest specification for a system was obtained by first describing a single instance of a resource, and the operations on it, and then using those descriptions to describe the behaviour of the system which contained a collection of named instances of the resource. Some promotions were not obviously required until both writer and reviewer found themselves struggling with expressions to describe the behaviour of a set of objects together, where the behaviour of the single object had not previously been dealt with. This is an example of the process of discovering the need for structure where it was not originally obvious. An interesting fact is that the most complex data structure demanded only three promotion steps. The Transactions and Principal Facilities specification [2] describes, at the top level, a system comprising multiple terminals and multiple transactions; the deepest of these is the multiple terminal system, each of whose individual terminals contains multiple data collections; in turn, each data collection contains multiple data elements. The structure is represented in the following tree:

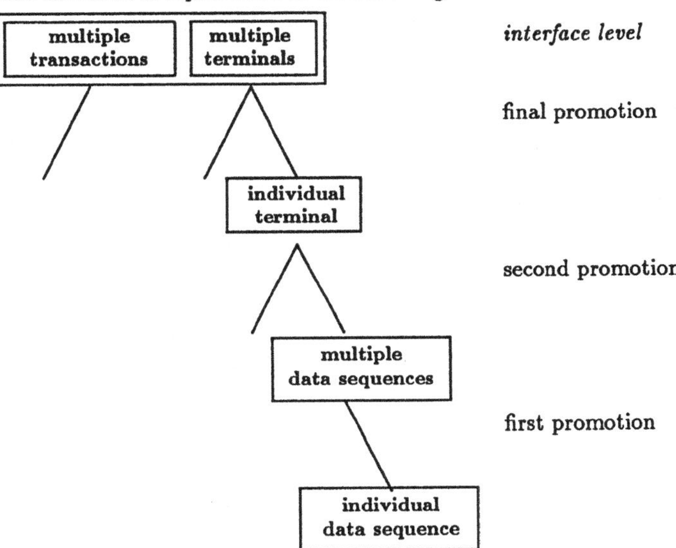

Interference and communications between states The ten separate specifications so far completed are modelled as more than ten separate but communicating systems. In some cases, to achieve the communication, two schemas are declared with a common component; when the schemas have been conjoined, this common component is hidden in much the same way as are the matching inputs and outputs of two schemas which are piped together. This communications component serves to describe the relationship between two pieces of separately described state. This sort of relationship frequently occurs in parts of the system that participate in some common actions but which are largely independent.

Choosing the behaviour to model

Not all the behaviour that a system exhibits is necessarily required by its specification. In some ways, modelling an existing system poses an opposite sort of problem to that of refinement. When a specification is refined, it is necessary to demonstrate that the concrete system has no less effect in no fewer situations than specified. When describing the existing CICS system, it was necessary to decide which behaviours were required of the interface, and which were simply accidental and so need not be described. In some cases, this caused considerable debate, but it was necessary, in the end, to include almost all of the existing system's behaviour in the specification, because experience has shown that at least some of the 30,000 customers of CICS rely upon behaviour that was not actually intended by its designers, but which occurred consistently nevertheless. However, to describe formally every (and possibly too complex to describe), and would give the CICS Service team a system to maintain whose behaviour is too complex to guarantee. Although some behaviour has been described which is very much more complex than would be provided in a new product, there are a few cases where the specification team has chosen not to require all implementations of CICS to behave as does, for example, the CICS/ESA implementation. Undoubtedly some of these choices will be proved to be wrong, but at least there is now a formal description of the behaviour of a guaranteed interface.

Lessons learnt

No project report would be complete without some reference to the mistakes that were made, or to the aspects of the work that could have been improved. So here are a few brief thoughts:

Tools About half-way through the project, a PS/2[3] based tool became available for use. This allowed parsing, type-checking and cross-referencing of formal text. Use of this tool caused a marked change in the nature of inspections: the writer could now be sure that his document was parsed and type-correct before the inspection. This allowed the inspectors to concentrate on the meaning of the mathematics, rather than its syntax. There was also a change in the way in which inspectors prepared for the meeting: instead of reading a hard copy of the document, they were able to use the tool's facilities for schema expansion and definition finding to help them navigate around the document. With hindsight, it would have been preferable to have had this tool available at the start of the project, because it greatly increased the productivity of both specifiers and inspectors. However, this was not possible at the time, because the development of the tool was not completed until after the project had started.

File Control One of the largest and most complicated parts of CICS is File Control. There are three different file access methods that have to be described, of varying degrees of complexity. A decision was taken by the specifier to describe the most complicated access method first, arguing that the other two would merely be simplifications of the first one. This now seems to have been a mistake—it would probably have been better to work on the simplest access method first, then extend this model to cover the more complex ones.

Interdependence of specifications The problem of finding the right modular structure for the API has already been mentioned. There were occasions when wrong decisions were made, which only came to light later: modules which were thought to be independent actually had some relationship. In some cases, the work on the module which was specified first had already been published, when it was realised that extra operations or more state variables were needed.

Conclusions

There is now considerable experience in the use of formal methods, particularly Z, at IBM Hursley Park. The CICS restructure project showed that it was possible to introduce Z into the development process, though only as a notation for recording specifications and designs, without any formal refinement. There are now very encouraging figures emerging about the quality of the product

[3]A trademark of the IBM Corporation

so produced. The benefits of the API specification work cannot be measured so directly. The specifications are intended to make explicit the contract between those supplying CICS products and those using them. Now that a large volume of API specifications has been published we can also hope that this will further stimulate interest in formal methods, particularly from those in the area of commercial software development.

References

[1] B.P. Collins, J.E. Nicholls, and I.H. Sørensen. Introducing formal methods: the CICS experience with Z. Technical Report TR12.260, IBM Hursley Park, December 1987.

[2] I.S.C. Houston. The CICS application programming interface: Transactions and principal facilities. Technical Report TR12.306, IBM Hursley Park, April 1991.

[3] IBM Corporation. *CICS/ESA Application Programmer's Reference.* SC33-0676.

A Debugger for a Meta-IV-like Meta-language

D. Kinnaes
dirkk@cs.kuleuven.ac.be

K. De Vlaminck
kdv@cs.kuleuven.ac.be

Department of Computer Science
Katholieke Universiteit Leuven
tel. +32(0)16–20 10 15, fax: +32(0)16–20 53 08

Abstract

The purpose of this paper is to report on the development of a debugging tool for a Meta-IV-like language. The tool consists of a static semantics checker and a debugger. The meta-language includes a subset of the DDC Meta-IV language, but with some simplifications and enhancements. A strong typing system was added to improve the static semantics checker. The debugger itself is quite powerful and includes features allowing (for example) invariants to be attached to breakpoints, objects and types. This paper explains why the debugger was developed, gives a short overview of the meta-language by comparing it to DDC Meta-IV, and presents some important features of the debugger.

1 Introduction

Generally, formal languages are intended and used to *specify* software systems, not to *develop* systems. Formal methods such as VDM [Jones 86] also support the development of systems by introducing concepts such as stepwise refinement and data reification.

Often however, it is also useful to derive a prototype of a system directly from its specification, or even to "execute" the specification itself.

We have developed a debugger for a Meta-IV-like language [Bjørner 78, DDC 85] with strong typing. There were at least two reasons for developing such a tool. First of all, we wanted to track errors in denotational definitions of programming languages. We did not only want to check the consistency of a denotational definition, but we also wanted to verify whether such a definition really defines the language one has in mind.

The other reason for developing this tool was to allow us to perform a non trivial case study for the Absynt [Craeynest 87] methodology and tools. Since this aspect falls somewhat outside the scope of the conference, we will only comment on it very briefly.

In this paper we will present some important concepts of our meta-language (only those which differ from DDC Meta-IV), and of our debugger.

2 The Meta-language

Our meta-language does not attempt to include the full DDC Meta-IV language. Of course, we had to restrict ourselves to an executable subset of Meta-IV, but other features such as exception handling were left out as well, at least in the current version. On the other hand, we wanted to improve the ability to detect more errors by a mere static analysis. This was done by providing strong typing. We also wanted to allow a *simple* type checking mechanism. To make this possible, additional type information has to be added to the metaprogram (in our case mostly denotational definitions).

2.1 Restrictions with respect to DDC Meta-IV

Because Meta-IV was developed as a specification language and not as a programming language, we had to restrict ourselves to an executable subset. Constructs which would be very hard to implement with reasonable efficiency were eliminated. In particular, the following restrictions with respect to Meta-IV apply:

- Recursive domain equations are allowed, but only objects with a finite representation can be created.
- Constructs requiring the enumeration of domains are only allowed for standard domains such as BOOL and INTG.
- Implicitly defined sets, maps and tuples are not allowed.
- Functions must be algorithmically specified, that is, a function cannot be specified by only giving a type clause or a pre- and postcondition.
- The fixpoint operator is not provided explicitly, but functions can be defined recursively.
- For certain nondeterministic constructs such as

  ```
  let a ∈ s in ...
  ```

  an arbitrary choice is made.

2.2 Types and Type Checking

In our meta-language, types are not *just* domains. A domain expression can be interpreted in two ways: it defines a domain as well as a type. Each domain constructor introduces a new type, disctinct from all other types (similar to a type definition in Ada). If we define

```
D1 = A | B
D2 = A | B
```

then D1 and D2 are the names of two different types, although the corresponding domains are the same. Also, a value of type A (or B) may not be used in a context where a value of type D1 (or D2) is expected, unless an explicit type conversion is applied. If a is of type A, it can be converted to type D1 by writing ↑D1(a). Likewise, if d is of type D1 or D2, it is converted to type A by writing ↓A(d).

The meta-language has been designed so as to allows a very simple type checking algorithm. Type checking can be performed bottom up, that is, the type of an expression can be determined uniquely by looking only at the types of its immediate constituents. In order to make this possible, additional type information must be provided at some places in the metaprogram.

For example, the empty set constructor {} has no immediate constituents, so its type cannot be determined by a bottom up type analysis. This is even so in the case of a non-empty set, e.g., {a}, because we could have

```
S1 = A-set
S2 = A-set
```

where a is of type A. To avoid this ambiguity, the set constructor must be preceeded by the type of the resulting expression, e.g., S1{a}. The same holds for other constructors (tuple, map, function, ...).

2.3 Example

To give the reader a general idea of the look and feel of our meta-language, we present a short example. This example is extracted from a denotational definition of a small programming language using continuation semantics [Gordon 79]. We have replaced some keywords by non-ASCII characters which are more widely used for writing denotational definitions.

```
...
Com = AssignCom | OutputCom | CallCom | IfCom | WhileCom | BlockCom;
AssignCom =    ::(sel-E1: Exp, sel-E2: Exp);
OutputCom =    ::(sel-E: Exp);
CallCom =      ::(sel-E1: Exp, sel-E2: Exp);
```

```
IfCom =        ::(sel-E: Exp, sel-C1: Com, sel-C2: Com);
WhileCom =     ::(sel-E: Exp, sel-C: Com);
BlockCom =     ::(sel-D: Dec, sel-C: Com);
...
𝒞 C r c = case C
  [ AssignCom: E1 ":=" E2 ]:
    ℰ E1 r
      (TestLoc (λl.ℛ E2 r (update ↓Loc(l) c) type Ec))
  [ OutputCom: "output" E ]:
    ℛ E r
      (λe s.↑Ans (mk-AnsList (↓Rv(e), c s)) type Ec)
  [ CallCom: E1 "(" E2 ")" ]:
    ℰ E1 r
      (TestProc (λp.ℰ E2 r (↓Proc(p) c) type Ec))
  [ IfCom: "if" E "then" C1 "else" C2 ]:
    ℛ E r
      (TestBool (λb.cond (𝒞 C1 r c) (𝒞 C2 r c) ↓Bool(↓(Rv(b))) type Ec))
  [ WhileCom: "while" E "do" C1 ]:
    ℛ E r
      (TestBool (λb.cond (𝒞 C1 r c) (𝒞 C r c) c ↓Bool(↓(Rv(b))) type Ec)
  [ BlockCom: "begin" D ";" C1 "end" ]:
    𝒟 D r
      (λr1.𝒞 C1 (addenv r r1) c type Dc)
...
```

Note that the lambda expressions are followed by a type name, and that explicit type converions are needed to convert to and from union types. The parts between double quotes are comments. Function application is denoted by juxtaposition of function and argument without parentheses. Functions can have only one argument, but higher order function are allowed. The meta-language has imperative constructs, but these are not used in this example.

3 The Debugger

The purpose of this section is to explain what the debugger does, and (briefly) how it was implemented.

3.1 What It Does

Before executing a metaprogram, the debugger performs a static analysis, reporting syntactic and static semantic errors (visibility errors, type errors). When no errors are detected during this static analysis, the debugger is ready to execute the metaprogram. During the execution phase the debugger provides many features found in currently available source level debuggers for various programming languages. Also, some new features are provided such as attaching invariants to types and objects. Here is a short overview:

- Breakpoints can be set on statements and functions. A condition can be added to a breakpoint, such that the breakpoint is only active when the condition is satisfied. Also, a statement can be added to a breakpoint. When the breakpoint is reached the statement is executed but the execution is not interrupted.
- Statements can be entered during the debugging phase. These statements are checked and executed immediately, exactly as if they would appear in the source text.
- The value of variables (or more generally: expressions) can be evaluated. Expressions are evaluated exactly as if they would appear in the source text.
- The call stack can be displayed.
- Invariants can be attached to types, objects and breakpoints. Normal execution is interrupted when such an invariant does not hold at some point during the execution. Invariants attached to an object are checked when the object is created (or changed, if possible). Invariants attached to a type are automatically attached to all objects of that type.

3.2 How It Is Implemented

The operation of the debugger consists of two consecutive phases. Firstly, the source text is parsed and a static semantic analysis is performed on the resulting parse tree, augmenting it with type information. Then the debugger goes into execution mode. This is the interactive mode in which the user can issue debugger commands and "run" all or parts of the specification. In the execution mode the debugger relies on an interpreter which manipulates the internal graph representation of the specification.

For debugger commands containing meta-language constructs (e.g. setting conditional breakpoints), parts of the parser and the static semantic analyser are called from within the execution mode of the debugger. To make this possible, all the symbol table information collected by the static semantic analyser is integrated into the graph representation during the static semantic analysis. Each applied occurrence of an identifier is replaced by a direct reference to the corresponding declaration.

With respect to the execution mechanism of the underlying interpreter we only want to mention that higher order functions are evaluated using strict evaluation, i.e. argument evaluation comes before function application.

As mentioned in the introduction, one of our intentions for developing the debugger was to have a non trivial case study for the Absynt methodology and tools.

Absynt is a language for describing intermediate representations of programs used in various language processing tools by means of an abstract syntax. It also provides operations to manipulate those intermediate representations (graphs or trees). Absynt has many features found in other programming languages, such as strong typing, (generic) modules, separate compilation and exceptions. Tool support includes an Absynt compiler (Absynt to Ada) and a source level debugger.

Our debugger was designed in an object oriented way. Several Absynt modules were isolated, e.g., statement, expression. Each module defines an object type by providing a type name and a number of operations on objects of that type. For our debugger the useful operations include—depending on the particular type—parsing, static semantic analysis (type and visibility checking), execution phase (execution, evaluation).

Since this section falls somewhat outside the scope of the conference, we will not elaborate on it any further.

4 Future Work

More work needs to be done mainly in three areas. The meta-language should be extended, introducing modules and exceptions, and the requirement to introduce typing information in several places in the specifications should be relaxed. Furthermore, some minor improvements are necessary to enhance the functionality of the debugger. Finally, the user interface of the debugger needs to be improved. We are currently developing a graphical user interface based on X-windows.

5 Conclusion

In this paper we have described a debugging tool for a Meta-IV-like language with strong typing. This tool was developed mainly to gain confidence in the correctness of denotational definitions of programming languages. The debugger is written in Absynt and translated automatically into Ada by our Absynt compiler, which makes it easily portable. Further work is still needed to enhance the meta-language and to improve the user interface of the tool.

References

[Bjørner 78] D. Bjørner and C.B. Jones, editors. *The Vienna Development Method: The Meta-Language. Lecture Notes in Computer Science no. 61*, Springer Verlag, Berlin, 1978.

[Craeynest 87] D. Craeynest, D. Kinnaes, W. De Bisschop, A. De Niel and K. De Vlaminck. *A Metaprogramming Language based on Abstract Syntax — Language Description.* CW report 57, Katholieke Universiteit Leuven, 1987.

[DDC 85] N. Bleech, N. Botta and I.Ø. Hansen. *Meta-IV Tool-set Abstract Syntax.* Technical Report DDC 164/RPT/4, Dansk Datamatik Center, June 1985.

[Gordon 79] M.J.C. Gordon. *The Denotational Description of Programming Languages*, Springer Verlag, New York, 1978.

[Jones 86] C.B. Jones. *Systematic Software Development using VDM. Series in Computer Science*, Prentice-Hall International, 1986.

[Stoy 77] J.E. Stoy. *Denotational Semantics: The Scott-Strachey Approach to Programming Language Theory.* MIT Press, 1977.

An Executable Subset of Meta-IV with Loose Specification*

Peter Gorm Larsen and Poul Bøgh Lassen
The Institute of Applied Computer Science (IFAD)
Munkebjergvænget 17, DK-5230 Odense M, Denmark
E-mail: peter@ifad.dk and poul@ifad.dk

Abstract

In ESPRIT project no. EP5570 called IPTES[1] a methodology and a supporting environment for incremental prototyping of embedded computer systems is developed. As a part of this prototyping tool an interpreter for an executable subset of a VDM dialect is developed. Based on a comparative study of different notations inspired by VDM we have now selected an executable subset of the BSI/VDM-SL[2] notation. This executable subset is interesting because it enables the designer to use loose specification. None of the executable VDM dialects which we have investigated contain as large a part of looseness as our subset does. In this article we will focus mainly on which constructs we have in this subset and how we have dealt with the looseness. Furthermore we will sketch the connection between the semantics of our subset and the semantics for the full BSI/VDM-SL.

1 Introduction

IPTES is an ESPRIT research project which aims at development of a methodology and a supporting environment for incremental prototyping of embedded computer systems. Initially a system is described by means of a high-level graphical specification and design language SA/RT[3] (see [Ward&85]) where BSI/VDM-SL (also called Meta-IV) is used in the so-called mini-specifications to specify sequential components. The SA/RT specifications are made executable by a transformation to high-level timed Petri nets (see [Ghezzi&91]), while the mini-specifications are interpreted by an interpreter which is going to conform to the operational semantics as described in this article. Parts of the specification can then gradually be transformed towards actual code, and in this way

*The work reported here is partially sponsored by the CEC ESPRIT programme under contract no. EP5570

[1]IPTES is an acronym for "Incremental Prototyping Technology for Embedded real-time Systems".

[2]BSI/VDM-SL is an acronym for "British Standards Institution/Vienna Development Method Specification Language". However, since the standardization effort is being carried forward within ISO it is possible that in the future this language will just be called VDM-SL.

[3]SA/RT is an acronym for the "Structured Analysis Real Time extension".

heterogeneous prototyping of the system can be performed. More information about the IPTES architecture can be found in [Leon&91].

We have chosen to use an executable subset of the BSI/VDM-SL. This language is developed in order to harmonize the different VDM dialects into one standard language. This standardization effort is currently done under the auspices of BSI and ISO and it involves the definition of a concrete syntax, an abstract syntax, a static semantics, and a dynamic semantics (see [BSIVDM91]). We have taken these four parts as our starting point and have selected a subset of BSI/VDM-SL with minor adjustments to make the language fit the IPTES architecture.

An important quality of BSI/VDM-SL is that it contains constructs which can be loosely specified. When a specification is deterministic it simply denotes one model (corresponding to the only valid implementation of the functionality of the specification). When a specification is loose it denotes a set of models (corresponding to the different valid implementations of the specification).

Our executable subset has an operational semantics (written using the complete version of the BSI/VDM-SL notation). When a specification written in BSI/VDM-SL contains looseness it will denote a set of possible models in the dynamic semantics. In our operational semantics an arbitrary of these models is returned. The relation between the dynamic semantics for BSI/VDM-SL and this operational semantics is further analysed in this article.

After this introduction we will explain the notion of loose specification. We will then present the constructs which we have selected for our subset. Then we will explain the semantics of the subset and shortly compare it to the standard dynamic semantics. This is followed by a few examples illustrating the expressiveness provided by the generality of the patterns in our subset. After that, we will compare our approach to some of the related work on executable subsets of VDM-SL. Finally we will give a few concluding remarks and identify future work.

2 Loose Specification

Loose specification occurs if a specifier wants to express that it does not matter which particular value an expression yields as long as it fulfills certain requirements. Thus, loose specification arises because a specification generally needs to be stated at a higher level of abstraction than that of the final code of the system. When loose specification is used, the question of how to interpret this looseness is often ignored. However, the interpretation is important, especially if a specification must be proven to implement another specification.

As shown in [Larsen&89], [Wieth89], and [Larsen90] there are at least two different ways of interpreting such loose specifications. These two different interpretations have been called 'nondeterminism' and 'underdeterminedness'. When a loosely specified construct is interpreted as underdetermined it denotes the set of all possible deterministic implementations of that construct. If the same construct is interpreted as nondeterministic instead, it denotes the set of all possible implementations of that construct (including the nondeterministic ones). In this work we have chosen to use the underdetermined interpretation, where we, by means of a deterministic algorithm, will select an arbitrary result (from the set of deterministic implementations) satisfying the specification. We have chosen the underdetermined interpretation in order to achieve the property of referential transparency. If the execution of a specification written in our executable subset of BSI/VDM-SL complies with the user's expectation, it means that there exists at least one model which is satisfactory. However, this is no guarantee that all the other models satisfy his requirements to the functionality. Thus, in general, it is not sufficient simply to give such a loose specification to somebody else for implementation. Some knowledge about which of the models that has been selected by means of the deterministic algorithm must also be taken into account.

3 Constructs in the Executable Subset

Not all BSI/VDM-SL constructs are executable. This applies to implicit function and operation definitions and all computations over infinite sets (types with infinitely many values). In addition to these constructs, a number of executable constructs have been excluded from our subset. An SA/RT specification gives a hierarchical and a graphical overview of the structure of a system. At the bottom level of such a specification, mini-specifications are used to specify how the input values are transformed to output values in a sequential way. In IPTES such algorithms will be described by means of an executable subset of BSI/VDM-SL which is presented in this article.

We have therefore analysed the expressive power that is necessary to describe the algorithms in the mini-specifications. The result of this analysis was that the individual mini-specifications are relatively small and have a simple structure. As a result of this, and the fact that we cannot expect industrial users of the IPTES tools to be familiar with functional programming, we have excluded advanced features like lambda expressions, polymorphism, locally defined functions, and recursive let expressions.

Included in the subset are state definitions, constant (value) definitions, type definitions, explicitly defined functions and operations. The full generality of patterns from BSI/VDM-SL and most of the expression and statement constructs are also included. In order to support a simple library facility including auxiliary functions, a subset of the module concept from BSI/VDM-SL is also adopted in the language.

3.1 Abstract Syntax

We will informally explain what is included, and use BSI/VDM-SL to describe selected parts of the abstract syntax for our subset. Most of these parts will be used in the semantic description in the following section.

Modules

A simple library facility is included in the subset by allowing modules with simple imports and exports. This has been restricted compared with the modules from BSI/VDM-SL so that state changing operations cannot be exported or imported. In the same way it is not allowed to have cyclic imports. Type information about the imported and exported entities enables type checking of a module without analyzing the imported modules.

Type Definitions

The type definitions contain a number of basic types and a number of type constructors. The basic types include Boolean, numeric types (natural numbers, integers, and reals), characters, and enumeration types (quote literals). The type constructors include a composite type constructor (producing records), a union type constructor, a product type constructor, an optional type constructor, a set type constructor, a sequence type constructor and a map type constructor. Thus all type constructors from BSI/VDM-SL are included except a few numeric types, the token type, the non-empty sequence type, the function type, and the injective map type. Invariants on the type definitions can also be used in the same way as in BSI/VDM-SL.

State Definitions

The state definition consists of a composite type (the components of the composite type can be considered as the global variables), possibly an invariant on the state type, and possibly an initialization function. This is equivalent to BSI/VDM-SL, except that the initialization function is not formulated as a truth-valued predicate like in BSI/VDM-SL but as an expression returning the initial value. This change is made to ensure executability in the general case.

Value Definitions

Constant (value) definitions are also included in the same way as in BSI/VDM-SL. Thus, the left-hand sides of the definitions can be general patterns.

Function Definitions

The function definitions are similar to a combination of explicit and implicit function definitions from BSI/VDM-SL. However, our abstract syntax differs from the explicit function definition part of BSI/VDM-SL by disallowing polymorphic functions and Curried functions, and by supporting a post-condition. The interpreter will then be able to check whether the arguments used in a function call satisfy the pre-condition and whether the result of the function also satisfies the post-condition.

Operation Definitions

The abstract syntax for operation definitions is similar to the abstract syntax for function definitions. The main difference is that the body is a statement instead of an expression. In addition, there is some information about which parts of the state are used by the operation. Finally it is possible to declare a number of local variables used in the operation.

Our abstract syntax differs from the explicit part of BSI/VDM-SL by allowing a post-condition to be connected to an explicitly defined operation. The locally defined variables are also dealt with differently in BSI/VDM-SL, where they can be defined inside any block statement. However, we have decided that we will permit only locally defined variables at the outermost level in operations. Thus, we have not included block statements.

Expressions

The expressions in our subset include all the expression constructs from BSI/VDM-SL except for the iota expression, the lambda expression and instantiation of polymorphic functions.

The major differences between the expressions in our subset and those in BSI/VDM-SL are:

- general bindings from BSI/VDM-SL (type bind and set bind) have been restricted to set bindings. This restriction is made in order to ensure executability.
- pattern matching cannot be constrained with additional type information.

In the following we will present the abstract syntax for those kinds of expressions we will use to illustrate the semantics with.

The abstract syntax for a let expression is:

$$\begin{aligned} \mathit{LetExpr} :: \; & \mathit{loc} : \mathit{Pattern} \xrightarrow{m} \mathit{Expr} \\ & \mathit{in} \;\; : \mathit{Expr} \end{aligned}$$

where the *loc* field contains a collection of patterns to be matched against the corresponding expressions. The let expression denotes the value of the *in* expression evaluated in an environment where the pattern matchings have been performed. However, it should be noted that we have restricted the collection of definitions to non-recursive ones because the mutually recursive definitions used in BSI/VDM-SL are not needed for the IPTES mini-specifications. Another difference from the standard is that we (for the same reason) have removed the possibility of defining local functions.

The abstract syntax for a let-be-such-that expression is:

$$\begin{aligned} \mathit{LetBeSTExpr} :: \; & \mathit{bind} : \mathit{SetBind} \\ & \mathit{st} \;\;\;\; : \mathit{Expr} \\ & \mathit{in} \;\;\;\; : \mathit{Expr} \end{aligned}$$

where the *bind* is a binding of a pattern to a finite set, *st*, is a predicate using the pattern identifiers from the *bind*. The expression denotes the value of the *in* expression in an environment where a successful pattern matching has been performed and the *st* predicate is satisfied. This abstract syntax is equivalent to the one used in BSI/VDM-SL except that the general binding has been restricted to a set binding for the reason explained in the beginning of this section. This expression may contain looseness and the next section illustrates how this looseness is dealt with.

The abstract syntax for quantified expressions ($\forall$ and $\exists$) is:

$$\begin{aligned} \mathit{AllOrExistsExpr} :: \; & \mathit{quant} : \mathit{AllOrExistsQuantifier} \\ & \mathit{bind} \;\; : \mathit{SetBind}\text{-}\mathbf{set} \\ & \mathit{pred} \;\; : \mathit{Expr} \end{aligned}$$

$$\mathit{AllOrExistsQuantifier} = \text{ALL} \mid \text{EXISTS}$$

This is equivalent to BSI/VDM-SL except that the general binding has been restricted to a set binding as explained above. However, the operational semantics differs from the BSI/VDM-SL semantics which will be discussed in the next section.

Patterns

All pattern constructs from BSI/VDM-SL have been included in our subset. Here we will only present the abstract syntax for a set union pattern because is the only pattern this construct which will be given semantics in the next section.

The abstract syntax for set union patterns is:

$$\begin{aligned} \mathit{SetUnionPattern} :: \; & \mathit{lp} : \mathit{Pattern} \\ & \mathit{rp} : \mathit{Pattern} \end{aligned}$$

where *lp* union *rp* are matched against a set value. The two patterns must be matched to two disjoint subsets of the set value. This construct is used when one wants to split a set into two disjoint sets and the resulting binding is therefore loosely specified.

Bindings

As explained above we have included only the set binding in order to make bindings executable.

Statements

We have included all the statements from BSI/VDM-SL except for the block statement, the non-deterministic statement, the identity statement, and the exit mechanism.

4 The Semantics of the Executable Subset

The semantics presented here is operational, and it is inspired by [Bjørner91] where a stack semantics of a Simple Applicative Language (SAL) is presented. However, we are only using a stack of environments, and not a stack of values. This difference is caused by the fact that the target for the development of the interpreter in [Bjørner91] was a stack machine, while our target is a high level programming language (C++).

The semantics of the executable subset of BSI/VDM-SL is itself described using the complete version of BSI/VDM-SL[4]. However, expressions in BSI/VDM-SL cannot have side-effects and therefore, operations cannot be called inside expressions. We have for notational convenience chosen to allow calls of operations, which do not change the state, inside expressions because these operations do not cause side-effects anyway.

[4]In order to increase the readability of the operational semantics we have chosen to indicate the block structure by means of indentation instead of grouping statements together in blocks by means of brackets. We have been able to do this because we have used the LaTeX macros produced by **Jan-Bert Oostenenk** (see [Oostenenk90]).

In this section we first present the semantic domains, and then we explain the principles of the evaluation functions illustrated by means of a few examples taken from the full definition of the operational semantics for our executable subset.

4.1 Semantic Domains

The semantic domains describe the type of the structures which will be used for specifying the operational semantics for the abstract syntax.

$$ENV_L = ENV^*$$

The main structure in the semantic domains is the environment. The environment ENV_L is organized as a stack of function application environments ENV. When a function is called, it must establish a local environment containing its own definitions such as the formal parameters.

$$ENV = BlkEnv^*$$

Expressions can define a local environment called a block environment (*BlkEnv*). For example a let expression will produce a local environment for which the scope is the body of the let-expression. The function application environment is therefore organized as a stack of block environments where the first block environment pushed on the stack contains the instantiation of the formal parameters. When the value of an identifier is looked up this will happen in a top down manner down through the block environments.

$$BlkEnv = IdVal^*$$

A block environment is a sequence of *IdVal*'s, each containing an identifier and its associated value. A *BlkEnv* could alternatively have been modeled as a map. Modeling it as a sequence allows a more controlled error recovery as illustrated by the function *UnionMatch* which is presented in section 4.2.2. Naturally, some auxiliary functions have been defined to manipulate the environment (e.g. *PushBlkEnv* and *PopBlkEnv*). They are called by the evaluation functions.

When possible, the values in the semantic domain are specified in terms of the corresponding BSI/VDM-SL constructs, except that they are all tagged.

$$VAL = BasicType \mid SET \mid \ldots$$

$$SET :: bd : VAL\text{-}\mathbf{set}$$

These tags are used by the interpreter for dynamic type checking.

4.2 Evaluation Functions

The evaluation functions in this operational semantics of our executable subset differ from the evaluation functions for the dynamic semantics of the BSI/VDM-SL. In order to take looseness into account, the evaluation functions from the dynamic semantics of the BSI/VDM-SL return all possible results of evaluating a syntactic construct in a given environment. In this work, an arbitrary one of the possible results will be returned when we deal with values. However, when we deal with pattern matching, all possible resulting binding environments are returned, and taken into account. This is necessary because there are situations (e.g. the let-be-such-that construct) where additional constraints are put on the matching afterwards. It is also important for quantified expressions where looseness in the pattern gives different binding environments which must all satisfy the predicate. Since the algorithm selecting an arbitrary value is deterministic, looseness of both functions and operations will be interpreted as underdeterminedness (i.e. if a function is loosely specified it will always return the same result given the same arguments). This will of course mean that two abstractly equal values (e.g. $\{1,2,3\}$ and $\{2,1,3\}$) are implemented so that they have the same concrete representation in the implementation.

All the evaluation functions use the state (and they ought therefore to be called operations in the BSI/VDM terminology). The state type in our operational semantics has as one of its components the stack of environments presented in the previous section:

$\Sigma :: \ldots$
  $env_l : ENV_L$

4.2.1 Expressions

The evaluation function for expressions uses the state, it takes a syntactic expression as argument and returns a semantic value. Thus, the signature of *EvalExpr* is:

$$EvalExpr : Expr \xrightarrow{o} VAL$$

where *VAL* is the type of an arbitrary value which the syntactic expression can evaluate to. The expressions contain patterns, and the patterns can be loosely specified. We will now describe the evaluation functions of a few expressions, starting with the let expression.

The semantics of the let expression is defined as:

$EvalLetExpr : LetExpr \xrightarrow{o} VAL$

$EvalLetExpr\,(mk\text{-}LetExpr(loc_m, in_e)) \triangleq$
  dcl $pat_{lp} : Pattern^* := [\,]$,
    $val_{lv} : VAL^* := [\,]$;
  for all $pat_p \in$ dom loc_m
  do $val_{lv} := val_{lv} \curvearrowright [EvalExpr(loc_m(pat_p))]$;
    $pat_{lp} := pat_{lp} \curvearrowright [pat_p]$;
  let $env_s = PatternListMatch(pat_{lp}, val_{lv})$ in
    if $env_s \neq \{\,\}$
    then let $env \in env_s$ in
        $PushBlkEnv(env)$;
        let $in_v = EvalExpr(in_e)$ in
          $PopBlkEnv()$;
          return in_v
    else error

The local definitions from loc_m are collected in two sequences; val_{lv} contains a sequence of semantic values and pat_{lp} contains a sequence of syntactic patterns. All possible ways of matching the patterns against the values are collected in env_s which is a set of binding environments where every binding environment contains the environment for one possible matching. If the matching fails an empty set is returned and the evaluation of the whole let expression fails. Otherwise, an arbitrary one of these resulting binding environments is chosen, and pushed on top of the environment stack. Even though this description states that any binding environment can be chosen, the implementation will ensure underdeterminism by returning the same binding environment given the same set env_s. Then the body expression is evaluated in the new context and the environment is popped off the stack again, before the resulting value is returned.

The operational semantics presented here corresponds (functionally) to the dynamic semantics of BSI/VDM-SL except that only one value is returned instead of the set of all possible values. Furthermore, as mentioned in the section about the abstract syntax we have chosen not to include mutually recursive definitions.

The semantics of the let-be-such-that expression is defined as:

```
EvalLetBeSTExpr : LetBeSTExpr -o-> VAL

EvalLetBeSTExpr (mk-LetBeSTExpr(bind_b, st_e, in_e)) ≜
  dcl env_s : BlkEnv-set := { };
  for all env ∈ EvalSetBind(bind_b)
  do PushBlkEnv(env) ;
     let st_v = EvalExpr(st_e) in
       if is-BOOL(st_v)
       then let mk-BOOL(b) = st_v in
              if b
              then env_s := env_s ∪ {env}
       else error;
     PopBlkEnv() ;
  if env_s ≠ { }
  then let env ∈ env_s in
         PushBlkEnv(env) ;
         let in_v = EvalExpr(in_e) in
           PopBlkEnv() ;
           return in_v
  else error
```

For all possible binding environments which can be constructed from the set bind ($bind_b$) the "such that" expression (st_e) is evaluated. The binding environments in which the st_e evaluates to **true** are collected, and an arbitrary one is selected and pushed on top of the stack. The body expression is then evaluated in this context and the environment is popped off the stack again before the resulting value is returned.

The definition above corresponds closely to the dynamic semantics of the complete version of BSI/VDM-SL. The only difference is that here only an arbitrary one of the possible values are returned, while all possible values are collected and returned in [Larsen90].

The semantics of the quantified expressions (∀ and ∃) is defined as:

```
EvalAllOrExistsExpr : AllOrExistsExpr ⥲ VAL
EvalAllOrExistsExpr (mk-AllOrExistsExpr(quant, bind_sb, pred_e)) △
  dcl env_s : BlkEnv-set,
      cont : B := true;
  env_s := EvalSetBindSet(bind_sb) ;
  while env_s ≠ { } ∧ cont
  do let env ∈ env_s in
        PushBlkEnv(env) ;
        let pred_v = EvalExpr(pred_e) in
          if is-BOOL(pred_v)
          then let mk-BOOL(b) = pred_v in
                  cases quant:
                    ALL    → cont := b,
                    EXISTS → cont := ¬ b
                  end
          else error;
        env_s := env_s − {env};
        PopBlkEnv() ;
   cases quant:
     ALL    → return mk-BOOL(cont),
     EXISTS → return mk-BOOL(¬ cont)
   end
```

For all possible binding environments which can be constructed from the set of bindings ($bind_{sb}$) the predicate expression ($pred_e$) is evaluated. It is then tested whether it is worth continuing (e.g. if it is a universal quantification we can leave the loop when we have found the first binding for which the predicate evaluates to **false**).

The dynamic semantics for BSI/VDM-SL is based on the three valued logic called LPF (Logic for Partial Functions) used in [Jones90]. This logic requires unbounded parallelism which naturally we cannot deal with when we are executing the specification. Thus, this operational semantics of the quantified expressions differs from the semantics of BSI/VDM-SL. The logic of the operational semantics can be considered as a conditional and/or between all the possible bindings. Thus, the two generalized forms of de Morgan's rule[5] still hold with our semantics, which we consider quite important.

4.2.2 Patterns

The general pattern matching operation *PatternMatch* uses the state and takes a syntactic pattern and a semantic value to match against the pattern as arguments, and returns the set of possible binding environments.

[5]The generalized forms of de Morgan's rule state that one of the quantifiers (universal or existential) over a predicate can be represented by negating the other quantifier with the negated predicate.

$PatternMatch : Pattern \times VAL \xrightarrow{o} BlkEnv\textsf{-set}$

A binding environment is a block environment which instantiate the unbound variables (pattern identifiers) introduced in the pattern. If a pattern matching fails an empty set will be returned. *PatternMatch* examines the syntactic pattern and calls the corresponding matching operation.

As an example we present *MatchSetUnionPattern* which matches a set union pattern to a set value.

$MatchSetUnionPattern : SetUnionPattern \times VAL \xrightarrow{o} BklEnv\textsf{-set}$

$MatchSetUnionPattern\ (mk\text{-}SetUnionPattern(lp_p, rp_p), val_v) \triangleq$
  dcl $envres_{sl} : BlkEnv\textsf{-set} := \{\};$
  if $is\text{-}SET(val_v)$
  then let $mk\text{-}SET(val_{sv}) = val_v$ in
      for all $(setl_{sv}, setr_{sv}) \in SetChop(val_{sv})$
      do let $envl_s = PatternMatch(lp_p, mk\text{-}SET(setl_{sv}))$,
          $envr_s = PatternMatch(rp_p, mk\text{-}SET(setr_{sv}))$ in
          if $envl_s \neq \{\} \wedge envr_s \neq \{\}$
          then $envres_{sl} := envres_{sl} \cup$
              $UnionMatch\ (\{EnvMerge(tmp_1, tmp_2) \mid$
                  $tmp_1 \in envl_s, tmp_2 \in envr_s\})$;
      return $envres_{sl}$
  else error

$SetChop : VAL\textsf{-set} \rightarrow (VAL\textsf{-set} \times VAL\textsf{-set})\textsf{-set}$

$SetChop\ (val_{sv}) \triangleq$
  $\{(setl_{sv}, setr_{sv}) \mid setl_{sv}, setr_{sv} \in \mathcal{F}\ val_{sv} \cdot$
      $(setl_{sv} \cup setr_{sv} = val_{sv}) \wedge (setl_{sv} \cap setr_{sv} = \{\})\}$

All possible disjoint pair of sets are chopped from the set value val_{sv} by *SetChop*. For all possible set-pairs, the sets are matched against two patterns lp_p and rp_p. This generates two sets of binding environments which, if both matchings succeed, are combined to obtain the joint set of possible binding environments. Before adding this set to the result it is filtered by *UnionMatch* which is defined as follows:

$UnionMatch : BlkEnv\textsf{-set} \xrightarrow{o} BlkEnv\textsf{-set}$

$UnionMatch\ (blk_{sl}) \triangleq$
  return $\{StripDoubles\ (blk_l) \mid blk_l \in blk_{sl} \cdot$
      $\forall\ (id, v_{1v}) \in \textbf{elems}\ blk_l, (id, v_{2v}) \in \textbf{elems}\ blk_l \cdot v_{1v} = v_{2v}\}$

UnionMatch filters a set of binding environments for inconsistency and redundancy. A binding environment is considered inconsistent if an identifier is associated with two different values. This situation can occur if repeated pattern identifiers have been used but are matched to different values. This is not a valid binding environment and is therefore removed. In *UnionMatch* this is done by returning only binding environments where possible identical pattern identifiers are associated to identical values.

If a pattern matching using repeated pattern identifiers succeeds (is consistent) it will result in duplicate entries in the binding environment which is redundant information. *StripDoubles* therefore removes all duplicate entries.

5 Examples

In this section we will present a few examples of patterns using loose specification and repeated pattern identifiers illustrating the expressiveness provided by the generality of the patterns in our subset.

To illustrate the use of loose specification we present a version of the *MergeSort* algorithm.

$MergeSort : \mathbb{N}\text{-set} \rightarrow \mathbb{N}^*$

$MergeSort\,(set) \triangleq$
  cases set :
    $\{\} \rightarrow [\,],$
    $\{e\} \rightarrow [e],$
    $set_1 \cup set_2 \rightarrow Merge(MergeSort(set_1), MergeSort(set_2))$
  end

$Merge : \mathbb{N}^* \times \mathbb{N}^* \rightarrow \mathbb{N}^*$

$Merge\,(seq_l, seq_r) \triangleq$
  cases (seq_l, seq_r) :
    $([\,], seq) \rightarrow seq,$
    $(seq, [\,]) \rightarrow seq,$
    $([e_l] \curvearrowright seq'_l, [e_r] \curvearrowright seq'_r) \rightarrow$ **if** $e_l < e_r$
      then $[e_l] \curvearrowright Merge(seq'_l, seq_r)$
      else $[e_r] \curvearrowright Merge(seq_l, seq'_r)$
  end

MergeSort takes a set of natural numbers and returns a sorted list of the elements in the set. If *set* contains more than one element it is split up, using the loosely specified union match, into two disjoint sets set_1 and set_2. These sets are sorted recursively and the results are merged by *Merge*.

If we wanted to ensure that set_1 and set_2 are of approximately the same cardinality, this could be done by the let-be-such-that expression which is also included in our subset. The last entry in the case expression in *MergeSort* should then be replaced with:

$s \rightarrow$ **let** $set_1 \cup set_2 \in \{s\}$ **be st abs** (**card** set_1 − **card** $set_2) \leq 1$ **in**
  $Merge(MergeSort(set_1), MergeSort(set_2))$

The let-be-such-that expression is still loosely specified as the pattern matching of the set union against *set* (the only element in the bind set $\{set\}$) can result in a number of possible binding environments. The difference from the original solution is the additional constraint (the such-that predicate) which is placed on the possible binding environments.

To illustrate the use of repeated pattern identifiers, we have specified an invariant for the type *PointSet*.

$$PointSet = (X \times Y)\text{-}\mathbf{set}$$

$$\mathbf{inv}\ ps \triangleq \forall (x, y_1) \in ps, (x, y_2) \in ps \cdot y_1 = y_2$$

This shows how the use of repeated pattern identifiers can describe, in a compact form, the condition on a set of type *PointSet*, that points which have the same the first coordinate must also have the same second coordinate.

6 Related Work

There exist a number of other executable languages which have been more or less inspired by VDM. In [Plat&89] an overview of existing tool support for VDM is presented. However, only two projects dealing with an executable subset of VDM-SL are given in that overview. These are the Meta-IV compiler project from Kiel University (see [Haß87]), and the EPROS project where both an interpreter and a compiler for a language called EPROL (strongly inspired by VDM) have been developed (see [Hekmatpour&88]). In addition to these two we have looked at 'me too' (see [Alexander&90]). The main difference between our executable language and the existing ones is the generality of the pattern matching.

None of the existing executable languages inspired by VDM which have been mentioned above contains more than pattern identifiers, tuple patterns, and record patterns. However, a number of languages for functional programming exist which also support sequence patterns. In addition, the pattern matching in all the existing languages is deterministic. However, it is clear that by taking an approach where we deal with loosely specified patterns we will lose some efficiency. On the other hand, the generality of the patterns we are using provides the user with much more flexibility in writing the (executable) specifications. For instance it would not be possible to write any of the examples from the previous section in any of the other executable languages inspired by VDM.

7 Concluding Remarks

We have defined an executable subset of a VDM dialect which is more powerful than any of the existing ones we are aware of. Even though the syntax has been selected specially to provide the necessary expressive power for the mini-specifications in IPTES, we hope to be able to implement it so that it can be used outside the IPTES environment as well. We hope to be able to do this because we feel that such an interpreter will be useful for other applications as well.

We also consider it a strength of the subset that it is as closely related to the forthcoming standard language (both BSI and ISO VDM-SL) as it is. Thus, the users of this interpreter will have plenty of existing literature at their disposal, because a lot of publications are expected to be using the standard notation.

We still have to finish the actual implementation of the interpreter according to the operational semantics presented here. The current state of the project (primo August 1991) is that we have finished the specification of the syntax and semantics. A parser which constructs abstract syntax trees have also been implemented and we are in the process of implementing C++ classes for the most common VDM-SL types. We hope that these classes and the operational nature of the semantics will allow us to design an interpreter which structure is closely related to the definition of the semantics, thereby achieving a short and reliable design in implementation phase. It is an open question how efficient our interpreter will be, due to the generality we have included. However, we expect to know much more about the efficiency at the time of the VDM symposium as the first version of the interpreter is planned to be completed in December 1991.

Acknowledgments

We would like to thank John Dawes, Stephen Bear, Hans Toetenel and especially Nico Plat and Jan Storbank Pedersen for valuable remarks on an earlier version of this article. In addition we have had constructive remarks from our colleagues at IFAD.

The IPTES consortium is formed by IFAD (Denmark), VTT (Finland), MARI (United Kingdom), CEA/LETI (France), ENEA (Italy), Synergie (France), DIT/UPM (Spain), Telefónica I+D (Spain), and Politecnico di Milano (Italy).

References

[Alexander&90] Heather Alexander and Val Jones. *Software Design and Prototyping using Me Too.* Prentice Hall, 1990.

[Bjørner91] Dines Bjørner. *Software Architectures and Programming Systems Design.* Submitted to publisher.

[BSIVDM91] *VDM Specification Language – Proto-Standard.* Technical Report, British Standards Institution, 1991. BSI IST/5/50.

[Ghezzi&91] Carlo Ghezzi, Dino Mandrioli, Sandro Morasca and Mauro Pezzé. A Unified High-Level Petri Net Model For Time-Critical Systems. *IEEE Transactions on Software Engineering*, 17(2), 1991.

[Haß87] Manfred Haß. Development and Application of a Meta IV Compiler. In *VDM – A Formal Method at Work*, Springer–Verlag, 1987.

[Hekmatpour&88] Sharam Hekmatpour and Darrel Ince. *Software Prototyping, Formal Methods and VDM.* Addison-Wesley, 1988.

[Jones90] Cliff B. Jones. *Systematic Software Development Using VDM (second edition).* Prentice Hall, 1990.

[Larsen&89] Peter Gorm Larsen, Michael Meincke Arentoft, Brian Monahan and Stephen Bear. Towards a Formal Semantics of The BSI/VDM Specification Language. In *Information Processing 89*, North-Holland, 1989.

[Larsen90] Peter Gorm Larsen. *The Dynamic Semantics of the BSI/VDM Specification Language.* Technical Report, August 1990.

[Leon&91] Gonzalo León, J.A. de la Puente, M.A. Ruz and E.W. Sink. *Definition of the IPTES Architecture.* Technical Report, May 1991.
IPTES Doc.id : IPTES-UPM-1-V2.3.

[Oostenenk90] Jan-Bert Oostenenk. *Typesetting VDM with VDMSL macros.* Technical Report, NPL, 1990.

[Plat&89] Nico Plat and Hans Toetenel. *Tool support for VDM.* Technical Report 89-81, Delft University of Technology, 1989.

[Ward&85] P.T. Ward and S.J. Mellor. *Structured Development for Real-Time Systems.* Yourdon Press, 1985.

[Wieth89] Morten Wieth. Loose Specification and its Semantics. In *Information Processing 89*, North-Holland, 1989.

Using VDM within an Object-Oriented Framework

Lynn S. Marshall and Linda Simon
Bell-Northern Research Ltd.
P. O. Box 3511 Station C
Ottawa, Ontario, Canada K1Y 4H7
ph: (613) 765-4856 / 765-4932
fax: (613) 763-4222 / 765-4920
e-mail: lynnmar@bnr.ca / ldsimon@bnr.ca

Abstract

The formal specification of OSI network management protocols presents a challenge as the structure and semantics of the information to be communicated across an interoperable interface is modelled as managed objects. It is necessary to integrate formal techniques into the specific object-oriented framework developed by the ISO management standards.

This paper examines the suitability of VDM as a candidate formal description method for use in specifying the behaviour of OSI managed objects. To investigate the suitability of incorporating object-oriented concepts such as inheritance within VDM, a case study of a simplified Log managed object class is examined.

1 Introduction

1.1 Background

The International Organization for Standardization (ISO) is developing a set of standards for managing Open Systems Interconnection (OSI)-based networks. These standards have adopted an object-oriented approach to the specification of management information as seen in protocol exchanges by open systems involved in management activities.

Within this approach, logical and physical resources (e.g. protocol state machines, modems, applications) to be managed by a remote system across a standardized interface are modelled as *managed objects*. Managed objects that share the same definition are instances of the same *managed object class*. A managed object class is defined in terms of: the *attributes* visible at the managed object boundary, the *operations* that may be applied to the managed object, the *notifications* which are emitted by the managed object when some event occurs, and the *behaviour* exhibited by the managed object.

Inheritance is an important concept of the OSI management object model. It provides a mechanism for incremental or relative specification, whereby a new managed object class (a subclass) may be derived from one or more existing managed object class(es) (refered to as its superclasses). The OSI management object model [9] defines a set of inheritance rules that ensure that every instance of a subclass is compatible with its superclass.

1.2 Motivation

The managed object class definitions specify the structure and semantics of the information which is conveyed in protocol exchanges between different systems, and hence represents standards which are the basis for the implementation of compatible OSI systems. It is therefore essential that these specifications be unambiguous, complete and concise.

A notation for describing the syntactical aspects of OSI managed objects has been developed [10], however, it does not provide a formal framework for defining the behaviour of managed objects.

The objective of this paper is to examine the suitability of VDM as a candidate specification technique for formally specifying the behaviour of managed objects. It is motivated, in part, by some earlier work reported in [13] which proposed defining managed object behaviour in terms of pre-conditions and post-conditions written in English. The VDM concepts of state and operations can be intuitively mapped onto the managed object concepts of attributes, and operations and notifications, respectively. Furthermore, work on interpreting the language Z in an object-oriented framework [4,11] suggest that object-oriented concepts including inheritance can be readily accommodated. Bear [2] has done some work on structuring VDM specifications, but he has not looked at inheritance.

To investigate the suitability of VDM as a candidate specification technique we take as a case study the Log managed object class, which is based on a simplified version of the OSI managed object class described in natural language in [6].

The remainder of this paper is organized as follows. An informal description of the Log managed object is given in Section 2. In Section 3, we discuss our experiences in developing a VDM formal description of the Log and a subclass of the Log. Section 4 provides an overview of the VDM specification itself. A discussion of the analysis of the specification can be found in Section 5. Section 6 presents our conclusions.

2 An Informal Description of the Log Managed Object

Here we present a simplification of the ISO Log control function. The Log managed object class is a conceptual repository for storing information about various events that have occurred. It also provides the ability for an external system to control which information is selected for logging.

Notifications emitted by managed objects within the local system are received by the conceptual log pre-processing function (see Figure 1). This function forms a *potential log record*.

Conceptually, a potential log record is distributed to all Logs that are contained within the local system. Each Log contains a *discriminator construct* attribute which specifies the characteristics a potential log record must have in order to be selected for logging.

If the discriminator construct evaluates to **true** for a potential log record and the Log is in the *unlocked* administrative state and in the *enabled* operational state, then a new log record will be created. Here we assume that the log has infinite capacity. This

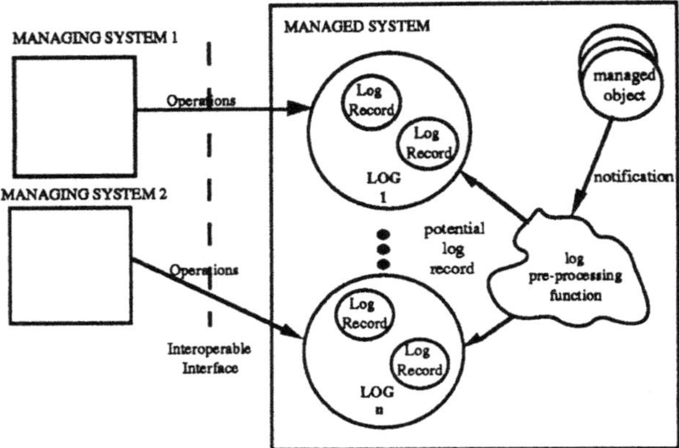

Figure 1: Log Conceptual Model

new log record will contain all of the information contained in the potential log record supplemented with additional information generated as part of the logging process (e.g. log record identifiers and logging time).

With the exception of the operational state (which represents the operational capability of a Log to perform its function), all attributes of a Log may be modified by a managing system by sending a *set* operation to that Log. The values of all attributes of a Log may be retrieved by sending a *get* operation to that Log.

A *create* operation may be sent by a managing system to request that the managed system create a Log managed object, thereby requesting new or additional logs be defined. A *delete* operation may be sent by a managing system to request the deletion of a Log (and its contained log records).

A Log generates an *attribute change* notification whenever one of its attributes is changed. An *object creation* notification and an *object deletion* notification are emitted by a Log when that Log is created and deleted, respectively.

3 Developing the VDM Specification

3.1 Issues Arising from the Informal Specification

Writing the formal description starting from an informal specification [6] turned out to be more difficult than originally expected. It required several iterations through reading the documentation, writing a formal description, and discussion, to reach an acceptable VDM specification of the simplified log. Many concepts became clear as the work progressed and the specification took shape. However, while trying to formalize the specification, many questions arose which are not answered by the documentation. The fact that formalizing an informal description always requires many iterations and raises many interesting questions shows how valuable this exercise can be.

For example, the ISO document [6] introduces an attribute, usage state, which reflects the ability of the Log to accommodate more *users*. This attribute is never referred to by the operations defined for the class.

The ISO Log managed object class includes a maximum log size which limits the size of the log file. In our simplified specification we assume the Log can be infinite. The size restriction is incorporated in a subclass and the concept of inheritance in VDM explored. It was determined that this subclass is not a strict extension of the superclass (i.e. does not follow the rules of inheritance).

3.2 Incorporating VDM Within the OSI Management Syntactical Framework

A primary objective was to use VDM within the syntactical framework provided by the standardized OSI Management *template* notation [10]. The *managed object class* (MOC) template specified in [10] forms the basis of the formal definition of a managed object. This template consists of a number of elements, one of which is the behaviour definition.

The behaviour definition may be documented by use of natural language text or by the use of formal description techniques; although, in practice only natural language has so far been used. Here, we propose that VDM be used for formally describing the behaviour of managed objects.

Data types referred to in the other elements of the MOC template are specified using Abstract Syntax Notation One (ASN.1) [7].[1] Since VDM specifications include both a data typing and a behavioural component, an issue concerns how to tie the ASN.1 data typing descriptions to formal VDM behaviour specifications. The specifications presented in this paper are given entirely in VDM. The approach taken was to manually translate the ASN.1 specifications to VDM types. Potential areas of future study include the automatic translation of ASN.1 to VDM and the ability to reference directly ASN.1 data descriptions within a VDM behavioural specification.

Syntactically, inheritance is achieved by including the names of the superclass(es) in the *derived from* element of the MOC template. This element is presumed to automatically import all characteristics from the superclass definition(s). Therefore, only the extended characteristics introduced by the subclass are documented in the other elements of the MOC template. A set of rules is specified in [10] for combining the inherited characteristics with those characteristics explicitly declared in the other elements of the MOC template.

Our objective is to specify only the extended behaviour in the MOC template and to enhance [10] to specify the rules for combining this VDM specification with the VDM specifications documented in the superclass(es) template. The rules for providing extensible behavioural specifications are discussed in the following subsection.

3.3 The VDM Style Appropriate for Inheritance

One of the key features of the ISO Standards for OSI Managed Objects is the notion of inheritance. While VDM is not an object-oriented formal method, it is possible to adopt

[1] ASN.1 is a notation for the description of data structures which was developed by ISO for the abstract specification of data types and values in OSI application protocols. ASN.1 is used to express the abstract syntax of the data types and values associated with managed object characteristics that are conveyed in OSI management protocols.

a VDM style appropriate for Managed Objects.

VDM provides the notion of *satisfiability* [12]. It provides a framework for showing that a concrete formal description is a valid implementation of (i.e. *satisfies*) a more abstract description. The *implementation* (concrete description) must meet the *specification* (abstract description) but may be defined on a larger domain and may be more determined (i.e. less non-deterministic). Thus for each operation the concrete pre-condition may be weaker and the post-condition may be stronger. This is exactly the concept necessary for inheritance in managed object terminology. A subclass must exhibit all the behaviour of the superclass, but may introduce additional (consistent) behaviour.

Thus a subclass specification of a managed object is derived from a superclass description by weakening the pre-condition and strengthening the post-condition of the applicable operations.

When expressing a subclass specification, only the additional information need be given. This will avoid repetition, aid in understandability, and tie in with the current OSI management template format. Thus a subclass is assumed to inherit the operations exactly as stated in the superclass unless an extension is given. If an extension is given, the new pre-condition is "or"ed ($\vee$) with the superclass pre-condition, and the new post-condition is "and"ed ($\wedge$) with the superclass post-condition. This will guarantee that the inheritance rules are met.

Taking the original log specification and attempting to derive a subclass for it, again required several iterations. To extend the behaviour of an operation by only weakening the pre-condition and strengthening the post-condition requires that the superclass operation be in an appropriate form. While this research has not yet disclosed exactly what this appropriate form might be, some conclusions can be drawn.

The split between the pre- and the post-condition is very important. Generally it seems to be best to put as much information in the pre-condition as possible. This seems to make extension go more smoothly. If the operation has a pre-condition of **true** (e.g. returns a flag indicating whether or not the operation was successful), it may be necessary to introduce a new operation which does have a pre-condition. The original operation may *quote* (VDM's equivalent to subroutine call) this new operation and the new operation will be extensible. It is also important that the post-condition be extensible. The **others** clause of the **case** construct and the **else** clause of the **if** construct should be avoided.

A further consideration is necessary when extending a managed object. The OSI management standard [9] allows subclasses to define new attributes as needed. This capability could be provided in VDM by leaving part of the top level state undefined and adding the necessary definitions in the subclasses. This is not very elegant and we have adopted the RAISE [5] approach[2], which allows extra fields to be added later with no mention of them in the original description.

In addition to adding new data types to a subclass, we may also add additional parameters to an operation. ISO management standards allow "holes" to be left in operation and notification signature definitions which can be filled in by the subclasses. An extend-

[2]RAISE stands for Rigorous Approach to Industrial Software Engineering. The RAISE Specification Language (RSL) supports model-oriented, algebraic, explicit, axiomatic, applicative, imperative, and concurrent styles. The RAISE Method is based on the stepwise refinement paradigm.

able definition is indicated in ASN.1 by providing a parameter of the "ANY DEFINED BY" type. To avoid the need for signature changes in the VDM specification it is best to structure the signature of such operations in such a way that the parameters are a set of parameter type and value pairs, instead of a list of parameter values whose type is determined by the signature. The function describing the valid types of the parameter set can be extended in the subclass definition.

3.4 Notifications and Triggers

In VDM we model both managed object operations and managed object notifications by VDM operations. An operation occurs if it is requested and the pre-condition is **true** (i.e. the pre-condition is a guard). A notification occurs whenever the pre-condition becomes **true** (i.e. the pre-condition is a trigger). To indicate a notification in the VDM specification we call the pre-condition a **trigger**. Whenever necessary this special operation will fire and issue a notification.

4 Overview of the VDM Specification

Only excerpts from the specification will be presented here. The authors will be pleased to provide copies of the complete specification upon request. Mario Wolczko's VDM LaTeX Macros [14] and the SpecBox Tool [1] were used to prepare the VDM specification.

4.1 Architecture

Since the *create* and *delete* operations have cross-object constraints, it is not possible to model a single Log in isolation. The specification is presented in two levels, or modules. The upper *Coordinator* level takes care of the creations and deletions, while most of the functionality is in the lower *Log* level.

The Coordinator level receives a request from outside the system, performs various checks, and then invokes (or, in VDM terminology, *quotes*) the corresponding Log level operation for the chosen Log(s).

4.2 Type and State Definitions

The Coordinator level state is:

compose *Logs* of
    loginfo : *Loginfo*
end

Log information is a map from Log id to Log.

Loginfo = map *Log-id* to *Log*

Log is defined in the Log module. The Log state contains the log information, the log records, and possibly an outgoing notification message.

compose *Log* of
info : *Log-info*
logrecs : *Log-records*
notif : [*Not-msg*]
end

Log information consists of: the log id, the construct describing the conditions that must be met for a message to be passed on, the administrative state (controlled by a manager), and the operational state (controlled by the local system). Other fields may be added later, as indicated by the keywords **at least**. This idea is inspired by RAISE (see section 3.3). We could express this concept in standard VDM, but this notation is more elegant and concise.

compose *Log-info* of at least
log-id : *Log-id*
disc-const : *Discriminator-construct*
admin-state : *Administrative-state*
op-state : *Operational-state*
end

The subclass definition then expands the Log information to include the maximum log size as follows:

extend *Log* with
maxrecs : *Maxnum*
end

4.3 Coordinator Behaviour

CREATE-LOGS creates a new log and invokes CREATE-LOG to trigger the OBJECTCREATION notification. The attributes given can include log id, discriminator construct, and administrative state. Those not supplied are given default values. Since *newlog* may have extra fields added in the future, we avoid the use of the *mk-* function.

CREATE-LOGS (*attrs*: *Attr-info*)
ext wr *loginfo* : *Loginfo*
pre $\mathrm{dom}\, attrs \subseteq \{LOGIDTYPE, DISCCONSTTYPE, ADMINSTATETYPE\} \wedge$
$LOGIDTYPE \in \mathrm{dom}\, attrs \;\Rightarrow\; attrs(LOGIDTYPE) \notin \mathrm{dom}\, loginfo$
post let $newlog \in Log\text{-}info$ in
$newlog.log\text{-}id = \text{if } LOGIDTYPE \in \mathrm{dom}\, attrs$
$\quad \text{then } attrs(LOGIDTYPE)$
$\quad \text{else } picklogid()$
$\wedge\; newlog.disc\text{-}const = \text{if } DISCCONSTTYPE \in \mathrm{dom}\, attrs$
$\quad \text{then } attrs(DISCCONSTTYPE)$
$\quad \text{else } EMPTY$
$\wedge\; newlog.admin\text{-}state = \text{if } ADMINSTATETYPE \in \mathrm{dom}\, attrs$
$\quad \text{then } attrs(ADMINSTATETYPE)$
$\quad \text{else } UNLOCKED$
$\wedge\; newlog.op\text{-}state = getopstate() \wedge$
$\exists log \in Log \cdot post\text{-}CREATE\text{-}LOG(mk\text{-}Log(newlog, \{\,\}, \mathrm{nil}), log) \wedge$
$loginfo = \overleftarrow{loginfo} \dagger \{newlog.log\text{-}id \mapsto log\}$

When extending this operation in the subclass we omit the signature since it is unchanged. orpre indicates the additional pre-condition which is "or"ed with the original, and **andpost** indicates the additional post-condition to be "and"ed with the original. Now we can also refer to the *maxrecs* field of *Log-info*.
CREATE-LOGS now possibly has a new attribute: the maximum size information.

CREATE-LOGS

$$
\begin{array}{l}
\textsf{orpre dom } attrs \subseteq \{LOGIDTYPE, DISCCONSTTYPE, \\
\quad ADMINSTATETYPE, MAXSIZE\} \wedge \\
\quad LOGIDTYPE \in \textsf{dom } attrs \Rightarrow attrs(LOGIDTYPE) \notin \textsf{dom } loginfo \\
\textsf{andpost } newlog.maxrecs = \textsf{if } MAXSIZE \in \textsf{dom } attrs \\
\qquad\qquad\qquad\qquad\quad \textsf{then } attrs(MAXSIZE) \\
\qquad\qquad\qquad\qquad\quad \textsf{else } 0
\end{array}
$$

Whenever a Log needs to produce a notification, NOTIFICATION-LOGS will fire.

NOTIFICATION-LOGS n: *Not-msg*

$$
\begin{array}{l}
\textsf{ext wr } loginfo \ : \ Loginfo \\
\textsf{trigger } \exists lid \in \textsf{dom } loginfo \cdot pre\text{-}NOTIFICATION\text{-}LOG(loginfo(lid)) \\
\textsf{post let } lid \in \textsf{dom } \overleftarrow{loginfo} \cdot \\
\qquad pre\text{-}NOTIFICATION\text{-}LOG(\overleftarrow{loginfo}(lid)) \textsf{ in} \\
\quad \exists lid \in Log \cdot post\text{-}NOTIFICATION\text{-}LOG(\overleftarrow{loginfo}(lid), log, n) \wedge \\
\quad loginfo = \overleftarrow{loginfo} \dagger \{lid \mapsto log\}
\end{array}
$$

4.4 Log Behaviour

We run into a problem when extending ADD-RECORD which adds a potential log record to the log if the necessary conditions are met. Now that there is a maximum size, the behaviour actually changes and cannot be extended within the inheritance framework. The original operation is:

ORIG-ADD-RECORD (*plr*: *Pot-log-record*)

$$
\begin{array}{l}
\textsf{ext wr } logrecs \ : \ Log\text{-}records \\
\quad\ \ \textsf{rd } info \quad\ : \ Log\text{-}info \\
\textsf{post if } shouldlog(plr, info) \\
\quad \textsf{then } \exists t \in Time \cdot gettime(t) \wedge \\
\qquad \exists rid \in Log\text{-}record\text{-}id \cdot pickrecid(info.log\text{-}id, rid) \wedge \\
\qquad logrecs = \overleftarrow{logrecs} \dagger \{rid \mapsto mk\text{-}Log\text{-}record(t, plr)\} \\
\quad \textsf{else } logrecs = \overleftarrow{logrecs}
\end{array}
$$

A new operation must be added to describe the subclass:
FINITE-ADD-RECORD now must check that the maximum size has not been reached.

FINITE-ADD-RECORD (*plr*: *Pot-log-record*)

$$
\begin{array}{l}
\textsf{ext wr } logrecs \ : \ Log\text{-}records \\
\quad\ \ \textsf{rd } info \quad\ : \ Log\text{-}info
\end{array}
$$

post if $info.maxrecs = 0 \vee info.maxrecs > \mathsf{card\ dom}\ \overleftarrow{logrecs}$
then $post\text{-}ORIG\text{-}ADD\text{-}RECORD(plr, \overleftarrow{logrecs}, info, logrecs)$
else $logrecs = \overleftarrow{logrecs}$

5 Analysis

Having completed the specification we can use the formal description to determine if certain properties hold. For example:

1. Will a locked Log always respond to an unlock request?
2. Is it true that a Log can only log records it receives (i.e. it can't invent records itself)?

The answer to these two questions (based on our model of the system) is yes. Examining the appropriate VDM operations allows us to easily answer questions such as these.

6 Conclusions

The perspective of our work differs from [2,4] in that our primary goal was not to propose extensions to an existing specification language (in our case VDM), to accommodate *object-orientation.* Rather, our main objective was to investigate whether an existing formal specification language could be used within a specific object-oriented framework developed for OSI management.

Based on the work presented in this paper, we conclude that VDM is well-suited for specifying the behaviour of OSI managed objects and can be used within the existing OSI management syntactical framework with minimal extensions. The proposed extensions to VDM are:

1. the use of the **trigger** keyword in VDM operation pre-conditions for describing the behaviour of OSI managed object *notifications.*
2. the use of special keywords and notation for explicitly identifying extensions to VDM operations and type definitions to accommodate the OSI management concept of inheritance.

Areas for future study identified in this paper include:

1. a formal treatment of the relationship between ASN.1 and VDM,
2. the development of general guidelines for structuring pre- and post-conditions to facilitate extensibility.

Our experiences reinforce the benefits of using formal specification techniques in standards development. In producing a formal description of the ISO Log managed object from an existing informal one, a number of ambiguities in the latter were identified and proposed changes to clarify these ambiguities were submitted to the appropriate ISO standards committee. Furthermore, given the formal specification we were able to prove a number of properties of the Log managed object, thus providing increased confidence in the correctness of the standard.

References

[1] Adelard. *SpecBox User Manual.* Coborn House Business Centre, London, UK, 1991.

[2] Bear, S. *Structuring for the VDM Specification Language*, in Proceedings VDM'88: VDM—The Way Ahead. Eds. R. Bloomfield, L. Marshall, R. Jones. Lecture Notes in Computer Science 328, September 1988, pp. 2–25.

[3] Cusack, E., Rudkin, S. and Smith, C. *An Object Oriented Interpretation of LOTOS.* Proceedings of the Second International Conference on Formal Description Techniques (FORTE '89), 5–8 December 1989, Vancouver, B.C., pp. 265–284.

[4] Duke, R., Rose., G. and Lee, A. *Object-Oriented Protocol Specification.* Proceedings of the Tenth International IFIP WG 6.1 Symposium on Protocol Specification, Testing and Verification, 12–15 June 1990, Ottawa, Ont., pp. 323–339.

[5] Eriksen, Kirsten E., and Prehn, Søren. RAISE Overview. Computer Resources International A/S, 1991.

[6] ISO. Systems Management—Part 6: Log Control Function. (ISO/IEC JTC1/SC21 N-4862), Output of the editing meeting held in Kyoto, Japan, May 1990.

[7] ISO. Final Text of IS 8824, Information Technology—Open Systems Interconnection —Specification of Abstract Syntax Notation One (ASN.1). (ISO/IEC JTC1/SC21 N-4720), April 1990.

[8] ISO. Formal Specification of the CMIP Protocol Machine. (ISO/IEC JTC1/SC21 WG4 N-1057), National Body Contribution from Australia, March 1990.

[9] ISO. Structure of Management Information Part 1—Management Information Model. (ISO/IEC JTC1/SC21 N-5252), Output of the editing meeting held in Paris, January 1990.

[10] ISO. Structure of Management Information Part 4—Guidelines for the Definition of Managed Objects. (ISO/IEC JTC1/SC21 N-4852), Output of the May 1990, Editing Meeting held in Kyoto.

[11] ISO. Architectural Semantics, Specification Techniques and Formalisms, Working Document. (ISO/IEC JTC1/SC21 N-4887), 1990.

[12] Jones, C. B. Systematic Software Development Using VDM. Prentice-Hall International, Second Edition, 1990.

[13] OSI/Network Management Forum. *J-Team Technical Report on Modelling Principles for Managed Objects.* Issue 1, Draft 8, December 17, 1990.

[14] Wolczko, Mario. *Typesetting VDM with* LaTeX. Department of Computer Science, University of Manchester, March 1988.

THE INTEGRATED SOFTWARE DEVELOPMENT AND VERIFICATION SYSTEM ATES

A. PUCCETTI
C.I.S.I. INGENIERIE
3 rue Le Corbusier, SILIC 232
F-94528 RUNGIS Cedex
FRANCE

ABSTRACT. This paper is a project report, presenting a few results of the ESPRIT project ATES, concerned with formal software development. A programming and proof system, based on a high level, abstract language, able to express the specifications necessary to develop reliable software, in a program-to-proof approach is described. Within this approach, we want to conceive a program and introduce the elements necessary for its proof, at the same time. (Those formal proof elements consist in logical assertions expressing mathematically what an algorithm does and logical properties of the function realized by the algorithm). Those proof elements will be used by the system, to verify the correctness of an algorithm, guided by an interactive proof checker.

1. INTRODUCTION

ATES is the number 1222 Esprit project, which has started in 1985 and finished in 1990. The following European partners are involved: CISI Ingénierie (France), Philips Research Laboratory Brussels, University of Liege (Belgium), University of Twente (The Netherlands), Université de Paris VII (France), and Commissariat à l'Energie Atomique (France). The objective of this project ([14]) was to establish the potential of the integration of a number of advanced techniques in the field of computer programming of software systems for scientific and technical applications and to provide an integrated environment to conceive and implement reliable software (the name of the project ATES being an acronym of "Advanced Techniques integration into Efficient scientific Software").

Using VDM ([11]), the development of a program consists of several steps of refinement and at each stage verifications should be carried out. The verifications are conducted within the framework provided by the proof rules, either formally or rigorously (i.e. by appealing to intuitive arguments) according to the cost-effectiveness of either approach within the context of the particular application. It is this approach to the entire development process, and the flexibility allowed, that make VDM a most attractive development method. However, the overheads involved in carrying out these various levels of refinement are considerable and any savings in effort would be beneficial. The RAISE ([6]) development method, based on the stepwise refinement paradigm, allows to develop software through a series of steps, where each step represents a refinement of the previous one. ATES suggests an alternative software development scenario, which is based on a methodology leading from a program to its proof: in a first step some algorithm is

written, jointly with its formal specifications, and finally the correctness of this algorithm is proved, guided by the interactive proof checker of the ATES system. Like RAISE, the ATES methodology offers support for the development phases from specification to implementation. The main difference is that it allows to built up software systems in a classical structured manner: at each level of the system decomposition, new operators may be written, specified, compiled and checked. Both methods include guidelines and substantial tool support for verification. However, the ATES method seems actually more practical for industrial use, in the sense that it still follows the quite natural "Structured Analysis and Decomposition" principle, that builds up programs progressively.
The ATES proof sub-system belongs to the same class of proof systems as System B ([1]), for it is based on rewriting rules and tactics. It has also some similarities with the LCF ([7]) proof system, in the sense that one can easily write well-suited or specialized proof strategies. The ATES proof system combines the advantages of most existing interactive proof systems, giving support to a variety of working styles.

In the present paper we will focus on the main ideas involved in the ATES method for program proof. This interactive method will make use of tactics and strategies, we shall describe in details. In a first part we introduce the basic elements of the ATES programming and specification languages, their main properties, and the guidelines for specifying mathematically algorithms, in such a way that the ATES system can prove them. Then, is explained how the ATES system establishes the correctness of an algorithm, given some formal specifications. A first experience with a theorem prover will be described, and a simplification tool proper to the ATES system and based on natural deduction, will be explained. In a third part, we describe the state of the ATES prototype, and mention some experiments carried through. Finally, some concluding remarks will be made, about the industrial interest of this system.

2. SHORT DESCRIPTION OF THE ATES LANGUAGE

The general programming language used in this system (see [2] and [3]), offers possibilities to express in a structured way the following kinds of components:

- The abstract headings of elementary ATES objects: operators and abstract data types. They give an external view of the elementary objects, without any relation to their internal representation, and also some syntactical notation for them.
Example: The heading of a function that solves a linear system of equations, of the form "A*x = B" where A is a squared lower triangular matrix (of dimension 100) and b is a vector (of the same dimension), can be expressed in the following way:

```
command gauss ( var x  : vector; const a : matrix; const b : vector)
        syntax gauss : a, b, x
```

- Implementation descriptions for operators and data types, using a Pascal-like syntax, named respectively algorithms and concrete data types.
Example:

```
algorithm gauss
```

```
var i, j, n : integer; inte : real
begin
   for i := 1 to 100
   do
   inte := 0.0;
   for j := 1 to i - 1
   do      inte := inte + a[i, j] * x[j]  od;
   x[i] := (b[i] - inte) / a[i, i]
   od
end
```

- Modules, describing the implementation choice for each operator and abstract data type by an algorithm or concrete data type. They generate executable code.

Example:

```
module gauss
        for operator gauss
        using algorithm gauss
```

- The axiomatic relative to the problem treated, introducing new mathematical objects: functions, sets and logical axioms. Functions model operators and sets model data types.

Example: The problem of solving the triangular system "A*x=B" can rise the following axiomatic, where "sum(j,i,a,x)" designates the mathematical quantity "$\Sigma_{1\leq k\leq j}$ $a_{i,k}$ * x_k", which represents the product of row number i of the matrix a by the vector b:

```
axioms gauss
        using axioms integer, real
var i, j: Int; a : Matrix; x: Vector
const sum : ( Int;Int;Matrix;Vector ) -> Real        << function definition >>
axiom sum_0 == sum(0, i, a, x) = 0.0                 << recursive definition of the sum >>
axiom sum_j == sum(j - 1, i, a, x) + a(i, j) * x(j) = sum(j, i, a, x)
end
```

- The pre and post-conditions of any operator (called its specifications), expressing the following property: if the pre-condition is satisfied before executing the operator in an algorithm, then the post-condition will be satisfied afterwards.

Example: Concerning the operator previously introduced, we can have the following specifications:

```
specif gauss
pre  diagonal_diff_0 == for k : { 1 .. 100 } then a(k, k) /= 0.0
                                  << The matrix must have non zero diagonal elements >>
post control_X == for k : { 1 .. 100 } then sum(k, k, a, x) = b(k)
                                  << x is a solution of the system >>
```

- Some additional information concerning the loop statements of an algorithm must be provided to do its proof. For each loop, we need a pre-condition, a post-condition, an invariance property and a monotonic decreasing function (these are named "proof elements" of the algorithm). In fact, the proof of an algorithm will be cut into smaller proof steps, by considering each loop of the algorithm to be proved as a separate operator, with its own pre-condition and post-condition. Then, once a loop is proved, it can be considered as an operator call included into some algorithm or other loop. In this way, the system builds a separate proof for each loop. This feature of the ATES system is essential, because of the necessity to keep the proofs manageable and understandable. The decreasing function will be used to prove the termination of the loop.

Example: A possible set of proof elements for our example can be written:

```
proofs gauss
  using axioms boolean, integer, real, gauss specifs boolean, integer, real, gauss
 proof gauss
    do 1 pre_loop_L1 : for ii : { 1 .. 100 } then a(ii, ii) /= 0.0
                    << pre-condition of internal loop >>
    do 1 post_loop_L1:
            a = a` and b = b`
            and (for k : { 1 .. 100 } then b(k) = sum(k, k, a, x))
                    << post-condition for internal loop >>
    do 1 inv_loop_L1:
            i <= 101 and a = a` and b = b`
            and (for k : { 1 .. i - 1 } then b(k) = sum(k, k, a, x))
            and (for ii : { 1 .. 100 } then a(ii, ii) /= 0.0)
                    << invariant for the same loop >>
    do 3 pre_loop_L2:
            inte = 0.0 and (0 < i and i <= 100)
    do 3 post_loop_L2:
            a = a` and x = x` and i = i` and inte = sum(i - 1, i, a, x)
    do 3 inv_loop_L2:
            i = i` and a = a` and x = x` and (0 < i and i <= 100)
            and j <= i and inte = sum(j - 1, i, a, x)
 end
end
```

where "1" (respectively "3") is the index of internal (resp. external) loop statement in the preceding algorithm, and a` (resp. b`) designate the values of a (resp. b) at the beginning of the loop statement.

To solve a given problem with the ATES language, it is necessary to write objects of each class (operators, algorithms, axioms, specifications and proof elements). According to their class and their range of application, these ones will be grouped into chapters. Further on, a collection of chapters around a certain theme will be grouped into larger entities, named "books". This structuring corresponds to the splitting of a given problem into sub-problems, and is left to the user. These chapters may use some external objects located in other chapters, which are imported by the "using" link.

3. PROVING THE CORRECTNESS OF ALGORITHMS

The correctness proof of an algorithm is done by the system, when introducing an associated proof chapter. In such a proof chapter, axioms and ATES-specifications are selected. In a first step the system will create an annotated algorithm according to Hoare's method, using the WP (weakest precondition) rules (see [5]) extended to the ATES features and the specifications of the operators used in this algorithm. Formally, the WP of some statement S and some predicate Q, denoted by "WP(S,Q)", is the weakest predicate P (in the sense of logical implication), verifying the property: if P is true before executing S, then Q will be true afterwards. In fact several separate annotations are generated: one for each loop, starting by the inner ones, and one annotation for the whole algorithm, loops excluded.

3.1. ANNOTATING AN ALGORITHM

This step consists in inserting between the elementary statements of an algorithm A, some predicates describing the successive states of the variables, during the computation, and their relations. To do this, the post-condition of A is placed at its end, then, moving upward through A with the WP rules (one for each kind of statements), the intermediate predicates are computed. The annotated algorithm represents in some way, the flow of informations through the instructions of A. The main WP rules we introduced are the following:

- WP of an assignment statement: *WP(x := e, P) = P [x/e],*

- WP of a conditional statement:*WP (if L then S1 else S2 fi, P) = if L then WP(S1, P) else WP(S2, P)*

- WP of an operator call: let O be an operator with formal input (resp. output) parameter "x" (resp. "y"), and "O(a,b)" be a call to this operator where "a" is an expression and "b" a variable name; let "pre_O" (resp."post_O") be the pre-condition (resp. post-condition) of O.
If "post_O" can be written "y = f(x`)", where "f" designates some function and "x`" represents the initial value of "x", then *WP(O(a,b), P) = P [b/f(a)] and pre_O [a/x,b/y],* otherwise, if O is not an explicit operator, then *WP(O(a,b)) = pre_O [x/a,y/b] and (post_O(x,y$) => P(x,y$))* where y$ designates a new free variable.

- WP of a loop statement: Let S be the loop statement "while L do S1 od" and pre_S (resp. post_S, inv_S) be its associated pre-condition (resp. post-condition, invariant). Let "In" be the set of variables used by the statement S but not modified by S, and "Out" the set of variables modified by S. The loop is considered as an operator call "O(In,Out)", and the operator O has pre and post-conditions respectively equal to pre_S and post_S. Then, if the following four conditions are satisfied,

pre_S and L => inv_S, *pre_S and not L => post_S,*
inv_S and L => WP(S1, inv_S), *inv_S and not L => post_S*

we get *WP(S, P) = WP (O(In,Out), P).*

3.2. EXAMPLE

The preceding example leads to the following annotation of the algorithm, where the loop statements are excluded and the top predicate, (1), is a verification condition:

```
algorithm gauss
  var i, j : integer;
      inte : real

{ (for k : { 1 .. 100 }
     then a(k, k) /= 0.0) => (for ii : { 1 .. 100 } then a(ii, ii) /= 0.0)
                         and (a$ = a and b$ = b                          ( 1 )
                           and (for k : { 1 .. 100 }
                                then b$(k) = sum(k, k, a$, x$))
                           => (for k : { 1 .. 100 }
                                then sum(k, k, a$, x$) = b$(k))) }
   begin

{ (for ii : { 1 .. 100 } then a(ii, ii) /= 0.0)
  and (a$ = a and b$ = b
    and (for k : { 1 .. 100 }
         then b$(k) = sum(k, k, a$, x$)) =>
       (for k : { 1 .. 100 } then sum(k, k, a$,x$) = b$(k)))  }

  i1:  for i := 1 to 100
        do
  i2:     inte := 0.0;
  i3:     for j := 1 to i - 1
           do
  i4:         inte := inte + a[i, j] * x[j]
           od
  i5:       x[i] := (b[i] - inte) / a[i, i]
        od

{ for k : { 1 .. 100 }
   then sum(k, k, a, x) = b(k) }

   end
```

As the algorithm only contains two loop statements, the following annotation is generated for the innermost one, by placing at the bottom of the loop its invariant and computing upward the WPs until the top is reached (predicates marked by "(2)", "(3)" and "(4)" are verification conditions):

```
      algorithm gauss
        var i, j : integer; inte : real
        begin
    i1:  for i := 1 to 100 do
    i2:       inte := 0.0;

{ inte = 0.0 and (0 < i and i <= 100) =>
    (1 <= i - 1 =>  ((0 < i and i <= 100) and 1 <= i
                         and inte = sum(1 - 1, i, a, x)))            (2)
          and (1 > i - 1 => inte = sum(i - 1, i, a, x))  }

{ j >= 1
  and (i = i` and a = a`  and x = x`
   and (0 < i  and i <= 100)  and j <= i
     and inte = sum(j - 1, i, a, x))
     and j > i - 1 => ( a = a` and x = x` and i = i`                 (3)
                    and inte = sum(i - 1, i, a, x)) }

{ j >= 1
  and (i = i` and a = a`  and x = x`
    and (0 < i and i <= 100) and j <= i and inte = sum(j - 1, i, a, x))
  and j <= i - 1 =>
           j > 0  and j <= 100
           and (i > 0  and i <= 100                                  (4)
            and (j + 1 >= 1
             and (i = i` and a = a` and x = x` and j + 1 <= i
                 and inte + a(i, j) * x(j) = sum(j + 1 - 1, i, a, x)))) }

   i3:       for j := 1 to i - 1 do

{ j > 0
  and j <= 100
  and (i > 0 and i <= 100
   and (j > 0 and j <= 100)
   and (j + 1 >= 1
   and (i = i` and a = a` and x = x` and j + 1 <= i
     and inte + a(i, j) * x(j) = sum(j + 1 - 1, i, a, x)))) }

   i4:            inte := inte + a[i, j] * x[j]

{ j + 1 >= 1
  and (i = i` and a = a` and x = x`
   and (0 < i and i <= 100) and j + 1 <= i
     and inte = sum(j + 1 - 1, i, a, x))  }

             od
   i5:          x[i] := (b[i] - inte) / a[i, i]
           od
       end
```

3.3. THE VERIFICATION CONDITIONS

The adequacy of the algorithm with its specification elements has now to be verified. This second task of the correction proof consists into proving formally the following correction property: *If the pre-condition is true before executing the algorithm and if this algorithm terminates, then the post-condition is true at the end.* This is equivalent to prove the two following assertions, given some algorithm A:

- The weakest precondition of the whole algorithm, with respect to its post-condition, must be deduced from its pre-condition. Formally this can be written: *pre_A => WP(A, post_A)*

- For each loop statement S of A, the associated invariant Inv_S (from the proof chapter) must be verified at each turn of the loop and must be true at the beginning and at the end of its execution, given some pre and post-conditions Pre_S and Post_S. Formally, in the case of some while-statement "while B do S od", these conditions can be expressed by the following assertions:

Pre_S => ((B => Inv_S) and (not B => Post_S))
Inv_S and B => WP(S, Inv_S)
Inv_S and not B => Post_S

Concerning our example, we need to prove the predicates (1) to (4); these have been inserted in the annotated algorithm too

4. THE FIRST EXPERIENCE

In a first experiment, it has been decided to orient the choice toward mechanical provers because in the last resort, the prover is to be integrated in a whole programming environment where the end user is to be, as much as possible, unaware of its existence. In any case, the final user will not converse directly with it because his prime worry is program proving and not theorem proving.
There is an overabundance of theorem provers, each with its own features, designed to answer specific requirements. However, they can be subdivided into two main classes: the interactive and the mechanical theorem provers. Interactive theorem provers act as proof checkers: a user writes the proof with or without the aid of tactics provided by the system. To this category belong LCF ([7]) and System B ([1]). Mechanical theorem provers, once a user has set some flags, apply their own strategies. To this category belong systems such as Plaisted's theorem prover ([13]), Boyer Moore's theorem prover ([4]), the Illinois Theorem Prover ([8]) and REVE ([12]). The chosen prover was a general theorem prover, called the Illinois Theorem Prover (I.T.P.) (see [8]). This prover has been integrated in the ATES environment, to perform the proof of the kinds of assertions previously mentioned.
The I.T.P. is based on unsorted first-order logic with equality, and whose basic mechanism is resolution. This consists in proving a given predicate by refutation, searching for a contradiction in the assertion *Axiom1 and Axiom2 and ... AxiomN and (not Predicate)* (where "Axiom1",...,"AxiomN" are the axioms collected in the proof chapter, and "Predicate" is a verification condition). The resolution method is applied to the new assertion, beforehand transformed into a clausal form.
But in concrete cases, the I.T.P. lacks at the following points: definition of proof methodology (because of the numerous heuristics embedded in the prover), addition of some strategies solving particular kinds of problems, handling of real size predicates (because of the high number of clauses produced), feedback of the prover in the case of an erroneous predicate, informations about the failure to prove some verification conditions, which seem correct, and performance slow down of the prover (when an incomplete axiomatization has been input).
Concerning our example, the proof of the predicates (1) to (4) can be performed by the system using the axioms about integers and reals. These axioms can be found in some basic axiom chapters called "integer"

and "real", linked to the proof chapter. But this task reveals to be tricky, because one has to choose the right axioms for the theorem prover and need to proceed tentatively, without any guidelines.

5. THE INTERACTIVE PROOF SYSTEM

Experience has shown that, with previous versions of the system, the proof of some algorithm is as much tedious and error prone as the programming task. Indeed, specifications, axioms and proof elements introduced into some book may reveal to be wrong, inadequate or even incomplete in the course of the proof. These problems have to be solved in the classical way, by modifying the source code and recompiling it, but these kinds of "errors" are difficult to find; contrarily to the algorithmic parts of a book, where the running of the executable code produced by the modules can help to find out errors, we need to perform the whole proof, to be convinced of the specification's correctness. In the previous version of the proof system, the algorithms were automatically annotated and the predicates to be proved were sent to the I.T.P. Thus the user had no control on the WP computations nor on the proof of the verification conditions, when running the prover. It was thought that a better understanding of the WP generation process and the on-line simplification of the predicates created were an efficient and important tool to find out the lacks and errors made in the formal specification elements. The availability of a simplification tool has another advantage: it reduces significantly the size of predicates, making in turn predicates easier to understand.

In the present paragraph, we introduce the main ideas of the ATES interactive simplifier and its user interface (see [3]).

For the proof or simplification of predicates, the proof system contains two programming languages: the first one, internal to the prover, called "tactics language", enables us to describe the elementary proof steps of a proof; the second one, called "strategies language", is used to describe the chaining of the different steps into subproofs or proofs. The informal idea of a tactic is to make the proof of a predicate equivalent to the (easier) proof of a list of sub-goals. A proof or a simplification being realized in a given context (i.e. with a list of axioms and hypotheses), the sub-goals are created combining parts of the contexts with the predicate and/or modifying the context. The informal idea of a strategy is to chain up the elementary proof steps (realized by tactics or other strategies), or to modify the context (for example, by restricting the axioms to a minimal set). The strategies serve to describe in a natural deductive way the proof of a predicate, using axioms and logical rules.

5.1. TACTICS

Axioms, along with pattern matching are used in a stepwise manner to reduce some goal to be proved into a new sub-goal. The tool provided by the ATES system provides a set of correct predicate transformation rules, based on rewriting.

From a given predicate, called the "current goal", a tactic generates a simpler sub-goal, such that the proof of the current goal amounts to prove the sub-goal. Given an initial predicate, the result of a tactic will be the predicate obtained by the proof of the sub-goal, joined with some error flag. The latter comes from the filtering of the input predicates by the goal pattern of the tactic. A context, called "theory", is associated to the input goal of a tactic: it consists of a list of axioms. The sub-goal's associated context becomes the input context, possibly modified by enabling or disabling some axioms. Indeed, the elements of such a context own an activation state, to restrict the search space of rewriting tactics (described later).

The following example shows a tactic handling conjunctive goals. It reduces a formula of the form "P and Q" into an equivalent sub-goal by substituting in Q every occurrence of P by "true". If no substitution can be performed, the tactic fails.

```
tactic reduce_conjunction
var P,Q : formula ; T : theory
goal T : (P and Q(P))
subgoal T : (P and Q(true))
```

The ATES proof system owns a set of predefined tactics, formalizing rules of first order logic. The main rules, along with their respective tactic, are the following ones:

- Rewriting rules:

```
tactic axiom_subst
var P, Q: formula; T: theory
goal T(Q): P(Q)
subgoal T : P(true)
```

```
tactic equivalence_subst
var P, Q, R: formula; T: theory
goal T(P<=>Q): R(P)
subgoal T : R(Q)
```

```
tactic substitution_1_2
var P: formula; t1, t2: term; T: theory
goal T(t1=t2): P(t1)
subgoal T : P(t2)
```

```
tactic reduce_conjunction
(see above)
```

```
tactic substitution_2_1
var P: formula; t1, t2: term; T: theory
goal T(t1=t2): P(t2)
subgoal T : P(t1)
```

```
tactic reduce_implication
var P, Q: formula; T: theory
goal T: P => Q(P)
subgoal T : P => Q(true)
```

```
tactic substitute_in_implication
var P: formula; t1, t2: term; T: theory
goal T: (t1=t2) => P(t1)
subgoal T : (t1=t2) => P(t2)
```

The tactic "axiom_subst" allows to substitute an occurrence of an axiom by "true". The rewriting tactics, namely "equivalence_subst" and "substitution_1_2", perform some rewriting on the goal, replacing one occurrence of the left hand side of an axiom by the right hand side of the axiom. It is clear that tactic "substitution_2_1" does the converse of the previous one. The tactic "reduce_implication" has already been described above. Next, tactic "reduce_conjunction" does the same kind of substitution as the previous one, but acts on conjunctions. Finally, tactic "substitute_in_implication" substitutes one occurrence of "t1" by "t2" in the right hand side of the predicate.

- Logical rules:

```
tactic implication_introduction
var P,Q,R: formula; T: theory
goal T (P => Q): (P => R)
subgoal T : P => (Q => R)
```

```
tactic specialization
var P: formula; S: set; x,y: S; T: theory
goal T : (for x : S then P(x))
subgoal T: (for x : S then P(x)) and P(y)
```

The tactic "implication_introduction" aims to include in the goal the right hand side of an axiom, whose left hand side matches with the goal's left hand side. The specialization tactic implements the well-known instantiation rule, concerning quantified expressions.

- Evaluation rules:

```
tactic eval_extended_function
var T: theory; S,U: set; x,y,e: S; f: [S -> U];
    P: formula
goal T : P((f  # [ x -> e]) (y))
subgoal T :  P( if y = x then e else f(y) fi)

tactic eval_lambda_exp
var T: theory; S,U: set; x,e: S; f: [S -> U];
    P: formula
goal T : P((lambda x:S . f(x))(e))
subgoal T :  P( f(e))

tactic eval_extended_function_by_lambda_exp
var T: theory; S,U: set; y: S; f,g: [S -> U];
    P: formula
goal T : P((f  # lambda x:S . g(x)) (y)
subgoal T :  P( if y : S then g(y) else f(y) fi)

tactic eval_let_exp
var T: theory; S,U: set; x,e: S; f: [S -> U];
    P: formula
goal T : P(let x = e in f(x))
subgoal T :  P( f(e))
```

These four tactics are relevant for evaluating some particular kinds of expressions. The two first tactics discard the “override” operator, denoted by a #-sign, from some expression, when the latter can be evaluated. The tactics "eval_lambda_exp" and "eval_let_expr" evaluate lambda-expressions and let-expressions, when possible.

5.2. STRATEGIES

The strategy language allows to give statements, explaining what should be done next in order to come closer to the goal. Questions that a strategy has to answer are: which tactic should be called next, which axioms should be enabled (added to the goal's context), what strategy should be called to perform a certain transformation? The basic commands are: the tactic call, the enabling/disabling call, the strategy call, the sequence, the alternative, the loop, and the negation. As tactics do fail or succeed, this information is used to decide what to do next in a given strategy. Therefore, the seven basic commands are functions which deliver a boolean result too: failure or success.
A strategy consists of a name and a body, which is a strategy command. In the following, we will briefly describe the semantics of all these constructions, along with their syntax, using some BNF-like syntax.

5.2.1. The tactic call

Syntax: *command ::=* ***tactic*** *{ tactic_name }+,*
The tactics are called sequentially, using the left to right order, until one of them succeeds. When a tactic succeeds, the others are skipped and the strategy is said to succeed; otherwise the tactic call fails.

5.2.2. The Enable/Disable call.

Syntax: *command ::=* ***enable*** *{ axiom_name}+,*
| ***disable*** *{ axiom_name}+,*

Axioms are either enabled or disabled in the prescribed order. Such an enable/disable call always succeeds.

5.2.3. The strategy call.

A strategy is called by indicating its name, and the result of the call is equal to the one of the called strategy.

5.2.4. The sequence

Syntax: *command ::= (command and { command }+and)*

A sequence consists of a list of commands, separated by the keyword "and". This represents just the normal sequence; the strategies are executed successively and the result is the one of the last executed strategy.

5.2.5. The alternative

Syntax: *command ::= (command or { command }+or)*

This construct works like the tactic call, but concerning strategies.

5.2.6. The loop

Syntax: *command ::= (do command od)*

The internal command is executed until it fails. Such a strategy fails if the loop body is just executed once, otherwise it succeeds.

5.2.7. The negation.

Syntax: *command ::= not command*

The result of the internal command is simply negated, i.e."fail" becomes "succeed" and vice-versa. These primitives allow to introduce other constructs, as the following one, expressing "if $strategy_1$ succeeds then execute $strategy_2$": *(if strategy1 then strategy2) == not (not strategy1 or not strategy2)*

In the light of this language, we have expressed a list of useful strategies for the simplification of intermediate predicates. They can be divided into four classes: the logical simplification strategies, the non-logical simplification strategies, the special simplification strategies and finally the general simplification strategies.

- The first class contains all strategies about logicals, and uses especially rewriting rules with the axioms located in the axiom chapter named "boolean".

First, one strategy is devoted to the elimination of logical constants, using appropriate axioms; for some given formula, it proceeds in a left to right traversal and performs rewritings and axiom substitutions. A second strategy performs structural transformations, whose result is not a constant value. Typical examples of axioms used are: "*(A and A) <=> A*", "*not (not A) <=> A*", "*(not (A) and not (B)) <=> (not (A or B))*". This strategy, called "structural_logical_simplifications", works in the same way as the preceding one.

These two strategies are chained up into a third more general one, performing structural transformations, whenever some constants have been extracted. It is written:

```
strategy logical_simplifications ==
( do ( if discard_logical_constants then
          structural_logical_simplifications ) od )
```

- The second class contains strategies mainly devoted to arithmetic simplifications.

First, there is some strategy to eliminate expressions containing only integer or real constants. This strategy works by calling a special tactic doing this job without any axiom. Another strategy is used for rewriting with axioms on integer or reals; once the "dangerous" axioms disabled, it runs in the same way as the strategy "discard_logical_constants". Indeed, some axioms may turn the system into an infinite loop, e.g. the ones expressing commutativity properties.

Next, there is some general strategy to reduce expressions made of equalities:

```
strategy simplify_equalities ==
( enable all and disable boolean)
and
( do (
        ( do tactic axiom_subst od)
    and
        ( disable commut_add, commut_mult, eq_terms,
                distrib, max_commut, min_commut, equal_commut,
                assoc_add, assoc_mult)
    and
        ( do tactic substitution_1_2 od)
    and
        ( enable commut_add, commut_mult, eq_terms,
                distrib, max_commut, min_commut, equal_commut,
                assoc_add, assoc_mult)) od)
```

The strategy above works as follows: first, it disables the uninteresting logical axioms, tries to substitute occurrences of enabled axioms and disables all "dangerous" axioms present in the "integer" and "real" axiom chapters to perform rewritings with the remaining ones.

- The third class contains strategies devoted to substitutions within implications and conjunctions. The following two main strategies are present.

```
strategy reduce_implications ==
( disable all )
and
( do tactic     reduce_implication, substitute_in_implications,
                substitute_eq_in_implications od)
```

Starting from the tactics described above, the strategy "reduce_implications" does all possible substitutions in this kind of expressions. For conjunctive expressions, a similar tactic is available. Both strategies are combined into the strategy "reduce_implications_and_conjunctions", not given here.

- Special simplification strategies exist in the system, to manage lambda-expressions and other special operators present in predicates (e.g the override operator, acting on functions, and the let operator, analogous to the ones of VDM). They are combined into a single strategy, named "special_simplifications".

- General simplifications strategies are integrated in the system to perform the simplifications belonging to the previous classes simultaneously.

A first strategy performs rewritings in an ordered manner: first, logical transformations are done; then arithmetical simplifications are made; next reductions within implications and conjunctions are performed; finally the special simplifications are done. Formally, this strategy can be written:

```
strategy simplify ==
( do (
        logical_simplifications and simplify_equalities and
        reduce_implications_and_conjunctions and
        special_simplifications ) od )
```

A second less general class of strategies provides single rewriting possibilities. They are useful when the user needs to simplify (by means of rewritings) a given expression with a precise list of axioms. The first strategy is the following:

```
strategy rewrite_with_selected_axioms ==
  ( disable all and enable X1, X2, ..., Xn)
  and
  ( do tactic axiom_subst, equivalence_subst, substitution_1_2 od)
```

It rewrites the initial expression using the list of axioms "X_1, ... X_n" input by the user beforehand. There is also a dual strategy, that uses axioms in the reverse direction.

Other strategies have been found by testing the rewriting strategies.

5.3. THE USER INTERFACE

Interaction with the proof checker is realized through a hierarchy of commands organized within a tree, with a menu at each node. Having successfully compiled a given book, the user enters the proof checker to perform the proofs. Successive menus show the lists of proof chapters, algorithms and elementary proofs (there is an elementary proof for the whole algorithm and for each loop contained in it: each one consists in computing some intermediate predicates and proving the verification conditions associated, as explained in paragraph 3.3). At each step one has to choose an item before entering the next menu. Selecting an elementary proof makes the system display the annotated algorithm. Depending upon the kind of elementary proof, the post-condition of the algorithm or of some loop has been placed in it. The system puts a mark in front of the post-condition and is now ready to perform progressive simplifications and WP computations (this mark will always indicate some location in the algorithm, containing the predicate we are allowed to access). At this point, one of the following commands can be entered: Compute intermediate predicates up to some other location, starting from the current location, Delete intermediate predicates between the current location and some previous one, Simplify the current predicate, and Return to the previous menu.

Using these commands, we can annotate in a stepwise manner some algorithm, by simplifying at each step the newly generated formula, reducing significantly the size of the intermediate predicates. When the simplification command is typed, a new menu appears, to handle the currently designated predicate. This menu offers the possibility to select a sub-predicate of the initial one, to perform simplifications on the desired part, without altering the entire formula. Then, a simplification can be carried out: first, the command "simplify" is chosen; the system displays some new menus, to select the strategy to be applied and, possibly, some axiom(s) to be used; finally, the strategy is executed, and the result is displayed. At each moment, the user may return to the previous menu, with the possibility to insert the result predicate in the algorithm. At each level of the command tree, the system reminds us of the state of the proofs, algorithms, proof chapters or book.

Among the several other facilities existing in the user interface, the handling of "journal" files should be underlined. These functions, necessary to most interactive software, permit to create, close and read some kind of logbook during the proof task.

6. THE ATES PROTOTYPE

Since the project has progressed for four years, a prototype running on a DEC-VAX 8350 under VMS is available, whose main subtools are the following ones:

- A compiler for ATES books (the book being the smallest unit of source code) performing three basic steps: syntactical and semantic analysis of all kinds of chapters, code generation, and production of annotated algorithms, starting from axioms, specifications and proof chapters.
- A management system adapted to a file, called the "master file", associated to the book, which contains all the information about its compilation, as the source code and the result of its syntactical and semantic analysis, and a special structure for managing the book in an efficient way, allowing selective, separate or system oriented compilation.
- A tool ordering the different compilation steps, leading the user to follow a program-to-proof methodology, in order to obtain a successfully compiled book. It keeps the book in a consistent state and reminds the compilation state of every chapter. This tool can also decide to recompile certain parts of a book and permits to modify chapters during the compilation task.
- A run-time environment, consisting of basic libraries, a memory manager and an exception handler.
- A interactive proof environment: as described previously, the proof checker provides the user with all the necessary features to perform the correctness proof of an algorithm. Within such a system, the user can easily follow the different proof steps and backtrack when necessary, leading in a comprehensive way to the proof.

A real-size application has been chosen and implemented, to validate the ATES system: this application deals with a finite element code applied to solve heat transfer equations.

A 2D and 3D version of this code (linear and steady-state case) has been written (about 50000 lines of source code). The major components of it are the following ones: computation on finite elements, solvers of linear equations systems, interfaces pre and post from and to a structure mechanical code (SAMCEF). This code has been extended to handle 3D cases, and an automatic 3D mesh generator has been realized, which notably increases the size of the code. The 1D version of the application (consisting of about 1000 lines of source code) has been formalized in terms of axioms, specifications and proof chapters and has been proved to be correct within 600 Men x Hours of work. The 2D version of this application has been tackled at the end of the project.

7. FINAL REMARKS

From a larger clearness inducing a better understanding of the specification steps, and with the help of the tools involved, ATES contributes to produce more reliable software.

The ATES system suggests an integrated approach for the formal development of medium and large-scale software, offering a safe, modular and progressive validation method and allowing to gain time by using a high-level programming and specification language during the programming task.

This system could be further improved by adding more general strategies and structuring them into chapters; the integration of a certain number of useful strategies, found by running the system on new medium-size examples, could be realized too. The ATES language being purely sequential in its current form, it seems easy to integrate parallelism primitives (at the algorithm level) increasing the power of the language with primitives whose semantic is clearly defined, and then to extend the proof method to this language.

Actually, the technology available for proving formally the correctness of programs seems to be mature for real use on medium scale sequential programs. Evidence is provided by the increasing use of such software environments for critical applications and the distribution of such commercial products (as MALPAS and SPADE ([17])).

Finally, the industrial interest of the ATES system is to build up a tool for the programming of reliable software. Indeed, most industries involved in safety critical software are highly interested in such tools. A first step toward the industrial use of such a system would be to add a front end translator to the system, such that ATES accepts programs written in classical programming languages too (as C, Fortran or Pascal). The translator should use the ATES language as a common description language. In this way, the system could be immediately employed for existing software in an industrial environment.

8. REFERENCES

[1] ABRIAL, J.R. (1988) 'The B tool' Proceedings of the conference "VDM 88: VDM the way ahead", Lecture Notes in Computer Science, 328, Springer Verlag.

[2] ATES Project (1987) 'Specifications of the programming language (revised version)', Report of the ESPRIT Project ATES 1222(1158), C.I.S.I. Ingénierie, FRANCE.

[3] ATES Project (1989) 'Proof user's manual' Report of the ESPRIT Project ATES 1222(1158), C.I.S.I. Ingénierie, FRANCE.

[4] BOYER, R.S. STROTHER-MOORE, J.(1979) 'A theorem prover for recursive functions: a user's manual', Report no. CSL-91, Computer Science Laboratory S.R.I. International, Menlo Park, California.

[5] DIJKSTRA, E.W. (1976) 'A discipline of Programming', Prentice Hall Series in Automatic Computation, Englewood Cliffs, N.J.

[6] ERIKSEN, K.E., PREHN, S. (1990) 'RAISE Overview', Computer Resources International A/S, Bregnerodvej 144, DK-3460, Birkerod, Ref. RAISE/CRI/DOC/9/V1.

[7] GORDON, M.J. MILNER, R. WADSWORTH, C. (1979) 'Edinburgh LCF', Lecture Notes in Computer Science, no. 78, Springer Verlag.

[8] GREENBAUM, S. (1986) 'Input transformations and resolution implementation techniques for theorem proving in first-order logic', PhD. thesis in Computer Science, University of Illinois at Urbana Champaign, USA.

[9] HASCOET, L. (1987) 'Un constructeur d'arbre de preuves dirigé par des tactiques', I.N.R.I.A. Report no. 770, FRANCE.

[10] HOARE, C.A.R. (1969) 'An axiomatic basis for computer programming', C.A.C.M. 12(10), pp. 576-583.

[11] JONES, C.B. (1980) 'Software development : A rigorous approach', Prentice Hall.

[12] LESCANNE, P. (1983) 'Computer experiments with the REVE term rewriting system generator', POPL Conference, Austin, Texas, USA.

[13] PLAISTED, D.A. (1981) 'Theorem proving with abstraction', Artificial Intelligence, 16, North Holland Publishing Company, pp. 47-108.

[14] PUCCETTI, A.P. (ed.) and al. (1991) 'The programming and Proof system ATES', Research Reports ESPRIT, Springer Verlag .(to be published)

[15] VANGEERSDAEL, J. (1988) 'A guided tour through theorem provers', Report of the ESPRIT Project ATES 1222(1158), Philips Research Laboratory Brussels, BELGIUM.

[16] RT&P Software Ltd. 'Validation et Vérification des Logiciels avec Malpas', Seminar on MALPAS, Paris june 29th (1990).

[17] Program Validation Ltd. 'SPADE, documentation of the product', Southampton, SO2 3FL, ENGLAND (1989).

Using RAISE — First Impressions from the LaCoS Applications

The LaCoS Consultants Group*

1 Introduction

LaCoS[1] is an ESPRIT II project aimed at demonstrating the feasibility of using formal methods for industrial development of software. The basis of LaCoS is the RAISE[2] method, language and associated tools produced as part of an ESPRIT I project. The "RAISE Overview" ([ErP91]) provides an introduction to the essential RAISE terms and concepts.

The partners in the LaCoS project are divided into *consumers* who are applying RAISE and *producers* who are further evolving RAISE based on the industrial experience gained by the consumers.

The consumers are Bull SA (France), Inisel Espacio SA (Spain), Lloyd's Register of Shipping (UK), Matra Transport SA (France), Space Software Italia SpA (Italy), BNR Europe Ltd. (England), and Technisystems Ltd. (Greece)

The producers are CRI A/S (Denmark), BNR Europe Ltd. (UK), and SYPRO A/S (Denmark)

During the LaCoS project a number of applications of RAISE are being conducted by the consumer partners within different industrial areas. The objective of these applications is to assess the utility of RAISE in real applications. Each application has an associated consultant who helps the consumer in using RAISE and gathers information on its use. The consumers document their experiences in a series of assessment reports. Additional information is provided in the form of course evaluation schemes, monthly

*D.L. Chalmers (BNR), B. Dandanell (CRI), J. Gørtz (SYPRO), J.S. Pedersen (CRI), E. Zierau (SYPRO)

[1] Large scale Correct Systems using formal methods

[2] Rigorous Approach to Industrial Software Engineering

management reports and an error reporting scheme for the tools. The collective experiences of the consumers and the consultants are presented in a series of experience reports; this document is a summary of the first of these. The full document is [Lcg91].

All the applications are summarised in section 2. Their objectives in participating in the project are briefly described in section 3. Section 4 presents the overall conclusions, and section 5 describes further development of the RAISE products.

2 Application summaries

There is a wide range of applications being undertaken. Some applications form all or part of new projects; some are parallel developments of parts of systems being developed by other teams; some are redevelopments of existing products.

2.1 Automated Train Protection — Matra Transport

This application will develop part of a fully automatic train system. The automated trains will run on a metro line in Paris called METEOR. The system is basically aimed at complete management-automation of trains that are conducted either automatically or by a train driver, using an already existing railway network.

The automatic train protection component that is being developed using formal methods is divided into two parts — a stationary part which is involved in train switching and track and signals management, and an embedded part which is involved in speed control, train position identification, alarm and emergency braking management.

The system must always guarantee a safe distance between the trains which are running, whether they are automatic or conventional. Furthermore, the system must be installed without impinging on the services provided by the existing system.

The use of formal methods for the critical software components of the system was recommended by the Paris Transit Authority and proposed by Matra Transport. The B method ([Nei90]) and tool were selected to develop the critical sequential software of METEOR. RAISE is being used to explore more advanced features which are not available in B (especially concurrency and modularisation).

2.2 Condition/Performance Monitoring Predictive System — Lloyd's Register of Shipping

The CPMPS, or Condition/Performance Monitoring and Predictive System, is an engine management advisory system for medium-speed four stroke diesel engines for ships. It is required to improve the availability and reliability of ship engines, provide facilities for integration into ship control systems, contribute towards a more efficient utilisation of engineers, and give advice on the optimisation of performance for ship engines.

It is a requirement of CPMPS that the software of the system is generic and modular and should be capable of being extended to be used for all designs of medium-speed four stroke diesel engines. This means that within certain limits, the engine can have any configuration of cylinders and sensors.

The basis for the design is an existing research prototype (written in C). The CPMPS will undergo a completely new development since it is an application of economic importance to both the client and the company.

2.3 Group Network Engineering Tool Set — BNR Europe

The Group Network Engineering Tool Set (GNETS) provides a range of computer-based planning and design tools for the development of communications networks. GNETS provides the network engineer with a graphical display — essentially just objects on a screen — together with applications packages for such things as cost analysis, configuration of equipment and other network engineering issues.

The basic architecture of GNETS is that of a layered system. The bottom layer is the database. Above this is a layer of database access routines. At the top is a layer devoted to the human-computer interface.

GNETS is already in existence and a new release has recently been provided to customers. However, future releases of GNETS will have enhanced functionality and performance. Consequently, redesign of certain localised areas is required to meet these needs. The LACoS application involves the redesign of part of the subsystem of GNETS which controls the display of network objects to the user (a network object can be e.g. a site where network traffic is routed to, or a duct carrying cable between sites, or a node where switching and branching of traffic takes place).

2.4 HyperWeb — Bull

HyperWeb is an environment and a user interface that enables the use of simultaneous applications on a workstation. HyperWeb also enables navigation inside documents related to these applications, switching when necessary from one application to another.

HyperWeb is based on a client-server approach. A server process manages the user interface and the communications between applications. (The X11 window manager is an example of such an approach.) The applications are the client processes of the server. Editors, compilers, debuggers and command shells are examples of applications within the HyperWeb environment.

The HyperWeb server is the centre of a star-network of applications. Messages from one application to another are sent through the server. The server has to keep information about clients, to check that they run correctly and to ensure sound communication. A suitable design of the server must ensure that the communication protocol is respected.

The HyperWeb server has been implemented in HyperLisp, an object-oriented dialect of Lisp which implements inheritance, message sending, and dynamic creation of objects.

Two teams are currently developing HyperWeb. One of the teams has built a prototype of the server. Another team, the one involved in the LaCoS project, is specifying the system in RSL. When the project began, a description of the prototype was presented to the LaCoS team as a reference document.

2.5 Image Exploitation — INISEL ESPACIO

An Image Exploitation Center is a system which is able to get, process, enhance and deliver remotely sensed images.

The system is made up of 3 subsystems — digital acquisition, image/data preprocessing and storage, and image dissemination.

The part that is subject to RAISE is the image/data preprocessing and storage subsystem. This processes the raw data image in order to store it and disseminate it to the user. An important component of this is the album, a set of reduced images that can be searched and processed.

The full application is being developed in parallel (using European Space Agency software engineering standards) by a team that also provides consultancy and support to the LaCoS team.

2.6 International Shipping Transaction — Technisystems

The ISTOS (International Shipping Transactions and Operating System) application aims at designing and developing an Office and Business System for transactional operations. The system will be applied and tested at a shipping company.

The office and business system will handle all day-to-day operations of the office worker, in particular all document filing and editing, information handling, communications and office procedural operations. The system focuses on the activities of the office worker who mainly handles business transactions.

RAISE will be used as the main platform for formal design of the ISTOS software. This concerns the specification of the general architecture, the concepts and the generic functional description.

2.7 Safe Monitoring and Control Systems — Lloyd's Register of Shipping

SMCS (Safe Monitoring and Control Systems) is a project which is being conducted by Transmitton, a member of the BICC plc Group, to develop a range of safe configurable controllers for mining environments. Transmitton, who specialise in the design, manufacture, and supply of computer-based telemetry and control equipment, are replacing their present range of programmable controllers with a new range. The SMCS project will design and implement a collection of configurable hardware and software building blocks, providing for the safe and easy configuration of these building blocks by using a suitable configuration language and support tools. In addition, the project will introduce relevant and recent standards and guidelines, and provide support for their implementation.

The present application is being conducted as part of the SMCS development. The objective of the application is to produce a top level RSL specification of the executive of the SMCS controller. The application will be an abstract investigation into the properties of executives for safety-critical control systems of the type under consideration. It is thus an exploratory study which will result in a clear, complete and consistent statement of requirements, accompanied by a formal specification in RSL.

2.8 Tethered Satellite System — Space Software Italia

In order to conduct gravity gradiometric and electrodynamics experiments in low earth orbit a satellite can be connected to the space shuttle by a tether.

The AMCS, or Attitude Measurement Control System, located on board the tethered satellite, provides control of the satellite in terms of three-axes attitude determination, yaw attitude and spin rate. The attitude data is transmitted during a telemetry session for off-line attitude determination on the ground. The ground system simulates the on-board system, investigates anomalous satellite behaviour and assesses proposed remedies.

The application is being developed in parallel with an SSI team that is using DSDM (Digital System Development Methodology). The application is being developed following an approach that is partly rigorous and partly formal.

3 Application objectives

All the consumer partners aim to evaluate RAISE — discover its strengths and weaknesses and assess its utility for their products in their particular application domains. At the same time, their continual feedback helps the producers improve the technology. More detailed aims are to evaluate

- the use of the RAISE language in requirements analysis and capture, including the discovery of errors, omissions and contradictions, the generation of better natural language requirements from specifications, and the use of specifications to assist in effective communication between client and developer
- the applicability of the RAISE method to their particular domain, including generating domain specific methodological guidelines, producing generic, reusable specifications and developments of them, and assessing appropriate and practical degrees of rigour
- the adequacy of the RAISE method and tools to produce good low level designs and target code, where typical quality attributes are maintainability, speed, reconfigurability, reliability, correctness and having good associated documentation
- the ease with which the RAISE language, method and tools can be learned by staff and assimilated into companies, which involves the relation of RAISE to existing standards, methods and tools
- the effect of RAISE on their productivity.

These items are not listed in order of importance — different partners have different priorities.

4 Conclusions

Practically all of the applications have realised their initial objectives, which is a substantial achievement. It is too early to pass comment on the longer term objectives, although work towards some of these has begun.

At the current stage of the project some of the applications have just finished constructing their initial specifications while others are still in the process of doing so. Therefore the experiences documented in this project report only relate to the process of learning RAISE, constructing initial specifications, and using the first release of the documentation and the tools.

To date, RAISE has shown itself to be a versatile approach to initial specification. However, there are detailed issues which have been raised as a result of the work over the current period. These are discussed below.

4.1 Method

In several cases it was found that, after committing to a particular set of requirements, development of the initial specification meant that certain requirements had to be updated. This meant backtracking to the requirements stage and committing to the new set of requirements. The significant amount of backtracking encountered suggests that requirements capture techniques were inadequate. Using RSL appears to be a good way of uncovering problems in requirements and of producing initial specifications.

It has been suggested that the method should include some mechanism whereby requirements can be tracked from the requirements document through the initial specification and beyond into the development stages.

A major issue which has been raised several times is that of guidelines to help users to produce *good* initial specifications. Many partners have created their specifications on a fairly ad-hoc basis, guided only by their consultant, examples in the manuals and their own personal experience. RAISE needs to specifically deal with this point; even if detailed universal guidelines can probably not be provided, specific problem domains could be addressed.

Several partners have started specification work at a fairly concrete level, then created another, abstract, specification. This seems to have been a good strategy for getting to understand the problem and for starting specification work, without being too worried initially about reaching the right level of abstraction. Such an approach should probably be dealt with more specifically in the method manual.

It was noted that the RAISE method and the tools force the designer to consider the overall structure of a system. This does not imply that parallel development of subsystems is impossible — on the contrary! — but the abstract design of a whole subsystem must be complete, together with interfaces, in order for the specification to proceed.

The RAISE method is centred around the notions of stepwise refinement and of separate development of subsystems. These in turn depend on a particular refinement relation between modules. The refinement relation in RAISE is very simple theoretically — it is theory extension — but in practice of course there are details one has to be careful about. So consumers have been particularly concerned about the effect of the structure and style of the initial specification on future designs, and with getting a better understanding of the refinement relation.

The fact that RAISE and formal methods in general are new to most organisations means that their use does not usually fit the quality procedures and the qualifications of their quality assurance staff.

4.2 RAISE Specification Language

In general, RSL has been found to be a rich and expressive language which has been more than adequate for the majority of the specifications in the applications. RSL presents few linguistic barriers to being very abstract, and allows specifiers to concentrate on the intellectual effort of abstraction itself.

The ease of learning was, not surprisingly, different for different people. Several partners already had formal methods experience before becoming involved in the LaCoS project — others had practically none. Although having experience of other formal methods is an advantage, it may not provide as much of a flying start as expected since the techniques and tricks used elsewhere may not map into RSL. This was particularly true of those people who had experience of model-based specification techniques (e.g. VDM) who had to come to terms with property-based specifications (i.e. using axioms). There was some difficulty regarding the semantics of RSL — there were several requests for a readable semantics document.

Many people felt that there is a good deal of peripheral material that needs to be assimilated before anyone can really start to learn RSL. Although many concepts in RSL may be familiar, a deep understanding of their meaning comes quite slowly. General computer science concepts also need to be familiar e.g. lambda abstraction, specification styles (imperative, applicative and concurrent would be a minimal set), abstract data types etc.

The language was felt to be very large. The rich structures available in the language allow seasoned users to work at their chosen level of abstraction. For more novice users, the bewildering choice of possible options is more a hindrance than a bonus. However, several partners only used a subset of the language, which made the learning task easier.

The most difficult parts seem to be concurrency and modularity. A few technical issues concerning the modelling of concurrency and object-orientedness have been raised. Some work-arounds have been found but the search for more adequate solutions continues.

As with all languages, RSL is best learned by actually *using* it. Courses and manuals have their place, but real understanding only comes about by trying to communicate with the language.

Only a limited number of external support techniques have been used in addition to RAISE (SADT at SSI and SASD at BNR). For these organisations, the techniques were already in place and were used to analyse and document systems, and to communicate with clients.

At present, RAISE must of necessity coexist with other analysis and design methodologies. Some consumers have indicated that graphical tool support for RAISE[3] might make RAISE more likely to supplant (at least parts of) these competing systems.

4.3 Products

Tools

Currently there exists a library for storing RSL modules, development relations between modules, theories and hints. Each of these library entities has a corresponding editor so that they can be created and changed. These editors perform syntax and type checking — they are all based on the Synthesizer Generator ([ReT88]). There are also translators from modules (using a subset of RSL) to Ada and C++, a pretty printer and tools for library inspection and manipulation.

Unfortunately, not all the partners received or installed the RAISE tools during the period covered by this report. Those who had didn't necessarily have the tools running on an optimal hardware platform. As a result some performance problems were noted and relayed to the tool developers.

Despite these teething troubles, the tools were generally found to be very useful. In particular, the syntax and type checking were a great help in getting to know the language.

Certain features of the tools drew some criticism, most notably the human-computer interface and the syntax-directed editor. It was noted that the strong link to the under-

[3] Such tools would support both the presentation of the library structure and the information contained in the modules in the library.

lying database had been inconvenient, and it would have been useful to have received a RAISE library containing reusable specifications with the tools. (A number of such reusable specifications are included in the RAISE Method Manual, [BrG90].)

Documentation

The *RAISE Method Manual* ([BrG90]) is currently pitched at users who are already familiar with formal methods and with the RAISE language. There needs to be some introductory material somewhere (possibly in another document) which will help with basic principles of software development, how to successfully translate from requirements to initial specification, which styles to use in what circumstances etc.

People were generally pleased with the *RSL Reference Manual* ([HaH90]) and felt it fulfilled its purpose, even though its use requires a good knowledge of RSL.

The *RSL Tutorial* ([Hav90]) was very popular and was consulted regularly by all the partners. It was found to be clearly laid out, understandable and very useful, often being used in preference to the *RSL Reference Manual.* There were, however, pleas for some discussion on which styles should be used for which problems, and how best to create initial specifications from requirements. In addition, an accessible and understandable account of RAISE semantics needs to be created (possibly in another document). As a tutorial it might also be useful if it contained some exercises and solutions.

In general the documents lacked glossaries and indexes.

Courses

Two 1-week courses, on the RAISE Specification Language in August/September 1990 and on the RAISE Method in November/December 1990, were given for all the LaCoS partners and were attended by most people involved. Both the language and method courses were found useful by the partners.

Unfortunately, many people were concentrating on their application requirements during the Autumn of 1990 and didn't begin specification work until 1991. This was found to be quite a long gap and much had been forgotten in the interim.

The statements of prerequisites which must be attained before attending the course were not found sufficiently precise, and the courses were felt to be too intense at only five days duration.

It was generally felt that too much time elapsed between the language and the method courses. This led to some feelings of discontinuity.

The RAISE Method Course should give advice on the translation of requirements into initial specifications as well the final design step before either manual or automatic translations can take place. Currently, the Method Course only deals with the design stage of the method.

The RAISE Method Course workshop example, although useful, was very detailed; time might have been better spent on a different, less detailed, problem which would have allowed more discussion about system modularisation and creation of initial specifications.

4.4 Consultancy

Each application has been assigned a consultant from a producer partner. Consultants have been involved in reviewing specifications, advising on use of the method, language and tools, advising on planning, providing feedback to the producers and keeping the consumers in touch with each other. Solutions to questions of general interest are being stored in a 'questions and answers' repository run by the consultants.

It is clear that the consultants are playing a vital role in two respects. They assist the consumers by providing experienced advice as and when required. They also, as a group, provide much of the project 'glue'; without it there would be strong tendencies for the consumers to concentrate only on their specific applications without learning from others and for the producers to build the products they felt like producing instead of those the consumers need.

5 Further Development of RAISE Products

One of aims of the LaCoS project is, of course, to develop the RAISE technology, and this has been progressing for the RAISE products while the applications have been assessing them.

5.1 Tools

Only one of the consumers was running release 1.2 when their first assessment reports were written, and this release corrected some of the errors reported against earlier releases. At the time of writing this report a release 1.2.1, consisting mainly of corrections to release 1.2, has just been made, correcting 90% of the reported errors. Further corrections and improvements in performance will be made in the next release, together with new tools, particularly in the area of justification.

5.2 Documentation

The RSL Tutorial and RSL Reference Manual have been amalgamated into a single volume ([Rlg91]). Apart from the correction of various minor errors and some clarifications, the main effort has been in producing a single and comprehensive index to the two parts. The lack of this was one of the main criticisms of the separate documents.

The Tools User Guide ([BDG91]) is being comprehensively revised: there is now an introduction to syntax directed editing and a separate section for each tool, making it more useful as a reference document.

The single RSL volume and the revised Tools User Guide was delivered with tools release 1.2.1. Work has also started on revising the RAISE Method Manual and on producing a 'Proof Rule Handbook' ([Pre91]).

5.3 Courses

The courses may not be re-run within the LACoS project — this will depend on what turnover of staff there is. But the comments made on the original courses will be useful when designing public courses later in the project and in the preparation of courses on justification (which has already started).

5.4 Further information

Requests for further information on LACoS should be directed to the Project Coordinator:

Chris George
CASE Systems Division
Computer Resources International A/S
Bregnerødvej 144
DK-3460 Birkerød
Denmark
tel: +45 45 82 21 00
fax: +45 45 82 17 11 or +45 45 82 17 66
e-mail: cwg@csd.cri.dk

References

[BDG91] Bruun, P.M. et al., RAISE Tools User Guide, LACOS/CRI/DOC/4, 1991

[BrG90] Brock, S., George, C., RAISE Method Manual, LACOS/CRI/DOC/3, 1990

[ErP91] Eriksen, K. E., Prehn, S., RAISE Overview, RAISE/CRI/DOC/9, 1991

[Hav90] Havelund, K., An RSL Tutorial, RAISE/CRI/DOC/1, 1990

[HaH90] Havelund, K., Haxthausen, A., RSL Reference Manual, LACOS/CRI/DOC/2, 1990

[Lcg91] The LaCoS Consultants Group, Experiences from Applications of RAISE — Report 1, LACOS/CRI/CONS/13, 1991

[Mil90a] Milne, R., Semantic Foundations of RSL, RAISE/CRI/DOC/4, 1990

[Mil90b] Milne, R., RSL Proof Rules, RAISE/CRI/DOC/5, 1990

[Nei90] Neilson, D., The Application of B to Process Control, The SafetyNet '90 Conference Proceedings pp. 8.1 - 8.19, The Royal Aeronautical Society, October 17, 1990

[Pre91] Prehn, S., The RAISE Proof Rule Handbook, LACOS/CRI/DOC/7 (draft), 1991

[ReT88] Reps, T.W., Teitelbaum, T., The Synthesizer Generator, Springer Verlag, New York, 1988

[Rlg91] The RAISE Language Group, The RAISE Specification Language, CRI/RAISE/DOC/1, 1991

A Specification of a Complex Programming Language Statement

P. McParland[1] P. Kilpatrick[2]

July 1991

Abstract

A formal specification of a complex programming language statement is presented. The subject matter was selected as being typical of the kind confronting a small software house. It is shown that formal specification notations may be applied, with benefit, to 'messy' problems. Emphasis is placed upon producing a specification which is readable by, and useful to a reader not familiar with formal notations.

1 Introduction

A frequently levelled criticism of formal specification techniques is that, when studied, their applicability is restricted to text book examples, or, where realistic cases are considered, the specification stops short of describing the lower level details of the problem under consideration. In an attempt to address this criticism, a local software company was asked to exhibit a problem typical of the kind confronting it in its everyday operations. The intention was to determine to what extent, if any, the use of a formal specification notation/technique could facilitate solution of the problem.

2 The Problem

A compiler for the data processing language HUBOL [4] is to be implemented. Compilers exist for this language but the software house hopes to produce a new implementation by tailoring an existing compiler (written in C) for a similar data processing language, UNIBOL/DIBOL. The only definition of the HUBOL language available is a natural language one. As an example of how a formal technique such as VDM [2] may be applied, it was proposed that a specification of the HUBOL *Input* statement be formally defined from the existing natural language specification.

The *Input* statement deals with the display and reading of various forms of data. It can also be used to control the passing of messages between user terminals. The overall system comprises a number of terminals operating separately, with occasional communication between them (message passing). To avoid the need to represent this concurrent activity, message passing is considered here from a current user's viewpoint only. (The work described is part of a larger project involving an investigation of the use of formal specification techniques applied to sequential systems: specification of concurrency is beyond the scope of the project.)

The aim of the project was to produce an *annotated* formal description of the HUBOL *Input* statement. Importance was placed on readability: the specification document should be useful to a reader not familiar with the formal notation used.

Before the style of the existing informal specification is presented and evaluated a brief description of the operation of the *Input* statement is given.

[1]Institute of Software Engineering, 30 Island Street, Belfast BT4 1DH

[2]Department of Computer Science, The Queen's University of Belfast, Belfast BT7 1NN

3 The Input Statement

The *Input* statement is used in a HUBOL program to :

- read input from a user's terminal ;
- display prompts, messages, etc. on a user's terminal ;
- facilitate message passing between a number of user terminals.

All of these activities may be intertwined within a single execution of an *Input* statement. For example, an invocation of the *Input* statement may display a prompt at a user's terminal screen and accept a response from the keyboard. The user types characters at the keyboard and these are processed by the *Input* statement. Associated with each user terminal is a message queue on which all messages received from other user terminals are placed. When the user types the special character, *Cmd_Print*, the top message on the queue (if any) is displayed.

The form of the *Input* statement is :

Input (Mode : Natural, Numexp : Natural)

where:

- *Mode* identifies the mode to be used ;
- *Numexp* defines the length of any data to be displayed.

The exact form of the *Input* statement's usage depends upon :

- the mode in which it is used. There are seven *Input* modes for reading and/or writing different forms of data and sending messages ;
- the state of a number of special variables. These are set by the user before an invocation of the *Input* statement. They determine the effect of the execution of the *Input* statement (by, for example, defining the length of prompts), record information about the usage of the *Input* statement (by, for example, counting the number of characters typed by a user) and store any data typed by the user.

There are seven different modes :

Mode	Functionality
0	text is displayed and if input is allowed (determined by the setting of one of the special variables) then a string of printable characters is read. When input is not allowed text only is displayed ;
1	numeric data is displayed and if input is allowed then a number is read which may contain spaces. The number read is formatted (to ignore unnecessary spaces) and re-displayed ;
2	text is displayed and if input is allowed then a string of printable characters is read but asterisks are echoed to the screen in place of the characters read. This mode is of use for reading passwords ;
3	message display is enabled for the current user's terminal to allow any messages received from another terminal to be displayed ;
4	a message (stored in one of the special variables prior to invocation of the *Input* statement) is sent to another user's terminal ;
5	a prompt is displayed and a 'Y' or 'N' is read as the response ;
6	numeric data is displayed and if input is allowed then a number is read which may not contain spaces.

4 The Informal Specification

The informal specification of the *Input* statement was developed by the local software house to improve upon the original description provided with the HUBOL language definition. The original description was considered "too informal". The current informal description, provided by the software house, is based upon the original description supplemented by information gained by experimentation with the *Input* statement running in the existing implementation. It consists of a description of the input modes and a description of the special variables.

The Input Modes

The bulk of the informal specification of the HUBOL *Input* statement consists of a description of the seven *Input* modes and the definition of the special variables. For each mode a description is presented which includes :

- a general description of the effect of the *Input* statement in this mode ;
- the updates to, and the use of, the special variables ;
- the I/O interface details.

However, there is no structure common to the individual mode descriptions. For example, to find the exact form of the I/O which occurs all of the description must be read in detail. Consider the description of *Input* mode 0 :

> 'In this mode the first *Numexp* characters of the *IN* special variable are displayed. Underline mode is used. If the *CE* special variable is set (i.e. non-zero), this number of extra characters is also displayed after the *Numexp* characters. Underline mode is not used for these extra characters and input is not allowed over these characters.
>
> If *PF* is zero, input is allowed; the input mode is alphanumeric. The cursor is returned to the beginning of the field. Any printing character is accepted and placed in the buffer *IN*.
>
> Printing characters are ASCII 32 to ASCII 126. Each printing character is echoed as it is accepted. Non-printing characters (other than the *DELETE* character) terminate input; they do not appear in the *IN* buffer or on the screen. The *DELETE* key deletes the last character entered (if any) from the buffer and moves the cursor left. If no characters have been entered, the *DELETE* key will terminate input.
>
> The *CHAR* special variable contains the last printing character input.'

There are a number of problems with this description :

- the reader is assumed to know a large amount of detail about the *Input* statement, such as the definition of the term *field* ;
- the use of mode 0 affects some of the special variables ; no reference is made to this in the description of mode 0 given ;
- the I/O detail (such as the description of the *DELETE* key) is not defined for each mode, i.e. in each successive mode definition the amount of description of the I/O detail varies. For example, the description of the *DELETE* character is not given elsewhere so it is assumed that the effect of the *DELETE* character is the same for all modes;
- there are some inaccuracies. For example, it is stated that *Input* is terminated by any non-printable character, except the *DELETE* character. A further exception is the *CMD_Print* character which is used to allow a user to have a message, received from another terminal, displayed.

A specification should be clear and precise. The above description of *Input* mode 0 is not clear unless the reader has a good understanding of the *Input* statement already. Nor is the informal description precise since the updates to all of the special variables are not described.

The other *Input* modes are described in a similar fashion.

The informal description of the *Input* statement lacks structure and clarity. For example, the form of the I/O detail is similar for each mode (e.g. the same conditions terminate input). Yet for each mode a different description of this I/O detail is presented. Each mode is treated as a different program statement, linked only by a common use of the special variables. This is particularly unnecessary when it is noted that some of the modes differ only slightly in their effect (modes 0 and 2 and modes 1 and 6).

The Special Variables

The special variables are used with the *Input* statement as follows :

PF Set to 0 when characters may be read from a terminal ;

AF Set to the maximum number of non-numeric printing characters which may be typed by a user ;

IN_Var This is a register which :

- stores any text to be displayed as a prompt to the user ;
- stores the valid portion of the characters typed by the user provided keyboard input is allowed (i.e. *PF* has value 0) ;

Char/DChar Holds the last character input to the *IN_Var* register;

CE Stores the number of extra characters, above *Numexp*, to be displayed as the prompt ;

CN Stores the number of valid characters input during an execution of the *Input* statement;

CI Stores the last special character used, e.g. *DELETE*, *TAB*, etc.;

DF Incremented by one each time an *Input* statement is executed and characters are accepted from the keyboard;

NUM In numeric modes the prompt displayed is the character representation of *NUM* and the resulting numeric input is placed in *NUM*.

5 The Formal Specification

A model of the environment of the *Input* statement is defined. An invocation of the *Input* statement is then described in terms of its effect upon this model.

The Data Types

The environment of the *Input* statement consists of the users and their terminals :

$System = Id \xleftrightarrow{m} Terminal$

For each user in the system there is a terminal composed of :

- a display screen ;
- a keyboard ;

- a message queue ;
- the special variables.

$$\begin{array}{lll} \mathit{Terminal} :: & \mathit{Display} & : \mathit{VDU} \\ & \mathit{Keyboard} & : \mathit{InputChars} \\ & \mathit{SpecialVars} & : \mathit{SpecialVariables} \\ & \mathit{MessageQueue} & : \mathit{Queue} \\ & \mathit{MessageAllowed} & : \mathit{Boolean} \end{array}$$

The display screen is represented as a sequence of lines and a cursor.

$$\begin{array}{lll} \mathit{VDU} :: & \mathit{Screen} & : \mathit{Line}^* \\ & \mathit{Cursor} & : \mathit{Position} \end{array}$$

where

The *Cursor* position is on the display (i.e. the *Cursor LineNo* is on the screen).

$$\mathit{inv\text{-}VDU}(\mathit{mk\_VDU}(s, c)) \;\triangleq\; \mathit{LineNo}(c) \in \mathrm{inds}\, s \land \mathit{CharNo}(c) < \mathit{ScreenWidth}$$

$$\begin{array}{lll} \mathit{Position} :: & \mathit{LineNo} & : \mathbb{N} \\ & \mathit{CharNo} & : \mathbb{N} \end{array}$$

$$\mathit{Character} = \{0, \ldots, 127\}$$

$$\mathit{Printable} = \{32, \ldots, 126\}$$

Each line is made up of printable ASCII characters :

$$\mathit{Line} = \mathit{Character}^*$$

where

$$\mathit{inv\text{-}Line}(r) \;\triangleq\; \mathrm{elems}\, r \subseteq \mathit{Printable}$$

The keyboard is represented as a sequence of characters, printable or otherwise :

$$\mathit{InputChars} = \mathit{Character}^*$$

The special variables are represented by a composite object :

$$\begin{array}{lll} \mathit{SpecialVariables} :: & \mathit{PF} & : \{0, 1\} \\ & \mathit{AF} & : \mathbb{N} \\ & \mathit{IN\_Var} & : \mathit{Register} \\ & \mathit{Char} & : \mathit{Character} \\ & \mathit{DChar} & : \mathit{Character} \\ & \mathit{CE} & : \mathbb{N} \\ & \mathit{CN} & : \mathbb{N} \\ & \mathit{CI} & : \{0 \ldots 7\} \\ & \mathit{DF} & : \mathbb{N} \\ & \mathit{Num} & : \mathit{Integer} \end{array}$$

where

$$\mathit{inv\text{-}SpecialVariables}(r) \;\triangleq\; \mathrm{elems}\, \mathit{IN\_Var}(r) \subseteq \mathit{Printable}$$

A register is a sequence of characters.

Register = *Character**

To allow messages to be passed between users each terminal has associated with it a message queue, *MessageQueue*. This queue stores each message received by a user's terminal until it is displayed. A sequence of messages, *MessageList*, is used to model this queue. Modifications to the message queue are defined in terms of the relationship between the initial and final lists of messages. However, during an invocation of the *Input* statement it is possible for a message to be received by a user terminal (and placed on *MessageList*) and immediately displayed (so removing it from *MessageList*). Such messages will not be included in the description of the message queue since they do not occur in the initial or final message lists. To include such messages in the description of the modifications to the message queue a history variable [1], *AllMessages*, is used to store every message received by a user's terminal. When a message is subsequently displayed it is not removed from *AllMessages*. Inclusion of this field allows statements to be made about messages received and displayed during execution of the *Input* statement.

Queue :: *MessageList* : *Message**
AllMessages : *Message**

where

MessageList (the current queue of messages to be displayed) is always equal to the end portion of the history variable, *AllMessages*.

$$inv\text{-}Queue(mk\text{-}Queue(MList, AList)) \triangleq$$
$$\exists Prefix: Message^* \cdot Prefix \frown MList = AList$$

Message = *Character**

The formal description of the *Input* statement is now presented. It uses the above model of the *Input* statement environment.

The *INPUTSTATEMENT* Operation

The *INPUTSTATEMENT* operation takes two parameters :

- *Mode* which defines the current Input mode;
- *Numexp* which determines, in association with the special variable *CE*, the length of any text which is displayed.

It must also reference the external variables :

- *Users* which is the *Input* statement environment;
- *CurrentUser* which identifies the user associated with the current invocation of the *Input* statement.

Its effect is determined primarily by its operation mode: this leads naturally to a specification in which details of the operation of the *Input* statement are abstracted according to *Mode*. Here the technique of employing pre- and post-conditions as predicates in the definition of other operations is used. The convention is that of [2]: for pre-conditions the order of parameters is: operation parameters, rd variables, wr variables; for post-conditions the order is: operation parameters, rd variables, hooked wr variables (before values), result variable, unhooked wr variables (after values).

INPUTSTATEMENT (*Mode*, *Numexp*: $\mathbb{N}$)
ext wr *Users* : *System*
rd *CurrentUser* : *Id*

pre

- the *CurrentUser* is a recognised user;
- the special variables have been initialised correctly;
- *Numexp* is greater than 0;
- the *CurrentUser*'s keyboard is initially empty.

$$CurrentUser \in \mathrm{dom}\ Users \wedge$$
$$SpecVarsInitialisedOK(SpecialVars(CurrentUser)) \wedge$$
$$Numexp > 0 \wedge KeyBoard(Users(CurrentUser)) = [\,]$$

post Depending upon the value of *Mode* the post-condition appeals to the operation description of that mode. Each mode description, except mode 4 (which is used to send a message to another user terminal so that the *CurrentUser*'s terminal is not affected), defines its effect in terms of the relationship between the initial and final states of the *CurrentUser*'s terminal. The variable, *UserTerminal*, is used to represent the final state of the *CurrentUser*'s terminal and it replaces the *CurrentUser*'s terminal in the final value of the *Input* statement environment, Users. If the mode is greater than 6 then it defaults to mode 0.

$$\exists\, UserTerminal \in Terminal \cdot$$
$$(mode > 6 \wedge$$
$$pre\_Mode\_0(Numexp, \overleftarrow{Users}(CurrentUser)) \wedge$$
$$post\_Mode\_0(Numexp, \overleftarrow{Users}(CurrentUser), Terminal))) \vee$$
$$\mathbf{cases}\ mode\ \mathbf{of}$$

$$0 \rightarrow (pre\_Mode\_0(Numexp, \overleftarrow{Users}(CurrentUser)) \wedge$$
$$post\_Mode\_0(Numexp, \overleftarrow{Users}(CurrentUser), UserTerminal))$$
$$1 \rightarrow (pre\_Mode\_1(Numexp, \overleftarrow{Users}(CurrentUser)) \wedge$$
$$post\_Mode\_1(Numexp, \overleftarrow{Users}(CurrentUser), UserTerminal))$$
$$2 \rightarrow (pre\_Mode\_2(Numexp, \overleftarrow{Users}(CurrentUser)) \wedge$$
$$post\_Mode\_2(Numexp, \overleftarrow{Users}(CurrentUser), UserTerminal))$$
$$3 \rightarrow (pre\_Mode\_3(Numexp, \overleftarrow{Users}(CurrentUser)) \wedge$$
$$post\_Mode\_3(Numexp, \overleftarrow{Users}(CurrentUser), UserTerminal))$$
$$4 \rightarrow (pre\_Mode\_4(Numexp, \overleftarrow{Users}(CurrentUser)) \wedge$$
$$post\_Mode\_4(Numexp, \overleftarrow{Users}(CurrentUser), UserTerminal))$$
$$5 \rightarrow (post\_Mode\_5(Numexp, \overleftarrow{Users}(CurrentUser), UserTerminal))$$
$$6 \rightarrow (pre\_Mode\_6(Numexp, \overleftarrow{Users}(CurrentUser)) \wedge$$
$$post\_Mode\_6(Numexp, \overleftarrow{Users}(CurrentUser), UserTerminal))$$
$$\mathbf{end}$$

$$\wedge$$
$$(Mode \neq 4 \;\Rightarrow\; Users = \overleftarrow{Users} \dagger \{CurrentUser \mapsto UserTerminal\})$$

From the above description it is clear that the effect of an invocation of the *Input* statement depends upon the mode in which it is used. This description presents a clear and uncluttered view of the *Input* statement. The definition has abstracted the I/O detail and the description of individual modes. Also, the pre-condition describes precisely the conditions under which the *Input* statement may be invoked.

Each of the formal descriptions of the *Input* modes uses one of the operations *DISPLAYTEXTANDCHECKINPUT*, *DISPLAYTEXT* or *CHECKINPUT* [3] to define the I/O details (such as the updates to the display and keyboard) which are common to all of the modes. To demonstrate this we consider the definition of mode 0.

Mode 0

This mode allows the display and/or reading of alpha-numeric data. Thus it must define the I/O detail concerned with updating the current user's terminal to allow for :

- the display of data ;
- the reading of data ;
- the reception and display of messages.

The operation *DISPLAYTEXTANDCHECKINPUT* is used to define much of this detail.

MODE_0 (*Numexp*: $\mathbb{N}$)
ext wr *CurrentTerminal* : *Terminal*
pre The length of the prompt in *IN_Var* is at least as long as the value in *Numexp*.

len $IN\_Var(SpecialVars(CurrentTerminal)) \geqslant Numexp$

post Uses the operation *DISPLAYTEXTANDCHECKINPUT* to display the prompt in *IN_Var* and read any *Input* into *IN_Var*. The information required by this operation is :

- the prompt which is the concatenation of the first *Numexp* characters in the special variable *IN_Var* and any extra characters defined by the special variable CE ;
- the data typed by the user (if any) which is equivalent to the final value of the special variable *IN_Var* ;
- the set containing those printable characters which constitute invalid input. This set is empty since all printable characters are acceptable in mode 0 ;
- the numeric value of the data *Input* by the user (which is only applicable in numeric modes i.e. modes which are used for reading/writing numeric data - modes 1 and 5) ;
- the initial and final states of the *CurrentTerminal*.

let $OldSpecials = SpecialVars(\overleftarrow{CurrentTerminal})$ in
let $Specials = SpecialVars(CurrentTerminal)$ in
post_DISPLAYTEXTANDCHECKINPUT(
$IN\_Var(OldSpecials)[1, \ldots, Numexp + CE(OldSpecials)]$,
$IN\_Var(Specials)$,
$[\,]$,
$Num(OldSpecials), \overleftarrow{CurrentTerminal}, CurrentTerminal)$

This operation specification defines the basic effect of the *Input* statement in mode 0 (to read and/or write alpha-numeric data) without presenting the I/O details or the updates to the message queue. This detail is defined in the operation *DISPLAYTEXTANDCHECKINPUT*. The definition of each mode is described in terms of this operation (or its related operations *DISPLAYTEXT* and *CHECKINPUT*). The complete specification is presented in [3].

6 Summary

The *Input* statement is very complex. This is because it is heavily overloaded to allow reading and writing of text and numeric data and also message passing. The nature of the given informal definition is not conducive to mastering this complexity. There is no common structure to the descriptions of the operation of the *Input* statement in its different modes.

In the formal description a formal model of the environment is defined. The definition of the *Input* statement is structured into levels:

- the description of the *Input* statement operation which shows the division of the definition by mode. It also defines the changes to the *Input* statement environment which are the result of the invocation of the *Input* statement;

- the description of the individual modes and the general nature of their interface with the current user's terminal ;

- the low level description of the updates to the current user's terminal.

The overlap between the *Input* modes has been identified, unified and hidden using abstraction (in operation *DISPLAYTEXTANDCHECKINPUT*). Thus the reader can identify clearly for each mode what influences the behaviour of the *Input* statement and what is modified.

7 Discussion

The aim has been twofold:

- to employ a formal specification notation in the solution of a *typical* problem of the software industry; and (if successful)

- to provide a specification which exhibits formality *and* which is readable/useful to one unfamiliar with formal notation.

The problem is certainly not a text book case study. The HUBOL *Input* statement is not an elegant construct. It is, however, representative of a class of complex input/output operations to be found in languages such as HUBOL. The formal specification is, correspondingly, not a model of elegance. However, many problems are inelegant by nature, and the structure and clarity of the presented formal specification is certainly of a different order from that of the informal one.

It could be argued that many of the structural benefits of the formal specification could be achieved by careful structuring of the informal one. This is the case. The point is that the use of a formal notation is *conducive* to clarity of structure by virtue of the abstraction and parameterization mechanisms available.

It may also be said that the structure of the formal specification could be improved. This may indeed be the case. But the law of diminishing returns comes into play. Small software houses can not afford the time to pursue elegance beyond the point where much benefit is obtained. The authors have attempted to simulate this *modus operandi*. Also, it was only as the specification was being constructed that the full complexity of the *Input* statement was appreciated. The structure of the specification reflects to some extent the way in which understanding of the informal specification developed in a bottom-up manner.

With regard to the second aim, care has been taken to embed the formal specification in a natural language surround. Pre- and post-condition and invariant comments have also been included within the formal text itself. It is likely that those software practitioners unfamiliar with formal specification notations will readily comprehend operation signatures by analogy with procedure/function headings in programming languages. A non-specialist can therefore read a specification of the kind provided in the appendix by concentrating on the signatures and the pre- and post-condition comments. In this way the specification retains the benefits of abstraction and parameterization while remaining palatable to one not comfortable with the predicate based notation.

The need for adequate annotation of formal specifications cannot be overstated. The annotation of the specification is required both to explain the mathematical statements used and to motivate the mathematical models (e.g. the data structures chosen) used. This case for documentation of formal specifications is the same as that for the documentation of programs (i.e. to record and explain decisions and to clarify complex definitions). Indeed, the case for documentation of formal specifications is perhaps even stronger than that for program annotation. A formal description forms the basis for all subsequent development of the problem being specified. As mistakes or misunderstanding as this level are likely to be more expensive than during any subsequent stage of development, it is crucial that peer reviewers and other developers have a clear understanding of the formal specification. Furthermore, it is much more likely that a formal specification will be read by persons without a strong background in the notation used than it is that a program will be read by someone unfamiliar with the programming language. Finally, it is the nature of formal notations that often very complex statements may be made very succinctly. It is important that this power of expression is accompanied by a commitment to making comprehensible the ideas expressed.

Acknowledgements

The authors wish to thank Software Ireland Ltd., Northern Ireland for providing the material for this case study and for their cooperation in its execution. The authors wish also to thank Stephen Gilmore for his help in the use of VDM and LaTeX, and Anne-Cèline McHugh, Donal Roantree and Paul Wray for their help with LaTeX.

References

[1] M. Clint and C. Vicent, "The Use of Ghost Variables and Virtual Programming in the Documentation and Verification of Programs", *Soft. Prac. and Exper.*, Vol. 14(8), pp. 711-737, 1984.

[2] C. Jones, *Systematic Software Development using VDM*, Second Edition, Prentice Hall International, 1990.

[3] P.McParland, *Software Tools to Support Formal Methods*, Ph.D. Thesis, The Queen's University of Belfast, 1989.

[4] "HUBOL *Input* Statement Specification", Internal Report, Software Ireland Ltd., Northern Ireland.

The PROSPECTRA System

Berthold Hoffmann and Bernd Krieg-Brückner
FB 3 Mathematik/Informatik, Universität Bremen
Postfach 330 440, D-2800 BREMEN 33
(UUCP: bkb%Informatik.Uni-Bremen.DE)

The PROSPECTRA Project (program development by specification and transformation) is a cooperative project between Universität Bremen, Universität Dortmund, Universität Passau, Universität des Saarlandes (all D), University of Strathclyde (GB), Syseca Logiciel (F), Computer Resources International A/S (DK), Alcatel S.E.S.A. (E), and Universitat Politècnica de Catalunya (E). It has been sponsored (February 1985 to 1990) by the CEC under the ESPRIT contracts no. 390/835.
The project has developed a rigorous methodology for developing *correct* software by transformation and implemented a comprehensive system for supporting all program development activities.

The PROSPECTRA System is a prototype environment for the development of correct software (see fig. 1). It is available on SUN Workstations under UNIX and X-Windows.
Its *user interface* is based on uniform principles of syntax-oriented editing and user interaction by menues and mouse. It has been constructed with the Synthesizer Generator of Cornell University and GrammaTech Inc. (see T. Reps, T. Teitelbaum: *The Synthesizer Generator*, Springer 1988).

Program development with the PROSPECTRA System starts with a formal requirements specification that is checked by the *specification editor*.

A development consists of stepwise refinements of this initial specification by interactive transformations, executed by a *transformer*, until an executable program is produced that can be submitted to a *compiler*. Interactive transformation is supported by a *proof editor* to verify applicability conditions for transformations, and a *completion subsystem* that helps transforming algebraic specifications into applicative programs.

Correctness-preserving transformations comprise re-usable programming knowledge. They integrate the tasks of program *construction* and *verification*, and break them down into manageable steps: by choosing a particular transformation, the developer takes a concious design decision, and, by verifying its applicability, proves the validity of each step. The resulting program is, by construction, *correct* w.r.t. the initial specification.

Transformation development is done analogously to program development: abstract transformation specifications are transformed into efficient transformation algorithms that are then submitted to a *transformation compiler*.

Re-usability is supported by a *library* and a *method bank* that store versions and configurations of programs, transformations, proofs, development histories and methods.

The Language Family supported by the PROSPECTRA System supports all development activities (see fig. 2).
The kernel of the language family is *PA^{nn}dA* (for PROSPECTRA Ada Anna), a wide-spectrum language for writing specifications and constructing programs. *Specification* is done in the algebraic framework, using parameterised modules, predicates, conditional equations, with partial and higher-order functions. *Program development* is oriented towards Ada, with other target languages such as C and ML as alternatives.

All other languages are sublanguages of PA^{nn}dA.

PA^{nn}dA-S is the sublanguage for specification: only requirements specifications can be edited, target programs are always derived by correctness-preserving transformations.

TrafoLa is a variant of PA^{nn}dA for meta-programming, i.e. the specification and development of transformation programs. Transformation and development tactics can be designed as higher-order functions. PA^{nn}dA program fragments, the objects of transformation, are represented as abstract syntax trees or concrete text.

ProofLa is a sublanguage for performing proofs (transformations of logical formulae) and the design of proof tactics.

ControLa is the sublanguage for interaction with the system. Each "command" denotes a transformation of some "program" in the system, eventually the tree structure of versions and configurations in the library. ControLa is the basis for abstraction from concrete developments to development methods.

The Uniform PROSPECTRA Approach to program, meta-program, proof and meta-proof development is perhaps the most important conceptual and methodological result of the PROSPECTRA project. It also has had some major practical consequences: the whole system interaction can be formalised this way and the approach leads to a uniform treatment of programming language, program manipulation and transformation language, proof and proof development language, and command language. This uniformity has been exploited in the PROSPECTRA system yielding a significant reduction of parallel work.

Challenges for the Future

Evaluation: Methodology and System still have to be evaluated for realistic large-scale applications.

Library: The Library needs to be populated with program modules, transformations and sample developments.

Goal-Orientation: The crucial selection in large libraries of transformations has to reflect the reasoning process in the development. A long-term research aim is the incorporation of goal orientation into the development process.

Further Reading

Krieg-Brückner, B.: Algebraic Specification and Functionals for Transformational Program and Meta Program Development. *in* Díaz, J., Orejas, F. (eds.): Proc. TAPSOFT '89 (Barcelona), Vol. 2. *LNCS 352* (1989) 36-59.

Krieg-Brückner, B.: PROgram development by SPECification and TRAnsformation. *Technique et Science Informatiques 9(2)*: Advanced Software Engineering in ESPRIT (special issue) (1990) 134-149.

Krieg-Brückner, B. (ed.): PROgram development by SPECification and TRAnsformation: Vol. I: Methodology, Vol. II: Language Family, Vol. III: System. PROSPECTRA Reports, Universität Bremen. approx. 1,200 pages (1990). To appear in *LNCS*.

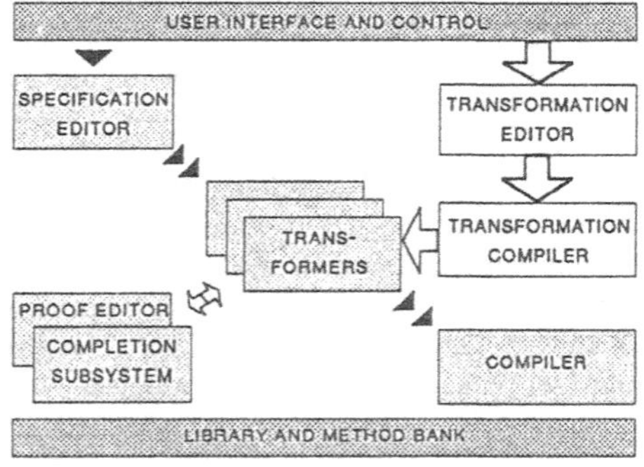

Figure 1: Structure of the PROSPECTRA System

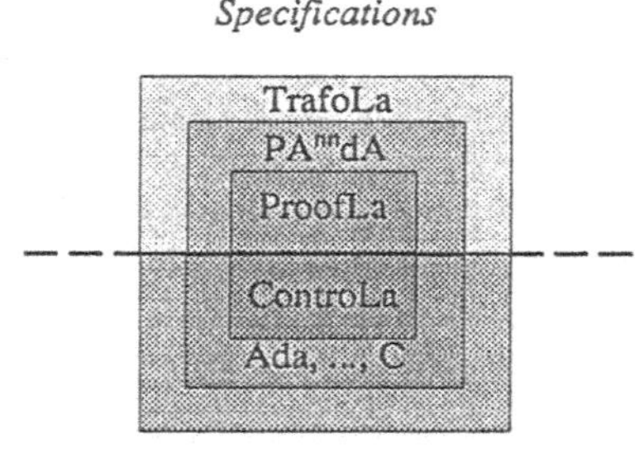

Figure 2: The PROSPECTRA Language Family

The Visual Presentation of VDM Specifications

Jeremy Dick, Jérôme Loubersac
Bull Corporate Research Centre,
Rue Jean-Jaurès, 78340 LES CLAYES-SOUS-BOIS, France

Motivation

Two barriers to the widespread industrialisation of formal methods are a lack of methodology, and the use of mathematical notations that are not easily understood by the non-specialist.

One way of addressing these problems is to use diagrams to visualise aspects of formal specifications. The approach adopted in "VDM through Pictures" (VtP) imposes a methodology on the early stages of system specification, and provides the analyst with a choice of notations, visual and non-visual, while maintaining an underlying formality. During the process of analysis, the notation most appropriate for the expression and communication of the concepts required can be selected.

Diagrams

Two sorts of diagram are used: Type-Structure Diagrams, and Operation-State Diagrams. The VtP tool consists of a diagram editor (the "Software through Pictures" Picture Editor from IDE), a VDM editor and type-checker, and a set of transformations to assist the analyst in moving between diagrams and VDM. Each diagram can be mapped onto parts of a common VDM specification, which forms the central underlying system description. Consistency can then be checked by type-checking the VDM specification.

Type-Structure Diagrams (TSDs)

TSDs portray VDM type definitions. A TSD for a binary tree is given overleaf, along side the corresponding VDM type definitions. The abstract syntax for TSDs is very close to that of BSI VDM ([BSI90a]), and any VDM type can be represented by a TSD.

Operation-State Diagrams (OSDs)

OSDs portray VDM operation definitions in terms of their pre- and postconditions. A style is encouraged whereby pre- and postconditions are expressed as predicates on the system state. The OSD for a timer is shown overleaf, along with the corresponding VDM operation definitions. (The auxiliary definitions for the predicates *timing* and *stopped* are also generated, but are not shown here.)

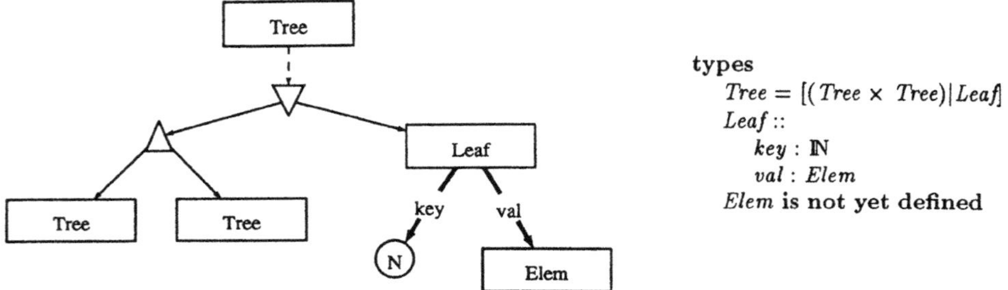

Figure 1: An example Type-Structure Diagram

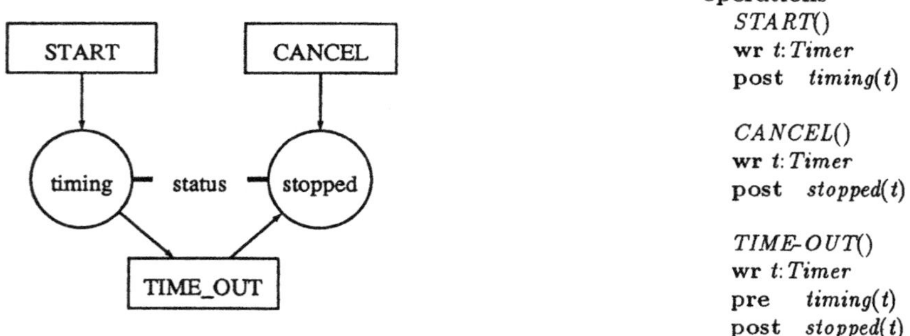

Figure 2: An example Operation-State Diagram

Acknowledgements

This work is partially supported by the ESPRIT project Atmosphere, Ref. #2565. The main partners are CAP Gemini Innovation (coordinator), Bull, Philips, Siemens, SNI and SFGL (contractor).

References

[BSI90a] British Standards Institute, *The BSI/VDM Proto-Standard*, Draft of 7 Sept 1990, Brian Richee (Ed.)

[DickLoub91] J. Dick, J. Loubersac, *A Visual Approach to VDM: Entity-Structure Diagrams*, Bull Research Center Report, DE/DRPA/DMA/91001, Jan 1991.

[Jones90] Cliff B. Jones, *Systematic Software Development using VDM*, Second Edition, Prentice Hall Int., 1990

mural and SpecBox

Richard Moore
Dept. of Computer Science
University of Manchester
Manchester M13 9PL
England

Peter Froome
Adelard
Coborn House Business Centre
3 Coborn Road
London E3 2DA
England

1 SpecBox

SpecBox is an interactive, window-based support tool for formal mathematical specifications written in the draft British Standard/ISO version of the VDM. It is composed of four main parts:

a syntax checker
The syntax checker is used to input specifications in the BSI/ISO draft syntax and check them for grammatical errors. SpecBox will import source files in the ASCII syntax, and the workstation and Windows 3 versions can be operated using either the ASCII or the mathematical syntax. It will prompt the user for either the terminals or the non-terminals of the grammar, and will automatically complete phrases.

a semantic analyser
The semantic analyser carries out checks on the well-formedness of the specification. Currently these checks include declaration scope, arity, use of state variables and hooked values, use of record types and constructor functions and use of 'is-expressions'.

a LaTeX generator
The LaTeX generator produces a source file for the LaTeX document preparation system that will print the specification in the BSI/ISO draft mathematical syntax. Line numbering and cross-references are supported.

a mural interface
The mural interface enables specifications checked by SpecBox to be passed to mural's VDM support tool and proof assistant for the generation and discharge of related proofs.

SpecBox is produced in the following versions:

- PC-AT (utilises up to 640k RAM)
- 386 PC (utilises all available RAM)
- 386 PC for Windows 3 (due Spring 1992)
- Sun 3 and Sun 4 with teletype interface
- Sun 3 and Sun 4 with SunView interface
- VAX/VMS with teletype interface

More detailed information can be found in P.K.D. Froome, B.Q. Monahan and R.E. Bloomfield: "SpecBox - a checker for VDM specifications", in Proceedings of Second International Conference on Software Engineering for Real Time Systems, Cirencester, UK, IEE 1989.

A run-time Prolog licence and a supported set of LaTeX macros for BSI/ISO-VDM are included with all versions. Prices range from £1,395 for the PC-AT to £4,995 for a multi-user workstation licence, inclusive of one year's maintenance and upgrades. Non-supported academic licences are available at substantial discounts.

2 mural

The mural system supports formal reasoning about specifications. It can be used to verify the internal consistency of a specification by discharging the appropriate proof obligations. It can also be used to validate a formal specification against an informal description of the system being specified by stating and proving properties of the system which its designer believes it should exhibit.

The main component of mural is a proof assistant. This is generic in that it can be instantiated to support reasoning about specifications written in a wide range of specification languages. It consists of a hierarchy of *theories*, each theory containing a set of declarations of the *symbols* which can be used to build valid mathematical expressions in that theory (e.g. : for type assignment, + for arithmetic addition, ∪ for set union, | for type union, $\mathbb{Z}$ for the type of integers, ∀ for universal quantification, etc.), a set of *axioms* stating those properties of these symbols which are assumed to hold without proof (e.g. substitutivity of equals, that the union of two sets is a set), and a set of *rules* stating other properties of the symbols (e.g. associativity of set union, distribution of multiplication over addition). Properties expressed by rules may be proved using axioms and other rules. Thus, the reasoning power of mural can be extended simply, either by adding new theories or by adding new rules to existing theories. A *tactic language* is also provided which allows the user to code and parametrize commonly used proof strategies.

In addition to the proof assistant, mural contains a VDM support tool. This allows the user to construct specifications in (a subset of) VDM, either by using the built-in structure editor or by directly reading a file generated from a specification checked for syntactic and semantic errors by SpecBox. The VDM support tool also allows a specification to be designated as a refinement of another specification.

Theories supporting reasoning about specifications and refinements stored in mural's VDM support tool can be generated automatically in (a VDM instantiation of) the proof assistant. This mechanism generates symbol declarations corresponding to the data-types, functions, etc. defined in the specification together with axioms describing their essential properties. In addition it generates the necessary proof obligations as rules to be proved by the user (satisfiability of operations, adequacy of retrieve functions for refinements, domain and result obligations for operation modellings, well-formedness conditions). The user can, of course, add additional rules to this theory, either to help with discharging these proof obligations or to support the process of validation of the specification.

In contrast to most other formal reasoning systems, mural has a sophisticated user interface which aims to make interaction with the system as natural and unconstrained as possible. This makes extensive use of windows, menus and buttons, and uses a full mathematical syntax. The basic philosophy behind its design is that it should be essentially user-driven but that it should maintain internal consistency. Thus, for instance, the system will, if so requested, provide a list of valid actions at any point, for example a list of those rules in some collection of theories which could be used in justifying some line in a given proof. On the other hand, mural doesn't force the user to complete a task before starting another one. One practical upshot of this is that it is possible to construct new rules and use them in the proofs of other rules without being forced to prove them first. Thus mural allows a notion of "rigorous" as opposed to fully formal proof, whereby a rule is proved modulo some set of unproven rules.

Further information on mural can be found in a recent book: "mural : A Formal Development Support System" by C.B. Jones, K.D. Jones, P.A. Lindsay and R. Moore (Springer Verlag, June 1991; ISBN 3-540-19651-X and 0-387-19651-X).

A large (at least 12Meg of memory) workstation running version 2.5 of Smalltalk-80 is required to run mural. Academic licences are available at a cost of £100. A selection of commercial licences is also available, ranging from a thirty day evaluation licence costing £100 to a full licence costing £15,000. A run-time licence for Smalltalk-80 can be supplied at an additional cost of around £350. Training and consultancy services based around mural are also available.

The VDM Domain Compiler
A
VDM Class Library Generator

Uwe Schmidt
Fachhochschule Wedel
Feldstr. 143
D-2000 Wedel/Holstein
FRG

Hans–Martin Hörcher
Deutsche System Technik
Edisonstr. 3
D-2300 Kiel
FRG

Description

The VDM Domain Compiler is a tool for supporting the development of efficient programs written in traditional programming languages from VDM specifications.

The system takes the domain equations of a specification (the abstract syntax and the semantic domains) as input and generates for every domain an abstract data type in the chosen programming language.

The VDM Domain Compiler works with a source code database. For every VDM domain constructor the database contains a collection of different implementations with different runtime and space characteristics. The user is forces to selet a suitable implementation for every domain equation. Furthermore the set of operators required from the specification must be given. With this extra implementation information, an efficient and small module for the abstract data types can be generated. The information about the set of operators allows to include the minimal set of routines in the generated library. So the programs do not contain superfluous code.

The functional specification must still be translated by hand into the programming language. But this can be done in an easy line by line transformation. All data types and associated operations from the specification are now directly available in the programming language via the generated library.

For programming languages without automatic storage management, the system generates routines for copying and deleting values (of arbitrary complex data structures). These routines are uniform for all data types.

The system stronly supports reuse of software. Experience has shown that about 2/3 of the source code of a program can be derived from the database. The transformation of functional specifications into programs becomes easier, testing and debugging time is significantly shortened. All pointer manipulations and storage allocation and deallocation is done in the libraries. Various storage allocation schemes can be selectet for the increase of efficiency and/or security.

Status

Two databases are available for C and Pascal implementation modules. Both contain about 40 different implementations for the domain constructors for sets, maps, tuples, trees, unions optionals and for elementary data types. Interface modules can be generated for C, Pascal and Modula.

The VDM Domain Compiler system runs on various Unix machines. Tested systems are Sun-3, Sun-4, Sun-386i, Interactive Unix, SCO-Xenix, Apollo-domain.

Future Development

Several further implementations for maps, sets and tuples are under construction including generic implementations for the support of code sharing for similar data structures.

An interface for C++ is planned to be ready in spring 92. This interface will enable the developer to use overloading and infix operators, such that the C++ code will look very much like a functional VDM specification.

References

[Moh91] Mohr,J.P.: *Erstellung eines Benutzerhandbuches zur Programmierung mit abstrakten Datentypen unter Verwendung einer Quellcode-Bibliothek mit verschiedenen Implementierungen am Beispiel von VDM*, Diplomarbeit, Fachhochschule Wedel, 1991

[Moh91a] Mohr,J.P.: *Programmierung mit abstrakten Datentypen unter Verwendung von VDM*, Handbuch, Fachhochschule Wedel, 1991

[ScH89] Schmidt,U.,Hörcher,H.-M.: *Systematische Programmentwicklung aus VDM-Spezifikationen mit automatischer Erzeugung von abstrakten Datentypen*, in: *GI Softwaretechnik-Trends*, Mitteilungen der Fachgruppe 'Software-Engineering', Band 9, Heft 3, 1989

[ScH90] Schmidt,U.,Hörcher,H.-M.: *Programming with VDM Domains*, Bjørner,D. et al. (eds.) : *VDM'90 VDM and Z*, LNCS 428, Springer, 1990

[WeW90] Weber-Wulff,D.: *A Buffering System Implemented in VDM*, to appear in Bjørner,D. et al. (eds.) : *VDM'90 VDM and Z*, LNCS 428, Springer, 1990

The Delft VDM-SL front-end

Nico Plat
Kees Pronk
Marcel Verhoef

Delft University of Technology
Faculty of Technical Mathematics and Informatics
P.O. Box 356, NL-2600 AJ Delft, The Netherlands
E-mail: {nico, kees, marcel}@dutiaa.tudelft.nl

1 Introduction

In this paper a short overview of the *Delft VDM-SL front-end* (front-end for short) is given. The front-end has been developed at Delft University of Technology. The tool is capable of checking syntactic and well-formedness properties of VDM specifications written in BSI/VDM-SL.

In this paper the functionality and characteristics of the front-end are described (section 2), an overview of its architecture is given (section 3), and an overview of the status of its development and perspectives are presented (section 4). An extensive overview of the front-end is given in [Plat 88].

2 Functionality and characteristics of the front-end

The Delft VDM-SL front-end has the following functionality:

- *Syntax checking.* The front-end accepts the standard ASCII syntax for VDM-SL [BSI/VDM]. Simple error recovery facilities are provided.
- *Static-semantics checking.* The major part of the static-semantic checks is type checking. The type system that has been implemented is described in [Plat 90]. Other checks include scope checking and various minor checks.
- *Generating an intermediate representation of the specification.* The front-end generates an abstract form of the original specification, which is called 'intermediate representation' because it is intended to be used by other tools, e.g. a pretty-printer or a prototyping tool. The form of the intermediate representation itself can be easily maintained by an in-house developed tool called *DIAS* [Langsæter 91].

The front-end is *batch-oriented*, so, as is the case with conventional compilers, the user must provide an input file with an ASCII VDM specification, which is then analyzed by the front-end. The user has the following options:

1. having only error messages (if any) generated by the front-end;
2. having a listing of the input generated, annotated with error messages;
3. using the front-end in combination with an editor, so that erroneous specifications can directly be changed, after which a new check-edit session can directly be started.

The front-end has been implemented on a number of UNIX-based platforms. Originally implemented on a VAX 11/750, then ported to a Sun 3/60, we are now in the process of porting the front-end to a Sun SPARC-2 platform, which will make a positive contribution to the front-end's performance (currently 10 lines of VDM-SL per second).

3 Architecture of the front-end

The implementation of the front-end is based on an *attribute grammar (AG)*. AGs were introduced by Knuth [Knuth 68] as a method for defining semantics of programming languages. An AG is based on a context-free grammar, in which both the terminal and nonterminal symbols can be augmented with *attributes*. An attribute is used to hold a semantical value associated with a symbol in the grammar. By defining relationships between attributes, semantic properties of the programming language can be defined.

A system capable of evaluating the attribute values for a specific programme (or in our case: a VDM specification) is called an *attribute evaluator*. For most classes of AGs such attribute evaluators can be automatically generated. We have used the *GAG* system [Kastens 82] for the implementation of the front-end. GAG is a member of a family of compiler construction tools originally developed at the University of Karlsruhe. GAG takes an AG written in the language ALADIN as its input, from which the attribute evaluator is constructed. GAG also generates a context-free grammar, suitable as input for the parser-generating system PGS, but we automatically transform this context-free grammar such that it is suitable as input for *yacc* instead.

The construction process of the front-end is shown in figure 1.

The execution of the front-end can be divided into two major phases (figure 2):

- In the first phase, the source file is scanned, parsed, and an internal representation is generated (the GAG tree) with initial values for the attributes. Error messages may, of course, be generated during scanning and parsing. The error messages are collected in an error message data base.
- In the second phase attribute evaluation is performed by executing a number of walks over the GAG tree during which attribute values are computed. In this way the static-semantic properties of the specification are checked. Error messages are collected in the error message data base, and the intermediate representation is generated which is written to a file.

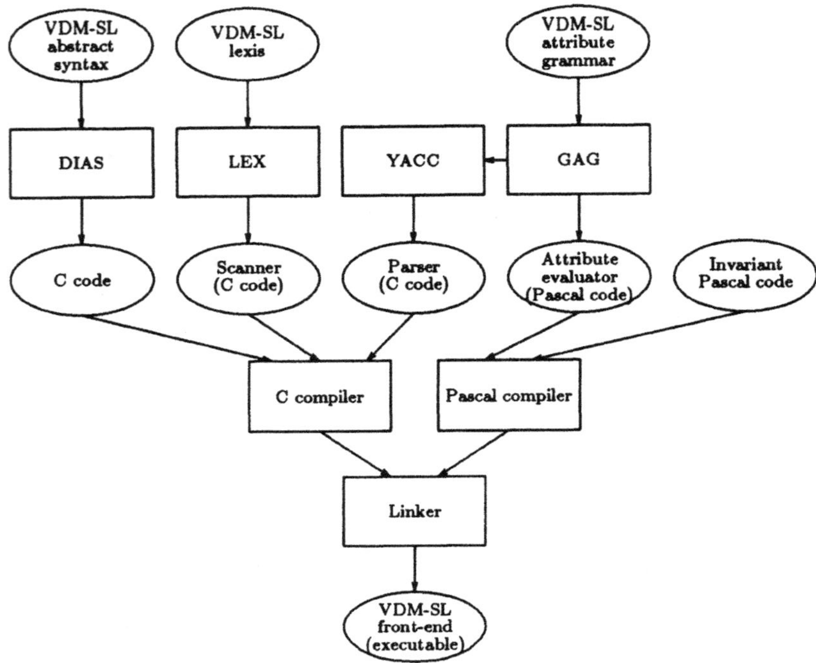

Figure 1: Construction process of the front-end

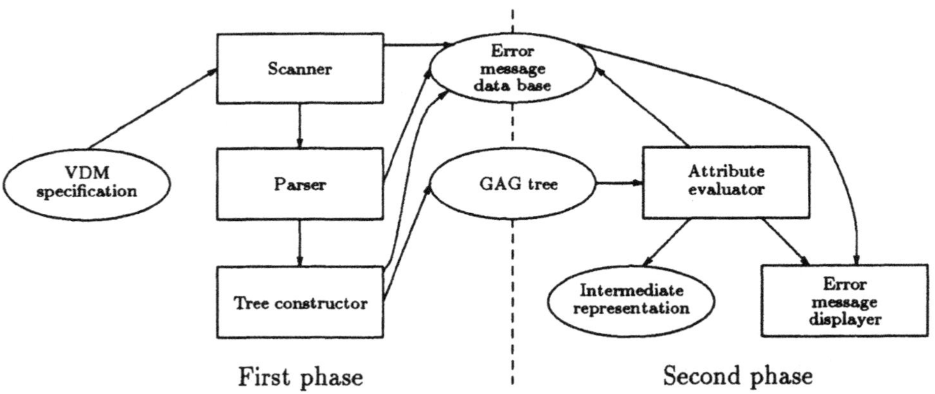

Figure 2: Architecture of the front-end

When the two phases have subsequently been executed, the main control part of the front-end makes the error messages available to the user.

4 Status and perspectives

The Delft VDM-SL front-end is not a commercial product. It grew out of an interest in both formal methods and techniques for constructing language processors. Nevertheless, as the front-end consumed more manpower and grew in size, and when the market situation for tool support for formal methods had been examined [Plat 89], it became clear that it might be worthwhile to make the front-end more widely available. In order to achieve this we are currently undertaking the following:

- *Extensive testing.* Testing and subsequent repair of the bugs found is essential in order to get the tool accepted by any user. The largest test case we are using is the proto-standard formal definition of Modula-2 [BSI/Modula-2], which has the additional benefit that the latter standard is checked as well.
- *Improving the user interface.* Currently, the user interface is rather old-fashioned. We are designing a window-oriented user interface under X-windows.
- *Providing auxiliary tools.* Specifications are usually written as part of a text document for which a text formatter is used. The de-facto standard for VDM specifications is LaTeX, therefore we are currently implementing a tool that is capable of generating ASCII specifications from LaTeX input, and a tool that is capable of generating LaTeX code from the intermediate representation generated by the front-end. A cross-reference generator is also under consideration.

The authors of this paper can be contacted to get more information on the front-end.

References

[BSI/Modula-2] JCT1/SC22/WG13. Draft Proposal DP 10514; Third Working Draft Modula-2 Standard.

[BSI/VDM] BSI IST/5/-/50. VDM Specification Language: Proto-Standard. March 1991.

[Kastens 82] U. Kastens, B. Hutt, E. Zimmermann. *GAG: A Practical Compiler Generator. Lecture Notes in Computer Science no. 141*, Springer Verlag, Berlin, 1982.

[Knuth 68] D.E. Knuth. Semantics of context-free languages. *Mathematical Systems Theory*, 2:127–145, 1968. Errata: 5:95-96, 1971.

[Langsæter 91] Jan Eivind Langsæter. *DIAS - An Interface-Generator for abstract syntaxes.* Master's thesis, Delft University of Technology, Faculty of Technical Mathematics and Informatics, P.O. Box 356, NL-2600 AJ Delft, The Netherlands, March 1991.

[Plat 88] Nico Plat. *Towards a VDM-SL Compiler.* Master's thesis, Delft University of Technology, Faculty of Technical Mathematics and Informatics, P.O. Box 356, NL-2600 AJ Delft, The Netherlands, December 1988.

[Plat 89] Nico Plat, Hans Toetenel. *Tool support for VDM.* Technical Report 89-81, Delft University of Technology, Faculty of Technical Mathematics and Informatics, P.O. Box 356, NL-2600 AJ Delft, The Netherlands, November 1989.

[Plat 90] Nico Plat, Ronald Huijsman, Jan van Katwijk, Gertjan van Oosten, Kees Pronk, Hans Toetenel. Type checking BSI/VDM-SL. In *VDM and Z; proc. of the 3rd VDM-Europe Symposium*, 1990.

PROTOTYPING WITH TEMPORAL VDM

A STATUS REPORT

Heping, H and H Zedan

Formal Systems Research Group
Department of Computer Science, University of York, England, UK
email:jorge@uk.ac.york.minster

1. $XVDM^T$ As A Formalism

VDM is extended by a *constructive* specification portion and *multiple assignement* statement.

The constructive portion of specification takes the form

fun <fun_name> (input_arg_name : <type_name>) : output_arg_name : <type_name>
pre <predicate_formula>
post <predicate_formula>
= <body>

where *body* represents a realization of the function implementation and **pre** and **post** are predicates over the system states in which the realization begin in a state where **pre** helds and terminates leaving the (prototype) system in a state where **post** is valid.

Multiple assignment is also introduced, denoted by Δ. Δ (x = 1, y = 2) which is equivalent to x,y := 1,2 . Multiple assignment is considered as an atomic operation on program's action in the sense that multiple assignment is only a single state transition.

VDM with its two simple extensions was integrated with temporal logic. The version of the logic is the where time is linear, discrete and infinite. If *w* is a well formed formula then the following are well formed formulae

$$\bullet w \mid \bullet^i w \mid \blacklozenge w \mid \Box w$$

with the normal first order logic operators built in, such that $\wedge$, $\vee$, $\rightarrow$, $\leftrightarrow$, $\exists$, $\forall$.

Here $\bullet$ can access any previous states and their values while i will denote the ith previous state.

2. The Structure of $XVDM^T$

$XVDM^T$ consists of a VDM language parser, a VDM pretty displayer, a VML implementor, a communication mechanism and a graphic behaviour exhibitor. The front end of $XVDM^T$ composed of two windows: the input and the output windows.

The parser reads VDM^T source lines from the input window or an input file, performs the syntax check and type check and interprets them into VML implementable codes and pass them to VML interpreter via the communication links. While the displayer displays the source lines in mathematical format in the input window; the VML interpreter executes the implementable codes, returns their values to the output window and optionally displays them in user defined wave forms.

Written in SML, the VML implementor builds up all the necessary functors for $XVDM^T$. The following diagram shows the implementation structure of $XVDM^T$.

Figure 1. Structure of $XVDM^T$

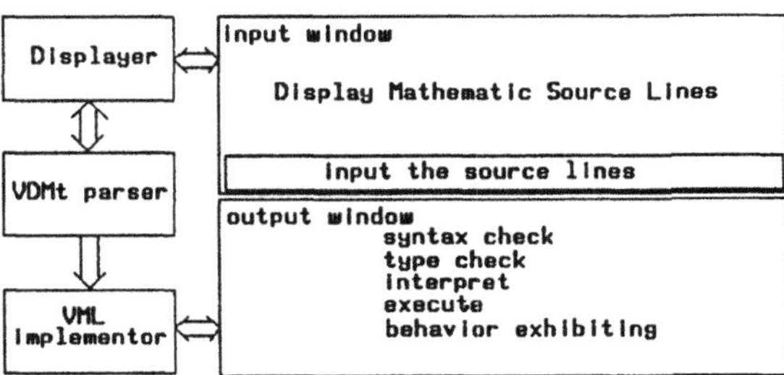

For further informations regarding formal semantics of integrated formalisms, user interface and case studies please contact the authors.

The ExSpect tool

K.M. van Hee L.J. Somers M. Voorhoeve

Department of Mathematics and Computing Science
Eindhoven University of Technology
Den Dolech 2, P.O. Box 513
5600 MB Eindhoven, the Netherlands
Email: wsinlou@win.tue.nl

Abstract

With the tool ExSpect one can design and simulate formal specifications of distributed systems by means of a formalism based on hierarchical colored Petri nets. A graphical tool set to support the specification process has been implemented. It consists of an editor that allows for hierarchical structuring, a type checker that verifies the rules of the type system and a simulator.

1 The model

ExSpect (EXecutable SPECification Tool) is a framework for executable formal specifications of distributed systems [Hee 89c]. It is based on a typed functional language to describe the state space and the transformations of a system. For the interaction structure it uses a variant of colored Petri nets, see e.g. [Jensen 91]. An example of an application of ExSpect can be found in [Aalst 90].

In ExSpect, the color sets of the places in a Petri net are specified by a *type*. The color of a token may represent a very complex datum (like a complete database) and the color sets are usually large (they may be countably infinite). The functions used to calculate the delays and values of the produced tokens stem from a sugared strongly typed lambda calculus.

The ExSpect framework is a *timed model*: time delays are associated with tokens. (Not with the places themselves as in place timed nets.) When a token is produced the transition also calculates a delay. Just as for the value, the delay of an output token is a function of the values of the input tokens only. The delay may not be negative, but zero delays are allowed. A token thus carries a value and a time stamp, the latter being equal to the global system time at its production plus the delay. A token may not be consumed before the (simulated) global system time is larger than or equal to its time stamp. The global system time only increases when there are no more firable transitions for the current system time.

The Petri nets constructed in ExSpect are *hierarchical*: at each level compound objects may occur. They stand for a subnet of transitions and places. At the bottom level one has only "pure" transitions.

For subnets a distinction is made between their definition and installation: once defined, such a subnet may be installed several times at different locations. This feature increases the *reusability* of specifications. Moreover, the subnets may be parametrized in various ways; types and functions, but also transitions and internal subnets, can be determined by the way such an object is installed.

Finally, ExSpect offers the possibility for standard Petri net *analysis* (S and T invariants) and temporal analysis (e.g. the calculation of the earliest arrival of tokens at each place).

2 The toolset

Basically the set of tools of ExSpect consists of a *shell* from which the different tools are controlled, a *graphical editor* to draw the places, transitions and (sub)nets, a *type checker* for checking the consistency, an *interpreter* for executing (and thus simulating) a specification and finally some supporting tools.

The tools run under UNIX on SUN hardware. The user interface is based on a set of window routines which are currently mapped on SUNVIEW. They are defined in such a way that it is straightforward to port them to any window system (like X-windows). The tools rely heavily on the parallelism offered by the UNIX operating system. For example, the interpreter is split into two UNIX processes, one for performing the simulation and one for asynchronously handling the user interaction.

The specifications, which consist of the definitions of types, functions, transitions and subnets are placed in files. These files contain plain ascii text and can be edited by the ExSpect graphical editor or any other editor which may be available.

The interpreter has an asynchronous user interface, called runtime interface. This interface allows the end-user to interact with the simulation while it runs. For example, the user can inspect and update the token contents of a place without having to stop the simulation. The runtime interface will present the value of a token in a default form which depends upon the type of the place the token belongs to. Furthermore, the designer can define his own forms. Such forms may contain for example headings or even subforms when the structure becomes very complex.

Tokens appearing in a place can be sent to or read from a file or another application. Such an application may be used for example for statistically analyzing results.

References

[Aalst 90] W.M.P.van der Alst and A.W.Waltmans, Modeling Logistic Systems with ExSpect, in: H.G.Sol, K.M.van Hee (eds.), Dynamic Modeling of Information Systems, North-Holland, 1991.

[Hee 89c] K.M.van Hee, L.J.Somers and M.Voorhoeve, Executable Specifications for Distributed Information Systems, in: E.D.Falkenberg, P.Lindgreen (eds.), Information system concepts: an in-depth analysis, North-Holland, 1989.

[Jensen 91] K.Jensen, Colored Petri Nets: A High Level Language for System Design and Analysis, in: G.Rozenberg (ed), Advances in Petri Nets 1990, Lecture Notes in Computer Science 483, Springer Verlag, 1991.

CADiZ – Computer Aided Design in Z

David Jordan
York Software Engineering
University of York, York, YO1 5DD, England

CADiZ

CADiZ is a UNIX[1] based suite of tools designed to check and typeset specifications produced in the Z specification language. CADiZ also supports previewing and interactive investigation of the properties of Z specifications. The main features of CADiZ are outlined in the paragraphs below.

Language Supported

CADiZ supports the standard Z core language and the mathematical toolkit. In addition CADiZ provides support for user defined operators, documents (which allow multi-part, structured, specifications to be handled), versions, fancy symbols and the automatic production of a specification index.

Checking

CADiZ will check a Z specification for syntactic, scope and type correctness. Comprehensive diagnostics are produced which may be related to a document by context using the interactive browsing facilities.

Typesetting

CADiZ is integrated with the *troff* family of document processing tools. The *troff* family is the *de facto* standard document processing tool set in the UNIX environment. In common with the rest of the *troff* family, CADiZ has its own special requests (essentially *troff* macros beginning with `.Z`). These are used to represent schemas, to import and export specification documents, and to control typesetting. The special Z symbols taken from CADiZ's own POSTSCRIPT[2] Z font are represented in input by simple ASCII abbreviations. CADiZ supports any POSTSCRIPT printer using TRANSCRIPT[3] software.

Interactive Browsing

Syntactically correct specifications may be previewed on a bit-map screen. Properties of the specification being previewed may be investigated interactively using a mouse. For example: errors reports can be related to the corresponding parts of schemas; types of variables and signatures of schemas can be inspected; use of declarations can be "tracked"; any schema calculus expression can be expanded; source text can be revealed.

Documentation

The comprehensive CADiZ documentation set includes: installation instructions; the CADiZ tutorial – a complete description of the facilities of CADiZ with many hands-on examples; quick reference guide – an *aide memoire* to CADiZ commands and the language supported; the CADiZ reference manual – an itemised description of all the Z operators and CADiZ requests; *troff* documentation – the standard documentation on *troff* and the associated tools; *The Z Notation: A Reference Manual* by J.M.Spivey – this book is the standard reference on Z. On-line help is also provided.

Configuration Requirements

To install CADiZ you require 8 Mbytes of file store. When running CADiZ, 2 Mbytes of main memory are required for non-interactive use; 4 Mbytes for interactive use.

Availability

CADiZ is currently available on Sun 3 and Sun SPARCstation platforms.

On-going Work

LaTeX support is under development.

Further Information

Please contact David Jordan at the above address.

---

1. UNIX is a registered trademark of UNIX System Laboratories Inc.
2. POSTSCRIPT is a registered trademark of Adobe Systems Inc.
3. TRANSCRIPT is a registered trademark of Adobe Systems Inc.

The HP-ST Toolset

Chris Dollin
Software Engineering Department, Hewlett-Packard Laboratories
Filton Road, Stoke Gifford
Bristol, Avon, BS12 6QZ
England
Email: kers@hplb.hpl.hp.co.uk

1 Summary

The HP-ST toolset allows a specifier to construct a *specification document* which contains mixed text and HP-SL specifications. The toolset can be used in either *batch mode*, when it is invoked as a collection of Unix commands, or in *interactive mode*, when it is invoked *via* an editing interface such as that provided by Emacs. Documents are LaTeX files with LaTeX-like annotations to control preprocessing.

2 The HP-SL language

HP-SL is a VDM-influenced specification language, retaining its model of function specification with pre- and post- conditions. However, it has departed substantially from its ancestor in several areas:

- The VDM record and union types have been completely redesigned.
- Higher-order functions and user-defined operators have been admitted into the language.
- There is no operator overloading; it has been replaced by ML-style polymorphism.
- There is no state; state changes must be modelled by relations on data-structures. (A specialised syntax can be used for declaring such relations.)
- A module structure (similar to those found in algebraic specification languages such as Clear) has been added on top of the language to control namespaces in large specifications.

3 Tool Functionality

The toolset provides three different kinds of functionality: *checking* of specifications, *incremental development* of specifications, and *printing* of specifications.

3.1 Checking

A document is checked by the tools extracting all the HP-SL fragments from it and checking the resulting single specification. (It is possible to mark specification fragments as "excluded", in which case they are not checked, but are still printed; this allows a document to contain examples of incorrect HP-SL (*eg*, for expository purposes) without interfering with the checking of the remainder of the document.)

Specifications can be checked for both syntactic and type correctness. Because subtypes can be specified with arbitrary predicates, full type correctness is not decidable, so the type-checking is restricted to base types (*ie*, what remains after all subtyping is stripped away). Thus integers, reals, and complexes are all treated as the same type.

To allow incremental development of specifications, the type-checker permits free variables, giving them "tentative" types which summarise all the types at which the variable has been used. It is also possible to save the binding of names to types in a *type environment*, which can be supplied to a later type-check, again to make it convenient to develop specifications incrementally.

3.2 Incremental Development

The Emacs interface to the toolset allows the user to write and check specifications incrementally. Individual fragments, regions, or entire buffers can be checked, and the resulting reports are displayed in another buffer.

When a checker has detected an error, it is possible to move directly to the text containing the error. Once a specification has been type-checked, is also possible to move from a *use* of a name to the *definitions* of that name, or to display the *type* of that name. This helps the user in browsing documents, finding definitions, and discovering types; there are browsing commands for all of these activities.

3.3 Printing

When a specification is printed, it is traditional to expect the full set of mathematical symbols for quantifiers, membership, mappings, *etc.* HP-SL is written using plain ASCII, with conventional names for the symbols (FORALL, IN, SUPER), and the toolset printer converts these into appropriate LaTeX incantations; this conversion is user-customisable. The printer also respects the users line-breaking and indentation.

Specification fragments can be framed (in the style of Z) and parts of specifications can be labelled and referred to from the non-specification part of the document.

As an example of both language and printing style, we present a definition for a higher-order function which maps functions over sets giving sets:

fn $(\!| A, B |\!)$ *setmap*: $(A \rightarrow B) \rightarrow Set\ A \rightarrow Set\ B$
is *setmap* $f\ s$
return s'
post $(\forall\ x \in s \cdot f\ x \in s')$
$\wedge\ (\forall\ x' \in s' \cdot (\exists\ x \in s \cdot f\ x = x'))$

4 Availability

The HP-ST toolkit is now in use in HP divisions and a number of other companies and universities. For more information, contact the author.

The RAISE Toolset

The CRI RAISE Tools Group

Computer Resources International A/S[1]

The RAISE Toolset is a comprehensive environment for writing, checking and verifying formal specifications and developments in RAISE[2].

The toolset is centered around the notion of a library, which maintains a version-controlled collection of *entities*. Entities may (currently) be RSL modules, development relations, theories, hints and justifications.

Entities are edited using interactive structure-oriented editors. These editors feature high-quality automatic unparsing and continuous type-checking. In addition to structure-oriented editing, which closely matches the documented syntax for RSL, the editors also support some amount of textual editing facilities, as well as the ability to load files prepared using other tools. The unparsing mechanism features full symbolic representation of RSL (including greek letters in identifiers), bolding of keywords, automatic indentation, automatic bracketing, etc. The continuous type-checking provide terse or verbose error messages (structurally linked to erroneous constructs), as well as error-message-only (overview) windows and editing windows with error messages suppressed.

In an entity, references may be made to other entities (which have been separately edited and checked). Entity editors have a context list, which establishes bindings of such references to particular versions in the library.

Modules are either objects or schemes, as defined in RSL. A module may refer to other modules stored in the library, via the context list.

Development relations are used to express a formal relationship between two modules. The relationship is expressed as an (RSL) predicate. However, the notion of predicate has been generalised in development relations to allow the formal notion of *implementation relation* to be stated.

Theories are used to express properties of a set of modules. These properties may be derived properties (which may be used in justifications), or expected properties (which should then be justified (i.e. validated)).

Hints may, in their context list, refer to an arbitrary set of entities. The contents of a hint is informal text, which is not interpreted by RAISE (but could be interpreted by some software engineering or project management tool).

Justifications are arguments why some justification conditions are believed to hold. Justification conditions may be *formal conditions* (theorems in a theory, or the predicate of a development relation) or *confidence conditions* (which are "warnings" about surpris-

[1]Bregnerødvej 144, DK-3460 Birkerød, Denmark. e-mail: raise@csd.cri.dk

[2]RAISE stands for Rigorous Approach to Industrial Software Engineering and comprises a wide-spectrum specification and design language RSL, a development method, a toolset and extensive documentation. RAISE has been developed and is continuously being enhanced through the RAISE and LaCoS ESPRIT projects. CRI A/S is further maturing and marketing RAISE as a product.

ing semantics of RSL written in modules, theories or development relations). A justification may be completely informal, or may be a formal proof (developed interactively by application of RSL proof rules, axioms which are in scope, or theorems from theories mentioned in the context list of the justification), or a mixture of informal and formal arguments. Justifications have a precise syntax (and semantics) and are manipulated, as other entities, by structural editing, automatic unparsing and continuous checking. The justification editor includes a *simplifier* which automatically makes (simple) inferences, and an *implementation condition expander* which may be used to break a stipulation of the implementation relation into smaller goals.

Pretty printers are used to generate LaTeX source for an entity. Such source may then be included in documents together with text, figures or any other related material. The resulting print-out is consistent with the unparsing displayed in the editors.

For the purpose of easily including fragments of RSL in LaTeX documents, the program RSLLaTeX may be used as a preprocessor on files in which such fragments have been written directly (using the ASCII-only representation of RSL).

Translators are used to produce source code from modules written in a suitable subset of RSL. Translators producing C++ and Ada exist. These are capable of translating substantial parts of executable RSL. The RSL-to-Ada translator is additionally capable of translating virtually all RSL modularisation constructs into Ada separate compilation and structuring constructs.

A library may be browsed and manipulated either by UNIX shell level tools, or by interactive tools. The interactive tools comprise a *list* tool for browsing the contents of a library; a *query* tool for chasing dependencies among entities in a library; a *delete* tool for purging entities in a dependency- and version-consistent manner, and a *change propagator* for automatic revision propagation over entity dependencies.

In addition to tools relying on the RAISE library, *stand-alone tools* (e.g., a module editor) are being developed. These use a simple UNIX file repository. They do not support a version concept, but do allow separate editing and checking. Some amount of consistency control and change propagation may be enforced by a make-based update mechanism.

The RAISE Toolset is currently running on Sun3 and Sun4 workstations, using the X11 or SunView window systems or even terminals (with degraded user interface), under SunOS 4.1. Open Windows will be supported in the very near future. The IBM RS6000/AIX platform will also be supported in the near future. At the time of writing, the justification tools are still being developed and enhanced, and are expected to be released in the near future.

For further information on RAISE, LaCoS or the RAISE Toolset, please use the address given above.

The IBM Z Tool

Iain Houston
IBM United Kingdom Laboratories Ltd *

The Z tool presented on Wednesday 23rd October is in use by the CICS[1] Development team at IBM's[1] United Kingdom Laboratories at Hursley. It was used in the writing of several of the specifications of the CICS application programming interface (API) mentioned in the project report "Experiences and results from the use of Z in IBM". It is used to provide basic document editing facilities, with syntax, scope and type checking of the formal paragraphs together with cross reference, schema expansion and facilities to navigate through the formal definitions of a document. The purpose of the tool is to enable users with different amounts of experience in Z to work efficiently when reading, writing or preparing to inspect Z specifications. It is not commercially available.

Basic Editing Facilities

These are provided by using the facilities of the LPEX[1] live parsing editor on OS/2[1]-based workstations. At Hursley, specifications are marked up with GML (general markup language) tags for formal and informal document elements and GML symbols for non-keyable characters. Different syntactic classes are recognised by their surrounding tags so that LPEX can selectively display say, just schema titles or the declarations of axiomatic boxes for example, as requested by the user. This is an unexpectedly useful facility for finding particular formal elements, checking names and naming conventions and even summarising the headings given to sections of informal text in the form of a table of contents.

Help is provided to allow the writer to pick from a symbol window and to quickly insert schema or other templates. In this way the formal part of a specification can be constructed with the minimum of interference from the underlying markup language.

Z-specific facilities

Several tools are available through the pull-down menus of the LPEX editor.

- "Type-check" results either in a message saying that the specification contains type-correct Z or in error messages that are inserted in the displayed document below incorrect expressions
- "Cross-reference" produces a target file produced from the source of the specification with embedded inline or global "where-defined" and "where-used" references

*IBM United Kingdom Laboratories Ltd, Hursley Park, Winchester, Hampshire SO21 2JN
[1]A trademark of the IBM Corporation

- "Expand schema" produces, in a pop-up window, an expanded schema that can be inspected or copied into the source or another document for later inspection
- "Find definition" and "Pop find(s)" allow the user to navigate through the inheritance path of formal definitions.

Experience with the tool

It is a great deal easier for an experienced writer of Z to manage a large specification than it was without the Z tool. Opportunities to rewrite unsatisactory parts of a specification would not have been so readily exploited without it. Although an invaluable tool, schema expansion can produce schemas with daunting predicate parts at the press of a button. This makes the user wish for rewriting facilities with which to calculate simpler predicates.

The VDM-SL Editor and Consistency Checker

Flemming M. Damm Hans Bruun Bo Stig Hansen

Department of Computer Science,
Technical University of Denmark,
Building 344, DK-2800 Lyngby

1 Introduction

As a part of the standardization of the VDM specification language (VDM-SL), the static semantics of VDM-SL is being defined. During this definition it has been found valuable to develop an editor and consistency checker for VDM-SL since the static semantics of VDM-SL is defined using VDM-SL itself. The aim of the tool is firstly to support the editing of the definition. Secondly, we want to be able to validate the consistency of the definition.

The editor is a so-called syntax directed editor. The attention is put on the abstract syntax tree and editing operations are performed on this tree. For this reason, the user can focus on what to specify and abstract from other aspects such as syntactical details and typographical layout details.

The editor does not only support editing of VDM-SL formulae but includes also facilities for merging VDM-SL formulae with regular text, sectioning, annotating specifications, generation and maintenance of symbolic references. Finally, it is possible to influence the layout (e.g. line breaking and indentation) of a specification.

During editing, the consistency checker operates in accordance with the static semantics [1]. Typical inconsistencies which may be detected are type errors and erroneous use of identifiers. Total consistency of VDM-SL specifications is, however, generally undecidable [2]. In accordance with the static semantics, the consistency checker generates proof obligations when it cannot verify consistency automatically.

2 An Overview

The VDM-SL Editor and Consistency Checker offers of a collection of different views. Each view displays a mapping of the abstract syntax tree. These mappings concern different aspects of the document edited. In some views, the aspects considered may be modified. In this way, the user can focus on one aspect at a time and abstract from other aspects.

The *logical document view* is useful when focusing on the abstract syntactical structure of the document. The tree-oriented editing operations offered with this view allow the user to concentrate on what to write rather than the appearance of the final document. Consequently, the user does not have to be concerned with line breaks, indentation and other layout specific things.

The layout of the document is controlled using the *layout view*. With this view it is possible to manually change the line breaking and indentation in VDM formulae.

In order to get an overview of the structure of the document being edited, an *outline view* may be used. The view shows the section headings of the document and with this it is possible to quickly shift attention to a new section since selection of a section heading in this view is reflected in the other views.

Two views are used in connection with consistency checking: one which displays inconsistencies and another which shows the proof obligations when a specification neither has been found erroneous nor could automatically be proved consistent.

At last, two views oriented towards system interface should be mentioned. One shows the document in a parsable form. The other shows the document in a representation which is suitable as input to the LaTeX typesetting system.

3 Availability

The editor is still under development. It is implemented using the Cornell Synthesizer Generator (CSG) [3]. The input to CSG is available free of charge. To make an editor from this input one must have the Cornell Synthesizer Generator. For further information contact the authors (email fmd@id.dth.dk).

References

[1] Hans Bruun, Bo Stig Hansen, and Flemming Damm. An approach to the static semantics of VDM-SL. This volume.

[2] Flemming Damm, Bo Stig Hansen, and Hans Bruun. Type checking in VDM and related consistency issues. This volume.

[3] Thomas W. Reps and Tim Teitelbaum. *The Synthesizer Generator. A System for Constructing Language-Based Editors*. Texts and Monographs in Computer Science. Springer-Verlag, 1989.

```
PROOF
  1  bvrb(x.y)                                                        SIDE CND
  2  ∀(x.y).(x inc y => f(x) inc f(y))                                HYP
  3    ∀(x.y).(x inc y => f(x) inc f(y))                              INHYP
  4    f(f¯) inc f¯                                                   3 r.4
  5    f(f(f¯)) inc f(f¯)                                             4 HYP.2
  6    f¯ inc f(f¯)                                                   5 r.3
  7  bvrb(x.y) & ∀(x.y).(x inc y => f(x) inc f(y)) => f¯ inc f(f¯)    DED
END OF PROOF
```

B-Tool

B-Tool provides the platform for solving the problem of specification and correct construction of software systems. It is a flexible inference engine which forms the basis of a computer-aided system for the formal construction of provably correct software. When used as a theorem proving assistant, B-Tool gives the software engineer the ability to verify the logical correctness of programs.

Origin and Background:

Development of B-Tool is a response to the demand for effective computer-aided tools to help prove mathematical theorems which arise in the process of applying formal methods to the development and verification of high-quality software. The aim was to develop a versatile and portable tool which would be of substantial use to practitioners in the field of formal methods based software development.

B-Tool has been used and tested in a number of medium scale formal software development projects, each of them typically requiring a few hundred mathematical theorems to be proved. B-Tool has demonstrated itself capable of coping with the theorem proving demand generated in the process of formal software development.

Description of B-Tool:

In essence, the B-Tool is a rule-based inference engine with rule-rewriting and pattern matching facilities. Its behaviour is controlled by rule bases known as "theories". The application of theories is guided by tactics. Specific proof strategies may be prescribed using appropriate combinations of theories and tactics. Given an appropriate combination of theories and tactics, a proof can be automated completely. Both forward reasoning and backward reasoning on a rule of the general form (A *op* B *op*.... => Y) are supported.

B-Tool has no pre-defined encoding of any logical laws; these are supplied in the form of theories and tactics wherever appropriate. As a result, B-Tool can be configured to support a large variety of different logics. However, B-Tool does have a number of basic mechanisms built in which are common to most formal proofs regardless of the underlying logic. These mechanisms support the idea of doing a proof *under certain hypotheses*, the notions of *variables and their scopes and freeness*, *quantifiers*, *substitution*, *equality* etc. The incorporation of these mechanisms greatly facilitates the practice of proving theorems encountered in the formal software development process without sacrificing B-Tool's generality and flexibility.

B-Tool is designed primarily to *assist* the software engineer in the *construction of formal proofs* to mathematical theorems arising from formal software development and verification. Although B-Tool can be configured (by supplying suitable theories and tactics) to behave like a *Proof Checker* or a *Theorem Prover*, it is not limited to such uses. Its practicality and flexibility set B-Tool apart from other theorem proving tools.

Major Advantages:

B-Tool enables the software engineer to put the theory of formal software development and verification into practice, with the resulting benefits of lower life-cycle costs, easy-maintenance, high productivity, precision and correctness.

B-Tool has the following features which have been identified in a recent MOD report† as desirable for a good theorem prover.

- A subgoaling approach which is natural for theorem proving
- A high degree of automation is possible
- Ability to use entirely new proof procedures where appropriate
- A portable user interface driven by nested menus
- Proven ability to integrate into a development environment
- High quality documentation
- Ease of use.

Other Uses:

The B-Tool is essentially an inference engine which can be driven by rules and tactics. As such it can be used in applications other than theorem proving, thus providing a common platform on which other tools may be built. One such application is automatic object code generation from detailed software designs. The rules necessary for such a process may be embedded in a rule base with appropriate tactics, with B-Tool acting as an interpreter. Another application is a verification condition generator which can be used to analyse a formal specification and design and generate the necessary verification conditions.

These and other applications form the basis of the B TOOLKIT which is a complete environment supporting the Abstract Machine Notation (AMN) style of software development from specification through design to automatic code generation. The components of the B TOOLKIT are packed into 4 separate tool packages, viz., (1) B-Proof Assistant, (2) B-AMN Specification and Design Assistant, (3) B-AMN Coding Assistant, and (4) AMN Environment Tools. Tool packages (1) to (3) rely on the B-Tool as their execution platform (hence the "B" prefix in their names). Tool package (4) provides an overall X-windows shell enveloping all the other tools.

Availability:

B-Tool is commercially available and comes with full documentation comprising an installation guide, a user manual, a tutorial, and a comprehensive technical reference manual. B TOOLKIT is currently in alpha-test phase and available free from BP Sunbury Research Centre to suitable alpha-test sites for evaluation. B-Tool is available on Unix and other platforms. For further details on the commercial availability of B-Tool please contact BP International's appointed distributor for B-Tool below:

The Distribution Manager,
Edinburgh Portable Compilers Ltd.,
17 Alva Street,
Edinburgh,
EH2 4PH.

Telephone:	031-225-6262
Fax:	031-225-6644
Email:	support@epc.ed.ac.uk

† Smith A., "Which Theorem Prover?", RSRE Memo No.4430, Procurement Executive, MOD, RSRE Malvern, Worcs., Oct. 1990.

A VDM Subset Compiler

Christoph Blaue
Christian-Albrechts-Universität zu Kiel
Preußerstr. 1-9, D-2300 Kiel
e-mail: cb@informatik.uni-kiel.dbp.de
phone: +49 4331 5604-33; fax: +49 4331 566143

Abstract

The VDM-COMPILER is able to process a subset of the VDM specification language as described in the BSI Proto Standard [PS91]. The compilation includes parsing, check of context conditions and code generation. The target language is an intermediate tree language [SC83, VO83] for which different code generation modules exist. Thus the VDM-COMPILER can produce code for various machines.

The Accepted Language

The compiler front end is generated automatically with a parser generator. The automatic generation enables us to maintain consistently different versions of the compiler (there is still a version in use, which accepts the language **META IV** as described in LNCS 61). The parser generates an abstract syntax tree, which is used for all subsequent processing.

Check of Context Conditions

The check of the static semantics usually has (among others) to ensure, that

- identifiers are used according to the visibility rules
- the numbers and types of parameters of functions can be coerced to those appearing in the declaration of the function
- the types of variables and constants in expressions and assignments "fit".

With **VDM** this is more difficult than in programming languages like PASCAL because arbitrary union types are allowed in **VDM** and the equality of types is not restricted to the syntactical identity.
Although it is not decidable at compiletime, whether union types are used correctly, the static semantics analyzer can check if the union type contains at least a subtype which meets the requirement. Restricting the language so that the direct access of subtypes is not possible has been rejected, because this would simplify the language too much.

The static semantics analyzer checks, whether the type equations can be converted to the same normal form or not. If they cannot, the types are said to be different.

Codegeneration

The Codegenerator handles most VDM-specific constructs, such as explicitely and implicitely defined sets, maps and sequences, patterns, quantified expressions, (recursive) lets, variables of functional types etc.
A more precise description can be found in [Ha87].

Applications

The compiler is running on Norsk-Data ND 5400, SUN-3 workstations and on IBM 386 under UNIX.
It has been used to produce several (small) compilers. The project started with PL/0, designed by N. Wirth. The VDM-COMPILER has further been used for the automatic generation of some compilers for PASCAL subsets with more complicated constructs.
The PASCAL-G language features GOTOs. The labels can be passed as parameters, which is far beyond of being simple. The PASCAL-P language features procedures and functions as parameters.
Although the generated compilers are rather slow, the code they produce is not: In terms of runtime and storage it is as good as that of a "handmade" compiler.

References

[BL90] C. Blaue, M. Haß: *A META IV Subset Compiler*
Technical Report, Kiel University, April 1990

[JU86] B. Juhl: *Überprüfung der Syntax und statischen Semantik von META IV*,
Master Thesis, CAU Kiel 1987

[SC83] U. Schmidt: *Ein neuartiger auf VDM basierender Codegenerator-Generator*,
PhD. Thesis, CAU Kiel 1983

[VO83] R. Völler: *Entwicklung einer maschinenunabhängigen Zwischensprache und zugehöriger Übersetzeroberteile für ein Mehrsprachenübersetzersystem mit Hilfe von VDM*,
PhD. Thesis, CAU Kiel 1983

[PS91] *VDM Specification Proto-Standard*
BSI IST/5/50 Document, Leicester, March 1991

[Ha87] M. Haß: *Development and Application of a Meta IV Compiler*
in LNCS 252: *VDM '87: VDM — A Formal Method at Work*
Springer-Verlag, Heidelberg 1987

Index of Authors

Lecture Notes in Computer Science

For information about Vols. 1–461
please contact your bookseller or Springer-Verlag

Vol. 462: G. Gottlob, W. Nejdl (Eds.), Expert Systems in Engineering. Proceedings, 1990. IX, 260 pages. 1990. (Subseries LNAI).

Vol. 463: H. Kirchner, W. Wechler (Eds.), Algebraic and Logic Programming. Proceedings, 1990. VII, 386 pages. 1990.

Vol. 464: J. Dassow, J. Kelemen (Eds.), Aspects and Prospects of Theoretical Computer Science. Proceedings, 1990. VI, 298 pages. 1990.

Vol. 465: A. Fuhrmann, M. Morreau (Eds.), The Logic of Theory Change. Proceedings, 1989. X, 334 pages. 1991. (Subseries LNAI).

Vol. 466: A. Blaser (Ed.), Database Systems of the 90s. Proceedings, 1990. VIII, 334 pages. 1990.

Vol. 467: F. Long (Ed.), Software Engineering Environments. Proceedings, 1989. VI, 313 pages. 1990.

Vol. 468: S.G. Akl, F. Fiala, W.W. Koczkodaj (Eds.), Advances in Computing and Information – ICCI '90. Proceedings, 1990. VII, 529 pages. 1990.

Vol. 469: I. Guessarian (Ed.), Semantics of Systems of Concurrent Processes. Proceedings, 1990. V, 456 pages. 1990.

Vol. 470: S. Abiteboul, P.C. Kanellakis (Eds.), ICDT '90. Proceedings, 1990. VII, 528 pages. 1990.

Vol. 471: B.C. Ooi, Efficient Query Processing in Geographic Information Systems. VIII, 208 pages. 1990.

Vol. 472: K.V. Nori, C.E. Veni Madhavan (Eds.), Foundations of Software Technology and Theoretical Computer Science. Proceedings, 1990. X, 420 pages. 1990.

Vol. 473: I.B. Damgård (Ed.), Advances in Cryptology – EUROCRYPT '90. Proceedings, 1990. VIII, 500 pages. 1991.

Vol. 474: D. Karagiannis (Ed.), Information Systems and Artificial Intelligence: Integration Aspects. Proceedings, 1990. X, 293 pages. 1991. (Subseries LNAI).

Vol. 475: P. Schroeder-Heister (Ed.), Extensions of Logic Programming. Proceedings, 1989. VIII, 364 pages. 1991. (Subseries LNAI).

Vol. 476: M. Filgueiras, L. Damas, N. Moreira, A.P. Tomás (Eds.), Natural Language Processing. Proceedings, 1990. VII, 253 pages. 1991. (Subseries LNAI).

Vol. 477: D. Hammer (Ed.), Compiler Compilers. Proceedings, 1990. VI, 227 pages. 1991.

Vol. 478: J. van Eijck (Ed.), Logics in AI. Proceedings, 1990. IX, 562 pages. 1991. (Subseries in LNAI).

Vol. 479: H. Schmidt, Meta-Level Control for Deductive Database Systems. VI, 155 pages. 1991.

Vol. 480: C. Choffrut, M. Jantzen (Eds.), STACS 91. Proceedings, 1991. X, 549 pages. 1991.

Vol. 481: E. Lang, K.-U. Carstensen, G. Simmons, Modelling Spatial Knowledge on a Linguistic Basis. IX, 138 pages. 1991. (Subseries LNAI).

Vol. 482: Y. Kodratoff (Ed.), Machine Learning – EWSL-91. Proceedings, 1991. XI, 537 pages. 1991. (Subseries LNAI).

Vol. 483: G. Rozenberg (Ed.), Advances in Petri Nets 1990. VI, 515 pages. 1991.

Vol. 484: R. H. Möhring (Ed.), Graph-Theoretic Concepts in Computer Science. Proceedings, 1990. IX, 360 pages. 1991.

Vol. 485: K. Furukawa, H. Tanaka, T. Fuijsaki (Eds.), Logic Programming '89. Proceedings, 1989. IX, 183 pages. 1991. (Subseries LNAI).

Vol. 486: J. van Leeuwen, N. Santoro (Eds.), Distributed Algorithms. Proceedings, 1990. VI, 433 pages. 1991.

Vol. 487: A. Bode (Ed.), Distributed Memory Computing. Proceedings, 1991. XI, 506 pages. 1991.

Vol. 488: R. V. Book (Ed.), Rewriting Techniques and Applications. Proceedings, 1991. VII, 458 pages. 1991.

Vol. 489: J. W. de Bakker, W. P. de Roever, G. Rozenberg (Eds.), Foundations of Object-Oriented Languages. Proceedings, 1990. VIII, 442 pages. 1991.

Vol. 490: J. A. Bergstra, L. M. G. Feijs (Eds.), Algebraic Methods II: Theory, Tools and Applicatlons. VI, 434 pages. 1991.

Vol. 491: A. Yonezawa, T. Ito (Eds.), Concurrency: Theory, Language, and Architecture. Proceedings, 1989. VIII, 339 pages. 1991.

Vol. 492: D. Sriram, R. Logcher, S. Fukuda (Eds.), Computer-Aided Cooperative Product Development. Proceedings, 1989 VII, 630 pages. 1991.

Vol. 493: S. Abramsky, T. S. E. Maibaum (Eds.), TAPSOFT '91. Volume 1. Proceedings, 1991. VIII, 455 pages. 1991.

Vol. 494: S. Abramsky, T. S. E. Maibaum (Eds.), TAPSOFT '91. Volume 2. Proceedings, 1991. VIII, 482 pages. 1991.

Vol. 495: 9. Thalheim, J. Demetrovics, H.-D. Gerhardt (Eds.), MFDBS '91. Proceedings, 1991. VI, 395 pages. 1991.

Vol. 496: H.-P. Schwefel, R. Männer (Eds.), Parallel Problem Solving from Nature. Proceedings, 1990. XI, 485 pages. 1991.

Vol. 497: F. Dehne, F. Fiala. W.W. Koczkodaj (Eds.), Advances in Computing and Information - ICCI '91. Proceedings, 1991. VIII, 745 pages. 1991.

Vol. 498: R. Andersen, J. A. Bubenko jr., A. Sølvberg (Eds.), Advanced Information Systems Engineering. Proceedings, 1991. VI, 579 pages. 1991.

Vol. 499: D. Christodoulakis (Ed.), Ada: The Choice for '92. Proceedings, 1991. VI, 411 pages. 1991.

Vol. 500: M. Held, On the Computational Geometry of Pocket Machining. XII, 179 pages. 1991.

Vol. 501: M. Bidoit, H.-J. Kreowski, P. Lescanne, F. Orejas, D. Sannella (Eds.), Algebraic System Specification and Development. VIII, 98 pages. 1991.

Vol. 502: J. Bārzdiņž, D. Bjørner (Eds.), Baltic Computer Science. X, 619 pages. 1991.

Vol. 503: P. America (Ed.), Parallel Database Systems. Proceedings, 1990. VIII, 433 pages. 1991.

Vol. 504: J. W. Schmidt, A. A. Stogny (Eds.), Next Generation Information System Technology. Proceedings, 1990. IX, 450 pages. 1991.

Vol. 505: E. H. L. Aarts, J. van Leeuwen, M. Rem (Eds.), PARLE '91. Parallel Architectures and Languages Europe, Volume I. Proceedings, 1991. XV, 423 pages. 1991.

Vol. 506: E. H. L. Aarts, J. van Leeuwen, M. Rem (Eds.), PARLE '91. Parallel Architectures and Languages Europe, Volume II. Proceedings, 1991. XV, 489 pages. 1991.

Vol. 507: N. A. Sherwani, E. de Doncker, J. A. Kapenga (Eds.), Computing in the 90's. Proceedings, 1989. XIII, 441 pages. 1991.

Vol. 508: S. Sakata (Ed.), Applied Algebra, Algebraic Algorithms and Error-Correcting Codes. Proceedings, 1990. IX, 390 pages. 1991.

Vol. 509: A. Endres, H. Weber (Eds.), Software Development Environments and CASE Technology. Proceedings, 1991. VIII, 286 pages. 1991.

Vol. 510: J. Leach Albert, B. Monien, M. Rodríguez (Eds.), Automata, Languages and Programming. Proceedings, 1991. XII, 763 pages. 1991.

Vol. 511: A. C. F. Colchester, D.J. Hawkes (Eds.), Information Processing in Medical Imaging. Proceedings, 1991. XI, 512 pages. 1991.

Vol. 512: P. America (Ed.), ECOOP '91. European Conference on Object-Oriented Programming. Proceedings, 1991. X, 396 pages. 1991.

Vol. 513: N. M. Mattos, An Approach to Knowledge Base Management. IX, 247 pages. 1991. (Subseries LNAI).

Vol. 514: G. Cohen, P. Charpin (Eds.), EUROCODE '90. Proceedings, 1990. XI, 392 pages. 1991.

Vol. 515: J. P. Martins, M. Reinfrank (Eds.), Truth Maintenance Systems. Proceedings, 1990. VII, 177 pages. 1991. (Subseries LNAI).

Vol. 516: S. Kaplan, M. Okada (Eds.), Conditional and Typed Rewriting Systems. Proceedings, 1990. IX, 461 pages. 1991.

Vol. 517: K. Nökel, Temporally Distributed Symptoms in Technical Diagnosis. IX, 164 pages. 1991. (Subseries LNAI).

Vol. 518: J. G. Williams, Instantiation Theory. VIII, 133 pages. 1991. (Subseries LNAI).

Vol. 519: F. Dehne, J.-R. Sack, N. Santoro (Eds.), Algorithms and Data Structures. Proceedings, 1991. X, 496 pages. 1991.

Vol. 520: A. Tarlecki (Ed.), Mathematical Foundations of Computer Science 1991. Proceedings, 1991. XI, 435 pages. 1991.

Vol. 521: B. Bouchon-Meunier, R. R. Yager, L. A. Zadek (Eds.), Uncertainty in Knowledge-Bases. Proceedings, 1990. X, 609 pages. 1991.

Vol. 522: J. Hertzberg (Ed.), European Workshop on Planning. Proceedings, 1991. VII, 121 pages. 1991. (Subseries LNAI).

Vol. 523: J. Hughes (Ed.), Functional Programming Languages and Computer Architecture. Proceedings, 1991. VIII, 666 pages. 1991.

Vol. 524: G. Rozenberg (Ed.), Advances in Petri Nets 1991. VIII, 572 pages. 1991.

Vol. 525: O. Günther, H.-J. Schek (Eds.), Advances in Spatial Databases. Proceedings, 1991. XI, 471 pages. 1991.

Vol. 526: T. Ito, A. R. Meyer (Eds.), Theoretical Aspects of Computer Software. Proceedings, 1991. X, 772 pages. 1991.

Vol. 527: J.C.M. Baeten, J. F. Groote (Eds.), CONCUR '91. Proceedings, 1991. VIII, 541 pages. 1991.

Vol. 528: J. Maluszynski, M. Wirsing (Eds.), Programming Language Implementation and Logic Programming. Proceedings, 1991. XI, 433 pages. 1991.

Vol. 529: L. Budach (Ed.), Fundamentals of Computation Theory. Proceedings, 1991. XII, 426 pages. 1991.

Vol. 530: D. H. Pitt, P.-L. Curien, S. Abramsky, A. M. Pitts, A. Poigné, D. E. Rydeheard (Eds.), Category Theory and Computer Science. Proceedings, 1991. VII, 301 pages. 1991.

Vol. 531: E. M. Clarke, R. P. Kurshan (Eds.), Computer-Aided Verification. Proceedings, 1990. XIII, 372 pages. 1991.

Vol. 532: H. Ehrig, H.-J. Kreowski, G. Rozenberg (Eds.), Graph Grammars and Their Application to Computer Science. Proceedings, 1990. X, 703 pages. 1991.

Vol. 533: E. Börger, H. Kleine Büning, M. M. Richter, W. Schönfeld (Eds.), Computer Science Logic. Proceedings, 1990. VIII, 399 pages. 1991.

Vol. 534: H. Ehrig, K. P. Jantke, F. Orejas, H. Reichel (Eds.), Recent Trends in Data Type Specification. Proceedings, 1990. VIII, 379 pages. 1991.

Vol. 535: P. Jorrand, J. Kelemen (Eds.), Fundamentals of Artificial Intelligence Research. Proceedings, 1991. VIII, 255 pages. 1991. (Subseries LNAI).

Vol. 536: J. E. Tomayko, Software Engineering Education. Proceedings, 1991. VIII, 296 pages. 1991.

Vol. 537: A. J. Menezes, S. A. Vanstone (Eds.), Advances in Cryptology – CRYPTO '90. Proceedings. XIII, 644 pages. 1991.

Vol. 538: M. Kojima, N. Megiddo, T. Noma, A. Yoshise, A Unified Approach to Interior Point Algorithms for Linear Complementarity Problems. VIII, 108 pages. 1991.

Vol. 539: H. F. Mattson, T. Mora, T. R. N. Rao (Eds.), Applied Algebra, Algebraic Algorithms and Error-Correcting Codes. Proceedings, 1991. XI, 489 pages. 1991.

Vol. 540: A. Prieto (Ed.), Artificial Neural Networks. Proceedings, 1991. XIII, 476 pages. 1991.

Vol. 541: P. Barahona, L. Moniz Pereira, A. Porto (Eds.), EPIA '91. Proceedings, 1991. VIII, 292 pages. 1991. (Subseries LNAI).

Vol. 543: J. Dix, K. P. Jantke, P. H. Schmitt (Eds.), Nonmonotonic and Inductive Logic. Proceedings, 1990. X, 243 pages. 1991. (Subseries LNAI).

Vol. 544: M. Broy, M. Wirsing (Eds.), Methods of Programming. XII, 268 pages. 1991.

Vol. 545: H. Alblas, B. Melichar (Eds.), Attribute Grammars, Applications and Systems. Proceedings, 1991. IX, 513 pages. 1991.

Vol. 547: D. W. Davies (Ed.), Advances in Cryptology – EUROCRYPT '91. Proceedings, 1991. XII, 556 pages. 1991.

Vol. 548: R. Kruse, P. Siegel (Eds.), Symbolic and Quantitative Approaches to Uncertainty. Proceedings, 1991. XI, 362 pages. 1991.

Vol. 550: A. van Lamsweerde, A. Fugetta (Eds.), ESEC '91. Proceedings, 1991. XII, 515 pages. 1991.

Vol. 551:S. Prehn, W. J. Toetenel (Eds.), VDM '91. Formal Software Development Methods. Volume 1. Proceedings, 1991. XIII, 699 pages. 1991.

Vol. 552: S. Prehn, W. J. Toetenel (Eds.), VDM '91. Formal Software Development Methods. Volume 2. Proceedings, 1991. XIV, 430 pages. 1991.